P9-AGD-043

Contents

Islamic architecture in Egypt colour section following p.152

Egyptian temple architecture colour section following p.312

Egypt's underwater world colour section following p.696

◄◄ The temple of Philae ◄ Camels at the Pyramids

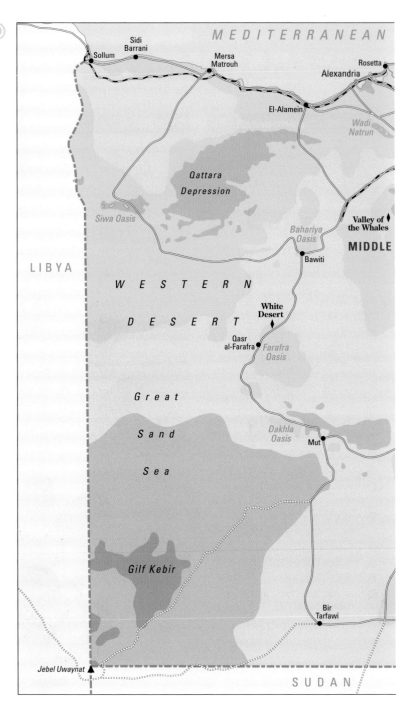

Karen Rush

The **Rough Gui**

Egypt

written and researched by

Dan Richardson and Daniel Jacobs

with additional contributions by

Lizzie Williams and Emma Gregg

ROUGH GUIDES

NEW YORK · LONDON · DELHI

www.roughguides.com

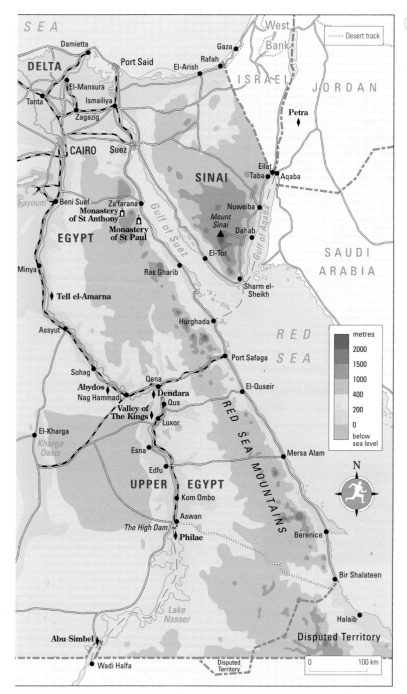

Introduction to
Egypt

Egypt is the oldest tourist destination on earth. Ancient Greeks and Romans started the trend, coming to goggle at the Cyclopean scale of the Pyramids and the Colossi of Thebes. During colonial times, Napoleon and the British looted Egypt's treasures to fill their national museums, sparking off a trickle of Grand Tourists that eventually became a flood of travellers, taken on Nile cruises and Egyptological lectures by the enterprising Thomas Cook. Today, the attractions of the country are not only the monuments of the Nile Valley and the souks, mosques and madrassas of Islamic Cairo, but also fantastic coral reefs and tropical fish, dunes, ancient fortresses, monasteries and prehistoric rock art.

The land itself is a freak of nature, its lifeblood the River Nile. From the Sudanese border to the shores of the Mediterranean, the Nile Valley and its Delta are flanked by arid wastes, the latter as empty as the former are teeming with people. This stark duality between fertility and desolation is fundamental to Egypt's character and has shaped its development since prehistoric times, imparting continuity to diverse cultures and peoples over seven millennia. It is a sense of permanence and timelessness that is buttressed by religion, which pervades every aspect of life. Although the pagan cults of Ancient Egypt are as moribund as its legacy of mummies and temples, their ancient fertility rites and processions of boats still hold their place in the celebrations of Islam and Christianity.

The result is a multi-layered culture, which seems to accord equal respect to ancient and modern. The peasants of the Nile and Bedouin tribes of the desert live much as their ancestors did a thousand years ago. Other communities include the Nubians of the far

> **Though most visitors are drawn to Egypt by its monuments, the enduring memory is likely to be of its people and their way of life.**

south, and the Coptic Christians, who trace their ancestry back to pharaonic times. What unites them is a love of their homeland, extended family ties, dignity, warmth and hospitality towards strangers. Though most visitors are drawn to Egypt by its monuments, the enduring memory is likely to be of its people and their way of life.

Where to go

Egypt's capital, **Cairo**, is a seething megalopolis whose chief sightseeing appeal lies in its **bazaars** and medieval **mosques**, though there is scarcely less fascination in its juxtapositions of medieval and modern life, the city's fortified gates, villas and skyscrapers interwoven by flyovers whose traffic may be halted by donkey carts. The immensity and diversity of this "Mother of Cities" is as staggering as anything you'll encounter in Egypt. Just outside Cairo are the first of the **pyramids** that range across the desert to the edge of the Fayoum, among

Fact file

• The Arab Republic of Egypt covers 1,001,450 square kilometres, of which 96.4 percent is **desert**; only the Nile Valley, its Delta and some oases are fertile.

• Egypt's **population** of 76 million is over twice that of the next most populous Arab country (Algeria) and a quarter of the population of the Arab world. Its ethnic profile is Eastern Hamitic and Semitic – Egyptians, Bedouins, Nubians and Berbers account for 99 percent – with tiny minorities of Greeks, Armenians and others. **Arabic** is spoken universally, Nubian around Aswan and Lake Nasser, and Siwi at Siwa Oasis. Islam is the national **religion**, with some 96 percent followers; almost all the rest are Coptic Orthodox Christians. Average **life expectancy** is 70 years.

• A **republic** since 1952, Egypt is divided into 26 governorates or *muhafazat*. President Hosni Mubarak has been head of state since 1981. The National Democratic Party invariably wins tightly regulated elections to the People's Assembly (Maglis al-Shaab) and Advisory Council (Maglis al-Shura). Opposition parties and independent MPs are outspoken, but powerless to change anything.

• **Tourism** is Egypt's largest money-earner, followed by tolls on the Suez Canal, and exports of oil, petroleum products, textiles and natural gas.

Hussein or Houssein?

There's no standard system of trans-literating Arabic script into Roman, so you're sure to find that the Arabic words in this book don't always match the versions you'll see elsewhere. Maps and street signs are the biggest sources of confusion, so we've generally gone for the transliteration that's the most common on the spot. However, you'll often need to do a bit of lateral thinking, and it's not unusual to find one spelling posted at one end of a road, with another at the opposite end. See p.819 for an introduction to Egyptian Arabic.

them the unsurpassable trio at **Giza**, the vast necropolis of **Saqqara** and the recently reopened pyramids at **Dahshur**. Besides all this, there are superb **museums** devoted to Ancient, Coptic and Islamic Egypt, and enough **entertainments** to occupy weeks of your time.

However, the principal tourist lure remains, as ever, the **Nile Valley**, with its **ancient monuments** and timeless river vistas – Nile **cruises** on a luxury vessel or a felucca sailboat being a great way to combine the two. The town of **Luxor** is synonymous with the magnificent temples of **Karnak** and the **Theban Necropolis**, which includes the **Valley of the Kings** where Tutankhamun and other pharaohs were buried. **Aswan**, Egypt's southernmost city, has the loveliest setting on the Nile and a languorous ambience. From here, you can visit the island **Philae temple of Isis** and the rock-hewn colossi at **Abu Simbel**, or embark on a cruise to other temples around **Lake Nasser**. Other sites not to be missed are **Edfu** and **Kom Ombo** between Luxor and Aswan, and **Abydos** and **Dendara** north of Luxor.

Besides monuments, Egypt abounds in natural wonders. Edged by coral reefs teeming with tropical fish, the **Sinai Peninsula** offers superb **diving** and **snorkelling**, and palm-fringed **beaches** where women can swim unmolested. Resorts along the Gulf of Aqaba are varied enough to suit everyone, whether you're into the upmarket hotels of **Sharm el-Sheikh** and nearby **Na'ama Bay**, or **Taba** further north, or cheap, simple living at **Dahab** and **Nuweiba**. From there it's easy to visit **St Catherine's Monastery** and **Mount Sinai** (where Moses received the Ten Commandments) in the mountainous interior. With more time, cash and stamina, you can also embark on **Jeep safaris** or **camel treks** to remote oases and spectacular wadis.

Egypt's **Red Sea coast** has more reefs further offshore, with snorkelling and diving traditionally centred around **Hurghada**, while barely touched island reefs further south from **Port Safaga** down to **Mersa Alam** beckon serious diving enthusiasts. Inland, the mountainous **Eastern Desert** harbours the **Coptic Monasteries of St Paul and St Anthony**, Roman quarries, and a host of pharaonic and **prehistoric rock art**, seen by few apart from the nomadic Bedouin.

While the Eastern Desert is still barely touched by tourism, the **Western Desert Oases** have been on the tourist trail for thirty years and nowadays host safaris into the wilderness. **Siwa**, out towards the Libyan border, has a unique culture and history, limpid pools and bags of charm. Travellers can also follow the "Great Desert Circuit" (starting from Cairo, Luxor or Assyut) through the four "inner" oases. Though **Bahariya** and **Farafra** hold the most appeal, with the lovely **White Desert** between them, the larger oases of **Dakhla** and **Kharga** also have their rewards once you escape their modernized "capitals". And for those into serious desert expeditions, there's the challenge of exploring the **Great Sand Sea** or the remote wadis of the **Gilf Kebir** and **Jebel Uwaynat**, whose prehistoric rock art featured in the film *The English Patient*. In contrast to these deep-desert locations are the quasi-oases of the **Fayoum** and **Wadi Natrun**, featuring the fossil-strewn **Valley of the Whales**, diverse ancient ruins and **Coptic monasteries**.

▼ A market at the Souk al-Tawfiqia, Cairo

The ibis

Images of ibises appear on temples, tombs and billboards all over Egypt. The white-bodied, black-billed sacred ibis that the Ancient Egyptians revered as an incarnation of Thoth, the god of knowledge, was last seen in Egypt in 1891 and is now only found as far north as Sudan – but in ancient times it was so abundant that literally millions were mummified at Tuna el-Gebel and other sites, despite it being a capital offence to kill one. Nowadays, the only species left in Egypt is the glossy ibis, which is sometimes seen near Aswan but doesn't breed there; in ancient tombs, it

was painted black, without its iridescent sheen. Another species depicted was the crested ibis, used as the hieroglyph for Akhu (part of the soul) and known as the Akhu bird. Today, the most striking waterbirds on the Nile are cattle and little egrets and the diving pied kingfisher (seen year-round in Aswan).

On the **Mediterranean**, Egypt's second city, **Alexandria**, boasts a string of beaches to which Cairenes flock in summer, and excellent seafood restaurants. Despite being founded by Alexander the Great and lost to the Romans by Cleopatra, the city today betrays little of its ancient glory; however, its magnificent new **library**, featuring statues raised from the sunken remains of **Cleopatra's Palace** and the **Lighthouse of Pharos** (which divers can explore) are restoring an air of majesty. Famous, too, for its decadence during colonial times, Alexandria still allows romantics to indulge in a nostalgic exploration of the city immortalized in Durrell's *Alexandria Quartet*, while further along the Mediterranean coast lie the World War II battlefield of **El-Alamein** and the Egyptian holiday resort of **Mersa Matrouh**. For divers, this coastline offers an array of sunken cities and wartime wrecks to explore.

The Nile **Delta**, east of Alexandria, musters few archeological monuments given its major role in Ancient Egyptian history, and is largely overlooked by tourists. However, for those interested in Egyptian culture, the Delta hosts colourful religious **festivals** at **Tanta**, **Zagazig** and other towns. Further east lies the Canal Zone, dominated by the Suez Canal and its three cities. **Port Said** and **Ismailiya** are pleasant, albeit sleepy places, where you can get a feel of "real Egypt" without tripping over other tourists. **Suez** is grim, but a vital transport nexus between Cairo, Sinai and the Red Sea coast.

When to go

gypt's traditional season runs from **late November to late February**, though in recent years Luxor and Aswan have only really been busy with tourists during the peak months of December and January. The Nile Valley is balmy throughout this winter season, although Cairo can be overcast and chilly. The season is also the busiest period for the Sinai resorts, while Hurghada is active year round. Aside from the Easter vacation, when there is a spike in tourism, **March or April** are also good times to visit, with a pleasant climate.

In **May and June** the heat is still tolerable but, after that, Egyptians rich enough to do so migrate to Alex and the coastal resorts. From **July to September** the south and desert are ferociously hot and the pollution in Cairo is at its worst, with only the coast offering a respite from the heat. During this time, sightseeing is best limited to early morning or evening – though August still sees droves of backpackers. **October into early November** is perhaps the best time of all, with easily manageable climate and crowds.

▼ Snorkelling at Dahab

Weather and tourism apart, the **Islamic calendar** and its related festivals can have an effect on your travel. The most important factor is **Ramadan**, the month of daytime fasting, which can be problematic for eating and transport, though the festive evenings do much to compensate. See "Festivals" in the Basics chapter for details of its timing.

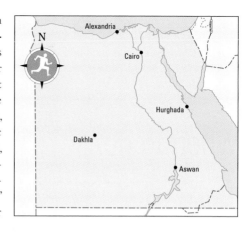

Average daily temperatures

	Jan	Mar	May	July	Sept	Nov
Alexandria *Mediterranean*						
Max/Min (°F)	65/51	70/55	79/64	85/73	86/73	77/62
Max/Min (°C)	18/11	21/13	26/18	29/23	30/23	25/17
Aswan *Southern Nile Valley*						
Max/Min (°F)	74/50	87/58	103/74	106/79	103/75	87/62
Max/Min (°C)	23/10	31/14	39/23	41/26	39/24	31/17
Cairo *Northern Nile Valley*						
Max/Min (°F)	65/47	75/52	91/63	96/70	90/68	78/58
Max/Min (°C)	18/8	24/11	33/17	36/21	32/20	26/14
Dakhla *Western Desert*						
Max/Min (°F)	70/41	82/47	99/68	104/74	96/70	82/53
Max/Min (°C)	21/5	28/8	37/20	40/23	36/21	28/12
Hurghada *Red Sea coast*						
Max/Min (°F)	70/50	74/61	86/70	90/77	86/74	77/59
Max/Min (°C)	21/10	23/12	30/21	32/25	30/23	25/15

Note that these are *average* daily maximum and minimum temperatures. Summer peaks in Aswan, Hurghada or Sinai, for example, can hit the 120°s F (low 50°s C) in hot years. The dryness of the air and absence of cloud cover makes for drastic fluctuations, though they do also make the heat tolerably unsticky outside Cairo and the Delta. The Mediterranean coast can be windy and wet in winter.

35

things not to miss

It's not possible to see everything that Egypt has to offer in one trip – and we don't suggest you try. What follows, in no particular order, is a selective taste of the country's highlights: outstanding temples and tombs, spectacular landscapes and opportunities for Nile cruises. They're all arranged in five colour-coded categories, so that you can browse through to find the very best things to see, do and experience. All highlights have a page reference to take you into the guide, where you can find out more.

01 **Aswan** Page **426** • Aswan has been Egypt's gateway to Nubia since ancient times, and its islands, bazaars and riverside restaurants can keep you happy in between excursions to sites such as Abu Simbel.

03 **Dahabiya cruises** Page **318** • These swanky nineteenth-century-style houseboats are perfect for cruising the Nile with a small group of friends.

02 **Mount Sinai** Page **714** • This awesome peak is revered as the site where Moses received the Ten Commandments from God.

04 **Jewellery** Page **249** • There's an endless choice of pharaonic, Classical, Islamic and contemporary designs in the bazaars of Cairo, as well as Luxor and Aswan, and oases such as Siwa.

05 **Diving and snorkelling** See *Egypt's underwater world* colour section • Amazing coral reefs, tropical fish and wrecks make the Red Sea a paradise for scuba divers and snorkellers, while Egypt's Mediterranean coast boasts ancient underwater ruins, sunken U-Boats and warships to explore.

06 **Dahab** Page **691** • Sinai chill-out zone, renowned for its diving, beach cafés, and camel and Jeep safaris into the rugged interior.

07 **The pyramids of Dahshur** Page **229** • Less famous than the Giza trio but no less fascinating – and far less crowded. The Bent Pyramid, resting place of Snofru, has a distinctive angled top.

08 **Moulids** Page **64** • Get swept up in the carnival atmosphere of popular religious festivals honouring Sufi or Christian saints, in Cairo, Luxor or the Delta.

09 **Juice bars** Page **50** • Most towns have a sprinkling of these, where you can quench your thirst with whatever's in season, from freshly-pressed oranges and mangoes to strawberries and sugar cane.

10 **Mezze** Page **49** • Dining in a restaurant, try *mezze*, consisting of many delicious, small dishes (particularly good for vegetarians).

11 **Bellydancing** Page **245** • The centuries-old tradition of raqs sharqi (oriental dance) is best seen at clubs frequented by locals, where the dancers and musicians will set your pulse racing.

12 **Islamic Cairo** Page **127** • City of a thousand minarets, teeming with life, and chock-full of architectural masterpieces and historic monuments. Head for Khan el-Khalili Bazaar, or the Citadel.

13 Ras Mohammed Page **676** • Egypt's oldest marine nature park boasts spectacular shark reefs and the wreck of the *Dunraven*.

14 The Pyramids and Sphinx at Giza Page **206** • The world's most famous monuments have inspired scholarly and crackpot speculations for centuries.

15 Siwa Oasis Page **550** • With its unique culture, hilltop citadel and spring-fed pools, Siwa is rated by many as the best of Egypt's oases.

16 **Al-Qasr** Page **524** • A labyrinth of shadowy lanes and covered passageways, dating back to medieval times, that was once the capital of Dakhla Oasis.

18 **White Desert** Page **511** • A tract of weird wind-eroded rock formations in Farafra Oasis, often visited on overnight safaris from the neighbouring oasis of Bahariya.

19 **Textiles and clothes** Page **251** • Cairo's bazaars sell rugs from Kerdassa and Harraniyya, hand-loomed Akhmim silks, embroidered robes from Sinai and the oases, and all kinds of kaftans, scarves and skullcaps.

17 **Street food** Page **48** • Sold from pushcarts or in sit-down diners, *taamiya*, *kushari*, *fuul* and *shawarma* are tasty, cheap and nourishing.

19

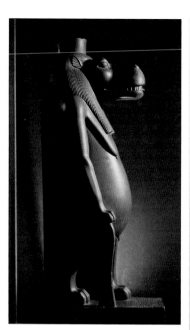

21 **Feluccas** Page **319** • These lateen-sailed boats can be hired for an afternoon lazing on the Nile, or a two- or three-day journey from Aswan, visiting the temples at Kom Ombo and Edfu.

20 **The Egyptian Antiquities Museum** Page **107** • A statue of Taueret, the pregnant hippopotamus-goddess of fertility, is just one of the highlights of this amazing collection, which includes Tutankhamun's treasures, monumental statues from the Old Kingdom and the Amarna era, and a dozen royal mummies.

22 **Abu Simbel** Page **463** • The monumental sun temple of Ramses II is the most spectacular of the Nubian antiquities that were relocated to higher ground on the shores of Lake Nasser.

23 Karkaday Page **50** • This infusion of hibiscus flowers makes a delicious hot or cold drink and tonic.

24 Birdwatching Page **490** • Wadi Rayan is a magnet for ornithologists, as are sites at Lake Nasser, Lake Manzala and the Sinai Peninsula.

25 Alexandria Page **570** • With its dazzling new library, and the chance to dive the ruins of Cleopatra's Palace and the Pharos Lighthouse, this Mediterranean port city founded by Alexander the Great is making waves again.

26 Catacombs of Kom es-Shoqafa Page **593** • Beneath the Karmous quarter of Alexandria are the spookiest tombs in Egypt, with a bizarre fusion of pharaonic, Greek and Roman funerary motifs, reflecting the city's ancient diversity.

27 Red Sea monasteries Page **727** • Secluded in the desert highlands, the monasteries of St Paul and St Anthony are the oldest in Egypt, if not the world, dating back to the dawn of Christian monasticism.

28 Abydos Page **322** • One of the most ancient cult-centres in Egypt, Abydos' mortuary temple of Seti I contains magnificent bas-reliefs, the finest to have survived from the New Kingdom.

29 Karnak Temple Page **359** • Dedicated to the ancient Theban Triad of Amun, Mut and Khonsu, this vast complex reached its zenith during the New Kingdom.

30 **Jeep or camel safaris** Pages **473, 686 & 702** • Make tracks into the dunes of the Western Desert or the canyons of Sinai – overnight trips or major expeditions are easily arranged.

31 **St Catherine's Monastery** Page **710** • Secluded beneath Mount Sinai, St Catherine's harbours the burning bush that appeared to Moses, and other holy relics.

32 **Na'ama Bay** Page **683** • Egypt's premier resort, teeming with bars, clubs and luxury hotels, and with magnificent coral gardens nearby.

33 **Great Sand Sea** Page **548** • This vast sea of dunes once swallowed up an entire Persian army, but you can safely explore its edge from Siwa Oasis, or join a deep-desert safari to traverse the Sand Sea.

34 **Valley of the Kings** Page **380** • The descent into the Underworld, the Judgement of Osiris and the rebirth of the pharaoh are vividly depicted on the walls and ceilings of the royal tombs.

35 **Balloon rides** Page **356** • Enjoy a magnificent view of the Theban Necropolis on Luxor's west bank.

Basics

Basics

Getting there

Although it is possible to get to Egypt by land via Israel or Jordan, most visitors will want to fly. Cairo is well served by international airlines, with direct scheduled flights from London and New York and a large choice of indirect routes from pretty much everywhere. Luxor and the main Egyptian resorts are also served by low-cost and charter flights from the UK.

The best air fares are available during the **low season**, November to March, excluding Christmas and New Year, which counts as **high season** along with June to the end of August. Note that flying at weekends can add significantly to the round-trip fare; price ranges quoted below are for the cheapest round-trip tickets including airport departure tax, and assume midweek travel. Many of them will be subject to restrictions such as fixed dates, which cannot be changed once the ticket is booked, and some may require advance purchase.

You can often cut costs by going through a **discount travel agent**. From the UK, you may even find it cheaper to pick up a bargain package deal to Luxor from one of the tour operators listed on pp.33–34. Some UK and European agents specialize in **charter flights**, which may be cheaper than anything available on a scheduled flight, but again departure dates are fixed and withdrawal penalties are high. Note that the maximum stay allowed in Egypt for visitors arriving on a charter flight is a month; attempting to circumvent this by buying two one-way tickets, with the return flight happening more than a month after the outbound date, can lead to your being barred from boarding the plane back.

If you're interested in visiting Egypt as part of a much wider journey, note that Cairo is unlikely to feature on the itineraries of the cheaper **Round The World** flight tickets, but can be visited on custom tickets issued by the airline consortiums Star Alliance (⒲www.staralliance.com) and One World Alliance (⒲www.oneworld.com). Alternatively, try the online build-your-own itineraries offered by companies like Airtreks (⒲www.airtreks.com).

Flights from the UK and Ireland

Flying time from the UK to Egypt is five to six hours nonstop. The best-value flights to Egypt are offered by a number of low-cost and charter airlines, including Thomsonfly, First Choice Airways, Flythomascook and XL Airways, who fly from the **UK** to **Luxor** and the main resorts – in particular **Sharm el-Sheikh** and **Hurghada**, though some flights to **Mersa Alam** and **Taba** are available. Many of these flights operate only once or twice a week (slightly more frequently in winter on some routes), but return fares are keen, starting from as little as £100. While the majority of flights depart from London Gatwick or Manchester, quite a few use other UK regional airports; Sharm is the destination with the best connections, being served from half a dozen or so British airports, including Birmingham and Glasgow. Some dive companies (see p.33) also offer cheap flight-only deals to Sharm, though these are usually not advertised, so you'll need to approach the company direct.

Among the full-price airlines, both EgyptAir and British Airways (BA) have daily scheduled flights to **Cairo** from London Heathrow. BA also flies four times weekly from Heathrow to Alexandria, while EgyptAir has weekly direct flights to Luxor and sometimes to Sharm. Most airlines flying indirectly to Egypt serve Cairo only, but Lufthansa, Olympic and Saudi Arabian Airlines also fly to Alexandria. Flights can cost as little as £270 return in low season, or £320 in high season.

Departing from **Ireland**, you can either make your own way to London and fly from there, or take an indirect flight, changing planes in London or another European hub. Fares to Cairo start at around €400

Fly less – stay longer! Travel and climate change

Climate change is the single biggest issue facing our planet. It is caused by a build-up in the atmosphere of carbon dioxide and other greenhouse gases, which are emitted by many sources – including planes. Already, flights account for around 3–4 percent of human-induced global warming: that figure may sound small, but it is rising year on year and threatens to counteract the progress made by reducing greenhouse emissions in other areas.

Rough Guides regard travel, overall, as a global benefit, and feel strongly that the advantages to developing economies are important, as are the opportunities for greater contact and awareness among peoples. But we all have a responsibility to limit our personal "carbon footprint". That means giving thought to how often we fly and what we can do to redress the harm that our trips create.

Flying and climate change

Pretty much every form of motorized travel generates CO_2, but planes are particularly bad offenders, releasing large volumes of greenhouse gases at altitudes where their impact is far more harmful. Flying also allows us to travel much further than we would contemplate doing by road or rail, so the emissions attributable to each passenger become truly shocking. For example, one person taking a return flight between Europe and California produces the equivalent impact of 2.5 tonnes of CO_2 – similar to the yearly output of the average UK car.

Less harmful planes may evolve but it will be decades before they replace the current fleet – which could be too late for avoiding climate chaos. In the meantime, there are limited options for concerned travellers: to reduce the amount we travel by air (take fewer trips, stay longer!), to avoid night flights (when plane contrails trap heat from Earth but can't reflect sunlight back to space), and to make the trips we do take "climate neutral" via a carbon offset scheme.

Carbon offset schemes

Offset schemes run by **climatecare.org, carbonneutral.com** and others allow you to "neutralize" the greenhouse gases that you are responsible for releasing. Their websites have simple calculators that let you work out the impact of any flight. Once that's done, you can pay to fund projects that will reduce future carbon emissions by an equivalent amount (such the distribution of low-energy lightbulbs and cooking stoves in developing countries). Please take the time to visit our website and make your trip climate neutral.

www.roughguides.com/climatechange

---

in low season, rising by at least €150 in high season.

If you're pushed for time, or want to make things easier, buying a **package holiday** makes a lot of sense. There are some amazing bargains to be had among the basic Luxor-plus-Cairo or Luxor-only packages. Besides these, many smaller independent operators feature felucca trips on the Nile, diving holidays on the Red Sea or camel trekking in Sinai.

Flights from the US and Canada

From the US, only EgyptAir flies direct to Cairo (daily from New York; 11hr), with fares

starting at around US$1000 in low season, rising to US$1600 in high season. Otherwise, a number of European and Middle Eastern airlines serve Cairo from a much wider range of departure points, though New York still offers by far the biggest choice of airlines. All West Coast flights are routed via the airlines' hub cities, so check that you won't have to wait overnight for your onward connection. By shopping around, you should be able to pick up a round-trip ticket for as little as $900 out of New York in low season, $1100 in high season. Flying from the West Coast, expect to pay at least $200 more.

From **Canada** there are direct flights to Cairo out of Montreal twice weekly in summer only with EgyptAir, who also offer through tickets from other cities via New York in combination with local airlines. Otherwise, many of the European carriers operate services via their hub cities from Toronto and Montreal. Fares start at around Can$1100 in low season, or Can$1800 in high season. Fares from Vancouver, with British Airways or Lufthansa, are Can$200–400 higher.

Flights from Australia, New Zealand and South Africa

A number of European, Middle Eastern and Asian carriers offer indirect flights to Egypt from **Australia** and **New Zealand**, changing planes at their hub airports. Cairo fares start at around A$1600 in low season, or A$2400 in high season from Australia, around NZ$2200 year-round from New Zealand. If flying into Dubai, you might want to investigate low-cost flights on Air Arabia (see p.30) from nearby Sharjah to Alexandria, Assyut and Luxor.

From **South Africa**, there are direct Cairo flights from Johannesburg with EgyptAir, or you can take an indirect flight with an East African airline such as Kenya Airways or Ethiopian Airlines, or a Middle Eastern Airline such as Emirates or Gulf Air. The ticket will set you back anything from R5000 to R7,500, with different airlines cheaper at different times of the year.

From Israel and the Gaza Strip

At the time of writing, most traffic between Israel and Egypt uses the border crossing at Taba near Eilat. The border crossing between Gaza and Egypt at Rafah is often closed by the Israelis. Entering Egypt via Taba, you're subject to an Israeli departure tax of US$15 (plus NIS3 if you pay at the border as opposed to the Post Office Bank) and an Egyptian entry tax of US$8. Travelling via Rafah, the corresponding taxes are US$32 and US$6.

Mazada Tours (141 Rehov Ibn Gvirol, Tel Aviv ⓣ03/544 4544; 19 Jaffa Road, West Jerusalem ⓣ02/623 5777; ⓦwww.mazada.co.il) runs **buses to Cairo** twice weekly (Sunday and Thursday) from both **Tel Aviv** and **Jerusalem**. One-way tickets are US$44 (plus border taxes totalling US$40), return tickets US$66 (plus US$55). It's best to book (and confirm return journeys) at least three days in advance. The company can apply for a visa for you on request, but the Egyptian Embassy is just around the corner from its office (see p.66 for the address), and it is cheaper to do it yourself.

Taba makes a fine jumping-off point for the Sinai coast resorts, St Catherine's Monastery or Cairo. From Eilat, a taxi or a #15 bus (which doesn't run on Shabbat) will get you to the Israeli checkpoint at Taba for an exit stamp; you then walk over to the Egyptian side, where Sinai-only visas can be obtained on the spot (for more on visas in general, see p.65). It usually takes a good hour to cross the border, longer at holiday times. A few banks in Sharm el-Sheikh and one or two banks and Forex bureaus in Cairo are the only places in Egypt where you can legally exchange Israeli shekels.

To reach **Rafah** under your own steam, take the daily Israeli Egged buses from Tel Aviv, Ashqelon or Beersheba. Otherwise the journey involves travelling to Erez at the northern entrance to the Gaza Strip, and by shared taxi through the Strip, changing at several points. Whether you can use this route will depend on the political situation in Gaza. When things are good, there are shared taxis (*sherut* in Hebrew) from Jaffa to Erez (Israeli buses from Tel Aviv and Ashqelon will leave you 4km short at Yad Mordecai), and from there to Gaza City and then on to Rafah. You may have to walk or charter a taxi for the 5km from Rafah to the border post. Once you're across the border, the Egyptian guards will examine your passport and visa (which cannot be issued at Rafah) and demand the entry tax.

You are not allowed to drive rented cars or 4WDs across the Israeli–Egyptian border. The Israeli Airports Authority website at ⓦwww.iaa.gov.il/Rashat/en-US/Rashot has further information on both the Rafah and Taba border crossings.

Finally, the Israeli airline El Al (ⓣ03/977 1111) **flies** from Ben Gurion (the airport serving Tel Aviv and Jerusalem) to Cairo twice a week, and EgyptAir subsidiary Air Sinai (ⓣ03/510 2481 to 4) does the same route three times weekly.

From Jordan

Royal Jordanian (☎06/567 8321) and EgyptAir (☎06/463 0011) operate expensive daily **flights** from Amman to Cairo. Royal Jordanian also fly from Amman to Sharm el-Sheikh, El-Arish and Alexandria.

Direct **buses** do the 21-hour journey **from Amman** to Cairo, but they are neither very pleasant nor very economical. The main operator is JETT, on King Hussein Street (☎06/569 6151), 900m north from Abdali station. At the time of writing, departures are at 6.30am, four days a week. Tickets costs US$58 one-way, not including the JD6 departure tax. Buses should arrive at Sinai bus terminal in Abbassiya, Cairo, but they sometimes terminate at Almaza in Heliopolis (see p.89). JETT's main competitor on the route is Afana, next door to JETT and at Abdali station (☎06/568 1560), whose buses leave from Middle East Circle (Duwaar ash-Sharq al-Aswat). Unless speed is of the essence, however (in which case flying is a better option), you'd do far better to break the journey at Aqaba or in Sinai.

From Aqaba, the quickest route to Egypt is by land via Eilat in Israel, using local buses. Disincentives are the telltale Taba border stamp (see box, p.66), and the hefty exit and entry taxes (totalling around US$47) which are payable at Taba. Alternatively, there are **ferries and catamarans** to Nuweiba in the Sinai operated by the Arab Bridge Maritime Company (ⓦwww .abmaritime.com.jo). The passenger catamaran takes just an hour to complete the crossing to Nuweiba (US$45), while the ferry (US$35), which can carry bicycles and motor vehicles, takes three hours but is notoriously unpunctual. You can buy tickets for either service from the company's offices in Amman (beside the Royal Jordanian building just off 7th Circle; ☎06/585 9554) or Aqaba (downtown near the *China* restaurant; ☎03/201 3237), from agents in Aqaba or up to an hour before departure at the passenger terminal itself, 9km south of Aqaba (open daily 24hr; ☎03/201 3891). The terminal is served by local buses from Aqaba's Corniche, or costs an exorbitant JD4 to reach by taxi.

Whether you're travelling by ferry or by catamaran, a tax of JD6 is payable on departure. On arrival in Nuweiba, you can obtain a Sinai-only visa at the port (for more on visas, see p.65).

From Libya and Sudan

It is possible to enter Egypt **from Libya**, by bus or service taxi direct from Tripoli or Benghazi (the service taxi drops you at Midan Opera in central Cairo, the bus at Almaza terminal in Heliopolis), or by taking a bus or service taxi from Benghazi to Al-Burdi, where there are vehicles to the border. On the Egyptian side, you can get a service taxi on to Sollum, from where there are service taxis to Mersa Matrouh, plus daily buses which continue to Alexandria.

From Sudan, there's a weekly ferry from Wadi Halfa up Lake Nasser to Aswan, which should connect with the train from Khartoum, though most Western travellers use the service in the opposite direction (see p.448). There is a road from Wadi Halfa to Aswan, and on the coast from Port Sudan to Halaib, but at the time of writing the Egyptian authorities do not allow foreigners to enter via either route. If you are coming north with a vehicle, you will have to arrange to take a barge from Wadi Halfa up to Aswan.

Airlines, agents and operators

Contact details for international companies in the listings below are given selectively, reflecting the territories from which they offer flights or tours to Egypt.

Online booking

ⓦ**www.ebookers.com** (in UK), ⓦwww.ebookers .ie (in Ireland).

ⓦ**www.expedia.co.uk** (in UK), ⓦwww.expedia .com (in US), ⓦwww.expedia.ca (in Canada)

ⓦ**www.opodo.com**

ⓦ**www.orbitz.com** (in US)

ⓦ**www.travelocity.co.uk** (in UK), ⓦwww .travelocity.com (in US), ⓦwww.travelocity.ca (in Canada), ⓦwww.zuji.com.au (in Australia), ⓦwww.zuji.co.nz (in New Zealand)

Airlines

Aer Lingus Ireland ☎0818/365 000, ⓦwww.aerlingus.com.

Air Arabia ⓦwww.airarabia.com.

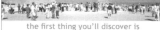
Air France US ☎1-800/237-2747, Canada
☎1-800/667-2747, UK ☎0870/142-4343, ⓦwww
.airfrance.com.
Air New Zealand New Zealand ☎0800/737 000,
ⓦwww.airnewzealand.com.
Alitalia US ☎1-800/223-5730, Canada
☎1-800/361-8336, UK ☎0870/544 8259, Ireland
☎01/677 5171, ⓦwww.alitalia.com.
American Airlines US ☎1-800/433-7300,
ⓦwww.aa.com.
Austrian Airlines US ☎1-800/843-0002,
UK ☎0870/124 2625, Ireland ☎1800/509 142,
Australia ☎1800/642 438 or 02/9251 6155,
ⓦwww.aua.com.
British Airways US and Canada ☎1-800/
AIRWAYS, UK ☎0870/850 9850, Ireland
☎1890/626 747, Australia ☎1300/767 177,
New Zealand ☎09/966 9777, ⓦwww.ba.com.
CSA (Czech Airlines) UK ☎0870/444 3747, Ireland
☎01 818 20 0014, ⓦwww.czechairlines.com.
Delta US and Canada ☎1-800/221-1212,
ⓦwww.delta.com.
EgyptAir US ☎1-800/334-6787 or 212/315-
0900, Canada ☎416/960-0009, UK ☎020/7734
2343, Australia ☎1300/309-767,
ⓦwww.egyptair.com.eg.
El Al US ☎1-800/223-6700 or 212/768-9200,
UK ☎020/7957 4100, Ireland ☎01/670 4731,
ⓦwww.elal.co.il.

Emirates US ☎1-800/777-3999, Australia
☎02/9290 9700, New Zealand ☎09/968 2200,
South Africa ☎0861/3647 2837, ⓦwww.emirates
.com.
Ethiopian Airlines US ☎1-800/445-2733, UK
☎020/8987 7000, South Africa ☎011/616 7624
ⓦwww.flyethiopian.com.
First Choice UK ☎0870/902 8021,
ⓦwww.firstchoice.co.uk.
Flythomascook.com UK ⓦwww.flythomascook
.com.
Gulf Air US and Canada ☎1-888/FLY-GULF,
UK ☎0870/777 1717, Ireland ☎0818/272 818,
Australia ☎1300/366-337, South Africa ☎011/202
7626; ⓦwww.gulfairco.com.
Iberia US ☎1-800/772-4642, UK ☎0870/609
0500, Ireland ☎0810/462 000, ⓦwww.iberia
.com.
Kenya Airways South Africa ☎011/881 9783,
ⓦwww.kenya-airways.com.
KLM US ☎1-800/225-2525, UK ☎0870/507
4074, ⓦwww.klm.com.
Lufthansa US ☎1-800/645-3880, Canada
☎1-800/563-5954, UK ☎0870/837 7747, Ireland
☎01/844 5544, Australia ☎1300 655 727, New
Zealand ☎09/303 1529, ⓦwww.lufthansa.com.
Malaysia Airlines Australia ☎13 26 27, New
Zealand ☎0800/777 747, ⓦwww
.malaysia-airlines.com.

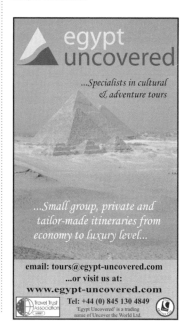

Malev Hungarian Airlines ☏1-212/566-9944, Canada ☏1-800 665-6363, UK ☏0870/909 0577, Ireland ☏01/844 4303, ⓦwww.malev.hu.

Olympic Airways US ☏1-800/223-1226, Canada ☏416/964-2720, UK ☏0870/606 0460, Australia ☏02/9251 2044, ⓦwww.olympic-airways.com.

Qantas Airways Australia ☏13 13 13, New Zealand ☏0800/808 767 or 09/357 8900, ⓦwww.qantas.com.

Qatar Airways South Africa ☏011/523 2928, ⓦwww.qatarairways.com.

Saudi Arabian Airlines US ☏1-800/4-SAUDIA, UK ☏020/7798 9898, ⓦwww.saudiairlines.com.

Singapore Airlines Australia ☏13 1011, New Zealand ☏0800/808-909, ⓦwwwsingaporeair.com.

Swiss US & Canada ☏1-877/FLY-SWIS, UK ☏0845/601 0956, ⓦwww.swiss.com.

Thomsonfly UK ☏0870/190 0737, ⓦwww.thomsonfly.com.

Tunisair UK ☏020/7734 7644, ⓦwww.tunisair.com.tn.

United Airlines US ☏1-800/241-6522, ⓦwww.united.com.

Agents and operators

Abercrombie & Kent US ☏1-800/554-7016, ⓦwww.abercrombiekent.com, UK ☏0845/070 0612, ⓦwww.abercrombiekent.co.uk, Australia ☏1300/851 800, ⓦwww.abercrombiekent.com.au, New Zealand ☏0800/441 638. Upmarket firm with a number of Egypt tours including some led by Egyptologists; also creates custom packages.

Ancient World Tours UK ☏020/7917 9494, ⓦwww.ancient.co.uk. In-depth archeological and historical tours led by experts. Claims to visit more sites in Egypt than any other operator, including several that no one else covers, and some that few tourists ever reach.

Crusader Travel UK ☏020/8744 0474, ⓦwww.crusadertravel.com. Experienced, specialist agent for diving holidays, which helps clients shop around the tour operators. Also does flight-only charter deals to Sharm, Hurghada, Mersa Alam and Luxor. Can be booked online from any country.

Discover Egypt UK ☏ 0870/755 8466, ⓦwww.discoveregypt.co.uk. Packages and tailor-made itineraries including Nile cruises and multi-centre holidays.

Egypt Tours US ☏1-800/TO-EGYPT, ⓦwww.egyptours.com. Packages ranging from a six-night highlights tour to a 23-night "In Depth" trip, as well as combined tours with Jordan and Israel.

Exodus UK ☏0870/240 5550, Ireland c/o Abbey Travel ☏01/804 7153, Australia and New Zealand c/o Peregrine (see below), US and Canada c/o GAP ☏866/732-5885, South Africa c/o Mask Expeditions ☏011/807 3333, ⓦwww.exodus.co.uk. A variety of overland adventure tours, including a fourteen-day "Egyptian Discoverer" tour with a Nile cruise from Aswan to Luxor, a day in Hurghada and two nights in Cairo; other options include diving and desert safaris.

Explore Worldwide UK ☏0870/333 4001, US c/o Adventure Center ☏1-800/227-8747, Canada c/o Trek Holidays ☏1-888/456 3522, Ireland c/o Maxwells Tours ☏01/677 9479, Australia c/o Adventure World ☏02/8913 0700, New Zealand c/o Adventure World ☏09/524 5118, South Africa c/o Shiralee Travel ☏028/313 0526, ⓦwww.explore.co.uk. Highly respected small-groups adventure-tour operator with several Egyptian programmes, including walking and trekking, cultural tours, desert adventures and a riverboat-based tour of the Temples of Middle Egypt.

Explorer Tours UK ☏0845/644 7090, ⓦwww.explorers.co.uk. Red Sea holidays with PADI courses from £425 including flight and lessons.

Guerba Expeditions UK ☏01373/826611, ⓦwww.guerba.co.uk. Long-established Africa-overland experts with a variety of Egyptian tours, and a three-month Cairo–Cape Town tour. Online bookings from any country.

Imaginative Traveller UK ☏0800/316 2717 or 01473/667 337, ⓦwww.imaginative-traveller.com. An assortment of tours, including an eight-day "Splendours of Egypt" tour and a four-day Cairo city break. Online bookings from any country.

Libra Holidays UK ☏0871/226 0446, ⓦwww.libraholidays.co.uk. Package tours and charter flights.

North South Travel UK ☏01245/608 291, ⓦwww.northsouthtravel.co.uk. Travel agency whose profits are used to support projects in the developing world, especially the promotion of sustainable tourism.

Oonasdivers UK ☏01323/648 924, ⓦwww.oonasdivers.com. Red Sea diving holidays, PADI courses, liveaboards and, for non-divers, the (cheaper) option of a beach holiday at the same resort.

Peregrine Adventures Australia ☏1300/854 444 or 03/8601 4444, UK 01635/872 300, ⓦwww.peregrine.net.au. A wide range of Egypt tours and Egypt/Jordan combinations. Their budget tour brand, Gecko's, offers adventure tours.

Regaldive UK ☏0870/220 1777, ⓦwww.regal-diving.co.uk. Dive packages at Dahab, El Gouna, Hurghada, Safaga, Sharm el-Sheikh and other bases, including courses for everyone from beginners to advanced, plus mini-safari add-ons and wreck trips.

Scubasnacks UK ☏0870/746 1266, ⓦwww.scubasnacks.co.uk. Seven-day packages based at Dahab, El-Quseir, Hurghada, Mersa Alam or Sharm el-Sheikh, plus liveaboard holidays.

Soliman Travel UK ☎ 0870/027 5230, ⓦ www
.solimantravel.co.uk. One of the longest-established
UK-based Egypt tour operators, with charter flights
and a large range of packages and tailor-made
holidays, mainly in five-star accommodation.
Somak Holidays UK ☎ 020/8423 3000, ⓦ www
.somak.co.uk. City breaks, Nile cruises and
combination packages.
STA Travel US ☎ 1-800/781-4040, ⓦ www
.statravel.com, Canada ☎ 1-888/427-5639,
ⓦ www.statravel.ca, UK ☎ 0870/1630-026,
ⓦ www.statravel.co.uk, Australia ☎ 1300/733
035, ⓦ www.statravel.com.au, New Zealand
☎ 0508/782 872, ⓦ www.statravel.co.nz, South
Africa ☎ 0861/781 781, ⓦ www.statravel.co.za.
Specialists in independent travel; also student IDs,
travel insurance, and more. Good discounts for
students and under-26s.
Swim with Dolphins UK ☎ 0845/345 9052,
ⓦ www.dolphinswims.co.uk. Luxury liveaboards on
the Red Sea and Sinai desert adventure safaris. Can
be booked online from any country.

Thomas Cook Canada ☎ 877/894-4333, ⓦ www
.thomascook.ca, UK ☎ 0870/750 5711, ⓦ www
.thomascook.com. Thomas Cook more or less
created tourism in Egypt with his first escorted
tour in 1869, and the country remains a speciality.
The firm offers a variety of deals in Cairo, Luxor
and several Red Sea resorts, as well as tours and
charter flights.
Trailfinders UK ☎ 0845/058 5858, Ireland
☎ 01/677 7888, Australia ☎ 1300/780 212,
ⓦ www.trailfinders.com. Well-informed and efficient
agent for independent travellers.
USIT Republic of Ireland ☎ 01/602 1904, Northern
Ireland ☎ 028/9032 7111, ⓦ www.usit.ie. Ireland's
main student and youth travel specialists.
Ya'lla Tours US ☎ 800/644-1595, ⓦ www
.yallatours.com. An interesting range of packages
including a "Footsteps of the Holy Family" tour to sites
of biblical significance, or four-night breaks in Cairo,
with optional add-ons to Alexandria, the Fayoum or
Mount Sinai.

Health

The majority of visitors to Egypt experience nothing worse than a bout or two of diarrhoea. Change of diet and climate accounts for most visitors' health problems. Some people adapt quickly, others take longer, especially children and older people. If you're only here for a week or two, it makes sense to be cautious, while for longer-staying visitors it is worth trying to acclimatize.

Unless you're coming from an area where yellow fever is endemic (in practice this means countries in sub-Saharan Africa), there are no compulsory **inoculations** for Egypt, though you should always be up to date with polio and tetanus. It's also worth being vaccinated against typhoid, which occasionally flares up in parts of Egypt. The cholera shot is generally acknowledged to be worthless. Vaccinations for onward travel to Asia or East Africa can be obtained in Cairo (see p.266). Visitors planning to stay a long time in Egypt or the Middle East should consider a Hepatitis A (Havrix mono-dose) shot; this can be expensive, but with a booster a year later it lasts for ten years.

Hepatitis B is transmitted like HIV, through body fluids, so you will be protected from it by the same precautions that you take against HIV; immunization is only really necessary for medical workers.

Health hazards

Tap water in Egyptian towns and cities is heavily chlorinated and mostly safe to drink, but is unpalatable and rough on tender stomachs. In rural areas, Sinai campsites and desert resthouses there's a fair risk of contaminated water. Consequently, most tourists stick to bottled mineral water, which is widely available and tastes better. However, excessive fear of tap water is unjustified and hard to sustain in practice if you're here for long. Once your stomach has adjusted, it's usually okay to drink it without going to the hassle of purifying it using Halazone tablets or iodine crystals, or by boiling.

What you should avoid is any contact with stagnant water that might harbour **bilharzia** (schistosomiasis) flukes. These minute worms, which breed in the blood vessels of the abdomen and liver (the main symptom is blood in the urine), infest irrigation canals and the slower stretches of the River Nile. Don't drink or swim there, nor walk barefoot in the mud, or even on grass that's wet with Nile water. The saline pools of desert oases are fine to bathe in.

Heat and dust

Many visitors experience problems with Egypt's intense heat, particularly in the south. Wear a hat and loose-fitting clothes (preferably not synthetic fabrics), and a high-factor sunscreen to protect yourself from **sunburn**, especially during summer (do wear a T-shirt when snorkelling, for the same reason). Try to avoid going out in the middle of the day. In non-air-conditioned environments, you might employ the traditional Egyptian method of sprinkling water on the ground to cool the surrounding area by evaporation – it also levels the dust.

Because sweat evaporates immediately in the dry atmosphere, you can easily become **dehydrated** without realizing it. Dehydration is exacerbated by both alcohol and caffeine. Drink plenty of other fluids (at least three litres per day; twice as much if you're exerting yourself) and take a bit of extra salt with your food.

Heat exhaustion – signified by headaches, dizziness and nausea – is treated by resting in a cool place and drinking plenty of water or juice with a pinch of salt. An intense headache, heightened body temperature, flushed skin and the cessation of sweating are symptoms of **heatstroke**, which can be fatal if not treated immediately. The whole body must be cooled by immersion in tepid water, or the application of wet towels, and medical assistance should be sought. If walking long distances in the sun, it is vital to carry drinking water. A sunhat can be drenched with water, wrung to stop it dripping, and worn

wet so that the evaporation of the water cools your head – you'll be amazed at how quickly it dries out.

Less seriously, visitors may suffer from **prickly heat**, an itchy rash caused by excessive perspiration trapped beneath the skin. Wearing loose clothing, keeping cool and bathing often will help relieve the symptoms.

Desert **dust** – or grit and smog in Cairo – may cause your eyes to itch and water. Contact-lens users should wear glasses instead, at least part of the time. If ordinary eye drops don't help, try antihistamine decongestant eye drops such as Vernacel, Vascon-A or Optihist. Persistent irritation may indicate trachoma, a contagious infection which is easily cured by antibiotics at an early stage, but eventually causes blindness if left untreated.

Spending time in the desert, you might find that your sinuses get painfully irritated by wind-borne dust. Covering your nose and mouth with a scarf helps prevent this, while olbas oil or a nasal decongestant spray (available at pharmacies) can relieve the symptoms.

Digestive complaints

Almost every visitor to Egypt gets **diarrhoea** at some stage. Rare meat and raw shellfish top the danger list, which descends via creamy sauces down to salads, juices, raw fruit and vegetables. Visitors who insist on washing everything (and cleaning their teeth) in mineral water are overreacting. Just use common sense, and accustom your stomach gradually to Egyptian cooking. Asking for dishes to be served very hot (*sukhna awi*) will reduce the risk of catching anything.

If you have diarrhoea, the best initial treatment is to simply adapt your diet, using drugs only as a last resort. Plain boiled rice and vegetables are the best things to eat, while greasy or spicy food, caffeine, alcohol, and most fruit and dairy products should be avoided (although some say that bananas and prickly pears can help, while yoghurt provides a form of protein that your body can easily absorb). Most importantly, keep your bodily fluids topped up by drinking plenty of bottled water. Especially if children are affected, you may also want to add **rehydration salts** (brands include Rehydran) to the water, or failing that, half a teaspoon of salt and eight of sugar per litre of water, which will help the body to absorb the fluid more efficiently.

Drugs like Imodium or Lomotil can plug you up, undermining your body's efforts to rid itself of infection, but can be handy to stabilize your gut if you have to travel or if symptoms aren't clearing after a couple of days. Avoid Enterovioform, which is still available in Egypt despite being suspected of damaging the optic nerve. Antinal (nifurox-azide) is widely prescribed against diarrhoea in Egypt, and available over the counter in pharmacies. Note that having diarrhoea can make drugs less effective if taken orally (contraceptive pills for example), as they can pass straight through your system without being absorbed.

If symptoms persist longer than a few days, or if you develop a fever or pass blood in your faeces, get medical help immediately, since diarrhoea can also be a symptom of serious infection. Accompanied by vomit-ing and fever, it may indicate **typhoid**, which responds well to antibiotics. Rarer is **cholera**, which requires urgent treatment with anti-biotics and rehydration fluids; it is marked by a sudden onset of acute diarrhoea and cramps, and tends to occur in epidemics rather than isolated cases. Except for the "rice-water shits" typical of cholera, similar symptoms occur with bacillary **dysentery**, which is treated with antibiotics. Amoebic dysentery is harder to shift and can cause permanent damage if untreated. The normal remedy is the heavy-duty antibiotic metro-nidazole (Flagyl), which should only be taken under medical supervision.

Rabies and malaria

Rabies is endemic in Egypt, where many wild animals (including bats, sometimes found in temples, tombs and caves) carry the disease. Avoid touching *any* strange animal, wild or domestic. Treatment must be given between exposure to the disease and the onset of symptoms; once these appear, rabies is invariably fatal. If you think you've been exposed, return home and seek help immediately.

Malaria, spread by the anopheles mosquito, does exist during the summer

months in the Fayoum, but not to the extent that warrants the use of malaria pills (unless you are staying for a while in that area). You should, nevertheless, take extra steps to avoid mosquito bites while you are there – use repellent and cover bare skin, espe-cially feet and ankles, after dusk (see below). The first signs of malaria are muscular sore-ness and a low fever; four to eight days later, the characteristic bouts of chills and fever appear. If you suspect that you have it, seek treatment immediately.

Mosquitoes and other bugs

Even without the risk of malaria, **mosquitoes** can make your life a misery. Horribly ubiqui-tous over the summer, these blood-sucking pests are never entirely absent. The only solution is total war, using fans, mosquito coils, rub-on repellent, and perhaps a plug-in vaporizer device, sold at pharmacies. A lot of people in Egypt use citronella oil, obtain-able from many pharmacies, as a repellent, but tests have shown it to be less effective (and to require more frequent applications) than repellents containing DEET (diethyltolu-amide), which are the ones recommended by medical authorities. Xgnat skin gel is an effective natural alternative. Don't forget to put repellent on your feet and ankles if they are uncovered when you go out in the evening. The best guarantee of a bite-less night's sleep is to bring a **mosquito net** to hang from above your bed (if you bring the sort that can be suspended from a single point, you can usually find ways of tying a string across the room to hang it from).

Equally loathsome – and widespread – are **flies**, which transmit various diseases. Only insecticide spray or air conditioning offers any protection. Some cheap hotels harbour fleas, scabies, mites, giant roaches and other bugs. Consult a pharmacist if you find yourself with a persistent skin irritation.

Scorpions and snakes

The danger from scorpions and snakes is minimal, as most species are nocturnal and generally avoid people. However, you shouldn't go barefoot, turn over rocks or stick your hands into dark crevices anywhere off the beaten track. Whereas the sting of larger, darker **scorpions** is no worse than a bad wasp sting, the venom of the pale, slender-clawed *Buthidae* is highly toxic. If stung, cold-pack the affected area and seek medical help immediately.

Egypt has two main types of poisonous snake. **Vipers** vary in colour from sandy to reddish (or sometimes grey) and leave two-fang punctures. The horned viper, Egypt's deadliest snake, is recognizable by its horns. Cobras are recognizable by their distinctive hood and bite mark (a single row of teeth plus fang holes). The smaller Egyptian **cobra** (coloured sandy olive) is found throughout the country, the longer black-necked cobra (which can spit its venom up to three metres) only in the south.

All snakebites should be washed immediately. Stay calm, as panicking sends the venom through your bloodstream more quickly, and get immediate medical help.

HIV and AIDS

Levels of HIV infection are low in Egypt, but so is **AIDS** awareness. One group of particularly vulnerable tourists are Western women going out with Egyptian gigolos in Luxor (see box, p.337), who may not be aware of just how much of an industry that is. Pharmacies in cities plus a few shops in Hurghada and Sinai are the only places in Egypt to sell **condoms** (*kabout*) – either Egyptian-made Tops (liable to rip) or US imports. It's best to bring your own supply.

Women's health

Travelling in the heat and taking antibiotics for an upset stomach make women much more susceptible to vaginal infections. The best precautions are to wash regularly with mild soap, and wear cotton underwear and loose clothing. **Yeast infections** can be treated with Nystatin pessaries (available at pharmacies), "one-shot" Canesten pessaries (bring some from home if you're prone to thrush), or douches of a weak solution of vinegar or lemon juice. Sea bathing can also help. Trichomonas is usually treated with Flagyl, which should only be taken under medical supervision.

Bring your own **contraceptives**, since the only forms widely available in Egypt are old-fashioned, high-dosage pills, the coil, and not too trusty condoms (see above). Cap-users should pack a spare, and enough spermicide and pessaries. If you're on the pill, beware that persistent diarrhoea can render it ineffective. **Sanitary protection** is available from pharmacies in cities and tourist resorts, but seldom anywhere else, so it's wise to bring a supply for your trip.

Medical resources for travellers

UK and Ireland

Hospital for Tropical Diseases Travel Clinic ℡020/7387 5000 or 0845/155 5000, ⊛www.thehtd.org.
MASTA (Medical Advisory Service for Travellers Abroad) ⊛www.masta.org or ℡0113/238 7575 for the nearest clinic.
Travel Medicine Services ℡028/9031 5220.
Tropical Medical Bureau ℡1850/487 674, ⊛www.tmb.ie.

US and Canada

CDC ℡1-877-394-8747, ⊛www.cdc.gov/travel. Official US government travel health site.
International Society for Travel Medicine ⊛www.istm.org. Has a full list of travel health clinics.
Canadian Society for International Health ⊛www.csih.org. Extensive list of travel health centres.

Australia, New Zealand and South Africa

Travellers' Medical and Vaccination Centre ⊛www.tmvc.com.au. Lists travel clinics in Australia, New Zealand and South Africa.

Medical services in Egypt

Pharmacies, found in every town, form the advance guard of Egypt's health service. Egyptian pharmacists are well trained, usually speak English and can dispense a wide range of drugs, including many normally on prescription. If they feel you need a full diagnosis, they can usually recommend a doctor – sometimes working on the premises.

Private **doctors** are just as common as pharmacies, and most speak English or French. They charge for consultations: expect to pay about £E100 a session, which doesn't include drugs, but should cover a follow-up visit.

If you get seriously ill, **hospitals** (*mustashfa*) that are privately run are generally preferable to public-sector ones. Those attached to universities are usually well equipped and competent, but small-town hospitals are often abysmal. Hospitals usually require a cash deposit of at least £E150 (it can go as high as £E1000) to cover the cost of treatment, and often require payment on the spot; you will then have to claim it back from your insurance provider. Despite several good hospitals in Cairo and Alexandria, Egypt is not a country to fall seriously ill in. In particular, if you need surgery, it's best to get back home for it if you can.

Getting around

Egyptian public transport is, on the whole, pretty good. There is an efficient rail network linking the Nile Valley, Delta and Canal Zone, and elsewhere you can travel easily enough by bus or collective (service) taxi. On the Nile you can indulge in feluccas or cruise boats, and in the desert there's the chance to test your camel-riding prowess. For those in a hurry, EgyptAir provides a network of flights.

While you can travel without restriction through most areas of Egypt, **travel permits** are required for the Red Sea Coast beyond Mersa Alam, for desert travel between Bahariya and Siwa oases (permits available in Siwa), and to Ain Della and the Gilf Kebir/Jebel Uwaynat (permits available in Cairo only). Applications for permits require two photos and photocopies of the identifying pages of your passport and your Egyptian entry visa, plus a good justification for your journey. Processing takes anywhere between four and fourteen days. Misr Travel at 1 Sharia Talaat Harb in downtown Cairo (☎02/393 0010, ✉misrtrav @link.com.eg) may be able to help obtain them for some restricted areas; otherwise you'll need to apply to the military, who are best approached via the tourist police. You should not need a permit to travel directly from Mersa Matrouh to the Libyan border, for example if taking a bus or service taxi to Benghazi or Tripoli, but the rules sometimes change, so it is wise to check first.

By rail

Covering a limited network of routes (from Cairo to Alexandria, the Delta and the Canal Zone, along the coast to Mersa Matrouh and up the Nile Valley to Luxor and Aswan, Cairo to Alexandria), Egypt's **trains** are best used for long hauls between the major cities, when air-conditioned services offer a comfier alternative to buses and taxis. For shorter journeys, however, trains are slower and less reliable.

Timetables are not available in leaflet or booklet form, but the Egyptian Railways' website (ⓦwww.egyptrail.gov.eg) allows you to look up schedules for its air-conditioned services. Schedules for sleeper services are available on the website of the company which operates them, Abela (ⓦwww.sleepingtrains.com).

Between Cairo and Alexandria, and between Cairo and Luxor or Aswan, both relatively fast **air-conditioned trains** (including sleepers, also called **wagons-lits**) and snail-like non-air-conditioned local-stop services operate. However, on the Cairo–Luxor/ Aswan route, foreigners are only allowed to use four "**tourist trains**" (one of which is a sleeper), whose compartments are guarded by gun-toting plainclothes cops. Originally this was for protection from "terrorists", but although the danger now seems to have passed, the restriction still applies. You might find yourself needing to circumvent this rule – for example if you got an Egyptian to buy your ticket, or by boarding an ordinary train without a ticket, and buying one from the conductor.

Buying tickets can get complicated at the largest stations, where separate queues eixst for different ticket classes.

Air-conditioned trains, including sleepers

Air-conditioned trains come in three varieties: Turbini, Spanish (or "speed") and French (or "express") services, in decreasing order of speed. They nearly nearly always have two classes of carriage. The most comfortable option is **first class** (*daraga awla*), which has waiter service, reclining armchairs and no standing in the aisles. Unfortunately for those trying to sleep, they also screen videos until midnight. **Second class superior** (*daraga tania mukayyifa*) is less plush and more crowded – but at two-thirds the price of first class it's a real bargain. Occasionally air-conditioned trains will be first or second class only. An ordinary first- or air-conditioned second-class carriage should be comfortable enough to allow sleeping on an overnight journey, at a fraction of the cost of a sleeper.

Seats are **reservable** up to seven days in advance. There is occasional double booking but a little baksheesh to the conductor usually sorts out any problem. One common difficulty is that return tickets can't necessarily be booked at the point of origin. The peak seasons for travel are summer for Alexandria and winter for Upper Egypt.

To give an idea of **fares**, a ticket from Cairo to Luxor costs around £E75 in first class, £E40 in air-conditioned second class, while Aswan to Luxor costs £E35 and £E21 respectively; minor variations occur depending on whether you're on a Turbini, Spanish or French train. **Students** with ISIC cards (see p.64) get at least a third off on all fares except on sleepers. Most travel agencies sell first-class tickets for a small commission, saving you from having to queue.

Wagons-lits (sleepers)

Many tourists cough up for snazzier *wagons-lits*, which may comprise an entire train, or be limited to a couple of carriages tacked on to a regular service. Fares are relatively hefty (though still cheaper than flying) at US$60 one-way from Cairo to Luxor or Aswan. Passengers get a comfortable two-bed cabin (a single traveller can book one exclusively for $80, or pay the normal fare and share with someone of the same sex) with a basin, plus breakfast and dinner, and access to a dining car, a bar and sometimes a disco.

Bookings for *wagons-lits* can be done through branches of Thomas Cook or American Express, or with Abela (Ⓦwww .sleepingtrains.com) or Hamis Travel (℡02/574-9275, Ⓦwww.hamis.com.eg).

Non-air-conditioned trains

Non-air-conditioned trains divide into **ordinary second class** (*daraga tania aadia*), which has padded bench seating, and **third class** (*daraga talata*), which is just wooden benches, with open doors and windows for ventilation. Both classes are invariably crowded, the rolling stock is ancient and often filthy, and schedules fanciful. Few foreigners use them, and the only reason to do so for a long journey is to save money, though on a few routes the only services are non-air-conditioned ones. Over short distances you might enjoy the funky disorder, with peasants and vendors getting on and off at every stop.

There is no advance booking for seats on these services and you needn't queue for a ticket at the station. You simply walk on and buy a ticket from the conductor, paying a small penalty fee (£E1–2).

By bus

Egypt's bus network is divided between three main operators, based in Cairo. The **Upper Egypt Bus Company** serves all points along the Nile Valley, the Fayoum and inner oases, and the Red Sea Coast as far down as El-Quseir. Sinai and the Canal Zone are covered by the **East Delta Bus Company**, whose livery is orange and white. The **West Delta Bus Company**'s vehicles are blue and serve Alexandria, Mersa Matrouh, Siwa Oasis and the Nile Delta. Key routes (from Cairo to Alexandria, Sharm el-Sheikh and Hurghada) are also covered by the **Superjet** company,

Road distances (in kilometres)

	Abu Simbel	Alexandria	Assyut	Aswan	Bahariya	Cairo	Dakhla	Fayoum
Abu Simbel	–	1363	756	290	1391	1145	906	1053
Alexandria	1363	–	607	1073	586	218	1023	311
Assyut	756	607	–	466	757	389	416	297
Aswan	290	1073	466	–	1101	855	616	763
Bahariya	1391	586	757	1101	–	368	485	441
Cairo	1145	218	389	855	368	–	805	113
Dakhla	906	1023	416	616	485	805	–	713
Fayoum	1053	311	297	763	441	113	713	–
Hurghada	800	676	471	510	826	458	598	388
Luxor	514	849	242	224	877	631	392	539
Mersa Alam	585	951	590	340	1347	733	1006	887
Mersa Matrouh	1631	268	875	1341	710	486	2152	579
Port Said	1407	258	651	1117	630	262	1067	375
Rafah	1500	504	744	1210	723	355	1160	468
Sharm el-Sheikh	1685	758	929	1395	908	540	1345	653
Siwa	1811	558	1165	1521	420	776	905	889
Suez	1278	351	522	988	501	133	938	246
Taba	1574	647	818	1284	797	429	1234	542

whose red, black and gold livery explains their nickname, the "Golden Arrows" or "Golden Rockets". Superjet is a subsidiary of the Arab Union Transport Company, which operates international services to Libya, Jordan, Syria and Saudi Arabia. Other operators such as **El Gouna** are entering the field.

Major routes are plied by air-conditioned buses, usually new(ish) and fast – while local routes usually have non-air-conditioned ones, generally old rattletraps. The former are invariably more expensive, but whether their air conditioning actually works depends on the company and the route. Superjet buses not only have air conditioning but also toilets, and they screen videos and sell expensive snacks.

Terminals and bookings

Though most towns have a single bus depot for all destinations, cities such as Cairo and Alexandria have several **terminals** (detailed in the guide). English- or French-speaking staff are fairly common at the larger ones, but rare in the provinces. **Schedules** – usually posted in Arabic only – change frequently, so information in the guide

should be verified in person. Bus information can also be obtained from hotels in Sinai and the oases, and the tourist offices in Luxor, Aswan and the oases.

At city terminals, **tickets** are normally sold from kiosks, up to 24 hours in advance for air-conditioned or long-haul services. In the provinces, tickets may only be available an hour or so before departure, or on the bus itself in the case of through-services, which are often standing-room only when they arrive. Passengers on air-conditioned services are usually assigned a seat (the number is written in Arabic on your ticket), but seats on "local" buses are on a first-come, first-served basis. **Fares** are very reasonable: Cairo to Alexandria costs £E12 by ordinary bus, £E25 on the deluxe Superjet service, while Cairo to Luxor is £E90.

By service taxi

Collective **service taxis** (known as *servees*) are one of the best features of Egyptian transport. They operate on a wide variety of routes and are generally quicker than buses and trains. On the downside, maniacal driving on congested roads calls for strong nerves; accidents are not uncommon. Note also that

Hurghada	Luxor	Mersa Alam	Mersa Matrouh	Port Said	Rafah	Sharm	Siwa	Suez	Taba
800	514	585	1631	1407	1500	1685	1811	1278	1574
676	849	951	268	258	504	758	558	351	647
471	242	590	875	651	744	929	1165	522	818
510	224	340	1341	1117	1210	1395	1521	988	1284
826	877	1347	710	630	723	908	420	501	797
458	631	733	486	262	355	540	776	133	429
598	392	1006	2152	1067	1160	1345	905	938	1234
388	539	887	579	375	468	653	889	246	542
–	286	275	944	579	665	764	998	357	653
286	–	288	1117	893	986	1171	1297	764	1060
275	288	–	1219	854	940	1273	1509	866	1162
944	1117	1219	–	526	772	1026	290	619	915
579	893	854	526	–	246	629	1038	222	518
665	986	940	772	246	–	415	1131	308	182
764	1171	1273	1026	629	415	–	1316	407	233
998	1297	1509	290	1038	1131	1316	–	909	1205
357	764	866	619	222	308	407	909	–	296
653	1060	1162	915	518	182	233	1205	296	–

tourists aren't allowed to use service taxis in the Nile Villey (see p.291 for more).

The taxis are usually big **Peugeot saloons** carrying seven passengers, or **microbuses** (sometimes called *meecros*) seating a dozen people. Most business is along specific routes, with departures more or less throughout the day on the main ones, while cross-desert traffic is restricted to early morning and late afternoon. You just show up at the terminal and ask for a service taxi to your destination (or listen out for drivers shouting out their destinations). As soon as the requisite number of people (or less, if you're willing to pay extra) are assembled, the taxi sets off. Fewer people travel after dark in winter or on Friday, when you might have to wait a while for a ride to a distant town; catching a service taxi to somewhere nearer, and then another one to your final destination, could be quicker.

On established routes, service taxis keep to **fixed fares** for each passenger, up to a third higher than the corresponding bus fare. You can ascertain current rates by asking at your hotel (or the tourist office) or observing what Egyptians pay at the end of the journey.

Alternatively, you can **charter a taxi** for yourself or a group – useful for day excursions or on odd routes. You will have to bargain hard to get a fair price (see entries in the guide).

By car

Driving in Egypt is not for the faint-hearted or inexperienced motorist. Cities, highways, backroads and *pistes* each pose a challenge to drivers' skills and nerve. Pedestrians and carts seem blithely indifferent to heavy traffic. Though accidents are less frequent than you'd think, the crumpled wrecks alongside highways are a constant reminder of the hazards of motoring.

The **minimum age** for driving in Egypt is 25 years, the **maximum age** 70. Foreigners require an International Driving Licence (obtainable from motoring organizations;) .The official **speed limit** outside towns is 90km per hour (100km on the Cairo–Alexandria Desert Road), but on certain stretches it can be as low as 30km per hour. Road signs are similar to those in Europe, but speed limits are posted in Arabic numerals (see box, p.822). Although driving on the right is pretty much universal, other **rules of the road** vary. Traffic in cities is relentless and anarchic, with vehicles weaving to and fro between lanes,

41

signalling by horn. Two beeps means "I'm alongside and about to overtake." A single long blast warns "I can't (won't) stop and I'm coming through!" Extending your hand, fingers raised and tips together, is the signal for "Watch out, don't pass now"; spreading your fingers and flipping them forwards indicates "Go ahead." Although the car in front usually has right of way, buses and trams always take precedence.

On **country roads** – including the two-lane east- and west-bank "highways" along the Nile Valley – trucks and cars routinely overtake in the face of incoming traffic. The passing car usually flashes its lights as a warning, but not always.

Most roads are bumpy, with deep potholes and all manner of traffic, including donkey carts and camels. Beware, especially, of children darting into the road. If you injure someone, relatives may take revenge on the spot. Avoid driving **after dark**, when Egyptians drive without lights, only flashing them on to high beam when they see another car approaching. Wandering pedestrians and animals, obstructions and sand drifts present extra hazards. During spring, flash floods can wash away roads in Sinai. On **pistes** (rough, unpaved tracks in the desert or mountains) there are special problems. You need a good deal of driving and mechanical confidence – and shouldn't attempt such routes if you don't feel your car's up to scratch. **Desert driving** is covered in detail on p.475.

One danger to be aware of is that of **unexploded mines** left over from the Middle East's many conflicts. Because of this, off-road driving is best avoided, especially in the Sinai and along the Red Sea coast. Minefields are usually surrounded by barbed wire (often old and rusty), but are not generally signposted.

Police checkpoints – signposted in English as "Traffic Stations" – occur on the approach roads to towns and oases and along major trunk routes. Foreign motorists are usually waved through, but you might be asked to show your passport or driving licence. In Middle Egypt the checkpoints are militarized, and Egyptian vehicles may be searched for weapons.

Car rental

Renting a car pays obvious dividends if you are pushed for time or plan to visit remote sites, but whether you'd want to drive yourself is another matter – it's not much more expensive to hire a car and driver. Any branch of Misr Travel (see p.38), and numerous local tour agencies, can fix you up with a car and **driver**. An alternative is simply to negotiate with local taxi drivers (see p.41). If you are driving your own vehicle, you are required to re-export it when you leave – even if the car has been wrecked.

A **self-drive car** can be rented through one of the big international rental chains, or with local companies in Egypt (addresses are given in the guide). It's worth shopping around for the best deal, since rates and terms vary considerably. At the cheaper end of the market, you can get a car with unlimited mileage for about £25/US$50 a day. Most companies require a hefty deposit, and not all accept credit cards. Note that you cannot bring a rented car across the border.

Before making a reservation, be sure to find out if you can pick up the car in one city and return it in another. Generally, this is only possible with cars from Hertz, Avis or Budget, found in the main cities and tourist centres. And before setting out, make sure the car comes with spare tyre, tool kit and full documentation – including insurance cover, which is compulsory with all rentals.

Car rental agencies

Avis US ☎1-800/230-4898, Canada ☎1-800/272-5871, UK ☎0870/606 0100, Republic of Ireland ☎021/428 1111, Australia ☎13 63 33 or 02/9353 9000, New Zealand ☎09/526 2847 or 0800/655 111, ⊛www.avis.com.
Budget US ☎1-800/527-0700, Canada ☎1-800/268-8900, UK ☎0870/156 5656, Australia ☎1300/362 848, New Zealand ☎0800/283 438, ⊛www.budget.com.
Hertz US & Canada ☎1-800/654-3131, UK ☎020/7026 0077, Republic of Ireland ☎01/870 5777, Australia ☎03/9698 2555, New Zealand ☎0800/654 321, ⊛www.hertz.com.

Fuel and breakdowns

Petrol (*benzin*) and diesel stations are plentiful in larger towns but few and far between in rural and desert areas. Replace oil/air filters regularly, lest impurities in the fuel, and Egypt's ubiquitous dust, clog up the engine.

Egyptian **mechanics** are usually excellent at coping with breakdowns, and all medium-sized towns have garages (most with a range of spare parts for French, German and Japanese cars). But be aware that if you break down miles from anywhere, you'll probably end up paying a lot to get a truck to tow you back.

Vehicle insurance

All car-rental agreements must be sold along with third-party liability insurance, by law. Though accident and damage insurance should be included, always make sure. In the case of an **accident**, get a written report from the police and from the doctor who first treats any injuries, without which your insurance may not cover the costs. Reports are written in Arabic.

Driving your own vehicle, you will need to take out **Egyptian insurance**. Policies are sold by the insurance companies Al-Chark (℡02/575-3265, Ⓦwww.alchark.com) and Misr Insurance (℡02/335-5350, Ⓦwww .misrins.com); offices are found in most towns and at border crossings. Premiums vary according to the size, horsepower and value of the vehicle.

Motorbikes and bicycles

Motorcycling could be a good way to travel around Egypt, but the red tape involved in bringing your own bike is diabolical (ask your national motoring organization and the Egyptian Consulate for details). It's difficult to rent a machine except in Luxor or Hurghada. Bikers should be especially wary of potholes, sand and rocks, besides other traffic on the roads.

Bicycles, useful for getting around small towns and reaching local sights or beaches, can be rented in Luxor, Aswan, Hurghada, Siwa Oasis and other places for a modest sum. Cycling in big cities or over long distances is not advisable. Traffic is murderous, the heat brutal, and foreign cyclists are sometimes stoned by children (particularly in the Delta). If you're determined to cycle the **Nile Valley**, you may do so only as part of

a convoy between Luxor and Aswan - if the police allow it

Most towns have a wealth of general **repair shops**, well used to servicing local bikes and mopeds. Though unlikely to have the correct spare parts for your make of bike, they can usually sort out some kind of temporary solution.

Hitching

The possibility of hitching is largely confined to areas with minimal public transport (where anything that moves is considered fair game) or trunk routes (if passing service taxis or scheduled buses are full). Since you'll probably end up paying anyway, there's no point in hitching unless you have to. Indeed, foreigners who hitch where proper transport is available may inspire contempt rather than sympathy. Women should never hitch without a male companion.

In the countryside and the desert, where buses may be sporadic or non-existent, it is standard practice for **lorries** (*camions*) and **pick-up trucks** (*bijous*) to carry and charge passengers. You may be asked to pay a little more than the locals, or have to bargain over a price, but it's straightforward enough. Getting rides from tractors is another possibility in rural areas.

Also noteworthy are **pilgrim convoys**, bound for the monasteries of Wadi Natrun, St Paul or St Anthony, or remoter sites to celebrate a festival such as the moulid of St Damyanah (p.636) or Sheikh al-Shazli (see box, p.756).

By air

In general, it's only worth flying if your time is very limited, or for the view – the Nile Valley and Sinai look amazing from the air, and the trip from Aswan to Abu Simbel (see p.463) is easiest by plane. **EgyptAir** flies between Cairo and Alexandria, Mersa Matrouh, Sharm el-Sheikh, Assyut, Hurghada, Luxor, Aswan and Abu Simbel, as well as between Aswan and Luxor and between Aswan and Abu Simbel. Details of flights and the addresses of local offices appear in the text.

Domestic **fares** are calculated in US$ but payable in Egyptian currency, backed by an exchange receipt. As a guide to prices, a one-way economy-class ticket from Cairo to

Luxor costs about £80/US$145; return fares are double the one-way fares. In the winter season, you would be lucky to get any kind of flight between Cairo and Luxor, Aswan, Abu Simbel or Sharm without booking at least a week ahead. Always reconfirm 72 hours prior to the journey, as overbooking is commonplace.

By boat

The colonial tradition of **Nile cruises**, familiar from films and novels, has spawned an industry deploying 240 steamers. Most boats start off in Luxor, sailing down to Aswan (others start here), with stops at Esna, Edfu and Kom Ombo, over three to five days.

The most reliable cruises are generally those sold in association with package holidays, and there are some excellent cut-price offers available for as little as £600 from the UK or US$2000 from North America for a week's cruise, including the air fare. In Egypt you can arrange a four-day trip on the spot for around £160/US$300. All these prices are per person, in a twin cabin. Prices escalate dramatically with the luxury quotient.

If looking around for a Nile cruise once you've arrived in Egypt, shop around and don't necessarily go for the cheapest deal – some boats leave a lot to be desired in terms of hygiene and living conditions. If at all possible, try to look around the vessel first. The luxurious boats with swimming pools can be wonderful, but not all offer value for money. The best deals are available from local agents (or directly from the boats) in Luxor and Aswan. Beware in particular the overpriced trips sold by touts and some hotels in Cairo (see box, p.88).

Feluccas, the lateen-sailed boats used on the Nile since antiquity, still serve as transport along many stretches of the river. Favoured by tourists for sunset cruises, they allow you to experience the changing moods of the Nile while lolling in blissful indolence. Many visitors opt for longer felucca cruises, stopping at the temples between Aswan and Luxor. While it's easy to arrange a cruise yourself (see pp.319–321), several tour operators do offer packages.

Local **ferries**, which are generally battered, crowded and cheap, cross the Nile and the Suez Canal at various points. There are also smarter tourist ferries between Luxor and the West Bank, but it's more fun to use the ordinary boats.

Long-distance services are confined to the Red Sea and the Gulf of Aqaba, where the slow boats of yore have been superseded by a **catamaran** that zips over from Hurghada to Sharm el-Sheikh four times a week, in just ninety minutes. The £25/US$45 fare isn't much more than is charged by the last of the old boats (which take over five hours), and is worth it to avoid the long overland journey via Suez, requiring the best part of a day. Another catamaran (plus an ordinary ferry) runs from Nuweiba to the Jordanian port of Aqaba.

City transport

Most Egyptian towns are small enough to cover on foot, especially if you stay in a hotel near the centre. In larger cities, however, local transport is definitely useful. Learn to recognize Arabic numerals and you can take full advantage of the cheap **buses**, **minibuses** and **trams** that cover most of Alexandria and Cairo (which also has river taxis and an excellent metro). Equally ubiquitous are four-seater **taxis,** which often operate on a shared basis, making stops to pick up passengers heading in the same direction.

To hail a cab, pick a major thoroughfare with traffic heading in the right direction, stand on the kerb, and wave and holler out your destination as one approaches. If the driver's interested he'll stop, whereupon you can state your destination again, in more detail. If the driver starts talking money, say "*maalesh*" (forget it) and look for another cab.

Don't expect drivers to speak English or know the location of every street; you may need to identify a major landmark or thoroughfare in the vicinity of your destination and state that instead. If your destination is obscure or hard to pronounce, get it written down in Arabic. Near the end of the journey, direct the driver to stop where you want (bearing in mind one-way systems and other obstacles) with "*hina/hinak kwayes*"(here/there's okay).

Calèches – horse-drawn buggies, also known as **hantoor** – are primarily tourist transport, and you'll be accosted by drivers in Alexandria, a few parts of Cairo, and most of all in Luxor and Aswan. Fares are high by the standards of local taxis and, despite supposed tariffs set by the local councils, are in practice negotiable. In a few small towns, mostly in Middle Egypt, the *hantoor* remains part of local city transport. Ask locals about fares before climbing on board, or simply pay what you see fit at the end. Some of the horses and buggies are in pristine condition; others painful to behold. Tourists can help by admonishing drivers who abuse their animals or gallop their horses, by not travelling more than four to a carriage, and by contributing to the Brooke Hospital for Animals (see box, right). Boycotting the worst offenders may work, but it would be wrong to judge all owners of neglected animals harshly, for many simply can't afford to take their horses off the streets.

A note on **addresses**: the words for street (*sharia*), avenue (*tariq*) and square (*midan*) always precede the name. Narrower thoroughfares may be termed *darb*, *haret*, *sikket* or *zuqaq*. *Bab* signifies a medieval gate, after which certain quarters

Founded in 1934, the **Brooke Hospital for Animals** (ⓦwww.thebrooke.org) provides free treatment for any animal brought to the clinic, and rescues abandoned ones. They have clinics in Cairo, Luxor, Edfu, Aswan, Alexandria and Mersa Matrouh, as well as in a number of other countries. Tourists are welcome to visit the Brooke clinics in Egypt (preferably by arrangement) and can send donations to the Brooke Hospital for Animals, Broadmead House, 21 Panton St, London SW1Y 4DR, UK. Another charity working in the same field is **Animal Care in Egypt** (ⓦwww.ace-egypt.org.uk), which has a clinic in Luxor.

are named (for example, Bab el-Khalq in Cairo); *kubri* a bridge; and *souk* a market. Whole blocks often share a single street number, which may be in Arabic numerals (see also p.822), but are commonly not shown at all.

Accommodation

The main tourist centres offer a broad spectrum of accommodation, with everything from luxury palaces – familiar from movies such as Death on the Nile – to homely pensions and flea-ridden dives. Even in high season, in Cairo, Sinai or the Nile Valley, you should be able to find something in your preferred range. Elsewhere, the choice is generally more limited, with only basic lodgings available in some of the desert oases. Cairo is generally more expensive for accommodation of all types.

Hotels

Egyptian hotels are loosely categorized into **star ratings**, ranging from five-star deluxe class down to one-star. Below this range, there are also unclassified hotels and *pensions*, some of them tailored to foreign backpackers, others mostly used by Egyptians.

Standards vary within any given category or price band – and from room to room in

many places. The categorizations tend to have more meaning in the higher bands; once you're down to one or two stars, the differences are almost negligible.

Deluxe hotels are almost exclusively modern and chain-owned (Sofitel, Mövenpick, Hilton, etc), with swimming pools, bars, restaurants, air conditioning and all the usual facilities. **Four-star** hotels can be

45

Accommodation price codes

All the establishments listed in this book have been graded according to the categories listed below, representing the cost, including tax, of the **cheapest double room** in high season (winter in Upper Egypt and Sinai, summer in Alexandria). For places that offer **dorm beds** or charge on a singles basis, rates per person are given in £E. Note that most hotels in categories ⑤ to ⑨ quote rates in US dollars, but will accept payment in £E. For the purposes of ready reckoning, we have taken the exchange rate as US$1 = £E6.

① **Under £E50** The rate for a basic room in a no-star hotel. Singles are rare, solo travellers may have to share with strangers or pay for a double room.

② **£E50–100** A reasonable unclassified or one-star hotel or *pension*, containing a mixture of rooms with shared and private facilities, and in most cases comfortable enough for a shortish stay.

③ **£E100–150** Mostly one- or two-star hotels, with the odd three-star place: the facilities may amount to no more than in the previous category, or be considerably better, depending on the age and location of the hotel.

④ **£E150–200** Largely three-star places, some rather aged, but there are many new ones in Hurghada, Luxor and Aswan. Rooms should have a/c, a phone, TV and fridge. There's almost certain to be a restaurant on the premises, and possibly a disco.

⑤ **£E200–300** Posher three-star places, which in Luxor, Sinai or Hurghada could well have a pool.

⑥ **US$50–75 (£E300–450)** Top three- and ordinary four-star hotels, at which you can usually take a pool and a/c for granted, although the odd place with neither may charge such rates for half- or full-board accommodation.

⑦ **US$75–150 (£E450–900)** Four-star or relatively low-priced five-star. There are scores along the Red Sea coast, where the deal may include half-board.

⑧ **US$150–250 (£E900–1500)** A deluxe hotel, with a gym, shops, several restaurants, a/c, room service and all the trimmings.

⑨ **Above US$250 (£E1500)** The very ritziest five-star hotels and holiday villages.

more characterful, including some famous names from the old tradition of Egyptian tourism: places like the *Old Cataract* in Aswan and the *Winter Palace* in Luxor. Again, all hotels in this class are air conditioned, with a pool, café and restaurant, etc. They merge into **three-star** hotels, among which there is again the odd gem, though most are 1970s-style towers, now becoming a little shabby. Facilities like plumbing and air conditioning get a lot less reliable, too.

Down at the **two- and one-star** level, you rarely get air conditioning, though better places will supply fans, and old-style buildings with balconies, high ceilings and louvred windows are well designed to cope with the heat. Conversely, some places can be pretty shabby and also distinctly chilly in winter, as they rarely have any form of heating.

Some of the cheaper hotels are classified as **pensions**, which makes little difference in terms of facilities, but tends to signify family ownership and a friendlier ambience.

At the cheap end of the scale, in the most popular tourist towns, like Luxor and Hurghada, you also get "**student hotels**", specifically aimed at backpackers. They are often quite well run and equipped, if a bit cramped. In some very cheap establishments however, standards of cleanliness may be suspect, and bedding limited to one sheet and a blanket.

Hotel touts

"Fishing" for guests (as Egyptians call it) is common practice in the main tourist centres, whereby new arrivals are approached by hotel **touts** at train and bus stations, airports and docks. Though some actually work in the hotel they're touting, most are simply hustling for commissions and quite prepared to use trickery to deliver clients to "their" establishment – swearing that other places are full, or closed, or whatever. In some cases, the hotel being touted may be agreeable, but all too often, it's the grotty or overpriced places that depend on touts. In any case, their commission will usually be added to your bill – another reason to avoid using them. In Cairo especially, some of these places exist purely for the purpose of housing foreigners so that they can be sold overpriced excursions or souvenirs.

Hostels

Egypt's youth hostels are cheap but their drawbacks are considerable. A daytime lock-out and nighttime curfew are universal practice; so, too, is segregating the sexes and (usually) foreigners and Egyptians (which you might appreciate when riotous groups are in residence). The most salubrious hostels are in Cairo, Sharm el-Sheikh and Ismailiya. These, however, are far from where the action is, as are grungier places in Alexandria and Luxor.

It seems to be up to individual hostels whether you need a **Hostelling International (HI) card**, and their rules change constantly. Non-HI members, if admitted, are usually charged £E2 extra per night. For more information, contact the Egyptian Youth Hostel Association in Cairo (1 Sharia el-Ibrahimy, Garden City, Cairo; ☎02/796-1448; annual membership £E25). There

are also a few **YMCA hostels**, which admit anyone. Most noteworthy is the Y in Assyut, which is much better value than most of the town's hotels.

Youth hostel associations

USA ☎301/495-1240, ⓦwww.hiayh.org.
Canada ☎1-800/663 5777, ⓦwww.hihostels.ca.
England and Wales ☎0870/770 8868, ⓦwww.yha.org.uk.
Scotland ☎01786/891 400, ⓦwww.syha.org.uk.
Ireland (Republic) ☎01/830 4555, ⓦwww.irelandyha.org.
Northern Ireland ☎028/9032 4733, ⓦwww.hini.org.uk.
Australia ☎02/9565-1699, ⓦwww.yha.com.au.
New Zealand ☎0800/278 299 or 03/379 9970, ⓦwww.yha.co.nz.
South Africa ☎021/788 2301, ⓦwww.hisa.org.za.

Camping

Such campsites as there are in Egypt tend to be on the coast, often shadeless and with few facilities, catering for holidaying Egyptian families. You'd have to be desperate to stay at these places. Rather better are the occasional campsites attached to hotels, which may offer ready-pitched tents with camp beds, plus use of the hotel shower and toilet facilities. As for camping rough, you should always check with the authorities about any coastal site – some beaches are mined, others patrolled by the military. In the oases it's less of a problem, though any land near water will belong to someone, so again, ask permission.

Food and drink

Egyptian food combines elements of Lebanese, Turkish, Syrian, Greek and French cuisines, modified to suit local conditions and tastes. In Alexandria, Mediterranean influences prevail, while Nubian cooking, from southern Egypt, is spicier than food in the north. Cairo offers every kind of cuisine in the world.

Opportunities for eating out divide into two categories. At a local level, there are cafés and diners and loads of street stalls, which sell one or two simple dishes. More formally and expensively, restaurants cater to middle-class Egyptians and tourists. The latter have menus (most cafés don't) offering a broader range of dishes, and sometimes specializing in foreign cuisine. They will also invariably add a service charge and taxes to your bill, which usually increases the total by about seventeen percent.

You are also expected to **tip**, roughly in proportion to the size of the bill; below ten percent in expensive places, more where the sums involved are trifling; see p.60 for more.

Cafés and street food

The staples of the Egyptian diet are bread (*'aish*, which also means "life"), *fuul* and *taamiya*. **Bread**, eaten with all meals and snacks, comes either as pitta-type *'aish shamsi* (sun-raised bread made from white flour) or *'aish baladi* (made from coarse wholewheat flour).

Fuul (pronounced "fool"; fava beans) is extremely cheap and can be prepared in several ways. Boiled and mashed with tomatoes, onions and spices, the beans are referred to as *fuul madammes*, a dish often served with a chopped boiled egg for breakfast. A similar mixture stuffed into *'aish baladi* constitutes the pitta-bread sandwiches sold on the street.

Just as inexpensive is **taamiya**, sometimes called falafel, deep-fried patties of green beans mixed with spices. Again, it's served in pitta bread, often with a snatch of salad, pickles and **tahina** (a sauce made from sesame paste, tahini), for which you can expect to pay the grand sum of £E1 or so.

Another cheap café perennial is **makarona**, a clump of macaroni baked into a cake with minced lamb and tomato sauce inside. It's rather bland but very filling. Similarly common is **kushari**, a mixture of noodles, rice, macaroni, lentils and onions, in a spicy tomato sauce (another sauce, made of garlic, is optional). It's served in small, medium and large portions (£E3–5) in tiled stand-up diners, also called *kushari*.

More elaborate, and pricier, are **fiteer**, a cross between pizza and pancake, and costing £E5–15 depending on size and ingredients. Served at café-like establishments known as *fatatri*, they consist of flaky filo pastry stuffed either with white cheese, peppers, mince, egg, onion and olives, or with raisins, jams, curds or just a dusting of icing sugar.

Most **sandwiches** are small rolls with a minute portion of *basturma* (pastrami) or cheese. Other favourite fillings include grilled liver (*kibda*) with spicy green peppers and onions; tiny shrimps; and *mokh* (crumbed sheep's brains).

A common appetizer is *torshi*, a mixture of pickled radishes, turnips, gherkins and carrots; luridly coloured, it is something of an acquired taste, as are pickled lemons, another favourite.

Lastly, there's **shawarma** – slices of marinated lamb, stuffed into pitta bread or a roll and garnished with salad and *tahina* – somewhat superior to the similar-looking doner kebabs sold abroad. A *shawarma* sandwich from a street stall can cost as little as £E2, while a plate of *shawarma* in a cheap diner will set you back around £E5.

On the **hygiene** front, while cafés and tiled eateries with running water are generally safe, street grub is highly suspect unless it's peelable or hot.

Restaurant meals

The classic Egyptian restaurant or café meal is either a lamb **kebab** or **kofta** (spiced mince patties), accompanied or preceded by a couple of dips – usually **hummus** (made from chickpeas), *tahina* and **babaghanoug** (*tahina* with aubergine). In a basic place, this is likely to be all that's on offer, save for a bit of salad (usually lettuce- and tomato-based), *fuul* and bread. However, you may also find other grilled meats. **Chicken** (*firakh*, pronounced "frakh" in Upper Egypt) is a standard, both in cafés and as takeaway food from spit-roast stands. **Pigeon** (*hamam*) is common too, most often served with *freek* (spicy wheat) stuffing. There's not much meat on a pigeon, so it's best to order a couple each. In slightly fancier places, you may also encounter pigeon in a **tageen** or *ta'gell*, stewed with onions, tomatoes and rice in an earthenware pot. A meal in an inexpensive restaurant should set you back around £E30 per person.

More expensive restaurants additionally feature a few, more elaborate dishes. Some places may precede main courses with a larger selection of dips, plus olives, stuffed vine leaves and so on – a selection known as **mezze**. Soups, too, are occasionally featured, most famously **molukhiyya**, which is made by stewing the herb Jew's mallow in chicken stock – a lot tastier than its disconcertingly slimy appearance suggests. Two common main dishes are **mahshi**, comprising stuffed vegetables (tomatoes, aubergines, etc), and **torly**, a mixed vegetable casserole with chunks of lamb or occasionally beef.

Fish (*samak*) also features on restaurant menus, particularly in Alexandria, Aswan, the Red Sea Coast and Sinai. There are many types, ranging from snapper to Nile perch; you're usually invited to pick your own fish from the ice box and it'll then be priced by weight. Fish is invariably grilled or fried, served with salad and chips, and usually very tasty. You may also find squid (calamari), shrimps (*gambari*) and octopus (*kaborya*).

One confusion you'll often run up against is the notion that **pasta**, **rice**, **chips** (French fries) and even **crisps** (potato chips) are interchangeable – order rice and you may get chips.

Snacks, sweets and fruit

You can supplement regular cooked meals with a variety of fare available from corner shops, delicatessens, patisseries and street stalls.

There are two main types of Egyptian **cheese**: *gibna beyda* (white cheese), which tastes like Greek feta, and *gibna rumi* ("Roman cheese"), a hard, sharp, yellow cheese. For breakfast you will often be given imported processed cheeses such as La Vache Qui Rit ("The Laughing Cow" – a popular nickname for President Mubarak).

Nut shops (*ma'la*) are a street perennial, offering all kinds of peanuts (*fuul sudani*) and edible seeds. *Lib abyad* and *lib asmar* are varieties of pumpkin seed, *lib battikh* come from watermelon, and chickpeas (hummus) are roasted and sugar-coated or dried and salted; all of these are sold by weight. Most nut shops also stock candies and mineral water.

Vegetarian eating

Most Egyptians eat vegetables most of the time – meat and fish are seen as luxuries. However, the concept of vegetarianism is incomprehensible to most people. It is possible to tell people that you are vegetarian (in Arabic, *ana nabati* if you're male, *ana nabatiya* if you're female) but they may not understand what you're getting at, and even if you do get across the idea that you don't eat meat (you could try telling people it's against your religious beliefs), you're as likely as not to be offered chicken or fish as a substitute.

Still, vegetarians and vegans will have no trouble feeding themselves in kushari and falafel joints, and *fatatris* offer reasonable pickings too, even for vegans (who can try ordering a veg or mushroom *fiteer* without cheese). Restaurants and hotels that cater particularly to tourists often feature a few vegetarian dishes on the menu, such as omelettes, vegetable tageens, pasta and salads.

Cakes are available at patisseries (some of which are attached to quite flash cafés) or from street stalls. The classics will be familiar to anyone who has travelled in Greece or Turkey: baklava (filo pastry soaked in honey and nuts – called *basbousa* in Upper Egypt, though elsewhere the term usually applies to syrup-drenched semolina cake; *katif* (similar but with shredded wheat); and a variety of milk- or cornflour-based puddings, like *mahallabiyya* (blancmange) and most famously Umm Ali (a cake, usually served hot and made with pastry, milk, sugar, coconut and cinnamon).

Fruits are wonderful in Egypt. In winter there are oranges, bananas and pomegranates, followed by strawberries in March. In summer you get mangoes, melons, peaches, plums and grapes, plus a brief season (Aug & Sept) of prickly pears (cactus fruit). Fresh dates are harvested in late autumn. Only apples are imported, and thus expensive. All are readily available at street stalls, or can be pressed into juice at juice bars (see below).

Drinks

As a predominantly Muslim country, Egypt gives alcohol a low profile. Public drunkenness is totally unacceptable, and in deference to the non-drinking Muslim majority, the sale of alcohol is prohibited on the Prophet Mohammed's birthday and the first and last days of Ramadan (if not during the whole month).

Tea, coffee and karkaday

Egypt's national beverage is **tea** (*shai*). Invitations to drink tea (*shurub shai?*) are as much a part of life in Egypt as they are in Britain, although the drink itself is served quite differently: tea is generally prepared by boiling the leaves, and served black and sugared to taste (though an increasing number of cafés use tea-bags and may supply milk). Tea with milk is *shai bi-laban*, tea-bag tea is *shai libton* – to avoid it ask for loose-leaf tea (*shai kushari*). Tea with a sprig of mint (*shai bi-na'ana'*) is refreshing when the weather is hot.

Coffee (*'ahwa*) is traditionally of the "**Turkish**" kind, served in tiny cups or glasses and pre-sugared as customers specify: *saada* (unsugared), *'ariha* (slightly sweetened), *mazboota* (medium sweet) or *ziyaada* (syrupy). In some places you can also get it spiced with cardamom (*'ahwa mahawega*). Most middle-class or tourist establishments also serve **instant** coffee, with the option of having it with milk (*'ahwa bi-laban*). Increasingly, however, five-star hotels and other upmarket places are investing in espresso machines.

Traditional **coffee houses** (called *'ahwa*) are usually shabby hole-in-the-wall places with chairs overlooking the street. Until very recently, it was unusual for women to frequent *'ahwas*, and unheard of to see them puffing away on a *sheesha*, but times change, and at least in more upmarket establishments younger, less inhibited women can now be seen with a waterpipe to their lips. Foreign women won't be turned away from *'ahwas* but may feel uneasy, especially if unaccompanied by a man. For a more relaxed tea or coffee, try one of the middle-class *'ahwas*, found in larger towns and often attached to patisseries.

A third drink, characteristic of Egypt, is **karkaday** (or *karkadé*), a deep-red infusion of hibiscus flowers. Most popular in Luxor and Aswan, it is equally refreshing drunk hot or cold. Elsewhere, they may use dehydrated extract instead of real hibiscus, so it doesn't taste as good. You may also enjoy other **infusions** such as *helba* (of fenugreek, bright yellow), *yansoon* (aniseed) or *'irfa* (cinnamon).

On cold winter evenings you might enjoy **sahleb**, a thick, creamy drink made from milk thickened with ground orchid root, with cinnamon and nuts sprinkled on top. In hot weather Egyptians imbibe **rayeb** (soured milk), which is something of an acquired taste.

Juice

Every main street has a couple of tiled, stand-up **juice bars**, recognizable by their displays of fruit. Normally, you order and pay at the cash desk, where you're given a plastic token or receipt to exchange at the counter for your drink.

Juices made from seasonal fruit include *burtu'an* (orange), *mohz* (banana; with milk *mohz bi-laban*), *manga* (mango), *farawla*

The sheesha

The **sheesha**, or waterpipe, is inseparable from Egyptian café society. It takes *ma'azil*, a special kind of tobacco mixed with molasses, which has a distinctive taste and aroma, guaranteed to take you right back to Egypt if you smell it again elsewhere. Posh coffee houses may also stock other flavours of tobacco (apple, strawberry, apricot, mint and so forth) and provide disposable plastic mouthpieces for the waterpipes. A *sheesha* is normally shared among friends, but you can decline to partake without causing offence.

The origin of the *sheesha* is something of a mystery. The name is Persian for "glass", a reference to the pipe's "vase". Another name is *nargila*, Persian for coconut, which shows what the vase was originally. Both names show that the waterpipe came to Egypt from Persia. But there were sophisticated waterpipes in Persia almost as soon as tobacco arrived in the seventeenth century, and some have suggested that they must have been in use there already. Possibly the Persians got the idea from trading with East Africa, where waterpipes were being used to smoke cannabis long before tobacco arrived. Despite these associations, don't call a *sheesha* a hubble-bubble, as the term in Egypt specifically refers to hashish, which is illegal.

(strawberry), *gazar* (carrot), *rummaan* (pomegranate), *subia* (coconut) and *'asab* (the sickly sweet, creamy, light-green juice of crushed sugar cane). You can also order blends; *nus w nus* (literally "half and half") usually refers to carrot and orange juice, but other combinations can be specified.

Street vendors also ladle out iced *'asiir limoon* (strong, sweet lemonade), bitter-sweet *er'a sous* (liquorice-water), and deliciously refreshing *tamar hindi* (tamarind cordial).

Soft drinks and mineral water

Despite this profusion of cheap fresh juices, the usual brands of **soda** are widely available, including Coca-Cola, Fanta, Sprite and 7-Up (referred to as "Seven"), all in both bottles and cans. There's also a local brand, Fayrouz, which offer unusual flavours such as mango or pineapple. Bottled sodas are normally drunk on the spot; you'll have to pay a deposit on the bottle to take one away.

If tourists request water, it's assumed that they mean bottled **mineral water** (*mayya ma'adaniyya*), which is widely available, particularly Baraka; the brands Siwa and Hyat (from Siwa Oasis) are less widely distributed. When buying, it's wise to check that the seal is intact; unsuspecting tourists may be palmed off with tap water – a favourite trick in the backpackers' resort of Dahab.

Tap water (*mayya baladi*) is safe to drink in major towns and cities, but too chlorinated for the average visitor's palate. People with sensitive stomachs should definitely stick to bottled water.

Alcohol

Alcohol can be obtained in most parts of Egypt, but the range of outlets is limited. In the Western Desert oases or Middle Egypt its sale is prohibited or severely restricted. If there are no bars, then hotels or Greek restaurants are the places to try; if you can't see anyone drinking it, there's none to be had. When you do manage to locate a drink, keep in mind that the hot, dry climate makes for dehydration, and agonizing hangovers can easily result from overindulgence.

Beer, whose consumption goes back to pharaonic times, is the most widely available form of alcohol. Native Stella beer is a light lager (4 percent ABV) in half-litre bottles, which is okay if it hasn't sat in the sun for too long, and also in cans. To check that bottled beer hasn't gone flat, invert the bottle before opening and look for a fizzy head. Stella retails in most places for £E6–10, though discos may charge as much as £E20 and cruise boats even more. Sakkara is a similarly light lager (4 percent) that most foreigners seem to prefer. Premium or "export" versions of both Stella and

Sakkara are available, which have a slightly fuller flavour. Also worth trying is lager, marketed under the Luxor name, which is ten percent alcohol by volume. There are also Egyptian versions of Heineken, Carlsberg, Löwenbrau and Meister, none of which is worth the extra cost, and kamikaze (7–10 percent) versions of Sakkara and Meister, which are worth avoiding. Marzen, a dark bock beer, appears briefly in the spring; Aswali is a dark beer produced in Aswan. Imported beer is the most expensive (£E15–20) and only appears in bars, flash hotels and restaurants. There is also Birrel, a non-alcoholic beer.

A half-dozen or so **Egyptian wines** are produced near Alexandria. The most commonly found are Omar Khayyam (a very dry red), Cru des Ptolémées (a decent dry white) and Rubis d'Egypte (an acceptable rosé). Obélisque offers a pretty good Red Cabernet Sauvignon, though the rosé and white are less so. In most restaurants these retail for about £E30 a bottle (but more like £E45 on a cruise boat). The latest addition to the wine scene is Chateau des Rêves, a classy red with complex flavours, which goes for £E55 and is best left to breathe for a while before drinking.

For serious drinking, Egyptians get stuck into spirits, usually mixed with sodas or fruit juice. The favoured tipple is **brandy**, known by the slang name of *jaz* (literally, "bottle"), and sold under three labels: Ahmar (the cheapest), Maa'tak (the best) and Vin (the most common). **Zibiba** is similar to Greek ouzo, but drunk neat. Avoid vile Egyptian-made **gin** and **whisky**, whose labels are designed to resemble famous Western brands; in fact they may even contain wood alcohol and other poisons, and can be dangerous if drunk to excess. If you prefer your drinks ready-mixed, a vodka-based alcopop called ID is also available, in various flavours, at liquor stores and in some bars and duty-free shops.

Foreigners can buy up to three litres of imported spirits (or two bottles of spirits plus a two-dozen-can carton of beer) at **duty-free** prices within 24 hours of arrival in Egypt, in addition to the two litres allowed in from abroad. There is a black market for duty-free booze (Johnny Walker Black Label is the most sought-after brand), and Egyptians may accost you in the street asking if you'll buy them some duty-free booze "for my sister's wedding", but beware: buying alcohol for someone is fine, but under no circumstances should you allow a stranger to be involved in the transaction inside the store. The paperwork for any duty-free purchase is filled out in Arabic, and some travellers have discovered on leaving Egypt that a TV or video has been bought duty-free with their passport. Being unable to produce the item for customs officials, they've had to pay duty on it, just as if they'd purchased and then sold it.

The media

The Egyptian press encompasses a range of daily papers and weekly magazines, chiefly published in English, French or Arabic. All are fairly heavily censored.

The **English-language** *Egyptian Gazette* (on Saturday, the *Egyptian Mail*) carries agency reports, articles on Middle Eastern affairs and tourist features, but it's pretty lightweight and you can read the whole thing in a few minutes flat. For more serious journalism, look out for the English weekly edition of *Al-Ahram*, which has interesting opinion pieces on politics, sociology and international affairs. The **French-language** counterparts of the *Egyptian Gazette/Egyptian Mail* are *Le Journal d'Egypte* and *Le*

Progrès Egyptien; there is also a French edition of *Al-Ahram*, called *Hebdo*.

Among the **Arabic** papers, *Al-Ahram* ("The Pyramids", founded in 1875 and thus Egypt's oldest newspaper), reflects official thinking, as do *Al-Akhbar* and *Al-Gomhouriya*. Other dailies with a party affiliation include the conservative *Al-Wafd* ("The Delegation"), the socialist *Al-Ahaly* ("The Nation") and *Al-Da'wa* ("The Call"), the journal of the Muslim Brotherhood.

Various British, US, French and German newspapers are available in Cairo, Alexandria, Luxor and Aswan, as are *Newsweek* and *Time* magazines. Elsewhere, however, you'll be lucky to find even the *Egyptian Gazette*.

Radio

If you have a short-wave radio, you can pick up the **BBC World Service** (Ⓦwww.bbc .co.uk/worldservice), the **Voice of America** (Ⓦwww.voa.gov) and other international broadcasters; check their websites for frequencies. You can also pick up the BBC on 1323kHz MW on the Mediterranean coast, in Cairo and, when conditions are right, as far south as Luxor or even Aswan.

Cairo has two privately run **music stations** which are worth a listen: Nogoum Radio

(100.6FM) plays mainly Arabic pop music, while Nile FM (104.15FM) plays Western pop. In addition, the state-owned Music Programme (89.0FM) plays folk and classical music, while the European Programme (94.5FM) has the news in English at 7.30am, 2.30pm and 8pm daily.

Television

Egypt has a plethora of terrestrial **television** channels, all state-controlled. Local football matches and Koranic recitations account for much of the programming, so it's not worth paying extra for a TV set in your hotel room unless it receives cable or satellite TV – and even then, chances are that half the channels will be Turkish or Kuwaiti.

Channels 1 and 2 often screen American films (generally after 10pm, or between midnight and 4.30am during Ramadan), and **Nile TV** has English subtitles on most programmes, most notably with classic old Egyptian movies, plus news in English and French. In addition to these, some hotels receive **satellite** channels like BBC World, CNN, Star Plus, Prime Sports, EuroNews, MTV and the Qatar-based news service Al Jazeera. Daily TV **schedules** appear in the *Egyptian Gazette*, whose Monday edition lists all the movies for the forthcoming week.

Festivals

Egypt abounds in holidays and festivals of all kinds, both Muslim and Christian, national and local. Coming across a local moulid can be one of the most enjoyable experiences Egypt has to offer, with the chance to witness music, dancing and other entertainments.

Most Islamic holidays and festivals follow the **Islamic calendar**. This is lunar-based, with twelve months of 29 or 30 days each, in the following sequence: Moharram, Safar, Rabi el-Awwal, Rabi el-Tani, Gumad el-Awwal, Gumad el-Tani, Ragab, Sha'ban, Ramadan, Shawwal, Zoul Qiddah and Zoul Hagga. The Islamic year is shorter than a solar year by

some ten or eleven days, so dates in the Muslim calendar move forward each year in relation to the Western calendar. Note that a day in the Islamic calendar begins at sundown, as a consequence of which Islamic festivals start on the evening before you'd expect.

Ramadan

Even if you're not interested in such festivals, it's important to be aware of the month of **Ramadan**, when most Muslims (which means ninety percent of Egyptians) observe a total fast from dawn to sunset for a month. This can pose big problems for travellers but the celebratory evenings are good times to hear music and to share in hospitality.

The ninth month of the Islamic calendar (for dates, see the box on p.72), Ramadan commemorates the time when the Koran began to be revealed to Mohammed. Ramadan, in a sense, parallels the Christian Lent; during Ramadan, Muslims observe a **fast**, involving abstention from food, drink, smoking and sex during daylight hours. Strict Muslims will even refrain from swallowing, lest they "drink" their own saliva.

With opening times and transport schedules affected (almost everything pauses at sunset so people can break the fast), and most local cafés and restaurants closing during the day (or remaining open, but not selling food), Ramadan is in many respects a bad time to travel. It is certainly no time to try camel trekking in the Sinai – no guide would undertake the work – and it is probably safer to travel by bus during the mornings only, as drivers will be fasting, too. (Airline pilots are forbidden to observe the fast.)

But there is a compensation in witnessing and becoming absorbed in the pattern of the fast. At sunset, signalled by the sounding of a siren and the lighting of lamps on the minarets, an amazing calm and sense of well-being fall on the streets, as everyone eats *fuul* and *taamiya* and, in the cities at least, gets down to a night of celebration and entertainment. Throughout the evening, urban cafés – and main squares – provide venues for live music and singing, while in small towns and poorer quarters of big cities, you will often come across ritualized *zikrs* – trance-like chanting and swaying.

If you are a **non-Muslim** you are not expected to observe Ramadan, but it is good to be sensitive about not breaking the fast (particularly smoking) in public. In fact, the best way to experience Ramadan – and to benefit from its naturally purifying rhythms – is to enter into it. You may not be able to last without an occasional glass of water, and you'll probably breakfast later than sunrise, but it is worth an attempt – and you'll win local people's respect.

Islamic holidays

At the end of Ramadan comes the feast of **Eid el-Fitr**. In Cairo it's a climax to the month's festivities, though in the villages it's observed more privately. Equally important in the Muslim calendar is **Eid el-Adha** (aka Eid el-Kabir or Korban Bairam – the Great Feast), which celebrates the willingness of Ibrahim (Abraham) to obey God and sacrifice his son. Both *eids* are traditional family gatherings. At the Eid el-Adha every household that can afford to will slaughter a sheep, often on the streets. For weeks prior to the event you see the sheep tethered everywhere, even on rooftops.

Eid el-Adha is followed, about three weeks later, by **Ras el-Sana el-Hegira**, the Muslim new year, on the first day of the month of Moharrem. The fourth main religious holiday is the **Moulid el-Nabi**, the Prophet Mohammed's birthday. This is widely observed, with processions in many towns and cities. For the approximate dates of these four festivals according to the Western calendar, see the box on p.72.

Moulids

Moulids are the equivalent of medieval European saints' fairs, popular events combining piety, fun and commerce. Their ostensible aim is to obtain blessing (*baraka*) from the saint, but the social and cultural dimensions are equally important. Moulids are an opportunity for people to escape the monotony of their hard-working lives in several days of festivities, and for friends and families from different villages to meet. Farming problems are discussed, as well as family matters – and marriage – as people sing, dance, eat and pray together.

With the exception of the Moulid el-Nabi, most moulids are localized affairs, usually centred around the mosque or tomb (*qubba*) of a holy man or woman. Most are scheduled according to the Islamic calendar, but certain moulids start (or finish) on a particular day (eg a Tuesday in a given month), rather than on any specific date. To complicate matters further, a minority of festivals occur at the same time every year, generally following the local harvest. If you're planning to attend a moulid, it's wise to verify the (approximate) dates given in this guide by asking local people or the tourist office.

If you are lucky enough to catch one of the major events, you'll get the chance to witness Egyptian popular culture at its richest. The largest events draw crowds of over a million, with companies of *mawladiya* (literally, "moulid people") running stalls and rides, and music blaring into the small hours. Smaller, rural moulids tend to be heavier on the practical devotion, with people bringing their children or livestock for blessing, or the sick to be cured.

The largest moulids are in Cairo, Tanta and Luxor. **Cairo** hosts three lengthy festivals in honour of El-Hussein, Saiyida Zeinab and the Imam el-Shafi'i (held during the months of Rabi el-Tani, Ragab and Sha'ban, respectively), plus numerous smaller festivals (see box on pp.258–259). Following the cotton harvest in October, the Moulid of El-Bedawi in **Tanta** starts a cycle of lesser **Nile Delta festivals** that runs well into November (see p.627). Equally spectacular is the Moulid of Abu el-Haggag in **Luxor**, held during the month of Sha'ban, and featuring a parade of boats (see p.358). Elsewhere, the procession may be led by camels or floats. Accompanying all this are **traditional entertainments**: mock stick fights, conjurers, acrobats and snake charmers; horses trained to dance to music; and, sometimes, bellydancers. All the longer moulids climax in a *leyla kebira* (literally "big night") on the last evening or the eve of the last day – the most spectacular and crowded phase; some moulids also have a corresponding big day.

Music and singing are a feature of every moulid and locals often bring tape recorders to make cassettes they can play back for the rest of the year. At the heart of every moulid

is at least one **zikr** – a gathering of worshippers who chant and sway for hours, striving to attain a trance-like state of oneness with God. Frequently, the *zikr* participants belong to one of the **Sufi brotherhoods**, which are differentiated by coloured banners, sashes or turbans, and named after their founding sheikh. The current incumbent of this office may lead them in a **zaffa** (parade) through town, and in olden times would ride a horse over his followers – a custom known as "the Treading".

Coptic festivals

Egypt's Christian Coptic minority often attend Islamic moulids – and vice versa. **Coptic moulids** share some of the social and market functions of their Islamic counterparts and, similarly, at their core is the celebration of a saint's name-day. As you'd expect, the major Christian events of the year are also celebrated.

The dates of **Christmas** (January 6/7), **Epiphany** (January 19) and the **Annunciation** (March 21) are as specified in the Julian calendar used by the Orthodox Church, but **Easter** and its related feast days are reckoned according to the solar Coptic calendar (ⓦwww.copticchurch.net has the dates), and therefore differ from both the Orthodox and Western dates by up to one month.

Major **saints' day events** include the Moulid of St Damyanah (May 15–20), the Feast of the Apostles Peter and Paul (July 12), and various moulids of the Virgin and St George during August. Many of these are celebrated at monasteries in Middle Egypt, the Delta and the Red Sea Hills.

Lastly, a Coptic festival (of pharaonic origin) celebrated by all Egyptians is the **Sham el-Nessim**, a coming-of-spring festival whose name literally means "Sniffing the Breeze". It provides the excuse for mass picnics in parks and on riverbanks throughout the country.

Sports and outdoor activities

Egypt's main spectator sport is football (soccer). As far as participation sports go, both horse- and camel-riding are popular, but the big draw for visitors is snorkelling and diving amid the Red Sea's magnificent coral reefs. Other aquatic activities, such as water-skiing, parasailing and windsurfing, are available on the Mediterranean coast. Despite Egypt's relative lack of greenery, golf is also possible, with several courses around Cairo as well as at Sharm el-Sheikh, Soma Bay, El Gouna and Luxor: details are available at Ⓦwww.touregypt.net/golfcourses.htm.

Football

Football (*kurat 'adem*) is Egypt's national sport. The two Cairo-based rivals, **Ahly** and **Zamalek**, are the major teams and contributed most of the country's squad which won the African Nations Cup in 2006. Clashes between the two teams can be intense – and have occasionally led to rioting – but games are in general relaxed: see p.264 for the details of games, tickets and stadium addresses. Should their team win, thousands of jubilant supporters drive around Cairo honking horns and waving flags attached to lances – beware of being run over or impaled.

Other popular teams include **Ismaily** from Ismailiya and **Masry** from Port Said, while **Santa Katerina** is a team composed entirely of Sinai Bedouin who train by running up Mount Sinai twice a day. Also noteworthy are a new wave of corporate-sponsored teams, such as Petrojet (funded by an oil company) and Cement Assyut.

Riding

Around the Pyramids and the major Nile sites, donkeys, horses and camels are all available for hire. **Horses** are fun if you want to ride across stretches of sand between the Pyramids or in the Sinai desert. **Donkeys** are best used for visiting the Theban Necropolis, where they traverse mountains that you'd never cross on foot, and enliven the trip no end. Elsewhere they have less appeal, but you might rent a *caretta* (donkey-drawn taxi cart) to explore the pools and ruins in Siwa Oasis.

Camels (the dromedary, or one-humped Arabian camel) make for pretty rigorous but exhilarating riding, and you'll probably want to try them at least once. They are good for short rides around Aswan, to the monastery of St Simeon, for example, but where they really come into their own is in Sinai or the Western Desert oases, where you can go trekking up wadis or across dunes that horses could never cope with. Trips – lasting anything from a half-day to a week – are easily arranged with local operators, or as part of "adventure holiday" packages before you set off.

Camel-riding is a real art, which gets a little easier on the body with experience. The mounting is done for you but be sure to hold on to the pommel of the saddle as the camel raises itself in a triple-jerk manoeuvre. Once on, you have a choice of riding it like a horse or cocking a leg around the pommel, as the Bedouin do. Be sure to use a lot of padding around the pommel: what begins as a minor irritation can end up leaving your skin rubbed raw.

Beware of being palmed off with a male (bull) camel that's in heat – they can be quite vicious. Bad signs are an inflated mouth sac, aggressive behaviour towards its mates, and lots of noise and slobbering. When enraged, camels can launch a fierce attack – they've been known to grip someone's neck and shake them like a rag doll, or crush the bones in a leg.

Snorkelling, diving and angling

Anybody who can swim can **snorkel**, and Egypt's Red Sea resorts have some of the world's most spectacular **coral-reef wildlife**, much of which requires nothing more than a mask and snorkel to see. For those who want to take it more seriously, Egypt is a very good place – and a relatively inexpensive one – to learn how to **dive**, or to go diving if you are already qualified. Dive centres are detailed throughout our chapters on the Sinai and the Red Sea coast.

If you do come to Egypt to dive, you are in for a treat, as the Red Sea's **coral and reef wildlife** puts even places like the Caribbean, the Indian Ocean and the South Pacific in the shade. Facilities are well developed, and on the Red Sea and Sinai coasts, dive safaris are a booming industry. Private charter boats ("liveaboards") take divers to remote reefs, the trips lasting from several days to two or three weeks. Most

are prebooked by groups, which may not welcome individuals joining them at the last moment, so it's better, and cheaper, to buy a package deal at home (see pp.33–34 for operators). Dive sites are covered in chapters seven and eight. Maps and detailed information on dive locations can be found at ⓦwww.goredsea.com.

For **fishing**, the place to come is Lake Nasser, the artificial lake behind the Aswan Dam, which is well stocked with massive and plentiful Nile perch, carp and tilapia. Fishing trips can be arranged in Aswan (see p.451) or booked through African Angler (Egypt ☎097/230-9748 or 010/342-410; Australia ☎02/9966 9316; ⓦwww.african-angler.co.uk).

Crime and personal safety

While relatively few in number, pickpockets are skilled and concentrate on tourists. Most operate in Cairo, notably in queues and on the crowded buses to the Pyramids. To play safe, keep your valuables in a money belt or a pouch under your shirt (leather or cotton materials are preferable to nylon, which can irritate in the heat).

Overall, though, **casual theft** is more of a problem. Campsites, hostels and cheap hotels often have poor security, though at most places you can deposit valuables at the reception (always get a receipt for cash). If you are **driving**, it goes without saying that you shouldn't leave anything you cannot afford to lose visible or accessible in your car.

Minefields (the Arabic for "mines" is *algham*, with the stress on the second syllable) still exist: from World War II along the Mediterranean coast, and from Israeli conflicts in the interior of Sinai and along the Red Sea coast (detailed in chapters 3, 4, 7 and 8). Don't take any risks in venturing into fenced-off territory, unless locals go there often.

Terrorism

During the 1990s, Egypt's image as a safe country to visit was shattered by a wave of terrorism. Islamist militants murdered tourists, police and government officials in a series of bombings and shootings. Middle Egypt became a no-go zone for foreigners and tourism expired nationwide after the Luxor massacre of 1997. Egyptians were so revolted by the atrocity that even the militant Gamaat Islamiya movement disowned it as an act by wayward members, and their imprisoned leadership announced an end to violence in 1998. Meanwhile, thousands were detained under the emergency laws until the state saw fit to release them, and the combination of force and inducements seemed to work in ending that spate of attacks.

Most Egyptians, of course, are horrified at these atrocities, and needless to say, the authorities take the situation very seriously. There are armed police at all tourist sites, stations and checkpoints, scanners in hotels, and plainclothes agents in bars and bazaars. Along the Nile Valley (see box, pp.280–281, for more), tourists travelling by rail can only use services designated for tourists, which have plainclothes guards riding shotgun. Tourist buses between Cairo and Israel, and from Aswan to Luxor or Abu Simbel, must travel in a **convoy** (*kol*) with a police escort. There is no ban on visiting once "risky" areas, but the local police will certainly keep a close eye on you and may insist on accompanying you to sites like Abydos or Dendara. In the event of real trouble, hit the deck or get off the streets immediately.

Of course the vast majority of tourists spend their stay in Egypt without encountering any kind of terrorist incident. Nonetheless, you should bear in mind that jihadist militants do see any non-Muslim foreigner as a potential target. Keep your ear to the ground (check government advisories before you travel – see p.74), be vigilant as regards unattended packages, suspicious behaviour and so on.

To reduce the risk of petty squabbles or misunderstandings developing, you should **respect local customs** in public; see opposite for more.

The police

Egypt has a plethora of police forces whose high profile in Cairo (which has more cops per thousand citizens than any other capital in the world) and at checkpoints on trunk roads strikes first-time visitors as a sign of recent trouble, although it has actually been the rule since the 1960s. Whereas Egyptians fear police brutality, foreign visitors are usually treated with kid gloves and given the benefit of the doubt unless drugs or espionage are suspected.

If you've got a problem or need to report a crime, always go to the **Tourist and Antiquities Police**. Found at tourist sites, museums, airports, stations and ports, they are supposedly trained to help tourists in distress, and should speak a foreign language (usually English). The ordinary ranks wear the regular khaki police uniform with a "Tourist Police" armband; officers wear black uniforms in winter and white in summer. The more senior the officer, the better the chance they'll speak English.

The **Municipal Police** handle all crimes and have a monopoly on law and order in smaller towns. Their uniform (khaki in winter, tan or white in summer) resembles that of the **Traffic Police**, who wear striped cuffs. Both get involved in accidents and can render assistance in emergencies. However, relatively few officers speak anything but Arabic.

The fourth conspicuous force is the **Central Security** force (dressed all in black and armed with Kalashnikovs), who guard embassies, banks and highways. Though normally genial enough, this largely conscript force will shift rapidly from tear gas to live rounds when ordered to crush demonstrations or civil unrest. Ordinarily, though, they are nothing to worry about. To guard vital utilities, there are also Electricity, Airport and **River Police** forces; the last is responsible for overseeing felucca journeys between Aswan and Luxor.

The **Military Intelligence** (the Mukhabarat) is only relevant to travellers who wish to visit remote parts of the Western Desert or travel south beyond Berenice on the Red Sea coast, for which you need travel permits (see p.38). Their offices in Mersa Matrouh and the oases are signposted in English and quite tourist-friendly, whereas in Sinai they have secret agents stationed in Dahab, Nuweiba, Na'ama Bay and Sharm el-Sheikh, whose brief includes watching Israeli tourists and Egyptians who visit Israel. Finally there is the **State Security**, who may take an interest in tourists in border areas or Middle Egypt, but are generally irrelevant as far as most tourists are concerned.

All of these forces deploy **plainclothes agents** who hang around near government buildings and crowded places, dressed as vendors or peasants – hence their nickname, the "Galabiyya Police". In hotels or bars, you might be disconcerted to find yourself chatting with a guy who suddenly announces that he's a cop. There are lots of them around.

Drugs

Egypt has its own **bango** (marijuana) industry, based in the Sinai (see p.693), whose output is supplemented by hashish from Morocco and, on a small scale, hash from Lebanon. A small amount of opium is also produced in the Sinai and Middle Egypt.

Despite a tradition of marijuana use stretching back to the thirteenth century, Egypt was one of the first countries in modern times to ban cannabis, back in 1879. The country now has draconian anti-drugs laws that make hanging or life imprisonment mandatory for convicted smugglers and dealers (which could be interpreted to mean somebody caught with a few sachets of the stuff), and the law against cannabis is much more strictly enforced than it ever used to be. Mere possession or use merits a severe prison sentence and a heavy fine, plus legal costs, upwards of US$1000. For trafficking, which includes bringing any illegal drug into the country, penalties can be as much as 25 years' hard labour, or even execution. Perversely, *bango* is popularly considered a worse drug than hashish, possibly because it is cheaper and thus more commonly used by members of society's lower strata; few people seem to be aware that both drugs come from the same plant.

In practice, the least you can expect if caught with a smoke is immediate deportation and a ban from ever visiting the country again. You may be able to buy your way out of trouble, but this should be negotiated discreetly and as soon as possible, while the minimum number of officers are involved: once you are at the police station, it will be a lot more difficult. Needless to say, your embassy will be unsympathetic. The best advice is to steer clear of all illegal drugs while in the country.

Culture and etiquette

If you want to get the most from a trip to Egypt, it is vital not to assume that anyone who approaches you expects to profit from the encounter. Too many tourists do, and end up making little contact with an extraordinarily friendly people.

Behaviour and attitude on your part are important. If some Egyptians treat tourists with contempt, it has much to do with the way the latter behave. It helps everyone if you can avoid rudeness or aggressive behaviour in response to insistent offers or demands. On another tack entirely, intimate behaviour in public (kissing and cuddling) is a no-no, and even holding hands is disapproved of.

Be aware, too, of the importance of **dress**: shorts are socially acceptable only at beach resorts (and for women only in private resorts or along the Gulf of Aqaba coast), while shirts (for both sexes) should cover your shoulders. Many tourists ignore these conventions, unaware of how it demeans them in the eyes of the Egyptians. Women wearing halter-necks, skimpy T-shirts, miniskirts and the like will attract gropers, and the disapproval of both sexes. If you're visiting a mosque, you're expected to be "modestly" dressed (men should be covered from below the shoulder to below the knee, women from wrist to ankle). It's also obligatory to remove shoes (or don overshoes).

When **invited to a home**, it's normal to take your shoes off before entering the reception rooms. It is customary to take a gift: sweet pastries (or tea and sugar in rural areas) are always acceptable.

One important thing to be aware of in Egypt is the different functions of the two hands. Whether you are right- or left-handed, the **left hand** is used for "unclean" functions, most importantly wiping your bottom, but also doing things like putting on and taking off shoes. This means that it is considered unhygienic to eat with your left hand. You can hold things like bread in your left hand in order to tear a piece off with your right hand, but you should never put food into your mouth with your left hand, and certainly never put it into the bowl when eating communally. You should also avoid passing things to people or accepting them with your left hand.

Egyptians are likely to feel very strongly about certain subjects – Palestine, Israel and Islam, for instance, and these should be treated diplomatically if they come up in conversation. Some Egyptians are keen to discuss them, others not, but carelessly expressed opinions, and particularly open contempt for religion, can cause serious offence.

Tipping and baksheesh

As a presumed-rich *khawaga* (the Egyptian term for a foreigner), you will be expected to be liberal with **baksheesh**, which can be divided into three main varieties. The most common is **tipping**: a small reward for a small service, which can encompass anything from being waited on to someone unlocking a tomb or museum room at one of the ancient sites. The sums involved are often paltry, but try to strike a balance between defending your own wallet and acquiescing gracefully when appropriate. There's little point in offending people over what are trifling sums for a Western tourist but often an important part of people's livelihood given that an average Egyptian's wage stands at about £E500 a month.

Typical tips might be 50pt–£E1 for looking after your shoes while you visit a mosque (though congregants don't usually tip for this), or £E2–5 to a custodian for opening up a door to let you enter a building or climb a minaret. In restaurants, you do not usually leave a percentage of the bill: typical tips (regardless of whether the bill claims to include "service") are as little as 50pt in an ultra-cheap place such as a *kushari* joint, £E2 in a typical cheap restaurant, or £E5 in a smarter establishment. Customers also usually give tips of 50pt in a café, and sometimes 25pt in a juice bar.

A more expensive and common type of baksheesh is for rewarding the **bending of rules** – many of which seem to have been designed for just that purpose. Examples might include letting you into an archeological site after hours (or into a vaguely restricted area), finding you a sleeper on a train when the carriages are "full", and so on. This should not be confused with bribery, which is a more serious business with its own etiquette and risks – best not entered into.

The last kind of baksheesh is simply **alms-giving**. For Egyptians, giving money and goods to the needy is a natural act – and a requirement of Islam. The disabled are traditional recipients of such gifts, and it seems right to join locals in giving out small change. Children, however, are a different case, pressing their demands only on tourists. If someone offers some genuine help and asks for an *alum* (pen), it seems fair enough, but to yield to every request might encourage a cycle of dependency that Egypt could do without.

Since most Egyptian money is paper, often in the form of well-used banknotes that can be fiddly to separate out, it can make life easier to keep small bills in a separate "baksheesh pocket" specifically for the purpose. If giving baksheesh in foreign currency, give notes rather than coins (these cannot be exchanged for Egyptian currency). Bringing a wad of one-dollar bills can be useful for this.

Women travellers

The biggest problem women travellers face in Egypt is the perception some Egyptian men have of women tourists as being "easy". Such views may be reinforced by the fact that many women visitors do a range of things that no respectable Egyptian woman would: dressing "immodestly", showing shoulders and cleavage; sharing rooms with men to whom they are not married; drinking alcohol in bars or restaurants; smoking in public; even travelling alone on public transport, without a relative as an escort. While well-educated Egyptians familiar with Western culture can take these in their stride, less sophisticated ones are liable to assume the worst. Tales of affairs with tourists, and the scandalous Russians of Hurghada, are common currency among Egyptian males. In Sinai, however, unaccompanied

Female genital mutilation

A little-known fact about Egyptian women is that the vast majority of them – up to 97 percent according to one survey – have been subjected to the horrific operation known euphemistically as "female circumcision", and more correctly as female genital mutilation (FGM). In this procedure, typically carried out on girls aged between 7 and 10, the clitoris and sometimes all or part of the inner vaginal lips are cut off. Obviously, this prevents the victim from enjoying sex.

FGM is an African rather than an Islamic practice, and in Egypt it is performed by Copts as much as by Muslims. Nonetheless, spurious religious reasons are given to justify it, including two disputed *hadiths* (quotations from Mohammed). In 1951, the Egyptian Fatwa Committee decreed that FGM was desirable because it curbs women's sex drive, and in 1981 the Sheikh of al-Azhar Mosque and University said that it was the duty of parents to have their daughters genitally mutilated.

The good news is that things have changed a little bit since then. Firstly, FGM is now, at least in theory, **illegal** – the government banned it in 1996 after a CNN documentary exposed the practice, and the Supreme Court threw out an attempt by Islamic fundamentalists to have the ban declared unconstitutional. On the other hand, the law is rarely enforced, and it would be hard for the government to enforce it, even if they really wanted to. Secondly, though some forty percent of victims still have the operation performed by a barber or similarly non-qualified person, and without anaesthetic, it is increasingly the case that FGM is performed by qualified medical practitioners under anaesthetic. Thirdly, the incidence of, and support for, FGM is beginning to decline, though still at high levels: a survey in 2000 found that 78 percent of 11- to 19-year-olds had been victims of FGM compared to 83 percent in 1995, and that support for the practice among Egyptian women had fallen from 82 percent to 75 percent. As for the religious authorities, both the current Sheikh of al-Azhar and the Coptic pope have stated that FGM is not a religious requirement, though of course that falls well short of a condemnation.

---

women experience few hassles, except from construction workers from "mainland" Egypt.

Without compromising your freedom too greatly, there are a few steps you can take to improve your image. Most important and obvious is **dress**: loose opaque clothes that cover all "immodest" areas (thighs, upper arms, chest) and hide your contours are a big help, and essential if you are travelling alone or in rural areas (where covering long hair is also advisable). On public transport (buses, trains, service taxis), try to sit with other women – who may often invite you to do so. On the Cairo metro and trams in Alexandria there are carriages reserved for women. If you're travelling with a man, wearing a wedding ring confers respectability, and asserting that you're married is better than admitting to being "just friends".

Looking confident and knowing where you're going is a major help in avoiding hassle. It's also a good idea to avoid making eye contact with Egyptian men (some women wear sunglasses for the purpose), and it is best to err on the side of stand-offishness, as even a friendly smile may be taken as a come-on. Problems – most commonly hissing or groping – tend to come in downtown Cairo and in the public beach resorts (except Sinai's Aqaba coast, or Red Sea holiday villages, which are more or less the only places where you'll feel happy about sunbathing). In the oases, where attractions include open-air springs and hot pools, it's okay to bathe – but do so in at least a T-shirt and leggings: oasis people are among the most conservative in the country.

Your reaction to **harassment** is down to you. Some women find that verbal hassle is best ignored, while others may prefer to use an Egyptian brush-off like *khalas* (finished) or *uskut* (be quiet). If you get groped, the best response is to yell *aram!* (evil!) or *sibnee le wadi* (don't touch me), which will shame any assailant in public, and may attract help.

On the positive side, spending time with **Egyptian women** can be a delight, if someone decides to take you under their wing. The difficulty in getting to know women is that fewer women than men speak English, and that you won't run into women in traditional cafés. However, public transport can be a good meeting ground, as can shops. If asking directions in the street, it's always better to ask a woman than a man.

Many women in relationships with Egyptian men choose to enter into so-called Orfi **marriages** (aka "Dahab marriages"), usually arranged by a lawyer, to circumvent the law that prohibits unmarried couples from sleeping under the same roof or public displays of affection. These allow couples to rent a flat without hassle from the Vice Squad and can be annulled without a divorce. However, it's as well to note that an Orfi marriage does not confer the same legal rights as a full marriage in a special registry office (Sha'ar el-Aqari) in Cairo, which is the only kind that allows women to bring their spouse to their own country or gives them any rights in child-custody disputes. Women can bolster their position by insisting on a marriage contract (pre-nuptial agreement). A useful factsheet, *Notes on Marrying an Egyptian*, is available from the British Embassy in Cairo. Note that, whatever you may be told, foreign women don't need to be married to an Egyptian to buy property or become a partner in a business. If you are considering this, however, it's vital to find a good lawyer, preferably one who has worked abroad and is familiar with Western ways.

Travelling with children

Children evoke a warm response in Egypt and are welcome more or less everywhere. It's not unusual to see Egyptian children out with their parents in cafés or shops past midnight. The only child-free zones tend to be bars and clubs frequented by foreigners. Most hotels can supply an extra bed and breakfast. Pharmacies sell formula milk, baby food and disposable nappies, and the last two may also be stocked by corner stores in larger towns. Things worth bringing are a mosquito net for a buggy or crib, and a parasol for sun protection.

From an adult minder's standpoint, most hazards can be minimized or avoided by taking due precautions. Traffic is obviously dangerous, while stray animals (possible disease carriers), fenced-off beaches (probably mined – see p.57), lifts with no inner doors (keep small hands away), and poisonous fish and coral in the Red Sea (see Egypt's underwater world colour section), are other potential hazards.

Children (especially young ones) are more susceptible than adults to **heatstroke** and **dehydration**, and should always wear a sunhat, and have high-factor sunscreen applied to exposed skin. If swimming at a beach resort, they should do so in a T-shirt, certainly for the first few days. The other thing that children are very susceptible to is an **upset tummy**. Bear in mind that antidiarrhoeal drugs should generally not be given to young children; read the literature provided with the medication or consult a doctor for guidance on child dosages.

If children baulk at unfamiliar **food**, outlets of all major American fast-food chains are always close at hand. Ice cream is cheap and ubiquitous, as is rice pudding and *mahalabiyya*.

On a more positive note, there are plenty of aspects to life in Egypt that children should enjoy, among them camel, horse and donkey rides, but choose carefully – AA Stables in

Cairo for example (see p.263) has a good reputation. Activities such as felucca rides, snorkelling and visiting a few of the great monuments can also be enjoyable. A number of activities in Cairo that will especially appeal to younger travellers are listed on pp.261–262.

Travel essentials

Ancient monuments

Egypt's ancient sites and monuments are maintained by the **Supreme Council of Antiquities** (SCA, formerly known as the Egyptian Antiquities Organization or EAO). Most are kept open on a daily basis, with caretakers on hand to unlock tombs and point you towards the salient features. Local opening hours are detailed in individual entries; for a few hints on baksheesh, see p.60.

Cigarettes

The vast majority of Egyptian men smoke, and offering cigarettes around is common practice. The most popular brand is Cleopatra (£E2.50; £E2.75 in a crush-proof pack). Locally produced versions of Marlboro, Rothmans and Camel (typically retailing at around £E7.50) have a much higher tar content than their equivalents at home; the genuine article can be found in duty-free shops. Matches are *kibreet*; a cigarette lighter is a *wallah*. Respectable women don't generally smoke, and certainly not in public, though nowadays wealthier young women may be seen smoking *sheeshas* in Cairo's posher establishments.

Costs

Once you've arrived, Egypt is an inexpensive and good-value destination – except perhaps for Sinai and Hurghada, which are pricier than other parts of the country. As a rule, though, providing you avoid luxury hotels or tourist-only services, costs for food, accommodation and transport are low by European standards.

Most of the prices in this book are given in Egyptian pounds (see p.70). The main exceptions to this rule – airfares, prices for top-flight accommodation and dive or safari packages – are given in US dollars or euros, depending on what the establishments themselves quote. Despite this, you can almost always pay in Egyptian pounds, according to the prevailing exchange rate.

If you're trying to keep expenses down, it is possible to get by on £15/$30 a day by staying in cheap hotels and eating street food, but you won't have much left over for sightseeing or activites. On £30/$60 a day, you can eat well and stay in a two- or even three-star hotel. If you want to stay in tiptop accommodation, you could be paying upwards of £100/$180 a night, but even if you travel everywhere by taxi and eat in the very best restaurants, you'll be hard put to add more than £20/$35 a day to that figure.

Although Egypt is generally fairly cheap, there are some hidden costs that can bump up your daily budget. Most restaurant and hotel bills are liable to a **service charge** plus **local taxes** (Cairo, Luxor and Hurghada have the highest), which increase the final cost by 17–25 percent (unless already included in the price). Visiting the Pyramids and the monuments of the Nile Valley entails spending a lot on **site tickets** (typically £E15–50, though holders of student cards get a discount of at least a third). The custodians of tombs and temples and the medieval mosques of Islamic Cairo also expect to be tipped.

Egyptian inflation is currently running at around five percent. Prices for luxury goods and services (ie, most things in the private sector) rise faster than for public transport, petrol and basic foodstuffs, the costs of which are held down by subsidies that the government dare not abolish.

Student and other discount cards

Full-time students are eligible for the **International Student Identity Card** (ISIC), which entitles to you to a fifty-percent discount on most of Egypt's museums and sites, a thirty-percent discount on rail fares and around fifteen percent on ferries. To obtain the card, you will need to provide a valid student ID card or proof of student status. ISICs can be bought at home (see ⓦ www .istc.org for details of outlets) or for E£70 at the Egyptian Student Travel Services at 23 Sharia el-Manial, on Roda Island in Cairo (☎ 02/531-0330, ⓦ www.estsegypt.com; daily except Fri 8am–6pm, Fri 9am–4pm); you can get there on foot from the El-Malek el-Saleh metro. An alternative available to anyone under 26 is the **International Youth Travel Card**, and teachers qualify for the **International Teacher Identity Card**, both at the same price, from the same places, and offering similar discounts.

At some of the budget hotels in Cairo, it may be possible to buy an ISIC card without presenting student ID, but this unofficial practice has been cracked down on in recent years. Obvious non-students brandishing student cards for reductions at archeological sites may end up having to explain themselves to the Tourist Police.

Disabled travellers

Disability is common in Egypt. Many conditions that would be treatable in the West, such as cataracts, cause permanent disabilities here because people can't afford the treatment. Disability carries no stigma, it is simply God's will, to be accepted – as Egyptians say, "Allah *karim*" (God is generous). On the other hand, disabled people are unlikely to get jobs (though there is a tradition of blind singers and preachers), so the choice is usually between staying at home being looked after by your family, and going out on the streets to beg for alms.

For a blind or wheelchair-using tourist, the streets are full of all sorts of obstacles that are hard to negotiate independently. If you walk with difficulty, you will find these obstacles and steep stairs hard going. Queueing, and the heat, will take it out of you if you have a condition that makes you tire quickly.

A light, folding camp-stool could be invaluable if you have limited walking or standing power. In that case, it's a good idea to avoid arriving in the summer months, when the scorching sun can really take it out of you.

For those who use a wheelchair, the **monuments** are a mix of the accessible and the impossible. Most of the major temples are built on relatively level sites, with a few steps here and there – manoeuvrable in a wheelchair or with sticks if you have an able-bodied helper. Your frustrations are likely to be with the tombs, which are almost always a struggle to reach – often sited halfway up cliffs, or down steep flights of steps. In the Valley of the Kings, for example, the only really straightforward tomb is that of Ramses VI. The Pyramids of Giza are fine to view but not enter, though the sound-and-light show is wheelchair accessible; Saqqara is difficult, being so sandy. Abu Simbel should be reasonably okay, provided you can cope with some rough surfaces. If you opt for a Nile cruise, bear in mind that you'll be among a large throng and will need to be carried on and off the boat if you depend on a wheelchair (often by people who don't understand English), an experience you may well not relish. In Aswan, it's not a good idea to stay on the islands if you use a wheelchair, because of the hassle of getting on and off ferries. In general, it's worth choosing accommodation within wheeling distance of the sites you wish to visit.

Cairo is generally bad news, especially Islamic Cairo, with its narrow, uneven alleys and heavy traffic, but with a car and helper, you could still see the Citadel and other major monuments. There's a lift in the Egyptian Antiquities Museum, and newer metro stations have lift access from street level to the platforms, though none of the older ones do, which unfortunately includes all those in the city centre. A number of hotels, all five-star, have rooms adapted for wheelchair users (these include the *Cairo Marriott*, *Conrad*, *Four Seasons*, *Grand Hyatt*, *Mena House Oberoi*, *Nile Hilton*, *Ramses Hilton* and *Semiramis Intercontinental*, all reviewed on pp.98–101).

Taxis are easily affordable and quite adaptable; if you charter one for the day, the driver is certain to help you in and out, and perhaps even around the sites you visit. If you employ a guide, they may well also be prepared to help you with steps and other obstacles. Some **diving** centres in Sinai and Hurghada accept disabled students on their courses, and the hotels in these resorts tend to be wheelchair-friendly.

Planning a holiday

There are **organized tours and holidays** specifically for people with disabilities, and some companies, such as Discover Egypt in the UK (see p.33), offer packages tailor-made to your specific needs. Egypt for All (in Egypt ✆012/396 1991; ✇www.egyptforall .com) run a range of tours – diving holidays, desert safaris, felucca trips, Nile cruises, etc – for people with disabilities, with programmes ranging from one-day excursions to two-week holidays.

If you want to be more **independent**, it's important to become an authority on where you must be self-reliant and where you may expect help, especially regarding transport and accommodation. It is also vital to be honest – with travel agencies, insurance companies and travel companions. A medical certificate of your fitness to travel, provided by your doctor, is also extremely useful.

It's a good idea to carry spares of any clothing or equipment that might be hard to find; if there's an association representing people with your disability, contact them early in the planning process.

Electricity

The current in Egypt is 220V, 50Hz. North American travellers with appliances designed for 110V should bring a converter. Most sockets are for round-pronged plugs, so you may need an adapter. Brief power cuts are quite common in Egypt.

Entry requirements

All visitors to Egypt must hold passports that are valid for at least six months beyond the proposed date of entry to the country. Citizens of most countries must also obtain tourist visas.

Regular **tourist visas** are available from Egyptian embassies abroad (see p.66). Most nationalities, including British, Irish,

Americans, Canadians, Australians, New Zealanders and all EU citizens, can also obtain visas on arrival at Cairo, Luxor and Hurghada airports. The process is generally painless and cheaper than getting one through an embassy, though note that visas issued at airports are valid for one month only, whereas embassies issue single-visit and multiple-entry visas entitling you to stay in Egypt for three months (the latter allow you to go in and out of the country three times within this period). Visas are *not* available at overland border crossings, or at Aswan, Suez or Nuweiba (apart from Sinai-only visas – see below).

Visa applications can be made in person or by post. If applying in person, turn up early in the day. Postal applications take between seven working days and six weeks to process. Don't be misled by statements on the application form indicating "valid for six months"; this simply means that the visa must be used within six months of the date of issue. When returning the form, you need to include a registered or recorded SAE, your passport, one photo, and a postal or money order (not a personal cheque).

Getting a standard visa on arrival costs US$17, irrespective of your nationality. The cost of getting a visa in advance of your trip varies according to your nationality, and from place to place. Some consulates may demand that you pay in US dollars instead of local currency, or ask you to supply extra photos. It's wise to allow for all these eventualities.

If you don't mind being limited to Sinai, you can obtain free **Sinai-only visas** at Taba on the Israeli–Egyptian border, St Catherine's Monastery or Sharm el-Sheikh airport, or the seaports at Sharm el-Sheikh and Nuweiba. Valid for fourteen days only, this visa restricts you to the Aqaba coast down to Sharm el-Sheikh, and the vicinity of St Catherine's; it is not valid for Ras Mohammed, the mountains around St Catherine's (except for Mount Sinai), or any other part of Egypt. It can't be extended, and there's no period of grace for overstaying. Note that neither regular nor Sinai-only visas are available at Rafah, the crossing between Gaza and Egypt.

Once in Egypt, carry your passport with you: you'll need it to register at hotels, change

Israeli stamps

At the time of writing, most Arab countries except Egypt and Jordan will deny entry to anyone whose passport shows evidence of a visit to Israel. Although Israeli immigration officials will usually give you an entry stamp on a separate piece of paper if you ask them to, an Egyptian entry stamp at Taba or Rafah in the Sinai will give you away – and the Egyptians insist on stamping your passport. So if you are travelling around the Middle East, be sure to visit Israel *after* you have been to Syria, Lebanon, or wherever. If you enter Egypt from Israel with the intention of travelling on to Libya or Sudan, you are going to have big problems trying to get an onward visa. Even if you have more than one passport, and apply for your Sudanese or Libyan visa on a passport with no Egyptian entry stamp, the embassy will want to know why it doesn't have one. Similarly, if you trade your old passport and get a new one issued by your embassy in Cairo, it is unlikely to pass muster with the Sudanese or Libyan authorities.

money, collect mail, and possibly to show at police checkpoints. If you're travelling for any length of time, you may find it worthwhile to register with your embassy on arrival in Cairo, which will help speed things up if you lose your passport. At the least, it's wise to photocopy the pages recording your particulars and keep them separately. If you are travelling to areas of the country that require permits (see p.38), spare sets of photocopies are useful for producing with your application.

Egyptian embassies and consulates

A lists of Egyptian embassies can be found on the Egyptian Foreign Ministry website (ⓦ www .mfa.gov.eg), and also on the Arab Net site at ⓦ www.arab.net/egypt/et_embassies.htm.
Australia 1 Darwin Ave, Yarralumla, ACT 2600 ☎ 02/6273 4437; Level 4, 241 Commonwealth St, Surry Hills, NSW 2010 ☎ 02/9281 4844; Level 9, 124 Exhibition St, Melbourne, Vic 3000 ☎ 03/9654 8869. Visa application forms are available at ⓦ www.egypt.org.au.
Canada 454 Laurier Ave E, Ottawa, ON K1N 6R3 ☎ 613/234 4931 or 4935; 1 Place Ville Marie, Suite 2617, Montreal PQ H3B 4S3 ☎ 514/866 8455 to 7, ⓦ www.egyptianconsulatemontreal.org.
Greece 3 Leoforos Vassilissis Sofias, 106-71, Athens ☎ 210 36 18 612 or 3.
Ireland 12 Clyde Rd, Ballsbridge, Dublin 4 ☎ 01/660 6566, ⓦ www.embegyptireland.ie.
Israel 54 Rehov Basel, Tel Aviv 62744 ☎ 03/546 4151 or 2; 68 Rehov Afrouni, Eilat ☎ 08/637 6882.
Jordan 14 Riyad Mefleh St, Amman (between 4th and 5th circles, next to the *Dove Hotel*) ☎ 06/560 5175 or 6; Al-Wahdat Al-Jarbiyya, Sharia al-Istiqlal, Aqaba ☎ 03/201 6171 or 81.

Libya Sharia el-Shatt, Tripoli ☎ 021/444, ⓔ egyemblib@hotmail.com; Sharia el-Awarsi, Western Fuwaihat, Benghazi ☎ 061/222 3099.
New Zealand c/o the embassy in Australia.
Palestine 204–55 Sharia Omar al-Mukhtar, Gaza City ☎ 07/282 4274 or 84 or 94.
South Africa 270 Bourke St, Muckleneuk, Pretoria ☎ 012/343 1590 or 91.
Sudan Sharia al-Gomhuria, PO Box 1126, Khartoum ☎ 03/1182 3666.
UK 2 Lowndes St, London SW1X 9ET ☎ 020/7235 9777, ⓦ www.egyptianconsulate.co.uk.
USA 3521 International Court NW, Washington DC 20008 ☎ 202/895-5400, ⓦ www.egyptembassy.us; 1110 Second Ave, Suite 201, New York, NY 10022 ☎ 212/759-7120 to 22, ⓦ www.egyptnyc.net; 3001 Pacific Ave, San Francisco, CA 94115–1013 ☎ 415/346-9700, ⓦ www.egy2000.com; 500 N Michigan Ave, Suite 1900, Chicago, IL 60611 ☎ 312/828-9162 to 4; 1990 Post Oak Blvd, Suite 2180, Houston, TX 77056 ☎ 713/961-4915 or 6.

Visa extensions and re-entry permits

Tourists who **overstay** their visa are allowed a fifteen-day period of grace in which to renew it or leave the country. After this, they're fined £E104 unless they can present a letter of apology from their embassy (which may well cost more).

Visa **extensions** cost around £E12, and are obtainable from the Mugamma in Cairo or from passport offices in governorate capitals such as Alexandria, Luxor, Aswan, Suez, El-Tor, Mersa Matrouh and Ismailiya (addresses are detailed in the guide). Depending on how long you wish to extend by, and on the whim of the official, you may have to produce exchange or ATM receipts proving that you've cashed sufficient hard currency during your stay, and you'll need to supply one or two photos. Procedures vary slightly from office to office, but shouldn't take longer than an hour outside Cairo.

If you have a single-entry visa and want to leave Egypt and return within the period of its validity, you will need a re-entry visa. Procedures for obtaining these are much the same as for a visa extension, and the cost is around £E50 for one entry, £E60 for two or more.

Gay and lesbian travellers

As a result of sexual segregation, male homosexuality is relatively common in Egypt, but attitudes towards it are schizophrenic. Few Egyptians will declare themselves gay – which has connotations of femininity and weakness – and the dominant partner in gay sex may well not consider himself to be indulging in a homosexual act. Rather, homosexuality is tacitly accepted as an outlet for urges that can't otherwise be satisfied. Despite this, people are mindful that homosexuality is condemned in the Koran and the Bible, and reject the idea of Egypt as a "gay destination" (although male prostitution is an open secret in Luxor and Aswan). The common term for gay men in Egyptian Arabic, *khawal*, has derogatory connotations.

Homosexuality is not illegal in Egypt, but that does not stop the authorities from persecuting gay men, usually on charges of "habitual debauchery". In 2001, a raid by Egyptian police on the *Queen Boat* floating disco hit the headlines worldwide. The venue was frequented by heterosexual couples as well as by gay Egyptian and foreign men, though only Egyptian men alone or with male partners were arrested. Most were tried for "habitual debauchery", and two for "contempt of religion". Those convicted received sentences of one to five years in jail.

One result of all this is that **meeting places** for gay men have gone underground, particularly in Cairo, and places that are well known as gay locales have become dangerous for Egyptians. Foreigners seem to be safe from such persecution, but if you have a gay relationship with an Egyptian man, be

aware that discretion is vital. **Lesbians** do not face this kind of state harassment, but they have never been visible in Egyptian society. As a Western woman, your chances of making contact are virtually zilch.

Online resources

Gay Egypt ⓦ www.gayegypt.com. Practical advice and contacts, but don't log on to it within Egypt, as the Security Police not only monitor the site but may also take an interest in computers which access it.
Globalgayz ⓦ www.globalgayz.com/g-egypt2. html. Their Egypt page has articles about the current situation facing gays in Egypt.
International Gay and Lesbian Human Rights Commission ⓦ www.iglhrc.org. Posts information about civil rights for gay people in Egypt.

Hiring guides

Professional guides can be engaged through branches of Misr Travel (see p.38), American Express and Thomas Cook, local tourist offices and large hotels. You can also hire them on the spot at sights such as the Egyptian Antiquities Museum in Cairo and the Pyramids of Giza. They normally charge a fixed hourly rate, though a tip would also be expected.

Such guides can be useful at major sites, like the Valley of the Kings, where they will be able to ease your way through queues at the tombs. If you feel intimidated by the culture, too, you might welcome an intermediary for the first couple of days' sightseeing. In general, however, there's no special need to employ anyone: they tend to have enough work already with tour groups.

Far more common are local, self-appointed guides, who fall into two main categories. At ancient sites, there are always plenty of hangers-on, who will offer to show you "secret tombs" or "special reliefs" or just present themselves in tombs or temples, with palms outstretched. They don't have a lot to offer you, and encouragement makes life more difficult for everyone following. You can usually get rid of them by reading aloud from a guidebook.

The other kind – most often encountered in a small town or village – are people, often teenagers, who genuinely want to help out foreigners, and maybe practise their English at the same time. Services offered could be escorting you from one taxi depot to another, or showing you the route to the souks or to a local site. The majority of people you meet this way don't expect money and you could risk offence by offering. If people want money from you for such activities, they won't be shy about asking.

Insurance

Travel insurance is well worth considering, providing useful cover in the event of unforeseen curtailment or cancellation of your trip, and for medical treatment you may need while in Egypt. Cover for lost or stolen baggage or valuables is often fairly minimal, but some "all risks" home insurance policies provide more generous backup cover. When choosing a policy, it's worth asking about whether you're covered to take part in so-called "dangerous sports" or other activities – in Egypt, this could mean, for example, camel trekking or scuba diving.

If you need to make a **claim**, you should keep receipts for medicines and medical treatment, and in the event you have anything stolen, you must obtain an official theft report from the police (called a *mahdar*). You may also be required to provide proof that you owned the items that were stolen, in the form of shop receipts or a credit-card statement recording the purchase.

Rough Guides has teamed up with Columbus Direct to offer you travel insurance that can be tailored to suit your needs. Products include a low-cost **backpacker** option for long stays; a **short break** option for city getaways; a typical **holiday package** option; and others. There are also annual **multi-trip** policies for those who travel regularly. Different sports and activities can be usually be covered if required.

See ⓦ www.roughguidesinsurance .com for eligibility and purchasing options. Alternatively, UK residents should call ☎ 0870/033 9988; US citizens should call ☎ 1-800/749-4922; Australians should call ☎ 1-300/669 999. All other nationalities should call ☎ +44 870/890 2843.

Internet

Internet access is available in almost all the main tourist destinations, with Internet cafés sprouting and hotels providing computers for guests to use. The charge is usually £E5–10 an hour, although five-star hotels may charge up to £E50.

Laundry

Wherever you are staying, there will either be an in-house laundry (*mahwagi*), or one close by to call on, charging piece rates: from £E4 for a dress, £E2 for a shirt or trousers. Some budget hotels in Luxor, Aswan and Hurghada allow guests to use their washing machine for a small charge, or gratis. You can buy washing powder at most pharmacies. Dry cleaners are confined to Cairo, Aswan and Hurghada.

Living in Egypt

Many foreigners make a living in Egypt, teaching English or diving, writing for the English-language media, or even bellydancing. Getting a work permit involves firstly getting a job offer, and then taking evidence of this to Mogamma in Cairo (see p.266), where you apply officially. So long as you have an offer of employment in a field where foreigners rather than Egyptians are needed, it is simply then a question of jumping through the necessary bureaucratic hoops.

Teaching in Egypt largely means working in Cairo or Alexandria, where there are many private language schools, generally catering to adults. There's quite a big market for people wanting to learn both conversational and business English. The British Council in Cairo (see p.263) may be able to supply a list of schools teaching English to approach.

Egypt has been the launch pad for several **journalistic** careers, for it's easy to place work with the local English-language media. *Egypt Today* takes travel articles and photos, while the *Egyptian Gazette* may need subeditors from time to time. International press agencies may also accept material and possibly employ stringers.

Though most jobs in **tourism** are restricted to Egyptian nationals, and locally based companies usually insist on a work permit, you can sometimes fix up a season's work with a foreign tour operator as a rep or tour guide. In Sinai, Hurghada and Luxor there may be a demand for people with foreign languages to sell dive courses or work on hotel reception desks. The most useful languages to have are German, French, Italian, Japanese or Russian (the last only on the Red Sea and Sinai coasts). Ask around dive centres or upmarket hotels if you're interested.

Divers with Divemaster or Instructor certificates can often find work with diving centres in Hurghada or Sinai, which may also take on less qualified staff and let them learn on the job, at reduced rates of pay or in return for free tuition. Dive centres commonly turn a blind eye to the lack of a work permit, or might procure one for a valued worker.

Foreign **bellydancers** are much in demand in nightclubs in Cairo, Alexandria, Luxor and Hurghada. The work can be well paid, but financial or sexual exploitation are real hazards. Aside from work, many foreign dancers come to Egypt to improve their art or buy costumes. Finding a teacher is surprisingly difficult, as there are no schools as such, but you might start by making enquiries at the *Berlin Hotel* in Cairo (see p.96), or at the specialist shops which sell bellydancing costumes, music tapes and videos (see p.252).

Studying

The **American University in Cairo** (℡02/794-2964, 🌐www.aucegypt.edu) offers year-abroad and non-degree programmes, a summer school and intensive Arabic courses. A full year's tuition (two semesters and summer school) costs roughly US$18,000. US citizens may apply to the Stafford Loan Program, at Office of Admissions, 420 Fifth Ave, 3rd Floor, New York, NY 10018-2729 (℡212/730-8800).

Foreign students may also attend one- or two-term programmes at **Egyptian universities**, such as Cairo (🌐www.cu.edu.eg), Ain Shams (🌐net.shams.edu.eg) and Al-Azhar (🌐www.alazhar.org). These are valid for transferable credits at most American and some British universities. In the US, you can get information on exchange programmes from the Egyptian Cultural and Educational Bureau, 1303 New Hampshire Ave NW,

Washington DC 20036 (℡202/296-3888, 🌐www.eceb.us) or AmidEast, 1730 M St NW Suite 1100, Washington DC 20036 (℡202/776-9600, 🌐www.amideast.org).

A number of schools in Cairo offer courses in **Arabic language**, both in colloquial Egyptian Arabic and Modern Standard Arabic; see p.265 for more.

Mail

Airmail letters sent from Egypt generally take around a week to ten days to reach Western Europe, and two to three weeks to North America or Australasia. It speeds up the delivery if you get someone to write the name of the country in Arabic. As a rule, around fifteen percent of correspondence (in either direction) never arrives; letters containing photos or other items are especially prone to go astray.

It's best to send letters from a major city or hotel; blue mailboxes are for overseas airmail, red ones for domestic post. Airmail (*bareed gawwi*) stamps can be purchased at post offices, hotel shops and postcard stands, which may charge a few piastres above the normal rate (£E1.50 for a postcard/letter to anywhere in the world). Registered mail, costing £E1 extra, can be sent from any post office. Selected post offices in the main cities offer an Express Mail Service. Private courier firms such as DHL and UPS are limited to a few cities, and a lot more expensive. To send a **parcel**, take it unsealed to a major post office (in Cairo, you'll need to use the one at Ramses Square) for customs inspection, weighing and wrapping (for which you may have to pay around £E5).

Post office hours are generally daily except Fridays from 8am to 6pm (Ramadan 9am–3pm), though in big cities post offices may stay open until 8pm.

If receiving mail, note that any package or letter containing goods is likely to be held, and you will have to collect it from the relevant post office, where you will have to pay customs duty; you should be informed that it has arrived and where you need to pick it up. **Poste restante** (general delivery) services exist, but are unreliable and best avoided if possible (you could have people write to you care of a hotel). If you do use the service, have mail addressed clearly, with the surname in capital letters, and bear in mind that even then, it may well be misfiled.

Maps

The best general **map** of Egypt is published by Rough Guides on a scale of 1:1,125,000, on tear-proof paper, with roads, railways and contours clearly marked; Freytag & Berndt's (1:1,000,000) is a good second-best. Kümmerly & Frey (1:950,000; published in Egypt by Lenhert & Landrock) makes a reasonable alternative, as does the more widespread Bartholomew map (1:1,000,000; also published in Egypt by Lenhert & Landrock), though this shows rather less detail.

Taken together, several local **city plans** cover Cairo in comprehensive detail (see p.89). Elsewhere, however, coverage is poor or non-existent. **Diving maps** of the Red Sea are available in Egypt, but some of these do not cover sites in the Sinai, which for most people is the main diving area.

Full-blown **desert expeditions** require detailed maps that can be obtained in Cairo from the Survey Office (*heyat al-misaha*) on Sharia Abdel Salam Arif at the corner of Sharia Giza (daily except Fri 9am–1pm; see map p.170 for location), though they may demand an official letter explaining why you need the maps. Geological maps can be obtained without bureaucratic obstruction (but bring your passport) from the Geological Survey and Mining Authority (*misaha wa geologia*) at 3 Sharia Salah Salem, Abbassiya, about 500m south of Midan Abbassiya and Sinai bus terminal (Mon–Thurs & Sun 9am–2.30pm; ☎02/628 8013).

Money

Egypt's basic unit of **currency** is the Egyptian pound (called a *ginay* in Arabic, and written £E or LE). At the time of writing, exchange rates were around £E11 to the pound sterling, £E5.80 to the US dollar, and £E7.50 to the euro. It is divided into 100 piastres, which are called *'urush* (singular *'irsh*) in Arabic.

Egyptian **banknotes** bear Arabic numerals on one side, Western numerals on the other, and come in denominations of 5pt, 10pt, 25pt, 50pt, £E1, £E5, £E10, £E20, £E50 and £E100, though the first two are uncommon. There are coins to the value of 5pt,

10pt, 20pt, 25pt, 50pt and £E1; some 25pt coins have a hole in the middle.

Many of the notes in circulation are so ragged that merchants refuse them. Trying to palm off (and avoid receiving) decrepit notes can add spice to minor transactions, or be a real nuisance. Conversely, some vendors won't accept high-denomination notes (£E20 upwards) due to a shortage of change. While some offer sweets in lieu of coins, others round prices up. Try to hoard coins and small-value notes for tips, fares and small purchases.

Carrying your money

The easiest way to access your money in Egypt is with **plastic**, though it's a good idea to also have some back-up in the form of cash or traveller's cheques. Using a Visa, MasterCard, Plus or Cirrus card, you can draw cash using ATMs at branches of the main banks in cities, major towns and tourist resorts. The machines are accessible at any time, as they're usually situated outside the banks and inside airports and some shopping centres. By using ATMs you get trade exchange rates, which are somewhat better than those charged by banks for changing cash, though your card issuer may well add a foreign transaction fee. Note also that there is a daily limit on ATM cash withdrawals, usually £E4000, and that some machines tend to jam and may swallow your card if you try to withdraw £E1000 at one go. If you use a credit card rather than a debit card, note also that all cash advances and ATM withdrawals obtained are treated as loans, with interest accruing daily from the date of withdrawal.

It's wise to make sure your card is in good condition and, before you leave home, make sure that the card and PIN will work overseas. Where there is no ATM, cash advances on Visa and MasterCard can be obtained at most branches of the Banque Misr on the same basis.

Credit cards are accepted for payment at major hotels, top-flight restaurants, some shops and airline offices, but virtually nowhere else. American Express, MasterCard and Visa are the likeliest to be accepted. Beware of people making extra copies of the receipt, to fraudulently bill you later; insist that the transaction is done before your eyes. American Express card-holders can cash personal cheques at the main Amex branches (see below).

If you are having **money wired** to yourself in Egypt, you can make use of Western Union (@www.westernunion.com; their agents are mainly branches of the Arab African International Bank) or Moneygram (@www.moneygram.com; via branches of the National Société Générale Bank, or NSGB).

Banks and exchange

Arriving by land or sea, you should have no trouble changing money at the border, and airport banks are open around the clock. It is illegal, and unnecessary, to import or export more than £E1000 in local currency.

The best exchange rates for cash can be found at **Forex bureaus**, which are private moneychangers found in large towns and tourist resorts, though they don't always take traveller's cheques, and will offer worse rates than the banks if they do. However, they are open longer hours and perform transactions more quickly than Egyptian banks, where forms are passed among a bevy of clerks and counters. Such extended transactions are less likely at foreign banks (found only in Cairo and Alexandria) or branches in hotels, or offices of **American Express** (branches in Alexandria, Luxor and Aswan) or **Thomas Cook** (branches in Cairo, Alexandria, Luxor, Aswan, Port Said, Hurghada and Sharm el-Sheikh). Among the main Egyptian banks are Bank of Alexandria, Banque Misr, Banque du Caire and National Bank of Egypt. **Commission** is not generally charged on currency exchange, but there might be 40pt stamp duty, which you can either pay or have them deduct from the amount issued.

Banking hours are generally Sunday to Thursday 8.30am to 2pm, or 9.30am to 1.30pm during Ramadan. Branches in five-star hotels may open longer hours, sometimes even 24/7. For arriving visitors, the banks at Cairo airport and the border crossings from Israel are open 24 hours daily, and those at ports whenever a ship docks.

US dollars, euros and English sterling notes are easy to exchange almost anywhere – though due to forgeries, banks are often unwilling to accept US$100 notes issued before 1992, or in less than mint condition. Aside from ordinary spending, hard cash (usually US$) may be required for visas, border taxes and suchlike. Forex bureaus will also change Canadian, Australian, Cypriot, Jordanian and Libyan currency (though notes must be in mint condition), and some banks will change all but the last – branches in five-star hotels are your best bet. Don't bring New Zealand dollars, or Scottish or Northern Irish sterling banknotes, which are not accepted. Sudanese pounds are extremely difficult to change in Egypt, and Israeli shekels can only be changed at the Taba border crossing, and at one or two banks (in five-star hotels) and some Cairo Forex bureaus.

From time to time there is a **black market** in foreign currency, but it seems to have gone into abeyance of late, and is always extremely clandestine. You're best advised to avoid illegal street moneychangers, who are very likely to be rip-off artists or *agents provocateurs*.

In theory you can change back up to £E1000 on departure (you may need to produce exchange receipts to prove that you obtained your Egyptian cash legally), but in practice you may find that airport banks are unwilling to supply hard currency. If you really need to change back any currency before leaving, a Forex bureau is your best bet.

Opening hours and public holidays

Offices tend to open Sunday to Thursday from 8.30am to 5pm. Shops are usually open from around 10am to around 8pm, sometimes later, with small places often closing briefly for prayers, especially Friday lunchtime between around noon and 3pm.

During the month of **Ramadan**, all these hours go haywire. Since everybody who keeps the fast will want to eat immediately when it ends at sunset, everything tends to close early to allow for this, and places may open early to compensate. Offices may open 7am–4pm, shops may simply close to break the fast, reopening afterwards, while banks open 9.30am to 1.30pm. Ramadan opening times are given, where available, throughout the text.

Islamic holidays

Islamic religious holidays are calculated on the lunar calendar, so their dates rotate throughout the seasons (as does the start of Ramadan, the dates for which are listed below). Approximate dates for the next few years are:

	2007	**2008**	**2009**	**2010**	**2011**
Eid el-Adha	Dec 20	Dec 9	Nov 28	Nov 17	Nov 6
Ras el-Sana el-Hegira	Jan 20	Jan 10 & Dec 29	Dec 18	Dec 7	Nov 25
Moulid el-Nabi	Mar 31	Mar 20	Mar 9	Feb 26	Feb 15
1st of Ramadan (not a holiday)	Sept 13	Sept 2	Aug 22	Aug 11	July 31
Eid el-Fitr	Oct 13	Oct 2	Sept 21	Sept 10	Aug 30

Public holidays are Coptic Christmas (Jan 7), Sinai Liberation Day (April 25), Labour Day (May 1), Evacuation Day (June 18), Revolution Day (July 23), Flooding of the Nile (Aug 15), Armed Forces Day (Oct 6), Suez Liberation Day (Oct 23), and Victory Day (Dec 23), plus the Islamic festivals in the box above, and Coptic Easter Monday (Sham al-Nassim: April 28, 2008; April 20, 2009; April 5, 2010; and April 25, 2011). Dates for other Coptic festivals appear on p.259.

Phones

All towns and cities have at least one 24-hour telephone and telegraph office (*maktab el-telephonat*, or *centraal*) for calling long-distance and abroad, but you can also buy a phonecard (issued by Menatel, Ringo or Egypt Telecom) from kiosks and grocery stores to use in street phone booths. Menatel is the main company – its latest rates can be found online at ⓦ www.menatel.com .eg. Outside peak time (8am–8pm) rates are around twenty percent lower.

Cards which have a scratch-off panel with a PIN underneath can be used from private phones by dialling a toll-free number, then the PIN on the card, and finally the number you wish to call. These usually work out cheaper than ordinary phonecards, and are available from the same places, but – annoyingly – they don't usually work from public telephones.

Mobile phones

If you want to use take your mobile phone with you, you'll need to check with your phone provider whether it will work in Egypt

and what the call charges are. You may get charged extra for international roaming to be activated, and to receive calls in Egypt. A mobile bought for use in the US must be GSM/triband to work in Egypt.

If you're planning to use your phone a lot in Egypt, especially for local calls, it's worth getting on to one of the Egyptian networks (if your phone is locked to your home network, you will need to pay a small fee to have it unlocked). You can then buy a SIM card from either of Egypt's two mobile providers, Mobinil (prefix ☎012) and Vodafone (☎010), both of which have retailers everywhere. A typical deal gives you a SIM card for around £E70, including £E50 of free calls. Top-up cards are available in denominations from £E10 to £E200 (plus 15 percent tax and a small mark-up for the retailer). Mobinil tends to have better coverage than Vodafone, especially in the Western Desert and on the Mediterranean coast.

Photography

Photography needs to be undertaken with care. If you are obviously taking a photograph of someone, ask their permission – especially in the more remote, rural regions where you can cause genuine offence. You may also find people stop you from taking photos that show Egypt in a "poor" or "backward" light. On a more positive front, taking a photograph of (and later sending it to) someone you've struck up a friendship with, or exchanging photographs, is often – in the towns at least – greatly appreciated. As ever, be wary of photographing anything militarily sensitive (bridges, train stations, dams, etc).

Useful codes and numbers

Egypt's country code is ☎20. If calling home, note that the initial zero is omitted from the area code when dialling the UK, Ireland, Australia and New Zealand from abroad.

US and Canada 00 + 1 + area code + number.
Australia 00 + 61 + area code + number.
New Zealand 00 + 64 + area code + number.
UK 00 + 44 + area code + number.
Republic of Ireland 00 + 353 + area code + number.
South Africa 00 + 27 + area code + number.

Emergencies and information
Directory enquiries ☎140 or 141
International operator ☎120
Police ☎122
Tourist police ☎126
Ambulance ☎123
Fire department ☎180

Religious buildings

Most of the **mosques** and their attached **madrassas** (Islamic colleges) that you'll want to visit are in Cairo and, with the exception of the El-Hussein and Saiyida Zeinab mosques, are classified as "historic monuments". They are open routinely to non-Muslim visitors, although anyone not worshipping should avoid prayer times, especially the main service at noon on Friday. Elsewhere in the country, mosques are not used to seeing tourists and locals may object to your presence. Tread with care and if at all possible ask someone to take you in.

At all mosques, dress is important. Shorts (or short skirts) and exposed shoulders are out, and in some places women may be asked to cover their hair (a scarf might be provided). Above all, remember to remove your shoes upon entering the precinct. They will either be held by a shoe custodian (small baksheesh expected) or you can just leave them outside the door, or carry them in by hand (if you do this, place the soles together, as they are considered unclean). A custodian who opens a place up, takes you into a tomb or lets you up a minaret rates £E5–10 (which you should pay after your visit).

Egyptian **monasteries** (which are Coptic, save for Greek Orthodox St Catherine's in Sinai) admit visitors at all times except during the Lenten or other fasts (local fasts are detailed in the guide where appropriate).

Similar rules of dress etiquette to those for mosques apply, though unless you go into the church itself you don't need to remove your shoes.

Shopping

Because prices in Egypt are generally so low, many things are worth buying there simply because they are cheap. Clothing and footwear falls into this category, for example. Souvenirs vary from tacky papyruses and (generally adulterated) perfumes, hawked everywhere tourists gather, usually at inflated prices, to bellydancing costumes and rugs, which require a little more serious shopping and price comparison. Most of these items are covered in our Cairo chapter (pp.249–257), where you'll find hints on how to check quality and avoid scams.

Haggling, needless to say, is *de rigueur*. Many Westerners are intimidated by this, but it really needn't be an ordeal. Know before you start what price you want to pay, offer something much lower, and let the shopkeeper argue you up, but not above your maximum price. If you don't reach an agreement, even after a lengthy session, nothing is lost. But if you state a price and the seller agrees, you are obliged to pay – so it is important not to start bidding for something you don't really want, nor to let a price pass your lips if you are not prepared to pay it. Haggling is, as much as anything else, a social activity and should be good-natured, not acrimonious, even if you know the seller is trying to overcharge you outrageously.

Don't be put off by theatrics on the part of the seller, which are all part of the game. Buyers' tactics include stressing any flaws that might reduce the object's value; talking of lower quotes received elsewhere; feigning indifference or having a friend urge you to leave. Avoid being tricked into raising your bid twice in a row, or admitting your estimation of the object's worth (just reply that you've made an offer).

One thing not to buy is any kind of supposed pharaonic **antiquity**. The export of antiquities is strictly prohibited, and you could end up in prison if caught trying to smuggle them out. Another thing to avoid is **ivory** products: their sale is legal, but Egypt has made the import of ivory illegal, leading to supplies being smuggled in from Sudan and Kenya, where poachers are decimating elephant herds. If that's not sufficient reason to boycott ivory products, almost all Western countries prohibit their importation. Inlaid or carved bone makes an acceptable, cheaper substitute.

Toilets

Public toilets are almost always filthy, and there's never any toilet paper (though someone may sell it outside). They're usually known as *toileta*, and marked with WC and Men and Women signs. Expect squat toilets in bus stations, resthouses and fleapit hotels; on sit-down toilets, beware of pranging yourself on the nozzle of the curly waterpipe, intended to assist the ablutions of devout Muslims. Though it's wise to carry toilet paper (£E1 per double roll in pharmacies) at all times, paper tissues, sold on the streets (50pt), will serve at a pinch.

Time

Egypt is on GMT+2 in winter, which means it is two hours ahead of the British Isles, seven hours ahead of the US East Coast (EST), eleven hours ahead of the US West Coast (PST), six hours behind Western Australia, eight hours behind East Australia and ten hours behind New Zealand. Egypt's clocks move forward for Daylight Saving Time on the last Friday in April and back again on the last Friday in September.

Tourist information

The Egyptian Tourist Authority (sometimes abbreviated as EGAPT; ⓦwww.egypt .travel) maintains general information offices in several countries, where you can pick up a range of pamphlets. However, most are simply intended to whet your appetite, and few hard facts can be gained from offices abroad. Their website gives a good overview of Egypt's tourist attractions, with sections on pharaonic and Coptic Egypt, as well as diving, golf, other sports and even health spas. Better still, ⓦwww.touregypt.net has quite a lot of useful information, including details of main tourist attractions, and listings of hotels, nightclubs and Internet cafés.

In Egypt itself, you'll get a variable response from local tourist offices (addresses are given throughout the guide). The most knowledgeable and helpful ones are in Luxor, Aswan, Sohag, Assyut, Minya, Alexandria and the oases of Siwa and Dakhla. Staff in Cairo are also well informed, but may need prodding. Elsewhere, most provincial offices are good for a dated brochure, if nothing else. As often as not, the level of knowledge and the quality of advice you receive may depend on who exactly you speak to: in some cases (detailed in the text), we recommend contacting a specific member of staff who speaks good English and is well informed.

Government travel advisory services

Australia Department of Foreign Affairs ⓦwww .dfat.gov.au, ⓦwww.smartraveller.gov.au.
Canada Department of Foreign Affairs ⓦwww .dfait-maeci.gc.ca.
Ireland Department of Foreign Affairs ⓦwww .foreignaffairs.gov.ie.
New Zealand Ministry of Foreign Affairs ⓦwww .mft.govt.nz.
UK Foreign & Commonwealth Office ⓦwww.fco .gov.uk/travel.
US State Department ⓦwww.travel.state.gov.

Egyptian tourist offices abroad

Canada 1253 McGill College Ave, Suite 250, Montreal, PQ H3B 2Y5 ☎514/861-4420, ⓔeta@total.net.
South Africa First Floor, Regent Palace Building, Mutual Gardens, Cradock Ave, Rosebank, Johannesburg, PO Box 3298 ☎011/880 9602.

UK 170 Piccadilly, London W1V 9DD ☎020/7493 5283, ⓦwww.gotoegypt.org.
USA 630 Fifth Ave, Suite 1706, New York, NY 10111 ☎212/332-2570, ⓔinfo@egypttourism .org; 8383 Wilshire Blvd, Suite 215, Beverly Hills, CA 90211 ☎323/653-8815, ⓔegypt@etala.com; 645 N Michigan Ave, Suite 829, Chicago, IL 60611 ☎312/280-4666, ⓔegyptmdwst@aol.com.

Travel agencies and hotels

Private travel agencies can advise on (and book) transport, accommodation and excursions, though their advice may not be unbiased. The most ubiquitous agency is the state-run Misr Travel, which operates hotels, buses and limos and can make bookings for most things. Its head office is in Cairo, with branches in other important cities, details of which are in the text. Misr Travel is also represented in London (second floor, 308 Regent St, W1B 3AT ☎020/7255 1087, ⓔmisrtravel@btclick.com) and New York (630 Fifth Ave, Suite 1460, New York, NY 10011 ☎212/332-2600 or 2601, ⓦwww .misrtravel.org). American Express and Thomas Cook also offer various travel services besides currency exchange. In Luxor, Hurghada and some of the Western Desert oases, most *pensions* double as information exchanges and all-round "fixers", as do campsites and backpackers' hotels in Sinai.

Tourist publications

The best guide to **what's on** can be found in the monthly magazine *Egypt Today*, which lists activities, entertainment and exhibitions in Cairo and Alexandria (it's sold in both), and events in Luxor and Aswan. Its features cover diverse aspects of Egyptian culture and travel in Egypt. Selected events are also listed in the daily *Egyptian Gazette*, and the weekly English-language edition of *Al-Ahram*, which are more widely available (see also p.52).

Useful things to bring

- **Binoculars** Perfect for observing reliefs high up on temple facades – or birdlife.
- **Earplugs** Help muffle the noise of videos on long-distance buses and trains, if you're trying to sleep.
- **Film/memory cards** Kodak and Fuji film is available in most towns and major resorts, but it may be old stock, so bring adequate supplies. If you use a digital camera, it doesn't hurt to bring more capacity in terms of memory cards than you think you'll need.
- **Mosquito net** The best guarantee of a mozzie-free night's sleep in the oases and the Nile Valley. Alternatively, buy a plug-in device (such as Ezalo) at any Egyptian pharmacy.
- **Sink plug** Few hotels (even relatively upmarket ones) have sink plugs, so pack an omnisize plug.
- **Sleeping bag** A decent bag is invaluable if you're planning to sleep out in the desert in spring or autumn, or in any low-budget hotel over winter. In the summer, a sheet sleeping bag or silk sleeping bag liner is handy if you're staying at cheap hotels, where just one (not necessarily clean) sheet is provided.
- **Snaps** of your family, home town, football team (or whatever) help bridge the language barrier. Locals will proudly show you their own.
- **Suitable clothes** Dress should be appropriate given Egypt's deeply conservative sensibilities (see p.59). Northern Egypt can be cold and damp in the winter, while the desert gets freezing at night, even in spring and autumn, so a warm sweater is invaluable, as are a solid pair of shoes: burst pipes are commonplace, and wandering around muddy streets in sodden sandals is a miserable experience.
- **Torch/flashlight** For exploring dark tombs, and for use during power cuts.

Guide

Guide

Cairo and the Pyramids

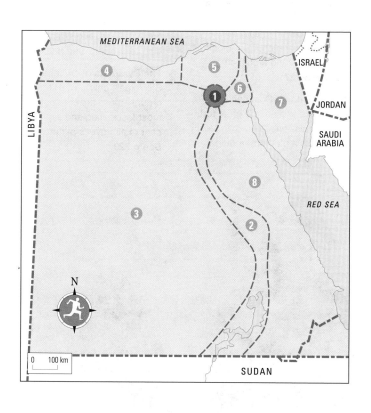

CHAPTER 1 # Highlights

✳ **The Museum of Egyptian Antiquities** One of the world's truly great museums, containing a massive collection of ancient statues, sarcophagi, frescoes, reliefs, and incredible treasures from the tomb of Tutankhamun. See p.107

✳ **Islamic Cairo** The medieval city of Salah al-Din (Saladin) is Cairo's true heart, teeming with life and chock-a-block with stunning architecture. See p.127

✳ **The Citadel** Dominating Cairo's skyline, the great fort commissioned by Salah al-Din boasts a plethora of quirky museums, a classic Ottoman mosque, and commanding views of the city. See p.154

✳ **Old Cairo** This compact quarter contains the city's most ancient Coptic churches and its oldest synagogue. See p.169

✳ **The Pyramids of Giza** The sole surviving wonder of the ancient world, and still stunning to this day. See p.206

✳ **The Pyramids of Dahshur** Still largely unknown to tour groups, these are some of the most fascinating and significant of all Egypt's pyramids. See p.229

△ The skyline of Islamic Cairo

1

Cairo and the Pyramids

The twin streams of Egypt's history converge just below the Delta at **Cairo**, where the greatest city in the Islamic world sprawls across the Nile towards the **Pyramids**, those supreme monuments of antiquity. Every visitor to Egypt comes here, to reel at the Pyramids' baleful mass and the seething immensity of Cairo, with its bazaars, mosques and Citadel and extraordinary Museum of Egyptian Antiquities. It's impossible, too, not to find yourself carried away by the street life, where medieval trades and customs coexist with a modern, cosmopolitan mix of Arab, African and European influences.

Cairo has been the largest city in Africa and the Middle East ever since the Mongols wasted Imperial Baghdad in 1258. Acknowledged as *umm dunya* or "**Mother of the World**" by medieval Arabs, and as Great Cairo by nineteenth-century Europeans, it remains, as Jan Morris writes in *Destinations*, "one of the half-dozen supercapitals – capitals that are bigger than themselves or their countries … the focus of a whole culture, an ideology or a historical moment". As Egypt has been a prize for conquerors from Alexander the Great to Rommel, so Cairo has been a fulcrum of power in the Arab world from the Crusades to the present day. The *ulema* of its thousand-year-old Al-Azhar Mosque (for centuries the foremost centre of Islamic intellectual life) remain the ultimate religious authority for millions of Sunni Muslims, from Jakarta to Birmingham. Wherever Arabic is spoken, Cairo's cultural magnetism is felt. Every strand of Egyptian society knits and unravels in this febrile megalopolis.

Egyptians have two names for the city, one ancient and popular, the other Islamic and official. The foremost is **Masr**, meaning both the capital and the land of Egypt – "Egypt City" – an Ur-city that endlessly renews itself and dominates the nation, an idea rooted in pharaonic civilization. (For Egyptians abroad, "Masr" refers to their homeland; within its borders it means the capital.) Whereas Masr is timeless, the city's other name, **Al-Qahira** (The Conqueror), is linked to an event: the Fatimid conquest that made this the capital of an Islamic empire that embraced modern-day Libya, Tunisia, Palestine and Syria. The name is rarely used in everyday speech.

Both archetypes still resonate and in monumental terms are symbolized by two dramatic **landmarks**: the **Pyramids of Giza** at the edge of the Western Desert and the great **Mosque of Mohammed Ali** – the modernizer of Islamic Egypt – which broods atop the Citadel. Between these two monuments

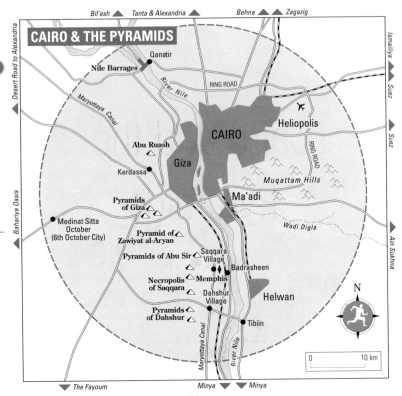

CAIRO & THE PYRAMIDS

sprawls a vast city, the colour of sand and ashes, of diverse worlds and epochs, and gross inequities. All is subsumed into an organism that somehow thrives in the terminal ward: medieval slums and Art Deco suburbs, garbage-pickers and marbled malls, donkey carts and limos, piousness and "the oaths of men exaggerating in the name of God". Cairo lives by its own contradictions.

This is a city, as Jan Morris put it, "almost overwhelmed by its own fertility". Its **population** is today estimated at around eighteen million and is swollen by a further million commuters from the Delta and a thousand new migrants every day. Today, one-third of Cairene households lack running water; a quarter of them have no sewers, either. An estimated half a million people reside in squatted cemeteries – the famous **Cities of the Dead**. The amount of green space per citizen has been calculated at thirteen square centimetres, not enough to cover a child's palm. Whereas earlier travellers noted that Cairo's air smelt "like hot bricks", visitors now find throat-rasping air **pollution**, chiefly caused by traffic. Cairo out-pollutes LA every day of the week: breathing the atmosphere downtown is reputedly akin to smoking thirty cigarettes a day.

Cairo's genius is to humanize these inescapable realities with **social rituals**. The rarity of public violence owes less to the armed police on every corner than to the *dowshah*: when conflicts arise, crowds gather, restraining both parties, encouraging them to rant, sympathizing with their grievances and then finally urging "*Maalesh, maalesh*" ("Never mind"). Everyday life is sweetened by flowery gestures and salutations; misfortunes evoke thanks for Allah's dispensation (after all, things could be worse). Even the poorest can be respected for piety; in the mosque, millionaire and beggar kneel side by side.

Extended-family values and neighbourly intervention prevail throughout the *baladi* quarters where millions of first- and second-generation rural migrants live, while arcane structures underpin life in Islamic Cairo. On a city-wide basis, the colonial distinction between "native quarters" and *ifrangi* (foreign) districts has given way to a dynamic stasis between rich and poor, westernization and traditionalism, complacency and desperation. Every year its polarities intensify, safety margins narrow and statistics make gloomier reading. The abyss beckons in prognoses of future trends, yet Cairo confounds doomsayers by dancing on the edge.

A brief history

Cairo is an agglomeration of half a dozen cities, the earliest of which came into existence 2500 years *after* ancient **Memphis**, the first capital of pharaonic Egypt, was founded (*c.*3100 BC) across the river and to the south. During the heyday of the Old Kingdom, vast necropolises developed along the desert's edge as the pharaohs erected ever greater funerary monuments, from the first Step Pyramid at **Saqqara** to the unsurpassable **Pyramids of Giza** (for their history, see pp.203–215). Meanwhile, across the Nile, there flourished a sister city of priests and solar cults known to posterity as **Ancient Heliopolis** (see p.200).

It took centuries of Persian, Greek and Roman rule to efface both cities, by which time a new fortified town had developed on the opposite bank. **Babylon-in-Egypt** was the beginning of the tale of cities that culminates in modern Cairo, the first chapter of which is described under "Old Cairo" (see p.169). Babylon's citizens, oppressed by foreign overlords, almost welcomed the army of Islam that conquered Egypt in 641. For strategic and spiritual reasons, their general, Amr, chose to found a new settlement beyond the walls of Babylon – **Fustat**, the "City of the Tent" (see "Old Cairo", p.169), which evolved into a sophisticated metropolis while Europe was in the Dark Ages.

Under successive dynasties of caliphs who ruled the Islamic Empire from Iraq, three more cities were founded, each to the northeast of the previous one, which itself was either spurned or devastated. When the schismatic Fatimids won the caliphate in 969, they created an entirely new walled city – **Al-Qahira** – beyond this teeming, half-derelict conurbation. **Fatimid Cairo** formed the nucleus of the later, vastly expanded and consolidated capital that Salah al-Din (Saladin) left to the Ayyubid dynasty in 1193. But the Ayyubids' reliance on imported slave-warriors – the Mamlukes – brought about their downfall: eventually, the Mamlukes simply seized power for themselves, ushering in a new era.

Mamluke Cairo encompassed all the previous cities, Salah al-Din's Citadel (where the sultans dwelt), the northern port of Bulaq and vast cemeteries and rubbish tips beyond the city walls. Mamluke sultans like Beybars, Qalaoun, Barquq and Qaitbey erected mosques, mausoleums and caravanserais that still ennoble what is now known in English as "Islamic Cairo". The like-named section of this chapter relates their stories, the Turkish takeover, the decline of **Ottoman Cairo** and the rise of Mohammed Ali, who began the modernization of the city. Under Ismail, the most profligate of his successors, a new, increasingly **European Cairo** arose beside the Nile (see "Central Cairo", p.102). By 1920, the city's area was six times greater than that of medieval Cairo, and since then its residential suburbs have expanded relentlessly, swallowing up farmland and desert. The emergence of this **Greater Cairo** is charted under "Gezira and the west bank" and "The northern suburbs".

Navigating this chapter

Arrival, information and city transport

Greater Cairo (see map pp.86–87) consists of two metropolitan governorates: **Cairo**, on the east bank of the Nile, and **Giza**, across the river. The **River Nile**

(*bahr en-nil*, or simply *en-nil*) is the prerequisite of their existence and fundamental to basic orientation. Bear in mind that it flows northwards through the city. The waterfront is dominated by the **islands** of Gezira and Roda and the **bridges** that connect them to the **Corniche** (embankment) on either side of the Nile. There are four major divisions of the city:

• **Central Cairo** (see map pp.104–105) spreads inland to the east of the islands. Its **downtown** area – between Ezbekiya Gardens and **Midan Tahrir** – bears the stamp of Western planning, as does **Garden City**, the embassy quarter further south. At the northern end of central Cairo (beyond the downtown area) lies **Ramses Station**, the city's main train terminal. Most of the banks, airlines, cheap hotels and tourist restaurants lie within this swathe of the city.

• Further east sprawls **Islamic Cairo**, encompassing **Khan el-Khalili** Bazaar, the Gamaliya quarter within the **Northern Walls**, and the labyrinthine Darb al-Ahmar district between the **Bab Zwayla** and the **Citadel**. Beyond the latter spread the eerie **Cities of the Dead** – the Northern and Southern cemeteries, and rising up beyond them, the **Muqattam Hills**, a barrier throughout history against Cairo's further eastward spread.

• The Southern Cemetery and the populous **Saiyida Zeinab** quarter merge into the rubbish tips and wasteland bordering the **ruins of Fustat** and the **Coptic quarter** of **Old Cairo**, further to the south. From there, a ribbon of development follows the metro out to **Ma'adi**, Cairo's plushest residential suburb, and **Helwan**, the city's heaviest industrial centre. Except for stylish **Heliopolis**, the **northern suburbs** hold little appeal for visitors.

• Across the river on the **west bank**, the residential neighbourhoods of **Aguza** and **Dokki** aren't as smart as nearby **Mohandiseen** or the high-rise northern end of **Gezira** island, known as **Zamalek**. The **Imbaba** district, just to the northeast, was once notable for its weekly **camel market**, but this has now moved out of town to Birqesh. The dusty expanse of **Giza** (which lends its name to the west bank urban zone) is enlivened by **Cairo Zoo** and the nightclub-infested **Pyramids Road** leading to the **Pyramids of Giza**.

Arrival

Setting foot in a big city can be a daunting experience, but you needn't worry too much about Cairo. Touts and taxi drivers at various arrival points might try to con you into taking an overpriced and second-rate hotel (see box, p.87), and taxi drivers may well try to overcharge you, but that really is the worst that is likely to happen. Elaborate swindles are rare, and robbery with violence is unheard of.

Cairo International Airport, about 15km northeast of the city centre, has two main terminals which are roughly 3km apart. **Terminal 1**, used by EgyptAir and other airlines, is known as the old airport, but has now been refurbished, and is actually more modern than **Terminal 2** (aka the new airport); to find out which terminal your airline uses, you'll have to ask. For **airport information** call ☏02/265-3333 or 5000 (Terminal 1), or ☏02/265-2222 or 2029 (Terminal 2), or check ⓦwww.cairo-airport.com.You'll find 24-hour currency exchange, ATMs as well as tourist offices at both terminals.

Emerging from customs, you'll be waylaid by taxi drivers who'll swear that they're the only way of **getting into town**. This isn't so, but you might prefer going by **taxi** anyway. Airport cab drivers will probably demand £E60; to get a taxi into town for £E30–40, head out beyond the airport car park and pick

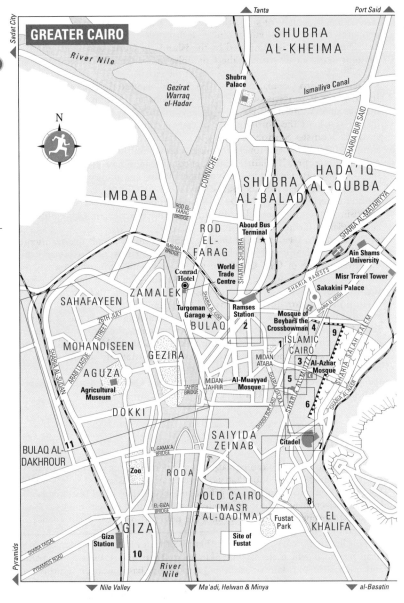

GREATER CAIRO

Sadat City ◄

Tanta ▲   Port Said ▲

SHUBRA
AL-KHEIMA

River Nile

Gezirat
Warraq
el-Hadar

Shubra
Palace

Ismailiya Canal

CORNICHE

SHARIA BUR SAID

N

HADA'IQ
AL-QUBBA

IMBABA

ROD EL-
FARAG
BRIDGE

ROD
EL-
FARAG

SHUBRA
AL-BALAD

SHARIA AL-MATARIYYA

IMBABA
BRIDGE

Aboud Bus
Terminal ★

SHARIA SHOBRA

Ain Shams
University

Conrad
Hotel ●

World
Trade
Centre

Misr Travel Tower

ZAMALEK

SHARIA AL-GISR

SHARIA RAMSES

Sakakini Palace

SAHAFAYEEN

Turgoman
Garage ★

Ramses
Station
2

Mosque of
Beybars the
Crossbowman 4

SHARIA EL-GEISH

9

26TH JULY
STREET

BULAQ

1

ISLAMIC
CAIRO

SHARIA SALAH SALEM

MOHANDISEEN

GEZIRA

MIDAN
ATABA

3

Al-Azhar
Mosque

ARAB LEAGUE

SHARIA AL-SUDAN

AGUZA

Agricultural
Museum

TAHRIR
BRIDGE

MIDAN
TAHRIR

Al-Muayyad
Mosque

SHARIA AL-MU'IZZ

SHARIA BUR SA'ID

5

SHARIA AL-NASR

DOKKI

6

BULAQ AL-
DAKHROUR

11

EL-GAMA'A
BRIDGE

SAIYIDA
ZEINAB

Citadel

7

Zoo

RODA

8

GIZA

EL-GIZA
BRIDGE

OLD CAIRO
(MASR
AL-QADIMA)

Fustat
Park

EL
KHALIFA

Giza
Station

10

Site of
Fustat

SHARIA FAISAL

PYRAMIDS ROAD

River
Nile

Pyramids ◄

▼ Nile Valley   ▼ Ma'adi, Helwan & Minya   ▼ al-Basatin

up a taxi outside its precincts (airport taxis add a surcharge as they pay a fee to enter the airport premises).

On one side of Terminal 1's forecourt is the parking area for **buses** and **minibuses** into the centre. The most comfortable of the bus services is the a/c bus #356 (£E2), which stops at Terminal 2 before continuing to Midan Ramses and Abdel Mouneem Riyad terminal by Midan Tahrir in downtown Cairo. This

Virgin's Tree ▲ & Obelisk ▲ Ismailiya

MATARIYYA / EL-ZEITUN

Buses for Cairo — Terminal 1 ★
Cairo International Airport
Terminal 2

HELIOPOLIS (MASR AL-GADIDA)

Merryland
MIDAN TRIOMPHE

Qubba Palace

SHARIA AL-HIGAZ

MIDAN ISMAILIYA
SHARIA AL-AHRAM

MIDAN ROXI
SHARIA MERGHANI
Urubah Palace

SHARIA AL-ORUBA

NOUZHA

Almaza Bus Terminal ★

Heliopolis Sporting Club
Baron Empain's Palace

SHARIA EN-NOZHA

Nasser's Tomb

SUEZ DESERT ROAD

October War Panorama

▸ Suez

ABBASSIYA

Cairo Stadium

SHARIA AL-NASR

Sadat's Tomb

Sinai Bus Terminal ★

MEDINET NASR

SHARIA RAMSES

MAP ENLARGEMENTS

1 Central Cairo (see pp.104–105)
2 Around Ramses Station (p.124)
3 Around Khan el-Khalili & al-Azhar (p.132)
4 To the Northern Gates (p.136)
5 Between Al-Azhar & the Bab Zwayla (p.143)
6 Between Bab Zwayla & The Citadel (p.151)
7 The Citadel (p.155)
8 Around Ibn Tulun & S. Cemetery (p.160)
9 The Northern Cemetery (p.167)
10 Old Cairo & Roda Island (pp.170–171)
11 Gezira & The West Bank (pp.188–189)

Muqattam   Hills   Petrified Forest

0   2 km

service runs from about 7am to 11pm, as does minibus #27 (50pt), which follows the same route. After hours, your choice is between bus #400 (25pt), which plies the same route round the clock, though it is less comfortable and takes somewhat longer to get downtown – easily over an hour in rush hour, about forty minutes at night. There is another 24-hour service – bus #948 – to Midan Ataba, on the northern edge of downtown. The airport terminals are connected to each other by a free EgyptAir **shuttle bus**, running all through the night. Besides the above

Hotel touts and excursion rackets

There's a racket going on in Cairo, and newly arrived tourists are the victims. It starts at the **airport and bus terminals**, the aim being to steer tourists into hotels which will pay a commission to the person bringing them, usually a taxi driver or street tout. The commission will of course be added to your bill. Most places in Cairo are reputable and above board, but it pays to know how to avoid the ones that aren't.

As soon as you arrive at **Cairo airport**, and before you even clear customs, you may be approached by "travel agents" wearing official badges with their photo, on which the only thing written in English is the words "Ministry of Tourism". This does not mean that they work for the ministry, simply that they have a licence to operate in the airport. They will probably try to dissuade you from going to the hotel you had in mind (by saying it's closed or no good), and they may even appear to call the hotel to check if there is a room. Don't believe it if a voice on the other end of the phone says, "Sorry, we are full." Likewise, don't believe similar stories from **taxi drivers** (especially those who accost you before you leave the airport), or any "friendly" stranger who gets talking to you on the bus into town. If a taxi driver tells you that the hotel you want has closed, take another taxi or, if you are already on your way into town, ask to be dropped off at Midan Tahrir or on Sharia Talaat Harb and walk the rest of the way, or insist on being taken to the supposedly closed hotel. Other touts may approach you on the street; some hang around on the stairs below popular hotels and may even claim to be the manager.

A number of hotels that work with touts also subject their guests to a sales campaign with the aim of getting them to buy souvenirs, horse and camel trips and, most of all, excursions to Luxor and Aswan. These hotels take a cut of whatever the tourist pays. Most hotels in town will of course sell sightseeing tours, but no reputable hotel will pressurize their guests to buy such tours, nor overcharge to the extent that some do, and large parts of these tours will be spent visiting shops (often billed as "museums") rather than the sites you came to see. The tour usually adapted and sold by dubious operators (not merely at budget establishments, but also at some quite reputable hotels) is that of Amigo Tours in Aswan, an unremarkable package frequently sold to unsuspecting tourists with a mark-up of 300 percent or more. The best advice is never to buy any tour without first shopping around (you'll get a better deal if you buy from operators such as First 24 Hours or Eastmar, p.265), and to check out of any hotel that starts putting pressure on you to buy a tour, or that allows in touts who will try to take you to papyrus or perfume shops. You may prefer not to pay for more than one night upfront, so that you can leave the next day if necessary.

For more on street touts, see p.103.

options, there's a **limousine taxi service** next to Terminal 1's Misr Travel stand; prices are fixed and posted, though higher than regular taxi rates.

By bus and train

Most buses from Jordan and Sinai arrive at the old **Sinai Bus Terminal** (aka Abbassiya Station), 4km from the centre. Taxis outside grossly overcharge newcomers (the fare into town is £E5–8); if you want to take a cab, your best bet is to cross the street outside the terminal (Sharia Ramses) and hail one that's passing. Alternatively, cross the street and catch a bus or minibus from the bus stop 100m to the right – buses #28, #310 and #710, and minibuses #1 and #998 serve Midan Ramses; buses #27 and #998 and minibus #30 serve both Midan Ramses and Midan Tahrir. However, if you turn left outside the terminal and walk 300m on past the flyover to the hospital, you have an even wider choice of buses and minibuses to Ramses, Tahrir and Ataba. Tickets on the buses and minibuses plying these routes cost 25pt–£E1.

Coming from Jordan or Libya on a Superjet bus, you'll arrive at their terminal in **Almaza**, at the back end of Heliopolis. A taxi into town from here costs £E15–20, but the terminal is served by bus #15 to Midan Ramses, or minibus #39 and bus #796 to Ramses and Tahrir. Alternatively, 300m north of the terminal along Sharia Abu Bakr al-Siddiq, under the flyover, you can pick up a tram (the Heliopolis metro; see p.201) from the stop across the tracks and to your right, which goes along Sharia Merghani direct to Midan Ramses: make sure you get the right tram, though – it's the long green one, not the short yellow one.

Certain buses from Alexandria and the Delta, plus Superjet services from Sinai will drop you at **Turgoman Garage**, in Bulaq. Transport from here into downtown Cairo is somewhat disorganized; the simplest option is to take a taxi (£E2–3 to Midan Ramses, £E3–5 to Midan Tahrir), unless you fancy walking, in which case it's straight ahead out of the gate and 600m down Sharia el Kolali to Midan Ramses (see map on p.124), or right out of the gate and on down Sharia Shahan to Orabi metro station (see map on p.104).

Other bus companies coming from Alexandria and the Delta and Upper Egypt arrive at **Aboud Terminal** in Shubra. By far the easiest way into town from here is to climb up the steps to the main road where microbus service taxis await to take you straight to Sharia Orabi by Ramses train station (see below and the map on p.104).

All **trains** into Cairo stop at **Ramses Station** (see map on p.87), which has a tourist office. There are hotels nearby, but most visitors prefer to head downtown. You can do this by metro (Mubarak Station is beneath Midan Ramses), taxi (£E3–5), or on a bus along Sharia Ramses. Alternatively, it's a ten- to fifteen-minute walk down Sharia Ramses, taking a left at Sharia Emad el-Din or Sharia Orabi, into the main downtown area, where most of the budget hotels are located.

Information and city transport

Cairo's downtown **tourist office**, at 5 Sharia Adly (daily 8.30am–7pm; ☎02/391-3454), can supply a rather useless free map and some brochures, and staff generally try to be helpful, but often do not have the information you need. There are also tourist offices at the airport's Terminal 1 (open 24hr; ☎02/265-4760) and Terminal 2 (open 24hr; ☎02/265-2223). Tourist information is also available at Ramses Station (daily 8.30am–9pm; ☎02/579-0767), Giza train station (daily 8am–11pm; ☎02/570-2233), and the Giza Pyramids (daily 8.30am–5pm; ☎02/383-8823). A new office is also due to open at Fustat.

The *New Handy Map of Cairo* is generally the best **map** of the city, with a street index and an inset covering Heliopolis. Cairo City Key's *Detailed Map of Greater Cairo* comes second, with maps of Heliopolis and Ma'adi on the back, though it doesn't have a street index or extend out to Medinet Nasr. Alternatives include the Cairo Engineering and Manufacturing Company's *Cairo Tourist Map*, which extends out to Heliopolis, and Lehnert & Landrock's map of the same name, which is better for downtown. A free map full of advertisements can be found at some upmarket hotels and tourist venues, containing reasonable plans of Heliopolis, Ma'adi, Mohandiseen, Zamalek and the downtown area. Of more use for longer stays are the American University in Cairo's (AUC) *Cairo: The Practical Guide Maps* (£E30), which contains a useful set of maps; the weighty and currently out-of-print *Cairo A–Z* (£E70 if you can find it); and the *Cairo City Key* (£E40). The best place to buy maps is at a bookshop such as Lehnert & Landrock (44 Sharia Sherif) and Shorouk (1 Midan Talaat Harb), but a shop by the name of Buccellati, at the northwest corner of the junction where Sharia Qasr el-Nil meets Sharia Mohammed Farid, may have maps that other places don't stock.

Don't expect Cairenes themselves to relate to maps; they comprehend their city differently. That said, however, people are remarkably helpful to visitors, going out of their way to steer them in the right direction; offer profuse thanks, but never baksheesh, which will offend in this situation.

City transport

Getting around Cairo is relatively straightforward; **Midan Tahrir** is the main transport hub, with several other terminals in the centre connecting up the city. The metro is simple to use, and taxis are inexpensive. Familiarize yourself with Arabic numerals (see p.822) and you can also use buses and minibuses, which reach most parts of the city. **Street names** are posted in English (or French) and Arabic in central Cairo and Zamalek, almost everywhere else in Arabic only, or not at all. The same goes for **numbers**, rendered in Western and Arabic numerals, or just the latter; a single number may denote a whole block with several entrance passageways – something to remember when you're following up addresses.

Walking in Cairo

The one advantage of Cairo's density is that many places of interest are within walking distance of Midan Tahrir or other transport interchanges. You can walk across downtown Cairo from Tahrir to Midan Ataba in fifteen to thirty minutes; the same again brings you to Khan el-Khalili in the heart of Islamic Cairo. The fascinating medieval quarter can really only be explored on foot, starting from Khan el-Khalili or the Citadel.

Arguably, walking is the best way to experience the city's pulsating **street life**. Though pavements are congested with vendors and pedestrians, they weave gracefully around each other, in contrast with the bullish jostlings of Western capitals. The commonest irritants are rubbish, noxious fumes and puddles, uneven pavements and gaping drains; in poorer quarters, the last two may not even exist. Women travellers must also reckon with gropers, who strike chiefly along Talaat Harb and around Khan el-Khalili. Close proximity to a male escort confers some immunity, but the best solution is to develop an instant response (see "Women travellers", p.61).

To make faster headway you can walk along the edge of the road – obviously, always facing oncoming traffic. **Traffic** is heavy from 8am to midnight, but dwindles away for a few hours before dawn. Its daytime flow only diminishes during Ramadan celebrations, major football matches, and the midday prayer on Fridays, when many side streets are carpeted over and used as outdoor mosques.

At all times, **crossing the road** takes boldness. Drivers will slow down to give people time to dart across, but dithering or freezing midway confuses them and increases the risk of an accident. A prolonged horn burst indicates that the driver can't or won't stop. Remember that motorists obey police signals rather than traffic lights, which were only installed in the 1980s and have still to acquire local credibility.

You might as well resign yourself to the fact that everyone here drives like participants in the Paris–Dakar Rally, but accidents are surprisingly rare, all things considered. The streets are busy from 8am to midnight, and, unless you enjoy sweltering in traffic jams, it's best to try and avoid travelling during **rush hours** (7–10am & 4–7pm).

The metro

Cairo's **metro** (for some background, see Ⓦ www.urbanrail.net/af/cairo.htm) works like nothing else in the city – it's clean and efficient, with a well-enforced

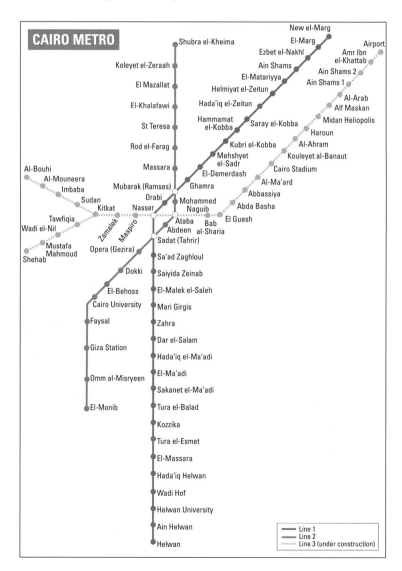

CAIRO METRO

Line 1
Line 2
Line 3 (under construction)

ban on littering and smoking. Trains run every few minutes from 5.30am to midnight; outside of the rush hours they're no more overcrowded than in other cities around the world. The front carriage of each train is reserved for women, worth keeping in mind if you're a lone female traveller.

Stations are signposted with a large "M"; signs and route maps appear in Arabic and English. **Tickets** are purchased in the station (£E1 flat fare, cheaper during Ramadan); twin sets of booths cater for passengers heading in opposite directions, sometimes with separate queues for either sex. Hang on to your ticket to get through the automatic barriers at the other end. Travelling without a ticket will result in a E£50 fine.

Line One connects the northeastern suburb of **El-Marg** with the southern industrial district of **Helwan** (via Mubarak, Sadat, Saad Zaghoul, Saiyida Zeinab, Mar Girgis and Maadi), with Line Two running from **Shubra** in the north to **El Monib** (via Mubarak, Ataba, Sadat, Opera and Giza). The new stations on Line Two are wheelchair accessible, but stations on Line One are not. Line Three is still at the planning stage, but should eventually run from the airport via the city centre (Ataba and Nasser) to Zamalek and Mohandiseen.

Taxis

The most common type of **taxi** is the black-and-white four-seater (Fiats or Ladas), which in peak hours may carry passengers collectively. Don't confuse regular cabs with larger special taxis (usually Peugeot 504s or Mercedes), which cost three times more and prey on tourists. If you do ride in a special, establish the price – and bargain it down – before you get in. For more on hailing taxis, see p.44.

Fares are determined by market rates rather than by meters (which are rarely switched on). Cairenes normally pay a £E2 minimum, £E3–5 for a down-town hop (for example, Midan Tahrir to Al-Azhar, Zamalek or Mohandiseen), and more if heading further out, especially to a prosperous area (for example £E15–20 to Heliopolis or the Pyramids). For each extra person, you pay 25 percent again. After midnight, fares are supposed to increase by 50–100 percent, but this usually goes by the board. Though foreigners can get away with local rates, drivers expect you to pay over the odds, especially if you are well dressed or staying in an expensive hotel: say £E5 minimum, £E5–8 across downtown or the Nile, and £E15–20 further out. The airport and the Pyramids are special cases (see p.85 and p.207). Fares given in the text are for a single person at **tourist rates**, unless indicated otherwise. Don't be alarmed by circuitous routes taken to avoid bottlenecks.

Useful metro stations

From a tourist's standpoint, there are six crucial stations:

MUBARAK, beneath Midan Ramses, is for reaching or leaving Ramses Station.

NASSER, two stops on, leads onto 26th July Street near the top end of Talaat Harb (take the High Court exit).

SADAT, the most used (and useful) station, is set beneath Midan Tahrir, and doubles as a pedestrian underpass.

SAIYIDA ZEINAB, two stops beyond Sadat, lies midway between the Saiyida Zeinab quarter and the northern end of Roda Island.

MARI GIRGIS is the best stop for Coptic Cairo and Amr's Mosque.

OPERA (GEZIRA) is by the Opera Complex in south Gezira.

At the end of your journey, ideally you'd hand over the correct fare, with a tip if you feel like it, say "*itfuddel, shukran*" (here you are, thank you) and that would be the end of it. If the driver protests, either he's trying it on and will back down if you invoke the police, or you've misjudged the fare and should pay more with good grace. Remember that taxi drivers don't generally deal with change so it's best to have the exact fare ready. Note also that taxi drivers who hustle tourists for business in the street do so with the intention of overcharging – always hail a taxi yourself rather than taking one which hails you.

A second type of taxi is the pricier **limousines**, usually Mercedes or Peugeot 406s. Operated by firms such as Limo Misr (℡02/685-6125) and Target Limousine (℡02/588-0095), they are stationed at five-star hotels and at the airport, with fixed fares (£E66 from the airport to downtown, for example), and rentable by the day as well as for set routes. A limo for the day (12 hours and 100km) costs £E340.

New in town is a third kind of taxi, **Cairo Cab**. Bright yellow in colour, Cairo Cabs, amazingly, actually use a meter. They are also generally more expensive than ordinary taxis, with a flagfall of £E3.50, plus another £E1-odd per kilometre, and a £E5-per-hour waiting fee. Drivers of metered cabs will have their own scams for increasing fares, such as taking the scenic route, or making sure to get caught up in heavy traffic, while the meter ticks away. One route on which Cairo Cabs are cheaper than ordinary taxis is to the airport, which costs around £E35, including the airport entry fee, but other cabs firms are starting to object to this, so it may not last. Cairo Cabs can be hailed in the street, and they also have ranks, including one on the west side of Midan Tahrir in front of Omar Makram Mosque, one on 26th July Street in front of the High Court building, and one at the northwest corner of Ezbekiya Gardens, or you can call them within Cairo on ℡19155.

Service taxis

Cairo has some 60,000 service taxis which transport over a million Cairenes to work every day, causing appalling pollution, traffic jams and accidents. Service taxis travel a set route (see box below for some of the most useful) and can be flagged down anywhere along it if there is space aboard. In town they are invariably **microbuses**, known as *arrabeya bin nafar* or just *servees*, and are more like buses than taxi cabs. **Fares** range from 50pt to £E1 per person, according to the distance travelled. They are especially useful for longer-distance journeys such as from town to the pyramids. Their main terminals are at **Abdel Mouneem Riyad** (behind the Museum of Egyptian Antiquities and in front of the *Ramses Hilton* hotel), and behind and around **Ramses station**. For Saqqara and Dahshur, they leave from a street off Maryotteya Canal near its junction with Pyramids Road (down the east bank of the canal and first left), the junction itself being easily reached on a pyramids-bound service taxi from Ramses or Abdel Mouneem Riyad.

Buses

Cairo's **buses** mainly operate from 5.30am to 12.30am daily (6.30am–6.30pm & 7.30pm–2am during Ramadan). Fares are cheap enough to be affordable for everyone, so buses are usually full and overflow during rush hour, when passengers hang from doorways. Though many foreigners are deterred from using buses by the crush, not to mention the risk of pickpockets and gropers, there's no denying that the network reaches virtually everywhere. Because buses tend to make slow progress against the traffic, however, service-taxi microbuses are generally a better option, where available, though there are **air-conditioned buses** on some routes to prosperous suburbs such as Heliopolis and Medinet Nasr, and to tourist sights such as the Pyramids.

Buses should have **route numbers** in Arabic numerals on the front, side and back. Those with a slash through the number (represented in this guide as, for example, #13/) may follow different routes from buses with the same number unslashed; some route numbers even have two slashes. **Bus stops** are not always clearly signposted (look for metal shelters, plaques on lampposts or crowds waiting), and buses often just slow down instead of halting, compelling passengers to board and disembark on the run. Some bus stops (at the time of writing, those on the west bank of the river, in and around Mohandiseen) have route information posted, but this is in Arabic only.

Most buses start from (or pass through) at least one of the main city-centre nuclei at Midan Tahrir, Abdel Mouneem Riyad terminal (behind the Museum of Egyptian Antiquities), Midan Ramses or Midan Ataba. At each of these locations, there are several bus stops, and where exactly you pick up your bus will depend on which direction it is going in and whether it starts there or is simply passing through. If possible, ask the conductor "*Rayih...?*" (Are you going to...?) to make sure.

Except at terminals, you are supposed to enter through the rear door (often removed to facilitate access) and exit from the front. Conductors sell **tickets** (the flat fare on most routes is 25pt, 50pt on longer routes, £E1 on newer, more comfortable vehicles, and £E2 on air-conditioned buses) from behind a crush-bar by the rear door. The front of the bus is usually less crowded, so it's worth squeezing your way forwards; start edging towards the exit well before your destination.

Useful bus and minibus routes

Abdel Mouneem Riyad and Midan Ramses to: Airport #356, #400 (24hr), minibus #27; Abbassiya and Heliopolis (Midan Roxi) #400, #400/, #500, minibuses #27, #35, #35/.

Abdel Mouneem Riyad to: Citadel (Bab Gabal) #951, minibus #105; Midan Salah el-Din #456, #955, minibus 35; Saiyida Zeinab and Ibn Tulun Mosque #72//, #102, #160; Imam al-Shafi'i minibus #154; Mohandiseen #337; Manashi #214; Muqattam Hills #951; Pyramids #30, #355, #357, #900; Sphinx #997; Haraniyya #337; Badrasheen #987.

Minibuses

Minibuses run along many of the bus routes, supplemented by privately run green minibuses on new routes. Besides making better headway through traffic and actually halting at stops (usually the same stops as used by ordinary buses), minibuses are far more comfortable than ordinary buses and never crowded, as standing is not permitted. Tickets (25pt–£E1) are bought from the driver. Minibuses should not be confused with service taxis (usually smaller micro-buses, see p.93). There are minibus **terminals** alongside the big bus stations in Midan Tahrir (by the *Nile Hilton* and near Arab League/Omar Makram Mosque) and Midan Ataba.

Trams and river-taxis

As the metro and minibus systems expand, Cairo's original **tram network** (built in colonial times) is being phased out. The Heliopolis tram system remains in use throughout that area (see "The northern suburbs", p.195, for details), but all the other lines into town have been withdrawn, though a few suburban lines still run. Like buses, the trams are cheap and battered, sometimes with standing room only; their Arabic route numbers are posted above the driver's cab.

River-taxis (aka waterbuses) are the most relaxing way to reach Old Cairo. They leave from the Maspero Dock outside the Television Building, 600m north of the Museum of Egyptian Antiquities. Boats run every hour from 7am to El Gama'a Bridge in Giza (see map on p.170), continuing early morning (7–8am) to Old Cairo; you can buy tickets (50pt flat fee) at the dock. On Fridays and Sundays, they also run up to the Nile barrages at Qanatir (£E5 each way; see "Excursions from Cairo", p.267).

Driving

The only thing scarier than **driving in Cairo** is cycling, which is tantamount to suicide. Dashes, crawls and finely judged evasions are the order of the day; donkey carts and jaywalkers trust in motorists' swift reactions. Any collision draws a crowd. Minor dents are often settled by on-the-spot payoffs, but should injury occur, it's wise to involve a cop right away. Multistorey car parks, such as the one on Midan Ataba, are ignored as motorists park bumper-to-bumper along every kerb, leaving their handbrakes off so vehicles can be shifted by the local *minaidy* (street parking attendant), whom they tip £E1 or so. Given all this, it's no surprise that few foreigners drive in Cairo. **Renting a car** with a driver costs around $20 a day more than doing the driving yourself; see p.263 for rental outlets.

Accommodation

Cairo is packed with **accommodation** to suit every tourist's taste and budget. When tourism is at its normal level, most hotels are busy or full throughout December and January, while the cheaper ones are flooded with backpackers over the summer. When tourism is down, however – as it invariably is following ructions in the Middle East – you can be certain of a vacancy almost anywhere, and **hotel touts** will compete more fiercely than ever (see box, p.88). Yet finding a room needn't be traumatic if you hop on a bus or hail a taxi and begin visiting downtown hotels.

Hotels and pensions

Cairo's hotels reflect the city's diversity: deluxe chains overlooking the Nile; functional high-rises; colonial piles and homely *pensions* with the same raddled facades as bug-infested flophouses. **Standards** vary within any given price range or star rating – and from room to room in many places. Try to inspect the facilities before checking in. Also establish the price and any service tax or extra charges (which should be posted in reception) at the outset. Hotels with three or more stars require payment in USdollar, or Egyptian currency backed by an exchange receipt. Officially, rates are the same all year, with an annual rise in early October.

Cairo has around thirty hotels with a **four- or five-star** rating, and all the international chains are represented. The regular rates for such places start at around $150 for a double, not including breakfast, though package tourists may get hefty reductions. **Mid-range** establishments chiefly comprise three-star hotels whose rooms have private bathrooms and a/c, perhaps also fridges, phones and TV. If facilities fall short of what's advertised (and charged for), you're entitled to raise a stink. However, a couple of places in the centre are (more or less) refurbished colonial edifices whose old-world charm makes up for any lack of modern gadgetry.

Inexpensive hotels and pensions tend to be located on the upper floors of downtown office buildings. Some feature Art Deco rooms with sweeping balconies, and all can provide bottled water, tea and soft drinks. Most are reached from street level via an alleyway and/or lobby serving the entire building; a few are locked at midnight, so if you arrive later you'll have to rouse the doorman (*bowab*), who will probably expect some modest baksheesh for his trouble. The budget establishments reviewed here are agreeable or conveniently located (a few combine both assets). Breakfast is included in the rate unless otherwise stated.

Central Cairo

Talaat Harb, Mahmoud Bassiouni and Qasr el-Nil streets offer the widest range of **budget** hotels. A few are excellent, a few really squalid, but the majority fall somewhere in between. Richer tourists can choose between comfortable modern hotels or a number of vintage establishments redolent of prewar high society. The hotels below are all marked on the map on pp.104–105.

Budget

Amin 38 Midan Falaki, opposite Bab al-Luq market ☎02/393-3813. Very reasonable rooms with fans on the sixth, seventh and tenth floors. It's worth paying a bit more for a room with private bathroom and constant hot water – the shared facilities aren't so clean. Breakfast not included. ❶

Berlin Fourth floor, 2 Sharia el-Shawarby ☎ & ℱ02/395-7502, ℰberlinhotelcairo @hotmail.com. A small hotel on the fourth floor, with lofty double and triple rooms, each with its own shower, quiet split-unit a/c, comfortable mattresses and Art Nouveau-style fittings. Services include laundry, Internet access, airport pick-up, and their own drivers to take you round the pyramid sites or elsewhere, at decent rates. ❷

Crown 9 Sharia Emad el-Din ☎020/591-8374, ℰcrowncairo@yahoo.com. Quite a well-kept place north of the main downtown area, and claiming Canadian management, though it isn't in evidence. The better rooms have a/c and private bathroom, but all are pretty decent. Breakfast not included. ❷

Dahab 26 Sharia Bassiouni ☎02/579-9104. The top budget choice, this is a Dahab tourist camp transported – surprisingly convincingly – to a downtown roof, with poky rooms, friendly staff and lots of backpackers. Plenty of vegetation and an open rooftop area to socialize in make it a pleasant hangout; facilities include a Bedouin-style café, kitchen, laundry service and 24hr hot water. Ignore the touts hanging around at the entrance. Breakfast not included. ❶

Garden City House Third floor, 26 Sharia Kamal al-Din Salah ☎ 02/794-8400, ⓦ www .gardencityhouse.com. Refurbished 1930s *pension* on the edge of the Garden City, behind the *Semiramis*. Some rooms have Nile views, some have en-suite bathrooms, and some have a/c. On the downside, the location is rather noisy. ❷

Happyton 10 Sharia Ali al-Kassar ☎ 02/592 8671 or 6. Two-star hotel with en-suite a/c rooms of variable sizes, all well kept. There's no bar, but you can buy beer in the lobby and drink it on the roof terrace. A TV in your room costs £E8 a night extra, so specify if you don't want one; a/c costs £E10. ❷

Ismailia House Eighth floor, 1 Midan Tahrir ☎ 02/796-3122, ⓔ ismahouse@hotmail.com. Advance booking is advisable for this cool, cheerful seventh-floor haven, with singles, doubles, triples and dorm beds (£E18), 24hr hot water and plenty of communal areas to hang out in. The Tahrir-facing rooms are noisy at night but have great views. ❷

King Tut Hostel Eighth floor, 37 Sharia Talaat Harb ☎ 02/391-7897, ⓔ king_tut_hostel@yahoo .com. Wonderful pharaonic decor in the entrance and public areas welcomes you to this well-kept hotel (not really a hostel, despite the name), all gleaming bright, and often full, so worth booking ahead. Rooms have a/c but bathrooms are shared. ❷

Lotus 12 Sharia Talaat Harb ☎ 02/575-0627, ⓦ www.lotushotel.com. Reception on the seventh floor, reached via an arcade. Staff are friendly and there's a restaurant and a bar, but avoid buying tours here. Some rooms have a/c and private baths. Hot water 6–10am and 6–10pm. ❷

Luna Fifth floor, 27 Sharia Talaat Harb ☎ 02/396-1020, ⓔ lunapension@hotmail .com. Well kept, with helpful staff and large a/c rooms, some en suite. It's worth asking for the Egyptian breakfast (*fuul* and falafel) in preference to the Continental. Free airport pick-up if you stay four days or more. ❷

New Hotel 21 Sharia Adly ☎ 02/392-7065, ⓕ 392-9555. A reasonable two-star place with a 24hr café and slightly worn, carpeted rooms, some with a/c and en-suite shower and toilet. ❸

Orient Palace Tenth floor, 14 26th July St ☎ 02/393-9375 or 6. A friendly place (use the right-hand lift to reach it), with some of the cheapest singles in town (£E20), but rather dingy rooms in general. There's a rooftop café; breakfast not included. ❷

Pensione Roma 169 Sharia Mohammed Farid ☎ 02/391-1088 or 391-1340, ⓕ 579-6243. The stylish 1940s ambience, immaculately maintained by Madame Cressaty, is highly recommended and it's wise to book in advance. Hot water is constant and there are some private bathrooms, and a laundry service. The entrance is around the side of the Gattegno department store. ❷

Select 19 Sharia Adly, beside the synagogue ☎ 02/393-3707, ⓔ hotelselect@yahoo.com. A bright little place, recently refurbished, with friendly staff and good views, some rooms en suite, eight floors up a 1930s building with period touches. ❷

Sultan ☎ 02/577-2258, **Safari** ☎ 02/577-8692, ⓔ safari_res@hotmail .com and **Venice** ☎ 02/575-1477, ⓔ venicehotelcairo@yahoo.com, all at 4 Sharia Tawfiqia. Trio of ultra-cheapies in a building opening onto a colourful market street near Midan Orabi, very handy for inexpensive eating and groceries, and just the right distance from the centre of downtown. All are friendly and offer hot water and use of kitchen facilities, but none is especially clean. The *Safari* has dorm beds only (the other two offer poky singles and doubles as well as dorms) and is the least appealing of the three. Dorm beds £E9 in the *Sultan* and *Safari*, £E15 with breakfast in the *Venice*. Rates at the *Sultan* and *Safari* do not include breakfast. ❶

Tulip 3 Midan Talaat Harb ☎ 02/393-9433, ⓔ tuliphotel@yahoo.com. Decent old-style place, now refurbished, facing *Groppi's*. The rooms, en suite and some with a/c, are bright and cheerful and the beds have firm mattresses. ❷

Mid-range

Carlton 21 26th July St ☎ 02/575-5022, ⓔ carltonhotelcairo@yahoo.com. Built in 1935 and still retaining some wood-panelled period charm, albeit rather worn around the edges. All rooms are a/c; pricier deluxe rooms have satellite TV and a minibar. There's a restaurant on the seventh floor and a very pleasant rooftop garden with coffee shop. ❹

Cosmopolitan 1 Sharia Ben Talaab, off Qasr el-Nil ☎ 02/392-3956, ⓕ 393-3531. This refurbished and rather grand monumental *belle époque* building has a European restaurant, English-style bar, bank and international calls facility, but avoid the tours sold at the travel desk. All rooms have a/c and private baths. ❻

Grand 17 26th July St ☎ 02/575-7801 to 5, ⓔ grandhotel@link.net. Characterful and very comfortable Art Deco edifice featuring original lifts and furniture, a fountain, coffee shop and old-fashioned, homely rooms with immaculately varnished wooden floors, attached to large, spotless, bright tiled bathrooms, though the plumbing can be temperamental. Entrance in the alley off Sharia Talaat Harb. Very good value. ⑤

Odeon Palace 6 Sharia Abdel Hamid Said ☎02/577-6637, ⓕ576-7971. Three-star tower with lots of wood panelling and a comfortable lived-in feel, as well as a restaurant and 24hr roof bar, just off Sharia Talaat Harb. Rate excludes breakfast. ⑤

Windsor 19 Sharia Alfi Bey ☎02/591-5810, ⓦwww.windsorcairo.com. This colonial hotel retains much character and one of the nicest bars in Cairo (the *Barrel Lounge*, see p.243), but has definitely seen better days and is rather overpriced. The patron's father, Ramses Wissa Wassef, founded Harraniyya's weaving school (see p.214). All rooms have a/c and satellite TV; all but the very cheapest have private bathroom. Offers fifteen percent discount for *Rough Guide* readers, but avoid buying tours here. ⑤

Expensive

Four Seasons 1089 Corniche el-Nil, Garden City ☎02/791-7000, ⓦwww.fourseasons.com. Sleek, sophisticated and luxurious to a fault, this branch of the *Four Seasons* chain is better suited to Western tastes than its gaudier sister establishment opposite the zoo in Giza. The rooms have a classic charm with little extras like a DVD player and high-speed Internet terminal. ⑨

Nile Hilton On the river right by Midan Tahrir and the Museum of Egyptian Antiquities ☎02/578-0444 or 0666, ⓦwww.hilton.com. If you want to be right in the centre of things, go for this refurbished 1950s building, boasting the biggest rooms in town and a range of cafés and restaurants. River-facing doubles cost slightly more than rooms overlooking Tahrir. ⑥

Ramses Hilton Corniche el-Nil ☎02/577-7444, ⓦwww.hilton.com. Cairo's tallest hotel, rooms on the upper stories giving excellent views over the city and as far as the Pyramids, but the *Ramses* plays second fiddle to the *Nile Hilton*, and the standard of service here is somewhat inferior. ⑥

Semiramis Intercontinental Corniche el-Nil ☎02/795-7171, ⓦwww.cairo.intercontinental.com. Slightly plusher than the two Hiltons, with spacious, elegant rooms, plus a gym, a pool, the *Haroun al-Rashid* nightclub (see p.246), and seven restaurants offering cuisine from around the world. Rooms on the upper floors give excellent views, and in fact the views over Cairo from the slightly cheaper city-side rooms are better than from the Nile side. ⑧

Shepheard Corniche el-Nil ☎02/792-1000, ⓦwww.shepheard-hotel.com. Nile-side version of the famous nineteenth-century establishment that stood on the present site in 1957, and still retaining a certain 1950s feel. Rooms on the quieter side facing the Muqattam Hills are cheaper than those facing the Nile. Facilities include two restaurants, a casino and the *Castle* disco (see p.247), but no swimming pool. ⑦

Downtown, near Ramses Station

These places are a little further from the centre, but still within striking distance, and handy if arriving late or leaving early from one of the terminals around Midan Ramses. They're marked on the map on p.124.

Big Ben 33 Sharia Emad el-Din ☎02/590-8881. Singles, doubles and triples with fans and soft beds, and private bath in some cases. A few rooms have balconies with a view of the mosque next door. Take the left-hand lift in the foyer to the seventh floor. Breakfast not included. ②

Fontana Off Midan Ramses ☎02/592-2321. Comfortable and well kept, with a small rooftop swimming pool (summer only), bar, restaurant, café, and a nightclub (see p.246). Rooms have TV, fridge and a/c, and some have views of the Citadel. ⑤

New Cicil Fourth floor, 29 Sharia Emad el-Din ☎02/591-3859. A cleanish place with a mainly Egyptian clientele, fans in the rooms, and shared hot-water bathrooms. Breakfast not included. ①

Venus Hotel Tenth floor, 38 Sharia Ramses ☎02/577-5186. The best budget option near Ramses. Rooms are comfortable, although small; some are en suite with a/c, and the staff are friendly. There's also a TV lounge, laundry service and luggage store. ②

Victoria 66 Sharia el-Gumhorriya ☎02/589-2290 to 94, ⓔinfo@victoria .com.eg. A three-star 1930s hotel once frequented by George Bernard Shaw. Lots of wood panelling, attractive a/c rooms (many with mahogany furniture), bar, restaurant and spacious lounge area make this one of the best deals in town. Takes Amex, MasterCard and Visa. ⑤

Islamic Cairo

Islamic Cairo rubs shoulders with its medieval past: noises, smells and insects penetrate hotel rooms, while outside, the quarter's customs demand recognition. Once numerous bug-ridden dives around Saiyida Zeinab and Khan el-Khalili are excluded, there are three hotels worth considering, marked on the map on p.132.

El-Hussein Muski, entered via a passage to *Fishawi's* ℡02/591-8089, ℻591-8479. Rooms overlooking the square are harangued by Cairo's loudest muezzins, while the upper floors shake from wedding parties in its rooftop restaurant (great views, awful food). Sleep is impossible during festivals (bring earplugs), when the square bops all night, but if you don't mind the noise, a balcony overlooking the square gives you a ringside view. Reservations advisable. ❷

El Malky 4 Sharia el-Hussein ℡02/589-0804. Behind the Saiyidna Hussein Mosque, with a mainly Muslim clientele, this is a well-kept hotel that's good value. It's well located in the heart of Islamic Cairo but out of the noise and bustle, with carpeted, a/c, en-suite rooms, generally comfortable though the beds are a bit on the hard side. ❷

Radwan Muski ℡02/786-5180 or 2, ℮said19480@yahoo.com. In an excellent location just across the Muski from the *El-Hussein*, so equally noisy, but with smaller rooms, less character and sporadic hot water, though bathrooms are en suite. Not advisable for women on their own. Rate excludes breakfast. ❷

Zamalek and Gezira

The northern half of Gezira Island is quieter and fresher than central Cairo, except along 26th July Street, where buses and service taxis shuttle between downtown and the west bank, with an elevated roadway for through traffic. Besides the *Cairo Marriott*, the island has a few modern three-star hotels, plus a couple of cheaper options. Also here are the former *El Borg*, acquired by the Accor Novotel chain, and the former *Gezirah Sheraton*, now part of the Sofitel chain; they are likely to open as, respectively, a four-star and a five-star hotel during the lifetime of this book. For the locations of the establishments reviewed, see the map on pp.188–189.

Cairo Marriott Sharia Saray al-Gezira, off 26th July St, Zamalek ℡02/735-8888, ℗www.marriott.com/caieg. Choose between garden rooms or slightly pricier tower rooms with a better view, all built around a lavish palace constructed to house Napoleon III's wife Empress Eugénie. There are fine restaurants and bars, a casino, nightclub (summer only) and pool; rooms have fast Internet connections and the hotel is WiFi-enabled throughout. ❽

🏃 **Longchamps** Fifth floor, 21 Sharia Ismail Mohammed ℡02/735-2311, ℗www.hotellongchamps.com. Spotless, quiet and well-run three-star hotel with a/c, satellite TV, Internet connection and a fridge in all rooms, plus a pleasant terrace and meals available. It's advisable to book at least a couple of weeks ahead, but if it's full, the similarly priced *Horus House* downstairs isn't a bad fallback. ❻

Mayfair 9 Sharia Aziz Osman, First floor above ground ℡02/735-7315, ℗www.mayfaircairo.com. Immaculate rooms, some en suite and a/c, all with balconies, in a quiet location, with a great Art Deco entrance lobby, a breakfast terrace overlooking the street. Ten percent discount for *Rough Guide* readers, but avoid buying tours here. ❸

Nile Zamalek 21 Sharia Aziz Abaza ℡02/735-1846, ℻735-0220. Spacious rooms with bath, phone, TV and a/c in this modern riverside two-star, some with a balcony overlooking the Nile. ❹

Pension Zamalek 6 Sharia Salah al-Din ℡02/735-9318, ℮pensionzamalek@msn.com. Very much a European-style *pension*: clean, quiet and secluded with a pleasant family atmosphere, and one bathroom to every two rooms. ❹

Roda Island

Grand Hyatt ℡02/365-1234, ℗www.cairo.grand.hyatt.com (see map on pp.170–171). A superior five-star at the northern tip of Roda Island, though best accessed via its own bridge from Garden City, with stylish rooms in a sumptuous new wing (north-facing ones offer killer views of central Cairo and the Nile), with all the facilities you'd expect – sauna, health club, business centre, two pools – plus no fewer than twelve restaurants, including a revolving restaurant with panoramic views (see p.263). ⑨

Elsewhere in the city

Conrad 1191 Corniche el-Nil, Bulaq ☎02/580-8000, ⓦwww.conradhotels.com (see map on pp.86–87). Run by the Hilton chain, but calmer and more sedate than its city-centre counterparts, with some of the most comfortable rooms in Cairo. It has international dining, palm trees

Long stays and flat-hunting

Should you decide to stay a while, it's worth remembering that many hotels reduce their rates after one or two weeks' occupation. Depending on demand for rooms and your rapport with the management, it may be possible to negotiate further discounts for long stays at pensions.

In the longer term, however, it's better to rent an **apartment**. Quietly spacious **Ma'adi** (see p.186) is home to most of Egypt's American community and mega-wealthy natives. **Zamalek** (see p.191) favoured by embassies and European expats, is likewise costly, but always has vacancies. Another focus for the foreign community is **Heliopolis** (see p.199). Rents here are lower than in downtown Cairo, where few flats are available at any price unless you move into **Bulaq** (see p.196) or the Qasr al-Aini side of **Garden City** (see p.124). Across the Nile, middle-class **Dokki** (see p.194) merges into *baladi* market quarters, while **Mohandiseen** (see p.192) parades blocks of flats and shopping centres along its shiny boulevards. Single males with a grasp of Arabic and Egyptian ways might enjoy living in **baladi quarters** (Islamic Cairo, see p.127; Bulaq; Imbaba), which are cheap and cheerful, unhygienic and noisy.

Given the range of localities and amenities, expect to look at half a dozen places before settling on one. Check the small ads in *Egypt Today*, the *Egyptian Gazette* and *Community Times* and expat community newssheets such as the *Maadi Messenger* or *British Community News*, and look at noticeboards at English-language institutes and cultural centres (see p.263), the *Bon Appetit* café in Sharia Mohammed Mahmoud (see p.232), and the American University. It's also possible to see what's available and check prices online via the websites such as E-dar (ⓦwww.e-dar.com) and Gomhoria (ⓦwww.algomhoria.com). A free listings paper called *al-Waseet* (ⓦwww.ewaseet.com), available at some upmarket hotels, carries ads for apartments, but doesn't give prices. The AUC's regularly updated *Cairo: the Practical Guide* contains much valuable wisdom on apartment rental and Cairo living in general.

Foreigners working or studying in Cairo often seek flatmates or want to sublet during temporary absences. Another way involves using a *simsar* (flat agent), who can be found in any neighbourhood by making enquiries at local shops and cafés. Unless you spend a long, fruitless day together, he's only paid when you settle on a place; ten percent of your first month's rent is the normal charge. Flat agencies in Ma'adi levy the same commission on both tenant and landlord. As a general guide to **prices**, you can rent a flat in the centre for £E1000–1500 per person per month; prices are a lot lower in winter than in summer. Additional "key money" is illegal, but often demanded.

Before signing a lease, check plumbing, water pressure, sockets, lighting, phone, stove and water-heater (*buta* gas cylinders need changing), and ask if power or water cuts are regular occurrences. Also determine whether utilities (phone, gas, electricity) and services (the *bowab*, rubbish collector) are included in the rent and are paid up to date when you move in (ask to see receipts if necessary). The flat's contents should be noted on an inventory, and the responsibility for repairs and the size of the deposit established. A flat without a phone isn't likely to acquire one, whatever the landlord promises.

in the lobby, a pool and health club, but not a nightclub. ❽

Mena House Oberoi Near the Giza Pyramids ☎02/383-3222, ⓦwww.oberoihotels.com (see map on p.204). Set in lush grounds (of which some rooms have a view), this one-time khedival hunting lodge witnessed Roosevelt and Churchill initiate the D-Day plan, and the formal signing of the peace treaty between Israel and Egypt. Its renovated arabesque halls and nineteenth-century rooms are delightful; the modern Mena Gardens annexe isn't so grand, though the rooms are plush enough. Facilities include the *Moghul* restaurant (the best Indian restaurant in Egypt; see p.238), pool, golf course and tennis courts. ❼

Hostels and camping

Hostelling and camping offer meagre rewards by comparison with downtown hotels, and any gains in clean air or seclusion tend to be negated by the extra travel involved in sightseeing from an outlying base. That said, the **HI youth hostel** near the El-Gama'a Bridge on Roda Island (☎02/364-0729, ⓕ368-4107; see map on pp.170–171) is readily accessible by #82 minibus from Tahrir. Buses #355 and #357 also run nearby, or you can catch a river-taxi to the Giza University stop and walk back across the bridge. There is a choice between three-person dorms (£E25.25 per bed including breakfast) or cheaper eight- to ten-person ones (£E11.30). Non-HI members pay £E2 extra, or can take out membership for £E25. Doors are closed midnight to 8am, so no carousing unless you aim to make a full night of it.

Salma Camping in Harraniyya, outside Giza (☎02/381-5062 or 010/145-7316; ❷; see map on p.204), is a bit run-down, but as Cairo's only campsite, it attracts tourists with camper-vans or bikes, and is handy for the Pyramid sites at Giza and Saqqara. Camping or caravanning, it charges £E25 per person, including electricity and free hot showers, with no extra tent or vehicle charge. Alternatively, you can rent a hut or even a double room at £E80 a night for two people; breakfast is not included, but there is use of a kitchen. It's reached by turning off Pyramids Road towards Saqqara at Maryotteya Canal (1km before the Pyramids), and then after 4km taking a signposted turn-off at Harraniyya village; continue for 100m, and the site is about 100m away on your right. Buses and service taxis run from town to the junction of Maryotteya Canal with Pyramids Road, where you can catch regular service taxis to the Harraniyya turn-off.

The City

With so much to see (and overlook, initially), you can spend weeks in **CAIRO** and merely scratch the surface. But as visitors soon realize, there are lots of reasons why people don't stay for long. The city's density, climate and pollution conspire against it, and the culture shock is equally wearing. Tourists unfamiliar with Arab ways can take little for granted, regular visitors expect to be baffled, and not even Cairenes comprehend the whole metropolis. The downside weighs especially on newcomers, since it's the main sights that generate most friction. A day at Khan el-Khalili bazaar can feel like a course in sales resistance and baksheesh evasion. Generally, however, Cairenes are the warmest, best-natured city dwellers going. They have to be to live in such a pressure cooker without exploding. Their sly wit and prying render pretension and secrecy impotent; their spirited ingenuity transcends horrendous conditions. Potential riots are defused by tolerance and custom; a web of ties resists alienation. Once you have something of the measure of this, Cairo feels an altogether different and more enjoyable place.

Central Cairo

Most people prefer to get accustomed to **central Cairo** before tackling the older, Islamic quarters, for even in this westernized downtown area known as *wust al-balad*, the culture shock can be profound. Beyond the sanctuary of the luxury hotels beside the Nile, crowds and traffic jostle for space in the fume-laden air; whistling cops direct weaving taxis and limousines, donkey carts and buses; office workers rub shoulders with *baladi* folk, Nubians and soldiers. The pavements and shadowy lobbies of cavernous Art Deco or Empire-style apartment buildings are a lifetime's world for many vendors and doormen – both major contributors to Cairo's grapevine. Above the crumbling pediments and hoardings, pigeon lofts and extra rooms spread across the rooftops – a spacious alternative to the streets below, forming a city above the city centre.

The area is essentially a lopsided triangle, bounded by **Ramses Station**, **Midan Ataba** and **Garden City**, and for the most part it's compact enough to explore on foot. Only the Ramses quarter and the further reaches of Garden City are sufficiently distant to justify using transport. At the heart of central Cairo is the broad, bustling expanse of **Midan Tahrir**, its most famous landmark the domed **Museum of Egyptian Antiquities**, which houses the finest collection of its kind in the world.

Midan Tahrir and around

The centre of modern Cairo is a concrete assertion of national pride, which threatens to burst as it pumps traffic around the city. Created on the site of Britain's Qasr el-Nil Barracks after the 1952 revolution, **Midan Tahrir** (Liberation Square) embodies the drawbacks of subsequent political trends. During the 1960s, two bureaucratic monoliths and several transport depots responsible for much of Egypt and all of Greater Cairo were concentrated here, as Nasser

---

Cairo's museums

Although Cairo has more than a dozen museums, most visitors limit themselves to the big three, devoted respectively to **Egyptian Antiquities** (see p.107), **Coptic art** (see p.172) and **Islamic art** (see p.147). The Islamic Art Museum was closed at the time of writing (the tourist office should know if it's reopened and, if so, what the the latest opening hours and prices are), but would otherwise make a fitting adjunct to exploring its quarter of the city; both it and the Coptic Museum can be comfortably seen in a couple of hours. The Egyptian Antiquities Museum, by far the largest of the three and the most popular, needs at least two visits to do it any kind of justice.

On a practical note, unless you're planning to buy a photo permit, it's best to leave your **camera** at the hotel. Otherwise you'll have to check it in at the entrance to all three main museums, a process which occasionally leads to the wrong cameras being returned to owners. For the smaller and more distant museums, given temporary closures and erratic opening hours, it's worth telephoning before setting out.

Tout trouble

Touts who pose as friendly strangers and attach themselves to tourists are common on the streets of downtown Cairo. They are petty crooks, mostly (but by no means all) young, whose aim is to work various scams on you, to persuade you to buy over-priced tours (see p.88), or to steer or follow you into shops, where they will tell the shopkeeper in Arabic that they are your guide and entitled to a commission on what-ever you buy, which you end up paying of course. Touts favour particular perfume and papyrus shops with whom they regularly deal, but they can accompany you into any shop, and in general the shopkeeper will go along with them to avoid trouble – you will be gone next week after all, but the tout will still be around. So long as you are aware of the situation from the start, you should be able to get rid of the tout relatively quickly, without an argument. It is illegal for touts to harass tourists, and you can expect ordinary Egyptians to take your side if you have any serious problems.

Each tout has their own opening line. Some will compliment you on your clothing, others will simply ask what you are looking for – if anyone asks you this when you are not obviously looking for anything, you can be sure they're a tout. Once they've gained your confidence they can be hard to shake off. Should you make the mistake of telling one of them your name and hotel, you may find them turning up there asking for you, or you may even be greeted on the street by name by a different tout (who may even say, "Don't you remember me?" as if you had met before), since they often work in teams.

How do you distinguish a tout from someone who's just being friendly? The first rule of thumb is there's no need to be rude: just smile and say hello, or nod, and carry on walking. An ordinary Egyptian will not be offended. Touts tend to come up behind you to start a conversation, which ordinary Egyptians do not usually do. A tout will probably try to stop you by demanding to know why you are in such a hurry, or may accuse you of being rude. Being noncommital is a good way to shake a tout off; if someone asks where you are going, for example, you can reply airily, "Nowhere."

Touts favour **specific areas**. One such is Sharia Talaat Harb, especially between Midan Tahrir and Midan Talaat Harb; outside *Felfela* is a favourite place, as are road junctions, where they will often accost you while you cross the street. Other places worked by touts include the Ghuriya and Spice Bazaar in Islamic Cairo, and the road from there to Bab Zuweila. Some also work Tahrir Bridge and Sharia Tahrir on Gezira Island. People who greet you in areas with few tourists are most unlikely to be touts, and indeed ordinary Egyptians are much more likely to take an interest in you in such areas.

adopted Soviet-style centralization. A decade later, Sadat rejected his mentor's "Arab Socialism" in favour of an Infitah (Open Door) to Western capital-ism, causing private car ownership to soar almost as fast as Cairo's population. Impending gridlock was only averted by digging a metro, in spite of which, buses and roads are still grossly overcrowded.

The entrances to **Sadat metro station** serve as pedestrian underpasses linking these depots and buildings with the main roads leading off Tahrir. Despite clear labelling in English, it's easy to go astray in the maze of subways and surface at the wrong location. Many Cairenes prefer to take their chances crossing by road – a nerve-wracking experience for newcomers. Though some **landmarks** are obvi-ous, rooftop billboards and neon signs flanking the end of streets like Talaat Harb or Qasr el-Nil also help with orientation. To watch the square over tea, try one of the Arab cafés between Talaat Harb and El-Bustan; the café nearest to Sharia Talaat Harb, the *Wadi el-Nil*, was bombed by Islamic radicals in 1993, apparently because they didn't like the Sudanese cannabis dealers who used to hang out in it.

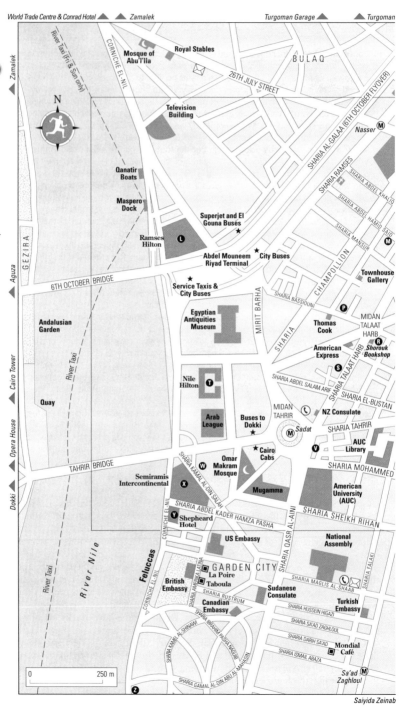

Saiyida Zeinab

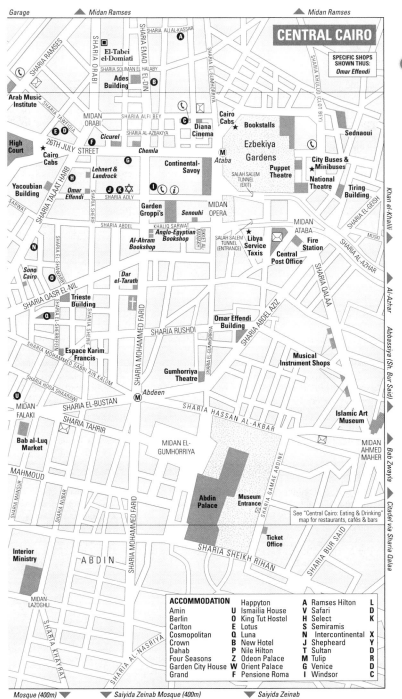

CENTRAL CAIRO

SPECIFIC SHOPS
SHOWN THUS:
Omar Effendi

Garage — Midan Ramses — Midan Ramses

SHARIA RAMSES
SHARIA ALI AL-KASSAR
SHARIA EMAD
SHARIA EL GUMHORIYA
SHARIA KHULUD (GLOT BEY)

El-Tabei
el-Domiati
SHARIA ORABI
SHARIA SOLIMAN EL HALABY
EL DIN

Ades
Building

Arab Music
Institute
SHARIA TAWFIQIA

MIDAN
ORABI
SHARIA ALFI BEY
SHARIA AL-AZBAKIYA

Cairo
Cabs ★
Diana
Cinema
Cairo
Cabs
Bookstalls

Ezbekiya
Gardens
Sednaoui

High
Court
26TH JULY
STREET
Cicurel
Chemla

Cairo
Cabs
Cairo Talaat Harb
Lehnert &
Landrock

Omar
Effendi
SHARIA ADLY
SHARIA SHERIF

Continental-
Savoy

Ataba
M
Puppet
Theatre

City Buses &
Minibuses ★
National
Theatre
Tiring
Building

SALAH SALEM
TUNNEL
(EXIT)

Yacoubian
Building
SHARIA TALAAT HARB
SARWAT

Garden
Groppi's
Senouhi
MIDAN
OPERA

SHARIA EL-SHARIF
SHARIA ABDEL
KHALIQ SARWAT
SIKKET AL-MANAKH

Anglo-Egyptian
Bookshop

Al-Ahram
Bookshop
Dar
el-Tarath
SALAH SALEM
TUNNEL
(ENTRANCE)

Libya
Service
Taxis

MIDAN
ATABA
Fire
Station

Central
Post Office

SHARIA EL-GEISH
MUSKI
Khan el-Khalili

Sono
Cairo
SHARIA QASR EL-NIL
SHARIA EL-SHERIFEEN

Trieste
Building
SHARIA SHERIF
SHARIA MOHAMMED FARID
SHARIA RUSHDI

Omar Effendi
Building
SHARIA ABDEL AZIZ
SHARIA QALAA
Al-Azhar
SHARIA AL-AZHAR

SHARIA MOHAMMED SABRI AIN KALOM

Espace Karim
Francis
SHARIA EL GUMHORIYA

Gumhorriya
Theatre

Musical
Instrument Shops
Abbassiya (Sh. Bur Said)

SHARIA HODA SHAARAWI

MIDAN
FALAKI
SHARIA EL-BUSTAN
Abdeen
M

SHARIA HASSAN AL-AKBAR

Islamic Art
Museum

Bab Zweyla

Bab al-Luq
Market
SHARIA TAHRIR
SHARIA MANSUR

MIDAN EL-
GUMHORRIYA

MIDAN
AHMED
MAHER
Citadel via Sharia Qalaa

MAHMOUD
SHARIA NUBAR
SHARIA GAMAE ABDINE

Abdin
Palace
Museum
Entrance

See "Central Cairo: Eating & Drinking"
map for restaurants, cafés & bars

Interior
Ministry
ABDIN

Ticket
Office
SHARIA BUR SAID

MIDAN
LAZOGHLI
SHARIA SHEIKH RIHAN

SHARIA KHAYRAT
SHARIA AL-NASRIYA

ACCOMMODATION				
Amin	U	Happyton	Ramses Hilton A	L
Berlin	O	Ismailia House	Safari V	D
Carlton	E	King Tut Hostel	Select H	K
Cosmopolitan	Q	Lotus	Semiramis S	
Crown	B	Luna	Intercontinental N	X
Dahab	P	New Hotel	Shepheard J	Y
Four Seasons	Z	Nile Hilton	Sultan T	
Garden City House	W	Odeon Palace	Tulip M	D
Grand	F	Orient Palace	Venice G	R
		Pensione Roma I	Windsor	D
				C

Mosque (400m) — Saiyida Zeinab Mosque (400m) — Saiyida Zeinab

Tahrir landmarks

West of the square, behind the former bus terminal (a building site at the time of writing), the blue-and-white **Nile Hilton** – the first modern "international" hotel built along the Corniche – adjoins a tan-coloured edifice, the secretariat of the **Arab League**, built during the 1960s and now a vestige of the time when Egypt was acknowledged leader of the "progressive" Arab cause. After Sadat's treaty with Israel, the headquarters of the League moved to Tunis and most of its members severed relations with Egypt. Mubarak's policy of rapprochement was finally rewarded in 1992, when the League returned to Cairo and, with it, posses of limos and gun-toting guards. Next to the Arab League Building, Tahrir Bridge runs between guardian lions towards Gezira Island and Dokki. Further down the Corniche, roughly opposite the *Shepheard Hotel*, was the site of the Thomas Cook landing stage, where generations of tourists embarked on Nile cruises and General Gordon's ill-fated expedition set off for Khartoum in 1883.

Across the Tahrir Bridge ramp from the Arab League Building, Egypt's Ministry of Foreign Affairs is less conspicuous than the **Omar Makram Mosque**, where funeral receptions for deceased VIPs are held in brightly coloured marquees. But dominating the southern end of Midan Tahrir is a concave office block that inspires shuddering memories: the **Mugamma**. A "fraternal gift" from the Soviet Union in the 1960s, this Kafkaesque warren of gloomy corridors, dejected queues and idle bureaucrats houses the public departments of the Interior, Health and Education ministries, and the Cairo Governorate. How many of the 50,000 people visiting El-Mugamma each day suffer nervous breakdowns from sheer frustration is anyone's guess; an African supposedly flung himself through a window several years ago (for advice on handling the Mugamma, see p.266). On the corner of Sharia Qasr al-Aini, opposite the Mugamma, a handsome pseudo-Islamic facade masks the old campus of the **American University in Cairo** (entered via Sharia Sheikh Rihan). Responsible for publishing some of the best research on Egypt in the English language, the AUC is also a Western-style haven for wealthy Egyptian youths and US students doing a year abroad, its shady gardens and preppy ambience seeming utterly remote from everyday life in Cairo. Visitors might experience a premonitory shiver that Iran's gilded youth probably looked pretty similar

Cairo's best views

The rooftop bar at the *Nile Hilton* (see p.98) is just one of several high points where you can take in a view over Cairo. Here you get great views of **Tahrir Square** that only the front rooms at the *Ismailia House* hotel can equal, and beyond the square you can see as far as the Citadel and the Muqattam Hills. The Citadel (see p.155) offers a good view over **Islamic Cairo**, while some of Islamic Cairo's minarets give you a vista as far as the Pyramids on a clear day if they are open (the Qalaoun Complex and the Blue Mosque are among the best; the al-Muayyad minarets atop Bab Zwayla also give a pretty good view). But the best and widest view over Islamic Cairo is from the high point in Al-Azhar Park (see p.169). For a vista over the chaos and mayhem that is **Midan Ramses**, the terrace café of the *Hotel Everest* (see p.240) is the place.

The Cairo Tower on Gezira (see p.190), with its sporadically revolving restaurant, is also great for views, as is the newer and more reliably revolving restaurant at the *Grand Hyatt* hotel on Roda Island (see p.99). The latter is high enough, and well enough placed, to offer what must rate as the very best Cairo view, encompassing the Pyramids, the Citadel, the Nile and most of downtown.

before the Islamic Revolution. Egyptian Marxists and Islamic fundamentalists regard the AUC as a tool of US and Zionist imperialism.

Five or so minutes' walk north from the main AUC entrance, near the University Library at **Midan Falaki** (or walk along Sharia Tahrir from the square), you'll find a pedestrian bridge of the kind that circumvented Midan Tahrir before its subways were dug. Off to the right, a broad street awash with fruit and vegetable stalls runs alongside the covered **Bab al-Luq market**. Not a place for the squeamish, and overpriced compared to other markets, it's still an interesting spot to watch haggling and gossiping over trussed poultry or tea and *sheeshas*. It also holds a number of extremely cheap eating places. A coffee merchant's store across on the north side fills the square with the fine aroma of cardamom-spiced *'ahwa mahawega*.

Moving on from Tahrir, you can continue south and east to explore the Garden City and the Abdin quarter (see p.124), or walk back to the square and take either Sharia Talaat Harb or Qasr el-Nil to head for the shops and restaurants of downtown Cairo (see pp.118–121).

The Museum of Egyptian Antiquities

However, downtown's biggest attraction is the Egyptian Museum, or to give it its full title, the **Museum of Egyptian Antiquities**, at the northern end of Midan Tahrir (daily 9am–6.45pm; Ramadan 9am–4pm; £E50, students £E25, no cameras allowed; ⓦ www.egyptianmuseum.gov.eg). Founded in 1858 by Auguste Mariette, who excavated the Serapeum at Saqqara and several major temples in Upper Egypt (and who was later buried in the museum grounds), it has long since outgrown its present building, which now scarcely provides warehouse space for the pharaonic artefacts. Allowing one minute for each, it would take about nine months to view its 136,000 exhibits. Forty thousand more items lie crated in the basement, where many have sunk into the soft ground, necessitating excavations beneath the building itself. A new Grand Egyptian Museum, which will house some or all the exhibits in the present one, is already under construction by the Pyramids of Giza, and is due to open in around 2015. Meanwhile, for all the chaos, poor lighting and captioning of the old museum, the richness of the collection makes this one of the world's few truly great museums.

A single visit of three to four hours suffices to cover the Tutankhamun exhibition and a few other **highlights**. Everyone has their favourites, but a reasonable shortlist might include, on the ground floor, the Amarna galleries (**rooms 3 and 8**), the cream of statuary from the Old, Middle and New kingdoms (**rooms 42, 32, 22 and 12**) and the Nubian funerary cache (**Room 44**); on the upper floor, the Fayoum Portraits (**Room 14**) and model figures (**rooms 37, 32 and 27**), and, of course, the Mummy Room (**Room 56**) – though it costs extra.

As you approach the museum, don't pay attention to people who may try to persuade you that the museum is briefly closed and that you should come to their shop ("papyrus museum") instead. The water lilies growing in the pond in front of the main entrance are the now-rare blue lotus, a psychoactive plant used as a drug by the Ancient Egyptians – which they are depicted using (by dipping the flowers into their wine) on several frescoes and reliefs. Also outside the museum, by the camera deposit, you'll probably be offered a **guided tour**, which generally lasts two hours (at £E50–80 per hour, depending on your bargaining skills), though the museum deserves at least six. The guides are extremely knowledgeable and they do help you to make sense of it all. Alternatively, you can rent headphones with a **recorded commentary** in English,

Arabic or French (£E20; you'll need your passport as a deposit), and numbers to press on a handset for each of the items covered. However, as the exhibits were already numbered on at least two different systems, the addition of new numbers for the digital commentary complicates matters still further, leading to some items now having three different numbers, and often no other labelling (in such cases, we have identified exhibits by their most prominent number).

The best published **guide** to the museum's contents is the AUC's *Illustrated Guide to the Egyptian Museum* (£E150), with lavish illustrations of the museum's top exhibits. It doesn't list the exhibits in order, but there is a room-by-room picture index at the back to help you find what you are looking at in the text, and it is certainly an excellent souvenir of the museum.

The museum's first-floor **café–restaurant** is entered via the souvenir shop from outside the museum.

Ground floor

Exhibits are arranged more or less chronologically, so that by starting at the entrance and walking in a clockwise direction round the outer galleries you'll pass through the Old, Middle and New kingdoms, before ending up with the

Late and Greco-Roman periods in the east wing. This approach is historically and artistically coherent but rather plodding. A snappier alternative is to proceed instead through the Atrium – which samples the whole era of pharaonic civilization – to the superb Amarna Gallery in the northern wing, then backtrack to cover sections that sound interesting, or instead head upstairs to Tutankhamun.

To suit either option, we've covered the ground floor in six sections: the Atrium, Old, Middle and New kingdom galleries, the Amarna Gallery, and the East Wing. Whichever approach you decide on, it's worth starting with the Atrium foyer (**Room 43**), where the dynastic saga begins.

The Rotunda and Atrium

The **Rotunda**, inside the museum entrance, kicks off with **monumental sculptures** from various eras, notably (in the four corners) three colossi of Ramses II (XIX Dynasty) and a statue of Amenhotep, son of the XVIII Dynasty royal architect Hapu. Also here, hidden away in the northwest corner, are sixteen small wooden and stone statues of a 24th-century BC official named Iby showing him at various stages in his life. Just to the left of the door as you enter sits the limestone **statue of King Zoser** (#106), installed within its *serdab* beside his Step Pyramid at Saqqara in the 27th century BC, and removed by archeologists 4600 years later.

The forging of dynastic rule is commemorated by a famous exhibit in **Room 43**, as you enter the Atrium. Two XII Dynasty **funerary barques** from the Pyramid of Senusert III at Dahshur stand on either side of the room, but the most interesting works are two decorative versions of the slate palettes used to grind kohl. The **Palette of Narmer** (#111) records the unification of the Two Lands (*c.*3100 BC) by a ruler called Narmer or Menes. One side of the palette depicts him wearing the White Crown of Upper Egypt, smiting an enemy with a mace, while a falcon (Horus) ensnares another prisoner and tramples the heraldic papyrus of Lower Egypt. The reverse face shows him wearing their Red Crown to inspect the slain, and ravaging a fortress as a bull; dividing these tableaux are mythical beasts with entwined necks, restrained from conflict by bearded men, an arcane symbol of his political achievement. Unlabelled in the case behind this is part of another palette (the top half is unfortunately missing), the **Libyan Tribute Tablet**, beautifully carved with trains of bulls, donkeys and goats, and a grove of olive trees. A century or so older than Narmer's palette, it seems to have been made to commemorate the payment of a tribute to the Upper Egyptian ruler by the Tjemehu tribe of Libya.

Descending into **Room 33**, the Atrium itself, you'll find **pyramidions** (pyramid capstones) from Dahshur, and more sarcophagi from the New Kingdom. Overshadowing those of Tuthmosis I and Queen Hatshepsut (before she became pharaoh) is the **sarcophagus of Merneptah** (#213), surmounted by a figure of the king as Osiris and protectively embraced from within by a relief of Nut, the sky goddess. But Merneptah's bid for immortality failed: when discovered at Tanis in 1939, his sarcophagus held the coffin of Psusennes, a XXI Dynasty ruler whose gold-sheathed mummy now lies upstairs.

At the centre of the Atrium is a **painted floor** from the royal palace at **Amarna** (XVIII Dynasty). It shows a river brimming with ducks and fish and framed by reeds where waterfowl and cows amble, a fine example of the lyrical naturalism of the Amarna period. For more of this revolutionary epoch in pharaonic history, head upstairs past the colossal statues of **Amenophis III**, **Queen Tiy** and **their three daughters**, which serenely presage Akhenaten and Nefertiti in the northern wing.

But first you must pass through **Room 13**, containing Merneptah's Victory Stele on the right, also called the **Israel Stele** (#134). Its name derives from the boast "Israel is crushed, it has no more seed", from among a list of Merneptah's conquests at the Temple of Karnak – the sole known reference to Israel in all the records of Ancient Egypt. Partly on the strength of this, many believe that Merneptah, son of Ramses II, was the Pharaoh of the Exodus (XIX Dynasty) – although this view has come under increasing criticism of late (see box, p.765). The other side carries an earlier record of deeds by Amenophis III (Akhenaten's father) in the service of Amun, whom his son later repudiated. On the threshold between here and Room 8 is a model of a **typical Egyptian house**, as excavated at Amarna, the short-lived capital of Akhenaten and Nefertiti – who are honoured with their own gallery in rooms 8 and 3 just ahead (see p.112).

Old Kingdom Galleries

The southwest corner of the ground floor is devoted to the **Old Kingdom** (*c.*2700–2181 BC), when the III–VI dynasties ruled Egypt from Memphis and built the Pyramids. Lining the central aisle of **rooms 46–47** are funerary statues of deceased VIPs and servants (the custom of burying retainers alive ended with the II Dynasty). On the north side of Room 47, six **wooden panels** from the tomb of **Hesy-Re** (#21) portray this senior scribe of the III Dynasty, who was also the earliest known dentist. Room 47 also displays statuettes of *shabti* (worker) figures, depicted preparing food (#52 and 53). To the north and south are three slate triads of **Menkaure flanked by Hathor** and the goddess of the Aphroditopolis nome, from the Mycenius valley temple at Giza. The pair of alabaster **lion tables** by the fourth pillar on the north side were probably used for sacrifices or libations towards the end of the II Dynasty.

Among the more striking exhibits in Room 46 are **statuettes** of the dwarf Khnumhotep, Overseer of the Wardrobe, a man with a deformed head and a hunchback afflicted by Pott's disease (#54 and 65). Fragments of the **beard of the Sphinx** are at the end of the hall (**Room 51**), to the left below the stairs (#6031). The British Museum in London possesses another metre-long chunk; the beard was probably five metres long before it was shot to pieces by Mamluke and Napoleonic troops during target practice. Also in Room 51, a sculptured head of V Dynasty pharaoh Userkaf (#6051) represents the earliest known larger-than-life-size statue in the world.

At the entrance to **Room 41**, **reliefs** from a V Dynasty tomb at Maidum (#25) depict a desert hunt and other rural activities. Ahead and to the left, another panel (#59), from a V Dynasty tomb at Saqqara, shows grain being weighed out, milled and graded, as well as glass being blown and statues carved. The women on these reliefs wear long chemises, the men loincloths or sometimes nothing (revealing them to be circumcised, according to Egyptian custom). **Room 42** boasts a superb **statue of Chephren**, his head embraced by Horus (#31). Carved from black diorite, whose white marbling emphasizes the sinews of his knee and clenched fist, the statue comes from Chephren's valley temple at Giza. Equally arresting on the left is the wooden **statue of Ka-aper** (#40), a plump figure with an introspective gaze, which Arab diggers at Saqqara called "Sheikh al-Balad" because it resembled their own village headman. One of the two newly restored wooden statues just beyond him could well be of the same man. The **statue of a scribe** (#43, to the right of the doorway as you enter), poised for notation with an open scroll across his knees, is also memorable.

On the walls of **Room 31** are sandstone reliefs from Wadi Maraghah, near the ancient turquoise mines of Sinai. Twin limestone **statues of Ra-Nufer** (#45 and 46) signify his dual role as Memphite high priest of Ptah and Sokar; aside from their wigs and kilts, they look virtually identical. Both were created in the royal workshops, possibly by the same artist.

Room 32 is dominated by life-size seated **statues of Prince Rahotep and Princess Nefert**, from their *mastaba* at Maidum (IV Dynasty). His skin is painted brick-red, hers a creamy yellow – a distinction common in Egyptian art. Nefert wears a wig and diadem and swathes herself in a diaphanous wrap; the prince is simply clad in a waist cloth. Look out for the **tableau of the dwarf Seneb and his family** on the left (#39). Embraced by his wife, this Overseer of the Wardrobe seems contented; his naked children hold their fingers to their lips. In the second niche on the left-hand wall hangs a perfectly observed, vividly stylized mural, known as the **Maidum Geese** (III/IV Dynasty). Although the heyday of the Old Kingdom is poorly represented by a **statue of Ti**, to the right as you enter (#49), its twilight era boasts the first known metal sculptures (*c*.2300 BC): two **statues of Pepi I and his son**, made by hammering sheets of copper over wooden armatures. Although these usually reside in Room 32, they had been away for restoration and, at time of writing, one of them, newly restored, was temporarily on display in the entrance lobby.

In **Room 37**, the **furniture of Queen Hetepheres** has been expertly reconstructed from heaps of gold and rotten wood. As the wife of Snofru and mother of Cheops, she was buried near her son's pyramid at Giza with a sedan chair, gold vessels and a canopied bed. Also in the room, in a cabinet of its own, is a tiny **statuette of Cheops** (#143), the only known likeness of the Great Pyramid pharaoh.

Middle Kingdom Galleries

With **Room 26** you enter the **Middle Kingdom**, when centralized authority was restored and pyramid-building resumed under the XII Dynasty (*c*.1991–1786 BC). A relic of the previous era of civil wars (termed the First Intermediate Period) sits on the right, glum-faced. Endowed with hulking feet to suggest power, and black skin, crossed arms and a curly beard to link it to Osiris, this **statue of Mentuhotpe Nebhepetre** was buried near his funerary shrine at Deir el-Bahri and discovered by Howard Carter – whose horse fell through the roof. If the Mummy of Dagi were still around, it could use the pair of "eyes" painted inside its sarcophagus across the hall to espy two **statues of Queen Nofret** wearing a sheath dress and a Hathor wig, flanking the entrance to Room 21.

The statuettes at the back of **Room 22** (#92) are striking for the uncharacteristic expressiveness of their faces, in contrast to the manic staring eyes of the wooden statue of Nakhti on the right-hand side of the room. Also around the room are likenesses of Amenemhet III and Senusert I, but your attention is grabbed by the **burial chamber of Harhotpe** from Deir el-Bahri, in the middle of the room and covered inside with pictorial objects, charms and texts. Surrounding the chamber are ten limestone **statues of Senusert** from his pyramid complex at Lisht, stiffly formal in contrast to his cedarwood figure in the case to the right as you enter the room (#88). The sides of these statues' thrones bear variations of the *sema-tawy* symbol of unification: Hapy the Nile-god, or Horus and Seth, entwining the heraldic plants of the Two Lands.

This basic imperative of statecraft might explain the unique **double statue of Amenemhat III** (#508) in **Room 16**. Personified as the Nile god bringing his people fish on trays, the dual figures may represent Upper and Lower Egypt, or the living king and his deified *ka*. On the left, five **lion-headed sphinxes with human faces** watch your exit from the Middle Kingdom; the anarchic Second Intermediate Period and the Hyksos invasion go uncommemorated.

New Kingdom Galleries

With **Room 11** you pass into the **New Kingdom**, an era of renewed pharaonic power and imperial expansion under the XVIII and XIX dynasties (*c*.1567–1200 BC). Egypt's African and Asian empires were forged by Tuthmosis III, who had long been frustrated while his unwarlike stepmother, Hatshepsut, ruled as pharaoh. From one of the Osiride pillars of her great temple at Deir el-Bahri comes a commanding crowned **head of Hatshepsut** (#6184), while on the right of the room stands an unusual wooden *ka* statue of Pharaoh Hor (#75), mounted on a sliding base to signify his posthumous wanderings. In **Room 12** you'll find a grey schist statue of **Tuthmosis III** (#62) and other masterpieces of XVIII Dynasty art. At the back of the room, the **Hathor Shrine** from Tuthmosis III's ruined temple at Deir el-Bahri contains a statue of the goddess in her bovine form, emerging reborn from a papyrus swamp. Tuthmosis stands beneath her cow's head, and is suckled as an infant in the fresco behind Hathor's statue, overshadowed by a star-spangled ceiling. To the right of the room is a block statue (#418) of Hatshepsut's vizier, Senenmut, with the queen's daughter Neferure, with a smaller statue of the same duo in the second recess on the right. The relationship between the queen, her daughter and her vizier has inspired much speculation. From the same period comes a section of the Deir el-Bahri "**Punt relief**" (#130, in the second niche on the left), showing the Queen of Punt, who suffered from elephantiasis, and her donkey, observed by Hatshepsut during her expedition to that fabled land.

To the right of the Punt relief stands a grey granite **statue of the god Khonsu** with a sidelock denoting youth and a face thought to be that of the boy pharaoh Tutankhamun, which was taken from the temple of the moon-god at Karnak. Flanking this statue and the Punt relief, two statues of a man named **Amenhotep** portray him as a young scribe of humble birth (#6014) and as an octogenarian priest (#98), honoured for his direction of massive works like the Colossi of Memnon.

Before turning the corner into the northern wing, you encounter two **lion-headed statues of Sekhmet**, found at Karnak. A **sphinx** with the head of Hatshepsut welcomes you to **Room 6**, where the first set of reliefs on the southern wall come from the Tomb of Maya at Saqqara. The tomb was uncovered in the nineteenth century but subsequently lost until its rediscovery in 1986. **Room 8** is largely an overflow for the Amarna Gallery (see below) but also contains a monumental **dyad of Amun and Mut**, smashed to pieces by medieval limestone quarriers and lovingly pieced together from fragments long lost in the vaults of the museum and at Karnak, where it originally stood. Those pieces that could not be fitted into the jigsaw are displayed in a case just behind it.

To the left of the stairs in **Room 10**, note the painted **relief** on a block from Ramses II's temple at Memphis, which shows him subjugating Egypt's foes. In a motif repeated on dozens of temple pylons, the king grabs the hair of a Libyan, Nubian and Syrian, and wields an axe. Ramessid pharaohs who never fought a battle were especially keen on such reliefs. The room is dominated by a pun (#6245): a **statue of Ramses II** as a child, finger to mouth, holding a plant while protected by the sun-god *Re* or *Ra*, which combines with the word for child (*mes*) and the word for the plant (*su*) to form his name. From Room 10 you can follow the New Kingdom into the East Wing (covered on p.113), or climb the stairs to the Tutankhamun galleries on the upper floor.

The Amarna Gallery

Room 3 and much of the adjoining **Room 8** focus on the **Amarna period**, a break with centuries of tradition which barely outlasted the reign of Pharaoh

Akhenaten (c.1379–1362 BC) and Queen Nefertiti. Rejecting Amun and the other deities of Thebes, they decreed the supremacy of a single god, the Aten, built a new capital at Amarna in Middle Egypt to escape the old bureaucracy, and left enigmatic works of art that provoke a reaction.

Staring down from the walls of **Room 3** are four **colossi of Akhenaten**, whose attenuated skull and face, flaring lips and nostrils, rounded thighs and belly are suggestive of a hermaphrodite or a primeval earth goddess. Because these characteristics are carried over to the figures of his wife and daughters on certain **steles** (such as those in case #169 in Room 8), **statuettes** (such as those in case #162 in Room 8) and tomb reliefs, it has been argued that the Amarna style pandered to some physical abnormality in Akhenaten (or the royal family) – the captions hint at perversions. Others retort that the famous head of Nefertiti, in Berlin, proves that it was just a stylistic device. Another feature of Amarna art was its note of intimacy: a **stele of the royal family** (#167 in Room 8) portrays Akhenaten dandling their eldest daughter, Meritaten, whilst Nefertiti cradles her sisters. For the first time in Egyptian art, breakfast was depicted. The Amarna focus on this world rather than the afterlife infused traditional subjects with new vitality – witness the freer brush strokes on the fragments of a **marsh scene**, displayed around the walls of Room 3. To the left of the entrance to the room, display case A contains some of the **Amarna Letters** (others are in London and Berlin), recording pleas for troops to aid the pharaoh's vassals in Palestine, the impact of his death, and Nefertiti's search for allies against those who pressed Tutankhamun to reverse the Amarna revolution. Originally baked into earthen "envelopes" for delivery, these cuneiform tablets were stored in the Foreign Office archives at Amarna.

Akhenaten's carnelian-, gold- and glass-inlaid **coffin** is in the middle of Room 3, the upper half displayed alongside the gilding from the bottom part of the coffin. This gilding disappeared from the museum at some time between 1915 and 1931, but resurfaced in Switzerland in the 1980s. It has now been restored and mounted on a Plexiglas cast in the presumed shape of the original coffin.

The East Wing

As an inducement to follow the New Kingdom into the East Wing, **Room 15** starts with, directly facing the statue of Ramses II as a child, a sexy statue of his daughter and consort Merytamun. The centrepiece of **Room 14** is a restored pink granite triple statue of Ramses III being crowned by Horus and Set, representing order and chaos respectively.

Waning with the XX Dynasty and expiring with the XXI, the New Kingdom was followed by the so-called **Late Period** of mostly foreign rulers. From this period, in the middle of **Room 30**, comes an alabaster **statue of Amenirdis**, whom the pharaoh made divine votaress of Amun to watch over the Theban priesthood. Dressed as a New Kingdom queen, Amenirdis wears a falcon head-dress crowned with *uraei*, originally topped by a Hathor crown bearing a solar disc and horns. Of the diverse statues of deities in **Room 24**, the most striking by far is that of **Taweret** (or Tweri), the pregnant-hippopotamus goddess of childbirth, on the left (#248). Very sleek, in smooth black slate, the statue was found in a sealed shrine at Karnak, which is why it is so well preserved.

Rooms 34 and **35** cover the **Greco-Roman Period** (332 BC onwards), when Classical art engaged with Ancient Egyptian symbolism. Facing you as you enter Room 34 is a coiled serpent, ready to strike, and to the left of it, in case D, an alabaster head of a very young-looking Alexander the Great. At the back of the room, on the right, a Roman fresco depicts the famously Freudian legend of King Oedipus, shown here killing his father, but not doing the other thing that he's famous for. The meld of Egyptian and Greco-Roman styles is typified by the bizarre statues and sarcophagi down the corridor in **Room 49**, especially the **statue of Alexander II** at the threshold of the room. Room 44, on your way, is used for temporary exhibitions.

Upper floor

The upper floor is dominated by the Tutankhamun galleries, which occupy the best part of two wings. Once you've seen Tut's treasures, everything but the Mummy Room and the display of masterpieces seems lacklustre – even though the other galleries feature artefacts just as fine as those downstairs. Come back another day and check them out.

Tutankhamun Galleries

The funerary impedimenta of the boy-king **Tutankhamun** numbers 1700 items and fills a dozen rooms. Given the brevity of his reign (*c*.1361–1352 BC) and the paucity of his tomb in the Valley of the Kings, the mind boggles at the treasure that must have been stashed with great pharaohs like Ramses or Seti. Tutankhamun merely fronted the Theban counter-revolution that

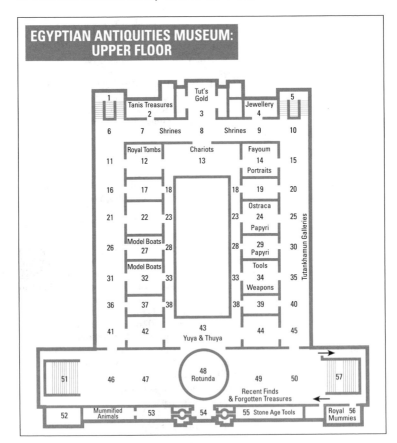

effaced Amarna and restored the cult of Amun and its priesthood to their former primacy. However, the influence of Amarna is apparent in some of the **exhibits**, which are laid out roughly as they were packed into his tomb: chests and statues (**Room 45**) preceding furniture (**rooms 40, 35, 30, 25, 20, 15 and 10**), shrines (**rooms 9–7**) and gold appurtenances (**Room 3**). Adjacent to this are jewellery (**Room 4**) and other treasures from diverse tombs (**rooms 2 and 13**). Most visitors make a beeline for the last four (2, 3 and 4 close fifteen minutes early), ignoring the sequence just outlined. If that includes you, skip ahead through the following rundown.

When Howard Carter's team penetrated the sealed corridor of the tomb in 1922 (see p.385), they found an antechamber, stuffed with caskets and detritus, that had been ransacked by robbers, and two life-size **ka statues of Tutankhamun** (flanking the doorway to **Room 45**), whose black skin symbolized his rebirth. Just beyond are golden **statues of Tutankhamun**, mostly depicting him hunting with a harpoon.

Room 35 is dominated by a **gilded throne** with winged-serpent arms and clawed feet (#179). Its seat back shows the royal couple relaxing in the rays of the Aten, their names given in the Amarna form – dating it to the time when Tutankhamun still observed the Amarna heresy. Among the other worldly goods that the boy pharaoh carried with him into the next world are an ebony and ivory **gaming set** for playing *senet*, a game similar to draughts or checkers (#49), and a host of **shabti figures** to fulfil any tasks the gods might set him (flanking the door to Room 34).

Room 30 has a case of "**Prisoners' Canes**" (#187), whose ebony- and ivory-inlaid figures symbolize the unity of north and south. A bust of the boy-king emerging from a lotus (#118) shows the continued influence of the Amarna artistic style during Tutankhamun's reign. The "**ecclesiastical throne**" (#181) in **Room 25** is a prototype for episcopal thrones of the Christian Church. Its seat back is exquisitely inlaid with ebony and gold, but looks uncomfortable. More typical of pharaonic design are the wooden Heb-Sed throne and footstools, and an ornate commode.

The king's clothes and unguents were stored in two magnificent **chests**. On the lid and sides of the "Painted Chest" (#186) in **Room 20**, he is depicted hunting ostriches and antelopes and devastating ranks of Syrians in his war chariot, larger than life; the end panels show him trampling other foes in the guise of the sphinx. In contrast to the warlike figures of Tutankhamun elsewhere in the gallery, the lid of the "Inlaid Chest" (#188) bears a gentle, Amarna-style vignette of Ankhesenamun (daughter of Nefertiti and Akhenaten) offering lotus, papyrus and mandrake to her husband, framed by poppies, pomegranates and cornflowers. The **golden shrine** covered in repoussé scenes of conjugal harmony once held statues of Tut and his wife Ankhesenamun that were stolen in antiquity.

From ivory headrests in **Room 15**, it's a natural progression to **gilded beds** dedicated to the gods whose animal forms are carved on their bedposts (#183, 221 and 732 in **rooms 9 and 10**). Beyond these is a **shrine of Anubis** (#185), carried in the pharaoh's cortège: the protector of the dead depicted as a vigilant jackal with gilded ears and silver claws. Next along, four alabaster canopic jars in an alabaster chest (#176) contained the pharaoh's viscera, and were themselves contained in the next exhibit, a golden **canopic chest** protected by statues of the goddesses Isis, Nephthys, Selket and Neith (#177). Ranged along **rooms 7 and 8** are four boxy **gilded shrines**, which fitted one inside another like Russian dolls, enclosing Tutankhamun's sarcophagus.

The always packed-out **Room 3** contains **Tutankhamun's gold**, some of which may be on tour abroad. Assuming it's in Cairo, the centrepiece is his haunting **funerary mask**, wearing a headdress inlaid with lapis lazuli, quartz and obsidian. The middle and innermost layers of his mummiform **coffin**, adorned with the same materials, show the boy-king with his hands clasped in the Osiride position, protected by the cloisonné feathers of Wadjet, Nekhbet, Isis and Nephthys. On Tutankhamun's mummy (which remains in his tomb at the Valley of the Kings) were placed scores of **amulets**, a cloisonné **corselet** spangled with glass and carnelian, gem-encrusted **pectorals** and a pair of golden **sandals** – all displayed here.

The **Jewellery Room** next door is almost as overpowering. A VI Dynasty golden **head of a falcon** (once attached to a copper body) from Hieraconpolis rates as the star attraction, but there's stiff competition from the **crown and necklaces of Princess Khnumyt** and the **diadem and pectorals of Princess Set-Hathor**. Buried near the latter at Dahshur were the **amethyst belt and anklet of Mereret**, another XII Dynasty princess. The ceremonial **axe of Ahmosis**, commemorating his expulsion of the Hyksos from Egypt, was buried in the tomb of his mother, Queen Ahhotep. From the same cache (found by Mariette in 1859) came a hinged bracelet of lapis lazuli and the bizarre **golden flies** of the Order of Valour – bug-eyed decorations for bravery.

From the XXI–XXII Dynasty, when northern Egypt was ruled from the Delta, comes the Treasure of 787, displayed in **Room 2**. Of the three royal caches unearthed by Montet in 1939, the richest was that of Psusennes I, whose electrum coffin was found inside the sarcophagus of Merneptah (which is downstairs). His gold necklace is made from rows of discs, in the New Kingdom style.

Between **Room 8** and the Atrium stand two wooden **chariots**, found in the antechamber of Tutankhamun's tomb. Intended for state occasions, their gilded stucco reliefs show Asiatics and Nubians in bondage; pharaonic war chariots were lighter and stronger.

Having finished with Tut, you can either head down the western wing to the Mummy Room, or tackle the other galleries.

Mummies

The southern end of the museum's upper floor harbours two rooms full of mummies. **Room 53** exhibits **mummified animals and birds** from necropolises across Egypt, evincing the strength of animal cults towards the end of the pagan era, when devotees embalmed everything from bulls to mice and fish. Modern Egyptians regard these relics of ancestral superstition with equanimity, but the exhibition of human remains offended many – hence Sadat's closure of the famous **Mummy Room** (previously Room 52) in 1981. Since then, the Egyptian Museum and the Getty Institute have been working to restore the badly decomposed royal mummies. The results of their work are now displayed in Room 56, where you have to buy another ticket (£E70, students £E35; closes 6.15pm) to see them – not really worth the expense unless you have a keen interest in mummies. In deference to the deceased, no guiding is allowed, and the low hum of *sotto voce* chatter is only broken by the attendant periodically calling for "Silence, please!"

Altogether eleven royal mummies are displayed here (clearly labelled and arranged chronologically anticlockwise around the room), including the mortal remains of some of the most famous pharaohs, in particular the great conquerors of the XIX Dynasty, Seti I and his son Ramses II, the latter looking rather slighter in the flesh than the massive statues of him at Memphis and elsewhere.

Also here is Ramses's son, Merneptah, whom many believe to be the pharaoh of the Biblical Exodus (see p.769). All the mummies are kept in sealed cases at controlled humidity, and most of them look remarkably peaceful – Tuthmosis II and Tuthmosis IV could almost be sleeping – and many still have hair. Queen Henuttawi's curly locks and handsome face suggest Nubian origin.

The mummies were found in the royal cache at Deir el-Bahri (see p.397) and in a spare chamber in the tomb of Amenophis II (see p.391), where they had been reburied during the XXI Dynasty to protect them from grave robbers. For a description of the mummification process, see p.382; and for a graphic demonstration of the hollowness of a mummy, take a look up Ramses V's right nostril – from this angle you'll be able to see straight out through the hole in his skull.

The other galleries

To view the other galleries in approximate chronological order you should start at Room 43 (overlooking the Atrium) and proceed in a clockwise direction, as on the ground floor. However, since most visitors wander in from Tut's galleries, we've described the western and eastern wings from that standpoint.

Starting with the **western wing**, along with other stone and faience jewellery in **Room 6**, notice the "**Heart Scarabs**" that were placed upon the throats of mummies, bearing a spell that implored the deceased's heart not to bear witness against him or her during the Judgement of Osiris. **Room 12**'s hoard of objects from **XVIII Dynasty royal tombs** includes the mummies of a child and a gazelle (Case I); priestly wigs and wig boxes (Case L); a libation table flanked by two leopards from the funerary cache of Amenophis II (#3842); and the chariot of Tuthmosis IV (#4113). **Room 17** holds the **contents of private tombs**, notably that of Sennedjem, from the Workmen's Village near the Valley of the Kings. With skills honed on royal tombs, Sennedjem carved himself a stylish vault; its door (#215) depicts him playing *senet*. The beautiful gold painted sarcophagus of his son Khonsu carries a design showing the lions of Today and Yesterday supporting the rising sun, while Anubis embalms his mummy under the protection of Isis and Nephthys.

While the corridor displays **canopic chests and coffins**, the inner rooms feature **Middle Kingdom models**. From Meketre's tomb at Thebes come marvellous domestic figures and tableaus in **Room 27**: peasants netting fish from reed boats (#75), as well as other boating scenes, and a tableau of cattle being driven past an estate-owner for counting (#76). In **Room 32**, compare the fully crewed model boats in Case F with the unmanned solar barques for voyaging through eternity in Case E. Model-soldier buffs will delight in the phalanxes of Nubian archers and Egyptian pikemen from the tomb of Prince Mesehti at Assyut, in **Room 37**.

The museum's **southern wing** is best seen at a trot. The middle section contains a **model of a funerary complex** showing how the pyramids and their temples related to the Nile (**Room 48**), and the cubic **leather funerary tent** of an XXI Dynasty queen, decorated in red-and-green checkered squares (#3848, by the southeast stairway in Room 50). More striking are two exhibitions in the central section: **recent finds and forgotten treasures**, which are showcased in **Room 49**; and in **Room 43**, objects from the **tomb of Yuya and Thuya**. The finest of these are Thuya's gem-inlaid gilded mask, their mummiform coffins and statues of the couple. As parents of Queen Tiy (wife of Amenophis III), they were buried in the Valley of the Kings; their tomb was found intact in the late nineteenth century. Hidden away by the entrance to Room 42 is a panel of blue faïence tiles from Zoser's burial hall at Saqqara (#17).

Also in Room 48, on the west side, is a display case (#155) containing a stone head of Akhenaten's mum Queen Tiy that prefigures the Amarna style, and "dancing dwarves" modelled on equatorial Pygmies. The same case also holds a beautiful, very lifelike wooden statuette of a Nubian woman, possibly Queen Tiy, with her hair in braids, looking strikingly modern. Next to it, another case (#82) holds a striking bright blue faïence hippopotamus.

Room 53, hidden away off the recess (Room 54) at the southern end of Room 48 contains an odd assortment of mummified animals, but is most worth popping into for a look at the **bird stele** from the Sun Temple of Userkaf at Saqqara. The relief on the stele is the first known example of natural scenes being used as decoration within a royal funerary edifice: a pied kingfisher, purple gallinule and sacred ibis are clearly recognizable.

If approached from the north, the **eastern wing** begins with **Room 14**, containing a couple of mummies and the superbly lifelike but sadly ill-lit "**Fayoum Portraits**" found by archeologist Flinders Petrie at Hawara. Painted in encaustic (pigments mixed into molten wax) while their sitters were alive, the portraits were glued onto Greco-Roman mummies (100–250 AD). The staggering diversity of Egypt's pantheon by the late pagan era is suggested by the **statues of deities** in **Room 19**. The tiny statuettes are worth a closer look, especially those of the pregnant hippo-goddess Sekhmet (in Case C), Harpocrates (Horus as a child), Ibis-headed Thoth and the dwarf god Ptah-soker (all in Case E), a couple of whose figurines (third shelf down, on the left), look almost Mexican, as do some of the statuettes of Bes in Case P. In the centre of the room, look out for the gold and silver image of Horus in Case V, apparently the case for a mummified hawk.

Room 24 next door, and Room 29 beyond that, are devoted to **ostraca and papyri**. Ostraca were limestone flakes or potshards, on which were scratched sketches or ephemeral writing; papyrus was used for finished artwork and lasting **manuscripts**. Besides the *Book of the Dead* (**rooms 1 and 24**) and the *Book of Amduat* (depicting the Weighing of the Heart ceremony; on the south side of **Room 29** above Cabinet 51), note the *Satirical Papyrus* (#232 in Cabinet 9 on the north side), showing mice being served by cats. Painted during the Hyksos period (see p.767), the cats represent the Egyptians, the mice their rulers, who came from countries that were part of Egypt's former empire, implying that rule of Egyptians by foreigners is not the natural order. Room 29 also displays a scribe's writing kit and an artist's paints and brushes (by the doorways at either end), while the next door **Room 34** contains musical instruments and statuettes of people playing them. In the corridor (**Room 33**), two interesting seats are displayed: an Amarna toilet seat in Case O by the 3door, and in Case S, a seat used for childbirth looking remarkably similar to those used today. **Room 39** has some Greco-Roman glassware, mosaics and statuettes, while **Room 44** displays, on its north side, Mesopotamian-like faïence panels from the palaces of Ramses II and III.

Downtown Cairo

The layout of **downtown Cairo** goes back to the 1860s, when Khedive Ismail had it rebuilt in the style of Haussmann's new Paris boulevards to impress dignitaries attending the inauguration of the Suez Canal. Cutting an X-shaped swathe through the area are the main thoroughfares of **Talaat Harb** and **Qasr el-Nil** (each about 1km long), which contain most of the city's budget hotels, airlines and travel agencies. Almost every visitor gravitates here at least once, while many spend a lot of time checking out the restaurants, shops and bars.

Kalashnikov-toting police and Central Security troops are ubiquitous in downtown Cairo, but never threatening.

Talaat Harb

Fifty years ago, Suleyman Pasha Street was lined with trees and sidewalk cafés, a gracious ornament to the Europeanized city centre built in the late nineteenth century. Since being renamed **Sharia Talaat Harb** (many Cairenes still use its old name), the street has seen its once elegant facades effaced by grime and neglect, tacky billboards and glitzy facings – yet its vitality and diversity have never been greater. Thousands of Cairenes come here to window-shop, pop into juice bars and surge out of cinemas. Imelda Marcos would drool over the profusion of shoe shops, some devoted to butterfly creations fit only for a boudoir.

Almost every tourist seeks a break from the crowds and culture shock at one of three places along the initial stretch of Talaat Harb. **Felfela's Restaurant**, just around the corner of Hoda Shaarawi, is followed shortly by the **Café Riche**, where the Free Officers supposedly plotted their overthrow of Egypt's monarchy; another version maintains that they communicated over the telephone in **Groppi's**, a famous coffee house on **Midan Talaat Harb**, at the intersection with Qasr el-Nil. Here stands a statue of Talaat Harb (1876–1941), nationalist lawyer and founder of the National Bank. While negotiating the six-way road junction, and avoiding the touts here, check out the fine Art Nouveau facade of the building on the north side (nos. 3–5), a reminder that this was once the heart of Cairo's elegant, colonial Ismailiya district.

Up to this point traffic runs both ways, but thereafter northbound vehicles are restricted to Qasr el-Nil; because the streets cross over at an acute angle, it's easy to take the wrong one by mistake if you're on foot. Between Midan Talaat Harb and 26th July Street, Talaat Harb abounds in takeaways, **cinemas** and cheap **hotels**. Number 34, next door to the Miami Theatre, is the **Yacoubian Building**, immortalized in Alaa Al Aswany's bestselling novel of the same name (see p.812), though the real building differs somewhat from the fictional version.

△ Midan Talaat Harb

Qasr el-Nil

Although the racecourse that once ran beside **Sharia Qasr el-Nil** disappeared in the nineteenth century, northbound traffic tries to rival bygone derbys, and the shops, though functional enough, play second fiddle to Talaat Harb's. Two blocks beyond Midan Talaat Harb, a side street on the right allows a glimpse of the carmine-and-gold Art Nouveau **Cosmopolitan Hotel** (see p.97), an elegant leftover from colonial times. Another is the **Trieste Building**, one block further on, though its lovely green-and-gold tilework has been unpleasantly marred by the careless placing of air-conditioning units. The building is still notable for its wonderful neo-Moorish balconies and window arches, and the dragon holding a flagpole that protrudes from its northwest corner.

Sharia Abdel Khaliq Sarwat and Sharia Adly

Other than the Khan el-Khalili bazaar, **Sharia Abdel Khaliq Sarwat** – the first major street you reach after the Midan Talaat intersection – has the city centre's highest concentration of **jewellers**, particularly around the Midan Opera end, where a street of goldsmiths called Sikket al-Manakh leads off to the south. Because their marked prices are higher, canny shoppers can use them as benchmarks when haggling for lower rates in the Khan (see p.250). At the corner of Sharia Mohammed Farid, no. 42 was once home to the elegant Venus Fashions ladieswear store, and still bears multiple likenesses of the Venus de Milo between the arches on its southern frontage, though the shop has long been closed.

A block north, on the north side of **Sharia Adly**, you'll see a buff, temple-like edifice like something out of a Cecil B. de Mille movie. This is the **Shaar HaShamayim Synagogue** (daily 10am–3pm, Fridays till 6pm; donations appreciated; bring your passport to get in), the main house of prayer for Cairo's now much reduced Jewish community (see p.180). Because of the threat of attack by Islamic fundamentalists, the synagogue is surrounded by armed police, who don't take kindly to tourists pointing cameras at it – which is a pity, because it's actually one of downtown Cairo's most photogenic buildings. Though it looks like a piece of Art Deco, the synagogue was actually built well before that era, in 1905. The palm trees on the facade are a symbol peculiar to Egyptian Jewry; the interior is also impressive, with its high dome, stained-glass windows and opulent marble fittings. Nowadays services are held only at the Jewish New Year (around September), and the Day of Atonement (Yom Kippur, ten days after the New Year).

One block along from the synagogue is Cairo's main **tourist office**. Across the road, **Garden Groppi's** spacious patio and panelled salon contrast with the *Groppi's* on Midan Talaat Harb. During World War II, this was one of the few posh establishments open to ordinary British troops – "other ranks", as they were called – who the military top brass had decided should not mix socially with officers. Its high prices nonetheless ensured that officers, Egyptian *pashas* and their fur-draped Levantine mistresses predominated. Nowadays it's frequented by courting couples, journalists and bourgeois matrons.

Another colonial institution that bit the dust still survives in moribund form north of Sharia Adly's termination at Midan Opera. Before World War I, tourists could buy, as James Aldridge put it, "anything from a boa constrictor to a fully grown leopard" outside the grandiose **Continental-Savoy Hotel** – where one scandalized missionary insisted on providing trousers to cover the genitals of a performing baboon. Orde Wingate, the eccentric military genius who liberated Abyssinia from Italian rule for Emperor Haile Selassie, attempted suicide in his room here. Unfortunately, the hotel has been largely disused for many years now, and its grand halls stand empty and neglected.

26th July Street and Sharia Alfi Bey

The busiest, widest thoroughfare of downtown Cairo is **Sharia Setta w'Ashreen Yulyu** – more easily rendered as **26th July Street** – which runs all the way from Ezbekiya Gardens across the Nile to Zamalek. It was once called Sharia al-Malik Fouad, a name still quite commonly used, after King Fouad (reigned 1917–36); the current name commemorates the date on which his son King Farouk abdicated in 1952, following a bloodless coup by the Free Officers three days earlier.

As well as a slew of hotels – most notably the *Grand* – this stretch of the street features a bevy of sleazy **nightclubs**, a couple of liquor stores, and almost as many shoe shops and pavement hawkers as Talaat Harb. Behind the Cicurel department store, which was expropriated from its Jewish owner in 1957, is a vintage Cairene restaurant, *El Haty*.

Better still for eating and drinking is **Sharia Alfi Bey**, two blocks north – known by locals as the Cairene Champs-Élysées. At one end is **Midan Orabi**, frequented round-the-clock by Cairenes noshing on *taamiya* and *shawarma* bought from one of the many takeaways here. Admirers of Art Deco might want to check out the picture palace at the eastern end of the street, formerly the Kursaal, now renamed the Diana, as well as the Ades Building with its stylish corner tower. A couple of blocks up Sharia Emad el-Din (the extension of Sharia Mohammed Farid), the Ades Building was originally, like Cicurel, a Jewish-owned department store. Also worth dropping into for tea is the rather kitsch *Umm Kalthoum* café on Sharia al-Azbakiya, to the south of Alfi Bey, entered between two large likenesses of the eponymous singing star, and dominated by another within, the walls decked with memorabilia of herself and her contemporaries.

Though perfectly safe even late at night, the backstreets between Alfi Bey and 26th July retain an aura of illicit goings-on. When Lawrence Durrell and his wife were evacuated from Greece to Cairo in 1941, they discovered that their refugee hotel here doubled as a brothel.

Midan Opera and Midan Ataba

During the 1860s, when Cairo's centre was rebuilt, an Opera House was also constructed; symbolically, the building faced west, overlooking **Midan Opera** and the modern city rather than Islamic Cairo. Although the opening night saw a lavish production of *Rigoletto*, it was surpassed a year later by the anniversary celebrations, when an opus that had been specially commissioned to have an imperial Egyptian theme was first performed – Verdi's *Aïda*. The square's centrepiece, an equestrian statue of Ibrahim Pasha, by Cordier, honours Ismail's father. Though still the sprucest bit of greenery in central Cairo, the square lost its namesake when the Opera House burned down in 1971; a multistorey car park now occupies the site.

Almost a century after Ismail mortgaged Egypt to foreign creditors, anti-colonial resentments exploded here on "**Black Saturday**" (January 26, 1952). The morning after British troops had killed native police in Ismailiya, demonstrators were enraged to find an Egyptian police officer drinking on the terrace of *Madame Badia's Opera Casino* (where the Opera Cinema stands today). A scuffle began and the nightclub was wrecked; rioting spread quickly, encouraged by the indifference of Cairo's police force. As ordinary folk looted, activists sped around in Jeeps torching foreign premises. Similarly, during the bread riots of 1977, nightclubs and boutiques were specifically targeted by a radical Islamist group.

Midan Ataba

Behind Midan Opera car park, a minibus depot and split-level thoroughfares render **Midan Ataba** just as Yusuf Idris described it in *The Dregs of the City*: "a madhouse of pedestrians and automobiles, screeching wheels, howling klaxons, the whistles of bus conductors and roaring motors". Originally called the Square of Green Steps, Ataba could justifiably be renamed the Square of Flyovers.

Midan Ataba is a good starting point for several **walking routes into Islamic Cairo** (see pp.127–169), but there is one attraction that you might want to visit in the square itself: the **Post Office Museum** on the second floor of the Central Post Office (daily except Fri 8am–1pm; 50pt; tickets sold in the post office at the commemorative stamps office, then go upstairs through the guarded entrance on the east side of the building). The museum houses exhibits from Egypt's postal service through the ages, with stamps galore (including the rare Suez Canal commemorative issue), Egypt's oldest mailboxes, and a picture of the Sphinx and Pyramids composed entirely of stamps bearing an image of the same.

There are also three wonderful **belle époque department stores** in the vicinity of Midan Ataba, though all are sadly shadows of their former selves. Only Sednaoui, just off Sharia Khulud (aka Sharia Clot Bey), continues to function as a single grand store, and it's worth popping in to check out the atrium with its huge chandeliers and spectacular glass ceiling. Omar Effendi on Sharia Abdel Aziz, and Tiring, just off Midan Ataba itself, have long been divided up into offices and smaller shops, but their early twentieth-century exteriors are still impressive.

Ezbekiya Gardens and north to Ramses

The **Ezbekiya Gardens**, to the north of Opera and Ataba squares, were laid out in the 1870s by the former chief gardener of Paris, forming a twenty-acre park. Subsequent extensions to 26th July Street reduced them to trampled islands amid a sea of commerce and traffic, but the western half has now been enclosed to preserve its magnificent banyan tree, while much of the eastern side remains a pitch for hawkers of Islamic arts, gewgaws and incense, as well as a market for secondhand books. Beyond the clothes stalls on the east side stands the **Cairo Puppet Theatre** (see p.261).

In medieval times a lake fed by the Nasiri Canal and surrounded by orchards existed here, but in 1470 the Mamluke general Ezbek built a palace, inspiring other beys and wealthy merchants to follow suit. During the French occupation Napoleon commandeered the sumptuous palace of Alfi Bey, and his successor Kléber promoted Western innovations such as windmills, printing presses, and a balloon launch which embarrassingly failed. Another novelty was *Le Tivoli* club, where "ladies and gentlemen met at a certain hour to amuse themselves" – unheard of in a society where men and women socialized separately.

During Mohammed Ali's time, visitors could still witness Cairenes celebrating the Prophet's Birthday here with unrestrained fervour. Sufi dervishes entranced by *zikrs* lay prostrate to be ridden over by their mounted sheikh in the famous Doseh (Treading) ceremony. However, snake-swallowing had already been ruled "disgusting and contrary to their religion" by the sheikh of the Sa'adiya, and under British rule popular festivals were discouraged and dispersed around the city. Hussein and other squares are more active during Moulid el-Nabi nowadays.

Though nothing remains of them today, two bastions of colonialism once overlooked Ezbekiya from a site bounded by Alfi Bey and El-Gumhorriya, where Scottish pipers once played. Here, *Shepheard's Hotel* (founded in 1841) once flourished alongside the Thomas Cook Agency, which pioneered tourist "expeditions" in the 1870s. Rebuilt more grandly in 1891, *Shepheard's* famous terrace, Moorish Hall, Long Bar and Ballroom (featuring "Eighteenth Dynasty Edwardian" pillars modelled on Karnak) were destroyed by Black Saturday rioters in 1952.

Between Ezbekiya and Ramses

When Mohammed Ali created a military high road to link the Citadel with Cairo's new railway station, and named it after the French physician Antoine Clot – whom he ennobled for introducing Western ideas of public health to Egypt – nobody foresaw that **Sharia Clot Bey** (spelt Klot Bek on some street signs, but now officially Sharia Khulud) and the fashionable area north of Ezbekiya would degenerate into a vice-ridden *wasa'a*, or "open land". By World War I, however, the quarter was full of honky-tonk bars, backstreet porn shows and brothels, shacks and plush establishments alike paying protection to Ibrahim el-Gharby, the fearsome transvestite "King of the *Wasa'a*". In the Mahfouz novel and classic Egyptian movie *The Beginning and the End*, the main character's hash-dealing brother set up shop here. During World War II, activities centred around Wagh el-Birket, known to troops as "**the Berka**": a long street with curtained alleys leading off beneath balconies where the prostitutes sat fanning themselves. Only after the killing of two Australian soldiers (who were notorious for throwing women and pianos out of windows) was the Berka closed down in 1942.

Nowadays the area is shabbily respectable, with cheap shops and cafés. A stroll up from the gardens along Sharia Khulud towards Ramses will take you past the hulking nineteenth-century **Cathedral of St Mark**, now superseded by the new Coptic cathedral in Abbassiya. The run-down porticoed Ottoman pile at no. 117 **Sharia el-Gumhorriya**, at the Ramses end of the street which runs up from the west side of the gardens, was the original premises of *Al-Ahram* ("The Pyramids"), the first and still the foremost newspaper in the Arab world.

Ramses Station and around

The Ramses Station area is the northern ganglion of Cairo's transport system. Splayed flyovers and arterial roads haemorrhage traffic onto darting pedestrians, keeping **Midan Ramses** busy round the clock. The square took its name from a red granite Colossus of Ramses II, moved here from Memphis in 1955. By 2006 it had become so corroded by pollution that it was relocated out by the Giza Pyramids, at the junction of Pyramids Road and the Alexandria Desert Road, despite lobbying from local Egyptologists to have it returned to its original site. In ancient times, when the Nile ran further east, Ramses was the site of Tendunyas, the port of Heliopolis. Renamed Al-Maks (the Customs Point) by the Arabs, it was incorporated within Cairo's fortifications by Salah al-Din, whose Iron Gate was left high and dry as the Nile receded westwards, and was pulled down in 1847 to make way for the station.

The square's main focus is **Ramses Station** itself, a quasi-Moorish shoebox to which a major **post office** and the **Egyptian Railways Museum** are appended. At the east end of the station, the museum (Tues–Sun 8am–2pm; £E10, £E20 on Fri & public holidays, camera £E10) houses model steam engines, stations, engineering works and even the odd aeroplane, plus a couple of real steam locomotives, most notably Khedive Ismail's private train. For a superb vista over the square, head to the terrace café of the otherwise rather down-at-heel fifteenth-floor *Everest Hotel*, open round the clock.

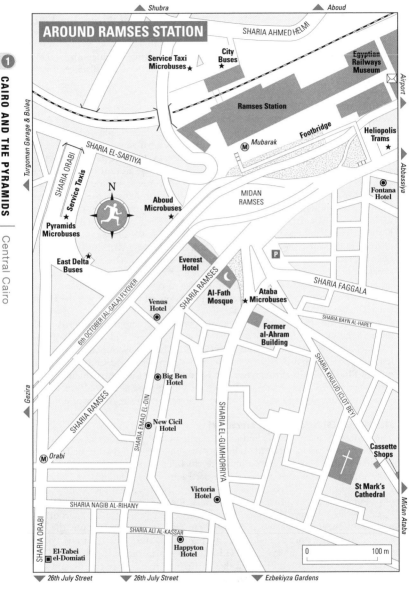

AROUND RAMSES STATION

▲ Shubra   ▲ Aboud

SHARIA AHMED HELMI

City Buses ★

Service Taxi Microbuses ★

Egyptian Railways Museum

Airport ▶

Ramses Station

SHARIA EL-SABTIYA

Turgoman Garage & Bulaq ◀

SHARIA ORABI

Service Taxis ★

Ⓜ Mubarak

Footbridge

Heliopolis Trams ★

Abbassiya ▶

MIDAN RAMSES

Fontana Hotel ⦿

N

Aboud Microbuses ★

Pyramids Microbuses ★

East Delta Buses ★

Everest Hotel

SHARIA RAMSES

Ⓟ

6th OCTOBER (AL-GALAI FLYOVER)

Venus Hotel ⦿

Al-Fath Mosque ☪

Ataba Microbuses ★

SHARIA FAGGALA

SHARIA BAYN AL-HARET

Gezira ◀

Former al-Ahram Building

⦿ Big Ben Hotel

SHARIA EMAD EL-DIN

⦿ New Cicil Hotel

SHARIA KHULUD (CLOT BEY)

SHARIA RAMSES

SHARIA EL-GUMHORRIYA

Cassette Shops

Ⓜ Orabi

St Mark's Cathedral ✝

Midan Ataba ▶

Victoria Hotel ⦿

SHARIA NAGIB AL-RIHANY

SHARIA ORABI

SHARIA ALI AL-KASSAR

El-Tabei el-Domiati ◼

Happyton Hotel

0   100 m

▼ 26th July Street   ▼ 26th July Street   ▼ Ezbekiyza Gardens

Garden City and the Abdin quarter

Spreading south from the square towards Old Cairo and the Islamic districts
are two very different, yet historically interlinked, quarters. Sharia Qasr al-Aini
divides the leafy winding streets of **Garden City** from Qasr al-Aini, the grid of
blocks where Egypt's ministries and parliament are located. On the other side
of Qasr al-Aini, the ex-royal, now presidential Abdin Palace lends its name to

the convoluted **Abdin quarter** that merges on its southern side into Saiyida Zeinab (see p.163).

Since Garden City, Qasr al-Aini and Abdin all meet around Midan Tahrir, each can claim to host Egypt's **National Assembly** (Maglis al-Shaab). During the late 1980s, Cairenes were agog over abusive exchanges and fisticuffs in parliament, as the hardline minister Zaki Badr replied to allegations of torture, wrongful arrest and bugging by the **Interior Ministry**, sited a couple of blocks to the east in Abdin. Badr has long since gone, but the ministry's repressive activities continue: Amnesty International reports cases of torture from Alexandria to Aswan. The road on which both buildings stand is barricaded at either end against suicide car bombers, floodlit at night and perpetually guarded by machine-gunners.

Garden City

When Ibrahim Pasha's al-Dubbarah Palace was demolished in 1906, British planners developed the site for diplomatic and residential use, laying down crescents and cul-de-sacs to create the illusion of lanes meandering through a **Garden City**. Until the Corniche road was ploughed through, embassies and villas boasted gardens running down to the Nile; nowadays, fishermen's shacks and vegetable plots line the river's edge.

Aside from the traffic, it's a pleasant walk along the Corniche towards Roda Island, past a cluster of **feluccas** available for Nile cruises (see p.264). Further inland, Art Deco residences mingle with heavily guarded **embassies** (for addresses, see p.263). Despite being outsized by the US – whose embassy here is the largest in the world – the British enjoy grander buildings with more spacious grounds, a legacy of their pre-eminence in the days of Lord Cromer and Sir Miles Lampson. The main artery, running south from Tahrir towards Old Cairo, is **Sharia Qasr al-Aini**, which goes from riches to rags, banks and villas yielding to cheap backstreet eating places near Manial Bridge. A bygone "Palace of the Spring" lends its name to Qasr al-Aini, the mixed neighbourhood between Garden City and the slaughterhouse district (see "Old Cairo", p.169), and to Cairo's largest public **hospital**, erected in the 1960s, where

War stories

During World War II, much of Garden City was commandeered by military organizations. The British Army's general headquarters was originally based at 10 Sharia Tolombat (referred to in secret despatches as "Grey Pillars" after the columns in its entrance hall), but rapidly outgrew these premises to fill an entire neighbourhood. It was here that **R.A. Bagnold** proposed the formation of the Long Range Desert Group (see p.546), whose daring raids (with David Stirling's SAS) behind enemy lines were the genesis of a martial legend.

On Sharia Rustrum, the Middle Eastern headquarters of the **SOE** (Special Operations Executive) plotted operations from Yugoslavia to Libya, involving Fitzroy McLean, Evelyn Waugh and Patrick Leigh Fermor, among others. At no. 13 Sharia Ibrahim Pasha Naguib, novelist **Olivia Manning** and her husband Reggie (the model for Guy Pringle in *Fortunes of War*) lived beneath Stirling's brother, Peter, who hosted wild parties in a flat crammed with captured ammunition.

British sang-froid only cracked once, when the Afrika Korps seemed poised to seize Alexandria and advance on Cairo. On "**Ash Wednesday**" (July 1, 1942) GHQ and the Embassy burned their files, blanketing Garden City with smoke. Half-charred classified documents were wafted aloft to fall on the streets, where peanut vendors twisted them into little cones.

the eminent short-story writer Yusuf Idris once practised as a doctor. **Roda Island** and the mainland **further south** are described under "Old Cairo" (see pp.169–186).

The Abdin Palace

With hindsight, several rulers must have regretted that Khedive Ismail moved the seat of state from the Citadel to what is now the **Abdin quarter**, where tenements surrounded the palace enclave long ago. The European-style **Abdin Palace**, flanked to the north by the Cairo Governorate building, is now the state headquarters of Egypt's president. During Ramadan a large tent is pitched outside in the middle of Midan el-Gumhorriya, in which virtuoso performers recite the Koran. The neighbourhood is still chiefly residential and working-class, and divided from the Saiyida Zeinab quarter by **Sharia Bur Said**, which marks the course of the Khalig al-Masri Canal that was filled in after the Aswan Dam reduced Cairo's dependency on Nile floodwater.

When, in the 1860s, Ismail began building the Abdin Palace, a worldwide scarcity of cotton had raised the value of Egypt's export crop to £25 million a year, and his own civil list was double that of Queen Victoria. After prices slumped and creditors gathered, the palace was bequeathed to his successors together with vast debts that reduced them – and Egypt – to near vassal status. The nadir of humiliation came in February 1942, when British armoured cars burst through the palace gates and Ambassador Lampson demanded that King Farouk sack the prime minister or abdicate. It was this that resolved Nasser to assemble the Free Officers, seize power and redeem Egypt. Ten years later, as Farouk displayed his long-awaited son at a magnificent reception, rioters burned downtown Cairo within earshot of the palace; six months afterwards, the Free Officers deposed him and declared a republic. Another mass protest – against Sadat's abolition of subsidies on bread and other essentials in January 1977 – took place on Midan el-Gumhorriya. Chanting "Thieves of the Infitah, the people are famished", crowds overwhelmed Central Security and rampaged against symbols of wealth and authority until the subsidies were restored.

The Palace Museum

At the back of the palace grounds is the **Abdin Palace Museum** (daily except Fri 9am–2.30pm; £E10, students £E5, camera £E10), devoted to a collection of guns and other weaponry. The entrance is behind the palace in Sharia Gamae Abdine, and tickets are sold just across the street. A souvenir booklet (£E15) is available at the entrance, though its commentary is not especially useful.

Begin by walking through the palace grounds to **Mubarak's Hall**, which contains an assortment of weapons presented to President Mubarak by foreign leaders, most notably a set of gold-plated automatic rifles given by Saddam Hussein. From here you cross a courtyard, past more cannons and Gatling guns and a shrine to local saint Sidi Badran, which predates the palace and was restored under King Fouad.

This brings you to the **Arms Museum**, entered between two suits of armour. Pavilion 2, on the right, is filled with **daggers**, including Rommel's, engraved with the slogan "Alles für Deutschland" (everything for Germany), and some gruesome-looking multi-bladed daggers used by India's Hindu Rajputs against the Muslim Mughals in the eighteenth century. Back in the main room, you pass Mamluk breastplates, chain mail and maces before getting down to the real business of the day, namely **guns**. While many of these will be of interest only to serious weapons enthusiasts, some will catch anybody's eye, among them an 1852 Beckwith percussion rifle with six revolving barrels and a display of unusually shaped revolvers. Nearby is a particularly mean-looking Apache-Dolene pin-fire revolver which doubles as a knuckleduster and a blade. In the same display case, a twenty-chamber Belgian revolver from the early twentieth century was no doubt handy for prolonged games of Russian roulette.

The next section is devoted to **medals and decorations** from around the world, but especially from early twentieth-century Europe. Also here, and a lot more interesting, are a set of Napoleonic enamel snuff and tobacco boxes, and King Farouk's personal *sheesha* pipes, plus a vial made from a giant crab claw. From here you move on to the **Gifts Museum** containing presents given to the president by various organizations and dignitaries, including (in gallery four) an abalone and mother-of-pearl model of Jerusalem's Dome of the Rock mosque from Yasser Arafat, and a silver plate bearing the images of President Mubarak's wife Suzanne and Akhenaten's wife Nefertiti, set against a map of Middle Egypt. The **Historical Documents** room, with treaties and decrees dating back to the nineteenth century, displays some fascinating letters of condolence sent to King Farouk on the death of his father King Fouad from the likes of Adolf Hitler, Japan's Emperor Hirohito, and Britain's ill-fated King Edward VIII.

The last part of the museum is devoted to **silverware, glassware and crockery**, including assorted dinner sets used by the Egyptian royal family, and a tea set belonging to King Fouad, complete with what would be a traditional English-style pair of teacups and saucers, except that they are made of solid silver instead of the more customary bone china.

Islamic Cairo

The core of the city itself was circumscribed by the river and hills of refuse, the castle, the aqueduct and the abandoned slums. Most of the bazaars lay in the densely packed quarters of the North-East, nestling in amongst and parasitic upon the rubble of the old Fatimid palaces, and behind the commercial streets one found small courtyards and large tenements, into which were crowded communities of closely knit creeds and tribes. … The city was like a disordered mind, an expression of archaic wishes and half-submerged memories of vanished dynasties.

Robert Irwin, *The Arabian Nightmare*

Islamic Cairo sustains fantasy and confounds certainty. Few foreigners enter its maw without equal measures of excitement and trepidation. Streets are narrow and congested, slimy underfoot with donkey shit and burst water mains, overhung with latticed balconies. Mosques, bazaars and medieval lanes abound; the smell of *sheeshas* and frying offal wafts through alleys where muezzins wail "Allahu akbar!" (God is most great) and beggars entreat "Ya mohannin, ya rabb" (O awakener of pity, O master) – as integral to street life as the artisans and hawkers. The sights, sounds, smells and surprises draw you back time after time, and getting lost or dispensing a little baksheesh is a small price to pay for the experience.

You can have a fascinating time exploring this quarter of the city without knowing anything about its history or architecture, but to describe Islamic Cairo one has to refer to both. Islamic architecture has its own conventions, terminology and stylistic eras, which we've attempted to cover in the separate colour section. The potted history section provides a general context, with many of the personalities and events mentioned in more detail under the appropriate monument. Most of these are named after their various founders; modern-day Islamic fundamentalists shun them as *masjid el-derar* – mosques built for self-glorification.

The 1992 **earthquake** caused a lot of damage in Islamic Cairo, though this has led to a great many of the mosques and monuments being gradually returned to their former glory after years of neglect, often with financial aid from organizations like the American Research Center and the World Monuments Fund. Unfortunately, this means that many of the Islamic Cairo's monuments are currently closed to the public. Even so, there is plenty to keep you busy, and you can happily spend days, even weeks, exploring the area without running out of new things to see.

A brief history of Islamic Cairo

Islamic Cairo is the sum total of half a dozen cities whose varied names, ages and locations make for an unusually complex urban history. One helpful constant is that new cities have invariably been constructed to the north of the old, for quite simple reasons: an east–west spread was constrained by the Muqattam Hills and the Nile (which ran further east than nowadays), while the prevailing northerly wind blew the smoke and smell of earlier settlements away from newer areas.

Approaching and exploring Islamic Cairo: practicalities

The best way **to explore Islamic Cairo** is by walking. Basically, you decide on a starting point that's readily accessible from downtown Cairo, and then follow an itinerary on foot from there. The most obvious **starting points** are Khan el-Khalili, the Bab Zwayla and the Citadel; see the beginning of each of these sections for details on getting there by public transport (also see the bus/minibus information on pp.94–95). Many of the itineraries given on the following pages can be linked up or truncated; the main limitations on how much you see are time and your own stamina. The streets of Islamic Cairo are labyrinthine and, while getting lost among them can result in the richest experiences, some visitors prefer to be shown round by a **guide**. The tourist office can put you in touch with authorized guides, and unofficial ones may accost you on the street.

There are four ways to approach Islamic Cairo on foot from **Midan Ataba** in downtown Cairo, using the Ataba post office and fire station for orientation:

SHARIA EL-GEISH Topped by a flyover, "Army Street" runs out towards Abbassiya and Heliopolis. The main reason for venturing beyond the Paper Market is to visit the Mosque of Beybars the Crossbowman on Midan Zahir, and the Sakakini Palace beyond.

THE MUSKI A narrow bazaar, identifiable by the crowds passing between the *El-Mousky* hotel and a clump of luggage stalls, this is the classic approach to **Khan el-Khalili**, though it takes slightly longer than Sharia al-Azhar. For more details, see "Around Khan el-Khalili and Al-Azhar", p.131.

SHARIA AL-AZHAR Overshadowed by a flyover running to the heart of Islamic Cairo, Sharia al-Azhar buzzes with traffic and cottage industries. It's a ten-to-fifteen-minute walk to **Al-Azhar Mosque** from Midan Ataba, crossing one of Cairo's few remaining tram routes at the Bur Said overpass.

SHARIA QALAA Across from the fire station, this runs directly to the **Citadel** (2km). The stretch down to Midan Ahmed Maher – where the **Islamic Arts Museum** is located – features musical instrument shops, all-night stalls and cafés.

Most of Islamic Cairo's **monuments** are self-evident and often identified by little green plaques with Arabic numbers; these correspond to the numbers on Lehnert

Thus when the Muslim troops of Amr conquered Egypt for Islam in 641 AD, they sited their city, **Al-Fustat**, just north of Coptic Babylon (see "Old Cairo", p.169). Here it grew into a powerhouse of religious conversion, surpassing Alexandria as Egypt's leading city, though remaining a mere provincial capital in the vast Islamic Empire ruled from Damascus by the caliphs, whose only direct contact occurred when the last of the **Umayyads** (661–750) fled to Al-Fustat, and then burned it. Their successors, the **Abbasids** (750–935), ordered the city to be rebuilt further north, and so Medinet al-Askar (City of Cantonments) came into being. More important in the long term was the Abbasid reliance on Turkish-speaking warriors, who were granted fiefdoms throughout the empire, including Egypt.

In 870, encouraged by popular discontent, the Abbasids' viceroy in Egypt asserted his independence and went on to wrest Syria from their control. Like his predecessors, Ahmed **Ibn Tulun** founded a new city, reaching from Medinet al-Askar towards a spur of the Muqattam. Inspired by the imperial capital of Samarra, it consisted of a gigantic congregational mosque, palace and hippodrome, surrounded by "the Wards" (Al-Qitai) or military quarters after which the city was named. However, when the Abbasids invaded Egypt in 905, Al-Qitai was razed and ploughed under, sparing only the great Mosque of Ibn Tulun, which stands to this day.

& Landrock's map of Cairo and the listings in the exhaustive *Islamic Monuments in Cairo: A Practical Guide*, published by the AUC. Although the area **maps** printed in this book should suffice, the AUC book and four fold-out maps published by SPARE (the Society for the Preservation of the Architectural Resources of Egypt) show even more detail. Al-Shorouk, AUC and Lehnert & Landrock (see p.256) are the best places to look for the SPARE maps, which are not always easy to come by.

Likewise, certain **books** can provide further detail and evocative accounts of time and place. Edward Lane's *The Manners and Customs of the Modern Egyptians* illuminates life during Mohammed Ali's time. The changes wrought last century underlie Naguib Mahfouz's *Midaq Alley* and *Cairo Trilogy*. Mamluke Cairo is the setting for Robert Irwin's surreal *The Arabian Nightmare*, whereas its fevered demise haunts *Zayni Barakat* by Gamal al-Ghitani. For straight – but never dull – history, try Max Rodenbeck's *Cairo: The City Victorious*, James Aldridge's *Cairo* or Desmond Stewart's *Great Cairo, Mother of the World*. All of these works are reviewed under "Books" in Contexts (pp.803–814) and a selection is available at the bookstores listed on p.256.

The buildings you will most want to visit are **mosques**, **madrassas** (theological schools) and **wikalas** (caravanserais, see p.830). On occasion, former private **mansions** are also open to the public. Most mosques and religious buildings don't charge admission, but unscrupulous custodians and other opportunists may try to charge visitors for entry. If this happens to you, demand an official ticket – if they have none, the charge is spurious and you should refuse to pay it. Of course, custodians generally expect baksheesh. **Opening hours** are roughly 9am to 7pm daily (where they're significantly different, specific details are given in the text), though places may well open up later, depending on when the guardian turns up, and they may close an hour or two earlier in winter. During Ramadan, you will not be able to visit after about 4pm. You will also not be welcome during **prayer times** and the Friday noon assembly, which lasts over an hour but should be finished by 2.30pm. A couple of mosques (indicated in the text) are permanently closed to non-Muslims.

The city regained a shadow of its former importance under the **Ikhshidids** (935–969), who seceded from the later Abbasid caliphs. But the impetus for its revival, and that of the Islamic empire, came from Tunisia, where adherents of Shia Islam had created their own theocracy, ruled by a descendant of Ali and Fatima – the dynasty of **Fatimids**. Aiming to seize the caliphate, they hit upon Egypt as an ill-defended yet significant power base, and captured it with an army of 100,000 in 969. The Fatimid general, Gohar (Jewel), a converted Greek, immediately began a new city where the dynasty henceforth reigned (969–1171).

By this time distinctions between the earlier cities had blurred, as people lived wherever was feasible amid the decaying urban entity known as **Masr**. The Fatimids distanced themselves from Masr by building their city of **Al-Qahira** (The Conqueror) further north than ever, where certain key features remain. It was at the Al-Azhar Mosque that Al-Muizz, Egypt's first Fatimid ruler, delivered a sermon before vanishing into his palaces (which, alas, survive only in name); the Mosque of Al-Hakim commemorates the caliph who ordered Masr's destruction after residents objected to proclamations of his divinity. Also surviving are the great Northern Walls and the Bab Zwayla gate. These date from 1092, when the Armenian-born army commander Al-Gyushi, having reconquered Al-Qahira for the Fatimids following its 1068 fall to the Seljuk Turks, expanded the city's defences northwards. But as the Fatimid city grew, Fustat began disappearing as people scavenged building material from its abandoned dwellings, a process that spread to Masr, creating great swathes of *kharab*, or derelict quarters.

The disparate areas only assumed a kind of unity after **Salah al-Din** (Saladin) built the **Citadel** on a rocky spur between Al-Qahira and Masr, and walls which linked up with the aqueduct between the Nile and the Citadel, so as to surround the whole. Salah al-Din promoted Sunni, not Shia, Islam and built *madrassa*s to propagate orthodoxy; he ruled not as caliph, but as a secular sultan. His successors, the **Ayyubids**, erected pepperpot-shaped minarets (only one remains, on Sultan Ayyub's Madrassa and Mausoleum; see p.137) and the magnificent tombs of the Abbasid caliphs and Imam al-Shafi'i (which still exist) in the Southern Cemetery, but they made the same error as the Abbasids: depending on foreign troops and bodyguards. When the sultan died heirless and his widow needed help to stay in power, these troops, the Mamlukes, were poised to take control.

With the support of the right amirs, the most ruthless Mamluke could aspire to being sultan. Frequent changes of ruler were actually preferred, since contenders had to spread around bribes, not least to arrange assassinations. The Mamluke era is divided into periods named after the garrisons of troops whence the sultans intrigued their way to power: the Qipchak or Tartar **Bahri Mamlukes** (1250–1382), originally stationed by the river (*bahr* in Arabic); and their Circassian successors, the **Burgi Mamlukes** (1382–1517), quartered in a tower (*burg*) of the Citadel.

Paradoxically, the Mamlukes were also renowned as aesthetes, commissioning mosques, mansions and *sabil-kuttabs* (Koranic schools featuring fountains) that are still the glory of today's Islamic Cairo. They built throughout the city, and although urban life was interrupted by their bloody conflicts, the city nevertheless maintained public hospitals, libraries and schools, commissioned and endowed by wealthy Mamlukes and merchants. The caravanserais overflowed with exotica from Africa and the spices of the East, and with Baghdad laid waste by the Mongols, Cairo had no peer in the Islamic world, its wonders inspiring many of the tales in the *Thousand and One Nights*.

But in 1517 the **Ottoman Turks** reduced Egypt from an independent state to a vassal province in their empire, and the Mamlukes from masters to mere overseers. When the French and British extended the Napoleonic War to Egypt they found a city living on bygone glories, introspective and archaic, its population dwindling as civil disorder increased. Eighteenth-century travellers like R.R. Madden were struck by "the squalid wretchedness of the Arabs, and the external splendour of the Turks", not to mention the lack of "one tolerable street" in a city of some 350,000 inhabitants.

The city's renaissance – and the ultimate shift from Islamic to modern Cairo – is owed to **Mohammed Ali** (1805–48) and his descendants. An Ottoman servant who turned against his masters, Mohammed Ali effortlessly decapitated the vestiges of Mamluke power and raised a huge mosque and palaces upon the Citadel. Foreigners were hired to advise on urban development, and Khedive Ismail's Minister of Public Works ordered Boulevard Mohammed Ali (now Sharia Qalaa) to be ploughed through the old city (asking rhetorically:"Do we need so many monuments? Isn't it enough to preserve a sample?"). As Bulaq, Ezbekiya and other hitherto swampy tracts were developed into a modern, quasi-Western city, Islamic Cairo ceased to be the cockpit of power and the magnet for aspirations. But as visitors soon discover, its contrasts, monuments and vitality remain as compelling as ever.

Around Khan el-Khalili and Al-Azhar

Khan el-Khalili Bazaar and the Mosque of Al-Azhar form the commercial and religious heart of Islamic Cairo, and the starting point for several walking tours. A taxi here from downtown Cairo (usually via the Al-Azhar flyover) shouldn't cost more than £E5, although drivers often try to overcharge tourists bound for Midan el-Hussein – the main square adjoining Khan el-Khalili that's best given as your destination. Bus #66 serves Al-Azhar from Abdel Mouneem Riyad bus station. If you walk from Midan Ataba, it's best to go via the Muski and return by Sharia al-Azhar, or vice versa.

The Muski

The Muski is a narrow, incredibly congested street running eastwards from Midan Ataba; look for the faded Arabic sign of the *El-Mousky Hotel* on the corner. Worming your way through the crowds, past windows full of wedding gear, tape decks and fabrics, and vendors peddling everything from salted fish to socks, beware of mopeds and other traffic thrusting up behind. Barrow-men still yell traditional warnings – "Riglak!" (your foot!), "Dahrik!" (your back!), "Shemalak!" (your left side!). Itinerant drinks-vendors are much in evidence: although the *saqi* (water-sellers) have been made redundant by modern plumbing, *susi* dispensing liquorice-water and *sherbutli* with their silver-spouted lemonade bottles remain an essential part of street life.

Halfway along the Muski you'll cross Sharia Bur Said, which you cannot cross directly (you'll have to take a right and dodge under the flyover). Beyond here the Muski turns touristy, with hustlers emerging as it nears Khan el-Khalili.

Midan el-Hussein

Midan el-Hussein, framed by an eclectic mix of architecture, is a central point of reference. To the north stands the tan-coloured **Mosque of Saiyidna Hussein**, where the Egyptian president and other dignitaries pray on special occasions; it's a sacred place, off-limits to non-Muslims. Its cool marble, green and silver interior guards the relic of a momentous event in Islamic history:

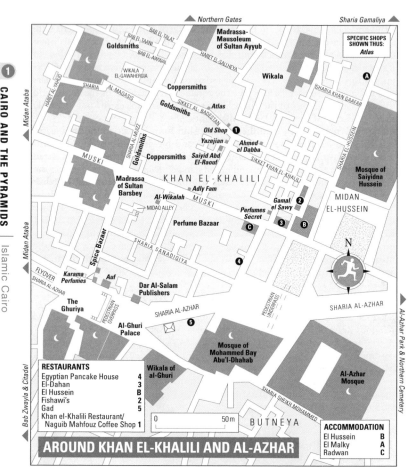

AROUND KHAN EL-KHALILI AND AL-AZHAR

the **head of Hussein**. The grandson of the Prophet Mohammed, Hussein was killed in Iraq in 680 by the Umayyads, who had earlier been recognized as Mohammed's successors against the claims of his son-in-law, Ali, Hussein's father. This generational power struggle over the caliphate caused an enduring schism within Islam. The Muslim world's Sunni ("followers of the way") majority not only recognized the Umayyad caliphate but forbade the office to anyone of Ali's line. Conversely, the Shia ("partisans of Ali") minority refused to accept any leader but a descendant of Ali, and revered Hussein as a martyr. In Egypt, whose Muslim population is almost completely Sunni, Hussein is nevertheless regarded as a popular saint, ranked beside Saiyida Zeinab, the Prophet's granddaughter.

Hussein's annual moulid is one of Cairo's greatest **festivals** – a fortnight of religious devotion and popular revelry climaxing on the *leyla kebira* or "big night", the last Wednesday in the Muslim month of Rabi al-Tani. Here the Sufi brotherhoods parade with their banners and drums, and music blares all night, with vast crowds of Cairenes and *fellaheen* from the Delta (each of whose villages has its own café and dosshouse in the neighbourhood). Midan el-Hussein is also a focal point during the festivals of Moulid al-Nabi, Eid al-Adha, Ramadan and Eid al-Fitr, all well worth seeing. A balcony room at the *El-Hussein Hotel* provides a perfect vantage point, but don't expect to get any sleep. The minarets, ablaze with neon lights (including green "Allahs"), boom sleepers into wakefulness around dawn with their amplified muezzins – and that's on ordinary nights of the year.

The Khan el-Khalili bazaars

Above all, the **Khan el-Khalili** quarter pulses with commerce, as it has since the Middle Ages. Except on Sundays, when most shops are shut, everything from spices to silk is sold in its bazaars. What follows is primarily a guide to the sights; for hard facts about merchandise, dealers and bargaining, see "Shopping", pp.248–257. Generically speaking, all the bazaars around here are subsumed under the name Khan el-Khalili – after Khalil, a Master of Horse who founded a caravanserai here in 1382. However, the *khan* itself is quite compact, bounded by Hussein's Mosque, Sharia al-Muizz and the Muski, with two medieval lanes (Sikket al-Badestan and Sikket Khan el-Khalili) penetrating its maze-like interior.

Most of the shop fronts conceal workshops or warehouses, and the system of selling certain goods in particular areas still applies, if not as rigidly as in the past. **Goldsmiths**, jewellers and souvenir-antique shops mostly congregate along the lanes, which retain a few arches and walls from Mamluke times. When you've tired of wandering around, duck into **Fishawi's** via one of the passages off the Muski or the square. Showing its age with tobacco-stained plaster and cracked gilded mirrors, this famous café has been open day and night every day of the year for over two centuries, an evocative place to sip mint tea, eavesdrop, and risk a *sheesha*.

South off the Muski, along Sharia al-Muizz, you'll find the Souk al-Attarin or **Spice Bazaar**, selling dried crushed fruit and flowers besides more familiar spices. On the corner of the same street, screened by T-shirt and *galabiyya* stalls, stands the **Madrassa of Sultan al-Ashraf Barsbey**, who made the spice trade a state monopoly, thus financing his capture of Cyprus in 1426. The *madrassa*, resplendent without in its red-and-white striped stonework, is full of wooden *mashrabiyya*-work within, where you can also check out the inlaid wooden *minbar*, and the tombs of Barsbey's wife and son.

Sharia Sanadiqiya (off Sharia al-Muizz) will take you into the **Perfume Bazaar**, a dark, aromatic warren sometimes called the Souk es-Sudan because much of the incense is from there; in the nineteenth century, Baedeker's *Guide for Travellers* also noted "gum, dum-plant nuts" and "ill-tanned tiger-skins" among the merchandise. Mamluke sultans appointed a Muhtasib to oversee prices, weights and quality. Empowered to inflict summary fines and corporal punishments, he was also responsible for public morals – "enjoining what is right and forbidding what is wrong". The first passage on your left off Sharia Sanadiqiya leads up a flight of steps to a tiny cul-de-sac. This is Zuqaq al-Midaq, or **Midaq Alley**, immortalized by Naguib Mahfouz in his novel of the same name, the film adaptation of which was shot here. There is no street sign apparent; it's kept in the tiny (and easy to miss) café, where they'll ask if you want to photograph it – for baksheesh, of course.

Al-Azhar Mosque

To the southwest of Midan el-Hussein, a pedestrian underpass leads towards the **Mosque of Al-Azhar** (pronounced "Al-*Az*har"), whose name can be translated as "the radiant", "blooming" or "resplendent". Founded in 970, as soon as the enclosure walls of Fatimid Al-Qahira were completed, Al-Azhar claims to be the world's oldest university (a title disputed by the Kairaouine Mosque in Fez, Morocco). For more than a millennium, though, Al-Azhar has provided students from all over the Muslim world with free board and with an education that, despite Nasserite reforms, remains largely as it was during the classical Islamic era. Students study every facet of the Koran and Islamic jurisprudence (*fiqh*); logic, grammar and rhetoric; and how to calculate the phases of the lunar Muslim calendar. Much of this involves listening in a circle at the feet of a sheikh, and rote memorization, but with greater knowledge, students may engage in Socratic dialogue with their teachers, or instruct their juniors.

Given this, and the status of the Sheikh of al-Azhar as the ultimate theological authority for Egyptian Muslims, it's unsurprising that the mosque has always been politically significant. Salah al-Din changed it from a Shi'ite hotbed into a bastion of Sunni orthodoxy, while Napoleon's troops savagely desecrated it to demonstrate their power. Omitting any mention of this, a nineteenth-century Baedeker guide cautioned visitors to this "fountain-head of Mohammedan fanaticism... not to indulge in any gestures of amusement or contempt". Al-Azhar was a nationalist stronghold from the nineteenth century onwards, and was chosen by Nasser as the venue for his speech of defiance during the Suez invasion of 1956. When Saudi King Fahd prayed here with Mubarak in 1989, it symbolized Egypt's return to the conservative Arab fold; yet, paradoxically, many of Al-Azhar's 90,000 students revere the blind fundamentalist sheikh Omar Abd al-Rahman, currently serving a life sentence in the US for his part in the 1993 bombing of the ill-fated New York World Trade Center.

The **mosque** itself (open Mon–Thurs & Sun 7.30am–7.30pm, Fri 7.30–11am & 3–5pm) is an accretion of centuries and styles, harmonious if confusing. You come in through the fifteenth-century **Barber's Gate**, where students traditionally had their heads shaved, onto a great **sahn** (courtyard) that's five hundred years older, overlooked by three minarets. The *sahn* facade, with its rosettes and keel-arched panels, is mostly Fatimid, but the latticework-screened *riwaqs* (residential quarters) of the *madrassas* on your right-hand side date from the Mamluke period. Unfortunately, these are rarely opened for visitors, but you can walk into the carpeted, alabaster-pillared prayer hall, where the *mihrab*, or niche facing Mecca, is located. The **roof** and minarets (closed to visitors at time of writing, but it's worth asking if you can go up) offer great views of Islamic Cairo's vista of crumbling, dust-coloured buildings that could have been erected decades or centuries ago, the skyline bristling with dozens of minarets.

Butneya

The warren of lanes and tenements behind Al-Azhar – an area known as **Butneya** – could be described as Cairo's "Thieves' Quarter", except that racketeering and drugs are more important. Until 1988, the main business was hashish: sold from "windows" and "green doors", it could be smoked with impunity in *ghorzas* (literally "stitches", small and hidden places) throughout the quarter. Local drugs barons like Kut Kut and Wilad Nasare entered Cairene folklore for their ostentatious wealth and devotion to their neighbourhood; Mustafa Marzuaa built a fifteen-room villa, with video recorders in every room, smack in the middle. After the great crackdown in December 1988, when scores of corrupt officials were arrested, the drugs "mafiosi" decamped to the suburbs, leaving Butneya to local racketeers. Some gangs cream off the profits from organized garbage collection and begging; others extort money from shops or restaurants, and one gang even specializes in weddings: families pay them to stay away rather than risk disturbances.

None of this should affect foreigners who stay outside the quarter (though you might be offered hashish, or even regaled with stories of the "good old days" when slabs were carved up on tables outdoors). In any case, the well-defined tourist trail leads elsewhere. Leaving Al-Azhar by the Barber's Gate, you can turn left down an alley to reach the Wikala of al-Ghuri and other monuments described in the next-but-one walking tour; or return to Midan el-Hussein and check out the following itinerary.

To the Northern Gates and back again

The itinerary described below covers an array of monuments from different eras, occupying the one-time heart of Fatimid Cairo. Although you can walk the route – from Midan el-Hussein to the Northern Gates and back again – within an hour, checking out the interiors of all the monuments could take half a day or more, so you might wish to be selective. If your time is limited, it's probably best to concentrate on the three big attractions: the Qalaoun–Al-Nasir–Barquq complex, Al-Hakim's Mosque and the Beit al-Sihaymi.

Midan el-Hussein to Bayn al-Qasrayn

Starting from Midan el-Hussein (see map on p.132), walk 200m west along the Muski to a crossroads with two mosques, and then turn right onto the north-ern extension of **Sharia al-Muizz**. Here, jewellers' shops overflowing from the Goldsmiths Bazaar soon give way to vendors of pots, basins and crescent-topped finials, after whom this bit of street is popularly called Al-Nahaseen, the **Coppersmiths Bazaar**.

△ The Coppersmiths Bazaar

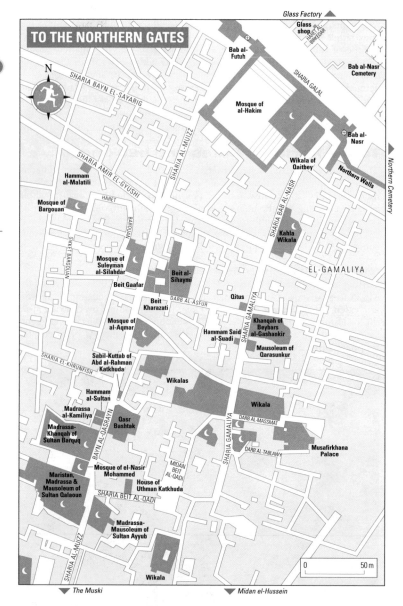

In Fatimid times this bazaar was a broad avenue culminating in a great parade ground between caliphal palaces – hence the name **Bayn al-Qasrayn** (Between the Two Palaces), which is still used today although traces of the palaces are long gone. Robert Irwin writes evocatively of the place as it was during the Mamluke era, when it was customary "for the men and even a few of the women to promenade in the cool twilight. Later, when respectable people had gone back to their homes, the streets were left to the lamplighters, carousing mamlukes, prostitutes and the sleepers." More recently, the street has given its name to the first novel of Naguib Mahfouz's *Cairo Trilogy*, where it is usually translated as "Palace Walk".

To the right of the bazaar, a minaret poking above a row of stalls gives away the unobtrusive **Madrassa and Mausoleum of Sultan Ayyub**, more interesting for its historical associations than anything else. Its founder, the last Ayyubid sultan, was responsible for introducing Mamlukes, an act pregnant with consequences for Egypt. As related under "Cities of the Dead" (p.163), the sultan's widow's daring bid for power made the Mamlukes aware that they were kingmakers – whence it was a short step to ruling Egypt themselves, as they did from 1250 onwards. From an architectural standpoint, Ayyub's *madrassa* (built 1242–50) was the first to incorporate *iwans* (teaching halls) dedicated to each of Sunni Islam's four juridical schools and to be linked to its founder's mausoleum, thus serving as the prototype for the Mamlukes' great mosque-*madrassa*-mausoleum complexes. Beneath the minaret, whose *mabkhara* (incense burner) or "pepperpot" crown is the sole example of this Ayyubid motif left in Cairo, an alleyway with a gate (on the left) leads into the courtyard of what used to be the *madrassa*. A sixteenth-century *sabil-kuttab* protrudes from the wall between the minaret and Ayyub's domed mausoleum (usually locked), further up the street.

The Qalaoun–Al-Nasir–Barquq Complex

Across the road from the *madrassa*, the medieval complex of buildings endowed by the sultans **Qalaoun**, **Al-Nasir** and **Barquq** – three of the most significant of the Mamlukes – forms an unbroken and quite breathtaking 185-metre-long facade. Each of these building groups was designed to serve several functions, yet to form a harmonious whole. All of them were severely damaged in the 1992 earthquake, and parts of them are still undergoing restoration, but it's worth trying to visit as much as is open.

The Qalaoun Complex

Influenced by the Syrian and Crusader architecture its founder had encountered while fighting abroad, **Sultan Qalaoun's Maristan, Madrassa and Mausoleum** arguably inaugurated the Burgi Mamluke style, which is typified by lavish ornamentation and execution on a grand scale. If modern visitors are impressed by the fact that these structures were completed in thirteen months (1284–85), Qalaoun's contemporaries were amazed.

The **Maristan** provided free treatment for every known illness (including cataract removals), storytellers and musicians to amuse the patients, and money to tide them over following their discharge. A modern eye clinic now occupies the site of Qalaoun's hospital, of which only three *liwans* remain; to see them, walk down the tree-shaded lane that starts opposite the *sabil-kuttab* mentioned above.

Further up the street, a main door clad in bronze with geometric patterns gives access to a corridor running between the *madrassa* and the mausoleum. The damaged **Madrassa** (entered to the left off this corridor) has a sanctuary *liwan* recalling the three-aisled churches of northern Syria, with Syrian-style glass mosaics around its prayer niche.

But the real highlight of the ensemble is Qalaoun's **Mausoleum**, across the corridor. First comes an atrium court with a *mashrabiya* doorway, surmounted by a beautiful stucco arch worked with interlocking stars, floral and Koranic motifs, as intricate as lace. Beyond is the tomb chamber, 30m high, with its soaring dome pierced by stained-glass windows in viridian, ultramarine and golden hues. Elaborately coffered, painted ceilings overhang walls panelled in marble, with mother-of-pearl mosaics spelling out "Mohammed" in abstract calligraphy. Until this century the *mihrab* was credited with healing powers, so supplicants could be seen "rubbing lemons on one of its pilasters, and licking up the moisture", while a stick hanging from the tomb's railings was used "to cure fools or idiots by striking them on the head".

Qalaoun himself was a handsome Qipchak, purchased for one thousand dinars during Ayyub's reign. He rose through the ranks due to the patronage of Sultan Beybars al-Bunduqdari, whose 7-year-old son he eventually deposed in 1279. Qalaoun's sonorous titles Al-Mansour and Al-Alfi ("the Thousand", after his high price) were mocked by his name, which sounds comical in Arabic; it's supposedly derived from the Mongolian word for "duck", or an obscure Turkish noun meaning "great ransom" or "rich present". A tireless foe of the Crusaders – he died en route to Acre Fortress in 1290, aged 79 – Qalaoun imported Circassians to offset Qipchak predominance among the Mamlukes, and founded a dynasty that ruled for almost a century (barring hiccups).

The Al-Nasir Complex

Qalaoun's second son, responsible for the **Mosque of Al-Nasir Mohammed** next door, had a rough succession. Only 9 years old when elected, he was deposed by his regent, then restored but kept in miserable conditions for a decade by Beybars al-Gashankir. He finally had Beybars executed and subsequently enjoyed a lengthy reign (1293–1340, counting interregnums), which marked the zenith of Mamluke civilization. Although the **mausoleum** here was intended for Al-Nasir, he actually lies next door in Qalaoun's mausoleum, his wife and son being buried in this one.

The building of thirty mosques, the great Aqueduct and a canal north of Cairo attests to Al-Nasir's enthusiasm for public works (matched apparently by his devotion to horses and sheep). The mosque's **minaret** is a superb ensemble of stuccoed Kufic and Naskhi inscriptions, ornate medallions and stalactites, probably made by Moroccan craftsmen.

The complex has been undergoing restoration work, but this is now almost complete, and it should open in the near future.

The Barquq Madrassa and Khanqah

Now restored to full glory following severe earthquake damage, the adjacent **Madrassa and Khanqah of Sultan Barquq** appears in a much-reproduced nineteenth-century drawing by Owen Carter, which also depicts the Sabil-Kuttab of Ismail Pasha, opposite Al-Nasir's mosque. Its broad facade, divided into shallow recesses, echoes Qalaoun's *madrassa*, although Barquq's complex (1384–86) has the taller dome. It also boasts a minaret, which you can ascend (second door on the right in the entrance passage and over the roof) for excellent views of Islamic Cairo, though it's a good idea to bring a torch as parts of the spiral staircase are very dark.

Barquq was the first Circassian sultan (1382–98), a Burgi Mamluke who seized power by means of intrigue and assassination. His name, meaning "plum" in Arabic, appears on the raised boss in the centre of the bronze-plated doors, behind which a vaulted passageway leads to an open court. The *madrassa's* sanctuary *liwan* (on the right as you enter) has a beautiful blue and gold ceiling supported by porphyry columns of pharaonic origin; upstairs are the cells of the Sufi monks who once inhabited the **khanqah** (monastery). To the north of the prayer hall, a splendid domed mausoleum upheld by gilded pendentives contains the tomb of Barquq's daughter.

The house of Uthman Katkhuda and Qasr Bashtak

The domestic architecture of the Mamlukes was no less sophisticated. Perfectly adapted to Cairene conditions, it offered greater comfort than contemporary European homes – for the well-to-do, at least. An example close at hand is the **house of Uthman Katkhuda**, so called after an eighteenth-century resident, although the mansion itself dates from 1350. You'll find it on Sharia Beit al-Qadi, which runs eastwards opposite Qalaoun's mausoleum; it's halfway along the north side of the street at no. 9. The facade has been restored, but the interior remains closed to the public, for the time being at least.

Back on Sharia al-Muizz, walk past Barquq's Complex (beyond which the street is known as Bayn al-Qasrayn; see p.136.) and cross the road, turning into a muddy alleyway on the right, where a door on the left (just before the archway straight in front of you) opens onto the fourteenth-century **Qasr Bashtak**. The entrance is round the side on Darb Kermez, just before the bend, but the palace is closed for restoration until at least 2008. Here the *qa'a* is upstairs, with *mashrabiya*-screened galleries that permitted ladies to witness the amir's parties, and similar devices overlooking the street. Amir Bashtak was married to Al-Nasir's daughter, so he could afford a five-storey palace with running water on every floor; alas, only a section has survived.

The Sabil-Kuttab of Abd al-Rahman Katkhuda

Back on Bayn al-Qasrayn and situated on a fork in the road just beyond the Qalaoun, Al-Nasir and Barquq Complex, the **Sabil-Kuttab of Abd al-Rahman Katkhuda** rises in tiers of airy wooden fretwork above solid masonry and grilles at street level. The *sabil* (public fountain), and *kuttab* (primary school) are common charitable institutions throughout the Islamic world, but uniquely in Cairo, they were usually combined. At one time there were some three hundred such *sabil-kuttabs* in the city, of which around seventy survive. This one, founded by an eighteenth-century amir who wanted to make amends for his roistering youth, betrays a strong Ottoman influence, notable in the floral carvings between the arches. As usual, the *sabil* is on the ground floor (where the Ka'ba at Mecca is depicted in Syrian tilework), with the *kuttab* upstairs. An old proverb suggests that teaching methods were simple: "A boy's ear is on his back – he listens when he is beaten." As for girls, they were not even deemed worthy of schooling.

The Mosque of Al-Aqmar

Taking the left-hand fork at the *sabil-kuttab* and walking 70m north along Sharia Bayn al-Qasrayn, you reach the **Mosque of Al-Aqmar**, on the right. Its most salient feature is the facade, whose ribbed shell hood, keel arches and stalactite panels were the first instance of a decorated mosque facade in Cairo. Built between 1121 and 1125 by the Fatimid caliph's grand vizier, the mosque gets its name – "the moonlit" – from the glitter of its masonry under lunar light. Notice the intricate medallion above the door; the way that the street level has risen well above the mosque's entrance; and the "cutaway" corner up the road, designed to facilitate the manoeuvring of loaded camels.

Beit al-Sihaymi and the Mosque of Suleyman al-Silahdar

One block further north, turn right into **Darb al-Asfur**. Years of restoration work have left it in such a pristine state that it no longer seems part of the surrounding district. In fact it looks more like a modern reconstruction than a genuine Gamaliya street. The first three houses on the left are all open to the public (daily 9am–5pm; £E20, students £E10), entered through the broad wooden door of no.19, **Beit al-Sihaymi**, which is the finest of the three. Its rooms surround a lovely courtyard filled with bird noises and shrubbery, overlooked by a *maq'ad* or loggia, where males enjoyed the cool northerly breezes; the ground-floor reception hall with its marble fountain was used during winter, or for formal occasions. The *haramlik* section, reserved for women, is equally luxurious, adorned with faïence, stained glass, painted ceilings and delicate latticework. From here, you pass through the similarly restored early eighteenth-century **Beit Kharazati**, to emerge via the smaller, nineteenth-century **Beit Gaafar** on the corner at no.25. The three houses offer a unique chance to see what lies behind the walls of these old-city streets, and view the interior of a traditional wealthy Cairene's home, although the family life that once filled it is missing.

Returning to the main street and continuing north brings you to the **Mosque of Suleyman al-Silahdar**, recognizable by its "pencil" minaret, a typically Ottoman feature. Built in 1839, the mosque reflects the Baroque and Rococo influences that reached Cairo via Istanbul during Mohammed Ali's reign – notably the fronds and garlands that also characterize *sabil-kuttabs* from the period. Shortly afterwards the street widens into a triangular square, beyond which it's busy with the colourfully painted carts of garlic- and onion-sellers who roll in through the mighty gate ahead.

Al-Hakim's Mosque and the Northern Gates

The **Mosque of Al-Hakim**, abutting the Northern Walls, commemorates one of Egypt's most notorious rulers. **Al-Hakim bi-Amr Allah** (Ruler by God's Command) was only 11 years old when he became the sixth Fatimid caliph, and 15 when he had his tutor murdered. His reign (996–1021) was capricious and despotic by any standards, characterized by the persecution of Christians, Jews and merchants and by a rabid misogyny: Al-Hakim forbade women to leave their homes (banning the manufacture of women's footwear to reinforce this) and once had a group of noisy females boiled alive in a public bath. His puritanical instincts were also levelled at wine, chess and dancing girls – all of which he prohibited – and all the city's dogs were exterminated as their barking annoyed him. Merchants found guilty of cheating during Al-Hakim's inspections were summarily sodomized by his Nubian slave, Masoud, while the caliph stood upon their heads – comparatively restrained behaviour from a man who once dissected a butcher with his own cleaver.

In 1020, followers proclaimed Al-Hakim's divinity in the Mosque of Amr, provoking riots which he answered by ordering Fustat's destruction, watching it burn from the Muqattam Hills, where he often rode alone at night. However, legend ascribes the conflagration to Al-Hakim's revenge on the quarter where his beloved sister, **Sitt al-Mulk** (Lady of Power), took her lovers. Only after half of Fustat-Masr was in ruins was she examined by midwives and pronounced a virgin, whereupon he surveyed the devastation and asked, "Who ordered this?" Allegedly, it was his desire for an incestuous marriage that impelled her to arrange Al-Hakim's "disappearance" during one of his nocturnal jaunts, though his body was never found.

By governing as regent for the child-caliph Zahir and dying peacefully in her bed, Sitt al-Mulk forfeited the eternal fame that later accrued to Shagar al-Durr, renowned as the only female ruler of Egypt since Cleopatra (see p.164). Meanwhile, Al-Hakim's follower Hamza Ibn Ali, and his disciple, Mohammed al-Durzi, persuaded many foreign Muslims that Al-Hakim was a manifestation of God similar to the Christian Messiah. This idea is the origin of the **Druze** faith, whose tightly knit communities still exist in Syria, Lebanon and Israel, and who subscribe to doctrines of which the details are secret. Conversely, the Copts maintain that Al-Hakim experienced a vision of Jesus, repented, and became a monk.

At all events, though, his huge **mosque** was thereafter shunned or used for profane purposes until 1980, when it was restored by a sect of Isma'ili Shi'ites from India who have dedicated themselves to looking after Cairo's Fatimid mosques. The sect's addition of brass lamps, glass chandeliers and a new *mihrab* outraged purists, but the original wooden tie-beams and stucco frieze beneath the ceilings remain. From the roof, you can gaze over Bab al-Nasr Cemetery (see below) and admire the mosque's minarets, which resemble bastions and are its only original features. One advantage of modernization is that the court-yard has some degree of wheelchair access, though there is still the odd step to negotiate.

The Northern Gates

In times past, the annual pilgrim caravan returning from Mecca would enter Cairo via the **Bab al-Futuh** (Open Gate), drawing huge crowds to witness the arrival of the Mahmal. This decorative camel litter once carried Ayyub's widow on her pilgrimage, but thereafter it symbolized rather than signified the sultan's participation. Islamic pageantry is still manifest during the **Moulid of Sidi Ali al-Bayoumi**, in early October, when the Rifai brotherhood parades behind its mounted sheikh with scarlet banners flying. The procession starts from El-Hussein, passes through the Bab al-Futuh and north along Sharia Husseiniya, where locals bombard the sheikh and his red-turbanned followers with huge sweets called *arwah*.

The **Northern Walls** are in principle accessible from Al-Hakim's Mosque, but closed at time of writing for restoration. When they reopen, you can gain admission to a **prison** in the dark interior, where the custodian will point out archers' slits and bombardiers' apertures, shafts for pouring boiling oil onto enemies entering through the Bab al-Futuh below, and bits of pharaonic masonry (featuring Ramses II's cartouche and a hippo) filched from Memphis. The ceiling of the two-hundred-metre tunnel is vaulted, which allowed mounted guards passage through. At its end lies a grim and cavernous judgement room where the condemned, if found guilty, were hanged immediately, their corpses unceremoniously dumped through a hole in the floor, into the waters of the moat.

Erected in 1087 to replace the original mud-brick ramparts of Fatimid Al-Qahira, the walls were intended to rebuff the Seljuk Turks, but never put to the test, although they later provided a barracks for Napoleonic, and then British, grenadiers. The French attempted to rename the bastions of Bab al-Futuh and the next gate along, **Bab al-Nasr** (Gate of Victory), and titles such as "Tour Julien" and "Tour Pascal" are still inscribed on them. Bab al-Nasr can be reached, like Bab al-Futuh, from the roof of Al-Hakim's Mosque. The gate's inscription – "No deity but Allah; Mohammed is the Prophet of God" – includes a defiant Shi'ite addition, "And Ali is the Deputy of God". It was after entering this gate in 1517 that the victorious Ottoman Sultan, Selim the Grim, had eight hundred Mamlukes decapitated and their heads strung on ropes on Gezira Island. Directly opposite the gate lies **Bab al-Nasr Cemetery**, nowadays so overbuilt with houses that you can hardly see the tombs. At the top end of Haret al-Birkhader, one of the small streets off Sharia Galal opposite Bab al-Futuh, is a traditional **glass factory** (daily except Fri 6am–3pm; free) where they hand-blow Muski glass, and are usually happy for tourists to pop in and have a look: if you can't find it, ask for directions in their shop at no. 10.

From Bab al-Nasr you could catch a taxi or walk 1500m east, following the Walls and then Sharia Galal, to reach Barquq's complex in the Northern Cemetery (see p.168).

Sharia Gamaliya and into El-Gamaliya

Re-entering Islamic Cairo along Sharia Bab al-Nasr you come into the heart of **El-Gamaliya**, whose name derives from the old camel road, Sharia Gamaliya, off which the quarter's alleys run; in one of them, Nobel prize-winning author Naguib Mahfouz was born in 1911. Immediately to your right stands the sturdy fifteenth-century caravanserai or **Wikala of Qaitbey**, largely derelict within following damage in the 1992 earthquake, though most of the facade remains intact. Such caravanserais naturally clustered near the city gates, and the facades of three more *wikalas* (the last reduced to a mere portal) are visible beyond a small domed mausoleum on the other side of Sharia Gamaliya.

Beyond these *wikalas* stands the **Khanqah of Beybars al-Gashankir**, with its unmistakably bulbous dome and stumpy minaret (closed for restoration, not expected to reopen before 2009). Founded in 1310, and thus the oldest Sufi monastery in Cairo, the *khanqah* is entered via a "baffled" corridor that excludes street noises from the inner courtyard. Without tiles or mosaics, the courtyard escapes severity by the variety of its windows: ribbed, S-curved or keel-arched in styles derived from the Fatimid era. Al-Gashankir's tomb (off the corridor) is spectacular by comparison, with sunbeams falling through stained glass onto marbled walls inset with radiating polygons, and his cenotaph within its ebony *mashrabiya* cage. Sultan for one year only, Beybars was dubbed Al-Gashankir (the Taster) to distinguish him from Beybars al-Bunduqdari (the Crossbowman), a mightier predecessor.

Opposite the *khanqah* on the corner of Darb al-Asfur (see p.139), is a *sabil-kuttab*, **Qitus**, built in 1630 and, like the rest of the street, now lovingly restored, though not open to the public. Continuing south along Sharia Gamaliya for 100m, you'll pass a ruined *wikala*, a fifteenth-century mosque built above shops (whose rent finances the mosque's maintenance), and then another couple of mosques. Immediately after this, turn left into Darb al-Tablawy, an alleyway that bends left around a high stone wall to reach the **Musafirkhana Palace**. Though semi-derelict and undergoing slow restoration, this eighteenth-century mansion (where Khedive Ismail was born) retains beautiful *mashrabiyas*, decorative ceilings, a fountain in the reception hall, and a peaceful atmosphere rarely disturbed by visitors. It's still closed to the public at the time of writing, but the custodian may let you in for a small tip.

Returning to the main street, you'll find that it narrows and forks as it runs south. Precise directions are difficult, but by turning right at one fork and passing through a medieval-looking gate, you should emerge onto a square with shops selling scrap metal and weighing machines, behind the El-Hussein Mosque.

Between Al-Azhar and Bab Zwayla

Some of the most arresting sights in Islamic Cairo cluster between **Al-Azhar Mosque** and the medieval gate known as **Bab Zwayla** – a fairly brief itinerary (20min–1hr) that can be followed in either direction. Bab Zwayla is the starting point for **longer walking tours** of the Qasaba and Darb al-Ahmar, winding up beneath the Citadel, as described in the section following.

BETWEEN AL-AZHAR AND BAB ZWAYLA

SPECIFIC SHOPS SHOWN THUS: Auf

Northern Gates

SHARIA AL-AZHAR

Auf

PEDESTRIAN OVERPASS

SHARIA AL-AZHAR

Al-Azhar & Khan el-Khalili

Mosque-Madrassa of Al-Ghuri

Al-Ghuri Palace

Rashidi

HARET AL-FAHHAMIN

Fez shop

AL-MUIZZ

Mausoleum of Al-Ghuri

Hamid Ibrahim Abdel Aal

Shahatta Talba Manna

SHARIA

Wikala of Al-Ghuri

Shoe Bazaar

SHARIA KHUSH QADAM

Islamic Arts Museum & Midan Ahmed Maher

House of Gamal al-Din al-Dahabi

HARET HOSH QADAM

Fakahani Mosque

SHARIA AL-MUIZZ

Sabil-Kuttab of Tushun Pasha

El-Muayyad Hammam

Mosque of al-Muayyad

Hammam al-Sukariya

SHARIA AHMED MAHER

Sabil-Kuttab of Nafisa al-Bayda

Bab Zwayla

SHARIA DARB AL-AHMAR

Fatimid Wall

N

0   75 m

Qasaba

Mosque of Salih Tala'i

Citadel

The Wikala, Mosque-Madrassa and Mausoleum of Al-Ghuri

Now restored, the **Wikala of Al-Ghuri** (daily 8am–7pm) is Cairo's best-preserved merchants' hostel (twenty such structures remain, mostly squatted or derelict, out of the two hundred active in 1835). Its upstairs rooms have been converted into artists' studios, which the custodian will be glad to show you around. With its stables and lock-ups beneath tiers of spartan rooms, the *wikala* is uncompromisingly functional, yet the rhythm of *ablaq* (striped) arches muted by the sharp verticals of shutters, and the severe masonry lightened by *mashrabiya*s and a graceful fountain, achieves elegance. On Wednesday and Saturday evenings, it is the venue for a free and spectacular performance of Sufi **dervish dancing** (see box, p.258), which you shouldn't miss if you are in town.

Although it was built in 1505, as the new Cape route to the East Indies was diminishing Cairo's role as a spice entrepôt, the *wikala* doubtless witnessed the kind of scenes described in *The Arabian Nightmare*:

The Muhtasib stood immovable, flanked by two huge Turks who carried lanterns on great staves. Black slaves staggered under trunks of merchandise that were being fought over. A party of men were unsuccessfully trying to persuade a camel to leave by the same gate that it had come in by. A sheep was being roasted in the centre of the compound.

Located on a side street off Sharia al-Azhar, the *wikala* can be reached by turning left on leaving the Mosque of Al-Azhar, then following the alley round past a market; or you can visit it after seeing the **Ghuriya** – the mausoleum and mosque-*madrassa* of Qansuh Al-Ghuri. Boldly striped in buff and white, this pair of buildings forms a set piece at the junction of Sharia al-Muizz and the Al-Azhar high road, plainly visible from the footbridge. To the right (west) of the bridge stands the **Mosque-Madrassa**, now restored to its full glory. The rooftop offers glimpses of the Spice Bazaar and a grand view of the neighbourhood – the door is diagonally opposite the entrance to the main part of the mosque, but is often closed, so you may have to ask a custodian for access. Across the way is Al-Ghuri's **Mausoleum** (closed for restoration), originally topped by a green-tiled dome, which collapsed in the early twentieth century. On the other side of the mausoleum is the **Al-Ghuri Palace**, now used to host occasional concerts (details from the Wikala of al-Ghuri).

Qansuh al-Ghuri was 60 years old when he became the penultimate Mamluke sultan in 1500, and he remained vigorous into his 70s, playing polo, writing poetry and discoursing with Sufis – not forgetting traditional pursuits such as intrigue, arbitrary justice and the construction of new buildings. Though not averse to filching marble for his mosque-*madrassa*, Al-Ghuri wished to be remembered for his strict enforcement of Koranic precepts. He berated judges for laxity, and once sentenced a dervish accused of "atheism, sorcery, and the use of milk for his ablutions and intimate toilet" to be paraded naked on a camel, and then hanged. In 1516 Al-Ghuri was killed fighting the Turks outside Aleppo; his body was never found and his intended tomb was occupied by his luckless successor, Tumanbey (see p.146). Gamal al-Ghitani's novel *Zayni Barakat* is a fictionalized account of this Mamluke twilight.

Towards Bab Zwayla

Named after the conquering Fatimid caliph, **Sharia al-Muizz** was the chief thoroughfare of Islamic Cairo, running from the Northern Gates down towards the Citadel, and meeting another main road – the Darb al-Ahmar – at the Bab Zwayla. Traditionally, each stretch of Al-Muizz had its own name, usually derived from the merchandise sold there. In olden times the stretch between the Ghuriya buildings was roofed over, forming the Silk Bazaar where carpets were sold, the subject of a famous drawing by David Roberts. Nowadays, shops along here sell mostly household goods, making fewer concessions to tourism than Khan el-Khalili.

On the west side of the street, less than 50m south of Al-Ghuri's Mosque, is the last **fez workshop** in Cairo, kept alive by sales to five-star hotels and tourists. Various grades of fez are available, the cheapest going for just £E10. The fez, or *tarboush fassi*, was originally a mark of Ottoman allegiance, which came to represent the secular, Westernized effendi, as opposed to the turbaned traditionalist. Under Nasser it fell from fashion, stigmatized as a badge of the old regime. Waiters and entertainers are the main wearers nowadays, but demand is so small that the craft of fez-making seems unlikely to survive.

Some 200m south, you'll find the "Fruit Seller" or **Fakahani Mosque**, whose arabesque-panelled doors are all that remain of the twelfth-century original after its reconstruction in 1735. The nearby **House of Gamal al-Din al-Dahabi**, at 6 Haret Hosh Qadam, was the home of seventeenth-century Cairo's foremost gold merchant. Its magnificent interior is still under restoration but is sporadically open to the public (in theory, daily 9am–7pm; £E10, students £E5, but depending on the work in progress, they may let you in unofficially for some baksheesh), and is full of beautiful stone inlay work and ornate wooden ceilings, especially in the first-floor portico overlooking the main courtyard.

South of the Fakahani Mosque, Sharia al-Muizz curves around the Rococo facade of the 1820 Ottoman-built **Sabil-Kuttab of Tusun Pasha** (daily 8am–8pm; £E10, students £E5), adorned with wrought-iron sunbursts, garlands and fronds. Inside, explanatory displays tell you about the building and its founder, a campaigner for tolerant Islam and against the austere and uncompromising Wahhabist movement of Saudi Arabia. Shortly afterwards, the street passes between two buildings structurally adjacent to Bab Zwayla, whose formidable outline dominates the view ahead. To the left, the wall of a *mashrabiya*-fronted *wikala* is preceded by an unobtrusive door (next to a jewellers' shop) that fronts the eighteenth-century **Al-Sukariya hammam** at no. 7, a traditional bathhouse that is currently closed for restoration. The fires that heated the water here were also used to cook *fuul madammes* for the neighbourhood's breakfast. The traditional extra allure of such baths was described by Flaubert in 1839: "You reserve the bath for yourself (five francs including masseurs, pipe, coffee, sheet and towel) and you skewer your lad in one of the rooms." Flaubert described the masseurs as "naked *kellaas* … turning you over like embalmers preparing you for the tomb". The reputation of bathhouses as gay brothels has endured, though the restoration of this and three other hammams in Islamic Cairo may mark their return to fashion as legitimate places to enjoy a steam bath (see p.264).

Across the way, the **Mosque of Al-Muayyad** – also known as the "Red Mosque" for the colour of its exterior – occupies the site of a prison where its founder was once incarcerated for plotting against Sultan Barquq. Plagued by lice and fleas, he vowed to transform it into a "saintly place for the education of scholars" once he came to power. When he did, 40,000 dinars were dutifully lavished on the mosque's construction (1415–22). The building is entered via a nine-tiered stalactite portal with a red-and-turquoise geometric frame around its bronze door, but is closed for repairs at the time of writing. Off the vestibule lies a mausoleum where Al-Muayyad and his son are buried in fittingly sized cenotaphs. The Kufic inscription on Al-Muayyad's reads: "But the god-fearing shall be amidst gardens and fountains: Enter you them, in peace and security" – which seems appropriate for the mosque's courtyard, half filled with palms and open to the sky. Beneath the roofed section, a thickly carpeted sanctuary precedes the *qibla* wall, niched and patterned with polychrome marble and mosaic. Its minarets are built atop the turrets of Bab Zwayla, the neighbouring city gate. Another old bathhouse, the **Hammam al-Muayyad**, can be found down a small alley behind the mosque, but has been derelict for a while.

Bab Zwayla

The Al-Muayyad's minarets, added four hundred years after the turrets were built, make **Bab Zwayla** look far mightier than the Northern Gates. The gate itself was constructed when the Fatimid city's defences (including sixty gates) were reinforced during the 1090s, using Anatolian or Mesopotamian Christian architects and Egyptian labour. Originally the main south gate, Bab Zwayla later became a central point in the Mamluke city, which had outgrown the

△ Mosque of Al-Muayyad

Fatimid walls and pushed up against Salah al-Din's extensions. Nevertheless, the practice of barring the gates each night continued well into the nineteenth century, maintaining a city within a city. There's a strikingly medieval passage just on the north side of the gate, but the full awesomeness of the Bab itself is best seen from the south side.

The gate was named after Fatimid mercenaries of the Berber al-Zwayla tribe, quartered nearby, whom the Mamlukes displaced. Through the centuries it was the point of departure for caravans to Mecca and the source of the drum rolls that greeted the arrival of senior "Amirs of One Hundred". Dancers and snake charmers also performed here, and from the fifteenth century onwards punishments provided another spectacle. Dishonest merchants might be hung from hooks or ropes; garrotting, beheading or impalement were favoured for common criminals; while losers in the Mamluke power struggles were often nailed to the doors. It was here that Tumanbey, the last Mamluke sultan, was hanged in 1517, after a vast crowd had recited the *Fatiha* (the first chapter of the Koran) and the rope had broken twice before his neck did. However, Bab Zwayla's reputation was subsequently redeemed by its association with Mitwalli al-Qutb, a miracle-working local saint said to manifest himself to the faithful as a gleam of light within the gatehouse.

The **western gatetower**, the **turret** and the **minarets** are now open to the public (daily 8.30am–5pm; £E10, students £E5) and can be visited via a door just next to the al-Muayyad Mosque. Finds from the site are on display, as well as votive offerings left by local residents for Mitwalli al-Qutb. You can also climb to the top of the two minarets for great views over Islamic Cairo and a bird's-eye perspective over the al-Muayyad and Salih Tala'i mosques below. Note the barbells high up on the western gatetower – a relic of medieval keep-fit enthusiasts.

Across the street from the entrance to the gate, the eighteenth-century **Sabil-Kuttub of Nafisa al-Bayda** has been restored and opened to the public (daily 8am–6pm; £E6, students £E3; tickets from the desk at Bab Zwayla), with accounts of the building and some of the artefacts found there, but nothing hugely compelling.

A whole slew of places to the south of the Bab are covered by the next itinerary (see p.150), but it's worth mentioning an alternative, heading westwards along Sharia Ahmed Maher towards the Museum of Islamic Art (see below). En route you'll pass stalls selling waterpipes and braziers, a nineteenth-century *sabil-kuttab* and a fifteenth-century mosque. Minibuses #68 and #75 run to the museum, but it's probably quicker to walk (about ten minutes). The neighbourhood between Bab Zwayla and the Abdin district is known as the **Bab el-Khalq quarter**, after a long-since-vanished medieval gate. On your right off Sharia Ahmed Maher, just before Sharia Bur Said (the entrance to the museum is off this street), is Darb es-Saada, a street of carpenters' workshops, which backs onto a local remand prison. Relatives of the inmates can often be seen on unofficial visits, lining the street and calling up to the windows of the cells.

The Museum of Islamic Art

The **Museum of Islamic Art** stands at the junction of Sharia Ahmed Maher, Sharia Bur Said and Sharia Qalaa, 600m west of Bab Zwayla (see "Central Cairo" map p.104–105). It is an unmissable collection, but like so many things in Islamic Cairo, was closed for refurbishment at the time of writing. If you are able to visit (the tourist office should be able to tell you if it's reopened), bear in mind that the layout of exhibits may have changed from those described below.

The museum is best visited midway through an exploration of Islamic Cairo, since the historic architecture lends meaning to the museum's artefacts, which, in turn, enhance your appreciation of the old city. It was the ruinous state of many of its mosques and mansions that impelled Khedive Tewfiq and the historians Herz and Cresswell to establish an Islamic collection in 1880. Pieces were stored in Al-Hakim's Mosque until 1902, when a museum was created on the ground floor of the imposing neo-Mamluke Dar al-Kutub (National Library) which houses it today.

Because Sunni Muslims extended the Koranic strictures against idolatry to any images of humans or animals, these are largely absent. Instead of paintings and statues, there are exquisite designs based on geometry, Islamic symbolism, plant motifs and Arabic calligraphy. Dates are given as AH, Anno Hegirae (the Hegira being Mohammed's flight from Mecca in 622 AD, the starting point of Islamic chronology).

Touring the museum

Some of the museum's most **recent acquisitions** are housed in **Room 1**. In **Room 2**, surrounded by Ottoman mosaics of polychrome marble, a single display case contains objects from the **Umayyad period** (661–750). Among them is a bronze ewer with a spout in the form of a crowing cockerel, which probably belonged to the last Umayyad caliph of the Arab Empire, Marwan II, who was slain near Abu Sir, just south of Cairo. On his death, the Umayyads were succeeded by the Abbasid dynasty, who moved the capital of the caliphate from Damascus to Baghdad.

Brassware from the **Abbasid** period in **Room 3** includes the figure of a deer, not an animal much associated with the Middle East. Also here are ninth- and tenth-century Persian imitations of Chinese ceramics, showing how Chinese art influenced the Islamic world. The examples of **stucco** on the walls here show how it was developed into a high art form under the Abbasids, especially in Iraq. From being deeply cut and crisply textured with relatively naturalistic

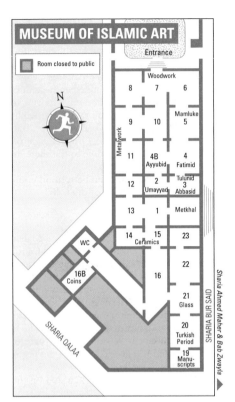

MUSEUM OF ISLAMIC ART

Entrance

■ Room closed to public

Woodwork

8   7   6

N

Mamluke
9   10   5

Metalwork

11   4B Ayyubid   4 Fatimid

12   2 Umayyad   Tulunid 3 Abbasid

13   1   Metkhal

14   15 Ceramics   23

WC

16B Coins   16   22

21 Glass

20 Turkish Period

19 Manuscripts

Sharia Ahmed Maher & Bab Zwayla

SHARIA BUR SAID

SHARIA QALAA

vines and acanthus scrolls, stucco panels became increasingly abstract and flowing, no longer carved but moulded. Meanwhile under **Tulunid** rule in Egypt (868–905), three different styles from Samarra in Iraq were also imitated in wood; compare the stucco panels with the woodwork from Al-Qitai.

Passing into **Room 4** through a huge door from Sultan Qalaoun's Maristan, you enter the **Fatimid era** (969–1171). As Shi'ites, the Fatimids had no doctrinal objection to depicting animals and birds (a theme popular among their co-religionists in Persia), as attested by **panels from the Western Palace**, one of the two palaces which once stood on Bayn al-Qasrayn (see p.136). Also exhibited are inlaid ivory and jewellery, rock crystal, painted **glassware**, and early **lustreware** ceramics from Fustat. On the southern wall, **frescoes** from a Fustat bathhouse depict people and animals, not yet taboo at this time in Islamic art. **Room 4B** (part of the main hall) is a lovely composite of Mamluke columns, an Ottoman fountain and floor, and intricate *mashrabiya* work from the **Ayyubid** period (1171–1250).

From Room 4, you enter **Room 5** under a collection of Ottoman-period stained-glass "moon windows" set in open plasterwork. Also in the doorway (on the right), a stone medallion once embedded in the wall of a building depicts a two-headed eagle and fire-breathing bull amid a confusion of animal forms that all seem to belong to one body. The room itself covers the **Mamluke period** (1250–1517) and centres upon a lovely sunken mosaic fountain. Round about are displayed **mosque lamps** and stucco *mihrabs*; woven and printed textiles of linen and cotton; inlaid metalwork, polychrome pottery and a wooden **cenotaph from the El-Hussein Mosque**. At the far end of the room is a wooden door from the Mosque of Sultan Ayyub, bearing square Kufic and cursive Naskhi inscriptions. The **glassware** here is noticeably more sophisticated, painted with ornate calligraphy.

A pair of doors from the Al-Azhar Mosque leads into **Room 6**, the first of three rooms devoted to **woodwork**, whose evolution paralleled that of stuccos. The deeply incised, naturalistic forms of Umayyad woodcarving gave way to interlocking arches and concentric circles under the Abbasids, followed by bevelled, stylized birds and animals in Tulunid times. Gradually confined to small areas during the Fatimid era, figures were then progressively simplified into arabesques by Ayyubid craftsmen. However, representational art could still be found under the early Mamlukes, as evinced by a **frieze from Qalaoun's Maristan**, which shows hunting, music and dancing. Also featured in Room 6 are carved panels from the Western Palace, the original *mihrab* from Saiyida Ruqayya's Mashhad (see p.165), and a portable prayer niche for use on military campaigns.

Room 7, opposite the entrance, contains a series of *mashrabiyas*, and a highlighted **object of the month**. Hanging from the ceilings of rooms 7 to 11 are examples of the brass lanterns traditionally hung in mosques, though out of use in these days of electricity.

Room 8's treasures include three wooden **minbars** (pulpits), a panelled ceiling and a case of pieces originally inlaid into the geometric designs of *minbars*, ceilings, doors and furniture. The objects in the room's other display cases include wooden combs, ivory boxes, and a beautiful bone-inlaid panel depicting a hawk attacking a hare. Among the wooden panels on the wall, a frieze in Hebrew commemorates the building of a synagogue in the twelfth century by one Ibrahim el-Amshati.

Wooden panels overspill into **Room 9**, where caskets inlaid with ivory and mother-of-pearl rather show up the shoddy workmanship of the goods nowadays sold to tourists in the Khan. Bronze **mirrors** and brass lamps inaugurate the museum's **metalwork** section, but the room's most striking pieces are a Persian brass candlestick in the form of two intertwined snakes and, among the **figurines** by the west wall, a little man on a horse in a "Look, no hands" pose. What looks like a horse-headed cigar-cutter in the same case is in fact a chopper for betel nut, a stimulant much used in India and Southeast Asia, but not in the Middle East.

Room 10, next door, reflects Ottoman tastes in interior design. Beneath an exquisitely **coffered ceiling**, guests could socialize around a graceful fountain, secretly overlooked by the women of the household. The furnishings in here date from the seventeenth and eighteenth centuries.

From Mosul in Iraq came the technique of inlaying copper or silver into bronze, which was to characterize Egyptian **metalwork**. A brass-plated door from the Mosque of Salih Tala'i stands at the entrance to **Room 11**. Inside you'll find candlesticks and caskets; incense burners inlaid with gold and silver (some with Christian symbols); a fourteenth-century hand-warmer; and a case of astrolabes, used by Muslim navigators.

Room 12 contains a fraction of the Mamluke **Armoury** (most of which was taken to Istanbul by Selim the Grim). Case 7, on the left of the door to Room 11, holds the swords of Mehmet II and Suleyman the Magnificent (the respective conquerors of Constantinople and the Balkans). Daggers on the west wall include one with an exquisite enamelled Persian scabbard of the fifteenth or sixteenth century.

Room 13 takes you back to the Fatimid period, with a display of lustreware decorated with people and animals in the main display case in the northeast corner. The relatively primitive nature of this decoration is shown up by the metallic blue Mina'i ware in the southwest case. In the northwest case, and on the west wall, tiny glass vessels are the ancestors of today's ornate perfume bottles.

Room 14 contains more ceramics, mainly Persian, including blue wall tiles. Ceramics in **Room 15** include tiles found at Fustat that originated in Tunisia, Andalusia and Christian Europe, showing the extent of the city's commercial reach, and including blue Delft tiles from Holland. Also here are **stone moulds** used for casting metal ornaments.

The dominant exhibit in **Room 16** is a blue-tiled nineteenth-century **Turkish fireplace**. At the southern end of the room, a section of an old **kuttab** (Koranic school) from Rosetta incorporates a niche for the teacher to sit beneath its *muqarnas* ceiling. Among the ceramics, notice the *ahlaq* (chokes) that were inserted in the necks of Fatimid water jars to regulate their flow, fretted with bird, animal and calligraphic motifs. The room also contains stucco *mihrabs* and nineteenth-century Turkish prayer rugs. A diversion from Room 16 takes you down a passage whose walls are decked with stone inscriptions, to **Room 16B**, used to display coins, weights, medals and glass seals.

At the museum's southern end, **Room 19** showcases **calligraphy and bookbinding**, including Persian and Indian illustrated manuscripts, but primacy is accorded to the word of God, with numerous medieval Korans from the collection of King Farouk. The first mass-produced Korans were made in Egypt following Napoleon's introduction of the printing press; Cairo is still the main publishing centre of the Arab world.

Room 20 is stuffed with **Ottoman material**, including seventeenth- and eighteenth-century wall tiles depicting the Kaaba at Mecca, Islam's holiest site, and the Prophet's Mosque at Medina, Mohammed's burial place. Among the room's less pious offerings is a beautifully made *sheesha* pipe from Istanbul.

Room 21 is devoted to Egyptian **glass**. Various techniques perfected in ancient times continued to be used; lustreware (a Fatimid speciality) and enamelled glass were the chief innovations in the Islamic period. Among the mosque lamps and eighth- to fourteenth-century perfume jars, a large hour-glass stands out as the most prominent exhibit.

Among the **Persian objects** of the ninth to seventeenth centuries in **Room 22** are three ceramic figurines of animals: a camel with a litter on its back by the west wall and a lion by the east wall, both in cobalt blue; plus, by the east wall, a hoopoe glazed in turquoise.

Like the neighbouring *metkhal* (entrance hall), **Room 23** is used for **temporary exhibitions**.

Between Bab Zwayla and the Citadel

There are two basic walking routes between Bab Zwayla and the Citadel: via the Qasaba, **Sharia al-Muizz** and Sharia Qalaa; or following the old **Darb al-Ahmar** (after which this quarter of Islamic Cairo is named). It's possible to get the best of both worlds by combining the Darb al-Ahmar with a detour into the **Qasaba** and **Saddlemakers Bazaar**, located on the other route, a total distance of about 1500m. Assuming you're starting from the Bab Zwayla as in the itinerary below, it's logical to visit the Qasaba before embarking on the Darb al-Ahmar, whereas the reverse holds true if you're coming from the Citadel. If that's what you're doing, you'll want to start with the "Blue Mosque" of Aqsunqur on Sharia Bab al-Wazir and backtrack through the text from there.

From Bab Zwayla into the Qasaba

Emerging from Bab Zwayla, you'll see a cluster of Islamic monuments across the street, which is often flooded by burst water mains. On the right-hand corner stands a Sufi establishment, the **Zawiya of Farag ibn Barquq** (currently closed for restoration), whose inlaid marble lintels and *ablaq* panels may be hidden by stalls. Opposite the *zawiya*, the **Mosque of Salih Tala'i** withdraws behind an elegant portico with five keel arches – a unique architectural feature. The last of Cairo's Fatimid mosques, the building shows an assured use of the motifs that were first employed on the Mosque of Al-Aqmar: ribbed and cusped arches and panels, carved tie-beams and rosettes. Notice the capitals, plundered from pre-Islamic buildings, and the "floriated Kufic" script around the arches.

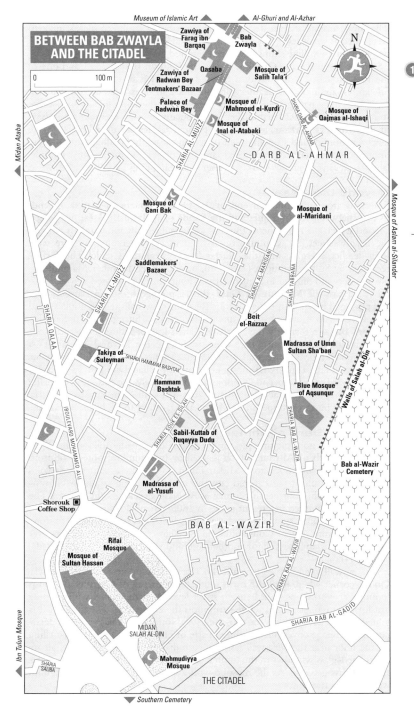

BETWEEN BAB ZWAYLA
AND THE CITADEL

Museum of Islamic Art ▲   ▲ Al-Ghuri and Al-Azhar

N

0   100 m

Zawiya of
Farag ibn
Barqaq

Bab
Zwayla

Qasaba

Mosque of
Salih Tala'i

Zawiya of
Radwan Bey
Tentmakers' Bazaar

Palace of
Radwan Bey

Mosque of
Mahmoud el-Kurdi

Mosque of
Qajmas al-Ishaqi

Mosque of
Inal el-Atabaki

DARB AL-AHMAR

SHARIA AL-MU'IZZ

SHARIA DARB AL-AHMAR

Mosque of
Gani Bak

Mosque of
al-Maridani

Midan Ataba ▲

Mosque of Aslam al-Silander ▲

Saddlemakers'
Bazaar

SHARIA AL-MARIDANI

SHARIA TABBANA

Beit
el-Razzaz

Takiya of
Suleyman

SHARIA HAMMAM BASHTAK

Madrassa of Umm
Sultan Sha'ban

Hammam
Bashtak

Walls of Salah al-Din

"Blue Mosque"
of Aqsunqur

SHARIA BAB AL-WAZIR

SHARIA QALAA

(BOULEVARD MOHAMMED ALI)

SHARIA SOUK ES SILAH

Sabil-Kuttab of
Ruqayya Dudu

Bab al-Wazir
Cemetery

Shorouk
Coffee Shop

Madrassa of
al-Yusufi

BAB AL-WAZIR

Rifai
Mosque

Mosque of
Sultan Hassan

SHARIA BAB AL-WAZIR

SHARIA BAB AL-GADID

Ibn Tulun Mosque ▲

MIDAN
SALAH AL-DIN

Mahmudiyya
Mosque

SHARIA
SALIBA

THE CITADEL

Southern Cemetery ▼

The shops around its base (whose rents contributed to the mosque's upkeep) were once at street level, but this has risen well over a metre since the mosque was built in 1408. The shops have been restored, but are as yet unoccupied.

Straight ahead lies the **Qasaba**, erected by Ridwan Bey in 1650, and one of the best-preserved examples of a covered market left in Cairo. Here colourful fabrics, appliqué and leatherwork are piled in dens ranked either side of a gloomy, lofty passageway, still rather rickety at the back following damage sustained in the 1992 earthquake. It's popularly known as the Khiyamiyya, or **Tentmakers Bazaar**, as colourful printed fabrics are used here to make tents for moulids and weddings and to screen unsightly building work – a big improvement on tarpaulins. Printed fabric is sold by the metre, quite cheaply; labour-intensive appliqué work is pricier (see "Shopping", p.248).

Beyond the Qasaba

Emerging from the southern end of the Qasaba, **Sharia al-Muizz** extends its path between two mosques and the facade of Ridwan Bey's former palace, beyond which the monuments thin out as vegetable stalls and butchers congest the narrow street. By Mamluke times most of the older quarters here were semi-derelict, merging into the "Tartar Ruins" near the Citadel. The Tartars, recruited by Sultan Kitbugha (1296–96), were despised by other Mamlukes as horse-eaters and billeted in a quarter that's long since disappeared. About 150m on you'll pass the **Mosque of Gani Bak**, a protégé of Sultan Barsbey, who was poisoned by rivals at the age of 25. Beyond, a few stalls selling donkey- and camel-wear constitute what remains of the Souk es-Surugiyyah, or **Saddlemakers Bazaar**, formerly the centre of Cairo's leather industry.

Assuming you don't turn back here to pursue the Darb al-Ahmar, it's a fairly mundane 350-metre walk to Al-Muizz's junction with **Sharia Qalaa**. The Sultan Hassan and Rifai mosques below the Citadel are plainly visible at the boulevard's southern end, 300m away. Alternatively, use bus services in the opposite direction to reach the Islamic Arts Museum, 1km up Sharia Qalaa. Some of the buses continue on to Midan Ataba, others to Abdin or Al-Azhar.

Along the Darb al-Ahmar

An alternative, more picturesque route towards the Citadel follows the "Red Road", or **Darb al-Ahmar**, which is plied by two minibus routes: #68 from Midan Ramses, and #75 from Midan Tahrir. Originally a cemetery beyond the southern walls of the Fatimid city, this quarter became a fashionable residential area in the fourteenth century, as Al-Nasir developed the Citadel. The thoroughfare acquired its present name in 1805, when Mohammed Ali tricked the Mamlukes into staging a coup before slaughtering them. Stuffed with straw, their heads were sent to Constantinople as a sign of his power; six years later the surviving Mamlukes fell for another ruse, and were massacred in the Citadel (see p.154).

Start by walking 150m east from Salih Tila'i's Mosque near the Bab Zwayla. On the corner where the Darb turns south, the **Mosque of Qajmas al-Ishaqi** looms over workshops sunk beneath street level. A marble panel with swirling leaf forms in red, black and white surmounts the entrance to a vestibule with a gilded ceiling; left off this is the mosque itself. Notice the *mihrab*'s sinuous decorations (incised grooves filled with red paste or bitumen) and the fine panelling on the floor near the *qibla* wall (ask the custodian to lift a mat). Best of all are the stained-glass windows in the tomb chamber occupied by one Abu Hurayba. A raised passage connects the mosque with a *sabil-kuttab* across the street; both were built in the 1480s.

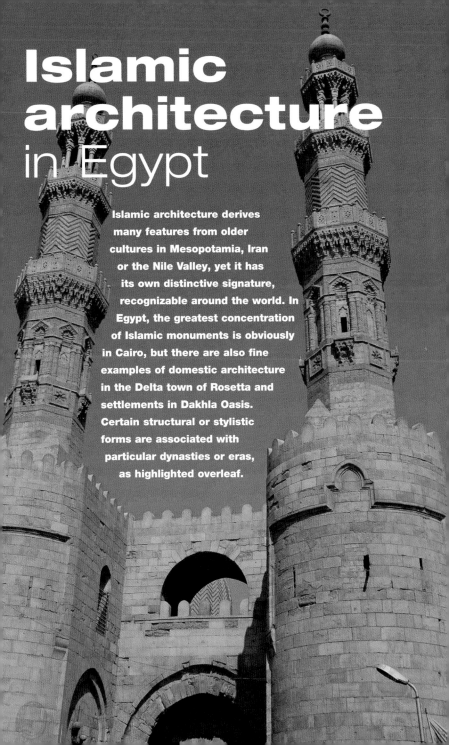

Islamic architecture
in Egypt

Islamic architecture derives many features from older cultures in Mesopotamia, Iran or the Nile Valley, yet it has its own distinctive signature, recognizable around the world. In Egypt, the greatest concentration of Islamic monuments is obviously in Cairo, but there are also fine examples of domestic architecture in the Delta town of Rosetta and settlements in Dakhla Oasis. Certain structural or stylistic forms are associated with particular dynasties or eras, as highlighted overleaf.

▲ The varied skyline of the Northern Cemeteries

Beginnings

The first mosque in Islam was the courtyard of the Prophet Mohammed's house in Medina – an enclosure with palm-roofed arcades shading the *qibla* wall facing Mecca, towards which worshippers prayed. These simple features have been replicated and elaborated ever since, alongside others introduced at an early stage in Islamic history: the mihrab, or niche in front of which the imam leading the prayer stands, may have originally just been a mark on the *qibla* wall; minarets date from the Arab conquest of Damascus in 636, when the call to prayer issued from the towers of the Church of St John before it was reconstructed as the Umayyad Great Mosque.

The Tulunids

Egypt's earliest extant example of a mosque is that of Ibn Tulun in Cairo, which follows the Umayyad tradition of the congregational mosque, with its great enclosure (*sahn*) flanked by arcades (*liwan*) and a fountain for ablutions. The Tulunid style was austerely monumental, the vast mosque deriving its impact from the rhythm of its arches and parapet mouldings, surrounded by a city of cantonments. Ibn Tulun was an Abbassid viceroy who founded a breakaway dynasty in Egypt; his distinctive spiral minaret is modelled on that of the mosque at Samarra in Iraq, where the Abbassids remained in power – and from where they would wreak revenge on the Tulunid city.

The Fatimids

In 969 Egypt was conquered by the Fatimids, Shia Muslims who founded a new capital near the ruins of Ibn Tulun's city. While the Fatimids' legendary palaces

▼ The Mosque of Ibn Tulun, with its spiral minaret

have not survived, their street plan and fortifications, including such gates as the Bab Zwayla, between the Northern Walls and the Citadel, still distinguish what is now called Islamic Cairo. Fatimid mosques had decorative facades with keel-shaped or scalloped arches, stucco rosettes and honeycombed *muqarnas* – motifs that became part of the lexicon of Islamic architecture. In frontier oases, the Fatimids encouraged *qasr* (fortress)-style villages, with twisting lanes and low-roofed passages to make life difficult for mounted invaders.

◄ ◄ The Bab Zwayla, one of several monumental gateways in the heart of Islamic Cairo

The Ayyubids

The Fatimids' successor Salah al-Din (Saladin) enlarged Cairo's Citadel and built an aqueduct from the Nile, but his most significant innovation was the madrassa or Islamic seminary, intended to roll back Shia "heresy". *Madrassas* were usually attached to mosques, often in a cruciform pattern to provide separate lodgings for each of the four schools of Sunni jurisprudence. Other contributions that Salah al-Din's Ayyubid dynasty made to Islamic architecture were the pepper-pot-style minaret that distinguishes twelfth- and thirteenth-century mosques in Cairo and the oases, and the technique of laying alternating courses of different coloured stone to achieve a striped effect on on walls and arches, known as ablaq.

▲ A fine portal in Islamic Cairo, featuring *ablaq* and topped by *muqarnas* work

The decorative arts

All this architecture stimulated decorative arts, from wood and stucco carving to glassblowing and calligraphy. The Fatimids developed bevelled carving to create monumental compositions of foliage, birds and animals, while the Ayyubids preferred to work with small polygonal panels or pieces of turned wood that were fitted together to form lattices for dividing halls or screening windows – such **mashrabiya** are a feature of traditional houses still to be seen in Cairo, Alexandria and Rosetta. Though the Fatimids loved animal motifs, later mosques respected Islam's rejection of figurative art as idolatrous; designs based on geometry, foliage or Arabic calligraphy and the text of the Koran adorned walls and ceilings. Vivid blue Iznik tiles were favoured in the Ottoman era (after 1517) and interiors were influenced by European Rococo under Pasha Mohammed Ali (1805–48).

▼ Decorative tiles at the Sabll-Kuttab of Abd al-Rahman Katkhuda

The Mamlukes

All these dynasties paved the way for the Mamlukes, a warrior caste drawn from far-off lands, which ruled Egypt from 1250 to 1517. Mamluke sultans such as Qalaoun and Beybars endowed Cairo with magnificent mosques and *madrassas*, while Qalaoun also built a hospital. Islam extolled cleanliness and education, so a ruler could also show his piety and court popularity by building a public bathhouse (*hammam*), fountain (*sabil*) or boys' school (*kuttab*), sometimes sited above a fountain to create a dual-purpose *sabil-kuttab*. Mamlukes vied to outdo their rivals with lavish materials and decorations – marble, imported tiles, cedar-wood and wrought iron.

▲ Carvings on the dome of Sultan Qaitbey's Mausoleum, in Cairo's Northern Cemetery

While early Muslims abhorred ostentatious graves, the Mamlukes built magnificent tombs in two quarters of Cairo, later known as the Cities of the Dead. The classic form was a cuboid structure crowned by a *qubba* (dome) whose surface was carved with patterns that shifted as the sun illuminated incised or raised parts of the design – exemplified by the Mausoleum of Qaitbey. Mausoleums were attached to mosques or *madrassas*, or a kind of dervish monastery called a *khanqah*, as can be seen in Cairo's Northern Cemetery. Simpler domed tombs like egg-boxes form vast cemeteries outside Minya in Middle Egypt.

Domestic architecture and town planning

Until the seventeenth century, Islamic **domestic architecture** was far ahead of Europe's. Wealthy Cairenes had mansions with running water and Turkish baths, cooled by a rooftop ventilator and an inner courtyard, and distanced from the noisy, dusty streets by a zigzag entrance passage. Rooms had high ceilings, panelled or tiled walls, *mashrabiya* screens and cooling fountains, but were not associated with specific functions; rather, people relaxed, ate or slept in whichever room was most comfortable according to the season or time of day. The crucial distinction was between the semi-public *salamlik* and the private family quarters, or *haramlik*, which Europeans misconstrued as harems.

Town planning strove to promote public hygiene, security and harmony. At one time, fortified walls not only enclosed cities but divided them into *mahala* or quarters whose gates were locked at night. Neighbourhoods were based on ethnic or religious affinity (many towns still have a Christian quarter), with commerce centred on the *souk* or bazaar, where professions considered clean and honourable (perfume makers, tailors, booksellers) congregated near mosques, and unclean crafts (tanners, dyers, blacksmiths) were relegated to the fringes – an arrangement that can still be seen at Khan el-Khalili in Cairo or Al-Qasreya in Assyut. Visiting merchants could store their goods and stay at caravanserais in the *souk* or near gates in the city walls, which might be called a *khan*, *funduq* or *wikala*. Surviving ones serve as workshops today.

▲ A *mashrabiya* window at Cairo's Beit al-Sihaymi mansion

Al-Silahdar's Mosque

If you're not pushed for time, consider detouring off the Darb to visit the **Mosque of Aslam al-Silahdar**. From Qajmas's Mosque, walk through the tunnel around the side and on past a shrine where the street forks (bear right); Al-Silahdar's Mosque lies 250m ahead. The marble panel outside is typical of exterior decoration during the Bahri Mamluke period; inside, the layout is that of a cruciform **madrassa**. Students used to live in rooms above the north and south *liwans*, behind an ornate facade of stucco mouldings and screened windows. The mosque's founder was a Qipchak Mamluke who lost his position as swordbearer after Sultan al-Nasir believed rumours spread by his enemies, and imprisoned him, only to reinstate Aslam as *silahdar* ("swordbearer") six years later. To return to the Darb, either retrace your steps or take the street running southwest off the square, which joins the Darb further south, beyond Al-Maridani's Mosque.

South along the Darb al-Ahmar

South from the Qajmas Mosque, the Darb al-Ahmar passes the **Mosque of Al-Maridani**, built in 1340 and still a peaceful retreat from the streets. The mosque is usually entered via its northern portal, offset by a stalactite frieze with complex patterns of joggled voussoirs and *ablaq* panels. Inside, a splendid *mashrabiya* screen separates the open courtyard from the prayer hall with its stained-glass windows and variegated columns (Mamluke, pre-Islamic and pharaonic). Because it was economical with wood and minimized the effect of warping in a hot, dry climate, *mashrabiya*-work was an ideal technique for Egyptian craftsmen. Architecturally speaking, the minaret marks the replacement of the Ayyubid "pepperpot" finial by a small dome on pillars, which became the hallmark of Mamluke minarets. Below the dome and above the *minbar*, arboreal forms in stucco may allude to the Koranic verse, "A good word is as a good tree – its roots firm, its branches in heaven".

Leaving via the southern entrance, you'll need to turn left to rejoin the Darb – or **Sharia Tabbana** as it's called at this point. Roughly 200m on, past a small Turkish mosque, stands the hulking **Madrassa of Umm Sultan Sha'ban**. Umm Sha'ban was the concubine of a son of Al-Nasir, whose own son erected the *madrassa* (1368–69) as a gesture of gratitude after he became sultan at the age of 10; murdered in 1376, he preceded her to the grave and was buried here since his own *madrassa* was unfinished. A wealth of *muqarnas* and *ablaq* rims the entrance, which is flanked by a *sabil* and a drinking trough. Watering animals was meritorious in the eyes of Islam; the Prophet himself had seen a prostitute give water to a thirsty dog, and promised her, "For this action you shall enter paradise". Behind the mosque, and entered through the neighbouring doorway (no. 56), lurks the **Beit al-Razzaz**, a rambling, derelict palace, also undergoing restoration, though they may let you in for a quick look (no photos allowed for the time being, however).

The Blue Mosque and the Hammam Bashtak

Further along the street, now called **Sharia Bab al-Wazir** after the Gate of the Vizier that once stood here, lies the **"Blue Mosque"** or **Mosque of Aqsunqur**. When originally built in 1347, the mosque was plainer, its *ablaq* arches framing a *sahn*, now battered and dusty, with a palm tree and chirping birds. The Iznik-style tiles (imported from Turkey or Syria) were added in the 1650s by Ibrahim Agha, who usurped and redecorated the fourteenth-century mosque. The indigo and turquoise tiles on the *qibla* wall – with cypresses, tulips and other floral motifs either side of the magnificently inlaid *mihrab* – were added at the same time. Along with similar tiles around the tomb of Ibrahim Agha in the mosque's southwest corner, they were probably made in Damascus, and explain the mosque's name and its popularity with tourists. The marble *minbar*, inlaid with green, grey, salmon and plum stone, is original, as is the recently restored circular minaret, which affords a superb **view** of the Citadel (on a clear day you can even make out the Pyramids).

The mosque's founder, Shams al-Din Aqsunqur, intrigued against the successors of Sultan al-Nasir, his father-in-law. Al-Nasir was succeeded in turn by eight of his sons, one of whom, Al-Ashraf Kuchuk, was enthroned at the age of 6, "reigned" five months, and was strangled by his brother three years later. The reign of another of Al-Nasir's sons, Al-Kamil Sha'ban (not to be confused with Sha'ban II, who erected the Madrassa of Umm Sultan Sha'ban) lasted a year, ending in a palace coup and the crowning of his brother-in-law, Muzaffar Hadji. Muzaffar, recalling how Aqsunqur had manipulated Kuchuk (who's buried just inside the mosque's entrance) and deftly organized the coup against Sha'ban, promptly had him garrotted.

A couple of hundred metres west of the Blue Mosque, the **Hammam Bashtak** was a bathhouse serving the Darb al-Ahmar quarter, many of whose tenements lack washing facilities, but like most of Islamic Cairo's traditional steam bathhouses, it's now closed. Its elaborate portal is worth a second glance, however, the ribbed keel arch bearing the napkin motif (later used for "diamonds" in a pack of playing cards) of a *jamdar* or "Master of Robes". In Mamluke society, this position ranked below the "Men of the Sword" (cabinet ministers, chosen from the Amirs of One Hundred), but was on a par with the sultan's Taster, Cup-Bearer, Slipper-Holder and Polo-Stick Keeper. Several Mamlukes who became sultans included their former rank (or slave price) among their titles.

To reach the Citadel from the hammam, walk 300m down **Sharia Souk es-Silah** (formerly the Weapons Bazaar, now a secondhand ball-bearings market), past the fenced-off gingerbread facade of the **Sabil-Kuttab of Ruqayya Dudu** at no. 41, and the **Madrassa of al-Yusufi**, whose founder was a Cup-Bearer.

The Citadel and around

The **Citadel** is the natural focus of a visit to Islamic Cairo; the area just below it, around Midan Salah al-Din, features two of the city's greatest monuments – the **Sultan Hassan** and **Rifai mosques**. You need a good half a day to do justice to these, and to the Citadel itself. Depending on how much time you have, you may want to visit only the Citadel, but it is well worth stopping in **Midan Salah al-Din** to take in the arresting mix of sounds and the views (see p.158).

To reach the Citadel area, you can either catch a taxi from downtown (£E5–8) or a bus (see p.97 for bus routes) – if you've got the energy, it's also an interesting walk. Any of these approaches will leave you beneath the Citadel, either on Midan Salah al-Din or lower down behind the Sultan Hassan and Rifai mosques. Note, however, that the actual **entrance** to the Citadel is over a kilometre's walk from Midan Salah al-Din, which is where most Cairenes will assume you want to go if you just ask for the Citadel (Al-Qalaa – usually pronounced "al-'alaa").

Of the various routes you could take from the Citadel, the shortest (covered below) takes you to the awesome Mosque of Ibn Tulun, while the longest ones (requiring transport, and covered on pp.165–168) involve the Cities of the Dead. To head back to Bab Zwayla from the Citadel, you could follow the text on pp.150–154 in reverse, picking up the trail at the Blue Mosque.

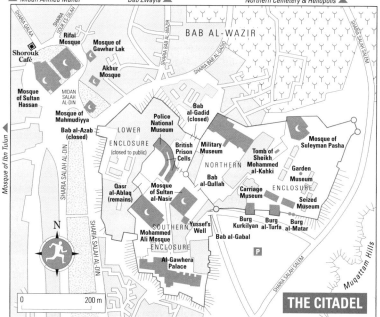

BAB AL-WAZIR

Shorouk Café

Rifai Mosque

Mosque of Gawhar Lak

Akhur Mosque

Mosque of Sultan Hassan

MIDAN SALAH AL-DIN

Mosque of Mahmudiyya

Bab al-Azab (closed)

Police National Museum

LOWER ENCLOSURE (closed to public)

Bab al-Gadid (closed)

British Prison Cells

Military Museum

NORTHERN

Bab al-Qullah

Tomb of Sheikh Mohammed al-Kahki

Mosque of Suleyman Pasha

Garden Museum

ENCLOSURE

Qasr al-Ablaq (remains)

Mosque of Sultan al-Nasir

Carriage Museum

Seized Museum

SOUTHERN

Mohammed Ali Mosque

ENCLOSURE

Yussef's Well

Bab al-Gabal

Burg Kurkilyan

Burg al-Turfa

Burg al-Matar

Al-Gawhera Palace

N

Muqattam Hills

0   200 m

THE CITADEL

Mosque of Ibn Tulun ◄

SHARIA SALAH AL-DIN

SHARIA SALAH SELIM

▼ Southern Cemetery

The Citadel

The Citadel (daily 8am–5pm; mosques closed Fri except for prayer; last entry to museums 30min before closing; £E35, students £E20) presents the most dramatic feature of Cairo's skyline: a centuries-old bastion crowned by the needle-like minarets of the great Mosque of Mohammed Ali. The entrance at Bab al-Gabal is on the opposite side of the Citadel from Midan Salah al-Din, but can be reached by minibus #154 from Abdel Mouneem Riyad terminal near Midan Tahrir, or by service-taxi microbuses from Ramses and Ataba along Sharia Salah Selim.

The whole fortified complex was begun by **Salah al-Din**, the founder of the Ayyubid dynasty – known throughout Christendom as Saladin, the Crusaders' chivalrous foe. Salah al-Din's reign (1171–93) saw much fortification of the city, though it was his nephew, Al-Kamil, who developed the Citadel as a royal residence, later to be replaced by the palaces of Sultan al-Nasir.

The main features of the Citadel as it is today, however, are associated with **Mohammed Ali**, a worthy successor to the Mamlukes and Turks. In 1811 he feasted 470 leading Mamlukes in the Citadel palace, bade them farewell with honours, then had them ambushed in the sloping lane behind the **Bab al-Azab**, the locked gate (now closed to the public) opposite the Akhur Mosque. An oil painting in the Manial Palace on Roda Island depicts the apocryphal tale of a Mamluke who escaped by leaping the walls on his horse; in reality he survived by not attending the feast.

On entering the Citadel, you keep the wall to your right and follow it round into the southern courtyard of the **southern enclosure**, most of whose buildings are currently closed for restoration, among them the former **Mint**. A passage from the courtyard's north side leads through to the central courtyard;

to the left of this passage, stairs lead up to the back of the Citadel's most dominant structure, the Mosque of Mohammed Ali.

Mohammed Ali's monuments

The **Mohammed Ali Mosque**, which so ennobles Cairo's skyline, disappoints at close quarters: its domes are sheathed in tin, its alabaster surfaces grubby. Nonetheless, it exudes *folie de grandeur*, starting with the ornate clock given by France's King Louis Philippe (in exchange for the obelisk in the Place de la Concorde, Paris), which has never worked; and the Turkish Baroque ablutions fountain, resembling a giant Easter egg. Inside the mosque, whose lofty dome and semi-domes are decorated like a Fabergé egg, the use of space is classically Ottoman, reminiscent of the great mosques of Istanbul. A constellation of chandeliers and globe lamps illuminates Thuluth inscriptions, a gold-scalloped *mihrab* and two *minbars*, one faced in alabaster, the other strangely Art Nouveau. Mohammed Ali is buried beneath a white marble cenotaph, behind a bronze grille on the right of the entrance. The mosque itself was erected between 1824 and 1848, but the domes had to be demolished and rebuilt in the 1930s.

Due south of Mohammed Ali's Mosque is the entrance to what remains of his **Al-Gawhara Palace**, also known as the Bijou ("Jewelled") Palace, where he waited while the Mamlukes were butchered. Its French-style salons contain a dusty display of nineteenth-century dress, royal furniture and tableware. The most notable exhibit, however, is a mother-of-pearl model of Jerusalem's Dome of the Rock mosque. Somewhere in this vicinity is the spot where St Francis of Assisi attempted to preach Christianity to the Ayyubid ruler Al-Kamil.

Medieval remains

For an idea of the Citadel's appearance before Mohammed Ali's grandiose reconstruction programme, descend from the Mohammed Ali Mosque's front entrance into the Citadel's central courtyard. On your right, at the end of the passage from the southern courtyard, is the **Mosque of Sultan al-Nasir** (also called the Mosque of Ibn Qalaoun, after Al-Nasir's father). Unlike other Citadel mosques, this one is open to sightseers on Fridays as it is not used for prayers.

The Mamlukes and the Mongols of Persia enjoyed good relations when the mosque was constructed (1318–35), and a Tabriz master mason probably designed the corkscrew minarets with their bulbous finials and faïence decorations, if not the dome, which, though rather unconvincingly restored, also smacks of Central Asia. Since Selim the Grim carted its marble panelling back to Turkey, the mosque's courtyard has looked ruggedly austere, with rough-hewn pillars supporting *ablaq* arches linked by Fatimid-style tie-beams – although the *mihrab* itself is a feast of gold and marble. Notice the stepped merlons around the parapet, and the blue, white and silver decorations beneath the sanctuary *liwan*.

If you leave the mosque, turn right and walk clockwise around it, you'll find a wasteland with barbicans at the far end. There, a locked gate prevents admission to **Yussef's Well**, which spirals down 97m to the level of the Nile, whence water percolates through fissures in the bedrock. Dug by prisoners between 1176 and 1182, this so-called "Well of the Snail" had its steps strewn with soil to provide a footing for the donkeys that carried up water jars. The Citadel's infamous Jubb dungeon, "a noisome pit where foul and deadly exhalations, unclean vermin and bats rendered the pitchy darkness more horrible", was blocked up by Al-Nasir in 1329, but reactivated under the latter-day Mamluke sultans.

The Police National Museum

On the northwestern side of the central enclosure, a gate leads through to another courtyard, at whose northern end is the **Police National Museum**. As you pass through the gateway, the door to your right (with a plaque that reads "Citadel's Prison Museum") leads to **cells** that were used when the Citadel was a prison. Famous detainees included Anwar Sadat, arrested by the British for wartime espionage (see p.193), as well as the Islamist Ayman al-Zawahiri, mentor to Osama Bin Laden. Although the cells are officially closed to the public, police at the entrance may offer to let you in for a look if you show an interest.

The quirky **exhibition** in the museum covers some of Egypt's most sensational murders and assassinations, although the most infamous of all – Anwar Sadat's – is conspicuously absent. The rooms of the main hall, taken clockwise, begin with one on Pharaonic Egypt, including weapons of the time and an explanation of the conspiracy to assassinate Ramses III. The next room, incongruously labelled "Islamic Period", shows photos taken after the assassination of Lord Moyne by members of the maverick Zionist paramilitary group, the Stern Gang, in Zamalek in 1944. Also featured here are 1940s Assyut gangster Al-Khott, and female serial killers Rayya and Sakina, whose grizzly murders of nearly thirty young girls for their jewellery led to the duo's execution in 1921. The next room has a scale model of Ismailiya barracks illustrating the 1952 Battle of Ismailiya (see box, p.651) that galvanized public opinion against the British occupation. The "Forgery and Counterfeiting" room contains the death mask of murderer Mahmoud Amin Mahmoud Soleiman, as well as a press for counterfeiting banknotes. Fake ancient coins appear in the "Confiscations" room, along with ancient artefacts seized from smugglers attempting to export them illegally.

There is a superb **view** of the entire city from the terrace outside the Police Museum, where you'll also find toilets and a **café**. At the southern end, in a pit, are the excavated remains of the **Qasr al-Ablaq**, or Striped Palace of Sultan al-Nasir. For many of the hapless boy-sultans chosen by the Mamlukes, the palace amounted to a luxury prison, and finally an execution cell. Nevertheless, the Citadel remained the residence of Egypt's rulers for nearly 700 years, and Mohammed Ali prophesied that his descendants would rule supreme as long as they resided here. Ismail's move to the Abdin Palace did indeed foreshadow an inexorable decline in their power.

The Northern Enclosure

Passing through the Bab al-Qullah, you'll enter the Citadel's northern enclosure, open to visitors despite a military presence. Straight ahead, beyond a parade of Soviet- and US-made tanks from four Arab–Israeli Wars, is Mohammed Ali's old Harim Palace, occupied by the **Military Museum**. Its vast exhibition devotes more space to ceremonial accoutrements than the savage realities of war, and even pacifists should enjoy the main salon, with its spectacular trompe l'oeil. While in a military vein, it's worth recalling that the Citadel fell to Mohammed Ali after he stationed cannons on the Muqattam heights. The military electronics that festoon them now are a reminder that strategic ground seldom loses its utility.

By turning right at the barracks near the enclosure entrance and following the lane around, you'll come out into a compound with a formal garden. This **"Garden Museum"** is unshaded but decorated with assorted columns, the odd nineteenth-century gateway, and – its centrepiece – the top of a minaret from the 1441 mosque of Qaitbey al-Jatkasi. To its south is the **Carriage**

Museum, with its row of horseheads. Inside are six royal carriages and two picnic buggies, one of them an infant prince's; the largest state carriage – heavy with gold – was presented as a gift to Khedive Ismail by Napoleon and his wife, Empress Eugénie.

Just beyond is the small **Seized Museum** (closed at the time of writing), displaying various pharaonic, Roman, Coptic and Islamic antiquities recovered from smugglers before they left Egypt. Exhibits in the first room include, in the first display case on the right, the mummy of an ibis before which sits a little man in supplication, plus whole sarcophagi from the late Pharaonic period. The second room contains Coptic icons, antique manuscripts, glassware and pistols, all charmingly labelled "misdemeanor no. 738", "misdemeanor no. 1296" and the like.

Behind here are two of the many bastions along the Citadel's ramparts, each with evocative names. Although the derivation of **Burg Kirkilyan** (Tower of the Forty Serpents) is unknown, the **Burg al-Matar** (Tower of the Place of Flight) probably housed the royal carrier pigeons. Neither can be entered, but it's worth visiting a neglected treasure at the other end of the compound. A cluster of verdigris domes and a pencil-sharp minaret identify the **Mosque of Suleyman Pasha** as an early sixteenth-century Ottoman creation, borne out by the lavish arabesques and rosettes adorning the interior of the cupola and semi-domes. Inside, cross the courtyard to find a **mausoleum** where the tombs of amirs and their families have *tabuts* indicating their rank: turbans or hats for the men, floral-patterned *lingam*-like rods for the women. Adjacent to the courtyard is a *madrassa* where students took examinations beneath a *riwaq* upheld by painted beams.

Midan Salah al-Din

Humdrum traffic islands and monumental grandeur meet beneath the Citadel on **Midan Salah al-Din**, where makeshift swings and colourful tents are pitched for local moulids. With an audience of lesser mosques on the sidelines, the scene is set for a confrontation of the square's two behemoths, given voice when the muezzins call. Both the **Rifai** and **Sultan Hassan mosques** have powerfully voiced muezzins whose duet echoes off the surrounding tenements. This amazing aural experience is best enjoyed from one of the seats on the sidewalk outside the **Shorouk coffee shop**, on the corner of Sharia Sultan Hassan and Sharia Qalaa; check prayer times in the newspapers or by asking around. From this vantage point you can survey both mosques, built so close as to create a knife-sharp, almost perpetually shadowed canyon between them. The dramatic angles and chiaroscuro, coupled with the great stalactite portal on this side of the Rifai, make this facade truly spectacular, although the view from the Citadel itself takes some beating. A few centuries ago, all this area would have been swarming with mounted Mamlukes, escorting the sultan to polo matches or prayers.

The Mosque of Sultan Hassan

Raised at the command of a son of Al-Nasir, the **Mosque of Sultan Hassan** (daily except Fri 8am–4.30pm, Fri 8–10am & 3–4.30pm; £E12, students £E6) was unprecedentedly huge in scale when it was begun in 1356, and some design flaws soon became apparent. The plan to have a minaret at each corner was abandoned after the one directly above the entrance collapsed, killing 300 people. Hassan himself was assassinated in 1391, two years before the mosque's completion. After another minaret toppled in 1659, the weakened dome collapsed; and if this wasn't enough, the roof was also used as an artillery platform during coups against sultans Barquq (1391) and Tumanbey (1517). But the mosque is big enough to withstand a lot of battering: at 150m in length, it covers an area of 7906 square metres, with walls rising to 36m and its tallest minaret to 68m.

The mosque is best seen when the morning sun illuminates its deep courtyard and cavernous mausoleum, revealing subtle colours and textures disguised by shadows later in the day. Entering beneath a towering stalactite hood, you're drawn by instinct through a gloomy domed vestibule with *liwans*, out into the central **sahn** – a stupendous balancing of mass and void. Vaulted **liwans** soar on four sides, their height emphasized by hanging lamp chains, their maws by red-and-black rims, all set off by a bulbous-domed ablutions fountain (probably an Ottoman addition). Each *liwan* was devoted to teaching a rite of Sunni Islam, providing theological justification for the cruciform plan the Mamlukes strove to achieve regardless of the site. At Sultan Hassan, four *madrassas* have been skilfully fitted into an irregular area behind the *liwans* to maintain the internal cruciform.

Soft-hued marble inlay and a band of monumental Kufic script distinguish the sanctuary *liwan* from its roughly plastered neighbours. To the right of the *mihrab* is a bronze door, exquisitely worked with radiating stars and satellites in gold and silver; on the other side is **Hassan's mausoleum**, cleverly sited to derive *baraka* from prayers to Mecca while overlooking his old stamping grounds. The mausoleum is sombre beneath its restored dome, upheld by stalactite pendentives. Around the chamber runs a carved and painted Thuluth inscription, from the Throne verse of the Koran. Note also the ivory-inlaid *kursi*, or Koranic lectern.

The Rifai and Amir Akhur mosques

Adjoining Sultan Hassan, the **Rifai Mosque** (daily except Fri 8am–4.30pm, Fri 8–10am & 3–4.30pm; £E12, students £E6) is pseudo-Mamluke, built between 1869 and 1912 for Princess Khushyar, the mother of Khedive Ismail. With the royal entrance now closed, you enter on the side facing Sultan Hassan. Straight ahead in a sandalwood enclosure lies the **tomb of Sheikh Ali al-Rifai**, founder of the Rifai *tariqa* of dervishes, whose mould occurs during Gumad el-Tani (see p.259). Off to your left are the *mashrabiya*-screened **tombs of King Fouad** (reigned 1917–36), his mother, the last **Shah of Iran** and **King Farouk** of Egypt (who likewise died in exile). The monumental sanctuary (on the left) is impressive, but after Ismail's chief eunuch had overseen its forty-four columns, nineteen types of marble, eighteen window grilles costing £E1000 apiece, and £E25,000 dispersed on gold leaf, dowdiness was scarcely possible: what it lacks is the power of simplicity embodied by the mosques of Ibn Tulun and Sultan Hassan.

Finally, facing the Citadel, you can't miss the **Mosque of Amir Akhur** (on the left), with its bold red-and-white *ablaq*, breast-like dome and double minaret finial, incorporating a *sabil-kuttab* at the lower end of its sloping site.

The Mosque of Ibn Tulun and the Saiyida Zeinab quarter

Two aspects of Islam are strikingly apparent in the great **Mosque of Ibn Tulun** and the quarter of the city named after Egypt's beloved saint, **Saiyida Zeinab**. The mosque evokes the simplicity of Islam's central tenet, submission to Allah, whereas the surrounding neighbourhoods are urban stews seething with popular cults. **Zeinab's moulid** is the wildest festival in Cairo, its high-octane blend of intense devotion and sheer enjoyment is also characteristic of other moulids

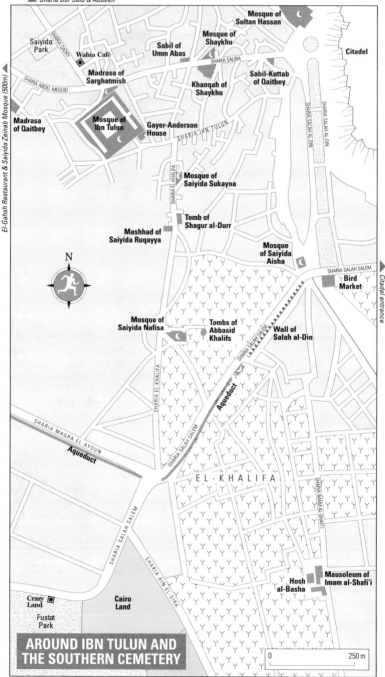

CAIRO AND THE PYRAMIDS | Islamic Cairo

El-Gahsh Restaurant & Saiyida Zeinab Mosque (500m) ◀

Mosque of
Sultan Hassan

Mosque of
Shaykhu

Saiyida
Park

Wahia Café

Sabil of
Umm Abas

SHARIA QADRY

SHARIA SALIBA

Citadel

Madrasa of
Sarghatmish

SHARIA ABDEL MEGUID

Sabil-Kuttab
of Qaitbey

Khanqah of
Shaykhu

Madrasa
of Qaitbey

Mosque of
Ibn Tulun

Gayer-Anderson
House

SHARIA IBN TULUN

SHARIA SALAH AL-DIN

N

Mosque of
Saiyida Sukayna

SHARIA EL KHALIFA

Tomb of
Shagur al-Durr

Mashhad of
Saiyida Ruqayya

Mosque
of Saiyida
Aisha

SHARIA SALAH SALEM

Bird
Market

Mosque of
Saiyida Nafisa

Tombs of
Abbasid
Khalifs

Wall of
Salah al-Din

SHARIA SALAH SALEM

Aqueduct

SHARIA EL KHALIFA

SHARIA MAGRA EL-AYOUN

Aqueduct

SHARIA SALAH SALEM

E L - K H A L I F A

SHARIA IMAM AL-SHAFI'I

Crazy
Land

Fustat
Park

Cairo
Land

SHARIA SALAH SALEM

SHARIA AIN EL-SIRA

Hosh
al-Basha

Mausoleum of
Imam al-Shafi'i

▶ *Citadel entrance*

**AROUND IBN TULUN AND
THE SOUTHERN CEMETERY**

0   250 m

▼ *Al-Basatin*

honouring Saiyida Nafisa, Ruqayya and Aisha, whose shrines lie between Ibn Tulun and El-Khalifa (the Southern Cemetery).

The following section covers only Ibn Tulun, Saiyida Zeinab and sites along Sharia Saliba. You could conceivably visit all of them in a single day. Buses #72// and #160/ provide the easiest access to Saiyida Zeinab **from Midan Tahrir**, running through the quarter past its namesake shrine and within sight of Ibn Tulun's Mosque, towards the Citadel, and on to the Mausoleum of Al-Shafi' in the Southern Cemetery. Alternatively, ride the metro to Saiyida Zeinab station, five minutes' walk from Midan Saiyida Zeinab at the heart of the quarter, or take bus #840 which runs **from Midan Ataba**.

Along Sharia Saliba

The fifteen-minute walk from the Mosque of Sultan Hassan to Ibn Tulun takes you along **Sharia Saliba**, past a prison that serves as a barometer of law and order: whenever there's been a crackdown you can see several arms thrust from each cell window. Next comes the lofty **Sabil–Kuttab of Qaitbey**, with its bold red, white and black facade, now beautifully restored and housing an Islamic Civilization Library. Further along, beyond the **Khanqah of Shaykhu** (currently under restoration), Sharia el-Khalifa turns off towards the Southern Cemetery, as described on p.164. By ignoring this and carrying on past the nineteenth-century **sabil of Umm Abbas**, with its blue-and-red panels and gilt calligraphy, you'll see the huge walls of Ibn Tulun's Mosque on the left. Its entrance is that way, too.

The portal on the main street belongs not to Ibn Tulun but to the neighbouring, recently restored **Madrassa of Sarghatmish**. Its courtyard, resplendent in white marble inlaid with red, black and green porphyry, is absolutely stunning, with a cool, light feel that makes a pleasant change from the rather heavy architecture of Cairo's classic mosques. It centres around a fountain surmounted with an *oba* (canopy), and surrounded by the cell-like quarters formerly used by its students. The Sarghatmish who had the *madrassa* built, a Mamluke commander assassinated on the orders of Sultan Hassan in 1358, is interred in a chamber adjoining the courtyard.

The Mosque of Ibn Tulun

Ibn Tulun's Mosque (daily 8am–5pm; no entry fee) is a rare survivor of the classical Islamic period of the ninth and tenth centuries, when the Abbasid caliphs ruled the Muslim world from Iraq. Their purpose-built capital, Samarra, centred upon a congregational mosque where the entire population assembled for Friday prayer, and this most likely provided the inspiration for the Ibn Tulun. You enter the mosque via a **ziyada**, or enclosure, designed to distance the mosque from its surroundings; to the left stands the Gayer-Anderson House (see p.162). It's only within the inner walls that the vastness of the mosque becomes apparent: the courtyard is 92m square, while the complex measures 140m by 122m.

Besides its sheer size, the **mosque** impresses by its simplicity. Its vast courtyard, open to the sky, has the grandeur of a desert where all of Allah's worshippers are prostrated equally beneath the sun. Ibn Tulun's architects understood the power of repetition – see how the merlons echo the rhythm of the arcades – and also restraint: small floral capitals and stucco rosettes seem at first glance to be the only decorative motifs. Beneath the arcades you'll find a sycamore-wood frieze over 2km long, relating roughly one-fifth of the Koran in Kufic script. The severely geometric ablutions fountain, an inspired focal point, was added in the thirteenth century, when the *mihrab* was also jazzed up with marble and glass mosaics – the only unsuccessful note in the complex.

Ibn Tulun and Al-Qitai

It was from Iraq that the Abbasids made **Ahmed Ibn Tulun** governor of Fustat in 868, and smarted as he declared his independence. Ibn Tulun (the "Son of Tulun", a Turkish slave) founded the Tulunid dynasty that ruled Egypt until 905, and established a new city to the northeast of Fustat. According to legends, Noah's Ark had come to rest on this site when the Flood receded; Moses confronted the pharaoh's magicians here; and Abraham had been ready to sacrifice his son on a nearby hillock. Unperturbed by this, nor by the existence of Christian and Jewish cemeteries on the site, he dictated the construction of **Al-Qitai** ("the Wards", so called after its division into military cantonments).

Ibn Tulun's performance on the polo field filled his doctors with foreboding, for in sickness he "refused to follow their orders, flouted their prescribed diet, and when he found himself still sinking, he had their heads chopped off, or flogged them till they died". But under his soft-living successor the Al-Qitai midan was converted into a garden with a silver lake, where the insomniac Khomaruya lolled on an airbed guarded by a blue-eyed lion. The Tulunids could afford such luxury, for their annual revenue amounted to 4,300,000 dinars.

When the Abbasids subsequently reconquered Egypt in 905, they destroyed everything here but the mosque, which became derelict. Exploited as a makeshift caravanserai and a hideout for bodysnatchers during the terrible famine of 1200, it was belatedly restored in 1296 by Sultan Laghin, who had hidden there as an amir suspected of murdering the sultan.

The **minaret** (entered from the mosque's outer courtyard) is unique for its exterior spiral staircase, which gives the structure a helical shape. Supposedly, Ibn Tulun twisted a scrap of paper into a spiral, and then justified his absent-minded deed by presenting it as the design for a minaret. But the great minaret at Samarra (itself influenced by ancient Babylonian ziggurats) seems a likelier source of inspiration. Expect to pay baksheesh to climb the minaret, and for looking after your shoes or providing shoe covers, but resist excessive demands, especially if you are told (falsely) that they are official charges.

The Gayer-Anderson House

From the *ziyada* of the Ibn Tulun Mosque, a sign directs you to the **Gayer-Anderson House** (daily 8.30am–4.30pm; £E30, students £E15, video camera £E20), otherwise known as the Beit al-Kritiliya ("House of the Cretan Woman"), which abuts the southeast corner of the mosque.

Gayer-Anderson was a retired British major who, during the 1930s and 1940s, refurbished two mansions dating from the sixteenth and eighteenth centuries, filling them with Oriental bric-a-brac. Among the many paintings here is a self-portrait of Gayer-Anderson wearing a pharaonic headdress. **Tours** of the house (the buildings are linked by a passage on the third floor) are conducted by charming curators. There are Persian, Chinese and Queen Anne rooms, and an amazing guest bedroom named after Damascus, whence its opulent wooden panelling originated. It's possible to sneak through a camouflaged *dulab* (wall cupboard) into the screened gallery overlooking the *salamlik*, as women did in olden days. With its polychrome fountain, decorated ceiling and kilim-covered pillows, this is the finest reception hall left in Islamic Cairo, and served as the set for a tryst and murder in the James Bond film *The Spy Who Loved Me*.

Saiyida Zeinab

The backstreets west of Ibn Tulun harbour another gem of Islamic architecture in the **Madrassa of Qaitbey**. Ignore the dust and grime and tip the curator to unlock the building, whose mosaic floors and *minbar* are superb examples of fifteenth-century craftsmanship.

Real aficionados can also track down other monuments in the area, as detailed in the AUC's *Islamic Monuments in Cairo* guide. Otherwise, head further west into the densely populated **Saiyida Zeinab quarter**, where Islamic and modern Cairo merge in a confusion of tenement blocks and **markets**. Midan Lazoghli, on the edge of the Abdin quarter, hosts a daily car spares and repairs souk, while a **bird market** is held beneath an overpass in the direction of Qasr al-Aini Hospital on Mondays and Thursdays – hence its name, the Souk Itnayn w Khamis. Like Saiyida Zeinab metro station, the market is on the quarter's periphery, where it merges with Garden City and Old Cairo (see map on p.170). To the northeast of the slaughterhouse district and the Al-Abdin Mosque, at 2 Sharia Bayram el-Tonsi, is the **Brooke Hospital for Animals** (see box, p.45; visits possible daily 9am–4pm; ☎02/364-9312).

The quarter's highlight is the annual **Moulid of Saiyida Zeinab**, which features parades of Sufi orders by day and nocturnal festivities that attract half a million people. Ecstatic devotion and pleasure rub shoulders (and other parts of the anatomy, if you're a woman) in this seething, mostly male crowd, transfixed by the music and spectacles. To see the *zikrs*, snake charmers, conjurers, nail-swallowers and dancing horses performing, you'll have to force your way through a scrum of people and tents – don't bring any valuables. The fifteen-day event takes place during Ragab, the seventh month of the Muslim calendar.

The focal point for these celebrations is the **Mosque of Saiyida Zeinab** (closed to non-Muslims), off Sharia Bur Said. Zeinab, born in 628 AD, was the Prophet's granddaughter; she emigrated to Fustat after the Umayyads slew her brother, Hussein, and died there shortly afterwards. For Egyptian Muslims, especially women, Zeinab is a protectress whose *baraka* is sought in matters of fortune and health – in other words, a popular saint. Although the Koran forbids the deification of mortals, the human urge to anthropomorphize religious faith seems irresistible. Every Muslim nation has its own "saints" (chosen by popular acclaim rather than a supreme authority) and respects bloodlines descended from the Prophet or his immediate kin. For the Shia, the martyrdom of Ali and Hussein is a parable of their own oppression, while Zeinab (whose moulid attracts foreign Shia) is honoured as their closest kinswoman.

Before heading back into town, you might want to try one of Saiyida Zeinab's many cheap but renowned **eating places**, for more on which see p.235. To return to downtown Cairo from here, catch a bus or minibus from Sharia Khayrat opposite Zeinab's Mosque, or ask for directions to the nearest metro entrance (ten minutes' walk). From Saiyida Zeinab or Saad Zaghloul (which is as near) you can take the metro north to Tahrir or Ramses, or south to Old Cairo (Mari Girgis station).

Cities of the Dead

It's thought that at least 500,000 Cairenes live amid the **Cities of the Dead**, two vast cemeteries that stretch away from the Citadel to merge with newer shantytowns below the Muqattam. The Southern Cemetery, sprawling to the southeast of Ibn Tulun's mosque, is only visible from the Muqattam, or at close quarters. The Northern Cemetery, by contrast, is an unforgettably eerie sight, with dozens of mausoleums rising from a sea of dwellings along the road from Cairo Airport.

Although tourists generally – and understandably – feel uneasy about viewing the cemeteries' splendid **funerary architecture** with squatters living all around or in the tombs, few natives regard the Cities of the Dead as forbidding places. Egyptians have a long tradition of building "houses" near their ancestral graves and picnicking or even staying there overnight; other families have simply occupied them. By Cairene standards these are poor but decent neighbourhoods, with shops, schools and electricity, maybe even piped water and sewers. The saints buried here provide a moral touchstone and *baraka* for their communities, who honour them with **moulids**.

Though these are generally not dangerous quarters, it's best to exercise some caution when **visiting**. Don't flaunt money or costly possessions, and be sure to dress modestly; women should have a male escort, and will seem more respectable if wearing a headscarf. By responding to local kids (who may request baksheesh) with the right blend of authority and affection, you can win the sympathy of their elders and seem less of an intruder; react wrongly, and you might be stoned out of the neighbourhood. You'll be marginally less conspicuous on Fridays, when many Cairenes visit their family plots; but remember that mosques can't be entered during midday prayers. At all events, leave the cemeteries well before dark, if only to avoid getting lost in their labyrinthine alleys – and don't stray to the east into the inchoate (and far riskier) slums built around the foothills of the Muqattam.

The Southern Cemetery

The older and larger **Southern Cemetery** is broadly synonymous with the residential quarter of **El-Khalifa**, named after the Abbasid caliphs buried amid its mud-brick tenements. The area is noted for drug dealing and quite unsafe after dark. Although the Abbasid tombs aren't half as imposing as those of the Mamlukes in the Northern Cemetery, one of the approach routes passes several shrines famous for their moulids. Another moulid is held at the beautiful **Mausoleum of Imam al-Shafi'i**, which is best reached by bus as a separate excursion. For this reason, we've described two different routes into what Egyptians call "the Great Cemetery" (Al-Qarafah al-Kubra).

Sharia Saliba to the Tomb of the Abbasid Khalifs

This walking route passes through one of the oldest poor neighbourhoods in Cairo, where it's thought that people started settling around their saints' graves as early as the tenth century. None of the tombs is remarkable visually, but the stories and moulids attached to them are interesting.

The trail begins where **Sharia el-Khalifa** turns south off Sharia Saliba, just after the Khanqah of Shaykhu (see map on p.160). This narrow street passes a succession of tombs. The second on the left, within a yellow-and-white mosque (currently undergoing refurbishment), is that of **Saiyida Sukayna**, a great-granddaughter of Mohammed, whose moulid (held during Rabi el-Tani) is attended by several thousand locals and features traditional entertainments like dancing horses and stick-twisters.

Such saintly graves invariably acquired an oratory (*mashhad*) or mosque, unlike the **Tomb of Shagar al-Durr**, 100m further on, a derelict edifice sunk below street level. Shagar al-Durr (Tree of Pearls) was the widow of Sultan Ayyub, who ruled as sultana of Egypt for eighty days (1249–50) until the Abbasid caliph pronounced "Woe unto nations ruled by a woman". This compelled her to marry Aybak, the first Mamluke sultan, and govern "from behind the *mashrabiya*". In 1257 she ordered Aybak's murder after learning that he sought another wife, but then tried to save him; the assassins cried, "If we stop halfway through, he will kill both you and us!" Rejecting her offer to marry Qutuz, their new leader, the Mamlukes handed Shagar al-Durr over to Aybak's former wife, whose servants beat her to death with bath clogs and threw her body to the jackals. Now totally gutted, her locked tomb once contained a *tabut* inscribed: "Oh you who stand beside my grave, show not surprise at my condition. Yesterday I was like you, tomorrow, you will be like me."

Slightly further down and across the street, the **Mashhad of Saiyida Ruqayya** commemorates the stepsister of Saiyida Zeinab, with whom she came to Egypt; the name of her father, Ali, adorns its rare Fatimid *mihrab*, and the devotion she inspires is particularly evident during Ruqayya's moulid.

Ruqayya's devotion doesn't, however, compare with that accorded to the **Mosque of Saiyida Nafisa**, 100m to the south, by a roundabout planted with grass and flowers. This, Egypt's third-holiest shrine, is closed to non-Muslims, though visitors can still appreciate the good-natured crowd that hangs around after Friday noon prayers, or during Nafisa's moulid (see p.259). Honoured during her lifetime as a descendant of the Prophet, a *hafizat al-Qur'an* (one who knows the Koran by heart) and a friend of Imam al-Shafi'i, Nafisa was famed for working miracles and conferring *baraka*. Her shrine has been repeatedly enlarged since Fatimid times – the Southern Cemetery possibly began with devotees settling or being buried near her grave – and the present mosque was built in 1897.

If you walk down the alley to its left, and through the passage beyond, a green-painted gate to the right (just before the street turns) leads to a compound enclosing the **Tombs of the Abbasid Caliphs** (daily 9am–5pm; the caretaker will let you in for a small consideration). Having been driven from Baghdad by the Mongols, the caliphs gratefully accepted Beybars' offer to re-establish them in Egypt, only to discover that they were mere puppets. Beybars appropriated the domed mausoleum (usually kept locked) for his own sons; the caliphs were buried outdoors in less than grandiose tombs. Notice the beautiful foliate Kufic inscription on the cenotaph of Khadiga, under the wooden shed. In 1517 the last Abbasid caliph was formally divested of his office, which the Ottomans assumed in 1538 and Ataturk abolished in the 1920s.

An alternative route back towards the Citadel passes the **Mosque of Saiyida Aisha**, whose **moulid** occurs during Sha'ban. To get there, retrace your steps to the junction just south of Ruqayya's shrine and take the road leading off to the right. It's roughly 500 metres' walk to Aisha's Mosque. From there, Sharia Salah Salem runs southwest alongside the medieval **Wall of Salah al-Din**, and northeast to the Citadel entrance at Bab al-Gabal, while Sharia Salah al-Din leads north to Midan Salah al-Din. If you happen to be here on Friday, consider making a detour to the **bird market** (Souk al-Asafeer or Souk al-Gom'a), held on a side street to the south of the Salah Salem overpass.

The Mausoleum of Imam al-Shafi'i

Imam al-Shafi'i, revered as the founder of one of the four Sunni schools of Islamic law, occupies a great mausoleum 2km from the Citadel. Other than by catching a taxi from there (for about £E3–5), you can reach the mausoleum on bus #81 or #89 from Midan Ataba, or bus #160 from Midan Ramses, or more comfortable #154 minibuses from Abdel Mouneem Riyad, which turn off Sharia Imam al-Shafi'i 100m short of the mausoleum. If you miss the turn-off, ride on to the terminal, have a glass of tea with the driver, and get dropped at the corner on the way back.

Recognizable by its graceful dome, crowned by a metal boat like a weather vane, the **Mausoleum of Imam al-Shafi'i** lurks beside a mosque at the end of the street. The largest Islamic mortuary complex in Egypt, it was raised in 1211 by Al-Kamil, Salah al-Din's nephew, a propagator of Sunni orthodoxy, like the imam himself (who died in 820). Al-Shafi'i's teak cenotaph – into which the faithful slip petitions – lies beneath a magnificent dome perched on stalactite squinches and painted red and blue, with gilt designs. The walls are clad in variegated marble, dating from Qaitbey's restoration of the building in the 1480s. In times past, the boat on the roof was filled with birdseed and water; boats are vehicles of spiritual enlightenment in Islamic symbolism, while birds are associated with souls. Al-Shafi'i's **moulid** (see p.259) attracts many sick and infirm people, seeking his *baraka*. More prosaically, the street leading northwards to the mausoleum from the Al-Basatin quarter is used for scrap, clothing and livestock **markets** every Friday morning.

By walking clockwise around the block in which the Imam's mausoleum is located, you'll find a five-domed complex directly behind it. Inside the courtyard are clumps of cenotaphs decorated with garlands and fronds, topped by a turban, fez or other headdress to indicate the deceased's rank. These constitute the **Hosh al-Basha**, where Mohammed Ali's sons, their wives, children and retainers are buried. The conspicuously plain cenotaph belongs to a princess with radical sympathies, who abhorred ostentation. In a separate room, forty statues commemorate the 470 Mamlukes butchered by Mohammed Ali in the Citadel (see p.155).

The Northern Cemetery

The finest of Cairo's funerary monuments – erected by the Burgi Mamlukes from the fourteenth to sixteenth centuries – are spread around the **Northern Cemetery**. The majority of tourists who venture in from Sharia Salah Salem are content to see three main sites, plus whatever crops up in between, over an hour or so.

Aside from catching a taxi (ask for the *al-qarafat ash-sharqiyyah* – Eastern Cemetery – in Arabic), the surest way of **getting there** is to walk from Al-Azhar. This will take around fifteen minutes, following the dual carriageway Bab al-Ghuriyab past university buildings and uphill to its roundabout junction with Salah Salem. Although the tombs of Anuk and Tulbey are among the nearby mausoleums, you might prefer to head 250m north along the highway to the Dirasa bus terminal – also accessible by minibus #102 **from Midan Tahrir** or minibus #10 **from Ramses and Ataba** – and then cut east into the cemetery. That way you start with Qaitbey's Mausoleum, whose ornate dome and minaret are clearly visible. Dirasa can also be reached by service-taxi microbus from Midan Ramses.

Sultan Qaitbey's Mausoleum

Sultan Qaitbey was the last strong Mamluke ruler and a prolific builder of monuments from Mecca to Syria; his funerary complex (depicted on £E1 notes) is among the grandest in the Northern Cemetery. His name means "the restored" or "returned", indicating that he nearly died at birth; as a scrawny lad, he fetched only fifty dinars in the slave market. The rapid turnover in rulers after 1437 accelerated his ascent, and in 1468 he was acclaimed as sultan by the bodyguard of the previous incumbent, an old comrade-in-arms who parted from Qaitbey with tears and embraces. His 28-year reign was only exceeded by Al-Nasir's, and Qaitbey remained "tall, handsome and upright as a reed" well into his eighties, still attentive to citizens' complaints at twice-weekly *diwaniyyas*.

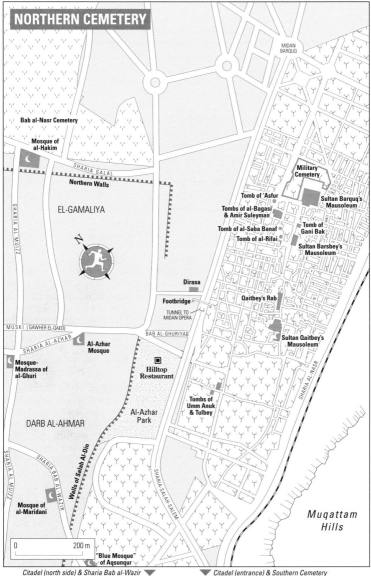

Abbassiya & Heliopolis ▲

NORTHERN CEMETERY

MIDAN
BARQUQ

Bab al-Nasr Cemetery

Mosque of
al-Hakim

SHARIA GALAL

Northern Walls

Military
Cemetery

Tomb of 'Asfur

Sultan Barquq's
Mausoleum

EL-GAMALIYA

Tombs of al-Bagasi
& Amir Suleyman

Tomb of al-Saba Banat

Tomb of
Gani Bak

Tomb of al-Rifai

Sultan Barsbey's
Mausoleum

SHARIA AL MUIZZ

N

Dirasa

Footbridge

Qaitbey's Rab

TUNNEL TO
MIDAN OPERA

MUSKI (GAWHER EL-QAED)

BAB AL-GHURIYAB

SHARIA AL-AZHAR

Al-Azhar
Mosque

Sultan Qaitbey's
Mausoleum

Mosque-
Madrassa of
al-Ghuri

Hilltop
Restaurant

SHARIA AL-NASR

DARB AL-AHMAR

Al-Azhar
Park

Tombs of
Umm Anuk
& Tulbey

SHARIA BAB AL-WAZIR

SHARIA AL MUIZZ

Walls of Salah Al-Din

SHARIA SALAH SALEM

SHARIA SALAH AL-DIN

Mosque of
al-Maridani

Muqattam
Hills

0   200 m

"Blue Mosque"
of Aqsunqur

Citadel (north side) & Sharia Bab al-Wazir ▼   ▼ Citadel (entrance) & Southern Cemetery

An irregularly shaped complex built in 1474, the **Mausoleum of Sultan Qaitbey** (daily 9am–5pm) is dynamically unified by the bold stripes along its facade, which is best viewed from the north. The trilobed portal carries one's eye to the graceful **minaret**, soaring through fluted niches, stalactite brackets and balconies to a teardrop finial. Inside, the *madrassa liwans*, floors and walls are a feast of marble and geometric patterns, topped by elaborately carved and gilded ceilings, with a lovely octagonal roof lantern. Qaitbey's **tomb chamber** off the prayer hall is similarly decorated, its lofty dome upheld by squinches. One of Mohammed's footprints, brought over from Mecca, is also preserved in the tomb chamber. Ask to climb the minaret for a close view of the marvellous stone carving on the dome's exterior: a raised star-pattern is superimposed over an incised floral one, the two designs shifting as the shadows change. From this minaret vantage point you could also plot a course to Barsbey's complex, further up the narrow, winding street.

The Barsbey and Barquq complexes

As the street jinks northwards from Qaitbey's Mausoleum it passes (on the left) the apartment building that Qaitbey deeded to provide income for the building's upkeep and employment for poor relations. Such bequests could not be confiscated, unlike merchants' and Mamlukes' personal wealth, which partly financed the **Mausoleum of Sultan al-Ashraf Barsbey** (daily 9am–8pm), 200m beyond the building. Barsbey was the sultan who acquired young Qaitbey at a knockdown rate. He himself had been purchased in Damascus for eight hundred dinars, but was "returned to the broker for a filmy defect in one of his blue eyes". Unlike other sultans, who milked the economy, Barsbey troubled to pay his Mamlukes regularly and the reign (1422–38) of this well-spoken teetotaller was characterized by "extreme security and low prices".

Based on a now-ruined *khanqah*, the complex was expanded to include a mausoleum and mosque-*madrassa* (1432) after Barsbey's funerary pile near Khan el-Khalili was found lacking. If there's a curator around, ask him to lift the mat hiding the marble mosaic floor inside the long mosque, which also features a superb *minbar*. At the northern end, a great dome caps Barsbey's tomb, its marble cenotaph and mother-of-pearl-inlaid *mihrab* softly lit by stained-glass windows, added at a later date. The stone carving on the dome's exterior marks a transition between the early chevron patterns and the fluid designs on Qaitbey's Mausoleum. Fifty metres up the street, another finely carved dome surmounts the **Tomb of Gani Bak**, a favourite of Barsbey's, whose mosque stands near the Saddlemakers Bazaar.

The third – and oldest – of the great funerary complexes can be found 50m further north, on the far side of a square with a direct through-road onto Sharia Salah Salem. Recognizable by its twin domes and minarets, the **Mausoleum of Sultan Barquq** (daily 9am–8pm) was the first royal tomb in a cemetery that was previously noted for the graves of Sufi sheikhs. Its courtyard is plain, with stunted tamarisks, but the proud chevron-patterned domes above the sanctuary *liwan* uplift the whole ensemble. Barquq and his son Farag are buried in the northern tomb chamber, his daughters Shiriz and Shakra in the southern one, with their faithful nurse in the corner. Both are soaring structures preceded by *mashrabiyas* with designs similar to the window screens in Barquq's *madrassa* on Sharia al-Muizz (see p.138). The sinuously carved *minbar* was donated by Qaitbey to what was then a Sufi *khanqah*; stairs in the northwest corner of the courtyard lead to a warren of dervish cells on the upper floors, long since deserted.

The complex was actually erected by Farag, who transferred his father's body here from the *madrassa*. Farag was crowned at the age of 10 and deposed and killed in Syria after thirteen years of civil strife: it's amazing that the mausoleum was finally completed in 1411.

Depending on your route out, you might pass the minor **tombs of Barsbey al-Bagasi and Amir Suleyman**, or those of **Princess Tulbey and Umm Anuk**, nearer Bab al-Ghuriyab and visible from the highway.

Across Sharia Salah Salem from the northern cemetery, its entrance about 200m south of Dirasa, and 500m north of the Citadel's Bab Gadid, is the new and very welcome **Al-Azhar Park** (daily: summer 9am–2am; winter 9am–midnight; £E10). Funded by a $45million grant from the Aga Khan Trust, the park is part of a regeneration project for the Darb al-Ahmar area, and was built on the site of a filthy and rather dangerous stretch of waste ground, used as a rubbish dump and the haunt of junkies. Now all that has changed: in its place is a scrupulously kept recreational area that has provided local employment and given one of Cairo's most deprived areas a new lease of life. Scattered around the park's lawns and fountains are trees, plants and shrubs from around the world, all labelled, while the western boundary includes a 1300-metre stretch of Ayyubid city wall, most of it newly uncovered during construction of the park, and whose bastions will be open to the public when work is complete. The park also contains a lakeside café and a classy **restaurant** (see p.235), and its highest point offers a panoramic view over Islamic Cairo, especially impressive at night when many monuments are illuminated.

Old Cairo, Roda Island and the southern suburbs

The southern sector of the city is divisible into three main areas, the most interesting of which is **Old Cairo** (Masr al-Qadima). Depending on whether it's broadly or narrowly defined, Old Cairo covers everything south of Garden City and Saiyida Zeinab – from the slaughterhouse district beside the Mamluke Aqueduct out to the ancient Jewish cemetery of Al-Basatin – or a relatively small area near the Mari Girgis metro station, known to foreigners as "Coptic Cairo". Cairenes themselves distinguish between the general area of Masr al-Qadima and specific localities such as Fumm al-Khalig (where you can see the **Aqueduct** which brought water to the Citadel) or Qasr el-Sham'ah, which was the fortress of **Babylon**, where the Holy Family is thought to have taken refuge from King Herod. This developed into a powerhouse of native Christianity, and today remains the heart of Cairo's Coptic community. Featuring several medieval churches, the superb **Coptic Museum** and an atmospheric synagogue, it totally eclipses the site of **Fustat** – Egypt's first Islamic settlement, of which little remains but the much-altered **Mosque of Amr** – or the largely uninteresting **southern suburbs** of Ma'adi and Helwan. Understandably, most tourists concentrate on Coptic Cairo, followed by a brief look at the Mosque of Amr.

Connected by bridge to Old Cairo – and so covered in this section, too – is **Roda Island**, which boasts a venerable Nilometer and the wonderfully kitsch Manial Palace. The Nilometer is best visited in combination with Coptic Cairo, but the palace is more easily accessible from central Cairo.

Coptic Cairo

Coptic Cairo recalls the millennial interlude between pharaonic and Islamic civilization and the enduring faith of Egypt's Copts (see box, pp.174–175). Though not a ghetto, the quarter's huddle of dark churches suggests a mistrust of outsiders – an attitude of mind that has its roots in the Persian conquest and centuries of Greek or Roman rule.

Perhaps as early as the sixth century BC, a town grew up in this area around a fortress intended to guard the canal linking the Nile and the Red Sea. Some

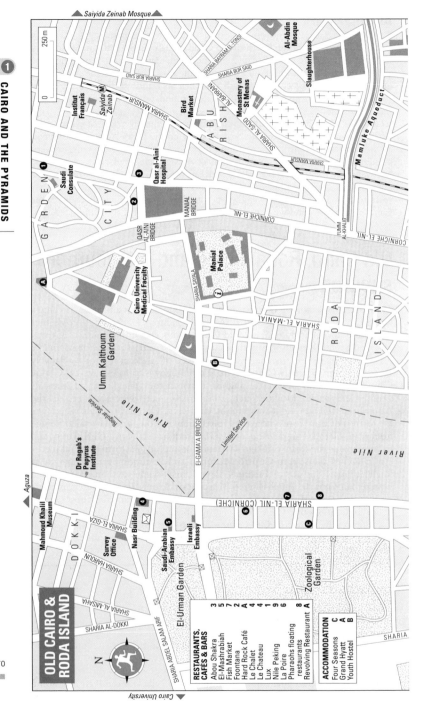

CAIRO AND THE PYRAMIDS

▲ Saiyida Zeinab Mosque ▲

250 m

0

Institut
Français

Saiyida
Zeinab Ⓜ

SHARIA BAYRAM EL-TONSI

SHARIA BUR SAID

SHARIA BUR SAID

Al-Abdin
Mosque

Slaughterhouse

Bird
Market

Monastery of
St Menas

A B U
R I S H

SHARIA MANSUR

AL-BARRANI

SHARIA AL-SAID

Mamluke Aqueduct

Ⓐ

G A R D E N

Saudi
Consulate

Ⓑ

C I T Y

Qasr al-Aini
Hospital

❸

❷

QASR
AL-AINI
BRIDGE

MANIAL
BRIDGE

CORNICHE EL-NIL

FUMM
AL-KHALIG

CORNICHE EL-NIL

SHARIA MANSUR

Ⓐ

Cairo University
Medical Faculty

Manial
Palace

ⓘ

SHARIA SAYALA

R O D A   I S L A N D

SHARIA EL-MANIAL

R O D A

Umm Kalthoum
Garden

Ⓑ

Regular Service

R i v e r   N i l e

Dr Ragab's
Papyrus
Institute

EL-GAMA'A BRIDGE

Limited Service

R i v e r   N i l e

▲ Aguza

Mahmoud Khalil
Museum

D O K K I

SHARIA EL-GIZA

Survey
Office

SHARIA HAROUN

Nasr Building

❹

❺

Saudi-Arabian
Embassy

Israeli
Embassy

SHARIA AL-MISAHA

SHARIA AL-DOKKI

SHARIA ABDEL SALAM ARIF

El-Urman Garden

SHARIA EL-NIL (CORNICHE)

❾

❼

❽

Ⓒ

Zoological
Garden

SHARIA

N

OLD CAIRO &
RODA ISLAND

**RESTAURANTS,
CAFÉS & BARS**
Abou Shakra 3
El-Mashrabiah 5
Fish Market 7
Foontana 2
Hard Rock Café A
Le Chalet 4
Le Chateau 4
Lux 1
Nile Peking 9
La Poire 6
Pharaohs floating
restaurants 8
Revolving Restaurant A

ACCOMMODATION
Four Seasons C
Grand Hyatt A
Youth Hostel B

▲ Cairo University

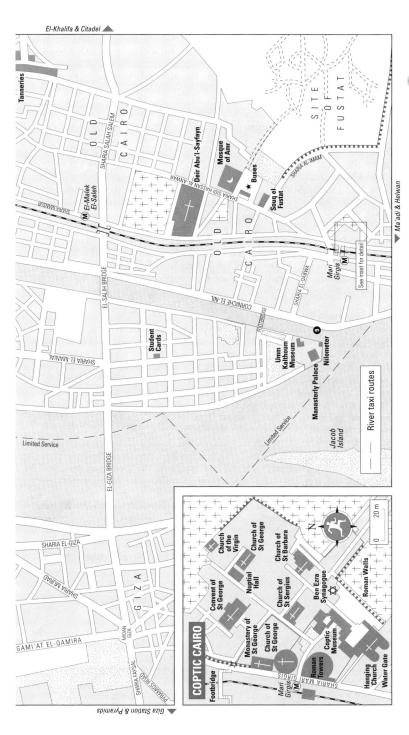

CAIRO AND THE PYRAMIDS

1

SITE OF FUSTAT

Tanneries

OLD CAIRO

SHARIA SALAH SALEM

SHARIA MANSUR

El-Malek El-Saleh Ⓜ

Deir Abu'l-Sayfayn

SHARIA SIDI HASSAN AL-ANWAR

Mosque of Amr

★ Buses

Souq el Fustat

SHARIA AL-IMAM

OLD CAIRO

Mari Girgis Ⓜ

SHARIA EL-QADRA

See inset for detail

▼ Ma'adi & Helwan

EL-SALIH BRIDGE

CORNICHE EL-NIL

Footbridge

SHARIA EL-MANIAL

Student Cards

Umm Kalthoum Museum

Manasterly Palace

Nilometer ⑨

Limited Service

Jacob Island

Limited Service

River taxi routes

EL-GIZA BRIDGE

SHARIA EL-GIZA

SHARIA MURAD

GIZA

MIDAN GIZA

GAMI'AT EL-QAMIRA

SHARIA FAYSAL

PYRAMIDS ROAD

COPTIC CAIRO

Footbridge

Mari Girgis Ⓜ

SHARIA MARI GIRGIS

Monastery of St George

Convent of St George

Church of St George

Nuptial Hall

Church of the Virgin

Church of St George

Church of St Sergius

Church of St Barbara

Ben Ezra Synagogue

Roman Towers

Coptic Museum

Roman Walls

Hanging Church

Water Gate

N

0   20 m

171

ascribe the name of this settlement – **Babylon-in-Egypt** – to Chaldean workmen pining after their home town beside the Euphrates; another possible derivation is Bab il-On, the "Gate of Heliopolis". Either way, it was Egyptian or Jewish in spirit long before Emperor Trajan raised the existing fortress in 130 AD. Many of Babylon's inhabitants, resentful of Greek domination and Hellenistic Alexandria, later embraced Christianity, despite bitter persecution by the pagan Romans. Subsequently, after the emperor Constantine's conversion, the community was further oppressed by Byzantine clerics in the name of Melkite orthodoxy. Thus when the Muslim army besieged Babylon in 641, promising to respect Copts and Jews as "People of the Book", only its garrison resisted.

The Coptic quarter is rapidly accessible by taking the **metro** from downtown Cairo to the **Mari Girgis** station (four stops from Midan Tahrir in the Helwan direction; 75pt). From 7am to 8am, you can also take a **river-taxi** (50pt) from Maspero Dock (see p.95), zigzagging southwards upriver – Mari Girgis is the fifth stop, but note that, aside from these early morning services, the river-taxis (aka water buses) only run as far as El-Gama'a Bridge. **Taxis** from downtown Cairo are reluctant to accept less than £E10 for the trip to Coptic Cairo, while **buses** from Tahrir and **minibuses** from Midan Ataba to Amr's Mosque are usually packed on the outward journey but fine for getting back.

The Roman fortress

Almost opposite the Mari Girgis (St George) metro station you'll see the twin circular **towers** of Babylon's western gate. In Trajan's day, the Nile lapped the base of this gate and was spanned by a pontoon bridge leading to the southern tip of Roda. Today, Babylon's foundations are buried under ten metres of accumulated silt and rubble, so the churches within the compound and the streets outside are nearly at the level of the fortress's ramparts. The right-hand tower is ruined, exposing a central shaft buttressed by masonry rings and radial ribs, which enabled it to withstand catapults and battering rams. Atop the other tower stands the Orthodox Church of St George (see p.178). Both towers are encased in alternating courses of dressed stone (much of it taken from pharaonic temples) and brick, a Roman technique known as *opus mixtum* or "mixed work". While exploring the Coptic quarter, you'll notice various sections of Babylon's Roman **walls**, rebuilt during the fourth and fifth centuries.

You should be able to walk from the Coptic Museum through the fortress's inner courtyard and down into the old **Water Gate** beneath the Hanging Church. The gate is partly flooded and, though its arches and walls are visible from precarious walkways, the interior is only accessible by a stairway behind the three stone piers supporting the back of the church (bring a torch). It was through this gate that the last Byzantine viceroy, Melkite bishop Cyrus, escaped by boat under cover of darkness before Babylon surrendered to the Muslims.

The Coptic Museum

Nestled between the Hanging Church and the Roman towers of Babylon, the **Coptic Museum** (daily 9am–5pm, closing at 3pm in Ramadan; £E30, students £E15; ⓦ www.copticmuseum.gov.eg) is one of the highlights of Old Cairo. Its peerless collection of Coptic artefacts is enhanced by the beautiful carved ceilings, beams and stained-glass domes inside its *mashrabiya*'d wings, which enclose peaceful gardens. Though spread over three floors, the collection can be seen in detail within a couple of hours, or covered at a trot in half that time (bear in mind that the layout may be different from that described here, as the museum has recently reopened after renovations). A gateway from the grounds gives access to the courtyard of the Hanging Church (see p.177).

Founded in 1908 under the patronage of Patriarch Cyril V and Khedive Kamil, the museum was intended to save Christian antiques from the ravages of neglect and foreign collectors, but soon widened its mandate to embrace secular material. With artefacts from Old Cairo, Upper Egypt and the desert monasteries, the museum traces the evolution of Coptic art from Greco-Roman times into the Islamic era (300–1000 AD). Notwithstanding debts to pharaonic and Greco-Roman culture, its spirit was refreshingly unmonumental: Stanley Stewart (see p.804) calls it "realistic, at times humorous", and notes that Coptic art reflected "plebian or agricultural concerns". It often seems homespun compared to pharaonic and Islamic craftsmanship and, appropriately enough, its finest expression was in textiles.

New Wing (ground floor)

If you enter the museum grounds from Sharia Mari Girgis, the **New Wing**, built in 1937, is straight ahead. The **ground floor** is arranged in chronological order in an anticlockwise direction, starting with Room 1. The other exit from this room leads into a garden containing tombstones and funerary steles, from where you can access stairs that lead down to the Water Gate beneath the Hanging Church and up into the old wing.

Centred upon a fountain from one of the old houses of the quarter, **Room 1** displays **pagan reliefs and statues** of figures from Classical mythology. The squat proportions and oversized heads make Aphrodite, Daphnae, Pan, Leda and the Swan look more African than Greco-Roman. The tendency to superimpose two flat layers, and the motif of a broken pediment with a shell, were both characteristic of proto-Coptic art. Artefacts in **Room 2** evince a shift towards Christian symbolism from the third century onwards. Pharaonic ankhs (see p.282) are transmuted into looped crosses, while true crosses appear on the shell pediments and coexist with Horus hawks on a basket-weave capital.

Coptic artistry reached its zenith between the sixth and ninth centuries, as exemplified by the stone carvings and frescoes from **Bawit Monastery**, near Assyut. In the middle of the righthand wall of **Room 3** is a splendid apse

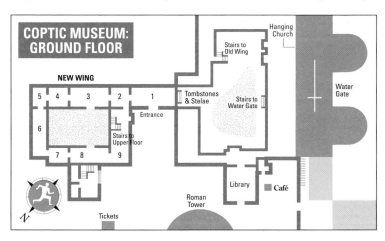

173

Coptic Christianity

While Egypt's **Copts** share a common national culture with their Muslim compatriots, they remain acutely conscious of their separate identity, and intercommunal marriages are extremely rare. Because of this, it's often said that the Copts are "purer" descendants of the Ancient Egyptians than the Muslims – overlooking the infusions of Nubian, Greek, Jewish and Roman blood that occurred centuries before the Arab conquest. Though some maintain that Copts have higher cheekbones or almond-shaped eyes, Copts are rarely recognizable other than by tokens of their faith (wearing a cross around their neck, or tattooed on their wrist) or by forenames such as Maria, Antunius (Antony), Girgis (George) and Ramses.

Coptic Christianity differs from the Eastern Orthodox and Roman churches over doctrine and ritual. The Coptic Orthodox Church and its pope (chosen from the monks of Wadi Natrun) are totally independent from the Vatican, which only recently agreed to disagree for the sake of ecumenical harmony. The Coptic Bible (first translated from Greek c.300 AD) antedates the Latin version by a century. While Coptic services are conducted in Arabic, portions of the liturgy are sung in the old Coptic language descended from Ancient Egyptian, audibly prefiguring the Gregorian chants of Eastern Orthodoxy.

Christianity in Egypt

Christianity reached Egypt early: tradition holds that **St Mark** made his first convert (a Jewish shoemaker of Alexandria) in 45 AD. From Jews and Greeks the religion spread to the Egyptians of the Delta – which teemed with Christian communities by the third century – and thence southwards up the Nile. The persecution of believers began under Emperor Decius (249–51) and reached its apogee under Diocletian, whom the Copts accuse of killing 144,000 Christians; the Coptic Church dates its chronology from his accession (284). During this **Era of** Martyrs many believers sought refuge in the desert. Paul of Thebes, Antony and Pacome – the sainted "**Desert Fathers**" – inspired a multitude of hermits and camp followers, whose simple communities became the first **monasteries**.

The Christian faith appealed to Egyptians on many levels. Its message of resurrection offered ordinary folk the eternal life that was previously available only to those who could afford elaborate funerary rituals. And much of the new religion's **symbolism** fitted old myths and images. God created man from clay, as did Khnum on his potter's wheel, and weighed the penitent's heart, like Anubis; Confession echoed the Declaration of Innocence; the conflict of two brothers and the struggle against Satan echoed the myth of Osiris, Seth and Horus. Scholars have traced the **cult of the Virgin** back to that of the Great Mother, Isis, who suckled Horus. The resemblance between early **Coptic crosses** and pharaonic ankhs has also led some to argue that Christianity's principal symbol owes more to Egypt than Golgotha.

niche depicting Christ enthroned between the creatures of the Apocalypse and the moon and sun; below, the Virgin and Child consort with Apostles whose homely faces can still be seen in any Egyptian city today. In **Room 4**, whose contents are described as "Miscellaneous", notice the eagle on the right, an early Christian symbol of resurrection (as was the peacock). **Room 5** is also filled with miscellaneous objects, its centrepiece a painted capital carved with sinuous acanthus leaves, a motif borrowed from the Greeks and Romans but apparently devoid of symbolic meaning for the Copts.

Entering **Room 6**, dedicated to objects from the **Monastery of St Jeremiah** at Saqqara, you walk between an avenue of capitals with acanthus leaves and grapevines that mingle with pharaonic palm fronds and lotus motifs. At the end is

Although Emperor Constantine converted to Christianity and legalized his adopted faith throughout the empire (313–30), Byzantine converts known as **Melkites** continued to oppress the Copts. Political tensions were expressed in bitter theological disputes between **Arius** and **Athanasius** of Alexandria, which the Nicene Council (325) failed to resolve. When the Copts rejected the compromise verdict of the Council of Chalcedon (451) that Christ's human and divine natures were both unmixed and inseparable, and insisted that his divinity was paramount, they were expelled from the fold for this **Monophysite heresy** (monophysite meaning "single nature", a misrepresentation of their stance on Christ's divinity).

Most Egyptians remained Christian long after the Arab conquest (640–41) and were treated justly by the early Islamic dynasties. Mass **conversions to Islam** followed harsher taxation, abortive revolts, punitive massacres and indignities engendered by the Crusades, until the Muslims attained a nationwide majority (probably during the thirteenth century, though earlier in Cairo). Thereafter Copts still participated in Egyptian life at every level, but the community retreated inwards and its monasteries and clergy stagnated until the nineteenth century, when Coptic reformists collaborated with Islamic and secular nationalists bent on overhauling Egypt's institutions. The association between Coptic Christianity and proto-nationalism was plain to Egypt's foreign rulers. Indeed "Copt" derives from the Greek word for Egypt, Aigyptos.

The Copts today

In recent decades the Coptic community has undergone a **revival** under the dynamic leadership of its current pope, **Shenouda III**. The monasteries have been revitalized by a new generation of highly educated monks; community work and church attendances flourish as never before. Undoubtedly, this Coptic solidarity also reflects alarm at rising Islamic fundamentalism: what frightens the Copts is the state's strategy of wooing Islamist opinion by discriminating against non-Muslims. Merely to open a new church requires presidential permission; in 1998, one in Ma'adi was closed by security forces backed up by armoured cars. Over two hundred converts to Christianity have been arrested under the National Security Act, and in 1999, sectarian Muslim mobs murdered 21 Copts at El-Qusiya in Middle Egypt (see p.310) while local police, already accused of torturing local Coptic residents, stood by and did nothing – some accounts even accuse them of participating.

Fortunately, it's relatively few Muslims who actively support this kind of sectarian repression – which is at least a source of comfort for Egypt's six million Copts and 200,000 Christians of other denominations (Greek Orthodox, Maronite, Armenian, Catholic, Anglican and Baptist).

the earliest known example of a stone pulpit, possibly influenced by the Heb-Sed thrones of Zoser's funerary complex. The fresco to its right, like the Bawit apse, subtly identifies the Virgin Mary with Isis. Other instances of recycled iconography can be seen around the corner in **Room 7**: a frieze of the grape harvest (a theme favoured by pharaonic nobles) and a small sphinx-like lion figure between two stylized versions of itself.

Room 8 moves on to **Biblical scenes** (Abraham and Isaac, Christ with angels) and **friezes** of animals offset in plant rondels – a motif that was later adopted by Fatimid woodcarvers. Entering **Room 9** you'll encounter on your right a tenth-century panel from Umm al-Birgat (in the Fayoum), depicting Adam and Eve before and after the Fall, for which he blames her in the latter scene while a serpent relishes the denouement. In the centre of the hall is an elaborate papyrus and lotus basket-weave capital, hollowed out to form a **baptismal font**.

New Wing (upper floor) and Old Wing

Climbing the staircase to the **upper floor**, you come to casefuls of *ostraca* (inscribed shards of pottery, stone, bone and wood) and manuscripts produced by monastic scriptoria, including several papyrus sheets from the **Gnostic Gospels of Nag Hammadi**, whose 1200 pages shed light on the development of early Christianity and its mystic tradition. The Gospels (translated from Greek into Coptic) were probably buried during the purges against Gnostics in the fourth and fifth centuries; farmers unearthed the sealed jar in 1945 (see box, p.327).

A 1600-year-old towel by the doorway to Room 11 – next to the oldest book ever to be found complete with its cover – presages a host of **textiles**. From the third or fourth century onwards, Coptic weavers (chiefly women) developed various techniques to a pitch of sophistication. Tapestry and pile-weave designs blended human and bird forms with plant motifs; tunics were appliquéd with bands and rondels. In **Room 12** there's a magnificent silk robe embroidered with pictures of the Apostles, dating from the eighteenth century.

Room 13 displays Alexandrian-style **ivorywork** and cruder efforts from Upper Egypt, alongside a selection of **icons** from Old Cairo, Aswan and Kharga Oasis. Some believe that the change from murals to painted icons resulted from the need to hide sacred treasures from hostile interlopers. The next three rooms showcase **metalwork**, ranging from crosses and censers to musical instruments and tools. In **Room 15** are patriarchal crowns, a lamp emblazoned with both a Christian cross and an Islamic crescent, and an eagle from the Fortress of Babylon.

The upper floor concludes with an exhibition in **Room 17** of **Christian paintings** salvaged during the 1950s and 1960s from villages about to be drowned by Lake Nasser. Like Isis-worship in ancient times, Christianity persisted as the dominant religion in Nubia for several centuries after it had

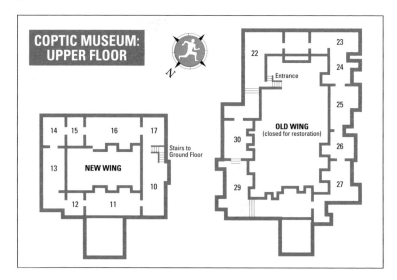

waned in Egypt. The figures depicted, being Nubian, are darker, with larger eyes and rounder heads than those in Coptic art from further north.

The **Old Wing**, entered via stairs from the sculpture garden, boasts even finer ceilings and *mashrabiyas*. On the left as you enter **Room 22** are the original **fourth-century altar** and a Fatimid-era dome from the Church of St Sergius nearby. In the other direction lie two halls full of Nubian wall paintings, plus a pair of lunettes (semicircular paintings) from Bawit Monastery (**Room 23**). Rounding the corner, an original screen from the Church of St Barbara inaugurates the **woodwork** section. Fragments in the following alcove show a similar mixture of Hellenistic mythology, pharaonic symbolism and Coptic naturalism to the stone-carving in the other wing, while later pieces feature human activities. A panel depicting **Christ's entry into Jerusalem**, taken from the Hanging Church, is the high point of **Room 25**.

Sharing **Room 26** with Coptic toys and domestic utensils are several **mummy portrait panels**, latter-day versions of the Roman "Fayoum Portraits" displayed in the Museum of Egyptian Antiquities (see p.107). In the far right-hand corner is a remarkable **early Coptic crucifix** (one of the few in existence), which combines a beardless Christ with a Horus hawk and sun disc. Byzantine and Sassanid (Persian) influences underlie the **friezes** of hunting scenes and fabulous creatures – motifs which continued into Islamic times until the Sunni restoration. The episcopal chairs in the annexe to **Room 27** are similar to the reception thrones used by wealthy amirs.

The last quarter of the wing displays **pottery**, arranged by type or form rather than antiquity. Ancient motifs such as fish, ducks and plants are widely employed. At the end of **Room 29** are **pilgrims' flasks** showing St Menas between two camels (see p.607). Among the later work in **Room 30** are lustreware pieces like those made by Muslim potters at Fustat, but here emblazoned with a Coptic fish or cross. The annexe beyond contains a small collection of **glassware**.

The Hanging Church

Built directly above the water gate, the **Hanging Church** (in Arabic Al-Mu'allaqah, "The Suspended"; daily 9am–5pm: Coptic Mass Fri 8–11am & Sun 7–10am) can be reached via an ornate portal on Sharia Mari Girgis. Ascending a steep stairway, you enter a nineteenth-century vestibule displaying cassettes and videos of Coptic liturgies and papal sermons. Above this are the monks' quarters; beneath it lies a secret repository for valuables, only discovered last century. Through the door and to the right, a glass panel in the floor of the church allows you to see that the church is indeed "suspended" bridge-like, above the water gate.

The main **nave** – whose ceiling is ribbed like an upturned boat or ark – is separated from the side aisles by sixteen pillars, formerly painted with images of saints. Behind the marble pulpit, beautifully carved screens hide three **haikals** (altar areas) from the congregation. Their star patterns, accentuated by inlaid bone and ivory, are similar to those found in mosques. Both pulpit and screens date from the thirteenth century, but the church was founded at least six hundred years earlier and may even have originated in the fourth century as a chapel for the soldiers of the bastion. Among its relics, the church once claimed to own an olive stone chewed by the Virgin Mary, to whom Al-Mu'allaqah is dedicated. The thirteen pillars holding up the pulpit represent Jesus and the twelve disciples: as is customary in Coptic churches, one of the pillars is black, for Judas, and another, perhaps rather unfairly, is grey for "doubting" Thomas.

The Monastery of St George and into the Old Quarter

Returning to the Coptic Museum and heading north, go through the first gateway beyond the Coptic Museum entrance (ignoring any demands for cash from "doormen") to reach the precincts of the **Monastery of St George**, now the seat of the Greek Orthodox Patriarchate of Alexandria. The monastery itself rarely admits tourists, but it's worth looking into the neighbouring **Church of St George** (daily 8.30am–4pm), built in 1904 after a fire destroyed the original tenth-century structure. The only round church in Egypt (it's so shaped because it's built atop one of the old Roman gateway towers), it has a dark interior perfumed with incense and pierced by sunbeams filtered through stained glass. A (barred) flight of steps descends into the bowels of the Roman tower, once believed to be "peopled by devils". Notwithstanding the church's Greek Orthodox allegiance, its **Moulid of Mari Girgis** (on St George's Day – April 23) is one of the largest Coptic festivals in Cairo.

A hundred metres up the main road, a **subterranean gateway** leads into the oldest part of Old Cairo, whose cobbled lanes flanked by high-walled houses wend between **medieval churches and cemeteries**. In 1929, Evelyn Waugh wrote disparagingly of a "constricted slum" whose Coptic residents hardly differed from their Muslim neighbours: "the only marked sign of their emancipation from heathen superstition was that the swarm of male and juvenile beggars were here reinforced by their womenfolk, who in the Mohammedan quarters maintain a modest seclusion". Since the late 1970s, the quarter has been gradually sanitized and tarted up for tourists, and now seems quite spruce compared to Islamic Cairo.

The most interesting of the churches is reached through the first gate on the left, after you pass through the subterranean gateway. This is the Coptic **Convent of St George** (Deir Mari Girgis; daily 9am–4pm), whose main building, still a nunnery, is closed to visitors. Underneath however, and usually open to visitors, though closed for restoration at last check, is a lofty hall that once belonged to a Fatimid mansion. The chapel beyond, with tall, narrow wooden doors, boasts a cedarwood casket containing relics of St George. To

△ The Church of St George

the left of this building, though not always open, is a small room used for the "**chain-wrapping ritual**", symbolizing the saint's persecution by the Romans. Several of the nuns speak English and welcome questions about their faith; they might even be prepared to wrap you in chains for a souvenir photo.

Upon leaving the convent, walk on to the end of the lane, where it meets another thoroughfare. At this intersection, turn right around the corner to the Church of St Sergius, or head left to explore the quarter's northern reaches.

North to the churches of St George and the Virgin

The north part of the Coptic quarter contains nothing special, but its solitude is refreshing and you might enjoy wandering around the overgrown **cemeteries** – so far unsquatted Cities of the Dead.

Fifty metres up the road from the intersection, an alley to the left leads to yet another **Church of St George**, founded in 681 by Athanasius the Scribe. Of the original foundation, only the Hall of Nuptials survived a conflagration in the mid-nineteenth century, after which the current structure was erected.

Beyond it, at the end of the road, stands the smaller **Church of the Virgin**, also known as Qasriyyat al-Rihan ("Pot of Basil") after the favourite herb of the Orthodox Church. Because Al-Hakim's mother was of that faith, the church was given to the Greek community for the duration of his reign, but later returned to the Copts. Largely rebuilt in the eighteenth century, it's chiefly notable for several icons painted by John the Armenian in 1778.

The churches of St Sergius and St Barbara

Heading right from the intersection beyond the convent, you pass a tourist bazaar before reaching the **Church of St Sergius** (Abu Serga; daily 8am–4pm), whose site below street level attests to its great age. Probably founded in the fifth century and continuously rebuilt since medieval times, Abu Serga retains the basilical form typical of early Coptic churches. The low ceiling and the antique columns topped with Corinthian capitals support the women's gallery, where you can inspect the thirteenth-century *haikal* screen and bits of frescoes and mosaics in the central apse. Steps to the right of the altar descend into a **crypt** where the Holy Family are believed to have stayed, a sojourn commemorated by a Coptic **festival** (June 1).

From St Sergius, you can wander along to the end of the lane where another thoroughfare leads to the Church of St Barbara (to the left) and Ben Ezra Synagogue (on the right). The eleventh-century **Church of St Barbara** (daily 8am–8pm) replaced an earlier Church of SS Cyrus and John, which was razed during Al-Hakim's assault on Fustat. Unlike others in the quarter, its wooden-vaulted roof is lofty, with skylights and windows illuminating a nave flanked by Arabic arches with Fatimid tie-beams. Its *minbar*-esque pulpit and inlaid *haikal* screen would not look amiss in a mosque. The western sanctuary contains the relics of *Sitt* Barbara. Tradition holds that she was the daughter of a pagan merchant who was murdered for preaching Christianity in the third century, but sceptics might note that her belated recognition followed another questionable case (see p.716).

The Ben Ezra Synagogue

Down the road, behind a wrought-iron fence, is the **Ben Ezra Synagogue** (daily 9am–4pm), a unique relic of Cairo's ancient Jewish community. Bereft of its former host of worshippers (see box, p.180), the synagogue would have crumbled away were it not for the efforts of one "Rabbi" Cohen, who shamelessly overcharged for souvenir postcards to fund repairs for twenty years, until

Egypt's Jewish community is nowadays much reduced, with only around two hundred practising *yahud*, living mainly in Alexandria or downtown Cairo. Twelve synagogues still exist, most in a state of disrepair (though they can be visited, if you are prepared to pay a substantial donation towards their upkeep – ask at Adly Street Synagogue if you are interested). Only Adly Street (p.120) and Ben Ezra in Old Cairo (p.179) are still used for services – Adly for the solemn "High Holidays" of Rosh HaShannah (Jewish New Year) and Yom Kippur (Day of Atonement), Ben Ezra for happier occasions such as Hannukah, the winter festival of lights.

Egypt's Jewish community is undoubtedly ancient. The **Old Testament** relates how the Israelites settled in the "Land of Goshen" (see p.633), where they "multiplied and waxed mighty" until a new pharaoh enslaved them to build "the treasure-cities, Pithom and Raamses". Their flight from Egypt to the Promised Land, described in Exodus, is supposed to have occurred during the Ramessid era (c.1320–1237 BC), but squaring it with Egyptian **history** presents difficulties. While numerous sites are suggestive of Pithom and Raamses, there's no mention of the Exodus in pharaonic records. Some evidence exists for the Prophet Jeremiah's foundation of a new community at Babylon-in-Egypt after the destruction of Jerusalem (585 BC), but there is no firm historical ground until the second century BC, when it is known that the Ptolemies encouraged an influx of Jews into Alexandria. The apocryphal (and misnamed) third book of Maccabees describes the Alexandrian community's struggle against anti-Semitism in Ptolemaic times.

In contrast to the Alexandrian fusion of Greek and Jewish culture, the Jews of "Babylon" were more like native Egyptians. Mutual sympathies were strengthened by the **Jewish revolt** against Roman rule (115–17 AD) and the Christian belief in the **Egyptian exile of the Holy Family**. Babylon's Jewish community would have been a natural haven for Mary, Joseph and the baby Jesus when Herod's wrath made Palestine too dangerous (it's harder to see why they should have hidden out near Assyut, as is also claimed).

As "People of the Book", Egypt's Jews were treated about as well (or badly) as the Copts **during the Islamic period**, acting as small traders, gold- and silversmiths, moneychangers or moneylenders. In Mohammed Ali's day, E.W. Lane (see p.803) estimated that they numbered about five thousand. Until the late nineteenth century, Cairo's Jews were concentrated in the Haret al-Yahud, off the Muski west of Sharia al-Muizz (see map on p.132), where the currently derelict Maimonides Synagogue incorporates a *yeshiva* (religious school, equivalent to a Muslim *madrassa*) founded in the twelfth century by the great Jewish philosopher whose name it bears, who was also Salah al-Din's personal doctor. Under colonialism, European Jews arrived, mainly merchants or professionals who settled in Alexandria or Cairo. A few families of this *haute Juiverie* – the Menasces, Rolos, Hararis and Cattauis – were financiers who moved in royal circles, and a number of businesses in the new downtown district, such as the Cicurel and Ades department stores (see p.121), were opened by Jewish entrepreneurs.

After the creation of **Israel** in 1948, Egypt's Jews found themselves in a tricky situation, and each war eroded their security further. By the time of the 1967 war their numbers had declined through emigration from 75,000 to 2600 (mostly living in Cairo), though the capital still had 26 working synagogues, until mobs attacked them for the first time during the conflict. Thereafter, most of the remaining Jews left, leaving the tiny community that remains today.

the American Jewish Congress and the Egyptian government stepped in to restore it. Today it is as good as new.

In form, the synagogue resembles a basilical church of the kind that existed here between the fourth and ninth centuries. Sold to the Jews in order that the

Copts could pay taxes to finance Ibn Tulun's Mosque, this church was either demolished or incorporated within the synagogue, which Abraham Ben Ezra, the Rabbi of Jerusalem, restored in the twelfth century. The inlaid marble and gilded stalactite niche date from around then, but most of the graceful mouldings and floral swirls are the result of nineteenth-century repairs, which unearthed a huge cache of medieval manuscripts (now dispersed around Western libraries), including a sixth-century Torah written on gazelle hide.

Nevertheless, Jewish and Coptic traditions invest the site with ancient significance. Here, the pharaoh's daughter found Moses in the bulrushes; Jeremiah gathered survivors after Nebuchadnezzar destroyed Jerusalem; and the temple named after him provided a haven for the Holy Family, who lived among the Jews of Babylon for three months. Moreover, the Copts believe that Peter and Mark pursued their apostolic mission in Egypt, whence Peter issued the First Epistle General. The rest of Christendom disagrees, however, arguing that the Biblical reference to Babylon (I Peter 5:13) is only a metaphor for Rome.

Around the back of the synagogue are a newly restored chunk of the Roman walls and a derelict Jewish Refuge founded by one Ralph Green.

The Mosque of Amr, Deir Abu'l-Sayfayn and Fustat

The Mosque of Amr and Deir Abu'l Sayfayn, plus the western part of Fustat (including its handicrafts souk), can easily be reached on foot from Coptic Cairo. Mari Girgis and El-Malek el-Saleh metro stations are within walking distance, while buses serve the mosque from Midan Tahrir (#27 or #134/), Ataba (#27 or #825) and Ramses (#27, #83, #94 or #134/).

The Mosque of Amr

To get a feel for what happened after Babylon and Egypt surrendered to Islam, return to Mari Girgis Street and follow it northwards, past the turning for Fustat and a small bus depot, to the **Mosque of Amr**. Though it was altered several times and doubled in size in 827, this boasts direct descent from Egypt's first-ever mosque, built in 641. A simple mud-brick, thatch-roofed enclosure without a *mihrab*, courtyard or minaret, it was large enough to contain the Muslim army at prayer. At its inauguration, **Amr Ibn al-As** told his 3500 Arab warriors:

The Nile floods have risen. The grazing will be good. There is milk for the lambs and kids. Go out with God's blessing and enjoy the land, its milk, its flocks and its herds, and take good care of your neighbours, the Copts, for the Prophet of God himself gave orders for us to do so.

Until the fratricidal struggle between Sunni and Shia, this injunction was honoured: aside from paying a poll tax, non-Muslims enjoyed equal rights. It was Ibn Tulun and Al-Hakim who introduced the discrimination (or worse), that later rulers either forswore on principle or practised for motives of bigotry, fear or greed. But on an everyday level, citizens of each faith amicably coexisted within the city of Fustat-Masr, as they do in modern Cairo.

The site of the mosque was indicated by Allah, who sent a dove to nest in Amr's tent while he was away at war; on returning he declared it sacrosanct, waited until the dove's brood was raised, then built a mosque. The existing building follows the classic congregational pattern, arched *liwans* surrounding a pebbled *sahn* centred on an ablutions well. Believers pray or snooze on fine carpets in the sanctuary *liwan*. When Amr introduced a pulpit, he was rebuked by Caliph Omar for raising himself above his Muslim brethren. The *mashrabiya*'d **mausoleum** of his son, Abdullah, marks the site of Amr's house in Fustat. A nearby column bears a gash caused by people licking it until their tongues bled, to obtain miraculous cures. The pair of columns on the left as you come in are said to part to allow the truly righteous to squeeze through, and another was whipped from Mecca by Omar. From the mosque's **well**, it is said, a pilgrim retrieved a goblet dropped into the Well of Zemzem in the Holy City.

Deir Abu'l-Sayfayn

If the Coptic quarter hasn't satisfied your curiosity about medieval churches, pay a visit to **Deir Abu'l-Sayfayn** (daily 8am–8pm), northwest of Amr's Mosque. This high-walled enclosure is entered via a humble wooden door, as the original iron-bound door is now in the Coptic Museum. Within the compound are several churches, including the **Church of St Mercurius**, first mentioned in the tenth century (when it served as a sugar-cane warehouse) but claiming older antecedence, and totally rebuilt after the burning of Fustat. Beneath its northern aisle you can descend into a tiny crypt where St Barsum the Naked lived with a snake until his death in 317; a special Mass is held here on his name day (September 10).

A doorway beside the crypt stairway leads through into the rest of the complex. The Upper Church, reached by steps, contains five disused chapels. Of more interest are the Small Church with its *haikal* dedicated to St James the Sawn-asunder, and the early seventh-century **Church of St Shenute** (Anba Shenouda; undergoing renovation but still open), featuring beautiful cedar-wood and ebony iconostases. From the same period comes the diminutive, icon-packed **Church of the Holy Virgin**, beyond which stands the **Convent of St Mercurius**, still inhabited by nuns. The liturgy is celebrated in all the churches (Wed 8am–noon, Fri 7–11am & Sun 6–10am). Adjacent to Deir Abu'l-Sayfayn are extensive Protestant and Maronite **cemeteries**, including a military cemetery for Commonwealth servicemen killed in World War II.

Fustat

Behind the Amr Mosque, and stretching all the way to the Citadel, the site of ancient **Fustat** is still partly occupied by rubbish tips and shantytown hovels, but the far side of it (accessible from Sharia Dalah Salem) has been grassed over and landscaped to create **Fustat Park** (see map on p.160; daily 11am–midnight; £E1). The transformation of the site continues, with plans for a Museum of Islamic Civilization and Fustat's own tourist office.

Fustat ("Tent") is the site of Cairo's very first Muslim city, founded by the victorious Arab general Amr Ibn al-As in 640, right by the Roman/Byzantine fortress of Babylon, which had just fallen to his troops. Originally a cluster of tribal encampments around Amr's Mosque, Fustat evolved into a mud-brick beehive of multistorey dwellings with rooftop gardens, fountains, and a piped water and sewage system unequalled in Europe until the eighteenth century. As the Abbasids, Tulunids and Ikhshidids also built their own cities ever further to the northeast, a great conurbation known as **Fustat-Masr** was formed. However, the Fatimids moved the administration to their newly-founded city of Al-Qahira, after which Fustat-Masr's decline began. In 1020, the mad caliph Al-Hakim ordered his troops to sack Fustat-Masr for reasons worthy of Caligula (see p.140). Yet even in 1168, what remained was so vast that Vizier Shawar decided to evacuate and burn it rather than let the Crusaders occupy the unwalled and defenceless old city outside Al-Qahira, upon which it would have been a useful base for attack. Set ablaze with 10,000 torches and 20,000 barrels of naphtha, Fustat smouldered for 55 days.

The area today boasts the newly constructed **Souq el Fustat**, on the corner of Sharia al-Imam, the road leading down into Fustat, and Sharia Hassan al-Anwar (daily 10am–10pm). This small market showcases handicrafts and objets d'art made by local artisans, who pay subsidized rents for shop space in exchange for teaching handicraft skills to local children. Such skills are much needed, as much of Fustat and the adjoining area remains a shantytown, inhabited by **potters** who slave over beehive kilns, churning out domestic ware for *baladi* households and piping for sewers and water mains, and *zebaleen* or **rubbish-gatherers**, who collect and sift Cairo's rubbish for anything edible or recyclable. The glass, cardboard, metal, rags and leather which they salvage are sold as raw materials to factories.

North to the Aqueduct

Travelling between Coptic and central Cairo by bus or taxi, you'll catch sight of the great **Aqueduct** that carried water to the Citadel. Originally a mere conduit supported by wooden pillars, it was solidly rebuilt in stone by Sultan al-Nasir in 1311 and subsequently extended in 1505 by Al-Ghuri to accommodate the Nile's westward shift, to a total length of 3405m. River water was lifted by the **Burg al-Saqiyya**, a massive hexagonal water-wheel tower near the Corniche. On its western wall can be seen Al-Ghuri's heraldic emblem and slots for engaging the six oxen-powered water wheels, which remained in use until 1872.

The site of this tower is known as **Fumm al-Khalig** ("Mouth of the Canal"), after the waterway that once ran inland to meet the walls of Fatimid al-Qahira. This Khalig Masri ("Egyptian Canal") supplied most of Cairo's water during Mamluke and Ottoman times, and was also linked to the ancient Nile Delta–Red Sea waterway, re-dug by Amr and Al-Nasir. In an annual ceremony to mark the Nile flood, the dike that separated it from the river was breached, sending fresh water coursing through the city. Pleasure boats were launched onto the lakes near Bab al-Luq and Ezbekiya, while fireworks heralded nocturnal revelries. But the taming of the Nile spelt the end of this practice, and after piped water was introduced early last century the canal was filled in to create Bur Said and Ramses streets.

Further inland

From the Fumm al-Khalig roundabout, Sharia al-Sadd al-Barrani runs up to Saiyida Zeinab (2km) past a swath of **Christian cemeteries**. Within the northernmost cemetery, high walls enclose the **Monastery of St Menas** (Deir Abu Mina), whose sunken basilical church has been endlessly rebuilt since 724. Having returned the holy remnants of St Menas to his desert monastery (see p.607), the church now gives pride of place to the relics of saints Behnam and Sarah, who were martyred by their own father. The monastery receives very few visitors and has no set opening hours.

Further south, the Aqueduct bestrides a medieval slum centred around a huge **slaughterhouse** and reeking **tanneries**. To outsiders, stark poverty seems all-pervasive; yet among those who live here, social distinctions are keenly felt. A slaughterhouse worker and his boss will both wear bloodstained *galabiyyas* during working hours, and possibly live on the same street – but the former can only speculate on what riches the latter keeps indoors. Conversely, people will salvage designer-label bags and boxes to flaunt on the streets as if they were returning with a purchase.

Unlike the tanneries of Morocco, this area is hardly on the tourist trail, although French writer Gustave Flaubert spent an afternoon here in 1850, shooting birds of prey and "wolf-like dogs". However, the odd tourist has been known to attend Saturday evening *zikrs* outside the **Mosque of Sidi Ali Zein al-Abdin**, on the periphery of the Saiyida Zeinab quarter (the area itself is described on pp.159–163).

Roda Island

The narrow channel between **Roda Island** and the mainland is bridged in such a way that the island engages more with Garden City than with Old Cairo – a reversal of historic ties. As the much-rebuilt **Nilometer** suggests, it was the southern end of Roda that was visited by ferries en route between Memphis and Heliopolis, and Roman ships bound for Babylon-in-Egypt. However, Roda reverted to agricultural use as Cairo's focus shifted northeastwards, and nothing remains of the Byzantine fortress that defied the Muslim invasion, nor the vaster Ayyubid *qasr* where the Bahri Mamlukes were garrisoned. The island's main sight, the **Manial Palace**, re-established a fashion for palatial residences early last century, though it wasn't until the 1950s that Roda experienced a building explosion similar to Zamalek's.

With Roda's tourist attractions sited 3km apart, choice of **transport** is a major consideration. The Nilometer is best reached on foot from Old Cairo via the footbridge from the Corniche. You can take a minibus or service taxi down the Corniche from the centre to Old Cairo; alternatively Mari Girgis metro station is just two blocks southeast of the footbridge. Should you settle for only one sight, make it the palace, which is easily accessible from central Cairo. Aside from a taxi (£E4–5), a #58 minibus is the fastest way of getting there from Midan Tahrir (Abdel Mouneem Riyad terminal), and minibus #56 heads there from Ramses; alight on Sharia Sayala, near the palace gates. Walking takes about half an hour from downtown Cairo, and on hot days can leave you totally bushed.

The closest bridge to downtown leads to the **Grand Hyatt Hotel**, a deluxe five-star job with some of the best views in Cairo. The next crossing, Qasr al-Aini Bridge, leads down to **Cairo University Medical Faculty**. By walking 150m south from here you can reach the palace gates without crossing the Manial Bridge, used by traffic heading for Giza.

The Manial Palace

Built in 1903, the **Manial Palace** (daily 9am–4.30pm; £E20, students £E10) is a Cairo must. Its fabulously eclectic architecture reflects the taste of King Farouk's uncle, Prince Mohammed Ali, author of *The Breeding of Arabian Horses* and the owner of a flawless emerald that magically alleviated his ill health (so legend has it). Each of the main buildings manifests a different style – Persian, Syrian, Moorish, Ottoman and Rococo – or mixes them together with gay abandon.

Having bought your ticket, make a beeline for the **Reception Palace** just inside the gateway. Its magnificent *salamlik*, adorned with stained glass, polychrome tiles and ornate woodcarving, prepares you for the opulent guest rooms upstairs; the finest is the Syrian Room, which was quite literally transplanted from Damascus. On the stairs you'll notice a scale model of Qaitbey's Mausoleum, made entirely of mother-of-pearl.

184

Leaving the Reception Palace and turning right, you come upon a pseudo-Moroccan tower harbouring the prince's **mosque**, whose lavish decor is reminiscent of the great mosque of his namesake in the Citadel. Further along, the grotesque **Hunting Museum** features scores of mounted ibex heads, gorgeous butterflies and ineptly stuffed fowl, a hermaphrodite goat, a table made from elephants' ears and a vulture's claw candlestick.

The **Prince's Residence**, deeper into the banyan-shaded garden, is richly decorated in a mixture of Turkish and Occidental styles. The drab-looking building out back contains a long **Throne Hall** (closed for restoration at last check) whose red carpet passes life-size royal portraits hung beneath a sunburst ceiling. Around the outside of this hall are the skeletons of the prince's horse and camel, and a stairway to the upper level (often closed). If accessible, visitors can admire the Obsidian Salon and the private apartments of the prince's mother, enriched by a silver four-poster bed from the Abdin Palace. Lastly, signs show the way to the **Private Museum** (also closed for restoration), a family hoard of manuscripts, carpets, glassware and silver plate, including some huge banqueting trays.

The Nilometer and Umm Kalthoum Museum

The southern tip of Roda Island features a **museum** dedicated to the life and work of Egypt's most popular singer, **Umm Kalthoum** (daily 10am–4pm; £E2). Through audiovisual clips, photos, press cuttings and a filmshow, the museum attempts to recreate the life of this giant of Arabic music (see p.797). Though she died in 1975, her songs, invariably backed by an orchestra of violins, remain massively popular throughout the Arab world. Exhibits include 78rpm wax records, letters from Egyptian and other Arab heads of state including Nasser, Sadat and King Farouk, and, most poignantly, her trademark pink scarf and dark glasses.

In the same compound is the **Nilometer** (daily 9am–5pm; £E6, student £E3), often locked, though the caretaker will turn out for rare visitors. From ancient times into the present century, Egyptian agriculture depended on the annual **flooding of the Nile**. Crop yields were predicted and taxes were set according to the river's level in August, as measured by Nilometers. A reading of 16 *ells* (8.6m) foretold the valley's complete irrigation; significantly more or less meant widespread flooding or drought. Public rejoicing followed the announcement of the Wafa el-Nil ("Abundance of the Nile"), while any other verdict caused gloom and foreboding.

Although the southern tip of Roda has probably featured a Nilometer since pharaonic times, the existing one dates from 861 and its Turkish kiosk is actually a modern replica, built in 1947 and recently restored. Its stone-lined shaft, descending well below the level of the Nile, was connected to the river by three tunnels (now sealed) at different heights – the uppermost is still accessible. Around the shaft's interior are Koranic verses in Kufic script, extolling rain as God's blessing; its central column is graduated into 16 *ells* of roughly 54cm each.

The neighbouring **Manasterly Palace** is a Rococo confection dating from 1850. Built as a conference centre, the palace is now open only for concerts and exhibitions.

The southern suburbs

South of Old Cairo, a ribbon of development follows the east bank of the Nile down to Helwan. Though easily reached by metro, these **southern suburbs** hold little attraction for tourists, notwithstanding Ma'adi's popularity as an expatriate residential area.

Less than a kilometre south of Coptic Cairo and Roda Island, on the Corniche northwest of Zahra metro station, the **Egyptian Geological Museum** (daily except Fri 9am–1pm; free) will interest fans of fossils, rocks and minerals. Pieces of dinosaur bone found in Egypt are displayed to the right of the entrance, with invertebrate fossils, mostly marine, down the right-hand side of the museum's single hall, and samples of different minerals on the left-hand side. At the end of the left-hand section are some prehistoric stone tools, and a piece of moon rock, displayed with an Egyptian flag that was flown round the moon on *Apollo 17* in 1972. It's the museum's middle section that's of most interest, containing the remains of prehistoric mammals, including the cast of a skeleton from an elephant ancestor called moeritherium.

Ma'adi to Helwan

With its Corniche boutiques and takeaways, and acres of villas, **Ma'adi** is unmistakably wealthy. Besides native millionaires and Gulf Arabs, most of Egypt's American community lives here, and it's also home to some trendy restaurants.

The **Military Hospital**, on the Corniche further north, is the largest of its kind in the Middle East. It was here that the ex-Shah of Iran died of cancer, and President Sadat was rushed by helicopter from the blood-soaked reviewing stand in Medinet Nasr. As a young officer during World War II, Sadat was actually stationed in Ma'adi when he became embroiled in a Nazi spy ring (see p.193). Ma'adi is directly accessible from Tahrir or Ramses by microbus service taxi or metro (25min).

The once-fashionable spa of **Helwan** is now grossly polluted by a gigantic **iron- and steelworks** that exploits power from the Aswan Dam and iron ore from the Western Desert. The steelworks wreak eco-death on a nineteenth-century **Japanese Garden** (ask for Ganenit el-Arbaine Harami; daily: summer 9am–midnight; winter 9am–10pm; £E2) – complete with Buddhas and a pagoda – five blocks east from Helwan metro station (turn left as you exit). One hundred metres south of Ain Helwan metro station (one stop back up the line from Helwan station) on the west side of the tracks, was a tacky but fun **Waxworks Museum** (*methaf sham*) portraying such moments in Egyptian history as the death of Cleopatra and Salah al-Din's meeting with Richard the Lionheart. Unfortunately, it was closed at last check, and its future seems uncertain. The sulphurous **Ain Helwan Baths** (daily 8am–5pm; £E4) are less than 100m northwest of Ain Helwan station, but are essentially just an open-air swimming pool, crowded with kids whenever school's out.

Gezira and the west bank

Flowing northwards through Cairo, the Nile divides into channels around the two major islands of Roda and Gezira. **Gezira**, the larger island, is further from the centre than Roda and notably more spacious and verdant than the rest of Cairo. Elevated highways bear cross-town traffic to diverse districts on the **west bank** of the Nile, collectively known as **Giza** and administered as a separate governorate, though transport and utilities are functionally integrated with Cairo's. **Imbaba** here is a working-class district, a world apart from the adjoining **Aguza**, with its Corniche nightlife, and even more at odds with the Dallas-style pretensions of **Mohandiseen**. Further south and east is **Dokki**, whose wealthy enclaves give way to *baladi* market quarters, the green lungs of

Cairo's zoo, and scattered university faculties, before the dusty expanse of Giza city extends to the Pyramids (see p.203).

Gezira and Zamalek

Gezira (literally "island") dominates the waterfront from Garden City to Bulaq, its three sets of bridges spanning the Nile. Nearly 4km long and 1km wide, the island is big enough to encompass two distinct zones. The southern half, featuring the Opera House complex, parks, a viewing tower and famous sporting clubs, is Gezira proper. **Zamalek** (pronounced "Za-*ma*-lek"), further north, is pure real estate – apartments, villas, offices and embassies – with a westernized ambience and nightlife. Both seem so integral to Cairo that it's hard to envisage their absence, yet the island itself only coalesced in the early 1800s and remained unstable until the first Aswan Dam regulated the Nile's flood in the 1900s. For more on the history and architecture of Gezira and Zamalek, check out Samir Raafat's website at ⓦ www.egy.com /landmarks.

Almost a third of the island belongs to the **Gezira Sporting Club** (see p.264), laid out by the British Army on land given by Khedive Tewfiq. The club's main pursuits were horse-racing and polo; "It is on the Gezira polo grounds that the officers of the Cavalry Brigade are tested for military efficiency and fitness for command", wrote C.S. Jarvis in the 1920s. Diplomats and selected upper-crust Egyptians also belonged to the club and, after Nasser decided against expropriation following the revolution, it soon acquired members from the new elite. The hefty membership fees still restrict access to its golf course, tennis courts, stables, gardens and pet cemetery; non-members are resolutely excluded.

Approaches to Gezira and Zamalek: the bridges

The **6th October Bridge**, high above the Sporting Club, is more of a direct link between Aguza and central Cairo than a viable approach to Gezira (though there are stairs down to both banks of the island). However, it does overlook the offices and former ground (now used only for training) of **Ahly FC**, one of Egypt's top football teams.

It's the southern bit of **Gezira**, however, that's most accessible and worth seeing. Despite heavy traffic, it's enjoyable to walk across the **Tahrir Bridge** (200m from Midan Tahrir), catching the breeze and watching barges and feluccas on the river. Gaining the island, you can strike 200m northwards past the former *El-Borg Hotel* and turn left down an avenue to reach the Cairo Tower (10min), or follow the traffic heading for Dokki, which brings you to the Cairo Opera House and several museums (5–10min). Alternatively, take a *calèche*, a horse-drawn carriage seating up to five people, on a circuit of Gezira – a short trip, around the Cairo Tower area, will cost around £E30, while a longer circuit, all the way round the Gezira Sporting Club, works out at about £E50. *Caleches* can be picked up on Sharia al-Gezira at the corner of Sharia el-Borg, or on Sharia Tahrir just before the Gala'a Bridge.

To get to **Zamalek** from central Cairo, save yourself a long walk and grab a taxi (which shouldn't cost more than £E5–8). Buses from Midan Tahrir to Zamalek will drop you on Sharia Gabalaya on the western side of the district, and there's no lack of minibuses heading west along **26th July Street** from Midan Ataba and Midan Ramses. Having traversed the island, 26th July Street crosses the **Zamalek Bridge** onto the west bank, where Midan Sphinx funnels traffic into Mohandiseen (see p.192).

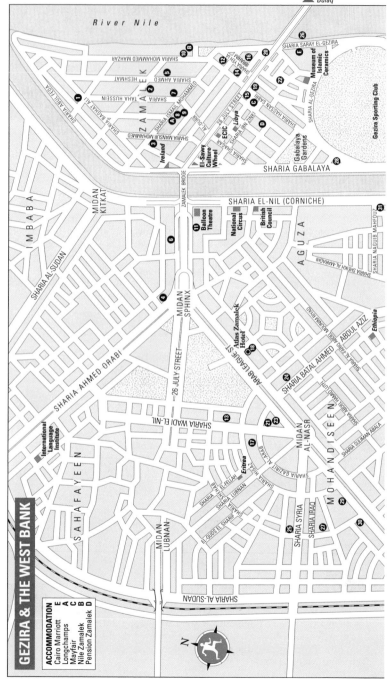

GEZIRA & THE WEST BANK

ACCOMMODATION
Cairo Marriott   E
Longchamps   A
Mayfair   C
Nile Zamalek   B
Pension Zamalek   D

River Nile

▲ Bulaq

Z A M A L E K

SHARIA MOHAMMED MAHZAR
SHARIA ABU'L FIDA
SHARIA BASHIR ALI
SHARIA AHMED HESHMAT
SHARIA TAHA HUSSEIN
SHARIA ISMAIL MOHAMMED
SHARIA MANSUR MOHAMMED

Ireland

El-Sawy Culture Wheel

ECIC
Libya

26 JULY STREET
SHARIA AL-FANN
SHARIA SHARIF IBN ZAKI

SHARIA SARAY EL-GEZIRA
Museum of Islamic Ceramics

SHARIA HASSAN SABRI
SHARIA AL-GEZIRA

Gabalaya Gardens

SHARIA GABALAYA

Gezira Sporting Club

SHARIA EL-NIL (CORNICHE)

ZAMALEK BRIDGE

Balloon Theatre

National Circus

British Council

A G U Z A

SHARIA NAGUIB MAHFOUZ

SHARIA SHEIKH AL-MARAGHI

MIDAN KITKAT

I M B A B A

SHARIA AL-SUDAN

MIDAN SPHINX

Atlas Zamalek Hotel

ARAB LEAGUE ST
26 JULY STREET

SHARIA FARID SEMEIKA MOHAMMED FARID
SHARIA ABDUL AZIZ

Ethiopia

SHARIA BATAL AHMED

SHARIA AHMED ORABI

S A H A F A Y E E N

International Language Institute

SHARIA WADI EL-NIL

MIDAN AL-NASR

M O H A N D I S E E N

SHARIA ABUL MAHASIN
SHARIA SULIMAN ABALA

Eritrea

SHARIA GAZIRET EL-ARAB

EL-QUDS EL-SHARIF
SHARIA LUBNAN
SHARIA EL-FELLAH
SHARIA HIGAZ

MIDAN LUBNAN

SHARIA SYRIA
SHARIA IRAQ

SHARIA AL-SUDAN

N

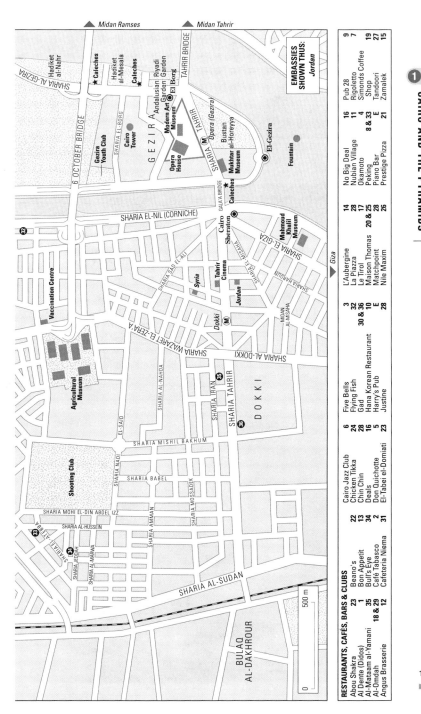

CAIRO AND THE PYRAMIDS

189

Cairo Tower

Rising 187m above Gezira, the **Borg al-Qahira** or **Cairo Tower** offers a stupendous view of the seething immensity of Cairo (daily: summer 9am–1am; winter 8am–midnight; £E60, video permit £E20); the entrance is to the north of the tower in Sharia el-Borg. Built between 1957 and 1962 with Soviet help, the tower combines pharaonic and socialist realist motifs within a latticework shaft of poured concrete that blossoms into a lotus finial.

On the fourteenth floor is an overpriced "Egyptian-style" restaurant (buy a £E100 ticket for entry and set-menu meal) that – when it's working – revolves for a 360° view; above it is a similarly styled cafeteria serving tolerable tea (entry plus drink is £E80), with a viewing room – complete with telescopes – upstairs from here. The real attraction, though, provided by the café, restaurant and a **viewing platform** at the top, is the panoramic **vista** of Cairo. East across the river, the blue-and-white *Nile Hilton* and the antenna-festooned Television Building delineate an arc of central Cairo. Beyond lies the medieval quarter, bristling with minarets below the Citadel and the serene Muqattam Hills. Roda Island and deluxe hotels dominate the view south (upriver); to the north are Zamalek, Shubra and the Nile Delta. Westwards, the city extends to meet the desert, with the Pyramids visible on the horizon on clear days. Come a while before sunset to witness Cairo transformed by nightfall, as a thousand muezzins call across the water.

The Opera House complex

Fans of postmodernist architecture should check out the **Cairo Opera House**, which is near Tahrir Bridge and directly connected to the Metro (the station is signed "Opera" but is marked as "Gezira" on the Metro map). Outwardly Islamic in style, it has an interior that melds pharaonic motifs with elements of the Baroque opera houses of the nineteenth century: an audacious blend of Oriental and Occidental by Japanese architect Koichiro Shikida. Built in 1988, the Opera House was a $30million gift from Japan, and belatedly replaces the old building on Midan Opera, which burned down in 1971.

△ Sunset on the Nile, with the Cairo Tower in the background

Off to the right as you walk towards the Opera House is the **Modern Art Museum** (Mon 5.30–10pm, Tues–Thurs, Sat & Sun 10am–2pm & 5.30–10pm; £E10, students £E5), which displays paintings, sculptures and graphics by Egyptian artists since 1908; there is always something new on show.

Following Sharia Tahrir towards the west bank, you'll pass the old Gezira Exhibition Grounds, whose dilapidated pavilions formerly housed the **Gezira Museum** (of objets d'art collected by the royal family) and a **Planetarium** – both closed for long-term renovation – and a **Museum of Egyptian Civilization**, illustrating national history from pharaonic to modern times, also closed, but due to reopen in a new venue at Fustat in 2008. Across the road to the south, just before the Gala'a Bridge, the **Mukhtar Museum** (daily except Mon 10am–1.30pm & 5–9pm; £E5) honours the sculptor Mahmoud Mukhtar (1891–1934), who is buried in the basement. Working in bronze and marble, he created several patriotic sculptures, including the *Renaissance of Egypt* monument that welcomes drivers into Dokki.

The 27-storey **El-Gezira Hotel** at the southern tip of the island has been bought by Sofitel, who were busy doing it up at last check, but it should reopen as a seriously swish establishment. On public holidays, a **fountain** in the middle of the Nile between Gezira and Roda shoots an immense jet of water into the sky.

Zamalek

Originally a very British neighbourhood, despite its Continental grid of tree-lined boulevards, **Zamalek** still has bags of social cachet: renting a flat here is the Cairene equivalent of moving into Manhattan. Unlike most parts of Cairo, the quarter feels very private; residents withdraw into air-conditioned high-rises or 1930s apartment buildings, and with so many foreign companies and **embassies** in the area, most of the streets are lifeless after dark. Somewhat paradoxically, Zamalek also features some of the trendiest **nightspots** in Cairo. Near the Aguza side of the Gezira Sporting Club on Sharia Hassan Sabry, the *Four Corners* complex contains, among others, a deluxe French restaurant, *Justine* (see p.236), and there are more bars and restaurants to be found in the *Marriott Hotel*. Other places congregate north of the 26th July flyover. For more on eating and drinking in Zamalek, see p.235 and p.243.

Zamalek has less to offer by day, though children may enjoy the **aquarium grotto** in **Gabalaya Gardens** (daily 9am–4pm; 35pt; see p.261), entered from Sharia Gabalaya. For more cultural pursuits, head for the other end of Sharia al-Gezira as it curves around the northern edge of the Sporting Club, where a graceful nineteenth-century villa houses the Museum of Islamic Ceramics (see p.192). The modern annexes of the adjacent **Cairo Marriott Hotel** screen what was originally a "madly sumptuous palace" built for Napoleon's wife Empress Eugénie, later sold to wealthy Copts in lieu of Ismail's debts and turned into a hotel. Non-residents can wander in and loll amid khedival splendour for the price of a drink.

Although Zamalek is pretty young by Egyptian standards, it isn't without its history. The portions of Sharia Shagar al-Durr and Sharia Mansur Mohammed south of 26th July Street were once home to nineteen **Edwardian villas** constructed by the British government in 1906–7 to house important official employees. Of the nine still standing, the grandest is at 20 Sharia Ibn Zinki (on the corner of Mansur Mohammed) with its imposing triple-arched portico. Further south, the *Four Corners* complex occupies the site of a villa where the UK's senior representative in wartime Egypt, **Lord Moyne**, was shot in 1944, along with his driver, by members of a far-right Zionist paramilitary group known as the Stern Gang. A more recent Zamalek murder, which shocked the Middle East as much, was that of Tunisian singer **Zikra** in November 2003, at her swanky apartment on Sharia Mohammed Mazhar. She was killed by her husband, apparently in a fit of jealousy, after refusing his demand that she give up her career. Having produced two pistols and a machine gun, he pumped Zikra with 25 rounds, then shot two of their friends, and finally himself. Thousands attended the singer's funeral.

Museum of Islamic Ceramics

Housed in a white-domed villa close to the *Cairo Marriott*, the **Museum of Islamic Ceramics** (daily except Fri 10am–2pm & 5–9pm; £E25, students £E12) is one of Cairo's most agreeable museums. Built by Prince Amru Ibrahim in the late nineteenth century, the structure itself is worth a look for its elaborate marble inlays and floors.

The collection contains pieces from Egypt, Persia, Syria, Turkey, Morocco, Iraq and Andalusia, ranging from the seventh century to the present. The illustrated guidebook (£E25) explains each piece in English and also gives a thorough account of the history of Islamic ceramics. Downstairs there's an art gallery (same hours; free) that exhibits original paintings and sculptures as well as prints by modern Egyptian artists such as Asraf and Alzamzami. All the works exhibited are for sale.

Imbaba

From Midan Kitkat, 300m north of Zamalek Bridge, Sharia al-Sudan arcs through the **Imbaba** district, whose overspill covers the site of the "**Battle of the Pyramids**" where Napoleon's army routed the Mamlukes on July 21, 1798, prior to taking Cairo. Unfortunately for Napoleon – who dreamed of "founding a religion, marching into Asia riding an elephant", bearing "the new Koran that I would have composed to suit my needs" – his strategic ambition to disrupt British power in India was literally scuppered when Nelson sank his fleet at Abu Qir Bay. Within eighty years, the Suez Canal had become a vital link between Britain and its empire "East of Suez", maintained by British naval supremacy but necessitating British control over Egypt. With the advent of aviation, flying boats on the famous Cape-to-Cairo run used the Nile, while most Imperial Airways flights used **Imbaba Airport**, now a flying school.

Mohandiseen

Laid out during the 1960s to house Egypt's new technocrats, Medinat Mohandiseen ("Engineers' City"), as the suburb was initially called, responded to an influx of business and media folk during the Sadat era by shortening its name to just **Mohandiseen** and emulating America. Nowhere else in Cairo can you cruise down a boulevard glittering with boutiques and junk-food outlets, squint and imagine that you're in LA. Even the palm trees seem to hail from Hollywood, rather than the Nile.

Most of the action occurs along Mohandiseen's main axis, **Arab League Street** (Sharia Gameat al-Dowal al-Arabiya), also known as "The Mall", which is bisected by palms and shrubbery for its three-kilometre length. You can look down it on a clear day and see the Pyramids of Giza in the distance. During summer Cairene families picnic here – an indication of how few green spaces are available. The avenue's main landmark is the **Atlas Zamalek Hotel**, 500m past Midan Sphinx.

To **reach the quarter** from central Cairo, you can catch buses from Midan Falaki, Midan Tahrir, Midan Ataba or Midan Ramses that end up on Sharia al-Sudan near Midan Lubnan. Alternatively, to get to Midan al-Nasr on Arab League Street, you can take buses from the Arab League Building in Midan Tahrir (#337), or from Midan Ataba (#17, #19 or #103). A faster way is to jump in a Zamalek-bound service-taxi microbus at Ramses or the corner of 26th July Street with Sharia al-Gala and get whisked to Midan Sphinx or Arab League Street.

Southwest beyond the Al-Sudan ring road lies **Bulaq al-Dakhrour**, an unplanned sprawl of ramshackle dwellings built by migrant *fellaheen* from Upper Egypt and the Delta. Bulaq al-Dakhrour ends at the **Maryotteya Canal**, beyond which the village of **Kerdassa** (see p.214) precedes another canal before the strip of luxury hotels (*Mövenpick*, *Pyramids Park*, *Sofitel*, *Oasis*) along the Desert Road to Alexandria.

Aguza and Dokki

A 100-metre-wide channel separates Zamalek and Gezira from the west bank districts of **Aguza and Dokki**. Being mainly residential and devoid of major "sights", they're only worth considering as a quieter place to stay than central Cairo, or for their nightlife, though in their time these prim-looking neighbourhoods generated as much scandal as the Clot Bey and Abdin quarters once did.

Aguza

Wedged between Mohandiseen and the Nile, **Aguza** ("Old Woman") stretches its legs **along the Corniche**. At the northern end of Sharia el-Nil, near the Zamalek Bridge, are the **Balloon Theatre** – a regular venue for the National and Reda dance troupes – and Egypt's **National Circus** (see p.261). A popular stopover for taxi drivers and nightclubbers is the 24-hour *Cafeteria Niema*, opposite the Police Hospital near the 6th October Bridge.

Fifty years ago the Corniche was a popular mooring place for houseboats, which saw their share of scandal. One was occupied by a famous belly dancer, Hekmet Fathy, who used to entice Allied staff officers aboard to inveigle secrets from them on behalf of the Nazis. Also involved was a young Egyptian officer, Anwar Sadat, who attempted to convey messages to Rommel and was subsequently jailed by the British for treason. Post-revolutionary Egypt was austere by comparison, but hardly innocent. In 1988 the government tried to suppress the memoirs of Eitimad Khorshid, a *femme fatale* who cut a swath through the Nasserite establishment of the 1950s, and promised to reveal all in what became an underground bestseller.

To reach any of the above locations, catch a taxi via the 6th October Bridge, an elevated extension of which pushes 500m inland towards the **Agricultural Museum** (daily except Mon 9am–2pm; 10pt) in the grounds of the Ministry of Agriculture; the entrance is on the south side of the estate. A group of six pavilions – some closed for renovation, others that could themselves almost be museum pieces – these solemnly dingy museums of yesteryear contain exhibits on ancient farming techniques, with stuffed animals and models of native village life. There are also quirky items such as prettily arranged displays of insects and a rather horrific demonstration of various animal diseases. One of the pavilions houses the **Cotton Museum** (closed Thurs & Fri), which gives the rundown on Egypt's main cash crop. For most visitors, however, the pleasant grounds are more of a draw than the dusty old museums. The Ministry of Agriculture marks the point where Aguza merges into Dokki.

Dokki

The social geography of **Dokki** (usually pronounced "Do'i", with a glottal stop in the middle) is more complex than Aguza's. Broadly speaking, the rich occupy the land nearest the river and the Dokki Sporting Club, with a phalanx of private hospitals, VD clinics and covert bordellos separating their villas and apartments from the poorer market quarter to the southwest.

Coming over the Galaa Bridge from Gezira Island, you'll see Mahmoud Mukhtar's **Renaissance of Egypt statue** and the twin towers of the **Cairo Sheraton**. From here, Sharia al-Sad al-Ali itself continues on to meet Suleyman Gohar, Dokki's vibrant **market quarter**. For **cinemas** and **restaurants**, look along Sharia Tahrir and Sharia al-Misaha, radiating west and southwest from the Galaa Bridge.

Two main roads head south from the *Sheraton*. Running one block inland, **Sharia el-Giza** passes the Russian Embassy and the former residence of President Sadat, where his widow, Jihan, still lives in guarded seclusion (photography is prohibited in this area). Another once-famous resident of Dokki was Field Marshal Amr, a long-time friend and ally of Nasser's who supposedly committed suicide after being accused of plotting a coup against him, and was posthumously scapegoated for Egypt's defeat in the 1967 War.

The main feature of interest on Sharia el-Giza, however, is the **Mahmoud Khalil Museum** (daily except Mon 10am–6pm; Ⓦwww.mkm.gov.eg; £E25, students £E12; wheelchair access), two blocks south of the *Sheraton*, housed in the refurbished mansion where Khalil, a prewar politician and Agriculture Minister, lived with his French-born wife, Emeline Hector. Together they built up this magnificent collection of art and sculpture, mostly French Impressionist and post-Impressionist works by the likes of Monet, Renoir, Gauguin and Pissarro, but also featuring artists such as Van Gogh, Delacroix and Rodin. There are information sheets on the artists in various languages, but the computer screens that tell you about the Khalils and their home are in Arabic only.

Running parallel to Sharia el-Giza is the **Corniche** (now officially Sharia Gamal Abdel Nasser). Three boats moored 200m south of the *Cairo Sheraton* house **Dr Ragab's Papyrus Institute** (daily 9am–9pm; free), demonstrating papyrus-making, an ancient craft which died out in the tenth century AD but was revived in modern times by Ragab. Although it's more of a papyrus emporium (and pricey) than a museum, visitors are not harassed to buy. Beyond the Papyrus Institute are Cairo's **Rowing Club** and **Yacht Club**, both citadels of privilege. A few blocks nearer Giza, the Nasr Building contains two excellent Swiss-owned **restaurants**: *Le Chalet* and *Le Château*.

Dokki is served by buses #15, #82, #194, #203 and #926, and minibuses #102 and #183, from in front of the Arab League Building on Midan Tahrir, all running along Sharia Tahrir. Dokki metro stop is also on Sharia Tahir.

Giza

In pharaonic times **Giza** lay en route between Heliopolis and Memphis and probably also housed the skilled corps of pyramid-builders. As Memphis declined during the Christian era, so Giza flourished, thanks to its proximity to the Fortress of Babylon, across the river; Amr's reopening of the ancient Delta–Red Sea Canal subsequently boosted its prosperity under Muslim rule. Giza's apogee coincided with the reign of Salah al-Din – the Moorish traveller Ibn Jubayr described it as a "large and important burgh with fine buildings" – when its Sunday market attracted vast crowds. But the area's vulnerability to floods caused stagnation, and it wasn't until Ismail laid the Pyramids Road, drained swamps and built a palace in the 1860s that Giza became fashionable again. By Nasser's time, however, expansion was proceeding virtually unchecked. As Giza's population topped a million, a tide of high-rise hovels, tacky nightclubs and roaring flyovers devoured crumbling villas, erstwhile farmland and desert, right to the Giza Plateau beneath the Pyramids.

The zoo and Midan Giza are not far from Faysal and Giza metro stations, and can also be reached by **bus** from Tahrir (#30, #355 and #357, minibuses #82 and #83), Ramses (#30 and minibus #83) and Ataba (#6, #9, #106 and #109), and from Ramses and Abdel Mouneen Riyad by service-taxi microbus.

Around Cairo Zoo and University

The extensive grounds which Deschamps laid out for Ismail's palace are now divided into Cairo's **Zoological Garden** – which is packed on Fridays and public holidays, but fun to visit at other times (see p.261) – and the smaller **El-Urman Garden** (daily 8.30am–4pm): along with the floating restaurants near the **El-Gama'a Bridge**, they're marked on the "Old Cairo and Roda Island" map (see pp.170–171). The bridge is named after **Cairo University**, which was founded in 1908 as a counterweight to traditionalist Al-Azhar but has never been any the less political. Access to its scattered faculties is controlled by Central Security, so foreigners may need a letter of introduction (or at least their passports) to pass beyond its gates. Morbid curiosity might inspire a visit to the Agricultural Faculty, near the bottom of Sharia Gameat al-Qahira and occupying a former palace of Mohammed Ali; its basement holds remnants of his torture chamber.

Midan Giza and Pyramids Road

West of the **El-Giza Bridge** and south of the university belt, Cairo's second largest **bus and taxi terminal** agitates **Midan Giza**. Its seething ranks include buses to the Pyramids; minibuses to Tahrir, Ramses and Heliopolis; and service taxis to Fayoum City, Beni Suef and the Red Sea coast. A few minutes' walk south is **Giza Station**. More flyovers funnel traffic onto the **Pyramids Road** (Sharia al-Ahram), which runs the gauntlet of **nightclubs** and tourist bazaars for 8km. A couple of kilometres before the Pyramids of Giza, Sharia al-Ahram crosses two canals in quick succession, which lead south to Saqqara and Dahsur; service-taxi microbuses for both can be found by the first of these two canals, Maryotteya. See pp.203–231 for details of both these and the Giza Pyramid site.

The northern suburbs

During the last century, Cairo's **northern suburbs** swallowed up villages and farmland and expanded far into the desert to form a great arc of residential neighbourhoods stretching from the Nile to the Muqattam. **Heliopolis**, with its handsome boulevards and Art Deco villas, is still favoured above the satellite suburbs that have mushroomed in recent decades, and retains a sizeable foreign community. Otherwise, tourists usually only venture into **Abbassiya** for the Sinai Bus Terminal, or to visit the Coptic Patriarchate and Sakakini Palace; and you have to be fanatically keen to bother hunting down the Virgin's Tree in **Matariyya**, Sadat's tomb in **Medinet Nasr**, or Mamluke edifices in **Bulaq**. For a guide to the location of these areas, see the "Greater Cairo" map on pp.86–87.

Bulaq, Shubra and Rod el-Farag

Bulaq and its neighbours **Shubra** and **Rod el-Farag** (northwest of central Cairo) are run-down and overcrowded, with ten times the population density of Garden City. More or less bereft of "sights", these quarters have a predominantly *baladi* ambience and might appeal to visitors fascinated by ordinary Cairene life. Shubra and Rod el-Farag are best reached by metro. Bulaq can be reached on foot, or by bus or microbus service taxi, along 26th July Street.

Bulaq

Immediately east of the 6th October flyover (see the "Central Cairo" map on pp.104–105) lies the oldest of the northern suburbs, **Bulaq**, whose name derives from the Coptic word for "marsh". During medieval times, the westward shift of the Nile turned a sandbank into an island, which merged with the east bank as the intervening channel silted up. As the Fatimid port of Al-Maks was left high and dry, Bulaq became the new anchorage in the 1350s, rapidly developing into an entrepôt after Sultan Barsbey re-routed the spice trade and encouraged manufacturing. When Mohammed Ali set about establishing a foundry, textiles factory and modern shipyards in the 1820s, Bulaq was the obvious site. Unfortunately, the Ottomans permitted free trade, enabling British manufacturers to undersell local industries and force Egypt back into its dependency on cotton exports to the Lancashire mills.

Since then, small workshops and apartment buildings have taken over Bulaq, while world affairs are handled in two towering landmarks along the Corniche: the **Television Building** and the twin towers of the **Cairo Plaza**. Inland of the latter is a one-time hostel for members of the Rifai order, next to the **Mosque of Sinan Pasha**, a sixteenth-century hybrid of Mamluke and Ottoman styles. More revered by locals for its namesake's *baraka* is the fifteenth-century **Mosque of Abu'l'Ila**, on 26th July Street just west of the Corniche. Nearby, and currently undergoing rennovation, stand the former **royal stables of Mohammed Ali**, which at one time housed the Royal Carriage Museum (now in the Citadel, see p.157).

Shubra

Two million Cairenes live in the sprawling beehive known as **Shubra**, the older part of which is called Shubra al-Balad to distinguish it from the newer outgrowth beyond the Ismailiya Canal, dubbed Shubra al-Kheima. Originally an island (its name, "Elephant", supposedly comes from a ship that ran aground), Shubra became attached to the mainland about the same time as Bulaq, but was given over to orchards and villages until the nineteenth century. In 1808, Mohammed Ali built a summer palace here that caused Europeans to snigger ("The taste, alas! of an English upholsterer"), where he later died insane. Other palaces were erected by Ismail, who also laid a carriage road to the original residence, planted with acacia and sycamore-fig trees, where Cairenes promenaded. The palace, which is inside the Ain Shems University's faculty of agriculture, has now been restored and is expected to open to the public shortly.

The 1891 edition of *Murray's Handbook* deemed **Sharia Shubra** "the most republican promenade in the world. No description of vehicle, nor manner of animal, biped or quadruped, is excluded, and the Khedive and his outriders are jostled and crossed in a most unseemly fashion by files of bare-boned and sore-covered mules and donkeys, whipped in by ragged urchins." Nowadays the avenue seems thoroughly proletarian, for Shubra has long since evolved from a garden suburb into densely packed quarters where educated Copts and Muslims rub shoulders with poor rural migrants.

Though self-help projects have improved some of the bleak low-rise estates in Shubra al-Kheima, dire poverty inclines a minority towards radical Islam, and reinforces the superstitions that most Cairenes at least half-believe. What psychologists might regard as mental illnesses are treated here as cases of demonic possession, possibly caused by deliberate cursing (one method of hexing is to recite the 33rd *sura* of the Koran backwards.) While certain moulids feature public **exorcisms**, most are private. Joseph McPherson, Cairo's secret police chief in the 1920s, witnessed a *zar* where celebrants whirled to ancient and Muslim incantations, cymbals clashed, and a ram, ganders, doves and rabbits were sacrificed, their blood being daubed on the participants, whose frenzy increased. When all concerned believe in the ritual's spiritual efficacy, the desired result is frequently achieved.

Rod el-Farag

During the 1950s, a slice of Shubra al-Balad was developed as a separate residential and commercial district, named "Farag's Orchard" after its previous role. The name remains appropriate, since **Rod el-Farag** hosts Cairo's largest **fruit and vegetable market**, Abu el-Farag. Like the others, it's the exclusive preserve of one or two cabals of wholesalers. In Rod el-Farag's case, they hail from the villages around the capital, whereas elsewhere Saiyidis from Upper Egypt may control trade. The modern **Port of Cairo** is another local source of wealth with a shady underside.

Abbassiya, Hada'iq al-Qubba and Medinet Nasr

In practice, the demarcation lines between these northeastern districts (which subdivide into other quarters) and Heliopolis are blurred by sheer density, overcrowding and interlocking transport networks.

Abbassiya

The sprawling **Abbassiya** district gets its name from a palace built by Mohammed Ali's grandson, Pasha Abbas I, who dreaded assassination during his brief reign (1848–54) and kept camels saddled here for rapid flight into the desert – to no avail, for he was murdered by his servants. Previously called Ridaniya, the area was the site of the last battle between the Mamlukes and the invading Ottoman Turks, who went on to take Cairo. Nearer the centre, the British established the Abbassiya Barracks (where the nationalist leader Orabi surrendered after his defeat at Tell el-Kebir), which vastly expanded during wartime. Like the Army GHQ (still located in Abbassiya), it was later seized by the Free Officers in a bloodless coup against Egypt's monarchy on the night of 22 July, 1952. Cairenes awoke next day to learn of a revolution led by General Naguib – a figurehead, since it was Nasser who had engineered it and secretly controlled affairs until his public emergence as leader.

Abbassiya today juxtaposes spacious institutions and crowded slums, marshalling yards and hospitals. Its main thoroughfare, Sharia Ramses, divides the oil-depot zone of Al-Sharabiyya from Gamra and El-Sakakini, two residential market quarters. On Sharia Sakakini, near Ghamra metro station, the ornate Rococo **Sakakini Palace**, built in 1898 for an Italian nobleman, is supposedly being restored and due to open to the public, though they have been saying this for years. In the meantime, it is still worth a look if you are in the area for its outrageously kitsch facade, and the caretaker may let you see the marvellous interior with its huge mirrors, murals, painted ceilings and antique elevator.

At the end of Sharia Sakakini, on Midan al-Zahir, the thirteenth-century **Mosque of Beybars the Crossbowman** was built in 1268, the first mosque to be located outside the city's walls. Covering ten thousand square metres, this is also one of Cairo's biggest mosques, its sturdy walls enclosing a vast open courtyard, surrounded by a rather heavy arcade. After it ceased to be a place of worship in the sixteenth century, it was subsequently used as a military store-house by the Ottomans, a barracks by Napoleon and a slaughterhouse by the British. Restoration started in the early 1990s but soon petered out, and the southeast side is now again in use as a mosque; the rest of it can be visited by tourists. A more conspicuous edifice is the curvaceous **Coptic Cathedral of St Mark**, the seat of the Coptic Patriarchate since it was raised in the 1970s. Visitors interested in joining pilgrim excursions to the Red Sea Monasteries should contact officials in the adjacent Church of SS Peter and Paul (Al-Batrus-siya), at 222 Sharia Ramses.

Other landmarks include the **Misr Travel Tower**, housing the Ministry of Tourism, 500m from the **Sinai Bus Terminal** near the junction of Salah Salem and Al-'Urubah, and a similar distance from the Engineering Faculty of **Ain Shams University**. Round about are sited numerous clubs (*nady*) and training schools belonging to professional unions, the police and military.

Buses (including #1, #4, #400, #400/, #500/, #611 and #973) and mini-buses (including #27, #35 and #35/) run to Abbassiya, from Tahrir's Abdel Mouneem Riyad terminal via Midan Ramses. Alternatively, you could use El-Demerdash station on the metro.

Hada'iq al-Qubba: Nasser's Tomb

Northeast of Abbassiya along Sharia al-Khalifa al-Ma'mun (a continuation of Sharia Abbassiya), a modern mosque stands beside a dusty shrine containing the **Tomb of Gamal Abdel Nasser**. When Nasser died in September 1969, a million Egyptians followed his bier through the streets of Cairo and the whole Arab world mourned. His cult was subsequently downplayed by Sadat (who feared comparisons) and in recent years most of the visitors to Nasser's shrine have been foreign admirers or gloating Israelis. Whatever Egyptians may think about Nasser's son, Khalid – who was finally acquitted of involvement in Thawraat Masri, a Libyan-backed group that attacked US and Israeli targets in the 1980s – his father's legend remains a potent one. Saddam Hussein's claim to be Nasser's "spiritual heir" was only the latest attempt by an Arab leader to metaphorically wrest the sword from the stone.

The tomb lies on the edge of **Hada'iq al-Qubba**, a district named after Ismail's **Qubba Palace**, now a presidential residence used for state conferences; it was here that the Shah of Iran spent the last days of his exile. Its four hundred rooms were inherited by Khedive Tewfik and later contained King Farouk's vast collection of rare stamps, coins and other treasures, ranging from medieval Korans to a Fabergé thermometer. The palace's walled grounds can be seen along the #420 bus route from Abbassiya; it and Nasser's tomb are best reached by metro (Saray el Kobba station and Kubri el Kobba station respectively).

Medinet Nasr

During the 1960s and 1970s **Medinet Nasr** was created as a new satellite suburb on the site of the Abbassiya Rifle Ranges, and many government departments were relocated to this "Victory City". Also here, alongside the Sharia al-Nasr boulevard, is a landscaped parade ground centred on a pyramid-shaped **Victory Memorial** to the 1973 October War. In 1981, Islamic radicals infiltrated the October 6 anniversary parade and blasted the reviewing stand with machine guns and grenades, fatally wounding President Sadat (Mubarak, who stood beside him, was unharmed). **Sadat's Tomb** is beneath the Victory Memorial.

North of Sadat's Tomb and the Victory Memorial, on Sharia al-Oruba, the huge **October War Panorama** was built on a suggestion made to Hosni Mubarak by Kim Il Sung of North Korea when the Egyptian president visited that country in 1983. Construction was supervised by North Korean technicians, and it shows: the building looks like a pavilion in some Communist theme park of the 1950s and is decorated with Maoist-style reliefs, but instead of East Asian peasants and workers striding purposefully forward, it's Egyptian soldiers in front of the Pyramids. Shows put on here (daily except Tues 9.30am, 11am and 12.30pm, plus in winter 5pm and 6.30pm, summer 6pm and 7.30pm; £E10, camera £E2) start with two rather silly dioramas illustrating the opening round of the October War, and culminate in a really quite impressive three-dimensional panorama of the war in Sinai, during which the audience is rotated around 360° to take it all in. The commentary (in Arabic, with an English version available via headphones) explains the action with such phrases as "the glorious minutes passed rapidly", and the whole thing is so over-the-top in its triumphalism that you might almost think the Egyptians had actually won the October War.

Travellers coming into Cairo from Suez will pass the Olympic-size **Cairo Stadium** off Sharia al-Nasr, where Cairo football clubs Ahly and Zamalek usually play their home matches, and where international ties and cup finals are also held (see p.264).

Heliopolis (Masr al-Gadida)

By the beginning of the twentieth century, the doubling of Cairo's population and the exponential growth of its foreign community had created a huge demand for new accommodation, which fired the imagination of a Belgian entrepreneur, Baron Édouard Empain, itching for new projects after his successful construction of the Paris Metro. Baron Empain proposed creating a garden city in the desert, linked to the downtown area by tram: a venture attractive to investors, since Empain's company would collect both rents and fares from commuting residents of the new suburb, which was named **Heliopolis** after the ancient City of the Sun nearby in Matariyya.

Laid out by Sir Reginald Oakes in radial grid patterns, the suburb's wide avenues were lined with apartment blocks ennobled by pale yellow Moorish facades and bisected by shrubbery. It soon acquired every facility from schools and churches to a racecourse and branch of *Groppi's*. Wealthy Egyptians settled here from the beginning; merely prosperous ones moved in as foreigners left in droves during the 1950s, when poorer quarters grew up around Heliopolis, ending its privileged isolation from Greater Cairo. During the 1970s, air-conditioned towers began to replace spacious villas, the racecourse was turned into a fun park, and burger joints proliferated. Today, visitors come for the restaurants and nightlife, or to admire the stylish architecture along its central boulevards; many foreigners also rent apartments or work in Heliopolis, known in Arabic as "New Cairo" (Masr al-Gadida).

Transport to Heliopolis

Heliopolis is between fifteen- and thirty-minutes' ride from downtown Cairo. You can get there by **bus** (#400, #400/ and #500) or **minibus** (#27, #35 and

Ancient Heliopolis, the Ennead and the cult of Re

Although Anthony Trollope scoffed "Humbug!" when he saw what little remained in 1858, the site of **Ancient Heliopolis**, near modern Matariyya, originally covered perhaps five square kilometres. The City of the Sun (called On by its founders, but better known by its Greek appellation) evolved in tandem with Memphis, the first capital of Dynastic Egypt. As Memphis embodied the political unification of Upper and Lower Egypt, so Heliopolis incarnated its theological aspect, syncretizing diverse local cults into a hierarchical cosmogony that proved more influential than other creation myths of the Old Kingdom.

Having been eclipsed by Karnak and Amun-worship during the New Kingdom, Heliopolis was devastated by the Persians in 525 BC. Once it was rebuilt, however, its intellectual reputation attracted fifth-century BC luminaries such as Plato, Eudoxus (who probably invented the sundial after studying Egyptian astronomy) and Herodotus. But as Alexandria became the new focus for science and religion, Heliopolis inexorably declined; the first-century geographer Strabo found it nearly desolate and the Romans totally ignored it. Today, the only tangible reminders of its existence are **Senusert's obelisk** and the **Spring of the Sun** in Matariyya, where Atum supposedly washed himself at the dawn of creation.

Cosmogony

▶ Shu, Nut and Geb

In the **Heliopolitan cosmogony**, the world began as watery chaos (Nun) from which Atum the sun-god emerged onto a primal mound, spitting forth the twin deities Shu (air) and Tefnut (moisture). They engendered Geb (earth) and Nut (sky), whose own union produced Isis, Osiris, Seth and Nephthys. Later texts often regarded this divine **Ennead** (Nine) as a single entity, while the universe was conventionally represented by the figures of Shu, Nut and Geb. Meanwhile (for reasons unknown), the primal deity Atum was subsumed by Re or Ra, a yet mightier aspect of the sun-god.

▶ Re

Re manifested himself in multiple forms: as hawk-headed Re-herakhte (Horus of the Horizon); the beetle Khepri (the rising sun); the disc Aten (the midday sun); and as Atum (the setting sun). The Egyptians believed that Re rose each morning in the east, traversed the sky in his solar barque and sank into the western Land of the Dead every evening, to voyage through the Duat (netherworld) during the night, emerging at sunrise. This journey inevitably linked Re to the Osirian myth, and from the V Dynasty onwards it became de rigueur for pharaohs to claim descent from Re by identifying themselves with Horus and Osiris. The **cult of Re** was exclusive, for only the pharaoh and priesthood had access to Re's sanctuary, whose daily rituals were adopted by other divine cults and soon became inextricably entangled with Osiris-worship (see p.325 & p.361). Ordinary folk – whose participation was limited to public festivals – worshipped lesser, more approachable deities.

#35/) from Tahrir and Ramses but, especially during the rush hour, these are slower than the suburb's original tram system, known as the **Heliopolis metro**, which begins at Midan Ramses. From there, its three tram lines follow the same track through Abbassiya, diverging shortly before Midan Roxi. Each has its own colour-coded direction boards:

• The **Abd al-Aziz Fahmi line** (destination written in blue) runs past Midan Roxi and along Sharia al-Ma'had al-Ishtiraki and Sharia al-Higaz, past Merryland and Heliopolis Hospital, to Midan Heliopolis, where it turns off up Abd al-Aziz Fahmi towards Ain Shams.

• More centrally, the **Nouzha line** (destination written in red) veers off Sharia Merghani near the Heliopolis Sporting Club, and follows Al-Ahram and Osman Ibn Affan to Midan Triomphe, then heads up Sharia Nouzha to Midan al-Higaz.

• Initially running alongside the Nouzha line, the **Merghani line** (destination usually written in yellow) follows the street of that name to Midan Triomphe, and out towards the Armed Forces Hospital.

Sights and activities

Nouzha-line trams run through the heart of Heliopolis, up **Sharia al-Ahram**, its handsome villas rich with flowery Art Nouveau and Neoclassical details. Here you'll find classy cafés like *Amphytryon* and of course *Groppi's*, where the bourgeoisie of the district's 1920s heyday would relax with a cake and a coffee, as indeed you can today. At the top of Al-Ahram, the tram sidles to the right to pass around the suburb's centrepiece, the Byzantine-style "jelly-mould" **Basilica**, which is also Baron Empain's last resting place.

Some of Heliopolis's finest neo-Moorish facades can be seen along the streets leading off from Al-Ahram, most notably **Sharia Laqqani**, which leads north

△ Baron Empain's Palace

to **Midan Roxi**, and **Sharia Ibrahimi**, which crosses Al-Ahram a couple of blocks before the Basilica; both streets are lined by arcades topped with Andalusian-style balconies and pantiles. At the start of Al-Ahram, where it branches off from Sharia Merghani, the wonderful neo-Moorish pile known as the **Urubah Palace** was formerly the *Heliopolis Palace Hotel*, but is now used as offices by the president, and out of bounds to the public.

The area's most famous and impressive landmark is further southeast, on Sharia al-'Urubah. Modelled on Hindu temples from Cambodia and Orissa, **Baron Empain's Palace** (known to locals as Qasr al-Baron) originally boasted a revolving tower that enabled its owner to follow the sun throughout the day. Although the building, completed in 1910, is now derelict within, its exterior has been spruced up, and is illuminated at night. As Sharia al-Oruba is the main road to the airport, you may see it on the way to or from taking a plane.

Heliopolis can be a good place to escape the summer heat, at the Heliopolis and Heliolido **sporting clubs**, both with swimming pools (see p.266), though they do not usually admit non-members on a Friday, when they tend to be full. Northeast of the Heliolido, on the "blue" tram route, **Merryland** is a green area where children can play (see p.262).

Matariyya and beyond

Northwest of Heliopolis, several former villages have evolved into ramshackle *baladi* suburbs. **El-Zeitun** (the Olives) merits a footnote in history as the site of Sultan Selim's defeat of the Mamlukes in 1517 and of conspiratorial gatherings of Free Officers during the early 1950s. The adjacent **Helmiya** quarter gets its name from yet another khedival palace built last century. But for actual sights you have to venture even further out, into **Matariyya**. Cairo's metro makes this sector of the northern suburbs readily accessible from the centre.

The modern suburb of Matariyya traces its antecedents way back to the Old Kingdom and claims later acquaintance with the infant Christ. As evidence of the former, the neighbourhood preserves a 22-metre-high, pink granite **Obelisk of Senusert I** (daily 8am–5pm; £E12, students £E6). Known locally as el-Misallah, it stands in a little garden in the middle of a large area of waste ground, about 600m northwest of Matariyya metro station (out of the exit from the northbound platform, take the street straight ahead of you for 200m until it forks, then follow the right-hand fork to the end and turn right). The obelisk, one of a pair raised to celebrate the pharaoh's Jubilee Festival (*c*.1900 BC), originally stood outside the Temple of Re, erected by Amenemhat I, Senusert's father, who founded the XII Dynasty. Another pair, belonging to the XVIII Dynasty ruler Tuthmosis III, was moved by the Romans to Alexandria, whence it ended up in New York's Central Park and on London's Victoria Embankment. However, the significance of this site and its cult of the sun-god are far older, dating back to the earliest dynasties.

The Spring of the Sun and the Virgin's Tree

Nowadays, the **Spring of the Sun** waters a famous Christian relic, the **Virgin's Tree** (daily 9am–5pm; £E10, students £E5). Located 500m south of the obelisk (from the metro, follow the street straight ahead to the fork, where you bear left down Sharia Shagaret Mariam, turning left at the end), and known locally as Shagaret Mariam, this gnarled sycamore fig is supposedly descended from a tree whose branches shaded the Holy Family during their Egyptian exile. Tradition has it that they rested here between Bilbeis and Babylon-in-Egypt (see p.180) and that Mary washed the clothes of the baby Jesus in the stone trough that still lies beside the tree. Early last century, according to James Aldridge, "Christian souvenir-hunting was so bad that the owner of the sycamore tied a knife to the tree and put up a notice begging people not to hack at it any more with axes, and to leave some of it for others". Now enclosed within a compound, it grows near the **Church of the Virgin**, a modern building on the site of far older churches.

The Pyramids

All things dread Time, but Time dreads the Pyramids.

Anonymous proverb

For millions of people the **Pyramids** epitomize Ancient Egypt: no other monument is so instantly recognized the world over. Yet comparatively few foreigners realize that at least 97 pyramids are spread across 70km of desert, from the outskirts of Cairo to the edge of the Fayoum. The mass of theories, claims and counterclaims about how and why the Pyramids were built contributes to the sense of mystery that surrounds them. Some of the recent contributions to this debate include *The Orion Mystery* (1994*)*, in which Robert Bauval asserts that the orientation of the Giza Pyramids corresponds to the three stars in Orion's Belt, and the "ventilation" shafts in the Geat Pyramid were aligned with Orion's Belt and the star Alpha Draconis. Graham Hancock took this a stage further in *Fingerprints of the Gods* (1995), arguing that the entire pyramid field corresponded to an astronomical map. In later books he says that the Sphinx and Pyramids are far older than reckoned and recall a vanished Ur-civilization that was destroyed in 12,000 BC, having left its stamp on Angkor Wat, the Maya and Easter Island. Egyptologists have since been lining up to refute these theories; meanwhile you can read up on the latest crop – including some involving Martians – on the Internet through links at Ⓦparanormal.about.com/cs/ancientegypt.

Most visitors are content to see the great **Pyramids of Giza** and part of the sprawling necropolis of **Saqqara**, both easily accessible from Cairo (tours to Saqqara often include a visit to the ruins of the ancient city of **Memphis**). Only a minority ride across the sands to **Abu Sir**, or visit the **Dahshur** pyramid field (see map on p.204 for the location of all these sites). Still further south, the dramatic "Collapsed Pyramid" of **Maidum** and the lesser Middle Kingdom pyramids of **Hawara**, **El-Lisht** and **Lahun** are easier to reach from the Fayoum, so for the sake of convenience we've covered them in Chapter 3. The Pyramid at **Abu Ruash**, to the west of Cairo, inaccessible and little more than a pile of sand, is only of interest to specialists, as are the remains of the Pyramid of Jifric (Cheops's Son) recently unearthed nearby (if you do want to find them, you can take one of the service taxis from Mansureya Canal by Pyramids Road to the nearby Abu Ruash industrial area).

If you are really determined, and very energetic, it is possible to visit the pyramid sites at Giza, Abu Sir, Saqqara and Dahshur all in one day, starting very early (say 7.30am from town). To do this, you will need to find a taxi driver who will take you, wait at each, and finally bring you back. Make sure the driver understands exactly what you want, and negotiate hard. In principle, you should

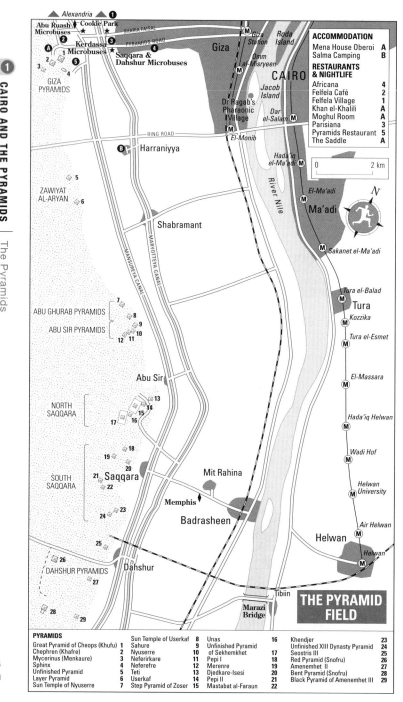

ACCOMMODATION
Mena House Oberoi   A
Salma Camping   B

RESTAURANTS
& NIGHTLIFE
Africana   4
Felfela Café   2
Felfela Village   1
Khan el-Khalili   A
Moghul Room   A
Parisiana   3
Pyramids Restaurant   5
The Saddle   A

THE PYRAMID FIELD

PYRAMIDS
Great Pyramid of Cheops (Khufu)   1
Chephren (Khafre)   2
Mycerinus (Menkaure)   3
Sphinx   4
Unfinished Pyramid   5
Layer Pyramid   6
Sun Temple of Nyuserre   7

Sun Temple of Userkaf   8
Sahure   9
Nyuserre   10
Neferirkare   11
Neferefre   12
Teti   13
Userkaf   14
Step Pyramid of Zoser   15

Unas   16
Unfinished Pyramid
  of Sekhemkhet   17
Pepi I   18
Merenre   19
Djedkare-Isesi   20
Pepi II   21
Mastabat al-Faraun   22

Khendjer   23
Unfinished XIII Dynasty Pyramid 24
Seostris III   25
Red Pyramid (Snofru)   26
Amenemhet II   27
Bent Pyramid (Snofru)   28
Black Pyramid of Amenemhet III   29

be able to visit all four sites for around £E100, or Giza, Saqqara and Dahshur for £E80, but £E120–150 would not be an unreasonable rate. Some hotels (the *Berlin*, for example) have their own drivers who are used to taking tourists on such excursions. Alternatively, you could opt for a guided tour (see p.217) that takes in both Giza and Saqqara in one day.

The Pyramids in history

The derivation of the word "pyramid" is obscure. *Per-em-us*, an Ancient Egyptian term meaning "straight up", seems likelier than the Greek *pyramis* – "wheaten cake", a facetious descriptive term for these novel monuments. Then again, "obelisk" comes from *obeliskos*, the Ancient Greek for "skewer" or "little spit".

Whatever, the Pyramids' sheer **antiquity** is staggering. When the Greek chronicler Herodotus visited them in 450 BC, as many centuries separated his lifetime from their creation as divide our own time from that of Herodotus, who regarded them as ancient even then. For the Pyramid Age was only an episode in three millennia of pharaonic civilization, reaching its zenith within two hundred years and followed by an inexorable decline, so that later dynasties regarded the works of their ancestors with awe. Fourteen centuries after the royal tombs of the Old Kingdom were first violated by robbers, the Sa'te (XXVI) Dynasty collected what remained, replaced missing bodies with surrogates, and reburied their forebears with archaic rituals they no longer comprehended.

The Pyramid Age began at Saqqara in the twenty-seventh century BC, when the III Dynasty royal architect Imhotep enlarged a *mastaba* tomb to create the first **step pyramid**. As techniques evolved, an attempt was made to convert another step pyramid at Maidum into a true pyramid by encasing its sides in a smooth shell, but it seems that the design was faulty and the pyramid collapsed at some time under its own weight. According to one theory, this happened during construction of what became the Bent Pyramid at Dahshur, necessitating a hasty alteration to the angle of its sides. The first sheer-sided **true pyramid**, apparently the next to be constructed, was the Red Pyramid at Dahshur, followed by the Great Pyramid of Cheops at Giza, which marked the zenith of pyramid architecture. After two more perfect pyramids at Giza, fewer resources and less care were devoted to the pyramid fields of Abu Sir and South Saqqara, and the latter-day pyramids near Fayoum Oasis, and no subsequent pyramid ever matched the standards of the Giza trio.

The Pyramids' **enigma** has puzzled people ever since they were built. Whereas the Ancient Greeks vaguely understood their function, the Romans were less certain; medieval Arabs believed them to be treasure houses with magical guardians; and early European observers reckoned them the Biblical granaries of Joseph. The nineteenth century was a golden era of discoveries by Belzoni, Vyse, Petrie, Mariette, Maspero and Lepsius, which all suggested that the Pyramids were essentially containers for royal tombs and nothing else. It was also the heyday of Pyramidologists like Piazzi Smyth and David Davidson, who averred that their dimensions in "pyramid inches" proved the supremacy of Christianity and the Jewish origin of the pyramid-builders.

Archeologists now agree that the Pyramids' **function** was to preserve the pharaoh's **ka**, or double: a vital force which emanated from the sun-god to his son, the king, who distributed it amongst his subjects and the land of Egypt itself. Mummification, funerary rituals, false doors for his **ba** (soul) to escape, model servants (*shabti* figures) and anniversary offerings – all were designed to ensure that his *ka* enjoyed an afterlife similar to its former existence. Thus was the social order perpetuated throughout eternity and the forces of primeval chaos held at bay, a theme emphasized in tomb reliefs at Saqqara. On another level of **symbolism**, the pyramid form evoked the primal mound at the dawn of creation, a recurrent theme in ancient Egyptian cosmogony, echoed in megalithic *benben* and obelisks whose pyramidal tips were sheathed in glittering electrum.

Although the limestone scarp at the edge of the Western Desert provided an inexhaustible source of building material, finer stone for casing the pyramids was quarried at Tura across the river, or came from Aswan in Upper Egypt. Blocks were quarried using wooden wedges (which swelled when soaked, enlarging fissures) and copper chisels, then transported on rafts to the pyramid site, where the final shaping and polishing occurred. Shipments coincided with the inundation of the Nile (July–Nov), when its waters lapped the feet of the plateau and Egypt's workforce was released from agricultural tasks.

Herodotus relates that a hundred thousand slaves took a decade to build the causeway and earthen ramps, and a further twenty years to raise the Great Pyramid of Cheops. Archeologists now believe that, far from being slaves, most of the workforce were actually peasants who were paid in food for their three-month stint (papyri enumerate the quantities of lentils, onions and leeks), while a few thousand skilled craftsmen were employed full-time on its **construction**. One theory holds that a single ramp wound around the pyramid core, and was raised as it grew; when the capstone was in place, the casing was added from the top down and the ramp was reduced. Other ramps (recently found) led from the base of the pyramid to the quarry. Apparently, pulleys were only used to lift the plug blocks that sealed the corridors and entrance; all the other stones were moved with levers and rollers. It is estimated that during the most productive century of pyramid-building, some 25 million tons of material were quarried.

Whether or not the Ancient Egyptians deemed this work a religious obligation, the massive levies certainly demanded an effective bureaucracy. Pyramid-building therefore helped consolidate the state. Its decline paralleled the Old Kingdom's, its cessation and resumption two anarchic eras (the First and Second Intermediate Periods) and the short-lived Middle Kingdom (XII Dynasty). By the time of the New Kingdom, other monumental symbols seemed appropriate. Remembering the plundered pyramids, the rulers of the New Kingdom opted for hidden tombs in the Valley of the Kings.

The Pyramids of Giza

Of the Seven Wonders of the ancient world, only the **Pyramids of Giza** have withstood the ravages of time. "From the summit of these monuments, forty centuries look upon you", cried Napoleon; "A practical joke played on History", retorted another visitor. The Great Pyramid of Cheops has inspired more learned and crackpot speculation than any monument on earth. For millions of people, the Giza Pyramids embody antiquity and mystery. Burdened with expectations, however, you may find the reality disappointing. Resembling small triangles from afar and corrugated mountains as you approach, their gigantic mass can seem oddly two-dimensional when viewed from below. Far from being isolated in the desert as carefully angled photos suggest, they rise just beyond the outskirts of Giza City. During daytime, hordes of touts and tourists dispel any lingering mystique, as do the Sound and Light shows after dark. Only at sunset, dawn and late at night does their brooding majesty return.

As site plans suggest, the Pyramids' **orientation** is no accident. Their entrances are aligned with the Polar Star (or rather, its position 4500 years

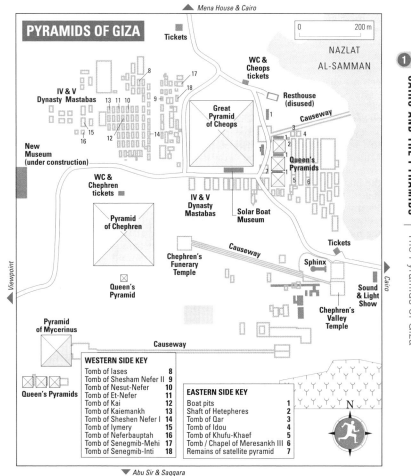

▲ *Mena House & Cairo*

PYRAMIDS OF GIZA

Tickets

NAZLAT
AL-SAMMAN

0   200 m

IV & V
Dynasty Mastabas   13 11 10

8

17

18

WC &
Cheops
tickets

Resthouse
(disused)

Causeway

Great
Pyramid
of Cheops

1

9

New
Museum
(under construction)

15
16   12   14

Queen's
Pyramids

2
3   4

1

2

5   6

WC &
Chephren
tickets

IV & V
Dynasty
Mastabas

Solar Boat
Museum

Pyramid
of Chephren

Chephren's
Funerary
Temple

Causeway

Tickets

Sphinx

Queen's
Pyramid

Viewpoint

Cairo

Sound
& Light
Show

Chephren's
Valley
Temple

Pyramid
of Mycerinus

Causeway

Queen's Pyramids

N

WESTERN SIDE KEY
Tomb of Iases	8
Tomb of Shesham Nefer II	9
Tomb of Nesut-Nefer	10
Tomb of Et-Nefer	11
Tomb of Kai	12
Tomb of Kaiemankh	13
Tomb of Sheshen Nefer I	14
Tomb of Iymery	15
Tomb of Neferbauptah	16
Tomb of Senegmib-Mehi	17
Tomb of Senegmib-Inti	18

EASTERN SIDE KEY
Boat pits	1
Shaft of Hetepheres	2
Tomb of Qar	3
Tomb of Idou	4
Tomb of Khufu-Khaef	5
Tomb / Chapel of Meresankh III	6
Remains of satellite pyramid	7

▼ *Abu Sir & Saqqara*

ago); the internal tomb chambers face west, the direction of the Land of the Dead; and the external funerary temples point eastwards towards the rising sun. Less well preserved are the causeways leading to the so-called valley temples, and various subsidiary pyramids and *mastaba* tombs. The entire site is being renovated by Egypt's Supreme Council for Antiquities (SCA) and continues to yield surprises.

Practicalities

The site is directly accessible from Cairo by the eleven-kilometre-long **Sharia al-Ahram** (Pyramids Road) built by Khedive Ismail for Napoleon III's consort, the Empress Eugénie. Though heavy traffic can prolong the journey, getting there is straightforward. Taxi drivers often quote upwards of £E20, but the proper fare is around £E15 for a one-way trip from town. A cheaper option is to take a/c bus #355 or #357 (£E2), or ordinary bus #900 (25pt), all from behind Ramses train station or on Midan Tahrir; minibus #183 from Midan

Ataba (50pt); or a microbus service taxi from Ataba (just south of the bus station), Ramses (by Sharia Orabi) or Abdel Mouneem Riyad (all 75pt; drivers heading for the Pyramids shout, "Al-Ahram, al-Ahram"). Bus #30 from Midan Ramses also runs more or less all the way to the site. An easier one-day, minimum-effort way to visit the Giza Pyramids, while also taking in Saqqara, is to go on a guided tour (see p.217).

Opposite the *Mena House* is a **tourist office** (daily 8am–5pm; ℡02/383-8823). To visit (daily: summer 8am–5pm; winter 8am–4pm) you must buy a **ticket** (£E50, students £E25) covering the site, the Sphinx and Chephren's Valley Temple – though tickets aren't rigorously checked. Extra tickets (only sold at the attractions themselves) are required for entry to the Solar Boat Museum (£E35), and for the Great Pyramid of Cheops (£E100), Chephren's Pyramid (£E20) and the Pyramid of Mycerinus (currently closed). Generally the interiors of two of the pyramids will be open, the third closed, and from time to time they rotate them, so it may in the future be Cheops's or Chephren's Pyramid that is closed.

Plan on spending half a day at the Pyramids, which are best entered early in the morning before the heat and crowds become unbearable (tour buses start arriving from 10.30am), or in the late afternoon. By 5pm most tour groups have left and people have yet to arrive for the nightly **Sound and Light Show**. There are three one-hour shows every night accompanied by a rather crass, melodramatic commentary in different languages. For schedules, call ℡02/385-2880 or 386-3469, or check *Egypt Today* or Ⓦwww.egyptsandl.com. Seats cost £E60, plus £E35 for a video camera; the Arabic version costs £E11, though non-Arab nationals are not allowed to buy tickets for it. Seats are on the terrace facing the Sphinx, which is wheelchair accessible. Bring a sweater, since nights are cold, even in summer.

In Baedeker's day, it was de rigueur for visitors to climb the Great Pyramid: while two Bedouin seized an arm apiece and hauled from above, a third would push from below. **Climbing the pyramids** is now forbidden and is undoubtedly very dangerous, although attempts are still made. Though **going inside** is quite safe, anyone suffering from claustrophobia or asthma should forget it. Clambering through all three shafts in the Great Pyramid will make your leg muscles ache the following day.

Behind the grandstand is a row of stables **renting horses and camels** that are generally in no better shape than the animals touted around the site by Nagama Bedouin. They usually demand £E50 for a brief camel ride, and you should beware of those offering rides at low rates – they have a tendency to lead you far out into the desert and then announce that the low rate was only for the outward journey and it will be £E50 per hour or more to get back. As the site is small enough to cover on foot, riding is more of an experience than a timesaver, and haggling with these guys just might ruin your visit, but if you do want to ride a horse or camel, get in touch with a reputable operator such as AA or KG (see p.263).

Ignore con men posing as ticket collectors or "special guides", who offer commentary along the lines of "Cheops Pyramid very old". Also ignore horse and camel touts on the way in who try to tell you that their stables are "government". Such nuisances are supposedly set to disappear under the "Giza Plateau Conservation Project", which will include an IMAX cinema and cultural centres. The isolation fence around the site is already nearly complete, much to the dismay of Nazlat al-Samman villagers, whom it will cut off not only from their local monument, but more importantly from their main source of employment.

The Great Pyramid of Cheops (Khufu)

The oldest and largest of the Giza Pyramids is that of the IV Dynasty pharaoh **Khufu** – better known as **Cheops** – who probably reigned between 2589 and 2566 BC. Called the "Glorious Place of Khufu" by the Ancient Egyptians, it originally stood 140m high and measured 230m along its base, but the removal of its casing stones has reduced these dimensions by three metres. The pyramid is estimated to weigh six million tons and contain over 2,300,000 blocks whose average weight is 2.5 tons (though some weigh almost 15 tons). This gigantic mass actually ensures its stability, since most of the stress is transmitted inwards towards its central core, or downwards into the underlying bedrock. Until recently, the pyramid was thought to contain only three chambers: one in the bedrock and two in the superstructure. Experts believe that its design was changed twice, the subterranean chamber being abandoned in favour of the middle one, which was itself superseded by the uppermost chamber. By the time archeologists got here, their contents had been looted long ago, and the only object left *in situ* was Khufu's sarcophagus. However, in April 1993, a German

▲ Cheops

team of scientists using a robot probe accidentally discovered a door with handles supposedly enclosing a fourth chamber, apparently never plundered by thieves, which might contain the mummy and treasures of Cheops himself. The head of the SCA, Dr Zahi Hawass, argues that there is no chamber, and that the "door" was a device for smoothing the inside of the shaft – but until investigations resume, the truth will not be known.

Inside the Great Pyramid

To keep down humidity inside the pyramid, the number of visitors allowed to enter is limited to 150 in the morning and 150 in the afternoon. If you want to buy **tickets** (£E100, students £E50, no cameras allowed), you will neeed to look sharp. In the morning, tour groups tend to snap up all of them before anyone else can get a look in; it is generally less difficult to get the afternoon tickets, especially if you can be at the ticket office as soon as they go on sale at 1pm, but be prepared to jostle for position (or, if you go in the morning, to sprint to the ticket office as soon as the main gate opens).

You enter the pyramid via an opening created by the treasure-hunting Caliph Ma'mun in 820, some distance below the original entrance on the north face (now blocked). After following this downwards at a crouch, you'll reach the junction of the ascending and descending corridors. The latter – leading to an unfinished chamber below the pyramid – is best ignored or left until last, and everyone heads up the 1.6-metre-high **ascending corridor**. According to medieval Arab chroniclers, intruders soon encountered an "idol of speckled granite" wreathed by a serpent which "seized upon and strangled whoever approached", but latter-day visitors are merely impeded by the 1:2 gradient of the passage, which runs for 36m until it meets another junction.

To the right of this is a **shaft** that ancient writers believed to be a well connected to the Nile; it's now recognized as leading into the subterranean chamber and thought to have been an escape passage for the workmen. Straight ahead is a horizontal passage 35m long and 1.75m high, leading to a semi-finished limestone chamber with a pointed roof, which Arabs dubbed the "**Queen's Chamber**". Petrie reckoned this was the *serdab*, or repository for the pharaoh's statue, while the eccentric Davidson saw it as symbolizing

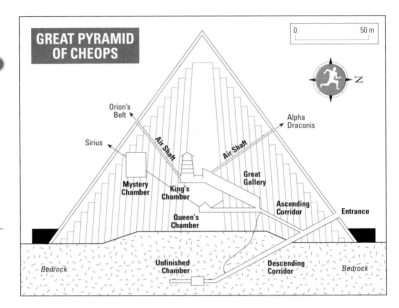

GREAT PYRAMID
OF CHEOPS

the ultimate futility of Judaism. Either way, there's no evidence that a queen was ever buried here. In the northern and southern walls are two holes made in 1872 for the purpose of discovering the chamber's ventilation shafts; it was through one of these that the robot probe discovered the "secret chamber", at the end of a 65-metre passageway only twenty centimetres high and the same distance wide, which is aligned with the Dog Star, Sirius (representing the goddess Isis).

However, most people step up into the **Great Gallery**, the finest section of the pyramid. Built of Muqattam limestone, so perfectly cut that a knife blade can't be inserted between its joints, the 47-metre-long shaft narrows to a corbelled roof 8.5m high. (Davidson believed that its length in "pyramid inches" corresponded to the number of years between the Crucifixion and the outbreak of World War I.) The incisions in its walls probably held beams that were used to raise the sarcophagus or granite plug blocks up the steep incline (nowadays overlaid with wooden steps). Though no longer infested by giant bats, as nineteenth-century travellers reported, the Great Gallery is sufficiently hot and airless to constitute something of an ordeal, and you'll be glad to reach the horizontal antechamber at the top, which is slotted for the insertion of plug blocks designed to thwart entry to the putative burial chamber.

The **King's Chamber** lies 95m beneath the apex of the pyramid and half that distance from its outer walls. Built of red granite blocks, the rectangular chamber is large enough to accommodate a double-decker bus. Its dimensions (5.2m by 10.8m by 5.8m) have inspired many abstruse calculations and whacky prophecies: Hitler ordered a replica built beneath the Nuremberg Stadium, where he communed with himself before Nazi rallies. To one side of the chamber lies a huge, lidless **sarcophagus** of Aswan granite, bearing the marks of diamond-tipped saws and drills. On the northern and southern walls, at knee height, you'll notice two air shafts leading to the outer world, aligned with the stars of Orion's Belt and Alpha Draconis (representing Osiris and the hippo goddess Rer respectively).

Unseen above the ceiling, five **relieving chambers** distribute the weight of the pyramid away from the burial chamber; each consists of 43 granite monoliths weighing 40 to 70 tons apiece. These chambers can only be reached by a ladder from the Great Gallery, and then a passage where Colonel Vyse found Khufu's name inscribed in red (the only inscription within the Giza Pyramids), but the flow of people normally rules this out.

On your way back down, consider investigating the 100-metre-long **descending corridor**, which leads to a crudely hewn **unfinished chamber** beneath the pyramid. There's nothing to see, but the nerve-wracking descent is worthy of Indiana Jones.

Subsidiary tombs

East of the Great Pyramid, it's just possible to discern the foundations of Khufu's funerary temple and a few blocks of the causeway that once connected it to his valley temple (now buried beneath the village of Nazlat al-Samman). Nearby stand three ruined **Queens' Pyramids**, each with a small chapel attached. The northern and southern pyramids belonged to Merites and Hensutsen, Khufu's principal wife (and sister), and the putative mother of Chephren, respectively; the middle one may have belonged to the mother of Redjedef, the third ruler of the dynasty. Between that and the Great Pyramid, the remains of a fourth satellite pyramid have recently been discovered, including its capstone, the oldest yet found, but the pyramid's purpose is so far unknown.

Just northeast of Queen Merites' Pyramid is a **shaft** where III Dynasty pharaoh Snofru's wife Queen Hetepheres' sarcophagus was found, having been stashed here following lootings at its original home in Dahshur. To the east of it are the tombs of Qar and his son Idou, which contain life-size statues of the deceased and various reliefs. To the east of Queen Hensutsen's Pyramid are the tombs of Cheops' son Khufu-Khaef, and Chephren's wife (also Hetepheres' daughter) Meres-ankh, the best preserved of all the tombs on the Giza plateau, complete with statues in the niches and reliefs showing scenes of daily life, with much of the paintwork intact. To get into these tombs, ask at the custodian's hut beside Hetepheres' shaft; naturally, the custodian will appreciate a tip for opening up.

To the west of the Great Pyramid lie dozens of **IV and V Dynasty mastabas**, where archeologists have uncovered a 4600-year-old mummified princess, whose body had been hollowed out and encased in a thin layer of plaster – a hitherto unknown method of mummification. Here are more **tombs** that until 1995 had been closed to the public since their discovery in the nineteenth century. In general, these are less interesting than those on the eastern side of the Great Pyramid, but that of Neferbauptah – almost parallel with the west side of Chephren's Pyramid – has a dinosaur fossil preserved in the fifth block from the right of the second row up on its north side. Should you want to enter any of these tombs, ask at the Inspectorate office to the north. Beware of deep shafts with no fences around them.

The Solar Boat Museum

Perched to the south of the Great Pyramid, across the road from another cluster of *mastabas*, is a humidity-controlled pavilion (daily: summer 9am–5pm; winter 9am–4pm; £E35, students £E20) containing a 43-metre-long **boat** from one of the five boat pits sunk around Khufu's Pyramid. (Another boat has been located by X-rays and video cameras, but for the present remains unexcavated.)

When the pit's limestone roofing blocks were removed in 1954, a faint odour of cedarwood arose. Restorer Hagg Ahmed Yussef subsequently spent fourteen years rebuilding a graceful craft from 1200 pieces of wood, originally held together by sycamore pegs and halfa-grass ropes. Archeologists term these vessels "solar boats" (or barques), but their purpose remains uncertain – carrying the pharaoh through the underworld (as shown in XVII–IX Dynasty tombs at Thebes) or accompanying the sun-god on his daily journey across the heavens are two of the many hypotheses.

The Pyramid of Chephren (Khafre)

Sited on higher ground, with an intact summit and steeper sides, the middle or **Second Pyramid** seems taller than Khufu's. Built by his son **Khafre** (known to posterity as Chephren), its base originally covered 214.8 square metres and its weight is estimated at 4,883,000 tons. As with Khufu's Pyramid, the original rock-hewn burial chamber was never finished and an upper chamber was subsequently constructed. Classical writers such as Pliny believed that the pyramid had no entrance, but when Belzoni located and blasted open the sealed portal on its north face in 1818, he found that Arab tomb robbers had somehow gained access nearly a thousand years earlier, undeterred by legends of an idol "with fierce and sparkling eyes" bent on slaying intruders.

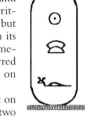
▲ Chephren

Inside the pyramid (£E20, students £E10, no current limit on numbers, no cameras allowed), you can follow one of the two entry corridors downwards, and then upwards, into a long horizontal passage leading to Chephren's **burial chamber**, where Belzoni celebrated his discovery by writing his name in black letters. This ebullient circus strongman-turned-explorer went on to find Seti I's tomb in the Valley of the Kings, and died searching for the source of the River Niger. Set into the chamber's granite floor is the sarcophagus of Khafre, who reigned *c.*2558–2533 BC. The square cavity near the southern wall may have marked the position of a canopic chest containing the pharaoh's viscera.

Chephren's Funerary Complex and the Sphinx

The funerary complex of Chephren's Pyramid is the best-preserved example of this typically Old Kingdom arrangement. When a pharaoh died, his body was ferried across the Nile to a riverside valley temple where it was embalmed by priests. After the process was complete, mourners gathered here to purify themselves before escorting his mummy up the causeway to a funerary (or mortuary) temple, where further rites preceded its interment within the pyramid. Thereafter, the priests ensured his *ka*'s afterlife by making offerings of food and incense in the funerary temple on specific anniversaries.

Chephren's **funerary temple** consists of a pillared hall, central court, niched storerooms and a sanctuary, but most of the outer granite casing has been plundered over centuries and the interior may not be accessible. Among the remaining blocks is a 13.4-metre-long monster weighing 163,000 kilos. Flanking the temple are what appear to be boat pits, although excavations have yielded nothing but pottery fragments. From here you can trace the foundations of a **causeway** that runs 400m downhill to his valley temple, near the Sphinx.

The **valley temple** lay buried under sand until its discovery by Mariette in 1852, which accounts for its reasonable state of preservation. Built of limestone and faced with polished Aswan granite, the temple faces east and used to open onto a quay. Beyond a narrow antechamber you'll find a T-shaped hall whose gigantic architraves are supported by square pillars, in front of which stood diorite statues of Chephren. Contrary to the widely accepted theory, a few scholars believe that mummification occurred at Memphis or Chephren's mortuary temple, this edifice being reserved for the "Opening of Mouth" ceremony, whereby the *ka* entered the deceased's body.

The Sphinx

This legendary monument, whose enclosure is entered through the Valley Temple, is carved from an outcrop of soft limestone that was supposedly left standing after the harder surrounding stone was quarried for the Great Pyramid; however, since the base stone was too soft to work on directly, it was clad in harder stone before finishing. Conventional archeology credits Chephren with the idea of shaping it into a figure with a lion's body and a human head, which is often identified as his own (complete with royal beard and *uraeus*, see p.282), though it may represent a guardian deity. Some thousand years later, the future Tuthmosis IV is said to have dreamt that if he cleared the sand that engulfed the **Sphinx** it would make him ruler: a prophecy fulfilled, as recorded on a stele that he placed between its paws. All these notions went unchallenged until 1991, when two American geologists argued that the Sphinx was at least 2600 years older than had been imagined: its bedrock was heavily weathered and eroded by water, probably during the Nabtian Pluvial era (3000–1200 BC). This argument is dismissed by SCA director Zahi Hawass, who cites an analysis of the Sphinx's bedrock by the Getty Institute, which concludes that the erosion was caused by the action of mineral salts within the plateau and/or the wind. The controversy delighted the maverick Egyptologist John West, who has long claimed that Egyptian civilization was the inheritor of a more Ancient, lost culture – the mythical Atlantis. The name "Sphinx" was actually bestowed by the Ancient Greeks, after the legendary creature that put riddles to passers-by and slew those who answered wrongly; the Arabs call it Abu el-Hol (the awesome or terrible one). During Sound and Light shows, the Sphinx is given the role of narrator.

Used for target practice by Mamluke and Napoleonic troops, the Sphinx lost much of its beard to the British Museum and was sandbagged for protection during World War II. Early modern repairs did more harm than good, since its porous limestone "breathes", unlike the cement that was used to fill its cracks. There is also the problem of chemical pollutants from sewage and fires in Nazlat al-Samman. A more recent **restoration project** (1989–98) involved hand-cutting ten thousand limestone blocks, to refit the paws, legs and haunches of the beast; the missing nose and beard have not been replaced, deliberately.

Three **tunnels** exist inside the Sphinx, one behind its head, one in its tail and one in its north side. Their function is unknown, but none goes anywhere. Other tunnels have been unearthed in the vicinity of the Sphinx; again, who built them or what they were for is unknown, but one suggestion is that they were created by later Ancient Egyptians looking for buried treasure.

The Pyramid of Mycerinus (Menkaure)

Sited on a gradual slope into undulating desert, the smallest of the Giza Pyramids speaks of waning power and commitment. Though started by Chephren's successor, **Menkaure** (called Mycerinus by the Greeks), it was finished with unseemly haste by his son Shepseskaf, who seemingly enjoyed less power than his predecessors and depended on the priesthood. Herodotus records the legend that an oracle gave Mycerinus only six years to live, so to cheat fate he made merry round the clock, doubling his annual quantum of experience. Another story has it that the pyramid was actually built by Rhodophis, a Thracian courtesan who charged each client the price of a building block (the structure is estimated to contain 200,000 blocks).

Because its lower half was sheathed in Aswan granite, this is sometimes called the Red Pyramid (a name also applied to one of Snofru's pyramids at Dahshur). Its relative lack of casing stones is due to a twelfth-century sultan whose courtiers persuaded him to attempt the pyramid's demolition, a project he wisely gave up after eight months. Medieval Arab chroniclers frequently ascribed

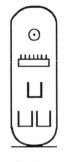
▲ Mycerinus

Kerdassa, Harraniyya and the Pyramids of Zawiyat al-Aryan

The villages of Kerdassa and Harraniyya have no connection with the Pyramids, but tour groups often pay one or both of them a visit. **KERDASSA**, roughly due west of Imbaba (but accessible by microbus from the junction of Pyramids Road with Sharia Mansureya), is where most of the scarves, *galabiyyas* and shirts in Cairo are made, plus carpets, which are sold by the metre. Although no longer a place for bargains, it's still frequented by collectors of ethnic textiles, particularly Bedouin robes and veils (the best-quality ones retail for hundreds of dollars). In times past, Kerdassa was also the starting point of the camel trail across the Western Desert to Libya.

Folks on guided tours are inevitably taken to **HARRANIYYA**, the site of the famous **Wissa Wassef Art Centre** (daily 10am–5pm; ☎02/381-5746, ⊛www.wissa-wassef-arts.com). Founded fifty years ago by Ramses Wissa Wassef, an architect who wanted to preserve village crafts and alleviate rural unemployment, the centre teaches children to design and weave carpets, and has branched out into batik work and pottery. The pupils, supervised by his widow and the original generation of students, produce beautiful tapestries which now sell for thousands of dollars and are imitated throughout Egypt. You can see them at work (except at lunchtime and on Fridays), and admire a superb collection in the museum designed by Hassan Fathy, a masterpiece of mud-brick architecture. To reach the Art Centre under your own steam, take a taxi or minibus 4km south along the Saqqara road (Maryotteya Canal, west bank) from Pyramids Road, or catch bus #334 from Abdel Mouneem Riyad terminal, and get off at Harraniyya.

Zawiyat al-Aryan

The **Zawiyat al-Aryan pyramid field** lies roughly midway between Giza and North Saqqara and about 3.5km from the Sun Temples of Abu Ghurab at Abu Sir (see p.216). Both its pyramids are sanded over, and are in any case in a military zone and closed to the public. The northerly **Unfinished Pyramid** makes extensive use of granite, suggesting that it might hail from the IV Dynasty, but never got beyond its foundations and enclosure wall – unfinished blocks and stone chippings are scattered all around. To the southeast lies a **Layer Pyramid** built of small stone blocks, which seems to have been intended as a step pyramid and thus presumably belongs to the III Dynasty. Should you have a special urge to see these pyramids, your best bet is either to pass by here on a horse- or camel-ride from the Pyramids of Giza, or else take a service taxi microbus from Maryotteya Canal at Pyramids Road to the nearby village of Shabramant and walk from there, but you will not be admitted to the site itself.

the Giza Pyramids to a single ruler, who supposedly boasted: "I, Surid the king, have built these pyramids in 61 years. Let him who comes after me attempt to destroy them in six hundred. To destroy is easier than to build. I have clothed them in silk; let him try to cover them in mats." The **interior** (currently closed to the public) is unusual for having its unfinished chamber in the superstructure and the final burial chamber underground. Here Vyse discovered a basalt sarcophagus later lost at sea en route to Britain, plus human remains that he assumed were Menkaure's, but which are now reckoned to be a XXVI Dynasty replacement and which rest in the British Museum.

The complex also features three subsidiary pyramids, a relatively intact funerary temple, and a causeway to the now-buried valley temple. Northwest of the latter lies the sarcophagus-shaped **Tomb of Queen Khentkawes**, an intriguing figure who appears to have bridged the transition between the IV and V dynasties. Apparently married to Shepseskaf, the last IV Dynasty ruler, she may have wed a priest of the sun-god after his demise and gone on to bear several kings who were buried at Saqqara or Abu Sir (where she also built a pyramid).

The best **viewpoints** over the pyramids are south of Mycerinus' Pyramid. Most tourists gather (along with touts and knick-knack sellers) along the surfaced road some 400m west of the pyramid, which is particularly popular in the late afternoon when the sun is in the right direction. In the morning, however, photos are better taken from the southeast, though it can often be hazy early on. For the best view of the Pyramids close together, the ridge to the south of Mycerinus' Pyramid is the place to head for.

Abu Sir and Abu Ghurab

A necropolis of V Dynasty (c.2494–2345 BC) pharaohs covers an arc of desert beyond the village of **ABU SIR**. The mortuary complexes here are smaller than the Giza Pyramids of the previous dynasty, suggesting a decline in royal power; their ruinous state and the effort required to reach them also mean that few tourists come here. Those who do often feel that Abu Sir's splendid isolation compensates for its monumental shortcomings. The site was closed to the public at the time of writing (when it opens, hours and prices should be daily: summer 9am–5pm; winter 9am–4pm; £E20, students £E10), but if you have a special interest, you may be able to persuade the custodian to let you in to look around.

The pyramids of Abu Sir are a ten-minute walk from the village of the same name, with a pair of sun temples nearby at **Abu Ghurab**. The village can be reached by service taxi microbus from Maryotteya Canal at Pyramids Road or by taxi from Abu Sir or Saqqara village (£E5–8). The boldest option, however, is to visit them **en route between Giza and Saqqara** by horse or camel, spending three hours in the saddle. Making a round trip **from North Saqqara** (see p.217) is less demanding, but still requires commitment. With the Pyramids clearly visible 6km away, you can either walk (1hr 30min–2hr) or conserve energy by renting a horse or camel from near the refreshments hut (£E60–100 for the round trip).

The pyramid complexes

The four pyramid complexes are ranged in an arc that ignores chronological order. At the southern end of the pyramid field a low mound marks the core of the unfinished **Pyramid of Neferefre**, whose brief reign preceded Nyuserre's. As the core is composed of locally quarried limestone and was never encased in finer Tura masonry, no causeway was ever built. However, the desert may yet disgorge other structures: during the 1980s, Czechoslovak archeologists uncovered another pyramid complex, thought to belong to Queen Khentkawes, the mother of Sahure.

Dominating the view north is the much larger **Pyramid of Neferirkare**, the third ruler of the V Dynasty, who strove to outdo his predecessor, Sahure. If finished, it would have been 70m high – taller than the third pyramid at Giza – but Neferirkare's premature demise forced his successor to hastily complete a modified version using perishable mud-brick. Although too dangerous to climb, its summit commands a view of the entire pyramid field, from the three at Giza and the four at Saqqara to the Red and Bent pyramids at Dahshur, and even the Collapsed Pyramid of Maidum on the distant horizon. The valley temple and grand causeway of Neferirkare's Pyramid were later usurped to serve the **Pyramid of Nyuserre**, further north. A battered mortuary temple with papyriform columns mocks the original name of this dilapidated pyramid, "The Places of Nyuserre are Enduring"; the pharaohs who followed him preferred burial at Saqqara. A cluster of mastabas to the northwest includes the **Tomb of Ptahshepses**. The tomb's most curious feature is the double room off the courtyard, which may have held solar boats. If so, the only other known example of this in a private tomb is that of Kagemni in North Saqqara. Ptahshepses was Chief of Works to Sahure, the first of the V Dynasty kings to be buried at Abu Sir.

The **Pyramid of Sahure** is badly damaged, but its associated temples have fared better than others in this group. A 235-metre-long causeway links the ruined valley temple to Sahure's mortuary temple on the eastern side of the pyramid. Though most of its reliefs (which were the first to show the king smiting his enemies, later a standard motif) have gone to various museums, enough remains to make the temple worth exploring. It's also possible to crawl through a dusty, cobwebbed passage to reach the burial chamber within the pyramid (whose original name was "The Soul of Sahure Gleams"). Just to the north of the causeway, a series of fascinating reliefs shows scenes from the building of a pyramid, notably of workers dragging a pyramidion (capstone) covered with white gold, while dancers celebrate the pyramid's completion.

The Sun Temples of Abu Ghurab

Just northeast of the Abu Sir pyramids is the site known as **Abu Ghurab** (if you are riding between Giza and Saqqara, you could ask the guide to stop here). Its twin temples were designed for worship of Re, the sun-god of Heliopolis, but their Jubilee reliefs and proximity to a pyramid field suggest a similar function to Zoser's Heb-Sed court at Saqqara.

Unlike the ruinous **Sun Temple of Userkaf**, 400m from Sahure's Pyramid, the more distant **Sun Temple of Nyuserre** repays a visit. At its western end stood a colossal megalith as tall as a pyramid, symbolizing the primordial mound – of which only the base remains. The great courtyard, approached from its valley temple by a causeway, is centred on an alabaster altar where cattle were sacrificed. From the courtyard's vestibule, corridors run north to storerooms and south to the king's chapel. The "Chamber of Seasons" beyond the chapel once contained beautiful reliefs; to the south you can find the remnants of a brick model of a solar boat.

North Saqqara

While Memphis (see p.227) was the capital of the Old Kingdom, Egypt's royalty and nobility were buried at **Saqqara**, the limestone scarp that flanks the Nile Valley to the west – the traditional direction of the Land of the Dead. Although superseded by the Theban necropolis during the New Kingdom, Saqqara remained in use for burying sacred animals and birds, especially in Ptolemaic times, when these cults enjoyed a revival. Over three thousand years it grew to cover 7km of desert – not including the associated necropolises of Abu Sir and Dahshur, or the Giza Pyramids. As such, it is today the largest archeological site in Egypt. Its name – usually pronounced "sa'-'ah-rah" by Cairenes, with the q's as glottal stops – probably derives from Sokar, the Memphite god of the dead, though Egyptians may tell you that it comes from *saq*, the Arabic word for a hawk or falcon, the sacred bird of Horus.

Besides the pyramids and mastabas seen by visitors, Saqqara has an incalculable wealth of monuments and artefacts still hidden beneath the windblown sands. In 1986, the **tomb of Maya**, Tutankhamun's treasurer, was discovered, stuffed with precious objects (it won't be open to the public for some time). Yet aside from Zoser's Pyramid, the site was virtually ignored by archeologists until Auguste Mariette found the Serapeum in 1851.

The Saqqara necropolis divides into two main sections: **North Saqqara** – the more interesting area (covered here) – and **South Saqqara** (see p.228). North Saqqara boasts a score of sights, so anyone with limited time should be selective. The **highlights** are Zoser's funerary complex, the Serapeum, and the Double Mastaba of Akhti- and Ptah-Hotep; if time allows, add the museum and some more tombs to your itinerary. To take in the whole site you would need several days.

Practicalities

North Saqqara lies 21km south of the Giza Pyramids as the camel trundles, or 32km from Cairo by road, being roughly opposite Helwan on the east bank of the Nile. The quickest way there by **public transport** (about an hour) is to take a bus or service taxi to Pyramids Road, get off at Maryotteya Canal (about 1km before the Pyramids), head down the east bank of the canal and take the first left, where you'll find service taxi microbuses to Saqqara village (20min; 75pt). An alternative route is to take bus #330 from Midan Giza to Saqqara village, or bus #987 from Midan Ramses or Midan Tahrir to El-Badrasheen, and then a microbus to Saqqara village (15min; 35pt), by way of Memphis. A final option is to take the metro to Helwan station (30min; 75pt), then a minibus to Tibiin, near the Marazi Bridge (15min; 65pt); another service taxi (often a Peugeot rather than a microbus) across to El-Badrasheen on the west bank (15min; 50pt); and finally one to Saqqara as above. One disadvantage of all these methods is that they leave you in Saqqara village, still over a kilometre from the site entrance, though the service taxi from Maryotteya will drop you slightly nearer the site entrance if you ask. Getting back to Cairo, it is wise not to leave too late, or you may not find transport in Saqqara village, and will have to either pay well over the odds for a taxi, or walk another 5km to El-Badrasheen (or at least to the Maryotteya Canal) to pick up a bus or microbus back to Cairo.

To save time and energy for the site, you could take a **tour**, such as the ones run by the affable Salah Mohammed Abdel Hafiez (☎02/298-0650 or 012/313-8446, Ⓔsamo@link.net). The tours leave around 8am in summer, 9am in winter. You'll be driven in an air-conditioned minibus to Memphis,

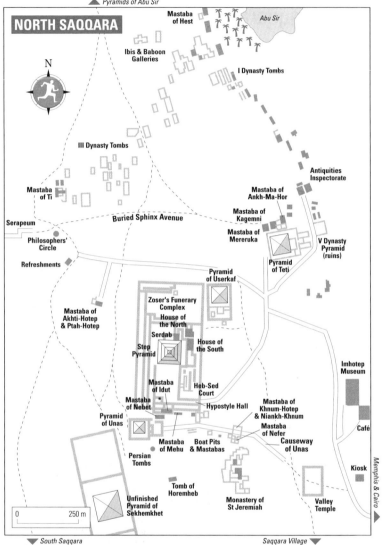

The map labels (as part of the image) include:

Pyramids of Abu Sir, Mastaba of Hest, Abu Sir, NORTH SAQQARA, Ibis & Baboon Galleries, I Dynasty Tombs, N, III Dynasty Tombs, Antiquities Inspectorate, Mastaba of Ti, Mastaba of Ankh-Ma-Hor, Serapeum, Mastaba of Kagemni, Buried Sphinx Avenue, Mastaba of Mereruka, V Dynasty Pyramid (ruins), Philosophers' Circle, Pyramid of Teti, Refreshments, Pyramid of Userkaf, Zoser's Funerary Complex, House of the North, Serdab, House of the South, Mastaba of Akhti-Hotep & Ptah-Hotep, Step Pyramid, Imhotep Museum, Mastaba of Idut, Heb-Sed Court, Mastaba of Nebet, Hypostyle Hall, Mastaba of Khnum-Hotep & Niankh-Khnum, Pyramid of Unas, Mastaba of Nefer, Café, Mastaba of Mehu, Boat Pits & Mastabas, Causeway of Unas, Persian Tombs, Kiosk, Tomb of Horemheb, 0 250 m, Unfinished Pyramid of Sekhemkhet, Monastery of St Jeremiah, Valley Temple, Memphis & Cairo, South Saqqara, Saqqara Village

North Saqqara, the Wissa Wassef tapestry school at Harraniyya and the Pyramids of Giza – all accompanied by an English-speaking Egyptologist – before returning to Cairo at 4–5pm. Be sure to ask to see the Mastaba of Ti during your trip. The price of the tour (£E50) doesn't include admission tickets, but *Rough Guide* readers who book direct get a £E5 discount, with a free airport transfer to your hotel on arrival also thrown in. Thomas Cook, Misr Travel and American Express also run tours to Saqqara for upwards of £E160 per person. Another option is to rent a **private taxi** for the day (£E60–80 for just Giza and Saqqara, £E80–120 if you add on Dahshur). Be sure to specify which sites are included and how long you expect to stay when you negotiate with the driver.

Lastly, you could plump for riding across the desert from the Pyramids of Giza by **horse** or **camel** (3hr). Although touts swear that the route takes you through the desert, past Zawiyet al-Aryan, the Sun Temples of Abu Ghurab and the Pyramids of Abu Sir, they will often ignore all such promises and guide you along a more direct village track on the edge of the cultivated area, supposedly due to military restrictions. Either way, the journey will leave you stiff for days afterwards (see p.56 for the rudiments of camel-handling). Most people opt for a one-way ride (£E120–150); return trips cost twice that, plus a negotiable sum for waiting time (around £E300–400 in all). Be warned that some guides threaten to abandon travellers in the middle of nowhere unless they receive hefty baksheesh; it's usually safe to call their bluff, but better to use a reputable firm such as AA or KG (see p.263).

Even if you don't emulate Lawrence of Arabia, bear in mind **conditions** at Saqqara. Over winter, the site can be swept by chill winds and clouds of grit; during the hottest months walking around is exhausting. Beware of deep pits, which aren't always fenced off. Bring at least one litre of water apiece, as vendors at Memphis and the refreshments tent at North Saqqara are grossly overpriced, like every restaurant along the Saqqara road; a packed lunch is also a good idea. Alternatively, the **Palm Club** just over the Mansureya Canal from the site entrance (℡02/819 1555 or 1999; daily 8am–6pm), has a swimming pool set amid pleasant gardens and charges £E65 for a day's access including lunch – definitely an option worth considering if you have kids in tow, or if you feel like a dip and a bite after a hard morning's trudge around the site.

Though **opening hours** are daily 8am to 5pm in summer, 8am to 4pm in winter, guards start locking up the tombs at least half an hour early. A kiosk on the approach road sells **tickets** (£E50, students £E25 including Imhopte Museum); on occasion this kiosk is closed, in which case tickets must be obtained at the Imhotep Museum (see below). It's a good idea to check at the kiosk which tombs are open – especially those further afield – as they often close due to restoration work. Some guards encourage unauthorized snapping in the tombs in the expectation of baksheesh, but aside from this you're not obliged to give anything unless they help with lighting or provide a guided tour. If you don't want a running commentary, make this clear at the outset.

To reduce foot-slogging around the site, consider **renting a camel** (£E40–50 per hour), **horse** (£E30–40 per hour) or **donkey** (£E25 per hour) from around the step pyramid or outside the refreshments hut near the Serapeum.

The Imhotep Museum

Just beyond the ticket kiosk, to the right of the main road leading onto the site, the **Imhotep Museum** (daily 9am–4pm, Ramadan until 3pm; £E15, students £E10) is named after the architect who started the whole pyramid building craze by designing the step pyramid for Pharaoh Zoser back in 2650BC or thereabouts. Visitors are first directed into a "Viewing Room", where they can see a nine-minute **film**, narrated by Omar Sharif, about Imhotep and Saqqara. From here, you can check out the museum itself, which contains a number of interesting items found at the site, and merits a fifteen-minute halt if you aren't pressed for time.

To the right of the entrance hall, the "Expedition Hall" has a prettily **painted mummy** from the Ptolemaic XXX Dynasty, as well as **Imhotep's wooden coffin** (his body has yet to be found, however), and some copper **surgical**

instruments from the tomb of a palace physician called Qar. The main hall, dominated by a reconstruction of the facade from Zoser's tomb, contains the original **green faïence panels** found by archeologists at the site, a **cobra frieze** similar to the one *in situ*, and a bronze statuette of Imhotep – no big deal, you might think, except that this one was made nearly a millennium after the great architect's death. The architect was revered throughout pharaonic history and was worshipped at Saqqara as a god of healing; the Ptolemies associated him with Asclepius, the Greek god of medicine.

To the right of the main hall is a room full of stone vessels and **wooden statues**, most notably two likenesses of a V Dynasty vizier named Ptahotep, modelling two different third-millennium BC hairstyles. The room on the other side of the main hall holds assorted tomb treasures, including the mummy of VI Dynasty pharaoh **Merenra I**, and a canopic jar containing his vital organs. Some of the smaller items are also worth a second glance, among them quite a dinky little XVIII Dynasty goldfish carved in red stone.

Zoser's funerary complex

The funerary complex of King Zoser (or Djoser) is the largest in Saqqara, and its **step pyramid** heralded the start of the Pyramid Age. When Imhotep, Zoser's chief architect, raised the pyramid in the 27th century BC, it was the largest structure ever built in stone – the "beginning of architecture", according to one historian. Imhotep's achievement was to break from the tradition of earthbound mastabas, raising level upon level of stones to create a four-step, and then a six-step pyramid, which was clad in dazzling white limestone. None of the blocks was very large, for Zoser's builders still thought in terms of mud-brick rather than megaliths, but the concept, techniques and logistics all pointed towards the true pyramid, finally attained at Giza.

Before it was stripped of its casing stones and rounded off by the elements, Zoser's Pyramid stood 62m high and measured 140m by 118m along its base.

△ Zoser's Step Pyramid

The original entrance on the northern side is blocked, but with permission and keys from the site's Antiquities Inspectorate you can enter via a gallery on the opposite side, dug in the XXVI Dynasty. Dark passageways and vertical ladders descend 28m into the bedrock, where a granite plug failed to prevent robbers from plundering the burial chamber of this III Dynasty monarch (*c*.2667–2648 BC).

Surrounding the pyramid is an extensive **funerary complex**, originally enclosed by a finely cut limestone wall, 544m long and 277m wide, now largely ruined or buried by sand. False doors occur at intervals for the convenience of the pharaoh's *ka*, but visitors can only enter at the southeastern corner, which has largely been rebuilt. Beyond a vestibule with simulated double doors (detailed down to their hinge pins and sockets) lies a narrow colonnaded corridor, whose forty "bundle" columns are ribbed in imitation of palm stems, which culminates in a broader **Hypostyle Hall**.

From here you emerge onto the **Great South Court**, where a rebuilt section of wall (marked ★ on our site plan) bears a **frieze of cobras**. Worshipped in the Delta as a fire-spitting goddess of destruction called Wadjet or Edjo, the cobra was adopted as the emblem of royalty and always appeared on pharaonic headdresses – a figure known as the *uraeus*. Nearby, a deep shaft plummets into Zoser's **Southern Tomb**, decorated with blue faïence tiles and a relief of the king running the Heb-Sed race. During the Jubilee festival marking the thirtieth year of a pharaoh's reign, he had to sprint between two altars representing Upper and Lower Egypt and re-enact his coronation, seated first on one throne, then upon another, symbolically reuniting the Two Lands. Besides demonstrating his vitality, the five-day festival confirmed the renewal of his *ka* and the obedience of provincial dignitaries.

Although the festival was held at Memphis, a pair of altars, thrones and shrines were incorporated in Zoser's funerary complex to perpetuate its efficacy on a cosmic timescale. The B-shaped structures near the centre of the Great Court are the bases of these altars; the twin thrones probably stood on the platform at the southern end of the adjacent **Heb–Sed Court**. Both shrines were essentially facades, since the actual buildings were filled with rubble. This phoney quality is apparent if you view them from the east: the curvaceous roof line and delicate false columns wouldn't look amiss on a yuppie waterfront development. Notice the four **stone feet** beneath a shelter near the northern end of the court.

Beyond this lies the partially ruined **House of the South**, whose chapel is fronted by proto-Doric columns with lotus capitals, and a spearhead motif above the lintel. Inside you'll find several examples of XVIII–IXX Dynasty tourist graffiti, expressing admiration for Zoser or the equivalent of "Ramses was here" – banalities which one scornful ancient graffitist likens to "the work of a woman who has no mind". Continuing northwards, you'll pass a relatively intact row of casing stones along the eastern side of Zoser's Pyramid. The **House of the North** has fluted columns with papyrus capitals; the lotus and the papyrus were the heraldic emblems of Upper and Lower Egypt.

On the northern side of the pyramid, a tilted masonry box or **serdab** contains a life-size statue of Zoser gazing blindly towards the North and circumpolar stars, which the ancients associated with immortality; seated thus, his *ka* was assured of eternal life. Zoser's statue is a replica, however, the original having been removed to Cairo's Egyptian Museum (see p.107). The ruined mortuary temple to the right of the *serdab* is unusual for being sited to the north rather than the east of its pyramid, and for the underground tunnel which originally led to Zoser's burial chamber.

South of the complex

South of Zoser's funerary complex are several tombs and other ruins, dating from various dynasties. During the Old Kingdom, nobles were buried in subterranean tombs covered by large mud-brick superstructures; the name "mastaba" (Arabic for "bench") was bestowed upon them by native workmen during excavations last century. Three such edifices stand outside the southern wall of Zoser's complex; they are often closed for no apparent reason, but it's usually just a question of locating and tipping the caretaker for opening them up. The **Mastaba of Idut** is the most worthwhile, with interesting reliefs in five of its ten rooms. Among the fishing and farming scenes, notice the crocodile eyeing a newborn hippo, and a calf being dragged through the water so that cows will ford a river. The chapel contains a false door painted in imitation of granite, scenes of bulls and buffaloes being sacrificed, and Idut herself. Idut was the daughter of Pharaoh Unas, whose pyramid stands just beyond the **Mastaba of Nebet**, his queen. The reliefs in Nebet's Mastaba are also worth seeing: in one scene, Nebet smells a lotus blossom.

The Pyramid of Unas

Although its frontal aspect resembles a mound of rubble, the **Pyramid of Unas** retains many casing stones around the back, some carved with hieroglyphs. A low passageway on the northern side leads into its **burial chamber**, whose alabaster walls are covered with inscriptions listing the rituals and prayers for liberating the pharaoh's *ba*, and the articles for his *ka* to use in the afterlife. These **Pyramid Texts**, forming the basis of the New Kingdom *Book of the Dead*, are the earliest-known example of decorative writing within a pharaonic tomb chamber, and speak of the pharaoh becoming a star and travelling to Sirius and other constellations. Painted stars adorn the ceiling, while the sarcophagus area is surrounded by striped, checked and zigzag patterns. Thomas Cook & Sons sponsored the excavation of the tomb by Gaston Maspero in 1881.

▲ Unas

Unas was the last pharaoh of the V Dynasty, so his pyramid follows those of Abu Sir, which evince a marked decline from the Great Pyramids of Giza. Given the duration of pharaonic civilization, it's sobering to realize that only 350 years separated the creation of the Step Pyramid from this sad reminder of past glories. Originally, it was approached by a one-kilometre **causeway** enclosed by a roof and walls. Reliefs inside the short reconstructed section depict the transport of granite from Aswan, archers, prisoners of war, and a famine caused by the Nile failing to rise. The ruins of a valley temple face the ticket office below the plateau. To the south of the causeway are two gaping, brick-lined **boat pits** that may have contained solar barques like the one at Giza, or merely symbolized them, since nothing was found when the pits were excavated.

Other tombs and ruins

A stone hut to the south of the Unas Pyramid gives access to a spiral staircase that descends 25m underground, to where three low corridors lead into the vaulted **Persian Tombs**. Chief physician Psamtik, Admiral Djenhebu and Psamtik's son Pediese were all officials of the XXVII Dynasty of Persian kings founded in 525 BC, yet the hieroglyphs in their tombs invoke the same spells as those written two thousand years earlier. The dizzying descent and claustrophobic atmosphere make this an exciting tomb to explore. Though often locked, it's not "forbidden" as guards sometimes pretend, hoping to wangle excessive baksheesh.

Further to the southeast lies the recently rediscovered **Tomb of Horemheb**. Built when he was a general, it became redundant after Horemheb seized power from Pharaoh Ay in 1348 BC and ordered a new tomb to be dug in the Valley of the Kings, the royal necropolis of the New Kingdom. Many of the finely carved blocks from his original tomb are now in museums around the world. Another set of paving stones and truncated columns marks the nearby **Tomb of Tia**, sister of Ramses II. The **Tomb of Maya**, Tutankhamun's treasurer, was found nearby in 1986 and is still under excavation. Due east lie the sanded-over mud-brick ruins of the **Monastery of St Jeremiah**, which the Arabs destroyed in 960, four hundred years after its foundation. Practically all of the monastery's carvings and paintings have been removed to the Coptic Museum in Old Cairo. Just to its north, on the causeway of Unas, are four mastabas belonging to nobles.

It's indicative of how much might still be hidden beneath the sands at Saqqara that the **unfinished Pyramid of Sekhemkhet** was only discovered in 1950. Beyond his monuments, nothing is known of Sekhemkhet, whose step pyramid and funerary complex were presumably intended to mimic those of his predecessor, Zoser, and may also have been built by Imhotep. The alabaster sarcophagus inside the pyramid (which is unsafe to enter) was apparently never used, but the body of a child was found inside an auxiliary tomb.

From Sekhemkhet's Pyramid and the monastery it's roughly 700m to the nearest part of South Saqqara.

Around the pyramids of Userkaf and Teti

While neither of these pyramids amounts to much, the mastabas near Teti's edifice contain some fantastic reliefs. If you're starting from Zoser's complex, it's only a short walk to the pulverized **Pyramid of Userkaf**, the founder of the V Dynasty, whose successors were buried at Abu Sir (see p.216). From here, a track runs northwards to the **Pyramid of Teti**, which overlooks the valley from the edge of the plateau. Excavated by Mariette in the 1850s, it has since been engulfed by sand and may be closed; in one of the funeral chambers (accessible by a sloping shaft and low passageway), the star-patterned blocks of its vaulted roof have slipped inwards.

Although most of the VI Dynasty kings who followed Teti chose to be buried at South Saqqara, several of their courtiers were interred in a **"street of tombs"** beside his pyramid, which was linked to the Serapeum by an Avenue of Sphinxes (now sanded over). To do justice to their superbly detailed reliefs takes well over an hour, but it's rare to find all of them open.

▼ Teti

The Mastaba of Mereruka

The largest tomb in the street belongs to **Mereruka**, Teti's vizier and son-in-law, whose 32-room complex includes separate funerary suites for his wife Watet-khet-hor, priestess of Hathor, and their son Meri-Teti. In the entry passage, Mereruka is shown playing a board game and painting at an easel; the chamber beyond depicts him hunting in the marshes with Watet-khet-hor (the frogs, birds, hippos and grasshoppers are beautifully rendered), along with the usual farming scenes. Goldsmiths, jewellers and other artisans are inspected by the couple in a room beyond the

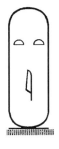

rear door, which leads into another chamber showing taxation and the punishment of defaulters. A pillared hall to the right portrays them watching sinuous dancers; a room to the left depicts offerings, sacrifices and birds being fed, with a serdab at the far end.

Beyond the transverse hall, with its tomb shaft, false door and reliefs of grape-treading and harvesting, lies the main offerings hall, dominated by a statue of Mereruka emerging from a false door. The opposite wall shows his funeral procession; around the corner are boats under full sail, with monkeys playing in their rigging. To the left of the statue, Mereruka is supported by his sons and litter-bearers, accompanied by dwarves and dogs; on the other side, children frolic while dancers sway above the doorway into Meri-Teti's undecorated funerary suite.

To reach **Watet-khet-hor's suite**, return to the first room in the mastaba and take the other door. After similar scenes to those in her husband's tomb, Watet-khet-hor is carried to her false door in a lion chair.

The Mastabas of Kagemni and Ankh-ma-hor

East of Mereruka's tomb and left around the corner, the smaller **Mastaba of Kagemni** features delicate reliefs in worse shape. The pillared hall beyond the entrance corridor shows dancers and acrobats, the judgement of prisoners, a hippo hunt and agricultural work, all rich in naturalistic detail. Notice the boys feeding a puppy and trussed cows being milked. The door in this wall leads to another chamber where Kagemni inspects his fowl pens while servants trap marsh birds with clap-nets; on the pylon beyond this he relaxes on a palanquin as they tend to his pet dogs and monkeys. As usual in the offerings hall, scenes of butchery appear opposite the false door. On the roof of the mastaba (reached by stairs from the entrance corridor) are two boat pits. As vizier, Kagemni was responsible for overseeing prophets and the estate of Teti's pyramid complex.

The **Mastaba of Ankh-ma-hor** is also known as the "Doctor's Tomb" after its reliefs showing circumcision, toe surgery and suchlike, as practised during the VI Dynasty. If the tomb is open, it's definitely worth a look, unlike the sand-choked **I Dynasty tombs** that straggle along the edge of the scarp beyond the **Antiquities Inspectorate**.

The Double Mastaba of Akhti-Hotep and Ptah-Hotep

This mastaba belonged to **Ptah-Hotep**, a priest of Maat during the reign of Unas's predecessor, Djedkare, and his son **Akhti-Hotep**, who served as vizier, judge and overseer of the granaries and treasury. Though it's smaller than Ti's mastaba, its reliefs are interesting for being at various stages of completion, showing how a finished product was achieved. After the preliminary drawings had been corrected in red by a master artist, the background was chiselled away to leave a silhouette, before details were marked in and cut. The agricultural scenes in the entrance corridor show this process clearly, although with the exception of Ptah-Hotep's chapel, none of these reliefs was ever painted.

Off the pillared hall of Akhti-Hotep is a T-shaped chapel whose inside wall shows workers making papyrus boats and jousting with poles. More impressive is the chapel of his father, covered with exquisitely detailed reliefs. Between the two door-shaped steles representing the entrance to the tomb, Ptah-Hotep enjoys a banquet of offerings, garbed in the panther-skin of a high priest. Similar scenes occur on the facing wall, whose upper registers show animals being slaughtered and women bringing offerings from his estates. The left-hand wall swarms with activity, as boys wrestle and play *khaki la wizza* (a leapfrog game still popular in Nubia); wild animals mate or flee from hunting dogs, while others are caged. A faded mural above the entrance shows the priest being manicured and pedicured at a time when Europe was in the Stone Age.

The Mastaba of Ti

Discovered by Mariette in 1865, this V Dynasty tomb has been a rich source of information about life in the Old Kingdom. A royal hairdresser who made an advantageous marriage, **Ti** acquired stewardship over several mortuary temples and pyramids, and his children bore the title "royal descendant".

Ti makes his first appearances on either side of the doorway, receiving offerings and asking visitors to respect his tomb **[a]**. The reliefs in the courtyard have been damaged by exposure, but it's possible to discern men butchering an ox **[b]**, Ti on his palanquin accompanied by dogs and dwarves **[c]**, servants feeding cranes and geese **[d]**, and Ti examining accounts and cargo **[e]**. His unadorned tomb (reached by a shaft from the courtyard) contrasts with the richly decorated interior of the mastaba.

Near his son's false door, variously garbed figures of

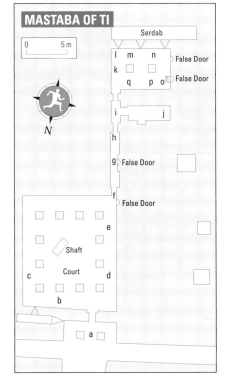

Ti **[f]** appear above the portal of a corridor where bearers bring food and animals for the sustenance of his *ka* **[g]**. Beyond a doorway **[h]** over which Ti enjoys the marshes with his wife, funerary statues are dragged on sledges above scenes of butchery, and his Delta fleets are arrayed **[i]**. Potters, bakers, brewers and scribes occupy the rear wall of a storage room **[j]**, while dancers shimmy above the doorway to Ti's chapel.

In the harvesting scene, notice the man twisting a donkey's ear to make it behave **[k]**. Further along, Ti inspects shipwrights shaping tree trunks, and sawing and hammering boards **[l]**. Goldsmiths, sculptors, carpenters, tanners and market life are minutely detailed **[m]**, like the musicians who entertain Ti at his offerings table **[n]**. Peer through one of the apertures and you'll see a cast of his statue inside its serdab. The original is in the Egyptian Museum.

Reliefs on the northern wall depict fishing and trapping in the Delta **[o]**; Ti sailing through the marshes while his servants spear hippopotami **[p]**; harvesting papyrus for boat-building; and ploughing and seeding fields **[q]**. The scene of hunting in the marshes is also allegorical, pitting Ti against the forces of chaos (represented by fish and birds) and evil (hippos were hated and feared). If you aren't claustrophobic and like cold, dark spaces, it is possible to squeeze down the steps of the shaft into the burial chamber below.

A cluster of **III Dynasty tombs** to the east of Ti's mastaba is now reckoned a likely site for the tomb of Imhotep, as yet undiscovered. Further northeast lie the **Ibis and Baboon Galleries** sacred to Thoth, which Flaubert visited in the 1840s: "We go down into a hole and then crawl along a passageway almost on our stomachs, inching over fine sand and

▲ Feeding cranes

fragments of pottery; at the far end the jars containing ibises are stacked like blocks of sugar at a grocer's, head to foot."

The Serapeum

Saqqara's weirdest monument (closed for restoration at the time of writing) lies underground near a derelict building downhill from the refreshments tent. Discovered by Mariette in 1851, the rock-cut galleries of the **Serapeum** held the mummified corpses of the Apis bulls, which the Memphites regarded as manifestations of Ptah's "blessed soul" and identified with Osiris after death. Having been embalmed on alabaster slabs at Memphis, the bulls were interred in sarcophagi weighing up to seventy tons apiece. Meanwhile, the priests began searching for Ptah's reincarnation amongst the sacred herd. Once a new bull had been chosen, it spent forty days at Nilopolis (across the river from Memphis), where women were allowed to approach it *only* to expose their vulvas (a practice believed to ensure fertility). After the full moon the bull was taken to its future residence in Memphis, where it had its own priestly attendants and a harem of cows.

The **cult of the Apis bulls** was assailed by Egypt's Persian conqueror, Cambyses, who stabbed one to disprove its divinity, whilst Artaxerxes I avenged his nickname "the donkey" by having a namesake beast buried here with full honours. But the Ptolemies encouraged native cults and even synthesized their own. "Serapeum" derives from the fusion of the Egyptian Osarapis (Osiris in his Apis form) and the Greeks' Dionysus into the cult of Serapis, whose temple stood in Alexandria.

Although robbers had plundered the galleries centuries before, Mariette found a single tomb miraculously undisturbed for four thousand years. The fingermark and footprints of the ancient workman who sealed the tomb were still visible, and Mariette also found a mummified bull and the coffin of Khamenwaset, son of Ramses II and high priest of Ptah. The oldest of the galleries dates from that era, and is now inaccessible; the second is from the Saite period, and the main one from Ptolemaic times.

Enormous granite or basalt **sarcophagi** are ranged either side of the Ptolemaic gallery, at the end of which is a narrow shaft whereby robbers penetrated the Serapeum. The finest sarcophagus squats on the right, while another one lies abandoned near the entrance to the Ramessid gallery. Sadly, none of the mummified bulls remains *in situ*.

En route to the Serapeum you'll notice a concrete slab sheltering broken statues of Plato, Heraclitus, Thales, Protagoras, Homer, Hesiod, Demetrius of Phalerum and Pindar – the **Philosopher's Circle**, now rather rubbish-strewn and neglected. The statues formerly stood near a temple that overlaid the Serapeum, proof that the Ptolemies juxtaposed Hellenistic philosophy and Ancient Egyptian religion with no sense of incongruity.

Memphis

Most tour excursions to Saqqara include a flying visit to the scant **remains of Memphis** in the village of **MIT RAHINA**. Sadly, these hardly stir one's imagination to resurrect the ancient city effaced over centuries by Nilotic silt, which now lies metres below rustling palm groves and oxen-ploughed fields. Although something of its glory is evident in the great necropolises ranged across the desert, and the countless objects in Cairo's Egyptian Museum, to appreciate the significance of Memphis you have to recall its history.

The city's foundation is attributed to Menes, the quasi-mythical ruler (known also as Narmer – and possibly a conflation of several rulers) who was said to have unified Upper and Lower Egypt and launched the I Dynasty around 3100 BC. At that time, Memphis was sited at the apex of the Delta and thus controlled overland and river communications. If not the earliest city on earth, it was certainly the first imperial one. Memphis was Egypt's capital throughout the Old Kingdom, regained its role after the anarchic Intermediate Period, and was never overshadowed by the parvenu seat of the XII Dynasty. Even after Thebes became capital of the New Kingdom, Memphis still held sway over Lower Egypt and remained the nation's second city until well into the Ptolemaic era, only being deserted in early Muslim times after four thousand years of continuous occupation.

Alas for posterity, most of this garden city was built of mud-brick, which returned to the Nile silt whence it came, and everyone from the Romans onwards plundered its stone temples for fine masonry. Nowadays, leftover statues and steles share a garden (daily 8am–4pm; £E30, students £E15) with souvenir kiosks. The star attraction, found in 1820, is a limestone **Colossus of Ramses II**, similar to the one that used to stand in Midan Ramses, but laid supine within a concrete shelter. A giant **alabaster sphinx** weighing eighty

---

The cults of Ptah and Sokar

In pre-Dynastic times, **Ptah** was the Great Craftsman or Divine Artificer, who invented metallurgy and engineering. However, the people of Memphis esteemed him as the Great Creator who, with a word, brought the universe into being – a concept that never really appealed to other Egyptians. Like most creator gods, he was subsequently linked with death cults and is shown dressed in the shroud of a mummy. The Greeks equated him with Hephaestus, their god of fire and the arts.

Another deity closely associated with Memphis is **Sokar**, originally the god of darkness but subsequently of death, with special responsibility for necropolises. He is often shown, with a falcon's head, seated in the company of Isis and Osiris. Although his major festival occurred at Memphis towards the end of the inundation season, Sokar also rated a shrine at Abydos, where all the Egyptian death gods were represented.

▲ Ptah

tons is also mightily impressive. Both these figures probably stood outside the vast Temple of Ptah, the city's patron deity.

By leaving the garden and walking back along the road, you'll notice (on the right) several alabaster **embalming slabs**, where the holy Apis bulls were mummified before burial in the Serapeum at Saqqara. In a pit across the road are excavated chambers from Ptah's temple complex; climb the ridge beyond them and you can gaze across the cultivated valley floor to the Step Pyramid of Saqqara.

South Saqqara

Like their predecessors at Abu Sir, the pharaohs of the VI Dynasty (*c.*2345–2181 BC) established another necropolis – nowadays called **South Saqqara** – which started 700m beyond Sekhemkhet's unfinished pyramid and extended for over 3km. Unfortunately for sightseers, the most interesting monuments are those furthest away across the site; renting a donkey, horse or camel (£E30–50 for the round trip) will minimize slogging over soft sand. It is also possible to walk from Saqqara village: just keep heading west until you emerge from the palm trees. If you stop to ask directions, bear in mind that, whatever you say (even if you say it in Arabic), the villagers will almost certainly assume you are looking for the Step Pyramid, and direct you accordingly.

Once you reach the site, two tracks run either side of several pyramids before meeting at the Mastabat al-Faraun. The western one is more direct than the route that goes via Saqqara village, set amid lush palm groves 2km from North Saqqara's ticket office. There is no official entrance fee to the site, and you probably won't see another tourist. Apart from the tranquillity, however, what you get here, with the pyramids of North Saqqara clearly visible to the north, and those of Dahshur to the south, is the feeling of being in the midst of a massive pyramid field, somewhere very ancient and vast.

The site

Heading south along either track, you'll pass a low mound of rubble identified as the **Pyramid of Pepi I**. The name "Memphis", which Classical authors bestowed upon Egypt's ancient capital and its environs, was actually derived from one of this pyramid's titles. To the southwest, another insignificant heap indicates the **Pyramid of Merenre**, who succeeded Pepi. French archeologists are excavating the latter's pyramid, but neither site is really worth a detour.

Due west of Saqqara village, sand drifts over the outlying temples of the **Pyramid of Djedkare-Isesi**. Known in Arabic as the "Pyramid of the Sentinel", it stands 25m high and can be entered via a tunnel on the north side. Although a shattered basalt sarcophagus and mummified remains were found here during the 1800s, it wasn't until 1946 that Abdel Hussein identified them as those of Djedkare, the penultimate king of the V Dynasty. Far from being the first ruler to be entombed in South Saqqara, Djedkare was merely emulating the last pharaoh of the previous dynasty, whose own mortuary complex is uniquely different, and the oldest in this necropolis.

Built of limestone blocks, the mortuary complex of Shepseskaf resembles a gigantic sarcophagus with a rounded lid; another simile gave rise to its local name, **Mastabat al-Faraun** – the Pharaoh's Bench. If you can find a guard, it's possible to venture through descending and horizontal corridors to reach the burial chamber and various storerooms. The monument was almost certainly commissioned by Shepseskaf, who evidently felt the need to distance himself from the pyramid of his father, Mycerinus. However, the archeologist Jequier doubted that the complex was ever used for any actual burial and Shepseskaf's final resting place remains uncertain.

Northwest of here lies the most complete example of a VI Dynasty mortuary complex, albeit missing casing stones and other masonry that was plundered in medieval times. The usual valley temple and causeway culminate in a mortuary temple whose vestibule and sanctuary retain fragments of their original reliefs. Beyond this rises the **Pyramid of Pepi II**, whose reign supposedly lasted 94 years, after which the VI Dynasty expired. A descending passage leads to his rock-cut burial chamber, whose ceiling and walls are inscribed with stars and Pyramid Texts. These also appear within the subsidiary pyramids of Pepi's queens, Apuit and Neith, which imitate his mortuary complex on a smaller scale. Various nobles and officials are buried roundabouts.

Dahshur

The **Dahshur pyramid field** (daily: summer 8am–5pm; winter 8am–4pm; last ticket sold an hour before closing; £E25, students £E15) contains some of the most impressive of all the pyramids, and some of the most significant in the history of pyramid-building. The easiest way to get to Dahshur is by taxi, but there are also service taxi microbuses to Dahshur village from Maryotteya Canal by Pyramids Road (the same yard as for Saqqara; see p.217) and from Saqqara village. Infrequent service taxis run the 2km to the site entrance from Dahshur village, but most people will find it easier to walk or take a private taxi. The latter is quite a good idea since the site is extremely spread out: it's another kilometre from the gate to the Red Pyramid, and another from there to the Bent Pyramid. A taxi should cost £E2 from the village to the Red Pyramid, but somewhat more if you also want to be driven around the site and back. Getting back to Cairo should not be left too late or you may find yourself stranded with the nearest public transport 5km away in Saqqara – transport from Dahshur tends to dry up at around 5pm.

The pyramids are in two groups. To the east are three **Middle Kingdom complexes**, dating from the revival of pyramid-building (*c.*1991–1790 BC) that culminated near the Fayoum. Though the pyramids proved unrewarding to nineteenth-century excavators, their subsidiary tombs yielded some magnificent jewellery (now in the Antiquities Museum). To the north, the pyramids of XII Dynasty pharaohs Seostris III and Amenenkhet II are little more than piles of rubble, but the southernmost of the three, the **Black Pyramid of Amenemhet III** (Joseph's pharoah in the Old Testament, according to some), is at least an interesting shape: though its limestone casing has long gone, a black mud-brick core is still standing (its black basalt capstone is in the Antiquities Museum). More intriguing, however, are the two **Old Kingdom pyramids** further into the desert, which have long tantalized archeologists with a riddle. Both of them are credited to **Snofru** (*c.*2613–2588 BC), father of Cheops and founder of the IV Dynasty, whose monuments constitute an evolutionary link between the stepped creations of the previous dynasty at North Saqqara and the true Pyramids of Giza.

The Red Pyramid

The first pyramid you come to if you follow the road past the ticket office is Snofru's northern **Red Pyramid**, which is named after the colour of the limestone it was built from. Despite its lower angle (43.5°) and height (101m), Snofru's Red Pyramid clearly prefigures Cheops's edifice, which is also the only pyramid that exceeds it in size, Snofru's Red Pyramid being larger than Chephren's Pyramid at Giza. It was probably Snofru's third attempt (see below) at pyramid building, but he was not laid to rest in any of the three burial chambers here – all were unused.

The Red Pyramid's **interior** is now open to the public, and you can climb up and descend into it to check out its three rather musty chambers. Electric lighting has been installed to illuminate them, but it sometimes fails, so it's a good idea to bring a torch (flashlight) if you have one. The first two chambers are roughly parallel to each other, but the third is on a higher level and perpendicular to the other two. One definite advantage of visiting the interior of this pyramid rather than those at Giza is that you will very probably be alone to absorb the rather eerie, if fetid, atmosphere.

The Bent Pyramid

From the Red Pyramid, a track leads south to the pyramid where Snofru was buried, the **Bent Pyramid**, which is not only the most intriguing of all the pyramids, but, because of its state of preservation, also the most breathtaking. What makes Snofru's final resting place different from all the other pyramids is its change of angle towards the top: it rises more steeply (54.3°) than the Red Pyramid or Giza pyramids for three-quarters of its height, before abruptly tapering at a gentler slope – hence its name. The explanation for its shape, and why Snofru should have built two pyramids only a kilometre apart, is a longstanding conundrum of Egyptology.

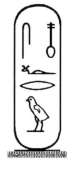

▲ Snofru

Mindful of the truism that a pharaoh required but one sanctuary for his *ka*, many reasoned that the Bent Pyramid resulted from a change of plan prompted by fears for its stability, and when these persisted, a second, safer pyramid was built to guarantee Snofru's afterlife. But for this theory to hold water, it's necessary to dismiss Snofru's claim to have built a *third* pyramid at Maidum as mere usurpation of an earlier structure; and the possibility that its sudden collapse might have caused the modification of the Bent Pyramid must likewise be rejected on the grounds that he needed only one secure monument.

In 1977, a professor of physics at Oxford University reopened the whole debate. Kurt Mendelssohn, arguing that Snofru did, indeed, build the "Collapsed Pyramid" at Maidum (whose fall resulted in changes to Dahshur's Bent Pyramid), overcame the "one pharaoh–one *ka*–one pyramid" objection by postulating a pyramid production line. As one pyramid neared completion, surplus resources were deployed to start another, despite the satisfaction of the reigning king's requirements. The reason for continuous production was that building a single pyramid required gigantic efforts over ten to thirty years; inevitably, some pharaohs lacked the time and resources. A stockpile of half-constructed, perhaps even finished, pyramids was an insurance policy on the afterlife.

Egyptologists greeted Mendelssohn's theory with delight or derision, but unlike the Great Pyramids, or the lives of Hatshepsut, Nefertiti and Akhenaten, the enigma of Snofru's pyramids has never excited much public interest. Nevertheless, of all the pyramids, the Bent Pyramid is probably the most visually stunning. The reason it seems so impressive lies in the fact that, although its corners have fallen away at the base, the pyramid's limestone casing is still largely intact, giving a clear impression of what it once looked like – smooth and white. All the Old Kingdom pyramids were originally clad in limestone, their surfaces smooth like this one, but they have almost all been stripped, the stone burned for lime. The Bent Pyramid escaped that fate because its narrower angle made it harder to remove the facing, though this has disappeared from much of the base.

In fact, the removal of the lowest courses of limestone cladding enables you to see not only how closely the blocks were slotted together, but something else too. On the ground at the northwest corner of the pyramid, pits and grooves have been carved into the bedrock. These were used to dress the pyramid, and presumably were carved before the pyramid was begun, indicating that construction began with the marking out of a base on the cleared bedrock. This is even clearer on the small satellite pyramid immediately to its south.

The Bent Pyramid is unusual in one final respect: it has two entrances, one on its west side as well as the more conventional one in its north face. The reason for this is unknown. To its south is a subsidiary queen's pyramid, possibly belonging to Snofru's wife Hetepheres (though some say Snofru himself was buried here). If it did belong to her, she didn't stay there too long: after robbers had entered both of Snofru's pyramids at Dahshur, Hetepheres' sarcophagus was moved to Giza for safekeeping, and hidden down a shaft next to the Great Pyramid of her son Cheops. The interior of the Bent Pyramid is unlikely to be open to the public in the near future, but you can see inside it on Ⓦ www .guardians.net/egypt.

Consumers' Cairo

As befits its size, Cairo has the most varied culinary scene, shopping and night-life in North Africa. Much of it developed in the Sadat era after decades of Nasserite austerity, and for those who can afford it, conspicuous consumption is very much the order of the day. As a visitor, you're well catered for, whether you're into sailing on the Nile, watching a belly dancer, or absorbing a whole world of popular culture at Cairo's religious festivals. For latest news and reviews on eating, drinking and nightlife in Cairo, check Ⓦ www.yallabina.com.

Eating

Don't fall into the trap of eating only in Cairo's tourist restaurants, or thinking that Egyptian food doesn't rise beyond *kofta* and kebab. You can satisfy most tastes if you know where to look. The options range from Arab cafés offering a few simple dishes to extravagant "food weeks" at deluxe hotels (advertised in *Egypt Today*).

Restaurants run the gamut from *nouvelle cuisine* salons to backstreet kebab houses and open-fronted tiled diners. The ones devoted to *kushari* or *fuul* and *taamiya* provide the cheapest nutritious meals going. *Fatatris* offer up *fiteer*, Egyptian pizzas which are tastier and cheaper than most Western-style pizzas available in Cairo. At the other end of the gastro-cultural spectrum, every hotel rated three stars or above has at least one restaurant and coffee shop that's accessible to non-residents. If familiar food and no hassle are top priority, **hotel dining** is usually a safe bet. For those who need them, there are several branches of *McDonald's*, *Pizza Hut* and *KFC* around the centre as well as in Mohandiseen and Heliopolis and along Pyramids Road. Surprisingly to Westerners, these chains are considered posh eating places by Cairenes, who may even dress up to go to them.

Between these extremes there's a huge variation in standards of cleanliness and presentation, and whether somewhere seems okay or grotty depends partly on your own values. Running water remains a crucial factor – anywhere without it is risky. A number of places off Ramses, Orabi, Ataba, Falaki, Lazoghli and Giza squares and midway down Sharia Qalaa function **all night**.

Restaurants and street food

The establishments reviewed have been categorized as follows: **inexpensive** means that you can get a full meal (starter, main course and soft drink) for £E30 or less, **moderate** means that a full meal costs £E30–75, and **expensive** will set you back over £E75 for a full meal – still cheap by Western standards. Many restaurants sell seafood and *kofta* and kebab by weight: a quarter of a kilo is one portion, while a full kilo is usually enough for three to four people. The majority of places reviewed have **menus** in English or French and staff who understand both, but others deal only in Arabic; fortunately, many of them display what's on offer, so you only have to point.

Increasingly, restaurants in Cairo, from fast-food joints through to posh eateries, offer **home delivery** (or hotel delivery, if your hostelry will allow it). Phone numbers are given for those places, and for establishments where a **reservation** is advisable.

Downtown Cairo

Aside from Egyptian restaurants, ranging from very upmarket establishments to cheap *kushari* diners, downtown Cairo has a fair number of different international cuisines to choose from, with several French, Levantine, Italian, Chinese and Korean eating places, and others offering a variety of Western dishes. All the restaurants below are marked on the map opposite unless otherwise stated.

Al-Haty 3 Sharia Halim, off 26th July St, behind the *Windsor Hotel*. Vintage decor, with mirrors and fans, and inexpensive, traditional and good-value fare, including *mezze*, roast lamb (*moza*), *kofta* and kebab. The chargrilled half-chicken is good. No alcohol. Inexpensive. Daily noon–11.30pm. There is another, more elegant branch with low tables and something approaching classic decor in the passage off no. 8, on the other side of 26th July St, open daily 11am–1pm.

Alfi Bey 3 Sharia Alfi Bey ☏02/577-1888. Another vintage restaurant, founded in 1938. Its panelling, chandeliers and gilt furniture have been there ever since it opened. Best for lamb dishes, chicken, or pigeon stuffed with rice and liver. No alcohol. Moderate. Daily noon–1am.

Arabesque 6 Sharia Qasr el-Nil ☏02/574-8677. French and Levantine cuisine, strong on soups and

meat dishes, but chiefly remarkable for its chic ambience and contemporary art gallery rather than the quality of the food. Licensed. Moderate. Daily noon–4pm & 7.30pm–midnight.

Bon Appetit Sharia Mohammed Mahmoud, opposite the AUC Library. Downtown branch of the Mohandiseen café-restaurant (see p.237), this one favoured by students from the AUC, with a free notice board advertising accommodation, Arabic lessons and sometimes even work. Moderate. Daily 9am–1am.

El-Guesh (aka Sayed Emara) 32 Midan Falaki, on the corner of Tahrir and Falaki streets. A family place serving *kofta* and kebab, stuffed pigeon, succulent lamb (*oka*), or more exotic offerings such as kidney and testicles. Inexpensive. Daily 11am–11pm.

Estoril 12 Sharia Talaat Harb, in the passage ☏02/574-3102. "Eat undescribable and

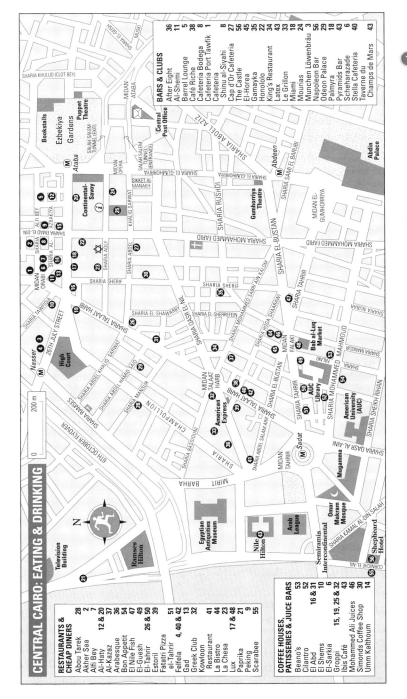

CENTRAL CAIRO: EATING & DRINKING

N

0   200 m

RESTAURANTS & CHEAP DINERS

Abou Tarek	28
Akher Saa	2
Alfi Bey	7
Ali-Haty	12 & 20
Al-Kazaz	37
Arabesque	36
Bon Appetit	54
El Nile Fish	47
El-Guesh	49
El-Tahrir	26 & 50
Estoril	39
Fatatri Pizza el-Tahrir	51
Felfela	4, 40 & 42
Gad	13
Greek Club	32
Kowloon Restaurant	41
La Bistro	44
La Chesa	23
Lux	17 & 48
Paprika	21
Peking	9
Scarabee	55

COFFEE HOUSES, PATISSERIES & JUICE BARS

Beano's	53
Cilantro	52
El Abd	16 & 31
El Shems	10
El-Sarkia	6
Groppi	15, 19, 25 & 32
Ibis Café	43
Mohammed Ali Juices	46
Simonds Coffee Shop	30
Umm Kalthoum	14

BARS & CLUBS

After Eight	36
Al-Shemi	11
Barrel Lounge	5
Café Riche	38
Cafeteria Bodega	8
Cafeteria Port Tawfik	1
Cafeteria	8
Shinu al-Siyahi	27
Cap d'Or Cafeteria	56
The Castle	45
El-Horea	35
Gamayka	22
Honololo	34
King's Restaurant	43
Latex	33
Le Grillon	18
Miami	24
Mourias	3
Munchen Löwenbräu	56
Napoleon Bar	29
Odeon Palace	18
Palmyra	43
Pyramids Bar	6
Scheharazade	40
Stella Cafeteria	43
Taverne du Champs de Mars	43

unpronounceable dishes at the oldest restaurant in downtown Cairo," its blurb says, though the dishes are French and Lebanese standards, and the restaurant dates only from 1959. You can eat here in quiet surroundings, and there's a vintage bar that merits a Bogart. Moderate. Daily noon–midnight.

Felfela 15 Sharia Hoda Shaarawi. A tourist favourite, offering Egyptian dishes in a long hall with funky decor. Sells beer. Service can be a little snooty if you're scruffily dressed, and there's nothing you can get here that wouldn't be cheaper elsewhere. Inexpensive. Daily 8am–midnight. *Felfela's* takeaway, around the corner on Talaat Harb (daily 7am–11pm), with another branch opposite the High Court on 26th July St (daily 6am–1am), does *shawarmas* and *taamiya* sandwiches, though again you'd pay less elsewhere.

Gad 13 26th July St ☏02/576-3353 or 3583. The modern and very popular takeaway downstairs is always crowded, as is the upstairs where you can get a sit-down meal. Excellent standards – *taamiya*, *fuul*, *shawarma* and burgers – plus delicious specialities such as *kibda skanderani* (Alexandrian-style liver with chilli), wonderful baked-on-the-premises Syrian-style pitta bread ('*aish shaami*), and some of the best *fiteers* in town. They also deliver. Inexpensive. Daily 24hr.

Greek Club Above *Groppi's* on Midan Talaat Harb; entrance on Sharia Bassiouni. The cuisine isn't particularly Greek, but the food isn't bad (fried squid and chips makes a change, or there are kebabs), and the summer terrace is pleasant. Serves alcohol, including ouzo. Moderate prices but you have to pay a temporary membership fee (£E5) to eat here. Daily 6pm–1.30am.

Kowloon Restaurant Entered via the *Hotel Cleopatra* on the corner of Midan Tahrir and Sharia el-Bustan ☏02/575-9831. Expensive but superb

Korean and Chinese food cooked by Korean chefs. The menu includes several pork dishes and the place is popular with East Asian expats. Daily 11am–11pm.

La Bistro 8 Sharia Hoda Shaarawi ☏02/392-7694. A bright little place serving reasonably good French food (sea bass in mustard sauce, beef tournedos in red wine sauce, crêpes, chocolate mousse), though the blue-and-white decor is a little jarring and the muzak can sometimes be excruciating. Moderate. Daily noon–midnight.

La Chesa 21 Sharia Adly ☏02/393-9360. Salubrious, Swiss-managed café serving good Western food, including fondues (cheese, meat, chocolate or "Chinese"), and Zurich-style veal slices in mushroom sauce, as well as Swiss breakfasts (£E27), scrumptious pastries and great coffee. Expensive but worth it. Daily 7am–midnight.

El Nile Fish 25 Sharia el-Bustan, just off Midan Falaki. Popular fish restaurant with choice of various denizens of the deep freshly caught and fried or grilled to order, served with salad, tahina and pickles. Moderate (unless you go for the king prawns). Daily noon–1am.

Paprika 1129 Corniche el-Nil, just south of the TV Building ☏02/578-9447. Serving a mix of Hungarian and Egyptian food – tasty paprika-based dishes and *mezze*. The speciality is goulash. Frequented by media folk (including Omar Sharif) and footballers, it's especially busy at weekends. Expensive. Daily noon–midnight.

Peking 14 Sharia Saray el-Azbakiya ☏02/591-2381, ⊛www.peking-restaurants.com. Central branch of a citywide chain of Chinese restaurants, nowhere near as authentic as the *Kowloon*, nor anything like as good (and the music is a bit much), but they do takeaways and delivery, and boast branches in Zamalek, Mohandiseen and Heliopolis, plus a floating restaurant (see p.239). Moderate. Daily noon–12.30am.

Very cheap options

Most of the really cheap diners are concentrated around Midan Orabi (especially along the first block of Sharia al-Azbakiya, the small street between the two patisseries) and Midan Falaki (especially on Sharia Mansur, outside Bab al-Luq market). They are not listed individually here, but worth a peruse. All of the following fall into the lower end of the inexpensive price band; you can fill up for well under £E10 at most of them.

Abou Tarek 40 Sharia Champollion, at the corner of Sharia Maarouf ⊛www.aboutarek.com. You can't miss this a/c diner on two floors as it's lit up like a Christmas tree. It serves the best *kushari* in Cairo, with rice pudding for afters. Daily 7am–11.30pm.

Akher Saa 8 Sharia Alfi Bey, next to the Nile Christian Bookshop. A very popular 24hr *fuul* and falafel takeaway with a sit-down restaurant attached. Not a bad place for breakfast either – *fuul*, omelette, bread and *tahina* for £E5.50.

Al-Kazaz 38 Sharia Abo Alaam. Clean, inexpensive 24hr diner, just off Midan Talaat Harb. Tasty *shawarma*, *taamiya* and other fried food, served in a tiny a/c dining room upstairs.

El-Tabei el-Domiati 31 Sharia Orabi, north of Midan Orabi ☎02/575-4391. Pick-and-mix *mezze* are the best thing in this souped-up *fuul* and *taamiya* diner, though it also does reasonable Egyptian puddings. The takeaway sandwiches, though, are less good. They also deliver. Daily 7am–1am.

El-Tahrir Sharia Tahrir between Midan Tahrir and Midan Falaki. A long-established place, with a second branch at 19 Sharia Abdel Khaliq Sarwat,

just off Sharia Talaat Harb. A rival to *Abou Tarek*, though most *kushari* freaks agree it plays second fiddle nowadays. Daily 6am–1am.

Fatatri Pizza el-Tahrir Sharia Tahrir, one block east of Midan Tahrir (look for the marble facade on the south side). *Fiteers* (with meat and egg) and crustier versions topped with hot sauce, cheese and olives make a delicious meal. Also pancake *fiteers* filled with apple jam and icing sugar. Daily 24hr.

Lux 26th July St, near the corner of Sharia Sherif; also south side of Midan Falaki. The original holder of the Cairo *kushari* title, but not as good these days as *El-Tahrir* or *Abou Tarek*. Daily 6am–2am.

Islamic Cairo and Saiyida Zeinab

Although every main street and square in **Islamic Cairo** features poky eating places serving cheap grub, most tourists stick to the places in Khan el-Khalili detailed below (see map on p.132). But for those inured to flies and roaches, there are discoveries to be made, like the hole-in-the-wall near the market on Sharia Qalaa, which does freshly grilled shrimp sandwiches. If you are prepared to wander into **Saiyida Zeinab**, you can find some excellent, and low-priced, traditional Egyptian food, especially at night; a couple of places are listed here.

Khan el-Khalili

Egyptian Pancake House Between Midan el-Hussein and Al-Azhar. Made-to-order savoury or sweet *fiteers* filled with meat, egg, cheese, or any combination of coconut, raisins, jam or honey. Soft drinks only. Inexpensive, but check for extraneous items on the bill. Daily 24hr.

El-Dahan On the Muski, beneath the *El-Hussein Hotel*. An excellent kebab house, where a quarter kilo of mixed kebab with salad and *tahina* costs £E24.50. There's also roast goat, but no alcohol. Inexpensive. Daily 11am–1am.

El-Hussein On the roof of the *El-Hussein Hotel*. Fantastic views over Islamic Cairo, but not very good food. They also have juices, teas and *sheeshas*. Used for wedding parties at least two nights a week. Inexpensive. Daily 7am–midnight.

Gad Sharia al-Azhar. See review opposite. Inexpensive. Daily 9am–2am.

Khan el-Khalili Restaurant 5 Sikket al-Badestan. An a/c café/restaurant managed by the *Mena House Oberoi*, near the old gate 40m west of El-Hussein's Mosque. Western and Egyptian snacks (£E14–25) and meals (main dishes from £E50) are served in the dining room (evening minimum charge £E30, plus £E1.20 "entertainment tax") as well as ice cream (£E19.50). Expensive. Daily 10am–2am.

Near the northern cemetery

Hilltop Restaurant Al-Azhar Park, Sharia Salah Salem (see map, p.167). Classy Egyptian eating, subtle background music, grills and kebabs, and on Friday and Saturday evenings, a £E93 eat-all-you-can buffet with soups, salads, half-a-dozen main dishes to sample, and a gluttonous choice of afters. And the toilets are spotless. Expensive. Daily 1–11pm.

Saiyida Zeinab

El-Gahsh A block along Sharia Abdel Meguid from Midan Saiyida Zeinab, on the way to Ibn Tulun Mosque (look for the mule-cart cartoon sign). It may not look much, but this insalubrious little takeaway diner is generally held to do the best *fuul* in Cairo. Best at night, when they lay out tables in the neighbouring streets. Inexpensive. Daily 24hr.

Rifai 37 Midan Saiyida Zeinab, opposite Saiyida Zeinab Mosque (hidden up an alley by the Sabil Kuttab of Sultan Mustapha, signposted "Mongy Destrict"). A renowned nighttime *kofta* and kebab joint – people are known to drive from Heliopolis for a takeaway. A quarter-kilo of *kofta* and kebab with tahina, cheese, salad and a glass of salad juice with chilli will set you back the princely sum of £E23. Inexpensive. Daily 7pm–6am.

Zamalek

As befits a high-rent, cosmopolitan neighbourhood, Zamalek boasts several upmarket restaurants devoted to foreign cuisine, plus trendy nightspots like *Matchpoint* and *Pub 28* (see "Drinking" p.243), the second of which does good food too. Most of them are within ten minutes' walk of 26th July Street. There's also a place that caters especially well for vegetarians, *L'Aubergine*. All the restaurants reviewed are on the map on pp.188–189, as is the Zamalek branch of the Chinese *Peking* chain (23b Sharia Ismail Mohammed ☎02/736-3894).

Al Dente (Didos) 26 Sharia Bahgat Ali ☎02/735-9117. Besides good pasta (choice of spaghetti, fettuccine, penne or fusili with a range of sauces, £E5–18.50), this little place also has excellent salads and specialities such as Portuguese-style fish. Delivers anywhere in central Cairo. Moderate. Daily 24hr.

Angus Brasserie 34 Sharia Yehia Ibrahim, inside the *New Star Hotel* ☎02/735-1865. Steaks, notably *asado* (Argentinian-style sirloin with chimchurri sauce), or fillet steak with a choice of mustard, blue-cheese or mushroom topping. Moderate. Daily 5pm–12.30am.

Chin Chin 4 Hassan Sabry, in the *Four Corners* complex ☎02/737-2119. Chinese restaurant whose specialities include Szechuan-style fish and roll-it-yourself crispy duck in pancakes with hoisin sauce. Moderate. Daily 7.30–11.30pm.

Don Quichotte 9a Sharia Ahmed Heshmat ☎02/735-6415. Small, elegant, lounge-style restaurant serving great cuisines of the world. The speciality of the house is *coquille bonne femme* (seafood in white wine sauce), and puddings include chocolate soufflé. Expensive. Reservations advisable. Daily 1pm–2am.

Five Bells Corner of Adil Abu Bakr and Ismail Mohammed ☎02/735-8970. It's worth dressing up for this swish Italianate joint, complete with garden and fountain. Specialities include meat fondue, grill-it-yourself charbonnade, and fish with squid and prawns in a choice of red or white sauce. Expensive. Daily noon–2am.

Hana Korean Restaurant Sharia Mohammed Mahzar ☎02/738-2972. Small, friendly place offering various Asian dishes. A huge portion of *sukiyaki* (do-it-yourself stir-fry seafood soup) costs £E38. Also does deliveries. Expensive. Daily noon–10.30pm.

Justine 4 Hassan Sabry, in the *Four Corners* complex, 2 blocks south of Gabalaya Gardens ☎02/737-2119. Probably the finest and one of the priciest restaurants in Cairo (count on £E100–200 per person including wine). French cuisine, soft lighting, music and formal dress. Expensive. Daily 1–3pm & 8–11pm.

On the same floor (same phone number also) are:

L'Aubergine 5 Sharia Sayed el-Bakri. Moderately priced with an adventurous menu, changed weekly and featuring a good variety of vegetarian dishes, such as mushroom and tomato crêpes, or halloumi-stuffed eggplant. The food is usually very good though some of the more ambitious dishes may disappoint. There's also a bar upstairs (see p.243). Daily 11am–2am. Breakfast served 11am–2pm.

La Piazza 4 Hassan Sabry, in the *Four Corners* complex ☎02/737-2119. A stylish Italian restaurant serving good pasta dishes (from £E30), and main courses such as fillet of sea bass, with crème brulée for afters. Expensive. Daily 12.30pm–12.30am.

Maison Thomas 157 26th July St, opposite the *Marriott Hotel* ☎02/735-7057. Deli-diner-takeaway place serving freshly made baguettes and pizzas as well as light meals (from £E35). They make their own pork sausages and mozzarella, as well as doing bacon-and-egg breakfasts (7am–11am; £E20). They will deliver to anywhere in central Cairo – even beer at £E6 a bottle. Branches in Heliopolis, Mohandiseen and Ma'adi. Moderate. Daily 24hr.

Zamalek Restaurant 118 26th July St, near the intersection with Sharia al-Aziz Osman. Takeaway and sit-down diner for *taamiya*, *fuul* and *tahina*. Inexpensive. Daily 7am–2am.

Mohandiseen, Aguza and Dokki

Mohandiseen has no shortage of fast-food outlets and chic restaurants, mostly situated along or just off Arab League Street (Sharia Gameat al-Dowal al-Arabiya, also nicknamed "The Mall") and Sharia Batal Ahmed Abdel Aziz, while cheap eating places abound in market quarters like Suleyman Gohar in Dokki. The west bank also has branches of several well-known Cairo chains, such as the Indian-influenced *Chicken Tikka*, at 47 Sharia Batal Ahmed Abdel Aziz (☎02/346-0393); the popular Chinese restaurant *Peking*, 26 Sharia el-Atebba (☎02/749-6713); downtown fast-Egyptian-food-favourite *Gad*, at 47a Arab League St (☎02/335-7237) and Sharia Tahrir; Zamalek deli *Maison Thomas*, 29 Sharia Shehab (☎02/303-6174); pick 'n' mix *mezze* diner *El-Tabei* *el-Domiati*, 17 Arab League St (☎02/304-1124), and the *kofta* and kebab chain *Abou Shakra* , also at 17 Arab League St (☎02/344-4767). All of the above restaurants will deliver within Mohandiseen/Dokki/Zamalek, and are keyed on the map on pp.188–189, as are those listed below.

Al-Mataam al-Yamani 10 Sharia al-Iran, Dokki. The name means "Yemeni restaurant", and it does just what it says on the tin (it's where Cairo's Yemeni community come to eat). It's worth popping in, especially round about lunchtime when the food's freshly prepared, for wonderful Yemeni bread (*sahawuq*), soup (*shorba*), lamb ribs (*okda*), or succulent lamb on the bone with rice (*mandi*). The menu is in Arabic only. Moderate. Daily 24hr.

Al-Omdah 6 Sharia al-Gaza'ir, around the corner from the *Atlas*. An island of pukka Egyptian food (*kushari* £E5–10; *kofta* and kebab £E35) in a sea of plastic fast-food joints. (There's a snazzier-looking branch at 17 Arab League Street, popular with Gulf Arabs, with outdoor dining and *sheeshas*, though the service isn't as good.) Moderate. Daily 9am–2am, a/c, with takeaway downstairs.

Bon Appetit 21 Sharia Wadi el-Nil. Café-restaurant with baguette sandwiches, salads, pasta, even chicken Kiev, plus all kinds of espresso-based coffees and ice-cream-based desserts including cassata and banana split. Moderate. Daily 9am–1am.

Cafeteria Niema 172 Corniche el-Nil, Aguza. The best takeaway *fuul* and *taamiya* sandwiches in Cairo – so taxi drivers swear. Hamburgers and *shawarma* rolls £E3. Inexpensive. Daily 24hr.

Flying Fish 166 Corniche el-Nil, Aguza ☎02/336-5111 (see map, p.189). Another Omar Sharif hang-out, this excellent and very classy seafood restaurant has specialities such as stuffed fish, squid and lobster (the latter priced by the kilo depending on season); also does home delivery. Moderate to expensive. Daily noon–1am.

Le Tirol 38 Sharia Gazirit al-Arab, just west off Sharia Wadi el-Nil ☎02/344-9725. Austrian-style chalet decor and tasty Central European cuisine, with a lot of beef and veal dishes, a smoked ham platter and, at lower prices, pasta and pizzas. Serves alcohol; also does home delivery. Expensive. Daily 9am–1am.

Nubian Village Midan Sphinx, Aguza. The main Nubian specialities here are spicy *kofta* and hot drinks (*karkaday*, of course, plus hot ginger and herbal teas called *hargel* and *haleban*). Otherwise, the menu is typical Egyptian, with a few European dishes. There's a £E15 minimum charge. Moderate. Daily 9am–3am.

Okamoto 7 Sharia Ahmed Orabi, off Midan Sphinx ☎02/346-5264. Excellent Japanese food, well worth the high prices; serves *sake*. Expensive. Last orders 30min before closing. Daily except Tues noon–2pm & 6–10.30pm.

Prestige Pizza 43 Gazirit al-Arab, just east of Sharia Wadi el-Nil ☎02/347-0383. A smart Italian restaurant with a more casual pizzeria attached for a choice of ambience – and price; also home delivery. Moderate to expensive. Daily noon–2am.

Tandoori 11 Sharia Shehab, 2 blocks west of Arab League St ☎02/748-6301. Run by an ex-employee of the *Mogul Room*, serving good Indian cuisine. Try the tandoori chicken, curried lamb (*kema*) or prawns (*jhinga*). Also has some European and Egyptian dishes. No alcohol. Takeaways and deliveries cost less. Moderate. Daily noon–midnight.

Garden City and Roda Island

The places reviewed here are mostly keyed on the map on pp.170–171.

Abou Shakra 69 Sharia Qasr al-Aini, opposite the hospital ☎02/531-6111, ⓦwww.aboushakra .com. Decorated in marble and alabaster, this famous establishment specializes in *kofta* and kebab sold by weight (£E69 per kilo), to eat in or take out. Despite the pretensions, the food here isn't as good as in *baladi* establishments such as *el-Dahan* or *Rifai* in Islamic Cairo. Moderate. Daily noon–midnight (Ramadan from 7pm).

Lux 68 Sharia Qasr al-Aini, Garden City. Traditional *kushari* joint. Inexpensive. Daily 6am–2am.

Revolving Restaurant Fortieth floor, *Grand Hyatt Hotel*, Roda Island ☎02/365-1234. "Semi-formal" dress is required (no T-shirts or jeans), and children under 12 are barred at this tip-top French restaurant with the best view in Cairo. Start with the likes of snails provençal or seafood bisque, follow with lobster in mustard sauce or duck with apple sauce, and finish with three varieties of crême brulée. Expensive. Daily 7pm–1am.

Taboula 1 Sharia Amerika Latina, Garden City ☎02/792-5261 (see map pp.104–105). One of Cairo's best Lebanese restaurants, with very grand decor, a massive choice of *mezze*, various preparations of *kofta*, and Lebanese *fattehs* (dishes made with toasted pitta pieces). Expensive but not outrageous. Does takeaways and home delivery. Daily noon–2am.

Giza and the Pyramids area

There are plenty of cheap eating places around Midan Giza, while overpriced kebab restaurants and hotel dining loom large along the Pyramids Road. Visitors with children should enjoy the **outdoor family restaurants** – such as *Felfela Village* – beside the Maryotteya Canal (bring mosquito repellent), or the floating restaurants near the El-Gama'a Bridge (see below).

El-Mashrabiah 4 Sharia Ahmed Nessim, opposite the El-Urman Garden, Giza ℡02/748-2801 (see map, p.170). Elegant Moorish decor and excellent Middle Eastern and Egyptian food, including lamb, *kofta* and turkey dishes. No alcohol. Expensive. Daily 12.30pm–1am (Ramadan nightfall–3.30am).

Felfela Café 27 Sharia Alexandria Desert Rd, 300m from junction with Pyramids Rd ℡02/376-3117 (see map, p.204). An offshoot of *Felfela's*, whackily adorned with fake birds and trees, with a similar menu and prices to the downtown branch. Moderate. Daily 7am–12.30am.

Felfela Village Maryotteya Canal ℡02/384-1515 or 1616 (see map, p.204). On a canal that crosses Pyramids Road, 1km north on the east bank, this rambling outdoor complex features a zoo and playground, and a show with camel rides, acrobats, puppets and bellydancers – even dancing horses. The show (1–7.30pm) is presented Fri & Sun in summer, Fri in winter. Standard Egyptian fare is available. Moderate. Restaurant daily 8am–1am.

Fish Market *Americana* boat, 26 Sharia el-Nil ℡02/570-9693 or 4 (see map pp.170–171). The main Cairo branch of the renowned Alexandria seafood restaurant (see p.599). Good, but not as good as in Alex. Expensive. Daily noon–2am.

Le Chalet Nasr Building, Giza ℡02/748-6270 or 761-0165; see map pp.170–171. Pleasant Swiss-run place with fine views of the Nile. Offers salads and pasta, hot meat or fish platters and delectable pastries and ice creams; also a children's menu. Moderate. Daily 8am–12.30am.

Le Chateau Nasr Building, Giza; same numbers as *Le Chalet*; see map pp.170–171. Plush restaurant upstairs from *Le Chalet*, offering rich main courses and scrumptious desserts; expect a lot of corporate diners. Expensive. Daily noon–2am.

The Moghul Room *Mena House Hotel* ℡02/377-3222 ext 6840 (see map, p.204). Cairo's top Indian restaurant. As the name suggests, north Indian Mughal dishes are the mainstay here, notably *rogan josh* (lamb curry with tomato), but they also do veg curries, and southern dishes such as vindaloo; they usually go easy on the chilli, so tell them if you want it spicy. Expensive. Daily 7pm–midnight.

Pyramids Restaurant 9 Sharia Abu el-Hol (see map, p.204). A plain honest-to-goodness chicken and kebab house with normal *baladi* prices (quarter-kilo *kofta* and kebab £E12.50, chicken £E16, salad and *tahina* cost extra), despite the plethora of tourists. Inexpensive. Daily 10am–2am.

Heliopolis

Heliopolis has plenty of decent options for a meal or a snack. In addition to the following, there are branches of the Zamalek deli *Maison Thomas* (114 Sharia Merghani), the Alexandrian fast-food chain *Gad* (99 Sharia Merghani), the *kofta* and kebab chain *Abou Shakra* (82 Sharia Merghani) and the Chinese *Peking* (115 Sharia Osman Ibn Affan, off Midan Triomphe).

Abou Haidar Sharia Laqqani. Shawarma sandwiches, burgers, juices and snacks to eat in or take away. Inexpensive. Daily 8am–1am.

L'Amphitryon 18 Sharia Ibrahim al-Laqqani (on the corner of Sharia al-Ahram). A restaurant with bar, takeaway and coffee terrace, founded in 1922, though its elegance of yesteryear is rather faded nowadays. Moderate. Daily 8am–1.30am.

Petit Palmyra 27 Sharia al-Ahram ℡02/417 1720. Quite a stylish restaurant, its walls decked with old photos of Heliopolis, serving Egyptian dishes such as pigeon stuffed with rice and nuts, at surprisingly reasonable prices, though European dishes, such as trio filet palme d'or (veal, beef and lamb with three different sauces), are a little more expensive. There's live piano music in the evenings. Moderate. Daily noon–1.30am.

Floating restaurants

Floating restaurants can be an agreeable way to enjoy the Nile, but as cruise schedules change, it is wise to phone and check, and it's worth booking, too.

Nile Maxim ℡02/738-8888. Docked in front of the *Marriott* (see map on pp.188–189), this runs dinner cruises (daily 7.30pm & 10.30pm), with an à la carte menu (main dishes from £E175, with free salad bar and dessert) and an impressive floor-show, including bellydancer Ketty.

Nile Peking ℡02/531-6388, ⊛www .peking-restaurants.com. Moored opposite the Nilometer, 200m west of Mari Girgis metro station (see map pp.170–171), this is the floating branch of the *Peking* chain of Chinese restaurants. The boat sails daily 7.30pm–9.30pm, also Wed & Thurs 10.30pm–12.30am, and Fri 3–5pm. The Wednes-day late cruise features a bellydancing show. Food is à la carte when moored, with a choice of four-teen set menus (£E50–100, including one vegetar-ian menu) when sailing. There's also an on-deck café serving afternoon tea. Alcohol is served, and there's a bar downstairs with DJs.

The Nile Pharaoh & Golden Pharaoh ℡02/570-1000. Pair of mock-pharaonic barges complete with scarab friezes, picture windows, and golden lotus flowers or figures of Horus mounted on the stern and prow. Moored 1km south of the El-Gama'a Bridge (see map pp.170–171) and operated by *Oberoi Hotels*, they cruise for lunch (3–5pm; £E110) and dinner (7–9pm and 7.45–9.45pm; £E150; or 9.45–11.45pm and 10.30pm–12.30am; £E165). You should check in half an hour before sailing. The dinner cruises feature music and a belly-dancer, while the lunch cruises have live Middle Eastern music.

Scarabee ℡02/794-3444. Docked on the Corniche near *Shepheard Hotel* (see map, p.233). Not as posh as the other floating restaurants, the *Scarabee* does two dinner cruises nightly (7.30–9.30pm & 10pm–midnight; £E145) with an "orien-tal" floor show, bellydancer and a dance band, plus Friday buffet lunch cruises (2.30–4.30pm; £E90) with a band and magician.

Coffee houses and tearooms

Cairene males have socialized in hole-in-the-wall **coffee houses** (*'ahwas*) ever since the beverage was introduced from Yemen in the early Middle Ages (for a rundown on coffee and tea drinking and preparation, see p.50). A few – such as *Fishawi's* in Khan el-Khalili and *El-Horea* in Midan Falaki (see p.243) – are larger and more sophisticated *'ahwas*, with high ceilings and tall mirrors. Certain *'ahwas* are the haunt of hobbyists – chess players at *Al-Shataranj* in Saiyida Zeinab and *El-Horea*, stamp collectors at the *Muktallat* at 14 Souq al-Khudar off Midan Ataba – or rural migrants (oasis folk frequent *Al-Wahia* on Sharia Qadry, off Sharia Bur Said), but most have an eclectic clientele. Although professional *qasas* (storytellers), once a mainstay of some coffee houses, have largely been supplanted by broadcast or taped music, other traditional diversions such as backgammon and dominoes are still popular, and smokers remain loyal to their waterpipes.

Some *'ahwas* are distinguished by their decor, notably the incredibly kitsch *El Shems*, near Midan Orabi in the passage by 4 Sharia Tawfiqia, and on Sharia al-Azbakiya, the *Umm Kalthoum* café, done out with memorabilia of the singer

Groppi's coffee house

Synonymous with Cairo's erstwhile European "café society", the classic **Groppi** chain now has five locations. The coffee itself is terrible in all of them, but the pastries are great. The once-palatial branch on Midan Talaat Harb (daily 7am–11pm) has lost much of its charm since renovation, but has a restful air-conditioned salon. The panelled interior of *Garden Groppi's* on Sharia Adly (daily 7am–9pm) hasn't changed much since World War II, but its patio is a letdown. There's a far nicer terrace attached to *Grop-pi's in Heliopolis*, at 21 Sharia al-Ahram (daily 8am–midnight). Lacking the style of the others are two downtown branches with the same name, *Groppi's Al'Americaine* at 44 Sharia Emad el-Din (daily 7am–midnight) and Sharia Talaat Harb (daily 8am–midnight), both on the corner of 26th July Street. All have a £E10 minimum charge.

△ Café chess

and other stars of her day. For football fans, *Mondial Café* at 4 Sharia Darih Sa'd (marked on the main central Cairo map on pp.104–105), is handy as one of the few places in town that can generally be relied on to show important English and European matches live. **All-night** *'ahwas* can be found around Midan Ramses and Sharia Qalaa; those around the Saiyida Zeinab end of Sharia Mohammed Farid and Sharia el-Nasireya show videos (sometimes in English) throughout the night. There are also modern all-night coffee shops in the *Intercontinental*, *Nile Hilton* and other deluxe hotels. Establishments where women can enjoy a *sheesha* without drawing stares include the terrace of the *Nile Hilton* hotel, the rooftop bar of the *Odeon Palace* hotel, and the Arab League Street branch of *Al-Omdah* in Mohandiseen (see p.237).

As *'ahwas* are numerous (the downtown ones mentioned above appear on the map on p.233), pretty standard, and do not sell food, the reviews below concentrate on the more upmarket Western-style coffee houses and tearooms. These serve selections of pastries, rice pudding, crème caramel and suchlike, and can provide a welcome alternative to the monotony of standard hotel breakfasts. Also reviewed here are the **breakfast buffets** offered by a range of deluxe hotels and open to non-residents. Finally, also covered below are the new generation of sophisticated – and pricey – coffee-shop chains catering for the modern taste in cappuccinos, lattes, frappés and the like. They're to be found both downtown and in prosperous expat-frequented areas like Zamalek, Heliopolis and Ma'adi. Here you can linger over your froth-and-chocolate-topped coffee creation with, should it so please you, a smoked turkey club sandwich or a Caesar salad, generally in air-conditioned coolness, and usually with free WiFi coverage.

Downtown
Marked on the map on p.233, unless otherwise stated.

Cilantro 31 Sharia Mohammed Mahmoud. All sorts of caffés, frappés, cappucinos and frappuccinos, plus quiches, toasties, club sandwiches and salads, or cakes and pastries if you want something sweet, but precious little for under £E10. Daily 7am–11pm. Branches in various upmarket suburbs.
Everest Hotel Midan Ramses (map, p.124). The fifteen-floor terrace café of an otherwise

unremarkable cheap hotel, whose coffee isn't the best in town, but you can take a tea or fruit juice and enjoy a view over Midan Ramses and as far as the Citadel and the Muqattam Hills. Daily 24hr. **Ibis Café** Ground floor, *Nile Hilton*. Breakfast buffet is open daily 5.30–11am (£E86); there's also an unlimited all-day salad bar (£E46), as well as lunches, suppers and snacks. Daily 24hr. **Simonds Coffee Shop** 29 Sharia Sherif. A downtown branch of Zamalek's French-style café (see below) with a vintage Gaggia espresso machine and pastries. Daily 9am–9pm.

Islamic Cairo
Marked on the map on p.132.

Fishawi's Behind the *El-Hussein Hotel* in Khan el-Khalili. Cairo's oldest tea house has been managed by the same family – and remained perpetually open – since 1773. Imbibe the atmosphere – cracked mirrors, battered furniture, haughty staff and wandering vendors – with a pot of mint tea and a *sheesha*. Prices are posted up in Arabic, but if you don't read it, expect to be overcharged. Daily 24hr.
Naguib Mahfouz Coffee Shop 5 Sikket al-Badestan. Upmarket a/c tourist café in the heart of the bazaar, serving snacks, coffee, mint tea and orange juice. Part of the *Khan el-Khalil Restaurant*. Daily 10am–2am.

Gezira and the West Bank
Marked on the map on pp.188–189.

Beano's 8 Sharia al-Marsafy, Zamalek. Hot and cold espresso-based coffee concoctions in a lovely a/c space that's cool in both senses, with free WiFi coverage to boot. Also serves crêpes, pastries, salads and sandwiches, but neither the coffee nor the snacks are cheap. Daily 7am–midnight. There's a downtown branch on Sharia Mohammed Mahmoud (map, p.233), but it's nothing like as good.
Café Tabasco 18b Sharia el-Marashly, Zamalek ☏02/735-8465. A sophisticated, Western-style coffee house, WiFi-enabled, where the TV (usually Eurosport) isn't obtrusive, there are magazines to read, and you can get coffee, juices, herb teas and food (salad, *mezze*, sandwiches, pasta, pizza and ice cream). A good place to hang out, and they even deliver within Zamalek. Daily 7am–3am. Also in Dokki (7 Sharia Mossadek).

No Big Deal Sharia Sayed el-Bakri, next to *Deals* bar. Small, San Francisco-style coffee shop, with home-made cakes and such exotic beverages as Earl Grey tea. Pleasant, but somehow not very Egyptian. Daily 7am–1am.
Rigoletto Yamaha Centre, 3 Sharia Taha Hussein, Zamalek. Espresso, cappuccino, cheesecake and by far the best ice cream in town (£E3.50 a scoop) – try the cinnamon flavour if you fancy something unusual. £E5 minimum charge to eat in. Daily 9am–midnight.
Simonds Coffee Shop 112 26th July St, near the Hassan Sabry intersection. The original French-style coffee shop, with cappuccino, hot chocolate, lemonade, fresh croissants and *ramequins* (cheese puffs). Daily 7am–10pm.

Pyramids of Giza

Khan el-Khalili Coffee Shop in the *Mena House Oberoi* (see map, p.204). Skip the paltry Continental breakfast at this luxurious a/c cafeteria, and go for the full-blown £E78 American or Egyptian version. They also have snacks and main meals including such unlikely dishes as mulligatawny soup, Indonesian *nasi goreng* and chicken Madagascar. Daily 24hr; breakfast served 3.30–10.30am.

Patisseries, juice bars and ice cream

More sophisticated coffee shops and the upmarket tearooms serve pastries, but they'll be cheaper at **patisseries**, where traditional sticky sweets such as baklava and *burma* (the latter being slices of syrup-drenched shredded wheat around a pistachio or hazelnut core) are normally sold by the kilo. Good downtown patisseries (see map on p.233) to try are *El Abd* at 25 Talaat Harb, and on the corner of 26th July and Sherif, and *El-Sarkia* on Sharia Alfi Bey. Even more renowned is the city-wide chain *La Poire*, of which the original and most central branch, at 1 Sharia Amerika Latina (not far from Midan Tahrir; see map pp.104–105), offers home-made baklava (£E48 per kilo) and eclairs (£E4 each); other branches can be found in Mohandiseen (see map on p.188), Giza (Sharia el-Nil, 100m south of the Gama'a Bridge), and Heliopolis (92 Sharia al-Higaz, near Midan Heliopolis). Many cafés and not a few kushari shops and cheap diners offer puddings such as *mahalabiyya* or rice pudding. One of the best places for the latter, topped if you like with *basbousa* (a confection made with semolina, nuts and syrup), is *Foontana* on Sharia Handusa opposite the north side of Qasr el-Aini Hospital (see map on p.170); it's signed in Arabic only, but look for the honey pots in the window).

As for **juice bars** (usually open 8am–10pm), the ones near the *Café Riche* and *Felfela* charge more than most, but they're never expensive. The best one in Cairo is *Farghaly Fruits*, 71 Arab League Street, in Mohandiseen (see map on p.188), but *Mohammed Ali* in Midan Falaki downtown (see map on p.233) is unrivalled for its huge selection, including a wonderful coconut milkshake. **Sobia**, usually sold in juice shops as a kind of rice milk, is available in its original form, as a gloopy dessert, from *Al-Rahmany*, at the corner of Khayrat and Mohedayan streets in Saiyida Zeinab.

Ice cream in Cairo is usually not very good, though you may find interesting flavours like guava and mango. One place that does really good ice cream is *Rigoletto* in Zamalek (see p.241).

Drinking

Besides restaurants and hotels, there are various **bars** in which to imbibe, the cheapest of which are rather rough male-only hard-drinking dens, usually open until around midnight. They're certainly not recommended for women on their own, and even with a male escort you'd be the object of much attention. Other bars are chiefly meeting places for men and prostitutes (the only Egyptian women found there). The more upmarket bars often have a minimum charge, often unadvertised (usually around £E10–20). Inevitably, there's also some overlap between bars and nightclubs (covered under "Nightlife and entertainment" on p.244). As throughout Egypt, the sale of alcohol is banned during Ramadan and other major Muslim festivals.

Downtown

Spit-and-sawdust **drinking dens** include the *Stella Cafeteria* on the corner of Sharia Talaat Harb and Sharia Hoda Shaarawi, by *Felfela's* takeaway, the *Cap d'Or Cafeteria* at 31 Sharia Abdel Khaliq Sarwat, the *Cafeteria Port Tawfik* in Midan Orabi on the corner of Sharia Ahmed Orabi, the *Mourias* at 4 Sharia Adly, and *Cafeteria Bodega* and *Cafeteria Shinu al-Siyahi* at 9 Sharia Alfi Bey. Beer is usually served with free nibbles and lots of drunken bonhomie. There are several sleazy **red-light bars** in the area, most notably the *Honololo* opposite the *Pensione Roma* on Sharia Mohammed Farid, which has live music some nights, and the *Al-Shemi* opposite the *Grand Hotel*, in a passage off Sharia Talaat Harb and 26th July Sreet. There's also the *Munchen Löwenbräu* behind *Felfela's* takeaway on 26th July Street, and *King's Restaurant* on Sharia Ibrahim el-Kabari (off Sharia Qasr el-Nil, 20m east of Midan Talaat Harb), which serves kebab as well as beer and whisky.

Women should be able to get a fairly hassle-free drink in all the bars listed below, except *Gamayka*, though in *Le Grillon*, *Hard Rock Café* and *Odeon Palace*, you may feel happier with a male escort. All the drinking places mentioned above and listed below are marked on the map on p.233.

Barrel Lounge On the first floor of the *Windsor Hotel*, Sharia Alfi Bey. Faded Anglo-Egyptian decor and charming ambience. Foreigners can buy alcohol during Ramadan. Native rum or brandy (best mixed with Coca-Cola) is the cheapest drink, followed by Stella and *zibiba*. Daily 10am–1am.

Café Riche 17 Sharia Talaat Harb. This was once a hangout for artists and intellectuals, and practically every Arab revolutionary of the last century has visited at least once – including Saddam Hussein. Although now strictly for tourists, it still oozes history. Have a chat with the owner, who can give you the full story; he was a pilot during the wars with Israel. Daily 8am–midnight.

El-Horea Midan Falaki. A mirrored, very 1930s café that's hardly changed since then, and serves beer as well as tea, coffee and *sheesha* pipes. Chess players meet here in the evening and people gather to watch them play – though drinking isn't allowed round the boards. Daily 9am–2am.

Gamayka Sharia el-Bank el-Ahly, a small street off Sheria Sharif. Named after the island of Jamaica (the owner's sister went there once), this cosy little dive is really just an ordinary bar, but a cut above the harder drinking dens mentioned above, and you can have a *sheesha* with your beer. Daily 24hr.

Le Grillon 8 Sharia Qasr el-Nil, down a small passage between Qasr el-Nil and Sharia Bustan.

A cosy, carpeted bar that also serves mediocre food and has a smoking garden in case you want a *sheesha*. Daily 11am–2am.

Napoleon Bar *Shepheard* hotel. One of the most comfortable bars in town, with Napoleonic prints on the walls, wood panelling and live music every night. Foreigners can buy alcohol here during Ramadan. Daily 5pm–2am.

Odeon Palace Hotel 6 Sharia Abdel Hamid Said. The 24hr rooftop bar here is a popular and very pleasant location for a bit of after-hours rooftop drinking, with a *sheesha* if you like. Minimum charge £E7 7am–9pm, £E10 9pm–7am.

Pyramids Bar Roof of the *Nile Hilton*. Quite a sleek and suave drinking locale, but what you really come here for is the view over Midan Tahrir and the Nile, and over the rooftops of town to the Citadel. Daily 11.30am–1am, with a £E35 minimum charge after 6pm.

Taverne du Champs de Mars Ground floor, *Nile Hilton*. Come evening this spendidly ornate *fin-de-siècle* Brussels tavern – its interior brought over from Belgium and reconstructed here – becomes a music bar, and has traditionally been a gay meeting place (though this role has faded given the state scrutiny of the city's gay scene). Draught Sakkara beer is £E27 a pint, and they also serve bar snacks and have live music in the evenings. Daily noon–1.30am.

Zamalek

Middle-class Cairenes and expats favour *Pub 28*, at the junction of Shagar al-Durr and Hassan Assim streets, and *Harry's Pub* at the *Marriott*. A younger crowd congregates at *Deals* bar and the neighbouring café on Sharia Sayed el-Bakry, and the *Café Tabasco* on Sharia al-Marashli (see p.241). All the places listed here are marked on the map on pp.188–189.

Deals 5 Sharia Sayed el-Bakri. One of Cairo's most congenial drinking spots, and one of the few with any kind of atmosphere; small, homely and popular among expats and Egyptians alike, with no hassling of women. There are pop videos, a range of cold beers, tasty and well-presented bar snacks. Branches in Mohandiseen (2 Sharia Gol Gamal, cosy and intimate) and Heliopolis (40 Sharia Baghdad). Daily 4pm–2am.

Harry's Pub *Marriott Hotel*. English-style bar known for its karaoke nights. Happy hour 6–7pm. Daily noon–3am.

Matchpoint Four Corners complex, 4 Sharia Hassan Sabry. A pseudo-American video bar,

frequented by rich young Cairenes attending the AUC. Officially couples only, though if you're smartly dressed and behave respectably there shouldn't be a problem. Daily 1pm–1am.

Piano Bar *Marriott Hotel*. More refined than *Harry's*, and, as its name suggests, offers live piano music to enhance the ambience. Much frequented by expats. Daily 6pm–2am.

Pub 28 28 Shagar al-Durr. A bar that's also popular as a place to eat, with a few different beers, *sangría* by the carafe, plus English coldcuts, *mezze*, grills and good steaks. Daily noon–2am.

Roda Island

Hard Rock Café *Grand Hyatt* hotel (see map, p.170). The Cairo branch of the international chain, popular with bright young things, and rather pricey by local standards (£E100 minimum charge after midnight weekdays, £E150 weekends). It's mainly notable for having Gamal Abdel Nasser's 1957 Ford suspended above the tables amid the usual pop paraphernalia. Daily noon–4am, with a DJ from midnight.

Nightlife and entertainment

Egyptians make a clear distinction between a **disco**, where you dance to records, and a **nightclub**, where you have dinner and watch a floorshow; should you wish to go "clubbing", it's a disco, not a nightclub, that you want. For current information about **what's on** at cinemas, concert halls and nightclubs, get hold of the daily *Egyptian Gazette* (on Saturday, the *Egyptian Mail*), the monthly *Egypt Today*, or the weekly English edition of *Al-Ahram* newspaper.

Music

Aside from in discos, tourist restaurants and at the Opera House, you're unlikely to hear much Western music, though a homegrown rock scene is beginning to emerge, as the city's occasional **SOS music festivals** (Ⓦ www.sosmusicfestival .com) bear out – quite a bold development in a country whose pop scene is dominated by manufactured Arabic sounds, and where heavy metal has been known to arouse the ire of police over alleged Satanic overtones. For contemporary Arabic music, by far the liveliest time of year is after the school and university exams, from late June to November; you'll need an Arabic-speaking friend to tell you what's happening, as none of it is advertised in the English press.

Contemporary and dance music

Contemporary Egyptian music can be categorized as either *shaabi*, the folk music of *baladi* Cairo, blending traditional *mawals* (laments) with raunchy, satirical lyrics; or *shababi*, a fusion of Nubian, Libyan and Bedouin rhythms with a disco beat, reflecting the tastes of upwardly mobile Cairene youth. *Shaabi* stars perform at nightclubs along Pyramids Road, at rich weddings and private parties. Hotel nightclubs, open-air venues at the Gezira and Heliopolis clubs or Cairo University (usually during summer vacation) are likelier venues for *shababi* stars. Up-and-coming performers might appear at downtown nightclubs.

The city's best music venue is *Cairo Jazz Club* at 197 26th July Street in Mohandiseen (daily noon–3am; ☏02/345-9939, Ⓦ www.cairojazzclub .com; see map on p.188), which often has live musicians – though only one night a week is dedicated to jazz – and also serves food. The lighting is soft, the seating comfortable and the crowd (couples aged over 25 only) friendly. There's no minimum charge, but a £E16.50 "entertainment tax" is added to your first-round bill. Another venue with live jazz is the sweaty, smoky *After Eight* at 6 Sharia Qasr el-Nil (daily 8pm–2am weekdays, 8pm–3am weekends; ☏010/339-8000, with low lights, cocktails and a £E40 "minimum charge" (£E60 at weekends), which often seems to mutate magically into an entry fee. Reservation is usually required to get in.

Folk, classical Arab and religious music

During the Nasser era, numerous troupes were established to preserve Egyptian folk music and dance in the face of urbanization. Despite this, folk music doesn't command a wide following today, but traditional rural numbers like *The Gypsy*

Dance or *The Mamluke* performed by the **National Troupe** and the **Reda Troupe** can often be seen at the **Balloon Theatre** on the Corniche in Aguza (℡02/347-1718; see map on p.188), which also stages performances of religious and other traditional music.

Another place that often hosts performances of Arabic folk and classical music is the **Abdel Monem el Sawy Culture Wheel** by Zamalek Bridge on Zamalek (℡02/736-8881, ⓦwww.culturewheel.com; see map on p.188), which holds regular concerts at low prices, advertised on its website. Performances, usually advertised in the weekly English edition of *Al-Ahram*, are also held at two downtown locations (see map pp.104–105): the **Gumhorriya Theatre** at 12 Sharia al-Gomhorriya (℡02/390-7707) and the **Arabic Music Institute**, 22 Sharia Ramses (℡02/574-3373). The Nile Music and Singing Troupe performs every Sunday at 7.30pm at Beit al-Sihaymi, on Darb al-Asfar in Gamaliya (℡02/591-3391, ⓦwww.cdf-eg.org; see map on p.136).

All the moulids listed on pp.258–259 feature **religious music** in the form of hypnotic Sufi chants, while few everyday sounds are more evocative than the call to prayer.

Bellydancing

A Marxist critique of **bellydancing** would point the finger at imperialism, and with good reason. The European appetite for exotica did much to create the art form as it is known today: a sequinned fusion of classical *raqs sharqi* (oriental dance), stylized harem eroticism and the frank sexuality of the *ghawazee* (public dancers, many of whom moonlighted as prostitutes during the nineteenth century). The association with prostitution has stuck ever since, notwithstanding the fact that most dancers today are dedicated professionals, and the top stars wealthy businesswomen. When Fifi Abdou (see p.246) bought an apartment in the deluxe Giza Towers, other tenants, such as the Saudi royal family, protested that she lowered the tone of the place. The Sheikh of Al-Azhar has even decreed that pilgrimages to Mecca undertaken by dancers and actresses are invalid unless they renounce their jobs. "They should give up their sins and return to God", he declared. Even though customers are strictly forbidden to touch the dancers, no matter how much they pay in tips, the increasing social stigma attached to bellydancing is deterring young Egyptian women from entering the profession, with the result that most up-and-coming bellydancers today are foreigners, and home-grown talent is getting thin on the ground.

For all that, Cairo nonetheless remains the most important bellydancing centre internationally, and every summer, usually in late June or early July, it hosts the world's premiere bellydancing event, the **International Oriental Dance Festival**, usually based at the *Mena House Oberoi* hotel. For the latest information on the festival, which features classes and workshops in the daytime and performances in the evenings, plus extra events such as bellydancing costume shows, check ⓦwww.raqiahassan.net. There is also a smaller and less prestigious rival festival, held three times a year; for further information check ⓦwww.nilegroup.net. If you're interested in **lessons**, Raqia Hassan (℡02/748-2338) is one of the very top (and most expensive) teachers; Hisham Youssef at the *Berlin Hotel* (see p.96) can arrange lessons with a number of teachers, including some of Cairo's top dancers, at various different levels and prices.

Pricey venues

To see top acts, the place to go is the nightclub of one of the **five-star hotels**. All of these provide a delicious four-course meal to tide you through the warm-up acts until the star comes on sometime between midnight and 3am. There's usually a minimum rate or flat charge (£E250–650) for the whole deal. Reservations and smart dress are required.

Of the **dancers** at these five-star venues, the big name nowadays is **Dina**, who performs at the *Semiramis Intercontinental Hotel* on Thursdays and Sundays. Back from retirement, an even bigger name – and one of the few remaining Egyptian belly-dance stars – is **Randa Kamel**, who performs Mondays and Thursdays at the *Impress* nightclub at the *Marriott Hotel*. Other names to look out for are the Brazilian **Soraya**, performing nightly at the *Cairo Sheraton*; the French **Ketty**, currently at the *Nile Maxim* (see p.239), and the Australian **Caroline**, who appears on Mondays and Wednesdays at the *Dabkha Restaurant* in the *Sheraton Heliopolis* (☎02/267-7730); call the venues to obtain performance times. There are a couple of other dancers to look out for, though both perform very rarely, having pretty much retired. **Fifi Abdou,** who exemplified the *bint balad*, or streetwise village girl in the big city, included circus tricks, vulgar posturing and rapping in her act. Now in her 60s, with several trips to the US for plastic surgery under her belt, she only makes very occasional appearances. Another well-known name, **Lucy**, also more or less in retirement, puts in the odd impromptu performance at the *Parisiana* club, which she runs with her husband.

The top venue at present is the *Haroun al-Rashid* at the *Semiramis Intercontinental* (Wed–Sun 11.30pm–4am; Thurs & Sun £E500–620, other days £E295–345, including dinner), especially on Thursdays and Sundays, when Dina performs. Other good options include the *Casablanca* restaurant at the *Cairo Sheraton* in Dokki (☎02/336-9700 or 9800), where Soraya performs, and the floating restaurants, in particular the *Nile Pharaoh* and *Nile Maxim* (see p.239).

Cheaper venues

A step down from this are the somewhat sleazy, rip-off nightclubs **along Pyramids Road**, where the entertainments are varied and sometimes good, but the food is usually poor. **Cheaper places**, with no food to speak of, lurk downtown. Most of these are far from pleasant and, if you intend to check them out, you need to be aware of how they operate. Most open their doors at around 10pm, but none really gets going until at least midnight. Most have an entry fee or minimum charge, sometimes both, but be warned that many will also endeavour to rip you off with **hidden charges and sharp practices**. Napkins, for example, may be placed on your table and then charged on your bill; nibbles may be placed on your table unordered, but they are far from free. You need to be on your toes to keep refusing these extras, as the clubs count on customers getting too drunk to notice. Venues may also add spurious taxes, or simply refuse to give change – even for a £E50 note.

Such practices have driven most Egyptian customers away, and a lot of these clubs are now pretty much dead midweek, only livening up, if at all, on Thursday nights and public holidays. The dancers who perform any time before the small hours of the morning are almost uniformly awful; if it's late enough and you're lucky, you might catch one who has a little rhythm. Women are unlikely to enjoy themselves at most of these places as the atmosphere is generally sleazy, drunken, lecherous and male. The only two **exceptions** in the list below are the *Palmyra* and the *Cancan*, where women can go, in a group or accompanied by men, and have a good time. All these venues are marked on the map on p.104–105, except where noted.

Cancan *Fontana Hotel*, off Midan Ramses ☎02/592-2321 (see map, p.124). A lower-priced version of the nightclubs in the five-star hotels. It's sufficiently upmarket to be a safe and respectable option. Thurs & Sun 8pm–2am (starts off as a disco; dancer from 11pm). Minimum charge £E38.50.

Miami In the passage at 16 26th July St. A small and spectacularly seedy venue, where the usual tricks are practised – just keep refusing the snacks and the napkins. The musicians are not bad as these places go. Daily 11pm–4am. Entry £E5; Stella £E15; no minimum charge.

Palmyra In the passage at 16 26th July St, next door to the *Miami*. Used to be free from sharp practices, but following a change of management has unfortunately become as bad as the rest. Daily 11pm–4am. Entry £E35 including one beer; Stella £E15 thereafter; no minimum charge.

Parisiana Pyramids Road, north side, just east of Maryotteya Canal ☎ 02/383-3911 (see map,

p.204). Run by bellydancer Lucy and her husband, this is just about the only half-decent nightclub on Pyramids Rd, and somewhat more upmarket than places in town. It's also pricier – £E323 including dinner – but only because it is open all night. Daily midnight–6am.

Scheharazade 1 Sharia Alfi Bey. The venue itself is a marvellous old vaudeville-style music hall, but unfortunately as sleazy as they come. The usual tricks are played, and waiters may even try to insist that snacks (lowest price £E20) are compulsory with every beer. The *New Arizona* opposite is to be avoided at all costs. Daily 11pm–6am. Minimum charge £E60.

Discos

Cairo has a fair number of **discos** but nowhere to rave about. The music is usually last year's hits back home or current Egyptian stuff; light shows are unsophisticated. But dance-floor manners are good, boozy boors are at a minimum and casual dress is acceptable at all but the ritziest places. More problematic is the trend towards a **couples-only policy**. Though you might imagine this is to prevent women from being swamped, locals say that it's to stop discos from becoming gay haunts or pick-up joints for prostitutes. In practice, women can usually get into discos without escorts, but men without women will have more difficulty. Call first to avoid disappointment.

Most **hotel discos** cater to rich foreigners and Westernized Egyptians, and none of them is very exciting. *Latex* at the *Nile Hilton* (daily except Mon 10pm–5am; minimum charge at weekends after midnight £E100 for men, £E50 for women, no minimum charge weekdays or before midnight) tries hard to be hip, and currently has soul on Mondays, R&B on Tuesdays, and house most other nights. Other venues include *The Castle* in the *Shepheard Hotel* (daily 9pm–4am; minimum charge £E25), and *The Saddle* in the *Mena House* (daily except Mon 10pm–3am; no minimum charge).

Less fastidious, **cheaper venues** include the *Fontana Hotel* disco (daily except Thurs & Sun when there is bellydancing, 8pm–2am; minimum charge £E22.50); and *Crazy House* at 1 Sharia Salah Salem, between Fustat Park and Cairo Land amusement park (☎ 02/366-1082; see map on p.160). *Africana*, about halfway along Pyramids Road in Giza (daily 11pm–4am; closed during Ramadan and religious holidays; £E50 entry including two beers), plays mostly **African and reggae music** to a largely African crowd, but has been growing progressively more seedy and doesn't really get going until at least 1am.

A couple of **bars** also have dance floors, including the *Hard Rock Café* at the *Grand Hyatt Hotel* (see p.244; daily noon–4am; DJ from midnight; minimum charge applies after midnight only, £E100 weekdays, £E150 weekends), and the *Bull's Eye* at 32 Sharia Jeddah in Mohandiseen (daily 6pm–2am; minimum charge £E50; see map on p.189).

Gay venues

In the past, venues such as *Harry's Bar* at the *Marriott* hotel and the *Taverne du Champs de Mars* in the *Nile Hilton* have been haunts for gay men, but fear is so prevalent in the gay community following the 2001 arrests at the *Queen Boat* (see p.67) that there are no really safe meeting places. Anywhere that becomes known as a gay venue is equally likely to be the haunt of undercover cops and blackmail artists (gay foreigners are unlikely to be arrested, but could easily be victims of blackmail or robbery if they pick up the wrong person). Most venues carefully avoid any reputation as a gay nightspot, and events that begin to attract a gay crowd (1980s retro nights may be worth checking out) are quickly closed. There are absolutely no venues for **lesbians** in Cairo, and you would be unlikely to even spot an all-female couple.

Opera, ballet and theatre

The **Cairo Opera House** on Gezira (℡02/739-8132 or 739-8144, ⓦwww .cairooperahouse.org) is the chief centre for performing arts. Its main hall hosts performances by prestigious foreign acts (anything from kabuki theatre to Broadway musicals) and the **Cairo Ballet Company** (Sept–June). The smaller hall is used by the **Cairo Symphony Orchestra**, which gives concerts there every Saturday from September to mid-June. During July and August all events move to the marble-clad open-air theatre where a programme of youth concerts includes everything from Nubian folk-dancing to Egyptian pop to jazz. Programme listings appear in *Egypt Today* and the *Al-Ahram* weekly, and are available in more detail from the ticket office. Tickets (£E25–75) should be booked several days beforehand (daily 10am–3pm & 4–8.30pm). A jacket and tie are compulsory for men attending events in the main hall. Some chamber-music concerts take place at the **Manasterly Palace** on Roda Island (℡02/363-1467, ⓦwww.manasterly.com)

Another venue for Western-style performing arts is the downtown **AUC Theatre** at the Falaki Academic Center on Sharia Falaki (℡02/797-6373, ⓔpva@aucegypt.edu), where most plays are performed in English. They are usually advertised at the entrance or on campus, though you'll need photo ID such as a passport to get in. For those who understand Arabic, the choice includes everything from serious heavyweight plays at the **National Theatre** on Midan Ataba (℡02/591-7783), to comedy just behind it at the **Thalia Theatre** (℡02/593-7948).

Shopping

Shopping in Cairo is a time-consuming process, which suits most locals fine; Cairenes regard it as a social event involving salutations and dickering, affirmations of status and servility. Excluding government stores, there are basically three types of retail outlet. **Department stores** (generally daily 10am–2pm & 6–10pm) have fixed prices and the tedious system where you select the goods and get a chit, pay the cashier and then claim your purchases from a third counter. **Smaller shops**, usually run by the owner, stay open till 9 or 10pm and tend to specialize in certain wares. Although most of them have fixed prices, tourists who don't understand Arabic price tags are liable to be overcharged in certain places (around the Khan el-Khalili bazaar and Talaat Harb, especially). If you know the correct price, attempts can be thwarted by handing over the exact sum (or as near as possible). In **bazaars** and **markets** bargaining prevails, so it's worth window-shopping around fixed-price stores before haggling (see p.73) for lower rates in bazaar stalls.

During **Ramadan** (see p.71), **shopping hours** go haywire, as some places close all day and operate through the night, while others open later and close earlier. Given that people splurge after sundown, Cairo's boutiques and bazaars are as busy then as Western stores before Christmas.

Souvenirs and antiques

Scores of shops in the Khan and central Cairo purvey **souvenirs**, mostly kitsch reproductions of pharaonic art – scarabs, statuettes of deities, busts of Nefertiti, eyes of Horus – which are cheaper to buy at source in Luxor or Aswan. Sheets of **papyrus** painted with scenes from temples or tombs are equally ubiquitous. Though sellers will tell you they're hand-painted, most of the papyri on sale are printed or partly printed, even if they have a signature. Prices range from around £E2 right up to £E80 and beyond, depending on size, intricacy, the quantity of gold paint used and where you're buying: around the Pyramids, in big hotels and the Khan, papyrus is sure to be extremely overpriced and most unlikely to be hand-painted. If you've got the stomach to bargain them down, itinerant street vendors give better deals. You can sometimes see **papyrus-making** demonstrated at Dr Ragab's Papyrus Institute (p.261), one of the few places where you can be sure of buying a genuine, hand-painted article.

Copies of **prints** by David Roberts and other nineteenth-century illustrators also make nice souvenirs. For cheap poster-size or postcard editions, check out Reader's Corner and Lehnert & Landrock (see p.256). Old Egyptian **stamps**, **coins** and **postcards** can be found downtown at Salon el Ferdaos, 33 Sharia Abdel Khaliq Sarwat (near the High Court), among other places, and there's often a man selling them on the pavement outside the main entrance to the post office in Midan Ataba.

Selling fake *antikas* (with spurious certificates) is an old tradition. Genuine pharaonic, Coptic or Islamic **antiques** cannot be exported without a licence from the Department of Antiquities. Old reproductions and foreign-made antiques are a safer bet. Dealers in the Khan include Old Shop and Ahmed el Dabba (both at 5 Sikket al-Badestan; see map on p.132).

Brass and copper ware

Egyptian craftsmen have been turning out **brass and copper ware** for over a thousand years, and aside from the tourist trade there's still a big domestic market for everything from banqueting trays to minaret finials. Among the items favoured as souvenirs are candlesticks, waterpipes, gongs, coffee sets, embossed plates and inlaid or repoussé trays (the larger ones are often mounted on stands to serve as tables). All of these are manufactured and sold within the Khan, particularly on Sharia al-Muizz in the **Coppersmiths Bazaar** (Souk al-Nahhasin).

Although the Khan offers the best range of decorative pieces, it's cheaper to buy **Turkish coffeepots** and hookah pipes between the Ghuriya and the Bab Zwayla, along Sharia Ahmed Maher west of Bab Zwalya, or from workshops on Sharia Khulud and other streets around Ramses. Be sure that anything you intend to drink out of is lined with tin or silver, since brass and copper react with certain substances to form toxic compounds. Remember also to test **waterpipes** for leaky joints. Shops on Sharia al-Muizz just north of the Barquq complex specialize in waterpipes, backgammon boards and other coffee house sundries; a passage on the left just before the Sabil-Kuttab of Abd al-Rahman is full of shops selling pipes. Prices range from £E15 to £E120, depending on the size; the ones with stainless steel rather than brass fittings are better made and more durable.

Jewellery and precious stones

Most Egyptians still regard **jewellery** as safer than money in the bank; for women, in particular, it constitutes a safety net in case of divorce or bereavement.

△ Copper ware on display in the souk

Pharaonic, Coptic and Islamic motifs, Bedouin, Nubian and oasis designs, work from Syria, Jordan, Yemen and Arabia – Cairo's jewellers stock them all, and can also make pieces to order.

Gold and silver are sold by the gram, with a percentage added on for workmanship. The current ounce price of gold is printed in the daily *Egyptian Gazette*; one troy ounce equals about 31 grams. Barring antiques, all **gold** work is stamped with Arabic numerals indicating purity: usually 21 carat for Bedouin, Nubian or *fellaheen* jewellery; 18 carat for Middle Eastern and European-style charms and chains. Sterling **silver** (80 or 92.5 percent) is likewise stamped, while a gold camel in the shop window indicates that the items are **gold-plated brass**.

Downtown jewellers are concentrated along Sharia Abdel Khaliq Sarwat and Sikket al-Manakh, near Midan Opera. In Islamic Cairo, the **Goldsmiths Bazaar** (Souk es-Sagha) covers Sharia al-Muizz between the Muski and Sultan Qalaoun's complex, and infiltrates the heart of the Khan via Sikkets al-Badestan and Khan el-Khalili. There are also several good **silversmiths** in the Wikala al-Gawarhergia.

The most popular souvenirs are gold or silver **cartouches**, with given names in hieroglyphics. The price depends on the quantity of metal used and whether the characters are engraved or glued on. A reliable jeweller who specializes in these is Yazejian, in the little lane opposite the *Khan el-Khalili Restaurant* on Sikket al-Badestan (see map on p.132). The price of the cartouche will depend on the size, which in turn will depend to a large extent on the number of syllables in the name you want to have put on it, but expect to pay around £E400–600.

Some jewellers offer **precious stones**, imported from all over (Egypt exhausted its own supply through centuries of mining). It's worth bearing the following points in mind if you're interested in buying. Most emeralds in Egypt are of poor quality (good ones are clear, dark green); very large or transparent "rubies" (from India and Burma) are almost certainly fake; and real sapphires should be opaque. True amber will float when put in salt water. Pearls (from the Gulf Emirates and Japan) should feel like glass if tapped against your teeth; German onyx should be opaque and make a sharp sound if dropped onto glass; and genuine turquoise (from Sinai, Iran or the USA) should contain streaks and impurities. To test the authenticity of Brazilian topaz, amethyst or aquamarine, place them on a sheet of white paper – genuine ones should have only two shades within the stone.

Carpets, appliqué and basketwork

Pure wool kilims and knotted carpets are an expensive (and bulky) purchase in any country, so serious buyers are advised to read up on the subject before spending hundreds of pounds on one. As most Egyptian **kilims** (pile-less rugs) and **knotted carpets** have half as many knots (16 per centimetre) as their Turkish counterparts, they should be significantly cheaper – especially the ones made from native wool rather than the high-grade imported stuff used in finer kilims. Prices posted in downtown stores like Omar Effendi (11 Sharia Adly/42 Sharia Sherif) or Sednaoui (on Sharia Khulud, 100m up from Midan Ataba) can give you an idea of what to aim for in the bazaar.

More affordable – and ubiquitous – are the **tapestries and rugs** woven from coarse wool and/or camel hair. These come in two basic styles. Bedouin rugs carry geometric patterns in shades of brown and beige and are usually loosely woven (often purely from camel hair). The other style, deriving from the famous Wissa Wassef School at Harraniyya (see p.214), features colourful images of birds, trees and village life. Beware of stitched-together seams and gaps in the weave (hold pieces up against the light) and unfast colours – if any colour wipes off on a damp cloth, the dyes will run when the rug is washed.

While the suburban village of Kerdassa (p.214) replicates every style imaginable, the only authorized outlet for genuine Wissa Wassef Harraniyya tapestries and batiks is **Senouhi**, 54 Sharia Abdel Khaliq Sarwat downtown (Mon–Fri 10am–5pm, Sat 10am–1pm; ☏02/391-0955). Crammed with carpets, jewellery, Bedouin embroidery, modern paintings, and some very high quality bric-a-brac, this small fifth-floor store is a fascinating place to browse, and its owner is happy to show you around. The best outlet in the bazaar is Haret al-Fahhamin, behind the Mosque-Madrassa of Al-Ghuri; here you can compare Rashidi and Shahatta Talba Manna (both at no. 11) with Hamid Ibrahim Abdel Aal (no. 5). These outlets are shown on the map on p.143, but you may have to ask directions as none of them is recognizably signposted (or even numbered).

Tent fabric and appliqué

The traditional Cairene crafts of tent-making and appliqué work are still practised in half a dozen tiny workshops inside the Qasaba, near the Bab Zwayla – hence its sobriquet, the **Tentmakers Bazaar** (Souk al-Khiyamiyya; see map on p.151). Colourful **appliqué work** comes in various forms: some designs are pictorial, based on pharaonic motifs or romantic Arab imagery; others are abstract, delicate arabesques (which tend to be dearer). A zippered pillowcase or cushion cover costs £E15–30; larger pieces, to be used as hangings, go for upwards of £E100, with bedspread-size ones starting at roughly £E450. A much cheaper alternative is the riotously patterned **printed tent fabric** used for marquees at moulids, or to screen unsightly building work. This costs about £E12 per metre, cut from a bolt of cloth roughly 1.6m wide; offcuts are cheaper still.

Another cheap souvenir is palm-frond **basketwork**, mostly from the Fayoum and Upper Egypt. Fayoumi baskets (for sewing, shopping or laundry) are more practical, but it's hard to resist the woven platters from Luxor and Aswan, as vibrantly colourful as parrots. You may also find baskets from Siwa Oasis, trimmed with tassels.

Clothing and leatherwork

As a cotton-growing country with a major textiles industry, Egypt is big on retail **clothing**. Smartly dressed Cairenes are forever window-shopping along Talaat Harb and 26th July Street (downtown), Sharia al-Ahram (Heliopolis) and Arab League Street (Mohandiseen), to name only the main clusters of **boutiques** (open till 9/10pm). Staider threads can be had in **department stores** like Chemla and Cicurel on the downtown section of 26th July Street, or Omar Effendi at 2 Talaat Harb (daily 10am–2pm & 5–9pm) and 11 Sharia Adly 42 Sharia Sherif (daily 10am–9pm). The cheapest outlets for clothes are **street vendors** along the Muski.

Egyptian clothes

Although few tourists can wear them outdoors without looking silly, many take home a kaftan or *galabiyya* for lounging attire. Women's **kaftans** are made of cotton, silk or wool, generally A-line, with long, wide sleeves and a round or mandarin collar (often braided). Men's **galabiyyas** come in three basic styles. *Ifrangi* (foreign) resembles a floor-length tailored shirt with collar and cuffs; the Saudi style is more form-fitting, with a high-buttoned neck and no collar; *baladi galabiyyas* have very wide sleeves and a low, rounded neckline. The fixed prices in downtown shops should be beatable by hard bargaining in the Khan, where there are also two fixed-price stores. Auf (pronounced "oaf"), on the north side of Sharia al-Azhar by the pedestrian bridge (see map on p.132), stocks a wide assortment of ready-mades at reasonable prices, including black dresses with Bedouin-style embroidery. Atlas, on Sikket al-Badestan, does made-to-order garments in handwoven fabrics with intricate braidwork, and can make slippers to order too (allow several weeks; keep all receipts). Their cheapest kaftans and *galabiyyas* are dearer than most garments in other shops.

Also fetching are the heavy, woven, fringed or tassled black **shawls** worn by *baladi* women, which are sold along the Muski for upwards of £E20, depending on their size and composition (nylon or silk); check for any snags or tears in the weave. If you want to go the whole hog, invest in a *melaya*, the flowing black ankle-length wraps that *baladi* women wear over their house dresses when they go outdoors.

Bellydancing costumes

Cairo is the cheapest place in the world to buy bellydancing costumes, and many foreign dancers come here just to buy all the gear. Forget the rubbish sold to tourists and look for one of the tiny specialist emporiums in Khan el-Khalili. The best one is Al-Wikalah at 73 Sharia Gawhar al-Qayid off the Muski (see map on p.132). Lavishly beaded and sequinned bras and hipbands, with a skirt and veil, cost £E1500–3000; the more you buy, the lower the price. There's a woman to help fit the costumes, and anything they don't have in stock they can make within a few days. If you're really serious, go to Amira el-Khattan, 27 Sharia Basra, Mohandiseen (☎02/749-0322), where a full tailor-made costume will set you back $300–400. For bellydancing tapes and videos of the great artistes, pay a visit to Gamal el-Sawy, on the left of the passage just before you reach *Fishawi's*.

Leatherwork

Egyptian **leatherwork** is nice and colourful, if not up to the standards of Turkey. Leather jackets cost upwards of £E100. You can get an idea of the range of products from several shops along Sikket Khan el-Khalili. Cheaper wallets, handbags and pouffes (tuffets) are sold throughout the Khan and central Cairo. Camel saddles are still made at a couple of places on Sharia Ahmed Maher, opposite the side wall of the Al-Muayyad Mosque (see map on p.143); a leather saddle will set you back around £E400.

Glass and ceramics

Primitive factories on Haret al-Birkedar just outside the Northern Gates still produce **Muski glass**, a form of hand-blown glassware popular in medieval times, which is nowadays made from recycled bottles. Recognizable by its air bubbles and extreme fragility, Muski glass comes in five main colours (navy blue, turquoise, aquamarine, green and purple) and is fashioned into inexpensive glasses, plates, vases, candle holders and ashtrays – sometimes painted with arabesque designs in imitation of enamelled Mamluke glassware. In the bazaar, the main stockist is Saiyid Abd el-Raouf (8 Sikket Khan el-Khalili; see map on p.132), but it's better to go to the factory, where you can see the glass being blown and also get a better price. The main one is called Al-Daour and can be found by leaving the walled city through Bab al-Futuh, crossing the main road (Sharia Galal; see map on p.136) and finding Haret al-Birkedar about 20m to your right behind the first row of shops; the factory is more or less at the end of it, and there's a retail outlet near the beginning of the street at no. 10.

A very different kind of glassware is represented by the elegant handmade **perfume bottles** sold in the bazaars. The cheaper ones (£E3–10) are made of glass and as delicate as they look. Pyrex versions cost about twice as much and are a little sturdier (they should also be noticeably heavier). A reasonable and hassle-free place to buy them in the bazaar is Perfumes Secret just off the Muski in the lane opposite the *Radwan Hotel* (see map on p.132).

Robust **household pottery** is sold outdoors near the Mosque of Amr in Old Cairo and along the Corniche between Cairo and Ma'adi to the south. For more refined **ceramics**, check out downtown department store Senouhi (see p.251), or Ceramica Cleopatra (36 Sharia Batal Ahmed Abdel Aziz) and Ceramica el Gawhara (35 Sharia Lubnan), both in Mohandiseen. Vases and sculptures made from **alabaster** are ubiquitous in Cairo's tourist marts, but you can get better deals at source, in Luxor.

Mashrabiya and inlay work

With little demand for the huge latticed screens that once covered nearly every window in Cairo, modern **mashrabiya work** is usually confined to decorative screens and table stands. Generally made of imported red birch or oak, they consist of scores or hundreds of turned wooden beads, joined by dowels and glue, without nails. The technique is also applied to Koran stands (which make splendid magazine racks), the fancier ones being embellished with mother-of-pearl, bone and other inlays.

Inlaid **boxes** come in all sizes, from cigar holders to multi-drawer jewellery caskets. Small boxes cost upwards of £E10; prices increase with size and quality of workmanship. Senouhi (see p.251) has some higher-quality inlaid boxes than those you'll find in the bazaar. **Backgammon boards** (*thowla* – pronounced "dow-la") come in two broad varieties: very simple, with minimal (often poor-quality or plastic) inlay, for around £E35; and larger sets made of hardwoods, intricately inlaid with mother-of-pearl, bone or ivory. A multiple box set can cost £E140 or more. Many backgammon sets have chessboards on the back; **chesspieces** in every style and material are widely available, but good backgammon counters are hard to find.

Spices, herbs and perfume

As the world's main spice entrepôt from Fatimid times until the eighteenth century, Cairo remains the largest market for perfumes and spices in the Arab world, with some of the business still conducted in bazaars. The Muski end of the **Spice Bazaar** is, however, disappointing, as such spice shops as remain cater almost exclusively to tourists. Even so, *'irfa* (cinnamon) and *simsim* (sesame), piled high and named in Arabic, are still evocative of distant lands. What is sold as saffron (*za'faraan*) is in fact safflower, which is why it seems ridiculously cheap compared with what you'd pay for the real thing – real saffron consists of fine red strands only, with no orange or yellow in it at all, though a recent wheeze has been to start dying safflower red to fool the tourist punters. Also sold here is *karkaday*, in various grades, though Aswan is really the place it. The top grade should consist of whole, healthy-looking flowers.

In fact, there are some excellent spice shops in Cairo, but you won't find them in the Muski, nor in the "Spice Bazaar" (Haret al-Fahhamin) behind the Mosque-Madrassa of Al-Ghuri (which nowadays sells only clothes and carpets). One good place is Rag Abdel Attar at 40 Sharia al-Azhar, 200m east of Midan Ataba.

The best spice shops are also **herbalists** (*etara*), whose remedies for ailments from impotence to constipation are widely used. There are several *etara* on and around al-Muizz near Barsbey's *madrassa*, but the most famous establishment is Abdul Latif Mahmoud Harraz at 39 Sharia Ahmed Maher, which has been run by the same family since 1885; it's opposite a *sabil* 200m west of Bab Zwayla in the Bab el-Khalq quarter. Another 100m west, at the next main junction, Abd El Rahman Harraz (1 Midan Bab el-Khalq) specializes in medicinal herbs.

Incense and perfume

Just as herbal medicine blends into folk magic (many stalls purvey amulets), both make use of **incense**. The Spice and Perfume bazaars offer the widest range of musks and resins, but you can also find Sudanese vendors squatting beside aromatic cones and medicinal roots in the Ezbekiya Gardens.

Alongside the northern half of the Souk al-Attarin lies a warren of covered alleys that forms the **Perfume Bazaar**. Egypt produces many of the **essences** used by French perfumiers, which are sold by the ounce to be diluted 1:9 in alcohol for perfume, 1:20 for eau de toilette and 1:30 for eau de cologne. Local shops will duplicate famous perfumes for you, or you can buy brand imitations (sometimes unwittingly – always scrutinize labels). Almost all the perfume shops overcharge and cheat – around Talaat Harb especially, but also in the Khan. Boasting that their "pure" essence is undiluted by alcohol, crooked salesmen will omit to mention that oil has been used instead, which is why they rub it into your wrist to remove the sheen. In fact, if you know what you want and you know its name in Arabic, you can buy it at source: the shop the perfume sellers all get their supplies from (note the queue of Egyptian customers) is Karama Perfumes at the corner of Sharia al-Muizz with the Muski, or better still, the shop of the same name two doors up al-Muizz. Essential oils such as rose or jasmine, for example, should cost around 50pt a gram here.

Markets

Although the bazaars deal in more exotic goods, Cairo's **markets** provide an arresting spectacle, free of the touristy slickness that prevails around the Khan el-Khalili bazaar in Islamic Cairo. Watch how people bargain over the humblest items (often recycled from other products), a paradigm of free enterprise in the gutter. What isn't apparent are the customs, guilds and rackets that govern business, as exemplified by the vast wholesale market at Rod el-Farag (see p.197), whence **fruit and vegetables** are distributed throughout the city. Street markets in central Cairo can be found at Bab al-Luq (on the south side of Midan Falaki), Sharia Tawfiqia (off Midan Orabi), at the eastern end of Sheikh Rihan (by Sharia Bur Said), and the northern end of Sharia Qalaa – all of which do business through the night, accompanied by local coffee houses. With the kilo price displayed on stalls, you shouldn't have to bargain unless they try to overcharge. Elsewhere haggling is de rigueur.

Secondhand clothing can be found in the **Imam al-Shafi'i Market**, which straggles for 1km along the road leading from Al-Basatin to the Imam's mausoleum in the area of the Southern Cemetery. On Sharia el-Geish near Midan Ataba there's a daily **paper market**, selling all types of paper, dyed leather and art materials, and for **fabrics** (from hand-loomed silk to cheap offcuts), **tools** and much else, you can't beat the daily **Wikalat al-Bulah**, on Sharia Abu'l'lla in the Bulaq district.

Canary and budgerigar fanciers may want to check out Cairo's **bird markets** (10am–2.30pm), which are named after the days on which they're held: Souk al-Ahad (Sun; Giza Station), Souk al-Gom'a (Fri; by the Salah Salem overpass, south of the Citadel, see map on p.160) and Souk Itnayn w Khamis (Mon & Thurs; in the Abu Rish area of Saiyida Zeinab, see map on p.170).

Musical instruments and recordings

Cairo is a good place to buy **traditional musical instruments** such as the *kanoon* (dulcimer), *oud* (lute), *nai* (flute), *rabab* (viol), *mismare baladi* (oboe), *tabla* (drum), *riq* and *duf* (both tambourines; the latter is played by Sufis). All of them are made and sold by around a dozen shops on the west side of **Sharia Qalaa** between Midan Ataba and the Islamic Art Museum (see map on p.105), which also deal in Western instruments and cheaper imitations from China. Traditional instruments are also sold by itinerant vendors, especially during moulids, when a favourite buy is a hand-held dummy that claps its cymbals together when squeezed (known as a Shoukoukou after the famous comic monologist).

As the centre of the Arab music world and a melting pot for every tradition (see "Music" pp.796–802), Cairo is a superb place to buy recordings. Authorized **cassettes and CDs**, and pirated versions of them, are sold from kiosks where it's quite acceptable (indeed, advisable) to listen before buying. Given that non-Arabic labelling is minimal, it helps to recognize labels like Sout el-Beirut (a green cedar-pine logo; Gulf and Levantine music), SLAM! (mostly *shababi* music) and the *shaabi* imprint Fel Fel Phone (which has a retail outlet on Sharia Khulud, near Midan Ramses; see map on p.124). The kiosks on Ezbekiya chiefly stock religious and folk cassettes (often cheap, inferior copies). For quality recordings of Umm Kalthoum, Abdel Wahaab and orchestral music, visit Sono Cairo on Sikket Ali Labib Gabr, between Qasr el-Nil and Talaat Harb, or at the northern end of the entrance arcade of the former *Continental-Savoy Hotel* on Midan Opera. CDs are less widely available than cassettes, but there's a good selection of Arabic music on CD at Deals Music Store next to *Deals* bar on Sharia Sayed el-Bakri in Zamalek (daily noon–midnight), and at Diwan bookshop (see p.256).

Books

Unlike most other places in Egypt, Cairo has plenty of **books in foreign languages**, chiefly English, French and German. Generally, bookshops charge the original cover price for imported editions – usually at an unfavourable rate. For a huge range of material on all things Egyptian, plus novels, travel guides and dictionaries, visit the American University in Cairo Bookshop at the back of the main campus (daily except Fri 9am–6pm; entrance on Sharia Mohammed Mahmoud downtown), though you'll need ID. There's another branch of the AUC bookshop at 16 Sharia Mohammed Ibn Thakib in Zamalek (Mon, Sat & Sun 10am–6pm, Tues–Thurs 10am–7pm, Fri 1–7pm). Another good place for fiction, Egyptology and local literature is Shorouk (1 Midan Talaat Harb), who also sell books online (ⓦwww .e-kotob.com). Other good downtown bookshops are Lehnert & Landrock (44 Sharia Sherif) and the Anglo-Egyptian Bookshop (169 Sharia Mohammed Farid), which specializes in Arab politics, history and culture, but has an excellent all-round collection. Al-Ahram (165 Sharia Mohammed Farid) also sells books in English. Most of these downtown bookshops are closed on Sunday. In Zamalek, there are a trio of bookshops worth checking: the biggest is Diwan at 159 26th July Street, on the corner of Sharia Ishaq Yaakoub (daily 9am–11.30pm), with a wide selection of books, CDs and DVDs, and a coffee shop. Two smaller places are along Sharia Shagar al-Durr: the Zamalek bookshop opposite *Pub 28*, and (better for maps) Romancia, on the corner of Sharia Ismail Mohammed.

The best place for **secondhand books** is the book market in the northeast corner of Ezbekiya Gardens by Midan Ataba, many of whose titles are in English. Other places selling secondhand books in English include the newsstand opposite the AUC entrance on Sharia Mohammed Mahmoud, and one outside the Algerian embassy on Sharia Brazil in Zamalek (mostly pulps).

Egypt is the world's largest publisher of Arabic books and newspapers, so almost any type of **Arab literature** is available in Cairo. Aside from magazine and paperback stalls along the downtown thoroughfares, good sources include Dar al-Kitab al-Masri wal-Loubnani, on the first floor of 33 Sharia Qasr el-Nil; and Dar al-Maaref, 27 Sharia Abdel Khaliq Sarwat. For Islamic heritage books, try Dar el-Tarath, 22 Sharia Gumhorriya, and the stalls at Ezbekiya Gardens. Islamic books, including some books and pamphlets in English, can be found at Dar al-Salam Publishers, opposite the Al-Ghuri Palace on Sharia al-Azhar (see map on p.143).

Booze and cigarettes

Downtown **liquor stores**, run by Greek or Maronite Christians, maintain a low profile. The biggest concentration of stores is around the junction of Sharia Talaat Harb with 26th July Street. Outlets include: Orphanides, at 4 Sharia Emad el-Din, and opposite the High Court on 26th July Street; Corinthos (sign in Arabic only) on 26th July, 20m west of Sharia Talaat Harb; Nicolakis, on the corner of Sharia Talaat Harb and Sharia Suq al-Tawfiqia; Gianacus, below the *Hotel Claridge* at 41 Sharia Talaat Harb. All stock Egyptian beer, wine, *zibib*, *raki*, brandy and most sell dubious lookalike brands which you wouldn't want to drink, such as Johnny Wadie Whisky (Red and Black labels) and Gardan's Gin. In Zamalek, Drinkie's on 26th July Street, three doors from Maison Thomas, is good for beer and wine. Most liquor stores are **open** from mid-afternoon till 8pm, Monday to Friday, and close down entirely during Ramadan and other major Muslim festivals.

You can buy your duty-free allowance of alcohol (see p.52) within 24 hours of arriving in Egypt, either at the airport, at the Egypt Free Store on Arab League Street in Mohandiseen, or at the *Sheraton* in Dokki, but you'll need your passport, as you'll get a stamp in it saying what you've bought.

With **cigarettes** available on every corner, only smokers addicted to certain foreign brands need hunt down specialist outlets. Babik, in the passage by 39 Sharia Talaat Harb, and Smoker's Corner, on Midan Talaat Harb, sell numerous brands of cigarette papers and other smokers' requisites. Refilling stalls all over the city can recharge your lighter (even if it's "non-refillable") for 50–75pt, or change flints for 25pt.

Contemporary art

Contemporary art is not something that most people think of buying when they visit Egypt, but as you'll know if you've visited Gezira Island's Modern Art and Mahmoud Mukhtar museums (see p.191), there are some fine artists working in Egypt today. Two of the best places to see (and buy) work by contemporary Egyptian painters and sculptors are the Zamalek Art Gallery on the second floor at 11 Sharia Brazil in Zamalek (daily except Fri 10.30am–9pm; ☎02/735-1240, ⓦwww.zamalekartgallery.com) and the nearby Safar Khan Gallery at no. 6 (daily except Sun 9.30am–1.30pm & 4.30–8.30pm; ☎02/735-3314, ⓦwww.safarkhan.com). Also in Zamalek is the Espace Karim Francis, on the third floor of Baehelers Mansions at 157 26th July Street (daily except Mon 4–11pm; ☎02/736-2183, ⓦwww.karimfrancis.com), whose website displays a good sample of its artists' work, while ECIC at 11 Sharia Shagar al-Durr (☎02/736-5410) and Abdel Monem el Sawy Culture Wheel by Zamalek Bridge (☎02/736-6178, ⓦwww.culturewheel.com) both host exhibitions by up-and-coming new talents.

Downtown galleries worth checking out include the Townhouse Gallery at 10 Sharia Nabrawy, off Sharia Champollion (Mon–Wed, Sat & Sun 10am–2pm & 6–9pm, Fri 6–9pm; ☎02/576-8086, ⓦwww.thetownhousegallery.com), and the Mashrabia Gallery for Contemporary Art on the first floor at 8 Sharia Champollion (daily except Fri 11am–8pm; ☎02/578-4494), both of which exhibit work by foreign as well as Egyptian artists. There's also a downtown branch of Espace Karim Francis at 1 Sharia el-Sherrefein, off Sharia Qasr el-Nil, 100m east of Midan Talaat Harb (daily except Fri 2–9pm; ☎02/391-6357).

Religious festivals and weddings

Though few foreign visitors frequent them, Cairo's **religious festivals** are quite accessible to outsiders – and a lot of fun. Many begin with a *zaffa* (parade) of Sufis carrying banners, drums and tambourines, who later perform marathon *zikrs*, chanting and swaying themselves into the trance-like state known as *gazb*. Meanwhile, the crowd is entertained by acrobats, stick dancers, dancing horses, fortune-tellers and other side shows.

Whereas most festivals are specifically Muslim or Christian, people of both faiths attend **moulids**, the birthday or name-day celebrations of holy persons with *baraka* (the power of blessing). The only problem in attending one, aside from the crowds (don't bring valuables, or come alone if you're a woman), is ascertaining the **dates**. Different events are related to the Islamic, Coptic or secular calendars, and sometimes to a particular day or week rather than a certain date, so details below should be double-checked locally.

Whirling dervishes

The Mowlawiyya are Arab adherents of a Sufi sect known to Westerners as the **whirling dervishes**, founded in Konya, Turkey, during the mid-thirteenth century. Their Turkish name, Mevlevi, refers to their original Master, who extolled music and dancing as a way of shedding earthly ties and abandoning oneself to God's love. The Sufi ideal of attaining union with God has often been regarded by orthodox Muslims as blasphemous, and only during Mamluke and Ottoman times did whirling dervishes flourish without persecution.

In modern Egypt the sect is minuscule compared to other Sufi orders, and rarely appears at moulids, but a tourist version of the famous whirling ceremony is staged at the Wikala al-Ghuri (see map on p.132). Free hour-long **performances**, sponsored by the government, are held on Wednesdays and Saturdays starting at 8pm; arrive early to get a good seat, and at least half an hour before the performance in any case. Photos are permitted but not videos.

Each element of the **whirling ceremony** (*samaa*) has symbolic significance. The music symbolizes that of the spheres, and the turning of the dervishes that of the heavenly bodies. The gesture of extending the right arm towards heaven and the left towards the floor denotes that grace is being received from God and distributed to humanity without anything being retained by the dervishes. The camelhair hats represent tombstones; the black cloaks the tomb itself; the white skirts shrouds. During the *samaa* the cloaks are discarded.

Muslim festivals

Below is a list of Islamic festivals, broken down by months of the Muslim calendar, dates which occur approximately eleven days earlier each year by the Western (Gregorian) calendar. One Muslim festival is unrelated to the Islamic calendar: the Moulid of Sidi Ali al-Bayoumi, in early October, when a colourful parade of dervishes proceeds from El-Hussein's Mosque to the Bab al-Futuh and thence into the Husseiniya quarter.

Moharram (Starts around Jan 10 in 2008). The first day of the month is the Islamic New Year, Ras el-Sana el-Hegira. The initial ten days of this first month are blessed, especially the eve of the tenth day (Leylat Ashura), which commemorates the martyrdom of Hussein at Karbala. Until well into the last century, it witnessed passionate displays by Cairo's Shia minority – the men would lash themselves with chains. Sunni Muslims observe the next day (Yom Ashura) with prayers and charity; the wealthy often feed poor families, serving them personally to demonstrate humility. But aside from *zikrs* outside Hussein's Mosque, there's little to see.

Safar and Rabi al-Awwal (In 2008 Safar begins around Feb 8, Rabi al-Awwal around March 9). In olden days the return of the pilgrims from Mecca (Nezlet el-Hagg) occasioned great festivities at Bab al-Futuh towards the end of Safar. Nowadays celebrations are localized, as pilgrims are feasted on the evening of their return, their homes festooned with red-and-white bunting and painted with hajj scenes. However, it's still customary to congregate below the Citadel a week later and render thanksgiving *zikrs* in the evening. Previously, these gatherings blended into celebrations of the Prophet's birthday (Moulid al-Nabi), which run from the third day of Rabi al-Awwal to the night of the twelfth, the last being most important. The eve of the twelfth – known as Leylat Mubarak (Blessed Night) – witnesses spectacular processions and fireworks, with *munshids* (singers of poetry) invoking spiritual aid while crowds chant "Allahu Hei! Ya Daim!" (God is Living! O Everlasting!). Midan el-Hussein, the Rifai Mosque and Ezbekiya Gardens are the best vantage points.

Rabi el-Tani (Starts around April 7 in 2008). The Moulid of El-Hussein gathers pace over a fortnight, its big day usually a Tuesday, its *leyla kebira* on Wednesday night. Hussein's Mosque in Khan el-Khalili is surrounded by crowds chanting "Allah mowlana!" (God is our Lord!), dozens of *zikrs* and amplified *munshids*, plus all the usual side shows. This month also sees the smaller Moulid of Saiyida Sukayna at her mosque on Sharia el-Khalifa (see map, p.160).

Gumad el-Tani (Starts around June 5 in 2008). On a Thursday or Friday in the middle of the month, Sufis of the Rifai order attend the Moulid of Al-Rifai at his mosque below the Citadel. Those carrying black flags belong to the mainstream Rifaiyah; subsects include the Awlad Ilwan (once famous for thrusting nails into their eyes and swallowing hot coals) and the Sa'adiya (snake charmers, who used to allow their sheikh to ride over them on horse-back). Dervishes are less evident at the Moulid of Saiyida Nafisa (on a Wed or Thurs mid-month, or a Tues towards the end of the month), but the event is equally colourful.

Ragab (Starts around July 4 in 2008). The month is dominated by the great Moulid of Saiyida Zeinab, Cairo's "patron saint", which lasts for fifteen days and attracts up to a million people on its big day and *leyla kebira* (a Tues & Wed in the middle of the month). A much smaller, "local" event is the Moulid of Sheikh al-Dashuti on Rajab 26, at his mosque near the junction of Faggala and Bur Said streets, 1km northwest of the Bab al-Futuh. The eve of Rajab 27 is observed by all Muslims as the Leylat el-Mirag or Ascension, with *zikrs* outside the Abdin Palace and principal mosques.

Sha'ban (Starts around Aug 2 in 2008). The week-long Moulid of Imam al-Shafi'i enlivens his mausoleum in the Southern Cemetery (see p.165). The starting date varies: normally it's the first Wednesday of the month, but if this falls on the first or second day of the month, the moulid is delayed

until the following Wednesday. Either way, it ends on Wednesday evening the following week. The eve of Sha'ban 15 is believed to be the time when Allah determines the fate of every human over the ensuing year, so the faithful hope to gain *baraka* by visiting the mausoleum at this time.

Ramadan (Starts around Sept 13 in 2007, Sept 1 in 2008). Ramadan is a month of fasting from sunrise to sunset, with festivities every night (see p.54 for more). *Zikrs* and Koranic recitations draw crowds to El-Gumhorriya and El-Hussein squares, while secular entertainments are concentrated around Ezbekiya and other areas. The Leylat el-Qadr (Night of Power) on the eve of Ramadan 27 was traditionally marked by whirling and howling dervishes at Mohammed Ali's Mosque at the Cita-del. The end of Ramadan heralds the three-day Eid al-Fitr, when people buy new clothes, visit friends, mosques, shrines and family graves.

Zoul Qiddah (Starts around Nov 11 in 2007, Oct 30 in 2008). Most pilgrims on the hajj depart during the month, with local send-offs that coun-terpoint the Nezlet al-Hagg.

Zoul Hagga (Starts around Dec 11 in 2007, Nov 29 in 2008). The twelfth month is notable for Eid al-Adha ("Feast of Sacrifice", also called Corban Bairam), which takes place throughout the city. It involves the mass slaughter of sheep and other livestock on the tenth, commemorating Ibrahim's willingness to sacrifice Isma'il to Allah (the Muslim version of the story of Abraham and Isaac).

Coptic festivals

Coptic festivals are primarily religious, with fewer diversions than Muslim ones; the feasts centred around Easter (see ⓦ www.copticchurch.net for dates), Christmas (January 7), Epiphany (January 19) and the Feast of Annunciation (March 21) have little to offer, unless you're into church services.

However, there's more to enjoy at two festivals in Old Cairo: the **Moulid of Mari Girgis** at the round Church of St George (April 23, St George's Day) and the **Moulid of the Holy Family** at the Church of St Sergius (June 1). Moreover, all Egyptians observe the ancient pharaonic-Coptic spring festival known as **Sham el-Nessim** (literally "Sniffing the Breeze"), held the day after Coptic Easter Sunday (see p.72 for dates), when families picnic on salted smoked herring, onions and coloured eggs in gardens and cemeteries.

Weddings

There's nothing bashful about Cairo **weddings** or the curiosity of spectators. On Thursday nights the city resounds with convoys of honking cars convey-ing guests to Nile-side hotels and casinos; and with ululations, drums and tambourines welcoming the newlyweds, whom relatives shower with rose petals. In poorer quarters all the bridal furniture is first displayed to admiring neighbours.

At the reception itself, the couple sit receiving congratulations ("*alf mabrouk*" is the formal salutation) while relatives and friends perform impromptu dances. Guests may be segregated, allowing both sexes to let their hair down: women can dance and smoke, men indulge in spirits (or hashish, in private homes). Although it's not uncommon for foreign onlookers to be invited into middle-class or *baladi* wedding parties, rich ones are predictably exclusive.

Parks and kids' stuff

Cairo is incredibly densely populated, with few green spaces. Even in prosperous Mohandiseen, people use the central reservations of the main boulevards for sitting out or picnicking. Most of Cairo's parks are more like gardens, being small with well-tended flowerbeds and strict keep-off-the-grass rules, and they all charge admission fees, though these are usually small; only prices in excess of £E2 are stated below.

The city's most impressive park by far is the new **Al-Azhar Park** on Sharia Salah Salem opposite the Northern Cemetery (see p.169). Also in Islamic Cairo, **Saiyida Park** on Sharia Qadry, close to the Ibn Tulun Mosque (see map on p.160; daily: summer 10am–9pm; winter 9am–6pm; free), is a public landscaped garden in traditional Arabic style, and a good place for a breather after a day's sightseeing.

In **Gezira** (see map pp.188–189), there are a number of small gardens open to the public, all open 9am–midnight in summer, 9am–10pm in winter, and charging £E2 entry to foreigners. They include the **Andalusian Garden** just south of Sharia el-Borg (which also has a more exclusive upper section, daily 9am–5pm; £E10), and the **Riyadi Garden** next door, by the river, complete with Cleopatra's Needle-style obelisk. Between them and the 6th October Bridge are two more gardens, the **Hadiket al-Mesala** and, to its north, the **Hadiket al-Nahr**. South of Sharia Tahrir, **Bustan al-Horeyya** is bigger, and decorated with statues.

On Roda Island (see map on p.170), there's the **Umm Kalthoum Garden** north of el-Gema'a Bridge (daily: summer 9am–midnight; winter 9am–10pm;

△ Musicians at Al-Azhar Park

£E2), while the **El-Urman Gardens** on Sharia Abdel Salam Aref near the zoo in Giza (see below) are a stately remnant of the Khedival Gardens laid out by the French. Other options include Gabalaya Gardens in Zamalek, the zoo in Giza, and Merryland in Heliopolis, all covered here.

Chiefly for children

Besides the following places, most children (and adults) should enjoy felucca and camel rides (see pp.263–264), the Pyramids Sound and Light Show, and theme restaurants like *Felfela Village* on Maryotteya Canal at Giza (see p.238). Most of the parks and pleasure grounds are on the islands or the west bank.

The aquarium and zoo

The **Aquarium Grotto** in Gabalaya Gardens in Zamalek (daily 9am–4pm; 35pt) displays assorted live and preserved tropical fish amid a labyrinth of passageways and stairs that children will love to explore. The entrance is on Sharia Galabaya, on the western side of the park.

Alternatively, the larger **Cairo Zoo** in Giza (daily 9am–5pm; 30pt, camera 25pt, also 25pt to walk across the hippo pond) can easily be reached from downtown by bus (#355 and #357 from Tahrir, #30 and #83 from Ramses, #6, #9, #106 and #109 from Ataba). As zoos go, it's reasonably humane, with quite large enclosures for most animals – the main exception is the lion house. You are greeted on entry by an impressive display of flamingoes, and children will enjoy helping to feed the camels or the elephants. Try to avoid Fridays and public holidays, when the zoo is packed with picnicking families, and don't bother with the small museum of stuffed reptiles.

Dr Ragab's Pharaonic Village

Dr Ragab's Pharaonic Village at 3 Sharia Bahr al-Azam (daily: summer 9am–9pm; winter 9am–6pm; £E119 at the gate, £E95 at the Papyrus Institute; ℡02/571-8675, ⓦinteroz.com/Egypt/Village) is a kitsch simulation of Ancient Egypt on Jacob Island, upriver from Roda. During the three-hour tour, visitors survey the Canal of Mythology (flanked by statues of gods) and scores of costumed Egyptians performing tasks from their floating "time machines", before being shown around a replica temple and nobleman's villa, and no less than ten mini-museums, dedicated to Hellenic, Coptic and Islamic civilization, ancient arts, mummification and (a little incongruously) Nasser, Sadat and Napoleon. All in all, it's a fun visit, and quite educational, demonstrating such activities as how papyrus is made and how the Ancient Egyptians put on their make-up.

You can reach the Pharaonic Village on one of the **boats** that operate half-hourly from the west bank Corniche, 2km south of the Giza Bridge. Alternatively, head there by taxi (£E8–10 from downtown) or metro (the Pharaonic Village is 1km north of El-Monib station).

The circus and the puppet theatre

Those who enjoy acrobats, clowns, magicians and trapeze artists should visit the **National Circus** (℡02/347-0612; £E10–30; box office Mon, Tues & Sat 5–11pm, Thurs & Fri 3–11pm) in Aguza, next to the Balloon Theatre near the Zamalek Bridge. Performances, in Arabic, run from 8pm to 11pm daily except Wednesday, sometimes with matinées (5–7.30pm) on Thursday and Friday. Another traditional diversion is the **Cairo Puppet Theatre** (Fri 10.30am, Thurs & Fri 7.30pm; ℡02/591-0954) in Ezbekiya Gardens downtown, which stages *Sinbad the Sailor*, *Ali Baba* and other favourites, or campy musicals, also in Arabic (Oct–May).

Rides and games

Fun rides and games are on offer at the **Cookie Amusement Park** near the Giza Pyramids, 400m up Mansoreya Canal from Pyramids Road (daily 10am–midnight; £E5), with dodgems, roundabouts and a big slide, at **Cairo Land** on Sharia Salah Salem (see map on p.160; daily: winter 9am–11pm, summer 5pm–1am; £E3 entry plus £E3–5 per ride), and the larger **Sinbad Amusement Park** near Cairo Airport, which has bumper cars, a small roller coaster and lots of rides for tots (☏02/624-4001 or 2; daily 5pm–midnight; £E5 entry plus £E3 per ride). **Merryland** on Sharia al-Higaz, off Midan Roxi in Heliopolis, is a safe environment to play, with a fun fair, pedalo lake and small zoo (daily 9am–11pm; £E1 at weekends, £E2 Fri & public holidays). Further out of the city, in 6th October City, 38km southwest of Cairo beyond the Giza Pyramids, is a larger amusement park, **Dreampark** (Ⓦ www.dreamparkegypt .com; daily except Fri 4pm–midnight, Fri noon–9pm, Ramadan 9pm–2am), with bigger and better rides and a view of the pyramids from the top of the two roller coasters.

Directory

Airlines Air Canada, c/o Imperial Travel Center, 26 Sharia Bassiouni ☏02/575-8939, Ⓔ itcsales @itcgroup.com; Air France, 2 Midan Talaat Harb ☏02/770-6262; Air New Zealand, c/o Lufthansa; Air Sinai, *Nile Hilton* arcade ☏02/576-0750; Alitalia, *Nile Hilton* arcade ☏02/578-5823–5; Austrian Airlines, 5th floor, 4D Sharia Gezira, Zamalek ☏02/735-2777; British Airways, corner of Sharia Bustan and Midan Tahrir ☏02/578-0741–6; CSA Czech Airlines, 9 Sharia Talaat Harb ☏02/393-0416; Cyprus Airways, 4th floor, 17 Sharia Qasr el-Nil T02/395-4770; Delta, 17 Sharia Ismail Mohammed, Zamalek ☏02/736-2039; EgyptAir, 9 Sharia Talaat Harb ☏02/393-2836, and 6 Sharia Adly ☏02/392-7649, and at *Nile Hilton* ☏02/579 9443 and *Cairo Sheraton* ☏02/335 4863; El Al, 1st floor, 5 Sharia el-Makrizi, just south of Zamalek Bridge, Zamalek ☏02/736-1795; Emirates, 18 Sharia Batal Ahmed Abdel Aziz, Mohandeseen ☏02/336-1555; Iberia, 15 Midan Tahrir ☏02/579-5700; KLM, 11 Sharia Qasr el-Nil ☏02/580-5700; Korean Air, Room 26, 2nd floor, *Nile Hilton* arcade ☏02/576-8255; Lufthansa, 6 Sharia Sheikh el-Marsafi, Zamalek ☏02/739-8339; Malaysia Airlines, *Nile Hilton* arcade ☏02/579-9713–5; Malev, 3rd floor, 5 Sharia Talaat Harb

☏02/391-5083; Olympic Airways, 23 Sharia Qasr el-Nil ☏02/393-1318; Royal Air Maroc, 9 Sharia Talaat Harb (entrance in Sharia el-Bustan) ☏02/392-2956; Royal Jordanian, 6 Sharia Qasr el-Nil ☏02/575-0905; Saudi Arabian Airlines, 5 Sharia Qasr el-Nil ☏02/574-1200; Singapore Airlines, *Nile Hilton* arcade ☏02/575 0276; Sudan Airways, 1 Sharia Abdel Salam Arif ☏02/578-7145; Swiss, 4 Mamar Behlar (between Talaat Harb and Qasr el-Nil) ☏02/396-1737; Syrianair, 25 Sharia Talaat Harb ☏02/392-8284; TAROM, c/o Red Sea Tours, 8a Sharia Qasr el-Nil ☏02/576-6655; Thai Airways, c/o Lufthansa; United, c/o Lufthansa.

Banks and exchange An increasing number of banks have ATMs that accept foreign cards, especially on the streets around Sharia Talaat Harb in the downtown area, but also in Zamalek, Mohandiseen, along Sharia Tahrir in Dokki, and in most commercial areas. Changing cash or traveller's cheques is usually quick and easy at the 24hr Bank Misr exchange bureaux in the *Nile Hilton* and the *Ramses Hilton*, and outside the *Shepheard*; or at branches in other major hotels, which are open daily till 8pm. Alternatively, there are Forex bureaux around town, including the Arab Group for Exchange at 9 Sharia Alfi Bey, and others at 6 Sharia el-Bustan, 29 Sharia

Emad el-Din by the *New Cicil Hotel*, on the corner of Sharia Qasr el-Nil and Sharia Sherif, three on Qasr el-Nil between Sharia Mohammed Farid and Sharia el-Gumhoriyya, El Sabah on Sharia Mohammed Sabri at the corner of Sharia Mohammed Mazloum, and a couple on the south side of Midan Opera, just off Sharia el-Gumhoriyya, which are your best bet for hard-to-change currencies such as Israeli, Syrian and Sudanese. Thomas Cook's main office is at 17 Sharia Bassiouni Ⓦ www.thomascookegypt .com (daily 8am–5pm), American Express at 15 Sharia Qasr el-Nil (daily except Fri 9am–4pm; Ramadan 9am–2.30pm). For international transfers, MoneyGram's agents in Cairo are Thomas Cook (who will issue the cash in Egyptian pounds or, with a one-percent commission, US dollars), and Sphinx Trading, 2 Sharia Sherif; Western Union's agents are Misr America Bank (most centrally at 4D Sharia el-Gumhoriyya or 19 Sharia Qasr el-Nil), or Intel Business Associates (1079 Corniche el-Nil, Garden City ℡ 02/797-1385 or 6; daily except Fri 9am–9pm).

Car rental A number of local agencies can be found on Sharia el-Misaha in Dokki. Avis (Ⓦ www .avisegypt.com) is at 16A Sharia Maamal el-Sukar, Garden City (℡ 02/794-7400), with branches at Midan Simon Bolivar, Garden City (℡ 02/703-2400), the airport (Terminal 1 ℡ 02/265-4249, Terminal 2 ℡ 02/265-2429) and at the *Nile Hilton* (℡ 02/579-2400). Budget is at 22 Sharia al-Mathaf al-Zira'i, Dokki (℡ 02/762-0518) and Terminal 2 (℡ 02/265-2395). Hertz (Ⓦ www.hertzegypt.com) is at 195 26th July St, Aguza (℡ 02/347-4172), at Terminal 2 (℡ 02/265-2430) and at the *Ramses Hilton* hotel (℡ 02/575 8914).

Cinemas Cheap downtown venues (£E10–15), mostly Art Deco picture palaces, include Cosmos, 12 Emad al-Din (℡ 02/574-2177); Diana, 17 Sharia Alfi Bey (℡ 02/592-4727); Metro, 35 Sharia Talaat Harb (℡ 02/393-7566); Rivoli, 26th July St opposite the law courts (℡ 02/575-5053). Plusher venues (up to £E25), with a/c and no-smoking, no-chattering rules, include Al-Tahrir, on Sharia Tahrir, Dokki (℡ 02/335-4726) and the mall opposite the *Ramses Hilton* (℡ 02/574-7435). For cinema listings, see the weekly English edition of *Al-Ahram*. The Cairo International Film Festival (Ⓦ www.cairofilmfest.com) is usually held in late autumn.

Courier services EMS, opposite the west side of Ataba post office, in Sharia al-Bedak, (daily 24hr) promises worldwide delivery in three to four working days. Private firms (faster but more expensive) include DHL, 38 Abdel Khaliq Sarwat (℡ 02/302-9801), with branches in Garden City and Heliopolis; and UPS, c/o Maadi Express Center, 8 Road 78, Ma'adi (℡ 02/750-8555 or 8777).

Cultural centres American Research Center in Egypt, 1st floor, 2 Midan Simon Bolivar, Garden City (℡ 02/794-8239, Ⓦ www.arce.org) organizes a programme of lectures and courses on subjects like Egyptology and Islamic art. The British Council, is at 192 Corniche el-Nil, Aguza, near the Circus (℡ 02/300-1666, Ⓦ www.britishcouncil.org.eg); use of their library costs £E200 for annual membership, or £E120 for six months. The Egyptian Centre for International Cultural Cooperation (ECIC), 11 Sharia Shagar al-Durr, Zamalek (℡ 02/736-5419, Ⓔ eg_center@hotmail.com; daily except Fri 10am–5pm); organizes Arabic classes, exhibitions, recitals and occasional tours. Maulana Azad Indian Cultural Centre, Mamor el Shay el Hendy, off Sharia Talaat Harb by no.21 (℡ 02/393-3396; Mon–Thurs & Sun 10am–5.30pm), has a library (borrowing for members only), and also offers yoga classes. The Netherlands–Flemish Institute, 1 Sharia Mahmoud Azmi, Zamalek (℡ 02/738-2527), has lectures in English about Egypt (Sept–June Thurs 6pm).

Dentists Dr Avedis Djeghalian, 6 Sharia Abdel Hamid Said ℡ 02/577-7909; Dr Emad Zaghloul, 12 Sharia el-Gehad, off Midan Loubnan, Mohandiseen ℡ 02/345 5429.

Desert riding Notwithstanding the pitfalls mentioned on p.219, riding in the desert is a fantastic experience. Unless you relish haggling, authorized stables are a safer bet than footloose Bedouin operators; in either case, check to see that your horse is in good condition and well looked-after. Stables behind the Sound and Light grandstand near the Sphinx include AA (℡ 012/373-1803 or 02/385-0531), which has very reasonable rates and is good for children, and KG Stables round the corner (℡ 02/385-1065).

Doctors Dr Naguib Badir, Anglo-American Hospital ℡ 02/735-6162–4; Dr Sharif Doss or Dr Emad Rushdi, *Nile Hilton* clinic ℡ 02/578-0444.

Embassies and consulates Some embassies only issues visas to people with letters of recommendations from their home country's embassy, which may charge for this service (details given where relevant). Australia, 11th floor, World Trade Centre, 1191 Corniche el-Nil, Bulaq, 200m north of the 26th July Bridge (℡ 02/575-0444, Ⓔ austremb@dfat.gov.au; Mon–Thurs & Sun 8.30am–noon & 1.30–4pm; letters of recommendation A$30); Canada, 26 Sharia Kamel el-Shenawi, Garden City (℡ 02/794-3110, Ⓦ www.cairo-gc.ca, Mon–Thurs & Sun 9am–2pm, letters of recommendation £E250); Eritrea, 6 Sharia el-Fellah, Mohandiseen (℡ 02/303-3503; Mon–Thurs & Sun 8–11am, no letter of recommendation required); Ethiopia, 2 Midan al-Misaha, Dokki (℡ 02/335-3696; Mon–Thurs & Sat 9am–noon, no letter of recommendation required); Ireland, 7th floor, Abu el-Feda Tower, just north of the Zamalek Bridge (☏02/735-8264; Mon–Thurs & Sun 9am–noon, letters of recommendation free); Israel, 6 Mohammed al-Durri, Giza, near the El-Gama'a Bridge (☏02/761-0458; Mon–Thurs & Sun 10.30am–12.30pm); Jordan, 6 Sharia Gohini (aka Sharia Bassem el-Kateb), Dokki, two blocks west of the *Sheraton* (☏02/749-9912; Mon–Thurs & Sun 9.30am–2.30pm); Libya, 7 Sharia Saleh el-Ayoub, Zamalek (☏02/735-1269; Mon–Thurs & Sun 9am–noon; no letter of recommendation required but visas usually issued to Egyptian residents only); New Zealand, c/o Emeco Travel Services, 4th floor, 2 Sharia Talaat Harb (☏02/574-9360; Mon–Thurs & Sun 9am–5pm; letters of recommendation £E66); Palestine, 33 Sharia el-Nahda, Dokki (☏02/338-4761; Mon–Thurs & Sun 8am–4pm); Saudi Arabia, 2 Sharia Ahmed Nessim, Giza (☏02/760-4560; Mon–Thurs & Sun 9am–noon); South Africa, 55 Rd 18, Ma'adi ☏02/359 4365; Sudan, 1 Sharia Mohammed Fahmi el-Sayed, Garden City (☏02/794-9661; Mon–Thurs & Sun 9am–4pm; letter of recommendation required for visa); Syria, 18 Sharia Abdel Raheem Sabry, Dokki (☏02/749-5210; Mon–Thurs & Sun 9am–2pm, no letter of recommendation required but visas usually issued to Egyptian residents only); UK, 7 Sharia Ahmed Ragheb, Garden City (☏02/794-0852, ⓦwww.britishembassy.org.eg; Mon–Thurs & Sun 9.30am–1.30pm, do not issue letters of recommendation, but can do you a letter explaining this for £E260); USA, 5 Sharia Amerika Latina, Garden City ☏02/797-2301, ⓦcairo.usembassy.gov; Mon–Thurs & Sun 8am–noon; letters of recommendation free, but not issued for travel to countries considered unsafe, in particular those with regimes opposed by the US government).

Felucca trips Most of the feluccas moored along the river bank opposite the *Shepheard* hotel and the northern tip of Roda can seat eight people and charge £E50 per hour. Bring a picnic and lots of mosquito repellent. For rather less cost, you can join one of the boats just south of Maspero Dock, which do round trips to the Nile barrages at Qanatir (£E10 per person). Shorter jaunts are available on boats from the quay just north of Tahrir Bridge on Gezira Island (£E2 for 30min). For an even cheaper no-frills ride on the Nile, catch a river-taxi (50pt) from Maspero Dock up to Giza or down to Qanatir (£E5 each way).

Film developing and photographic equipment Developing typically costs £E2–3 per film, and there is sometimes a surcharge of 50pt–£E1 per print, depending on how quickly you need your pictures. Downtown, try Photo Greenwich,

16 Sharia Adly (Mon–Thurs & Sat 9am–8pm, Sun 9am–2pm; ☏02/360-6990), which also sells tripods and lenses; Kodak Shop, 20 Sharia Adly (daily 9am–9pm); Mitry Colour, 3rd floor, 127 Sharia Ramses, at the corner of Sharia Khan el-Khouly (Mon–Sat 10am–10pm).

Football Of the city's spectator sports, football (soccer) is the most exciting. During the season (Sept–May), premier league teams Ahly and Zamalek take on challengers like Ismailiya, Mahalla and Masri at the Cairo Stadium in Medinet Nasr (Fri: usually 7pm in summer; 3pm in winter; £E5–25). The most exciting fixture of the season is the derby between Ahly and Zamalek, when rivalry runs high and tickets sell out well in advance.

Golf Cairo and the surrounding region have a number of golf courses, of which the most central is the 18-hole course at the Gezira Sporting Club (☏02/735-6000; £E50 plus day membership of £E20–30). The *Mena House Oberoi* by the Pyramids (☏02/377-3222 or 3444) also has an 18-hole course (£E150 for non-residents), and there are a couple more around the ring road out past Heliopolis: the 18-hole course at Katameya Heights (☏02/758-0512 or 17, ⓦwww.katameyaheights .com), and an 18-hole course at the *JW Marriott Hotel* (☏02/409-1464, ⓦwww.miragecitygolf .com). You'll find further information on Cairo's golf courses at ⓦwww.touregypt.net/golfcourses.htm.

Gyms There are gymnasiums in the *Ramses Hilton* (£E40), *Nile Hilton* (£E60) and other five-star hotels. The Community Services Association, 4 Road #21, Ma'adi (☏02/358-5284), runs a fitness centre with a weight room.

Hammams Almost gone from Cairo is the *hammam*, a traditional steam bath in which you proceed through a cold room to a hot room, where you sweat the dirt out of your pores and then rub it off (preferably with a loofah – loofahs are often sold in street markets). Some baths serve men in the morning and women in the afternoon; others assign them separate days, or only admit one sex. With no mixed bathing, Egyptian women can ignore taboos and talk frankly; foreigners may be adopted into their circle, which usually includes children being scrubbed. Male baths have been linked to gay prostitution since Ottoman times, so many men avoid them. The only bathhouse now open in Islamic Cairo is Hammam al-Malatili at 40 Sharia Emir el-Gyushi (women 9am–5pm, men 6pm–9am; see map, p.136), dating from the sixteenth century and none too salubrious. Under restoration, with the possibility of opening in the future, are the fifteenth-century Hammam al-Sultan on Sharia Muizz opposite Qasr Bashtak (see map, p.136), the Hammam al-Sukariya on Sharia al-Muizz opposite al-Muayyad Mosque (see map, p.143), and Hammam Said al-Suadi on Sharia Gamaliya (see map, p.136). A good option, in the Wikalet al-Balah district of Bulaq, is the Hammam el Arbaa at 5 Sharia el-Ansari (aka Sharia al-Hammamat; ☏ 010/579-0760; daily women 10am–5pm, men 6pm–midnight). The street is on the left (west) side 300m up Sharia Bulaq al-Gadid, which runs north from 26th July Street opposite the Abu'I'Ila Mosque. Less traditional venues include the saunas and Turkish baths at the *Nile Hilton* (£E60) and the *Ramses Hilton* (£E50).

Hospitals Anglo-American Hospital by Cairo Tower, Gezira ☏ 02/735-6162-4; Al-Salam International Hospital, on the Corniche in Ma'adi ☏ 02/524-0250 or 0077; Cairo Medical Centre, on Sharia al-Ansari, just off Sharia Higaz by Midan Roxi, Heliopolis ☏ 02/450-9800. For any of these, you can use the private Al-Salam ambulance service (same phone numbers as the hospital). Public ambulances offer free transport to whichever hospital is the nearest: call ☏ 123.

Internet access Hany, 16 Abdel Khaliq Sarwat (daily 10am–8pm); 4U, 5 Midan Talaat Harb (daily 8am–midnight); Five Stars, 3 Sharia Talaat Harb (daily 8am–2am); Zamalek Center, 25 Sharia Ismail Mohammed, Zamalek (daily 8am–midnight); *Café Paris*, in the Bustan Centre, Sharia Bustan (daily 8am–10pm).

Language schools Arabic lessons are offered by: AUC Public Service Division room #110, 28 Sharia Falaki (☏ 02/797-6872 or 3, ✉ arabcace @aucegypt.edu), which is well respected though its teaching methods may not be as up-to-date as at Kalimat or the ILI; the Egyptian Centre for International Cultural Cooperation (ECIC), 11 Sharia Shagar al-Durr, Zamalek (☏ 02/736-5410, ✉ eg_center @hotmail.com); International Language Institute (ILI), 4 Sharia Mahmoud Azmi, Sahafayeen (north of Mohandiseen) (☏ 02/346-3087, ⊛ www .arabicegypt.com); Kalimat Language and Cultural Centre, 22 Sharia al-Koroum, behind Mohammed Mustafa Mosque, Mohandiseen (☏ 02/761-8136, ⊛ www.kalimategypt.com), which was set up by former British Council teachers. For private tutors, check the notice boards at AUC and at *Bon Appetit* in Sharia Mohammed Mahmoud (see p.232), or ask the British Council for its list of Arabic teachers. The lowest-priced courses are those offered by ECIC, at £E950 for an eight-week course with 48 hours' tuition, while ILI charges $320 for 40hr of tuition over four or five weeks.

Newspapers Foreign newspapers and magazines can be found in the bookshops of the five-star hotels. The best downtown newsstand is on Sharia Mohammed Mahmoud, opposite the AUC entrance and by *McDonald's*, which carries British dailies (usually one day late), the *International Herald Tribune*, *USA Today* and even sometimes the *New York Times*. The two bookshops on Sharia Shagar al-Durr in Zamalek also stock British papers.

Nile cruises Luxury cruises operated by the *Hilton*, *Sheraton* and *Mena House Oberoi* are prohibitively expensive. Budget travellers may consider less ritzy boats run by agencies such as Eastmar Tours, in the passage of 13 Sharia Qasr el-Nil (☏ 02/574-5024, ⊛ www.eastmar-travel.com), which charges – depending on season – $85–150 a night per person for a four-to-seven-night cruise. Be aware, however, that better deals could well be available from local agents in either Luxor or Aswan. For more on Nile cruises, see pp.316–318; for details of felucca trips in Cairo, see p.264.

Passport photos Mitry Colour, charges £E15 for eight photos while you wait, but only £E5 for a dozen photos plus one large print ready the next day. The Kodak Shop, 20 Sharia Adly charges £E12 for eight photos ready in half an hour. For the addresses of both stores, see "Film developing", p.264. There's an automatic booth in room #99 on the ground floor of the Mugamma (eight photos for £E15 while you wait).

Pharmacies These are plentiful around town, with some 24hr outlets, including: Al-Esa'af, 27 26th July St, at the junction with Sharia Ramses (☏ 02/574-3369); Atalla, 13 Sharia Sherif, at the junction with Sharia Mohammed Sabri (☏ 02/393-9029); El-Ezaby, in Ramses station (☏ 02/575-6272) and citywide; and Abdallah, 2 Sharia Tahar Hussein, Zamalek (☏ 02/738-1988). In cases of emergency, these pharmacies will also deliver medicines.

Police An alleyway to the left of the Sharia Adly tourist office gives access to the headquarters of the tourist police (open 24hr; ☏ 02/390-6028). Other tourist police stations can be found at Ramses Station (☏ 02/579-0767), the Giza Pyramids (☏ 02/385-0259), Khan el-Khalili (☏ 02/590-4827) and Manial Palace (☏ 02/363-6707).

Post offices The central post office is on Midan Ataba (daily except Fri 8am–8pm, Ramadan 9am–3pm), with branches (daily except Fri 8am–6pm, Ramadan 9am–3pm) citywide, including one on Sharia Tahrir by Midan Falaki, one on Sharia Ramses by the junction with 26th July Street, one in Ramses station, and one on Sharia al-Azhar near Al-Azhar Mosque. Letters posted in the lobby of the *Nile Hilton* are said to arrive faster than those dropped in ordinary mailboxes. For Express Mail see "Courier services" p.263. Poste restante (general delivery) is in Sharia al-Bedak, round the corner from the main entrance to Ataba central post office, on the west side of the building – go to the last door, signposted "Private boxes", and it's inside at counter #10 (Mon–Thurs, Sat & Sun, Ramadan 8am–4pm, Fri 10am–noon; bring your passport). Mail should be addressed to you, with surname in capitals and underlined, at Poste Restante, Post Office Ataba, 11511 Cairo. Letters are held for a month, but are often filed under the wrong name. Amex customers can have mail sent c/o American Express on Sharia Qasr el-Nil (see p.263). Parcels can only be mailed abroad from the Ramses Square post office, round the back (the north side of the building), in an office marked "Export Section for Foreign Parcels" (daily except Fri 9am–2.30pm). To receive a parcel, go to the main entrance (east side) of the same building, fourth floor.

Running The expat Hash House Harriers (@www .cairohash.com) is one of several clubs organizing street running, best done on Gezira, Roda or the west bank Corniche, before 8am or after 10pm to avoid heavy traffic and air pollution.

Swimming pools Best of the hotel pools is at the *Semiramis Intercontinental* (£E110), with alternatives at the *Nile Hilton* (£E230 for two people, including use of a poolside cabin), and *Cairo Marriott* (£E110). The rooftop pool of the *Fontana Hotel*, off Midan Ramses (summer only, £E15), is OK for dipping but barely big enough for a swim. For more serious swimmers, the Ahli Club (☏02/735-2202; monthly membership $100) behind the Opera House on Sharia Om Kalthoum offers an Olympic-size pool and women-only sessions. In Heliopolis, there's a choice between the Heliolido on Sharia al-Mahad al-Ishtiraki, just off Midan Roxi (☏02/258-0070; £E20) and the nearby Heliopolis Sporting Club on Sharia Merghani (☏02/417-0061–3; £E25 entry, £E5 for a swim), which has a larger pool. Further afield, there's the naturally heated spa pool at Ain Helwan (see p.186), but it tends to be full of school-kids during school holidays and at weekends. At Saqqara, there's the Palm Club (see p.219).

Telephone and fax offices Phone calls can be made, and faxes sent and received, at the following telecom offices: 8 Sharia Adly (☏02/393-3909); Sharia Alfi Bey by the *Windsor Hotel* (☏02/589-7635); Sharia Ramses, opposite Sharia Tawfiqia (☏02/578-0977); 13 Midan Tahrir; Midan Ataba by the National Theatre (☏02/578-0979). All are open 24hr. Faxes can also sent and received at the EMS office by Ataba post office (☏02/390-4250; daily 24hr). American Express clients can receive faxes free at their office (☏02/574-7997). EMS and the phone offices will inform you of your fax's arrival if your name and phone number are at the top of the page.

Translation services Fouad Nemah, 2nd floor, 37 Sharia Qasr el-Nil ☏02/392-2124, @fouad _nemah@hotmail.com, or 14a Sharia Sherif, Heliopolis ☏02/450-6219; both offices open Mon–Thurs & Sun 9.30am–3pm.

Travel permits Permits to travel in restricted areas are usually issued by Military Intelligence (Mukaharabat 26), whose office is in Sharia Manshia el-Bakry in Heliopolis. Rather than apply to them directly however, your first approach should be to Misr Travel at 1 Sharia Talaat Harb (☏02/393 0010, @misrtrav@link.com.eg), who may be able to help you obtain certain permits, or to the tourist police at 5 Sharia Adly, see p.38. For more on travel permits, see p.38.

Vaccinations The Public Health Vaccination Centre (daily except Fri 10am–7pm), at the rear of the lobby of the largely disused *Hotel Continental-Savoy* on Midan Opera, does yellow fever jabs (£E75.50, including the certificate), and cholera (£E15.50), but no others. The Egyptian Organization for Biological Products and Vaccines (Vacsera), 51 Sharia Wazart el-Zaraa (☏02/761-1111; daily 24hr), 100m north of the 6th October Bridge/Agricultural Museum intersection (take the first right inside the gate, then go round the side of the first building on the left), has vaccines against cholera (£E21), typhoid (£E10), meningitis (£E61) and yellow fever (£E34), but cannot issue the yellow fever vaccination certificate you'll need if travelling to countries south of the Sahara. There's a second branch of Vacsera in Midan Giza opposite the metro station.

Visa extensions Extending your visa entails visiting the Mugamma, that bureaucratic behemoth on Midan Tahrir (daily except Fri 8am–2pm). To avoid the crush, arrive first thing in the morning or during the evening shift. Unless you're certain which numbered "window" is currently appropriate (details below may become outmoded), check with the information desk upstairs on the first floor, before going through the door on your left. For a tourist visa extension, go to windows #13–14 of the immigration section – accessed via entrance 4 on the same floor, and down the corridor to the end – and pick up a form. You need to provide a passport photo plus a photocopy of the page in your passport with your photo and personal details, and also the page which carries your original visa – there are copying facilities on the ground floor. Take your form to window #43 to get a stamp (£E8), and then back to window #13 or #14 where your new visa will be issued. This may be done the same day or the next day, or it may take as long as two weeks, depending on your nationality and the length of stay you ask for. Re-entry visas are handled at windows #1–4. You should apply before 1.30pm, collecting the visa the following day at 2pm. In case of lost or stolen passports, replacement entry stamps are obtainable from window #42; however, these may not pass muster with the Libyan or Sudanese consulates. Display patience and good humour when dealing with the Mugamma; only stage a tantrum or nervous breakdown as a last resort.

Excursions from Cairo

The Nile Valley – most people's target after Cairo – is too distant for a **day excursion** from the city. Elsewhere, however, you can choose between such possibilities as a jaunt to the seaside or remoter pyramids, a river trip or desert monasteries – and still be back in Cairo the same night.

Those without the time to organize their own excursions might consider taking a set or **tailor-made tour**. There are plenty of disreputable tour operators about, so beware; those worth trying include First 24 Hours (☎012/313-8446, ⓦwww .first24hours.com) c/o Noga Tours, 26 Sharia Quday, Shubra; or Eastmar Tours, in the passage of 13 Sharia Qasr el-Nil (☎02/574-5024, ⓦwww.eastmar-travel .com), and for desert excursions, Humdinga Safaris (☎010/106-7673, or c/o Noga Tours). Eastmar also offers Nile cruises (see p.265).

The Nile barrages at Qanatir

Roughly 20km downriver from Cairo, the Nile divides into two great branches which define the Delta, whose flow is controlled by the **Nile barrages** at **Qanatir**. Decoratively arched and turreted, this splendid piece of Victorian civil engineering is surrounded by shady parks and lush islets – an ideal spot for a picnic. Providing you don't come on Friday, when the area is ridiculously crowded, the barrages make a pleasant excursion.

Originally conceived by Mohammed Ali's French hydro-engineer, Mougel Bey, the barrages were later realized as part of the nationwide hydrological system designed by Sir Colin Scott-Moncrieff. At the eastern end of the 438-metre-long Rosetta Barrage lies the Istarahah al-Qanatir or **Presidential Villa** that Islamic Jihad once considered attacking with an anti-aircraft cannon from the garden of one of their member's homes, across the river. Egypt's **State Yacht** (originally King Farouk's, on which he sailed into exile) is often moored at the quay.

Qanatir is accessible by bus #210 from the Abdel Mouneem Riyad terminal on Midan Tahrir, or by ferry from the Maspero Dock (hourly 8–10am, returning 2–4pm; £E5)in front of the Television Building, or by pleasure boat (daily round trips departing around 9am; £E6) from just north of the Maspero Dock. Travelling by felucca is slow, since the mast has to be lowered at every bridge.

The Muqattam Hills and Wadi Digla

The **Muqattam Hills** plateau, rising beyond Cairo, are seldom visited by tourists but readily accessible by #951 bus from Abdel Mouneem Riyad, or #401 from Midan Ataba. Zigzagging up the hillside past caves and quarries, ruined shrines and guarded outposts, buses terminate at **Medinet Muqattam**, an upmarket suburb whose avenues are flanked by villas and casinos. The Muqattam Corniche, circling the edge of the plateau, offers spectacular views across the Citadel and most of Cairo – an unforgettable vista at sunset.

People planning desert expeditions might consider a few training runs below the Muqattam. Victorian travellers used to engage a dragoman to lead them to the **Petrified Forests** – two expanses littered with broken, fossilized trunks, thought to date from the Miocene Period. The larger one (marked on the map of Greater Cairo) is really only accessible with a guide, but would-be explorers can easily find the "Little Forest" on the Jebel el-Khasab plateau, north of the Digla–Ain Sukhna road.

The **Digla–Ain Sukhna road** turns east off the Nile Valley expressway near a *zebaleen* village beyond Ma'adi. Roughly 25km from the turn-off, you'll pass the Jebel el-Khasab on the left; if you keep on, you'll notice various tracks leading off to the right, which eventually converge on a main desert track running east–west. By following it west, back towards Digla, you'll pass through several meandering *wadis* before the way is blocked by **Wadi Digla**. This miniature canyon is good for **rock-climbing** and **bird-watching**; bring water, food and shade.

Birqesh Camel Market

Held 60km north of the city at **Birqesh**, (pronounced "Bir'esh"), Cairo's **Camel Market** is a twice-weekly feast of drama and cruelty. Beaten into defecating ranks, the hobbled camels are assessed by traders who disregard their emaciation – caused by a month-long trek from northwestern Sudan to Aswan, followed by an overnight truck ride to Cairo – and concentrate on other features.

Strength and speed are discernible in the legs, chest, eyes, ears and position of the hump, while teeth reflect age; the clearly knackered are evaluated for their meat and hide. During rutting season, signs of irritation (an inflated mouth sac, ferocious slobbering and gurgling) often herald a kick or bite from an enraged bull camel. Docile females are generally preferred as mounts. They're also exchanged for goats and other livestock, while Bishari herdsmen and Egyptian merchants gossip over tea, unperturbed by throat-slittings and disembowelments near the piles of saddlery and tack. In an adjacent compound is a furniture and bric-a-brac market, not unlike a car-boot or yard sale.

The Souk el-Gamal (pronounced "Gah*mell*") lasts from dawn till early afternoon every Friday (and also Monday, when the market is smaller), but is busiest between 6am and 8.30am; tourists pay a £E20 entry fee. To get there by taxi will cost around £E60–80 for the round trip. Alternatively, you can catch the #214 bus from Abdel Mouneem Riyad to Manashi by the Nile barrage at Qanatir (45min) and take a service taxi microbus from there, or you can get a service taxi microbus from Sharia Sabtiya, off Midan Ramses, changing vehicles at Imbaba. Going back into town, you may be able to find a microbus that will take you all the way to Ramses.

The Fayoum

Fayoum Oasis, 100km southwest of Cairo, is another place to escape to; see pp.483–497. The **ruins of Karanis** (see p.492) lie just off the Fayoum–Cairo road; the dramatic **"Collapsed Pyramid" of Maidum** (see p.495) is a short ride from El-Wasta. Either makes a good day excursion, but you should bring food and drink and be on your way by mid-morning. Service taxis from Midan Giza, El Mouneeb, or Sharia Orabi near Ramses station, are the fastest way of reaching Fayoum City (2hr): see p.483 for details. The Maidum Pyramid can be reached by service taxi from El-Wasta station, which is served by trains that leave pretty much hourly from Ramses, stopping at Giza station (where there are also a few extra services), and taking an hour and a half to reach El-Wasta.

Alexandria and the Monasteries of Wadi Natrun

Alexandria (see Chapter 4) is only three hours from Cairo. It can be reached by bus from Aboud terminal (departures every 45min), train from Ramses station (2hr 10min on the Turbini), or service taxi from either of those (Aboud has more departures): for details, see pp.270–271. The Desert Road to Alex passes the turn-off for the fortified **Monasteries of Wadi Natrun**, (see p.477), the most accessible of which are **Deir Anba Bishoi** and **Deir al-Suryani**, 10km from the rest stop on the highway (which can be reached by bus or service taxi from Cairo). To visit all four, it's best to rent a taxi or car for the day, either in Cairo or at the rest stop, which is roughly midway between Alexandria and Cairo. Unless you start very early or have a car, it's not really feasible to visit both Alexandria and the monasteries in one day.

Ismailiya, Ain Sukhna and the Red Sea Monasteries

The canal city of **Ismailiya** (see p.648) can be reached by bus from Turgoman Garage or service taxi from Sharia Orabi near Ramses station (2–3hr). Cairenes with transport visit **Ain Sukhna** (see p.730) on the Gulf of Suez for its **beaches** and offshore coral reefs. If you fancy swimming and **snorkelling**, it's worth renting a car for the day rather than switching buses at Suez and having to hitch back. Bring food and drink (plus snorkel if required), since they're not obtainable there. Don't wander into areas ringed by barbed wire, which are still mined. Ain Sukhna is approachable via Suez (3hr) or by the Digla–Ain Sukhna desert road. Further south and high inland are the **Red Sea Monasteries** of St Paul and St Anthony (see p.727). With a car, you could combine a visit to St Anthony's with a swim at Ain Sukhna, but unless you leave at the crack of dawn it's impossible to get to both monasteries and return the same night.

Moving on from Cairo

Cairo is the linchpin of Egypt's transport network and its main link to the outside world. Many parts of the country are accessible from the capital by several forms of transport.

Trains

All trains depart from **Ramses Station** (Mahattat Ramses), a cavernous beehive seemingly designed to bemuse. Almost all trains to points south halt at **Giza Station**, 15min after leaving Ramses. Entering Ramses Station from Midan Ramses, you'll find the **tourist office** (☎02/579-0767), tourist police and sleeper booking offices on the left; to your right are platforms 1–4, serving Alexandria, the Delta and Canal Zone. Tickets for air-conditioned services to these destinations are sold at the far end of the main hall, directly opposite the main entrance from Midan Ramses, but if you want to use a slow, non-air-conditioned train, you'll find the ticket office outside, through the doorway to the left of the a/c ticket office.

To the right of the a/c ticket office is the doorway through to platforms 8–11, where southbound trains depart for Middle and Upper Egypt. All tickets for trains on this route, bar sleepers, are sold from offices alongside platform 11 (the furthest platform, accessible via an underpass). Note that foreigners travelling to Upper Egypt are only allowed to use certain services (see below).

Timetables are not available in leaflet or booklet form, but can be looked up online at ⓦ www.egyptrail.gov.eg. Train times are posted up, in Arabic only, at various points around the station, most prominently by the round **information kiosk** (ⓣ 02/575-3555) opposite platform 4. Staff here should in theory be able to advise on departures, schedules and any problems you may have with ticket buying, but you may need to fall back on the tourist office. There is a **left luggage** office by platform 1, open 24/7 and charging £E2.50 per item per day.

Buying tickets is rarely easy. The two non-sleeper ticket offices both have separate windows for 1st class/2nd class superior seating (which is reservable) and ordinary 2nd class/3rd class (which isn't). You have to find the right queue and get your requirements (it helps to have them written down in Arabic) across to clerks who may not give a damn. Tickets can be booked up to a week in advance and should be booked at least a day in advance; 1st and 2nd class superior seats sell out first.

Regular services

There are two kinds of services to **Alexandria**: air-conditioned and not. Thirteen trains a day are air-conditioned, which also means fast with limited stops, and require reservations. The seven or so daily Turbini trains are the best (2hr 20min), followed by the four daily Spanish trains, which are also nonstop (2hr 40min). Slightly cheaper and slower than the Spanish and Turbini services are the fourteen daily French trains, which stop at Benha, Tanta and Damanhur, reaching Alexandria in three hours. Lastly, there are some forty non-air-conditioned trains to Alexandria every day, composed of 2nd and 3rd class carriages only. These trains cost a fraction of the price of the air-conditioned services, stop everywhere, and can take four hours or more to reach Alexandria.

Apart from the sleeper service, there are nine daily departures for **Aswan** (14–17hr) and five more for **Luxor** (11–12hr). Tourists are allowed to use three of these trains (departing at 7.40am, 10pm and 12.30am). Fares for ordinary seats (not sleeping berths) are £E67 in 1st class and £E35 in 2nd for Luxor, £E81 and £E45 for Aswan.

Direct services to **Mersa Matrouh** only run in summer: there's a thrice-weekly sleeper, and a daily a/c service leaving early in the morning. Failing this, it is far better to travel by bus from Cairo or Alex than to endure the interminable journey in ordinary 2nd or 3rd class from Alexandria.

Sleeper services

There are daily **wagon-lit services** (8pm) to Upper Egypt. The cost per person for a double cabin including dinner and breakfast is $60 one-way to Luxor or Aswan (you can stop over at Luxor and continue to Aswan on the same ticket). Solo travellers can reserve the entire cabin for $79, or consent to share it with a stranger of the same sex and pay the normal fare. From mid-June until mid-September, there are also three weekly sleeper trains to Mersa Matrouh (Mon, Wed & Sat 11pm, arriving 6am).

You can book at the sleeper office (cash only; daily 9am–3pm; ⓣ 02/574-9474) until 6pm on the day of departure, but you're best off reserving a sleeper a few days in advance if possible. This can be done at the station or through Abela, who operate the sleeper trains (ⓣ 02/574-9274, ⓦ www.sleepingtrains .com). Tickets can also be booked through Hamis Travel, whose office is just outside the station, in the building by the 3rd class ticket office for Alexandria

(℡ 02/574-9275, Ⓦ www.hamis.com.eg). As well as taking Visa and MasterCard, they also accept euros and US dollars. Their staff tend to be somewhat more helpful than those in the station sleeper office. Bookings can also be made for a small premium at the Carlson Wagon Lit office by the *Shepheard* hotel.

Inter-city buses

Inter-city buses reach most parts of Egypt, often faster than trains. Services depart from four main terminals: Turgoman Garage (which handles the majority of bus departures to destinations within Egypt, especially to the Canal Zone, Aboud (especially to Alexandria, the Delta, Middle and Upper Egypt), Sinai Terminal (aka Abbassiya Terminal; services to the Sinai) and El Moneeb (especially to Middle Egypt). A number of buses that start at Aboud and Turgoman may stop at El Mouneeb or Sinai Terminal, and at Almaza Terminal in Heliopolis (see p.89). A few buses also leave from Sharia al-Galaa near the *Ramses Hilton*, and one or two services from Aboud may be picked up off Sharia Orabi near Ramses station. Some destinations may be served by buses from more than one departure point, notably Alexandria (Aboud, Turgoman and the *Ramses Hilton*), Hurghada (*Ramses Hilton*, Aboud and El Moneeb), Sharm el-Sheikh (Sinai and Turgoman), and Fayoum, Beni Suef and Minya (Turgoman and El Moneeb).

Unless stated otherwise, all services below run daily, though schedules are liable to change. None of the bus companies will take bookings over the phone – tickets must be purchased at the terminal (or, in the case of Mansura and Damietta, from the old Koulali terminal off Sharia Orabi).

Turgoman Garage

Turgoman Garage in Bulaq – 600m west of Ramses Station on Sharia Shanan – is not really served by local public transport, but it's an easy walk from Ramses station or from Sharia Ramses by Orabi metro. A taxi from Midan Tahrir should cost around £E3, and certainly not more than £E5.

In the old part of the garage (the first part you come to if approaching from Ramses), the first booth is for East Delta services to **Suez** (every 30min 6am–8.30pm; 2hr; £E7.25) and **Ismailiya** (every 20min 6.30am–8pm; 2hr; £E7.25). The second booth sells tickets for East Delta services to **Mansura** (every 20 mins 6am–8pm; 2hr; £E8.50–9) and **Damietta** (16 daily; 3hr 30min; £E14–15). These latter two can also be picked up in town at the old Koulali terminal by Sharia Orabi north of Sharia Ramses (see map on p.124), and both destinations are in any case better served from Aboud (see below). The third booth is for West Delta buses to **Alexandria** (1–2 per hour 5am–11.30pm; 3hr; £E18) and **Mersa Matrouh** (4 daily; 6hr; £E40). The booth after that is run by the Middle Delta Bus Co, serving **Tanta** (hourly 7am–10pm; 1hr 30min; £E6.50) and **Mahalla** (hourly 7am–10pm; 2hr; £E7.50), but again there are more frequent departures to these places from Aboud.

From the new part of Turgoman, which is behind the old part and will eventually take over all its functions, there are Superjet buses to **Hurghada** (3 daily; 5–6hr; £E60) and **Sharm el-Sheikh** (4 daily; 5hr; £E70–85), as well as West Delta services to **Alexandria** (hourly 6am–10pm; 3hr; £E16).

Aboud Bus Terminal

The **Aboud Bus Terminal**, 3km north of Ramses station, up Sharia Ahmed Helmi by the Sharia Shubra intersection, is most easily reached by service taxi microbus from Ramses station (75pt). A taxi will cost around £E3 from Ramses Station, £E5–6 from downtown.

The Delta is from here served by three companies, of which the West Delta Bus Co (☎02/431-6742) runs buses to **Alexandria** (every 45min 7am–8.30pm; 3hr; £E12) and **Damanhur** (every 45min 7am–11pm; 2hr; £E9), while Middle Delta Bus Co serves **Tanta** (half-hourly 7am–9pm; 1hr 30min; £E6), **Mahalla el-Kubra** (every 30min; 2hr 30min; £E7) and **Kafr el-Sheikh** (every 30min; 3hr; £E7). East Delta Bus Co covers **Benha** (every 30min 6am–8pm; 1hr; £E2.50), **Zagazig** (every 20–30min 7am–9.30pm; 1hr 30min; £E5), **Faqus** (every 45min 7.30am–8.15pm; 2hr; £E8), **Mansura** (half-hourly 7am–8pm; 2hr; £E9), **Damietta** (hourly 7am–8pm; 3hr 30min; £E14) and, in summer (June–Sept), **Ras el-Bahr** (every 45min; 3hr; £E17).

For destinations southwards up the Nile Valley, the Upper Egypt Bus Co (☎02/431-6723) has departures to **Fayoum** (every 30min 6am–7pm; 2hr; £E8), **Minya** (hourly 6am–1am; 4hr; £E15), **Mellawi** (every two hours 7.15am–1.30am; 4hr 30min; £E17), **Assyut** (hourly 7am–1am; 6–7hrs; £E12–15), **Sohag** (hourly 7am–11pm; 8–9hrs; £E30), **Qena** (hourly 7am–11pm; 9–10hrs; £E30), **Luxor** (1 daily; 9hr; £E90) and **Aswan** (1 daily; 12hr; £E90). The last two destinations, however, are more comfortable by train.

Sinai (Abbassiya) Terminal

The **Sinai Bus Terminal** (Mahattat Seena), 4km from the centre in Abbassiya, can be reached by bus from Abdel Mounem Riyad (#27 and #998, and minibus #30) or Midan Ramses (#28, #310 and #710, and minibuses #1 and #998), with more buses to Midan Abbassiya, a short walk away. A taxi will cost £E5–8 from downtown.

Buses from here are operated by the East Delta Bus Co, and serve **El-Arish** (2 daily; 5hr £E26.50–37), **Taba** (3 daily; 10hr; £E55–75), **Dahab** (4 daily; 9hr; £E62–75) and **Sharm el-Sheikh** (10 daily; 5hr; £E55–65). All these buses stop additionally at Almaza Terminal (see p.89), and there are also Superjet services to Sharm from Turgoman Garage (see p.271).

El Moneeb Bus Terminal

The **El Moneeb Bus Terminal**, under a flyover 300m north of El-Monib metro station, is the terminal for the Upper Egypt Bus Co's services to Middle Egypt and the western desert oases (but not Siwa, which is reached from Mersa Matrouh or Alexandria). Here you'll find departures for **Fayoum City** (every 30min; 2hr; £E5), **Beni Suef** (28 daily; 2hr; £E6.50) and **Minya** (5 daily; 4hr; £E13.50), as well as **Bahariya** (5 daily; 6hr; £E20), **Farafra** (3 daily; 8–10hr; £E27) and **Dakhla** (3 daily; 14–16hr; £E40). Superjet services to Hurghada and Upper Egypt services to Luxor and Aswan also call here.

Ramses Hilton departures

Superjet runs deluxe buses to **Alexandria** (hourly 6am–11pm; 3hr; £E25) from Sharia al-Galaa near the *Ramses Hilton* hotel (see map on p.104). A few doors down, El Gouna runs seven daily buses to **Hurghada** (5–6hr; £E40–65).

International buses

Buses to **Tel Aviv** and **Jerusalem** take fourteen hours, usually routed the long way round, via Taba and Eilat, to avoid the Gaza Strip. At the time of writing, two buses a week depart from the *Cairo Sheraton* in Dokki (Thurs & Sun 6am; $55 one-way, $75 return, plus border taxes of around $20 each way). For tickets and information, contact Misr Travel at the *Cairo Sheraton* (☎02/335-5470).

East Delta has four weekly services to **Amman** in Jordan and **Damascus** in Syria, travelling via the Nuweiba–Aqaba ferry. Buses leave the Sinai Terminal

(Mon, Wed, Thurs & Sun at 7.30am); the fare is $80 plus £E50 to Amman (15hr), $65 plus £E50 to Damascus (30hr). Superjet also runs twice weekly (Tues & Sun; $70 plus £E50) buses to Amman from their terminal at **Almaza** at the far end of Heliopolis, which can be reached by buses #39 and #796 from Abdel Mouneem Riyad, buses #15, #39 and #796 from Midan Ramses, or on the Heliopolis metro (the Merghani line; see p.201), from Ramses to the junction of Sharia Merghani with Sharia Abu Bakr al-Siddiq (under the flyover), following the latter street 300m right (south) to the terminal.

Also from the Almaza Terminal, Superjet runs buses to Libya: to **Benghazi** (daily except Sun at 7am; 17hr; £E150) and **Tripoli** (daily except Wed & Sat; 36hr; £E270).

Inter-city service taxis

If you don't mind a slightly cramped and definitely hair-raising journey, **service taxis** (*servees*), whether Peugeots or microbuses, are usually the fastest way to reach a host of destinations. Their biggest advantage is that they leave as soon as they're full; just turn up, and you'll probably be away in 15min (morning and late afternoon are prime times).

Fares generally work out 20–30 percent above the bus fare, though they are occasionally cheaper. Drivers are unlikely to overcharge you, but watch what Egyptians pay and you can hardly go wrong. If you're alighting halfway (for example, at Wadi Natrun, along the Desert Road to Alex), it's normal to pay the full fare.

For **Alexandria and the Delta**, the best place to pick up a service taxi is Aboud terminal, where you'll find vehicles to Alex, Baltim, Benha, Damanhur, Damietta, Faqus, Kafr el-Sheikh, Mahalla, Mansura, Tanta and Zagazig, with very frequent departures and a direct route out of town. Vehicles to several of these destinations, in particular Alex and Tanta, can sometimes be picked up around Ramses rail station too, especially during rush hours, but they may take a roundabout route out of town, and end up taking longer than taxis from Aboud.

Service taxis for **Suez** and **Ismailiya** leave from Sharia Orabi near Ramses Station (see map on p.124). For **Fayoum**, the best place to pick up a service taxi is at Midan Giza (see p.195 for local bus connections), though you can also get them from Sharia Orabi near Ramses Station (see map on p.124). Service taxis to Fayoum, and also to **Beni Suef** and **Middle Egypt**, also leave from a depot opposite El Mouneeb bus station.

International service taxis

In addition to domestic runs, there are international service taxis to **Libya** run by Wikala Suessi on Midan Opera (℡02/395-4480; see map on p.105). These leave daily from there at around 8pm bound for Benghazi and Tripoli. It's wise to book your place a day or two ahead if possible.

Depending on the current political situation, it is also possible to get to **Palestine and Israel** by service taxi in stages. The route to the Gaza Strip is inadvisable at time of writing due to the situation in Palestine, and in any case the Israelis frequently close the border for days or weeks at a time. Should things settle down, you can take a service taxi from Sharia Orabi near Ramses Station (see map on p.124) to Suez, where you should be able to get one to the Rafah border crossing. On the other side of the border, you may have to take a "special" (i.e. a private taxi) to Khan Yunis, where there are service taxis to Gaza City and thence to the Israeli border at Erez. If you do this, you will need to set out early to avoid being stranded at Khan Yunis, where there is no accommodation. There is also transport from Rafah directly into Israel. Alternatively, there are a couple of buses from Suez (at 3 & 5pm) to the Israeli border at Taba (5hr; £E35) via Nuweiba.

Domestic flights

Domestic flights leave from Terminal 1, the "old airport" (*al-mataar al-qadima*), which can be reached by bus, minibus or taxi (£E50 is the going rate, though drivers may demand more). Both airport terminals are served by air-conditioned bus #356, minibus #27 and 24-hour bus #400, all from Abdel Mouneem Riyad Terminal (in front of the *Ramses Hilton*) and Midan Ramses, and also by 24-hour bus #948 from Midan Ataba. During rush hour, and especially by bus, the journey can take well over an hour, so always allow plenty of time.

EgyptAir (for information ☎ 02/265-7244 or 0900/70000) has flights to Abu Simbel (2 daily, both very early morning; 2hr 45min; $210), Alexandria (at least 6 weekly; 50min; $50), Assyut (2 weekly; 1hr; $75), Aswan (6–8 daily; 1hr 20min; $160), Hurghada (3–4 daily; 1hr; $120), Luxor (5–8 daily; 1hr 5min; $115), Mersa Matroah (alternative days; 1hr) and Sharm el-Sheikh (4–6 daily; 55min; $120). All these prices are subject to tax (currently £E110).

In addition, the oil company Salit Khadramaat Betrol, based at 45 Akfit al-Mahdi, off Sharia al-Azhar (☎02/392-1674) run a weekly flight on Sundays for their personnel from Cairo airport's old terminal to Kharga Oasis, which will take passengers for £E470 if there is room.

International flights

Many airlines (see p.262 for contact details) make Cairo a stopover between the Near and Far East, or between Europe and sub-Saharan Africa, ensuring a competitive market in fares, student and youth discounts – but also heavy demand for flights. Don't leave buying tickets until the last moment. Especially during August, you should book weeks in advance on Eastern European airlines (which often have the cheapest flights to Western Europe, the British Isles and North America) or for popular long-haul destinations like Nairobi and Delhi.

All reservations should be reconfirmed 72 hours before departure. Also check which terminal you are flying from: some airlines, including EgyptAir, KLM and the more down-at-heel African and East European companies, use Terminal 1 (*al-mataar al-qadima*, "the old airport"); others use Terminal 2 (*al-mataar al-gadida*, "the new airport").

Agents such as Spring Tours (3 Sharia Sayed el-Bakry, Zamalek ☎02/736-5972, ⓦwww.springtours.com) and Travco (13 Sharia Mahmoud Azmi, Zamalek ☎02/736-2042, ⓦwww.travco-eg.com), may offer discounts and can often find seats when the airline itself swears that none exist. Some agents and airlines may accept credit card payments for tickets, but don't bank on it.

Ferries

The **Hurghada–Sharm el-Sheikh catamaran** is operated by International Fast Ferries, whose Cairo office is on the second floor at 46 Sharia Suriya in Mohandiseen (☎02/794-8927 or 8). Tickets can also be purchased from downtown travel agents such as De Castro Tours (12 Sharia Talaat Harb ☎02/574-3213, ⓔdecastrotours@link.net). Arab Bridge Maritime, who run ferries from **Nuweiba** and **Sharm el-Sheikh to Aqaba** in Jordan (see p.704 for details), have a downtown office at 7 Sharia Abdel Khalaq Sarwat (☎02/419-8657). For details of the ferry service from **Aswan to Wadi Halfa** in Sudan, see p.448; for information on ferries from **Suez to Jeddah** in Saudi, see p.648.

The Nile Valley

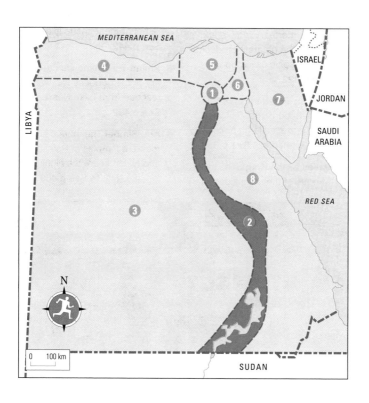

CHAPTER 2 # Highlights

✳ **Dahabiyas** Cruise the Nile in style, aboard a chartered houseboat sailing between Esna and Aswan. See p.318

✳ **Feluccas** A timeless way to view the Nile's scenery and temples, sailing downriver from Aswan to Edfu. See p.319

✳ **Abydos** The carvings in Seti I's mortuary temple are among the greatest produced by pharaonic civilization. See p.322

✳ **Karnak Temple** It took 1300 years to construct this vast cult centre, as large as ten great cathedrals. See p.359

✳ **Valley of the Kings** The most famous of the magnificent burial complexes and mortuary temples that make up the Theban Necropolis. See p.380

✳ **Aswan's bazaar** This wonderful marketplace sells all kinds of handicrafts, souvenirs and spices. See p.434

✳ **Nubian music and dance** Exuberant and haunting by turns, they're best enjoyed on Sehel or Elephantine Island. See p.442

✳ **Philae** This island sanctuary of the goddess Isis was rescued from Lake Nasser. See p.452

✳ **Abu Simbel** The monumental rock-cut temples of Ramses II and Nefertari are the highlights of Lake Nasser. See p.463

△ A jeweller's shop in Aswan's bazaar

The Nile Valley

E gypt has been called the gift of the Nile, for without the river it could not exist as a fertile, populous country, let alone have sustained a great civilization five thousand years ago. Its character and history have been shaped by the stark contrast between the fecund **Nile Valley** and its Delta (covered in Chapter 5), and the arid wastes that surround them. To the Ancient Egyptians, this was the homeland or Kemet – the Black Land of dark alluvium, where life and civilization flourished as the benign gods intended – as opposed to the desert that represented death and chaos, ruled by Seth, the bringer of storms and catastrophes.

Kemet's existence depended on an annual miracle of rebirth from aridity, as the Nile rose to spread its life-giving waters and fertilizing silt over the exhausted land during the season of inundation. Once the flood had subsided, the *fellaheen* (peasants) simply planted crops in the mud, waited for an abundant harvest, and then relaxed over summer. While empires rose and fell, this way of life persisted essentially unchanged for over 240 generations, until the Aswan Dam put an end to the inundation in 1967 – a breathtaking period of continuity considering that Jesus lived less than eighty generations ago.

This continuity and ancient history is literally underfoot. Almost every Nile town and village is built upon layers of previous **settlements** – pharaonic, Ptolemaic, Roman and Coptic – whose ancient names, modified and Arabized, have often survived. When treasure-hunting "archeologists" first turned their attention to the ancient temples and tombs in the 1830s, they had to sift through metres of sand and debris before reaching their goal. Yet the centuries of burial preserved a panoply of ancient bas-reliefs and carvings that would otherwise have been defaced by Coptic or Muslim iconoclasts, who hacked away at the pagan gods on the accessible friezes, pillars and ceilings, and plundered masonry for their own churches and mosques.

After a century and a half of excavation by just about every Western nation – and by the Egyptians since independence – the Nile's **monuments** constitute the greatest open-air museum in the world. Revealed along its banks are several thousand **tombs** (over 900 in Luxor's Theban Necropolis alone) and scores of **temples**: so many, in fact, that most visitors feel satiated by just a fraction of this legacy.

To enjoy the Valley, it's best to be selective and mix sightseeing with felucca rides on the river, roaming around bazaars and camel markets, or attending the odd moulid. Most visitors succeed in this by heading straight for **Upper Egypt**, travelling by train or air to **Luxor** or **Aswan**, then making day-trips to the sights within easy range of either base – most notably the cult temple at **Edfu** – in addition to exploring the New Kingdom temples and tombs of **Karnak** and the

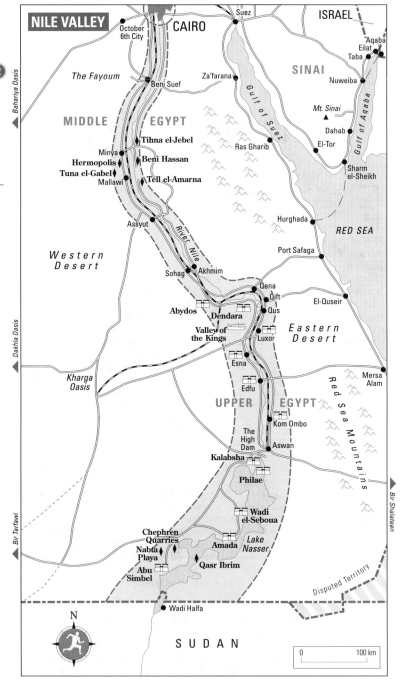

THE NILE VALLEY ②

Theban Necropolis from Luxor. Prices for **Nile cruises** have never been lower, whether you shop around before you leave (see Basics, pp.316–321); at travel agents in Cairo, Luxor and Aswan; or on the boats moored at Aswan, which is also the point of departure for felucca cruises to Kom Ombo and Edfu (see pp.319–321 for details). Further north, **Middle Egypt** is chiefly known for its temples at **Abydos** and **Dendara**, but independent travellers and adventure tour groups also visit the tombs of **Beni Hassan** and the ruins of Akhenaten's capital at **Tell el-Amarna**.

And lastly, a word on the **terms from Egyptology** that fill this chapter: many may be unfamiliar and need a fuller explanation than a glossary allows (see p.826), hence the boxes at intervals in the text: on statehood and symbolism on p.382; funerary beliefs and practices under "The Valley of the Kings" (pp.382–383); and gods and goddesses under their respective cult temples (see the main index for a list). Temple architecture is featured in its own colour section.

The river, its gods and pharaohs

The **Nile** is the world's longest river (6695km), originating in the highland lakes of Uganda and Ethiopia, which give rise to the White and Blue Niles. At Khartoum in Sudan these join into a single river which flows northwards over a series of cataracts through the Nubian desert, before forming Egypt's Nile Valley and Delta, through which it travels 1545km to the Mediterranean Sea. The river's northward flow, coupled with a prevailing wind towards the south, made it a natural highway.

As the source of life, the Nile influenced much of Ancient Egyptian **society and mythology**. Creation myths of a primal mound emerging from the waters of chaos reflect how villages huddled on mounds till the flood subsided and they could plant their crops. Even more crucially, the need for large-scale irrigation works in the Valley and the consequent mobilization of labour may have engendered the region's system of centralized authority – in effect, the state.

Both the Valley and its Delta were divided into **nomes** or provinces, each with a **nomarch** or governor, and one or more **local deities**. As political power ebbed and flowed between regions and dynasties, certain of the deities assumed

Travel restrictions and routes into the Nile Valley

Setting out from Cairo or the Red Sea coast, you are faced with a variety of approaches to the Valley, but you need to bear in mind certain travel restrictions, imposed in response to the terrorist attacks on tourists in the Valley in the 1990s, and more recently in Sinai. The system relies on police checkpoints to filter traffic and ensure that tourists respect the restrictions listed below. Officially, tourists can visit any place in the Valley providing they get there in a way that stays within the rules, but in reality it can be hard, if not impossible, to reach some places. Whereas tourists are unbothered by controls within the security "bubble" of Luxor and Aswan, in **Middle Egypt** the police insist on **escorting** them on excursions, or around town. While you have little choice but to comply and should certainly never get angry, the system is sufficiently inconsistent and fallible enough that you can sometimes persuade them to cut you some slack.

Bear in mind that you're a privileged visitor but also a nuisance to the police, who want you off their turf as soon as possible and preferably into another governorate's territory. Each governorate fine-tunes the rules for their territory without reference to its neighbours, sometimes resulting in weird inconsistencies. The following rules and exceptions **specifically apply to the Nile Valley**:

• **Trains** Travelling between Cairo's **Ramses Station and Luxor or Aswan**, tourists may only use three regular trains (guarded by plainclothes cops with Uzis) or the deluxe *wagons-lits* service. Clerks will simply refuse to sell tickets for other trains. In **Middle Egypt**, however, you can usually buy a ticket for any train at the station kiosk with no difficulty, while travelling from Aswan to Luxor (but not the other way) you're allowed to use six trains, not just the three authorized for long-distance travel. For details of ticket classes and other rail information, see p.269.

• Foreigners cannot **drive** a car or motorbike through Middle Egypt. To reach Luxor from Cairo (or vice versa) they must use the Red Sea highway via Hurghada and Port Safaga, or travel through the Western Desert via Kharga. This rule also applies to **cyclists**.

• In Upper Egypt, **tourist buses and hired taxis** must travel in **convoys** escorted by the police. There are three daily between Luxor and Aswan and Luxor and Hurghada; two from Aswan to Abu Simbel, and one from Luxor to Abydos. Local

national significance and absorbed the attributes of lesser gods in a perpetual process of religious mergers and takeovers. Thus, for example, Re, the chief god of the Old Kingdom, ended up being assimilated with Amun, the prime divinity of Thebes during the New Kingdom. Yet for all its complexity, Ancient Egyptian religion was essentially practical and intended to get results. Its pre-eminent concerns were to perpetuate the beneficent sun and river, maintain the righteous order personified by the goddess Maat, and achieve resurrection in the afterlife.

Abundant crops could normally be taken for granted, as prayers to Hapy the Nile-god were followed by a green wave of humus-rich water around June. However, if the Nile failed to rise for a succession of years there ensued the "years of the hyena when men went hungry". Archeologists reckon that it was **famine** – caused by overworking of the land, as well as lack of the flood waters – that caused the collapse of the Old and Middle Kingdoms, and subsequent political anarchy. But each time some new dynasty arose to reunite the land and re-establish the old order. This remarkable conservatism persisted even under foreign rule: the Nubians, Persians, Ptolemies and Romans all continued building temples dedicated to the old gods, and styled themselves as pharaohs.

drivers should know where and when the convoy departs from its assembly point and arrive early.

• **Buses** from Cairo's Aboud, El Moneeb and Turgoman terminals to Luxor and Aswan are routed via the Red Sea coast rather than Middle Egypt. Buses to Beni Suef, Minya, Assyut and Sohag in Middle Egypt do exist, but tourists trying to buy tickets for these may be refused. If you do reach Middle Egypt by train, local cops may tolerate you using inter-city buses within the region or heading south to Luxor, from which point on you may use any bus – providing there aren't more than four tourists aboard the vehicle. Even this limit doesn't seem to apply to buses to Hurghada. Since few tourists use buses at present, in practice you can probably rely on being able to catch any bus – though finding a seat may be another matter, as many buses arrive already full (standing is allowed).

• Tourists aren't allowed to use **service taxis** anywhere along the Nile Valley. However, as the rule isn't always observed between Luxor and Aswan (though it is *in* Luxor and Aswan), or in Middle Egypt, we've included some details of routes under town accounts, in case the restriction is lifted.

General travel practicalities

Planes are the fastest way to travel from one end of the Nile Valley to the other. Depending on demand, there can be from two to a dozen flights a day from Cairo to Luxor, Aswan and Abu Simbel, affording amazing views over the Valley's green belt of cultivated land. You can also fly from Aswan to Abu Simbel, and Luxor to Hurghada or Sharm el-Sheikh.

Package tours booked abroad are generally good value, but visitors buying tours in Cairo often pay over the odds for substandard hotels and excursions. Many have complained about touts selling or adapting itineraries from Amigo Tours at huge mark-ups; for more on this racket, see p.88. If you *do* want a tour, talk to Salah Mohammed (p.217) or Eastmar Travel (p.265) in Cairo – Eastmar also does cruises between Luxor and Aswan and on Lake Nasser, and has offices in Luxor and Aswan.

For details of **tickets**, **prices** and **departure** and **journey times** from Cairo, see the "Moving on" section at the end of Chapter 1.

The people of the Nile Valley

Although the Nile Valley and its Delta represents a mere four percent of Egypt's surface area, it is home to 95 percent of the country's population. While Cairo and Alexandria account for about a quarter of this, the bulk of the people still live in small towns and villages and, as in pharaonic times, the **fellaheen** or peasant farmers remain the bedrock of Egyptian society.

Most **villages** consist of flat-roofed mud-brick houses, with chickens, goats, cows and water buffalo roaming the unpaved streets, and elaborate multistorey pigeon coops (the birds are eaten and their droppings used as fertilizer). The plastered outside walls of the houses are often painted light blue (a colour believed to ward off the Evil Eye), and if the householder has made the pilgrimage to Mecca, they will be decorated with characteristic hajj scenes (recalling the journey with images of ships and charter jets, lions and the sacred Kaaba shrine). Children begin work at an early age: girls feed the animals, fetch water and make the dung patties which are used for fuel (though primus stoves are increasingly popular), while by the age of 9 or 10, boys are learning how to farm the land that will one day be theirs.

Rural life might appear the same throughout the Nile Valley, but its character changes as you go further south. The northern part of the Valley is wider and

Much of the symbolism of Ancient Egypt referred to the union of the **Two Lands**, the **Nile Valley** (Upper Egypt) and its **Delta** (Lower Egypt; in native usage and current administration there's no such area as Middle Egypt). The establishment of this union was what marked the onset of the Old Kingdom (c.3100 BC) – unless you buy the theory advanced by one Egyptologist that the Two Lands were actually the east and west banks of the Nile (which seems unlikely).

▲ Winged sun-disc

Each Land had its own deity – the Delta had **Wadjet**, the cobra goddess, while the Valley had **Nekhbet**, the vulture goddess. With union, their images were combined with the sun-disc of the god Re to form the **winged sun-disc**, which often appeared on the lintels of temple doors. Another common image was that of the Nile-god, **Hapy**, binding together the **heraldic plants** of the Two Lands, the papyrus of the Delta and the lotus of the Valley.

▲ Hapy binding the two lands

Much the same process can be observed in the evolution of **pharaonic crowns**. At state rituals, the pharaoh customarily wore first the **White Crown** of Upper Egypt and then the **Red Crown** of Lower Egypt, although by the time of the New Kingdom (c.1570 BC) these were often subsumed into the **Combined Crown**. Pharaonic crowns also featured the **uraeus** or fire-spitting cobra, an incarnation of Wadjet believed to be a guardian of the kings.

Another image that referred to the act of union (an act which had to be repeated at the onset of the Middle and New Kingdoms) was the **Djed pillar**, a symbol of steadfastness. Additional symbols of royal authority included the **crook** (or staff) and the **flail** (or scourge), which are often shown crossed over the chest – in the so-called Osiride position – on pharaonic statues. A ubiquitous motif was the **ankh**, symbolizing breath or life, which pharaohs are often depicted receiving from gods in tombs or funerary texts.

However, the archetypal symbol of kingship was the **cartouche**, an oval formed by a loop of rope, enclosing the hieroglyphs of the pharaoh's **nomen** and **prenomen**. Traditionally a pharaoh's title consisted of five names: four adopted on accession to the throne (Horus name, Nebty name, Golden Horus name and prenomen) and a birth name (nomen), roughly corresponding to a family name. The prenomen was introduced by a group of hieroglyphs meaning "He who belongs to the sedge and the bee" and was nearly always compounded with the name of Re, the sun-god. The nomen – the name by which pharaohs are known to posterity – was likewise introduced by an epithet, "Son of Re".

White crown   Red crown   Combined crown   Uraeus   Djed pillar   Crook   Flail   Ankh

greener, unconstrained by the desert hills; its people have a reputation for being quietly spoken and phlegmatic. By contrast, Egyptians characterize the **Saiyidis** of Upper Egypt as mercurial in character, alternating between hot-blooded passion and a state known as kismet – a kind of fatalistic stasis. To non-Saiyidis, they are also the butt of jokes mocking their stubbornness and stupidity. A further ethnic contingent of the southern reaches of the Valley are the black-skinned **Nubians**, whose traditional homeland stretching far into Sudan was submerged by Lake Nasser in the 1960s.

Nile wildlife

The exotic Nile wildlife depicted on ancient tomb reliefs – hippos, crocodiles, elephants and gazelles – is largely a thing of the past, though you might just see a croc near Aswan. However, the Valley has a rich diversity of **birds**. Amid the groves of palms (dates all along the Valley and dom palms south of Assyut), fruit and flame trees, sycamores and eucalyptus, and fields of *besoom* (Egyptian clover) and sugar cane, you can spot hoopoes, turtle- and laughing-doves, bulbuls, bluethroats, redstarts, wheatears and dark-backed stonechats. Purple gallinules, egrets and all kinds of waders are to be seen in the river, while common birds of prey include a range of kestrels, hawks and falcons.

Middle Egypt

It was nineteenth-century archeologists who coined the term **Middle Egypt** for the stretch of river between Cairo and the Qena Bend. It's a handy label for a region that's subtly distinct from Upper Egypt, further south (in this guide, the Middle Egypt account ends at Sohag; the sites to the south – at Abydos and Dendara – are dealt with in the Upper Egypt account as the best access to them is from Luxor). Owing little to tourism, the towns are solidly provincial, with social conservatism providing common ground for those wanting to preserve peaceful relations between the Muslim majority and Middle Egypt's Coptic community (about twenty percent of the local population, roughly double the national average). During the 1990s this was badly strained by Islamic militants, whose attacks on Copts, the security forces and tourists made the region a no-go zone for foreigners. Though adventure-tour groups are returning, few independent travellers have followed, and the restrictions intended to ensure tourists' security can be off-putting even though the risk of danger has receded.

Even before this, most tourists rated Middle Egypt a low priority, as towns like **Minya** and **Sohag** lack the romance of Aswan or the stupendous monuments of Luxor, for all that the local antiquities have fascinated scholars. The rock tombs of **Beni Hassan** and the necropolis of **Tuna al-Gabel** are well-preserved relics of Middle Kingdom artistry and Ptolemaic cult-worship, while the desolate remains at **Tell el-Amarna** stand as an evocative reminder of the "heretic" Pharaoh Akhenaten. All these sites may be visited with a police escort.

Beni Suef

Beni Suef is one of Egypt's poorest governorates, with high unemployment due to a shortage of arable land. Many welcome the siting of five **cement factories** on the east bank, despite the pollution they cause, as the only other

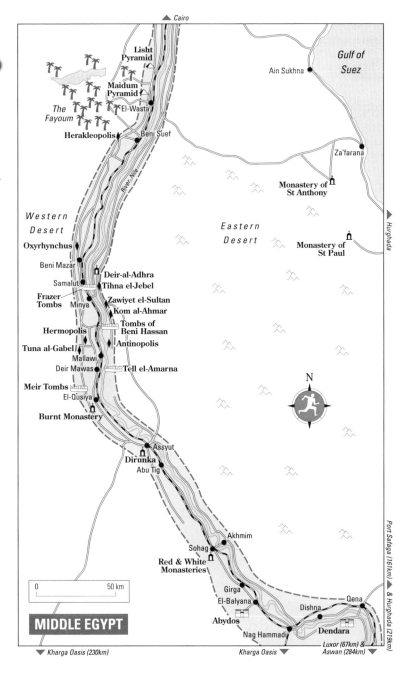

work is quarrying for marble – a job that has killed or crippled scores of men. Hopes for a better life rest on exploiting the **natural gas** fields beneath the Western Desert, with the new Kuraymat power-station as the hub of a future grid of pipelines running to October 6th City, Assyut, Qena and Aswan. Another contributor to environmental pollution is the airbase that hosts Egypt's "Top Gun" **fighter pilots school**, whose students dogfight in the skies above the governorate.

There's no reason to visit the governorate's ramshackle capital, also called **BENI SUEF**, except to switch transport for the Red Sea coast, the Fayoum or the Pyramid of Maidum. Should this mean **staying** overnight, your best option is the two-star *Semiramis Hotel* (☎082/232-2092, ⒻF 232-6017; ❷) behind the **telephone** and **post** offices, just north of the **train station**. By carrying on to a bridge and turning right, you'll find a **bank** on Sharia Sa'ad Zaghloul. Alternatively, cross the canal and carry on for 200m then turn right, and you'll reach the depot for **minibuses** and pick-ups to El-Wasta, from where a service taxi can get you within range of the Pyramid of Maidum (see p.495). Hourly **buses** to Minya and the Fayoum, and one daily to Za'farana on the Red Sea – running past the turn-off for St Anthony's Monastery (see p.727) – leave from the bus station on Sharia Bur Said, 400m south of (and on the other side of the canal from) the train station. For **eating**, there's a choice between kebab or chicken at the *Semiramis*, or the *kushari*, *fuul* or *taamiya* outside the station.

Forgotten cities: Herakleopolis and Oxyrhynchus

Though nothing remains of them, two ancient cities once flourished along this stretch of the Nile Valley. **Herakleopolis** is marked by a huge mound of rubble near the village of Ihnasya el-Medina, 15km from Beni Suef. Founded early in the Old Kingdom and long the capital of the twentieth nome, its rise coincided with the decline of the VIII Dynasty, which barely controlled the region around Memphis by 2160 BC. While anarchy reigned throughout the Two Lands, **Achthoes**, the nomarch of Herakleopolis, forged a new dynasty. Although his successors never achieved control of southern Egypt, their reassertion of centralized authority in the north paved the way for the XII Dynasty and the Middle Kingdom.

Of similarly academic interest, **Oxyrhynchus**, 9km northwest of Beni Mazar, was the capital of the nineteenth nome. It's noted for the discovery of numerous papyri – including third-century fragments of the gospels of Matthew and John; portions of plays by Sophocles, Euripides and Meander; and summaries of the lost books of Livy. More frivolously, it deserves to be remembered for revering the elephant-snout fish, which the Ancient Egyptians believed ate the penis of Osiris after his dismemberment by Seth (see box on p.325).

Minya and around

The best archeological sites in Middle Egypt are around **Minya**, 229km (and 3hr 30min by train) from Cairo, and **Mallawi**, 47km further south. This area was the epicentre of the conflict between Islamic militants and the security forces in the mid-1990s, when canefields were burned to deny the militants cover, and armoured cars patrolled the streets of Minya and Mallawi. Since the militants were flushed out or ceased fighting in 1998 there have been no reported acts of violence, and locals point out that, even in the worst years, no tourists were attacked in Minya. Even so, the police are omnipresent and expect tourists to conform to security restrictions. This generally means **visiting the sites in private taxis**, with a police escort, rather than using local buses or service taxis – which makes trips costlier – although for **inter-city travel** you may use any train up or down the Valley, and there's always a chance that you'll be able to pick up a bus or service taxi when the police aren't looking, or decide to turn a blind eye just to get you off their turf as fast as possible.

The main attractions are the rock tombs of **Beni Hassan**, roughly midway between the towns; these contain the finest surviving murals from the Middle Kingdom. Nearer to Mallawi on the west bank are the ruins of **Hermopolis** and its partially subterranean necropolis, **Tuna al-Gabel**, while the rock-cut temples of **Tihna el-Jebel** and the Coptic **Monastery of the Virgin** lie across the river to the north of Minya. Minya's bridge provides easy access to the east bank of the Nile, where Beni Hassan is the main attraction, followed by the **Frazer Tombs**, Tihna el-Jebel and Deir al-Adhra. Minya's tourist office can arrange trips to all these sites. As the east bank road doesn't extend as far south as **Tell el-Amarna**, 12km south of Mallawi, this is best visited on a separate trip (hence it's covered in its own section on p.297), though it can be combined with Hermopolis and Tuna al-Gabel.

Minya

Known as the "Bride of Upper Egypt" (Arous al-Sa'id), **MINYA** derives considerable charm from its elegant villas built by Italian architects for Greek and Egyptian cotton magnates – now picturesquely decaying amid overgrown gardens – and from its people, known in Egypt for their warmth and honesty. The only sign that it was once embroiled in a struggle between Islamic militants and the security forces are the concrete gun-towers at strategic locations – nowadays mostly unmanned. Tourists may wander about town without an escort, but the police will want to know where you're staying and to accompany you on any excursions to the surrounding sites.

△ Detail of the former villa of a cotton magnate, Minya

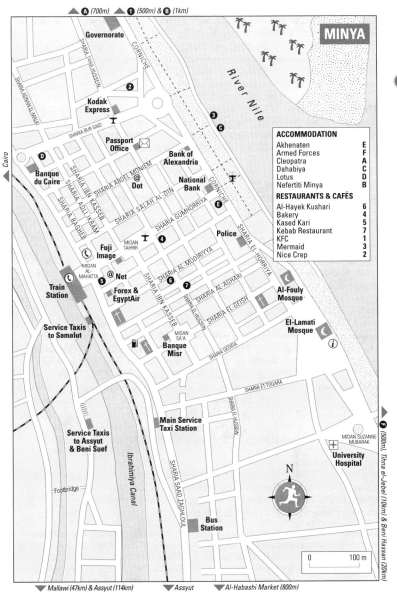

ACCOMMODATION

Akhenaten	E
Armed Forces	F
Cleopatra	A
Dahabiya	C
Lotus	D
Nefertiti Minya	B

RESTAURANTS & CAFÉS

Al-Hayek Kushari	6
Bakery	4
Kased Kari	5
Kebab Restaurant	7
KFC	1
Mermaid	3
Nice Crep	2

Outside the train station, Midan al–Mahatta is a square redolent of an ex-colonial *ville* in North Africa. From here Sharia Gumhorriya leads to the palm-shaded **Midan Tahrir**, whose most elegant villa is the governor's residence. Minya's **bazaar** stretches southwards along Sharia el-Hussein as far as Midan Sa'a, bustling from mid-morning to midnight, as is the adjacent Sharia Ibn Khasseb, lined with Coptic jewellers and pharmacies. The

Corniche is quiet by comparison, with a park affording views of the striated hills of the Eastern Desert across the Nile.

Minya's annual **City Festival** on March 8 features a military band on the Corniche in commemoration of the fierce local resistance to British rule during the 1919 revolution, while the weekly **Al-Habashi Market** (Mon) in the south of town has been a fixture since Ottoman times.

Practicalities

Though microbuses (25pt) and taxis (£E2) are widely used, Minya is compact enough for walking, with its local and long-distance transport depots fairly close together. The **tourist office** (daily 9am–5pm; ☎086/237-1521) beside the El-Lamati Mosque on the Corniche is keen to help, with English-speaking Hussein Farag (☎010 129-9479, ✉lindshussien@aol.com) and his sidekick Mahmoud Abd el-Samir (☎010 123-5343) able to arrange taxi **excursions** to any of the archeological sites in the vicinity for £E20 an hour, and can supply an English-speaking **guide** for £E150 a day, allowing you to dispense with the otherwise obligatory escort from the **tourist police** (☎086/236-4527). Another possible guide is Habashy Soliman of the Tourist Friends' Association (☎086/262-3423).

As in other towns in Middle Egypt, the police prefer you to use **trains** to reach Cairo, Assyut, Luxor or Aswan, and don't seem to mind which of the dozen or so daily services you catch. Foreigners may also use inter-city **buses** to Assyut (hourly; 4hr) and Cairo (every 2hr; 5hr), leaving from the bus station on Sharia Sa'ad Zaghloul.

A 24-hour **telephone office** beside the station sells phonecards for use in booths around town. The main **post office** (daily except Fri 8am–2pm), one block north of Sharia Abdel Moniem, has a **passport office** (daily except Fri & Sat 8am–2pm) on the floor above that can extend visas. For cash, use the Forex (daily 10am–10pm) beside EgyptAir or banks with ATMs: Banque Misr does cash advances on Visa cards, and the National Bank changes traveller's cheques. The University **hospital** (☎086/236-6743) on Midan Suzanne Mubarak is the best in the region. Dot on Sharia Abdel Moniem and Net in an alley behind Midan al-Mahatta both offer **Internet access** (daily 11am–midnight).

Accommodation

None of the old-fashioned hotels near the train station want foreign guests, so visitors are limited to the places listed below. Most have cops outside, who'll ask where you're going whenever you leave and become nervous if you're out late after dark. Breakfast is included in the rates.

Akhenaten On the Corniche ☎086/236-5918 or 012 115-6875, ✉kingakhenaton@hotmail.com. Friendly staff, comfy en-suite a/c rooms with satellite TV, and a fine view of the Nile from its sixth-floor restaurant. Their breakfast is better than most. ❸

Armed Forces Across the bridge on the east bank ☎ & ℱ086/236-6283. Open to civilians, this palatial complex has spacious a/c rooms with TV, fridges and sun terraces; its enormous suites ($65) sleep four. Amenities include a pool, sauna, bowling and squash. ❺

Cleopatra Sharia Taha Hussein ☎086/237-0800, ℱ237-0901. A 20min walk from the centre, this high-rise hotel has a fabulously kitsch lobby, cosy a/c en-suite rooms and a bar on the seventh floor. ❸

Dahabiya Moored on the Nile ☎086/236-0096. A vintage houseboat owned by a Coptic evangelical organization, with four cabins with washbasins and heaters, sharing a bathroom with hot water. Recently refurbished, it's clean and atmospheric. ❶

Lotus 1 Sharia Bur Said ☎086/236-4500. In a quiet-ish part of town, ten minutes' walk from the centre. Decent a/c rooms with showers and TV, and a top-floor restaurant serving alcohol. ❷

Nefertiti Minia On the Corniche 1km north of the Governorate building ☎086/234-1515,

Eating, drinking and entertainment

If it's not too windy, you can enjoy the view of the Nile over a plate of grilled fish or chicken aboard the *Mermaid* outdoor restaurant, moored alongside the Corniche. Other **restaurants** with a view are on the top floors of the *Akhenaten* and *Lotus* hotels – though food is better at the restaurant in the *Armed Forces Hotel*. For cheaper eats, try *Al-Hayek Kushari* or the nameless kebab restaurant in the bazaar, where customers share a table. Failing that, there's a *KFC* on the Corniche 500m past the Governorate building, or *Nice Crep* (for sweet or savoury pancakes) near Sharia Bur Said. Ice cream and cakes are served at the *Kased Kari* patisserie on Midan al-Mahatta, and there's a 24-hour **bakery** just off Midan Tahrir.

Two hotel **bars** serve Egyptian beer, wine and spirits. The *Cleopatra*'s is popular with courting couples and even pious Muslims on account of its cheery decor and tasty food, unlike the deadbeat bar in the *Lotus*. For entertainment, pay £E6 to enter the manicured grounds of the *Armed Forces Hotel*, whose amenities include **bowling** (daily 9am–midnight; £E10 a game), **squash** (£E20), a **gym** (£E6/hr), a **sauna** and **Jacuzzi** (£E8 per person), a fair-sized **swimming** pool (£E3), a **cinema** (£E6), a children's playground and sun-loungers overlooking the river.

The Frazer Tombs and Tihna el-Jebel

Six kilometres north of Minya, a turning east onto a side road leads towards some cliffs, where fallen rocks as big as houses mark the start of a path to the **Frazer Tombs** (daily 9am–5pm; free). Named after their excavator, Gary Frazer, these V and VI Dynasty rock-cut tombs are reached by sunken passageways. The two that are open to visitors once belonged to two dignitaries both named Nika-Ankh. The first contains damaged statues of Nika-Ankh, his wife, their children and grandson, interspersed by hieroglyphs. The effigies in the second tomb are better preserved; note the finely carved pleats on the kilt of Nika-Ankh's statue.

Two kilometres further north, another spur road runs to the village of **TIHNA EL-JEBEL**, beside mounds of earth and the mud-brick **ruins** of the pharaonic town of Dehenet (Forehead), known to the Greeks as Acoris. A long stairway once flanked by altars and statues leads to a craggy massif with two unfinished **rock-cut temples** dedicated to Amun and Suchos (the Greek name for the crocodile-god Sobek). In the penultimate chamber of the first temple are two niches that originally held mummified crocodiles: if you carefully circumvent a deep shaft right outside, you can see a remaining croc in a chamber beyond the second temple. Further round the cliff-face, a chapel to the goddess Hathor is so high it seems unbelievable that it was ever used for offerings.

Deir al-Adhra: the Monastery of the Virgin

Beyond Tihna the main road hugs the base of the cliffs, where men cut limestone boulders into kerb-stones, and a flight of 166 steps ascends to the cliff-top village of **Gabel et-Teir**, nowadays also accessible by road. The village is renowned for its **Monastery of the Virgin** (Deir al-Adhra in Arabic), otherwise once known as the Monastery of the Pulley, after a hoist that was the only means of access before steps were cut into the cliff.

A simple nineteenth-century edifice encloses a **rock–hewn church**, reputedly founded in 328 AD by Helena, mother of the Byzantine emperor Constantine. Its sanctity derives from a tiny **cave** where the Holy Family is believed to have hidden for three days, that now contains an icon of the Virgin credited with miraculous powers. Similar tales surround an icon of St Damyanah and the Forty Virgins (see p.636) and a baptismal font carved into one of the church's Greco-Roman columns. Usually only visited by local villagers, the church receives thousands of pilgrims during the week-long **Feast of the Assumption**, forty days after the Coptic Easter: during the festival, minibuses run here directly from Minya.

The Church of Aba Hur, Zawiyet el-Sultan and Kom al-Ahmar

Four kilometres south of Minya, the road to Beni Hassan runs past the predominantly Coptic village of **AL-SAWADAH**, where a sign in English welcomes visitors to the **Church of Aba Hur**. You can't miss the modern church that stands in front of a tunnel leading to its subterranean rock-hewn namesake. A blacksmith's son who was born in 310 AD and originally named Baghoura, Aba Hur became a hermit at the age of 20 and took up residence in a disused Ptolemaic temple a year later; his faith under torture converted the Roman governor of Pelusium to Christianity. Should you arrive at prayer-time the saint's shrouded body can be seen behind the iconostasis, wreathed in incense smoke.

On July 6, hordes of pilgrims attend the **Moulid of Aba Hur**, camping out in the **cemetery** beyond Al-Sawadah. This vast cemetery, called **Zawiyet el-Sultan** (after the next village) or Zawiyet el-Mayyiteen, consists of thousands of domed mausolea in confessional enclaves, the Coptic ones topped by a forest of crosses. Local people can direct you to the **Hosh al-Basha** in the Muslim section, an austere edifice with an inlaid door, containing the tomb of **Hoda Shaarawi**, an early-twentieth-century feminist who campaigned for women's liberation and was the first woman to publicly remove her veil (in Cairo's Ramses station). Traditionally, locals visit their ancestral tombs during the Muslim months of Shawwal, Ragab and Zoul-Hagga, at the time of the full moon.

Beyond this the road passes **Kom al-Ahmar** (daily 9am–5pm; free), the site of ancient Hebenu, capital of the Oryx nome. The name Hebenu comes from the Ancient Egyptian word *hbn*, meaning to kill with a knife, and refers to the revenge of the god Horus on his father's murderer, Seth. The site's most interesting feature is a ruined III Dynasty **pyramid** whose symbolic tomb was never used as such, unlike another tomb dating from the New Kingdom, containing the defaced funerary statue of a local nomarch, Nefer-Skheru. The site was once crowned by a Greco-Roman temple reached by a flight of steps, to the right of which lies a chunk of masonry carved with the face of an unidentified Ptolemaic queen.

Beni Hassan, Speos Artemidos and Antinopolis

Some 20km south of Minya, barren cliffs on the east bank harbour the **rock tombs of Beni Hassan** (daily 8am–5pm; £E20), named after an Arab tribe that once settled hereabouts. The vivid murals in this necropolis shed light on the Middle Kingdom (2050–1800 BC), a period when provincial dignitaries

△ The entrance to a tomb at Beni Hassan

showed their greater independence by having grand burials locally, rather than at Saqqara. Beni Hassan is also memorable for the stark contrast between the fertile banks of the Nile and the desert. A path links the tombs to the isolated temple of **Speos Artemidos**, 3km away.

At present, the only way of visiting the tombs is by **private taxi** from Minya, escorted by a policeman or a guide from the tourist office (see p.288). A new road along the east bank enables cars to get there directly in 25 minutes. Alternatively, you can combine Beni Hassan with Tuna al-Gabel and Hermopolis in a longer excursion, travelling via Abu Qirkus on the west bank and taking a ferry across the Nile. In this case, the taxi will drop you at the ferry stage 3km from Abu Qirkus and wait for your return from Beni Hassan; the **ferry** (daily 8am–5pm) takes fifteen minutes and costs £E6 for up to six people, or 50pt each for more than six.

The ticket office at Beni Hassan is 300m from the landing stage, with a resthouse selling soft drinks. A guard will accompany you up the steps to the tombs and unlock them: a tip is expected at the end. As at all the sites in the Nile Valley, there is a heavy police presence.

The tombs of Beni Hassan

Most of Beni Hassan's 39 tombs are unfinished. The four shown to visitors evince a **stylistic evolution** during the XI–XII Dynasties, their variously shaped chambers representing a transitional stage between the lateral *mastaba* tombs of the Old Kingdom and the deep shafts in the Valley of the Kings, gradually acquiring porched vestibules and sunken corridors to heighten the impact of the funerary effigies at the back. The actual mummies were secreted at the bottom of shafts, accompanied by funerary texts derived from the royal burials of the Old Kingdom. Pharaonic iconography and contemporary reportage are blended in the **murals**, whose innovative wrestling scenes

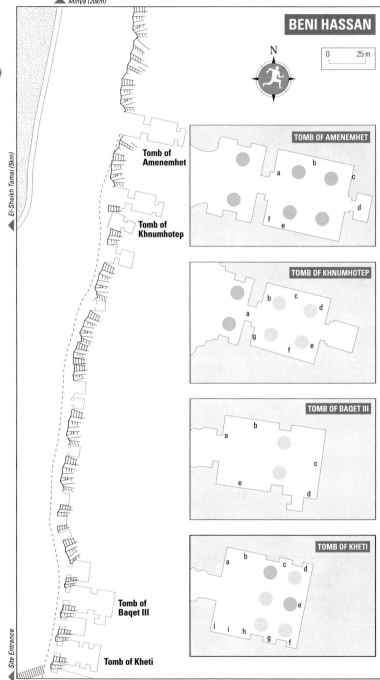

presaged the battle vistas of the New Kingdom. Though battered and faded in parts, their details reward careful study; the following descriptions are keyed to the tomb plans on p.292. To prevent further fading, **photography** is no longer allowed inside the tombs.

Tomb of Kheti (#17)

Of the many chambers hewn into the cliff-side, the first you'll come to is the **Tomb of Kheti**, which retains two of its papyrus-bud columns, painted in places – the colours are quite fresh. As in most tombs of Ancient Egyptian dignitaries, its images are arranged in "registers" (rows), whose height above floor level reflects their spatial relationship. Thus, Nile scenes go below those involving the Valley, above which come desert vistas, the highest ones most distant.

In the murals, hippopotami watch the papyrus harvest **[a]**, as desert creatures are hunted **[b]** above registers of weavers, dancers, artists and *senet* players (*senet* was a bit like draughts or checkers) observed by Kheti and his wife **[c]**, to whom minions bring offerings of gazelles and birds **[d]**.

The rear (east) wall features a compendium of wrestling positions **[e]**, thought to emphasize efforts to defend Egypt against invaders from the east; a now-vanished scene of warriors storming a fortress once explicitly made the point. Don't miss the man standing on his head and in other yoga positions, near the scenes of wine-making **[f]** and herding cattle **[h]**. Ploughing **[i]** is another task overseen by Kheti in his role as nomarch, attended by his dwarf and fan-bearers **[g]**. Notice Kheti's boats, and bulls locking horns, in the corner **[j]**.

Tomb of Baqet III (#15)

Kheti inherited the governorship of the Oryx nome from his father, buried in the **Tomb of Baqet III**. Its imagery is similar to that in Kheti's tomb, with some scenes better preserved, others not. While the mural of papyrus-gathering in the marshes **[a]** is quite faded, the desert hunt **[b]** is rich in details: notice the copulating gazelles near the left-hand corner. Ball players, women spinning and fullers beating cloth appear below. Nearly two hundred wrestling positions are shown on the rear wall **[c]**, with a lovely pair of birds above the funerary niche **[d]**. The south wall **[e]** is covered with episodes from the life of this XI Dynasty nomarch. In the second register from the top, his underlings count cattle and beat tax defaulters with sticks.

Tomb of Khnumhotep (#3)

Columned porticos and a niche for statues (which replaced the Old Kingdom *serdab* or secret chamber) are hallmarks of the XII Dynasty tombs, 150m north. The **Tomb of Khnumhotep** is framed by proto-Doric columns and hieroglyphs praising this nomarch, who was also governor of the Eastern Desert. His funeral cortege appears inside the entrance **[a]**. Servants weigh grain and scribes record its storage in granaries **[b]**, while beneath the desert hunt **[c]**, Semitic Amus from Syria in striped tunics pay their respects, their alien costumes, flocks and tribute all minutely detailed – the governor is shown accepting eye paint.

In the niche, images of Khnumhotep's children are visible on the walls but only the plinth of his statue remains. Elsewhere are vivid scenes of Khnumhotep netting birds, hunting with a throwing stick **[d]**, and spearing fish from a punt in the marshes **[e]**. After the usual offerings **[f]**, he inspects boat-building timber from a litter and then sails to Abydos **[g]**. Higher and lower registers portray bare-breasted laundrywomen, weavers and other artisans. The hieroglyphic text beneath these scenes has yielded clues about the political relationship between the nomarchs and pharaohs of the XII Dynasty.

Tomb of Amenemhet (#2)

The **Tomb of Amenemhet** belongs to Khnumhotep's predecessor, whose campaign honours are listed beside the door near a text relating the death of Senusert I. Proto-Doric columns uphold a vaulted ceiling painted with checkered reed-mat patterns. A mural **[a]** of armourers, leatherworkers (at the top) and weavers (below) precedes the customary hunting scene **[b]**, beneath which Amenemhet collects tribute from his estates. Note the scribes berating defaulters on the second register from the bottom. Below the wrestling and siege tableaux, boats escort him towards Abydos **[c]**. The niche **[d]** contains mutilated effigies of Amenemhet, his mother and his wife Heptet, who sits at her own table to receive offerings **[e]**. Fish are netted and spit-roasted above a painted false door flanked by scenes of music making, cattle fording and baking **[f]**.

Speos Artemidos

The cliffside path at Beni Hassan affords a fine view of the Nile and the abrupt transition from cultivation to desert. If the police let you, follow it for 2.5km past the Tomb of Kheti and turn 500m up a wadi to find the small rock-hewn **temple of Speos Artemidos**. Begun by Queen Hatshepsut, whose claims to have restored order after Hyksos misrule are inscribed above its door (to be usurped by Seti I, who slapped his cartouche on top, thereby crediting the deed to himself), the temple has only roughed-out Hathor-headed columns, and its sanctuary – dominated by a statue of the lion-goddess Pakht – is largely unfinished. However, scenes of Hatshepsut making offerings to the gods have been executed in the hall. Just before the site there's a small **grotto** (*speos*), whence comes the temple's Greek name. Further into the desert are early Christian **hermit cells**, after whom the wadi was called the Valley of the Anchorites.

Antinopolis

The ancient city of **Antinopolis**, 10km south of Beni Hassan, deserves a mention for its origins alone. Touring Egypt with his lover Antinous in 130 AD, the Roman emperor Hadrian was warned by an oracle to expect a grievous loss, whereupon Antinous drowned himself in the Nile to prevent a greater calamity befalling his master. In grief, Hadrian deified the youth and founded a city in his honour before continuing south to Thebes with his unloved wife Plotina. Today, little remains but some fine red-granite columns; most of the **ruins** were used to build the neighbouring village of Sheikh Abadah, or turned into cement in the nineteenth century.

Hermopolis and Tuna al-Gabel

Across the river on the west bank are two further sites whose remains are less dramatic than their mythical associations. According to one tradition, Creation began on a primordial mound near **Hermopolis**, where two giant stone baboons recall the long-vanished Temple of Thoth. More impressive is the city's necropolis, **Tuna al-Gabel**, where thousands of sacred baboons and ibises were buried in catacombs in the desert.

Due to travel restrictions, both sites are only accessible **by private taxi**, escorted by a policeman or tour guide. Reckon on six or seven hours to see either Beni Hassan or Tell el-Armana, in conjunction with Tuna al-Gabel and Hermopolis – it's not feasible to do them all in a single day excursion.

The ruins of Hermopolis

The pulverized ruins of Hermopolis spread beyond the village of **ASHMUNEIN**, 8km from Mallawi. Turning right off the village's main street you'll come to an

Thoth and the Hermopolitan Ogdoad

In Egyptian mythology, **Thoth** was the divine scribe and reckoner of time, the inventor of writing and the patron god of scribes. His cult probably originated in the Delta, but achieved the greatest following in Middle Egypt; later, by association with Khonsu, he acquired the attributes of the moon-god and mastery over science and knowledge. Though usually depicted with a man's body and the head of an ibis (his sacred bird), Thoth also assumed the form of a great white baboon, invariably endowed with an outsize penis. Baboons habitually shriek just before dawn, and the Egyptians believed that a pair of them uttered the first greetings to the sun from the sand dunes at the edge of the world.

▲ Thoth

Thoth's role is rather more complex in relation to the Hermopolitan cosmogony, which ordained that the chaos preceding the world's creation had four characteristics, each identified with a pair of gods and goddesses: primordial water (Nun/Nanuet), infinite space (Heh/Hehet), darkness (Kek/Keket) and invisibility (Amun/Amunet). From this chaos arose the primeval mound and the cosmic egg whence the sun-god was hatched and proceeded to organize the world. While stressing the role of this **Hermopolitan Ogdoad** (company of eight), Thoth's devotees credited him with laying the cosmic egg in the guise of the "Great Cackler", so it's difficult to know who got star billing in this Creation myth. By the New Kingdom it had generally succumbed to the version espoused at Heliopolis (see p.200), but Thoth's cult continued into Ptolemaic times.

outdoor **museum** (free) of antique stone-carvings, fronted by two **giant sandstone baboons** that once sported erect phalluses (hacked off by early Christians) and upheld the ceiling of the Temple of Thoth. Built by Ramses II using masonry from Tell el-Amarna, the temple stood within an enclosure covering 640 square metres, the spiritual heart of the city of the moon-god.

Hermopolis was a cult centre from early Dynastic times, venerated as the site of the primeval mound where the sun-god emerged from a cosmic egg. Like Heliopolis (which made similar claims) its priesthood evolved an elaborate cosmogony, known as the Hermopolitan Ogdoad (see box above). Though Ancient Egyptians called the city Khmunu, history remembers it as **Hermopolis Magna**; its Ptolemaic title reflects the Greek association of Thoth with their own god Hermes. However, none of the mounds of rubble that remain seem credible as the site of Creation, and there's little to see except 24 slender granite **columns** further south, which were re-erected by archeologists who mistook the ruins for a Greek *agora*. The columns previously supported a fifth-century Coptic basilica, but originally belonged to a Ptolemaic temple.

Tuna al-Gabel

From Ashmunein, a surfaced road continues to the village of **TUNA AL-GABEL**, which takes its name from the ancient **necropolis** (daily 8am–5pm; £E20) 5km further on into the desert. Along the way, notice the **boundary stele** on a distant cliff, marking the edge of the agricultural land that was claimed by Tell el-Amarna, across the river (see p.297). The name "Tuna" may derive from the Ancient Egyptian *ta-wnt* (the hare) or *ta-hnt* (a place where many ibis birds gather). For millennia it was a cult-centre where pilgrims gave homage to Thoth by paying the priests to embalm ibises – over two million were sacrificed, mostly bred for the chop. Today this necropolis is awash with sand, wind-rippled drifts casting its angular mausolea into high relief, but obscuring other features.

Past the resthouse at the entrance (which sells drinks and has smart toilets), a path to the right leads to the **catacombs**, which some believe stretch as far as Hermopolis. The accessible portion consists of rough-hewn corridors with blocked-off side passages, where the mummified baboons, which were sacred to Thoth, and ibises were stacked (a few bandages remain). A shrine near the ladder contains a baboon fetish and a pathetic-looking mummy. You can also see the limestone sarcophagus of a high priest of mummification.

Further along the main track are several mausolea excavated by Gustav Lefebvre in 1920. The finest is the **Tomb of Petosiris**, High Priest of Thoth (whose coffin is in the Cairo Antiquities Museum), dating from 350 BC. Its vestibule walls depict traditional activities such as brick-making, sewing and reaping (left), milking, husbandry and wine-making (right) – with all the figures wearing Greek costume. Inside the tomb are colourful scenes from the *Book of Gates* and the *Book of the Dead*. The most vivid scene (on the right-hand wall near the back) shows nine baboons, twelve women and a dozen cobras, each set representing a temporal cycle. Notice the Nubians at the bottom of the opposite wall.

Another mausoleum contains the **Mummy of Isadora**, a young woman from Antinopolis who drowned in the Nile around 120 BC. Victims of the life-giving river acquired posthumous sanctity, but due to slapdash mummification and an infestation of termites her mummy is no longer fit to show.

In the desert off to the right you'll spot some columns from the Temple of Thoth that once dominated the site. You can also see the brick superstructure of a **well** that used to supply the necropolis and its sacred aviary with fresh water, drawn up from 70m below the desert by a huge **waterwheel** which still exists, though it no longer works. A spiral staircase gives access to the well-head.

Mallawi

MALLAWI has gone to the dogs ever since Minya supplanted it as the regional capital in the 1960s. Many streets are still unpaved, and hovels are more prevalent than villas. To Egyptians, it is best known as the birthplace of President Sadat's assassin, Khalid al-Islambouli, and his brother Shawky, who fought with the Afghan *mujahadin* and later formed his own terrorist group in Egypt. Mallawi bore the brunt of the state's counter-insurgency campaign in the mid-1990s, which crippled its economy. Needless to say, the local police want foreigners to pass through as quickly as possible, but will tolerate a visit to the small **museum** on Sharia Banque Misr (daily except Wed 9am–4pm; £E6), exhibiting artefacts from Hermopolis and Tuna al-Gabel, and maybe a quick look at the derelict Hindu-Gothic-style **feudal palace** on a parallel street a few blocks away.

Mallawi's terminals are dispersed on either side of the Ibrahimiya Canal that runs through the middle of town. On the east bank are the **train station** and, further south, the depot for **service taxis** to all points south of Mallawi. North-bound taxis leave from a depot 200m north of the canal bridge. On the other side of this is the main drag, Sharia Essim, along which buses and service taxis shuttle between Minya and Assyut. Across the road from the station on Sharia Bank Misr (aka Sharia Gala'a) is a **restaurant** serving *kofta* and a Banque Misr. To reach the **post office** (daily except Fri 8.30am–2pm), follow the dirt road to the left of the bank and turn left after 100m.

Tell el-Amarna

TELL EL-AMARNA is the familiar name for the site where **Pharaoh Akhenaten** and **Queen Nefertiti** founded a city dedicated to a revolutionary idea of God, which later rulers assailed as heretical. During their brief reign, Egyptian art cast off its preoccupation with death and the afterlife to revel in human concerns; bellicose imperialism gave way to pacifistic retrenchment; and the old gods were toppled from their pedestals. The interplay between personalities, beliefs and art anticipates the Renaissance – and their story beats Shakespeare for sheer drama.

The remains of Akhenaten's city lie on the east bank of the Nile, 12km from Mallawi and roughly halfway between Minya and Assyut, and spread across a desert plain girdled by an arc of cliffs. Away from the palm groves beside the Nile, the site is utterly desolate, a tawny expanse of low mounds and narrow trenches littered with potshards. These fragments of pale terracotta, cream and duck-egg blue-glazed pottery seem more tangible links to the city's past than its vestigial remains. Because the city was created from scratch and deserted soon after Tut moved the court back to Thebes, its era of glory lasted only twelve years, and much of the building was never completed, so don't expect to find imposing ruins or statues, as everything of value has been removed to museums. Only the faintest outline of the city is discernible, while the reliefs in its rock-cut tombs have been badly mutilated (initially by reactionaries, who defaced the images of Akhenaten and his deity). However, over a century of archeological research has identified the city's salient features, assisted by pictures found in contemporary tombs. The site strikes some visitors as intensely evocative: a place of mystery whose enchantment grows the more you know about it.

The story of Akhenaten and Nefertiti

Few figures from ancient history have inspired as much conjecture as Akhenaten and Nefertiti, as scholars dispute even fundamental aspects of their story – let alone the interpretation of the events. The tale begins with Pharaoh **Amenophis III**, who flouted convention by making Tiy, his Nubian concubine, Great Wife, despite her lack of royal blood. **Queen Tiy** remained formidable long after Amenophis entered his dotage and their eldest son ascended the throne as **Amenophis IV**. Some believe this event followed his father's death, others that mother and son ruled jointly for twelve years. To square the former theory with the period of his reign (*c.*1379–1362 BC) and his demise around the age of 30 would mean accepting that Amenophis Jr embarked on his religious reformation between the ages of 9 and 13, though a marriage at 13 is quite likely.

The origins of Amenophis's wife, **Nefertiti**, are obscure. Her name – meaning "A Beautiful Woman Has Come" – suits the romantic legend that she was a Mesopotamian princess originally betrothed to Amenophis III. However, others identify her as Amenophis III's child by a secondary wife, or as the daughter of his vizier **Ay**, whose wife, **Tey**, was almost certainly Nefertiti's wet nurse. The pharaonic custom of sister–brother and father–daughter marriages allows plenty of scope for speculation, but the fair-skinned bust of Nefertiti in the Berlin Museum suggests that she wasn't Tiy's child, at any rate. (Amid all the fuss about Cleopatra being black, nobody seems to have noticed that Queen Tiy – and therefore her son, Amenophis IV – were indubitably so.)

Early in his reign, Amenophis IV began to espouse the **worship of Aten** (see p.298), whose ascendancy threatened the priesthoods of other cults. The bureaucracy was equally alarmed by his decree that the spoken language

Aten-worship and Amarna art

Many scholars herald **Aten-worship** as a breakthrough in human spirituality and cultural evolution: the world's first monotheistic religion, thus representing "a peak of clarity which rose above the lowlands of superstition". Aten was originally just an aspect of the sun-god (the "Globe" or "Disc" of the midday sun), ranking low in the Theban pantheon until Amenophis III privately adopted it as a personal deity. Then Akhenaten publicly exalted Aten above other gods, subsuming all their attributes into this newly omnipotent being. Invocations to Maat (representing truth) were retained, but otherwise the whole cast of underworld and celestial deities was jettisoned. Morbid Osirian rites were also replaced by paeans to life in the joyous warmth of Aten's rays (which are usually shown ending in a hand clasping an ankh), as in this extract from the famous *Hymn to Aten*:

When you rise from the horizon the earth grows bright; you shine as the Aten in the sky and drive away the darkness; when your rays gleam forth, the whole of Egypt is festive. People wake and stand on their feet, for you have lifted them up … Then the whole of the land does its work; all the cattle enjoy their pastures, trees and plants grow green, birds fly up from their nests and raise their wings in praise of your spirit. Goats frisk on their feet and all the fluttering and flying things come alive.

Similarities between the *Hymn* and *The Song of Solomon* (supposedly written 500 years later) have encouraged speculation about the influence of Atenism on early Jewish monotheism. In *Moses and Monotheism*, Freud argued that Moses was an Egyptian nobleman and the Biblical Exodus a "pious fiction which a remote tradition has reworked in the service of its own biases". Conversely, a book by Ahmed Osman advances the theory that Akhenaten's deity derived from tales of the Jewish God

▲ Nefertiti and Akhenaten

related to him by his maternal grandfather Yuya, the Joseph of the Old Testament (see p.809).

Equally intriguing is the artwork of the Amarna period and the questions it raises about Akhenaten. **Amarna art** focused on nature and human life rather than the netherworld and resurrection. Royal portraiture, previously impersonally formalized, was suffused by naturalism (a process which began late in the reign of Amenophis III, as evinced by the stele depicting the obese king listlessly slumped beside Tiy). While marshes and wildlife remained a popular subject, these scenes no longer implicitly associated birds and fish with the forces of chaos. The roofless Aten temples made new demands on sculptors and painters, who mixed sunk- and bas-relief carving to highlight features with shifting shadows and illumination.

Most striking is the rendering of **human figures**, especially Akhenaten's, whose attenuated cranium, curvaceous spine and belly, and matronly pelvis and buttocks (evident on the colossi in the Cairo Museum) have prompted speculation that the pharaoh may have suffered from Marfan's syndrome – a rare genetic disorder that leads to feelings of alienation and a slight oddness in physical appearance – or was possibly a hermaphrodite. Some argue that the Amarna style was essentially an acquiescence to Akhenaten's physiognomy, others that such distortions were simply a device that could be eschewed, as in the exquisite bust of Nefertiti. Advocates of the "Akhenaten was sick" theory point out that this was the only time when vomiting was ever represented in Egyptian art; however, Amarna art also uniquely depicted royalty eating, yet nobody asserts that other pharaohs never ate.

should be used in official documents, contrary to all tradition. To escape their influence and realize his vision of a city dedicated to Aten, the pharaoh founded a **new capital** upon an empty plain beside the Nile, halfway between Memphis and Thebes, which he named **Akhetaten**, the "Horizon of the Aten". It was here that the royal couple settled in the fifth year of their reign and took Aten's name in honour of their faith. He discarded Amenophis IV for **Akhenaten** (Servant of the Aten) and vowed never to leave the city, while she took a forename meaning "Beautiful are the Beauties of the Aten", styling herself **Nefernefruaten–Nefertiti**. Her status surpassed that of any previous Great Wife, approaching that of Akhenaten himself. Bas-reliefs and stelae show her participating in state festivals, and her own cartouche was coupled with Aten's – an unprecedented association. Tableaux from this period depict an idyllic royal family life, with the couple embracing their daughters and banqueting with Queen Tiy. Yet some believe that Tiy tried to persuade Akhenaten to return to Thebes and Amun-worship, and took against Nefertiti because of her fervent Atenism.

There's no sign that their happiness was marred by his decision to take a second wife, **Kiya**, for dynastic ends; nor of the degenerative condition that supposedly afflicted Akhenaten in later life. However, the great ceremony held at Akhetaten in their twelfth regnal year marked a turning point. Whether or not this was Akhenaten's true coronation (following his father's death), he subsequently launched a **purge against the old cults**. From Kom Ombo to Bubastis, the old temples were closed and their statues disfigured, causing widespread internal unrest. Although this was quelled by Akhenaten's chief of police, **Mahu**, his foreign minister apparently ignored pleas from foreign vassals menaced by the Hittites and Habiru, and the army was less than zealous in defending Egypt's frontiers. Akhenaten was consequently blamed for squandering the territorial gains of his forefathers.

What happened in the last years of Akhenaten and Nefertiti's reign is subject to various interpretations. The consensus is that Nefertiti and Akhenaten became estranged, and he took as co-regent **Smenkhkare**, a mysterious youth married to their eldest daughter, **Meritaten**. While Nefertiti withdrew to her Northern Palace, Akhenaten and his regent lived together at the other end of the city; the poses struck by them in mural scenes of the period have prompted suggestions of a homosexual relationship. Whatever the truth of this, it's known that Smenkhkare ruled alone for some time after the **death of Akhenaten** (c.1362 BC), before dying himself. Nefertiti's fate is less certain, but it's generally believed that she also died around the same time. To date, none of their mummies have been found (or, rather, definitely identified).

In the 1970s, a novel solution to the puzzle of Smenkhkare's identity and the **fate of Nefertiti** was advanced by Julia Samson of the Petrie Museum in London. Samson argued that Smenkhkare *was* Nefertiti, who, far from being spurned by Akhenaten, finally achieved pharaonic status, adopting Smenkhkare as her "throne name". Since the faces on the stelae depicting Akhenaten and his co-regent have been obliterated, only their cartouches identify them; and previous hypotheses have never satisfactorily explained why Smenkhkare's should be coupled with "Nefernefruaten", Nefertiti's Aten-name. Conversely, the youth shown with a princess isn't identified as her husband, nor by name, but he does wear the royal *uraeus*, or cobra. Unfortunately, this figure looks too old to be the famous boy-king who succeeded Smenkhkare at the age of 9 – known to posterity as **Tutankhamun**.

Tut's own genealogy is obscure (some hold that his parents were Amenophis III and his half-sister Sitamun; others favour Ay and Tey, or Akhenaten and Kiya), but it's certain that he was originally raised to worship Aten, and named Tutankh*aten*. By renouncing this name for one honouring Amun, he heralded a return to Thebes and the old gods, fronting a **Theban counter-revolution** executed by Vizier Ay and General Horemheb. Some think this was relatively benign while Tut and his successor Ay ruled Egypt, blaming **Horemheb** and Seti I for a later, ruthless extirpation of Atenism. Certainly, in time-honoured tradition, Seti plundered the abandoned city of Akhetaten for masonry to build new temples, ordered its site cursed by priests to deter reoccupation, and excised the cartouches of every ruler tainted with the "Amarna heresy" from their monuments and the List of Kings. So thorough was this cover-up that Akhenaten and Nefertiti remained unknown to history until the nineteenth century.

The site

While tour groups are now visiting Tell el-Amarna, independent travellers are still rare and presently only allowed access **by private taxi** from Minya or Assyut, accompanied by a police escort or tour guide. The east bank road from Minya peters out 15km beyond Beni Hassan (see p.290), so access to Tell el-Amarna is via the west bank, using a car ferry 9km from Mallawi. To visit both sites on the same day, you must double back to Minya, or use another car ferry between El-Sheikh Tamai (4–5km south of Beni Hassan) and the west bank,

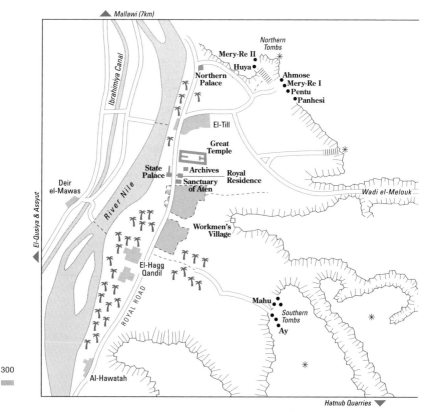

before proceeding to Mallawi to cross back over to the eastern side. Mallawi's landing stage has a choice of craft: a car ferry (£E16 per vehicle with passengers; retain the ticket for the return journey); a green motor-launch (£E6 for up to six people, or 50pt each for more than six); and an occasional blue tourist boat – all landing at **El-Till**, on the east bank. Here a kiosk sells **tickets** for the site (daily 8am–5pm; £E1), and there's a **car with a driver** (£E50) for anyone arriving without their own vehicle. The tourist police will assign a cop to ride with you to the main ticket office near the Northern Tombs, and a custodian to ride with you to the Royal Tomb if you wish to visit it. The main office sells separate **tickets** for the Northern and Southern Tombs (£E20) and the Royal Tomb (£E20).

The City

The dirt track running south from El-Till follows the old **Royal Road** that formed ancient Akhetaten's main axis, and is known locally as the Sikket es-Sultan, the Road of the Sultan. Alongside is a Muslim cemetery, which overlies part of a rectangle stretching eastwards towards the ridge. This was once the **Great Temple of Aten**, whose northern wall incorporated the Hall of Foreign Tribute where emissaries proffered treasure (as depicted in tombs). Unlike traditional temples, which got darker as one approached the sanctuary, Aten's was roofless, admitting the rays of its namesake. It's thought that Horemheb ordered the temple's destruction after Akhenaten's death, and Ramses II quarried its

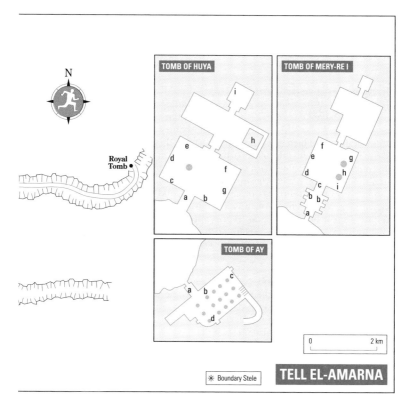

foundations for his temples at Hermopolis, across the Nile. Today, replicas of a complete and a partial lotus-bundle **column** (erected by Barry Kemp of the Tell el-Amarna Project, who has been working here for decades) tower incongruously above the low walls.

Further south (and hard to distinguish beneath shifting sands) are the remnants of the Foreign Office **Archives**, where the **Amarna Letters** were discovered. Written in the Akkadian script used for diplomatic correspondence with Asiatic states, these clay tablets have revealed much about the period. Over 360 letters have been found, but more were undoubtedly lost, leaving an incomplete puzzle for archeologists to piece together and argue over.

Next come three excavated rectangles that were once the **Royal Residence**. Their private apartments were separated from the stately reception halls that ran through the centre of the huge palace compound. When Flinders Petrie excavated Nefertiti's suite, he found wall tiles decorated with fruit and flowers, and a painted floor depicting fish, birds and insects (later smashed by a farmer who resented tourists walking across his fields). Across the Royal Road stood an even larger **State Palace**, with a dock for the royal barge. Both palaces were connected by a covered "flyover" spanning the road (part of one pylon remains), into which was set the **Window of Appearances**, whence Nefertiti and Akhenaten showered favoured courtiers with gold collars and other rewards.

To the south of their residence lay the **Sanctuary of Aten**, probably used for private worship by the royal family, and the home of the High Priest, Panehsi. Beyond spread the city's **residential quarters**: the richest homes beside the road, the poorest hovels backing onto desert. Also in this quarter was the workshop of the sculptor Tuthmosis, where the famous bust of Nefertiti was uncovered in 1912, before being smuggled to Berlin's Ägyptisches Museum.

Outlying palaces and stelae

The best-preserved outline of an Amarna building is Nefertiti's **Northern Palace** or summer residence, 1500m from El-Till. Low walls and hollows delineate rooms and courtyards grouped around a garden which once contained a pool that cooled the palace by evaporation. Like all Amarna residences, it was divided into public and private quarters, with north-facing doors to catch the prevailing wind. Rooms were plastered and painted, lit by oil lamps hung from pegs or set in niches, and warmed by braziers over winter. Fitted toilets and bathrooms also featured in the homes of the well-to-do. A magnificent painted floor depicting wildfowl and fish was found here, and is now in the Egyptian Antiquities Museum in Cairo. Unlike traditional marsh

▲ Akhenaten

scenes, Amarna tableaux rarely feature hunting, suggesting that Akhenaten abjured the sport of kings.

In summer, Akhenaten and Nefertiti would ride in their electrum-plated chariot to the other end of the Royal Road, where another palace called Maru-Aten stood near the modern-day hamlet of Al-Hawatah. Alongside this **Southern Palace** lay a pleasure lake surrounded by trees and shrubs, which fed smaller pools within the palace. The walls of its columned hall were painted with flowers and inlaid with figures and Aten symbols. It was here that Petrie found hundreds of glazed pieces and flakes of paint adhering to blocks that bore Meritaten's cartouche superimposed over another, assumed to be that of Nefertiti – the rather shaky basis upon which archeologists devised the theory of Nefertiti's rejection in favour of Smenkhkare. In 1974, however, John Harris re-examined the fragments and concluded that the hidden cartouches really belonged to Kiya, whose existence had been unknown to earlier scholars. From this point on, Samson developed her theory that Nefertiti and Smenkhkare were one and the same.

Akhetaten's periphery was defined by **boundary stelae** carved high up on the cliffs, erected over successive years; their inscriptions and family portraits have enabled archeologists to deduce many events during Akhenaten's reign. Fine alabaster for the temples and public buildings was dragged from the **Hatnub Quarries**, 10km southeast of the city (only accessible by donkey or 4WD car). On the way up the wadi are the remains of workmen's huts and pottery from diverse periods.

The Northern Tombs

Some visitors are content to see just the **Northern Tombs**, 4km from El-Till. Bring a **torch** to spotlight uneven floors and to study the reliefs and paintings (now less clear than the copies made by Norman de Garis Davies in the 1900s). Tombs #1 and #2 lack electric lighting and are only shown to visitors who insist. **Photography** is not allowed in any of the tombs.

Tomb of Huya (#1)

As Steward to Queen Tiy and Superintendent of the Royal Harem, **Huya** is shown praying at the entrance, with the text of the *Hymn to Aten* alongside **[a]**. In the following banqueting scene **[b]**, involving Tiy, the royal couple and two princesses, it may be significant that the dowager queen is merely drinking (which was acceptable by Theban standards of decorum), whereas the Amarna brood tuck in with gusto (an act never hitherto portrayed of royalty). Across the way they imbibe wine, *sans* princesses **[c]**, and then make a royal procession to the Hall of Tribute, where emissaries from Kush and Syria await Akhenaten and Nefertiti **[d]**.

On the rear wall, Akhenaten decorates Huya from the Window of Appearances (notice the sculptor's studio, lower down **[e]**), who displays his awards **[f]** on the other side of the portal, the lintel of which portrays three generations of the royal family, including Amenophis III. Along the east wall, Akhenaten leads Tiy to the temple built for his parents **[g]**. Huya's mummy was stashed in a burial shaft **[h]** below the transverse hall, beyond which is a shrine painted with offerings, containing an unfinished statue of Huya **[i]**.

Tomb of Mery-Re II (#2)

The last resting place of **Mery-Re II**, Overseer of the Two Treasuries, is similar in shape to Huya's tomb, but was constructed late in Akhenaten's reign, since his cartouches have been replaced by Smenkhkare's, and Nefertiti's by Meritaten's. Beyond the entrance (whose adoration scene and *Hymn to Aten* are largely destroyed), the inner walls portray Nefertiti straining a drink for the king, who is seated beneath a sunshade (to the left); and Mery-Re receiving a golden crown, followed by a warm welcome from his household (right). The rear wall bears an unfinished scene of Mery-Re being rewarded by Smenkhkare and Meritaten, drawn in black ink.

Tomb of Ahmose (#3)

This battered tomb is one of the four that visitors usually see. The entrance walls show **Ahmose**, Akhenaten's fan-bearer, praying to Aten, with a now-illegible inscription enjoining the deity to ensure "that there is sand on the shore, that fishes in the stream have scales, and cattle have hair. Let him sojourn here until the swan turns black and the raven white". Inside, you can just discern Ahmose carrying an axe and a fan, his official regalia. On the left-hand wall are bas-reliefs of shield-bearers and pikemen, crouched and moving, followed by an outsized horse and chariot outlined in red pigment (presumably intended to represent Akhenaten leading his army into battle, which never happened). In the transverse hall are two false doors, a deep vertical shaft, and a defaced, life-size statue of Ahmose in a niche.

Tomb of Mery-Re I (#4)

High Priest **Mery-Re I** (father of Mery-Re II) rated a superior tomb, with a coloured cornice around its entrance **[a]** and false columns of painted flowers at the rear of the vestibule **[b]**. Reliefs of Mery-Re and his wife, Tenro, at prayer flank the portal **[c]** into the main chamber, which retains two of its original papyrus-bud columns. Proceeding clockwise round the room, you see Mery-Re's investiture with a golden collar **[d]**, the royal family leaving the palace **[e]**, and Akhenaten in a chariot (his face and the Aten symbol have been chiselled out, as usual). Scenes of offerings **[f]** and Aten-worship **[g]** flank the left side of doorway into the unfinished rear chamber, which lacks any decoration. More interesting is the eastern wall **[h]**, depicting Akhenaten and the Great Temple (which has helped archeologists visualize the city's appearance). Notice the sensitive relief of blind beggars awaiting alms, low down in the corner **[i]**.

Tombs of Pentu (#5) and Panehsi (#6)

The third tomb in this cluster belongs to **Pentu**, the royal physician. Its papyrus-bundle columns retain traces of paint with chariots visible on the right-hand wall, but there's little else to see. It's better to head 300m south along the cliff path to the isolated tomb of **Panehsi**, overseer of the royal herds and granaries. Unlike most of the others, its decorative facade has remained intact, but the interior has been modified by Copts who used it as a chapel. To the left of the entrance, the royal family prays above their servants. The painted, apse-like recess in the main chamber is probably a Coptic addition – notice the angel's wings. In one corner of the inner chamber, steps spiral down into an underground sarcophagus chamber containing broken urns. Lower down the cliff are strata of rubble and potshards – vestiges of a medieval Coptic village.

The Royal Tomb

It's an easy ten-minute drive to the subterranean **Royal Tomb**, in a desolate ravine 5.5km from the plain. A custodian will ride with you to unlock the tomb and fire up the generator to provide lighting. The tomb, dug into the bed of the wadi (which now has drainage canals to carry flash floods away), was the first from the XVIII Dynasty to run directly from a corridor to a burial chamber. Its burial scene and text were virtually obliterated by Amun's priests, and no mummies were ever found there, but in a chamber off the first descending passage, fragmentary bas-reliefs (now being clumsily "restored") depict the funerary rites of one of the royal daughters (either Meketaten or Ankesbaten), and a granite sarcophagus bearing Tiy's cartouche was found, suggesting this might have been a family vault. No one knows whether Akhenaten and Nefertiti were interred in the main burial chamber beyond a deep pit (and perhaps dragged out to rot a few years later) or in the Valley of the Kings. Some believe that the mysterious mummy found in tomb KV55 is Akhenaten's (see p.394), or that Nefertiti's has been discovered in tomb KV35 (see p.391).

The Southern Tombs

From El-Hagg Qandil beyond the ancient Workmen's Village, a poorly surfaced road runs between palm-groves to the **Southern Tombs**, scattered over seven low hills in two clusters: #7–15 and #16–25. Amarna notables buried here include Tutu, the foreign minister, and Ramose, Steward of Amenophis III, but the ones to see are Ay and Mahu.

Tomb of Ay (#25)

Ay's Tomb was never finished, since he built himself a new one at Thebes after the court returned there under Tutankhamun, but such carvings as were executed show the Amarna style at its apogee and the ceiling of its central aisle is painted with a fetching checkerboard pattern.

Both sides of the tomb's vestibule **[a]** are decorated. On the left, the king and queen, three princesses, Nefertiti's sister Mutnedjmet and her dwarves lead the court in the worship of Aten. Across the way is a superb relief of Ay and his wife Tey rendering homage and the most complete text of the *Hymn to Aten*; every fold of their skirts and braid in their hair are meticulously depicted. The really intriguing scenes, however, are in the main chamber. On the left side of the entrance wall, Ay and Tey are showered with decorations from the Window of Appearances, acclaimed by fan-bearers, scribes and guards **[b]**. Palace life is depicted in ink or sunk-relief: a concubine has her hair done, while girls play the harp, dance, cook and sweep. The depth of bowing by courtiers is the most servile ever found in Egyptian art **[c]**. Along the rear wall are a ruined door-shaped stele **[d]** and a stairway leading to an unfinished burial shaft.

Ay and Tey are mysterious figures, honoured as "Divine Father and Mother", but never directly identified as being royal. Some reckon Ay was a son of Yuya and Thuya, Akhenaten's maternal grandparents; others that Tey was Nefertiti's wet nurse, or that both conceived Tutankhamun. Certainly, Ay was vizier to Amenophis III, Akhenaten and Tutankhamun, and reigned briefly himself (1352–1348 BC). He was ultimately buried in the Western Valley of the Theban Necropolis (see p.394).

Tomb of Mahu (#9)

Ten minutes' walk away, the **Tomb of Mahu**, Akhenaten's chief of police and frontier security, opens with a rough-cut transverse hall featuring a scene of Mahu standing before the vizier with two intruders, whom he accuses of being "agitated by some foreign power", as minions heat irons in a brazier for their torture (to the left as you enter). Further in are two more chambers at different levels, linked by a winding stairway – mind your head on the low ceiling.

Assyut and around

ASSYUT (pronounced "As-*yoot*") was the first part of Middle Egypt to become a no-go zone for tourists in the 1990s, as local Islamic militants targeted foreigners as well as the security forces in their war against the state. The city endured nearly a decade of curfews and arrests as the conflict spread south before fizzling out, leaving Assyut with an overwhelming police presence and the mother of bad reputations. So it's not surprising that citizens – and the Christian population especially – rejoiced at **apparitions** of the Virgin Mary that occurred (so people swear) in 2000 and 2005, in the form of a light above two churches. Another cause for optimism is the upturn in

Assyut's militant tradition

In the late 1970s, **Assyut University** became a stronghold of **Gama'at Islamiya**, bent on turning Egypt into an Islamic republic. They got music and co-ed drama banned, and cafeterias segregated by sex; violations were punished by club-wielding militants. The authorities turned a blind eye until 1981, when Sadat cracked down on religious extremism after years of tolerating it as a counterweight to the Left. In response, members of the secret group **Al-Jihad** assassinated Sadat in Cairo and stormed Assyut police HQ the following day, hoping to launch a revolution. Two days of rioting ensued, causing 55 deaths.

Among those later indicted at the "Trial of the Jihad 302" was the blind university theologian **Sheikh Omar Abd el-Rahman**, their "spiritual leader". Acquitted but exiled to the Fayoum, the Sheikh later moved to the US, where in 1995 he was sentenced to life imprisonment for conspiring to blow up the World Trade Center. By that time many of his followers had joined forces with al-Qaida, whose own attack on the Twin Towers was reputedly undertaken in Abd el-Rahman's name. His son, Ahmed, was later captured by US forces in Afghanistan, fighting with the Taliban.

The 1997 **Luxor massacre** (see p.395) was also related to the sheikh and Assyut; the splinter group responsible reportedly consisted of six students from Assyut University, and a letter found on one of the terrorists claimed that they meant to seize hostages in a bid to bargain for Abd el-Rahman's release from prison. Yet some suspect that the killers' true identity and aims were deliberately obscured; an autopsy found that four of them were uncircumcised, which hardly fits the profile of radical Islamists.

The insurgency and hardships of the 1990s fostered organized crime, personified by **Izzat Hanafi**, based 10km upriver from Assyut in the village of **El-Nekheila**. With its drug plantations and arsenals, El-Nekheila was "like Columbia". The state tolerated it in return for Hanafi's help penetrating Islamist networks, till he outlived his usefulness and became too brazen. In 2004, 200 armoured cars surrounded the village where he was protected by gunmen and cooking-gas cylinders wired to explode. Residents alleged that up to seventy people died in the fighting; the police stated that only a single gang member was killed. The government later built a school and hospital to alleviate local resentment and stationed a large police garrison to ensure that El-Nekheila didn't slip back into the hands of criminals. In 2007 Hanafi and his brother were hanged for kidnapping and drugs trafficking.

the economy and the success of the city's **football** team Cement Assyut, sponsored by the cement factory across the river. Residents are more ambivalent about the fame of Assyut-born sex bomb Ruby – whose pop-videos make Britney Spears look like a nun – and local Mafioso Izzat Hanafi (see box above). Volatile, god-fearing, polluted and decrepit, Assyut is Naples on the Nile or Palermo with chadors.

Aside from the atmospheric **bazaar** and a **Governorate Festival** (April 18) commemorating the defeat of French forces by local villagers in 1799 – marked by folklore shows and a flotilla of boats on the Nile – the only reasons to come here are a couple of monasteries and tombs within the governorate. As in Minya, supervision by the **police** can be off-putting – though in Assyut they're weirdly inconsistent, giving you a motorcycle escort one time and totally ignoring you the next.

Arrival, information and accommodation

While the **train and bus stations** are both central, **service taxis** use the Arba'in terminal beside the El-Mallah Canal on the edge of the old quarter (£E5 by taxi from the centre). Assyut's **tourist office** (daily except Fri & Sat

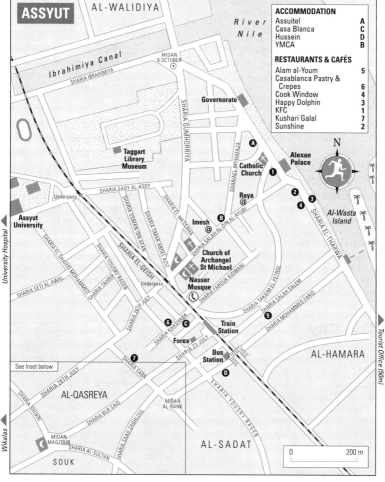

Assyut Barrage & Lillian Trasher Orphanage

ASSYUT

AL-WALIDIYA

River Nile

2

THE NILE VALLEY | Assyut and around

ACCOMMODATION
Assuitel	A
Casa Blanca	C
Hussein	D
YMCA	B

RESTAURANTS & CAFÉS
Alam al-Youm	5
Casablanca Pastry & Crepes	6
Cook Window	4
Happy Dolphin	3
KFC	1
Kushari Galal	7
Sunshine	2

Ibrahimiya Canal

SHARIA IBRAHIMIYA

MIDAN 6 OCTOBER

Governorate

SHARIA GUMHORRIYA

Taggart Library Museum

Underpass

SHARIA GADY AL-ASDY

Assyut University

SHARIA EL-SHAHID MOHAMMED

SHARIA SETI AL-AWAL

SHARIA OSMAN IBN AFFAN

SHARIA YOUSSEF FAGEB

SHARIA TAHIRIYA

SHARIA 26TH JULY

University Hospital

SHARIA EL-GEISH

SHARIA TAKSIM ABDEL AZIZ

Underpass

Catholic Church

SHARIA EL-MESSAHA

SHARIA EL MOHAFAZA

SHARIA SALAH AL-DIN AL-AYUBI

Raya @

Imesh @

Church of Archangel St Michael

Nasser Mosque

SHARIA FAROUK KIDWANI

SHARIA TAKSIM EL-PETROL

SHARIA SALAH SALEM

SHARIA MOHAMMED FARID

Alexan Palace

N

Al-Wasta Island

SHARIA EL-THARWA

Tourist Office (50m)

Train Station

Forex

SHARIA KHASHABA

SHARIA 23 JULY

Bus Station

SHARIA YOUSSEF FAGEB

AL-HAMARA

See Inset below

SHARIA SABR

SHARIA 26TH JULY

AL-QASREYA

SHARIA SHUKRI

SHARIA BUR SAID

SHARIA SAAD ZAGHLOUL

MIDAN MAGZOUB

SHARIA AL-SULTAN

MIDAN AL-BANK

AL-SADAT

0   200 m

SOUK

Wikalas

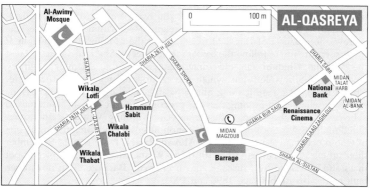

AL-QASREYA

0   100 m

Al-Awimy Mosque

SHARIA 26TH JULY

SHARIA SHUKRI

SHARIA AL-QASREYA

Wikala Lotfi

Hammam Sabit

Wikala Chalabi

Wikala Thabat

SHARIA 26TH JULY

MIDAN MAGZOUB

SHARIA SABR

MIDAN TALAT HARB

MIDAN AL-BANK

National Bank

Renaissance Cinema

SHARIA BUR SAID

SHARIA SAAD ZAGHLOUL

Barrage

SHARIA AL-SULTAN

Arba'in Taxi Station (600m)

8.30am–8pm; ☎088/230-5110) on the Corniche will send someone to meet you at the train station, given a day's notice. Manager Ramadan Osman (☎012 346-2601) or Mohammed Abd el-Hamid can arrange excursions to Deir el-Muharraq and the Meir Tombs or the convent at Dirunka (see p.310). There are two **Internet** cafes on Sharia Salah al-Din (Imesh is open 24hr); the 24-hour **telephone exchange** and main **post office** are near the train station. You can change **money** on Midan al-Bank, where National Bank and Banque Misr have ATMs; the latter does cash advances on Visa and MasterCard. Assyut University's Ga'ama **hospital** (☎088/235-6235) has some English-speaking doctors.

Accommodation

Many **hotels** don't want foreign guests because of the hassle they entail: police are posted at the entrance and tourists can only step outside after an escort has been arranged. The few places willing to accept foreigners are mostly overpriced and within a few blocks of the train station.

Assiutel Sharia el-Tharwa ☎088/231-2121, ☎231-2122. The best choice if you can afford it, this faded three-star on the Corniche has a/c, satellite TV and fridges, a bar and restaurant. Breakfast included. ❺
Casa Blanca Sharia Khashaba ☎088/233-7662. A few blocks from the train station, this overrated three-star charges way too much for dingy rooms. Breakfast included. ❹

Hussein Sharia Mohammed Farid ☎088/234-2532. A small, fairly basic hotel near the bus station, handy for transport but noisy. ❷
YMCA Sharia Salah al-Din al-Ayubi ☎088/232-3218. The only decent budget option, it has simple rooms with fridges (£E30 with a/c), a large garden and basketball courts, used by Coptic youth groups. Reservations advised; manager Attiyah speaks English. ❶

The City

A dusty metropolis seething with traffic pouring off elevated freeways, **Assyut** has largely erased its own history. Scores of rock tombs west of town are the only sign of pharaonic Sawty, a nome capital which the Greeks renamed Lycopolis ("Wolf-town") after the local god, **Wepwawet**, "Opener of the Ways". Represented as a wolf or jackal of the desert, he was an apt symbol for a city which later prospered from slavery, for it was here that survivors of the Forty Days Road (see p.425) emerged from the desert to be traded wholesale. Trafficking may have continued until 1883, although Amelia Edwards saw nothing amiss a decade earlier, when she enthused over the "quaint red vases" and "bird-shaped bottles" in Assyut's souks.

The **bazaar** quarter – known as **Al-Qasreya** – is a must-see: a web of shadowy lanes between sharias 26th July and Bur Said, smelling of incense and offal. To find it, walk along Bur Said till you reach Midan Magzoub, with its remains of a **Nile Barrage** from the reign of Mohammed Ali. Enter the narrow continuation of Bur Said to the left of the mosque and turn right at the first crossroads, to follow the bazaar's main artery – Sharia al-Qasreya – past the **Wikala Chalabi** (an old caravanserai) and other Mamluke edifices, emerging on Sharia 26th July, which you can follow back towards the centre.

From there, take a stroll along Sharia Salah al-Din al-Ayubi (aka Sharia al-Namees), where each evening Assyutis **promenade** past fairy-lit boutiques to a breezy **Corniche** lined with private clubs hosting weddings and other functions. This was once inhabited by cotton magnates and foreign consuls, one of whom occupied the now-derelict **Alexan Palace**. From May to September there are pleasure **cruises** (£E5–10) to **Al-Wasta Island** – a lush picnic spot that's also accessible by felucca – and the **Assyut Barrage**, 2km downriver, built by the British between 1898 and 1903.

This era also saw the founding by American missionaries of a boys' college (now the co-ed Al-Salaam School), off Midan 6th October: its Taggart Library **museum** (daily except Fri, Sun and school vacations 8am–2pm; free) displays such curios as mummified dogs and fish, and pharaonic soldiers' dog-tags. Across the river, the **Lillian Trasher Orphanage** (Malga Trasher) is the largest, best-known institution of its kind in Egypt (there's another famous one in Tanta, funded by pop star Mohammed Tharwat). Founded in 1911 by Florida-born Lillian Trasher, who came to Egypt at the age of 23 and died in her adopted homeland in 1961, the orphanage is a source of pride for Assyut's Copts, and visitors are welcome (as are donations). Microbuses (50pt) from the centre stop nearby, or you can get a taxi (£E5).

Eating, drinking and nightlife

The Corniche offers the best choice for **eating**, with the *Happy Dolphin* floating restaurant serving grilled fish or meat alfresco; the *Cook Window* and *Sunshine Restaurant* burgers, pizzas and *shawarma* indoors; and a *KFC* up the road – all open till midnight. Downtown, *Casablanca Pastry and Crepes* does takeaway pizzas and pancakes (savoury or sweet), *Alam al-Youm* is the place for kebabs, or you can dig in at *Kushari Galal* (till 1am or later). There are coffee-houses and juice-bars all over the centre, but you can only **drink** alcohol in the lifeless mock-Tudor bar of the *Assuitel* (which doesn't do takeaways). Aside from promenading, **nightlife** is limited to whatever's on at the Renaissance cinema on Sharia Bur Said, or hanging out in coffeehouses.

Moving on from Assyut

The police prefer tourists to leave town by train, so they don't restrict them to any particular service. About nine **trains** a day run to Cairo (5–7hr), stopping at Mallawi (2hr), Minya (3hr) and Beni Suef (5hr) along the way, and a dozen trains call at Sohag (2hr), Qena (4hr) and Luxor (6hr) en route to Aswan (12hr). Tourists are presently allowed to use **buses** running more or less hourly to Cairo (6–7hr; £E25) and Sohag (2hr; £E8); every two hours to Minya (2–3hr; £E8); twice daily to Qena (noon & 1pm; 4hr; £E15); Alexandria (7am & 7pm; 10hr; £E35) and Hurghada (9am & 8pm; 8hr; £E25); and once to Sharm el-Sheikh (3pm; 12hr; £E40), Luxor and Aswan (at 8am; 6–9hr; £E25–40). Additionally, there are four buses daily to Kharga (4hr; £E8) between 7am and 10pm, two of which run on to Dakhla Oasis (7–8hr; £E20). Although **service taxis** run to every town along the Valley from Minya to Qena, foreigners may only take them to Kharga Oasis (4hr; £E8). EgyptAir, in the Governorate building (℡088/231-5228; daily except Fri 9am–3pm), operate **flights** to Cairo (Tues & Thurs; £E180 one-way).

Around Assyut

Two **monasteries** in the vicinity of Assyut testify to the roots Christianity put down in this region in the fourth century. Copts believe that these and other sites were actually visited by the **Holy Family** during the four years that Mary, Joseph and the infant Jesus stayed in Egypt to escape King Herod's massacre of the first-born. Although the Bible says little about this period, details of their wanderings were revealed in a dream to Patriarch Theophilus in AD 500, and Copts have made much of this tradition ever since. Indeed, most tourism in the Assyut region involves Copts from other parts of Egypt, making pilgrimages on holy days – although Assyut's tourist office hopes to lure foreigners with the little-visited **Meir Tombs**.

Dirunka: the Convent of the Virgin

Copts believe that the Holy Family sought refuge in caves at **DIRUNKA**, 12km outside Assyut – as did later Christians. From such troglodyte origins, the present **Convent of the Virgin** (aka Deir el-Adhra, or Santa Maria) on the site has grown into what resembles a fortified campus – cynics might say a refuge for Assyut's Coptic population, should the worst ever occur.

The expansion is justified by the nearly one million pilgrims who attend the **Moulid of the Virgin** (August 15–30). This occasions the parading of icons around the spacious cave church where they stand for most of the year. Coptic altars face east because it's from there that Jesus will return, but also because he is "the sun" of their religion. Pilgrims are photographed against a huge portrait of the Virgin, or the verdant plain overlooked by the convent's terrace, below which is a Coptic village where nuns operate a dispensary. About fifty nuns and monks live in the convent.

As the police might wish to escort visitors and may frown on you travelling by minibus (50–75pt) from Assyut, a private taxi (£E30–35 round-trip with 1hr waiting) is the best way of **getting there**, and saves you a fifteen-minute uphill slog from the roadside. If you don't retain your taxi, returning minibuses can be flagged down on the main road.

En route to Dirunka you'll pass a range of barren hills riddled with the **Tombs of the Nobles** (normally locked, but sometimes accessible by prior arrangement with the tourist office). Mostly from the Middle Kingdom, they provide virtually the only record of events during the First Intermediate Period (2160–2050 BC). The Tomb of Djefaihapy I contains some of the oldest surviving legal documents anywhere (required reading for Egyptology students), while hundreds of votive stelae and figurines were found in the Tomb of Djefaihapy III, that was uniquely used as a popular shrine long after his death.

El-Qusiya: the Burnt Monastery and the Meir Tombs

It's the police who decide whether foreigners can enter the area around El-Qusiya. If you get the go-ahead, the tourist office can arrange an excursion **by private taxi** to both the Burnt Monastery and the Meir Tombs for £E120.

EL-QUSIYA, 42km north of Assyut, has a troubled recent history. In 1998, thousands of local Copts were tortured by state security, seeking to "solve" the murders of two Coptic youths while excluding any Islamist involvement. Though arrests ceased after Bishop Wissa alerted the world's media (he was later charged with "endangering national unity"), no police were ever punished. On New Year's Eve, 1999, a fatal quarrel between a Coptic merchant and a Muslim customer was followed by a wave of shootings and arson that left twenty Copts and one Muslim dead, which the police did nothing to stop for two days.

Five kilometres outside town, the **Burnt Monastery** (Deir el-Muharraq) stands near the desert's edge. Its tinderbox surroundings explain the name and protective walls; the crenellated inner rampart is still blackened from a conflagration that occurred during the **Moulid of the Virgin** (June 21–28) over a decade ago. Visitors are shown around the thriving modernized establishment, except on fast days. Many of the hundred students at its Theological College will become monks when they turn 25. Within the compound are grouped the Abbot's residence, a fourth-century keep and two churches. Believers maintain that the **cave sanctuary** of the **Church of the Anointed** (El-Azraq) once hid the Holy Family for six months and ten days, and that the church was one of the first in the world, foretold in the Old Testament as "an altar to the Lord in the midst of the land of Egypt" (Isaiah 19:19–21). It's also said that what is now the altar stone was once used to block the cave's entrance. When an abbot ordered its replacement, the mason's hand was paralysed and a vision of Jesus appeared, intoning "Leave it alone." The icon of the Virgin and Child is said to be painted by St Luke; the apostles in the **Church of St George** come from Ethiopia. Remember to remove your shoes before entering the churches.

The **Meir Tombs** are further north, 6km from the village of **Meir** (or Mayr), reached by a secondary road. This rock-hewn necropolis belonged to the rulers of the fourteenth nome, whose capital Qis or Cusae was the ancestor of El-Qusiya. Nine of its seventeen tombs are open to the public (daily except Thurs & Fri 9am–2pm; £E16), several of them still vividly coloured. Tombs #1 and #2 are inscribed with 720 deities, defaced by the Christian hermits that once dwelt there, while in tomb #4 you can see the original grid drawn on the wall to help the artists execute their designs. Best of all are the splendid desert hunting scene in the tomb of **Senbi-Sa-Ukh-hotep**, and the women's fashions of the XII Dynasty depicted in Chancellor **Ukh-hotep**'s tomb. Model boats from these tombs are exhibited in the Luxor Museum.

Sohag

Set on a rich agricultural plain bounded by the hills of the Eastern and Western deserts, **SOHAG** (pronounced "So*haj*") is a city of 221,000 people with a large Christian community and a small university. Before the troubles of the 1990s, tourists used it as a base for visiting the nearby **Red and White monasteries** or **Abydos** Temple, further away (see p.322). Today, the government is trying to woo back visitors by building an archeological museum and touting a colossal statue of an Ancient Egyptian princess in **Akhmim**, across the Nile.

While hotels and stations are on the west bank, the tourist office and museum are over the river in **Medinet Nasr**. Akhmim is 3km further east: a statue of a princess with a harp marks the municipal boundary. For visitors, this entails shuttling back and forth, hampered by the tourist police. The **museum** is intended to showcase some five thousand artefacts found within the governorate, from the Middle Kingdom until Greco-Roman times – to be joined by finds from ongoing excavations in Akhmim. Alas, when last seen, only the temple-like exterior was finished, and its inauguration has been set back to 2008.

Meanwhile, Sohag's attractions are episodic. Its weekly Souk el-Itnayn (Mon 6am–noon) is a huge **animal market**, held just off the Girga road. The whole city celebrates the **Moulid of Al-Aref** – Sohag's patron saint – a few weeks before the nationwide feast of Eid al-Adha. Among other deeds, Al-Aref is remembered for hiding Murad Bey, the only Mamluke to escape the infamous massacre at the Citadel, who fled to Upper Egypt. **City Day** (April 10), commemorating a local victory over Napoleon's troops in 1799, sees a parade of folk-dancers and soldiers at the stadium, otherwise shared by three football clubs – all hopeless, locals admit.

Practicalities

Arriving at the train station, you'll be detained by the **tourist police** and assigned an escort for the duration of your stay. The police will probably insist that you travel everywhere by **taxi** (Medinet Nasr costs £E2, Akhmim £E10), rather than minibuses or service taxis (50pt) from depots on either side of the river – though you may be able to use them on the way back. The inconsistency arises because each municipality has its own police command; private taxis may have to wait for a change of escort cars at the "border".

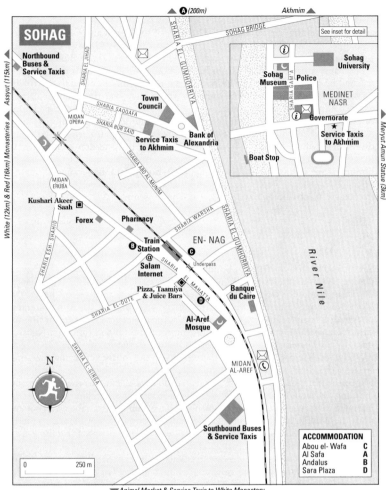

White (12km) & Red (16km) Monasteries ◄ | *Assyut (115km)* ◄ | ▲ **Ⓐ** *(200m)* | *Akhmim* ▲ | ► *Meryut Amun Statue (3km)*

SOHAG

Northbound
Buses &
Service Taxis

SHARIA EL-JIHAD

SOHAG BRIDGE

See inset for detail

Sohag
University

MIDAN
NASR

Sohag
Museum Police

Governorate

Service Taxis
to Akhmim

Boat Stop

SHARIA EL-GUMHORRIYA

SHARIA SAQQAFA

Town
Council

MIDAN
OPERA

SHARIA BUR SAID

Service Taxis
to Akhmim

Bank of
Alexandria

SHARIA ABD AL-MUNIM

MIDAN
ERUBA

Kushari Akeer
Saah

Forex

Pharmacy

❸ Train
Station
@
Salam
Internet

SHARIA WARSHA

EN- NAG

Ⓒ

Underpass

SHARIA ESH-SHAHID

Pizza, Taamiya
& Juice Bars

SHARIA EL-OUTE

SHARIA EL MAHATTA

Ⓓ

Banque
du Caire

River Nile

Al-Aref
Mosque

SHARIA EL-GIRGA

N

MIDAN
AL-AREF

Southbound Buses
& Service Taxis

ACCOMMODATION
Abou el- Wafa   **C**
Al Safa   **A**
Andalus   **B**
Sara Plaza   **D**

0 _____ 250 m

▼ *Animal Market & Service Taxis to White Monastery*

At the **tourist office** (daily except Fri 9am–9pm; ☎093/460-4453), where Hassan Rifat (home ☎093/232-2249, ✉hassan79_2003@yahoo.com) can arrange excursions by taxi to the monasteries or Abydos – call him the day before you arrive. It's easier to change **money** at the Forex (daily 10am–10pm) on Sharia al-Mahatta than at banks on the Corniche, where a **post** and **telephone office** is also located. There's another telephone office in the station, with Salam **Internet** (24hr) across the road. The University **hospital** (☎093/231-9101) and **police** (☎122) are in Medinet Nasr.

As for **moving on**, the police prefer you to travel by **train** to Luxor (4hr), Cairo (8–10hr) or anywhere else, and set no restriction on which train you take. If you're allowed to use them, there are seven **buses** daily to Minya and Cairo (5am–10pm), plus regular buses and **service taxis** to Qena, from where others run on to Luxor. Assyut (1hr 30min; £E5) is the furthest destination for northbound service taxis, while Qena (1hr; £E10) is the normal limit for southbound vehicles.

Egyptian
temple
architecture

Two types of temple were built in Egypt from the earliest times. Mortuary temples were devoted to the worship of a dead king, whereas cult temples were dedicated to the principal god or goddess of a region, and were regarded as the pr-ntr or "house of the god", whose effigy was cosseted with daily rituals and periodically taken to visit its divine spouse in another temple. Most temples embody centuries of work by successive kings, some of whom added major sections while others merely decorated a wall or carved their name on another pharaoh's statue, usurping it for their own glory. Ancient Egyptian style made waves in Europe once Western scholars arrived to study (and plunder) the temples and tombs: Art Deco was influenced by pharaonic motifs following the discovery of Tutankhamun's tomb, as the French Empire style had been by Napoleon's expedition over a century earlier.

▶ The Hypostyle Hall at Karnak

Temple layout

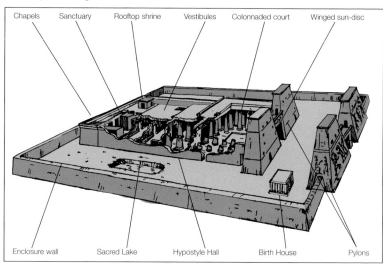

Chapels | Sanctuary | Rooftop shrine | Vestibules | Colonnaded court | Winged sun-disc

Enclosure wall | Sacred Lake | Hypostyle Hall | Birth House | Pylons

The general form and layout of temples hardly changed over millennia, and were still being imitated during Ptolemaic and Roman times. Most temples were surrounded by high mud-brick **enclosure walls** (still intact at Karnak and Medinet Habu) which defined the holy precincts. Generally inaccessible to commoners, these contained priestly residences, workshops, storehouses and a **Sacred Lake** for ritual ablutions.

▼ Obelisk, colossi and pylon at Luxor Temple

In Greco-Roman times, there was also a **Birth House** or *mamissi* containing scenes asserting the king's divine ancestry, while at certain "healing" temples – notably Dendara and Karnak – ordinary folk could submit prayers to **Chapels of the Hearing Ear** by the outer rear wall, featuring carvings of medical instruments or human ears and deep gouges left by pilgrims seeking "blessed" dust from the temple.

Entering the temple proper meant passing through massive stone **pylons**, whose tapering facades bore giant reliefs of the pharaoh making offerings to the gods and smiting Egypt's foes. Whether categorized as Nubians, Asiatics or Sea Peoples, they were depicted begging for mercy or with their amputated hands and genitals being tallied by royal scribes, even if the pharaoh credited with the triumph was only descended from the real victor, as with Ramses III at Medinet Habu. Some temples also had **obelisks**

▲ Door lintel motif symbolizing the union of the Two Lands, Medinet Habu

with tips sheathed in gold or electrum (an alloy of gold and silver), guardian **colossi** representing a pharaoh or a deity, and open **courts** flanked with **colonnades** of Osiride pillars.

Another pylon (or a screen wall surmounted by open columns) divided the court from a **Hypostyle Hall**, whose forest of columns was intended to resemble a papyrus thicket, dimly illuminated by shafts of sunlight penetrating apertures in the roof. Beyond lay a series of **vestibules** or antechambers (often preceded by a smaller Hypostyle Hall), climaxing in the **sanctuary** where the deity's idol and gilded boat-shaped shrine, or barque, reposed. Smaller **chapels** for worshipping subsidiary deities were grouped near the sanctuary; from the Late Period onwards a secret **crypt** underneath served for hiding sacred treasures from invaders – as you can see at Dendara's Temple of Hathor, erected in Greco-Roman times directly on top of a far older shrine.

Some temples had a **rooftop shrine** for an annual ritual celebrating the resurrection of Osiris, which revitalized the temple's effigy. Enshrined in a barque, it was carried to the roof to be touched by the sun at dawn on New Year's Day. The best preserved rooftop shrine is at Dendara, which depicts Isis restoring Osiris to life by copulating with his mummy.

Because temples were envisaged as a progression from this world into the realm of divine mysteries, halls got darker and lower, thresholds rose and doors narrowed the closer they were to the sanctuary. In accordance with this convention, halls or pylons added subsequently had to increase in size as they grew more distant from the sanctuary, and the architecture is generally older the further in you venture.

Pillars and columns

Pillars and columns evolved from two basic types. Square-sectioned **pillars** were faced with a statue of the pharaoh as a god (usually Osiris, hence the term Osiride pillars) or crowned with the head of the goddess Hathor (occasionally with a cow's face, but more often with cow's ears). **Columns** derived from plant forms, with different permutations of shafts and capitals. Palm columns had a plain shaft and leafy capital, while papyrus columns chevron

▲ A Hathor-headed pillar, with cow's ears

markings and an open (flowering) or closed bud capital, while lotus columns had a shaft resembling a bundle of stems. In Ptolemaic times, capitals resembled Baroque bouquets and established forms were mixed to create so-called composite columns.

▲ Detail of the astronomical ceiling at Dendara

Decoration

As in Ancient Greece and Rome, temples were whitewashed and painted all over, looking far gaudier than today, when a bit of **colour** makes an exciting change from monochrome masonry – the skin of gods or goddesses might be red or yellow, their garments cobalt blue or turquoise. Virtually every wall is covered in **reliefs**, either carved proud (bas-reliefs, the most delicate and time-consuming method), recessed into the surface (sunk-reliefs) or simply incised (the quickest form to execute) in rows called "registers". The festival procession of the deity's shrine is depicted on the walls of courts and Hypostyle Halls, along with coronation scenes and other events in a king's reign.

Hieroglyphs and **cartouches** (ovoid frames, each containing a pharaoh's name) are carved everywhere, lauding whoever founded or enlarged the temple, the rituals of its consecration or the myth of its deity; all are vital sources of information for Egyptologists. For example, the Gallery (or List) of Kings at Abydos is an invaluable record of 34 rulers starting with Menes, mythical unifier of the Two Lands (the Nile Valley and its Delta), and ending with the XIX Dynasty ruler Seti I, omitting pharaohs deemed heretics or usurpers. In the Greco-Roman era, when rulers frequently came and went, stonemasons at distant temples in Nubia left cartouches blank, to be filled in at a later date.

Imagery often refers to the union of the Two Lands – the Nile Valley and its Delta – represented by the vulture-goddess Nekhbet and the cobra-goddess Wadjet combined with a sun-disc on the lintels of doorways; by their heraldic plants, the sedge and lotus; and by the ribbed Djed pillar, symbolizing stability. Some Ptolemaic temples feature **astronomical ceilings** combining Ancient Egyptian and Babylonian cosmology, with the sky-goddess Nut swallowing and giving birth to the sun, planets and stars juxtaposed with bulls, scorpions and other zodiac symbols.

▼ Sunk-relief of a festival procession, at the Ramesseum

Accommodation

The hotels listed below are willing to take foreigners. It's wise to **reserve** in advance through the tourist office (few hotel staff speak English). Breakfast is included in the price.

Abou el-Wafa Behind the train station ☏ 093/231-6222 or 012 3924884. The best budget option: an illuminated high-rise whose small, clean rooms with a/c, TV, fridge and bathroom aren't as noisy as you'd imagine. Reception is on the fifth floor. ❷

Al Safa Sharia el-Gumhorriya, 150m north of Sohag Bridge ☏ 093/220-7703, ☏ 220-7704. Sohag's ritziest hotel has large carpeted a/c rooms with satellite TV and balconies facing the Nile, a pleasant restaurant and riverside terrace. ❻

Andalus Unsigned on Sharia al-Mahatta, diagonally opposite the station ☏ & ☏ 093/233-4328. Its small en-suite rooms are a bit shabby, but come with fridges, fans and a/c, and are cheaper than other places in the same price band. ❷

Sara Plaza Sharia al-Mahatta ☏ 093/234-1320. Entered via an alley, with reception on the fifth floor, it has similar amenities to *Abou el-Wafa*, but could do with a lick of paint. ❷

Eating and drinking

The *Al Safa Hotel* has the best **restaurant** in town, serving fish, grills and pizzas; a full meal here costs about £E50. For cheaper eats try the late-night *Kushari Akeer Saah* or the nameless pizza, *fuul* and *taamiya* joints further down Sharia al-Mahatta, where's there's also a juice bar. Or you could buy a spit-roast chicken to take back to your room from a rotisserie near the *Andalus Hotel*. You can buy Egyptian beer and spirits at low-key **alcohol** shops on Midan Opera, to drink in your room.

Akhmim

The sixteenth-century Moorish geographer-historian Leo Africanus reckoned **AKHMIM** "the oldest city in Egypt". Akhmimis have built on the rubble of their ancestors since pre-Dynastic times; the town, the ancient capital of the ninth nome, rests on a mound of remains, with a maze-like street plan little changed since medieval times. Its name comes from the Coptic "Khmim", recalling a local fertility god, Khente-Min, often represented by a giant **phallus**. Legend has it all the town's men were killed at war, except for one lucky youth who had to re-stock the population and was later deified. The Greeks called the town Panopolis, after their own priapic god, Pan. Egyptologists also associate it with the Akhmim Tablet, a kind of worksheet for scribes, defining mathematical units. Akhenaten's mother, Tiy, was born here, and Herodotus noted that the town was famed for its sorcerers.

In 1981 excavations to build a school uncovered a colossal **statue of Meryut Amun** (daily 7am–6pm; £E20), now displayed in a pit. **Service taxis** that shuttle between Akhmim and Sohag (many are lovely vintage cars from the 1930s and 1940s) drop you at an intersection in Akhmim's centre known as Sitta Aziza; from here, follow a road leading north towards the market and the Al-Amri Mosque, to find Meryut Amun's statue a bit further on. By buying a ticket, you can examine the statue's finely carved wig and skirt and the cartouches that identify it as Meryut Amun (or Meryetamun). Nefertari's eldest daughter, she had to marry her father, Ramses II, after the death of his second wife, Istnofret (as did her half-sister). Some, however, date the statue to the earlier Amarna period, evidenced by its almond-shaped eyes and blocks inscribed with Aten symbols, found beneath its base (now piled under a shelter). When found, the eleven-metre-tall limestone figure had rouged lips, but the colour has since faded.

Across the street behind her head, another pit reveals the plinth and legs of a seated **colossus of Ramses II**. The colossus is reckoned to weigh 700 tonnes and be nearly as large as the ones at Abu Simbel; it probably stood at the entrance to a vast temple whose ruins awed the Arab explorer Ibn Batuta, which is thought to lie beneath the town's Muslim cemetery. Alas, most of the £E35 million allocated to move the cemetery and excavate the temple has been "spent" with nothing to show for it, yet antiquities are being unearthed at building sites all over town and smuggled abroad.

Having seen the plinth, you can visit a **weaving factory** in the building with green gates, to the right. It's one of four built in the 1900s, using power-looms from England, that nearly wiped out the local hand-weaving industry – a tradition going back to the pharaohs, who were buried in shrouds of Akhmim silk. Hand-weaving was only preserved by a missionary-inspired **Women's Cooperative** (Rahabaat), whose tapestries are now sold as works of art. The weavers forgo celebrity in order not to irritate their menfolk, so visitors are unwelcome. The factory, however, may let you see its (male) weavers at work and has a shop downstairs, selling tablecloths, sheets and cuts from bolts of silk or cotton – all in 1950s' patterns, nothing like the Rahabaat's work (sold in Cairo and Luxor).

Monasteries near Sohag

The **Red and White monasteries** (daily 8am–8pm) to the south of Sohag are both small and dilapidated, yet their near-desolation seems more evocative of the early Christians who sought God in the desert than busier establishments like Dirunka. Only a handful of acolytes tend the chapels, timeworn stones and plastic medallions attesting to the thousands of Copts who visit them during Shenoudi's moulid in the first two weeks of July, when dozens of minibuses shuttle in the pilgrims.

Although local service taxis run to the White Monastery (12km), the police will make you take a **private taxi** (arranged by the tourist office for £E15–20, including one hour waiting time), which enables you to also visit the Red Monastery, 4km further on. There's no admission charge for the monasteries, but baksheesh is expected.

The White Monastery

Across the plain from Sohag, high limestone walls enclose the **White Monastery** (Deir al-Abyad), named for the colour of its masonry, mostly taken from pharaonic or Roman buildings. Supposedly founded by St Helena on her way back from Jerusalem, the monastery once possessed the greatest Coptic library in Egypt (now dispersed among 23 museums worldwide) and was home to over two thousand monks. Today it has only four residents, and its courtyard is flanked by ruined cloisters and cells. Despite its fortress-like walls – which are much thicker at the base and topped with a Cavetto cornice in the ancient Egyptian style – the monastery was often sacked by marauders. When the artist Denon passed by with Napoleon's troops in 1798, it was still smouldering after a raid by the Mamlukes.

Remove your shoes before entering the **Church of St Shenoudi**, a lofty basilica admitting breezes and birdsong, observed by a stern-faced Christ Pantokrator. Note the monolithic granite pulpit halfway along the northern wall, Roman columns in the apses, and pharaonic hieroglyphics on the outer rear wall.

The monastery is also known as Deir Anba Shenouda after its fifth-century founder, who enforced the monastic rule with legendary beatings – on one occasion, fatally. Shenoudi condemned bathing as an upper-class luxury maintained by the sweat of the poor; early monks cleansed themselves by rolling naked in the sand. During **Shenoudi's moulid** (which reaches its climax on July 14), childless women roll down nearby hills in sacks, hoping to obtain divine intervention.

The Red Monastery

Down the road past walled Coptic and Muslim cemeteries, a straggling village conceals the **Red Monastery** (Deir al-Ahmar) in an unobtrusive cul-de-sac. Built of dark red brick, the monastery is attributed to St Bishoi, a penitent armed robber who became Shenoudi's disciple (retaining his club as a reminder); hence its other sobriquet, Deir Anba Bishoi.

The monastery's principal **church** is darker than Shenoudi's, its blackened tenth-century murals less remarkable than the finely carved tiers of niches. Whereas purloined Roman columns and the White Monastery's pharaonic-style corvetto cornice betray artistic debts, the intricate floral capitals inside the outer gate show that Coptic architecture soon transcended mere imitation. In the courtyard's far corner squats the smaller **Red Church**, whose inner sanctum is barred to women. Notice the intricate peg-locks on the doors.

Upper Egypt

In antiquity, **Upper Egypt** started at Memphis and ran as far south as Aswan on the border with Nubia. Nowadays, with the designation of Middle Egypt, borders are a bit hazy, though the **Qena Bend** is generally taken as the region's beginning and **Aswan** is still effectively the end of the line.

Within this stretch of the Nile is the world's most intensive concentration of ancient monuments – temples, tombs and palaces constructed from the onset of the Middle Kingdom (*c.*1990 BC) up until Roman and Byzantine times. The greatest of the buildings are the **cult temples** of **Abydos**, **Dendara**, **Karnak**, **Esna**, **Edfu**, **Kom Ombo**, **Philae** and **Abu Simbel**, each conceived as "homes" for their respective deities and an accretion of centuries of building. Scarcely less impressive are the multitude of tombs in the **Theban Necropolis**, most famously in the **Valley of the Kings**, across the river from **Luxor**, where Tutankhamun's resting place is merely a hole in the ground by comparison with those of such great pharaohs as Seti I and Ramses II.

Monuments aside, Upper Egypt marks a subtle shift of character, with the desert closing in on the river, and dom palms growing alongside barrel-roofed houses, designed to reflect the intense heat. One of the greatest pleasures to be had here – indeed one of the highlights of any Egyptian trip – is to absorb the river-scape slowly from the vantage point of a **felucca**. This is easily arranged in Aswan, whence you can sail downriver with no fear of being becalmed; Nile **cruise boats** and **dahabiyas** provide a more luxurious experience. While cruises can be booked at short notice in either city, better deals are usually available in Aswan.

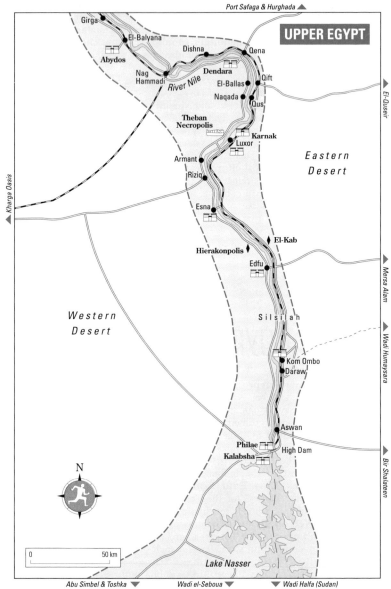

Nile trips

Some people love **Nile cruise boats**, others hate them. On the plus side they offer the chance to travel the river with all the comforts of a four- or five-star hotel. The downside is that you'll visit temples with hundreds of other tourists according to a rigid timetable, amid much noise and air pollution wherever dozens of boats are moored alongside each other – which is hardly surprising when there are over 250 cruisers plying the river between Luxor and Aswan.

For those with money to burn, a **dahabiya** cruise is everything a journey on the Nile should be, recalling a leisurely age of tourism before steamer tours, and as more *dahabiyas* take to the Nile, prices are dropping. At the other end of the scale, **felucca** journeys between Aswan and Luxor are a uniquely Egyptian experience which many travellers rate as the highlight of their visit – though tales of misery aren't uncommon either.

Nile cruise boats

The indubitable advantage of Nile cruises is that they're cheap. **Package tours** from Europe with a return flight and a cruise often cost far less than flights and hotels booked independently. Peak times are Christmas, New Year and Easter, when most (but not all) tour operators raise their prices. In Britain, you can search for deals at Nile Cruises Direct (Ⓦ www.nilecruisesdirect.com). **Independent travellers** can find bargains in Luxor or Aswan (Cairo is risky unless you deal directly with the company owning the boat). Budget hotels like Luxor's *Happy Land* (see p.342) can book a double cabin in a five-star boat for $70 a night, or a three-star ship for $55 (except in December, when boats may well be unavailable), while local travel agencies offer **deals** on some of the ritzy ships listed below. Alternatively, you can put on smart clothes and go hunting along the Corniche, where boats are moored three or four abreast. The boat manager is likely to quote a lower rate than travel agencies, especially if the boat is near its sailing time and only half full, or you have a bottle of Johnny Walker Black Label to throw into negotiations.

There are two basic **itineraries**: seven nights to Aswan and back starting from Luxor, or a briefer trip commencing at either end, which means two nights' sailing if you start from Luxor or a one-night cruise from Aswan, both journeys including stopovers at the temples of Edfu and Kom Ombo. In both cases, there's an indeterminate wait to pass through the **locks at Esna**, which makes it unwise to rely on getting back to Luxor or Cairo in time for a flight home. When the locks are **closed** for a fortnight's maintenance in June and the first half of December, passengers are bussed from Esna to sites up to three hours' distant. These routes aside, there are also cruises on Lake Nasser (see p.451).

Choosing a boat

You'll be told that all the **boats** rate five stars, which the Ministry of Tourism has indeed awarded them, though **standards** vary from bog-average three-star up to the palatial. Even an average vessel will have a/c cabins with en-suite bathrooms, a restaurant, bar, sun deck and swimming pool; superior boats have double beds, large bathrooms, patio doors and balconies. Try to avoid getting a cabin on the lowest deck, where your view of the passing scenery may be restricted by riverbanks.

Though some tourists expect (and pay for) ultraviolet water sterilization, it is basic hygienic controls that will determine your health – and which are most likely be skimped on boats where costs are cut to the bone. A recent investigation revealed fecal contamination of cabin surfaces, pool water and meals, which suggested that lax cleaning was to blame rather than a bug in the water system. Rather than **tip** your cabin cleaner at the end of the voyage, do so at the beginning as an incentive; cleaners are paid less than £E20 a day.

Other things to consider are the quality of **meals** (included in the price, but ranging from mediocre to sumptuous), the inflated cost of **alcohol** (many people smuggle booze aboard despite prohibition), seating arrangements (independent travellers are obliged to eat at the same table) and **moorings**. Boats in Luxor and Aswan are gradually being moved to new berths outside town, but those belonging to chains like Sonesta, Sofitel and Mövenpick may continue to dock by their respective hotels.

Boats grossly overcharge for **onshore excursions**, such as £E150 to visit Karnak Temple from nearby berths in Luxor. The management won't mind if you find a cheaper way unless you tell other passengers about it.

The following cruise boats are a cut above the rest – and costlier.

Philae Ⓦwww.oberoihotels.com. Like a Mississippi paddle-steamer, with teak panelling and antiques galore, this Oberoi-managed boat has all mod cons, including the latest water filtration system and is unusual in that each cabin has its own balcony. Rates for two people sharing are $3000 for four nights, $4500 for six nights, with a $150 surcharge per person at Christmas, New Year and Easter.

Radamis I & II Ⓦwww.nile-cruises.net. Managed by the Mövenpick chain, these two boats have large cabins, ample views and top-class facilities. The cost per person for a three- or four-day cruise starts at $310/420 from Luxor/Aswan in low season; in high season prices can virtually double.

St George I Ⓦwww.sonesta.com. The flagship of the Sonesta fleet, this state-of-the-art boat has a full-service spa and fitness centre, nightly entertainment, and over-the-top decor. Cruises start at $300 per person per day. The Sonesta also runs the *Star Goddess* – whose cabins are all suites (from $600 a night, single or double occupancy) – *Moon Goddess* (from $290 per person per night) and *Sun Goddess* (from $260), which are less opulent but still extremely comfortable.

Shehrayar and Shehrazad Ⓦwww .luxurynilecruises.com. Also managed by the Oberoi chain but marketed separately from the

Philae (see above), these two boats each have forty spacious cabins and all the usual amenities. Two people pay $840/1120/1960 for three, four or seven nights, plus $150 each at peak times.

Sudan Ⓦwww.steam-ship-sudan.com. Commissioned in 1885 for Cook's fleet, this vintage paddle steamer once belonged to King Fouad and was later used as a set in *Death on the Nile* before being left to rot until 2001. With only 22 cabins, it has bags of character, which makes up for the lack of a pool. No children under 7. Four or five-day cruises from €660 per person.

Sun Boat III Ⓦwww.akegypt.com. This luxurious boat, managed by Abercrombie & Kent, carries only 36 passengers, with a more intimate ambience than on *Sun Boat IV*, carrying 80 passengers, or the *Nile Adventurer* and *Nile Intrepid*, both sleeping 68 guests. On all these boats, mobile phones and smoking are prohibited indoors. Their three-, four- or seven-day cruises have an Egyptologist on board and enjoy private moorings at Luxor, Aswan and Kom Ombo.

Triton Bookable through Ⓦwww.capecairo.com and other upmarket, mainly foreign, agencies. Perhaps the ritziest boat on the Nile, this behemoth has an indoor and outdoor pool, a spa, a steward for each of its twenty double cabins, and a gourmet á la carte restaurant.

Dahabiyas

Egypt's pharaohs loved their pleasure-barges: Cleopatra and Julius Caesar spent *nine months* sailing round Egypt escorted by four hundred ships. Some of this luxury rubbed off on the houseboats that conveyed Ottoman officials up and downriver, dubbed **dahabiya** (from the Arabic for "gold") after their gilded railings. Despite the advent of Cook's tours in the 1860s, some Europeans still preferred to choose one of the two hundred *dahabiyas* for hire at the Cairo port of Bulaq (taking the precaution of first submerging it to kill any vermin), but by the 1900s steamers and railways had relegated them to Cairo love nests, which later went to the scrap-yard or were left to rot in the 1960s.

Thirty years later, a few entrepreneurs began refurbishing *dahabiyas* to run exclusive cruises. These proved so successful that replicas are now being built in the Delta with the traditional configuration of two lateen sails, and decor out of *Death on the Nile*. Though sometimes rented to tour groups, they are often **chartered** for a private cruise by newlyweds, families or friends. Passengers enjoy personalized service and are less constrained by schedules and moorings than on cruise boats, making it feasible to visit sites at quiet times or where larger ships can't moor, so besides the temples at Esna, Edfu and Kom Ombo, you get to explore **El–Kab** and **Silsilah**, which are otherwise difficult to reach (see p.420).

A typical *dahabiya* has a spacious salon; wood-panelled cabins ventilated by sliding louvres, with brass fittings and tiled bathrooms; and an upper deck where meals are eaten, whose awning can be rolled back for sunbathing. Besides sightseeing and stopovers there is backgammon, a library of books and CDs, and maybe live music or dancing after supper for entertainment. Meals are lavish, with lots of fresh fish and salads, washed down with fruit juices, beer or cocktails. Filtered water and rigorous hygiene mean that sickness is seldom a problem.

Three- to eight-day **itineraries** start or end in Esna or Aswan. Passengers arriving at (or flying home from) Luxor are transferred by bus, as the police prohibit *dahabiyas* sailing to Luxor. The **price** usually includes transfers, meals and soft drinks, excursions and tickets to the temples en route (but not necessarily in and around Aswan and Luxor) – read the small print carefully. All the boats below are recommended.

Assouan and El-Nil ⊛ www.nourelnil.com. Two replica antique boats equipped with state-of-the-art plumbing, water filtration, and power storage so the generator needn't be run at night. At 47m, *El-Nil* is the largest *dahabiya* on the Nile, accommodating twenty passengers. The cost per person for a six-day cruise runs from €1000/1250 (low/high season) for a regular cabin up to €1500/1750 for a luxury suite with French windows; or you can charter the boat for €22,000/27,000. On the smaller *Assouan*, sleeping up to sixteen, the rates are €1000/1250 for a cabin, €1250/1500 for a suite and €16,000/20,000 to charter the boat.
El-Bey (His Lordship), **El-Hanem** (Her Ladyship), **Nesma** (Breeze) and **Zahra** (Flower) ⊛ www.nubiannilecruises.com. Four replica antique vessels, each 38m long and sleeping up to twelve passengers in six cabins. An eight-day cruise costs from €1910 for a cabin (single or double occupancy) and exclusive boat hire from €11,000, depending on the time of year.
Neferu-Ra ⊛ www.museum-tours.com. Built for Omar Pasha in 1910, this 23m-long vessel, owned by a US tour company, sleeps up to five in three single cabins and one suite (small compared to other boats). Three-, four- or five-night cruises cost

$2000/2500/3000 for up to three people, $600/800/1000 for each extra passenger.
Royal Cleopatra ⊛ www.nubiannilecruises.com. A converted *sandale* (cargo felucca) rather than a proper *dahabiya*, so the owners call it a "yacht", which is what it looks like, with a bar, salon and two staterooms which can each be configured for up to three guests. The crew includes an Egyptologist guide for the sites between Esna and Aswan (7 days for about $1825 per person; shorter tours available).
Vivant Denon ⊛ www.dahabeya.net. Restored by ex-hotel manager Didier Caille, this 30m-long craft built in 1889 (named after the artist on Napoleon's expedition to Egypt) sleeps up to six passengers in four cabins. The ten cruises a year from October to April are mainly booked by French tourists, though Didier and his crew also speak English. Exclusively for chartering; a week's cruise costs €5500.
Zarafa (Giraffe) Built in 1835 for Egyptian royalty and owned by 1950s film stars, this large *dahabiya* carries eighteen passengers. Often chartered to foreign tour companies like Vintage Egypt (⊛ www.vintage-egypt.com; £200 sterling per person per day) or Travel in Style (⊛ www.travelinstyle.com; cabin $5500, entire boat $38,500).

Feluccas

Whether your **felucca** trip is blissful or boring, tragicomic or unpleasant depends on a host of factors. Conditions on the river are crucial. Nights are freezing in winter and otherwise cool and damp except in summer, when days are scorching. Nile breezes may be cooling, but winds from the desert can suck you dry and the effect of ultraviolet rays is magnified by water.

As the wind nearly always blows south, travelling downstream (towards Luxor) involves constant tacking, unless you simply drift with the sluggish current, but there's no chance of being becalmed, unlike sailing upriver, where the cliffs

△ Feluccas on the Nile near Aswan

between Esna, Edfu and Kom Ombo block the wind – which is why most journeys start **from Aswan**. The usual trips on offer are to Kom Ombo (two days, one night); Kom Ombo and Edfu (three days, two nights); or a two-day jaunt where you sail from noon to sunset and an hour next morning before being driven to Kom Ombo, Edfu and Luxor, which many tourists prefer to a three-day journey. Few care to sail all the way to Esna (four days, three nights), nor will crews agree to go as far as Luxor. Short daylight hours in winter and the low water level between October and May (when inexperienced pilots may run aground on sandbanks) can cause schedules to slip.

Establish beforehand where the journey ends. Tourists intending to disembark at **Edfu** often find themselves 30km short of town (in the villages of Hammam, Faris or Al-Ramady) or even at **Kom Ombo**, where minivans are on hand to drive them to Edfu temple and on to Luxor and whichever hotel the captain has a deal with. (The proper fare is £E10 per person, payable on arrival in Luxor.)

Many of the felucca captains come from villages outside Aswan and will take you there for tea at some point. Feluccas are prohibited from sailing after 8pm, so most stop at sunset for an evening round a campfire, enlivened by singing and drumming. You sleep either ashore after the boat has tied up, or on mattresses aboard. Each day will be different from the last: stow your watch and take things as they come.

Note that it's also possible to hire a felucca for a half-day outing or day-trip, as detailed in the accounts of Luxor and Aswan.

Arranging a felucca trip

Typically, a vessel has an English-speaking Nubian captain and carries six passengers (the largest boats take ten). Arranging a trip through a hotel is easier than doing it yourself, and reputable hotels are choosy about which feluccas they use, minimizing the chance of you getting a bad one. On the other hand, in the event of a dispute it will be harder to recover any cash from the captain, since the hotel will have already taken its cut.

To arrange a trip independently in Aswan, first find fellow travellers to share the cost by asking around in the Corniche restaurants or responding to messages posted in the tourist office. Women will benefit from teaming up with some men for the duration: an all-female group might have problems. Agree on the number of passengers before you go and don't be talked into accepting others later on, downriver, or food supplies and space will be more limited than you'd expected. Take your time **choosing a captain**; candidates can be "interviewed" at *Emy*, *Salah al-Din* and other cafés in Aswan – ignore any recommendations from the city's tourist office.

Would-be voyagers are entitled to a free cruise around Aswan "bay" to check out the boat and its crew in action. Some captains have been guilty of taking tourists for a jaunt on a smart boat, and then substituting an inferior vessel (or crew) on the day of departure. If this happens, refuse to set sail and report it to the tourist office, who'll act as an intermediary between you and the tourist police.

The **cost** is calculated according to the duration of the journey, but also varies with demand. For a group of six, the tourist office quotes £E36 per person for a trip to Kom Ombo, £E69 for Esna and £E70 for Edfu – but you'll have to settle a price with the captain. Hotels are less inclined to haggle and factor their commission into the price – for example, Aswan's *Keylany* hotel (see p.432) charges £E85 per person for a two-day trip making landfall just short of Kom Ombo and travelling the rest of the way to Luxor by minibus, visiting two temples en route. If you hire your own captain, don't pay the whole sum up front, lest the boat "break down" and curtail the trip prematurely, and be sure that all passengers know what has been negotiated, to ensure solidarity in the event of a dispute with the crew.

Don't hand over your **passport**; captains or middlemen like to collect them as proof that they've got some passengers in the bag while they go hunting for more. A photocopy of the page(s) with your personal details and photograph suffices for registration with the **River Police**, which is mandatory. This can be arranged by felucca captains or hotels – which charge £E5 per person for the effort, though there is no official fee.

Blankets are provided but seldom enough to keep you warm at night – a sleeping bag is essential. Ensure that the boat has a canvas awning (it will protect you from the sun and double as a tent at night), adequate mattresses, a jerry can for water, a kerosene stove and lamp, proper cutlery and a padlocked luggage hold. Few carry life-jackets, so passengers who can't swim must bring their own.

Food and hygiene

Meals, prepared on a campfire or primus stove, consist of *fuul*, rice, bread, feta cheese and salad, washed down with tea. Any treats you want should be bought beforehand, and some groups prefer to agree on a price without food and do their own shopping.

There's a real risk of you getting sick if **hygiene** precautions aren't observed. Be sure to buy plenty of bottled water, or the crew may dip into the Nile for drinking or cooking purposes. Bring extra-strong sterilizing tablets to purify the jerry can of Nile water used for washing up (one tablet per 25 litres); also purchase carbolic soap and be sure that everyone uses it (food is mostly eaten with fingers); burn rubbish and bury excrement (the Nile's banks are badly littered) – few captains will bother with any health precautions unless pressed. Also essential are a hat, sunscreen and bug repellent (the shallows swarm with mosquitoes).

Abydos

As Muslims endeavour to visit Mecca once in their lifetimes and Hindus aspire to die at Benares, the Ancient Egyptians devoutly wished to make a pilgrimage to **ABYDOS** (pronounced "Abi-dos"), cult centre of the god Osiris. Those who failed to make it hoped to do so posthumously; relatives brought bodies for burial, or embellished distant tombs with scenes of the journey to Abydos (represented by a boat under sail, travelling upriver). Egyptians averred that the dead "went west", for the entrance to the underworld was believed to lie amid the desert hills beyond Abydos. By bringing other deities into the Osirian fold, Abydos acquired a near monopoly on death cults, which persisted into Ptolemaic times. Its superbly carved **Temple of Seti I** has been a tourist attraction since the 1830s, and many rate its artwork as the finest in Egypt.

Practicalities

A daily tourist **convoy** to Abydos and Dendara leaves Luxor at 8am. In Luxor, Karnak Travel, Thomas Cook and other agencies offer **bus excursions** to both sites for £E335–550 per person (including tickets), while hotels like *Happy Land* and *Nefertiti* can arrange a taxi (£E200) or minibus (£E300) – the group price doesn't include tickets. An excursion to Abydos can also be arranged from **Sohag** (see p.311).

The convoy schedule allows visitors slightly over an hour at Abydos – long enough to explore Seti's temple and the Osireion, but nothing else. To stay longer at Abydos involves taking a **train** from Luxor (or Qena) to the town of **EL-BALYANA**, 10km from Abydos. On leaving the train, go back 30m to a railway crossing, turn right and after 300m you should find a **police** checkpoint, where the cops will summon a taxi and escort you to the temple and back for a fair price. This works out better than bargaining with taxi drivers at the station, who try to overcharge.

The **site of Abydos** (daily 8am–5pm; £E25) is reached by a well-surfaced country road which terminates at the village of **AL-ARABA EL-MADFUNA**, where a ticket kiosk, outdoor café and souvenir stalls lead towards the temple. Should you care to **stay**, the *Abydos Hotel* (☎010 413-1800; ❷) has cleanish rooms, preferable to the grungy *Seti I Resthouse* (☎093/489-2852; ❶) across the road, which can rustle up basic **meals** and beer.

The Temple of Seti I

While the temples of Karnak and Deir el-Bahri at Luxor are breathtaking conceptions executed on a colossal scale, it is the exquisite quality of its bas-reliefs that distinguishes Abydos' **Temple of Seti I**. The reliefs are among the finest works of the New Kingdom, harking back to Old Kingdom forms in an artistic revival that mirrored Seti's political efforts to consolidate the XIX Dynasty and recover territories lost under Akhenaten. The official designation of Seti's reign (1318–1304 BC) was "the era of repeating births" – literally a renaissance.

▲ Seti I

It was in fact Seti's son, Ramses II (1304–1237 BC), who completed the reconquest of former colonies and the construction of his father's temple at Abydos. Strictly speaking, the building was neither a cult nor a funerary temple in the ordinary sense, for its chapels contained shrines to a variety of deities concerned with death, resurrection and the netherworld, and one dedicated to Seti himself. Its purpose was essentially political: to identify the king with these cults and with his putative "ancestors", the previous rulers of Egypt, thus conferring legitimacy on the Ramessid Dynasty, whose ancestors had been mere Delta warriors a few generations earlier.

The temple's spell has endured through the ages, as New Age pilgrims follow in the footsteps of Dorothy Eady – known as **Umm Seti** (Mother of Seti) – who lived at Abydos for 35 years until she died in 1981, believing herself to be the reincarnation of a temple priestess and lover of Seti I. Her trances and prophetic gifts are related in Jonathan Cott's biography, *The Search for Omm Sety* – available at souvenir stalls here.

The forecourt and Hypostyle Halls

The temple's original **pylon** and **forecourt** have almost been levelled but you can still discern the lower portion of a scene depicting Ramses II's dubious victory at Qadesh **[a]**, women with finely plaited tresses **[b]**, and Seti making offerings to Osiris (in a niche, nearby). From the damaged statues currently stored in the upper, second court, your eyes are drawn to the square-columned **facade**, where tiny birds inhabit fissures in the wall behind pillars covered with scenes of Ramses greeting Osiris, Isis and Horus **[c]**. Originally, the temple was entered by seven doors (corresponding to the shrines within), but Ramses ordered all except the middle one blocked up. The upper part of the facade has been crudely rebuilt in concrete.

The ponderous sunk-reliefs in the **outer Hypostyle Hall**, completed by Ramses after Seti's death, suggest that he used second-rate artists, having redeployed Seti's top craftsmen on his own (now destroyed) temple. The entrance wall portrays Ramses measuring the temple with the goddess Selket and presenting it to Horus on Seti's behalf, while on the wall to your right Ramses offers a falcon-headed box of papyrus to Isis, Horus and Osiris, and is led to the temple by Horus and Wepwawet (the jackal-headed god of Assyut) to be doused with holy water (represented by the interlinked signs for life and purity) **[d]**. On one of the roof-lintels is a cartouche which has achieved mythical status on the Internet; purportedly, it shows a helicopter and a submarine – though archeologists deride the "**Abydos helicopter**" as a simple case of palitation (the superimposition of one cartouche upon another, combining with erosion to produce an unusual shape), and the digitally enhanced image on the Web is far clearer than the murky original.

The deeper **inner Hypostyle Hall** was the last part of the temple decorated before Seti's death, and some sections were never finished, but others are exceptional. On the right-hand wall Seti stands before Osiris and Horus – who pour holy water from garlanded vases – and makes offerings before the shrine of Osiris, who is attended by Maat and Ronpet (the goddess of the year) in front, with Isis, Amentet (goddess of the west) and Nephthys behind **[e]**. Seti's profile is a stylized but close likeness to his mummy (in the Cairo Antiquities Museum). The east and west walls are of sandstone, the north and south of limestone. Two projecting piers **[f]** near the back of the hall depict Seti worshipping the Djed pillar while wearing the crown of Upper or Lower Egypt. The reliefs along the rear wall – showing him being anointed and crowned by the gods – are still brightly coloured. Best of all is a scene of Seti kneeling before Osiris and Horus, with the sacred persea tree in the background, which appears above head height on the wall between the sanctuaries of Ptah and Re-Herakhte **[g]**.

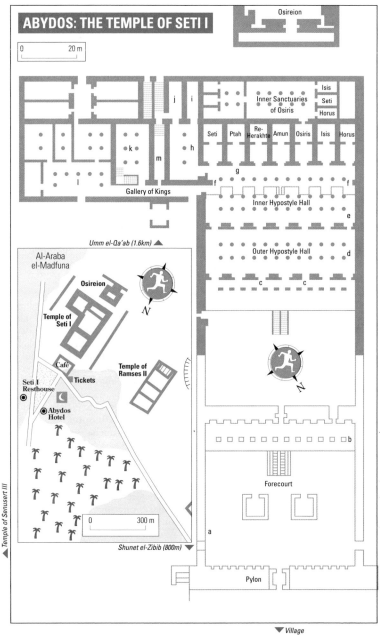

ABYDOS: THE TEMPLE OF SETI I

Osireion

0   20 m

Isis
Seti
Horus

j i

Inner Sanctuaries
of Osiris

Seti   Ptah   Re-   Amun   Osiris   Isis   Horus
              Herakhte

k

h

m

g

l

f   f

Gallery of Kings

Inner Hypostyle Hall

e

Umm el-Qa'ab (1.6km) ▲

Outer Hypostyle Hall

d

c   c

Al-Araba
el-Madfuna

Osireion

N

Temple of
Seti I

Café

Tickets

Temple of
Ramses II

Seti I
Resthouse
◉

☾

◉ Abydos
Hotel

N

🏃

🏃

b

Forecourt

0   300 m

a

Shunet el-Zibib (800m) ▼

Pylon

◀ Temple of Senusert III

◀ Temple of Ramses II (300m; see inset)

▼ Village

The sanctuaries

The finest **bas-reliefs** at Abydos are inside the sanctuaries dedicated to Seti and six deities. Though retaining much of their original colouring (showing how most temple reliefs once looked), their graceful lines and subtle moulding are best appreciated on the unpainted reliefs. Seti's classical revival eschewed both Amarna expressionism and the bombastic XVIII Dynasty imperial style, which his son embraced and raised to new heights of megalomania. The seven sanctuaries are roofed with false vaults carved from rectangular slabs, and culminate in false doors (except for Osiris's chamber, which leads into his inner sanctuaries).

To Ancient Egyptians, these chambers constituted the abode of the gods, whom the king (or his priests) propitiated with daily rituals, shown on the walls. Having opened the shrine, the pharaoh would offer the god sacrifices and wash and dress its statue, which was then purified and presented with gifts. After further offerings before the god's barque, he would scatter sand on the floor, sweep away his footprints and withdraw, leaving the deity alone till next morning.

An exception to this rule is the **Sanctuary of Seti**, which emphasizes his recognition by the gods, who lead him into the temple and ceremonially unite the Two Lands along the northern wall. Below the barque near the back of the left-hand wall, Seti receives a list of offerings from Thoth and the High Priest Iunmutef, wearing the leopardskin and braided sidelock of his office. Finally, Seti leaves the temple, his palanquin borne by the souls of jackal-headed deities

---

The cult of Osiris

Originally the corn-god of Busiris in the Delta, **Osiris** attained national significance early in the Old Kingdom, when he was co-opted into the Heliopolitan Ennead. According to legend, Re (or Geb) divided the world between Osiris and his brother Seth, who resented being given all the deserts and murdered Osiris to usurp his domain. Although the god's body was recovered by **Isis**, the sister-wife of Osiris, Seth recaptured and dismembered it, burying the pieces at different locations and feeding the penis to a crocodile. Aided by her sister Nephthys, Isis collected the bits and bandaged them together to create the first mummy, which they briefly resurrected with the help of Thoth and Anubis. By transforming herself into a hawk, Isis managed to conceive a child with Osiris before he returned to the netherworld to rule as lord and judge of the dead. Secretly raised to manhood in the Delta, their child **Horus** later avenged his father and cast Seth back into the wilderness (see p.419).

▲ Osiris

Abydos, as the "place of the head" of Osiris (the meaning of its ancient name, Abdjw), was the setting for two annual **festivals**. The "Great Going Forth" celebrated the search for and discovery of his remains, while the Osiris Festival re-enacted his myth in a series of Mystery Plays. In one scene, the god's barque was "attacked" by minions of Seth and "protected" by **Wepwawet**, the jackal-headed god of Assyut. This marked the final stage in a process of religious mergers, for it was Wepwawet who supplanted **Khentamenty**, the original death-god of Abydos, as the "Foremost of the Westerners", before his own assimilation into the cult of Osiris. The total identification of Abydos with **death cults** was completed by its association with **Anubis**, the jackal-headed god of embalming, always present in funerary scenes.

from the Upper Egyptian town of Nekhen and hawk-headed gods from the Delta capital of Pi-Ramses.

The fine unpainted reliefs of Seti and seated deities in Re-Herakhte's chamber make interesting comparison with similar painted scenes in the sanctuaries of Ptah, Amun, Osiris and Isis. On the side wall just outside the Sanctuary of Horus, the pharaoh presents Maat to Osiris, Isis and Horus, a XIX Dynasty motif symbolizing righteous order and the restoration of royal legitimacy.

The **inner sanctuaries of Osiris** boast three side chapels whose colours were still fresh and shiny in the 1980s, but are now blackened by mould – a rapid rate of deterioration affecting many of the temples and tombs in the Nile Valley.

The southern wing

From the inner Hypostyle Hall you can enter the southern wing of Seti's temple. The portal nearest his sanctuary leads into the columned **Hall of Sokar and Nefertum**, two deities of the north representing the life-giving forces of the earth and the cycle of death and rebirth, who were integrated into the Osirian cult by Seti's time. Reliefs on the right-hand wall depict Seti receiving a hawk-headed Sokar **[h]**; Nefertum is shown on the opposite wall in both his human and leonine forms (crowned with a lotus blossom). In the **Chapel of Sokar [i]**, Osiris appears in his bier and returns to life grasping his penis (near the back of the right-hand wall), while Isis hovers over him in the form of a hawk on the opposite wall. The **Chapel of Nefertum** is next door **[j]**.

The other portal leads through into the **Gallery of Kings**, so called after the list of Seti's predecessors carved on the right-hand wall – the earliest (Zoser) on the far left of the top row, with Seti at the far end of the bottom register. For political reasons, the Hyksos pharaohs, Hatshepsut, Akhenaten and his heirs have all been omitted, and Seti has recorded his own name as *Menmare Osiris-Merneptah* (rather than *Menmare Seti-Merneptah*) to distance himself from his namesake Seth, the killer of Osiris. Nonetheless, the list has proved immensely useful to archeologists, naming 34 kings (chiefly from the VI, VII, XII, XVIII and XIX dynasties) in roughly chronological order.

Running off from the gallery are the **Sanctuary of the Boats [k]**, where the deities' barques were kept on platforms; the **Hall of Sacrifices [l]** (closed); and a corridor **[m]** with vivid sunk-reliefs of Seti and Ramses harnessing a bull to present to Wepwawet, and hauling birds in a net. This will bring you out through a rear door to the Osireion, behind the temple.

The Osireion and other remains

The **site of Abydos** covers a huge area, with ruins and mounds scattered across the edge of the desert. Few visitors have the time to wander far even if the police would let them, but it's worth investigating the structure directly behind Seti's temple.

When Flinders Petrie excavated Abydos in the early twentieth century, he uncovered numerous *mastabas* which he belived to be royal tombs, but which later Egyptologists held to be cenotaphs or Osirian burial places – dummy tombs, built to promote a closer association between the pharaoh's *ka* and Osiris, while his mummy reposed elsewhere. Seti's Cenotaph, known as the **Osireion**, is the only one now visible, albeit half-buried and rendered partly inaccessible by stagnant water. Built of massive blocks, it once enclosed a room containing a mound surrounded by a moat (symbolizing the first land arising from the waters of Chaos at the dawn of Creation), where a pseudo-sarcophagus awaited resurrection. Nearby is a long underground passage that once led to the cenotaph.

Some 300m northwest is a ruined **Temple of Ramses II**, Seti's father, where fragments of scenes of the Battle of Qadesh (see p.466) can be discerned on the enclosure walls and pillared courtyard.

Other sites further afield give insights into **predynastic history**. The German Archeological Institute (Ⓦ www.dainst.org) has been excavating the Early Dynastic royal cemetery at **Umm el-Qa'ab** since 1977, and more recently funerary enclosures at **Shunet el-Zebib**. The complex of Khasekhemwy, last king of the II Dynasty, who died about 2686 BC, was surrounded by walls up to 11m high and 5.5m thick, 122m long and 65m wide. Dr Gunter Dreyer believes that the pyramids at Saqqara evolved from the enclosure of sunken brick-lined tombs at Abydos, where hieroglyphic writing predating Saqqara's has been found, suggesting the existence of a predynastic king Hor or Horus, who conquered the Delta and united the Two Lands a century before Narmer. In 1991, six **Solar Boats** were found buried within Khasekhemwy's enclosure, which are thought to date from the reign of the I Dynasty ruler Aha (*c.*2920–2770 BC). All this raises the possibility that the Early Dynastic burials attributed to Saqqara may have occurred at Abydos instead, and that an intact royal tomb might one day be found here.

Nag Hammadi and Dishna

At **NAG HAMMADI** (pronounced "Naja Ham*maad*i"), 40km south of El-Balyana, the Nile sweeps into the "**Qena Bend**", and the main road and train tracks transfer from the west bank to the other side of the river. Other than its historic association with the Gnostic Gospels (see box below), Nag Hammadi is only notable for its cement factory, hydroelectric barrage, and comfortable *Aluminium* **hotel** (Ⓣ & Ⓕ 096/659-0001; Ⓢ), 3km south of town.

Across the river, **Dishna** looks like any farming town in the Valley, but is infamous throughout Egypt for its **vendettas**. While blood-feuds (*al-tar* in Arabic) are common in Upper Egypt, the one between two villages here lasted generations, obliging every adult male to carry a gun at all times. The police seldom left their fortified post and never got involved in fights: after dark, gunmen roamed freely and held up cars on the highway. Peace was only achieved after mediation by eminent sheikhs in 2004, though even now the police sometimes suspend traffic to the east bank after dark. During the day, however, the road is perfectly safe and Dishna folk are actually renowned for their hospitality to strangers – their hostility is reserved for their neighbours.

The Gnostic Gospels

The **Nag Hammadi Codices** – better known as the **Gnostic Gospels** – were found near the town, below the caves of Jebel et-Tur, in 1945. The gospels are fourth-century Coptic translations of second-century Greek originals, although the Gospel of Thomas might date from 50–100 AD, and therefore be as early as – or even older than – the gospels of Matthew, Mark, Luke and John.

The Gnostics (from *gnosis*, Greek for "knowledge") were early mystics who believed that God could only be known through self-understanding and that the world was illusory. Regarding self and the divine as one, they saw Jesus as a spiritual guide rather than the crucified son of God, pointing to his words in the Gospel of Thomas: *"If you bring forth what is within you, what you bring forth will save you. If you do not bring forth what is within you, what is within you will destroy you."* But the official church thought otherwise and condemned Gnosticism as a heresy; hence the burial of these codices (some of which can be seen today in Cairo's Coptic Museum).

Dendara and Qena

The **Temple of Hathor** at **Dendara** lacks the sublime quality of Seti's edifice at Abydos, but its astronomical ceiling and rooftop sanctuaries offer a unique insight into the solar rituals at other cult sites where they have not survived. Dendara also shows how Egypt's Greek and Roman rulers identified themselves with the pharaohs and deities of Ancient Egypt by copying their temples, rituals and icongraphy down to the last hieroglyph – though they did tinker with a few details of reliefs and murals. Goddesses and queens became bustier, and the feet of royalty were shown with all their toes (instead of only the big toe, as the Ancient Egyptians did).

Most tourists visit Dendara in conjunction with the temple at Abydos (see p.322), travelling in a convoy from Luxor – which limits you to an hour at Dendara. To stay longer at Dendara you'll have to get there by public transport via **Qena** (8km away), which is a bit of a hassle under the current travel restrictions. If you're setting off from Luxor, note that not all northbound trains stop at Qena, so it's advisable to catch an early-morning bus if you want to visit Dendara and then continue by train towards Abydos.

Dendara – the Temple of Hathor

Across the Nile from Qena, fields of onions and clover recede towards the cliffs of the Western Desert and the Temple of Hathor near the village of **DENDARA**. One of the few Egyptian temples with an intact and accessible rooftop, it offers fantastic views of the surrounding countryside.

The daily **convoy** from Luxor to Dendara and Abydos leaves the city at 8am. Thomas Cook, Karnak Travel and other agencies' **coach excursions** to both sites are a lot dearer than minibus trips arranged by budget hotels in Luxor (see p.357). Alternatively, the *Lotus Boat* and *Tiba Star* run **day cruises** from Luxor to Dendara on Tuesdays, Fridays and Sundays: tickets are sold through Thomas Cook (£E350), the *Iberotel* (£E355) and Karnak Travel (€40) three days in advance. Coming **by public transport** is only worth the effort if you want to stay longer at Dendara – trying to combine this with a visit to Abydos means starting at the crack of dawn: see "Practicalities" under Qena (p.334) for details.

The **site** (daily: summer 7am–6pm; winter 7am–5pm; £E25) is surrounded by high mud-brick walls and sufficiently large that few visitors venture far from the temple – even if the convoy schedule allowed more time. There is a café for refreshments, but the toilets are awful.

The Temple of Hathor

Although there have been shrines to Hathor, the goddess of joy, at Dendara since predynastic times, the existing **Temple of Hathor** is a Greco-Roman creation, built between 125 BC and 60 AD. Since the object of the exercise was to confer legitimacy on Egypt's foreign rulers, it emulates the pharaonic pattern of Hypostyle Halls and vestibules preceding a darkened sanctuary, "a progression from the light of the Egyptian sun to the mystery of the holy of holies" (T.G.H. James). Surrounding the complex are vast mud-brick enclosure walls.

The temple **facade** is shaped like a pylon, with six Hathor-headed columns rising from a screen. Here and inside, Hathor appears in human form rather than her bovine aspect (see p.331). Because this section was built during the reign of Tiberius, its reliefs depict Roman emperors making offerings to the gods, namely Tiberius and Claudius before Horus, Hathor and their son Ihy **[a]**,

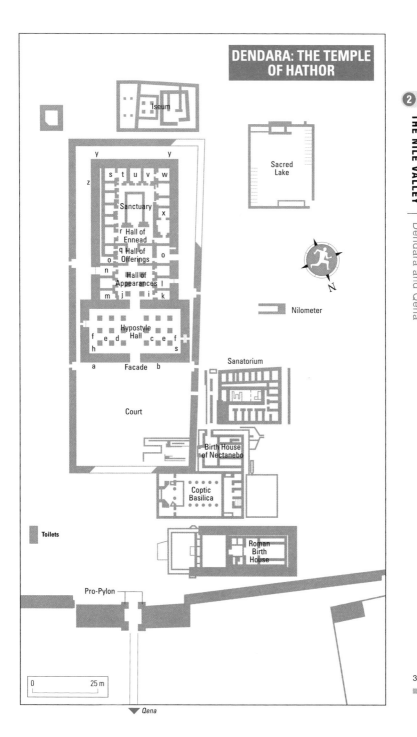

DENDARA: THE TEMPLE OF HATHOR

Iseum

Sacred Lake

Sanctuary

s t u v w
z
x
r Hall of Ennead
q Hall of Offerings
o   o
n
Hall of Appearances
l
m j   i k

y   y

Hypostyle Hall
f e d   c e f
h   s
a   Facade   b

Court

N

Nilometer

Sanatorium

Birth House of Nectanebo

Coptic Basilica

Roman Birth House

Toilets

Pro-Pylon

0   25 m

▼ Qena

and Tiberius as a sphinx before Hathor and Horus **[b]**. Nineteenth-century engravings show the temple buried in sand almost to the lintel of its portal, which explains why its upper sections bore the brunt of Coptic iconoclasm.

The Hypostyle Hall

Entering the **Hypostyle Hall** with its eighteen Hathor-headed columns, you'll need to let your eyes grow accustomed to the gloom before examining its famous **astronomical ceiling**, which retains much of its original colouring. This is not a sky chart in the modern sense, but a symbolic representation of the heavenly bodies, the hours of the day and night, and the realms of the sun and moon. Although the Qena Bend dictates a north–south orientation rather than the customary east–west axis (since temples always faced the Nile), the ceiling maintains the traditional dichotomy between the northern and southern halves of the sky.

Above the central aisle, a row of flying vultures and winged discs separates the left-hand bays representing the southern heavens from those to the right, dedicated to the northern sky. Here, the first row **[c]** begins with the Eye of Re in its barque, above which appear the fourteen days of the waning moon. Beyond the full moon in the centre come the fourteen stages of the waxing moon (each with its own deity), culminating in the full disc worshipped by Thoth, and lastly the moon as Osiris, protected by Isis and Nephthys. Souls in the form of jackals and birds adorn Re's barque as it journeys across the sun's register **[d]**.

Following these are two bands **[e]** showing the planets, the stars of the twelve hours of the night, and the signs of the zodiac (adopted from Babylonia). The end rows **[f]** are dominated by Nut, who gives birth to the sun at dawn and swallows it at dusk. On one side, the rising sun Khepri (the scarab beetle) is born **[g]**; on the other, the sun shines down on Hathor **[h]**.

The Hall of Appearances

The Ptolemaic section of the temple begins with the six-columned **Hall of Appearances**, where Hathor consorted with fellow deities before her voyage to Edfu (see opposite). With a torch, you can examine reliefs on the entrance wall depicting offerings **[i]**, and the foundation of the temple and its presentation to the gods **[j]**. Notice the "blank" cartouches, which attest to the high turnover of rulers in late Ptolemaic times, when stonemasons were loath to inscribe the names of Ptolemies who might not last for long – there were times when they wouldn't even know who actually reigned in Alexandria. Nonetheless, rituals continued at Dendara, where the priests kept holy objects of precious metal in the Treasury **[k]** and drew water for purification ceremonies from a well reached by the so-called Nile Room **[l]**.

Corresponding chambers across the hall include the laboratory **[m]**, where perfumes, incense and unguents were mixed and stored (notice the reliefs showing recipes, and bearers bringing exotic materials from afar); and another room for storing valuables **[n]**. A liturgical calendar listing festivals celebrated at the temple appears on the inner side of its doorway. The Egyptian calendar had 360 days – the five "missing" days were named after gods and devoted to feasting. Notice the bases of columns from an older temple, exposed by the flagstones in the corner.

The Hall of Offerings and the Hall of Ennead

Beyond lies the **Hall of Offerings**, the entrance to the temple proper, with twin **stairways** to the roof (see p.329) up which sacrificial animals were led **[o]**.

The cult of Hathor

Worshipped from the earliest times as a cow goddess, **Hathor** acquired manifold attributes – body of the sky, living soul of trees, goddess of gold and turquoise, music and revelry – but remained essentially nurturing. Her greatest role was that of wet nurse and bedmate for **Horus**, and giver of milk to the living pharaoh. In her human aspect (with bovine ears and horns), the goddess paid an annual visit to Horus at his temple in **Edfu**. Her barque, escorted by priests and cheered by commoners, proceeded upriver, where Horus sailed out to meet her on his own boat. After much pomp and ritual, the idols were left alone to reconsummate their union while the populace enjoyed a **Festival of Drunkenness**, which led the Greeks to identify Hathor with their own goddess of love and joy, Aphrodite.

▲ Hathor

However, drunkenness at other times drew condemnation, as in this timeless rebuke to a lager lout: "You trail from street to street smelling of beer, you have been found performing acrobatics on a wall, people run from your blows. Look at you beating on your stomach, reeling and rolling about on the ground covered in your own filth!"

A list of offerings appears on the rear wall **[p]**, across the way from a relief showing the king offering Hathor her favourite tipple **[q]**.

Next comes the **Hall of the Ennead**, where statues of the gods and kings involved in ceremonies dedicated to Hathor once stood. Her wardrobe was stored in a room to the left, where reliefs show the priests carrying the chests that held the sacred garments. Just outside the sanctuary you can see the text of the Hymns of Awakening. The **Sanctuary** housed Hathor's statue and ceremonial barque, which priests carried to the riverside and placed upon a boat that worshippers towed upriver to Edfu for a conjugal reunion with Horus. Reliefs depict the daily rituals (described on p.325) and the king presenting Maat to Hathor, Horus and Harsomtus (rear wall).

Side chapels

Two corridors with side chapels run alongside (and meet behind) the sanctuary. Above the doorway into the Corridor of Mysteries, Hathor appears as a cow within a wooden kiosk mounted on a barque **[r]**. Past the chapels of Isis, Sokar and the Sacred Serpent, you'll find the "Castle of the Sistrum" (Hathor's musical instrument), where niches depict her standing on the sky, and the coronation of Ihy as god of music **[s]**. This is entered via the darkened Per-Nu chapel **[t]**, whence Hathor embarked on her conjugal voyage to Edfu during the New Year festival (which fell on July 19 in ancient times).

The New Year procession began from the Per-Ur chapel **[u]**, where a shaky ladder ascends to a small cache chamber containing reliefs of Hathor, Maat and Isis. In the Per-Neser chapel **[v]**, one of the custodians will lift a hatch and guide you down into a low-ceilinged **crypt** carved with cobras and lotuses. The chapel itself shows Hathor in her terrible aspect as a lioness, for by Ptolemaic times she had assimilated the leonine goddess Sekhmet and the feline goddess Bastet. The temple's most valuable treasures were stored underneath the Chapel of Re **[w]**.

If you haven't already stumbled upon it, return to the Hall of the Ennead, bear left through an antechamber and then right, to find the "Pure Place" **[x]** or **New Year Chapel**, whose ceiling is covered by a relief of Nut giving birth to the sun, which shines on Hathor's head. It was here that rituals were performed prior to Hathor's communion with the sun on the temple's roof. Check out the rooftop shrines (see below) before leaving the temple and walking round to the rear wall, where two defaced sunk-reliefs **[y]** of Cleopatra and her son Caesarion feature in a procession of deities. The chubby face below the Hathor crown is so unlike the beautiful queen of legend that most people prefer to regard this as a stylized image rather than a lifelike **portrait of Cleopatra**. The lion-headed **waterspouts** below the cornice were a Roman innovation.

One last bit of iconography worth noting is the array of royal **crowns** – 22 different kinds appear on the third register of the east wall **[z]**.

Rooftop sanctuaries

From either side of the Hall of Offerings, a stairway ascends to the roof of the temple; the scenes on the walls depict the New Year procession, when Hathor's statue was carried up to an open kiosk on the rooftop to await the dawn; touched by the rays of the sun, Hathor's *ba* (soul) was revitalized for the coming year. Besides the sun kiosk there are two suites of rooms dedicated to the death and resurrection of Osiris, behind the facade of the Hypostyle Hall. Although such **rooftop sanctuaries** were a feature of most temples, those at Dendara are uniquely intact.

The one on the left (as you face south) is notable for the reliefs in its inner chamber, which show Osiris being mourned by Isis and Nephthys, passing through the gates of the netherworld, and finally bringing himself to erection to impregnate Isis, who appears as a hovering kite. The other suite contains a plaster cast of the famous **Dendara Zodiac** ceiling filched by Lelorrain in 1820 and now in the Louvre. Upheld by four goddesses, the circular carving features a zodiac which only differs from our own by the substitution of a scarab for the scorpion and the inclusion of the hippo goddess Taweret. The zodiac was introduced to Egypt (and other lands) by the Romans, who copied it from Babylonia. Mind your head on the low doorway.

Best of all is the magnificent **view** of the temple and the countryside from the rooftop. Also notice the **graffiti** left by French troops in 1799, including the names of their commander Desaix and the artist Denon, who sketched frenziedly at Dendara as the Mamlukes drew nearer, melting down bullets for lead when he ran out of pencils.

Outlying buildings

Surrounding the temple are various other structures, now largely ruined. Ptolemaic temples were distinguished by the addition of *mamissi* or Birth Houses, which associated the pharaoh with Horus, the deified king. When the Romans surrounded the temple with an enclosure wall, it split in two the **Birth House of Nectanebo** (XXX Dynasty), compelling them to build a replacement. The **Roman Birth House** has some fine carvings on its south wall, and tiny figures of Bes and Tweri on the column capitals and architraves. Between the two *mamissi* lies a ruined, fifth-century **Coptic Basilica**, built with masonry from the adjacent structures; notice the incised Coptic crosses.

As a compassionate goddess, Hathor had a reputation for healing and her temple attracted pilgrimages from the sick. In the **Sanatorium** here patients were prescribed cures during dreams, induced by narcotics. Water for ritual ablutions was drawn from a **Sacred Lake** now drained of liquid and full of palm trees and birds.

Nearby stands a ruined **Iseum** used for the worship of Isis and Osiris, built by Cleopatra's mortal enemy, Octavian, after he became Emperor Augustus.

△ Hathor suckling Horus in the Roman Birth House

Qena

QENA (pronounced "*Gena*") has long played second fiddle to Luxor in terms of tourism and investment, a grievance which might explain why it was the site of the first attack on tourists, in 1992. Like Sohag and Assyut, it suffered an

333

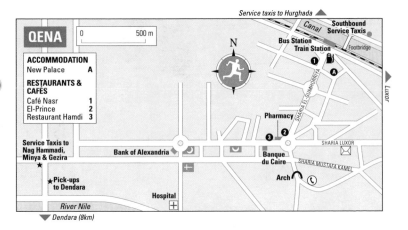

QENA

0   500 m

N

Canal   Southbound
         Service Taxis
Bus Station
Train Station   Footbridge

ACCOMMODATION
New Palace   A

RESTAURANTS &
CAFÉS
Café Nasr   1
El-Prince   2
Restaurant Hamdi 3

Luxor

Pharmacy

SHARIA EL GUMHORIYA

Service Taxis to
Nag Hammadi,
Minya & Gezira

Pick-ups
to Dendara

Bank of Alexandria

Banque
du Caire

SHARIA LUXOR

SHARIA MUSTAFA KAMEL

Arch

River Nile

Hospital

Dendara (8km)

economic nose-dive during the Islamist insurgency. Then, in 2000, a new governor – Adel Labib (now in charge of Alexandria) – began improving municipal services with such energy that Qena later won an international certificate of good governance. As the only city in Egypt where every road is paved, its streets are not only spotless but have flowerbeds and mosaics. Where women were once stuck indoors, there are now parks and cafés for family outings, a girls' sports centre and football team. Qenawis are proud that people from Luxor come here to enjoy its café society, yet the police still discourage foreigners from lingering.

Tourists in the convoy pass hundreds of roadside portraits of Mubarak, but only glimpse Qena's riverside cafés and two illuminated mosques that are local landmarks. The older mosque (with one minaret) contains the tomb of a twelfth-century Moroccan Sufi, who is honoured by the **Moulid of Abdel Rahim al-Qenawi**, featuring *zikrs*, dancing horses and horse races. The festival starts on Sha'ban 14 and finishes the day before the start of Abu el-Haggag's moulid in Luxor (see p.355). Qena's **City Day** (March 8) festival commemorates a series of battles in 1799, when local villages sank a French flotilla of a dozen vessels.

Due to the Qena Bend, the banks of the Nile lie north and south, rather than east and west of the river: the town is on the north bank, with a bridge to Dendara on the south bank.

Practicalities

Qena is a **transport** hub, with Superjet buses to Cairo (7am & 8pm) and regular ones to Port Safaga, Hurghada and Suez (hourly), El-Quseir and Mersa Alam (11am & 5.30pm). Middle Egypt and Luxor are better reached by train; **trains** to and from Luxor take around forty minutes, but you may be restricted to certain services.

Arriving at Qena train station or at the bridge over the canal, 200m further west, you're sure to be spotted by the police, who'll order a **taxi** (£E20) to take you straight to Dendara, where their colleagues will ensure a ride back. For Abydos, you could catch the #981 train, which departs Qena at 10.40am, to El-Balyana.

Despite several **hotels** under construction and the revamped *New Palace* (☎096/532-2509; ❷), foreigners are actively discouraged from staying. **Eating** is slightly better: the *Restaurant Hamdi* serves full meals of soup, chicken or *kofta*, rice and vegetables, as does *El-Prince* (which also occasionally sells beer), while *Café Nasr* also does cheaper veggie dishes.

There are two **banks** (daily except Fri 8am–2pm) for changing cash and traveller's cheques. The **post office** (daily except Fri 8.30am–2pm) and the 24-hour **telephone exchange** are a short walk from the main intersection, while the **police** can be found in the train station.

Between Qena and Luxor

While the police make it impossible for tourists to visit any of the sites **between Qena and Luxor**, you're likely to catch a fleeting glimpse at least, and some are important in Egyptian history.

Along the east bank

Crowded with traffic for Luxor, the east bank road passes through **Qift**, ancient Kebt or Koptos, a mining depot which became a commercial entrepôt once a route to the coast was found. The 216-kilometre road from here to **El-Quseir** on the Red Sea, well-paved, with resthouses, petrol station – and some ancient rock inscriptions – is described on p.759.

South towards Luxor, a factory for converting *bagasse* – the waste product of sugar refining – into paper presages **Qus**, which was second only to Cairo during Fatimid and Mamluke times, when it served as a place of exile for deposed sultans. A relic of its former status is the eleventh-century **Al-Amri Mosque**.

Further south, the Coptic community of **GARAGOS** is renowned for its **ceramics** and **textiles,** sold in Luxor. Approaching Luxor, look out for **EL-MADAMUD**, whose **ruined Temple of Mont** has a Ptolemaic–Roman avenue of sphinxes and monumental gateway like Karnak's, but overgrown and undisturbed.

Along the west bank

Close to Qift but on the West Bank, 23km from Qena, **El-Ballas** has manufactured white earthenware jars since antiquity; they are sold at Qena's **pottery** market alongside the town's own traditional wares, the porous water jars that women carry on their heads from childhood. South of here lay ancient Ombos, whose crocodile-worshipping residents never forgave the people of Dendara for eating one – a grudge reaffirmed at every Festival of Drunkenness (see box on p.331).

Further south, the predominantly Coptic village of **Naqada** lends its name to two **pre-Dynastic cultures** that are reckoned to have existed between around

The primal alphabet

During ancient times there was a road between Abydos and Luxor through the Western Desert, which followed the **Wadi el-Hol**. In 1999 a team under John Darnell of Yale University identified two **rock inscriptions** there as the earliest known examples of a **phonetic alphabet**. The alphabet was previously thought to have been developed by Semitic-speaking people in ancient Palestine around 1600 BC; the Wadi el-Hol inscriptions date from two or three centuries earlier and may have been a "shorthand" based on Egyptian hieroglyphics, developed by Semitic merchants living in Egypt. For example, "A" was the pictogram for a bull's head, turned upside down; the semitic for bull is *Aleph*, the first letter of the Hebrew alphabet, pronounced with the same "aah" sound as the Latin letter. It is possible that other symbols may be the precursors of the letters "L", "M", "T" and "R".

4000 and 3000 BC: Naqada I (early) and Naqada II (late). Look out for the **Pigeon Palace** in a field 200m west of the main road, which enables ten thousand birds to recuperate from their flight over the Western Desert; food is provided – and in turn the keepers eat their resident charges.

Luxor

LUXOR has been a tourist mecca ever since Nile steamers began calling in the nineteenth century to view the remains of Thebes, Ancient Egypt's New Kingdom capital, and its associated sites – the concentration of relics in this area is overwhelming. The town itself boasts **Luxor Temple**, a graceful ornament to its waterfront and "downtown", while a mile or so north is **Karnak Temple**, a stupendous complex built over 1300 years. Across the river are the amazing tombs and mortuary temples of the **Theban Necropolis**, and as if this wasn't enough, Luxor also serves as a base for trips to Esna, Edfu, Dendara and Abydos temples, up and down the Nile Valley.

In a town where **tourism** accounts for 85 percent of the economy, it's hardly surprising that you can't move without being importuned to step inside a shop or rent a *calèche*. Hassled at every turn, some tourists react with fury and come to detest Luxor. Provided you keep your cool and sense of humour, it's possible to find genuine warmth here. Once you get to know a few characters and begin to understand the score, Luxor becomes a funky soap opera with a cast of thousands, whose dealings and misunderstandings are as intriguing as the monuments. Read the box opposite for an idea of how things are.

Most foreigners come between October and February, when the **climate** is cooler than you might imagine, with chilly nights and early mornings. Around the end of March the temperature shoots up 10°C, making April the nicest time of the year to visit, though the weather remains agreeable until May, after which the daytime heat is brutal till late October, when the temperatures start mellowing out to April levels. During the summer tourism is well down, and the locals have time to sleep by day and party at night.

A little history

The name Luxor derives from the Arabic El-Uqsur – meaning "the palaces" or "the castles" – a name which may have referred to a Roman *castrum* or the town's appearance in medieval times, when it squatted amid the ruins of **Thebes**. This, in turn, was the Greek name for the city known to the Ancient Egyptians as Weset, originally an obscure provincial town during the Old Kingdom, when Egypt was ruled from Memphis. After power ebbed to regional overlords in the First Intermediate Period, Weset/Thebes gained ascendancy in Upper Egypt under Mentuhotpe II (*c.*2100 BC), who reunited Egypt under the Middle Kingdom. Though this dissolved into anarchy, the town survived as a power base for local princes who eventually liberated Egypt from the Hyksos invaders, reunited the Two Lands and founded the XVIII Dynasty (*c.*1567 BC).

As the capital of the **New Kingdom**, whose empire stretched from Nubia to Palestine, Thebes enjoyed an ascendancy paralleled by that of **Amun**, whose cult temple at Karnak became the greatest in Egypt. At its zenith under the XVIII and XIX dynasties, Thebes may have had a population of around a million; Homer's *Iliad* describes it as a "city with a hundred gates". Excluding the brief **Amarna Period** (*c.*1379–1362 BC), when the "heretic" Akhenaten

Package tours have become so cheap that there's little financial incentive to go for independent travel, and transport, catering and shopping are being monopolized by major tour operators. Consolidation is such that some tour guides even warn tourists that they should only shop in outlets recommended by the tour operator (which owns them).

Whether you come on a tour or independently, try to consider transactions **from the locals' standpoint** rather than expecting to get the cheapest price as a matter of right. Hoteliers, felucca captains and salesmen earn good money one day, then little or nothing for ages. The hotel touts who swear that your place of choice is closed or dirty know that most hotels in Luxor are half empty – so every guest counts. At **no-star hotels**, the price often depends on how full they are, how many there are of you, and at what time you arrive – it's negotiable. Be fair and realistic, even if you're on a tight budget. To get a double room with a shower and toilet for £E25–50 is a good deal by any standards.

Where hotels (and foreign tour operators) make their money is on **tours**. Although it's wise not to take the first deal offered, also bear in mind that the lowest price may not necessarily be a good deal: you could end up with someone who's so bad that they have to undercut better guides in order to get any work. It also helps to take a relaxed attitude towards **street hustlers** and react to such lines as "Hey – remember me?", "You've dropped your wallet", or "I know what you need" with a humorous rebuff (*Fil mish mish* – "In your dreams" – works well). You'll actually get hassled *less* once they recognize that you know the score – including the old ploy of asking you to translate a letter from abroad, as a way to lure you into conversation.

That said, it's best to be forewarned about a few **scams**. Watch out for the street hustlers who offer to exchange euros or dollars and rip you off by sleight of hand, and for the possibility of having an extra purchase added to the bill in a duty-free shop (see p.52). A bigger problem for tourists is that tour guides, touts, taxi and *calèche* drivers get **commission** on every transaction they facilitate – which is deftly added to your bill. Don't go shopping in the bazaar with a driver or a guide.

Over the past decade, **sex tourism** has quietly become a way of life in Luxor, a "hidden" industry that turns many of the stereotypes of the sex trade inside out. Egyptian women and foreign heterosexual males are left on the sidelines as local men and boys get together with foreign women and gays in feluccas, bars and discos. Thousands of women have holiday romances in Luxor every year and word has got home, encouraging others to come. The exchange of sex for cash usually occurs under the guise of true love, with misled women spending money on their boyfriends or "husbands" until their savings run out and the relationship hits the rocks – but enough foreigners blithely rent toyboys and settle into the scene for locals to make the point that neither side is innocent. Morality aside, it isn't just their money that foreigners are risking or that Egyptians are bringing home to their families. HIV now exists on both sides of the river and **AIDS** could easily spread fast if nothing is done. Yet locals are in denial about the problem and tourists hardly aware that it even exists. There has, at least, been a crackdown on foreign paedophiles in 2006.

Hissed invitations and whiffs of smoke by the Nile attest to a smoking subculture that's stronger in Luxor than anywhere else in Egypt except Dahab. **Bango** (marijuana) and **hashish** are easy to obtain if you know where to ask, and smoking shouldn't cause any problems if it's done discreetly; several budget hotels have a liberal atmosphere in this respect.

moved the capital northwards and forbade the worship of Amun, the dynasty's – and city's – supremacy lasted some five hundred years. Even after the end of the Ramessid line, when the capital returned to Memphis and thence moved to the Delta, Thebes remained the foremost city of Upper Egypt, enjoying a final fling as a royal seat under the **Nubian** rulers of the XXV Dynasty (*c.*747–645 BC).

Though Thebes persisted through **Ptolemaic** into **Roman** times, it retained but a shadow of its former glory, and might have been abandoned like Memphis were it not for Christian settlements. During Muslim times its only claim to fame was the tomb of Abu el-Haggag, a twelfth-century sheikh. However, Napoleon's expedition to Egypt awakened foreign interest in its **antiquities**, which were gradually cleared during the nineteenth century and have drawn visitors ever since.

To be fair, not every visitor to Luxor has been unequivocally impressed by its ancient monuments: during the filming of *Death on the Nile*, Hollywood icon Bette Davis famously remarked that "In my day we'd have built all this at the studio – and better". In a sense she had a point: the temple was half hidden by ramshackle bazaars, and downtown was a mess. Now a **transformation** is underway, spearheaded by Governor Samir Farag, an ex-general who previously managed Cairo's Opera House. The train station has been handsomely refurbished, Sharia al-Mahatta widened to create a view of Luxor Temple, and shops demolished to reveal more of the Avenue of Sphinxes. Traders have been relocated to malls beside the station while the dusty old bazaar on Sharia al-Souk has been made over. The authorities are also moving cruise boat moorings away from Luxor Temple to the New Corniche beyond the *Mövenpick*, to reduce air pollution. All this is only the first stage of Farag's masterplan for developing Luxor and the west bank, which has been pledged $600 million by UNESCO.

Arrival, orientation and information

Arriving in Luxor can be stressful, especially at the **train station**, where you're mobbed by hotel touts thrusting cards under your nose and bad-mouthing rival establishments. As most places are less than fifteen minutes' walk away, it is fine to strike out towards your preferred option without further ado. Arriving **by bus** is also a headache: the terminal is way east outside town and taxis demand £E25–30 for a ride into Luxor. From **Luxor Airport**, the cost of a taxi into town is officially £E20–25 depending on the size of the car and your destination, but few drivers will agree to under £E40; Hamdi Ebaid charges £E30 if you book ahead (☎012 365-4018, hamdi_ebaid@hotmail.com). Travellers who've come up **from Aswan by felucca** are dependent on minibuses or taxis from Edfu or Kom Ombo, whose drivers may well rendezvous with hustlers at the checkpoint south of Luxor and steer you to their hotels. **Cruise boat** passengers may find themselves moored within walking distance of Luxor or Karnak temples – or at the New Corniche far outside town (£E15–20 by taxi).

Orientation

Luxor spreads along the east bank of the Nile, its outskirts encroaching on villages and fields. For a general layout of the town along with Karnak and the Theban Necropolis, see the **map** on p.372–373; a detailed street plan appears on pp.340–341. **Orientation** in central Luxor is simplified by a relatively compact tourist zone defined by three main roads. **Sharia al-Mahatta** runs 500m from the train station towards Luxor Temple, where it meets **Sharia el-Karnak**, the main drag heading north to Karnak Temple (2.5km). Karnak is also accessible via the riverside **Corniche**, though tourists generally stick to the 1500-metre stretch between Luxor Museum and the *Winter Palace Hotel*. The "circuit" is completed by a fourth street, known as **Sharia al-Souk** after its bazaar.

In the last two decades Luxor has expanded south towards the village of Awmia, with dozens of hotels and other facilities along **Sharia Khalid Ibn Walid** (running 3km from the *Iberotel* to the *Sheraton*) and **Television Street** (named after its TV tower), which now constitute extensions of the tourist zone. The "suburbs" of **New Karnak** (between Karnak Temple and the *Hilton*) and **New Luxor** (at the far end of Mohammed Farid and Television streets) are both neighbourhoods with flats for rent.

Information

It's a good idea to visit the **tourist office** (daily 8am–8pm; ☏095/237-2215 or 237-3294) south of Luxor Temple to discover the latest official rates for taxis, *calèches*, feluccas or anything else you might be interested in. Confusingly, there are two offices next door to each other; you want the one signposted "Egyptian Tourist Authority", not "Luxor City Information". There's also a branch at the airport (☏095/237-2306) and another at the train station (generally open daily 8am–8pm).

The **tourist police**'s "front" office lies across the way from the tourist office, while their headquarters is upstairs, around the back of the building (daily 24hr; ☏095/237-3845 or 237-6620). They also have a branch in the station (daily 8am–8pm).

Transport

Although you can easily explore central Luxor **on foot**, it takes some time to get used to the traffic (a balletic mix of bikes, cars, carts and minibuses) and being importuned at every step. **Calèches** are fun to ride and useful if you're burdened with luggage, but a bit pricey for regular use. Fares are set by the authorities but drivers charge whatever they can get. Expect an argument if you pay the official rate (£E30/hr); rides to Karnak are a special case (see p.360). **Taxis** serve for trips to outlying hotels (£E10) or the airport, but are fairly superfluous around the centre (£E5), except for getting back from a disco. It's better to pay what's right at the end rather than haggle over the price at the beginning.

Surprisingly few visitors take advantage of the fleet of blue-and-white **minibuses** that shuttle between outlying points, constantly passing through the centre along Sharia el-Karnak. Northbound minibuses either turn off towards the taxi depot (*mogaf*) at the end of Sharia al-Mathari, or run straight on to Karnak and the *Nile Hilton*. Heading in the opposite direction, they terminate at the public hospital (*mustashfa*) far down Television Street, or at Awmia, out near the *Sheraton*. The *mustashfa*-bound ones detour inland via the train station, while Awmia buses stick to Sharia Khalid Ibn Walid. The tactic is to wave down any minibus heading in the right direction, holler "*Hilton*" (or whatever), and hop in if they're going there. There's a flat fare of 25pt on all routes.

While cycling in Luxor isn't advisable, many tourists rent **bicycles** to use on the west bank, for getting around the Theban Necropolis (see p.369). They can be carried on local ferries. Shops on Sharia al-Mahatta and Television Street, and many low-budget hotels, rent them from £E10 a day. Most bikes are one-speed only and may be defective in some respect (though bikes at *Happy Land* get daily maintenance), so it's always wise to check the machine and do a short test ride. A passport, student card or other ID is generally required as security. You can also rent **motorbikes** from several places, including the *Sherief Hotel* (ask for Ziggy; ☏010 527-8297): a 150cc bike costs £E50/day, 500cc £E75/day.

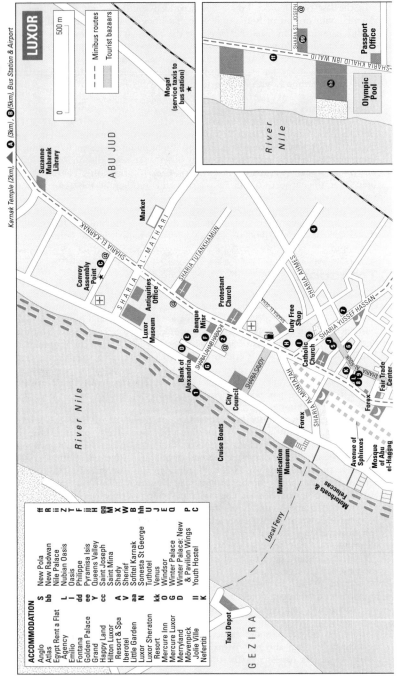

Karnak Temple (2km), ▲ (3km), Ⓐ (3km), Ⓑ (5km), Bus Station & Airport

LUXOR

– – – Minibus routes

Tourist bazaars

0   500 m

ABU JUD

Suzanne Mubarak Library

Convoy Assembly Point ★

Antiquities Office @

Luxor Museum

Market

SHARIA EL-KARNAK

SHARIA AL-MATHARI

SHARIA TUTANKHAMUN

Mogaf (service taxis to bus station) ★

River Nile

SHARIA KHALID IBN WALID

SHARIA ST-JOSEPH

Passport Office

Olympic Pool

River Nile

Protestant Church

Banque Misr

Bank of Alexandria

Duty Free Shop

SHARIA AHMES

SHARIA YUSSEF HASSAN

Catholic Church

City Council

SHARIA SAVOY

SHARIA AL-MONTAZA

Forex

Cruise Boats

Mummification Museum

Avenue of Sphinxes

Mosque of Abu el-Haggag

Motorboats & Feluccas

Fair Trade Center

Forex

River Nile

Local Ferry

Taxi Depot

GEZIRA

ACCOMMODATION

Anglo	**S**	New Pola	**ff**
Atlas	**bb**	New Radwan	**R**
Egypt Rent a Flat Agency	**L**	Nile Palace	**ii**
		Nubian Oasis	**Z**
Emilio	**I**	Oasis	**T**
Fontana	**dd**	Philippe	**F**
Golden Palace	**ee**	Pyramisa Isis	**jj**
Grand	**Y**	Queens Valley	**ii**
Happy Land	**cc**	Saint Joseph	**gg**
Hilton Luxor Resort & Spa	**A**	Saint Mina	**M**
		Shady	**X**
Iberotel	**V**	Sherief	**W**
Little Garden	**N**	Sofitel Karnak	**B**
Luxor Sheraton Resort	**aa**	Sonesta St George	**hh**
		Tuthotel	**U**
Mercure Inn	**O**	Venus	**J**
Mercure Luxor	**G**	Windsor	**E**
Merryland	**D**	Winter Palace	**Q**
Mövenpick	**II**	Winter Palace: New & Pavilion Wings	**P**
Jolie Ville		Youth Hostel	**C**
Nefertiti	**K**		

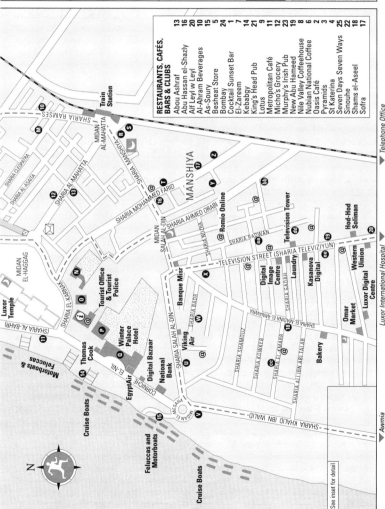

RESTAURANTS, CAFÉS, BARS & CLUBS

Abou Ashraf	13
Abu Hassan el-Shazly	16
Aif Leyl w Leyl	20
Al-Ahram Beverages	10
As-Soury	15
Besheat Store	5
Bombay	24
Cocktail Sunset Bar	1
El-Zareem	7
Kebabgy	14
King's Head Pub	21
Lotus	9
Metropolitan Café	11
Micho's Grocery	12
Murphy's Irish Pub	23
New Abu Hameed	19
Nile Valley Coffeehouse	8
Nubian National Coffee	6
Oasis Café	2
Pyramids	3
St Katerina	4
Seven Days Seven Ways	25
Shams el-Aseel	22
Sinouhe	18
Sofra	17

Accommodation

The cost and availability of **accommodation** varies with the time of year and fluctuations in tourism. Officially, there are just "high" (Nov–May) and "low" (June–Oct) **seasons**. In practice, prices rise or fall depending on **demand**, which is affected both by the number of tourists and competition from cruise boats. When tourism is healthy, peak time coincides with the Egyptian school vacation (Dec 10–Jan 10), but in a depressed market, hotels will cut their prices even then, if necessary. Many low-budget places employ **hotel touts**, who refer to netting tourists as "fishing" and happily poach them from rivals by telling outrageous lies.

If you haven't booked, the scope for **bargaining** varies. Three-star hotels may waive taxes, particularly new places that haven't yet got many customers or older ones threatened by better competitors. No-star hotels rarely charge tax anyway, and may shave a few pounds off the price. Outside of four-star hotels, **breakfast** is usually much the same everywhere, but a **restaurant** with a good cook and a licence to sell **alcohol** are definite assets. Staff are crucial, too, as hotels that were good can become bad (or vice versa) just because the manager or receptionist changes – especially low-budget hotels leased on one-year contracts.

The following hotels are all in **Luxor** itself. It's also worth considering staying on the **west bank**, where there are some great hotels (see p.376).

Inexpensive hotels and hostelling

Inexpensive hotels and real cheapos are concentrated around **Sharia al-Souk**, **Mohammed Farid** and **Television** streets. The biggest selection is around Television Street, no more than fifteen minutes' walk from Luxor Temple or the station. Despite its littered backstreets, this is an up-and-coming area that's safe to stay in and quieter than the centre of town. Unless stated otherwise, you should be sure of getting hot water and breakfast.

With hotels so cheap, you won't save money staying at the **youth hostel** (℡095/237-2139) near the Luxor Museum, and you'll have to endure its noise and daytime lock-out. Packed with Egyptian teenagers in winter and closed over summer, it has gender-segregated dorms with bunks (for Egyptians only) and "lux" rooms with three beds, for £E11 a head; HI membership is obligatory, but there's no age limit.

Anglo Sharia al-Mahatta ℡ & ℻095/238-1679. Being so close to the train station is a drawback, but the rooms are a/c and en suite (if a bit claustrophobic), and the hotel has an alcohol licence. ❶

Atlas Off Sharia Ahmed Orabi ℡095/237-3514. About five minutes' walk from the station, this hotel has simple rooms (£E25) with fan or a/c and private bath. Guests can use the washing machine for a fee. Breakfast not included. ❶

Fontana Sharia Radwan, off Television St ℡095/238-0663. A longtime backpackers' favourite: clean and well furnished, with a noticeboard, library and free washing machine; it's worth paying £E10 more for an a/c room with a bathroom. Prices for rooms and tours go up and down like a yo-yo, so compare notes with other guests before agreeing to anything. Sells ISIC cards. ❶

Grand Off Sharia Mohammed Farid ℡095/238-2905, ℮grandhotelluxor@yahoo.com. This quiet no-star run by schoolteacher Nobi has simple rooms with fans (£E20) or a/c (£E5 extra), decent bathrooms and a rooftop terrace. Hires bikes (£E10/day). ❶

Happy Land Sharia el-Kamrr, off Sharia el-Madina el-Minarwa ℡095/237-1828, ℻237-1140, ℗www.luxorhappyland.com. An established favourite, known for its cleanliness, honesty and fixed prices. All rooms with fans, some a/c and en suite, from £E20 per person; towels and mosquito-zappers provided. The stylish new rooftop restaurant will soon have a Jacuzzi. Breakfast includes cornflakes and fruit. Internet access and bike rental available. They offer excursions to Dendara and Abydos, Edfu, Kom Ombo, Abu Simbel, and the west bank, plus balloon trips and Nile cruises at competitive prices. ❶

Merryland Sharia Nefertiti, between Luxor Temple and the museum ☏ & ⓕ095/238-1746. Clean and quiet, with a fine view of the Nile from its rooftop. Rooms are a/c and en suite but on the gloomy side – which could be a bonus in the summer. ❷

🏃 **Nefertiti** Off Sharia el-Karnak ☏ & ⓕ095/237-2386, ⓦwww.nefertitihotel .com. A small, friendly hotel in the heart of town, with a/c en-suite rooms, a rooftop overlooking Luxor Temple, a pool table, Internet access and an above-average breakfast. There's also a sleek restaurant, *Al-Sahaby Lane*, serving traditional fare. Besides local trips, the management can organize safaris to the Western Desert oases and free transfers for guests with bookings. ❷

🏃 **Nubian Oasis** Sharia Mohammed Farid ☏095/236-2671 or 012 292-9445. Recently spruced up, with all rooms en suite, a free washing machine and kitchen and a generous breakfast, this is a good deal for £E10 per person (£E10–15 extra for a/c and satellite TV). ❶

Oasis Sharia Mohammed Farid ☏010 380-5882, ⓔbob2@yahoo.com. Spacious rooms with fans and shared facilities on two floors and a/c and private bathrooms on another, for £E10 per person. Excursions to the west bank and Valley temples, safaris to the oases or rides to Hurghada are available. Manager Tito also rents apartments in New Karnak (see p.345). ❶

Saint Mina Sharia Cleopatra ☏ & ⓕ095/237-6568, ⓔminahotel@hotmail.com. Friendly, clean, no-hustle hotel on a quiet backstreet in the Coptic quarter; its small, simple a/c rooms have bathrooms or share facilities with two other rooms. ❶

Sherief Sharia Badr, off Television St ☏010 527-8297, ⓔsheriefhotel@hotmail.com. A quiet, friendly backstreet hotel, with fans or a/c and shared or en-suite bathrooms (the latter £E10 extra). Chill out over a beer on their Bob Marley-themed rooftop, which has a view of the Nile. Bicycles and motorbikes for rent; competitively priced excursions. ❶

Venus Sharia Yussef Hassan ☏095/237-2625 or ☏012 171-3599, ⓔvenushotel@hotmail.com. Just off the bazaar, quite noisy and funky, with a louche bar. Rooms are faded and mostly a/c, with showers and tiny balconies. They offer Internet access, ISIC cards and donkey trips to the west bank (£E55). ❶

Mid-range hotels

Mostly rated with three stars, Luxor's mid-range hotels feature private bathrooms, air conditioning, phone and TV in the rooms, and a restaurant, bar and maybe also a pool on the premises. There the similarity may end, however, as each differs in its location, decor, atmosphere, clientele and rates. Although breakfast is included in the deal, don't expect anything fancier than you'd get in a budget hotel.

🏃 **Emilio** Sharia Yussef Hassan ☏095/237-6666, ⓕ237-0000, ⓦwww.emiliotravel .com. Freshly refurbished, this highly central, Euro-tour-group oriented hotel has comfy a/c rooms with fridge and satellite TV; a rooftop pool, bar and disco, Sunday buffet and dance show. Reservations essential. Accepts major credit cards. ❹

🏃 **Little Garden** Sharia Radwan ☏095/238-9038 or 012 1038441, ⓦwww .littlegardenhotel.com. A little gem: spacious and dazzlingly clean, with comfy a/c rooms (a private terrace costs €5 extra), a rooftop with sunbeds and showers, and a garden. Prebooked guests can take advantage of transfers from the airport or bus station (€8). ❸

Golden Palace 600m down Television St ☏ & ⓕ095/238-2974. Shabby if comfy rooms reached by a dodgy lift, plus a faux-Babylonian kidney-shaped pool, billiards and Internet access. ❸

Luxor Sharia el-Karnak, near Luxor Temple ☏095/238-0018 or ☏010 1176627. Locally known as the *Wena*, this decrepit pile has long been snarled up in a legal dispute. Its Arabesque lobby and billiard room were semi-refurbished for a BBC docu-drama, but the high-ceilinged rooms and overgrown garden are still in limbo. ❶

Mercure Inn Sharia el-Karnak, near Luxor Temple ☏095/238-0721, ⓕ237-0051, ⓦwww .accor-hotels.com. Popular with tour operators, this faded 1970s three-star (locally known as the *Egotel*) has rooms with fridge and satellite TV in ample grounds with a largish pool. Breakfast included. Accepts Diners, MC and Visa cards. ❺

🏃 **New Pola** Sharia Khalid Ibn Walid ☏095/236-5081, ⓦwww.newpolahotel .com. An excellent deal for the price, with spotless a/c rooms, a rooftop with a small pool and fabulous Nile views, and agreeably kitsch decor throughout. Ask for a room facing the river. ❺

New Radwan Sharia Manshiya ☏ & ⓕ095/238-5501. The a/c rooms are decent, but the pool is a bit murky, and the location noisy. Laundry service; sells beer. ❸

Philippe Sharia Labaib Habachi, near the Corniche ☏095/237-2284, ⓕ238-0050, ⓦwww .creativephilippe.com. Clean, carpeted rooms with fridges and a rooftop pool and sun terrace make this a favourite with adventure tour operators. Independent travellers may find the hotel rather impersonal. ❹

Queens Valley Off Sharia Yussef Hassan ☎095/237-0085, ℻238-1738, ⓦwww.queens-valley.net. Directly behind the *Emilio* (see p.343), this new hotel makes an acceptable fallback – rooms are spacious and a/c, the pool is a bit small but the views from the rooftop are great. ❸

🏃 **St Joseph** Sharia Khalid Ibn Walid ☎ & ℻095/238-1707, ⓔsihiev2002@hotmail.com. A popular three-star with a rooftop pool and bar facing the Theban Hills. They hold Saturday night Saiyidi parties with snake-dancing and a buffet. Friendly staff, and an excellent buffet breakfast. ❺

Shady Television St ☎095/238-1337, ℻237-4859, ⓔshady-hotel@hotmail.com. This hotel (whose name is pronounced "Shar-dy") has small, dark a/c rooms, a pool out back, a big rooftop with sunloungers and a view of the Theban Hills, and Internet access. ❸

Tuthotel Sharia Salah al-Din ☎095/237-7990, ⓦwww.partner-hotels.com. Rated four-stars, with an inviting lobby, but its rooms and rooftop pool are dirty, and service is awful. The *Regina* disco in the basement is popular with locals, however. ❹

Windsor Sharia Nefertiti, near the Corniche ☎095/237-5547, ℻237-3447, ⓦWindsor@click.com.eg. A step down from the *Philippe*, it has friendly staff but the rooms are dark and shabby, and the pool in the courtyard is tiny. ❸

Upmarket hotels

Luxor's **upmarket hotels** mostly deal with tour groups or rich Egyptians, who pay far less than the rack rates by booking in advance. Look for discounts on the Internet; the prices given below are published rates for the least expensive (garden- or street-facing) rooms in high season (most places charge more for Nile-view rooms). Non-residents may use hotel restaurants, if not other facilities, too. Some places are quite a distance from downtown Luxor.

Hilton Luxor Resort & Spa 4km north of Luxor Temple and 1.5km from Karnak Temple (see map on p.373) ☎095/237-4933, ⓦwww.hilton.com. Due to reopen in the summer of 2007 as a deluxe spa hotel, it should be worth investigating. ❽

Iberotel Midan el-Mesaha, 1km south of Luxor Temple ☎095/238-0925, ⓦwww.iberotel-eg.com. This former *Novotel* (still widely known as that) has a large atrium, and a pool and terrace overlooking the Nile; a Nile-view room costs $23 extra. Rooms are small and bland, but the location is excellent. ❼

Luxor Sheraton Resort Sharia Khalid Ibn Walid, 4km south of Luxor Temple ☎095/237-4544, ⓦwww.sheraton.com/luxor. Tranquilly secluded at the end of Khalid Ibn Walid, not too far from restaurants and shops, the *Sheraton* has good facilities and service. Go for a room in the main building rather than a garden one; "Nile-view" rooms only live up to their billing on the upper floors. Access by free bus from the Luxor Museum seven times daily, taxi (£E10) or by minibus as far as Midan el-Salam. ❼

Mercure Luxor Corniche el-Nil, between Luxor Temple and the museum ☎095/238-0944, ⓦwww.accor-hotels.com. Still known to locals as the *Etap*, this anodyne 1970s four-star is used by European tour operators, but anyone paying rack rates will get more for their money at the *Pyramisa Isis* or the *Sheraton*. ❼

🏃 **Mövenpick Jolie Ville** Crocodile Island, 4km south of Luxor ☎095/237-4855, ⓦwww.movenpick-luxor.com. Ideal for families,

with 320 bungalows in luxuriant grounds, tennis courts, a pool, playground and mini-zoo. There are hourly buses to the *Winter Palace* in town, and a motorboat three times daily. All major cards. ❽

Nile Palace Sharia Khalid Ibn Walid, 2km from Luxor Temple ☎095/236-6999, ⓦwww.nilepalacehotel.com. Awash with fake marble, this five-star behemoth overlooks a heated pool beside a Nile terrace, with disabled access throughout. Rooms facing the inner courtyard are noisy at night. All major cards. ❼

Pyramisa Isis Sharia Khalid Ibn Walid ☎095/237-2750, ⓦwww.pyramisaegypt.com. Near the end of the avenue, backing onto lush grounds with superb views of the river, this five-star complex is owned by President Mubarak's son, Ala. It boasts Italian and Chinese restaurants, and a large pool. Visa cards only. ❼

Sofitel Karnak Sharia el-Zinia Gebly, 5km north of Luxor, 3km from Karnak Temple ☎095/237-8025, ⓦwww.sofitel.com. Remote from town (see map on p.373), amid palms and bougainvilleas, this stylish new hotel has bungalows, a big heated Nile-side pool, tennis, squash, a sauna and Jacuzzi. Free shuttle bus or ferry to the *Winter Palace* in Luxor; £E15 by taxi. Takes Visa cards. ❼

🏃 **Sonesta St George** Sharia Khalid Ibn Walid ☎095/238-2575, ⓦwww.sonesta.com. The fanciest five-star on the street, with oodles of marble, Japanese and Italian restaurants, a heated pool by the Nile, and great service. Amex, MC, Visa. ❽

Winter Palace On the Corniche, 100m from Luxor Temple ℡095/238-0422, Ⓦwww.accor-hotels .com. The doyen of Luxor's hotels, founded in 1887, has played host to heads of state, Noël Coward and Agatha Christie (parts of *Death on the Nile* were written and filmed here). Now part of the Sofitel chain, it combines old-fashioned elegance with mediocre service. Rooms overlook the Nile or a vast garden with a pool (from $196 for a standard garden view up to $950 for the royal suite). The *New* and *Pavilion* wings are cheaper but lack character, and guests are no longer entitled to use the facilities at the *Winter Palace*. Buffet breakfast (£E75–90) not included. Amex, MC and Visa. ❼ for *New* and *Pavilion* Wings, otherwise ❽

Apartments

Renting an **apartment** in Luxor is easy; many regular visitors prefer this to staying at a hotel, for more privacy or to save money. Two reputable local **agencies** are Flats in Luxor (℡010 356-4540, Ⓦwww.flatsinluxor.co.uk) – which owns several fully equipped flats near the *Pyramisa Isis* and deluxe flats with a pool and Jacuzzi on the west bank (from £150 sterling per week) – and Egypt Rent a Flat (℡095/236-0205 or ℡010 6142722, Ⓦwww.egypt-rentaflat .com; daily except Sun 9am–8.30pm) on Sharia Sidi Mahmoud, in the bazaar quarter, with dozens of properties on both sides of the river, from two-bedroom apartments (from €70 a week) to deluxe mansions. Or you can deal directly with **landlords** such as Moamen (℡ & Ⓕ095/235-9804 or ℡010 440-1753, Ⓔmoamen-aicha@hotmail.com), who has several lovely deluxe three-bedroom flats near the *Golden Palace Hotel* on Television Street for £E1500 a week, or Tito (℡010 5494647, Ⓦwww.luxor-apartment.de), with four air-conditioned flats in New Karnak opposite the *Hilton*, featuring two or four double rooms, two bathrooms, kitchen, lounge and satellite TV, from £E80 a night or about £E1000 a month for four (including transfer from the airport).

Luxor Temple

Luxor Temple (daily: May–Sept 6am–10pm; Oct–April 6am–9pm; Ramadan 6am–6.30pm & 8–11pm; £E40, student £E20) stands aloof in the heart of town, ennobling the view from the waterfront and tourist bazaar with its grand colonnades and pylons, which are spotlit at night till 10pm. Though it's best explored by day – when its details can be thoroughly examined in a couple of hours – you could come back after dark to imbibe its atmosphere and drama with fewer people around.

Dedicated to the **Theban Triad** of Amun-Min, Mut and Khonsu (see p.361), Luxor Temple was the "Harem of the South" where Amun's consort Mut and their son Khonsu resided. Every spring a flotilla of barques escorted Amun's effigy from Karnak Temple to this site for a conjugal reunion with Mut in an Optet, or fertility festival, noted for its public debauchery.

Whereas Karnak is the work of many dynasties, most of Luxor Temple was built by two rulers during a period when New Kingdom art reached its apogee. The temple's founder was **Amenophis III** (1417–1379 BC) of the XVIII Dynasty, whose other monuments include the Third Pylon at Karnak and the Colossi of Memnon across the river. Work halted under his son Akhenaten (who erased his father's cartouches and built a sanctuary to Aten alongside the temple), but resumed under Tutankhamun and Horemheb, who decorated its court and colonnade with their own reliefs. To this, **Ramses II** (1304–1237 BC) of the XIX Dynasty added a double colonnaded court and a great pylon flanked by obelisks and colossi. Despite additions by later pharaohs and the rebuilding of its sanctuary under Alexander the Great, the temple has a coherence that reproaches Karnak's inchoate giganticism. When the French army first sighted it in 1799, the troops spontaneously presented arms.

The clarity of its **reliefs** is due to the temple having been half-buried by sand and silt, and overlaid by Luxor itself. Nineteenth-century visitors found a "labyrinthine maze of mud structures" nesting within its court; colonnades turned into granaries where dishonest merchants were hanged by their ears. "So stirs a mini-life amid the debris of a life that was far grander", wrote Flaubert. When the French wanted to remove an obelisk, and archeologists to excavate the temple, they had to pay compensation for the demolition of scores of homes.

In 2006, a massive underground ring-**drainage** system was installed to deal with the rising groundwater that had been damaging the temple; the adjacent park at the end of Sharia al-Mahatta was replaced by a paved viewing area and surrounding buildings were demolished to reveal more of the **Avenue of Sphinxes** leading to Karnak and provide an unobstructed view of the temple from all sides. Work is scheduled to be completed by 2008.

Approaching the temple

The ticket office is on the Corniche side, where the gradual slope inside the entrance obscures the fact that the site lies several metres below street level – a measure of the debris that accumulated here over centuries. At the end of the ramp, to your left, is a restored **Chapel of Seraphis** dedicated by the Roman emperor Hadrian on his birthday in AD 126. Beyond this, the courtyard opens into an **Avenue of Sphinxes** with human faces that once led to Karnak Temple – a XXX Dynasty addition by Nectanebo I.

The temple gateway proper is flanked by massive pylons and enthroned colossi, with a single **Obelisk** soaring 25m high. Carved with reliefs and originally tipped with electrum, this was one of a pair until its mate was removed in 1835, taken to France and re-erected on the Place de la Concorde. The four dog-faced baboons at the base of each obelisk also sported erect phalluses until prudish Frenchmen hacked them off. Behind loom three of the six **colossi of Ramses II** that originally fronted the pylon (four seated, two standing). The enthroned pair have Schwarzenegger physiques and double crowns; reliefs of the Nile-god binding the Two Lands adorn their thrones.

The **Pylon** is 65m wide and once stood 24m high; it is notched for flagpoles and carved with scenes of Ramses' supposed victory over the Hittites at Qadesh. You can see Ramses consulting his commanders in the Egyptian camp **[a]**, before charging his foes and battling them until reinforcements arrive **[b]**. Centuries later, Nubian and Ethiopian kings left their mark: notice the relief of Pharaoh Shabaka running the *heb* race before Amun-Min, high up on the left as you walk through the pylon **[c]**.

Courts and colonnades

Beyond the pylon lies the **Court of Ramses II**, surrounded by a double row of papyrus-bud columns, once roofed over to form arcades. The courtyard is set askew to the temple's main axis, doubtless to incorporate the earlier **barque shrines** of Tuthmosis III, dedicated to Khonsu (to the right as you enter), Amun (centre) and Mut (nearest the river).

Incongruously perched atop the opposite colonnade (which is still bricked up to its capitals), the **Mosque of Abu el-Haggag** is a much-rebuilt Fatimid edifice bearing the name of Luxor's patron saint, whose demolition the townsfolk refused to countenance when the temple was excavated. Its interior juxtaposes Islamic motifs with pharaonic hieroglyphs; if suitably dressed, non-Muslims might be invited in to see them (ask at the top of the stairway from Midan el-Haggag).

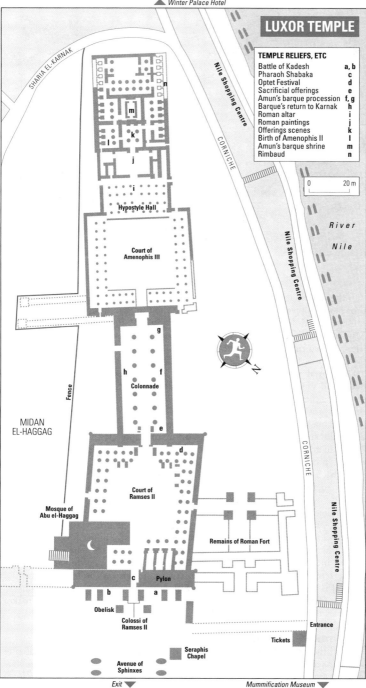

Winter Palace Hotel

LUXOR TEMPLE

TEMPLE RELIEFS, ETC

Battle of Kadesh	**a, b**
Pharaoh Shabaka	**c**
Optet Festival	**d**
Sacrificial offerings	**e**
Amun's barque procession	**f, g**
Barque's return to Karnak	**h**
Roman altar	**i**
Roman paintings	**j**
Offerings scenes	**k**
Birth of Amenophis II	**l**
Amun's barque shrine	**m**
Rimbaud	**n**

SHARIA EL-KARNAK

Nile Shopping Centre

CORNICHE

0   20 m

River

Nile

Hypostyle Hall

Court of Amenophis III

Nile Shopping Centre

N

g

h   f

Colonnade

Fence

MIDAN EL-HAGGAG

e

d

CORNICHE

Court of Ramses II

Mosque of Abu el-Haggag

Remains of Roman Fort

Nile Shopping Centre

c   **Pylon**

b   a

Obelisk

Colossi of Ramses II

Entrance

Tickets

Seraphis Chapel

Avenue of Sphinxes

Exit ▼

Mummification Museum ▼

△ Colonnade of Amenophis III with statue of Ramses II at Luxor Temple

In the temple itself, you can locate the lower half of a frieze depicting Amun's procession approaching the temple during the Optet festival, when the god was presented with lettuces, symbolizing his fertility **[d]**. Ramses makes offerings to Mut and Mont (the Theban war god), observed by his queen and seventeen of the hundred or so sons that he sired over ninety years. Notice the bullocks in the corner of the wall.

The portal itself is flanked by black granite statues of Ramses, their bases decorated with bound prisoners from Nubia and Asia. Beyond lies the older section of the temple, inaugurated by the lofty **Colonnade of Amenophis III**, with its processional avenue of giant papyrus columns whose calyx capitals still support massive architraves. Its scale is so vast that you can hardly take it in. On the walls are more damaged scenes from the Optet festival, intended to be "read" in an anticlockwise direction. After sacrifices to the boats at Karnak **[e]**, Amun's procession **[f]** arrives at Luxor Temple **[g]**, returning to Karnak 24 days later **[h]**. The pharaoh shown here is Tutankhamun, who had the colonnade decorated, but the cartouches honour his successor, Horemheb.

At the end of the colonnade lies the great **Court of Amenophis III**, surrounded on three sides by colonnades of papyrus-bundle columns with bud capitals – the most elegant form devised by the Ancient Egyptians. Its decorations include artwork from the time of Alexander and Philip of Macedon, with some traces of colour still visible on the eastern colonnade. The southern one merges into a **Hypostyle Hall** with 32 papyrus columns, serving as a vestibule to the temple proper. Between the last two columns on the left of its central aisle **[i]** is a Roman altar dedicated to Emperor Constantine, before his conversion to Christianity. On either side of the hall's rear wall, Amenophis makes offerings to the gods.

The inner sanctums

Beyond the hall lies a columned **portico** or antechamber, whose central aisle was flanked by the barque shrines of Mut and Khonsu. Roman legionaries later plastered over the pharaonic reliefs and turned it into a chapel where local

Christians were offered a choice between martyrdom or obeisance to the imperial cults. Paintings of Roman emperors are visible near the top of the walls, and around the niche on the south wall **[j]**; elsewhere the stucco has fallen away to reveal Amenophis offering sacrifices to Amun. In the smaller, four-columned **Hall of Offerings**, beyond, reliefs show the pharaoh leading sacrificial cows and presenting incense and sceptres **[k]**.

More interesting reliefs occur in the **Birth Room** of Amenophis III, whose north wall **[l]** emphasizes his divine paternity, since he was not of direct royal descent. The ravaged lower register shows Amun, Hathor and Queen Mutemuia embracing; and Thoth leading Amun (disguised as Tuthmosis IV) into the queen's bedchamber, where, the accompanying hieroglyphic caption states, "his dew filled her body". Examined from left to right, the middle register depicts Thoth foretelling Amenophis's birth; Mutemuia's pregnancy and confinement; Isis presenting the child to Amun; and the god cradling his son. Along the top register, Amenophis and his *ka* are nurtured by deities and presented to Amun; in the far right corner, Amenophis becomes pharaoh.

If the Birth Room is inaccessible from the Hall of Offerings you can reach it via the next hall, which Alexander the Great converted into the **Sanctuary of Amun's Barque** by removing four columns and installing a granite shrine **[m]**. Though its "doors of acacia inlaid with gold" are no more, some of the reliefs on the walls bear traces of their original colouring.

The remaining chambers to the south constituted the private apartments of the gods, reached by a transverse hall. However, this section of the temple is badly damaged and really only notable for the name Rimbaud, carved high up on the wall near the river **[n]**. Rimbaud spent the last sixteen years of his life roaming the Near and Far East; while living in Ethiopia he was feared dead, so Verlaine published his poems (all written by the age of 21), which took Paris by storm and inspired the Decadent movement.

Outside the walls, assorted pharaonic, Roman and Christian **stonework** is stored near the spot where, in 1989, workers uncovered a cache of 26 New Kingdom statues, sixteen of which are now on show in the Luxor Museum.

Mummification Museum

At the northern end of the Nile Shopping Centre below the Corniche, Luxor's **Mummification Museum** (daily: summer 9am–10pm; winter 9am–9pm; £E40, student £E20; no photography) devotes more space to the beliefs surrounding death and the afterlife than to the actual practice of mummification (see pp.382–383) and hardly breaks new ground. It does, however, display a spoon and spatula used to remove the deceased's brain, which was discarded by the Egyptians as an unimportant organ, unlike the viscera, which were preserved in canopic jars. A statue of Anubis, the jackal god of mummification, watches over the collection of reptile and bird mummies and a well-preserved XXI Dynasty official, Maserharti.

In wintertime on Saturdays at 7pm there is a free **archeological lecture** by such experts as Kent Weeks (studying tomb KV5 in the Valley of the Kings), Houry Souralzin (excavating the mortuary temple of Amenophis III) and Zbigniew Szafranski (of the Polish Mission at Deir el-Bahri). Visitors can consult the museum's Egyptology reference **library** (daily 9am-6pm; free).

Luxor Museum

Luxor Museum (daily: summer 9am–4pm & 5–10pm; winter 9am–9pm; £E70, student £E35), at the northern end of the Corniche, complements the town's monumental assets with a superb collection of statues and funerary goods from the Theban Necropolis and various temples. The museum is wheelchair-accessible, well laid out and labelled in English, though some names are rendered differently from those in this book (for example: Amenhotep for Amenophis). Photography is not allowed inside the museum, but illustrated guides are on sale at the bookshop. There is an overpriced café attached.

To the right as you enter is a ramp down to the sunken **Cachette Hall**, displaying sixteen of the statues found beneath Luxor Temple in 1987. It's uncertain whether they were hidden at the start of the Roman occupation or nine hundred years earlier, when Egypt was invaded by the Assyrians, who sacked Thebes in 664 BC. They include an alabaster sphinx of Tutankhamun; Amenophis III and Horus enthroned, in basalt; a headless cobra poised to strike in the name of the Nubian pharaoh Taharqa; Horemheb kneeling before the god Atum; and a processional effigy of Amenophis III, its rose quartzite left unpolished to highlight the texture of his kilt, armbands and Combined Crown.

The **first level** opens with a sensitive-faced statue of the adolescent Tutankhamun and a gilded head of the cow deity Mehit-Weret from his tomb in the Valley of the Kings. A colossal head of Amenophis III, found on the west bank in 1957, leads you on to a raised level showcasing more works in stone. Compare the careworn face of Sesostris II and the watchfulness of bureaucrat Yamo-Nedjeh with the serenity of the boy Tut beside the crocodile god Sobek, or the diorite head of Sekhmet from a colossal statue in the Precinct of Mut at Karnak.

A new extension entitled "Thebes Glory" displays artefacts related to the **New Kingdom war machine** (see box on p.654). Tut's war chariot, a relief of Amenophis II target-shooting, and royal bows (some recurved and composite) show how the Egyptians mastered the tactics and technology of the Hyksos invaders. A statue of Horemheb and his wife from their unfinished tomb at Memphis, a granite head of Ramses II and a super-sized alabaster Seti I recall the hard men of the XVIII and XIX dynasties. Notice the head of Nakhtim, a general under Tut and Ay (whose son he might have been), ousted by Horemheb; and the effigy of Nebre, commander of a Mediterranean fort, holding a staff topped by an effigy of the war-goddess Sekhmet.

Best of all, there are two **royal mummies**. That of **Ahmosis I** has a surprisingly delicate physique for the ruler who expelled the Hyksos. His gold-and-electrum axe (found at Dra' Abul Naga on the west bank) and a gold collar with Flies of Valour, from the tomb of Queen Ahhotep (who may have led the Theban army when Ahmosis was a child), are exhibited nearby. The other mummy was returned to Egypt from a museum at Niagara Falls, and might belong to **Ramses I** (see p.393).

On the **top level** are model boats from the Meir Tombs at Assyut, gilded *shabti* figures from Tut's tomb, and architects' tools from the Workmen's Village at Deir el-Medina. Between two haunting heads of **Akhenaten** from his Aten temple at Karnak is a **wall** from the same temple, made of small blocks known as *talatat*, that were later used as filler for the Ninth Pylon, wherein they were discovered in the 1960s. Reassembled, the painted sunk-reliefs depict Akhenaten's Sed festival, with the king and Queen Nefertiti in a litter surrounded by fan-bearers. Their figures have the strange physiognomy associated with Akhenaten's reign (see box on p.298).

Eating and drinking

Luxor's culinary scene is less diverse than Cairo's, but there's no shortage of places to eat. Upmarket **hotel restaurants** offer cuisines such as Chinese (at the *Pyramisa Isis*), Japanese (at the *Sonesta St George*), Italian or French (most places). Elsewhere you'll mainly find pizzas, kebabs, omelettes and other tourist fodder. Menus are generally written up outside and most waiters know English, so it's easy to order. Be prepared for the additional service charges and tax (up to 22 percent), though many places don't actually levy them.

All the usual **street food** can be found along El-Karnak, Ramses and Yussef Hassan streets. A 24-hour **bakery** near the corner of Sharia al-Mahatta and the souk turns out pretzels and rolls, while *Twinky*, at the station end of Sharia el-Manshiya, sells sticky confectionery. If you're self-catering, there's no shortage of small **grocery shops** selling canned goods, cheeses, olives, fruit yogurts and juices, which can be combined with fresh fruit and bread from the souk to make a wholesome meal. For a wider range of imported goods, check out the self-service **mini-markets** on Sharia el-Madina el-Minarwa – Omar Market is the best. There's a 24-hour bakery 50m up the road and another near the junction with Television Street.

Restaurants and cafés

Most of the **restaurants** and **cafés** below are inexpensive by Western standards, and open from mid-morning (or earlier) till 9–10pm (or later), though the range of meals diminishes as the evening wears on. Unless otherwise stated, they don't sell **alcohol**. Additionally, there åre some excellent places to eat on the **west bank**, near the ferry landing stage in Gezira. See p.371 for details.

1896 Restaurant *Winter Palace Hotel*, Corniche el-Nil ☎095/238-0422. Its grand colonial decor and starchy silver service are more alluring than the pallid Continental cuisine (three-course dinner for €20). Reservations and smart dress required (they'll lend men a tie if needed). Serves alcohol.

Abou Ashraf Sharia al-Mahatta. Brightly lit takeaway and sit-down diner, serving roast chicken, *kofta*, *shawarma* and *kushari*, with a counter of sweet pastries for dessert. Inexpensive, but prone to creative accountancy. Open till midnight.

Abu Hassan el-Shazly Sharia el-Manshiya. A kerbside *kofta* joint with indoor seating in the spice and hardware souk. Authentically *baladi*; if you enjoy bazaar-watching and badinage, it's worth trying. *Abu Hagger*, almost next door, serves similar fare at similar prices.

As-Soury Corniche el-Nil, near the *Iberotel*. A spacious Nile-side retreat that's less polluted by cruise boats than other places on the Corniche. Come to drink chilled wine rather than eat; most of the dishes on the menu aren't available.

Bombay Sharia Khalid Ibn Walid ☎010 665-9505. Aimed at curry-loving Brits, with a good value lunchtime set menu for two (£E80); main dishes cost £E25–40. A bit smarter than the *Taj Mahal* (see below). Sells beer and wine.

El-Zareem Sharia Yussef Hassan. A busy sitdown diner and takeaway serving *taamiya*, *kofta* or shrimp

sandwiches, *kushari* and other Egyptian staples, all freshly cooked and inexpensive. Daily 24hr.

Kebabagy Nile Shopping Centre, near Luxor Temple. At the southern end of the mall below the Corniche, this popular bistro serves kebabs, seafood, pizzas, stuffed pigeon, wine, beer and ice cream on a terrace beside the cruise-boat moorings, with big screen TV sports indoors.

La Mama *Sheraton Luxor Resort*, Sharia Khalid Ibn Walid ☎095/237-4544. For those with kids, this Italian restaurant is a good choice, with a tame pelican for amusement, and pizza and pasta dishes just like you'd get at home, served on a spacious terrace.

Lotus Sharia al-Souk. Overlooking the bazaar, with a/c, the *Lotus* has Egyptian, Continental and even a few Dutch/Indonesian dishes on its menu, at fairly reasonable prices.

Metropolitan Café Nile Shopping Centre, below Luxor Temple. Like *Kebabagy*, it has a view across the Nile and breezes from the river (which may be spoilt by diesel-belching cruise boats). Serves pizzas (£E25–35), club sandwiches, ice creams and beer on outdoor wicker tables.

Miyako *Sonesta St George Hotel*, Sharia Khalid Ibn Walid ☎095/238-2575. Luxor's only Japanese restaurant is worth a splurge. Set meals of meat (£E125) or seafood (£E180), à la carte grills (£E55–120), sushi (£E25–40) or sashimi

(£E40–100). Smartish dress expected. Serves alcohol. Most cards accepted. Daily 5–11pm.

Oasis Café Sharia Labaib Habachi ⓦ www .oasiscafeluxor.com. A restful retreat (think *Casablanca*) with recorded jazz and 1940s vocals, exhibitions and foreign-language magazines, smoking and non-smoking sections. Tuck into a muffin and a latte, a steak platter, the chef's Nepali specials, or the all-day brunch. No cards. Daily 10am–10pm.

Pink Panda *Pyramisa Isis Hotel*, Sharia Khalid Ibn Walid ⓣ 095/237-2750. One of Luxor's poshest restaurants, serving a bland approximation of Szechuan cuisine. Appetizers £E20–26, soups £E10, main dishes from £E35. Sells alcohol. Most credit cards accepted. Daily noon–11pm.

Pyramids Sharia Yussef Hassan. A small eatery devoted to *fiteer*, savoury or sweet, prepared to order.

Seven Days Seven Ways Sharia Khalid Ibn Walid, near Midan al-Salam, ⓣ 095/236-6264. A haven

for expat Brits, serving caff food and Sunday roast (5.30pm, 7.30pm & 9pm; £E30; reservation required). The *Royal Oak Pub* and *Showtime Lounge* (both 4pm–2am), upstairs, are for boozing or watching sports and film channels on TV. Daily 9am–11pm.

Shams el-Aseel Sharia el-Kmarr, off Television Street. If you're dying for a tasty doner, this nearly round-the-clock *shawarma*, burger, salad, *fuul* and *taamiya* takeway fits the bill, and has a few tables upstairs. Daily 6am–2am.

Sofra Sharia Mohammed Farid ⓣ 095/235-9752, ⓦ www.sofra.com.eg. A *sofra* is a round brass table, which typifies the decor of this romantic restaurant in the backstreets, serving delicious mezze and other Middle Eastern specialities. Enjoy a *sheesha* on the rooftop terrace, or reserve a private room for an intimate dinner. Daily 11am–midnight.

Coffee houses

The chief diversion for Luxor males is playing backgammon (*thowla*) or dominoes in **coffee houses.** Though café life is exclusively masculine, foreign women can usually feel comfortable in the places listed below. Otherwise, there are several all-night places on Sharia Ramses.

Alf Leyl w Leyl Television Street. With its private booths hung with Arabesque tent-fabric, its fresh juices and big choice of *sheesha* flavours, the "Thousand and One Nights" is popular with Egyptian newlyweds and families.

Nile Valley Sharia el-Karnak. Recognizable by a large portrait of the singer Umm Kalthoum, this shabby if tranquil coffee house is well used to the odd tourist seeking a break from the bazaar. Try *helba*, the bright yellow tea made from fenugreek.

Nubian National Coffee Sharia al-Souk. This funky tearoom decorated with blankets and fake boulders is the place to hear Nubian sounds and meet guys from Aswan. Try the coffee spiced with cardamom or the juices.

Victoria Lounge *Winter Palace Hotel*, Corniche el-Nil. The pleasure of being served cucumber sandwiches, fruit cake and tea here, as if the sun had never set on the British Empire, was restricted to hotel guests at the time of writing – but might not be in the future. £E35 per person; daily 4–6pm.

Drinking and duty-free shops

If you don't mind paying £E25–35 plus tax, the classiest places to **drink** a cold Stella beer are the Nile-side terraces of the *Sheraton*, *Pyramisa Isis*, or *Sonesta St George*, which all have fabulous views. In the centre of town, the Nile Shopping Centre below the Corniche has two places serving beer but the view (and fresh air) may be spoilt by cruise boats moored alongside. Otherwise, hotel **bars** are seldom anything special, but there are a couple of fun **pubs** and a cool riverside cocktail bar to enjoy.

Cheap imported booze can be bought at **duty-free shops** within 24 hours of arrival, in the arrivals lounge at Luxor airport and the duty-free shop on the street behind the *Emilio Hotel* (daily 10am–3pm & 7pm–midnight). You'll need your passport, in which the transaction(s) will be noted. Otherwise, fall back on Egyptian beer, wine or spirits (often labelled to resemble imported brands), sold at low-profile **outlets** like Besheat Store on Sharia al-Souk, Al-Ahram Beverages on Sharia Ramses or Micho's Grocery on Sharia al-Mahatta. They tend to open from 10am to midnight, and as most are run by Christians, they close during Easter as well as Ramadan and on Sundays.

Cocktail Sunset Bar Corniche el-Nil, near the *Mercure Luxor*. A chic, ultra-relaxed floating ice-cream parlour with a cocktail bar upstairs, retro decor, mood music and a fine view of the Nile. They serve cocktails and spirits (around £E35), beer (£E20), wine (£E25) and fresh juices (£E18), but the only things to eat are cheese snacks or Swiss ice cream. Daily 11am–midnight.

King's Head Pub Sharia Khalid Ibn Walid. The king in question is Akhenaten, this place looks and feels like an English pub, offering toasted sandwiches, soups, chips and a Sunday lunch of roast beef and Yorkshire pud. Its beer and cocktails are as cheap as anywhere, and there's billiards and satellite TV. Owner Gomaa Abu el-Fadl is a novelist, journalist and activist who enjoys a deep conversation. Daily noon–2am (later if there are customers).

Murphy's Irish Pub Sharia al-Gawazat, off Sharia Khalid Ibn Walid. Don't be misled by the deadsville eating area downstairs – upstairs is often livelier than the *King's Head*, with singalongs, Mexican waves, pool matches and sports TV, cheered on by boisterous Brits. There's also a small disco in the basement. Daily noon–2am or later.

Nile Terrace Café & Bar *Winter Palace Hotel, Corniche el-Nil*. When last heard this was restricted to residents, but if you can find a "sponsor", the hotel's lofty terrace is an elegant vantage point to watch the sun set over the Theban Hills, while quaffing a G&T or a cold Stella. Smartish dress expected (no shorts), and a minimum charge of £E35 per person.

Venus Bar *Venus Hotel*, Sharia Yussef Hassan. A downtown joint with bargirls to attract *baladi* clients, that's also popular with resident foreign gays. Sells Luxor beer, Egyptian wine and spirits. Daily till midnight, later if there are customers.

Nightlife

Luxor's nightlife is a paler shadow of Hurghada's, if only because most tourists are too tired from sightseeing to fancy clubbing. Many **discos** are empty, and even at the most popular ones local men outnumber foreigners. The *Sabil* disco (from 10.30pm) in the *Mercure Luxor* has the hottest DJ, plus a bellydancer from 12.30am, and levies a cover charge of £E30 (including one drink). The *Regina* disco in the *Tuthotel* on Sharia Salah al-Din has a reputation for punch-ups, while *Sinouhe*, on Sharia Khalid Ibn Walid, rarely gets going before 2am (when revellers leave the *King's Head or Murphy's*). Both are open till 5am every night, with no minimum charge.

Most top hotels feature a **bellydancer** who struts her stuff for half an hour or so. At some this is just an interlude in the disco, at others, part of a show of **Saiyidi music** and **folk dancing** (stick-fights or whirling dervishes). Outsiders can enjoy them for free (but must buy drinks) at the *Pyramisa Isis* disco (Wed & Sun 10.30pm) or the patio of *Le Meridien* (nightly 7.30–10.30pm), while the *Emilio's* Sunday night show includes a buffet meal (£E50 per person), as does the *Iberotel's* on Saturday (£E75) – reservations are advisable. Ask at the *Mercure Inn* about folkloric shows that occasionally feature a **snakecharmer**, at the outdoor *Dar al-Umda* restaurant.

The alternative is to visit a **real Egyptian nightclub**, where the decor is seedy, the clientele raucous (women are best off going with male companions), and the music brilliant. You have to stay through till dawn to savour the build-up, as the dancers tease local businessmen into throwing £E5 notes around, which are collected in a box at the end of each act and split equally among the dancer, the bandleader and the club. Rival big-spenders often come to blows over a woman and exit the club with their cronies, leaving the next dancer bereft of profitable customers. Luxor has two such clubs: *St Katerina*, off Sharia Ahmes in the centre, and *New Abu Hameed* on Television Street. The dancing starts at 1am and runs through till 5am if enough patrons are still spending. It's best to go with an Egyptian friend to get past the doorman who might claim there's an entry charge, or to argue if they add it to your bill – there isn't one; you should only pay for drinks (£E10–15 for Stella beer, £E100 upwards for spirits).

Shopping

Under the governor's masterplan, many tourist shops are being relocated to air-conditioned **malls** (beside the train station and city council), and the traditional **bazaar** around Sharia al-Souk has been refurbished, with overhead trellises to provide shade. At the time of writing it all looked a little raw, but will hopefully bed down in time.

Fixed-price shops are rare, but provide a benchmark for bargaining at other places. **Crafts** include humble handmade clay cooking pots, sold near the exit from Luxor Temple, Garagos pottery, wooden bowls from Hegaza and textiles from Akhmim. **Alabaster** and **papyrus** are generally cheaper on the west bank, where the Nefertari Papyrus Institute is one of the few fixed-price shops. **Gold and silver** are usually sold by weight and so real prices are roughly fixed. Other buys include *karkaday* (often better here than in Aswan), *duom* (gingerbread shell, to nibble or make tea), fresh cumin and vegetable dyes. Food, spices and clothing stalls cluster on Sharia Ahmes. On Tuesdays and Sundays there's a **fruit and veg market** on Sharia el-Madina el-Minawra, off Television Street, and a proper market hall is set to open on Sharia al-Mathari.

Most non-tourist shops close for a **siesta** (2–5pm).

Fair Trade Center Sharia el-Karnak, near Midan el-Haggag ☎095/238-7015, ✆www.egyptfairtrade .com. The local outlet for a Cairo-based NGO marketing the work of nine handicrafts coopera-tives, including Hegaza bowls carved from lemon, orange or tamarisk wood; Garagos pottery; beadwork from Sinai; recycled paper from Cairo; and cottons, silks and linens from Akhmim (see p.314). Daily 9am–10pm.

Marina's Shop Beside the *Dar al-Umda* restau-rant in the grounds of the *Mercure Inn*. High quality *galabiyyas*, kaftans and other cottons, at decent prices.

Mohammed Abdel Aziz Sharia al-Souk. The owner is always willing to discuss the finer points

of the carpets, embroidered robes and other textiles he stocks.

Radwan Bazaar Sharia Khalid Ibn Walid, opposite the *Pyramisa Isis Hotel*. This place stocks probably the widest choice of styles of jewellery in Luxor. Prices are nominally fixed, but they'll negotiate over sizeable orders.

Winter Akhmeen Gallery Corniche el-Nil, beside the stairway to the *Winter Palace Hotel* ☎095/238-0422. This small shop is stuffed with hand-woven cotton, silk and linen from the women's weaving cooperative in Akhmim (p.314). Prices are £E50–150 per metre, reflecting the high quality. They also make *galabiyyas* and shirts to order.

Festivals

Provided the whole year's programme of tourist events isn't abruptly cancelled due to some terrorist atrocity, wintertime visitors have a chance of witnessing the **West Bank marathon** (February 16), starting and finishing at Deir el-Bahri – the tourist office will have details. Contractual problems saw plans to stage Verdi's **opera** *Aïda* at Luxor Temple go awry at the last moment in 2005, to the disappointment of music lovers and local merchants, but on a brighter note, the new Suzanne Mubarak Library on Sharia el-Karnak might host drama, concerts and exhibitions in the future, like the Library at Alexandria.

Moulids reliably take place each year according to the Islamic calendar, generally during the two months preceding Ramadan; locals can rarely tell you the exact date, but always know when one is due. Foreigners are welcome to attend, but beware of pickpockets and gropers.

The largest, most famous is the **Moulid of Abu el-Haggag** (pronounced "Hajjaj"), honouring Luxor's patron sheikh, whose mosque overlooks the temple. Yussef Abu el-Haggag was born in Damascus (*c.*1150), moved to Mecca in his forties and finally settled in Egypt, where he founded a *zawiyah* in Luxor and met with other Sufi sheikhs such as Al-Mursi and Al-Shazli. Many of his descendants still live in the area, and the tradition of venerating local sheikhs is strong in villages around Luxor. During the festival, giant floats move through the densely packed streets, some dedicated to trades (the *calèche* drivers' bears a carriage), others to the sheikh himself. The parading of a large **boat** (or even three boats) is often compared to the solar barque processions of pharaonic times, though in Islamic symbolism boats represent the quest for spiritual enlightenment. Vast crowds attend the *zikrs* outside Abu el-Haggag's Mosque, and revel in traditional entertainments. There are **stick fights** (*tahtib*) to the music of drums and *mizmars* (a kind of oboe), and **horse races** (*mirmah*) where the riders gallop hell for leather, halting in a flurry of dust just before they plough into the crowd. The festival runs during the first two weeks of Sha'ban, the month before Ramadan. During **Ramadan** itself, townsfolk compensate for its daytime rigours by gathering to hear *zikrs* and dance outside Abu el-Haggag's Mosque in the evenings.

The moulid of **Sheikh Ali Musa of Karnak** lasts a week, its *leyla kebira* falling on Rajeb 6. Sheikh Ali Musa was actually born in another village, and when he died the villagers demanded that his body be buried there. The Karnakis said, "Let the sheikh decide", so his coffin was borne to the crossroads, whereupon it turned to face Karnak and was taken back in triumph. During the moulid you can't miss the music, swings and lights around his tomb, near the entrance to Karnak village.

About the same time, on the other side of town, Awmia village honours its own **Sheikh Ahmed al-Adasi** – who is known for appearing in the dreams of Egyptians working in Italy and Morocco – with a week-long festival, whose curtain raiser is a day of stick fights, horse and **camel races** on a nearby wasteground. For the moulid itself, Awmia's main street is enclosed by a tent, where *munshids* sing at ear-splitting volume; further in are fairground rides and a tent of Sufis in a *zikr*. Following the *leyla kebira* on Rageb 14, there's a final day of celebrations called Ed-Dara, when camels and horses are paraded through the streets and villagers throw candies at each other.

Other moulids occur across the Nile, at Gurna Ta'rif (p.379) and Riziq (p.413).

Activities

Sailing on the river in a **felucca** is a relaxing way to spend an afternoon, while a sunset cruise is the perfect way to end the day. Although the tourist office maintains that two people should pay £E10 an hour for a "local" cruise or £E70 for a three-hour trip to Banana Island, boatsmen will scoff at these rates if business is brisk.

Banana Island (Gezira el-Moz), 4km upriver, is a title loosely applied to two banana plantations either side of the river, whose owners charge visitors £E5 each to land. It's enjoyable to wander through the cool, shady groves of mature banana trees, with their vaulting fronds and pendant flowers; a handful of bananas are included in the price. The round trip takes between two and three hours depending on the wind, or about half-an-hour each way by **motorboat**. You should be able to rent one for £E50 an hour by negotiating with boatmen.

A little nearer town, **Crocodile Island** is great for **bird-watching**, with Nile sunbirds, glossy ibises, purple herons, pied kingfishers, African rock martins, Sardinian warblers, hooded wheatears and black and whiskered terns in its reed-beds and coves. The *Mövenpick's* bird-watching guide, Abdou Yussef (☏012 239-5467), can show you the best spots in his boat.

Luxor's public Olympic **swimming** pool on Sharia Khalid Ibn Walid (daily 9am–5pm; £E10) is the largest in town, but lacks the sunbeds and amenities found at hotels whose pools are open to non-residents. The *Shady* charges £E15; *Tuthotel*, £E25; the *Mercure Luxor and Iberotel*, £E50, including a snack lunch. For those staying a long time, the *Mövenpick* offers three months' unlimited use of its gym and pool for £E500. Non-residents may be allowed to use the **tennis** courts at the *Hilton Luxor Spa & Resort*, while **horse-riding** on the west bank can be arranged through stables in Gezira (see p.374). **Golf**-lovers can play the 18-hole desert course (set to be upgraded to 42 holes) at the luxurious Royal Valley Golf Club (☏012 246-5037, ⓦwww.golfluxor.com), out near the airport. For **meditation** or spiritual healing, contact Iris Meijer (☏010 189-1319, ⓦwww.energiesofegypt.com).

Finally, there's the experience of drifting over the Theban Necropolis in a **hot-air balloon**, which affords an awesome view of the temples, villages and mountains. Cruising at 300m, you can smell the cooking fires and donkeys and overhear conversations below, in an eerie silence punctuated by the roar of the balloon's gas-burners. The course is determined by meteorological conditions and the skill of the pilot, so each flight is different – but you'll probably spend 40–60 minutes aloft. Compare quotes from Magic Horizon Balloons (Sharia Khalid Ibn Walid, below *Sinouhe* disco; ☏095/236-5060 or ☏012 226-1697, ⓦwww.magic-horizon.com), Hod Hod Soliman (Television Street; ☏ & ⓕ095/237-0116), Sky Cruise (110 Sharia Khalid Ibn Walid, with desks in the *Sonesta St George* and *Isis*; ☏095/236-0407), Viking Air (Sharia Salah al-Din, with desks at the *Mercure Luxor* and *Sofitel Karnak*; ☏095/235-7211, ⓦwww.vikingairegypt.com) and Sindbad Balloons (37 Sharia Abdel Hamid el-Omda, off Television St; ☏095/236-1960, ⓦwww.sindbadballoons.com) with the discounted deals on offer at the *Happy Land* and *Nefertiti* hotels – you can pay as little as $70/£E390. The deal should include an early-morning transfer from your hotel to the launch site. There are no flights from June to September.

Directory

American Express In the arcade outside the *Winter Palace*. Changes money and traveller's cheques, makes cash advances on Amex cards, sells cheques and holds mail for Amex cardholders (daily except Fri 9am–5pm; ☏095/237-8333, ⓕ237-2862, ⓔluxor@aexp.com).

Banks and exchange The Forex bureaux (daily 8am–8pm) on Sharia al-Montazah and Sharia el-Karnak have better rates and faster service than Luxor's banks. There are ATMs outside Banque Misr (daily 8.30am–9pm, Fri closed 11.30am–3pm) and the Bank of Alexandria (daily except Fri & Sat 8am–2pm, Ramadan 10am–1.30pm) on Sharia Labaib Habachi, and the National Bank of Egypt (daily: summer 8.30am–10pm; winter 8.30am–9pm) and Banque du Caire on the Corniche (daily except Fri & Sat 8am–1pm & 2–4pm).

Barbers Men can get a sharp haircut and shave plus the full facial exfoliation that Egyptians prefer at a barber shop on Sharia Kowkeb off Television St, for £E30.

Books and newspapers Gaddis (Mon–Sat 9am–10pm), in the bazaar near the tourist office, is the finest bookshop in Upper Egypt, with heaps of Egyptology, repro prints, guide books and novels. A kiosk on the grass verge near the tourist office sells foreign newspapers.

Dentist Dr Moneer el-Shaoly, on Sharia al-Mahatta ☏095/237-3710.

Doctors Dr Hosam el-Arab's clinic on Television St (Tues, Thurs & Sun 7am–11pm, Fri 10am–3pm; ☏095/237-0032 or ☏010 694-4022, ⓔhosam_elazab@yahoo.com) will treat patients with insurance without charging upfront. Other practitioners include paediatrician Dr Bernaba El-Malah, Sharia Ramses ☏095/236-9125; dermatologist Dr Selim Fakhri ☏095/237-2028; and urologist Dr Samy Fakhri ☏095/237-4964.

EgyptAir In the arcade outside the *Winter Palace* (daily 8am–8pm; ☏095/238-0580 or 238-0581); at Luxor airport (☏095/238-0588). See "Flights" on p.359.

Hospitals Luxor International, off Television St (☏095/238-7194) is hardly up to European standards but is the best in Upper Egypt, with consultants from Cairo and annual surgical visits by Sir Magdi Yacoub. Foreigners pay £E120 for an ambulance call-out; dial ☏123.

Internet access Downtown, you can go online at the *Nefertiti* or *Venus* hotel, or Aboudi's bookshop on Sharia el-Karnak, and there are many Internet cafés around Television Street, most open daily 10am–11pm.

Pharmacies These exist all over town and have a rota for working nights, posted in Arabic. Many close for a siesta, and on Sundays.

Photo processing Places in the tourist bazaar can develop and print in an hour or two. Digital Bazaar (daily 8am–11pm) on the Corniche can burn photos onto a CD (£E25) or print images on a T-shirt (£E45–60); Kodak Express (daily 9am–midnight) on Television St also burns CDs.

Post office At the temple end of Sharia al-Mahatta (Mon–Thurs & Sun 8am–2pm), with a branch in the station (daily 8am–8pm). Street post boxes are only emptied when they're full, so it's better to post letters from a top-notch hotel. Don't use *poste restante*; have letters sent c/o American Express (if you're an Amex customer) or your hotel. A reliable courier firm is Aramex (daily except Fri 8am–8pm), next door to Western Union (see below).

Telephone Menatel, Nile and Ringo phonecards are sold at shops and kiosks and useable in booths all over town – though finding one in a quiet location can be a challenge. The 24hr state telecom office is on Sharia Orabi in New Luxor to the south of the centre. Hotels get away with charging £E35 (minimum 3min) for international calls.

Thomas Cook Outside the *Winter Palace*. Changes currency, sells traveller's cheques, does tours and reservations (daily 8am–8pm; ☏095/237-2402, ✉tcluxor@thomascook.com.eg).

Visa extensions The passport office is on Sharia Khalid Ibn Walid (Mon–Thurs & Sat 8am–2pm; ☏095/238-0885). Visa extensions require one photo plus a photocopy of your passport.

Western Union Television St (daily 8.30am–10pm, Fri 3–10pm; ☏095/238-7187).

Excursions from Luxor – and moving on

With Karnak Temple and the Theban Necropolis in the immediate vicinity, it'll be a while before you start considering **excursions** to other sites up and down the Nile Valley. However, the **temples of Esna**, **Edfu** and **Kom Ombo** are spaced along the way to Aswan, and bolder tourists may also hanker after **Abydos** and **Dendara**, around Qena. Any of these sites makes a feasible day excursion from Luxor.

Travel restrictions for foreigners are strictly enforced but rather illogical; some places are readily accessible by one form of transport but not by another, and certain journeys can be made in one direction but not the other. All tourist coaches, taxis and private cars bound for **Aswan** are obliged to travel in one of the **convoys** leaving Luxor at 7am, 11am and 3pm, which are scheduled to allow stops at Edfu and Kom Ombo (Esna is often omitted), while vehicles heading north towards **Dendara** and **Abydos** are restricted to a single convoy, leaving at 8am. There are also convoys to **Hurghada**, at 8am, 2pm and 6pm. However, almost all these places may also be reached by public buses that run at other times, so you needn't feel entirely bound by convoy schedules.

Many hotels offer **taxi or minibus excursions**, the cost usually split between passengers. *Happy Land* (see p.342) can do Edfu and Kom Ombo with a night in Aswan (£E200 by taxi; £E300 by minibus), or Abydos and Dendara returning to Luxor (for similar rates), and the *Atlas*, *Nefertiti*, *Fontana* and *Sherief* hotels are also competitive. **Day cruises** to Dendara on the *Lotus Boat* or *Tiba Star* (Tues, Fri & Sun) involve five hours on the river (with lunch) and an hour at the temple: tickets are sold by the *Iberotel* (£E355), Thomas Cook (£E350) and Karnak Travel (€40), and should be bought three days in advance.

With the road to **Kharga Oasis** open until 4pm daily, a few operators offer **small-group safaris** as far as the White Desert (see p.511). The cost per person depends on the size of the group, and includes meals and camping gear. In Luxor, talk to Aladin at the *Nefertiti Hotel* (℡010 601-6132, tours @nefertitihotel.com) or Abu El Naga Gabriel (℡010 124-0080, ⓦwww.egypt-westerndesert.com), whose tours range as far as the Gilf Kebir and Jebel Uwaynat. On the west bank, try Azab Safari (℡095/231-1014) at the *Restaurant Mohammed*, or Hamada El-Khalifa at the *Nile Valley Hotel* (℡012 796-4473, ⓦwww.nile-valley.nl). Otherwise, you should be able to hire a **taxi** to drive to Kharga for £E300–500.

Buses

The **bus station** (℡095/232-3218) is 5km east out of town. Anyone buying tickets at the Upper Egypt Bus Co. **kiosk** (℡095/237-2118) downtown (outside the train station at the time of writing, though it may move west to Midan el-Haggag) has been able to pay a £E5 surcharge for a **minibus transfer** (leaving 40min before the bus departs) as an alternative to getting there by taxi (£E25–30) or public transport (take a green-and-white minibus from the *mogaf* to El-Zanagta village, then a yellow-and-white one – it only costs 50pt but isn't worth the hassle).

The unwritten rule that no more than four tourists can travel on the same bus unless it goes in a convoy doesn't seem to be strictly enforced on buses heading for the Red Sea. Of the seven daily air-conditioned services to **Port Safaga** (4hr; £E20–25), **Hurghada** (4–5hr; £E25–30) and **Suez** (10hr; £E46–55), the 7pm and 9pm buses carry on to **Cairo** (£E85; 12–15hr), while the 8pm bus goes to **Port Said** (12hr; £E70). Avoid buses that travel the narrow desert road to Safaga after dark, as accidents are common. In winter, this includes the 5pm bus to **Sharm el-Sheikh** (15–17hr; £E70) and **Dahab** (£E120; 16–18hr), which takes hours longer than advertised and stops at costly roadside cafeterias. Services to **Aswan** are unreliable and often arrive full from Qena, so you're better off taking the train; buses to **Qena** (6.30am, 8am, 10.30am, 2.30pm, 7pm & 9pm; £E5) are equally uncomfortable.

Trains

Foreigners can only buy tickets for six trains to **Cairo** (12–14hr). On #981 (departing at 9.15am), #1903 (at 9.15pm) and #997 (at 11.10pm), air-conditioned first- (£E62–67, student £E40–45) and second class (£E35–40, student £E27–32) seats are comfortable enough to sleep in, so there's no real need to take sleeper train #83 (at 8.15pm) or #85 (at 9.30pm) – payment for which is in dollars or euros only (€53/$73). The overnight services are more popular than the daytime one. A similar restriction applies to trains to **Aswan** (3hr; first-class £E26–30, student £E18–23; second-class £E16–21/£E13–17), but here the #996 (7.15am) and #1902 (9.30am) are busier than the #980 (5pm). Additionally, there's a little-used third-class train to **Kharga Oasis** in the Western Desert (Thurs 7am; 7–11hr; £E11), that may not run for weeks on end due to sand dunes on the tracks. It's far easier to reach Kharga by road (see above).

Service taxis

In the event that restrictions are lifted, **service taxis** will provide tourists a quick and easy way of reaching most sites in Upper Egypt, including **Esna**

(1hr), **Edfu** (1hr 30min), **Kom Ombo** (2hr 30min) and **Aswan** (3hr 30min). The **depot** is beside the bus station; the twelve-seater minivans wait beneath a sign in English for each destination.

Flights

Luxor Airport (☏095/237-4655) is 6km southeast of town (£E30–40 by taxi). The latest domestic schedules can be obtained from **EgyptAir** (daily 8am–8pm; ☏095/238-0580) near the *Winter Palace*. Destinations include **Cairo** (daily; £E727), **Aswan** (daily; £E375), **Hurghada** (Mon & Wed; £E375), **Sharm el–Sheikh** (Tues, Thurs & Sat; £E548); all fares quoted are one-way. Book as far ahead as you can or try for last-minute cancellations. There may also be vacant seats on **charter flights to Europe**. Ask reps at the airport and big hotels, or travel agencies in Luxor. Travellers who overstay the four-week limit on charter return tickets may not get past check-in at the airport.

Karnak

The temple complex of **Karnak** beats every other pharaonic monument bar the Pyramids of Giza. Built on a leviathan scale to house the gods, it comprises three separate temple enclosures, the grandest being the **Precinct of Amun**, dedicated to the supreme god of the New Kingdom – a structure large enough to accommodate ten great cathedrals.

Karnak's magnitude and complexity is due to 1300 years of aggrandizement. From its XII Dynasty core, Amun's temple expanded along two axes – west towards the river and south towards the **Temple of Mut** – while its enclosure wall approached the **Temple of Mont**. Though Pharaoh Akhenaten abjured Amun, defaced his images and erected an Aten Temple at Karnak, the status quo ante was soon restored at the behest of Amun's priesthood.

At the zenith of its supremacy Karnak's wealth was staggering. A list of its assets during the reign of Ramses III includes 65 villages, 433 gardens, 421,662 head of cattle, 2395 square kilometres of fields, 46 building sites, 83 ships, and 81,322 workers and slaves. The Egyptologist T.G.H. James likened it to an industrial giant "which generated a mass of business subsidiary to the practice of the cults and a huge army of officials and working people". Yet ordinary folk were barred from its precincts and none but the pharaoh or his representative could enter Amun's sanctuary. The whole area was known to the Ancient Egyptians as Ipet-Isut, meaning the most perfect or esteemed of places.

Visiting Karnak

The **site** of Karnak covers nearly half a square kilometre, 2.5km north of central Luxor. The only part that's readily accessible is the Precinct of Amun (daily: summer 6am–6.30pm; winter 6am–5.30pm; £E50, students £E25), which hosts nightly Sound and Light shows. This alone requires at least two hours for a quick look round, three or four hours for a closer examination. As there's little shade, make sure you wear a hat and bring water. Usually the temple is busy with tour groups from 9am to mid-afternoon, so come early or late to beat the crowds. A café by the Sacred Lake sells tea and soft drinks, and toilets can be found near the grandstand and the open-air museum. A separate ticket (£E20) for the open-air museum is sold at the main ticket office and just outside the museum itself.

There are two **approaches** from town: via the Corniche, which turns inland further north, or along Sharia el-Karnak, roughly following the **Avenue of Sphinxes** that once connected Luxor and Karnak temples, past the towering **Gateway of Euergetes II** and the precinct's **enclosure wall**. You could cycle or walk, but it's best to conserve your energy for the site. The cheapest way there (and back) is by local **minibus** (25pt per person): services returning to Luxor follow the road nearest the river. The official rates for a one-way **taxi** (£E10) or **calèche** (£E10) ride provide a benchmark for haggling with drivers; for a **return** trip (£E30 including 2hr waiting time), be sure to agree a price first, and remember their licence number.

Expect to pay slightly more for rides to the **Sound and Light Show** (£E55, students £27; sold at the Karnak ticket office). Many find the show a letdown – the commentary is bombastic and the lights half-hearted – but in any case, spectators should come armed with mosquito repellent and a torch to light their footsteps. There are three or four shows each night, at least one of them in English. Schedules are posted in the tourist office, and (less accurately) on ⓦ www.egyptsandl.com. Go for the later ones to avoid an aural conflict with local muezzins around sunset.

The Temple of Amun

The great **Temple of Amun** seemingly recedes towards infinity in an overwhelming succession of pylons, courts and columned halls, obelisks and colossi. Compared by T.G.H. James to "an archeological department store containing something for everyone", it bears the stamp of dozens of rulers, spanning some thirteen centuries of ancient history. Half-buried in silt for as long again, the ruins were subsequently squatted by *fellaheen*, before being cleared by archeologists in the mid-nineteenth century. The Karnak thus exposed was far more ruinous than today, with columns and colossi lying amid piles of rubble and frogs croaking from the swampy enclosure. Since major repairs in the nineteenth century, the temple has been undergoing slow but systematic restoration, epigraphic study and (in some places) excavation.

Making sense of its convoluted layout isn't easy, with the ruins getting denser and more jumbled the further in you go. To simplify **orientation**, we've assumed that the temple's alignment towards the Nile corresponds with the cardinal points, so that its main axis runs east–west, and the subsidiary axis north–south.

It's worth following the main axis all the way back to the **Festival Hall**, and at least seeing the **Cachette Court** of the other wing. A break for refreshments by the lake is advisable if your itinerary includes the **open-air museum** or the **Temple of Khonsu**, off the main circuit.

Entering the temple

Walking towards the Precinct of Amun from the ticket office, and crossing over a dry moat, you'll pass the remains of an **ancient dock**, whence Amun sailed for Luxor Temple during the Optet festival. Before being loaded aboard a full-size boat, his sacred barque rested in the small **chapel** to the right, which was erected (and graffitied by mercenaries) during the brief XXIX Dynasty. Beyond lies a short **Processional Way** flanked by ram-headed sphinxes (after Amun's sacred animal) enfolding statues of Ramses II, which once joined the main avenue linking the two temples.

Ahead of this rises the gigantic **First Pylon**, whose yawning gateway exposes a vista of receding portals, dwarfing all who walk between them. The

Amun and the Theban Triad

Originally merely one of the deities in the Hermopolitan Ogdoad (see p.295), **Amun** gained ascendancy at Thebes shortly before the Middle Kingdom, presumably because his cult was adopted by powerful local rulers during the First Intermediate Period. After the expulsion of the Hyksos (*c*.1567 BC), the rulers of the XVIII Dynasty elevated Amun to a victorious national god, and set about making Karnak his principal cult centre in Egypt.

As the "Unseen One" (whose name in hieroglyphic script was accompanied by a blank space instead of the usual explicatory sign), Amun assimilated other deities into such incarnations as **Amun-Re** (the supreme Creator), **Amun-Min** (the "bull which serves the cows" with a perpetual erection) or ram-headed **Auf-Re** ("Re made Flesh"), who sailed through the underworld revitalizing the souls of the dead, emerging reborn as Khepri. However, Amun most commonly appears as a human wearing ram's horns and the twin-feathered *atef* crown.

His consort, **Mut**, was a local goddess in predynastic times, who became linked with Nekhbet, the vulture protectress of Upper Egypt. Early in the XVIII Dynasty she was "married" to Amun, assimilated his previous consort Amunet and became Mistress of Heaven. She is customarily depicted wearing a vulture headdress and *uraeus* and the Combined Crown of the Two Lands.

Amun and Mut's son **Khonsu**, "the Traveller", crossed the night sky as the moon-god, issued prophecies and assisted Thoth, the divine scribe. He was portrayed either with a hawk's head, or as a young boy with the sidelock of youth.

Karnak was the largest of several temples consecrated to this **Theban Triad** of deities.

▲ Amun

▲ Mut

▲ Khonsu

43-metre-high towers, composed of regular courses of sandstone masonry, are often attributed to the Nubian and Ethiopian kings of the XXV Dynasty, but may have been erected as late as the XXX Dynasty (when Nectanebo I added the enclosure wall). Although the northern tower is unfinished and neither is decorated, their 130-metre width makes this the largest pylon in Egypt. Karnak's vital statistics and the distances to other temples in Upper Egypt have been inscribed high up on the right as you walk through the pylon, by Napoleonic surveyors.

The **Forecourt** is another late addition, enclosing three earlier structures. In the centre stands a single papyriform pillar from the **Kiosk of Taharqa** (an Ethiopian king of the XXV Dynasty), thought to have been a roofless pavilion where Amun's effigy was placed for its revivifying union with the sun at New Year. Off to the left stands the so-called **Shrine of Seti II**, actually a way station for the sacred barques of Amun, Mut and Khonsu, built of grey sandstone and rose granite.

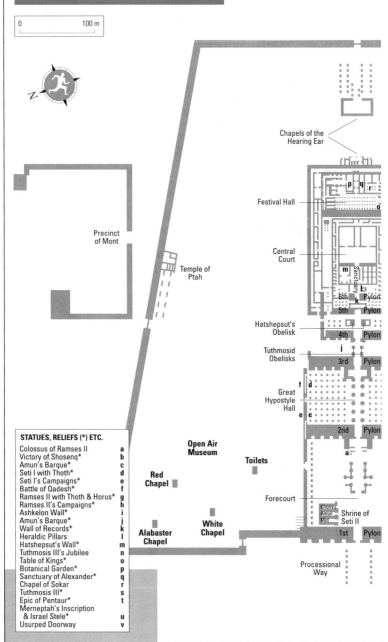

KARNAK: THE PRECINCT OF AMUN

0   100 m

Chapels of the
Hearing Ear

p   q   r

Festival Hall

o

Precinct
of Mont

Central
Court

Temple of
Ptah

m   Sanctuary

6th   Pylon

k

5th   Pylon

Hatshepsut's
Obelisk

4th   Pylon

Tuthmosid
Obelisks

j

3rd   Pylon

Great
Hypostyle
Hall

f   d

e   c

2nd   Pylon

**Open Air
Museum**

a

Toilets

**Red
Chapel**

Forecourt

Khonsu
Amun
Mut

Shrine of
Seti II

**White
Chapel**

**Alabaster
Chapel**

1st   Pylon

Processional
Way

STATUES, RELIEFS (*) ETC.

Colossus of Ramses II	a
Victory of Shosenq*	b
Amun's Barque*	c
Seti I with Thoth*	d
Seti I's Campaigns*	e
Battle of Qadesh*	f
Ramses II with Thoth & Horus*	g
Ramses II's Campaigns*	h
Ashkelon Wall*	i
Amun's Barque*	j
Wall of Records*	k
Heraldic Pillars	l
Hatshepsut's Wall*	m
Tuthmosis III's Jubilee	n
Table of Kings*	o
Botanical Garden*	p
Sanctuary of Alexander*	q
Chapel of Sokar	r
Tuthmosis III*	s
Epic of Pentaur*	t
Merneptah's Inscription & Israel Stele*	u
Usurped Doorway	v

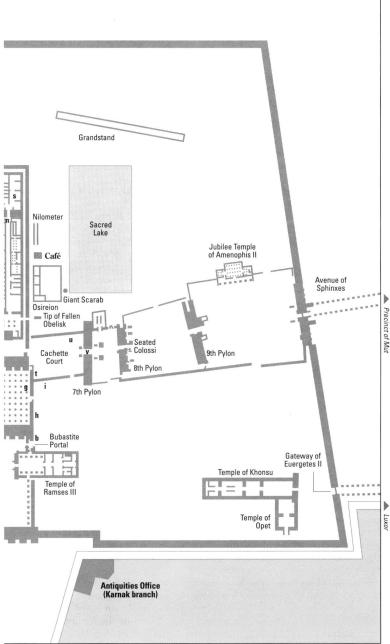

Grandstand

Nilometer

Sacred Lake

■ **Café**

Giant Scarab

Osireion

Tip of Fallen Obelisk

Cachette Court

Seated Colossi

8th Pylon

9th Pylon

Jubilee Temple of Amenophis II

Avenue of Sphinxes

7th Pylon

Bubastite Portal

Temple of Ramses III

Temple of Khonsu

Gateway of Euergetes II

Temple of Opet

Antiquities Office (Karnak branch)

▶ Precinct of Mut

▶ Luxor

Ticket Office ▼

The Temple of Ramses III to the Second Pylon

The first really impressive structure in the precinct is the columned **Temple of Ramses III**, which also held the Theban Triad barques during processions. Beyond its pylon, flanked by two colossi, is a festival hall with mummiform pillar statues, behind which are carvings of the annual festival of Amun-Min. A Hypostyle Hall precedes the darkened barque shrines of the temple, whose dedication reads in part: "I built and sheathed it with sandstone, bringing great doors of fine gold; I filled its treasuries with offerings that my hands had brought."

Though the pink granite **Colossus of Ramses II** beside the vestibule to the Second Pylon **[a]** is an immediate attention-grabber, it's worth detouring round the side of his temple to pass through the **Bubastite Portal**, named after the XXII Dynasty that hailed from Bubastis in the Delta. En route you'll pass some holes in the Second Pylon, where in 1820 Henri Crevier uncovered a host of statues and blocks from the demolished Aten Temple (including the colossi of Akhenaten in the Luxor and Cairo museums), which Horemheb used as in-fill for his pylon.

Pass through the Portal and turn left to find the **Shoshenk relief**, commemorating the triumphs of the XXII Dynasty Pharaoh Shoshenk. Traditionally, scholars have identified him as the Biblical Shishak (I Kings 14:25–26) who plundered Jerusalem in 925 BC, thus establishing a crucial link between the chronologies of Ancient Egypt and the Old Testament – an orthodoxy challenged by David Rohl's book, *A Test of Time* (see p.765). Although Shoshenk's figure is almost invisible, you can still see Amun, presiding over the slaughter of Rheoboamite prisoners in Palestine **[b]**. The scenes further along the wall are best seen after visiting the Great Hypostyle Hall.

To reach this, return to the forecourt and pass through the **Second Pylon**, one of several jerry-built structures begun by Horemheb, the last king of the XVIII Dynasty. The cartouches of Seti I (who completed the pylon) and Ramses I and II (Seti's father and son) appear just inside the doorway.

The Great Hypostyle Hall

The **Great Hypostyle Hall** is Karnak's glory, a forest of titanic columns covering an area of 6000 square metres – large enough to contain both St Peter's Cathedral in Rome and St Paul's Cathedral in London. Its grandeur is best appreciated early in the morning or late in the afternoon, when diagonal shadows enhance the effect of the columns. In pharaonic times the hall was roofed with sandstone slabs, its gloom interspersed by sunbeams falling through windows above the central aisle.

The hall probably began as a processional avenue of twelve or fourteen **columns**, each 23m high and 15m round (requiring six people with outstretched arms to encircle their girth). To this, Seti I and Ramses II added 122 smaller columns in two flanking wings, plus walls and a roof. All the columns consist of semi-drums, fitted together without mortar. The central ones have calyx capitals that once supported a raised section of the roof incorporating clerestory windows (the stone grilles of several remain in place), elevated above the papyrus-bud capitals of the flanking columns. Some of the lintels are still painted, as in ancient times.

Their **carvings** show the king making offerings to Theban deities, most notably Amun, who frequently appears in a sexually aroused state. Some Egyptologists believe that the temple priestesses kept Amun happy by masturbating his idol, and that the pharaoh did his bit to ensure the fertility of Egypt by ejaculating into the Nile during the Optet festival. Similar cult scenes decorate the side and end walls of the hall, which manifest two styles of carving. While Seti adorned the northern wing with bas-reliefs, Ramses II favoured cheaper sunk-reliefs for the southern wing. You can compare the two styles on the Hypostyle Hall's entrance wall, which features nearly symmetrical scenes of Amun's barque procession.

In Seti's **northern wing**, the procession begins on the north wall with a depiction of Amun's barque, initially veiled, then revealed **[c]**. Thoth inscribes the duration of Seti's reign on the leaves of a sacred persea tree **[d]** just beyond the doorway. By walking out through this door you'll come upon **Seti I's battle scenes**, whose weathered details are best observed in the early morning or late afternoon. One section **[e]** relates the capture of Qadesh from the Hittites in Syria (lower rows), and Seti's triumphs over the Libyans (above). Depicted elsewhere **[f]** are his campaigns against the Shasu of southern Palestine and the storming of Pa-Canaan, which the Egyptians "plundered with every evil".

Returning to the Hypostyle Hall, you can find similar reliefs commissioned by Ramses II in the **southern wing**, retaining traces of their original colours. Beyond the barque procession on the inner wall, Ramses is presented to Amun and enthroned between Wadjet and Nekhbet, while Thoth and Horus adjust his crowns **[g]**. On the outer wall are **Ramses II's battle scenes**, starting with the second Battle of Qadesh (*c.*1300 BC) **[h]**. Though scholars reckon it was probably a draw, Ramses claimed total victory over the Hittites. The text of their **peace treaty** (the earliest such document known) appears on the outer wall of the Cachette Court **[i]**.

This is known as the **Ashkelon Wall** after one of the four battle scenes flanking the treaty; another may depict a fight with the Israelites. Rohl argues that the enemy chariots in this scene contradict established chronology, since the Israelites didn't develop them until King Solomon's reign, but Ramses is conventionally supposed to have been the Pharaoh of the Oppression in the time of Moses, centuries earlier. Other clues from the Ashkelon Wall, Shoshenk's reliefs and the Israel Stele (see p.110) led Rohl to surmise that the Biblical Shishak was not Shoshenk, but Ramses II, and that the established synchronicity between Biblical and Egyptian history is three centuries out, due to an overestimation of the duration of the Third Intermediate Period (dynasties XXI–XXV). See p.765 in the Contexts section for more about Rohl's New Chronology hypothesis.

Pylons and obelisks

Beyond the XIX Dynasty Hypostyle Hall lies an extensive section of the precinct dating from the XVIII Dynasty. The **Third Pylon** that forms its back wall was originally intended by Amenophis III to be a monumental gateway to the temple. Like Horemheb forty years later, he demolished earlier structures to serve as core filler for his pylon. Removed by archeologists, these blocks are now displayed – partly reassembled – in the open-air museum. Two huge reliefs of Amun's barque appear on the far wall of the pylon **[j]**.

The narrow court between the Third and Fourth pylons once boasted four **Tuthmosid obelisks**. The stone bases near the Third Pylon belonged to a pair erected by Tuthmosis III, chunks of which lie scattered around. Of the pink-granite pair erected by Tuthmosis II, one still stands 23m high, with an estimated weight of 143 tonnes. Once tipped with glittering electrum, the finely carved obelisk was later appropriated by Ramses IV and VI, who added their own cartouches.

At this stage it's best to carry on through the **Fourth Pylon** rather than get sidetracked into the Cachette Court on the temple's secondary axis. Beyond the pylon are numerous columns which probably formed another hypostyle hall, dominated by the rose-granite **Obelisk of Hatshepsut**, the only woman to rule as pharaoh. To mark her sixteenth regnal year, Hatshepsut had two obelisks quarried in Aswan and erected at Karnak, a task completed in seven months. The standing obelisk is more than 27m high and weighs 320 tons, with a dedicatory inscription running its full height. Its fallen mate has broken into sections, now dispersed around the temple. After Hatshepsut's death, the long-frustrated Tuthmosis III took revenge, defacing her cartouches wherever they occurred and hiding the lower part of her obelisks behind walls – which inadvertently protected them from further vandalism during the Amarna Period.

The carved **tip** of Hatshepsut's fallen obelisk can be examined near the Osireion and Sacred Lake. On the way there, you'll pass a granite bas-relief of Amenophis II target-shooting from a moving chariot, protruding from the **Fifth Pylon**. Built of limestone, this pylon is attributed to Hatshepsut's father, Tuthmosis I. Beyond it lies a colonnaded courtyard with Osiride statues, built by one of the Tuthmosid pharaohs and possibly part of a large inner court surrounding the original Middle Kingdom temple of Amun.

Though the **Sixth Pylon** has largely disappeared, a portion either side of the granite doorway remains. Its outer face is known as the *Wall of Records* **[k]** after its list of peoples conquered by Tuthmosis III: Nubians to the right, Asiatics to the left. Beyond the latter is a text extolling the king's victory at Megiddo (Armageddon) in 1479 BC. By organizing tribute from his vanquished foes rather than simply destroying them, Tuthmosis III was arguably the world's first imperialist.

Around the Sanctuary

The section beyond the Sixth Pylon gets increasingly confusing, but a few features are unmistakable. Ahead stand a pair of square-sectioned **heraldic pillars**, their fronts carved with the lotus and papyrus of the Two Lands, their sides showing Amun embracing Tuthmosis III **[l]**. On the left are two **Colossi of Amun and Amunet**, dedicated by Tutankhamun (whose likeness appears with them) when orthodoxy was re-established after the Amarna Period. There's also a seated **statue of Amenophis II**.

Next comes a granite **Sanctuary** built by Philip Arrhidaeus, the cretinous half-brother of Alexander the Great, on the site of a Tuthmosid-era shrine which similarly held Amun's barque (whose pedestal is still *in situ*). The interior bas-reliefs show Philip making offerings to Amun in his various aspects, topped by a star-spangled ceiling. On the outside walls are sunk-reliefs depicting his coronation, Thoth's declaration of welcome, and Amunet suckling the young pharaoh, some still brightly coloured.

Around to the left of the Sanctuary and further back is a wall inscribed with Tuthmosis III's victories, which he built to hide a wall of reliefs by Queen Hatshepsut, now removed to another room **[m]**. **Hatshepsut's Wall** has reopened after lengthy restoration, as has the facing portion, where Tuthmosis replaced her image by offerings tables or bouquets, and substituted his father's and grandfather's names for her cartouches.

Beyond here lies an open space or **Central Court**, thought to mark the site of the original temple of Amun built in the XII Dynasty, whose weathered alabaster foundations poke from the pebbly ground.

The Jubilee Temple of Tuthmosis III

At the rear of this court rises the **Jubilee Temple of Tuthmosis III**, a personal cult shrine in Amun's back yard. As at Saqqara during the Old Kingdom, the

Theban kings periodically renewed their temporal and spiritual authority with jubilee festivals. The original entrance **[n]** is flanked by reliefs and broken statues of Tuthmosis in *hed-seb* regalia. A left turn brings you into the **Festival Hall**, with its unusual tentpole-style columns, their capitals adorned with blue-and-white chevrons. The lintels – carved with falcons, owls, *ankhs* and other symbols – are likewise brightly coloured. During Christian times the hall was used as a church, hence the haloed saints on some of the pillars.

A chamber off the southwest corner **[o]** contains an eroded replica of the **Table of Kings** (the original is in the Louvre), depicting Tuthmosis making offerings to previous rulers – Hatshepsut is naturally omitted from the roll call. Behind the hall are further chambers, mostly ruinous. The so-called **Botanical Garden** is a roofless enclosure containing painted reliefs of plants and animals which Tuthmosis encountered on his campaigns in Syria **[p]**. Across the way is a roofed chamber decorated by Alexander the Great, who appears before Amun and other deities **[q]**. The **Chapel of Sokar** constitutes a miniature temple to the Memphite god of darkness **[r]**, juxtaposed against a (now inaccessible) shrine to the sun. A further suite of rooms is dedicated to Tuthmosis **[s]**.

Chapels of the Hearing Ear

Excluded from Amun's Precinct and lacking a direct line to the Theban Triad, the inhabitants of Thebes used intermediary deities to transmit their petitions. These lesser deities rated their own shrines, known as **Chapels of the Hearing Ear** (sometimes actually decorated with carved ears), which straddled the temple's enclosure wall, presenting one face to the outside world. At Karnak, however, they became steadily less approachable and were finally surrounded by the present enclosure wall.

Directly behind the Jubilee Temple is a series of chapels built by Tuthmosis III, centred upon a large alabaster statue of the king and Amun. On either side are the bases of another pair of obelisks erected by Hatshepsut, of which nothing else remains. Still further east lie the ruined halls and colonnades of a Temple of the Hearing Ear built by Ramses II. Behind this stands the pedestal of the tallest obelisk known (31m), which Emperor Constantine had shipped to Rome and erected in the Circus Maximus; it was later moved to Lateran Square, hence its name, the **Lateran Obelisk**. As the Ancient Egyptians rarely erected single obelisks, it was probably intended to be accompanied by the Unfinished Obelisk that lies in a quarry outside Aswan, abandoned after the discovery of flaws in the rock.

Around the Sacred Lake

A short walk from Hatshepsut's Obelisk or the Cachette Court brings you to Karnak's **Sacred Lake**, which looks about as holy as a municipal boating pond, with the grandstand for the Sound and Light Show at the far end. The main attraction is a shady (and pricey) **café** where you can take a break from touring the complex and imagine the scene in ancient times. At sunrise, Amun's priests would take a sacred goose from the fowl-yards which now lie beneath the mound to the south of the lake, and set it free on the waters. As at Hermopolis, the goose or Great Cackler was credited with laying the Cosmic Egg at the dawn of Creation; but at Karnak the Great Cackler was identified with Amun rather than Thoth. During the Late Period, Pharaoh Taharqa added a subterranean **Osireion**, linking the resurrection of Osiris with that of the sun. The **giant scarab beetle** nearby represents Khepri, the reborn sun at dawn.

The north–south axis

The temple's **north–south axis** is sparser and less variegated than the main section, so if time is limited there's little reason to go beyond the Eighth Pylon. The Gate of Ramses IX, at the southern end of the court between the Third and Fourth pylons, gives access to this wing of the temple, which starts with the Cachette Court.

The **Cachette Court** gets its title from the discovery of a buried hoard of statues early in the twentieth century. Nearly 17,000 bronze statues and votive tablets, and 800 figures in stone, seem to have been cached in a "clearance" of sacred knick-knacks during Ptolemaic times. The finest statues (dating from the Old Kingdom to the Late Period) are now in the Luxor and Cairo museums. The court's northwest corner incorporates a mass of hieroglyphics known as the *Epic of Pentaur* **[t]**, which recaps the battles of Ramses II depicted on the outside of the Great Hypostyle Hall. Diagonally across the court are an eighty-line inscription by Merneptah and a copy of the **Israel Stele [u]** that's in Cairo, which contains among a list of conquests the only known pharaonic reference to Israel: "Israel is crushed, it has no more seed". Rohl argues that the stele has been misread and really relates the achievements of Merneptah's father and grandfather, Ramses II and Seti I.

More proof of the complexities of Egyptology is provided by the **Seventh Pylon**, which was built by Tuthmosis III, but decorated and usurped during the XIX Dynasty, a century or so later, when the cartouches on its door jambs **[v]** were altered to proclaim false ownership. It is fronted by seven statues of Middle Kingdom pharaohs, salvaged from pylon cores. On the far side are the lower portions of two **Colossi of Tuthmosis III**.

Although repair work has closed the **Eighth Pylon**, you might be able to walk around the edge for a distant view of its **four seated colossi**, or pay some baksheesh to be sneaked in for a closer look. The most complete figure is that of Amenophis I. Beyond a featureless court rises the **Ninth Pylon**, one of three erected by Horemheb and stuffed with masonry from the demolished Aten Temple, which is currently being rebuilt. Flanking the east wall of the final court is the ruinous **Jubilee Temple of Amenophis II**, which fulfilled a similar function to Tuthmosis III's temple in the main wing. The mud-brick houses of Karnak village are visible beyond the **Tenth Pylon**, from where an **Avenue of Sphinxes** once led to the Precinct of Mut.

The temples of Khonsu and Opet

Located in the southwest corner of Amun's Precinct are two smaller temples related to his cult. The **Temple of Khonsu** is dedicated to the son of Amun and Mut. Mostly built by Ramses III and IV, with additions by later kings, it is well preserved but crudely carved and dark inside. Many of the reliefs depict Herihor, first of Thebes' priest kings, who ruled Upper Egypt after the Ramessid pharaohs moved their capital to the Delta. This shift in power is also evident on the pylons, which show Pinundjem, another high priest, worshipping the gods as a king.

Alongside stands a smaller **Temple of Opet**, the hippopotamus-goddess traditionally believed to be the mother of Osiris. The temple is not always open, but if it is, check out the reliefs, which are finer than Khonsu's and date from Ptolemaic and Roman times. The towering **Gateway of Euergetes I**, with its winged sun-disc cornice, was raised in Ptolemaic times and is currently shut.

The open-air museum

The northern sector of Amun's Precinct contains an **open–air museum**, for which a separate ticket (£E20) must be bought before entering. Its prime

Sekhmet

Sekhmet – "the Powerful" – was the violent counterpart of the Delta goddess Bastet (see p.631). As the daughter of Re, she personified the sun's destructive force, making her a worthy consort for Ptah, the Memphite creator-god. In one myth, Re feared that humanity was plotting against him and unleashed his avenging Eye in the form of Sekhmet, who would have massacred all life had not Re relented and slaked her thirst with red beer, which the drunken goddess mistook for blood.

With the rise of Thebes and Amun's association with Ptah, a corresponding relationship was made between their consorts, Mut and Sekhmet. The New Kingdom pharaohs adopted Sekhmet as a symbol of their indomitable prowess in battle: the statues of the goddess at Karnak bear inscriptions such as "smiter of the Nubians". As "Lady of the Messengers of Death", Sekhmet could send – or prevent – plagues, so her priestesses also served as healers and veterinarians.

▲ Sekhmet

attractions are two early barque shrines, reassembled from blocks found inside the Third Pylon. From the XII Dynasty comes a lovely **White Chapel**, carved all over with bas-reliefs. While most depict Djed columns, ankhs and other symbols, it's the scenes of Senusert I embracing a priapic Amun-Min that you remember. The plainer **Alabaster Chapel** of Amenophis I contains more innocuous scenes of the pharaoh making offerings to Amun and his barque. Along the way you'll pass rows of blocks from Hatshepsut's **Red Chapel**, which archeologists have been unable to reconstruct since each block features a self-contained design rather than a segment of a large relief. This hasn't deterred Egyptologists from trying the same feat with the **Shrine of Tuthmosis III**, with more success. You'll also notice some granite **statues of Sekhmet**, taken from a small **Temple of Ptah** alongside Karnak's enclosure wall, whose ruins aren't much reward for a three-hundred-metre trek across broken ground, though the finest statues of Sekhmet are now in the Luxor Museum.

The Theban Necropolis

Across the Nile from Luxor, the **Theban Necropolis** testifies to the same obsession with death and resurrection that produced the Pyramids. Mindful of how these had failed to protect the mummies of the Old Kingdom pharaohs, later rulers opted for concealment, sinking their tombs in the arid Theban Hills while perpetuating their memory with gigantic mortuary temples on the plain below. The Necropolis straddled the border between the lands of the living and the dead, verdant flood plain giving way to boundless desert, echoing the path of the dead "going west" to meet Osiris as the sun set over the mountains and descended into the underworld.

Though stripped of its treasures over millennia, the Necropolis retains a peerless array of funerary monuments. The grandest of its tombs are in the **Valley of the Kings** and the **Valley of the Queens**, but there's also a wealth of vivid detail in the smaller **Tombs of the Nobles**. Equally amazing are the mortuary temples which enshrined the deceased pharaoh's cult: among these, **Deir el–Bahri** is timelessly magnificent and **Medinet Habu** rivals Karnak for grandeur, while the shattered **Ramesseum** and **Colossi of Memnon** mock the pretensions of their founders. On a humbler level, but still executed with great artistry, are the funerary monuments of the craftsmen who built the royal tombs, and the ruins of their homes at **Deir el-Medina**.

Beside its monuments, the west bank is interesting by way of contrast with Luxor: more rural than urban, and making fewer concessions to foreigners. Many of the Egyptians that you'll meet in Luxor actually come from villages on the west bank, and a lot of the money made in Luxor is invested there. The symbiosis between the two communities is underscored by the fact that, when speaking English, locals invariably refer to the west bank as "**the other side**". People living there also jokingly liken it to "Palestine", living under the rule of "Israel", due to land disputes between the villagers and Luxor City Council.

Visiting the Necropolis

Spread across wadis and hills beyond the edge of the cultivated plain, the Theban Necropolis is too diffuse and complex to take in on a single visit. Even limiting yourself to the Valley of the Kings, Deir el-Bahri and one or other of the major sites, you're likely to feel overwhelmed by the end of the day. Most people favour a series of visits, taking into account the climate and crowds – both major factors in the enjoyment of a trip. In **winter**, mornings are pleasantly hot, afternoons baking but bearable, and most coach tours are scheduled accordingly, making the principal sites crowded between 9am and 2pm. As lots of people come early "to beat the crowds", the royal tombs are actually emptiest in the late afternoon. In **summer**, it's simply too hot throughout the afternoon, and you should get here as early as possible.

The **opening hours** of the sites may change with the season and security restrictions, but are generally from 7am to 5pm daily, except for the Valley of the Kings, which opens at 6am year round, and closes at 4pm in the winter. Making a full tour of the Necropolis is expensive – although a **student card** entitles you to a fifty percent discount. If you wanted to see all the sites in the Necropolis, you'd end up spending around $80 on tickets at the full rate; most people are satisfied to see far less than that.

Guided tours, typically featuring the Colossi of Memnon, the valleys of the Kings and Queens and Deir el-Bahri, are bookable through any hotel or travel agency. The cost per person for an air-conditioned coach tour with Karnak Travel or Thomas Cook (€30–40 including admission tickets) exceeds the group rate for a trip, booked through one of the budget hotels, for up to eleven people sharing a minibus (£E120–150, excluding tickets). Even if you like the idea of a tour, don't sign up for the first one offered – at least, not without an idea of what's available elsewhere and the scope for **independent travel** (see p.371). Virtually all tours include a visit to a papyrus or alabaster "factory" where your guide stands to earn a commission on **sales**; some agencies own the shops where they send their clients. There's no point in getting indignant about this unless you end up spending more time there than at the sites. If you want to hire a **guide**, try Abu El Naga Gabrail (☎010 124-0080, ⒲www .egypt-westerndesert.com) or Kawsar Tawfik (☎010 524-7832).

Useful **things to bring** include a torch, plenty of water and small change. If you're planning to cycle or donkey it, a hat and double rations of water are vital. A snack, too, is a good idea, as the choice of food and drink is limited, and prices are higher than in Luxor.

Photography is now prohibited in the tombs to protect their fragile murals, which are widely reproduced in print and on the Theban Mapping Project website (⒲www.kv5.com) anyway. Dusk and early morning are the best times to capture the landscape and temples of the west bank.

Crossing the Nile

There are several ways of crossing **from Luxor** to the west bank. Since the opening of **Luxor Bridge**, 7km south of town at Bogdadi, all coaches, minibuses and taxis from Luxor use this circuitous route, which can take an hour if traffic is heavy. Some operators get round this by sending the vehicle on ahead, to meet passengers taken across the Nile by motorboat – and crossing by boat remains by far the most pleasant option.

A shabby **local ferry** sails frequently during daytime, hourly after 6pm and sporadically after midnight from the landing stage on the Corniche signposted "National Ferryboat", to dock near **Gezira village** on the west bank. Locals pay 25pt for the ride, tourists £E1. Crowded with villagers and baggage, the ferry psyches you up for the day ahead. Alternatively, dozens of **motorboats** and **feluccas** inveigle for custom by the water's edge, charging £E5 per boatload (£E10 for more than six passengers) after a brief haggle. Motorboats (called "lunches" in English or *zobak* in Arabic) are the fastest way to cross the river and may land or leave from anywhere along either riverbank, whereas crossing the Nile by **felucca** is more of a leisurely experience than a quick journey.

You should be able to take **bicycles** for free on all these vessels, but **motorbikes** can only be carried aboard the local ferry. Keep **safety** in mind: overcrowded boats or waterways at night are a recipe for disaster, as was proved during the festival of Abu el-Haggag in 2001, when 35 passengers drowned after a ferry hit their motorboat in the dark. Stepping across rickety wharfs after dark is a more mundane hazard – watch out for mooring lines and gaps in the planking.

West bank transport and activities

Once across the Nile, how you choose to get around will depend on the time of year and what you plan to see, your budget and your sense of adventure. If you intend to visit the Necropolis more than once, try using various modes of transport.

It's quite feasible to explore the Necropolis **on foot**, utilizing public transport. From the taxi depot in Gezira, **pick-ups** shuttle passengers to Old Gurna (known to drivers as Gurna Foq), bringing you within fifteen minutes' walk of Medinet Habu, the Valley of the Queens or the Ramesseum, for only 25pt per person. Many run on to Dra' Abu Naga, leaving you closer to the Tombs of the Nobles or Deir el-Bahri. Pick-ups can also be engaged **as taxis**, to whisk up to six passengers from one site to another for £E5 without paying for the driver to hang around while you explore.

Hiring a **private taxi** is the easiest way of visiting sites according to your own itinerary, but you may feel constrained about hiking over the hills between the

---

Short itineraries around the Necropolis

For those who like to linger over every carving, the tombs and temples on the west bank could easily fill three or four days. If you're forced to cram the highlights into **half a day**, a minimalist schedule might run: Valley of the Kings (1hr 30min), Deir el-Bahri (20min), the Tombs of the Nobles (30min–1hr), Medinet Habu (30min), and/or the Ramesseum (30min). If you have a **full day**, catch a taxi to the Valley of the Kings before 9am, spend a couple of hours there and then walk over the hills to Deir el-Bahri, arranging to be met there for another ride to Medinet Habu or Deir el-Medina and the Valley of the Queens. Alternatively, you could spend time at the Tombs of the Nobles and the Ramesseum before returning to the landing stage.

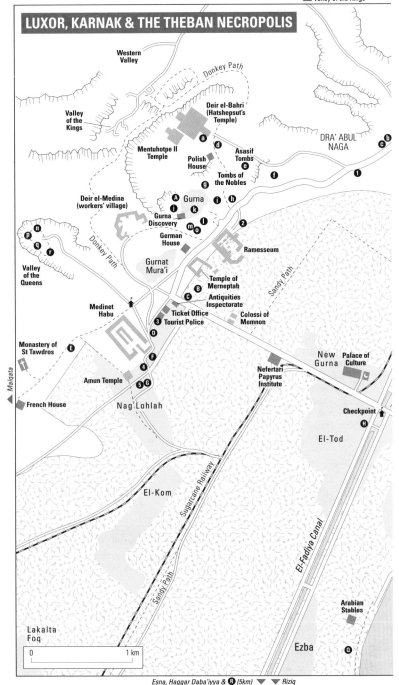

LUXOR, KARNAK & THE THEBAN NECROPOLIS

▲ Valley of the Kings

Western Valley

Donkey Path

Valley of the Kings

Deir el-Bahri (Hatshepsut's Temple)

DRA' ABUL NAGA

Mentuhotpe II Temple

Polish House

Asasif Tombs

Tombs of the Nobles

Deir el-Medina (workers' village)

Gurna

Gurna Discovery

German House

Gurnat Mura'i

Ramesseum

Valley of the Queens

Donkey Path

Sandy Path

Temple of Merneptah

Antiquities Inspectorate

Medinet Habu

Ticket Office
Tourist Police

Colossi of Memnon

Monastery of St Tawdros

New Gurna

Palace of Culture

▲ Malqata

Amun Temple

Nag Lohlah

Nefertari Papyrus Institute

French House

Checkpoint

El-Tod

New Gurna

Sugarcane Railway

El-Kom

El-Fadiya Canal

Sandy Path

Arabian Stables

Lakalta Foq

0   1 km

Ezba

Esna, Haggar Daba'iyya & R (5km) ▼ ▼ Riziq

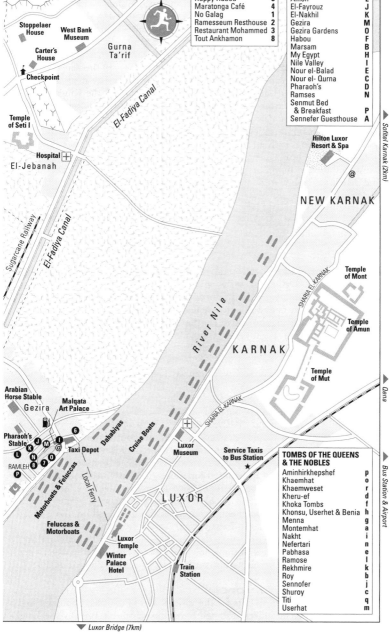

Sun Temple ▲   ▲ *Qena*

Gurna
Jedid

RESTAURANTS, CAFÉS & NIGHTLIFE

Africa Restaurant	6
Casablanca	7
Happy Habou	5
Maratonga Café	4
No Galag	1
Ramesseum Resthouse	2
Restaurant Mohammed	3
Tout Ankhamon	8

ACCOMMODATION

Al-Moudira	R
Al-Salam Camp	Q
Amenophes	G
Amon	L
El-Fayrouz	J
El-Nakhil	K
Gezira	M
Gezira Gardens	O
Habou	F
Marsam	B
My Egypt	H
Nile Valley	I
Nour el-Balad	E
Nour el- Qurna	C
Pharaoh's	D
Ramses	N
Senmut Bed & Breakfast	P
Sennefer Guesthouse	A

Stoppelaer
House

West Bank
Museum

Gurna
Ta'rif

Carter's
House

Checkpoint

Temple
of Seti I

Hospital
El-Jebanah

El-Fadiya Canal

Sugarcane Railway

El-Fadiya Canal

Hilton Luxor
Resort & Spa

@

NEW KARNAK

▶ *Sofitel Karnak (2km)*

River Nile

SHARIA EL KARNAK

Temple
of Mont

Temple
of Amun

KARNAK

Temple
of Mut

▶ *Qena*

Arabian
Horse Stable

Gezira

Malqata
Art Palace

Dahabiyas

Pharaoh's
Stable

@

Taxi Depot

RAMLEH

Cruise Boats

Luxor
Museum

SHARIA EL KARNAK

Service Taxis
to Bus Station
★

▶ *Bus Station & Airport*

TOMBS OF THE QUEENS & THE NOBLES

Aminhirkhepshef	p
Khaemhat	o
Khaemweset	r
Kheru-ef	d
Khoka Tombs	f
Khonsu, Userhet & Benia	h
Menna	g
Montemhat	a
Nakht	i
Nefertari	n
Pabhasa	e
Ramose	l
Rekhmire	k
Roy	b
Sennofer	j
Shuroy	c
Titi	q
Userhat	m

Motorboats & Feluccas

Local Ferry

LUXOR

Feluccas &
Motorboats

Luxor
Temple

Winter
Palace
Hotel

Train
Station

373

▼ *Luxor Bridge (7km)*

Valley of the Kings and Deir el-Bahri (see p.394), and will pay for waiting time in any case. Taxis are usually hired for four to six hours, at £E15–20 an hour.

Cycling and motorbiking

Assuming that you're reasonably fit, the cheapest way – after walking – to cover the Necropolis is by **cycling**. Bicycles (*ajila*) can be rented in shops and hotels in Luxor or on the west bank for £E10 a day. Test your bike before hiring; many have no gears, which makes any uphill stretch against a headwind murder. A day's touring might involve cycling 30km: for example, 3km from the river bank to the main ticket kiosk, 8km from there to the Valley of the Kings (beware of traffic), and 3km from Deir el-Bahri to Medinet Habu. The main drawback is that you can't then walk over the hills from the Valley of the Kings to Deir el-Bahri. Roads vary from smooth surfaces to stony *pistes*. In winter, you'll feel cool when riding but start sweating once you stop. Cycling during summer is a lot more demanding, so it's imperative to take the gradual uphill stretch to the Valley of the Kings early in the morning, allowing you to coast back downhill in the afternoon heat. Guard against heatstroke and keep swigging water. There are workshops for bicycle **repairs** on the road between the main ticket office and Medinet Habu, near the *Nour el-Gurna Hotel*, and in the village of El-Jebanah.

Alternatively, you could ride a **motorbike**. Several bike shops in Luxor rent them by the day for £E50–75. Be especially careful of children and livestock when riding on the west bank.

Riding and ballooning

Travelling by **donkey** offers the thrill of riding up the Theban Hills as mist cloaks the plain, skirting precipices and abandoned tombs before you descend into the Valley of the Kings, and returning via Deir el-Bahri and the Tombs of the Nobles – with fantastic views denied to other travellers. However, it's a physically gruelling five-hour trip, starting at 5am, that's not for anyone with vertigo, nor children. Light relief is provided by the donkeys, which disobey commands of *Hoosh!* ("stop") or *Hatla!* ("faster") whenever they encounter another beast on heat, or anything edible. As "mountain" donkeys know the trail, mishaps are more comical than serious. A more laid-back donkey option is a **village tour** of Beirat, using farm trails and backroads, which can be lovely if it's not too hot. Few Luxor hotels offer donkey trips nowadays besides the *Sherief* and *Venus* (see p.343), but you can hire beasts and a guide from Tayeb Khalifa in Gezira (℡095/231-2955 or ℡012 743-8266, ✉kingofluxor66 @hotmail.com), who supplies donkeys to adventure-tour companies.

Though **horses** or **camels** aren't any use for exploring the Necropolis, they're great fun to ride in the desert beyond Medinet Habu, or through the west bank villages. They can be hired for about £E30 an hour from Pharaoh's Stables (℡095/231-2263 or ℡010 632-4961) or the Arabian Horse Stable (℡095/231-0024 or ℡010 504-8558) in Gezira, owned by rival brothers, Bakri and Nobi. Both will collect clients from hotels in Luxor. A third, more rustic set-up is the Arabian Stables in Ezba village.

While it's no substitute for visiting the tombs and temples, a **hot-air balloon flight** gives a majestic view of the whole Necropolis. This amazing experience is worth a splurge and prices have never been lower – see p.356 for details.

Tickets for the Necropolis

Confusingly for visitors, **tickets** for the various sites in the Necropolis are sold at four or five separate offices, scattered across the west bank. Broadly speaking, tickets for all the mortuary temples (except Deir el-Bahri), Deir el-Medina and most of the Tombs of the Nobles are sold at the main office beside the tourist police HQ. The Valley of the Kings office sells tickets for itself and Ay's Tomb in the Western Valley; tickets for Tutankhamun's Tomb are sold at a separate kiosk within the Valley of the Kings. A third office at Deir el-Bahri sells tickets for Hatshepsut's Temple and some tombs in the vicinity, and there's yet another ticket office for the Valley of the Queens.

Prices are detailed below; rates for card-carrying **students** are roughly half the quoted price. It's unlikely that you'll use more than six or seven tickets in a day's outing. Tickets are only valid for the day of purchase, with no refunds for unused ones.

Main office (with a separate hatch for students)

#1	Medinet Habu (Temple of Ramses III)	£E25
#2	Ramesseum	£E25
#3	Tombs of Nakht and Menna	£E20
#4	Tombs of Rekhmire and Sennofer	£E20
#5	Tombs of Ramose, Userhat and Khaemhat	£E25
#6	Deir el-Medina (any two tombs)	£E25
#7	Khokha Tombs	£E20
#8	Temple of Seti I	£E25
#9	Tombs of Khonsu, Userhet and Benia	£E12
#10	Tombs of Roy and Shuroy (Dra' Abul Naga)	£E12
#11	Tomb of Peshedu (Deir el-Medina)	£E10
#12	Temple of Merneptah	£E10

Deir el-Bahri office

Deir el-Bahri (Hatshepsut's temple)	£E26
Asasif Tombs (Kheru-ef, Ankh-hor)	£E26
Tomb of Pabhasa	£E20

Valley of the Kings office

Valley of the Kings (any three tombs)	£E70
Tomb of Tutankhamun (sold inside the valley)	£E80
Tomb of Ay (Western Valley)	£E20

Valley of the Queens office

Valley of the Queens (excluding Nefertari's tomb)	£E25

West bank practicalities

You can find most things on Gezira's main street; **bicycle rental** (£E10 per day), **Internet access** (there's no broadband on the west bank), and a **dry cleaners** further up the street. If you need medical treatment, go to Luxor's International Hospital rather than the **hospital** in the west bank village of El-Jebanah. There are no currency exchanges on the west bank, but most hotels will **change money** unofficially.

Generally, the **police** leave tourists alone, but the checkpoint at the El-Fadiya Canal won't allow traffic to pass up the road to the Necropolis before 6am – which spoils things for donkey-groups hoping to catch the sunrise, unless they sneak through the fields – and service taxi drivers at Gezira's depot have been told not to take foreigners beyond the west bank **security zone**, which ends at Haggar Daba'iyya (to the south) and Gurna Ta'rif (to the north). After dark, even travel to Haggar Daba'iyya is regarded with suspicion, as the village is reputedly a den of dope dealing. Plainclothes cops often visit bars and restaurants in all the west bank villages, to enjoy free hospitality, collect a bribe and keep an eye on the clientele.

Accommodation

Staying on the west bank, you experience far less hassle and noise than in Luxor, and some places afford superb views of Luxor Temple or the Theban Hills. Gezira is only five minutes by motorboat from Luxor Temple and on the road to the Theban Necropolis, while other west bank localities are close to a variety of tombs and temples.

While the newest **hotels** are air conditioned and en suite throughout, some of the older ones out near the temples are old-fashioned and basic – but the pleasure of staying beside an ancient ruin may outweigh the discomfort. Though prices are comparatively higher than in Luxor, the view or ambience more than compensate. Unless stated otherwise, all the following have rooms with private bathrooms and include breakfast in the price. There's also a **campsite** in a rural setting, to the south of Gezira. See the **map** on p.372–373 for locations, and phone ahead before crossing the Nile with your baggage. Those hotels that aren't within walking distance of the ferry docks in Gezira village are accessible by pick-up or private taxi.

Some five hundred foreigners live on the west bank, so renting and selling **apartments** is big business – especially in the Ramleh district of Gezira. Mohammed El-Qadi (ⓣ010 666-9462) owns several blocks of air-conditioned flats with nice bathrooms and simple kitchens, some sharing a rooftop with fine views, or a garden: a two-bedroom flat costs £E800 a week. Many other apartments or villas – some with pools and Jacuzzis – are available through Egypt Rent a Flat or Flats in Luxor (see p.345). The *Restaurant Mohammed* (see p.378) rents clean, simple rooms (£E60) with a shared kitchen and bathroom.

Hotels

Gezira and around

Al-Salam Camp By the Nile 1600m from the ferry dock ⓣ010 682-4067, ⓦwww.luxor-westbank.com/camp. A Dahab-style campground with six huts (£E20 per person) and a clean washroom, enlivened by rock music and beer. Almost cut off by water when the Nile rises, it exists in a zonked-out world of its own. ❶

Amon At the back of Gezira ⓣ095/231-0912 ⓣ010 6394585, ⓕ095/231-1205. Two en-suite blocks flanking a lush garden; the south-facing one has bigger rooms with corner balconies. On the top floor are three triple rooms (£E230). Guests may use the kitchen, order beer or meals. The hotel can arrange transfers as far away as Hurghada. ❸

El-Fayrouz ⓣ095/231-2709 or 012 277-0565, ⓦwww.elfayrouz.com. A salmon-pink tower of spacious rooms with fans (some are a/c) and balconies, with a gorgeous garden and a rooftop overlooking the Theban Hills. There's Internet access, and meals and alcohol are available. ❸

El-Nakhil On the edge of Gezira ⓣ & ⓕ095/231-3922 or ⓣ012 382-1007. A Moorish array of comfortable a/c chalets (one equipped for disabled guests), with a pretty garden and a view of fields outside the wall. Gezira's most restful hotel, it's deservedly popular. Rates in euros. ❺

Gezira ⓣ095/231-0034, ⓦwww.el-gezira.com. Down the first turning off the main street, this pleasant hotel has a/c en-suite rooms with balconies, an attractive rooftop and terrace. Guests get £E5 discount on the pool at *Gezira Gardens*. Meals, beer and wine served. ❷

Gezira Gardens Off the waterfront ⓣ095/231-2505, ⓕ095/231-2506, ⓦwww.el-gezira.com. Owned by the same family as the *Gezira*, this mini holiday village has a/c rooms or self-catering apartments sleeping up to four ($55) with balconies overlooking the Nile or the swimming pool. Facilities also include two bars and restaurants, billiards and table tennis, laundry service and satellite TV. Buffet breakfast, and a Saiyidi show on Sunday. ❺

Nile Valley Near the ferry dock and taxi depot ⓣ095/231-1477 or ⓣ012 796-4473, ⓦwww.nilevalley.nl. Their rooftop restaurant boasts the world's finest view of Luxor Temple. Mostly en-suite a/c rooms with balconies; the ones at the back are quieter. A pool in the garden is due

soon. Well managed and friendly, with live music and a buffet on Sunday evenings. Sells beer, wine and spirits; organizes trips as far afield as Cairo. ❸
Ramses ☎095/231-2748 or ☎010 184-2083, ✉mamdouhsid@yahoo.com. Across the street from the *Gezira*, this hotel has mostly a/c rooms, and a fine view of Luxor from its roof. Owner Mamdouh has a boat with three cabins, called the *Sindbad*, which he charters for cruises between Aswan and Edfu. ❷

🛏 **Senmut Bed & Breakfast** Ramleh, on the edge of Gezira ☎095/231-3077 or ☎012 736-9159, 🌐www.senmut-luxor.com. This family-friendly B&B in an upmarket villa quarter has soothing rooms with or without a/c and bathrooms, a communal living room with a library and satellite TV; kitchen, free service wash and meals cooked to order; and a flowery rooftop overlooking the river. ❸

Near the temples

Amenophes Nag Lohlah ☎ & ℻095/231-1228, ✉sayedm25@hotmail.com. Pleasantly faded a/c rooms with TV and balconies, a few minutes' walk from Medinet Habu; the view from its shady rooftop is marred by houses. Takes MasterCard and Visa. ❹
Habou Nag Lolah, opposite Medinet Habu temple ☎095/231-1611 or 012 358-0242. Immortalized in Critchfield's *Shahhat*, this seedy mud-brick labyrinth has stuffy barrel-vaulted rooms, but the shared bathrooms are clean and there's a fabulous view of the temple from the rooftop. Bike rental. ❷

🛏 **Marsam** Gurnat Mura'i, off the road to the Tombs of the Nobles ☎095/237-2403 or 010 342-6471, ✉marsam@africamail.com. Built for US archeologists and later owned by Sheikh Ali Abdul Rasoul, who helped discover the tomb of Seti I, this west-bank institution is now managed by Czech-Australian Natasha. Its peaceful ambience and delicious meals compensate for the simple mud-brick rooms with fans (a private shower costs £E40 extra) and lack of alcohol. There's also a decent library and the odd archeologist in residence. Reservations essential Dec–Feb. ❷
My Egypt El-Tod, near the checkpoint ☎095/206-0787 or ☎010 332-8041, 🌐www.myegypt.co.uk. A small hotel with a rooftop restaurant facing the Theban Hills. New a/c en-suite rooms, some sleeping two adults and two children (£E160).

Optional half board for £E20 per person. Tours arranged. ❸
Nour el-Balad On the edge of the desert beyond Medinet Habu ☎095/242-6111 or 010 129-5812. Casbah chic rules in this mud-brick palace of "rustic" rooms with cotton duvets, mosquito nets and fancy bathrooms. Upstairs rooms cost £E50–100 more, rooftop suites £E450–500 (which seems a lot for a view of the Theban Hills). Its isolation is its main drawback (or selling point). ❸
Nour el-Qurna Gurnat Mura'l ☎095/231-1430 or 010 129-5812. The *Nour el-Balad*'s little sister hotel lurks in a palm grove across the road from the Antiquities Inspectorate. The mud-brick rooms have palm-frond beds with cotton duvets, mosquito net, stereo and tiled bathrooms. The vibe is friendly and quirky. Room rates vary according to the view. ❸
Pharaoh's Nag Lohlah, near Medinet Habu ☎095/231-0702 or 010 613-1436, ✉pharaohshotel@hotmail.com. Cosy rooms (most with a/c and bathrooms); the roof has a few larger ones costing £E60 more, and a side view of the temple. Serves beer and meals on a shady patio, plagued by mozzies in the summer. ❸
Sennefer Guesthouse Gurna, near the tomb of Sennofer ☎ & ℻095/231-0395 or ☎010 576-4317, 🌐www.senneferhotel.com. An unlicensed place with an owner known as "Snake", set amid the Tombs of the Nobles, overlooking the Ramesseum. Rooms have fans, and some showers (the shared facilities are clean), but are overpriced, given their austerity. ❹

Elsewhere on the west bank

🛏 **Al-Moudira** Haggar Daba'iyya, 5km from Medinet Habu and 5km from Luxor Bridge ☎012 325-1307, ℻012 322-0528, 🌐www.moudira.com. Simply the best hotel in Egypt, it resembles an Ottoman palace, with exquisite courtyards, vast gardens and pool, a Mediterranean/Middle Eastern restaurant, a bar, and horse-riding. Its 54 individually-styled a/c suites are furnished with antiques, mosquito nets, satellite TV and CD player; some have a fountain and a sunken Turkish *hammam*. The only drawback is that it is miles from anywhere; a taxi from Luxor or to the Necropolis costs around £E60. There's a twenty percent surcharge at Christmas and New Year. ❽

Eating and drinking

You can get a decent **meal** of *kofta* or chicken with rice and salad at almost any of the hotels on the west bank for £E25–30. Two that deserve a special mention are the 🍴 *Nile Valley* – which has a splendid view of Luxor Temple and a delicious buffet (£E55) with a dervish show at 7pm on Sundays – and the cooking at the 🍴 *Marsam*, which generally serves hearty Egyptian fare but sometimes experiments with vegetarian tempura and the like. Otherwise, check out the 24-hour ⚔ *Restaurant Mohammed* near the main ticket office, which is great for stuffed pigeon or homemade goat's cheese, and has spotless toilets and a garden with a 600-year-old acacia tree. By the temples, the *Maratonga Café* does a mean *tageen* (not on the menu), *Happy Habou* is dazzlingly clean and offers quiche and cakes besides hot food, while the *Ramesseum Resthouse* sells beer and wine. In Gezira, the *Africa Restaurant* near the taxi depot serves fresh fish and veggie dishes on its peaceful patio, and there are two places on the waterfront. *Casablanca*, on the corner of the sidestreet to *Gezira Gardens*, specializes in fish, while *Tout Ankhamon* serves impossibly vast set meals of coconut curry or duck with rosemary, spicy lentil and vegetable stews, with *baklava* or watermelon for dessert – but demands £E10 for a doggy bag to take away leftovers.

For a more restful scene, drop into the German-owned **Malqata Art Palace** in Gezira (daily except Mon 11.30am–3pm & 5.30–10.30pm; closed June–Aug; ⓦwww.luxor-westbank.com) to look at vintage photographs of Egypt and contemporary Egyptian paintings over freshly brewed coffee, civilized conversation and foreign-language newspapers. They also serve tasty meals.

The sale of **alcohol** is limited to the *Al-Moudira*, *Amon*, *El-Fayrouz*, *Gezira*, *Gezira Gardens*, *Nile Valley*, *Ramses* and *Pharaoh's* hotels, the *Africa* restaurant and the *Ramesseum Resthouse*. The *Nile Valley* has the liveliest **nightlife**, especially on Tuesdays and Sundays when it features Saiyidi musicians and Dervish dancers. A similar show plus a bellydancer may occur at *Gezira Gardens* on Sunday evening, when there's also live *rababa* music at the Rastafied *No Galag* rooftop in Dra' Abul Naga.

The west bank villages

The **west bank villages** are incidental to most tourists visiting the Theban Necropolis, but integral to the landscape and atmosphere. Their fields stretch from the river banks to the temples on the desert's edge; their goats root amid the Tombs of the Nobles. Though land remains paramount, almost every family is involved in tourism, either renting out donkeys or making souvenirs on the west bank, commuting to hotel jobs in Luxor, or sailing motorboats or feluccas on the Nile. Family and village ties bind them together and help them exploit the stream of rich visitors that flows across their land. Crafty, warm-hearted and proud, west-bankers are worth getting to know. Richard Critchfield's *Shahhat* (sold in most Luxor bookshops) gives a fascinating glimpse into their lives two generations ago, before tourism really changed things.

Your first encounter will be with **GEZIRA**, where ferries disgorge villagers returning from Luxor, and tourists arrive in motorboats. The depot for private and service **taxis** to villages on the west bank is up the slope; floodlit at night, it proclaims the urbanization of Gezira. Traditionally Gezira's role in tourism was to ferry tourists about or guide them on donkeys through the Necropolis, but the village now also has half-a-dozen hotels and flats for rent, among other amenities. During the last decade, Luxor Council tried to claim all the land along the waterfront but met fierce resistance from locals who'd built houses and hotels there, as well as from foreigners who'd bought apartments in the chic new district of **Ramleh**. Some only escaped demolition after the matriarch of the Khalifa family lay down in front of the bulldozers – after which Ramleh was nicknamed "Ramallah".

Gezira straggles the El-Fadiya Canal, where **EL-TOD** begins. Its inhabitants call the canal "the Nile", and those residing on either side of it regard themselves as superior to folks on the other, although they live similar lives and intermarriage is common. Across the main road lies **NEW GURNA**, built in the 1940s with government funds to wean villagers away from Old Gurna in the hills. Designed by Hassan Fathy, a leading advocate of creating architecture suited to local conditions, the settlement contains two superbly proportioned public buildings – the **mosque** and **Palace of Culture** – made of Fathy's favourite material, mud-brick. However, the village failed to attract many Gurnawis, and others moved in instead, to find that Fathy's houses were too small for their extended families, obliging them to add breeze-block extensions.

Beyond the Colossi of Memnon, the barren, windswept foothills are pockmarked with the Tombs of the Nobles and the sad remains of **Old GURNA** (often spelt "Qurna" but pronounced with a "G"). For generations this ramshackle village supplied the workforce for archeological digs while quietly **robbing tombs** directly beneath its own homes – a Faustian bargain that led to many unreported deaths through cave-ins, and deprived the villagers of piped water, obliging women and girls to collect water by donkey. After years of protests, the authorities finally forced people to move out in 2006, and bulldozed all but 27 buildings, a sanitized vestige of the village that once thrived amid the dead, whose history is related in the Gurna Discovery exhibition (see p.398).

The road runs on past **DRA' ABUL NAGA**, another largely demolished village whose remaining houses squat in an arid moonscape glittering with light reflected off mica and alabaster dust. Traditionally, it manufactured the statues and ashtrays sold in tourist shops throughout Egypt, in **alabaster workshops** decorated with garish murals. When the authorities had all buildings north of the road demolished, practically every house affected claimed to be an alabaster factory in order to get compensation.

At this point a spur road turns off towards Hatshepsut's temple, while the main one carries on to a crossroads beside a cemetery, where the road to the Valley of the Kings begins. The mud-brick complex on the hilltop was **Howard Carter's house** during his search for Tutankhamun's tomb. There was talk of turning it into a museum, but nothing happened. Nearby is another archeological residence called the **Stoppelaer House**, designed by Hassan Fathy. Japanese, French, German and Polish Egyptologists also have their residences on the west bank.

The wasteland at the crossroads near Gurna Tarif is the site for the annual **Moulid of Abu Qusman** on Sha'ban 27, commemorating a local holy man known for his miracles and outspokenness, who died in 1984. On one occasion Abu Qusman supposedly crossed the Nile on his handkerchief after the ferry refused to take him because he lambasted the tourists on board for immorality. His moulid used to last all night, but nowadays they wind it up at midnight.

A new **West Bank Museum** is due to open in 2007, to display antiquities from SCA storerooms; resembling a prison with watchtowers, it stands 500m beyond the checkpoint, on the road to **Gurna Jedid**, a sprawling township built to house the evicted inhabitants of Old Gurna and Dra' Abul Naga. Gurna Jedid was feared as a dumping ground until governor Farag strove to reconcile people to moving by upgrading its housing, encouraging extended families to buy adjacent properties, and installing civic amenities as good as Luxor's. To compensate those who earned a living at the Tombs of the Nobles, there will be shops selling handicrafts to coach parties – or so the plan has it.

The Colossi of Memnon

A kilometre or so beyond New Gurna the main road passes the **Colossi of Memnon**, looming nearly 18 metres above the fields. This gigantic pair of enthroned statues originally fronted the mortuary temple of Amenophis III, once the largest complex on the west bank, and possibly even larger than Karnak – which later pharaohs plundered for masonry until nothing remained but the king's colossi. Both have lost their faces and crowns, and the northern one was cleaved to the waist by an earthquake in 27 BC. Subsequently, this colossus was heard to "sing" at dawn – a sound probably caused by particles breaking off as the stone expanded, or wind reverberating through the cracks. The phenomenon attracted many visitors during antiquity, including the Roman emperors Hadrian (130 AD) and Septimus Severus, who gave orders to repair the statue in 199 AD, after which it never sang again.

Previously, the sound had been attributed to the legendary Memnon (whom Achilles killed outside the walls of Troy) greeting his mother, Eos, the Dawn, with a sigh. The Greeks identified the colossi with Memnon in the belief that his father, Tithonus, had been an Egyptian king. Before this, the colossi had been identified with Amenhotep, Steward of Amenophis III, whom posterity honoured as a demigod long after his master was forgotten. This association had some grounds in truth, since it was Amenhotep who supervised the quarrying of the monoliths at Silsilah, and their erection on the west bank. He was also probably responsible for Amenophis III's section of Luxor Temple.

Standing beside the barrier rope you can appreciate what **details** remain on the thrones and legs of the sandstone colossi. On the sides of the nearer one, the Nile-gods of Upper and Lower Egypt bind the heraldic plants of the Two Lands together. The legs of each colossus are flanked by smaller statues of Queen Tiy (right) and the king's mother, Mutemuia (left). They are covered in graffiti, including Roman epigrams, as high as you can reach.

Behind them, the long-lost **Mortuary Temple of Amenophis III** is being excavated to form a new archeological park and is currently off-limits to the public.

The Valley of the Kings

Secluded amid the bone-dry Theban Hills, removed from other parts of the Necropolis, the **Valley of the Kings** (daily: summer 6am–5pm; winter 6am–4pm) was intended as the ultimate insurance policy on life eternal. These secretive tombs of New Kingdom pharaohs were planned to preserve their mummies and funerary impedimenta for eternity. While most failed the test, their dramatic shafts and phantasmagorical murals are truly amazing. The descent into the underworld and the fear of robbers who braved the traps is still imaginable in the less crowded, darker tombs.

Royal burials in the "Place of Truth" (as the Ancient Egyptians called it) date from the early XVIII to the late XX dynasties. The first to be buried here was probably Tuthmosis I (1525–1512 BC). Until the time of Ramses I, queens and royal children were entombed here. The tombs were hewn and decorated by skilled craftsmen (known as "Servants at the Place of Truth") who dwelt at nearby Deir el-Medina. Work began

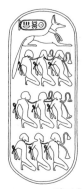

▲ Seal of the Valley of the Kings

early in a pharaoh's reign and never exceeded six years' duration; even so, some tombs were hastily pressed into service, or usurped by later kings. Broadly speaking, there are two types: the convoluted, split-level ones of early XVIII Dynasty rulers such as Tuthmosis I and Amenophis II, and the straighter, longer tombs of the XIX and XX dynasties.

The weaker rulers of the XX Dynasty were unable to prevent **tomb-robbing** on a massive scale. Both the vizier and police chief of Thebes were implicated

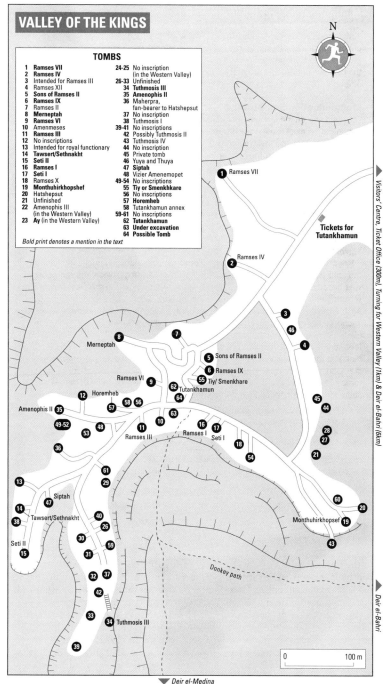

VALLEY OF THE KINGS

TOMBS

1	**Ramses VII**	24-25	No inscription
2	**Ramses IV**		(in the Western Valley)
3	Intended for Ramses III	26-33	Unfinished
4	Ramses XII	**34**	**Tuthmosis III**
5	**Sons of Ramses II**	**35**	**Amenophis II**
6	**Ramses IX**	36	Maherpra,
7	Ramses II		fan-bearer to Hatshepsut
8	**Merneptah**	37	No inscription
9	**Ramses VI**	38	Tuthmosis I
10	Amenmeses	39-41	No inscriptions
11	**Ramses III**	42	Possibly Tuthmosis II
12	No inscriptions	43	Tuthmosis IV
13	Intended for royal functionary	44	No inscription
14	**Tawsert/Sethnakht**	45	Private tomb
15	Seti II	46	Yuya and Thuya
16	**Seti I**	47	**Siptah**
17	Seti I	48	Vizier Amenemopet
18	Ramses X	49-54	No inscriptions
19	**Monthuhirkhopshef**	**55**	**Tiy or Smenkhkare**
20	Hatshepsut	56	No inscriptions
21	Unfinished	**57**	**Horemheb**
22	Amenophis III	58	Tutankhamun annex
	(in the Western Valley)	59-61	No inscriptions
23	**Ay** (in the Western Valley)	**62**	**Tutankhamun**
		63	**Under excavation**
		64	**Possible Tomb**

Bold print denotes a mention in the text

1 Ramses VII

Tickets for Tutankhamun

2 Ramses IV

3

46

4

8 Merneptah

7

5 Sons of Ramses II

6 Ramses IX

55 Tiy/ Smenkhare

9 Ramses VI

62 Tutankhamun

64

12 Horemheb

57 **58** **56**

63

Amenophis II **35**

49-52

53 **48**

36

11 **10** **16** **17**

Ramses III Ramses I Seti I

18

54

45

44

28

27

21

61

29

13

47 Siptah

14

38 Tawsert/Sethnakht

Seti II

15

40

26

30

31

59

32 **37**

42

33

34 Tuthmosis III

39

60

20

Monthuhirkhopsef **19**

43

Donkey path

0	100 m

▼ *Deir el-Medina*

▶ *Visitors' Centre, Ticket Office (300m), Turning for Western Valley (1km) & Deir el-Bahri (6km)*

▶ *Deir el-Bahri*

THE NILE VALLEY | The Theban Necropolis

The **funerary beliefs** manifest in the Valley of the Kings derive from two myths, concerning Re and Osiris. In that of **Re**, the sun-god descended into the underworld and voyaged through the hours of night, emerging at dawn to sail his barque across the heavens until sunset, when the cycle began anew. **Osiris**, king of the underworld, offered hope of survival in the afterlife through his death and resurrection.

Mummification and burial

To attain the afterlife, it was necessary that the deceased's name (*ren*) and body continued to exist, sustaining the *ka* or cosmic double that was born with every person and inhabited their mummy after death. **Mummification** techniques evolved over millennia, reaching their zenith by the New Kingdom, when embalmers offered three levels of mummification. The deluxe version entailed removing the brain (which was discarded) and the viscera (which were preserved in canopic jars); dehydrating the cadaver in natron salts for about forty days; packing it to reproduce lifelike contours, inserting artificial eyes and painting the face or entire body red (for men) or yellow (for women); then wrapping it in gum-coated linen bandages, and finally cocooning it in mummiform coffins. On the chest of the mummy and its coffin were placed heart scarabs, designed to prevent the deceased's heart from bearing witness against him during the judgement of Osiris.

Royal burials were elaborate affairs. Escorted by priests, mourners and musicians, the coffin was dragged on a sledge to the Valley of the Kings, where the sarcophagus was already occupied by a *sem* (death) priest, who performed the **Opening of the Mouth** ceremony, touching the lips of the mummy with an adze and reciting spells. As the mummy was lowered into its sarcophagus, priests slashed the forelegs of sacrificial animals, whose limbs were burned as the tomb was sealed. The tomb's contents (intended to satisfy the needs of the pharaoh's *ka* in the afterlife) included food, drink, clothing, furniture, weapons, and dozens of *shabti* figures to perform any task that the gods might require. Then the doors were walled up, plastered over and stamped with the royal seal and that of the Necropolis. To thwart robbers, royal tombs featured deadfalls and false burial chambers; however, none of these devices seem to have succeeded in protecting them.

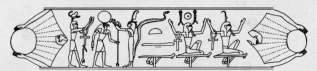

The Journey of Re
From right to left: Sunset; Year; Eternity; Everlasting; Maat (justice); Re; Heka; Sunrise

in the disposal of treasure, while many of the robbers were the workmen who had built the tombs, embittered over arrears in pay. In desperation, the priests reburied many sarcophagi and objects in two **secret caches** that were only discovered in the late nineteenth century (see p.391 & p.397).

The exploration of the Valley began in earnest with a series of **excavations** sponsored by Theodore Davis in 1902–14, when more than thirty tombs and pits were cleared (sometimes all too literally). In 1922, Howard Carter's discovery of Tutankhamun's tomb made headlines around the world. Nothing more was found till 1995, when clues from a papyrus in Turin led Kent Weeks

The journey through the underworld and judgement of Osiris

Funerary artwork dwelt on the journey through the underworld, whose pictorial representation inverted the normal order, so that each register was topped by sand instead of sky. The **descent** into the underworld (Duat), echoed that of a sarcophagus into its tomb, involving ramps, ropes and gateways. Each of the twelve **gates** was personified as a goddess and guarded by ferocious deities (for example, the "Lady of Duration" and the "Flame-eyed" serpent at the fifth gate). In the darkness between them lay twelve **caverns** inhabited by beings such as the jackal-headed gods who fed on rottenness at the first cavern, or the wailing goddesses with bloody axes who waited at the tenth.

It was Maat's Feather of Truth that was weighed against the deceased's heart (believed to be the seat of intelligence) during the **Judgement of Osiris**. With Anubis operating the scales and Thoth waiting to record the verdict, the deceased had to recite the **negative confession** before a tribunal of 42 **assessor gods**, each attuned to a sin. While the hearts of the guilty were devoured by crocodile-headed Ammut, the righteous were pronounced "true of voice" and led into the presence of Osiris to begin their **resurrection**, which paralleled **Re's passage through the underworld**. Voyaging through the twelve *decans* (hours or "divisions") of the night in his solar barque, Re had to overcome the serpent Apopis and other lesser denizens of **primeval chaos**, which threatened the **righteous order** personified by the goddess Maat. Re, helped by Anubis, Isis and Nephthys (often shown as serpents), Aker the earth-god (whose back bore Re's barque) and Khepri the scarab beetle, achieves rebirth in the fifth hour, and is fully restored to life by the tenth. Here the two myths part company, for whereas Re emerges from the body of the sky-goddess Nut to travel the heavens again, the Osirian journey (that of the righteous deceased) concludes by passing through the reedy **Fields of Yaru** (an Ancient Egyptian metaphor for death, also synonymous with fertility).

Since many of the scenes were supplemented by papyri buried with the mummy, funerary **artwork** is categorized in literary terms. The *Book of the Dead* is the name now given to the compendium of Old and Middle Kingdom Pyramid Texts and Spells, known in the New Kingdom as the *Book of Coming Forth*. Other **texts** associated with the New Kingdom include the *Book of Gates*, *Book of Caverns*, *Book of Hours*, *Book of Day and Night* and *Book of Amduat* (That Which is in the Underworld).

The Judgement of Osiris
From left to right: Anubis escorts the deceased and weighs his heart before Ammut and Thoth; then Horus leads him to Osiris, Isis and Nephthys

to clear the debris from tomb **KV5** – which Carter had dismissed as looted in antiquity – and uncover the entrance to a mass tomb for the **sons of Ramses II,** reckoned to contain one hundred and fifty chambers, some huge. While inscriptions suggest that fifty of Ramses' one hundred or so sons were meant to be interred here, the remains of only four adults have been found so far and the excavation is set to run for years (see the Theban Mapping Project website,Ⓦ www.kv5.com, for news plus images of other royal tombs).

More recently, in 2006, Otto Schaden uncovered an XVIII Dynasty tomb designated **KV63**, containing empty child-coffins and embalmers' gear

(🌐www.kv-63.com). Nicholas Reeves of the Amarna Royal Tombs Project had detected it six years earlier using ground-penetrating radar, but kept it secret. He has since announced that another, as-yet uncovered tomb exists near Tutankhamun's, which he calls **KV64** and which he believes to be a royal tomb from the post-Amarna period (see 🌐www.valleyofthekings.org).

Meanwhile the Valley of the Kings remains acutely vulnerable. Flash **floods** present a grave danger to the tombs, but clearing the wadis of debris and digging drainage channels risks destroying evidence that might point to undiscovered tombs. The SCA and foreign donors have already spent millions tackling an expanding sub-stratum of grey shale which ruptured several tombs in the 1990s, and installing glass screens and dehumidifiers to reduce the harm caused by **tourism** (the average visitor leaves behind 2.8g of sweat to corrode the murals).

The upshot is that some tombs are perpetually **closed** and the rest open according to a rota system, with only ten accessible at any one time. Though frustrating for visitors, this may be the only way to preserve the tombs' fragile artwork for future generations, and it's everyone's duty to refrain from touching the walls. **Photography** is no longer allowed inside any of the tombs; you can buy images of all of them if you want.

Visiting the tombs

The main **approach** to the valley (known as Biban el-Melouk, "Gates of the Kings" in Arabic) is via a serpentine road that follows the route of ancient funeral processions. Before the road, when donkeys were the only means of travel, its silence and emptiness were striking ("White earth; sun; one's rump sweats in the saddle", noted Flaubert). Nowadays, you'll only get this feeling on the trail across the hills from Deir el-Medina, which is still travelled by donkeys (see p.394).

Just before the ticket office is a new **visitors' centre** (free), whose centrepiece is a scale model of the valley, exquisitely crafted from glass to show each tomb's depth and alignment in relation to the others. Here you can also watch a brief film of the official opening of Tutankhamun's tomb in 1922, and access the Theban Mapping Project's website on laptops. Beyond this are a cloakroom for stashing video-cameras (free) and an office selling **tickets** for the Valley of the Kings and Ay's tomb in the Western Valley (see p.394 for prices). Beyond this, you can walk or ride an open-sided *tuf-tuf* train (£E1) 500m to the site entrance, just inside which is another kiosk selling tickets for Tutankhamun's tomb.

The valley is surrounded by limestone crags, the loftiest of which was the abode of Meretseger, snake-goddess of the Necropolis. The site is a natural suntrap, hot even in winter, the heat permeating the deepest tombs, whose air is musty and humid. New signs and maps make the **tombs** easier to find than before. They are **numbered** in order of their discovery, starting with the tomb of Ramses VII (known in antiquity) – #1 – and ending with the most recent discovery, #63. Egyptologists assign them the prefix KV (short for Kings Valley) to distinguish them from other numbered tombs in the Valley of the Queens. When you've had enough of royal tombs you might enjoy **hiking** over the ridge to Deir el-Bahri, for a matchless view of Hateshepsut's temple (see box on p.394).

Tomb of Ramses VII (#1)

Set apart near the entrance to the valley, the short tomb of **Ramses VII** lay wide open for millennia, and is now glassed over. Greek and Roman graffiti mars its sunk-reliefs and vivid colours (red, yellow and blue on white), whose freshness is due to restoration. Amid the standard imagery are odd details like the figures entombed in cartouches on the walls of the final corridor, while the hippo-goddess Tweri is prominent in the nocturnal pantheon on the ceiling of the burial chamber, whose sarcophagus is veined with blue imagery. Other Ramessid tombs are finer, however.

Tomb of Ramses IV (#2)

The next tomb, created for **Ramses IV**, is more of a crowd pleaser. Its cheerful colours make amends for the inferior sunk-reliefs and abundant Greek and Coptic **graffiti** (notice the haloed saints on the right near the entrance). The ceiling of the burial chamber is adorned with twin figures of Nut. On the enormous pink-granite **sarcophagus** are magical texts and carvings of Isis and Nephthys, to protect the mummy from harm. When these seemed insufficient, the priests stashed Ramses in the tomb of Amenophis II, whence the now empty sarcophagus has been returned. Notice the Coptic graffiti in the end storage room beyond the burial chamber. As for Ramses himself, his mummy in the Cairo Museum shows him to have been a short, bald man with a long nose. He became pharaoh in his forties after the failure of a conspiracy to usurp the throne (see p.409), and recorded the "testament" of his illustrious father, Ramses III, in the Great Harris Papyrus.

Tomb of Ramses IX (#6)

The tomb of **Ramses IX** belonged to one of the last rulers (1140–1123 BC) of the XX Dynasty, towards the end of the New Kingdom. It's indicative of waning majesty that the initial scenes in sunk-relief soon give way to flat paintings, akin to drawings. The walls of its stepped corridor (originally bisected by ramps, for moving the sarcophagus) depict Ramses before the gods and symbolic extracts from the *Book of Caverns*. Notice the solar barques bearing crocodiles, heads and other oddities, on the left-hand wall. The burial chamber is memorable for its *Book of Night* in yellow upon a dark blue background. Two sky-goddesses stretch back-to-back across the ceiling, encompassing voids swirling with creatures, stars and heavenly barques. While the king's sarcophagus pit gapes empty, his resurrection is still heralded on the walls by Khepri, the scarab incarnation of the reborn sun at dawn.

Tomb of Tutankhamun (#62)

One of the world's most famous tombs, the tomb of **Tutankhamun** is neither large nor imposing by the standards of the Valley of the Kings, reflecting Tut's short reign (*c.*1361–1352 BC; see p.299) as an XVIII Dynasty boy-pharaoh. Its renown stems from its belated discovery and its amazing hoard of treasures (now mostly in the Cairo Museum). After archeologist **Howard Carter** had dug in vain for five seasons, his backer, **Lord Carnarvon**, was on the point of giving up when the tomb was found on November 4, 1922. Fears that it had been plundered were dispelled when they broke through the second sealed door – officially on November 26, though in fact Carter and Carnarvon secretly entered the previous night, stole several items and resealed the door. Otherwise, the tomb was cleared meticulously. Each of its 1700 objects was documented, drawn and photographed *in situ* before being removed to an improvised labora-tory in the tomb of Seti II, for stabilizing and cleaning by Arthur Mace. Unpacking everything took nearly ten years, the whole process being recorded in more than 1800 superb photographs by Harry Burton, who converted an empty tomb into a darkroom. As for the tomb itself, it is now glassed over to

△ Howard Carter opening the tomb of Tutankhamun

protect its paintings, and the number of visitors has been reduced by a steep admission charge (you might well decide that the tomb isn't worth the £E80 fee); **tickets** for Tut's tomb are available at a separate kiosk within the entrance to the Valley of the Kings.

In 1922, Carter found the door at the bottom of the stairway **[a]** walled up and sealed with Tut's cartouche and the seal of the Necropolis, but signs of repairs, the detritus in the corridor **[b]** and another resealed door at the end indicated that robbers had penetrated the antechamber **[c]** during the XX Dynasty. Most of the funerary objects now in the Cairo Museum were crammed into the undecorated chambers **[c, d** (now walled up) and **e]**. Another wall (now replaced by a barrier) enclosed the burial chamber, which was almost filled by four golden shrines packed one inside another, containing Tut's stone sarcophagus and triple-layer mummiform coffin, of which the innermost, solid **gold coffin** and **Tut's mummy** remain. In 2005 the mummy was CAT-scanned *in situ*, revealing a broken leg that might have given rise to a fatal infection, casting doubt on the theory of a head injury that some had attributed to murder.

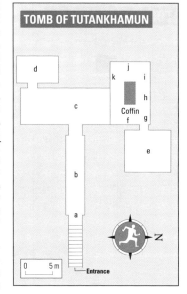

The colourful **murals** run anticlockwise, starting with the funeral procession where nine friends and three officials drag Tut's coffin on a sledge **[f]**. Next, his successor Ay performs the Opening of the Mouth ceremony **[g]** and makes sacrifices to the sky-goddess Nut **[h]**. The deceased king embraces Osiris, followed by his *ka* (in the black wig) **[i]**. His solar boat and sun-worshipping baboons appear on the left wall **[j]**. On the hard-to-see entrance wall, Anubis and Isis escort Tutankhamun to receive life from Hathor **[k]**.

The curse of Tutankhamun

Lord Carnarvon's death in Cairo from an infected mosquito bite in April 1923 focused world attention on a warning by the novelist Marie Corelli, that "dire punishment follows any intruder into the tomb". (At the moment of Carnarvon's death, all the lights in Cairo went out.) The **curse of Tutankhamun** gained popular credence with this and each successive "mysterious" death. The US magnate Jay Gould died of pneumonia resulting from a cold contracted at the tomb; a famous Bey was shot by his wife in London after viewing the discovery; a French Egyptologist suffered a fatal fall; Carter's secretary died in unusual circumstances at the Bath Club in London; and his right-hand man Arthur Mace sickened and died before the tomb had been fully cleared. However, of the 22 who had witnessed the opening of Tut's sarcophagus, only two were dead ten years later. Howard Carter died in 1939 at the age of 64, while others closely involved lived into their 80s (not least Dr Derry, who performed the autopsy which suggested that Tut died from a blow to the head, aged about 19).

Notwithstanding this, a new explanation for the "curse" was advanced by a scientist at Cairo University in 1991. Professor Thebat believes that Carnarvon and Mace were fatally weakened by radioactivity emanating from an unknown substance used as part of the mummification process, which had accumulated in the tomb over 3000 years; he also claims to have detected radioactivity in seventeen of the mummies in the Egyptian Museum.

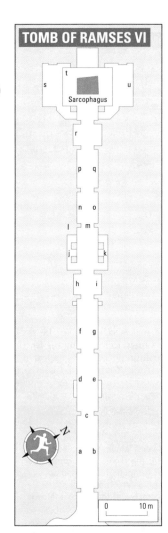

TOMB OF RAMSES VI

Tomb of Ramses VI (#9)

One reason why Tut's tomb stayed hidden for so long was that it lay beneath mounds of rubble from the tomb of **Ramses VI** (1156–1148 or 1151–1143 BC), which has been a tourist attraction since antiquity, when the Greeks called it the "Tomb of Memnon". The first two corridors have suffered from centuries of graffiti, but far worse occurred in 1992, when the ceiling fell down and had to be glued back on in nearly one thousand pieces.

The tomb was begun by Ramses V but usurped and enlarged by his successor, whose offering of a lamp to Horus of the Horizon opens the *Book of Gates* **[a]**, which faces other sunk-reliefs from the *Book of Caverns* **[b]**. Its astronomical ceiling continues through a series of corridors (note the winged sun-disc over the lintel and Ramses' cartouches on the door jambs **[c]**). Where the *Book of Gates* reaches the Hall of Osiris **[d]**, a flame-breathing snake and catfish-headed gods infest the *Book of Caverns* **[e]**. As Re's barque approaches the Seventh Gate, beyond which twelve gods hold a rope festooned with whips and heads **[f]**, the *Book of Caverns* depicts a procession of *ka* figures **[g]**. From here on, the astronomical ceiling features an attenuated sky-goddess and the *Book of Day and Night*.

The eighth and ninth divisions of the *Book of Gates* **[h]** and fifth division of the *Book of Caverns* **[i]** decorate the next chamber, originally a vestibule to the hall beyond, which marked the limits of Ramses V's tomb. This contains the concluding sections of the *Book of Gates* **[j]**, the seventh division of the *Book of Caverns* **[k]** and a summary of the world's creation **[l]**. The rear wall also features a scene of Ramses VI making offerings and libations to Osiris. On the pillars, he makes offerings to Khonsu, Amun-Re, Meretseger, Ptah-Sokar, Ptah and Re-Herakhte **[m]**.

The descent to the next corridor is guarded by winged serpents representing the goddesses Nekhbet and Neith (left), Meretseger and Selket (right). On the corridor walls appear the introductory **[n]** and middle sections **[o]** of the *Book of Amduat*; on the ceiling, extracts from the *Books of Re* and the *Book of Day and Night*. Scenes in the next corridor relate the fourth and fifth **[p]** and eighth to eleventh **[q]** chapters of the *Book of Amduat*. The small vestibule beyond contains texts from the *Book of Coming Forth by Day*, including the "negative confession" **[r]**. On the ceiling, Ramses sails the barques of Day and Night across the first register, while Osiris rises from his bier in the second.

Lovely back-to-back versions of the *Book of Day* and *Book of Night* adorn the ceiling of Ramses VI's burial chamber, where his image makes offerings at either end of one wall **[s]**. The rear **[t]** and right-hand walls carry portions of the *Book of Aker*, named after the earth-god of the underworld who fettered the coils of Apopis, safeguarding Re's passage. Incarnated as a ram-headed beetle, the sun-god is drawn across the heavens in his divine barque **[u]**.

The king's black granite **sarcophagus** was smashed open by treasure hunters in antiquity, and his mummy left so badly damaged that the priests had to pin the body to a board to provide the remains with a decent burial in another tomb.

Tomb of Merneptah (#8)

Merneptah (1236–1223 BC), the fourteenth son of Ramses II, didn't become pharaoh until his 50s, having outlived thirteen brothers with prior claims on the throne. On the evidence of his mummy, he was afflicted by arthritis and hardening of the arteries, and underwent dental surgery in old age. Many scholars hold, on the strength of his "Israel Stele" at Karnak and the identification of his father as the Pharaoh of the Oppression, that Merneptah was the Pharaoh of the Exodus (although this is disputed by Rohl; see p.767).

Like other tombs of the XIX Dynasty, his descends in corridors, with a total length of about 80m. In the first corridor, Merneptah is welcomed by Re-Herakhte and Khepri **[a]**, the *Litany of Re* **[b]** unfolds opposite the sixteen avatars of Osiris **[c]**, Re's barque is pulled through the underworld **[d]**, and Nekhebkau leads his soul towards Anubis **[e]**. Beyond a pit watched by Thoth and Anubis **[f]**, another corridor decorated with the *Book of Amduat* **[g]** leads to an antechamber with images of Osiris and Nephthys **[h]**, and Merneptah as Imutef **[i]**.

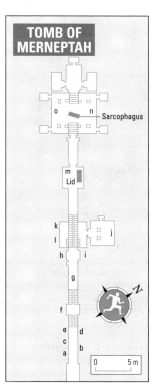

TOMB OF MERNEPTAH

The next hall is a false burial chamber (a trick that seldom fooled robbers) decorated with hymns to Osiris **[j]** and scenes from the *Book of Gates*. Notice the binding of the Serpents of Chaos **[k]**, a tug-of-war over a "rope" of human souls **[l]**, and the Osirian avatars above the lintel. The final corridors are largely bare, but for the outer **lid** of Merneptah's sarcophagus – left there by thieves – and the faint image of a monkey **[m]**.

In the real burial chamber, the gods voyage through the night across the ceiling, while murals show the metamorphosis of Khepri into Re, encircled by bird-men requesting the deceased's *ba* (soul) **[n]**, and Khnum piloting a boat with the pharaoh's mummy floating above **[o]**. There is a carving of the sky-goddess Nut inside Merneptah's massive granite **sarcophagus**.

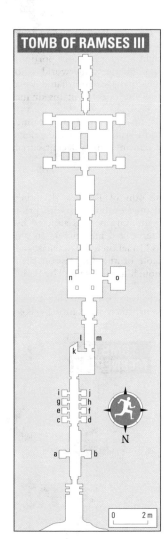

TOMB OF RAMSES III

N

0   2 m

Tomb of Ramses III (#11)

The grandest of the Ramessid tombs is that of **Ramses III**. His 31-year reign (1198–1166 BC) marked the heyday of the XX Dynasty, whose power declined under the later Ramessids. Like his temple at Medinet Habu, the tomb harks back to the earlier glories of the New Kingdom. Uniquely for royal tombs, its colourful sunk-reliefs include scenes of everyday life. From another vignette derives its popular name, the Tomb of the Harpers.

Off the entrance corridors lie ten side chambers, originally used to store funerary objects. Within the first pair are fragmentary scenes of butchery, cooking and baking **[a]**, and ships setting sail, those with furled sails bound downriver **[b]**. Next, Hapy blesses grain-gods and propitiates snake-headed Napret, with her escort of aproned *uraei* **[c]**. The bull of Meri (right) and the cow of Hesi (left) coexist with armoury scenes **[d]**, while hermaphrodite deities bring offerings **[e]** to a treasury **[f]**. Ramses owns cattle and minerals **[g]**, and from his boat inspects peasants working in the Fields of Yaru **[h]**. In a famous scene, two harpists sing to Shu and Atum, while Harsomtus and Anhor greet the king; the lyrics of the song cover the entrance wall **[i]**. The twelve forms of Osiris **[j]** are possibly linked to the twelve divisions of the night.

The dead-end tunnel **[k]** shows where diggers accidentally broke into a neighbouring tomb, at which point the original builder, Pharaoh Sethnakht, abandoned it and appropriated Tawsert's (see p.391). When construction resumed under Ramses, the tomb's axis was shifted west. The corridor has scenes from the fourth **[l]** and fifth **[m]** hours of the *Book of Amduat*. Part of the *Book of Gates* specifies four races of men: Egyptians, Asiatics, Negroes and Libyans (along the bottom) **[n]**. On the facing wall, the pinioned serpent Apopis is forced to disgorge the heads of his victims, in the fifth chapter of the *Book of Gates*. In the side room **[o]** are scenes from the *Book of Amduat*. The rest of the tomb has been barred since its ceiling fell down. Ramses III's mummy (in the Cairo Museum) was the model for Boris Karloff's figure in the 1930s film *The Mummy*.

Tomb of Horemheb (#57)

General **Horemheb** was the power behind the throne of Tutankhamun and his aged successor Ay, and finally became pharaoh himself. His reign (1348–1320 BC) marked the height of the Theban counter-revolution against the Amarna heresy and the last gasp of the XVIII Dynasty, and was spent shoring up the crumbling empire bequeathed by his predecessors. He died without leaving an heir (though Rohl thinks that he gave his daughter as a bride to King Solomon) and was succeeded by a military deputy called Paramessu, who took the throne name Ramses and founded the Ramessid dynasty.

The tomb's layout prefigures Seti's (see p.393), with a long, steep descent through undecorated corridors to a well room which depicts Horemheb with deities, highly detailed and coloured. Hathor, Isis, Osiris, Horus and Anubis reappear in the anteroom before the burial chamber, whose entrance is guarded by Maat. Its unfinished scenes range from stick-figure drawings to fully worked carvings; the *Book of the Dead* begins to your left and runs clockwise round the chamber, whose huge sarcophagus is carved with a relief of Nut. In the second room to the left, Osiris appears before a Djed pillar. An empty red granite sarcophagus remains; Horemheb's missing mummy has not been identified in the two caches of royal mummies.

Tomb of Amenophis II (#35)

One of the deepest tombs in the valley lies at the head of the wadi beyond Horemheb's tomb. Built for **Amenophis II** (1450–1425 or 1427–1400 BC) midway through the XVIII Dynasty, it has more than ninety steps and gets hotter and stuffier with each lower level. When the tomb was discovered in 1898, the body of the king was still in its sarcophagus and nine other royal mummies were found stashed in another chamber. The tomb's defences included a deep pit (now bridged) and a false burial chamber to distract robbers from the lower levels (which would have been sealed up and disguised).

From a pillared vestibule, steps descend into the huge chamber. On its six square pillars, Amenophis is embraced and offered ankhs by various gods. Beneath a star-spangled ceiling, the walls are painted pale beige and inscribed with the entire *Book of Amduat*, like a continuous scroll of papyrus. Notice the preliminary pen sketches to the left of the left-hand niche. When found in his quartzite sarcophagus (still *in situ*), the king's mummy had a floral garland around its neck. The second chamber on the right served as a **cache** for the mummies of Tuthmosis IV, Merneptah, Seti II, Ramses V and VI and Queen Tiy, after their original tombs proved insecure.

In 2006, Joann Fletcher re-discovered three mummies that had been catalogued, sealed up and forgotten in 1898. Fletcher believes that one might be the mummy of Akhenaten's queen, **Nefertiti**; a theory other Egyptologists dismiss as wishful thinking.

Tomb of Tawsert/ Sethnakht (#14)

Located en route to Seti II's tomb, this one is unusual for having two burial chambers. It originally held the mummy of Seti's wife, Queen **Tawsert**, but was usurped by Pharaoh **Sethnakht** (*c.*1200–1085 BC) after his own tomb

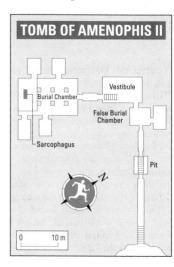

TOMB OF AMENOPHIS II

Burial Chamber

Vestibule

False Burial Chamber

Sarcophagus

Pit

0   10 m

(now Ramses III's) ran into difficulties. In the first corridor you find Sethnakht making offerings to Horus and Isis, and Osiris enshrined. Further on, a ram-headed god with a knife is followed by Anubis and Wepwawet. Texts from the *Book of the Dead* cover what was meant to be Tawsert's tomb chamber beyond which steps lead down towards Sethnakht's vault.

At the bottom of the stairs, the pharaoh's soul attains harmony with Maat, cherishing the Papyrus and Lotus of the Two Lands, while Anubis embalms his mummy in a side chamber further on. A hall of texts from the *Book of Caverns* and the Opening of the Mouth ceremony precede the burial chamber, whose pillars show the gods greeting Sethnakht, while the walls depict the resurrection of Osiris and Re's journey through the night.

Tomb of Siptah (#47)

Siptah (1194–1188 BC) was the only son of Seti II, born not of Queen Tawsert, but of a Syrian concubine, Sutailja. Since he was only a boy, with an atrophied leg, Tawsert ruled as regent in alliance with an official named Bay (also of Syrian origin). After Siptah came of age, Tawsert married him; some believe that his death six years later was orchestrated by Tawsert and Bay. His one recorded achievement was to have led a campaign in Nubia, but it is more likely that he had it sent in his name. To complete his run of bad luck, Siptah's tomb was usurped by a later pharaoh, its contents smashed up in antiquity, and his mummy ended up in the tomb of Amenophis II. There it was found in 1905, when it was determined that he probably had cerebral palsy or polio as an infant. However, his tomb looks impressive, with a finely dressed Siptah mingling with the gods in the *Litany of Ra* and floating through scenes from the *Book of Amduat*.

Tomb of Seti II (#15)

At the end of the wadi lies the tomb of **Seti II** (1216–1210 BC), which Arthur Mace used as a storage and restoration area during the excavation of Tutankhamun's tomb. Its long, straight corridors are typical of the XIX Dynasty, decorated with colourful scenes. Due to Seti's abrupt demise, however, there was only time to carve sunk-reliefs near the entrance, and the rest was hastily filled in with paintings or outline drawings. The king's mummy was later hidden in tomb #35 and replaced by that of an anonymous dignitary, which was plundered by thieves, who left only the sarcophagus lid. His mummy indicates that he suffered from arthritis, but had good teeth, which was unusual for that time.

Tomb of Tuthmosis III (#34)

Likewise secreted in a separate wadi, high up in a cleft, the tomb of **Tuthmosis III** (1504–1450 or 1479–1425 BC) is one of the oldest in the valley. Its concealment and (futile) defences make this tomb especially interesting, though some are disappointed by its artwork. Having ascended a wooden stairway to the cleft, you descend through several levels, crossing a pit by footbridge to reach a vestibule. The walls depict 741 deities as stick figures, in imitation of the format used on papyrus texts from the Middle Kingdom onwards, which was favoured for murals early in the New Kingdom. Reduced to their essentials, the ramps and shafts that led into the underworld, and Khepri's role in pulling Re's barque, are clearly visible.

The unusual rounded burial chamber is also decorated with outline figures and symbols. Although the yellow background simulates aged papyrus, the texts were only painted after Tuthmosis had been laid to rest; there's a crossed-out mistake on the "instruction" fresco.

Elsewhere you'll notice double images (as at Abu Simbel), believed by some archeologists to have been meant to suggest motion, and others to be the result of overcarving. On one of the pillars, Tuthmosis's mother stands behind him in a barque; the register below shows three wives and a daughter, to the right of which a tree-goddess suckles the young king. By shining a torch inside the quartzite sarcophagus, you can admire a lovely carving of Nut, whose arms would have embraced his mummy before priests removed it to a safer hiding place near Deir el-Bahri.

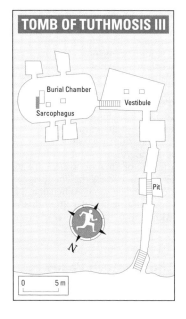

Tomb of Seti I (#17)

The tomb of **Seti I** is the finest in the valley, but despite a decade spent restoring damage wrought by the rising water table and tourists, and the installation of dehumidifiers, it is still too fragile to expose (though there is talk of allowing entry to VIP groups, like Nefertari's tomb in the Valley of the Queens). Discovered in 1817, it is the longest in the valley (over 120m) and has superlative carvings and gilded paintings comparable to those in Seti's temple at Abydos. It was Seti I (1318–1304 BC) who consolidated the XIX Dynasty, regained the colonies lost under Akhenaten, and paved the way for his second son, Ramses II, to reach new heights of imperialism. His tomb fared badly at the hands of European collectors: some of its reliefs are now in the Louvre and the Turin Museum, while Seti's sarcophagus lies in the Sir John Soane Museum in London.

Tomb of Ramses I (#16)

Buried next door to Seti is his father, **Ramses I**, founder of the XIX Dynasty, who was not of royal blood, but the son of a commander from Avaris. During his one-year reign (1320–1318 or 1295–1294 BC), Ramses campaigned in Asia, reopened the turquoise mines of Sinai, and married Sitre, the daughter of another soldier from the eastern Delta, siring an heir to continue the dynasty. His tomb has the shortest entrance corridor of any in the valley, leading to a small, finely painted burial chamber, the colours still bright against a blue-grey background. On the left wall are nine black sarcophagi in caverns, above twelve goddesses representing the hours of the night, from the *Book of Gates*. Elsewhere, Ramses appears with Maat, Anubis, Ptah, Osiris and other deities. In 1999, the royal **mummy** was traced to the Niagara Falls Museum, where it had supposedly lain, unidentified, since it was dubiously acquired in 1850. Since being returned to Egypt in 2004, it has been in the Luxor Museum, though the SCA is not convinced that it actually is Ramses.

Tomb of Monthuhirkhopshef (#19)

Sited high up a side-wadi, the seldom-visited tomb of **Monthuhirkhopshef** casts light on the life of princes – in this case, a son of Ramses IX, named "The

Arm of Montu is Mighty". Monthuhirkhopshef died in his teens – before his father – for he wears the blue-and-gold sidelock of youth, a finely pleated linen skirt and elaborate make-up, as he makes offerings to deities in the entrance corridor of his tomb. Eye make-up was worn by both sexes in Ancient Egypt; it's thought that some of the ingredients helped to prevent eye diseases such as glaucoma.

Tomb of Tiy or Smenkhkare (#55)

Identifying mummies isn't easy if the tomb was left undecorated and later looted – or the excavation was botched. The tomb designated **KV55** has been a conundrum ever since Theodore Davis failed to record its contents before removing the decrepit mummy in 1907, which he attributed to **Queen Tiy** – the wife of Amenophis III – due to its pelvic shape and "feminine" position (left arm bound across the chest, right arm alongside the body), and a gilded panel depicting her with Akhenaten. Later forensic analysis identified the bones as those of a man under 26 with signs of hydrocephalus, which seemingly fitted **Akhenaten**, until another examination in 2000 identified a man no older than his early twenties with a skull similar to Tutankhamun's, which many think was his mysterious predecessor, **Smenkhkare.**

The Western Valley and the Sun Temple of Thoth

A neglected offshoot of the Valley of the Kings, the **Western Valley** (Biban el-Gurud) contains only four tombs (two of them royal), of which just one is open. The **Tomb of Ay** (#23) was built for Tutankhamun's successor, who had earlier been Akhenaten's vizier and prepared himself a tomb at Tell el-Amarna (see p.305). His crypt in the Western Valley is notable for the blend of royal and noble imagery in the burial chamber, where the *Book of Amduat* is juxtaposed with a typical nobles' vignette of the deceased spearing fishes and birds. Given the distance by road off the main route to the Valley of the Kings (the Western Valley is clearly signposted), you can only get there by car or with a trail bike – **tickets** are sold at the entrance to the Valley of the Kings.

Locals call the valley "Wadi Monkey", after the caches of mummified baboons found there, probably connected with a remote **Sun Temple of Thoth** (baboons were sacred to Thoth). Uniquely for an Egyptian temple, this structure – which isn't open to tourists – is sited 400m above the Nile, on a spur of the

---

Hiking across the hills to Deir el-Bahri

This wonderfully scenic hike is easiest over winter but feasible at other times so long as you guard against heatstroke. Though the hike can be done in thirty minutes, it's worth taking it slowly once you've shaken off the souvenir vendors who wait above the start of the trail, where the donkey guides rest up. If you're tempted to be rude, remember that the vendors only come here because they can't afford to bribe the police to let them work in the Valley of the Kings.

When the path forks, take the left-hand track running flat along the top of a rock "loaf", before crossing the ridge to behold the Nile Valley. Directly beneath the sheer cliff lies Hatshepsut's temple; to see it, walk right for a bit before peering *carefully* over the edge. To descend, follow the path alongside the trampled fence till you reach a crag where the trail divides. Ignore anyone who tries to lure you down the steepest trail, to render "help" for baksheesh – the slightly less precipitous left-hand path is the one to take. Hiking along **other trails** in the Theban Hills is likely to be firmly discouraged by the police.

Theban range that the ancients called the "Crown of Thebes". The mud-brick temple built by Mentuhotpe II in the XI Dynasty overlays a stone temple from the Archaic Period – the oldest known one in Upper Egypt. The temple is distantly visible at the start of the road to the Valley of the Kings, but can only be reached on foot or by donkey (1hr 30min–2hr) by a steep five-kilometre path starting from near Howard Carter's house.

Deir el-Bahri

Of all the sites on the west bank, none can match the breathtaking panache of **Deir el-Bahri** (see below for ticket details). Set amid a vast natural amphitheatre in the Theban Hills, the temple rises in imposing terraces, the shadowed verticals of its colonnades drawing power from the massive crags overhead. Its great ramps and courts look modern in their stark simplicity, but in ancient times would have been softened and perfumed by gardens of fragrant trees. The reliefs that cover its colonnades and chapels bespeak of an extraordinary woman and dynastic intrigues.

Deir el-Bahri ("Northern Monastery") is the Arabic name for the **Mortuary Temple of Hatshepsut** (pronounced "Hat-Cheap-Suit"), the only woman ever to reign over Egypt as pharaoh (1503–1482 BC). A daughter of Tuthmosis I, married to his successor Tuthmosis II, Hatshepsut was widowed before she could bear a son. Rather than accept relegation in favour of a secondary wife who had produced an heir, Hatshepsut made herself co-regent to the young Tuthmosis III and soon assumed absolute power.

To legitimize her position, she was depicted in masculine form, wearing a pharaoh's kilt and beard; yet her authority ultimately depended on personal willpower and the devotion of her favourite courtier, Senenmut, who rose from humble birth to the stewardship of Amun's estates, before falling from grace for reasons unknown. When Tuthmosis came into his inheritance after her death, he defaced Hatshepsut's cartouches and images, consigning her memory to oblivion until her deeds were rediscovered by archeologists.

In 1995, the temple was used to stage Verdi's *Aïda*, which was a financial flop due to poor promotion and colossal expenditure, not least on building a road to the Nile so that VIPs could arrive by boat from Karnak, which has hardly been used since. However, dozens of coach parties arrive along the road from Dra' Abul Naga, making this one of the busiest sites in the Necropolis.

Tragically, in November 1997 Deir el-Bahri made headlines when 58 tourists and four guards were shot or stabbed to death by terrorists on the temple's Middle Terrace. The killers might have escaped in a hijacked coach if the driver hadn't deliberately crashed it near the Valley of the Queens and if they hadn't been chased by villagers, for the police took an hour to reach the scene. The day is vividly remembered on the west bank, especially by the donkey guides who witnessed the **massacre** from the clifftop above.

Ever since then, all the sites have been heavily guarded; at Deir el-Bahri a series of fences and checkpoints provides a security cordon. **Tickets** are sold at a kiosk just outside the coach parking lot; beyond the last security barrier, a free *tuf-tuf* transports visitors the final 300m to the temple.

Hatshepsut's temple

Hatshepsut called her temple **Djeser Djeseru**, the "Splendour of Splendours". In ancient times an avenue of sphinxes probably ran from the Nile to its **Lower Terrace**, which was planted with myrrh trees and cooled by fountains (the stumps of two 3500-year-old trees remain near the final barrier). At the top and bottom of the ramp to the next level were carved pairs of lions (one of each is still visible). Before ascending the ramp, check out its flanking **colonnades**, whose reliefs were defaced by Tuthmosis III, and later by Akhenaten. While Hatshepsut's image remains obliterated, those of Amun were restored after the Theban counter-revolution. Behind the northern colonnade (right of the ramp) can be seen a cow-herd, wildfowl and a papyrus swamp; reliefs in the southern (left) colonnade show the transport by river of two obelisks from Aswan – doubtless the pair that Hatshepsut erected at Karnak.

The **Middle Terrace** once also boasted myrrh trees, which Hatshepsut personally acquired from the Land of Punt in a famous expedition that's depicted along one of the square-pillared colonnades flanking the ramp to the uppermost level.

The Birth and Punt colonnades

To the right of the ramp is the so-called **Birth Colonnade**, whose faint reliefs assert Hatshepsut's divine parentage. Starting from nearest the ramp, its rear walls show Amun (in the guise of Tuthmosis I) and her mother Queen Ahmosis (seated on a couch), their knees touching. Next, bizarre deities lead the queen into the birth chamber, where the god Khnum fashions Hatshepsut and her *ka* (both represented as boys) on his potter's wheel. Her birth is attended by Bes and the frog deity Heqet; goddesses nurse her, while Thoth records details of her reign. The sensitive expressions and delicate modelling convey a sincerity that transcends mere political expediency.

At the far end of the colonnade, steps lead down into a **Chapel of Anubis** with fluted columns and colourful murals. Tuthmosis III and a falcon-headed sun-god appear over the niche to the right; a yellow-skinned Hathor on the facing wall; offerings by Hatshepsut and Tuthmosis to Anubis on the other walls. As elsewhere, the images of Hatshepsut were defaced after her death by order of Tuthmosis. Notice the friezes of cobras in the central, barrel-vaulted shrine.

On the other side of the ramp is the famous **Punt Colonnade**, relating Hatshepsut's journey to that land (thought to be modern-day Somalia). Though others had visited Punt to obtain precious myrrh for temple incense, Hatshepsut sought living trees to plant outside her temple. Alas, the faintness of the reliefs (behind a guard-rail) makes it difficult to follow the story as it unfolds (left to right). Commissioned by Amun "to establish a Punt in his house", the Egyptian flotilla sails from the Red Sea coast, to be welcomed by the king of Punt and his wife. In exchange for metal axes and other goods, the Egyptians depart with myrrh trees and resin, ebony, ivory, cinnamon wood and panther skins; baboons play in the ships' rigging. Back home, the spoils are dedicated to Amun and the precious myrrh trees bedded in the temple gardens.

The Punt Colonnade leads into a larger **Chapel of Hathor**, whose face and sistrum (sacred rattle) form the capitals of the square pillars. In the first, roofless, pillared chamber, the goddess appears in her bovine and human forms, and suckles Hatshepsut (whose image has not been defaced here) on the left-hand wall. The next chamber features delicate reliefs of festival processions (still quite freshly coloured) on the right-hand wall. Peering into the gated sanctuary, you can just about make out another intact Hatshepsut worshipping the divine cow (left), and an alcove (right) containing a **portrait of Senenmut**, which would have been hidden when the doors were open. Apocryphally, it was this claim on the pharaoh's temple that caused his downfall. After fifteen years of closeness to Hatshepsut and her daughter Neferure (evinced by a statue in the Cairo Museum, which some regard as proof of paternity), Senenmut abruptly vanished from the records late in her reign. When archeologists excavated the sanctuary in the early twentieth century they found it stacked with baskets full of wooden penises, seemingly used in fertility rituals.

The Upper Terrace

Reached by a ramp with falcon statues at the bottom, the **Upper Terrace** has emerged from decades of research and restoration work by Polish and Egyptian teams. Eight giant statues of Osiris front its portico and a red granite portal into a courtyard flanked by colonnades and sanctuaries. Bodyguards and oarsmen rowing the royal barque are depicted on the inside wall to the left as you enter. On the far wall are eight niches for votive statues, carved with hieroglyphs that rival the delicacy of Seti's reliefs at Abydos.

You can peep into (but not enter) the **Sanctuary of Amun**, dug into the cliff aligned towards Hatshepsut's tomb in the Valley of the Kings on the other side of the mountain. In Ptolemaic times the sanctuary was extended and dedicated to Imhotep and Amenhotep, the quasi-divine counsellors of Zoser and Amenophis III. Beneath it lies another burial chamber for Hatshepsut, presumably favoured over her pro forma tomb in the Valley of the Kings, since it was dug at a later date.

Other sites

From the heights of Hatshepsut's temple you can gaze southwards over the ruins of two similar edifices. The **Mortuary Temple of Tuthmosis III** was long ago destroyed by a landslide, but a painted relief excavated here can be seen in the Luxor Museum; more remains of the far older **Temple of Mentuhotpe II**, the first pharaoh to choose burial in Thebes (XI Dynasty). Unlike his XVIII Dynasty imitators, Mentuhotpe was actually buried in his mortuary temple; his funerary statue is now exhibited in the Cairo Museum.

Whereas Mentuhotpe's remains weren't discovered till modern times, many of the New Kingdom royal tombs were despoiled soon after their final burial in the Valley of the Kings. Towards the end of the XXI Dynasty, the priests hid forty mummies in a **secret cache** in the next hollow to the south above Mentuhotpe's temple, which the villagers of Gurna found in 1875 and quietly sold off for years until rumbled by the authorities, who forced them to reveal the cache's location. Amongst the mummies recovered were Amenophis I, Tuthmosis II and III, Seti I and Ramses II and III. As the steamer bore them downriver to Cairo, villagers lined the banks, wailing in sorrow or firing rifles in homage – a haunting scene in Shady Abdel Salem's film *The Mummy*, a classic of Egyptian cinema (1975).

How much may still lie undiscovered is suggested by the **Tomb of Montemhat**; Montemhat was mayor of Thebes under Amenophis II. Presently being excavated by the University of Tübingen, the tomb has a courtyard as big as a tennis court, flanked by giant carvings of heraldic plants, visible 20m beneath the desert's surface – be careful peering over the edge of the pit. You can see a long underground ramp leading to the tomb beside the *tuf-tuf* terminus of Hatshepsut's temple.

The Asasif Tombs

Midway between Deir el-Bahri and the Tombs of the Nobles lies a burial ground known as the **Asasif Tombs**, currently being studied by several archeological teams. While some of its 35 tomb chapels date from the XVIII Dynasty, the majority are from the Late Period (XXV–XXVI Dynasty), when Thebes was ruled by Nubian kings, and then from the Delta. **Tickets** for these tombs are sold at the Deir el-Bahri ticket office.

The most likely to be open is the **Tomb of Pabasa (#279)**, the steward to a Divine Votaress of Amun during the XXVI Dynasty. His tomb reflects the Saïte Dynasty obsession with the Old Kingdom, having a similar design to tombs at Saqqara. Its massive gateway leads into a pillared court with scenes of hunting, fishing and viticulture (note the bee-keeping scene on the central column). A funeral procession and the voyage to Abydos appear in the vestibule.

Also worth noting is the **Tomb of Kheru-ef (#192)**, a steward of Queen Tiy during the Amarna period. His scenes depict a Jubilee Festival, Tiy and Amenophis III, musicians, dancers and playful animals – as lyrical as those in Ramose's tomb (see p.399).

The Tombs of the Nobles

The **Tombs of the Nobles** are a study in contrasts to their royal counterparts. Whereas royalty favoured concealed tombs in secluded valleys, Theban nobles and high officials were ostentatiously interred in the limestone foothills overlooking the great funerary temples of their masters and the city across the river. The pharaohs' tombs were sealed and guarded; the nobles' were left open, for their descendants to make funerary offerings. Whereas royal tombs are filled with scenes of judgement and resurrection, the nobles' chosen artwork dwells on earthly life and its continuation in the hereafter. Given more freedom of expression, the artists excelled themselves with vivid **paintings** on stucco (the inferior limestone on this side of the hills militates against carved reliefs). One detail found in all these tombs is the blue lotus, which one Swedish Egyptologist reckons was a drug used for sexual rituals, containing bioflavonoid compounds similar to gingko extract.

The **tombs' layout** marks a further evolution in funerary architecture since the Middle Kingdom tombs of Beni Hassan. Most are entered via a courtyard, with a transverse hall preceding the burial shrine with its niche containing an effigy of the deceased (or statues of his entire family). Strictly speaking, they are tomb chapels rather than tombs, since the graves themselves lie at the bottom of a shaft (usually inaccessible).

All the tombs open to visitors cluster amid the remains of the village of Old Gurna, where they're divided into four groups (each requiring a separate ticket from the main ticket office), namely: **Rekhmire and Sennofer**; **Ramose, Userhat and Khaemhat**; **Nakht and Menna**; and **Khonsu, Userhat and Benia**. The first two lie furthest west and back from the road; the next trio downhill towards the Ramesseum; and the last two sets of tombs to the northeast, closer to Deir el-Bahri. With the demolition of many houses, the tombs are set to become more accessible as paths are upgraded – but visitors will no longer find the juxtaposition of life and death that used to characterize Gurna.

As visiting all the tombs plus the museum would take two hours or so, most people limit themselves to a single group or the highlights from each (marked ★ in the accounts following).

Gurna Discovery

On the way uphill from the main road to Sennofer's tomb you'll pass the **Gurna Discovery** museum (daily except Tues 8am–noon & 2–5pm), in one of the few buildings that remain since Gurna was bulldozed. Originally the Gurnawis were Bedouin who moved up from the plain to dig for treasure, but as European scholars sought papyri, potshards and other items formerly discarded as worthless, tomb-robbing became a wholesale business that thrived for generations. Trafficking was covertly encouraged by foreign museums and collectors, while archeologists deplored it. Reputedly, one person a week died from tomb-robbing accidents that were never reported. The exhibition is illustrated with photographs and copies of drawings by Robert Hay (the originals are in the British Library), showing the village as an integral part of the Necropolis.

Tomb of Rekhmire (#100)

Located off to the right of a mosque, the richly decorated tomb of **Rekhmire** casts light on statecraft and foreign policy under Tuthmosis III and Amenophis II, whom Rekhmire served as vizier. The badly damaged murals in its transverse hall show him collecting taxes from Upper **[a]** and Lower **[b]** Egypt, and inspecting temple workshops, charioteers and agricultural work **[c]**. Around the corner from his ancestors **[d]**, grapes are trod in large tubs and the juice is strained and stored in jars **[e]**.

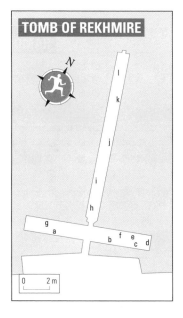

TOMB OF REKHMIRE

Along the rear wall are depicted a desert hunt **[f]** and a famous scene of Rekhmire receiving tributes from foreign lands **[g]**. Among the gifts shown are vases from Crete and the Aegean Islands (fourth row); a giraffe, monkeys and elephant tusks from Punt and Nubia (third row); and chariots and horses from Syria (second row).

Growing in height as it recedes towards the false door at the back, the long corridor is decorated with scenes of work and daily life. Slaves store grain in silos **[h]**, whence it was later disbursed as wages to armourers, carpenters, sculptors and other state-employed craftsmen **[i]**. An idealized banqueting scene with female musicians **[j]** merges into an afterworld with a lake and trees **[k]**. Also note Rekhmire's funeral procession and offerings to sustain him in the afterlife **[l]**.

Tomb of Sennofer (#96)

From Rekhmire's tomb, slog 50m uphill to the left to find another colourful tomb, in better condition. Entered by a low, twisting stairway, the tomb of **Sennofer** is known as the "Tomb of Vines" after the grapes and vines painted on the textured ceiling of the antechamber. As mayor of Thebes and overseer of Amun's estates under Amenophis II, Sennofer had local viticulture among his responsibilities. The walls of the burial shrine depict his funeral procession (left), voyage to Abydos (back, right) and mummified sojourn with Anubis (right). Its square pillars bear images of Hathor, whose eyes follow you around the room. A small tree-goddess appears on the inner side of the rear left-hand pillar.

Tomb of Ramose (#55)*

Down a dirt road to the southeast lies the tomb of **Ramose**, who was vizier and governor of Thebes immediately before and after the Amarna revolution.

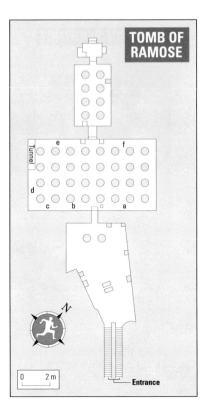

TOMB OF RAMOSE

Tunnel

e   f
d
c   b   a

N

0   2 m

Entrance

His spacious tomb captures the moment of transition from Amun- to Aten-worship, featuring both classical and Amarna-style reliefs, the latter unfinished since Ramose followed Akhenaten to his new capital. Besides its superb reliefs, the tomb is notable for retaining its courtyard – originally a feature of all these tombs.

Along the entrance wall of its pillared hall are lovely carvings that reflect the mellowing of classicism during the reign of Amenophis III, Akhenaten's father. Predictable scenes of Ramose and his wife **[a]**, Amenophis III and Queen Tiy **[b]** making offerings come alive thanks to the exquisite rendering of the major figures, carried over to their feasting friends and relatives **[c]**. The sinuous swaying of mourners likewise imparts lyricism to the conventional, painted funerary scene **[d]**, where Ramose, wife and priests worship Osiris.

The onset of Aten-worship and the Amarna style is evident in the reliefs at the back, despite their battered condition. Those on the left **[e]** were carved before Amenophis IV changed his name to Akhenaten and espoused Aten-worship, so the pharaoh sits beneath a canopy with Maat, the goddess of truth, receiving flowers from Ramose. (At the far end, note the red grid and black outlined figures by which the artist transferred his design to the wall before relief-cutting took place.) However, the corresponding scene **[f]** depicts the pharaoh as Akhenaten, standing with Nefertiti at their palace window, bathed in the Aten's rays. Ramose is sketched in below, accepting their gift of a golden chain; his physiognomy is distinctly Amarnan, but rather less exaggerated than the royal couple's (see p.298).

By a quirk of Egyptian security, a low wall bars access to Ramose's inner shrine, but there is nothing to prevent you from venturing into a dark tunnel leading off the hall, which suddenly plummets into his grave, 15m below – beware.

Tomb of Userhat (#56)

Immediately south of Ramose's tomb lies that of **Userhat**, a royal scribe and tutor in the reign of Amenophis II. Although some of the figures were destroyed by early Christian hermits who occupied the shrine, what remains is freshly coloured, with unusual pink tones. The tomb is also interesting in that it's still illuminated by means of a mirror reflecting sunlight inside, just as it was when the artists decorated the tomb.

Along the entrance wall of the antechamber are scenes of wine-making, harvesting, herding and branding cattle, collecting grain for the royal storehouse **[a]**, and the customary offerings scenes **[b]**. On the rear wall are reliefs of baking, assaying gold dust, and – lower down – a barber trimming customers beneath a tree **[c]**. The funerary feast scene **[d]** was extensively damaged by hermits, particularly the female figures. The inner hall contains paintings of Userhat hunting gazelles, hares and jackals from a chariot in the desert **[e]**; fowling and fishing amid the reeds **[f]**; and funerary scenes **[g]**. In a niche at the end is a headless statue of the deceased's wife.

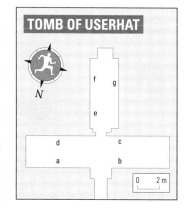

Tomb of Khaemhat (#57)
Next door is the tomb of **Khaemhat**, royal scribe and inspector of granaries under Amenophis III, which is reached via a forecourt off which two other tombs, now locked, once led. Flanking its doorway outside are battered reliefs of Khaemhat worshipping Re, and the complete set of instruments for the Opening of the Mouth ceremony (right). In the transverse antechamber with its red and black patterned ceiling, the best reliefs are on the left as you enter. Although Renenet the snake-headed harvest-goddess has almost vanished, a scene of grain boats docking at Thebes harbour is still visible nearer the niche containing statues of Khaemhat and Imhotep. In the bottom row to the left of the door into the corridor, Hathor breastfeeds a boy-king, surrounded by sacred cows.

Fishing, fowling and family scenes decorate the right-hand wall of the corridor, leading to a triple-niched chapel containing seated statues of Khaemhat and his family.

Tomb of Nakht (#52)*
Northeast of Ramose's tomb lies the burial place of **Nakht**, whose antechamber contains a small museum with drawings of the reliefs (which are covered in glass) and a replica of Nakht's funerary statue, which was lost at sea en route to America in 1917. Nakht was the overseer of Amun's vineyards and granaries under Tuthmosis IV, and the royal astronomer, but stargazing does not feature among the activities depicted in his tomb. The only decorated section is the transverse antechamber, whose ceiling is painted to resemble woven mats, with a geometric frieze running above the brilliantly coloured murals.

To one side, Nakht supervises the harvest in a scene replete with vivid details **[a]**. In the bottom register, one farmer fells a tree, while another swigs from a waterskin; of the two women gleaning in the row above, one is missing an arm. Beyond a stele relating Nakht's life **[b]** is the famous banqueting scene **[c]**, where sinuous dancers and a blind harpist entertain friends of the deceased, who sits beside his wife, Tawi, with a cat scoffing a fish beneath his chair; sadly, their figures have been erased.

The defacement of Nakht's image and Amun's name is usually ascribed to Amarna iconoclasm, but the gouging out of his eyes and throwing sticks in the

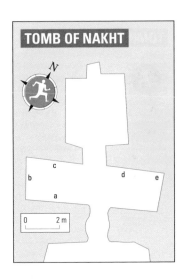

TOMB OF NAKHT

N

0   2 m

hunting scene **[d]** suggests a personal animus. Happily, this has not extended to the images in the corner **[e]**, where peasants tread grapes in vats, and birds are caught in clap-nets and hung for curing (below). The plain inner chamber has a false door painted to resemble Aswan granite, and a deep shaft leading to the (inaccessible) burial chamber.

Tomb of Menna (#69)

More scenes of rural life decorate the nearby tomb of **Menna**, an XVIII Dynasty inspector of estates. Accompanied by his wife and daughter, Menna worships the sun in the entrance passage. In the left wing of the first chamber, he supervises field labour (notice the two girls pulling each other's hair, near the far end of the third row), feasts and makes offerings with his wife. Across the way they participate in ceremonies with Anubis, Osiris, Re and Hathor. Though chiefly decorated with mourning and burial scenes, the inner chamber also features a spot of hunting and fishing, vividly depicted on the right-hand wall. The niche at the end contains the legs of Menna's votive statue.

Tombs of Khonsu, Userhet and Benia

This trio of small tombs near those of Nakht and Menna was opened to the public in 1992. The themes are standard, with scenes of offerings, hunting, fishing and funerary rites. In the tomb of Userhet (not to be confused with the Userhat in tomb #56), the guard may produce a mummified head for baksheesh.

Khoka Tombs

Set apart from the others – accessible by a track leaving the main road opposite the El Sheikh Abd El Gurna alabaster workshop – the **Khoka** (or, as locals say, "Hookah") tombs were built for a trio of New Kingdom officials. **Neferonpet** (known as Kenro) was a treasury scribe; the tomb's inner chamber depicts him assessing deliveries of gold and food, and the work of sculptors and weavers. The golden-yellow, red and blue murals, the brightly patterned ceilings and the votive statues of the deceased and his wives (badly disfigured) are also characteristic of the tomb of **Nefersekheru**, next door. Here, the wives enjoy greater prominence, flanking Nefersekheru pictorially (to the right as you enter) and sculpturally (in niches), and known to posterity as Maatmou, Sekhemui and Nefertari. Their mummies were buried in a shaft off the rear corridor, which leads into the adjacent tomb of Dhutmosi (now inaccessible).

Tombs of Roy and Shuroy

Theset two tombs have been opened on the edge of Dra' Abul Naga, just over 1km from the Khoka Tombs by road. You can get there by pick-up heading towards El-Jebannah; get off when you see a billboard with Mubarak's face and follow the signposted slip-road beyond it to the left.

The colours in both tombs are remarkably fresh. High priest **Roy** from the time of Horemeheb has a small rectangular tomb (#255), whose scenes of wailing mourners, sacrificial bulls and funerary offerings are offset by a ceiling checkered with yellow, red, black and white crosses. His near namesake **Shuroy** was a brazier-bearer at Amun's temple during the XIX Dynasty and has a larger T-shaped tomb (#13). Here, the murals are fragmentary or merely sketched in, though there's a fine frieze of dwarves along the top of the wall to the left inside the transverse hall.

The Ramesseum

The **Ramesseum** or mortuary temple of Ramses II was built to awe the pharaoh's subjects, perpetuate his existence in the afterlife and forever link him to Amun-United-with-Eternity (one of Amun's many avatars). Had it remained intact, the Ramesseum would doubtless match his great sun temple of Abu Simbel for monumental grandeur and unabashed self-glorification. But by siting it beside an earlier temple on land that was annually inundated, Ramses unwittingly ensured the ruination of his monument, whose toppled colossi would later mock his presumption, inspiring Shelley's sonnet *Ozymandias*:

I met a traveller from an antique land
Who said: Two vast and trunkless legs of stone
Stand in the desert … Near them on the sand,
Half sunk, a shattered visage lies, whose frown,
And wrinkled lip, and sneer of cold command
Tell that its sculptor well those passions read
Which yet survive, stamped on these lifeless things,
The hand which mocked them, and the heart that fed.
On the pedestal these words appear:
'My name is Ozymandias, King of Kings:
Look upon my works ye Mighty, and despair!'
Nothing beside remains. Round the decay
Of that colossal wreck, boundless and bare
The lone and level sands stretch far away.

Nineteenth-century writers knew the ruins as the Memnonium. Their present name only caught on late in the nineteenth century, by which time the Ramesseum had been plundered for statuary – not least the seven-tonne head of one of its fallen colossi, now in the British Museum. Yet its devastation lends romance to the conventional architecture, infusing it with the pathos that moved Harriet Martineau to muse how "violence inconceivable to us has been used to destroy what art inconceivable to us had erected". As bus parties seldom intrude, the Ramesseum seems peaceful, its tranquillity enhanced by a group of trees near the First Pylon, which offer a pleasant contrast to the desolation of other sites in the Necropolis.

▲ Ramses II

Half an hour suffices to see the famous colossi and the best reliefs, but you may care to linger. The nearby *Ramesseum Resthouse* sells cold drinks and hot meals; the owner's grandfather, Sheikh Hussein Abdul, was a teaboy at Carter's excavation in 1922 and photographed wearing a jewelled collar from Tut's tomb. Remember to buy a **ticket** for the site at the main ticket office before you come here.

The site

Like other mortuary temples in the Theban Necropolis, the Ramesseum faces towards the Nile and was originally entered via its **First Pylon**. Wrecked by the earthquake that felled the colossi, the pylon stands marooned in the scrub beyond a rubble-strewn depression that used to be the **First Court**. In 1983, Rohl found evidence for his "New Chronology" in an inscription on a block balanced atop the pylon, asserting that during the eighth year of his reign,

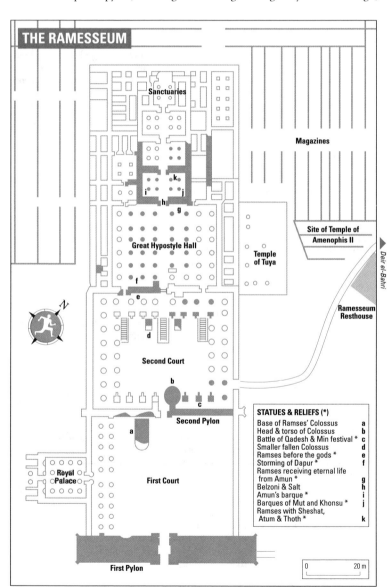

THE RAMESSEUM

Sanctuaries

Magazines

Great Hypostyle Hall

Site of Temple of Amenophis II

Temple of Tuya

Deir el-Bahri

Ramesseum Resthouse

N

Second Court

Second Pylon

STATUES & RELIEFS (*)

Base of Ramses' Colossus	a
Head & torso of Colossus	b
Battle of Qadesh & Min festival *	c
Smaller fallen Colossus	d
Ramses before the gods *	e
Storming of Dapur *	f
Ramses receiving eternal life from Amun *	g
Belzoni & Salt	h
Amun's barque *	i
Barques of Mut and Khonsu *	j
Ramses with Sheshat, Atum & Thoth *	k

Royal Palace

First Court

0   20 m

First Pylon

Ramses plundered a city named "Shalem", which Rohl thinks was Jerusalem in the time of King Solomon (see p.765).

Visitors enter the temple via the northern side of its **Second Court**, to be confronted by the awesome **fallen colossus of Ramses II**. This seated megalith once towered over the stairs from the first into the second court **[a]**; over 18m tall and weighing about 1000 tons, it was only surpassed by the Colossi of Memnon thanks to their pedestals. When it toppled some time after the first century AD, its upper half smashed through the Second Pylon into the court, where its head and torso lie today **[b]**, measuring 7m across the shoulders; the cartouche on its bicep reads: "Ruler of Rulers". In the lower court are other fragments, notably feet and hands. As Dean Stanley wrote in 1852, "You sit on his breast and look at the Osiride statues which support the porticos of the temple, and they seem pygmies before him".

Behind the chunky Osirian pillars rises what's left of the **Second Pylon**, whose inner face bears scenes from the second Battle of Qadesh, surmounted by a register depicting the festival of the harvest-god Min **[c]**. At the far end of the second courtyard, where three stairways rise to meet a colonnaded portico, is a **smaller fallen colossus** of Ramses **[d]**, more fragmented, though its face has suffered merely nasal damage. Originally there were two colossi, but the other – dubbed the "Young Memnon" – was seized for Britain in 1816 by the treasure-hunter Belzoni. The name "Ozymandias" arose from the Ancient Greeks' misreading of one of the king's many titles, User-Maat-Re.

Beyond here, the core of the Ramesseum is substantially intact. The first set of reliefs worth noting occurs on the front wall of the **portico**, between the central and left-hand doorways **[e]**. Above a bottom row depicting eleven of his sons, Ramses appears with Atum and Mont (who holds the hieroglyph for "life" to his nose), and kneels before the Theban Triad (right) while Thoth inscribes his name on a palm frond (centre). The top register shows him sacrificing to Ptah and making offerings to Min, whose outsize erection is decorously termed "ithyphallic" by Egyptologists.

The **Great Hypostyle Hall** had 48 columns, of which 29 are still standing. The taller ones flanking the central aisle have papyrus shafts and turquoise, yellow and white lotus capitals, supporting a raised section of roof, while the lower side columns have papyrus-bud capitals. On the wall as you come in, reliefs depict Egyptian troops storming the Hittite city of Dapur, using shields to protect themselves from arrows and stones **[f]**. At the back of the hall, incised reliefs **[g]** show lion-headed Sekhmet (far right) presenting Ramses to an enthroned Amun, who gives him the breath of eternal life from an ankh; along the bottom are depicted some of the king's hundred sons. Notice the names of Belzoni and his patron, the British consul Henry Salt, carved on the right-hand door jamb **[h]**.

Beyond this lie two **smaller Hypostyle Halls**. The first retains its astronomical ceiling, featuring the oldest known twelve-month calendar (whether lunar or solar months is debatable). Notice the barques of Amun, Mut and Khonsu (**[i]** & **[j]**), and the scene of Ramses beneath the persea tree with Atum, Sheshat and Thoth **[k]**. "Pukler Muskau" is the oddest of the many names scrawled on the columns over millennia. The ruined **sanctuaries** were presumably dedicated to Amun, Ramses the god and his glorious ancestors, for the edifice stood alongside an earlier temple of Seti I, which itself contained shrines to Seti and his father, Ramses I, both of whom were linked to Amun. Its scant remains lie to the northeast of the portico and Hypostyle Hall.

The whole complex is surrounded by mud-brick **magazines** that once covered about three times the area of the temple and included workshops, storerooms and servants' quarters, that has survived far better than the **royal** palace and **Temple of Tuya** that once adjoined the temple, of which only stumps of walls and columns remain. Nearby, the Italian mission is excavating the remains of the **Temple of Amenophis II**.

Other mortuary temples

In ancient times, the Ramesseum was one of half a dozen mortuary temples ranged along the edge of the flood plain with no regard for chronological order. The **Temple of Merneptah**, built by Ramses' thirteenth or fourteenth son, lies just southwest of the Ramesseum, intruding onto the edges of, and reusing masonry from, the vast complex of Amenophis III that once spread to the Colossi of Memnon. Recently opened to the public after thirty years' study and restoration by Swiss Egyptologists, the site consists of fragments and portions of the temple, placed in their original positions and supported by modern stonework.

The entrance is reached by walking past the *Marsam Hotel*, and represents the original position of the first pylon. An informative **museum** exhibits stone-carvings from the site (forty percent of them originally belonging to Amenophis III's temple or Deir el-Bahri) and records its excavation (1971–2001). Further in to the left stands a copy of the famous **Israel Stele** also replicated at Karnak, which features the earliest reference to Israel outside of the Bible (see p.110). Guards can unlock another section, containing the remains of a monumental gateway from Amenophis III's temple, clearly reused to build Merneptah's edifice.

While nothing remains of the temples of Tuthmosis IV, Tuthmosis II, Ay and Horemheb that once extended towards Medinet Habu, there is a substantial **Temple of Seti I** near the village of Gurna Ta'rif (accessible by pick-ups from old Gurna or Gezira). The site is still being excavated by German Egyptologists, but you can enter the temple, with its crude reliefs dedicated to Amun, Seti and Ramses I. Again, you must buy a ticket in advance at the main ticket office.

Deir el-Medina: the Workers' Village

Deir el-Medina, the **Workers' Village**, housed the masons, painters and sculptors who created the royal tombs in the Valley of the Kings. Because many were literate and left records on papyrus or *ostraca*, we know such details as who feuded with whom, their sex lives and labour disputes. As state employees, they were supposed to receive fortnightly supplies of wheat, dried meat and fish, onions, pulses and beer, corresponding in value to the price of a bull. When these failed to arrive as often happened during the ramshackle XX Dynasty, the workers downed tools, staged sit-ins at Medinet Habu, or demonstrated in Luxor.

Normally they worked an eight-hour day, sleeping in huts near the tombs during their ten-day shift before returning to their families at Deir el-Medina – a pattern followed over generations, as most occupations were hereditary. In their spare time craftsmen worked for private clients or collaborated on their own tombs, built beneath man-size pyramids. Their own murals appropriated imagery from royal and noble tombs, which was parodied in the famous *Satirical Papyrus*, showing animals judging souls, collecting taxes and playing *senet,* and humans having sex (see box on p.407).

Anyone taking the donkey trail to the Valley of the Kings can get a fine **overview** of the village from the hillside – but the real attraction is its tombs. Visitors should bear in mind that the Deir el-Medina **ticket** (#6) doesn't cover the tomb of Peshedu, which needs a separate ticket (#11) – both available only from the main ticket office. You can easily walk to Deir el-Medina from the main road; it's also feasible to do so from the Valley of the Queens or Medinet Habu.

The nearest pyramid to the entrance marks the **Tomb of Sennedjem** (or Sennutem), whose vaulted burial chamber is reached by steep flights of steps and two antechambers. Its colourful murals feature ithyphallic baboons (right end wall), Osiris and the Fields of Yaru, and Anubis ministering to Sennedjem's mummy (facing wall, far left). The **Tomb of Ankherha** (#359) has a similar design, with an antechamber whose ceiling is decorated with intricate abstract patterns. On the left wall of the burial chamber, Ankherha appears with Wepwawet and Khepri; Anubis breathes life into his mummy; his wife adores Horus as a falcon; and his naked daughters make libations. In the **Tomb of Peshedu** (#3), one can see the deceased praying beneath the tree of regeneration, below which flow the waters of the Amuntit, the "Hidden Region" where souls were judged. Unusually for Deir el-Medina, the **Tomb of Iphy** (#217) eschews ceremonial scenes and deities for tableaux from everyday life. The **Tomb of Iri Nefer** (#219) isn't officially open, but can be seen for baksheesh.

Just north of the village stands a **Ptolemaic temple** dedicated to Maat and Hathor, whose head adorns the pillars between the outer court and naos. Each of its three shrines is decorated with scenes from the *Book of the Dead*; near the back of the left-hand shrine, a hyena-like "Devourer of Souls" awaits those who fail the Judgement of Osiris. Ancient Greek graffiti is scrawled around the temple's entrance. Early in the Christian era, the temple and the workers' village were occupied by monks – hence the site's Arabic name of Deir el-Medina ("Monastery of the Town").

The Valley of the Queens

The **Valley of the Queens** is something of a misnomer, for it also contains the tombs of high officials (who were interred here long before the first queen was buried in this valley during the XIX Dynasty) and royal children. Polygamy and concubinage produced huge broods whose blood lines were further entangled by incestuous marriages between crown princes and their sisters, in emulation of Osiris and Isis. Princes were educated by priests and scribes, taught swimming, riding and shooting by officers, and finally apprenticed to military commands around the age of 12. Less is known about the schooling of princesses, but several queens were evidently well versed in statecraft and architecture.

Originally named the "Place of Beauty", but now known in Arabic as Biban el-Harem ("Gates of the Harem"), the valley contains nearly eighty tombs, most of which are basically just pits in the ground. Although the finest murals rival those in the Valley of the Kings for artistry, many have been corroded by salt deposits or badly vandalized, and the tomb of Nefertari is so fragile that it has been closed to the public: small corporate or VIP groups can book in advance to see it at a cost of $4000. **Tickets** for the other tombs are sold at the entrance to the valley; it takes fifteen minutes to walk there from Deir el-Medina or the main ticket office.

Tomb of Amunhirkhepshef (#55)

After Nefertari's, the best tomb in the valley belongs to **Amunhirkhepshef**, a son of Ramses III who accompanied his father on campaigns and perhaps died in battle at the age of 9. He is shown wearing the royal sidelock of youth, in lustrous murals where Ramses conducts him through funerary rituals, past the Keepers of the Gates, to an unfinished burial chamber containing a granite sarcophagus. A glass case displays a mummified foetus that his mother aborted through grief at Amunhirkhepshef's death, and entombed with her son.

Tomb of Queen Titi (#52)

Sited along the well-trodden route to Amunhirkhepshef's tomb, this cruciform structure was commissioned by **Queen Titi**, wife of one of the Ramessid pharaohs of the XX Dynasty. A winged Maat kneels in the corridor (where Titi appears before Thoth, Ptah and the sons of Horus) and guards the entrance to the burial chamber with Neith (left) and Selket (right).

The burial chamber itself boasts jackal, lion and baboon guardians, plus three side chambers, the finest being the one to the right. Here, Hathor emerges from between the mountains of east and west in her bovine form, while the tree-goddess pours Nile water to rejuvenate Titi, who reposes on a cushion across the room. Sadly, most of these murals are faded or damaged.

Tomb of Prince Khaemweset (#44)

This colourfully painted tomb is reached via a separate path. **Prince Khaemweset** was one of several sons of Ramses III who died in a smallpox epidemic, and the murals in his tomb give precedence to images of Ramses, making offerings in the entrance corridor and worshipping funerary deities in the side chambers. In the second corridor, decorated with the *Book of Gates*, Ramses leads Khaemweset past the fearsome guardians of the Netherworld to the Fields of Yaru, bearing witness for him before Osiris and Horus in the burial chamber. Notice the four sons of Horus on the lotus blossom.

Tomb of Queen Nefertari (#66)

Queen Nefertari was the principal wife of Ramses II, who praised her figure ("The buttocks are full, but her waist is narrow") and conceded her almost equal status by the end of his reign. Her ascendancy was signified by the appearance of her image beside the king's on the pylon of Luxor Temple; the dedication of a shrine within the Ramesseum to Nefertari and the Queen Mother, Tuya; and finally by a massive temple at Abu Simbel, which identifies her with the goddess Hathor. After Ramses' death, Nefertari may have retired to a palace near the Fayoum or died herself, for no more is heard of her.

Her **tomb**, the most illustrious in the valley, was found in 1904 by an Italian archeologist, Ernesto Schiaparelli. Its extreme fragility and the damage caused by its plaster dehydrating, and salt crystals forming beneath its paintings, kept the tomb closed for decades while a solution was debated; eventually restoration began in 1986. It took five years and $6 million to clean the murals and re-adhere paint and stucco to the walls, without altering or adding any colours. To avoid the humidity that causes salt crystallization, visitors were supposedly limited to 150 a day, but this was so often ignored that the murals visibly deteriorated within a few years – hence the policy of restricting access to small numbers of big-spending VIPs and corporate groups.

Medinet Habu

Medinet Habu ("Habu's Town") is the Arabic name for the gigantic **Mortuary Temple of Ramses III**, a structure second only to Karnak in size and complexity, and better preserved in its entirety. Modelled on the Ramesseum of his illustrious ancestor, Ramses II, this XX Dynasty extravaganza deserves more attention than it usually gets, being the last stop on most tourists' itineraries. The site itself was hallowed long before Ramses erected his "House of Millions of Years" and is still imbued with magical significance by the local *fellaheen*. Its massive enclosure walls sheltered the entire population of Thebes during the Libyan invasions of the late XX Dynasty and for centuries afterwards protected the Coptic town of Djeme, built within the great temple.

▲ Ramses III

The temple precincts

The entire complex was originally surrounded by mud-brick **enclosure walls**, sections of which rise at intervals from the plain. Its front facade is quite asymmetrical, with a jutting **Ptolemaic Pylon** whose winged sun-disc glows with colour since its recent restoration, overshadowing the entrance to the temple precincts. This **Migdol Gate** is named after the Syrian fortress that so impressed Ramses with its lofty gatehouse that he built one for his own temple, and often relaxed with his **harem** in a suite above the gate (inaccessible), decorated with reliefs of dancers in slinky lingerie. As social conditions worsened during the latter years of his reign, a secondary wife, Tiy, hatched a harem conspiracy to murder him during the Optet festival, so that her son, Pentwere, could inherit – but the conspirators were discovered and forced to commit suicide, and Ramses' chosen heir eventually succeeded him. The two grey-green diorite statues of Sekhmet by the gate's entrance may have served to transmit the prayers of pilgrims to Amun, who "dwelt" within the temple.

To the north stands the **Small Temple**, reputedly where the primeval mound arose from the waters of Chaos, preceding the creator-god Re-Atum of the Hermopolitan Ogdoad. The existing structure was built and partly decorated by Hatshepsut, whose cartouches and images were erased by Tuthmosis III. Akhenaten did likewise to those of Amun, but Horemheb and Seti replaced them. Some defaced reliefs **[a]** show Tuthmosis presiding over the foundation ceremonies, "stretching the cord" before the goddess Seshat, "scattering the gypsum" and then "hacking the earth" before a priapic Min.

Whereas the Small Temple antedates Ramses' work by three centuries, the **Chapels of the Votaresses** are Late Period additions. Several date from the XXV Dynasty of Nubian kings, who appointed these high priestesses of Amun and de facto governors of Thebes. The best reliefs are in the forecourt **[b]** and shrine of Amenirdis, sister of King Shabaka, whose alabaster funerary statue is now in the Cairo Museum. Ironically, these chapels remained objects of

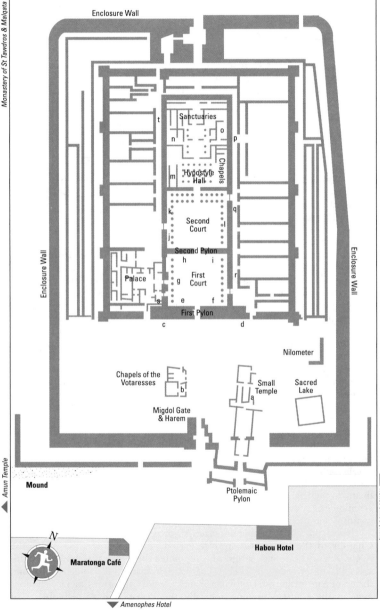

MEDINET HABU

Enclosure Wall

Sanctuaries

t

n o p

Chapels

m Hypostyle
Hall

k

Second
Court

j

Second Pylon

h

First
Court

g

s

e f

First Pylon

c d

Nilometer

Chapels of the
Votaresses

b

Small
Temple

a

Sacred
Lake

Migdol Gate
& Harem

Palace

q

r

Enclosure Wall

Enclosure Wall

Amun Temple

Mound

Ptolemaic
Pylon

N

Maratonga Café

Habou Hotel

Ticket office (1km)

Amenophes Hotel

410

veneration long after Ramses' temple had been abandoned. Notice the granite altars for offerings.

In the right-hand corner of the enclosure are the remains of a **Sacred Lake** where childless local women came to bathe at night and pray to Isis for conception. Behind this lies a dank **Nilometer**, once fed by a canal from the river. Originally, this whole area was a garden.

Entering the Mortuary Temple of Ramses III

Like Deir el-Bahri and the Ramesseum, this mortuary temple was a focus for the pharaoh's cult, linking him to Amun-United-with-Eternity. The effigies of Amun, Mut and Khonsu paid an annual visit during the Festival of the Valley, while other deities permanently resided in its shrines. Ramses himself often dwelt in the adjacent palace, his Libyan and Sardinian bodyguard billeted nearby. Aside from its lack of freestanding colossi, the sandstone temple gives a good idea of how the Ramesseum must have looked before it collapsed.

Had it not lost its cornice and one corner, the **First Pylon** would match Luxor Temple's in size. For baksheesh, a guard may unlock a stairway to the top, which offers a panoramic view of the temple, Theban Hills and Nile Valley. Reliefs on the outer walls (copied from the Ramesseum) show Ramses smiting Nubians **[c]** and Syrians **[d]**, though he never warred with either. Those on the inner wall relate genuine campaigns with Ramessid hyperbole. An outsized Ramses scatters hordes of Libyans in his chariot **[e]**. Afterwards, scribes tally the severed hands and genitals of dead foes (third row from the bottom) **[f]**.

Until the nineteenth century, the ruined houses of Coptic Djeme filled the **First Court**, now cleared to reveal its flanking columns. Those on the right bear chunky Osiride statues of the king, attended by knee-high queens. The other side of the court abuts the royal palace (now ruined and entered from outside). In the middle of this wall was a Window of Appearances **[g]** flanked by sunk-reliefs of prisoners, whence the king rewarded loyal commanders with golden collars. Yet more scenes of triumph cover the outside of the **Second Pylon**, where Ramses leads three rows of prisoners to Amun and Mut **[h]** (those in the lowest row are Philistines) and a long inscription lauds his victories in Asia Minor **[i]**. The vultures on the ceiling of the pylon's gateway are still coloured.

Halls and sanctuaries

During Coptic times most of the Osiride pillars were removed to make room for a church, and a thick layer of mud was plastered over the reliefs in the **Second Court**. Now uncovered, these depict the annual festivals of Min **[j]** and Sokar **[k]**, with processions of priests and dancers accompanying the royal palanquin. Elsewhere, the events of Ramses' fifth regnal year are related in a long text lower down the wall **[l]**. The lotus-bud columns of the rear arcade are coloured blue, red and turquoise.

The now-roofless **Hypostyle Hall**, beyond, once had a raised central aisle like the Great Hall at Karnak, and still has some brightly coloured pillars at the back. To the right lie five **chapels** dedicated to Ramses, his XIX Dynasty namesake, Ptah, Osiris and Sokar. On the opposite side are several (locked) treasure chambers whose reliefs show the weighing of myrrh, gold, lapis lazuli and other valuables bestowed upon the temple **[m]** – also visible on the outer walls.

Beyond this lie two **smaller halls** with rooms leading off. To the left of the first hall is the funerary chamber of Ramses III **[n]**; notice the lion-headed deity on the right-hand wall. The other side – open to the sky – featured an altar to Re. On the lintels that once supported the roof **[o]**, Ramses and several baboons worship Re's barque. The central aisle of the next level is flanked by red granite statues of Ramses with Maat or Thoth. At the back are three **sanctuaries** dedicated to the Theban Triad of Mut (left), Amun (centre) and Khonsu (right).

Along the outer walls

Some of the best reliefs at Medinet Habu are on the **outer walls** of the temple, involving a fair slog over broken ground. As most are quite faint, they're best viewed early or late in the day, when shadows reveal details obscured at midday. The famous **battle reliefs of Ramses II** run along the temple's northern wall, starting from the back. Although you'll encounter the last or middle scenes first, we've listed them in chronological order, as Ramses intended them to be seen. The first section **[p]** depicts the invasion of land-hungry Libyans, early in his reign. In the vanguard of the battle are Ramses, a lion, and the standard of Amun. Afterwards, scribes count limbs and genitals to assess each soldier's reward in gold or land. Yet despite this victory, Ramses was soon beleaguered on two fronts, as the Libyans joined with the Sea Peoples (Sardinians, Philistines and Cretans) in a concerted invasion of the Nile Delta. A giant Ramses fires arrows into a melee of grappling ships, in the only Egyptian relief of a sea battle **[q]**. A third invasion by the Libyans **[r]** was also thwarted, but their descendants would eventually triumph and rule Egypt as the XXIII and XXIV dynasties.

On the other side of the temple behind the First Pylon is a dramatic relief of Ramses hunting antelopes in the desert and impaling wild bulls in a marsh **[s]**, near a ruined **Palace** where he resided during visits. A calendar of festivals appears at the far end of the temple **[t]**, which is surrounded on three sides by mud-brick **storehouses**, eroded into worm-like shapes.

Other sites on the west bank

The village of **NAG LOHLAH** beside Medinet Habu will be familiar to readers of Richard Critchfield's *Shahhat* as the birthplace of its eponymous hero and the irascible Hagg Ali, owner of the *Habou Hotel* (which still exists, though Hagg is deceased). Most families have one foot in tourism and the other in farming, so that one finances the other as fortune allows. While Medinet Habu brings customers to their doorsteps – the *Maratonga Café* is ideal for cooling off – few visitors realise there's also an **Amun Temple** in someone's backyard (no set hours; baksheesh expected). Though small and knocked about, its reliefs retain some of the white background that has faded in other temples.

Monastery of St Tawdros

If it's not too hot, the **Monastery of St Tawdros** in the desert beyond Medinet Habu makes an interesting excursion. You can walk there from Medinat Habu in about twenty minutes, or cycle; even better, go riding in time for sunset. Be sure to cover your head and bring plenty of water; the unpaved track from Medinet Habu to the French House is easy going, but has no shade at all.

Roughly 200m right off the track into the desert, the monastery is easily identified by its beehive domes. Pharaonic, Greek and Roman masonry is incorporated into the low-vaulted church, whose shrines are dedicated to the Coptic martyrs Tawdros, Elkladius and Foktor. Tawdros (295–306 AD) was a leader in the Roman army before his conversion to Christianity, hence the monastery's alternative name, El Muharrib ("The Warrior"). The day of his martyrdom (January 20) and Easter see crowds of Copts descending on the monastery, but at other times the nuns who live there receive few visitors and seem pleased if anyone rings the bell.

Malqata

Further on, the **French House** stands guard over the scant **remains of Malqata**. This legendary pleasure palace built by Amenophis III had an artificial harbour linked to the Nile, for the royal family to arrive on its barge, *Aten Gleams*. Today the only visible remains are a long depression flanked by parallel mounds and low foundation walls, but archeologists from Waseda University have analyzed thousands of flakes of paint and stucco, to visually reconstruct the paintings on the walls and ceilings of the king's bedroom and harem chambers (see ⓦ www.waseda.ac.jp/projects/egypt).

Riziq

Travelling further afield is difficult, as police checkpoints seldom let tourists stray outside the security zone surrounding the Necropolis. However, many of the service taxis that carry pilgrims from Gezira to the **Moulid of St George** in the town of **RIZIQ** (aka "Razagat") – 15km south – travel by a desert track that avoids the checkpoints. Attended by Copts and Muslims alike, the moulid isn't for the squeamish; the circumcision of infants and the slaughter of animals play a major role in events. Held in and around the town's **Monastery of St George** (Deir Mari Girgis), it lasts for nearly a week, climaxing on November 11. Otherwise, Riziq is the start of the **road to Kharga Oasis**, which can't be used after the checkpoint closes at 1pm.

Esna

Small-town life and ancient stone are boldly juxtaposed at **ESNA**, on the west bank of the Nile 54km south of Luxor and 155km north of Aswan. A huge pit in the centre of Esna exposes part of the **Temple of Khnum**, but some visitors are disappointed by what they find: the only part to have been excavated is the Hypostyle Hall, whose somewhat inferior reliefs detract from the forest of columns and lofty astronomical ceiling. That said, Esna is worth a stopover en route to the fabulous **temple at Edfu** if you can arrange it, but unless you care to visit the early Saturday morning **animal market**, there's no reason to linger after seeing the temple, which takes less than an hour.

Visible just north of Esna are two **barrages** that act as bridges over the Nile. The one nearer town was built by the British in 1906 as part of a grand scheme to tame the Nile, with barrages at four points along its length. In the 1990s, the river was further exploited by an Italian-built hydroelectric barrage, known to locals as the "Electricity Bridge". Both barrages have **locks** to allow vessels to pass through, whose capacity is being doubled to reduce waiting time. Now that cruise boats no longer moor on Esna's Corniche, salesmen wait at the locks to throw their wares on to the decks for sunbathing tourists to buy.

Esna is the "border" between the Qena and Aswan governorates, whose respective **police** forces pass over the responsibility for escorting convoys here (hence the delay). Their reaction to independent travellers is hard to predict. It may depend on which direction you're travelling in, since Esna's police are more concerned with foreigners on Qena governorate territory than tourists entering the Aswan governorate.

The Temple of Khnum

When Amelia Edwards visited Esna, the **Temple of Khnum** (daily: summer 7am–5pm; winter 7am–4pm; £E15) was "buried to the chin in the accumulated

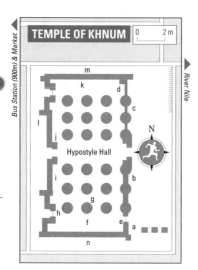

TEMPLE OF KHNUM

0   2 m

Bus Station (900m) & Market

River Nile

m

k   d

c

l

j

Hypostyle Hall

N

i

b

g

h

f   e

a

n

rubbish of a score of centuries" and built over with houses. To minimize their destruction, only a portion was excavated in the 1860s. Now 10m below ground level, the temple resembles a pharaonic Fort Knox, its boxy mass fronted by six columns rising from a screen, the open space above them covered with wire mesh to discourage nesting birds.

Arriving in Esna by bus, you can head to the temple by *calèche* (£E5) on the main road near the bus station, or walk there in about twenty minutes. The easiest way to do this is to follow the Corniche south past old *mashrabiya'*d houses and empty cruiser berths. Alternatively, join the flow of the crowd through the souk till you see a police station, backtrack one block and turn right down a side street, to emerge at the temple. The **ticket office** is a riverside kiosk beyond the covered tourist bazaar, which runs between the temple and the river, five minutes' walk from the souk.

The site

The temple, a Ptolemaic-Roman replacement for a much older structure dedicated to the ram-headed creator-god of ancient myth, faced eastwards and probably rivalled Edfu's for size. Since what you see is merely the Roman section (dating from the first century AD), the **facade** bears the cartouches of Claudius **[a]**, Titus **[b]** and Vespasian **[c]**, and the battered sun-disc above the entrance is flanked by votive inscriptions to these emperors.

As you enter the lofty **Hypostyle Hall**, your eyes are drawn upwards by a forest of columns that bud and flower in variegated capitals. Their shafts are covered with festival texts (now defaced) or hieroglyphs in the form of crocodiles **[d]** or rams **[e]**. One is a *Hymn of Creation* that acknowledges Khnum as the creator of all, even foreigners: "All are formed on his potter's wheel, their speech different in every region … but the lord of the wheel is their father too."

The hall's **astronomical ceiling** rivals Dendara's for finesse and complexity, but gloom, soot and distemper render much indiscernible. However, the zodiac register **[f]** visibly crawls with two-headed snakes, winged dogs and other creatures. Notice the pregnant hippo-goddess Tweri (whom the Greeks called Thoeris), and the scorpion in the next aisle **[g]**. Registers on the walls below show Septimus Severus, Caracalla and Geta before the gods.

The last Roman emperor mentioned is Decius **[h]**, whose persecution of Christians (249–51) anticipated the "Era of Martyrs" under Diocletian. Further along **[i]** is the cartouche of Ptolemy VI Philometor (Mother Lover), whose father began the construction of Esna temple. To the right of the portal, Decius makes offerings to Khnum, including a potter's wheel **[j]**. The liveliest reliefs are near the foot of the northern wall **[k]**, where Khnum, Horus and Emperor Commodus net fish and malignant spirits. To the left of this tableau stands an ibis-headed Thoth; to the right, Sheshat, goddess of writing. Around the outer

Khnum and Hapy

In Upper Egypt, **Khnum** was originally the ram-headed creator-god who moulded man on a potter's wheel, and the guardian of the Nile's source (which myth assigned to the caves just beyond the First Cataract, although the Ancient Egyptians must have known better). Later, however, Khnum was demoted to an underling of Amun-Re and shared his role as river deity with **Hapy**, god of the Nile in flood, who was also believed to dwell in an island cavern near the First Cataract. Shown with a blue-green body and a female breast, wearing a crown of lotus or sedge (the heraldic plants of Upper and Lower Egypt), he should not be confused with Horus's son, Hapi, the ape-headed deity of canopic jars.

▲ Khnum

▲ Hapy

walls of the temple are texts dedicated to Marcus Aurelius **[l]** and stiffly executed scenes of Titus, Domitian and Trajan smiting Egypt's foes before the gods **[m** and **n]**. Several stone blocks from an early Christian church lie in front of the temple.

Practicalities

Sadly for the local economy tourism tends to bypass Esna, as **cruise boats** merely pass through the locks, while travellers on **feluccas** from Aswan disembark 30km short of Esna to drive directly to Luxor, and budget hotels in Luxor no longer feature it on day excursions to Edfu and Kom Ombo. If you're still determined, expect to pay about £E150–200 for a four-seater cab from Luxor, and be sure to check beforehand which (if any) of the tourist convoys include a stop at Esna.

Getting here by **train** is awkward, as the station is on the east bank of the Nile, far from the temple, and not all trains stop at Esna anyway. **Buses** are handier, with four a day from Luxor and Aswan, which drop you in the centre of town, just under 1km from the temple.

The **tourist police** are near the temple ticket booth, and there's a **bank** (daily except Fri 8.30am–2pm; during Ramadan 10am–1.30pm) and a **post office** (daily except Fri 7am–2pm) further north along the Corniche. A humble place on the corner by the temple serves **meals**, and street food is sold in the souk.

Edfu and around

Situated on the west bank of the Nile, roughly equidistant from Luxor (115km) and Aswan (105km), the provincial town of **EDFU** boasts the best-preserved **cult temple** in Egypt, dedicated to the falcon-headed god **Horus**. Though actually built in the Ptolemaic era, this mammoth edifice respects all the canons of pharaonic architecture, giving an excellent idea of how most temples once looked. In terms of sheer monumental grandeur, it ranks alongside Karnak and Deir el-Bahri as one of the finest sites in the Nile Valley. A must-see for tourists (and on every cruise boat or felucca itinerary), it has saved Edfu from the fate of Esna.

The same can't be said of other sites, which had few visitors even before travel restrictions made getting there more difficult, but if deserted ruins are your thing, **El-Kab** fits the bill; **Silsilah** makes an interesting stopover on felucca or *dahabiya* cruises between Aswan and Edfu; and **Kom al-Ahmar** deserves a mention even if visits aren't permitted.

Practicalities

Edfu is most easily reached on **excursions** arranged by hotels or travel agencies. In Luxor, Thomas Cook charges £E650 per person for Edfu, Kom

△ One of the Horus statues at the Temple of Horus

Ombo and Philae (see p.452), returning from Aswan by train; budget hotels ask £E200–300 (shared between passengers) for Edfu and Kom Ombo, ending in Aswan.

The **train station** is on the east bank of the Nile, 4km from the temple. **Buses** travelling between Aswan and Luxor drop passengers either there or on the highway, from where you'll need to catch a covered pick-up to the bridge and then another into town (each costs 25pt), or rent one for the entire journey to the main square (about £E5), five minutes' walk from the temple. Arriving by river is a different story, as **cruise boats** moor far from the temple, to be met by *calèches*. The ride costs £E15–20, depending on your bargaining skills. **Feluccas** are also moored away from the centre, so their passengers may have to use *calèches* too.

Sharia al-Maglis, Edfu's main street, leads past a **police** station and a **bank** (Mon–Thurs & Sun 8.30am–2pm) to a circular junction named **Temple Square**. Further along, the temple lies off the tourist bazaar; the **tourist police** are based at the site entrance. Edfu's fruit and vegetable souk occupies an area of Tahrir and Gumhorriya streets, with the former continuing south into a textiles souk, while Gumhorriya carries on past the **post office** (daily except Fri 8am–2.30pm).

Avoid staying in Edfu, as the *El-Madina* **hotel** (☎097/471-1326; ●) is utterly basic, though its owner is proud of his generous breakfasts. The *Zahrat el-Medina* **restaurant** on Sharia al-Maglis serves basic chicken and vegetable dishes, while *fuul* and grilled fish are available in the fruit and vegetable market.

Leaving Edfu, you can catch a **bus** from the terminal off Sharia Tahrir to Luxor (2hr; £E10) or Aswan (1hr 40min; £E7). Buses to Mersa Alam pick up passengers at a café by the start of the east bank desert road at 7.30am and 8.30am.

The Temple of Horus

The site of the **Temple of Horus** (daily: summer 6am–5pm; winter 7am–4pm; £E40) is a huge excavated compound overlooked by mud-brick houses and catcalling children. Ahead stretch the sandstone enclosure walls and towering pylon of the temple, which lay buried to its lintels until the 1860s, when Auguste Mariette cleared the main building; a splendid drawing by David Roberts shows the courtyard full of sand and peasant houses built atop the Hypostyle Hall. Yet the mammoth task of excavation was nothing compared to the temple's construction, which outlasted six Ptolemies, the final touches being added by the twelfth ruler of that dynasty. The reliefs and **inscriptions** on the walls include the myth of the struggle between Horus and Seth and an account of the temple's foundation-rituals, known to Egyptologists as the Edfu texts. You

417

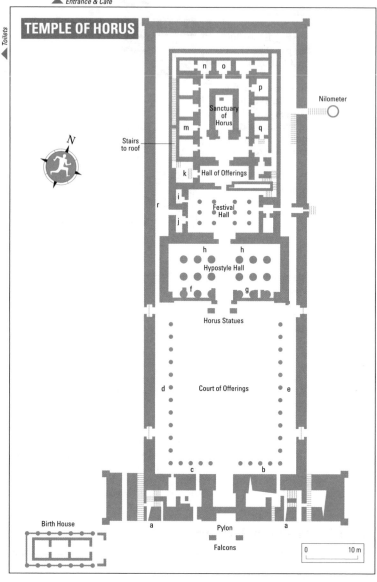

TEMPLE OF HORUS

Nilometer

n   o

p

Sanctuary
of
Horus

m   q

Stairs
to roof

k   Hall of Offerings

i

r   Festival
        Hall

j

h   h

Hypostyle Hall

f   g

Horus Statues

d   Court of Offerings   e

c   b

Birth House

a   Pylon   a

Falcons

0   10 m

can read them *in situ* using Dieter Kurth's annotated text, *Edfu Temple: A Guide by an Ancient Egyptian Priest* (see "Books" in Contexts).

Modern-day visitors approach the temple from the rear and have to walk its full length in order to enter through a gate in the pylon, fronted by two giant black-granite **falcons**. The **Pylon** was erected by Ptolemy IX before he was ousted from power by his brother Alexander, who was later usurped by another ruler, Neos Dionysos, depicted smiting foes before Horus the Elder **[a]**.

Entering the immense **Court of Offerings**, you can study the festival reliefs on the inner walls of the pylon, which continue around the court along the bottom of the wall. In the *Feast of the Beautiful Meeting*, Horus's barque tows Hathor's to the temple, where the deities retire to the sanctuary after suitable rituals **[b]**. Later they emerge from the temple, embark and drift downstream to the edge of the Edfu nome, where Horus takes his leave **[c]**. Beneath the western colonnade, Ptolemy IX makes offerings to Horus, Hathor and Ihy **[d]**; his successor appears before the Edfu Triad across the way **[e]**. However, most visitors are content to photograph the pair of **Horus statues** outside the Hypostyle Hall. One hawk stands higher than a man, the other lies legless in the dust.

The great **Hypostyle Hall** dates from the reign of Ptolemy VII (145–116 BC), known to his contemporaries as "Fatty". With a torch, you can examine two small rooms in the entrance wall: the Chamber of Consecrations, where the king or his priestly stand-in dressed for rituals **[f]**; and a Library of sacred texts adorned with a relief of Sheshat, the goddess of writing **[g]**. The reliefs showing the foundation of the temple and the deification of Horus **[h]** have been mutilated by iconoclasts. From here on you encounter the oldest section of the

The cult of Horus

Originally the sky-god of the Nile Valley, whose eyes were the sun and moon, the falcon deity **Horus** was soon assimilated into the Osirian myth as the child of Isis and Osiris (see p.454 and p.325). Raised in the swamps of the Delta by Isis and Hathor, Horus set out to avenge his father's murder by his uncle **Seth**. During their titanic struggle at Edfu, Horus lost an eye and Seth his testicles. Despite this, Seth almost prevailed until Isis intervened on her son's behalf and Osiris pronounced judgement upon them from the netherworld, exiling Seth back to the wilderness and awarding the throne to Horus. Thus good triumphed over evil and Osiris "lived" through his son.

▲ Horus

All pharaohs claimed to be the incarnation of Horus the "living king" and reaffirmed their divine oneness in an annual **Festival of Coronation**. A live falcon was taken from the sacred aviary, crowned in the central court and then placed in an inner chamber where it "reigned" in the dark for a year as the symbol of the living king. Another event, sometimes called the **Festival of Triumph**, commemorated the Contendings of Seth and Horus in a series of Mystery Plays. At the equally lavish **Feast of the Beautiful Meeting**, his wet nurse and wife Hathor sailed from Dendara aboard the *Lady of the Lake* to be met near Edfu by his own barque, *The First Horus*. Public ceremonies preceded their conjugal encounters in the privacy of the temple's sanctuary. Besides these festivals, Horus also underwent a reunion with the sun-disc at New Year, similar to Hathor's at Dendara.

To complicate the cult of Horus still further, he was also associated with the Divine Ennead of Heliopolis and another variant of the Creation myth. The Egyptians, having distinguished the Osirian Horus from the Heliopolitan deity by terming the latter **Horus the Elder**, split him into archetypes such as **Herakhte** (often conjoined with Re), **Hariesis** (stressing his kinship to Isis) and **Haroeris** (see p.422). His priesthood asserted a place for Horus in the Creation myth by crediting him with building the first house amid swamps at the dawn of the world, or even laying the Cosmic Egg whence the sun-god hatched. In rituals associated with the **Myth of the Great Cackler**, they launched a goose onto the sacred lake near Edfu Temple, whose egg contained air and the potential for life – crucial elements in the world's creation.

temple, begun by Ptolemy III in 237 BC and completed 25 years later by his son, who styled himself Philopator (Father Lover).

Try to imagine the shadowy halls during the annual festivals rhapsodized in temple texts, when the **Festival Hall** was decorated with faïence, strewn with flowers and herbs and perfumed by myrrh. Incense and unguents were blended according to recipes inscribed on the walls of the Laboratory **[i]**. Nonperishable offerings were stored in the room next door **[j]**, while libations, fruit and sacrificial animals were brought in through a passageway connected to the outside world.

The sacred barques of Horus and Hathor appear in glorious detail on either side of the doorway into the **Hall of Offerings**. During the New Year Festival, Horus was carried up the ascending stairway **[k]** to the rooftop; after being revitalized by the sun-disc, his statue was returned to the sanctuary via the descending stairway **[l]**. The ritual is depicted on the walls of both stairways, but you'll need a torch, and locked gates may prevent you from going far. Otherwise, carry on to the **Sanctuary of Horus**, containing a shrine of polished black granite and an offerings table. Reliefs on the lower half of the right-hand wall show Philopator entering the sanctuary and worshipping Horus, Hathor and his deified parents.

There are several chambers worth noting off the corridor surrounding the sanctuary. The Linen Room **[m]** is flanked by chapels to Min and the Throne of the Gods, while a suite nominally dedicated to Osiris contains colourful scenes of Horus receiving offerings **[n]**, a life-size replica of Horus's barque **[o]** and reliefs of his avatars **[p]**. Equally arresting is the **New Year Chapel**, with a blue-coloured relief of the sky-goddess Nut stretched across its ceiling **[q]**.

Returning to the Festival Hall, you can gain access to an external corridor running between the inner and outer walls, where the priesthood tallied tithes assessed on the basis of readings from the temple's own **Nilometer**. On the other side are tableaux from the Triumph of Horus over Seth, depicting Mystery Plays in which Seth was cast as a hippopotamus, lurking beneath his brother's boat **[r]**. At the end of the play, the priests cut up and ate a hippo-shaped cake, to destroy Seth completely.

On your way out, drop in at the colonnaded **Birth House**, a focus for the annual Coronation Festival re-enacting the divine birth of Horus and the reigning pharaoh. Around the back of the building are reliefs of Horus being suckled by Isis, both as a baby (low down on the rear wall) and as a young man (on the inside of the columns).

Around Edfu: El-Kab, Kom al-Ahmar and Silsilah

Fifteen kilometres downriver from Edfu, the east bank road between Luxor and Kom Ombo passes the site known as **EL-KAB**, once the ancient city of Nekheb, dedicated to the vulture-goddess of Upper Egypt. Opened to tourists in the late 1980s, the scattered ruins are less spectacular than other sites. Tickets are sold from a kiosk by the highway, which bisects the site. Buses from Aswan or Luxor can drop you there on request, but convoys don't stop there, and getting a ride out later could be difficult. If you happen to be aboard a felucca or *dahabiya*, ask to be let ashore to visit.

The most conspicuous part of the site (daily 7am–5pm; £E30) lies towards the Nile, where the vast mud-brick **walls** that once enclosed the city stand, along with the conjoined **temples** of Nekhbet and Thoth, now reduced to stumps of painted columns and a series of **crypts** (notable for a scene of baboons dancing to the rituals of Mut). Across the road and up the slope from the ticket office, other ruins are scattered eastwards across the desert. You may not fancy hiking 3.5km to a small

Chapel of Thoth and a Ptolemaic Temple of Nekhbet, but there are four **tombs** dug into the nearest ridge of hills. The best preserved is that of **Daheri**, royal scribe and tutor, and son of Tuthmosis I, which features ranks of lotus-sniffers and field workers. Next door are the tombs of commander **Ahmose**, who took part in the war to expel the Hyksos from Egypt and left a long account of his bravery; **Setau**, high priest of Nekhbet; and superintendent **Renini**.

On the far side of the Nile lies another site – **off-limits** to tourists – known as **Kom al-Ahmar** (Red Mound), which the Ancient Egyptians called Nekhen and the Greeks **Hierakonopolis** (City of the Falcon). As its names suggest, the city was closely associated with Horus and an earlier, local falcon-god, Nekheny. It flourished during the late predynastic and early dynastic periods (*c.*4000–2686 BC) and may have been the first administrative capital of the Two Lands, judging by such famous artefacts as the Palette of Narmer and the Scorpion Macehead – though vital evidence was lost during the first, poorly recorded excavation, which subsequent archeologists have tried to recover from other digs. Finds include Egypt's earliest cult-temple (a timber-framed structure fronted by cedar-wood pillars) and brewery (beer was one of the "four libations" offered to the gods). For news of current excavations by Reneé Friedman of the British Museum, see Ⓦwww.hierakonopolis.org and Ⓦwww.archaeology.org.

Travelling between Edfu and Kom Ombo by river, you'll pass a succession of ancient quarries, most notably at **Silsilah**, where the river is constricted by sheer cliffs and the bedrock changes from Egyptian limestone to Nubian sandstone. The site's ancient name, Khenu ("Place of Rowing"), suggests that rapids once existed here during the season of inundation. Feluccas and *dahabiyas* moor to let passengers explore the **quarries** on the east bank, reached by a narrow defile down which cut stones were dragged to waiting barges. Workmen's graffiti covers the rocks, while two formal inscriptions record the cutting of stone for Aten's temple at Karnak, and the reopening of the quarry in the 1900s to provide stone for the Esna Barrage. Across the Nile are 32 rock-hewn **shrines** dedicated to officials, priests, and pharaohs Merneptah and Horemheb – spotlit at night for the benefit of passing cruise boats.

Kom Ombo

Thirty kilometres before Aswan, the arid hills of the Eastern Desert recede from the river banks and bumper crops of sugar cane are harvested on reclaimed land. Many of the **Nubians** displaced by Lake Nasser have settled here around the town of **KOM OMBO**. In ancient times this stood at the crossroads of the caravan route from Nubia and trails from the gold mines of the Eastern Desert; under Ptolemy VI (180–145 BC), it became the capital of the Ombos nome and a training depot for African war elephants, which the Ptolemies required to fight the pachyderms of the Seleucid Empire.

While modern-day Kom Ombo is known to the *fellaheen* for its sugar refinery and felucca-building yards, tourists associate it with the Ptolemaic **Temple of Haroeris and Sobek**. Unlike other temples in the valley, this still stands beside the Nile, making the approach by river one of the highlights of a felucca journey or Nile cruise.

Practicalities

Kom Ombo lies along the east bank "highway" between Luxor (170km) and Aswan (45km), roughly 60km south of Edfu. Since the temple is 4km south of town, it's best to travel there directly in the convoy or arrive on a felucca or cruise boat. **Getting there** by public transport is a hassle; buses from Aswan (4–5 daily) can drop you at the signposted turn-off before town, from where you can walk or hitch 1700m to the temple. Otherwise, covered pick-ups (25pt) run from Kom Ombo to a ferry landing stage 800m north of the temple, or you can get a private taxi from town to the site for about £E10.

The local **police** aren't keen on tourists wandering around town and try to confine boat passengers to the vicinity of the temple, so **staying** in Kom Ombo is out of the question. In town, the *Restaurant El-Noba*, near the taxi depot, provides an alternative to **eating** at *fuul* and *taamiya* stands; near the temple are two outdoor tourist cafeterias. *Rural Home* has waterwheel irrigation, henna-tattooing and other diversions, while *Cafeteria Venus* serves burgers, *kofta* and beer. There's a kiosk by the Nile with **Internet** access and international phone lines.

The Temple of Haroeris and Sobek

The **Temple of Haroeris and Sobek** stands on a low promontory near a bend in the river whose sandbanks were a basking place for crocodiles in ancient times. This proximity to the Nile has both preserved and damaged the site (daily: summer 6am–5pm; winter 7am–4pm; £E25), covering the temple with sand which protected it from Coptic iconoclasts, but also washing away its pylon and forecourt, and undermining columns in the temple. What remains was aptly described by Amelia Edwards as a "magnificent torso"; truncated and roofless, it is still imposing, with traces of its original paint.

However, its main characteristic is its bisymmetry, with twin entrances and sanctuaries, and halls that are nominally divided down the middle. The left side is dedicated to the falcon-headed Haroeris, the "Good Doctor" (a form of Horus the Elder) and his consort Ta-Sent-Nefer, the "Good Sister" (an aspect of Hathor). The crocodile-god Sobek (here identified with the sun as Sobek-Re), his wife (another form of Hathor) and their son Khonsu-Hor are honoured on the right side of the temple.

Visitors approach the temple at right angles to its main axis, via an entrance by the **Gate of Neos Dionysos**. Only half of this gateway still stands and its provenance is obscure, as scholars disagree over the number, order and dates of the various Ptolemies, each of whom adopted a title such as Soter (Saviour), Euergetes (Benefactor) or Philometor (Mother Lover). Some identify Neos Dionysos as Ptolemy XII, others as Ptolemy XIII; however, there's general agreement that he fathered the great Cleopatra, had an interrupted reign (80–58 and 55–51 BC) and was nicknamed "The Bastard".

Before entering the temple you can pop into the **Chapel of Hathor** to see three **mummified crocodiles**, found nearby during roadworks in the 1970s.

The facade and Hypostyle Halls

With the forecourt (added by Trajan in 14 AD) reduced to low walls and stumps of pillars, your eyes are drawn to the **facade** of the Hypostyle Hall. Rising from a screen wall, its surviving columns burst in floral capitals beneath a chunk of cavetto cornice bearing a winged sun-disc and twin *uraei* above each portal. Bas-reliefs on the outer wall show Neos Dionysos being purified by Thoth and Horus **[a]**, and yet again in the presence of Sobek, whose face has been chiselled away **[b]**.

Wandering amid the thicket of columns inside the **outer Hypostyle Hall**, notice the heraldic lily of Upper Egypt or the papyrus symbol of the Delta carved on their bases. On the inner wall of the facade are splendid carvings of

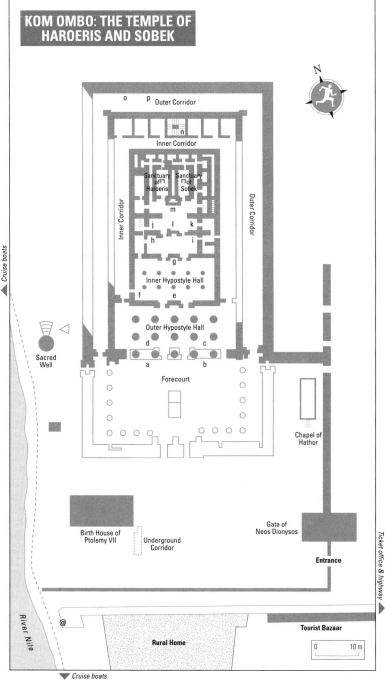

KOM OMBO: THE TEMPLE OF HAROERIS AND SOBEK

o   p   Outer Corridor

n

Inner Corridor

Sanctuary of Haroeris   Sanctuary of Sobek

Inner Corridor

m

j   l   k

h   i

g

Inner Hypostyle Hall

f   e

Outer Hypostyle Hall

d   c

a   b

Outer Corridor

Forecourt

Sacred Well

Cruise boats

Chapel of Hathor

Birth House of Ptolemy VII

Underground Corridor

Gate of Neos Dionysos

Entrance

Ticket office & highway

River Nile

@

Rural Home

Tourist Bazaar

0   10 m

Cruise boats

Neos Dionysos's coronation before Haroeris, Sobek, Wadjet and Nekhbet (the goddesses of the north and south) **[c]**, and his appearance before Isis, Horus the Elder and a lion-headed deity **[d]**. Neos Dionysos makes offerings to the same deities at the back of the hall, whose right side retains much of its roof, decorated with flying vultures.

Entering the older, **inner Hypostyle Hall**, you'll find a relief of Sobek in his reptilian form between the portals **[e]**. Ptolemy II receives the *hps* (sword of victory) from Haroeris (accompanied by his sister Cleopatra and his wife of the same name) in the southwest corner of the hall **[f]** and makes offerings to gods on the shafts of the pillars, while his elder brother does likewise to Haroeris at the back of the hall, where a list of temple deities and festivals appears between the doors **[g]**.

Vestibules and sanctuaries

Beyond lies the first of three, now roofless, **vestibules** (each of which sits a little higher than the preceding one) decorated by Ptolemy VI. Scenes at the back depict the foundation of the temple, with Sheshat, goddess of writing, measuring its dimensions **[h]**; and offerings and libations to Sobek **[i]**. To maintain the temple in a state of purity, these rituals were periodically repeated. Only priests were admitted to the next vestibule, which served as the **Hall of Offerings**. The ruined chamber to the right once held vestments and sacred texts, as at Edfu and Dendara. Offerings to Haroeris **[j]**, a description of the temple and an address to Sobek **[k]** appear on the southern wall, which also features a tiny relief of a woman giving birth, at roughly chest height **[l]**. Notice the painted vultures on the ceiling, too.

A fine relief between the doors of the sanctuaries **[m]** shows Ptolemy and his sister-wife being presented with a palm stalk from which hangs a Heb-Sed sign representing the years of his reign. Khonsu does the honours, wearing a blue crescent and red disc, followed by Haroeris and Sobek (representing air and water, respectively); Ptolemy himself sports a Macedonian cloak. Because so little remains of the **sanctuaries**, you can glimpse a secret corridor between them, whence the priests would "speak" for the gods; it's accessible via an underground crypt in one of the **shrines** behind the inner corridor **[n]**.

The outer corridor and precincts

In the **outer corridor** between the Ptolemaic temple and its Roman enclosure wall, pilgrims scratched graffiti on the pavements to while away the time before their appointment with the Good Doctor, who was represented by a statue in the small niche behind the central chapel. The carved ears heard their pleas and the eyes symbolized the health they sought. Though these carvings have been gouged away by suppliant fingers, other reliefs are in better shape. One shows Marcus Aurelius offering a pectoral cross to Ta-Sent-Nefer, the Good Sister (aka Sennuphis) **[o]**. The other testifies to sophisticated surgery nearly 2000 years ago, depicting instruments such as scalpels, suction cups, dental tools and bone saws **[p]** – though some scholars dismiss them as mere ritual instruments.

Finally, you can wander around the temple grounds, where other rituals were once enacted. The most intriguing structure is a finely built **Sacred Well** with two stairways descending to its depths (now out of bounds), which drew its water from the Nile. The small **pool** nearby was used for raising sacred crocodiles. Another curiosity is the partially exposed **underground corridor** leading to the **Birth House of Ptolemy VII** – or what's left of it since half the ruins fell into the Nile in the nineteenth century. A few reliefs are faintly visible, notably the scene of Ptolemy IX and two gods in a papyrus thicket, observed by an ithyphallic Min-Amun-Re clutching lettuces (which symbolize fertility).

Darow

Traditionally, **DAROW** (pronounced "De-*rao*") marks the point where Egypt shades into Nubia, a distinction underlined by its **camel market**, attended by tribesmen from the northern deserts of Sudan, and by a remarkable Nubian house called the **Beit al-Kenzi**. Darow itself is a ramshackle sprawl of mud-brick compounds either side of the highway and railway line. Though it's not a stopover for convoys or taxi excursions, **getting there** is straightforward, as almost all trains except sleepers call here. Private taxis in Darow might agree to take you to Kom Ombo Temple and back for £E20–30.

Darow Camel Market

The **Camel Market** (Souk el-Gamal) happens every Tuesday throughout the year, and maybe also on Sundays or Mondays over winter. Although hours (7am–2pm) remain constant, with activities winding down after 11am, the location of the market changes seasonally. Over winter, it's often held in two dusty compounds on the eastern outskirts of Darow (fifteen minutes' walk from the main intersection; cross the bridge, walk on past the cane fields and turn right down a lane flanked by mud-brick walls). During summer, it may take place on the other side of town beyond the fruit, vegetable and poultry souk – just follow the crowds. The giveaway is truckloads of camels bumping hither and thither along a dusty lane.

At the end you'll find several hundred camels with their forelegs hobbled in the traditional manner, and scores of drovers and buyers drinking tea and smoking *sheeshas* beneath awnings. As the principal camel market between Dongola and Cairo, Darow is a good place to do business. The camels spend two days in quarantine before being sold to *fellaheen* who need a beast of burden, or merchants who plan to sell the camels for a profit at Cairo's Birqesh market. Many are destined to end up on the dinner tables of the poor, or in a knackers' yard.

The Souk el-Gamal coincides with a **livestock market** where donkeys, sheep and cows jostle for space with people and trucks amid trampled mud

---

The last Forty Days Road

The camel trail from northern Sudan to Upper Egypt is one of the last great desert droving routes still active. The camels are reared in Sudan's Darfur and Kordofan provinces and herded 300–400km eastwards across the Libyan Desert to Dongola on the Nile, whence they follow the river into Egypt. Herdsmen call this month-long route the **Forty Days Road** (Darb al-Arba'in), perhaps from folk memory of the old slave trail from Kobbé to Assyut (see p.538), which was even longer and harder.

Now, as then, the drovers are usually Bishari or Rizayqat nomads, who sometimes appear at Egyptian markets in their traditional garb of flowing trousers, woollen cloak, dagger and sword. The camel owners are town-dwelling Sudanese merchants who fly up to supervise the sale, on which they can expect to make a profit of 500 percent. Some traders manage to avoid paying import tax by smuggling camels into Egypt and feeding them marijuana to keep them quiet while sneaking past border patrols.

and dung. In summer, the two markets are often held side by side, with **handicrafts** (as well as saddlery) also sometimes sold at the camel market throughout the winter.

Beit al-Kenzi

A cooler attraction is the **Beit al-Kenzi** – a fabulous house in the traditional Nubian style, built of mud-bricks and dom palms, with beehive domes, inner courtyards and spacious rooms divided by reed-lattice partitions, to allow air to circulate. Its rooms are furnished with Nubian artefacts and the exterior decorated with geometric patterns and ceramic plates. The house was built in 1912 by the grandfather of its present occupant so that his descendants would retain something of the ancestral village that was sacrificed to the first Aswan Dam. Its owner, Aid Mohammed Hassanein, is happy to show visitors around and talk about Nubian culture – indeed, he regrets that more tourists don't come. The house is beside the Gar Rasoul Mosque on Sharia al-Kunuz; turn right outside the train station, walk along the road and head left to find it.

Aswan and around

Egypt's southernmost city and ancient frontier town has the loveliest setting on the Nile. At **ASWAN** the deserts close in on the river, confining its sparkling blue between smooth amber sand and rugged extrusions of granite bedrock. Lateen-sailed feluccas glide past the ancient ruins and gargantuan rocks of Elephantine Island, palms and tropical shrubs softening the islands and embankments till intense blue skies fade into soft-focus dusks. The city's **ambience** is palpably African; its Nubian inhabitants are lither and darker than the Saiyidis, with different tastes and customs.

Although its own monuments are insignificant compared to Luxor's, Aswan is the base for **excursions** to the **temples of Philae and Kabasha**, near the great dams beyond the First Cataract, and the Sun Temple of Ramses II at **Abu Simbel**, far to the south. It can also serve for day-trips to Darow Camel Market, Kom Ombo, Edfu and Esna – the main temples between here and Luxor. But the classic approach is to travel upriver by felucca, experiencing the Nile's moods and scenery as travellers have for millennia – or on a luxurious cruise. The ins-and-outs of **felucca journeys**, **dahabiyas** and **Nile cruises** are described on pp.316–321. However, Aswan itself is so laid-back that one could easily spend time here hanging out, never mind going anywhere – though many people try to pack everything into two days. The local **tourism** scene is similar to that in Luxor, though rather more straitlaced (see box on pp.337).

Situated near the Tropic of Cancer, Aswan is hot and dry nearly all the time, with average daily **temperatures** ranging from a delicious 23–30°C in the winter to a searing 38–54°C over summer. In late January and early February, hordes of Egyptians visit Aswan, block-booking hotels and seats on trains from Luxor and Cairo. Late autumn and spring are the perfect times to visit, being less crowded than the peak winter period, yet not so enervating as summer (May–Oct), when long siestas, cold showers and air conditioning are essential and nocturnal **power cuts** not only deprive you of cooling and lighting, but mean that food may go bad in fridges overnight.

Some history

Elephantine Island – opposite modern Aswan in the Nile – has been settled since remotest antiquity, and its fortress-town of Yebu became the border post between Egypt and Nubia early in the Old Kingdom. Local governors, or "Guardians of the Southern Gates", were responsible for border security and trade with Nubia, for huge quarries for fine red granite, and mining of amethysts, quartzite, copper, tin and malachite in the desert hinterland. Military outposts further south could summon help from the Yebu garrison by signal fires and an Egyptian fleet patrolled the river between the First and Second Cataracts.

Besides this, Yebu was an important cult centre, for the Egyptians believed that the Nile welled up from subterranean caverns at the **First Cataract**, just upriver (see p.447). Its local **deities** were Hapy and Satet, god of the Nile flood and goddess of its fertility, though the region's largest temple honoured Khnum, the provincial deity (see p.415).

During settled periods, the vast trade in ivory, slaves, gold, silver, incense, exotic animal skins and feathers spawned a **market town** on the east bank (slightly south of modern Aswan, its linear descendant), but the island remained paramount throughout classical times, when it was known by its Greek appellation, Seyene. In the Ptolemaic era, the Alexandrian geographer **Eratosthenes** (276–196 BC) heard of a local well into which the sun's rays fell perpendicularly at midday on the summer solstice, leaving no shadow; from this he deduced that Seyene lay on the Tropic of Cancer, concluded that the world was round and calculated its diameter with nearly modern accuracy – being only 80km out. (Since that time, the Tropic of Cancer has moved further south.)

The potency of the **cult of Isis** at nearby **Philae** (see p.452) made this one of the last parts of Egypt to be affected by **Christianity**, but once converted it became a stronghold of the faith. From their desert Monastery of St Simeon, monks made forays into Nubia, eventually converting the local Nobatae, who returned the favour by helping them to resist Islamic rule through Fatimid times, until finally subjugated by Salah al-Din. However, Bedouin raiders persisted through to 1517, when Sultan Selim garrisoned an entire army here, by which time the town's name had changed from Coptic Sawan to its present form, and the population had embraced **Islam**.

From the early nineteenth century onwards, Aswan was the base for the conquest of the Sudan and the defeat of the Mahadist Uprising (1881–98) by Anglo-Egyptian forces. As British influence grew, it also became the favourite **winter resort** of rich, ailing Europeans, who flocked to Aswan for its dry heat and therapeutic hot sands, luxurious hotels and stunning scenery, spiced with the thrill of being "at the edge of civilization". Its final transformation into the Aswan of today owes to the building of the **High Dam**, 15km upriver, which flooded Nubia, compelling its inhabitants to settle in new villages built around Kom Ombo and Aswan itself, which is now predominantly Nubian. To assert its identity, the city has established an **Africa University** for the study of African science and culture, and a **Nubia Museum** tracing the Nubians' history.

Arrival, information and transport

From **Aswan airport**, 23km south of town, you can get a taxi into the centre for about £E25 (agree the price first). The **train station** is in the north of town, five minutes' walk from the Corniche or the bazaar quarter. The inter-city **bus station** and main **service taxi** depot are both 3km north of town,

Nubia and the Nubians

Nubia and Egypt have been neighbours since time immemorial. The Egyptians called Nubia Ta-Seti (Land of the Bow), after the weapons for which the Nubians were renowned, while its modern name is thought to derive from *nbw*, the ancient word for gold, which was mined there until Greco-Roman times.

A Nilotic people living between the First and Sixth Cataracts of the Nile (roughly from Aswan to Khartoum) may have been the forerunners of Egypt's civilization. Archeologists have found exquisite figurines and other funerary objects at sites dating from at least 8000 BC – predating prehistoric finds in Egypt by three thousand years – and the **world's oldest solar calendar** of standing stones, dating from around 6000 BC, at **Nabta Playa**, 100km from Abu Simbel (see box on p.462). Pharaonic and Ancient Nubian civilization seem to have evolved in similar ways until 3500 BC, when Egypt's unification raised the Old Kingdom to a level from which it could exploit Nubia as a source of **mineral wealth**, exotic goods and **slaves** – a pattern that was to last nearly 5000 years. Although the collapse of centralized authority allowed Nubia to reassert its independence during the First Intermediate Period, the onset of the Middle Kingdom saw the annexation of Lower Nubia – the land between the First and Second Cataracts of the Nile – and a chain of mud-brick **fortresses** built to safeguard trade; while under the New Kingdom, Nubia was divided into nomes and ruled by a viceroy entitled the King's Son of **Kush** (Kush being its southern province), aided by the priesthood of cult-**temples**. It was only in the Third Intermediate Period that Nubia got its own back, as the local rulers of **Napata** took advantage of Egypt's disunity to invade and establish their own **Kushite Dynasty** of pharaohs (747–656 BC), who reigned as their Egyptian predecessors had done until the Assyrian invasion of Egypt in 671 BC.

Re-consolidating itself beyond the Fourth Cataract, the Kushite **Kingdom of Meröe** marked the apogee of Nubian civilization; its remarkable pyramids are only now being studied properly. Meröe maintained amicable relations with most of the Ptolemies but angered the Romans by supporting an Egyptian revolt against Emperor Augustus. In 23 AD the Romans invaded Lower Nubia and garrisoned it as the pharaohs had. While this posed little threat to Meröe, the Roman exit-strategy proved fatal. Before withdrawing in 272, they invited warriors whom they called the **Nobatae** (perhaps Nuba from the Red Sea Hills of Sudan) to fill the vacuum. The Nobatae not only held their new land but seized more, as Meröe was unable to resist both them and fierce desert tribes known as the **Blemmyes** (maybe the ancestors of today's Beja) who raided Egypt as far north as the Fayoum. As Meröe declined, a new principality called **Ballana** arose circa 350 and endured until about 700; its tumuli contain both mummified horses and human sacrifices. In the seventh century the Nobatae were converted to Christianity by monks from Aswan's Monastery of St Simeon, and subsequently became the main bulwark against attacks by the Islamic rulers of Egypt during the twelfth and thirteenth centuries, until in 1315 the last Christian king was replaced by a Muslim one and most of the population accepted Islam.

Caliphs, sultans and Mamlukes made little attempt to control Nubia so long as it remained a "corridor to Africa" and supplied the ivory, slaves and exotica that they prized, until **Mohammed Ali** visited devastation on Nubia when he sent his son Ibrahim to enslave its male population as cannon fodder for his new army. Resentment smouldered through the reigns of khedives Abbas, Ismail and Tewfiq, drawing in the **British**, who began by supporting their forces and ended up underwriting an

near the Nile, a short ride by minibus (25pt) or taxi (£E5). As in Luxor, **cruise boats** currently dock along the Corniche in the centre, but will eventually be shifted to new moorings to the north of town.

Anglo-Egyptian government in 1899, when the border between Egypt and Sudan was drawn 40km north of Wadi Halfa and Nubia was divided, yet again.

Meanwhile, the **Nubians** remained true to their ancestral homeland. Traditional life centred round **villages** of extended families, each with its own compound of domed houses. The people made a livelihood farming the verges of the river, planting date palms, corn and *durra* melons, as well as fishing and transporting trade goods. Socially and spiritually, the Nile formed the basis of their existence. The whole village celebrated births, weddings and circumcision ceremonies with Nile rituals and, despite converting first to Christianity and then to Islam, retained a belief in water spirits, petitioning them for favours, while also brewing beer and date wine.

This way of life – which had existed pretty much unchanged for five millennia – was shattered by the **Aswan Dams**. The first dam, built in 1902 and successively raised, forced the Nubians to move onto higher, unfertile ground. Unable to subsist on agriculture, many of the menfolk left for Cairo and the cities, sending back remittances to keep the villages going. With construction of the High Dam, the Nubians' traditional homeland was entirely submerged, displacing the entire 800,000-strong community. Around half of them moved north, settling around Aswan and Kom Ombo, where the government provided homes and assistance with agriculture and irrigation. The rest were repatriated to Sudan, where many ended up in the Kassala/ New Halfa area, 1500km to the south. Meanwhile the **ancient monuments** of Nubia were moved to higher ground or foreign museums, under a huge program co-ordinated by UNESCO.

In Egypt, the **Nubian community** has done well. Many have taken advantage of higher education and business opportunities, making their mark in government, commerce and tourism. Others from the first wave of emigration continue to provide the backbone of Cairo's janitors and servants; Nubians as a whole have always been noted for their honesty and reliability. Remarkably, the community has maintained its cultural identity, with the resettled villages (which took their old names) acting as guardians of tradition.

The Nubian **language** is still spoken, but not written; its ancestor Old Nubian was recorded in a modified Greek alphabet (also used for Old Coptic texts, though the two languages were quite different). Some scholars maintain that the Nubian alphabet has 26 letters, others 30. Among **websites** are devoted to Nubian history and culture are ⓦwww.homestead.com/wysinger/nubians.html (for prehistory and the pyramids of Nubia), ⓦwww.thenubian.net (for cultural commentaries) and ⓦwww.napata.org (with recordings of spoken Nubian, contemporary and traditional music).

A few Nubian phrases

In the list below, accents indicate stress.

Er raigráy? or *er-minnabóu?*	How are you? (to a man or woman)
Ai raigérry	I'm fine
Ekináira?	What's your name?
Aigi …	My name is … (followed by -*era*)
Er fárdiray?	Are you busy?
Tégus	Sit down
Er wenáyseso	I am honoured
Asálgi	Tomorrow
Ena fiadr	Goodbye

The **tourist office** (daily: summer 8am–3pm & 7–9pm; winter 8am–3pm & 6–8pm; Ramadan 10am–2pm & 7–9pm, closed midday Fri; ⓣ & ⓕ097/231-2811) is housed in a domed Nubian-style building outside the station. Shukri

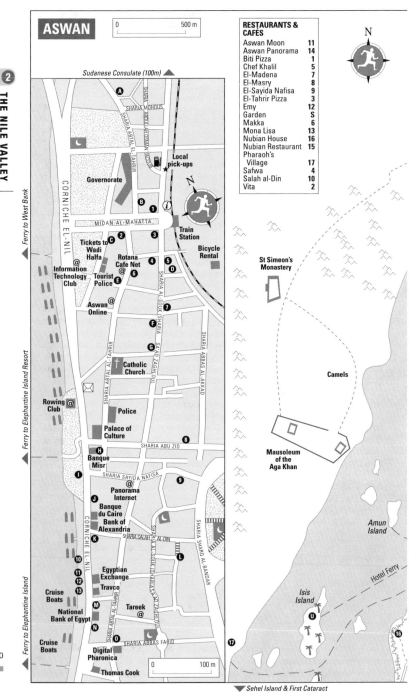

ASWAN

0   500 m

RESTAURANTS & CAFÉS

Aswan Moon	11
Aswan Panorama	14
Biti Pizza	1
Chef Khalil	5
El-Madena	7
El-Masry	8
El-Sayida Nafisa	9
El-Tahrir Pizza	3
Emy	12
Garden	S
Makka	6
Mona Lisa	13
Nubian House	16
Nubian Restaurant	15
Pharaoh's Village	17
Safwa	4
Salah al-Din	10
Vita	2

N

Sudanese Consulate (100m)

SHARIA MOHDUS.

SHARIA ABDUL ATOSMAN

SHARIA ABTAL EL-TAHIR

A

Ferry to West Bank

CORNICHE EL-NIL

Governorate

Local pick-ups

N

B **1**

i

MIDAN AL-MAHATTA

C **2** **3**

Tickets to Wadi Halfa

@

Information Technology Club

Rotana Cafe Net

@

Tourist Police

E

4 **5**

D

Train Station

Bicycle Rental

St Simeon's Monastery

@

Aswan Online

6

SHARIA AL-SOUK

F **7**

SHARIA SAAD ZAGHLOUL

SHARIA ABBAS AL-AKKAD

G

Catholic Church

SHARIA ABTAL AL-TAHIR

Ferry to Elephantine Island Resort

Rowing Club

@

Police

Palace of Culture

SHARIA ABU ZID

8

Camels

H

Banque Misr

SHARIA SAYIDA NAFISA

@

Panorama Internet

9

Mausoleum of the Aga Khan

I

J

Banque du Caire

Bank of Alexandria

SHARIA SALAH AL-DIN

SHARIA AL-SOUK (SHARIA AL-ZAGHLOUL)

SHARIA SHARQ AL-BANDAR

K

L

Amun Island

CORNICHE EL-NIL

10

Egyptian Exchange

11

12

Travco

13

Cruise Boats

National Bank of Egypt

M

Tareek

@

SHARIA ABTAL AL-TAHIR

N

Hotel Ferry

Isis Island

Cruise Boats

O

SHARIA ABBAS FARID

17

0   100 m

Digital Pharonica

Thomas Cook

U

16

Ferry to Elephantine Island

Sehel Island & First Cataract

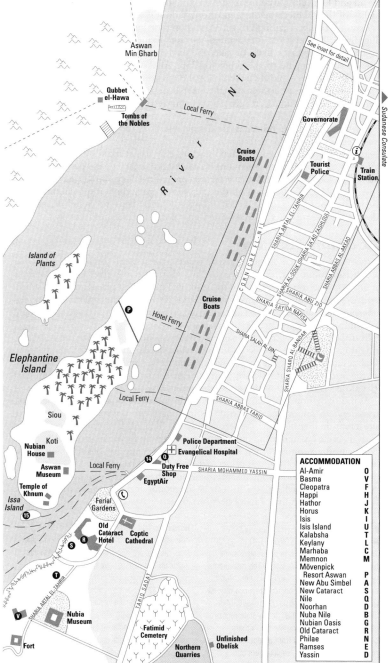

Aswan
Min Gharb

Qubbet
el-Hawa

Tombs of
the Nobles

Local Ferry

Governorate

Sudanese Consulate

Cruise
Boats

Tourist
Police

Train
Station

R
i
v
e
r
N
i
l
e

CORNICHE EL-NIL

SHARIA ABTAL EL-TAHRIR

SHARIA AL-SOUK (SHARIA SAAD ZAGHLOUL)

SHARIA ABBAS AL-AKKAD

Island of
Plants

Cruise
Boats

Hotel Ferry

SHARIA ABU ZID

SHARIA SAYIDA NAFISA

Elephantine
Island

SHARIA SALAH AL-DIN

SHARIA SHARDI AL-BANDAR

Local Ferry

SHARIA ABBAS FARID

Siou

Koti

Nubian
House

Aswan
Museum

Police Department

Evangelical Hospital

Temple of
Khnum

Issa
Island

Local Ferry

Duty Free
Shop

EgyptAir

SHARIA MOHAMMED YASSIN

14

Q

Ferial
Gardens

Old
Cataract
Hotel

Coptic
Cathedral

S

R

T

15

V

Nubia
Museum

SHARIA ABTAL EL-TAHRIR

TARIQ SADAT

Fort

Fatimid
Cemetery

Northern
Quarries

Unfinished
Obelisk

ACCOMMODATION	
Al-Amir	O
Basma	V
Cleopatra	F
Happi	H
Hathor	J
Horus	K
Isis	I
Isis Island	U
Kalabsha	T
Keylany	L
Marhaba	C
Memnon	M
Mövenpick	
Resort Aswan	P
New Abu Simbel	A
New Cataract	S
Nile	Q
Noorhan	D
Nuba Nile	B
Nubian Oasis	G
Old Cataract	R
Philae	N
Ramses	E
Yassin	D

431

Sa'ad and Hakeem Hussein can answer just about any question, but the impartiality of their felucca recommendations is doubtful.

Aswan is compact enough to get around on foot, but if you are burdened with luggage or bound for a distant hotel, you may want to rent a **taxi** or **calèche** (£E5; agree the price first), or take one of the **minibuses** that run from one end of the Corniche to the other for 25pt. All Aswan's nearby attractions are accessible by river – mostly by felucca – though you may want to rent a **bicycle** from the *Mona Lisa* on the Corniche, or the shop on the far side of the railway footbridge, for about £E15 a day, to cycle out to the Unfinished Obelisk or the Sculpture Park.

For better or worse, **feluccas** are inseparable from the Aswan experience. It's wonderfully relaxing to drift downstream while egrets swoop overhead, or tack between rocky islands; on the downside, it's easy to get irked by boatmen who fritter away time before demanding baksheesh, or weary of the persistent touts along the Corniche. The *Keylany Hotel's* charge for felucca hire (£E20/hr) is as low as you'd get by haggling on the spot; prices are highest at the landing stage beneath the *Old Cataract Hotel*. (Longer felucca trips to Sehel Island, or downriver towards Luxor, are covered on p.446 and p.319 respectively.)

Accommodation

Aswan's hotel scene is quite static; many places seem stuck in the 1970s. **Location** counts for much: hotels on the Corniche may have fabulous views, if not from the rooms, then from the rooftop. The poshest places are at the south end of the Corniche, or on private islands. Hotels in the bazaar tend to be cheaper and noisier. The least attractive area is north of the train station, though a couple of the hotels here are fine.

Standards vary within the same category; a hotel with two (or no) stars might be better than a place with three. Most hotels on the Corniche charge a higher rate for Nile-view rooms, which tend to be larger and better than rooms at the back. **Air conditioning** (or at least a fan) is an essential in summer. **Breakfast** is included in the rate unless otherwise stated.

As in Luxor, hotels face stiff competition from **cruise boats**, and independent travellers are importuned by **touts** (some board the train at Kom Ombo, to pre-empt their rivals). The squeeze is only felt (if at all) from mid-December to early February, when some hotels are booked up by Egyptian groups; the nadir comes in the summer, when most places are desperate for business and many offer **reductions** of up to fifty percent after a bit of haggling.

In many budget hotels guests are subjected to **pressure** to sign up for minibus or felucca trips. Such excursions can be an economical way to see the sites, but don't be railroaded into a hasty decision.

Budget

Happi Off the Corniche ☎097/231-4115, ⓕ230-7572. Decent a/c rooms with bathrooms; some have TV, balconies and Nile views. The restaurant, which faces Elephantine Island, sells beer. Guests can use the *Cleopatra's* pool for a reduced rate. ❷

Hathor Corniche el-Nil ☎097/231-4580. Midway along the Corniche, this has 36 en-suite rooms of varying sizes, some facing the Nile, others gloomy; a/c is controlled from reception. The rooftop has a small pool, sunloungers and splendid Nile views. ❷

Horus Corniche el-Nil ☎ & ⓕ097/231-3313. Their renovated Nile-facing rooms have bathrooms and fans; the rest are much tattier. The bar-restaurant, nightclub and rooftop have great views, but you might be kept awake by bellydancing after midnight. ❷

🏃 **Keylany** Sharia Keylany ☎097/231-7332 or 012 786-6940, ⓦwww.keylanyhotel .com. This friendly hotel off the bazaar has rooms with fans, a/c, soft beds and spotless bathrooms; WiFi, an Internet café and an attractive rooftop with a tiny pool, where pancakes are served for breakfast and Columbian coffee brewed to order. Their felucca trips and excursions are good value. ❷

Memnon Corniche el-Nil, above the National Bank; entrance via a back alley ☏ 097/230-0483. A cleanish two-star, with a/c, soft beds and a small pool on the roof, which lacks shade. ❷

New Abu Simbel Sharia Abtal al-Tahrir ☏ 097/230-6096. In the northern part of town, a 10min walk from the station. Carpeted a/c rooms with baths and hard beds; some have Nile views and balconies, fridges, TV or double beds. The large garden is a bonus. ❷

Noorhan Off Sharia al-Souk ☏ 097/231-6069. Five minutes' walk from the station, this much-hustled place has shabby, clean-ish rooms with fans, or a/c and bathrooms (£E10 extra). Internet access and beer available; breakfast not included. Staff aggressively promote tours. ❶

🏃 **Nuba Nile** Off Midan al-Mahatta ☏ 097/231-3267, ✉ nobanile_hotel @hotmail.com. A good option near the station, family-run and ultra clean. Its en-suite rooms come in all shapes and sizes – ask to see a few before choosing. Most have a/c. ❷

Nubian Oasis Off Sharia al-Souk ☏ 097/231-2123 or 012 248-7175, ☏ 097/231-2124, ✉ nubianoasis_hotel_aswan@hotmail.com. A multistorey backpackers' haunt with grungy a/c rooms (bathroom £E5 extra), Internet access, laundry service and tepid beer. Guests are hassled to sign up for excursions. ❶

Philae Corniche el-Nil ☏ 097/231-2090, ☏ 232-4089. This could be a good choice once renovations on the upper floors are finished; the first floor suffers from street noise. Private bathrooms and a/c throughout; Nile-facing rooms cost £E10 extra. No rooftop. ❷

🏃 **Ramses** Sharia Abtal al-Tahrir ☏ 097/230-4000, ☏ 231-5701. This centrally located tower block covered in mock-pharaonic carvings has small en-suite rooms with a/c and satellite TV (some overlooking the Tombs of the Nobles), plus a restaurant, bar and laundry service. ❷

Yassin Off Sharia al-Souk ☏ 097/230-7753. Next door to the *Noorhan*, this rival no-star is a bit smarter, but within earshot of the train tracks. The best rooms (with a/c and bathroom) are on the third floor. Laundry service. Staff can be pushy about selling tours. ❶

Mid-range

Al-Amir Sharia Abbas Farid ☏ 097/231-4732, ☏ 230-4411. One street back from the Corniche, this small three-star hotel is mainly aimed at Gulf Arabs, who presumably don't mind being awoken

by the mosque next door. The rooms are comfy, with a/c and phone. ❸

Cleopatra Sharia al-Souk ☏ 097/231-4001, ☏ 231-4002, ⓦ www.cleopatraaswan.com. Centrally located, with a rooftop pool (overlooked by taller buildings), but rooms are dingy and overpriced compared to such nearby rivals as the *Ramses* (see above) or *Marhaba* (see below). ❻

Kalabsha Sharia Abtal al-Tahrir ☏ 097/230-2666, ☏ 230-5974, ✉ kalabshahotel@yahoo.com. Uphill from the southern end of the Corniche, this tower block is far less classy than its four-star neighbours, though it does have a small pool and some rooms with a superb view of the First Cataract. ❼

🏃 **Marhaba** Off the Corniche near Midan al-Mahatta ☏ 097/233-0102, ☏ 233-0105, ✉ marhabaaswan@yahoo.com. A mock-pharaonic pile with tastefully decorated a/c rooms facing the Nile, and a fabulous rooftop. Their buffet breakfast is a treat. ❻

🏃 **Nile** Corniche el-Nil, near EgyptAir ☏ & ☏ 097/231-4222. The best-value option in this range, its spacious a/c rooms have Nile views, satellite TV and fridges. Internet access and book exchange. ❸

Upmarket

🏃 **Basma** On the hillside above the *Old Cataract* ☏ 097/231-0901, ☏ 231-0907, ⓦ www.basmahotel.com. This four-star complex has a large heated pool and a garden terrace with stunning views of the southern end of Elephantine, but is best avoided during the sculpture symposium due to the noise outside. Disabled access. Free bus from the *Isis* at quarter past every hour. ❼

Isis Midway along the Corniche ☏ 097/231-5100, ☏ 231-5500. A shabby mini-resort with faded a/c bungalows in a small garden with a pool, plus an Italian restaurant and a nightclub with bellydancing. Its best feature is its prime location facing Elephantine Island. ❼

🏃 **Isis Island** Upriver from Aswan ☏ 097/231-7400, ☏ 231-7405, ⓦ www.pyramisaegypt .com. Owned by Ala Mubarak, the President's elder son, this five-star colossus was built beside a nature reserve containing the only primordial Nilotic vegetation left in Egypt. It has rooms and chalets, two pools, a health club, mini-golf and a kids' zoo. It's reached by a 24hr launch from the docks near EgyptAir. ❼

🏃 **Mövenpick Resort Aswan** Elephantine Island ☏ 097/230-3455, ⓦ www .movenpick-hotels.com. It looks like an airport control tower, but the gardens and views are lovely, and the pool and spa worthy of its five-star rating. Nile-view rooms from $90, deluxe villas from $370.

Reached by a 24hr free ferry done up like a pharaonic barge, from near the *Isis*. ❼
New Cataract By the Ferial Gardens ☎097/231-6000, ⓕ231-6011. This refurbished a/c block (built by the Soviets in the 1960s) features a disco, bar, restaurants and shops, tennis courts and a big pool. ❼
Old Cataract By the Ferial Gardens ☎097/231-6000, ⓕ231-6011, ⓦwww.sofitel.com. A splendid Edwardian-Moorish relic, tastefully refurbished and jealously guarded against interlopers. Its river-facing rooms have glorious views and the others overlook a fine garden with a heated pool, but many complain that the food and service don't match the high prices (from $230). ❽

The Town

Ignoring the residential and industrial suburbs (as every tourist does) greatly simplifies **orientation**. Although Aswan's **Corniche** follows the river bank for more than 4km, most things worth noting lie along the 1500-metre stretch between the Rowing Club and **Ferial Gardens,** where the road swings inland past the *Old Cataract Hotel* and uphill to the **Nubia Museum**. Otherwise, the main focus of interest is **Sharia al-Souk**, the **bazaar** that runs two to three blocks inland all the way from the train station down to Sharia Abbas Farid, roughly paralleled by **Sharia Abtal al-Tahrir**, which is far less touristy; lined with grocers' stores, bakeries and cafes, it gets leafier by the colonial-style police station near Sharia Abu Zid, the main intersection leading to the Nile. Beyond this it shrinks to a narrow backstreet before transforming itself into the avenue to the Nubia Museum. Note that not all the streets off the bazaar appear on our map of town, and some areas are being demolished to create wider roads.

The bazaar and Corniche

Aswan's **bazaar** is renowned as the best in Egypt outside Cairo, both for its wares and its atmosphere. Unlike Luxor's bazaar, it has retained its character after a recent makeover, with tiled paving instead of broken cobblestones, more uniform shopfronts, and fewer street vendors to impede tourists. Souvenirs, jewellery, basketwork and piles of spices vie for attention starting a few blocks from the train station, all the way down to Sharia Saiyida Nafisa, beyond which fruit and veg sellers, ironmongers and other merchants take over. Popular buys include colourful **Nubian skullcaps** or long scarves; heavier, woven **shawls**; or **baskets** and **trays**, some semi-antique and others new. **Galabiyyas** and embroidered Nubian robes can be bought off the peg or tailored to order; try Metry Tawdros Mansour on Sharia Saiyida Nafisa. For contemporary and antique Bedouin and Nubian **jewellery**, check out the Butterfly Bazaar at 208 Sharia al-Souk. Pyramids or baskets of **spices** and dyes are another eye-catching feature; dried **hibiscus** (used to make *karkaday*), indigo dye and what is labelled as "saffron" are common tourist purchases. Aswan is also famous for its peanuts and its **henna** powder, sold in different grades.

Aswan's **Corniche** is the finest in Egypt, less for its architecture than for the superb vista of Elephantine Island, and feluccas gliding over the water like quill pens across papyrus, with the tawny wastes of the Western Desert on the far bank. If the view from riverside restaurants is spoilt by diesel-belching cruise boats moored alongside, you can enjoy the sunset from the rockbound **Ferial Gardens** (daily 9am–11pm; £E5) or the terrace of the **Old Cataract Hotel** (featured in the movie *Death on the Nile*), which afford a sublime view of the southern end of **Elephantine Island** and the smaller islands beyond – although the hotel relegates non-residents to a lower terrace and levies £E55 minimum charge to discourage rubberneckers.

△ Dates and other foodstuffs on sale in the bazaar

2

THE NILE VALLEY | Aswan and around

The Nubia Museum

Aswan's **Nubia Museum** (daily: summer 6am–10pm; winter 9am–1pm & 5–9pm; Ramadan 9am–3pm; £E35) has been widely acclaimed, delighting its sponsors, UNESCO, and posthumously crowning the career of its architect, the late Mohammed al-Hakim. Opened in 1998 after fifteen years on the drawing board, it's housed in an impressive modern building, loosely based on traditional Nubian architecture and faced in limestone, surrounded by landscaped grounds. It displays some 5000 artefacts, excellently organized and clearly labelled in English, making it a "must see" introduction to the history and culture of the Nubians; for a preview check out ⓦ www.numibia.net/nubia.

At the entrance to the main hall, a scale model of the Nile Valley shows the magnitude of the Nilotic civilizations and their architectural achievements. The exhibits lead you from prehistory through the kingdoms of Kush and Meröe into Christian and Islamic eras, until the drowning of Nubia beneath Lake Nasser and the salvage of its ancient monuments by UNESCO. Among the highlights are a quartzite statue of a Kushite priest of Amun, an eight-metre-high Ramses II, horse-armour from the Ballana tombs and frescoes from the Coptic churches of Nubia. There are also life-size models of traditional Nubian

435
▬

houses and photographs of the mud-brick fortresses, churches and cemeteries that were abandoned to the rising waters of Lake Nasser as the temples were moved to higher land.

In the grounds are further monuments and exhibits, including the mausoleum of 77 *wali* (sheikhs), a traditional Nubian house, and a cave containing prehistoric rock art removed from now inundated areas. An artificial watercourse runs through the corner of the grounds nearest the main road, attractively spotlit at night.

The museum is about 500m uphill beyond the *Old Cataract*, about thirty minutes' walk from the town centre (£E10 by taxi). If you've still got some energy after the museum, you can trek uphill past the *Basma Hotel* to find a derelict mud-brick **fort** with a watchtower, built in Mohammed Ali's time (now off-limits as a military zone), and a vantage point overlooking the Fatimid Cemetery (see p.445).

Elephantine Island

Elephantine Island takes its name from the huge black rocks clustered around its southern end, which resemble a herd of pachyderms bathing in the river. From a felucca you can see cartouches and Predynastic inscriptions carved on the rock faces, which are too sheer to view from the island. Elephantine's spectacular beauty is marred only by the towering *Mövenpick Resort Aswan*, reached by its own private ferry and cut off from the rest of the island by a lofty fence. (An even larger hotel lies abandoned at the far end of the island, after investors pulled out.)

Further south, two **Nubian villages** – **Siou** and **Koti** – nestle amid lush palm groves, their houses painted sky-blue, pink or yellow and often decorated with hajj scenes. Chickens peck in the dust and goats chew garbage in mudbrick alleys twisting past walled gardens, where the only concession to tourism is a signposted **Nubian House**, whose owner sells tea and handicrafts and arranges henna-painting (see "Entertainments and activities",

△ Rocks at Elephantine Island

p.442). Public **ferries** (every 15min 6am–11pm; £E1) sail to Elephantine from the landing stages near Thomas Cook and EgyptAir (boats from the latter dock conveniently close to the Aswan Museum). Alternatively you can get there by felucca (about £E5).

The Aswan Musuem

The small **Aswan Museum** (daily 8am–4pm; £E10, ticket also valid for the Nilometer and ruins further south) casts light on the island's past, when its southern end was occupied by the town of Yebu or Abu (meaning both "elephant" and "ivory" in the Ancient Egyptian language). Most of the museum's best exhibits have been moved to the Nubia Museum, but a mummified gazelle and jewellery found at the island's Temple of Satet are worth a look, as is the new **Annex**, whose highlights include a life-size granite statue of a seated Tuthmosis III, a colobus monkey embracing a pillar, and a pre-nuptial agreement from the reign of Nectanebo II. The museum was originally the villa of Sir William Willcocks, who designed the first Aswan Dam, and is set amid fragrant subtropical **gardens**. Come back and enjoy them once you've visited the Nilometer and the ruins of Yebu.

The Nilometers

In ancient times the Nilometers at Aswan were the first to measure the river's rise, enabling priests to calculate the height of the inundation, crop yields over the next year and the rate of taxation (which peasants paid in kind). There are two on the island, built at the tail end of pharaonic civilization but based on far older practice and used for centuries afterwards.

The easier to find is the **Nilometer of the Satet Temple**, by the riverside; ninety enclosed rock-cut steps lead down to a square shaft with walls graduated in Arabic, Roman and (extremely faint) pharaonic numerals, reflecting its usage in ancient times and during the late nineteenth century. Notice the names of Roman prefects on the left-hand wall. To get there from the museum, follow the path southwards for 300m to find a sycamore tree (the pharaonic symbol of the tree-goddess, associated with Nut and Hathor), which shades the structure. Should you approach it by river, notice the rock embankments to the south, which bear **inscriptions** from the reigns of Tuthmosis III, Amenophis III and the XXVII Dynasty ruler Psammetichus II.

The **Nilometer of the Temple of Khnum** is further inland amid the remains of Yebu. Built in the XXVI Dynasty, it consists of stairs leading down to what was probably a basin for measuring the Nile's maximum level; a scale is etched by the stairs at the northern end.

The ruins of Yebu

The southern end of the island is littered with the **ruins** of the ancient town, which covered nearly two square kilometres by Ptolemaic times. You can follow a trail from the Aswan Museum past numbered plaques identifying structures excavated or reconstructed by German and Swiss archeological teams working on Elephantine. The German mission's excellent guidebook, *Elephantine: The Ancient Town*, describes its 4400-year history and monuments.

A massive platform and foundation blocks (#6, #12 and #13) mark the site of the **Temple of Khnum**, god of the Aswan nome. The temple was founded in the Old Kingdom (when it accounted for two-thirds of the town's area) but entirely rebuilt during the XXX Dynasty. On its north side are the remains of pillars painted by the Romans, and Greek inscriptions; to the west stands the imposing gateway added by Alexander II, shown here worshipping Khnum.

Immediately to the north lies a Greco-Roman **Necropolis of Sacred Rams** (#11), unearthed in 1906, while further northwest stands the small **Temple of Hekayib**, a VI Dynasty nomarch buried in the Tombs of the Nobles (see p.398) who was later deified; the stelae and inscriptions found here by Labib Habachi in 1946 revealed much about Aswan during the Middle Kingdom.

Due east lies a **Temple of Satet** where excavations continue to produce discoveries. Built by Queen Hatshepsut around 1490 BC, it was the last of more than thirty such temples on this site, dating back four millennia, dedicated to the goddess who incarnated the fertile aspect of the inundation. Beneath the temples, German archeologists have found a shaft leading 19m into the granite bedrock, where a natural **whirl hole** is thought to have amplified the sounds of the rising water table (the first indication of the life-giving annual flood) and was revered as the "Voice of the Nile". Although the High Dam has since silenced its voice, a half-buried statue near the temple still draws new brides and barren women longing for the gift of fertility.

To the southwest of Khnum's temple, the layered **remains of ancient houses** have yielded Aramaic papyri attesting to a sizeable **Jewish colony** on Elephantine in the sixth century BC. A military order by Darius II permitting the Yebu garrison to observe Passover in 419 BC suggests that they defended the southernmost border of the Persian Empire. Although nothing remains of their temple to Yahweh, the Germans used leftover blocks from Kalabsha (see p.457) to reconstruct a **Ptolemaic sanctuary** with decorations added by the Nubian Pharaoh Arkamani in the third century BC, at the southern tip of the island.

The other islands

On the far side of Elephantine, almost hidden from the town by its bulk, the **Island of Plants** (Geziret an-Nabatat) is still commonly referred to by tourists as "Kitchener's Island". Consul-General Kitchener, presented with the island in gratitude for his military exploits in Sudan, indulged his passion for exotic flora, importing shrubs and seeds from as far afield as India and Malaysia. Today this island-wide **botanical garden** (daily 7am–sunset, 5/6pm in summer; £E10) is quite rundown but still a fine place to spend a quiet afternoon (except on Fridays), with lots of **birdlife**. The island is accessible by rowing boat or felucca from the west bank or Elephantine for about £E5.

The craggy strait between Elephantine and Amun islands looks its best from a felucca. If you're not already waterborne, the surrounding coves are frequented by lads who'll happily sail you to any of the islands or the west bank. **Amun Island** harbours a reclusive Club Med reached by private ferry from a landing stage near the telephone office; the hotel on **Isis Island** is accessible by private ferry from a signposted landing stage across the road from EgyptAir. Just north of this is another jetty used by boats to **Issa Island** – whose *Nubian Restaurant* has a huge palm garden for sitting out in the summer – and to the *Pharaohs' Village* on the west bank of the river (see p.442 for details of both).

The west bank

The main sights on the **west bank** of the river are the **Mausoleum of the Aga Khan** (only visible from outside) and the desert **Monastery of St Simeon**. When negotiating a price for a felucca here, be sure to establish how long you plan to spend on the west bank. Unless you're prepared to hike for more than 2km across the hills, the more northerly **Tombs of the Nobles** are best visited as a separate excursion, like the **Western Quarry** and its

Unfinished Obelisk, which can only be reached by camel. A new tourist zone with a golf course is being laid out beyond the village of Aswan Min Gharb, scheduled for completion in 2009.

The Aga Khan's Mausoleum

Just uphill from the embankment is a walled estate with a riverside garden and a stairway ascending the hillside to the **Mausoleum of the Aga Khan**. Modelled on the Fatimid tombs of Cairo, its marble sarcophagus enshrines Aga Khan III, the 48th Imam of the Isma'ili sect of Shiite Muslims, who was weighed in jewels for his diamond jubilee in 1945. Initially drawn to Aswan by its climate and hot sands, which relieved his rheumatism, he fell in love with its beauty, built a villa and spent every winter here till his death in 1957. Until she was buried beside him in 2000, his widow ensured that a fresh red rose was placed on his sarcophagus every day; legend has it that when none was available in Egypt, a rose was flown in by private plane from Paris on six successive days. The compound has been **closed** since her death but remains an imposing sight.

The Monastery of St Simeon

Unless you walk across the desert from the Tombs of the Nobles (see below), the ruined **Monastery of St Simeon** (Deir Anba Samaan; daily 8am–4pm; £E20) must be approached from the valley below. You can either scramble uphill through soft sand (30min) or negotiate hiring a **camel** near the landing stage (about £E30 for an hour; tell the driver beforehand if you want to stay longer), but either way, bring water.

Founded in the seventh century and rebuilt in the tenth, the monastery crowns the head of a desert valley, which used to be cultivated down to the river's edge. Built like a fortress, it was originally dedicated to Anba Hadra, a local saint of the fourth century who encountered a funeral procession the day after his wedding and decided to renounce the world for a hermit's cave before the marriage was consummated. From here, monks made evangelical forays into Nubia, where they converted the Nobatae to Christianity. After the Muslim conquest, the Nobatae used the monastery as a base during their incursions into Egypt, until Salah al-Din had it wrecked in 1173.

One of the custodians will show you around the split-level complex, whose lower storeys are made of stone, the upper ones of mud-brick. The now-roofless **Basilica** bears traces of frescoes of the Apostles, their faces scratched out by Muslim iconoclasts. In a nearby chamber with a font is the place where St Simeon used to stand sleeplessly reading the Bible, with his beard tied to the ceiling so as to deliver a painful tug if he nodded off. The central **Keep** has room for three hundred monks sleeping five to a cell; graffiti left by Muslim pilgrims who camped here en route to Mecca can be seen in the last room on the right. You can also explore a refectory, bathhouse, ovens and bakeries (notice the millstones). At sunset the surrounding desert turns madder-red and violet; foxes emerge to hunt and hawks soar aloft.

The Tombs of the Nobles

Relatively few tourists bother with the **Tombs of the Nobles** (daily 8am–4pm; £E20) hewn into the hillside further up the west bank, whose artwork has an immediacy and concern for everyday life that makes a refreshing change from royal art. If you're curious, **local ferries** ply between the station end of the Corniche and the landing stage of the west bank village of **Aswan Min Gharb** (every 30min 6am–11pm; £E1). To combine a visit with the monastery and mausoleum, start early at the tombs, then ascend to the domed hilltop

Muslim shrine known as **Qubbet el-Hawa** (Tomb of the Wind), and walk across the desert to St Simeon's (45min).

The Tombs of the Nobles lie at different heights (**Old and Middle Kingdom** ones uppermost, **Roman** tombs nearest the waterline), and are numbered in ascending order from south to north. Taking the path up from the ticket kiosk, you reach the high-numbered ones first.

Tomb of Sirenput I (#36)

Turn right at the top of the steps and follow the path downhill around the cliffside to find the tomb of **Sirenput I**, overseer of the priests of Khnum and Satet and Guardian of the South during the XII Dynasty. The six pillars of its vestibule bear portraits and biographical texts. On the left-hand wall he watches bulls fighting and spears fish from a papyrus raft, accompanied by his sandal-bearer, sons and dog. On the opposite wall he's portrayed with his mutt and bow-carrier, and also sitting above them in a garden with his mother, wife and daughters, being entertained by singers; the lower register shows three men gambling. Among the badly damaged murals in the hall beyond, you can just discern fowlers with a net (on the lower right wall), a hieroglyphic biography (left), and a marsh-hunting scene (centre). Beyond lies a chapel with a false door set into the rear niche; the corridor to the left leads to the burial chamber.

Tombs of Pepi-Nakht (#35) and Harkhuf (#34)

To reach the other tombs from Sirenput I, return to the top of the steps and follow the path southwards. Among a cluster of tombs to the left of the steps are two rooms ascribed to Hekayib (whose cult temple stands on Elephantine), called here by his other name, **Pepi-Nakht**. As overseer of foreign troops during the long reign of Pepi II (VI Dynasty), he led colonial campaigns in Asia and Nubia, which are related on either side of the door of the left-hand room.

A bit further south is the tomb of **Harkhuf** (#34), who held the same position under Pepi I, Merenre and Pepi II. An eroded biography inside the entrance relates his three trading expeditions into Nubia, including a letter from the eight-year-old Pepi II, urging Harkhuf to bring back safely a "dancing dwarf from the land of spirits" (thought to be a pygmy from Equatorial Africa), whom Pepi desired to see "more than the gifts of Sinai or Punt". The tiny hieroglyphic figure of a pygmy appears several times in the text.

Tombs of Sirenput II (#31)

The largest, best-preserved tomb belongs to **Sirenput II**, who held the same offices as his father under Amenemhat II, during the apogee of the Middle Kingdom. Beyond its vestibule (with an offerings slab between the second and third pillars on the right) lies a corridor with six niches containing Osiride statues of Sirenput, still vividly coloured like his portraits on the four pillars of the chapel, where the artist's grid lines are visible in places. Best of all is the recess at the back, where Sirenput appears with his wife and son (left), attends his seated mother in a garden (right), and receives flowers from his son (centre). Notice the elephant in the upper left corner of this tableau.

Tombs of Mekhu (#25) and Sabni (#26)

At the top of the double ramps ascending the hillside (up which sarcophagi were dragged) are the adjacent tombs of a father and son, which are interesting for their monumentality – a large vestibule with three rows of rough-hewn pillars, flanked by niches and burial chambers – and for their story. After his father **Mekhu** was killed in Nubia, **Sabni** mounted a punitive expedition that recovered the body. As a sign of respect, Pepi II sent his own embalmers to mummify the corpse; Sabni travelled to Memphis to personally express his thanks with gifts, as related by an inscription at the entrance to his tomb. Both tombs are crudely constructed and decorated, with small obelisks at their entrances, and twin vestibules that form a single rectangular room. Sabni's chapel has columns painted with fishing and fowling scenes.

The Western Quarry

The ancient **Western Quarry** in the desert behind the Tombs of the Nobles is harshly evocative of the effort to supply stone for pharaonic monuments. Huge blocks were prised from the sandstone of Gebel Simaan and dragged on rollers towards the Nile for shipment downriver; the stone for the Colossi of Memnon may have come from here. An **Unfinished Obelisk** with hieroglyphs extolling Seti I was abandoned by the wayside after a flaw in the rock was discovered. This desolate site is seldom visited (beware of snakes) and can only be reached **by camel** with a guide from the ferry landing by the tombs (for £E50–60); the ride takes half an hour each way. If that seems too arduous, another unfinished obelisk south of Aswan is easier to reach (see p.445).

Eating and drinking

Eating out in Aswan offers the pleasures of fresh fish and Nubian dishes such as okra in spicy tomato sauce, in riverside **restaurants** that are great on balmy nights but empty when it's cold. You won't find any Chinese food, and European cuisine other than pizzas is limited to a few big hotels. The bazaar is good for **street food**, with *fuul* and sandwiches sold near the station end of the street, and fruit and nuts on every corner. There are simple **cafés** for chicken and fish meals or *kushari*, and the usual juice bars and coffee houses.

All the Corniche places are **open** till around midnight (later if there is custom); cafés in the bazaar may close an hour or two earlier. Phone numbers are only given where **reservations** are advisable. Unless stated otherwise, **alcohol** is not available.

Restaurants, cafés and bars

1902 Restaurant *Old Cataract Hotel*, Corniche el-Nil ☏097/231-6000. The only restaurant in Aswan with a dress code. Its palatial colonial decor beats its Euro-Levantine set menu (€30 excluding drinks). Beer, wine and cocktails available. Reservations are obligatory. Daily 7.30–10pm.

Aswan Moon Corniche el-Nil, near the *Horus Hotel*. A spacious floating restaurant hung with colourful tent fabric, serving fish, chicken, vegetable dishes, pizzas and pasta (£E20–25 plus tax). Try *douad basha*, meatballs in tomato sauce, in an earthenware pot.

Aswan Panorama Corniche el-Nil, near the duty-free shop. Another riverside place, with similar prices to the *Aswan Moon*. Their *tageens* are better than their *kofta* or kebabs. Try the rice pudding with nuts and rosewater for dessert. Closes at 9pm.

Biti Pizza Midan al-Mahatta. Tourists are given an English menu of Western-style pizzas (£E25) rather than an Arabic one with more combinations,

including *fiteer*, which they only serve after 3pm. The upstairs dining rooms are a/c, with a view of the square.

Chef Khalil Sharia al-Souk. This small a/c café near the train station serves delicious fried and grilled fish with rice, salad and *tahina* (£E25–35; crab £E50; mixed seafood platter £E100). It's worth waiting for a table.

El-Madena Sharia al-Souk. A share-a-table diner with set meals (£E20–25) of liver, chicken or kebab with salad, *tahina*, vegetable stew, rice and bread.

El-Masry Sharia Abu Zid. This simple, clean a/c restaurant serves set meals (£E25–30) based around fish, kebab, pigeon or stuffed courgettes, with a rapid turnover of Egyptian clients that ensures that the food is always fresh.

El-Sayida Nafisa Off Sharia Sayida Nafisa. Named after a popular Cairene saint, this café is well regarded by locals for its cheap meals of grilled chicken, salad, rice and soup.

El-Tahrir Pizza Midan al-Mahatta. A cheery, inexpensive rival to *Biti* offering sweet *fiteer* as well as savoury ones and Western-style pizzas, plus Egyptian desserts such as *muhalabiyya*, *basboosa* and *Umm Ali* (unusually served cold, though you can ask for it hot).

Emy Corniche el-Nil. A haunt for felucca captains and expats, *Emy* (pronounced "Ee-me") has a double-decker boat section with views of Elephantine Island, and an enclosed part that's cooler in summer. Meals £E15–30, plus Egyptian beer and wine, as cheap as you'll find in Aswan.

🏃 **Garden** *New Cataract Hotel*, Corniche el-Nil ☎097/231-6002. Generous portions of *mezze* followed by chicken, lamb or fish cooked in clay pots, served in a trellised gazebo that's delightful in cool weather but too hot in summer. A full meal costs about £E70.

Makka Sharia Abtal al-Tahrir. Highly rated by locals yet seldom visited by tourists, they use better cuts of meat and fresher fish than similar places in town, and accordingly charge a bit more.

Mona Lisa Corniche el-Nil. This shabby haunt of courting couples and solitary beer drinkers features handpainted Cairo bazaar scenes on the walls. Try the fish with cloves or a *tageen* from the menu.

🏃 **Nubian House** Uphill from the *Basma Hotel* ☎097/236-6226. Not to be confused with the *Nubian House* on Elephantine or the *Nubian Restaurant* on Issa Island, this is worth a taxi ride (£E10) for its amazing views over Elephantine Island and the First Cataract, as well

as its Nubian meals (£E35–40). There are sometimes Nubian folklore shows, with music, in the evenings. Open 9am–1am, or from sunset on major holy days.

Nubian Restaurant Issa Island ☎097/230-2465. Geared towards tour groups, for whom a buffet and folk show are laid on, it's lacklustre at other times, though its palm garden is a delightful place to relax over a *sheesha* on summer evenings. Free boat from the dock opposite EgyptAir.

Pharaohs' Village On the west bank of the Nile. This laidback outdoor place by an orchard on the edge of the desert serves tasty Nubian food and can lay on live music if enough people are interested. Their motorboat leaves from beside the Judges Club near EgyptAir.

Safwa Off Sharia al-Souk. A two-storey *kushari* diner that also does "quiches" of macaroni with meat, and *muhalabiyya* for dessert. There's a smaller branch near the southern end of Sharia Abtal al-Tahrir, inland from the *Memnon Hotel*.

🏃 **Salah al-Din** Corniche el-Nil. Alongside the *Aswan Moon*, this multi-level restaurant offers the usual menu at slightly higher prices than its Corniche rivals, plus Egyptian beer and wine. Like *Emy*, it's a hang-out for felucca captains.

Vita Midan al-Mahatta. An ice-cream parlour boasting twenty flavours, of which a dozen are available at any time. They taste great, despite being short on cream.

Entertainments and activities

Traditional Aswani diversions include **promenading** along the Corniche and bazaar, meeting friends in riverside **restaurants** and listening to Nubian **music**. Most tourists spend their days sightseeing, and when not attending the **Sound and Light Show at Philae** (see p.453) usually opt for an early night.

If you're craving some excitement, there's **bellydancing** at two seedy venues on the Corniche, the *Lalampola Disco* in the *Isis Hotel* (12.30–4.30am) and the fifth-floor nightclub in the *Horus* hotel (midnight–4am). Alternatively, the *Isis Island* hosts a fairly bland nightly Nubian show, dancer and band (10.30pm–1am). All three levy a minimum charge of £E45 for drinks (which are cheaper at the first two). Bellydancing is suspended during *eids*, Sha'ban and other Muslim holy days.

Nubian music and weddings

Nubian music ranges from traditional village songs backed by drums and handclapping to urban sounds reflecting the influence of jazz, funk, trance or even classical music. The one thing that all these forms have in common is that they're sung in Nubian. While famous abroad thanks to the late masters Ali Hassan Kuban and Hamza al-Din, in Egypt Nubian music isn't widely popular outside the far south. Nubian CDs and cassettes are sold in Aswan, but contemporary Nubian stars seldom hold public concerts there. As with the jobbing musicians who sometimes play in the Ferial Gardens or a park near the Coca Cola factory outside town, their main income derives from performing at weddings or other private functions.

Nubian weddings are celebrated on a lavish scale, with musicians costing as much as £E30,000. The bridegroom recoups the expense by inviting hundreds of guests and charging them £E20 each, which makes summer – the wedding season – an expensive time for locals. The wedding ceremony is followed by a week of celebrations, culminating in "pigeon nights" when guests devour quantities of pigeon to increase their sexual potency. As guests from foreign lands are held to be auspicious, tourists are often invited to attend weddings in the villages around Aswan.

Nubian music is often accompanied by stick-dancing and other folk dances, which can be seen at venues that lay on a **folklore show** (often with a whirling dervish thrown in for good measure); try the *Nubian House* overlooking the First Cataract, the *Nubian Restaurant* on Issa Island (see p.442 for details of both) or the Kenzi House on Sehel Island (see p.447). Events are organized for tour groups or if enough people are interested. The cost (£E45–65 per person) includes food, entertainment and transport by boat if required.

Henna designs, spas and swimming

Elaborate **designs in henna** on the hands and feet of brides are a feature of Nubian culture. Foreign women can be "tattooed" by Madame Rahmat (℡097/230-1465) at her home, or by local women at the Nubian House (℡097/232-6226) on Elephantine; men wanting designs must go to guys in the bazaar such as Mahmoud Wahish (℡097/230-2651). Expect to pay £E20–50, depending on the size and complexity of the design. Another beauty treatment is "**sugaring**" – a traditional form of waxing using syrup; the *Keylany Hotel* offers a full-body exfoliation for £E120.

The *Mövenpick Resort Aswan* has various **spa** packages including the use of its sauna, gym and steam bath, massages, immersion in **hot sand** (good for arthritis and rheumatism) and a whirlpool bath. Similar facilities are available at the *Isis Island* resort. Contact either hotel for details.

Some hotels let non-residents use their **swimming pools**: *Cleopatra* is cheapest (£E20); *Isis Island* has both heated and cold pools (£E50); while the *Mövenpick* makes outsiders rent a pool cabin (£E250 for up to three people). Though local boys bathe in the Nile, tourists seldom do for fear of bilharzia, which is a problem near the riverbanks and islands that impede the water's fast flow. If you're still keen, there are some lovely bathing spots out at the First Cataract.

Festivals

Aswan's main event is a three-month international **Sculpture Symposium** starting in late January or early February, when you can see sculptors at work on the terrace of the *Basma Hotel*, before their creations are sent to the Sculpture Park (see "Excursions from Aswan", p.444). On **Aswan Day** (January 15), the Corniche witnesses a good-natured parade of civic and military hardware; fire engines and ambulances follow Jeep-loads of perspiring frogmen and rubber-suited decontamination troops. To appreciate the joke, catch the orgy of drilling and polishing that takes place outside the Police Department and the Governorate building the previous day.

Directory

Airlines EgyptAir on the Corniche (daily 8am–8pm; ℡097/231-5000) and at the airport (℡097/248-0568).

American Express Corniche el-Nil (daily except Fri 9am–5pm; ℡097/230-6983, ℻230-2909, ✉aswan.tso.@aexp.com). Will exchange currency and traveller's cheques, hold client mail and organize travel.

Banks and exchange The Egyptian Exchange bureau (daily 8am–8pm) offers slightly better rates than the banks along the Corniche. There are ATMs outside Banque Misr (daily except Fri 8am–9pm) and the National Bank of Egypt (Mon–Thurs & Sun 8.30am–2pm). You can change traveller's cheques at Banque du Caire (daily except Fri 8.30am–2pm & 3–10pm) or Bank of Alexandria (Mon–Thurs & Sun 8am–2pm). MasterCard and Visa cash advances are available from Banque Misr.

Books and newspapers You can find a wide range of AUC books in various languages, plus repro vintage postcards and prints at fixed prices, at the Rowing Club on the Corniche. Novels and Egyptology books are also stocked in the *New Cataract*. Street vendors sell the *Egyptian Gazette*, *Al-Ahram Weekly* and the odd foreign newspaper near the *Horus* and *Hathor* hotels.

Dry cleaners Off Sharia al-Souk, on the ground floor of the *Nubian Oasis Hotel*.

Duty Free Southern end of the Corniche (daily 9am–2pm & 6–10pm). The only retail outlet in Aswan selling alcohol, it's poorly stocked and fusty. Imported booze must be paid for in hard currency; domestic wine and spirits cost more than in Luxor. Takes Diners Club cards.

Hospitals The Evangelical Hospital off the Corniche (☎097/231-7176) charges £E120 for a consultation (Mon–Sat 7am–noon & 4–6pm), but for serious problems you're better off at the Mubarak Military Hospital on Tariq Sadat (☎097/231-7985). Aswan's tourist office can recommend doctors or dentists.

Internet access The Information Technology Club on the Corniche has the cheapest rates (£E5/hr), but you'll get faster connections at the *Keylany Hotel* (£E10/hr) or no-frills outfits like Tareek, Panorama Internet, Aswan Online or the Rowing Club (open till midnight or later).

Pharmacies El-Nile, next to the Banque du Caire on the Corniche (daily 8am–1am, Fri closed 1–5pm;

☎097/230-2674); Galal, next to the *Happi Hotel* (daily 7am–3pm & 6pm–midnight; ☎097/230-3011). Others are dotted all over town – ask at your hotel for the nearest.

Photo processing Photo Sabry on the Corniche near EgyptAir (Mon–Thurs, Sat & Sun 10am–1am, Fri 4pm–1am) prints photos and sells film. You can burn digital photos onto a CD at the *Keylany Hotel* (£E25) or Digital Pharonica on Sharia Abbas Farid (£E45).

Police The tourist police (☎097/230-3436) are based near the Corniche beside Misr Travel, with a branch in the train station; both are open round the clock. For serious cases, try to deal with the boss, Sayed Abu Hamed (☎097/231-4393). The Aswan Governorate's Police Department occupies a grand modern tower on the Corniche, and there's another, colonial-style police station on Sharia Abtal el-Tahrir.

Post office Main GPO (daily except Fri 8am–2pm) near the Rowing Club; the section for poste restante (same hours) is on Sharia Abtal el-Tahrir, one block inland behind the Bank of Alexandria.

Sudanese Consulate Off Sharia Abdullah Osman Yacoub, in the north of town (daily except Fri 9am–4pm ☎097/230-7231, ☎232-4563). Sudanese visas ($50–100) can be issued here with a letter of recommendation from your embassy, which could be faxed from Cairo.

Telephones International calls can be made from the 24hr telephone office near EgyptAir, or Menatel card booths all over town.

Thomas Cook On the Corniche near the Police Department (daily 8am–2pm & 5–8pm; ☎097/230-4011, ☎230-6839). Changes money, sells cheques and arranges tours to Abu Simbel.

Visa extensions The passport office is on Corniche el-Nil, in the Police Department (Mon–Thurs & Sun 8am–2pm & 6–8pm; ☎097/231-7006). Use the side entrance to the north and head for the second floor; you'll need a photocopy of your passport details and one photo.

Excursions from Aswan

Aswan is a base for **excursions** to many sites, some also accessible from Luxor. Many visitors cram the highlights into two long day-trips: south to Abu Simbel and Philae; and north to Kom Ombo, Edfu and Esna. Aswan's budget hotels offer trips in cramped minibuses with dodgy air conditioning, for a modest cost (not including tickets for the sites), but many tourists opt to pay more for a comfortable trip with Thomas Cook or American Express (whose rates include tickets), especially to Abu Simbel. Details of **Nile trips** from Aswan are covered on pp.317–321.

Convoys to **Abu Simbel** leave Aswan at 4.30am and 11am – but everyone sticks to the early one since the round-trip takes nine hours on agency tours (about €75/\$95 per head including admission ticket) and up to twelve hours on excursions that visit the Unfinished Obelisk (£E45 per person) or Philae and the High Dam (£E55–75) on the way back – the cost doesn't include tickets. The only reason to take a public bus (see p.463) is to travel outside of convoy hours or stay overnight at Abu Simbel. Alternatively – and more expensively – you can get there by **flying** (see p.463), or on a four-day **cruise on Lake Nasser** departing from the High Dam (see box on p.451).

A less arduous half-day excursion is to **Philae Island** with its lovely Temple of Isis, situated in the lake between the **Aswan Dams**. Travel agencies charge from \$30 per person, so it's far cheaper to hire a taxi to take you to the Philae launch dock, then the dams and back to Aswan, visiting the **Unfinished Obelisk** and the **Fatimid Cemetery** en route. For a four-hour tour, the group rate is about £E40 for a four-seater taxi, £E65 for a larger car. For £E70–80, you can probably persuade them to extend the tour to include **Kalabsha Temple**, which otherwise entails a separate trip.

The other main circuit takes in one or more of the **temples between Aswan and Luxor**. Using public transport, you could maybe combine **Kom Ombo** with **Edfu**, but to see **Esna** as well requires a taxi. Expect to pay about £E150–200 for a four-seater or £E275–300 for a larger car to take you to each site and then on to Luxor, on the **convoy** leaving at 7.30am. Alternatively, you could visit Kom Ombo and Edfu   · felucca or a cruise boat.

Descriptions of the sites nearer town follow: for accounts of the Aswan Dams, Philae, Kalabsha Temple and Abu Simbel, see the subsequent sections.

The Fatimid Cemetery, the Unfinished Obelisk and the Sculpture Park

Some 500m from the grounds of the Nubia Museum, you'll see a green metal fence surrounding hundreds of mud-brick tombs ranging from simple enclosures to complex domed cubes. This veritable lexicon of Islamic funerary architecture is known as the **Fatimid Cemetery** (daily 24hr; free), though the majority of tombs date from Tulunid times. Some of the domes are built on a drum with the corners protruding like horns, a design unique to Upper Egypt. Most tombs had marble inscriptions attached until a freak rainstorm washed them off, and they were taken to Cairo in 1887 without any record of their original locations, leaving the tombs starkly unadorned. While not as grand as the mausolea in Cairo's Cities of the Dead – or inhabited by squatters – they're an eerie sight. It's possible to walk through the cemetery to emerge on the road to the Northern Quarries.

The **Northern Quarries** (daily 8am–4pm; £E25) are the best known of the many quarrying sites in the hills south of Aswan, which supplied the Ancient Egyptians with fine red granite for their temples and colossi. Its fame derives from a gigantic **Unfinished Obelisk**, roughly dressed and nearly cut free from the bedrock, before being abandoned after a flaw in the stone was discovered. Had it been finished, the obelisk would have weighed 1168 tons and stood nearly 42m high. It's reckoned that this was the intended mate for the so-called Lateran Obelisk in Rome, which originally stood before the temple of Tuthmosis III at Karnak and is still credited as being the largest obelisk in the world. From chisel marks and discarded tools, archeologists have been able to deduce pharaonic quarrying techniques, such as soaking wooden wedges to split fissures, and using quartz sand slurry as an abrasive. A visitors' trail runs through the quarries past some **pictographs** of dolphins and ostriches, painted by ancient quarry workers.

While it's just about feasible to walk to the Northern Quarries, you definitely need wheels to reach the **Sculpture Park** near the **Southern Quarries** out towards the Old Dam. The park displays sculptures by artists attending Aswan's international Sculpture Symposium (see p.443), who spend a month on the terrace of the *Basma Hotel* creating works that are either judged fit to grace the streets of Aswan (eg the "Tottering Skyscraper" on the roundabout near the Coptic Cathedral), or join the others in the park. Besides the sheer variety and imaginativeness of the sculptures, the park enjoys a wonderful **view**, especially at sunset. Be sure to get a taxi whose driver knows what you mean by "*El Mathaf el-Maftouh*" and a rough idea of the route (about thirty minutes' journey). Take the road for the Old Dam, but turn off onto an uphill road rather than towards the Shellal docks (for ferries to Philae). Continue until you reach the top; the sculptures are on the right, the quarries to the left.

While **taxi tours** often briefly stop at the obelisk and the cemetery on the way back to Aswan, they ignore the park since few tourists ask to visit it. If your fellow passengers agree, it shouldn't be hard to persuade the driver to make the brief detour for £E10 extra. Otherwise, hire a taxi in Aswan for a few hours to visit all three sites in one trip (£E25–30).

Sehel Island and the First Cataract

Travellers enamoured of felucca journeys should visit **Sehel Island**, 4km upriver from Aswan. With a strong wind behind you it can be reached in an hour or so. The recommended rate for a three-hour trip is £E50. Bring water and a hat, and come well shod: although the river is cool, the rocks and sand are

△ A view over a part of Sehel Island

scorchingly hot. En route, look out for the bougainvillea-festooned villa of the pop star Mohammed Mounir, on the east bank of the river.

Landing on Sehel you may be mobbed by kids wanting to take you to its **Nubian village**, where the **Kenzi House** offers music and meals by arrangement with Gelal Mohammed Hassan (☎012 415-4902), who can otherwise be found outside Aswan's *Panorama* restaurant. Gelal can also arrange felucca cruises as far downriver as Edfu.

Kids are also keen to lead you to the "ruins", two hills of fenced-off jumbled boulders that dominate the island. Here are over 250 **inscriptions** from the Middle Kingdom until Ptolemaic times, "bruised" rather than carved into the weathered granite. Most record Egyptian expeditions beyond the First Cataract or prayers of gratitude for their safe return, but atop the eastern hill you'll find a Ptolemaic **Famine Stele** (#81). Backdated to the reign of Zoser, it relates how he ended a seven-year famine during the III Dynasty by placating Khnum, god of the cataract, with a new temple on Sehel and the return of lands confiscated from his cult centre at Esna, which had provoked Khnum to withhold the inundation.

The summit provides a superb view of the **First Cataract**, a lush, cliff-bound stretch of river divided into channels by outcrops of granite. Before the Aswan Dams, the waters foamed and roiled, making the cataract a fearsome obstacle to upriver travel. Until early last century, it was necessary to offload cargo and transport it overland while the lightened boats risked rowing against the rapids. Amelia Edwards described "the leap – the dead fall – the staggering rush forward", waves and spray flooding the boat and the oars audibly scraping the rocks on either side.

In ancient times the cataract was credited as being the source of the Nile (which was believed to flow south into Nubia as well as north through Egypt) and the abode of the deity who controlled the inundation (either Hapy or Khnum, or perhaps both working in tandem). The foaming waters were thought to well up from a subterranean cavern where the Nile-god dwelt. Offerings continued to be made at Sehel even after the cavern's putative location shifted to Biga Island during the Late Period or Ptolemaic times (see "Philae", p.452).

Moving on from Aswan

The convoy rule definitely applies to **private taxis** to points north of Aswan, so if you're renting one for an excursion, be prepared to start with the 8am convoy. A second convoy at 1.30pm runs directly to Luxor without any stopovers. Convoys assemble by the Officers Club, 1km north of the Governorate building.

Seats on **buses** between Aswan and Luxor (5 daily; 3hr; £E15) can't be booked in advance, and schedules are uncertain. Overnight buses to **Cairo** (13hr; £E85) leave at 7pm and 8.30pm. Travellers bound for the Red Sea or Sinai can take the 8am or 3pm bus to **Hurghada** (7hr; £E40) or **Suez** (12hr; £E85), or the 6am service to **Mersa Alam** (5hr; £E25). There are two daily buses to **Abu Simbel** (4hr; £E20). To reach the bus station, catch a pick-up (25pt) from near the tourist office.

As for **trains**, tourists may catch six daily services to **Luxor** (3hr; first class £E30, a/c second class £21), stopping at Darow, Kom Ombo, Edfu and Esna en route. However, for **Cairo** (15hr; first class £E77, a/c second class £E43) on trains #981 (6am), #1903 (6pm) and #997 (8pm), plus the two sleeper trains, #83 and #85, leaving at 8.15pm and 9.30pm.

Finally, EgyptAir flies from Aswan to **Luxor** (45min; £E375), **Cairo** (1hr 30min; £E987) and **Abu Simbel** (30min; £E995). The prices quoted are one-way fares, except for Abu Simbel, which is usually visited on a day-return ticket that includes transfers between the temple and .the airport.

The Aswan Dams

Under a good administration the Nile gains on the desert; under a bad one the desert gains on the Nile.

Napoleon

The **Aswan Dams** attest that Egypt's fundamental dilemma is more intractable than suggested by John Gunther's pithy diagnosis: "Make more land. Make fewer people. Either solution would alleviate the problem, but neither is easy." Although each dam has brought large areas under cultivation, boosted agricultural productivity and provided hydroelectricity for industry, the gains have been eroded by a population explosion – impelling Egypt to undertake yet more ambitious irrigation projects.

Ever conscious of the dams' significance, Egyptians are inclined to view them as a tourist attraction, whereas most foreigners simply regard the edifices as a route to the temples of Abu Simbel, Philae and Kalabsha, which were reassembled on higher ground following the construction of the High Dam. Views from the top of the dams are spectacular, though, so don't begrudge obligatory stopovers on tours.

The Old Dam

Just upriver from the First Cataract stands the old **Aswan Dam**, built by the British (1898–1902) and subsequently twice raised to increase its capacity. Once the largest dam in the world, it stands 50m tall, 2km long, 30m thick at the base and 11m at the top. Now that its storage and irrigation functions have been taken over by the High Dam, the dam chiefly serves to generate hydroelectricity for the nearby Kima factory, producing chemical fertilizers. Driving across, you'll notice the 180 sluice gates that used to be opened during the inundation and then gradually closed as the river level dropped, preserving a semi-natural flood cycle. **Philae** is visible among the islands to the south of the

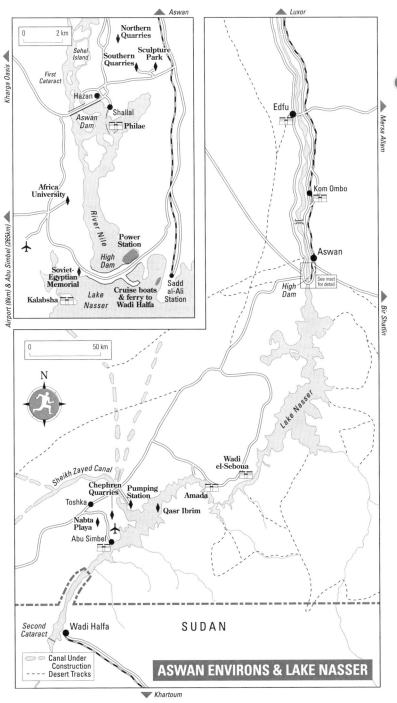

ASWAN ENVIRONS & LAKE NASSER

dam. Near the eastern end of the dam lies a residential colony for hydro-engineers, called **Hazan**, where colonial villas nestle amid verdant gardens.

The High Dam

By 1952 it was apparent that the Aswan Dam could no longer satisfy Egypt's needs nor guarantee security from famine. Nasser pledged to build a new **High Dam** (Al-Sadd al-Ali) 6km upstream, which would secure Egypt's future, power new industries and bring electricity to every village. When the World Bank reneged on its promised loan under pressure from the US, Nasser nation-alized the Suez Canal to generate revenue for the project and turned to the Soviet Union for help. The dam's construction (1960–71) outlasted his lifetime and the era of Soviet–Egyptian collaboration. When Egypt decided to install more powerful turbine generators in the late 1980s, they bought them from America – only to find that the Russian ones caused fewer problems. Today, Western European contractors are involved in a vast new project at Toshka, which one described as an "Engineer's Playground".

The most visible consequence of the High Dam is **Lake Nasser**, which backs up for nearly 500km, well into Sudan. Over 180m deep in places, with a surface area of 6000 square kilometres, the lake is the world's largest reservoir, and seems more like an inland sea. During the decade of drought that saw the Nile fall to its lowest level in 350 years, it saved Egypt from the famine that wracked Ethiopia and Sudan. When heavy rainfall caused the Nile to flood in 1988, the High Dam prevented Aswan from being inundated like Khartoum. Since a dam burst would wash most of Egypt's population into the Mediterranean, its security is paramount. The surrounding hills bristle with radar installations and anti-aircraft missiles; threats to bomb the dam made by Israel during the 1967 and 1973 wars, and by Gaddafi in 1984, have not been forgotten.

Environmental consequences

As Lake Nasser rose behind the High Dam, flooding ancient Nubia, an inter-national effort ensured that mud-brick fortresses and burial grounds were excavated and photographed, before being abandoned to the rising waters. Half a dozen temples and tombs were salvaged to be reassembled on higher ground or in foreign museums. Since then, however, many temples in Upper Egypt have been affected by damp and salt encrustation, blamed on the rising water table and greater humidity.

Although the human, cultural and environmental costs are still being evaluated, the dam has delivered most of its promised **benefits**. Egypt has been able to convert 3000 square kilometres of cultivated land from the ancient basin system of irrigation to perennial irrigation – doubling or tripling the number of harvests – and to reclaim more than 4200 square kilometres of desert. The dam's turbines have powered a thirty percent expansion of industrial capacity, too; humming pylons carry megavolts to Aswan's chemical and cement factories, the Helwan Iron and Steel Mill, and the refineries of Suez. Fishing and tourism on Lake Nasser have developed into profitable industries, and the new Toshka pumping station and the Sheikh Zayed Canal are set to turn more desert into farmland as the **Toshka Project** progresses (see box on p.467).

While the main losers have been the **Nubians**, whose homeland was submerged by the lake (see box on pp.428–429), other environmental conse-quences are still being assessed. Evaporation from the lake has caused haze, clouds

Cruises and fishing safaris on Lake Nasser

Cruise boats began operating on the lake in 1993 thanks to Mustafa al-Guindi, a Cairo-born Nubian who launched the opulent *Eugénie* and *Qasr Ibrim*. There are now four more boats run by different companies, mostly with five-star ratings. Each follows a similar **schedule**, departing from the High Dam (four days) or Abu Simbel (three days), taking in the otherwise inaccessible sites of **Wadi el-Seboua**, **Amada** and **Qasr Ibrim** (see pp.459–463) plus **Abu Simbel** and **Kalabsha** temples. Most passengers book through companies abroad, but trips can also be arranged in Egypt, sometimes at short notice. Rates are lowest in the summer, highest over Christmas/New Year and Easter.

Besides antiquities, Lake Nasser is renowned for its **fishing** – for **Nile perch** (the largest caught weighed 176kg, just short of the world record), huge **tilapia**, piranha-like **tigerfish** and eighteen kinds of **giant catfish**. After tilapia (at the bottom of the food chain) spawns in mid-March, perch and catfish thrive in depths of up to 6m till late September, after which big fish are caught in deeper water until February by trolling over submerged promontories or islands. The best fishing grounds are in the north of the lake – beyond Amada the fish get eaten by crocodiles. Anglers base themselves on mother ships and fish in twos or threes off smaller boats. Fishing packages includes meals, soft drinks and transfers from Aswan in the price; specialist rods can be hired if needed.

Cruises

Eugénie ☎02/516-9653, ⊛www.eugenie.com.eg. Managed by Belle Époque Travel in Cairo and named after the empress who opened the Suez Canal, this magnificent boat is modelled on a *khedival* hunting lodge, with a Turkish steam bath, French *haute cuisine*, cocktails and classical music at Abu Simbel to please its guests.

Nubian Sea ☎02/404-8902, ✉nubiansea@mist-net.net. Its 70 cabins and pool are nothing special, but the buffet meals are superior to all the boats on Lake Nasser except the *Eugénie* and *Qasr Ibrim*. Cruises are sold abroad by Viking.

Prince Abbas ☎02/738-3384, ✉nilxplor@rite.com. Operated by the Cairo-based Nile Exploration Corp. and marketed abroad by Bales and Viking, this has 55 cabins, billiards, a mini gym, Jacuzzi and a plunge pool on the sundeck.

Qasr Ibrim ☎02/516-9653, ⊛www.kasribrim.com.eg. With its lavish 1930s Art Deco interiors and haute cuisine, this boat is as grand as the *Eugénie*. Managed by Belle Époque Travel.

Queen Abu Simbel ☎010 1407753, ⊛naggar.4mg.com. Run by Naggar Travel, and featuring a sauna, Jacuzzi and Turkish bath.

Tania Luxor ☎095/237-6445, Aswan ☎097/231-6393, ⊛www.travco-eg.com. With a four-start rating, this is less fancy than the other boats.

Fishing safaris

African Angler ☎097/230-9748, ✉a-angler@link.net, ⊛www.african-angler.co.uk. One- (€185), six- (€900–1140) or thirteen-day (€1635–2035) fishing trips, organized by former Kenyan safari guide Tim Bailey. Rates highest early October to late December.

El-Temsah ☎012 3343203, ✉crocodile2004@hotmail.com. Run by Aladdin Temsah in Aswan, this simple houseboat sleeping six can be used for fishing, bird-watching or duck-hunting, for around £E650 per person a day.

Lake Nasser Adventure ⊛www.lakenasseradventure.com. Nubian fisherman Nekrashi (☎012 3503825, satellite phone ☎+88216 333 601 38) and his partner Steven (☎012 1040255 or ☎+88216 333 601 04) have three mother ships on the lake almost all year round. Prices depend on the time of year.

and even rainfall over previously arid regions and the water table has risen. Because the dam traps the silt that once renewed Egypt's fields, farmers now rely on chemical fertilizers, and the soil salinity caused by perennial irrigation can only be prevented by extensive drainage projects, which create breeding grounds for mosquitoes and bilharzia-carrying snails. And with no silty deposits to replenish it, the Delta coastline is being eroded by the Mediterranean.

It's estimated that the lake itself may be filled by silt within five hundred years. But whereas some reckon that the Nubian Desert may have reverted to its prehistoric lushness by then, others fear international conflicts over water resources in the future. When Ethiopia commissioned a study on damming the Abbai River (the source of the Blue Nile), Cairo warned that any reduction of Egypt's quota of Nile water, fixed by treaty at 59 billion cubic metres annually, would be seen as a threat to national security, and that Egypt would, in fact, be needing a larger share in the future.

Visiting the High Dam

Many tours to Abu Simbel from Aswan include a brief stopover at the High Dam, which is only 13km from the city and can be crossed anytime between 7am and 5pm. All vehicle passengers are charged a £E8 **toll**. Along the western approach stands the **Soviet-Egyptian Memorial**, a giant lotus-blossom tower built to symbolize their collaboration and the dam's benefits, as depicted in heroic, Socialist Realist bas-reliefs. A lofty **observation deck**, reached by elevator, allows four people at a time to see how the dam's concrete is crumbling and be stricken by vertigo. Off the road at the east end of the dam is a **visitors' pavilion** (daily 7am–5pm), which the curator will unlock for baksheesh. Exhibits include a fifteen-metre-high model of the dam, plans for its construction (in Russian and Arabic), and a photo narrative of the relocation of Abu Simbel.

However, unless you ask to visit the tower (*burg*) or "model" (*mekat*), taxis will only **stop midway across the dam** for a brief look. From this vantage point the dam's height (111m) is masked by the cantilever, but its length (3830m) and width at the top (40m) and base (980m) are impressive. From the southern side of the dam you can gaze across Lake Nasser to Kalabsha Temple. The **view** northwards includes the huge 2100-megawatt power station on the east bank and the channels through which water is routed into the Nile, rushing out amid clouds of mist, sometimes crowned by a rainbow. **Philae** lies among the cluster of islands further downriver.

As foreigners may not use service taxis from Aswan, the only public transport to the High Dam is a third-class train (hourly 6am–4pm; £E1) which terminates at **Sadd al-Ali Station**, 5km south of the eastern end of the dam, near the **docks** for the **ferry to Wadi Halfa** and Lake Nasser **cruise boats** (see the boxes on p.448 & p.451). Tourists disembarking there are allowed to catch a service taxi from outside the station into Aswan (£E2).

Philae

The island of **PHILAE** and its **Temple of Isis** have bewitched visitors since Ptolemaic times, when most of the complex was constructed. The devout and curious were drawn here by a cult that flourished throughout the Roman Empire well into the Christian era. Although the first Europeans to "rediscover" Philae in the eighteenth century could only marvel at it from a distance after their attempts to land were "met with howls, threats and eventually the spears of the natives living in the ruins", subsequent visitors revelled in this mirage from antiquity. "If a procession of white-robed priests bearing aloft the veiled ark of the God were to come sweeping round between the palms," mused Amelia Edwards, "we would not think it strange."

After the building of the first Aswan Dam, rising waters lapped and surged about the temple, submerging it for half the year, when tourists would admire its shadowy presence beneath the translucent water. However, once it became apparent that the new High Dam would submerge Philae forever, UNESCO and the Egyptian authorities organized a massive operation (1972–80) to **relocate** its temples on nearby **Aglika Island**, which was landscaped to match the original site. The new Philae is magnificently set amid volcanic outcrops, like a jewel in the royal blue lake, but no longer faces Biga Island, sacred to Osiris, whence its holiness derived.

Most people visit Philae on minibus or taxi **tours from Aswan** (see p.445), which is the only easy way of getting there and back. Taxis drop you at the **Shallal** motorboat dock, 2km from the eastern end of the Old Dam, where you can buy site **tickets** (daily: winter 7am–4pm; summer 7am–5pm; £E40). Having agreed on a price for a **motorboat** to the island (officially £E27 return per boat-load), you shouldn't pay anything until you're back on shore, obliging the boatman to wait while you explore; if you linger more than an hour, *baksheesh* is in order. There's nowhere to buy food or drink on the island.

Philae's **Sound and Light Show** is better than the one at Karnak. There are two or three performances nightly; check the schedules at Aswan's tourist office. As at Karnak, the show consists of an hour-long tour through the ruins, whose floodlit forms are more impressive than the melodramatic soundtrack. By manoeuvring yourself into the front row, you can enjoy a panoramic view of the entire complex without having to swivel your head during the second act. **Tickets** (£E55; no student reductions) are sold at the dockside just before the first show begins. You'll need to rent a **taxi** from Aswan to take you there and back; expect to pay £E25–30 for a four-seater cab (including waiting time), plus the cost of the motorboat ride there and back.

The Temple of Isis

Philae's cult status dates back to the New Kingdom, when Biga Island was identified as one of the burial places of Osiris – and the first piece of land to emerge from the primordial waters of Chaos. Since Biga was forbidden to all but the priesthood, however, public festivities centred upon neighbouring **Philae**, which was known originally as the "Island from the Time of Re".

Excluding a few remains from the Late Period, the existing **Temple of Isis** was constructed over some eight hundred years by Ptolemaic and Roman rulers who sought to identify themselves with the Osirian myth and the cult of Isis. An exquisite fusion of Ancient Egyptian and Greco-Roman architecture, the temple complex harmonizes perfectly with its setting, sculpted pillars and pylons gleaming white or mellow gold against Mediterranean-blue water and black Nilotic rock.

Approaching the temple

Motorboats land near at the southern end of the island. In ancient times, on the original Philae, visitors ascended a double stairway to the **Vestibule of Nectanebo** at the entrance to the temple precincts. Erected by a XXX Dynasty pharaoh in honour of his "Mother Isis", this was the prototype for the graceful kiosks of the Ptolemaic and Roman era. Notice the double

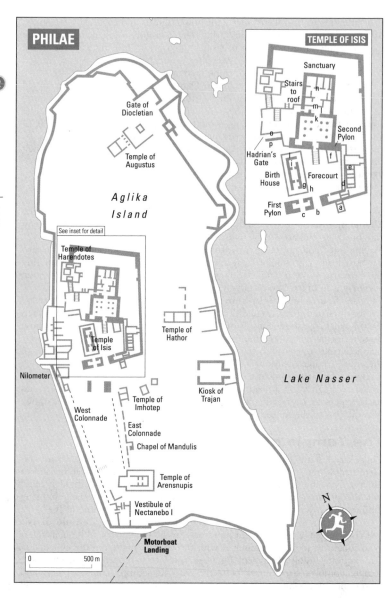

PHILAE

Gate of Diocletian

Temple of Augustus

Aglika Island

See inset for detail

Temple of Harendotes

Temple of Isis

Nilometer

West Colonnade

Temple of Imhotep

East Colonnade

Chapel of Mandulis

Temple of Arensnupis

Vestibule of Nectanebo I

Motorboat Landing

0   500 m

Temple of Hathor

Kiosk of Trajan

Lake Nasser

N

TEMPLE OF ISIS

Sanctuary

Stairs to roof

n

m

k

Second Pylon

o

p

Hadrian's Gate

Birth House

Forecourt

First Pylon

i

f

e

g   h

d

c   b

a

capitals on the remaining columns, traditional flower shapes topped with sistrum–Hathor squares that supported the architrave. The screens that once formed the walls are crowned with cavetto cornices and rows of *uraeus* serpents, a motif dating back to Zoser's complex at Saqqara, nearly three thousand years earlier.

Beyond the vestibule stretches an elongated trapezoidal courtyard flanked by colonnades. The **West Colonnade** is the better preserved, with finely carved capitals, each slightly different. The windows in the wall behind once faced Biga, the island of Osiris; the one opposite the first two columns is topped by a relief of Nero offering two eyes to Horus and Isis. The plainer, unfinished **East Colonnade** abuts a succession of ruined structures. Past the foundations of the **Temple of Arensnupis** (worshipped as the "Good Companion of Isis" in the Late Period) lies a ruined **Chapel of Mandulis**, the Nubian god of Kalabsha. Near the First Pylon, an unfinished **Temple of Imhotep** honours the philosopher-physician who designed Zoser's Step Pyramid and was later deified as a god of healing. Its forecourt walls show Khnum, Satis, Anukis, Isis and Osiris, and Ptolemy IV before Imhotep.

The Pylons and Forecourt

The lofty **First Pylon** was built by Neos Dionysos, who smites enemies in the approved fashion at either corner, watched by Isis, Horus and Hathor. Set at right angles to the pylon, the Gate of Ptolemy II **[a]** is probably a remnant of an earlier temple. The pylon's main portal **[b]** is still older (dating from the reign of Nectanebo II) and was formerly flanked by two granite obelisks; now only two **stone lions** remain. Inside the portal are inscriptions by Napoleon's troops, commemorating their victory over the Mamlukes in 1799. The smaller door in the western section of the pylon leads through to the Birth House and was used for rituals; the entrance depicts the personified deities of Nubia and the usual Egyptian pantheon **[c]**. On the back of the pylon are scenes of priests carrying Isis's barque.

Emerging into the **Forecourt**, most visitors make a beeline for the Birth House or the Second Pylon, overlooking the colonnade to the east. Here, reliefs behind the stylish plant columns show the king performing rituals such as dragging the barque of Sokar **[d]**. A series of doors lead into six rooms which probably had a service function; one of them, dubbed the Library **[e]**, features Thoth in his ibis and baboon forms, Maat, lion-headed

---

The cult of Isis

Of all the cults of Ancient Egypt, none endured longer or spread further than the worship of the goddess **Isis**. As the consort of Osiris, she civilized the world by instituting marriage and teaching women the domestic arts. As an enchantress, she collected the dismembered fragments of his body and briefly revived him to conceive a son, Horus, using her magic to help him defeat the evil Seth and restore the divine order. As pharaohs identified themselves with Horus, the living king, so Isis was their divine mother – a role which inevitably associated her with Hathor, the two goddesses being conflated in the Late Period. By this time Isis was the Great Mother of All Gods and Nature, Goddess of Ten Thousand Names, of women, purity and sexuality.

By a process of identification with other goddesses around the Mediterranean, **Isis-worship** eventually spread throughout the Roman Empire (the westernmost Iseum or cult temple extant is in Hungary). The nurturing, forgiving, loving Isis was Christianity's chief rival between the third and fifth centuries. Many scholars

▲ Isis

believe that the cult of the Virgin Mary was Christianity's attempt to wean converts away from Isis; early Coptic art identifies one with the other, Horus with Jesus, and the Christian cross with the pharaonic ankh.

Tefnut and Sheshat, the goddess of writing. At the northern end stands a ruined chapel **[f]**, which the Romans erected in front of a granite outcrop that was smoothed into a stele under Ptolemy IV and related his gift of lands to the temple.

Set at an angle to its forerunner, the **Second Pylon** changes the axis of the temple. A large relief on the right tower shows Neos Dionysos placing sacrifices before Horus and Hathor; in a smaller scene above he presents a wreath to Horus and Nephthys, offers incense and anoints an altar before Osiris, Isis and Horus. Similar scenes on the other tower have been defaced by early Christians, who executed the paintings in the upper right-hand corner of the pylon passageway, leading into the temple proper.

The Birth House

The western side of the forecourt is dominated by the colonnaded **Birth House** of Ptolemy IV, which linked his ancestry to Horus and Osiris. Most of the exterior reliefs were added in Roman times, which explains why the Emperor Augustus shadows Buto, goddess of the north, as she plays a harp before the young, naked Horus and his mother at one end of the central register, behind the Hathor-headed colonnade **[g]**. Further south and higher up, the Roman reliefs overlie inscriptions in hieroglyphs and demotic characters that partly duplicate those on the Rosetta Stone **[h]**. Inside, a columned forecourt and two vestibules precede the sanctuary, which contains the finest scenes **[i]**. Although iconoclasts have defaced the goddess suckling the child-pharaoh on the left-hand wall, you can see Isis giving birth to Horus in the marshes at the bottom of the rear wall. Around the back of the sanctuary behind the northern colonnade is a corresponding scene of Isis nursing Horus in the swamp **[j]**.

Inside the Temple of Isis

Immediately behind the Second Pylon lies a small open court that was originally separated from the **Hypostyle Hall** by a screen wall, now destroyed. A lovely drawing by David Roberts shows this "Grand Portico" in its rich original colours: the flowering capitals are in shades of green with yellow flowers and blue buds; crimson and golden winged sun-discs are seen flying down the central aisle of the ceiling, which elsewhere bears astronomical reliefs. The unpainted walls and column shafts show the hall's builder, Ptolemy VII Euergetes II, sacrificing to various deities. After the emperor Justinian forbade the celebration of Isis rituals at Philae in 550 AD, Copts used the hall for services and chiselled crosses into the walls. On the left-hand jamb of the portal **[k]** into the vestibule beyond, a piece of Roman graffiti asserts *B Mure stultus est* ("B Mure is stupid").

As at other temples, the **vestibules** get lower and darker as you approach the sanctuary. By a doorway **[l]** to the right of the first vestibule, a Greek inscription records the "cleansing" of this pagan structure under Bishop Theodorus, during the reign of Justinian. On the other side of the vestibule is a room giving access to the **stairs** to the roof (see below). The next vestibule has an interesting scene flanking the portal at the back **[m]**, where the king offers a sistrum (left) and wine (right) to Isis and Harpocrates. On the left-hand door jamb, he leaves offerings to Min, a basket to Sekhmet and wine to Osiris, with the sacred bull and seven cows in the background. In the partially ruined transverse vestibule, the king offers necklaces, wine and eye paint to Osiris, Isis, Hathor and Nephthys, outside the sanctuary **[n]**.

Dimly lit by two apertures in the roof, the **sanctuary** contains a stone pedestal dedicated by Ptolemy III and his wife Berenice, which once supported the goddess's barque. On the left wall, the pharaoh faces Isis, whose wings protectively enfold Osiris. Across the room, an enthroned Isis suckles the infant Horus (above) and stands to suckle a young pharaoh (below, and now defaced). The other rooms, used for rites or storage, contain reliefs of goddesses with Nubian features.

The Osirian Shrine

Try to persuade a guard to unlock the stairway to the roof, where a series of sunken rooms dwells on the resurrection of Osiris. After scenes of lamentation in the vestibule of this **Osirian Shrine**, you can see Isis gathering up his limbs, and the slain god lying naked and tumescent upon a bier (as always, the phallus has been vandalized). Mourned by Isis and Nephthys, Osiris revives to impregnate his sister-wife, while Selket and Douait reconstruct his body for its solar rebirth. Cast as the hawk-headed Sokar, Osiris is borne away to a papyrus swamp by the four sons of Horus, to be anointed with holy water with Anubis in attendance.

Hadrian's Gate

By leaving the temple through the western door of the first vestibule you'll emerge near **Hadrian's Gate**, set into the girdle wall that once encircled Philae Island. Flanking your approach are two walls from a bygone vestibule, decorated with notable reliefs. The right-hand wall **[o]** depicts the origin of the Nile, whose twin streams are poured forth by Hapy the Nile-god from his cave beneath Biga Island, atop which perches a falcon. To the right of this, Isis, Nephthys and others adore the young falcon as he rises from a marsh.

Above the door in the opposite wall **[p]**, Isis and Nephthys present the dual crowns to Horus, whose name is inscribed on a palm stalk by Sheshat (right) and Thoth (left). Below, Isis watches a crocodile drag the corpse of Osiris to a rocky promontory (presumably Biga). Around the gate itself, Hadrian appears before the gods (above the lintel) and the door jambs bear the fetishes of Abydos (left) and Osiris (right). At the top of the wall, Marcus Aurelius stands before Isis and Osiris; below he offers Isis grapes and flowers.

North of the gateway lie the foundations of the **Temple of Harendotes** (an aspect of Horus), built by the emperor Claudius.

Elsewhere on the island

To complete the cast of deities involved in the Osirian myth, a small **Temple of Hathor** was erected to the east of the main complex. Aside from two Hathor-headed columns *in situ* and fragmented capitals out back, the ruined temple is only notable for a relief of musicians, among whom the god Bes plays a harp. More eye-catching and virtually the symbol of Philae is the graceful open-topped **Kiosk of Trajan**, nicknamed the "Pharaoh's Bedstead". Removed from its watery grave by a team of British navy divers, the reconstructed kiosk juxtaposes variegated floral columns with a severely classical superstructure; only two of the screen wall panels bear reliefs.

Last in order of priority come the ruined **Temple of Augustus** and the **Gate of Diocletian**, which shared the northern end of old Philae with a mud-brick Roman village that was so eroded by repeated soakings that it was left to be submerged by the lake.

Kalabsha

The hulking **Temple of Kalabsha** broods beside Lake Nasser near the western end of the High Dam, marooned on an island or strung out on a promontory, depending on the water level. Between the site and the dam lies a graveyard of boats and fishy remains, enhancing its mood of desolation. The main temple originally came from Talmis (later known as Kalabsha), 50km to the south of Aswan; in a German-financed operation, it was cut into 13,000 blocks and reassembled here in 1970, together with other monuments from Nubia. Strictly speaking, "Kalabsha" refers to the original site rather than the temple itself, which is named after the god Mandulis, and has no historic connection with two smaller monuments in the vicinity, relocated here from other sites in Nubia.

Taxis are the best way of getting to Kalabsha and back. Official rates for a round trip from Aswan are £E25 for a four-seater taxi, £E35 for a seven-seater Peugeot. Better still, include Kalabsha in a half-day taxi tour taking in Philae, the dams and the Unfinished Obelisk (see p.445). **Motorboats** will take you over to Kalabsha and back for £E30 (for the whole boat; 6–8 people) with an hour at the site (daily: summer 7am–5pm; winter 7am–4pm; £E20), which is sufficient; tickets are sold at the temple itself.

The Temple of Mandulis

The **Temple of Mandulis** is a Ptolemaic-Roman version of an earlier XVIII Dynasty edifice dedicated to the Nubian fertility god Marul, whom the Greeks called Mandulis.

By Ptolemaic times, Egypt's Nubian Empire was a token one, dependent on the goodwill of the powerful kingdom of Napata ruled from Meröe near the Fourth Cataract, about 400km south of Abu Simbel. Having briefly restored old-style imperialism, the Romans abandoned most of Nubia during the reign of Diocletian, falling back on deals with local rulers to safeguard Egypt's southern border. As the linchpin of the last imperial town south of Aswan, the temple bears witness to this patronage and the kingdoms that succeeded the Napatan state, which disintegrated under the onslaught of marauding Blemmye (*c*.550 AD), a group of nomadic tribes who were perhaps the ancestors of the modern Beja.

The causeway, court and facade

Approaching the sandstone temple from behind, you miss the dramatic effect of the great stone **causeway** from the water's edge, used by pilgrims in the days when Kalabsha was a healing temple, like Edfu and Dendara. For reasons unknown, its chunky **pylon** is skewed at a slight angle to the temple, a blemish rectified by having a trapezoidal **courtyard** whose pillars are set closer together along the shorter, southern side.

The first batch of reliefs worth a mention occurs on the **facade** of the Hypostyle Hall at the back of the court. While Horus and Thoth anoint the king with holy water in a conventional scene to the left of the portal, the right-hand wall bears a decree excluding swineherds and their pigs from the temple (issued in 249 AD); a large relief of a horseman in Roman dress receiving a wreath from the winged Victory; and a text in poor Greek lauding Siklo, the Christian king of the Nobatae, for repulsing the Blemmye.

The Hypostyle Hall and Sanctuary

The now roofless **Hypostyle Hall** is distinguished by columns with ornate flowered capitals, and some interesting reliefs along the rear wall. Left of the portal, a Ptolemaic king offers crowns to Horus and Mandulis, while Amenhotep II (founder of the XVIII Dynasty temple) presents a libation to

Mandulis and Min. Across the way, a nameless king slays a foe before Horus, Shu and Tefnet.

Within the **vestibules** beyond, look for figures personifying the Egyptian nomes, below a scene of the king offering a field to Isis and Mandulis and wine to Osiris (near the stairs off the *pronaos* or outer vestibule); and a rare appearance by the deified Imhotep (low down on the left-hand wall of the *naos* or inner vestibule).

The **Sanctuary** is similar in size to the vestibules and, like them, once had two columns. Along its back wall you can identify (from left to right) the emperor offering lotuses to Isis and the young Horus, and milk to Mandulis and Wadjet; then incense to the former duo and lotuses to the latter. Although the god's cult statue has vanished, Mandulis still appears at either end of the scene covering the temple's **rear wall**: in his royal form, with a pharaonic crown, sceptre and ankh sign (right); and as a god whose ram's-horn crown is surmounted by a solar disc, *uraeus* and ostrich plumes (left).

From the *pronaos*, you may be able to ascend a stairway to the **roof**, which features an abbreviated version of the Osirian shrines found at other complexes. The **view** of Lake Nasser and the High Dam, over the temple courtyards, is amazing. A passageway between the temple and its enclosure wall leads to a well-preserved **Nilometer**.

The Kiosk of Qertassi and Beit al-Wali

Re-erected near the lakeside at the same time as Kalabsha Temple, the **Kiosk of Qertassi** resembles a knocked-about copy of the "Pharaoh's Bedstead" at Philae, but actually came from another ancient settlement, 40km south of Aswan. Aside from its fine views of Lake Nasser, this Ptolemaic-Roman edifice is chiefly notable for two surviving Hathor-headed columns, which make the goddess look more feline than bovine. In the forecourt, notice the women pleading for mercy as Ramses seizes their menfolk, and the Nubians paying tribute in the form of gold, ivory, leopard skins, feathers, and even an ostrich.

The oldest monumental relic from Nile-inundated Nubia is a temple dug into the hillside behind Kalabsha Temple. Originally hewn under Ramses II, who left his mark throughout Nubia, this cruciform rock-cut structure is known by its Arabic name, **Beit al-Wali** (House of the Holy Man). The weathered reliefs flanking its narrow court depict the pharaoh's victories over Nubians and Ethiopians (left), Libyans and Asiatics (right). By contrast, scenes in the transverse hall are well preserved and brightly coloured. Here, Ramses makes offerings before Isis, Horus and the Aswan Triad (Hapy, Satet and Khnum), and is suckled by goddesses inside the sanctuary, whose niche contains a mutilated cult statue of three deities.

Wadi el-Seboua, Amada and Qasr Ibrim

At the time of writing, the three reconstructed sites known as **Wadi el-Seboua**, **Amada** and **Qasr Ibrim** can only be seen while **cruising on Lake Nasser** (detailed in the box on p.451), but spur roads to Wadi el-Seboua and Amada have been built, so access might improve if security restrictions are eased. Meanwhile, cruise boats provide their passengers with motorboat rides to Wadi el-Seboua and Amada, moor tantalizingly close to Qasr Ibrim (where you can't land), and start or end their tours at Abu Simbel or Kalabsha.

Wadi el-Seboua

Cruise boats departing from the High Dam must sail nearly half the length of Lake Nasser before they reach **Wadi el-Seboua**. They usually moor there after dark for passengers to enjoy an awesome floodlit vista of three temples, joined by what appears to be a long processional avenue, which is revealed next morning to be a track across a desert of tan-coloured sand and grey rocks. The landscape is dotted with a few swaths of grass and a half-submerged crane that was used to transport the main temple from its original location, 4km away. **Admission** to the site costs £E20.

Wadi el-Seboua means "Valley of the Lions" in Arabic and refers to the **avenue of sphinxes** leading to the **temple** of that name. It was built during the reign of Ramses II by his viceroy of Kush, Setau, using Libyan prisoners of war, who also worked on Abu Simbel. Like Abu Simbel, it was dedicated to Amun-Re, Re-Herakhte and the deified pharaoh, whose role as a conqueror is emphasized by images of Libyan and Asiatic captives carved on the pedestals of the statues of the king that flank its gateway. In the second court, the human-headed sphinxes give way to falcon-headed ones, representing the four forms of Horus. Archeologists have discerned a subtle attempt to "rehabilitate" Seth – the reviled murderer of Osiris – by using red sandstone for the steps and base of the temple proper. (Red was the colour associated with Seth, who was the patron deity of the Delta city of Avaris, whence the Ramessid dynasty originated.)

Beyond the temple **pylon** is an **open court** with columns fronted by Osiride statues of Ramses, notable for their thick legs. Scholars disagree whether this reflected his physique or was merely to make him look stronger, but this feature occurs on all statues of Ramses, whose virility is further attested to by images of his numerous progeny (53 princes and 54 princesses) below the offering scenes on the walls. The remainder of the temple is cut from rock and once served as a Christian church; its **reliefs** retain much of their scarlet, white and yellow paint due to being covered by plaster for centuries. The best-preserved ones are in the transverse vestibule, including an unusual portrayal of Hathor with a woman's body and a cow's head. You can also see Ramses making offerings to his own sphinx, above and behind the doorway into the sanctuary, where a votive niche contains remnants of the Christian murals that once covered the walls, resulting in a surreal tableau of Ramses offering flowers to St Peter.

Temple of Dakka

From Wadi el-Seboua, passengers can walk or ride a camel (£E35) 1500m across the desert to the hilltop **Temple of Dakka** that once stood 40km north of its present site. Its most striking feature is an elegant freestanding **pylon**, which is over 12m tall; visitors are sometimes allowed to climb it, which affords them a fantastic view of the area. You may also see **hawks**, hovering on thermals above the pylon. There isn't much carving on the walls but the gateway is crowned by a winged sun-disc, and on its left-hand side is graffiti in Meröitic script thought to have been left by Nubian soldiers, retreating from Aswan in 23 AD.

The temple itself was started by **Arkamani**, one of the rulers (218–200 BC) of the Kingdom of Meröe – which at that time controlled Lower Nubia – and was added to by his contemporary, **Ptolemy IV**, and decorated by later Ptolemies. You can see the Hellenistic influence in the composite capitals (combining Greek and Egyptian forms) and scenes in the *pronaos*, where Isis sports big breasts in the Greek style. Also notice the four sacred cobras, carved in the corners of the entrance wall. On many of the reliefs in the temple the king performing the rituals is simply identified by a cartouche reading "Pharaoh", as the masons didn't know who was in power at the time in Alexandria, or didn't want to inscribe the name of a Ptolemy who wouldn't be on the throne for long – though this wasn't the case for Ptolemy IV and his sister-wife Arsinöe, who are shown offering a Maat (truth) figure to Thoth and Wepset on the lintel of the doorway into the vestibule.

At the back of the vestibule is a passageway and stairs leading to the **roof**, which affords a stunning view, while beyond lies the **Chapel of Arkamani** that originally served as the temple's sanctuary. Here, Arkamani makes offerings to the gods beneath a frieze of his cartouche interspersed with falcons and ibises, while on the rear wall is an interesting relief of Thoth as an ape adoring Tefnut, who is shown as a lioness. The temple was dedicated to a local form of Thoth called Thoth of Pnubs (Pnubs being a sycamore-fig tree), his consort Tefnut and their "offspring" Arensnupis, a Nubian god of the Meröitic era whom the Egyptians called "The Good Companion of Isis". A baboon worshipping a lion can also be seen in the side-passage leading off the chapel, while another ape consorts with a cow beneath a persea tree low down in the near right-hand corner of the sanctuary, which was built and decorated under the Roman emperors Augustus and Tiberius. On leaving the temple, walk around the east wall to see a **waterspout** in the shape of a lion's head.

Temple of Maharraqa

A short way downhill back towards the shore stands the small **Temple of Maharraqa**, taken from a site 50km north of its present location, which was the southern frontier of Egypt in Greco-Roman times. Its floral capitals and reliefs were left unfinished – in some places only roughly sketched in reddish-brown paint. The temple's most interesting feature, leading up to the roof, is the **spiral staircase**, the only one known in an Ancient Egyptian building. The temple was probably dedicated to Seraphis.

Amada

Beyond Wadi el-Seboua, Lake Nasser describes an S-shaped curve that takes it past another set of temples in one of the loveliest parts of Nubia, where the rocky desert shoreline is fringed with acacia scrub. Cruise passengers are ferried to **Amada** here by motorboat, and all three monuments are covered by one **ticket** (£E20). Bring a **torch** for examining the reliefs inside the temples.

Temple of Amada

The site is named after the **Temple of Amada**, which is the oldest surviving structure on Lake Nasser and contains some of the finest relief-carving to be seen on any of the Nubian monuments. It was built by the XVIII Dynasty pharaohs Tuthmosis III, Amenophis II and Tuthmosis IV, and restored and decorated during the XIX Dynasty. Like most of the Nubian temples, it was dedicated to Amun-Re and Re-Herakhte, who appear with various pharaohs in the usual offerings scenes. Amada Temple originally stood 2.6km from its present site, and was moved there on flatcars by French engineers in a race against the rising waters of the lake.

For archeologists, the temple is particularly interesting for two historic **inscriptions**: the first, carved on a stele on the left side of the entrance, describes the Libyan invasion of Egypt in the fourth year (1232 BC) of

Merneptah's reign; while the other, on the back wall of the sanctuary, dates from the second year (1423 BC) of Amenophis II's reign, and relates how he dealt with seven leaders of a revolt in Syria, whose heads and limbs were hung on the gates of Thebes as a warning to other would-be rebels.

When Amelia Edwards visited Amada in 1873 she found the temple "half-choked" with sand, so that she had to crawl into the sanctuary on all fours; judging by the **camels** drawn by Bedouin and pilgrims on the cornice of the facade, it was buried so in medieval times. The inner part of the temple consists of a vestibule and sanctuary with a small cult-chamber on either side, whose **reliefs** are as lapidary as any produced during the XVIII Dynasty. The ones in the right-hand room depict the foundation and consecration of the temple; Tuthmosis III and Amenophis II make offerings to the gods in the other chamber.

Temple of Derr

A few minutes' walk from Amada is the smaller **Temple of Derr**, once located on the east bank of the Nile (the only one in Nubia on that side of the river). With its gateway gone and its pillared forehall reduced to stumps, the temple now confronts visitors with a rugged portico featuring four square pillars and statues of Ramses II only roughed-out up to waist-level. The interior of the temple was entirely hewn from rock, with few straight lines or right angles, and its sunk-reliefs finished in stucco with painted details. On the side walls of the pillared hall, Re-Herakhte's sacred barque is carried in a procession on the shoulders of priests, as Ramses walks alongside wearing a leopard-skin cloak; the white background and the yellow of the barque and cloak are still visible. More colours survive on the walls of the sanctuary, where Ramses burns incense and pours a libation to the barque before annointing Re-Herakhte with his little finger (right). At the back, the four cult-statues that originally represented Ramses, Amun-Re, Re-Herakhte and Ptah were hacked away by Christian iconoclasts.

Tomb of Pennut

Leaving Derr temple, it's worth hurrying on ahead to get to the **Tomb of Pennut**, as it's only large enough to hold a few people. Pennut (or Penne) was a high official in Lower Nubia during the reign of Ramses VI, whose tomb was originally dug into a hillside at Aniba, 40km south of its present site. Sunk-reliefs in the rectangular offerings chamber show Pennut and his wife before the gods, mourners at his funeral, and Pennut worshipping the cow-goddess Hathor in the Western Mountains. Upon leaving the tomb, its custodian delves into a bucket to extract a baby **crocodile**, which he offers to tourists for a photo opportunity. The shallows of Lake Nasser beyond Amada are home to many crocodiles and monitor lizards, but they avoid spots frequented by tourists and are mainly seen by the 5000 fishermen who spend up to six months at a time in small rowing boats, collectively harvesting up to 50,000 tonnes of fish a year from the lake.

Qasr Ibrim

Qasr Ibrim – the last stop on the cruise before Abu Simbel – is unique for being the only one of the Nubian sites to remain *in situ*, albeit nowadays on an island rather than the summit of a hill. This continuity has allowed the Egypt Exploration Society to carry out **excavations** every two years since 1961 and establish that Qasr Ibrim was occupied throughout successive periods from the late New Kingdom until the early nineteenth century, when it was inhabited

In the desert off the road to Abu Simbel are two ancient sites of great significance. **Nabta Playa** is a large, kidney-shaped depression that trapped water during the wet phase of Saharan prehistory (8000–6000 BC). Settlements flourished, leaving the basin strewn with ostrich eggs, animal bones, pottery and structures. A circle of **megaliths** weighing up to 1.5 tonnes each is thought to be the world's earliest **astronomical calendar** (a millennium older than Stonehenge), used to mark the summer solstice shortly before monsoons brought rainfall. Nine **tombs** containing ritually sacrificed cattle may represent an early form of Ancient Egypt's cult of the cow-goddess Hathor. The site was found by chance in 1973 by a passing archeologist, Fred Wendorf, who has studied it ever since.

The **Chephren Quarries** were also discovered by accident, by a British patrol lost in a sandstorm in 1932. It was soon realized that this was the answer to a long-standing riddle: the source of the blueish diorite used for the **funerary statue of Khafre** (Chephren) that was briefly used in the Old Kingdom but never again. Other gneiss rocks and quartz were quarried here during the Middle Kingdom to make funerary vessels. About seven hundred quarries (forty of them large) are spread over nearly one hundred square kilometres, with ramps, stalls for watering animals, a bakery and thousands of hieroglyphic inscriptions. The SCA has declared part of it a historic monument, but the rest may be lost to canals as the Toshka Project (see box on p.466) enters its next phase.

by Bosnian mercenaries of the Ottoman Empire, who married into the local Nubian community. Before the Bosnians' arrival in the sixteenth century, Qasr Ibrim was one of the last redoubts of Christianity in Lower Nubia, as it had previously been the last area to forsake paganism, abandoning the worship of Isis two hundred years after the rest of Egypt. Qasr Ibrim's unusual name is derived from the ancient Pedme, which became Primis in Greek, Phrim in Coptic and finally Ibrim in Arabic (which has no sound for "p").

The ruined sandstone **cathedral** dates back to the eighth century and overlies a temple of Isis built by the Nubian XXV Dynasty pharaoh Taharka; as many as six temples once existed here. The cathedral's broken vaults rise amid a muddle of dry-stone and cut-masonry walls, riddled with portals, niches and cavities, attesting to the age and complexity of the site. Due to its fragility and the ongoing excavations, tourists are not allowed to land here, but boats moor so close to the shore that the ruins can easily be seen, or closely examined with **binoculars**.

Abu Simbel

The great **Sun Temple** of **Abu Simbel** (literally "Father of the Ear of Corn") epitomizes the monumentalism of the New Kingdom during its imperial heyday, when Ramses II (1304–1237 BC) waged colonial wars from the Beka'a Valley in Lebanon to the Fourth Cataract. To impress his power and majesty on the Nubians, Ramses had four gigantic statues of himself hewn from the mountainside, whence his unblinking stare confronted travellers as they entered Egypt from Africa. The temple he built here was precisely oriented so that the sun's rays reached deep into the mountain to illuminate its sanctuary on his birthday and the anniversary of his coronation. The deified pharaoh physically overshadows the sun-god **Re-Herakhte**, to whom the temple is nominally dedicated, just as his queen, **Nefertari**, sidelines **Hathor** in a neighbouring edifice, also hewn into the mountain.

The first European to see Abu Simbel since antiquity was the Swiss explorer Burckhardt, who found the temples almost completely buried by sand drifts in 1813. Although Belzoni later managed to clear an entrance, lack of treasure discouraged further efforts and the site was soon reburied in sand so fine "that every particle would go through an hourglass" – a process repeated throughout the nineteenth century. After Robert Hay took a cast of the face of the northern colossus, leaving it disfigured by lumps of plaster, Amelia Edwards ordered her sailors to remove the residue and tint the white stains with coffee, dismaying the vessel's cook, who had never "been called upon to provide for a guest whose mouth measured three feet and a half in width". Finally cleared, the temple became the scenic highlight of Thomas Cook's Nile cruises.

It was the prospect of losing Abu Simbel to Lake Nasser that impelled UNESCO to organize the salvage of Nubian monuments in the 1960s. Behind the temporary protection of a coffer dam, Abu Simbel's brittle sandstone was stabilized by injections of synthetic resin and then hand-sawn into 1041 blocks weighing up to thirty tons apiece. Two years after the first block was cut, Abu Simbel was reassembled 210m behind (and 61m above) its original site, a false mountain being constructed to match the former setting. The whole operation (from 1964 to 1968) cost $40 million.

Visiting Abu Simbel

Abu Simbel lies on the west bank of Lake Nasser, 280km south of Aswan and 40km north of the Sudanese border. A road runs there from Aswan, used by tourist vehicles travelling in a convoy, and public buses at other times. The site can also be reached by air or water – notably on the **luxury cruises** (p.451) that also visit other sites on Lake Nasser (see Wadi el-Seboua, Amada and Qasr Ibrim, on p.459). Although most tourists visit Abu Simbel on a **day-trip** from Aswan, it's quite feasible to spend a night in Abu Simbel town.

From Aswan, Thomas Cook and other agencies offer daily **excursions** by comfy air-conditioned minibus (€75/$95), while budget hotels pack trippers into minivans for £E35–55 per head. The **convoy** leaves at 4.30am, arrives at Abu Simbel three and a half hours later, and starts the return journey at 10am. This schedule makes sense given the heat of the desert, but means that hundreds of tourists arrive at the same time, packing out the temples. If you want to enjoy them in privacy and stay longer at Abu Simbel, there are currently two public **buses** (4hr; £E20) a day from Aswan, at 8am and 4pm, which start back at 1.30pm and 6am next day. Although there's supposed to be a limit of four tourists per vehicle, it isn't enforced.

For those with more cash, **flying** saves time and provides a unique view of Lake Nasser and Abu Simbel. EgyptAir flights from Aswan and Luxor are scheduled according to demand, with a dozen flights a day at busy times, and around three when tourism is low. Most people opt for a same-day return flight from Aswan (£E995, including airport transfers); if you want to stay overnight you are obliged to use the 11.15am flight.

Cruise-boat passengers provide most of the audience at the nightly **Sound and Light Show** (£E60; no student discount; ⓦwww.egyptsandl.com), starting at 6.30pm, 7.45pm and 9pm in the winter and one hour later in summer. Don't worry about which language the show is in, as they provide headphones for simultaneous translation and, in any case, the images projected onto the temple facades are more arresting than the soundtrack. Tickets are sold at the temple ticket office.

Abu Simbel town

The new town of **ABU SIMBEL** looks a desolate place as you roll in past the airport, but once beyond the main square it becomes quite picturesque as it straggles around rocky headlands dotted with beehive-domed houses and crimson oleander bushes. From the junction with its row of **cafés**, you can follow the main road as it curves around towards the temple, 1km away. This takes you past a **telephone office**, a **pharmacy** and three **banks** (none with ATMs; all closed Fri & Sat), followed by a **post office** with the **tourist police** (℡097/340-0277) around the corner, before you pass the town council and reach the souvenir arcade that precedes the visitors' centre and ticket office for the temples – about fifteen minutes' walk in all.

Few tourists **stay** at Abu Simbel. The *Abu Simbel Village* (℡097/340-0092; ❸), 200m from the main junction in the opposite direction from the temples, has simple vaulted rooms with bathrooms. A better option is the traditional Nubian-style *Eskaleh* (℡012 3680521, ✉fikrykachif@genevalink.com; ❺), run by musician Fikry Kachif, which doubles as a Nubian culture centre with a library and occasional performances of music and dance; five en-suite rooms, a restaurant and a roof terrace facing the lake. At the top of the heap is the five-star *Seti Abu Simbel* (℡097/340-0720, ⓦwww.setifirst.com; ❸), with a/c chalets in a lush garden with three pools, also overlooking Lake Nasser.

You're best off **eating** at *Eskaleh*, whose meals (£E30–40) are made from organic produce from its garden, or at *Seti Abu Simbel* (£E45–65), which serves **alcohol**. The *Wady El Nile* and other cafés on the main street serve decent tea, but the food may not be fresh.

The local **hospital** (℡097/349-9237) has a surgeon but no anaesthetist, and probably only exists because President Sadat had a holiday villa built at Abu Simbel. Tourists on cruise boats may feel like VIPs themselves, insofar as it's hard to go far from the boats (which moor nearby, but just out of sight of, the temples) without an armed police escort.

The Sun Temple of Ramses II

Having checked out the **Visitors' Centre**, which relates how the temples were moved to their present location, visitors walk around the hill to be confronted by the great **Sun Temple** (daily 7am–5pm, later if planes land in the evening; £E80, student £E35), seemingly hewn from the cliffs overlooking Lake Nasser. Its impact is perhaps a little diminished by familiarity (the temple

---

Bird-watching at Abu Simbel

Due to its location on a large body of water surrounded by desert, near the Tropic of Cancer, Abu Simbel sustains both indigenous African and migrant species of bird. Among the rarer species are pink-backed pelicans, yellow-billed storks, long-tailed cormorants, African skimmers and pied wagtails, and pink-headed doves. While serious twitchers will haunt the coves with binoculars, casual birdspotters can see quite a few dazzling birds in the grounds of the visitors' centre or the *Eskaleh* and *Seti Abu Simbel* hotels. The best time for bird-watching is during the **breeding season** in late January/early February. Mohammed Orabi from Aswan (℡012 334-0132) is a recommended bird-watching **guide**.

has been depicted on everything from T-shirts to £E1 notes): the technicolour contrast between red rockscape and aquamarine water is more startling than the clean-swept facade, which looks less dramatic than the sand-choked Abu Simbel of nineteenth-century engravings. For all the meticulous reconstruction and landscaping, too, it's hard not to sense its artificiality ... but gradually the temple's presence asserts itself, and your mind boggles at its audacious conception, the logistics of constructing and moving it, and the unabashed megalomania of its founder.

The colossi and facade

Although Re-Herakhte, Amun-Re and Ptah are also carved on the facade as patron deities, they're clearly secondary to Ramses II, the pharaoh-god whom courtiers feared as "a powerful lion with claws extended and a terrible roar". He ruled for 67 years, dying at the age of 96, having sired scores of sons, most of whom predeceased him. The temple facade is dominated by four enthroned **Colossi of Ramses II**, whose twenty-metre height surpasses the Colossi of Memnon at Thebes (though one lost its upper half following an earthquake in 27 BC). Their feet and legs are crudely executed but the torsos and heads are finely carved, and the face of the left-hand figure is quite beautiful. Between them stand figures of the royal family, dwarfed by Ramses' knees. To the left of the headless colossus is the pharaoh's mother, Muttuy; Queen

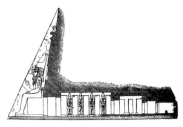
▲ Cross-section of the Sun Temple

Nefertari stands on the right of the colossus, Prince Amunhirkhepshef between its legs. On the right leg of this same figure, an inscription records that Greek mercenaries participated in the Nubian campaign of the Saïte king Psammetichus II (*c.*590 BC).

The **facade** is otherwise embellished with a niche-bound statue of **Re-Herakhte**, holding a sceptre and a figure of Maat. This composition is a pictorial play of words on Ramses' prenomen, User-Maat-Re, so the flanking sunk-reliefs of the king presenting the god with images of Maat actually signify Ramses honouring his deified self. Crowning the facade is a corvetto cornice surmounted by baboons worshipping the rising sun. On the sides of the colossal thrones flanking the temple entrance, twin Nile-gods entwine the heraldic papyrus and sedge around the hieroglyph "to unite". The rows of captives depicted beneath them are divided between north and south, so that Asiatics feature on the northern (right-hand) throne, Nubians on its southern (left-hand) counterpart.

The Hypostyle Hall and Sanctuary

This schematic division reappears in the lofty rock-cut **Hypostyle Hall**, flanked on either side by four pillars fronted by ten-metre-high statues of Ramses in the Osiris position, carrying the crook and flail (the best is the end figure on the right). Beneath a ceiling painted with flying vultures, the walls crawl with scenes from his campaigns, from Syria to Nubia. On the entrance walls, Ramses slaughters Hittite and Nubian captives before Amun-Re (left) and Re-Herakhte (right), accompanied by his eight sons or nine daughters, and his *ka*. But the most dramatic **reliefs** are found on the side walls (all directions here are as if you're facing the back of the temple).

The right-hand wall depicts the **Battle of Qadesh** on the River Orontes (1300 BC), starting from the back of the hall. Here you see Ramses' army marching on Qadesh, followed by their encampment, ringed by shields. Acting on disinformation tortured out of enemy spies, Ramses prepares to attack the city and summons his reserve divisions down from the heights. The waiting Hittites ford the river, charge one division and scatter another to surround the king, who single-handedly cuts his way out of the trap. The final scene claims an unqualified Egyptian triumph, even though Ramses failed to take the city. Notwithstanding this, the opposite wall portrays him storming a Syrian fortress in his chariot (note the double arm, which some regard as an attempt at animation), lancing a Libyan and returning with fettered Nubians. Along the rear wall, he presents them to Amun, Mut and himself (left), and the captured Hittites to Re-Herakhte, lion-headed Wert-Hekew and his own deified personage (right).

The eight **lateral chambers** off the hall were probably used to store cult objects and tribute from Nubia, and are decorated with offering scenes. Reliefs in the smaller **pillared hall** show Ramses and Nefertari offering incense before the shrine and barque of Amun-Re (left) and Re-Herakhte (right).

Walk through one of the doors at the back, cross the transverse vestibule and head for the central **Sanctuary**. Originally encased in gold, its four (now mutilated) cult statues wait to be touched by the sun's rays at dawn on February 22 and October 22. February 21 was Ramses' birthday and October 21 his coronation date, but the relocation of Abu Simbel has changed the timing of these **solar events** by one day. Perhaps significantly, the figure of Ptah "the Hidden One" is situated so that it alone remains in darkness when the sun illuminates Amun-Re, Re-Herakhte and Ramses the god. Before them is a stone block where the sacred barque once rested.

The Toshka and East Oweinat irrigation projects

Inaugurated by President Mubarak in 1997, the **Toshka Project** is a huge twenty-year venture whose goal is to cultivate 5700 square kilometres of desert northwest of Abu Simbel, and settle six million people there. The alluvial soil is potentially fertile and experimental farms have already successfully grown crops such as cotton, watermelons, grapes and wheat. To irrigate the land, the Egyptians have spent $1 billion creating the world's largest **pumping station** to extract five billion cubic metres of water from Lake Nasser annually, and digging the **Sheikh Zayed Canal**, named after the president of the United Arab Emirates (a big investor). The main canal – completed in 2002 – is 50km long, 30m wide and 6m deep; work is now underway on four branch canals totaling 159km in length, as well as auxiliary pumping stations. The government plans to deliver water to the edge of each property, leaving the owner to distribute it across his land. So far, the land has mainly been leased by big investors, such as Saudi Prince Alwaleed Bin Talal, whose farm is visible on the way to Abu Simbel.

Toshka's critics claim that the Egyptian government will end up footing most of the cost of the project – rather than twenty percent, as envisaged – and the total bill has been projected to be a staggering $66 billion. Besides the pumping station and the canal, there is a network of new roads linking Toshka to another irrigation project at **East Oweinat** in the Western Desert (see p.542), using aquifer water. Some fear that these projects are too ambitious and may turn out to be white elephants, though supporters point out that the same was said of the High Dam, without which Egypt could not sustain itself today.

The Hathor Temple of Queen Nefertari

A little further north of the Sun Temple stands the smaller rock-hewn **Temple of Queen Nefertari**, identified here with the goddess Hathor, who was wife to the sun-god during his day's passage and mother to his rebirth at dawn. As with Ramses' temple, the rock-hewn facade imitates a receding pylon (whose corvetto cornice has fallen), its plane accentuated by a series of rising buttresses separating six **colossal statues of Ramses and Nefertari** (each over 9m tall), which seem to emerge from the rock. Each is accompanied by two smaller figures of their children, who stand knee-high in the shadows. A frieze of cobras protects the door into the temple, which is simpler in plan than Ramses', having but one columned hall and vestibule, and only two lateral chambers; it runs 24m into the hillside.

The best **reliefs** are in the hall with square, Hathor-headed pillars whose sides show the royal couple mingling with deities. On the entrance wall Nefertari watches Ramses slay Egypt's enemies; on the side walls she participates in rituals as his equal, appearing before Anuket (left) and Hathor (right). In the transverse vestibule beyond, the portal of the sanctuary is flanked by scenes of the royal couple offering wine and flowers to Amun-Re and Horus (left), Re-Herakhte, Khnum, Satet and Anuket (right). The **Sanctuary** niche contains a ruined cow-statue of Hathor, above which vultures guard Nefertari's cartouches. On the side walls, she offers incense to Mut and Hathor (left), while Ramses worships his own image and that of Nefertari (right). The predominance of yellow in the paintings may allude to Hathor's title, "The Golden One".

The Western Desert Oases

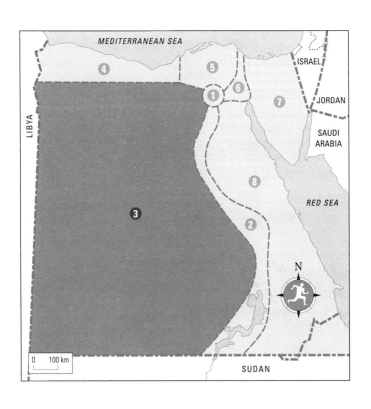

CHAPTER 3

Highlights

✳ **Jeep safaris** Whether you spend a night in the White Desert, or two weeks in the Great Sand Sea and the Gilf Kebir, you'll never forget the experience. See p.473

✳ **Bird-watching** Senegal coucals, kestrels, kites and herons are among the many species at Wadi Rayan. See p.490

✳ **White Desert** A surreal landscape of wind-eroded *yardangs* shaped like falcons, camels, lions and mushrooms, in Farafra Oasis. See p.511

✳ **The Ghard Abu Muhar-rik** Dune piled upon dune for hundreds of kilometres, beyond the stalactite cave of El-Qaf. See p.516

✳ **Al-Qasr** This fantastic labyrinth of mud-brick dwellings dating back to the tenth century is one of several once-fortified *qasr* villages in Dakhla Oasis. See p.524

✳ **Prehistoric rock art** *The English Patient* cast a spotlight on the Cave of the Swimmers in the remote Gilf Kebir, and there are many other sites at Jebel Uwaynat. See p.542

✳ **Siwa Oasis** Its citadel, palm groves, rock tombs and salt lakes make Siwa a must for travellers. See p.550

✳ **Hot springs** The best bathing spot is Bir Wahed in the outer dunes of the Great Sand Sea, near Siwa Oasis. See p.563

△ A view over Siwa Town

3

The Western Desert Oases

F or the Ancient Egyptians civilization began and ended with the Nile Valley and the Delta, known as the "Black Land" for the colour of its rich alluvial deposits. Beyond lay the "Red Land" or desert, whose significance was either practical or mystical. East of the Nile it held mineral wealth and routes to the Red Sea coast; west of the river lay the Kingdom of Osiris, Lord of the Dead – the deceased were said to "go west" to meet him. But once it was realized that human settlements existed out there, Egypt's rulers had to reckon with the **Western Desert Oases** as sources of exotic commodities and potential staging posts for invaders. Though linked to the civilization of the Nile Valley since antiquity, they have always been different – and remain so.

Siwa Oasis, far out near the Libyan border, is the most striking example: its people speak another language and have customs unknown in the rest of Egypt. Its ruined citadels, lush palm groves, limpid pools and golden sand dunes epitomize the allure of the oases. The four "inner" oases of **Bahariya**, **Farafra**, **Dakhla** and **Kharga** lie on the "**Great Desert Circuit**" that begins in Cairo or Assyut – a Long March through the New Valley Governorate, where modernization has affected each oasis to a greater or lesser extent. While Bahariya and Farafra remain basically desert villages, living off their traditional crops of dates and olives, Dakhla and Kharga have become full-blown modern towns. The appeal of the latter two is stronger in the journeying – across hundreds of miles of awesome barrenness, most of it gravel pans rather than pure "sand desert".

Much nearer to Cairo (and suitable for day excursions) are two quasi-oases: the Fayoum and Wadi Natrun. The **Fayoum** is more akin to the Nile Valley than the Western Desert, with many ancient ruins to prove its importance since the Middle Kingdom. Though a popular holiday spot for Cairenes, it doesn't attract many foreign tourists except for hunters and ornithologists. **Wadi Natrun** is significant mainly for its Coptic monasteries, which draw hordes of Egyptian pilgrims but, again, comparatively few foreigners.

The desert

Much of the fascination of this region lies in the desert itself. It's no accident that Islam, Judaism and Christianity were forged in deserts whose vast scarps and

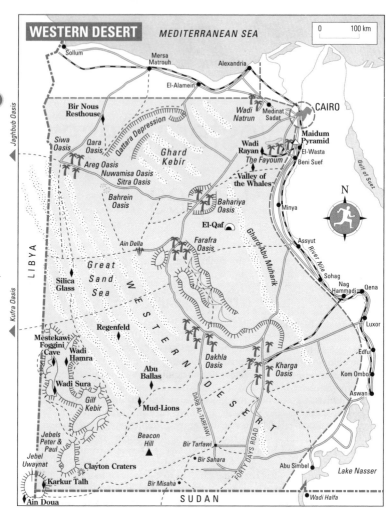

depressions displayed the hand of God writ large, with life-giving springs and oases as manifestations of divine mercy in a pitiless landscape. Although much of this landscape was once savanna, it was reduced to its current state millennia ago by geological processes and overgrazing by Stone Age pastoralists.

The **Western Desert**, which covers 681,000 square kilometres (over two-thirds of Egypt's total area), is merely one part of the Sahara belt across northern Africa. Its anomalous name was bestowed by British cartographers who viewed it from the perspective of the Nile – and, to complicate matters further, designated its southern reaches and parts of northwestern Sudan as the "Libyan Desert". Aside from the oases, its most striking features are the **Qattara Depression**, the lowest point in Africa, and the **Great Sand Sea** along the Libyan border, an awesome ocean of dunes that once swallowed up a whole army. Further south, the **Gilf Kebir** and **Jebel Uwaynat** feature some of the

Dunes

The true life of the desert is not made up of the marches of tribes in search of pasture, but of the game that goes endlessly on. What a difference in substance between the sands of submission and the sands of unruliness! The dunes, the salines, change their nature ... as the code changes by which they are governed.

Antoine de Saint-Exupéry, Wind, Sand and Stars

③

Though gravel plains, limestone pans and scarps account for sixty percent of Egypt's Western Desert, it is **dunes** that captivate the imagination. Lifeless yet restless, they shift and reproduce, burying palm groves, roads and railways in their unstoppable advance. Their shape is determined by prevailing winds, local geology and whatever moisture or vegetation exists. Where sand is relatively scarce and small obstructions are common, windblown particles form **crescent-shaped** *barchan* dunes, which advance horns first, moving over obstacles without altering their height. Baby dunes are formed downwind of the horns, which produces parallel lines of *barchans* with flat corridors between them, advancing up to 20m each year. *Barchans* can grow as high as 95m, extend for 375m, and weigh up to 450 million kilos. However, their mass is nothing compared to **parallel straight** dunes, or *seif* dunes (from the Arabic word for "sword"); some in the Great Sand Sea are 140km long. Formed by a unidirectional wind, they have slipfaces on both sides and a wavy, knife-edged crest along the top. When *seif* dunes fall over an escarpment they reform at the bottom as crescent dunes, which is why *barchans* are the prevailing form in Dakhla and Kharga. Occasionally, they pile one on top of another to create mountainous **whalebacks** or mega-*barchans*. *Seif* and whaleback dunes can combine to form huge **sand seas** or *ergs*. Egypt's Great Sand Sea extends from Siwa Oasis to the Gilf Kebir and far into Libya, where it merges with the Calanscio Sand Sea. When the wind direction alters constantly, it can even form **star-shaped** dunes. These are rare in Egypt, but one has been recorded at Wadi al-Bakht in the Gilf Kebir. Another type of formation is the flat, hard-packed **sand-sheet**, found in the Darb al-Arba'in Desert.

Much of the science of dune formation was discovered by the explorer Bagnold, whose classic book *The Physics of Blown Sand and Desert Dunes* (1939) later helped NASA to interpret data from its Martian space probes. The book was written with the benefit of five years' experimentation with a home-made wind tunnel and builder's sand; after his desert journeys of the 1920s, Bagnold felt "it was really just exploring in another form".

most magnificent prehistoric rock art in Egypt, and were the setting for the events in the book and film *The English Patient*.

All the **practicalities** of visiting the oases (including the best times to go) are detailed under the respective entries in this chapter. The most comprehensive source of historical, ethnographic and geographical **information** is Cassandra Vivian's *The Western Desert of Egypt: An Explorer's Handbook* (last updated in 2000; a new edition is due in 2007), which includes many useful maps and GPS waypoints, and is available from good bookshops in Cairo.

Visiting the desert: safaris

Organized desert safaris are the easiest and often the only way to reach some of the finest sites in and beyond the oases. There are **local operators** in all the oases, whose contact details appear in the text. As more are based in **Bahariya** (see p.507) than anywhere else, this is the best place to arrange safaris at short notice, particularly to the White Desert. Longer trips (4–19 days) to remoter sites such as the Great Sand Sea, the Gilf Kebir or Jebel Uwaynat must be booked weeks or months ahead. Safaris to the Gilf and Uwaynat are restricted to spring and autumn and may sell out six months beforehand.

Sadly, some safari outfits fail to respect the **environment**, leaving rubbish behind or encouraging tourists to remove flint arrowheads or spray water on rock paintings so that they look clearer in photos. All those we recommend below have good environmental credentials and can be booked in advance from Cairo or from abroad.

Amr Shannon ☎02/519-6894, ✆ashannon @internetegypt.com. Amr, an artist, desert explorer and TV presenter, takes small groups on tailor-made itineraries, particularly around Kharga Oasis; his wife navigates. Clients may drive their own vehicles.

Ancient World Tours ⓦwww.ancient.co.uk. This British firm specializing in archeological and desert travel does a sixteen-day tour featuring Nabta Playa, Uwaynat, the Gilf, the Great Sand Sea and Siwa (£2000), and a twelve-day tour including El-Qaf, Ain Amur and the Golden Mummies of Bahariya (£1600). Flights from Britain and deluxe accommodation in Cairo and Luxor are included in the price.

AquaSun Desert Safaris ☎02/337-2898 or 010 188-1368, ⓦwww.clubaquasun.com. Based in Cairo, Sinai and Farafra Oasis, rally driver Hisham Nessim's outfit offers five Western Desert or Sinai safaris of 7–14 days (including self-drive), plus tailor-made itineraries.

Badawiya Safari Flat 66, 22 Sharia Talat Harb, Cairo ☎02/575-8076, ⓦwww.badawiya.com. The sales office for an outfit in Farafra (see p.514), running 4WD, camel and walking treks all over the Western Desert. They visit Wadi Sura, the Mestekawi-Foggini Cave, Karkur Talh, the Selima

Sand Sheet and Regenfeld over 14–19 days ($150 per person per day).

Egypt Off-Road ⓦwww.egyptoffroad.com. Peter Gaballa runs fourteen-day expeditions to the Gilf paired with Uwaynat or the Sand Sea, plus three-day desert driving courses, outside Cairo. Peter speaks English, French, German and Arabic.

Fliegel Jerzerniczky Expeditions ⓦwww .fjexpeditions.com. This Hungarian company, run by Sahara expert András Zboray, mounts two or three expeditions a year to the Gilf and Uwaynat, sometimes venturing into Libya or Sudan. András speaks English and German.

Pan Arab Tours 5 Saudi Egyptian Building, Sharia el-Nozha, Heliopolis ☎02/418-4409, ☏291-3506, ⓦwww.panarabtours.com. A highly experienced Cairo-based agency with a sales office in Germany. Offers 4WD tours of the oases and tailor-made safaris to the Gilf and Uwaynat, the Chephren Quarries and Nabta Playa.

Zarzora Expedition 5 Sharia Tahrir, Mut, Dakhla Oasis ☎010 100-1109, ☏02/735-9435, ⓦwww .zarzora.com. Desert experts Wael Abed and former colonel Ahmed Mestekawi run a sixteen-day tour of the Gilf, Uwaynat and the Clayton Craters, and a nineteen-day Gilf, Sand Sea and oases safari.

Visiting the desert: self-drive excursions

An increasing number of visitors are driving themselves, even to sites beyond the inhabited oases of the Western Desert. The advice below should be borne in mind even if you're going to stick to main roads. For motorists considering more ambitious trips, you'll need a much more detailed handbook: see "Books", p.803, for recommendations, and p.70 for details of the best **maps** for exploring the oases. Novices will benefit from a three-day course in desert driving, offered by Egypt Off-Road in Cairo (see the "Safaris" section).

Permits

Motorists can drive to most places in the Western Desert without permission, with the following exceptions. Travel along the road **between Siwa and Bahariya** needs a permit which is easily obtained in Siwa or Bahariya. Travel to **Ain Della** requires a permit (applications should be made at least two weeks before your intended departure date), as does travel to everywhere south of Dakhla or Kharga oases – specifically the **Gilf Kebir** and **Jebel Uwaynat** – where all expeditions must be accompanied by an Egyptian soldier; applications here should be submitted at least six weeks in advance. Permits for all these places can be arranged through Badawiya Safari in Farafra (see p.474) or Misr Travel in Cairo (see p.38), who are used to dealing with the branch of Military Intelligence responsible for the surveillance of foreigners. You'll need to submit the names and passport numbers of everyone travelling, two photocopies of the main page and Egyptian visa in their passports, and the route and dates of travel.

Vehicles

The desert is a potentially lethal environment, so it's crucial to get the right vehicle. Some local safari operators swear by Libyan army-surplus Toyotas or Ford trucks, which are robust and easy to fix and handle well in the desert – though these don't have air conditioning or the other extras that are standard on the 4WD Landcruisers used by Cairo-based firms (or available for rental in Cairo). Mechanical reliability, high ground clearance and four-wheel-drive are vital; non-automatic gears, a water-cooled engine and an electrical fuel pump are strongly advised. Desert travel is extremely hard on tyres, so they must be in good condition; always carry two spare wheels, a tyre pump and pressure gauge, levers and a jack. A fire extinguisher, vital spares and a full tool/repair kit are also essential.

If you're renting a car, weigh the pros and cons of **diesel versus petrol** engines. Diesel fuel is roughly half the price of *benzin* – a significant difference if you're planning an expedition that requires thousands of litres of fuel; but diesel pumps and ignition systems are much harder to repair if there's a breakdown, so you'll need to carry replacements for all the critical parts. Fuel purity is also an issue: fuel sold in the oases is often adulterated with water, so anyone planning a major expedition should fill their jerry cans in Cairo.

Equipment

You can never carry too much **water** (in metal or heavy-duty polythene jerry cans, securely fixed to brackets) or **fuel** – travelling off-track can reduce a car's normal mileage by half. Even staying within the limits of an oasis depression, it's vital to be able to orient yourself. A vehicle-mounted **compass** must be adjusted to the car's magnetic field, which will also distort readings on hand-held compasses if you stand too close (as do ferrous rocks in Bahariya Oasis).

An increasing number of expeditions rely on **GPS** (Global Positioning System) for navigation. GPS sets can be hand-held or mounted on a dashboard to give your exact position in latitude and longitude, your compass-bearing, and record "Waypoints" so that routes can be retraced. While GPS ensures that you know *where* you are and can plot a course to any given point, it doesn't take any account of obstacles that might prove insurmountable – so choosing the best route still depends on knowing the terrain, whether it's the lie of dune "lanes" or the fragility of saltpans. **Mobile phones** can only receive a signal within 25km of towns or telecommunications masts; Mobinil has better coverage than Vodafone.

Desert driving

Decide from the start whether you plan to travel on paved roads, unpaved tracks, or through trackless open desert. It's safe to travel alone by road, as the check-points at either end (and at intervals along major routes) will raise the alarm if you fail to arrive. Always **travel in pairs** of vehicles if you're going off-road (though locals often drive alone on familiar territory). Never set off – or keep going – during **sandstorms**; should you get caught in one, shelter in the lee of cliffs or palm trees and turn the car's rear end towards the wind, lest it sand-blast the front windscreen and headlights into opacity.

Driving at **night** is likewise taboo: potholes are vicious and it's easy to crash or get lost. The **best times** for driving are early morning and late afternoon, when there's less risk of overheating or misjudging the terrain. During the middle of the day, the details of the landscape are lost in the glare, making it harder to judge **distances and scale**. Both are distorted by the desert, where drivers often perceive near-vertical slopes as level ground, or discarded jerry cans as villages. These optical illusions are commoner than **mirages** of shimmering "lakes".

If you are driving cross-country, stay alert for **changes in the desert's surface**, often indicated by a shift in colour or texture. Wheel ruts left by other vehicles can also yield clues: a sudden deepening and widening usually means softer sand (another sign of which is vegetation around the edges of dunes). Generally speaking, gravel plains provide a firm surface, while salt flats and dunes are the most unstable. Deflating one's **tyres** increases their traction on soft sand, but also their surface temperature and the car's fuel consumption, so keep a conservative speed.

There's no substitute for experience of **dunes**, but a few points need making. Dunes become softer in the summer, firmer in winter. When deflating tyres for better traction, do this just before you drive onto sand, and pump them up again before gaining firm ground. Shifting into a lower gear should also be done in advance. If stuck in soft sand, revving the engine will only dig you in deeper. Stop at once, change into low gear and try driving out slowly. If this fails, deflate the tyres as far as possible (or put traction mats, brushwood, rocks, etc beneath the rear wheels) and try again.

Never crest a dune at high speed, in case the far side has collapsed, leaving a slipface. If you *do* go over, accelerate hard (which tends to lower the rear of the vehicle), charge down the slope and hope to butch it out. Braking or slewing sideways is likely to somersault or roll the car over the edge. It's far safer to make a controlled descent in second gear and speed up as you reach the bottom.

Health care and emergencies

Dehydration, heatstroke and sunburn are the main **health** hazards. You can monitor your own water-level by watching your urine – if it starts to turn deep yellow, drink more water. Wear loose, light clothing and keep your head covered (a Bedouin headscarf works far better than a baseball cap, and can be used to veil your face against dust or grit). Use sun block and skin cream, particularly if you're travelling to the super-arid Gilf Kebir. Some travellers find air conditioning a mixed blessing, since alternating between a chilled interior and a furnace-hot environment causes passengers to catch colds.

While the odds that you'll be sleeping out when a sandstorm strikes are remote (if so, hunker down behind your rucksack), getting stuck, breaking down or crashing in the desert can be fatal if you compound the misfortune by acting wrongly. If you're driving solo, *never leave your own vehicle* unless you're within 5km of a plainly visible settlement or major highway. Otherwise, stay put, keep cool (literally) and try to attract attention. By day you can burn oil-soaked sand or bits of rubber to produce thick black smoke; at night, make a fire. A vehicle, smoke or fire are hard enough for search parties to locate; a person on their own is virtually impossible.

Other **emergencies** arise simply through drivers getting lost. The moment you suspect this, stop and try to get oriented using a compass or the sun; take your time calculating how much water and fuel remain, then decide on a course of action. The worst thing to do is simply drive on by instinct – it's a sure way of wandering even further in the wrong direction.

Although proper spares are obviously preferable, **improvised materials** can serve for vital **repairs**: nylon tights make a substitute fan belt and chewing gum can plug holes in fuel tanks or radiators. Lastly, spare a thought for the luckless **soldiers** at remote checkpoints, marooned there for forty days at a stretch. They're not seeking baksheesh, but certainly appreciate Arabic newspapers, fresh fruit or candy – and such gifts will smooth your way through the inevitable licence- and permit-checks. These guys are here to ensure that if a car breaks down in the desert, its passengers will be missed and a search launched, so it's only fair to look out for them, too.

Wadi Natrun

The quasi-oasis of **Wadi Natrun**, just off the Desert Road between Cairo and Alexandria, takes its name – and oasis stature – from deposits of natron salts, the main ingredient in ancient mummifications. Wadi Natrun's most enduring legacy, however, is its **monasteries**, which date back to the dawn of Christian monasticism, and have provided spiritual leadership for Egypt's Copts for the last 1500 years. Their fortified exteriors, necessary in centuries past to resist Bedouin raiders, cloak what are today very forward-looking, purposeful monastic establishments. Coptic monasticism experienced a revival during the 1980s, twenty years after an English writer dismissed the monasteries as "of little interest except to the specialist".

In the 1950s, model villages, olive groves and vineyards were planted here to reclaim 25,000 hectares of land from the desert, a project initially financed by the sale of King Farouk's stamp collection and other valuables. After decades of patient land reclamation, palms, flowers and hothouse vegetables now grow beside the **Desert Road** to Alex, spreading further as you travel north. Not far beyond Giza you'll pass the glass pyramids and post-modern edifices of **MEDINET SADAT** (Sadat City), a dormitory suburb, science park and film studio that represents Egypt's high-tech aspirations for the twenty-first century. On the other side of the highway, motels have sprung up around the turn-off for Wadi Natrun, which runs via the ramshackle township of **BIR HOOKER** (named after Mr Hooker, an early manager of the Egyptian Salt & Soda Co.) into the Natrun Valley.

Getting there

Wadi Natrun makes a memorable day excursion from Alex or Cairo. The easiest way to get there is to **rent a car**, or take a **taxi** (£E150–200 depending on how many monasteries you visit). By public transport, reaching the monasteries is a two-stage process. From Cairo, West Delta **buses** leave from the Turgoman terminal (hourly 6.30am–6.30pm; £E5) and terminate at Bir Hooker, where you should be able to hire a taxi to tour the monasteries for £E50–70. Otherwise, you can get a **service taxi** from Cairo (Aboud terminal) or Alex (Sidi Gaber) to the **Wadi Natrun Resthouse** at km 105 on the Desert Road – a bunch of gas stations and cafés where non-express inter-city buses also stop. From here, you can negotiate a private taxi ride to the nearest monastery, or hope to be offered a lift by one of the busloads of Coptic pilgrims that come this way. **Returning** to Cairo or Alex by bus or service taxi from the Resthouse, you'll probably have to pay the full inter-city rate. There are hourly buses to Cairo until 7pm; departures for Alex are fewer and further between, with perhaps only two buses in the afternoon, when people are most likely to be leaving after having visited the monasteries.

Alternatively there are **tours** out of Alexandria run by Alexandra Dive (see p.603), which combine a visit to Deir al-Baramus and Deir al-Suryani with Birket al-Hamra, the petrified mangrove forest and big dunes out near Omar's Wells (see p.482), for $250 per person per day, all-inclusive.

The monasteries of Wadi Natrun

Christian monasticism was born in Egypt's Eastern Desert, where the first Christian hermits sought to emulate St Anthony, forming rude communities; however, it was at Wadi Natrun that their rules and power were forged, during the persecution of Christians in urban areas under Emperor Diocletian. Several thousand **monks** and hermits were living here by the middle of the fourth century, harbouring bitter grudges against paganism, scores which they settled after Christianity was made the state religion in 330 by sacking the temples and library and murdering scholars in Alexandria. E.M. Forster judged them "averse to culture and incapable of thought. Their heroes were St Ammon, who deserted his wife on their wedding eve, and St Anthony, who thought bathing was sinful and was consequently carried across the canals of the Delta by an angel". The Muslim conquest and Bedouin raids encouraged a siege mentality among the monks, who often lapsed into idle dependence on monastic serfs. Nineteenth-century foreign visitors unanimously described them as slothful, dirty, bigoted and ignorant – the antithesis of the monks here today.

The four **Wadi Natrun monasteries** have all been totally ruined and rebuilt at least once since their foundation during the fourth century; most of what you see dates from the eighth century onwards. Each has a high wall surrounding one or more churches, a central keep entered via a drawbridge, containing a bakery, storerooms and wells, enabling the monks to withstand siege, and

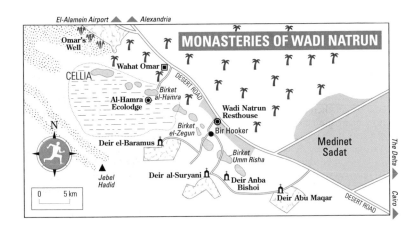

MONASTERIES OF WADI NATRUN

El-Alamein Airport · Alexandria

Omar's Well

Wahat Omar

CELLIA

DESERT ROAD

Birket al-Hamra

Al-Hamra Ecolodge

Wadi Natrun Resthouse

Birket el-Zegun

Bir Hooker

N

Deir el-Baramus

Medinet Sadat

Birket Umm Risha

Jebel Hadid

Deir al-Suryani

Deir Anba Bishoi

Deir Abu Maqar

DESERT ROAD

The Delta · Cairo

0 · 5 km

diverse associated chapels. Their low doorways compel visitors to humbly stoop upon entry (don't forget to remove your shoes outside). Their **churches** – like all Coptic chapels – are divided into three sections. The *haikal* (sanctuary) containing the altar lies behind the iconostasis, an inlaid or curtained screen, which you can peer through with your escort's consent. In front of this is the choir, reserved for Coptic Christians, and then the nave, consisting of two parts. *Catechumens* (those preparing to convert) stand nearest the choir, while sinners (known as "weepers") were formerly relegated to the back.

Practicalities: visiting the monasteries

Visiting hours vary from monastery to monastery, as does the extent to which each closes during the five seasons of **fasting**: 43 days before the Nativity, three days in commemoration of Jonah in the Whale, 55 days preceding Lent, the fast of the Holy Apostles (from Pentecost to July 12), and fifteen days marking the Assumption of the Virgin Mary (August 7–22). Fasts are posted on the Patriarchal website (ⓦ www.copticpope.org). Deir Anba Bishoi alone is open every day of the year; Deir al-Suryani and Deir el-Baramus have regular opening times but close during most of the feasts; while Deir Abu Maqar will only admit those with a letter of introduction from the Coptic Patriarchate in Cairo (next to the Cathedral of St Mark, 222 Sharia Ramses, Abbassiya; ☏02/282-5374) or Alexandria (in the Cathedral of St Mark on Sharia al-Kineesa al-Kobtiyya; ☏03/483-5522). The Patriarchate can verify the opening dates of specific monasteries. Fridays, Sundays and public holidays are best avoided, as the monasteries are often swarmed by Coptic pilgrims from all over Egypt.

Men wanting to **stay in a monastery** must get written permission from the appropriate "residence" in Cairo: Deir Anba Bishoi (☏02/592-4448); Deir al-Suryani (☏02/592-9658); Deir el-Baramus (☏02/592-2775); Deir Abu Maqar (☏02/577-0614). As other guests are devout pilgrims, you should make at least a token effort to attend prayers, and leave a donation in return for the tea and bread that's provided. Women are not allowed to sleep in any of the monasteries.

Comfier **accommodation** can be found at motels (❹–❺) near km 110 on the Desert Road, or the delightful *Al-Hamra Ecolodge* (☏02/346-8565; ❷) on the western side of Birket al-Hamra. With eight chalets and several rooms in the main building, it charges £E50 per person B&B, £E85 full board. The *Wahat Omar* **restaurant** at km 112 on the Desert Road serves tasty Egyptian and Italian dishes, with an adjacent mini-zoo to entertain kids.

The monastic rule and working day

All Egyptian monasteries are **cenobitic**, meaning that the monks share food and possessions and unconditional submission to the rule of their abbot (a word that derives from the Arabic *abd*, "father"). The **monastic day** begins at 3am with an hour of silent prayer in individual *laura* (cells), before two hours of collective worship in the chapel, followed by unrelenting labour until the main meal of the day at noon. Afterwards, the monks work until 5pm, assemble for prayers and then return to their tasks until sheer exhaustion forces them to bed.

Work and prayer are seen as equal holy obligations, and many of the younger monks and novices are qualified engineers or scientists. Black garments symbolize their death to the world of bodily desires; their hoods (possibly representing the "helmet of salvation" in Ephesians 6) are embroidered with twelve crosses, after Christ's disciples.

Deir al-Suryani

The loveliest of the monasteries is **Deir al-Suryani** (summer Mon–Fri & Sun 9am–7pm, Sat 9am–5pm; winter Mon–Fri & Sun 9am–6pm, Sat 9am–3pm) – a compact maze of honey-coloured buildings. Its tranquility belies its fractious origins: the monastery was founded by monks who quit St Bishoi's due to a sixth-century dispute over the theological importance of the Virgin. After they returned to the fold it was purchased for a group of Syrian monks, hence its name – the "Monastery of the Syrians". It was here that Robert Curzon came searching for ancient manuscripts (the ostensible reason for his tour of Balkan and Levantine monasteries in the 1830s), and found them lying on the floor or serving as covers for jars, all "well begrimed with dirt". The keep's oil cellar held a "mass of loose vellum pages", while the consistory of Abyssinian monks contained a library of Aramaic texts, hanging from pegs in individual leather satchels. Nowadays, the monastery's antique volumes are lovingly maintained in a modern **library**, including a cache of manuscripts up to 1500 years old. The monastery also boasts the remains of some twelve saints and a lock of hair from Mary Magdalene.

Deir al-Suryani's principal **Church of the Virgin**, built around 980, contains a *haikal* with stucco ornamentation, and a superb ebony "**Door of Prophecies**", inlaid with ivory panels depicting the disciples and the seven epochs of the Christian era, culminating in the split with the Orthodox Church and the Coming of Islam. Some lovely Byzantine-style **murals** dating back to the church's foundation have been uncovered by restorers. A dark passageway at the back of the church leads to the **cave** where St Bishoi tied his hair to a chain hanging from the ceiling to prevent himself sleeping for four days, until a vision of Christ appeared. The marble basin in the nave is used by the abbot to wash the feet of twelve monks on Maundy Thursday, emulating Christ's act during Passion week.

Outside, the large **tamarind tree** enclosed by walls is said to have grown from the staff of St Emphram, who, as a monk, thrust it into the earth after his fellows

△ A mosaic at Deir al-Suryani

criticized it as a worldly affectation. As Coptic pope, he established cordial relations with the Fatimid caliph in 997.

Deir Anba Bishoi

Deir Anba Bishoi (daily: summer 7am–8pm; winter 7am–6pm) is the largest of the four monasteries. Over 150 monks and novices live here, and the monastery receives a constant stream of pilgrims. The legend of **St Bishoi** suggests he was one of the earliest monks at Wadi Natrun. An angel told the saint's mother that he was chosen to do God's work even before his birth in 320; two decades later he moved here to study under St Bemoi alongside John "the Short". Adopting a rather imaginative chronology, the legend also recalls that Bishoi later met Christ as an old man, carried him to church, washed his feet and was allowed to drink the water as a reward. Whatever the truth, since Bishoi's death in 417 his body has reportedly remained uncorrupted within its casket, which is carried in procession around the church every year on July 17. Next to him lies Paul of Tammuh, who was revered for committing suicide seven times.

St Bishoi's is the oldest of the five **churches** in the monastery, its *haikals* dating from the fourth, ninth and tenth centuries. The **keep**, built three to four hundred years later, has chapels at ground level (around the back) and on the second storey, one floor above its drawbridge. There's also a fifth-century **well** where Berber tribesmen washed their swords after massacring the 49 Martyrs of Deir Abu Maqar (see below).

The multi-domed building furthest from the entrance is the **residence of Shenouda III**, the Coptic pope. He uses it as an occasional retreat, though he was exiled here for some years by Sadat, and sometimes ostentatiously secludes himself here to protest at the mistreatment of Copts. Most of the Coptic popes have been chosen from the monks of Wadi Natrun, and Deir Abu Maqar in particular.

Deir Abu Maqar

Enclosed by a circular wall ten metres high, **Deir Abu Maqar** requires visitors (with the requisite letter of introduction; see p.479) to pull a bell rope; in times past, two giant millstones stood ready to be rolled across to buttress the door against raiders. Its founder, **St Makarius**, died in 390 "after sixty years of austerities in various deserts", the last twenty of which were spent in a hermit's cell at Wadi Natrun. He's said to have been so remorseful over killing a gnat that he withdrew for six months to the marshes, getting stung all over until "his body was so much disfigured that his brethren on his return only knew him from the sound of his voice". A rigorous faster, his only indulgence was a raw cabbage leaf for Sunday lunch.

Over the centuries, thirty Coptic patriarchs have come from the monastery; many are buried there, together with the 49 Martyrs killed by Berbers in 444. In 1978, monks discovered what they believed to be the **head of John the Baptist**; however, this is also claimed to be held in Venice, Aleppo and Damascus. Since its nadir in 1969, when only six monks lived here, the monastery has acquired over a hundred brethren, a modern printing press and a farm employing six hundred workers. The monks have mastered pinpoint irrigation systems and bovine embryo transplant technology in an effort to meet their abbot's goal of feeding a thousand laypersons per monk.

Deir el-Baramus

Deir el-Baramus (daily: summer 9am–6pm; winter 9am–5pm) is likewise surrounded by orchards and fields. The monastery was founded by St Makarius in 340, making it the oldest of the four that remain in Wadi Natrun, and has has eighty monks and novices, one of whom will show you around.

Visitors are greeted outside by a picture of St Moses the Black, a Nubian robber who became a monk under the influence of St Isidore. The monastery's name derives from the Coptic Pe Romios ("House of the Romans"), referring to Maximus and Domidus, two sons of the Roman emperor Valentinus who died from excessive fasting; the younger one was only 19 years old. Their bodies are reputedly buried in a crypt below the **Church of the Virgin**, whose principal altar is only used once a day, since Mary's womb begot but one child. An adjacent altar, normally curtained off, serves the "Immaterial Fathers": the spirits of bygone saints and abbots who occasionally leave droplets of water sprinkled there. The relics of Moses and Isidore are encased in glass; pilgrims drop petitions into the bier. Notice the photo of a T-shirt bearing a bloody cross, the relic of an exorcism performed at the monastery in the 1980s, where the departing spirit left a lurid sign as it was expelled from the body of the possessed victim.

Restoration work has revealed layers of medieval **frescoes** in the nave, the western end of which incorporates a fourth-century **pillar** with Syriac inscriptions. It was behind here that St Arsanious prayed with a pebble in his mouth, grudging every word that he spoke (including a statement to that effect). The ninth-century church, with belfries of unequal height (symbolizing the respective ages of Maximus and Domidus), shares a vine-laden courtyard with a **keep** and four other churches.

Birket al-Hamra and Cellia

Beyond Deir al-Baramus are numerous **salt lakes** rimmed by crusts of **natron**, a mixture of sodium carbonate and sodium bicarbonate, which the Ancient Egyptians used for dehydrating bodies and making glass. **Birket al-Hamra** ("Red Lake") is magenta-hued and highly saline, with a "miracululous" sweetwater **spring** in the middle – Copts believe that the Virgin Mary quenched her thirst here. You can wade out to the spring (enclosed by an iron well) and taste it for yourself; the mud on the lake-bed is reputedly good for various afflictions.

The local *Al-Hamra Ecolodge* can arrange **horse-riding**, **camel trekking** and **bird-watching** (look out for spur-winged plovers, crested larks, jacksnipes and sandpipers). The lakes harbour Egypt's last surviving wild **papyrus**, a dwarf subspecies of the plant that once flourished throughout the Nile Valley, but gradually became extinct; the last large papyrus (which could reach 6m) was found in the Delta in the mid-nineteenth century. Today it exists only on plantations, thanks to Dr Rageb (see p.261), who rediscovered the lost technique of making papyrus paper. There are also petrified mangroves from the Eocene Period – thick, fallen trunks, rather than the petrified roots found at Wadi al-Hitan (see p.491).

Further out, the **ruins** of some five hundred **hermitages** are spread over an area known as **Cellia** or El-Muna. St Anthony is said to have told monks at Wadi Natrun who wished to live as hermits, "Let us take food at the ninth hour and then go forth and pass through the desert and consider the place." It's thought that Cellia maintained links with the pilgrim city of Abu Mina (see p.607) until their freshwater springs dried up. In 1995 archeologists unearthed the Monastery of St John, plus traces of five subterranean monasteries that had been lost since they were found in 1930 by Prince Omar Tousoum, who proved the ubiquity of freshwater beneath the desert by drilling **Omar's Wells**. Tall dunes stretch as far south as **Jebel Hadid**, visible on the horizon from Wadi Natrun.

Birket al-Hamra can be reached by turning off the Desert Road at km 111, just before the *Wahat Omar* restaurant. Exploring Cellia requires a 4WD vehicle.

The Fayoum

Likened in Egyptian tradition to a bud on the stem of the Nile and an "earthly paradise" in the desert, the **Fayoum** depends on river water – not springs or wells, like a true oasis. The water is distributed around the depression by a system of canals going back to ancient times, creating a lush rural enclave of palm trees dividing cotton and clover fields, orchards, and carefully tended crops of tomatoes and medicinal plants in the sandier outlying regions. Pigeons nest in mud-brick coops shaped like giant Victorian trifles, blindfolded cattle turn threshing machines and water buffalo plod home for milking. Along one shore of Lake Qaroun are fishing communities, while on the periphery are encampments of semi-nomadic Bedouin. Almost three million people live in the oasis, 500,000 in Fayoum City and the rest in four towns and 158 villages.

Despite easy access from Cairo, foreign tourists are thin on the ground. The main reason why is the Governorate capital, **Fayoum City**, which has all of Cairo's drawbacks and few of its advantages. Most of the **antiquities** require a car to reach them, and baksheesh-hungry locals pester visitors to **Lake Qaroun**. To enjoy the **birdlife**, local **moulids** or **desert safaris** needs pre-arranging, without which a day-trip will probably discourage further contact.

Winters are warmer and drier than in Cairo, summers milder than in Upper Egypt; however, cold winds in spring – known as the *khamseen* – coat everything with dust. At other times, the clarity of the air causes the sun's rays to burn more strongly than you'd expect.

Getting there

The **road from Cairo** to the Fayoum starts near the Pyramids of Giza, whose silhouettes sink below the horizon as the road gains a barren plateau dotted with army bases, then (76km later) reaches the edge of the Fayoum depression. Here, you'll pass the Ptolemaic-Roman site of Kom Oshim (on the left) before you sight Lake Qaroun and cruise down through Sinnuris into Fayoum City, driving past the Obelisk of Senusert I.

Buses from Cairo's Aboud (every 15min 6am–8pm; £E6) and El Moneeb (every 30min 6am–7pm; £E5) terminals do the one-hundred-kilometre journey in two to three hours; advance bookings are usually only necessary from midday Thursday till late on Saturday, or during Ramadan, Fayoumi moulids and public holidays. Alternatively, you can take a **service taxi** from Midan Orabi, Midan Ramses, Midan Giza or the El Moneeb terminal. These seven-seater Peugeots or pack-'em-in minibuses run practically nonstop from early morning to late at night, charging £E5–7 for a stomach-churning high-speed ride past the wrecks of previous crashes, reaching Fayoum City in about two hours. From the Nile Valley, catch one of the half-hourly buses or service taxis (£E1–2) **from Beni Suef**, which reach Fayoum City in an hour. The road runs through a cultivated strip beside the Bahr Yussef, so there's little sense of entering an oasis; en route it passes the start of tracks to the Lahun and Hawara pyramids. Buses and service taxis coming from this direction terminate at the Hawatim depot in the southwest of town.

Fayoum City

A kind of pocket-size version of Cairo, with the Bahr Yussef Canal in the role of the Nile, **FAYOUM CITY** makes a grab at the wallets of middle-class Cairenes who come to bask beside Lake Qaroun during summertime. The few foreigners that venture here tend to be whisked through in buses and remain immured in hotels, so independent travellers draw attention – especially women. Mosquitoes swarm from every nook and waterway, making evenings a misery. Add makeshift buildings, weaving traffic and malodorous canals and you've got half a dozen reasons not to linger. On the plus side, the city serves as the jumping-off point for almost everywhere you might consider visiting in the oasis. It also musters a pleasant **souk**, a couple of venerable **mosques** and some colourful **moulids** in the middle of the month of Sha'ban.

The city's official title is **Medinet el-Fayoum**, but it's known colloquially as El-Fayoum or Fayoum. The word "Fayoum" probably derives from Phiom, the Coptic word for "sea", although folklore attributes it to the pharaoh's praise of the Bahr Yussef: "This is the work of a thousand days" (*alf youm*).

Arrival, information and accommodation

Trains from Cairo terminate at the **station** in the centre of town, while buses and service taxis end up at the **Masr** depot on Sharia Gamal Abdel Nasser (£E2 by taxi to or from the centre). Coming from Beni Suef you arrive at the **Hawatim** depot south of the old town – a taxi or horse-drawn cab (*hantour*) shouldn't cost over £E10. If you're feeling adventurous and can read Arabic numerals,

take one of the green-and-white minibuses (25pt) that shuttle between outlying depots or suburbs and downtown (*wust al balad*). Minibuses #1, #2, #3 and #7 run from the Hawatim depot to the train station.

Downtown, most things worth seeing can be reached on foot, with the Bahr Yussef Canal facilitating **orientation**. The **tourist office** kiosk (daily 9.30am–3pm; ☎084/634-7298) near the four waterwheels has brochures on Fayoumi crafts, wildlife and eco-tourism, but its staff are a bit tongue-tied; to arrange anything, contact the director general of tourism, Mohammed Kamal Ahmed (☎084/634-2313, ✉mohamedkamal@yahoo.com), in the Governorate building north of the centre.

On checking into a hotel, you'll be assigned an escort from the **tourist police** (☎084/630-7298), who'll accompany you around or outside the city, preferably by taxi. They probably won't speak English but if you can muster a little Arabic they might prove helpful rather than a hindrance.

You can **change money** at any of the banks beside the Bahr Yussef (all have ATMs) or the Forex bureau near the corner of Sharia er-Ramla. The main **post office** (daily except Fri & Sat 8am–2pm) and 24-hour **telephone** exchange are on the south side of the canal, off which is DoubleClick **Internet** (daily 10am–7am; £E2/hr) on Sharia Khaled Pasha – look out for the green awning above a phonecard shop. Patients at the **hospital** on Sharia Sa'ad Zaghloul, 1km north of the centre, must pay cash up front.

Accommodation

Outside of Er-Rubi's festival, there shouldn't be any difficulty finding a room in town, though none of the hotels is great. Other options exist at Shakshuk and Tunis, near Lake Qaroun (see pp.489–490).

Honeyday 105 Sharia Gamal Abdel Nasser ☎084/634-0105, ☎634-1205. Near Masr bus depot, this high-rise hotel (whose name is pronounced "honey-die") has attractive a/c rooms with TV and fridge, a restaurant and a sleazy bar. Breakfast included. ❸
Palace Sharia Horriya ☎084/635-1222. Look out for the sign facing the Bahr Yussef; the entrance

is an alleyway, behind some kiosks. Its rooms are decent and have optional baths and a/c; the manager speaks English. ❷
Queen Sharia Munsha'at Lotfallah ☎084/346-189, ☎346-233. Spacious en-suite rooms with satellite TV (a/c costs extra) in a quiet neighbourhood, a 15min walk from the centre. Breakfast included. ❹

The City

Fayoum City's most central landmark is the four large wooden **waterwheels**, symbolic of Fayoumi agriculture, that groan away behind the tourist kiosk. The Fayoum has about two hundred such waterwheels, introduced by Ptolemaic engineers in the third century BC. Because Nile water enters the sloping Fayoum depression at its highest point, gravity does half the work of distribution, and the waterwheels act as pumps. Sluices at El-Lahun, at the entrance to the depression, regulate the current, which is strong enough to power the waterwheels for lifting irrigation water – except during January, when the whole system is allowed to dry out for maintenance; the waterwheels have a working life of ten years if properly tarred and maintained.

Coptic and Muslim folklore ascribes the **Bahr Yussef** (River of Joseph) to its Biblical namesake, who's believed to have been the pharaoh's vizier and minister for public works. Originally a natural waterway branching off the Nile near Beni Suef, it was regulated from the XII Dynasty onwards, and since the building of the Ibrahimiya Canal in the nineteenth century, has drawn water from the Nile at Dairut, nearly 300km further south. Baskets, pots and other **handicrafts** are sold on the north bank of the Bahr Yussef near the four waterwheels.

Walking west alongside the canal and crossing the fourth bridge from the tourist kiosk, you can follow a street with a wooden roof into the **Souk al-Qantara**, a labyrinth of tiny shops selling copperware and spices, grain and pulses, clothing and other goods – all without a hint of tourism. **Sharia es-Sagha**, the Street of Gold-smiths, is crammed with jewellers' shops, mostly owned by Christians. Fayoum City has a substantial Christian minority – mainly Copts, but also Anglicans and Catholics – whose churches are ranged along Sharia 26th July. The oldest is the **Church of the Virgin**, dating from the 1830s, which contains an altar dedicated to the local saint Anba Abram (1829–1912), Bishop of Fayoum and Giza, who was reputedly able to transport himself across distances in a miraculous fashion.

Near the souk you'll also find three historic mosques. The **Mosque of Ali er-Rubi** is dedicated to a local sheikh whose renown among the Fayoumis eclipses even Anba Abram's. His mausoleum, down some steps from the courtyard, is surrounded by an enormous *darih* or carved box-frame, and people muttering supplications to the saint. Further west beside the canal, the **Mosque of Qait-bey** is the oldest in the Fayoum, built (or perhaps restored) by the Circassian Mamluke Sultan Qaitbey (see p.166). Ancient columns from Kiman Faris (see box on p.488) uphold its dome, while the stone carving around the doorway, and the ebony *minbar* inlaid with Somalian ivory, are distinctly Mamluke. Qaitbey was also responsible for building the twin-arched **bridge** nearby, which was once named after his favourite concubine, Khwand Asl Bey (as was the mosque), but is now known as Bridge of the Gate of Farewells because it leads to a cemetery.

Crossing the bridge, you can head along the riverside to find the **Hanging Mosque**, so called because its north frontage is upheld by five arches, once occupied by artisans' workshops. Alternatively, delve into the backstreets near the cemetery to visit the Tuesday **pottery market** off Sharia el-Mudaris. Most of the red, pink or unglazed pots here are made at the village of Nazla, south of Ibshaway. There's also a **farmers' market** on Friday mornings.

East of the train station, the **Palace of Culture** is Fayoum City's newest landmark, an inverted pyramid housing a cinema, theatre and library. Behind it stands the **Gamal Abdel Nasser Mosque**, one of many that Nasser had built in provincial towns in the 1960s, and which bear his name.

The Seven Waterwheels and the Obelisk of Senusert I

For a pleasant half-hour's walk in the morning or evening, follow the right bank of the Bahr Sinnuris northwards out of town for 3km to reach the **Seven Water-wheels** (not to be confused with the four by the tourist kiosk). First comes a single wheel near a farm; slightly further on, a quartet revolves against a backdrop of mango trees and palms; the final pair is a little way on, near a crude bridge.

Entering or leaving town by the Cairo road, you'll pass the thirteen-metre-high red-granite **Obelisk of Senusert I**, the only obelisk in Egypt to have a rounded tip. Senusert was the second king of the XII Dynasty, who displayed a special fondness for the Fayoum and was the first to regard it as more than just a hunting ground, building the Lahun and Hawara pyramids, Medinet Madi and Qasr es-Sagha. Following the XII Dynasty (1991–1786 BC), interest in the Fayoum declined and didn't properly revive until the advent of the Ptolemies, fourteen centuries later.

Eating and drinking

Don't expect any fancy **restaurants** in Fayoum – the closest you'll get is the one in the *Queen Hotel*, which is nicely decorated and has a longish menu.

Besides the places listed below (all open till midnight or later), there are dozens of juice bars, teahouses and *fuul* and *taamiya* outlets within a few blocks' radius of Sharia er-Ramla – all basically the same, with no identifying signs or menus in English. The only place selling **alcohol** (local beer and spirits) is the bar in the *Honeyday Hotel*, which is frequented by prostitutes.

Hassouna Sharia Al-Sadd al-Ali. One of the few cafés with signs in English, it serves kebabs, *shawarma*, *fuul* and *taamiya*, grilled chicken and salad, to eat in or take away.

Milano Sharia Al-Sadd al-Ali, by the Bahr Sinnuris. Sells freshly squeezed juices, ice cream and crème caramel.

Omar Khayam Sharia Al-Sadd al-Ali. This vintage teahouse opposite *Hassouna* has a pleasant shady garden. Try the cold *sahleb*, which comes topped with slices of banana.

Festivals

It's worth visiting Fayoum City for its **festivals**, as many local farmers do. Hotels overflow during **Ali er-Rubi's moulid** in Sha'ban, when the alleys around his mosque are crammed with stalls selling sugar dolls and horsemen, and all kinds of amusements can be tried, while the devout perform *zikrs* in the courtyard.

The other big occasion is the "viewing" (*er-ruyeh*) of the new moon that heralds **Ramadan**. This calls for a huge procession from the Gamal Abdel Nasser Mosque: a parade of carnival floats represents the different professions (it's headed by the security forces, imams and sheikhs), and bombards spectators with "lucky" prayer leaflets.

During Ramadan, there's a small moulid at the domed white tomb of **Sheikha Mariam** (between the sluice of the Bahr Sinnuris and the four waterwheels). The **Great Feast** (starting on the tenth of Zoul Hagga) is a more private occasion, with most eateries closed.

On the Monday after the movable **Coptic Easter**, locals and day-trippers from Cairo picnic along the canalsides in the popular festival of "Smelling the Breeze" (Sham el-Nessim); many others celebrate it on the shore of Lake Qaroun.

Around the oasis

Lake Qaroun is readily accessible from Fayoum City, but reaching **Wadi Rayan** or the seldom-visited **ancient sites** on the periphery of the oasis is trickier, so don't undertake a trip lightly or without adequate water and food for the day. The oasis's other populous centres – Sinnuris, Ibshaway, Itsa and Tamiya – hold little interest, while Nazla is unsafe to visit.

Your freedom of movement may be impeded by the **tourist police**, who might insist that you use a private car or taxi to go any farther than Lake Qaroun – or allow you to use **public transport**. Having your own transport certainly makes life easier, and some sites are inaccessible without it. You should be able to hire a **taxi** for the day for £E200; Mohammed Ismail (☎084/820-306 or 010 692-7621) is a reliable driver. If you do **drive** yourself, stay alert for tractors, children and livestock on roads, and follow the advice on desert driving at the beginning of this chapter.

Lake Qaroun

Short of tankers gliding between the sandbanks of the Suez Canal, Egypt has no weirder juxtaposition of water and desert than **Lake Qaroun** (Birket

Sobek and Crocodilopolis

Kiman Faris (Horseman's Mounds) is the local name for a site on the northern outskirts of Fayoum City, rapidly disappearing beneath new colleges. Although nothing remains to justify a visit, it is the **site of Crocodilopolis** (later renamed Arsinoë after Ptolemy II's sister-wife), the Fayoum's ancient capital and centre of the **crocodile cult**. This supposedly began with Pharaoh Menes, the legendary unifier of Upper and Lower Egypt, whose life was saved by a croc while he was hunting in the Fayoum marshes. Crocodiles infested the lake beyond Kiman Faris (which was much larger in ancient times), so an urge to propitiate the creatures is understandable.

The crocodile deity, **Sobek**, was particularly favoured by Middle Kingdom rulers but assumed national prominence after he became identified with Re (as Sobek-Re) and Horus. He was variously depicted as a hawk-headed crocodile or in reptilian form with Amun's crown of feathers and ram's horns. At the Sacred Lake of Crocodilopolis, reptiles were fed and worshipped, and even adorned with jewellery, by the priests of Sobek.

▲ Sobek

Qaroun), where fishing boats bob against a backdrop of arid hills and the immensity of the Western Desert. Known to locals as "The Pond" (El-Birka), the lake's name may derive from the horn (*qorn*)-shaped peak on an island in the middle, but Fayoumis believe that it's named after a character in

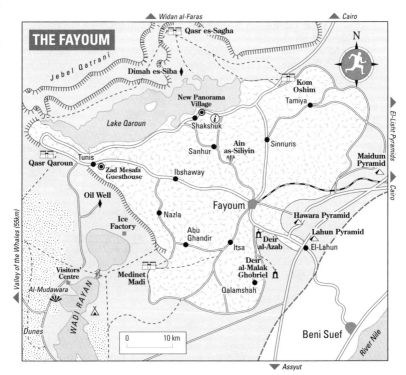

THE FAYOUM

the Koran, who was swallowed up by the earth as a punishment for being "exultant in his riches". Folklore also has it that he was a sorcerer who turned the land barren, or a Jew whose treasure still lies at the bottom of the lake. Although "glassy and brooding, surrounded by beaches encrusted with salts, the recipient of all the drainage canals in the region" (as one nineteenth-century guidebook described it), the lake is favoured by Cairenes as a **bathing resort**, undeterred by the beach of broken shells and saline gunk (keen swimmers may be glad to note that, though foul-tasting, the water is at least free of bilharzia). The "season" runs year-round, but from January to April it's too cold to swim.

The shore has partly been embanked after floods inundated the **Auberge du Lac-Fayoum**, a hotel that was once King Farouk's hunting lodge, where Allied and Arab leaders met after World War II to carve up the Middle East. Though supposed to reopen "soon", don't be surprised if it's still derelict. With binoculars, you can observe the lake's prolific **birdlife**: 88 species, including flamingos, which have a colony on **Horn Island** (Geziret el-Qorn). If the police don't object, you can hire a fisherman's **boat** near the *Auberge* or *New Panorama Village*, to enjoy the view from the water (£E80/hr for up to four people).

The lake itself covers 214 square kilometres, at 45m below sea level, a fraction of its size when the Nile first broke into the wind-eroded Fayoum depression seventy thousand years ago, forming a lake 40m above the current level. Egyptian mythology identified this with Nun, the waters of chaos and primeval life; from the Stone Age onwards people lived around the lake, which had shrunk considerably by Dynastic times.

Although the Middle Kingdom emerged at nearby Herakleopolis, it wasn't until Pharaoh Amenemhat I moved his capital from Upper Egypt to Lisht that the Fayoum became important. He had canals dug and the channel to the Nile deepened, draining parts for agriculture and submerging a greater area with what the ancients called **Lake Moeris**. It was this that the Ptolemies lowered to reclaim land for their settlements, whose decline by the end of the Roman period matched the lake's drop to 36m below sea level. Increasing salinity was a problem by medieval times, and after the lake came into equilibrium with the water sheet 40m beneath the Western Desert in 1890, it became too salty for freshwater fish; since the 1970s, ten new marine species have been introduced, including eel, mullet, sole and shrimp. In recent years the water table has risen again, flooding buildings and fields beside the lake.

Practicalities

To reach Lake Qaroun without private transport, take a service taxi (£E1) from the depot on Sharia Sadd al-Ali to the industrial town of Shakshuk. Depending on which route it takes, you'll pass the lakeside east or west of town, and can get off wherever looks promising. The only place to stay is the three-star *New Panorama Village* (☎084/683-0746; ❺) just east of Shakshuk, which has a/c chalets and a small pool. Of the lakeside **eating** spots, the *Café Gabal el-Zinah*, 1km further east, serves meals of fish or duck from the lake and has children's play areas. There is a small **tourist office** (daily 9.30am–3pm; ☎084/698-0707) near the *Auberge du Lac-Fayoum*.

West of Shakshuk, the holiday villas and timeshares of wealthy Cairenes spread out along the road that ultimately leads to **Qasr Qaroun** and **Wadi Rayan** (see p.490). If you've got a car, keep going, since local women and children pester you remorselessly for baksheesh.

Qasr Qaroun and Tunis

QASR QAROUN (daily 9am–4pm; £E32), the best-preserved of the Fayoum's Ptolemaic temples, lies on the northwestern rim of the oasis. Located 45km from Fayoum City, it can be reached by taking a service taxi to Shakshuk (£E1), and then another to the village of Qaroun (£E1–2), but it's easier to hire a car to visit the site in conjunction with Wadi Rayan and/or the Valley of the Whales.

Not a palace as its Arabic name suggests, Qasr Qaroun is actually a temple – outwardly plain but inwardly labyrinthine. You'll need a torch to explore its warren of chambers, stairs and passageways at different levels; beware of scorpions, bats, snakes and lizards – the last resemble miniature crocodiles, as befits a temple dedicated to Sobek. Round about are the **ruins of Dionysias**, a Ptolemaic-Roman town believed to have been abandoned in the fourth century AD when the lake shrank (it's now 45 minutes' walk away), leaving desiccated stalks of vegetation. Early European travellers undertook nine-hour horse rides to this site, believing that it was the famous Labyrinth described by Herodotus and Strabo (see "Hawara Pyramid", p.494). West of the temple is an even more ruinous **fortress**, constructed during the reign of Diocletian against the Blemmye (an indication of how far north these Nubian raiders went).

En route to or from Qasr Qaroun you'll pass through **TUNIS**, a hilltop farming village turned **artists' colony** of houses built in the vernacular style. In the 1970s the Swiss potter Evelyne Porret founded a **pottery school** (☎084/682-0405) for local children; Abdel Sattar (☎084/682-0827), Mahmoud Sherif (☎084/682-0851 or 010 554-2649) and Rawaya Abdel Kader Salem (☎084/682-0911) now have their own **workshops**, viewable by appointment, like the school itself. Down the lane, the eco-friendly *Zad Mesafa Guest House* (☎084/682-0180, ✉abdogobair48@maktoob.com; ❶) has simple, pleasant **accommodation**, a restaurant, playground and small pool.

Wadi Rayan and the Valley of the Whales

Wadi Rayan is a separate depression 15km outside the oasis, which has become a man-made wildlife haven and beauty spot. The idea of piping excess water from the Fayoum into the wadi was first mooted by the British but only put into practice in 1966, when three lakes and a waterfall were created, vegetation flourished and the area became a major nesting ground for birds. It is now a **nature reserve** harbouring the world's sole known population of slender-horned gazelles, eight other species of mammal, thirteen species of resident bird and 26 migrant and vagrant ones – not to mention the unique fossils in the **Valley of the Whales**. Squaring conservation with economic development and tourism hasn't been easy; routing the 2000 Paris–Dakar–Cairo rally through Wadi Rayan was a blunder, but a new fishing industry (served by an ice factory) and drilling for oil have created jobs without so far harming the environment.

As no public transport goes anywhere nearby, you can only **get there** by car (about £E200 from Fayoum City, £E100–150 from Shakshuk, including a quick visit to the Valley of the Whales). The route is easy: leave the lakeside road at a signposted turning 28km west of the *New Panorama Village*, and follow it to the entrance gate, where foreigners are charged an **admission fee** of $5 each plus £E5 for the vehicle. The open desert beyond gets sandier the closer you get to the azure **lakes**, where a track leads to the **waterfalls** (*shallalat*). The only ones in Egypt, they've appeared in countless videos and films despite being only a few metres high. Hordes of visitors descend here on Fridays and holidays, to sunbathe and play ghetto-blasters on the beach, which has several cafés.

Beyond the car park, a well-designed **Visitors' Centre** (daily 11am–3pm, Fri & Sat 10am–3.30pm; free) covers the wildlife, geology and prehistory of Wadi Rayan; curator Mohammed Hwihi is happy to answer any questions. About 10km on the road passes a hill known as **Al-Mudawara** (The Lookout), which you can hike up for a spectacular **view** of the reed-fringed lake and desert scarp beyond. Soon afterwards is the turn-off for the Valley of the Whales, followed by a signposted turning to a **bird-watching** site by the shore. Besides the ubiquitous cattle egrets, grey herons and little bitterns, there are hard-to-spot wagtails, skylarks, kestrels, kites and coucals from Senegal. Serious spotters should engage a **guide** such as Khalid Abdel Sattar (☎012 368-0198) or Abdalla Farrag (☎012 368-0197), charging £E30 per person for three to four hours.

Further on, magnificent *seif* **dunes** 30m high parallel an inlet fringed by tamarisks, with three sulphur **springs** nearby. Thereafter, the road crosses a boring stretch of desert to return to the oasis. All of this route can be done in a 2WD car.

The Valley of the Whales

No more the land that time forgot, the **Valley of the Whales** (Wadi al-Hitan) can be accessed by a surfaced road laid 50km into the desert, useable by 2WD cars if it isn't covered by windblown sand. In the valley itself, vehicles are restricted to marked tracks, and an Italian NGO is laying out walking trails between the fossilized remains strewn over several acres. The **fossils** consist of amphibious mammals deposited by the swirling waters and marine life stranded when the sea receded forty million years ago; today they have fallen from (or remain embedded in) hillocks shaped like giant whelks or filigreed slugs, part of the Qasr es-Sagha Formation created by the ancient Tethys Sea.

In 1877, geologist George Schweinfurth found two hundred fossilized skeletons of what he believed was a reptile named Basilosaurus (King Lizard), later reclassified as a seven-tonne mammal with a slender body 18m long and small but fully developed hind feet. It's thought that this **zeuglodon** was a dead-end in the evolution of whales that began when some land mammals migrated into the sea, and that another shark-eating creature, **dorudon** ("spear-toothed"), may be the ancestor of modern whales. New skeletons are being discovered all the time – over five hundred have been logged – and there are fossilized **mangrove roots** from a time when the valley resembled the Florida Everglades.

Egyptian Environmental Affairs Agency (EEAA) rangers urge visitors to respect the rules: look, photograph, but don't touch anything; anyone breaking the rules can be heavily fined.

Accommodation and safaris

Unless you have a tent to pitch at the designated camping spots beside the lake and the entrance to the Valley of the Whales, the nearest accommodation is in Tunis (see opposite). Marzouk Desert Cruises, based in Cairo (1 Midan Ibn Sandar, Hammamat al-Qubba; ☎ & 🖷02/258-8083, ✉mmarzouk2001 @yahoo.com), run Jeep safaris to the Valley of the Whales and camel-trekking to Bahariya Oasis via the Darb al-Rayan. Shorter treks can be arranged through Omar Mohammed Ahmed (☎084/368-5318) or Mohammed Saleh (☎010 370-4987) in Shalaan village, or Mohammed Someida (☎084/677-1231 or 010 116-0210) in Khalta (£E100 per person for 3–4 hr).

Medinet Madi

Medinet Madi is another temple site in the desert, roughly 35km southwest of Fayoum City. Getting there entails catching the El-Qasmiya bus from the Hawatim depot and riding on through Itsa, El-Minia and Abu Gandir. Ask to be dropped off at Menshat Sef, roughly an hour's drive from Fayoum City. From this bridge it's about an hour's walk to the temple. Turn right, follow the canal to the next bridge, cross over and take a narrower canal path past a small village on your left, aiming for a stone hut on the rise ahead, beyond which lies the site.

The **temple**, squatting in a sandy hollow where excavations are revealing an avenue of sphinxes and lions (one of them ruffed and bearded like a Renaissance grandee), was built for the XII Dynasty pharaohs Amenemhat III and IV, and dedicated to twin deities. Sobek appears in relief on the outside of the rear wall, while Renenutet the serpent-goddess (also associated with harvests) can be seen in the left-hand room of the limestone edifice. Ptolemaic additions include two female winged sphinxes and the **ruined town** of mud- and fired bricks to the southeast. Although legend attributes its destruction to a tribe of eleventh-century Nejd warriors enraged by the town's refusal of hospitality, the real cause of its blight was probably the shrinking of the lake. What looks like an embankment north of the temple was actually the storm beach of the lake in ancient times, 68m above its present level.

To return to Fayoum City, catch the bus from Menshat Sef in the same direction, as the route is circular.

Kom Oshim (ancient Karanis)

The most accessible of the ancient sites in the Fayoum is **Kom Oshim** (daily 8am–4pm), 30km north of Fayoum City, where the Cairo road descends into the depression. Ask a bus or taxi driver to drop you at Mat'haf Kom Oshim, the small **museum** by the road, where admission **tickets** are sold (£E16 for the museum; £E32 for the site). Its curator speaks good English and is keen to explain details. Pottery and glassware, terracotta figures used for modelling hairstyles and two lifelike "Fayoum portraits" (see p.494) convey the wealth and sophistication of the ancient frontier town, whose ruins lie behind the museum.

The **ruins of ancient Karanis** clearly show the layout of this Ptolemaic-Roman town, founded by Greek mercenaries and their camp followers during the third century BC, which had a population of three thousand or so until the fifth century AD. Although the mud-brick houses have been reduced to low walls, two stone **temples** are better preserved – no thanks to the nineteenth-century Antiquities Department, which allowed contractors to destroy Roman buildings for their bricks. The larger one was built towards the end of the first century BC and dedicated to two local crocodile gods, Petesouchos and Pnepheros.

Geneticist Scott Woodward believes that the population of Fayoum Oasis was more genetically diverse than anywhere else in Ancient Egypt. Of the bodies buried at Karanis, 85 percent of the upper strata are blond-haired (northern Mediterraneans) and couples are genetically dissimilar, whereas lower layers contain evidence of many brother-sister marriages. Scott attributes the change to the advent of Christianity (with its taboo on incest) in the Fayoum, which seems to have happened in the first century AD, two hundred years earlier than was previously thought.

If you phone a day ahead (☎084/501-825), the museum can usually provide a **guide** for excursions to Qasr es-Sagha and Dimeh es-Siba (see opposite). To return to Fayoum or Cairo, flag down any passing bus or service taxi – though it may be a while before one with a vacant seat comes by.

Qasr es-Sagha, Dimeh es-Siba and Widan al-Faras

For those with a 4WD and a hankering to explore the desert, there are several satisfyingly remote sites to the **north of Lake Qaroun**. Though the sites are unguarded, you'll have to tell the police your itinerary and it's advisable to take a guide from the Karanis museum, as the track to Qasr es-Sagha (40km) isn't always apparent and may have patches of soft sand, though the initial stretch is clear enough and busy with trucks coming from a nearby quarry.

The small Middle Kingdom temple known as **Qasr es-Sagha** (Palace of the Jewellers) nestles inconspicuously halfway up an outlying scarp of the Jebel Qatrani. Although lacking any friezes or inscriptions, it's remarkable for its masonry, which is unlike that of any other Egyptian temple. The blocks are irregularly shaped, with odd angles and corners fitting together like a jigsaw; the overall effect is of an Inca edifice transplanted from the Andes. Notice the enigmatic dead-end **passage** built into the front wall of the temple.

Lake Qaroun once lapped at the temple's base but now lies 11km away, beyond the ruins of **Dimeh es-Siba**, a Ptolemaic town that pegged out as the lake shrank. To reach this you drive 9km south past hundreds of giant egg-shaped boulders that have fractured into halves or slices due to the baking heat. It's hard to imagine that a town of well-fed Greek soldiers and courtesans once flourished here. The ruins, starkly visible against the desert, are ringed by a mud-brick wall up to 10m high and 5m thick. In the centre is a rough-hewn, ruined stone temple that was dedicated to Soknopaios, a form of Sobek (see p.488); the hill on which it stands was originally an island in the crocodile-infested lake. Approaching from that direction – a 2.5-kilometre walk – you'll come first to a 400-metre-long road (flanked by stone lions as recently as the nineteenth century), running past ruined houses into the temple enclosure. The ruins are frequented by **owls**, and occasionally **jackals**.

Gung-ho 4WD types can also follow an ancient road (8km) from Qasr es-Sagha to the Old Kingdom **quarries** of **Widan al-Faras**. Here, the basalt used to make pots and statues simply fell off the hillside, to be loaded onto sledges and dragged down the escarpment to barges at Qasr. The quarry road, the Rali Al-Farainah, is perhaps the world's oldest paved road, made four thousand years ago from stones and chunks of fossilized wood (akin to the Petrified Forest in the Muqattam Hills outside Cairo). It has been used by scientists to measure the erosion of the desert, for the road is now almost 1m above the desert's surface, meaning that the wind strips away 3cm per century. Widan al-Faras itself is a mountain extruded from the **Jebel Qatrani** range, whose fossil-rich sandstone and clay beds from the Eocene era are capped with a thick layer of black basalt. Guides who really know their stuff can navigate across the trackless desert from the Cairo–Bahariya highway 70km from Bawiti (the capital of Bahariya Oasis), and descend the nearly sheer escarpment into the Fayoum at one point.

Pyramids around the Fayoum

The Fayoum is associated with four separate **pyramid sites**, two of them beyond its limits, the other pair more conveniently sited off the Beni Suef road. The latter, at **Lahun** and **Hawara**, both date from the XII Dynasty, which governed Egypt – and ordered the waterworks that transformed the Fayoum – from its capital Itj-tway (Seizer of the Two Lands). This lay 30km to the northeast, near **El-Lisht**, where the dynasty's founder Amenemhat I built his own pyramid.

The fourth site, **Maidum**, is unconnected with the others (which it predates by seven centuries), but its dramatic-looking "Collapsed Pyramid" marks an evolutionary step between the pyramids at Saqqara and Giza.

Hawara Pyramid

Hawara (Great Mansion) may have stood on the shores of Lake Qaroun when it was built during the XII Dynasty, and later became the finishing point of a one-hundred-kilometre **desert endurance race** instituted by Pharaoh Taharqa (690 BC) to train his troops, revived as an event in 2001. Other than during the race, held every November, Hawara gets few visitors, for its 54-metre-high **Pyramid of Amenemhat III** (daily 9am–4pm; £E32) has degenerated into a mud-brick mound since its limestone casing was removed in antiquity. Unlike most pyramids, its entrance was on the south side: one of many ruses devised to foil tomb-robbers. Alas, due to rising

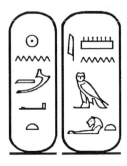

▲ Amenemhat III

ground water, you can't go inside to examine such features as the stone portcullises that sealed the corridor or the roof block that was lowered into place once the sarcophagus was in the burial chamber, both operated by sand. None of them saved the body of the pharaoh (1842–1797 or 1855–1808 BC) from being looted and burned centuries before Petrie rediscovered his sarcophagus alongside that of his daughter, Nefru-Ptah, which was stored here while her own tomb was being constructed. It was found intact with her treasures in 1956. East of the pyramid (the direction from which visitors approach) lies a bone- and bandage-littered necropolis, with deep shafts to ensnare the unwary.

To the south, towards and beyond the canal, a few column stumps and masses of limestone chippings mark the **site of the Labyrinth**. All that's known about this fabled building comes from Strabo, Herodotus and Pliny. Herodotus wrote that it contained over three thousand chambers hewn from a single rock, surpassing all the "great works of the Greeks . . . put together", while Strabo maintained that it had as many rooms as there were provinces, so that each could be represented by officials at ceremonies. Most archeologists think that it was Amenemhat III's mortuary temple, although Rohl argues that it may have been an eternal representation of the bureaucracy and waterworks that Joseph devised to prepare Egypt for the seven years of famine foretold by the pharaoh's dream (Genesis 41:1–4).

During the early excavations at Hawara in the nineteenth century, Petrie unearthed 146 brilliantly naturalistic **"Fayoum Portraits"** (100–250 AD) in the Roman cemetery to the north of the pyramid. Executed in beeswax-based paint while their sitters were alive, they were cut to size and stuck onto the bandaged cadavers, whose mummification was perfunctory compared to the embalming of Dynastic times. One such portrait graces the Karanis museum (see p.492); others can be admired in Cairo's Egyptian Antiquities Museum (see p.118).

Getting there involves a service-taxi ride (50pt) from Fayoum City's Hawatim depot to the village of Hawaraat al-Makta, where you cross the Bahr Yussef by a bridge, turn right at the T-junction beyond the village and walk on for about 1500m until the pyramid appears. From its summit (easily reached by climbing the southwest corner) you should be able to see the Lahun Pyramid on the southeastern horizon.

Lahun Pyramid

Ten kilometres beyond Hawara, the incoming Nile waters pass through El-Lahun, where modern sluices stand just north of the **Qantara of Sultan Qaitbey**, the thirteenth-century equivalent of the regulators installed by Amenemhat III. (Photographing these installations is forbidden.) Lahun gets its name from the ancient Egyptian Le-hone ("Mouth of the Lake"), and gives it to the Pyramid of Senusert II sited 5km away. Most of the service taxis from the Hawatim depot to El-Lahun stop where the track leaves the main road; it's well over an hour's walk to the pyramids from there. Part of the route follows a massive **embankment** thought to have been part of Amenemhat I's original barrage to divert water into the Fayoum. It ends at the desert's edge, where visitors buy an admission ticket for the site and pick up a police escort to walk the final kilometre to the pyramid.

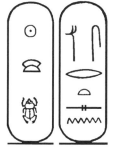

▲ Senusert II

Built seven or eight centuries after the Pyramids at Giza, the **Pyramid of Senusert II** (daily 9am–4pm; £E32) employed a new and different technique, devised by the architect Anupy. The core consists of a rock knoll on which limestone pillars were based, providing the framework for the mud-brick overlay, which was finally encased in stone. Mindful of flooding, Anupy surrounded the base with a trench full of sand and rolled flints, to act as a "sponge".

The subsequent removal of its casing stones left the mud-brick pyramid exposed to the elements, which eroded it into its present mess. When Petrie entered the pyramid and found Senusert's sarcophagus it had been looted long ago; however, Brunton discovered the jewellery of Princess Sat-hathor, which is now divided between Cairo's museum and the Metropolitan Museum of Art in New York.

Senusert II (1897–1878 or 1880–1874 BC), Amenemhat III's grandfather, ordered eight rock-cut *mastabas* for his family to the north of his pyramid; east of them is the shapeless so-called **Queen's Pyramid**, apparently lacking any tomb.

Maidum Pyramid

Although technically outside the limits of the Fayoum, the **"Collapsed Pyramid" of Maidum** (daily 9am–4pm; £E32) can be reached from there, or from Cairo. Take an early-morning train to El-Wasta from Fayoum or from Cairo's Ramses Station (1hr 30min), and then a service taxi to the village of Maidum (10–15min). From the far end of the village it's a short walk across the fields and two canals into the desert; beware of potholes and skulls underfoot. The pyramid is visible from the Nile Valley road, and during the last stage of the train journey. Tickets include admission to two *mastabas* and a ruined mortuary temple. Ask to see them or you won't get into either.

Standing isolated and truncated amid the sands "with much of its outer layers collapsed into piles of rubble, it looks more like the keep of a medieval castle than a proper pyramid", as T.G.H. James observed. The pyramid rises in sheer-walled tiers above mounds of debris: a vision almost as dramatic as the act of getting inside used to be, when "visitors had to hang by their hands from the ledge above and drop into the entry guided by a guard". Nowadays you climb a thirty-metre stairway on the north side, descend 75m to the bedrock by a steep passageway and then ascend to the airless **burial chamber** (bring a torch). Two new chambers were recently found using an endoscope; they have not been entered yet, but may have served to relieve the weight on the burial chamber. Round about the pyramid are unfinished *mastabas*, reduced to ruinous lumps, where the exquisite "Maidum Geese" frieze and the famous statue of Prince Ra-Hotpe and his wife Nofret were found (both can now be seen in the Cairo Egyptian Museum).

Archeologists ascribe the pyramid to **Snofru** (see p.229), the first king of the IV Dynasty (*c*.2613–2494 BC), or to **Huni**, the last ruler of the preceding dynasty. Partisans of Huni argue that Snofru is recognized as having built the Red and Bent pyramids at Dahshur, and would therefore not have needed a third repository for his *ka*. Mendelssohn's *The Riddle of the Pyramids* advances the contrary theory that Maidum was started by Snofru as a step pyramid (like Zoser's at Saqqara), and then later given an outer shell to make it a "true" pyramid. But the design was faulty, distributing stresses outwards rather than inwards, so that its own mass blew the pyramid apart. Mendelssohn argues that Snofru had already embarked on another pyramid at Dahshur, whose angle was hastily reduced (hence the Bent Pyramid), and that the Red Pyramid was a final attempt to get things right. He postulates that pyramids were built in production-line fashion, whether there were pharaohs to be buried in them or not; thus, kings who died before the completion of their own pyramid could be allotted one from the "stockpile".

El-Lisht Pyramids

The **Pyramids of El-Lisht** are the most inaccessible and ruined of the Fayoum collection, with little claim to anyone's attention. The larger of them, the **Pyramid of Amenemhat I** (1991–1962 BC), commemorates the founder of the XII Dynasty, whose capital, Itj-tway, was somewhere in the vicinity. Slightly to the south and harder to reach is the **Pyramid of Senusert I**, Amenemhat's son.

Fayoumi monasteries

Tradition has it that St Anthony personally inspired the first hermits in the Fayoum during the fourth century, and within two hundred years the depression held 35 monastic communities. As elsewhere in Egypt, Coptic monasticism gradually declined after the Muslim conquest, and only started to revive during the last century. But the habit of pilgrimage never faded, and still ensures visitors to monasteries that are virtually deserted except on holy days.

Deir al–Azab (Bachelor's Monastery), the nearest monastery to Fayoum City, is reached by heading 5km out along the Beni Suef road, and turning left at a fork; the monastery is on the right after just over a kilometre. Founded during the twelfth century and recently rebuilt *sans* style, it no longer houses monks, but draws many Coptic visitors on Fridays and Sundays, and also holds the **Moulid of the Virgin** (August 15–22). It's the burial place of St Abram, the revered Bishop of Fayoum and Giza between 1882 and 1914, whose portrait is said to reach out and shake hands with blessed visitors.

The remoter, more picturesque **Deir al–Malak Ghobriel** (Monastery of the Archangel Gabriel) squats on a desert hillside overlooking the cultivated lowlands. Pilgrim buses may turn up for the **Moulid of Archangel Gabriel** (December 18), but otherwise it's very quiet. Wolves have been known to make their dens in the hillside caves; from the ridge you can see the Lahun gap, and sometimes the Lahun and Hawara pyramids. Service taxis bound for Qalamshah from Fayoum City's Hawatim depot run past a yellow stone barn in the village of **Qalhana**, whence a dirt track leads to the monastery (5km; 1hr walk). Its

church dates from the tenth or eleventh century and contains some superb medieval **frescoes** found during restoration work in 1991, plus the naturally mummified "**Naqlun Martyrs**" – unknown monks, women and children murdered at some time in the distant past. Their corpses aren't on show, but the monastery's shop sells gory photos.

The Great Desert Circuit

The **Great Desert Circuit** is one of the finest journeys Egypt has to offer. Starting from Cairo, Luxor or Assyut, it runs for over 1000km through a desert landscape pocked by dunes and lofty escarpments. En route, amid wind-eroded depressions, **four oases** are sustained: Bahariya, Farafra, Dakhla and Kharga. Unlike Siwa, these "inner oases" have been almost continuously under the control of the Nile Valley since the Middle Kingdom, ruled by the pharaohs, Persians, Romans, Mamlukes, Turks and British, who've left behind temples, aqueducts, forts, mosques or roads. Since Nasser's time, an ambitious development programme known as the **New Valley** (see box, below) has transformed the oases.

Although each oasis has a central focus, the differences between them are as marked as their similarities. **Bahariya** and **Farafra** both score highly on their

---

The New Valley

The four "Great Desert Circuit" oases are situated along a dead, prehistoric branch of the Nile, and depend on springs and wells tapping the great aquifer beneath the Libyan Desert. In 1958 Nasser's government unveiled plans to exploit this, irrigate the desert, and relocate landless peasants from the overcrowded Nile Valley and Delta to the "**New Valley**" (El-Wadi el-Jedid). This was vital for social reasons, but was also intended to forestall landless *fellaheen* from emigrating to Syria, which was at that time joined with Egypt in the United Arab Republic, and relatively underpopulated. Nasser set up a Desert Authority which found the oases to be isolated, with no roads or modern facilities, and many of their ancient wells and canals blocked. From this emerged a five-year plan and a New Valley Governorate to run Kharga, Dakhla and Farafra oases, in collaboration with the Giza Governorate, which administers Bahariya Oasis.

Since work began in the 1970s, the project has been through ups and downs, as investments proved costlier than expected and doubts surfaced about the subterranean water table. Previously it was thought to be replenished by underground seepage from Lake Chad and Equatorial Africa, whereas now it's believed to be a finite geological legacy, sufficient for between one and seven hundred years. The water table has fallen dramatically in all the oases except Siwa; boreholes must be deeper and the groundwater pumped to the surface is hotter. Although the government has initiated **new projects** to bring Nile water to Kharga Oasis by the **Sheikh Zayed Canal** and exploit the groundwater beneath the desert at **East Oweinat**, many of the new settlements are still half empty, and advertisements urging farmers to settle there no longer appear on television. Hopes of prosperity and fears of decline still turn on the caprices of hydrology and the wits of the oasis-people, as they have since ancient times.

hot springs and palm groves, but Bahariya is influenced by Cairene ways and a major centre for **desert safaris**, whereas Farafra is more rural and traditional. In **Dakhla** and **Kharga** the modern centres are less appealing than the ancient ruins and villages on their peripheries, redolent of historic links with the Nile Valley or caravan routes from Sudan. Staying overnight in the haunting **White Desert** between Bahariya and Farafra is a must; while for those with more time and money there are safaris to remoter sites like the **El-Qaf** stalactite cave, or the uninhabited oases along the desolate road to **Siwa Oasis**, which allows die-hard travellers to visit all the Western Desert oases in a mega-circuit of over 1400km. Due to red tape, however, this journey is far easier in the other direction, starting from Siwa.

Relying on **public transport**, it's likely to take the best part of a week to visit all four New Valley oases. If you only have a few days, Bahariya and Farafra are the obvious destinations to aim for from Cairo; starting from Luxor and travelling in the opposite direction, if you're pushed for time it would make sense to ride straight on to Dakhla rather than stop in Kharga. But it would be a shame to rush the oases, when lazing around is part of their appeal.

Visiting the oases

While it's possible to tour the oases in comfort, don't expect to find fancy restaurants or bright lights – though you can look forward to Bedouin parties round a campfire. All the oases have a range of **accommodation**, from air-conditioned hotels to thatched huts on the edge of the desert. Most double as safari operators, offering tours of other oases as well as their own. Getting around using public **transport** is manageable, though you may have to stand during long bus journeys. If you decide to rent your own vehicle, you'll have to contend with potholed roads and very few petrol pumps, hundreds of kilometres apart. Always keep your **passport** handy in case the police want to see it at checkpoints. There are **banks** in the "capitals" of Bahariya, Dakhla and Kharga oases (though only Kharga's has an ATM), and all the oases now have **telephone** (if not Internet) links with the outer world.

Broadly speaking, the oases share the **climate** of Nile Valley towns on the same latitude – Bahariya is like Minya, and Kharga like Luxor – but the air is fresher (although the dust sometimes causes swollen sinuses). Winter is mild by day and near freezing at night (bring a sleeping bag); in summer temperatures can soar to 50°C at midday and hover in the 20°s after dark. Spring and autumn are the **best times** to visit the oases, with the orchards in bloom or being harvested and enough fellow travellers around to make sharing costs easy.

Tourism is in the hands of local officials and entrepreneurs whose competence and honesty varies. In Bahariya there are numerous safari operators competing for business, whereas Farafra has far fewer outfits and no tourist office. Dakhla's tourist office will help visitors get a fair deal with local drivers or safari operators, while in Kharga, staff at the tourist office and museum run their own excursions as a sideline. As always, it pays to check out different sources and compare what they're offering. But don't let over-suspicion sour things, since you really need local help to get the best from the oases and will have to strike a deal with somebody in the end.

Visitors should respect local values by dressing modestly and observing the conventions on bathing in **outdoor springs** (mostly concrete tanks, fed by a pipe or water percolating up from below). The ones nearest town are always used by local men; if women bathe there, it is only after dark, never when males are present, and only fully covered by a *galabiyya*. Tourists can avoid these restrictions by bathing in more isolated spots, but most **women** cover up anyway. Women on their own should beware of entering palm groves or gardens – behaving thus is regarded here as an invitation to sex.

Transport to the oases

Starting **from Cairo**, you'll need to book seats a day beforehand at the Moneeb bus terminal in Giza. There are six **buses** daily to Bahariya (5–6hr; £E21), two of which continue on to Farafra (8–10hr; £E40) and Dakhla (13hr; £E50). Kharga (7–8hr; £E40–55) is served by four overnight buses, routed via the Desert Road that parallels the Nile Valley. All Upper Egypt and Superjet buses running these routes have air conditioning, but whether it works is another matter.

If you fancy **flying** over the Western Desert and don't mind starting the Circuit at Kharga Oasis, an Egyptian petroleum company operates a weekly flight on Wednesday at 8am, which takes an hour to reach the oasis. Tickets are sold in Cairo at 45 Akfit al-Mahdi, off Sharia Al-Azhar (☏02/392-1674); a one-way ticket costs $120.

The journey **from Luxor** to Kharga is just two hours' drive. Some hotels in Luxor can arrange a **car** (£E350–500) and safaris as far as Dakhla or the White Desert (see p.358). Finding other travellers to split the cost might take a few days, but is preferable to relying on the **train**. Since a "tourist train" made its inaugural journey in 1998, with celebrities like Michael Palin aboard, the reality has been a third-class train that hardly anybody uses. It supposedly leaves Luxor every Thursday at 7am (7–12hr; £E10), but may not run for weeks due to sand on the line. It was moving sand dunes that scuppered the British-built railway from the Nile Valley (see p.536), and as the Ghard Abu Muharrik forges southwards, the new line is also in jeopardy. Kharga is also accessible **from Assyut** in Middle Egypt, by bus or service taxi (4–5hr; £E8).

Travellers hoping to combine the Great Desert Circuit with Siwa are at the mercy of arbitrary rulings by the military in Cairo. Currently, fixing the paperwork in Siwa is simple, whereas it can take days in Bahariya – so it's easier to muster a group to split the cost of a **car** (at least £E800) **from Siwa** to Bahariya than it is going the other way. However, this may change, so consult safari outfits in Bahariya (see p.507) and Siwa's tourist office (p.554) before deciding which direction to take.

Bahariya Oasis

Bahariya Oasis is the smallest of the four depressions, only 94km long and 42km wide, its desert floor and lower escarpments formed of Cretaceous sandstone, overlaid by limestone and basalt from the Eocene period. In the Late Cretaeous era, 94 million years ago, the environment resembled the Florida Everglades, with mangrove swamps inhabited by dinosaurs such as the plant-eating paralititan and the carnivorous carcharodontosaurus, whose bones have been found at Jebel el-Dist and Jebel el-Fagga. The oasis is known to have been under pharaonic control by the Middle Kingdom, when Zezes (as the oasis was known) exported wine to the Nile Valley. During the Late Period Bahariya thrived as an artery between Egypt and Libya, while throughout Islamic times, Arab armies, merchants and pilgrims passed through. Today, it is tourists who come here to enjoy the hot springs and palm groves, or undertake safaris into the dunes and rock formations of the Western Desert.

Although Bahariya covers 1200 square kilometres, less than one percent is actually cultivated, with date palms, olive and fruit trees, vegetables, rice and corn. Since the 1930s, when 32 springs dried up, 63,900 palm trees died and thousands migrated to Cairo, the population has risen again to 60,000, including over 5000 settlers from the Fayoum; most of the oasis families who have lived there for generations are of Saiyidi ancestory or descended from Senussi refugees from Libya (see p.552). Ominously, where groundwater was once tapped at a depth of 30m, they must now bore 1000m underground; fruit trees have suffered from being irrigated by hotter water, raising fears for Bahariya's future sustainability.

The **journey from Cairo** (360km) begins with the Pyramids of Giza visible as you enter the Western Desert. Not long afterwards you'll pass **6th October City**, one of the satellite cities meant to reduce Cairo's congestion. To relieve the tedium of traversing flat, featureless desert, vehicles stop at a grubby halfway **resthouse** (with biscuits, *fuul*, soft drinks and toilets). Running alongside is a **railway** for transporting ore to the steel mills at Helwan, supplied by a vast open-cast iron **mine** that imparts a ferrous hue to the surrounding desert. Soon after entering Bahariya Oasis the road passes a gravel track to the outlying settlement of El-Harra, and subsequent side roads to the villages of Mandisha and Agouz. Don't get off if the bus calls at any of these places – wait for the end of the line at the oasis "capital", **Bawiti**.

Due to its proximity to Cairo the oasis comes under the Giza Governorate. Mobile phone reception varies: Mobinil has widespread coverage in the oasis but Vodafone is limited to a five-kilometre radius of Bawiti.

Bawiti

BAWITI harbours a picturesque nucleus of old houses on a ridge overlooking luxuriant palm groves, but that's not what you see on arrival. The lower ground beside the Cairo–Farafra road is littered with half-finished New Valley projects, disrupting donkey traffic but not the ramshackle shops and cafés that enliven Bawiti's **main street**, Sharia Masr/Sharia Gamal Abdel Nasser. Buses

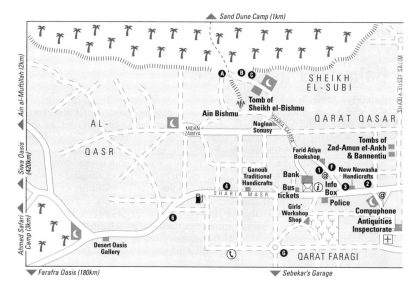

from Cairo or Farafra drop you right in the centre, where you'll immediately be besieged by touts from rival outfits who'll try to get you to stay at their place or sign up for trips.

Before terminating at the bus ticket kiosk, buses from Cairo may be boarded by tourist police who ask foreigners where they're staying in the oasis – just give the name of any hotel or campground and they'll be satisfied.

Arrival and information

Arriving by bus, you'll be dropped near the post office, just along from the low-key **tourist office** on the ground floor of the government building (daily except Fri 8.30am–2pm and sometimes also 5–8pm; ☏02/847-3039, ✉mohamed_kader26@hotmail.com), where Mohammed Abd el-Qader is an alternative source of information to Bahariya's safari operators (see p.507). The **tourist police** are based 1km up the main drag from here (daily 8am–8pm; ☏02/847-3900).

The National Bank for Development (Mon–Thurs & Sun 8am–2pm) is behind the post office: it can change **money** but not traveller's cheques, and doesn't have an ATM. When it's closed, Peter Wirth at the *International Hot Spring Hotel* changes money at good rates. The **post office** (daily except Fri 8am–2pm) is around the corner from two **Internet** kiosks, InfoBox and M&N Internet (both 9am–2pm & 5–10pm). Compuphone (daily 9am–1pm & 2pm–midnight), on Sharia Gamal Abdel Nasser, can burn digital photos onto CDs (£E20). There's a **telephone** office (daily 8am–midnight) near the *Alpenblick Hotel*. Bawiti has two **pharmacies** and a **hospital** (☏02/847-2390), but you'd be better off travelling to Cairo if there's a serious problem.

Accommodation

Hotels and campgrounds cater for every taste and budget and are rarely full, so it's a buyers' market. Decide whether you want desert seclusion or the "facilities" of Bawiti close at hand, and what kind of scene you fancy in the evenings. While locals make music and party on some of the campgrounds, the hotels

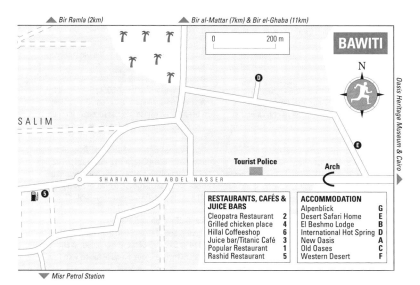

▲ Bir Ramla (2km)   ▲ Bir al-Mattar (7km) & Bir el-Ghaba (11km)

BAWITI

0   200 m

N

SALIM

Oasis Heritage Museum & Cairo

Tourist Police

Arch

SHARIA GAMAL ABDEL NASSER

RESTAURANTS, CAFÉS & JUICE BARS		ACCOMMODATION	
Cleopatra Restaurant	2	Alpenblick	G
Grilled chicken place	4	Desert Safari Home	E
Hillal Coffeeshop	6	El Beshmo Lodge	B
Juice bar/Titanic Café	3	International Hot Spring	D
Popular Restaurant	1	New Oasis	A
Rashid Restaurant	5	Old Oases	C
		Western Desert	F

▼ Misr Petrol Station

tend to be devoid of nightlife. Also, most campgrounds will provide free transport out from town, and usually into town too, while for some of the hotels you might have to rely on taxis or rent a bicycle.

The term **campground** doesn't specifically refer to somewhere you pitch a tent (though you can), but to a place that rents palm-thatch or mud-brick huts with sleeping platforms and mattresses – or proper rooms with beds and showers on the fancier sites. Most can rustle up a meal even if they lack a restaurant. If you're staying a long time, consider renting a one- or two-bedroom **flat** in the village of Agouz, 2km from Bawiti, for £E50 or £E100 a night respectively: contact Yehiya Kandil for details (☏02/849-6754 or 012 321-6790, ⓔ yahiakandil@yahoo.de).

For locations of places reviewed outside Bawiti, see the Bahariya Oasis map on p.509. All rates quoted include **breakfast** unless stated otherwise.

Bawiti

Alpenblick Qarat Faragi ☏02/847-2184, ⓔ alpenblick@hotmail.com. Bahariya's oldest hotel is quiet and centrally located, with a nice garden, but suffers from poor maintenance and hands-off management. ❷

Desert Safari Home On the eastern edge of town ☏02/847-1321 or 012 731-3908, ⓔ desertsafarihome@hotmail.com. Large en-suite rooms (a/c £E25 extra), dorm beds (£E10) and a restaurant. ❷

El Beshmo Lodge Ain Bishmu ☏02/847-3500, ⓦ www.beshmolodge.com. One of three hotels with a superb view of the palm groves, it has cosy en-suite rooms, a spring-fed swimming pool, and a restaurant, but no garden. Rates twenty percent lower in summer. ❸

International Hot Spring On the edge of town ☏ & ⓕ 02/847-2322 or ☏012 321-2179, ⓦ www.whitedeserttours.com. A comfy German-managed spa hotel with a/c rooms and chalets around a thermal pool; gym, sauna, playground and restaurant; plus a palm tree growing out of a deep hole in the ground. Rates include half board (children under 5 free, fifty percent off for under-12s). ❻

New Oasis Ain Bishmu ☏02/847-3030 or ☏012 104-4606, ⓔ max_rfs@hotmail.com. Shabbier and mustier than the neighbouring *Old Oases* and *El Beshmo Lodge*, it has a garden and spring-fed pool. ❸

Old Oases Ain Bishmu ☏02/847-3028 or 012 2324425, ⓕ 02/847-1855, ⓦ www .oldoasissafari.4t.com. The best of the three hotels overlooking Bawiti's palm groves, with rooms linked by walkways, plus a large garden, a spring-fed pool and table tennis. A/c costs £E60 extra. ❸

Sand Dune Camp 1km from Ain Bishmu ☏012 756-5643 or 012 336-0255, ⓔ hamouda@hotmail .com. A 15min walk through the palm groves, this free campground has a large communal hut

for sleeping, toilets and a hot spring nearby, but that's it.

Western Desert Right in the centre ☏ & ⓕ 02/847-1800 or ☏012 433-6015, ⓔ western deserthotel@hotmail.com. This new hotel, facing the *Popular Restaurant,* has large en-suite rooms with fans and a/c, satellite TV and balcony, plus Internet access, billiards and a rooftop with panoramic views. ❹

Around the oasis

Agouz and the Black Mountain

Bedouin Village Agouz, 2km from Bawiti ☏02/849-6811, ⓦ www.bedouinvillage.com. Behind the school, 200m from the highway, this shadeless campground has friendly staff, small clean rooms with fans and bathrooms (£E30 per person), mud huts (£E15 per person) and a reed tent for parties. Owner Abd el-Sadaq is a fantastic player of the banjo-like *simsimiya*. ❶

Camel Camp 2km from town, by the highway ☏02/847-3666 or ☏012 710-7965, ⓦ www. camelcamp.com. Several comfy, musty rooms with clean bathrooms, tacked onto the Oasis Heritage Museum (see p.503). ❷

Oasis Panorama 2km from town, halfway up the Black Mountain ☏02/847-3354, ⓕ 847-3896, ⓦ www.oasispanoramahotel.com. Resembling a beach hotel whose sea has receded, this has cool en-suite rooms with fan or a/c, and mosquito nets. ❺

Palm Village Between Agouz and Zabu, 5km from town ☏02/849-6272 or 012 468-1024, ⓕ 02/849-6271. Attractively laid out, with fine views of the Black Mountain, large a/c rooms, horse-riding ($20/hr) and billiards. Reductions May–Sept. ❻

Ain al-Muftillah and Tibniya

Ahmed Safari Camp 4km from town ☏02/847-1414 or 012 492-5563, ⓕ 847-2090, ⓔ ahmed _safari@hotmail.com. En-suite rooms with fans or a/c (£E30 extra), a garden with table tennis, billiards, rabbits, goats, turkeys and pigeons. Close to Alexander's Temple but otherwise remote, they promise free transport into town. ❸

Golden Valley 3km from town, by the Farafra highway ☏02/847-3031 or ☏012 497-2143, ⓦwww.craweentours.i8.com. Barrel-vaulted en-suite rooms without fans or a/c, and reed huts (£E40 per person) with a view of the desert. Its owner plays the *simsimiya* on music nights. ❹

Towards Bir al-Mattar

Badr's Sahara Camp 3km from town on the Bir al-Mattar road ☏02/847-2955 or 012 792-2728, ⓔbadrygoo@hotmail.com. A nice view of the palms, clean bathrooms, cafeteria and shaded seating area, but its huts (£E20 per person) lack protection against mosquitoes. ❶

Kasr el-Bawiti 2km from town on the same road ☏012 258-2586, ⓔinfo@qasrelbawiti.com. A fancy complex of stone-built en-suite chalets and huge suites with superb views (but too hot in summer), facing a terraced garden with two spring-fed pools. Obligatory half board included. ❻

Ain-Gufar

Eden Garden Camp 10km from Bawiti ☏02/847-3727 or 012 731-1876, ⓦwww.edengardentours .com. Friendly, well-run site in a mini-oasis with a hot spring, cold pool, cosy huts (£E20 per person), two a/c en-suite double rooms (£E50) and an outdoor lounge where you can sleep for £E5 (breakfast not included). Perfect for chilling out or partying, with meals and beer. Free transport into town; transfers to or from Cairo airport. ❶

Bir el-Ghaba

Nature Camp 11km from town ☏02/347-3643 or 012 450-4012, ⓔnaturecamps@hotmail.com. A lovely camp with thatched huts (£E40 per person) equipped with mosquito nets. There's also a library, great views of Jebel el-Dist and amazing meals cooked to order. ❷

Pyramid Mountain Safari Camp 11km from town ☏02/847-2184 or 010 441-9934. An offshoot of the *Alpenblick Hotel* in Bawiti, this has fifteen huts with mattresses (£E50 per person), but isn't as attractive as *Nature Camp*. Meals should be ordered in advance. ❷

Lake Mazafa

Minamar 11km from town ☏02/705-7586 or 012 255-3510, ⓦwww.minamar.com. A holiday village of spacious en-suite rooms with a/c, fridge and satellite TV, overlooking the azure, palm-fringed Lake Mazafa. Still being built but already crumbling. ❹

Oasis Heritage Museum

Bawiti's most visible "sight" is the **Oasis Heritage Museum** created by Mahmoud Eed, a self-taught artist inspired by Badr in Farafra (see p.514). Some feel that his fired-clay statues are more expressive than Badr's, but Mahmoud has yet to enjoy the same success abroad. Both artists portray a way of life that's almost disappeared in the oases, for the men at least, whose job it once was to hunt gazelles and weave mats; clothes and bread were made at home (women's roles haven't changed so much). A supine Bedouin drinking *arak* and a barber-doctor operating on a squirming patient are reminders that life wasn't so bucolic. You can't miss the museum, 1km beyond the town limits; a hilltop stockade with a pigeon tower and beehive domes, signposted "Camel Camp" (see p.502). Mahmoud can usually be found at museum or contacted by phone (☏02/847-3666 or 012 710-7965).

Bawiti's Antiquities Trail

All the **antiquities** officially open to the public (the tombs of Zad-Amun ef-Ankh, Bannentiu and Amunhotep Huy; the Temple of Alexander; the chapels of Ain al-Muftillah) are covered by a single **ticket** (£E30) and **photo permit** (£E25) sold at a kiosk downhill from the Antiquities Inspectorate in the centre of town. This also includes admission to the Inspectorate's makeshift museum, displaying three of the famous "Golden Mummies". However, as several of the sites are outside Bawiti, you'll need transport to realize the full value of the ticket – at least to reach Ain al-Muftillah and Alexander's Temple.

Antiquities Inspectorate

The unobtrusive **Antiquities Inspectorate** near the hospital displays three **mummies** from the huge cache found outside Bawiti. All are encased in gilded and painted *cartonage* (linen pasteboard) and have sculpted stucco masks, two of them gilded – hence their sobriquet "The Golden Mummies". Poignantly, the child was buried with its parents, and the female mummy had its head inclined towards her husband's. Her "chest plate" is sculpted with tiny triangular breasts – a funerary fashion in Greco-Roman times. In this era mummification was often perfunctory, as you can see from the sad, natron-soaked bundle that was once a child. Almost all the mummies removed from the earth have deteriorated – some previously on display here are no longer fit to be shown.

The tombs

From the Antiquities office you can walk downhill and cross the road to reach **Qarat Qasr Salim**, a dusty ridge harbouring two tombs that were opened to the public a few years ago. Both belonged to local merchants of the XXVI Dynasty, whose wealth enabled them to construct **tombs** of a kind previously reserved for high officials. That of **Zad-Amun ef-Ankh**, Bahariya's governor in the reign of the XXVI Dynasty pharaoh Amasis, is sunk in a steep-sided pit; its hall has rounded pillars (unusual for Bahariya) and is decorated with deities (notice the people bringing gifts, to the left), painted in ochre, brown and black upon a white background. He was buried in an alabaster sarcophagus enclosed within a limestone one, which are thought to have been quarried near Tell el-Amarna and Giza, shipped along the Nile and then dragged 200km overland to Bawiti. Nearby is the tomb of his son, **Bannentiu**, at the bottom of a ten-metre shaft – mind your head on the steel grating and the low entrance to its votive hall. Here the pillars are square and the murals are in brick red, golden yellow, pale blue and black upon white, and some of the deities have only been sketched in, but there's a fine solar barque at the back, and the embalming process is shown on the right-hand wall.

Strange as it sounds, several tombs found by Ahmed Fakhry in the 1930s were later lost, choked by sand and built over by villagers. That of Zad-Khonsu ef-Ankh was only rediscovered in 2000, beneath houses in the Sheikh el-Subi quarter. Since then, three more tombs have been found, belonging to the Badi-Isis family of oasis governors; two contain sarcophagi and mummies. While these tombs won't be accessible for some time yet, it's possible to visit a tomb belonging to **Amunhotep Huy**, a XVIII or XIX Dynasty governor. This lies on a ridge called **Qarat Hilwa**, 3km from town to the northwest of the Farafra road, though it's hard to find without a guide and not really worth the effort.

Bawiti's old quarter, Ain Bishmu and Al-Qasr

Bawiti's **old quarter** is in the centre of town, a huddle of mud-brick homes and mausolea flanking a main street where elders sit and gossip on mastabas. To appreciate its commanding position, follow the alley winding off to **Ain Bishmu**, a craggy fissure in the bedrock where a spring was hewn in Roman times, gushing hot water (35°C) into a natural basin, to flow into the **palm groves** below. Sadly, the ravine is now disfigured by a pumping station, although the three hotels that have been built here try not to mar the breathtaking view of the palm groves. The gardens look especially lovely spangled with apricot blossom in spring. Nearby is the dovecote-shaped **Tomb of Sheikh el-Bishmu**.

The old quarter's main street runs into **Al-Qasr**, an older village built directly over the capital of the oasis in pharaonic times and continuously inhabited since then – though many of the houses are now abandoned or used as livestock pens. Narrow alleys snake past secretive courtyards and walled gardens, abruptly ending or joining up with other lanes – making it easy to go astray. Some of the houses incorporate stones from a bygone XXVI Dynasty temple, and a Roman triumphal arch that survived until the mid-nineteenth century.

Ain al-Muftillah and the Temple of Alexander

The ancient town once extended 3km to **Ain al-Muftillah**, a spring that's now almost lost on the outskirts of the desert. It's feasible to cycle but better to get there by car, as the route is not signed or easy to explain. Look out for a barbed-wire enclosure containing four **ruined chapels** excavated by Steindorff and Fakhry. Built during the XXVI Dynasty, they don't conform to the canons of temple architecture and are built of local sandstone, streaked with ochre and sienna, which makes them look unusually colourful but is liable to flake. One of the temples was dedicated to Bes, the patron deity of musicians and dancers, but all that remains of his image is a foot and a tail. By crossing the rise and a dune beyond, you can enjoy a **panoramic view** of Al-Qasr, Bawiti, and the springs and mountains described below.

Further out in the locality of Tibniya, ask at *Ahmed Safari Camp* for directions to the **Temple of Alexander**, 400m away via a sandy track. Built of the same stone as the chapels, its reliefs have suffered from being sandblasted by the wind for centuries, and nothing remains of the face and cartouche of Alexander the Great that archeologists recorded in the 1930s – though you can still discern Amun, receiving offerings from the pharaoh. This is (or was) the only temple in Egypt to bear Alexander's figure and cartouche, and it is thought to have been founded by Alexander when he passed through the oasis en route from Siwa to Memphis.

Valley of the Golden Mummies

In May 1996, a donkey owned by one of the guards at Alexander's Temple stumbled into a hole in the desert, thus alerting its master to what turned out to be the **largest cache** of mummies ever found in Egypt. Surveys have since shown that the necropolis covers ten square kilometres and may contain 10,000 mummies, stacked in family vaults. Whereas some were simply wrapped in linen, others were in terracotta coffins adorned with human faces, their bodies covered in gilded *cartonage* and their faces with stucco masks. The **Golden Mummies** caught the imagination of the public, and TV networks bid $3 million to film the opening of a burial chamber in 1999. Coins and other artefacts buried with the mummies show that they date from Greco-Roman times, when the oasis was a thriving exporter of wine and wheat, ruled by an expatriate elite.

Hopes that DNA testing would reveal the mummies' ethnicity were called into question by Dr Eskander – the first forensic examiner, later sacked – who claimed that body parts were mixed up, and the cadavers so poorly mummified that they had deteriorated into mere skeletons and organic dust. Others note that, at the last televised tomb opening in 2004 (when another twenty mummies were unearthed), neither SCA boss Dr Zaki Hawass or the film crew wore gloves or masks to prevent contamination. After it became clear that most of the mummies started decomposing once removed from their graves, excavations were indefinitely suspended. The main **excavation** site at "Kilo Setta" (km 6) is off limits without a permit from Dr Hawass, but you can see how the mummies look *in situ* on ⓦwww.guardians.net/egypt and ⓦwww.mummytombs.com.

Handicrafts and natural healing

Despite a living crafts tradition in the oasis, Bawiti's handicrafts **shops** give more space to things made elsewhere than to homegrown products – with the honourable exception of the Girls' Workshop Shop. Ganoub Traditional Handi-crafts on Sharia Masr (closed Tues) has some oasis robes and jewellery among its stock, while New Newasha Handicrafts next to the Titanic Café sells woven baskets and platters. For naïve paintings and sculptures, visit the shop of self-taught artist Naglaa Sonusy (T02/847-3610 or 012 429-5299) on Sharia Safaya, or the Desert Oasis Gallery beyond the bazaar. The Farid Atiya Bookshop near the Western Desert Hotel sells photo books, prints and posters of the oases.

Meditation groups are a lucrative sideline for local safari outfits like Khalifa Expeditions, and eco-spiritual tourism has put down roots in Bahariya in the form of **Elysium** (Wwww.elysium.nu), a biodynamic farm 4km southwest of town, with guest rooms that can be hired by people seeking to re-energize themselves in harmony with nature. Contact Corien Elstgeest in advance to discuss your requirements.

Moving on from Bahariya

Although there's a direct **road to Siwa Oasis** (420km), the practical obstacles can be formidable. All travellers need a **permit** ($5 per person; $100 for ten or more; plus a fee of £E11 per person), which can currently only be obtained from Cairo by the safari operator that's taking them. Each person must submit a photocopy of their passport and visa, and the process takes at least 24 hours. If you are intent on travelling this route, try and do it in the other direction, as the paperwork is done much more easily in Siwa: see p.566 for a description of the oases along the way.

Eden Garden Tours (see p.507) quotes £E600 for the journey, including lunch; other outfits ask at least £E1100 (£E1400 to stay overnight in the desert if the army allows), the **cost** shared between passengers. People driving their own car should exercise caution; there are no facilities (only checkpoints) along the road, the first 200km of which is in atrocious condition. The drive takes six or seven hours, more if there's a lot of sand on the road.

Five buses daily run to **Cairo** (5 hr; £E21). You can book seats on the 6am, 10am and 3pm services departing from the ticket kiosk (9am–1pm & 7–11pm) near the post office, but not on through-buses from Farafra and Dakhla, which collect passengers from the ticket kiosk and the *Hillal Coffeeshop* between 11.30am and noon, and midnight and 1am. Alternatively, hire a Peugeot (£E125) or minibus (£E250) to drive you to Cairo – call Fadl (T012 117-9516) if you're interested.

While most people visit the **White Desert** on safaris (see p.512), it is possible to get there by **bus**, using the service that leaves between noon and 1pm. For a group aiming to reach Farafra directly it may be worth hiring an eight-seater **service taxi** (£E200). The 180-kilometre journey takes about three hours; **motorists** hoping to reach the White Desert before sunset should allow time to set up camp. Fill up on **fuel** as there are no pumps until Farafra: use the Misr petrol station in the backstreets behind the hospital, whose *benzin* is less likely to be adulterated than at other filling stations; you can only buy 80-octane in Bahariya. The journey requires about a hundred litres of fuel, of which twenty litres are consumed by the off-road section between Crystal Mountain, Agabat and the White Desert. Sebekar's **garage** (T012 275-2644) in Bawiti is the best place in the oases to fix Toyota Landcruisers.

Desert safaris from Bahariya

Bawiti is the main departure point for **safaris** in the Western Desert, ranging from forays into Farafra's White Desert to long-range expeditions to the remote Gilf Kebir and Jebel Uwaynat (p.539). For **overnight** trips to the White Desert, most safaris leave Bahariya in the morning, to visit the Black Desert and Crystal Mountain before reaching the White Desert to set up camp by nightfall. Most trips are priced on the basis of four passengers, but some firms quote a group rate while others charge per person. Desert safaris can also be organized from Farafra (see p.512 for details), but tend to be pricier, as there is far less competition.

While local outfits and freelancers vie for business, price shouldn't be the only consideration, for the farther you go into the desert the more vital their competence becomes. Anyone offering **4WD** trips should provide at least one jeep as logistical support for the car carrying tourists. In the case of **camel treks**, the supply-car stays out of sight and only appears to set up camp when needed, as trekkers alternate between riding and walking. While local teenagers can handle the White Desert by 4WD (so they boast), trips to Siwa or Dakhla – never mind the Gilf or Uwaynat – require guides that know the route and how to travel off-road by 4WD or camel. Although **GPS** satellite navigation can be invaluable, really expert guides don't need it, having memorized tracks and landmarks from experience.

Safari operators

Salah Abdallah ☎ & ⊕02/847-3038 or ☎012 232-4425. From the *Old Oases Hotel*, Salah does the White Desert (£E750 group-rate), a four-day trip to Wadi Rayan and expeditions to the Gilf Kebir.

Magdy Ali Ahmed ☎012 117-8636, ⓔmagdygo@hotmail.com. A teacher knowledgeable about the geology and fauna of the oases, Magdy offers safaris for £E250 per person per day.

Bedouin Safari Tours ☎02/847-2636 or 012 276-5188, ⓔm_lateefsafari@yahoo.com, ⓦwww.bedouiunsafaritours.nl. Mohammed Abdel Latif (aka "Bodadi") is a great driver and all-round entertainer. His Jeep or camel trips are sure to be fun, but perhaps not the most organized or fit to venture far beyond the White Desert.

Desert Safari Home ☎02/847-1321 or 012 731-3908, ⓔkhozamteego33@hotmail.com. Badry Khozam runs Jeep and camel safaris to the White Desert, Agabat and Magic Spring, for £E150 per person per day.

Desert Ship Safari ☎02/849-6754, mobile ☎012 321-6790, ⓦwww.desertshipsafari.com. Yehiya Kandil is an expert guide and driver who can take you anywhere from El-Qaf to the Gilf by Jeep (€50 per person per day), or arrange camel trekking.

Eden Garden Tours ☎02/847-3727 or 012 731-1876, ⓦwww.edengardentours.com. Talat Mulah at *Eden Garden Camp* organizes off-road tours (€50 per day per person), camel treks and walking tours as far south as Dakhla Oasis, or a night in the White Desert for €35 each. His well-trained crew ensures that the food and music rocks and the logistics run like clockwork. Minibus transfers to/from Cairo by arrangement.

Kareem El-Abed ☎012 756-2226, ⓔkareim69@yahoo.com. A driver/drummer known as the

"Desert Lion", who runs overnight excursions to the White Desert for £E150–250 per person.

Mohammed Hamedtay ☎02/847-1747 or 012 731-9512, ⓦwww.bahariyaexpedition.com. Hamada offers safaris to the Gilf and the Great Sand Sea ($140 per person per day), El-Qaf, the Valley of the Whales and the White Desert.

Esam Hdoota ☎02/847-2296 or 012 531-2659, ⓔasamhdoota@hotmail.com. The "Desert Tiger" charges £E600 group rate for an overnight excursion into the White Desert.

Khaled Kandeel ☎02/847-2835 or 012 716-0782, ⓔwestern_desert2000@yahoo.com. Safaris to El-Qaf, the Valley of the Whales or Bir Dikkur (£E125 per person by day, £E250 overnight; minimum six people).

Khalifa Expeditions ☎02/847-3260 or 012 321-5445, ⓦwww.khalifaexp.com. Khaled and Rose-Maria Khalifa do Jeep safaris to the Gilf, the Great Sand Sea and El-Qaf, camel trekking and meditation in the White Desert and painting tours to Ain Umm Dabadib in Kharga Oasis.

Ashraf Lotfi ☎02/347-3643 or 012 165-3037, ⓔnaturecamps@hotmail.com. From *Nature Camp*, Ashraf leads Jeep, camel or walking tours (€50 per person per day) and expeditions to the Gilf (€100 per person per day). The food provided is especially good.

Oasis Panorama Tours ☎02/847-3354 or 012 495-8438, ⓦwww.oasispanoramahotel.com. Tours of Bahariya Oasis (£E200), day trips (£E600) and overnight safaris, priced per group; meals cost extra. Run from the *Oasis Panorama Hotel*.

Oasis Safari ☎02/847-1886 or 012 337-7269, ⓔsafarioasis@yahoo.com, who owns the *InfoBox* Internet kiosk in Bawiti, offers day-trips to the White Desert for £E500 per car-load.

Ahmed Abd el-Rahim ☎ & ⊕02/847-1414 or ☎012 492-5563, ⓔahmed_safari@hotmail.com.

Ahmed Safari Camp offers the White Desert and long-range destinations including the Gilf, and camel trekking (minimum five people).

Lotfi Abd el-Sayed ☏ & ⓕ 02/847-3500, ⓦ www.beshmolodge.com. Based at *El-Beshmo Lodge*, Lotfi does the White Desert (£E650 group-rate), El-Qaf and Wadi Rayan.

Samy Safari ☏ 02/849-7260 or 012 368-2070, ⓔ samy_ba@hotmail.com. Samy Badry El-Badrmany, of the Bedouin family that owns all the camels in Bahariya, leads camel and walking tours, and may invite you to go walkabout in the desert for a month with his family in July. Samy doesn't speak much English, but Ashraf Lotfi (see previous page) can facilitate contact.

Mohammed Senussi ☏ & ⓕ 02/847-3439 or ☏ 012 224-8570, ⓔ aisha_kosa@yahoo.de. A highly experienced guide and driver, "Kosa" can take you anywhere in the Western Desert for €50 per person a day.

Mohammed Uosrri ☏ 012 158-1352, ⓔ mohameduosrri@yahoo.com. The "Desert Man" does Siwa, Dakhla and the White Desert off-road.

Western Desert Safari ☏ & ⓕ 02/847-1800 or 012 433-6015, ⓔ safari@westerndeserthotel.com. The White Desert overnight, plus Wadi Rayan, El-Qaf and other destinations.

White Desert Tours ☏ 02/847-2322, ⓕ 847-3014, ⓦ www.whitedeserttours.com. Peter Wirth guides self-drive and tailor-made Jeep safaris all over the Western Desert, and motorbike tours by arrangement (minimum four people). Peter speaks English and German, and his wife, Miharu, speaks Japanese.

Zaki Mohammed Zaki ☏ 012 963-9086, ⓔ desert_wolf642@yahoo.com. Bahariya and Farafra by Jeep (£E150 per person a day) or by camel (€350 a day for four people).

Around the oasis

If they're not busy taking people to the White Desert, some safari operators may do **half-day tours** of the oasis, visiting the Black Mountain, Jebel el-Dist and Bir el-Ghaba to the northeast of Bawiti. Priced per Jeep (four or five passengers), trips costs £E150–300, depending on whom you ask. Alternatively, you could **rent a bicycle** for £E25 a day from New Newasha Handicrafts and cycle out to Bir el-Ghaba – about 25km round-trip – or settle for exploring the palm groves, springs and villages nearer town.

Northeast of Bawiti

The nearest spring to Bawiti is **Bir Ramla**, a nice two-kilometre walk from Bawiti past palm and fruit orchards, but too hot (45°C) for most and quite public. Males can bathe here in shorts, women only at night, in full-length opaque clothing. Similar rules apply to **Bir el-Negba**, 1km further on, and **Bir al-Mattar**, another concrete tank of faintly sulphurous water (25°C), 7km from Bawiti. This "Well of the Airport" gets its name from an abandoned wartime airstrip, visible en route. Skirting palm groves, the road becomes a track leading on to **Bir el-Ghaba** (Well of the Forest), in a eucalyptus grove. Though private at night, the pool is rather hot (40°C) for comfort (try the irrigation canals instead) and the pump is turned off at 10pm. There are two campgrounds nearby (see p.503).

Visiting Bir el-Ghaba by day affords a view of mountains and hills that can be excursions in themselves. **Jebel el-Dist** (Mountain of the Pot) is more accurately described by locals in the tourist trade as "Pyramid Mountain", and the ever-changing play of light across it has inspired another name, "Magic Mountain". Alas, tours don't stop for long enough for you to reach the mountain, whose **dinosaur beds** have been picked bare (see p.499), but the fields and acacia groves nearer Bir el-Ghaba abound in insects and **birdlife** – most noticeably wheatears, which semaphore to each other with their black-and-white tails. You'll also see **camels** belonging to a Bedouin family that goes walkabout in the desert in July, when the oasis is plagued by camel-ticks. Samy Safari (see above) can arrange camel rides in the locality.

En route to all these sites you'll pass the aptly named **Black Mountain**. Its dolomite and volcanic basalt mass is crowned by a ruined look-out post

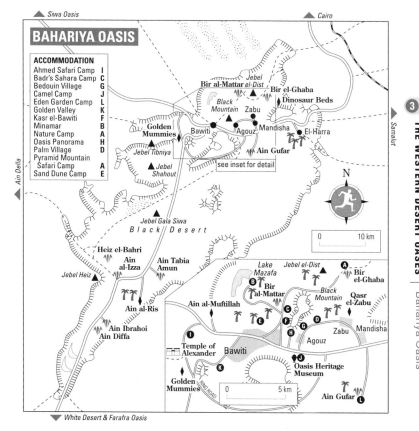

used by Captain Williams to monitor the Senussi in 1916, for which it is nicknamed Jebel el-Ingleez, the "English Mountain". Most of the inhabited parts of the oasis are visible from its summit, whose rocks have an oddly sticky texture and smell faintly of biscuits. Cars usually halt in a wadi not far below the summit.

East of Bawiti

Most tourists pay little heed to the **villages** outside Bawiti, whose people are friendly and hospitable. It's feasible to walk to **AGOUZ**, only 2km from town, off the Cairo highway. Agouz is reputedly inhabited by the descendants of families banished from Siwa Oasis for the loose morals of their womenfolk, but they would rather forget this slur on their ancestors. Following the link road towards **Mandisha**, you'll pass a field of dunes that threatens neighbouring **Zabu**, where houses and palm groves have been drowned in sand. Behind the gardens at the back of the village, facing towards the escarpment, you can follow a track into a canebrake to find **Qasr el–Zabu** – a giant sandstone boulder where Libyan nomads and other travellers have carved **inscriptions** since the twelfth century. Besides petroglyphs and sun symbols, you can see horses, a charioteer, a woman with her arms akimbo, and the name of the explorer Hyde.

South of Bawiti

The southern part of the oasis is generally seen by tourists bound for the White Desert on 4WD safaris. While some make a cursory detour off-road into the **Black Desert** (Sahara Suda) of charred outcrops and table-top rocks, others swing around the far side of **Jebel Gala Siwa** to see a lovely **dune** that has formed in the lee of the escarpment – which you can "ski" down. These tours sometimes stop for lunch at **Heiz el-Bahri**, where tamarisk-mounds and palms surround a cold spring, one of several fertile enclaves in the locality called El-Heiz. Unfortunately tours seldom visit **Ain al-Ris**, to the south of the highway, where Roman and Christian ruins attest to its settlement in ancient times (Ahmed Fakhry reckons that this was the "fourth oasis" described by texts in the temple at Edfu). This may change in the future if the SCA allows access to the **Church of St George**, one of the few surviving Christian monuments in the oasis; Copts believe that one of Christ's apostles, St Bartholomew, visited Bahariya before his martyrdom, and perhaps even died there. Ain al-Ris also harbours a mud-brick **Roman fortress** and remnants of an ancient **date-wine brewery**. Sticking to the highway, instead, you may notice a white **tomb** in the desert roughly 30km from Bawiti: a monument to Swiss René Michel, a pioneer of tourism to Bahariya, who died here from heatstroke in 1986. At km 56 are a checkpoint and the *Oasis Cafeteria*.

The Bahariya and Farafra depressions are separated by a limestone **escarpment** where gigantic drifts of sand flank the road as it traverses the **Naqb es-Sillum** (Pass of the Stairs), and two microwave masts relay signals between the oases (there's a first-aid post with an ambulance by the mast nearest Bahariya). From here on, many safari groups head off-road to reach Agabat and the White Desert, as described under Farafra Oasis (see below).

Eating, drinking and nightlife

Eating out in Bawiti is wholesome but unexciting, as in most of the oases. Hot meals can be had at most hotels and campgrounds (the best food is at Nature Camp), but few visitors leave without sampling the *Popular Restaurant*, which cooks one set meal a day of soup, vegetable stew, lamb, rice and salad (£E25), sells beer, and acts as the nerve centre of gossip and tourism in the oasis. Diagonally across are a juice bar and the *Titanic Café*, serving soft drinks. On Sharia Masr, the *Cleopatra Restaurant* does grilled chicken, *fuul* and *taamiya*, while the *Rashid* is better for desserts and *sheeshas*. In the bazaar are more tea and *sheesha* dens, including the *Hillal Coffeeshop* which doubles as a bus stop, plus a humble grilled chicken place. As well as at the *Popular Restaurant*, **beer** is sold at the *Oasis Panorama*, *International Hot Spring* and *Palm Village* hotels (which also sell wine and spirits) and *Eden Garden* and *Bedouin Village* campgrounds.

Night-time entertainment consists of **Bedouin parties**, which most campgrounds and hotels will arrange if enough tourists are staying. Conducted in a tent or round a fire, the singing, drumming and dancing are intoxicating even without beer (£E15–20) or hashish. Abdel Sadaq at the *Bedouin Village* charges £E25 to attend his parties, which happen several nights a week accompanied by the mellow, hypnotic sound of the *simsimiya*.

Farafra Oasis

Farafra Oasis is renowned for its **White Desert**, which many tourists visit on safaris from Bahariya rather than from the oasis "capital", Qasr al-Farafra, a one-horse town if ever there was. Historically, **Farafra Oasis** was the least populous, most isolated of the four oases. When camels were the only means of

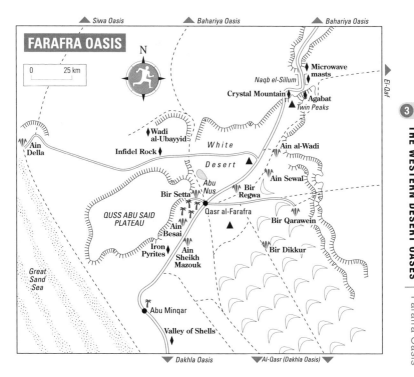

travel, the Farafrans had less contact with Bahariya (a journey of four days) than with Dakhla, which was tenuously connected to the Forty Days Road. Fakhry relates how the villagers once lost track of time and could only ascertain the right day for Friday prayers by sending a rider to Dakhla. Before the paved road was built in 1978 it took 4WD and a winch truck a whole day to climb the Bahariya escarpment. Yet the oasis had dealings with the Nile Valley as early as the V Dynasty, when it was called Ta-ihw, the "Land of the Cow". Even today, Farafra's cows are of the same breed as those depicted in ancient tombs and temples (though no pharaonic monuments have been found in the oasis).

Qasr al-Farafra was the only village in the oasis before the New Valley scheme seeded a dozen hamlets across the depression, now inhabited by 15,000 settlers from the Assyut region or the Delta. Qasr has remained a tight-knit community of four extended families and is noted for its piety, apparent during Ramadan, when the mosque overflows with robed imams and sheikhs. Compared to Bahariya few people are involved in **tourism** so there's almost no hustling – but little to do at night either. Farafra is the sleepiest of all the oases and few tourists stay longer than a night in Qasr.

Mobile phones only work within 25km of Qasr al-Farafra, unless you climb up on top of a *yardang* to get a stronger signal.

Crystal Mountain, Agabat and the White Desert

Coming from Bahariya, you'll enjoy a succession of fantastic views as you enter the Farafra depression. Many safaris stop at Jebel al-Izaz or the **Crystal**

Mountain, sited beside the highway shortly before the Naqb es-Sillum starts its descent into the oasis. This ridge is entirely composed of quartz crystal and has a human-high natural arch through the middle, which is why locals call it Hagar al-Makhrum, the "Rock with a Hole". Small crystals lie all around, and there are lumps the size of footballs farther from the road. At this point, 4WDs may turn off onto tracks leading to Agabat, or continue along the highway, past the landmark **Twin Peaks** at the end of the range of hills on the left.

Agabat is the name given to scores of rock sugarloaves surrounded by soft sand and powdered chalk. The sand can easily entrap vehicles that try to reach it from the direction of the highway, so it's easier to approach it off-road from the Crystal Mountain, whence a steep, dramatic descent into Agabat is possible.

This spectacularly rugged terrain merges into the famous **White Desert** (Sahara el-Beida) on either side of the highway. Here, the wind has eroded chalk monoliths into surreal forms resembling skulls, ostriches, hawks, camels, mushrooms and leopards, looming above a dusty pan strewn with shells, crystals and iron pyrites shaped like sea urchins or twigs. The chalk *yardangs* glint pale gold in the midday sun, turn violet and pink around sunset, and resemble icebergs or snowdrifts by moonlight – while **gazelles** may be glimpsed at daybreak as they forage for a few hours. Safari outfits distinguish between the "Old" and "New" White Deserts to the east of the highway and the larger inselbergs near the western escarpment – but you're sure to be entranced whatever the locality.

Practicalities

Try to preserve this wonderful landscape by ensuring that no rubbish is left behind. Though nominally an EEAA Protected Area, there are no controls at present; a $5 entry fee, park rangers and a visitors' centre are mooted for the future.

It can be hard to find a spot to camp out of sight of other groups at Christmas or Easter, when many people travel down from Cairo. Also keep **safety** in mind; several tourists have got lost and nearly died in the White Desert. Don't wander far from camp at night (it's easy to get disoriented by the *yardangs*). Women invited for a "Bedouin massage" should think twice. It's wise to pay at the end of a safari, not upfront.

Although the White Desert is in Farafra Oasis, many tourists visit it with safari outfits from Bahariya (see pp.499–510), whose excursions are competitive, with the scenic bonus of the Black Desert and Naqb es-Sillum en route. From Farafra, the *White Desert Hotel* quotes £E250 for two people to sleep overnight and return to Farafra next day, or £E350 to go on to Bahariya; the *El-Waha*, £E400 for two, returning to Farafra. Badawiya Safari quotes $60–80 per person a day by Jeep or **by camel**; AquaSun's rates are similar.

Most of the White Desert is accessible by **2WD** vehicles, providing that the driver can distinguish between soft sand and firmer ground. You can hire a **taxi** or pick-up in Farafra to drive you there and back for £E80–100 (which only allows a brief look by day). Lastly – and somewhat riskily – you can take a **bus** from Bahariya to Farafra (or vice versa) and ask to be dropped off in the desert, catching another bus out next day. Not to be tried during summer or the *khamseen*, this approach requires lots of water, a sleeping bag, food and firewood. Ask someone to raise the alarm if you don't reach the next oasis, and always stay oriented in relation to the highway.

Between Agabat and Bir Regwa

There are endless ways of combining Agabat and the White Desert with springs and wadis to the east of the highway. One follows a track from Agabat to **Bir Regwa** (aka Bir al-Akhbar), a hot spring beside the highway, 33km from Qasr al-Farafra. Starting from Agabat, you pass through the desolate **Wadi Hinnis** (Valley of John) to enter a small depression called **Ain al-Wadi**, whose golden sand is dotted with shrubs and palms and has recently been used to grow watermelons. For geologists, the wadi is significant for containing the oldest exposed bedrock in the Farafra depression, formed 66 million years ago. From there you travel to the ancient watering hole of **Ain Hadra**, recognizable by a single palm tree rising from a clump of fronds on a sandy hillock, surrounded by potsherds from Roman, Coptic and medieval times. Beware of camping here, as there are not only mosquitoes but **horned vipers**, which usually sleep in the winter but will wake up if disturbed. A short way beyond lies **Wadi Sunt**, otherwise known as "Acacia" after the venerable tree that shades the spot, whence the trail carries on past picturesque *yardangs* nicknamed the **Tents**, the **Ice Cream Cones** and the **Mushrooms**.

Qasr al-Farafra

The low ground in **QASR AL-FARAFRA** has been colonized by modern infrastructure, which obscures the view of the hilltop village, backing onto palm groves. Even there, development is apparent, with sewage mains being laid

Aqua Sun Hotel & Bir Setta ▲ (6km)   Badawiya Hotel (300m), Hospital (400m), White Desert Hotel (450m) & ▲
Bahariya Oasis (180km)

SHARIA BIR SETTA

N

Badr's Museum

SHARIA MADRASSA

SHARIA MADRASSA

Fortress

El Waha Hotel

SHARIA AL-BOSTA

SHARIA GAMAL ABDEL NASSER

Town Council

Men's Bathhouse

Tourist Police

SHARIA AL-BOLIS

Shops, Teahouses & Bakery

Bir Qarawein (62km) ►

Samir Restaurant

El Waha Restaurant

SHARIA AL-BALAD

QASR AL-FARAFRA   0   50 m

Dakhla Oasis (310km) ▼

and old houses replaced by breeze-block homes with proper bathrooms. The traditional mud buildings have an austere beauty, their low windowless facades topped by flowing pediments or crenellations, but are disliked by locals for being dusty, shabby and old-fashioned.

Their new houses maintain the pattern of extended-family compounds but allow more privacy for newlyweds or grandparents – and dispense with the traditional mastaba, or street bench, for neighbours to gather. Yet everyone knows each other and their lineage: many of the villagers are of Libyan ancestry and bear the surname Senussi. The first census of the oasis in 1892 recorded only 542 inhabitants, and its population rose slowly while agriculture was limited to the nearby palm groves and a few outlying springs. Though Qasr's population has shot up to 5000 in the last twenty years due to better healthcare, its shops and market are still meagre and frugality is the order of the day, despite a few wealthy locals who've built villas on the edge of town.

Arrival and information

While a triumphal arch welcomes traffic from Dakhla, buses from Bahariya pass the *Badawiya Hotel* on the outskirts before dropping passengers at the fuel station and shops down the road. On **arrival**, local police may enquire about your nationality, but shouldn't trouble you after that. The **post office** (daily 8.30am–2.30pm) and **telephone exchange** (24hr) are behind the Town Council. The **hospital** (☎092/751-0047) is out past the *Badawiya*. In the absence of a bank, you may be able to change small amounts of **cash** at the hotels.

As there isn't a tourist office, visitors rely on hotels and safari operators for **information**, with the Ali family being the main players: Atif Ali manages the *Badawiya* hotel; Hamdy Ali leads Badawiya Safari trips and Sa'ad runs its Cairo office; while their artist brother Badr has a local museum and gallery.

Accommodation

Your choice of accommodation may decide which safari operator you travel with (or vice versa), as the hotels expect their guests to sign up for safaris, and regard it as bad form for them to go elsewhere.

AquaSun Bir Setta, 6km from town ☎ & ☎02/337-2898 or ☎012 813-9372, ⌨www .clubaquasun.com. Accessible by taxi (£E10), this quiet hotel has a/c chalets with satellite TV and a warm pool, fed by a hot spring outside the grounds. Their safari outfit is run by rally driver Hisham Nessim. Rates include half board. ❻

Badawiya ☎092/751-0060 or 012 214-8343, ☎751-0400, ⌨www.badawiya.com. Located on the edge of town, this attractive desert-palace-style complex has split-level rooms with raised beds and mosquito nets, and a spring-fed pool. Breakfast included. ❹

El-Waha ☎012 720-0387, ⌨wahafarafra@yahoo .com. This small hotel in Qasr has basic rooms, some with bathrooms (£E15 extra). Some women travellers have reported sexual harassment by the *El-Waha*'s safari crew. ❶

White Desert ☎012 255-7263. A spartan ex-government resthouse just beyond the hospital; rooms lack fans, and en-suite facilities cost £E10 extra. ❶

The village

Behind the school you'll find **Badr's Museum**, the creation of a self-taught artist who has successfully exhibited in Germany, France and Britain. His museum resembles a Disneyfied desert mansion, with reliefs of camels and farmers decorating its walls, and an antique wooden lock on the door. Its dozen-odd rooms exhibit Badr's rustic sculptures and surreal paintings, stuffed wildlife, weird fossils and pyrites. The Farafrans find his desert garden incomprehensible, but relish his portraits of local people. The museum opens when Badr wishes; there's no admission charge, but donations are appreciated.

Otherwise, you can investigate the mud-brick **fortress** (*qasr*) that gives the village its name (though the full appellation is rarely used in everyday speech). Until early in the twentieth century, the Farafrans would retreat inside when invaders came; each family had a designated room, where, during normal times, provisions were stored and guarded by a watchman. Damaged by heavy rainfall, the fortress began to crumble in the 1950s; the less damaged parts are now home to a few families, and blend into the surrounding houses.

You can also wander around the **palm groves** behind the village, which look especially lovely an hour before sunset. They are divided into walled gardens planted with olive and fruit trees as well as date palms (whose branches are used to fence the land). You can walk the paths freely, but shouldn't enter the gardens uninvited; for single women to do so is regarded as provocative. Likewise, avert your eyes from the **men's bathhouse** on the edge of the village, where youths splash around in a concrete tank fed by a pipe gushing warm water. Foreigners are expected to bathe at other springs.

Come nightfall, there's little to do but hang out in teahouses or maybe wallow in the hot spring at Bir Setta (see below), unless you happen to chance upon a *zikr* in somebody's home. **Zikrs** play an important role in the religious and social life of Farafra; foreigners of both sexes are welcome, providing they respect that they are guests at a religious ritual, not spectators at a tourist attraction – which means modest dress and behaviour.

Local excursions

Besides the White Desert, there are other beauty spots around Farafra. **Bir Setta** is a concrete tank of sulphurous hot water that's good for wallowing but stains clothes brown. Three kilometres away, the turquoise lake of **Abu Nus** has only formed in the last ten years, but draws all kinds of wildlife. Further afield are **Ain Besai**, a cold pool beside the rock tombs and chapels of a settlement abandoned in Christian times; the small, uninhabited oasis of **Ain el-Tanien**; and **Ain Sheikh Mazouk**, a hot sulphur spring feeding a tank where local men bathe. While Bir Setta is accessible by taxi from town, and Ain Sheikh Mazouk is close enough to the highway to be reached by bus, the others require a Jeep. This is also true of two sites of geological interest, namely an area of desert (known to safari guides) strewn with flower-shaped **iron pyrites**, and the **Valley of Shells** (Wadi el-Khawaka) out beyond Abu Minqar.

Eating and drinking

It doesn't take long to sample the culinary delights of Farafra. The *Badawiya* and *AquaSun* hotels serve decent spaghetti bolognese, *kofta*, kebab and salad, at higher prices than the humble **restaurants** in town which do omelettes, *fuul*, grilled chicken, salad or soup till 7pm. The *Samir* and *El-Waha* (no connection with the hotel) are family-run, clean and friendly. For *sheeshas*, tea or coffee, there are a few joints (one of which doubles as a bus stop) among the shops on the main street, where you'll also find a **bakery**. Nowhere in Farafra sells **alcohol**, nor is dope to be found. Only one shop (at the far end of the row) sells cigarettes.

Moving on from Farafra

Buses to Bahariya (2–3hr; £E20) and **Cairo** (8–10hr; £E40) leave around 10am and 10pm daily, with an extra bus to Cairo on Monday, Wednesday and Friday at 9am. You buy tickets on board and there's usually no problem getting a seat, but be sure to arrive in good time, as the bus may leave before its scheduled departure time. Otherwise, there's a chance of **minibuses** to Bahariya, or lifts from cars that have just deposited tourists after a night in the White Desert. The going rate for a full minibus is £E200.

Buses to Dakhla Oasis (4hr; £E20) leave between 1pm and 2pm and 1am and 2am. Minibuses also cover the route, maybe once or twice a day. In a fully-loaded vehicle, passengers pay about £E18 each; fewer individuals pay more. If you're planning to do this, spread the word so drivers know that you're interested. Buses both ways can be flagged down outside the *Badawiya Hotel* (the police there will do it for you) and also stop at the teahouse among the shops in town for a few minutes.

El-Qaf and the Ghard Abu Muharrik

Some safari operators in Farafra and Bahariya run trips to **El-Qaf** – also known as Gara or Djara – a remote stalactite **cave** near the great sand barrier of the Ghard Abu Muharrik. Though doubtless known to Bedouin long before it was "discovered" by Gerhard Rohlfs in 1873, its whereabouts were forgotten until it was rediscovered by Carlo Bergmann in 1989. Bergmann believes that it was an important prehistoric settlement; archeologists have since found stone arrowheads and knives predating similar tools in the Nile Valley by 500 years, suggesting that Neolithic technology originated in the desert. The cave was formed some 100,000 years ago but its limestone formations stopped growing when the rains ceased about 5000 BC, since when it has filled with sand to a depth of 150m – what's visible today is a fraction of its totality. Some of the pure white stalactites and veil-formations are six metres tall; each one resonates with a different note if gently tapped at its point. Bring lighting – the cave isn't lit by electricity.

Equally impressive is the **Ghard Abu Muharrik** or "Dune with an Engine", which passes within 20km of El-Qaf on its way to Kharga Oasis. As Abu Muharrik consists of three stretches 100–125km long, separated by high, rocky ground, pedants dismiss its claim to be the longest dune in Africa, but it's still an awesome sight, dune piled upon dune from horizon to horizon. You can visit it after spending the night at El-Qaf, which is six or seven hours' drive from Bahariya or Farafra, though many safaris include detours to Agabat or the White Desert that extend the excursion over two or three days.

Ain Della

Only 120km from Farafra by road, the humble **Ain Della** (Spring of the Shade) has played an epic part in the history of the Western Desert as the last waterhole before the Great Sand Sea, used by raiders and smugglers since antiquity, motorized explorers in the 1920s and 1930s, and the Long Range Desert Group in World War II. It now has a small Egyptian Intelligence garrison that chases smugglers using 4WD instead of camels, as in the days of the Frontier Camel Corps, which once pursued a caravan of hashish all the way across the desert to Giza.

Visiting Ain Della requires special **permission** from Cairo, which Badawiya Safari in Farafra can arrange with two weeks' notice. The road to Ain Della starts at a checkpoint in the White Desert, and has great rock formations for most of the way. At 53km into the journey to Ain Della, you'll pass the so-called **Infidel Rock** or "Church of the Spirits of the Lost Persian Army", an anthropomorphic rock formation on a hillock, that locals believe marks the last known location of the fabled Lost Army of Cambyses (see box opposite). Further north, Italian archeologists are investigating a prehistorical village and a cave containing **rock art**, at **Wadi al-Ubayyid**.

The road to Dakhla

Relatively few vehicles follow the 310-kilometre road **between Farafra and Dakhla Oasis**. Once you're past Ain Sheikh Mazouk, the desert shifts from white stone to gravel and sand until you reach **Abu Minqar** (Father of the Beak). A green smudge in the wilderness, where wells have been sunk and houses built in an effort to attract settlers, it is the westernmost point on the Great Desert Circuit, and an obligatory tea-stop. Beyond lie more gravel pans, where golden orioles flit across the highway as it veers towards the escarpment that delineates Dakhla Oasis, where you'll pass through Al-Qasr and Mut Talatta before reaching Mut, Dakhla's main centre.

Off-road to Dakhla Oasis

If you've got time to spare, this is an amazing journey that deserves several days, with constantly varying scenery. A paved road starting in Qasr al-Farafra runs out to **Bir Qarawein**, whose ancient well has now been supplemented by boreholes, allowing watermelons to be grown here (and *bango*, until the plantation was spotted by chance by an army helicopter). By turning off the road halfway to Qarawein, you can follow a track to the sweetwater spring of **Bir Dikkur**, marked by two palms and a camel's skeleton, and into the **dune lanes** that run parallel in a southeasterly direction. Some have trees protruding from their crests, where the dunes have buried whole palm groves on their relentless march towards Dakhla. Further on lie the **Black Valley**, whose floor is covered

---

The Lost Army of Cambyses

One of the most famous tales in the *Histories* of Herodotus is of the Persian conqueror **Cambyses** (525–522 BC), son of Cyrus the Great, who sent an army across the desert to destroy the Siwan Oracle. According to Herodotus, the 50,000-strong **army** marched from Thebes (Luxor) for seven days to an "oasis", and thence towards Siwa – which leaves room for doubt as to whether the oasis was Kharga or Farafra. Depending on which story you favour, their last watering hole was Ain Amur or Ain Della, beyond which the army ran out of water and perished in the Great Sand Sea after a sandstorm blew up from the south, scattering and burying the weakened troops. Some ascribe this disaster to the Persians miscalculating their longitude, while others blame their ignorance of the environment.

Human bodies have been preserved by the desert for 5000 years, but no indubitably Persian corpse has been found yet. The mystery of where the army disappeared to tantalized explorers such as László Almássy (see p.545), who claimed to have found the site but never disclosed its location. In 2000 Dr Ali Barakat, a geologist from Helwan University, announced he had found the Lost Army after discovering bronze arrowheads and human skeletons north of Wadi al-Ubayyid, but failed to convince anyone. Others theorize that the army numbered far less than 50,000 (Persian sources routinely overestimated the size of armies), perhaps no larger than 5000 soldiers.

Whatever the fate of his "Lost Army", Cambyses seems to have been a disastrously incompetent general, for while the Siwan expedition was marching towards its death, he was personally leading another army up the Nile to invade Ethiopia, which ran out of food in the Nubian Desert and resorted to cannibalism to survive. News of these two disasters caused disaffected nobles in Persia to unite behind his son and stage a revolt, and it was en route to recover his throne that Cambyses accidentally stabbed himself in the thigh with his own dagger and died of gangrene in Syria. For an invader who had wantonly desecrated the Serapeum and sought to destroy the Oracle of Amun (said to control desert storms), these misfortunes must have seemed divine punishment for his hubris.

3

THE WESTERN DESERT OASES | Farafra Oasis

517

in iron pyrites, and the **Marble Labyrinth**, whose sharp stones are equally hard on tyres. Mobile phones don't work beyond Bir Dikkur. The route ends with a steep **descent** from the plateau to Al-Qasr (see p.524) in Dakhla.

Eden Garden Tours in Bahariya combines this route with Agabat and the White Desert on a four-day Jeep safari, while Nasser in Dakhla (see below) can do it in reverse **by camel** in five to eight days.

Dakhla Oasis

Verdant cultivated areas and a great wall of rose-hued rock across the northern horizon make a feast for the eyes in **Dakhla Oasis**. Partitioned by dunes into more or less irrigated, fertile enclaves, the oasis supports 75,000 people living in fourteen settlements strung out along the Farafra and Kharga roads. Although it's the out-lying sites that hold most attraction, the majority of travellers base themselves in or near **Mut**, Dakhla's "capital", which has better facilities. Minibuses between Mut and the villages enable you to see how the Dakhlans have reclaimed land, planted new crops, and generally made the best of New Valley developments.

Most **villages** have spread down from their original hilltop maze of medieval houses and covered streets, into a roadside straggle of breeze-block houses, schools and other public buildings. Besides Islamic architecture, Dakhla has pharaonic, Roman and Coptic antiquities, dunes, palm groves and hot springs to explore. As in Bahariya, there's a niche market in spiritual tourism and **natural healing**, represented by Nasser and his wife at Sheikh Wali (see p.526), who offer massage, herbal medicine and Islamic prayers and charms for diverse afflictions.

Mut

Dakhla's capital, **MUT** (pronounced "moot"), was branded a miserable-looking place by travellers early in the nineteenth century, but it has come on apace since the 1950s, as the Dakhlans have subverted or embraced planned modernity accord-ing to their needs and tastes. The architect of Mut's already crumbling low-rise flats is unlikely to have foreseen their balconies being converted into extra rooms or pigeon coops, and the four-lane Sharia al-Wadi that snakes through town rarely carries anything heavier than cyclists. Yet the locals welcome the hospital and schools and big capital investments such as the Fish Pond wastewater project.

Arrival and information

Arriving by bus, you can get off at Midan Tahrir or Midan Gam'a, the latter being where services terminate. Don't mistake the conspicuous State Informa-tion Office on Midan Tahrir for the **tourist office** (daily 8am–2pm, and maybe 6–9pm; ☎092/782-1686 or 012 179-6467, ✉desertlord@hotmail.com), 250m west, where Omar Ahmed is usually at his desk, and if not, can be contacted at home (☎092/782-0782). Well-informed and helpful, he is the best man to see about excursions. Besides Omar, **safari operators** include Nasser (who owns *Nasser Hotel & Camp* in Sheikh Wali and whose brothers own the *Ahmed Hamdy*, *Hamdy* and *Abu Mohammed* restaurants), the gofers at the *Anwar Hotel*, and Hagg Abd el-Hameed and Yosef Zeydan of the *Bedouin Camp* in El-Douhous. All are useful sources of information, though bear in mind that they'll try to persuade you to sign up for an excursion.

Mut's Banque Misr (daily except Fri 8am–2pm) can change **money** or travel-ler's cheques and give advances on Visa, and the tourist office also exchanges cash. Menatel card-phones all over town can be used for international calls if

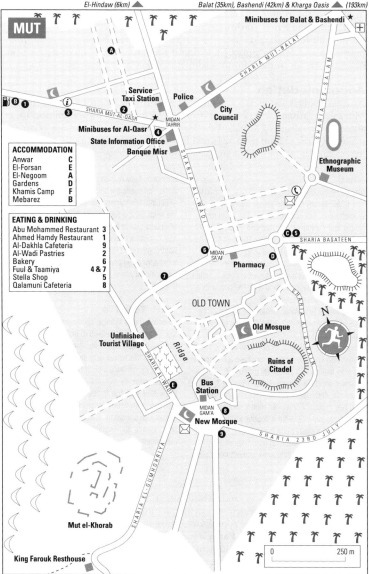

El-Hindaw (6km) ▲   Balat (35km), Bashendi (42km) & Kharga Oasis ▲ (193km)

MUT

Minibuses for Balat & Bashendi ★

Mut Talatta (3km), Bedouin Camp (7km), Al-Qasr (32km) & Farafra Oasis (310km)

SHARIA MUT-BALAT

SHARIA ES-SALAM

Ⓐ

Service
Taxi Station   Police

Ⓑ ①   ⓘ
③

SHARIA MUT-AL-QASR

②

MIDAN
TAHRIR

Minibuses for Al-Qasr
State Information Office
Banque Misr

④

City
Council

Ethnographic
Museum

ACCOMMODATION
Anwar   C
El-Forsan   E
El-Negoom   A
Gardens   D
Khamis Camp   F
Mebarez   B

SHARIA AL-WADI

☎
✉

Ⓒ⑤   SHARIA BASATEEN

EATING & DRINKING
Abu Mohammed Restaurant 3
Ahmed Hamdy Restaurant 1
Al-Dakhla Cafeteria   9
Al-Wadi Pastries   2
Bakery   6
Fuul & Taamiya   4 & 7
Stella Shop   5
Qalamuni Cafeteria   8

⑥   MIDAN
SA'AF

Ⓓ

Pharmacy

⑦

OLD TOWN

SHARIA AL-TAHAIN

Old Mosque

N

Unfinished
Tourist Village

Ridge

SHARIA AL-WALI

Ruins of
Citadel

Ⓔ   Bus
Station

MIDAN
GAM'A   ⑧

New Mosque
✉
⑨

SHARIA 23RD JULY

Mut el-Khorab

SHARIA EL-GUMHORIYA

0   250 m

King Farouk Resthouse

Ⓕ (1km) ▼   ▼ Ⓕ (2km), Airport (8km) & Jebel Uwaynat

you can't be bothered to queue at the **telephone exchange** on Sharia es-Salam (24hr). There are **post offices** on Midan Gam'a and beside the telephone exchange (daily except Fri 8am–2pm), and **Internet access** at the *Abu Mohammed* restaurant (£E15/hr) and *El-Forsan Hotel* (£E10/hr).

Mut's Central **hospital** (☏092/782-1555), 1500m from Midan Tahrir along Sharia Mut-Balat, is well equipped by the standards of the Western Desert.

You'll pass the **police** (☎092/782-1500) en route to the hospital, and tyre-repair shops and a **fuel station** along the road to Mut Talatta. Anyone filling up for the Gilf Kebir should check the purity of their fuel before paying for it, by pouring a sample into a glass jar, letting it sit and seeing if liquids separate out or sediment falls to the bottom – adulteration has been reported.

Accommodation

As oases go, Dakhla offers a fair range of **accommodation** in Mut itself or at Mut Talatta springs (3km north; see map on p.519), with more possibilities further afield in the village of Sheikh Wali (5km; see p.526), in El-Douhous (7km; see p.523), Al-Qasr (32km; see p.524), and by the hot springs at Bir el-Gabel (37km; see p.523). All except the last are fairly easily accessible by minibus.

Mut

Anwar Sharia es-Salam ☎092/782-0070 or 010 531-9355. Mostly en-suite rooms with fans or a/c. Women might feel uncomfortable. The hotel runs safaris and minibuses to Luxor, and sells beer. ❶

El-Forsan Sharia al-Wadi ☎092/782-1343, ℗782-1347, ℮elforsan1@yahoo.com. Decent rooms with fans; en-suite costs £E22 more, a/c another £E15. There's also Internet access, a hilltop garden with a playground and a coffeeshop with a view. Breakfast not included. ❶

El-Negoom A few blocks behind the tourist office ☎092/782-0014, ℗782-3084. Perhaps the best choice in Mut: quiet, clean and welcoming, with a large garden and patio. Most rooms have a/c, phones and en-suite facilities, or share a bathroom and a TV lounge with two other rooms. ❷

Gardens Sharia Al-Ganain ☎092/782-1577, ℮khamis_camp@yahoo.com. This shabby, friendly hotel has mosquito-screened rooms with fans and lumpy beds (only £E16 for a double; £E25 with shower), and a dusty palm garden. ❶

Khamis Camp Off the airport road, 2km south of Mut ☎012 106-8192, ℮khamis_camp@yahoo.com.

A moribund site of mud huts (£E15 per person). Hot water and meals are unlikely and you'll need a bike to get into town unless you take a short cut across the fields to King Farouk's Resthouse. ❶

Mebarez Sharia Mut-Al-Qasr ☎ & ℗092/782-1524. Clean a/c rooms with soft beds; a private bathroom costs £E20 extra. The best feature is a tepid spring-fed pool at the back. Restaurant, international phone line, and satellite TV in the lobby. ❷

Mut Talatta

Bedouin Oasis Village 1500m from Mut, towards Mut Talatta ☎092/782-0070 or 012 357-7749, ℮Bedouin.oasis.valleg@hotmail.com. Known as the *Badia*, this hilltop *qasr*-style complex suffers from an inexplicable lack of fans, and slapdash management. ❹

Sol y Mar Mut Inn ☎092/782-1530, ⊛www .solymar-hotels.com. Small en-suite chalets and rooms with shared facilities, around a circular hot pool, open to non-residents (£E5). Nice but rather overpriced. ❺

The Town

With its low-rise blocks and whitewashed trees, the **New Town** which compromises most of present-day Mut presumably once looked good on a drawing board but has little appeal for visitors, though locals are friendly. Sharia al-Wadi runs past **Hassan Fathy**'s pioneering design for a **tourist village**, signposted as a national monument (never finished, it later inspired similar complexes all over Egypt), but there are no directions to the Old Town behind the ridge. Mut originated as a hilltop *qasr* or citadel of windowless facades and twisting passages, its interior divided into quarters separated by gates that were locked at night; and was still a fortified town when Harding-King saw it in 1909. Though the summit is in ruins, the lanes below are still bustling with life and fun to explore (though perhaps not for women on their own). You can enter from the north and exit on to Midan Gam'a (aka New Mosque Square), using the Old and New **mosques** as landmarks. **Midan Gam'a** used to be the hub of social life but is pretty sleepy nowadays, despite its role as a bus and service taxi terminus.

Off to the south you can glimpse the remains of **Mut el-Khorab** ("Mut the Ruined"), an ancient city dedicated to the Theban goddess Mut. Fennec foxes dwell in burrows in the sides of pits left by treasure-hunters, emerging to hunt at dusk, and can be seen on the way back from enjoying the sunset over the **dunes** that rise beyond the fields. This is the most accessible dune field in Dakhla, but not the finest. A bit further down the road to the airport is a modest colonial-style villa that was once **King Farouk's Resthouse**, now used to lodge visiting VIPs.

By arrangement with Omar at the tourist office, you can also visit Mut's **Ethnographic Museum** (£E3), arranged like a family dwelling, with household objects on the walls and a complex wooden lock on the palm-log door. Its seven rooms contain clay figures posed in scenes from village life, by the Khargan artist Mabrouk. Notice the gazelle-hide receptacle for carrying fat on long camel journeys, and the spiked basket that Dakhlans hid beneath the sand to ensnare gazelles. Preparing the bride and celebrating the pilgrim's return from Mecca are two scenes that remain part of oasis life today.

Eating and drinking

Most **restaurants** in Mut offer similar menus of soup, pasta or rice, vegetable stew, chicken, *kofta* or kebab, for £E20–30 all in. The *Abu Mohammed* restaurant on Sharia Mut-Al-Qasr comes in just ahead of the *Ahmed Hamdy* nearby; if you're looking for pizza or spaghetti, the *Anwar Hotel* is the place. The *Qalamuni Cafeteria* on Midan Gam'a does a few dishes, too, unlike the nearby *Al-Dakhla*, which just serves drinks. Otherwise, you can buy *fuul* and *taamiya* off Midan Tahrir and on Sharia al-Wadi; hot rolls from the **bakery** on Midan Sa'af; fruit at the **market** on Tahrir; or freshly-baked *fiteer* (sweet, or with cheese if you bring some along) at *Al-Wadi Pastries* on Sharia Mut-Al-Qasr. Anyone buying supplies for an expedition should know that no meat is sold on Sundays. **Beer** is only available at the Stella shop on Sharia Basateen (open in the evening) and the *Abu Mohammed* restaurant (for £E15) – though you can enjoy a beer (£E19) or a bottle of wine (£E97) around the hot pool at Mut Talatta.

Moving on from Mut

Upper Egypt **buses** leave Mut for **Kharga** (3hr; £E10-12) daily at 6am, 8.30am and 10pm, continuing on to **Assyut** (8hr; £E20). For **Farafra** (4hr; £E20), **Bahariya** (6hr; £E30) and **Cairo** (13hr; £E50) the bus departs at 6.30am and 6pm. There are also a/c Superjet buses to Cairo (13hr; £E48–55) at 7pm and 8pm daily, plus a Herz Co. bus at 7pm (leaving from the service taxi depot), routed via Kharga. Tickets to Cairo should be purchased the day before. All buses except Herz Co. leave from Midan Gam'a, where tickets are sold; by buying them the day before you can board at Midan Tahrir or Al-Qasr if it's easier. **Minibuses** and **service taxis** also run from Midan Gam'a to the other New Valley oases and charge similar rates to the buses providing they are full. The tourist office or the *Anwar Hotel* can arrange a minivan to **Luxor** (10hr) for about £E400–500. Before leaving Mut, **motorists** should fill up with fuel, as there's no more petrol until Kharga or Farafra. Though their local office has been closed since the weekly flight to Cairo was scrapped, bookings on **EgyptAir** flights from other airports can be confirmed through the tourist office.

Around the oasis

Transport around Dakhla is hit and miss, depending on your destination. **Taxis** are the priciest option – bargain hard if you want the driver to wait at sites and then return to Mut, or try Omar at the tourist office, who can fix a taxi for a decent rate, with no hassle, or a **minibus** or **4WD**, with driver.

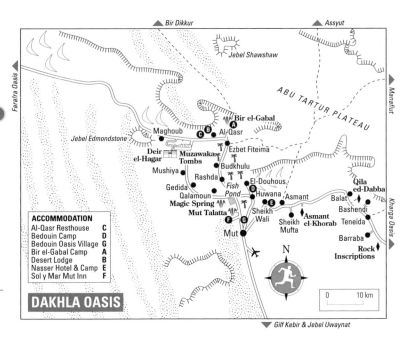

Bir Dikkur ▲   Assyut ▲

Jebel Shawshaw

Farafra Oasis ◄   Manaflut ►

ABU TARTUR PLATEAU

Bir el-Gabal 🅐
Maghoub   🅒 🅑 Al-Qasr
Jebel Edmondstone
Deir   Ezbet Fiteima
el-Hagar   Muzawaka
          Tombs   Budkhulu
Mushiya
          Rashda   El-Douhous   🅓
Gedida   Fish   Huwana   🅔   Asmant   Balat
Qalamoun   Pond   Qila
Magic Spring   ed-Dabba
Mut Talatta   🅕 🅖 Sheikh   Bashendi
                    Wali   Asmant   Teneída
                    Sheikh   el-Khorab
                    Mufta   Barraba
Mut   Rock
                    N   Inscriptions

Kharga Oasis ►

ACCOMMODATION
Al-Qasr Resthouse   **C**
Bedouin Camp   **D**
Bedouin Oasis Village   **G**
Bir el-Gabal Camp   **A**
Desert Lodge   **B**
Nasser Hotel & Camp   **E**
Sol y Mar Mut Inn   **F**

0   10 km

DAKHLA OASIS

Gilf Kebir & Jebel Uwaynat ▼

Public transport consists of green-and-white **minibuses**, running out towards both ends of the oasis. Minibuses to Al-Qasr (75pt) and other western villages pick up passengers near the corner of the Al-Qasr road and Midan Tahrir, while vehicles for Balat (£E1) leave from a depot near the bus station. Between 2 and 3pm, you're unlikely to get a ride as all the minibuses are full of schoolkids travelling home.

Local farmers get around in covered **pick-ups**, which usually charge minibus rates, though you may get a free lift or, conversely, be expected to pay "special" rates. Cycling is feasible in winter and **bikes** can be rented from the *Abu Mohammed Restaurant* or *Gardens Hotel* for £E15 a day. You need to be fit, though, since visiting outlying villages will involve a round trip of at least 60km.

As some places are hard to reach, and it takes local knowledge of natural beauty spots to get the best from Dakhla, organized **excursions** can be a good idea. Omar at the tourist office can arrange half-day trips either to the east or the west (£E75–100 for the car) or a full day-trip to both (£E120–150), while other tours combine Al-Qasr and Muzawaka with the Magic Spring and some dunes: *Nasser Hotel and Camp* charges £E200/£E400 for a half-/full-day 4WD tour (group rate), or £E200 per person per day by camel; *Bedouin Camp* charges £E150 per person for a day's camel trekking; and the *Anwar Hotel* £E300 per person by Jeep or camel. All three also do **overnight** Jeep excursions into the escarpment north of the oasis, or the dunes to the southwest: Nasser charges £E600 per night group rate (£E550 after five nights); the *Anwar* charges £E500 per head and the *Bedouin Camp* $100 group rate (up to six people). Although the first two are fine for **Bir Dikkur** or the **White Desert**, only the *Bedouin Camp* can take people to the **Gilf Kebir**, on a ten- to twelve-day expedition (€150 per person a day): it needs six weeks' notice to arrange the paperwork in Cairo.

North of Mut

Most visitors are initially drawn to the western part of the oasis by the village of **Al-Qasr**, which is deservedly renowned for its old town, an abandoned enclave of medieval mud-brick architecture. Should they ever reopen, the colourful **Muzawaka Tombs** are also within striking distance, as is the restored Roman temple of **Deir al-Hagar**, which lies further from the main road. To cover more ground than this requires days to spare or private transport. Shop around the various safari operators in Mut for trips to other villages, or **springs** and **dunes** you can reach by camel at sunset (staying overnight if desired).

There are two **routes** to Al-Qasr via different villages, so, if you can, it's worth following one out and the other one back. Most traffic leaves Mut by the main road (and shorter route; 32km), with minibuses stopping at the villages of Rashda and Budkhulu; while along the secondary loop road (45km) they call at Qalamoun, Gedida and Mushiya. On the way you'll pass the **hot springs** and resort at **Mut Talatta** (3km from Mut; 24hr; £E5) and the drainage lake for irrigation water known as the **Fish Pond** – great for **bird-watching** (avocet, stilt and coot). With private transport, try a brief initial **detour** along the desert road via **Huwana**, to see the domed and coffin-shaped tombs of an **Islamic cemetery** between Huwana and the Bedouin village of **EL-DOUHOUS**, 1km from the junction where the desert road joins the highway and the loop road begins. El-Douhous is home to the *Bedouin Camp* (T092/785-0480 or 010 622-1359, Wwww.dakhlabedouins.com; **①**), a hillside retreat of thatched huts with fans and mosquito nets (£E20 per person), and spacious "houses" (**③**) with en-suite facilities: meals are served or you can bring your own food and cook. They run Jeep and camel **safaris**.

The main road and Bir el-Gabel

Back on the main road beyond El-Douhous, olive groves and orchards presage the clifftop village of **Rashda**, set far back from the highway. The local custom that when he marries, a man must build a new house for his bride, accounts for Rashda's modern appearance. A nicer stopover is **BUDKHULU**, where new buildings flank an **old quarter** of covered streets and houses with carved lintels, surrounding a ruined **Ayyubid mosque** with a pepperpot minaret and a palm-frond pulpit. Visible on a hill as you approach the old quarter is a **Turkish cemetery** with scores of tombs shaped like bathtubs or grave markers in the form of ziggurats, plus a dozen *qubbas*: the freshly painted one belongs to a revered local sheikh, Tawfiq Abdel Aziz. During the Islamic era, Budkhulu was a customs post on the caravan routes between Kharga, Assyut and Farafra.

Shortly before Al-Qasr, a road turns off the highway to **Bir el-Gabal** (6km), a large, enclosed, spring-fed warm **pool** (no set hours; T092/772-6288) that charges £E15 admission, or £E10 to guests at the agreeable *Bir el-Gabal Camp* nearby (T092/772-6600 or 012 106-8227, Eelgabalcamp@hotmail.com; **②**), which can arrange **camel trekking** (£E120 per person per day). With a bicycle (£E5 a day), the campground is a feasible base for visiting Al-Qasr.

The loop road

Tourists are often taken to bathe at the **Magic Spring**, a warm, deep waterhole fringed by palms, that's so-named because bubbles rising up from below make it impossible to touch the bottom. The spring is just off the **loop road** to Al-Qasr, which links three villages interspersed by stagnant pools and desert. **Qalamoun** dates back to pharaonic times, and many families are descended from Mamluke and Turkish officials once stationed here, whereas the next village is only 200 years old – hence its name, **GEDIDA** (New). Mut's tourist office can arrange a visit to the **mashrabiya factory**, a source of employment in a village whose men have traditionally worked in Cairo, taking it in turns to share the same job with a friend back home. Shortly before reaching **Mushiya**, the road passes **Bir Mushiya**, a keyhole-shaped tank fed by a tepid spring, where tourists are also taken to bathe. The loop road joins the highway between Al-Qasr and the turn-off for the Muzawaka Tombs (see opposite), opposite a golden **dune field**. Originating as longitudinal dunes on the plateau above the escarpment, they cascade down the cliff to reform as crescent dunes below, and continue their way southwards. Tourists are brought here by Jeep or camel to enjoy rolling down the dunes and to take in the view at sunset. The dunes have occasionally been heard to "sing" in a slow rhythm which locals have traditionally attributed to spirits, and which scientists explain as the friction of one layer of sand slipping over another.

Al-Qasr

AL-QASR (or Al-'Asr, as locals say) is a must – an amazing Islamic settlement built upon Roman foundations, that may be the longest continually inhabited site in the oasis and was indubitably Dakhla's medieval capital. Work on the site is being carried out by the SCA and the Dakhla Oasis Project – a multinational venture combining archeology and conservation that's been working in the oasis some thirty years; both bodies are taking pains to restore the town while maintaining its integrity. The old town crowns a ridge above palm groves and a salt lake, set back from sprawling New Qasr beside the highway, built with money earned by local men working in Kuwait. The "border" is marked by **handicrafts** sellers beside the New Mosque and a **tour centre** (daily 9am–5pm) where you can pick up a guide to lead you around and unlock certain houses. Pay him at the end – £E10 per group seems fair.

Alternatively, for an agreeably spooky experience, you can go exploring alone. Beyond the twelfth-century **Nasr el-Din Mosque**, whose 21-metre-high **minaret** has a "pepperpot" finial typical of Ayyubid architecture, you enter a maze of high-walled alleyways and gloomy **covered passages**. Many of the houses here have acacia-wood **lintels** whose cursive or Kufic inscriptions name the builders or occupants (the oldest dates from 1518): look out for **doorways** with Pharaonic stonework and arabesque carvings, **archways** with *ablaq* brickwork, and a **frieze** painted in one of the passageways. Near the **House of Abu Nafir** – built over a Ptolemaic temple, with hieroglyphics on its door jambs – is a donkey-powered **grain-mill**.

Another interesting feature is the rooftop *mala'af* or **air-scoop**, incorporated into an especially long T-shaped passage to convey breezes into the labyrinth. Beyond here is a tenth-century **madrassa** (school and court), featuring painted *liwans*, niches for legal texts, cells for felons, and a beam above the door for whippings. The maze of alleyways also harbours a restored **blacksmith**'s forge and an antique **waterwheel** (*saqqiya*). For more information on these and other facets of the old way of life, check out the **Ethnographic Museum**, (daily 10am–5pm; £E3) near the tour centre, founded by the anthropologist Aliya Hussein and containing artefacts and photos from all of the oases in the Western Desert.

If you fancy **staying**, the cheapest option is the fly-blown but friendly *Al-Qasr Resthouse* beside the main road (☎092/787-6013 or 010 201-7158; ❶). Its few rooms have clean shared bathrooms and erratic water, or you can pay £E5 to sleep on the roof, where you'll get fantastic views of old Al-Qasr. Its proprietor, Mohammed Hussein, can arrange **camel trekking** for £E120 per person and rents **bicycles** for £E5 a day in tandem with *Bir el-Gabal Camp*, which he

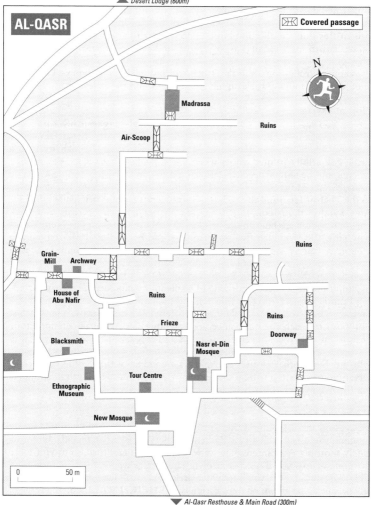

Desert Lodge (600m)

AL-QASR

▷◁ **Covered passage**

N

③

Madrassa

Ruins

Air-Scoop

Grain-
Mill Archway

Ruins

House of
Abu Nafir

Ruins

Blacksmith

Frieze

Nasr el-Din
Mosque

Ruins

Doorway

Ethnographic
Museum

Tour Centre

New Mosque

0   50 m

Al-Qasr Resthouse & Main Road (300m)

THE WESTERN DESERT OASES | Dakhla Oasis

also owns. Alternatively, there's the classy *Desert Lodge* (☎092/772-7062 or 012 734-5960, ⓦwww.desertlodge.net; ❼) on a hilltop behind old Al-Qasr, with ravishing desert views, a restaurant, Internet access, library, outdoor chess and **classes** in yoga or Arabic calligraphy. Rates don't include breakfast.

The Muzawaka Tombs

Five kilometres west along the highway from Al-Qasr, a signpost indicates the track to the **Muzawaka Tombs**, a twenty-minute walk or a slow drive through the silent desert, past rock buttes gouged with empty tombs. Of the three hundred or so recorded by Egyptologist Ahmed Fakhry in 1972, two deserve his exclamation "Muza!" (Decorations) from which their name derives. Sadly, both have been **closed** for years as restoring them has proved far harder than anticipated due to their clay composition – but tour groups often come anyway to see the eerie-looking site, and the curator is ready to produce a pair of **mummies** from another tomb for a photo opportunity (baksheesh expected).

The **Tomb of Petosiris** is vividly painted with Roman-nosed blonds in pharaonic poses, curly-haired angels and a zodiac with a bearded Janus figure on the ceiling. Cruder murals in the **Tomb of Sadosiris** show Anubis, Osiris and another Janus, looking back on life and forward into the hereafter.

Deir al-Hagar

Unless you've chartered a taxi, getting to **Deir al-Hagar** (daily 8am–5pm; £E20) demands commitment. The trail begins 2km further west along the highway, where an unmarked road runs south past some Roman ruins to a small, colourfully painted village (1km); beyond here a track crosses a ridge, whereupon the temple becomes visible on the right. Notwithstanding its Arabic name, "Stone Monastery", Deir al-Hagar is actually a Roman temple dedicated to the Theban Triad and the god of the oasis, Seth, and was originally called Est Ah ("Land of the Moon"). Its sandstone Hypostyle Hall, sanctuary and brick enclosure wall were built in the first century AD, under emperors Nero, Vespasian, Titus and Domitian (whose cartouches can be seen) and later served as a Coptic monastery (notice the mural of Christ, the lion and the lamb, in a niche to the left of the pylon), until a huge dune consumed it, collapsing the roof and leaving only the tops of the columns visible. One is inscribed with the names of almost every explorer who visited Dakhla in the nineteenth century, including Edmondstone, Drovetti, Cailliaud, and the entire Rohlfs expedition. It was they who named Dakhla's only mountain **Jebel Edmondstone**, after the first European to reach the oasis since ancient times; Sir Archibald Edmondstone beat his French rival, Drovetti, by ten days, in February 1819, to "discover" it in the name of England. Such notions were incomprehensible to the oasis people, who attributed other motives to explorers; legend has it that Rohlfs sacrificed a servant to the spirits guarding the temple's treasury, in order to rob it. Trumpeting finches and other **birds** frequent the locality.

East of Mut

Villages on the east side of the oasis are more or less accessible from Mut by minibus; some halt at Balat or Bashendi, others go as far as Teneida. Unfortunately, most places of interest are some way off the main road, so to visit more than one or two you'll need your own transport, as well as food and water.

Heading out of town, you'll see where irrigation canals have enabled wheat, rice and peanuts to be grown on once barren land. **SHEIKH WALI** is on the verge of becoming a suburb of Mut, yet backs onto desert, with olive groves and goat-pens surrounding a Biblical **waterwheel**, while dunes swell in the distance. It's home to the compound of the *Nasser Hotel & Camp* (℡092/782-2727 or 010 682-6467; ➊), whose adobe rooms, with fans and shared bathrooms, lie beneath a lukewarm rooftop pool fed by spring-water. Travellers pay £E25 each, or £E20 to pitch a tent. Nasser and his wife offer **natural healing**, by prior arrangement.

Asmant, 6km on, has the usual sprawl of modern buildings by the roadside and a high-walled **old village** on the hill further back. A **museum** to exhibit antiquities from Dakhla is set to be built on the Teneida side of Asmant.

Asmant el-Khorab

Asmant lends its name to an ancient site 9km further east and 1km off the highway. **Asmant el-Khorab** ("Asmant the Ruined") is the local name for the **ruins of Kellis**, a Roman and Coptic town inhabited for seven centuries.

Its two cult temples and three churches mark the shift from pagan Rome to Byzantine Christianity, with one of the **churches** dating back to the end of the first century AD.

Kellis is one of several sites being studied by the Dakhla Oasis Project (see p.524). Besides temples and churches, they've unearthed the remains of aqueducts, farmhouses and tombs, including 34 mummies and wooden codices, casting light on religion and daily life in the third century AD. The site is **off-limits** while excavations continue.

Balat and Qila ed-Dabba

After the swath of desert beyond Asmant one welcomes the casuarina-tree-lined road through **BALAT**, whose teahouse is a *de facto* bus stop. Cross the road to explore the old village beyond the TV mast, with its 300-year-old **mosque** upheld by palm-trunks, and a maze of twisting **covered streets** that protect the villagers from sun and sandstorms and once prevented invaders from entering on horseback. Painted oxblood, salmon, terracotta or pale blue, with carved lintels and wooden peg-locks, its mud-brick **houses** are only slightly less impressive than the ones in Al-Qasr, with many still inhabited. Although the oldest dates from Mamluke times, Balat was a town and a governors' seat (its name means "Palace of the Lord") way back in the Old Kingdom, when it prospered through trade with Kush (ancient Nubia).

There's proof of this in Balat's ancient necropolis, known to the locals as **Qila ed-Dabba** (or just Ed-Dabba), where five mud-brick mastabas, once clad in limestone but long ago reduced to lumps, mark the **tombs of VI Dynasty governors**. In 1977, French archeologists discovered an intact one from the reign of Pepi II (2292–2203 BC) by excavating a deep pit resembling an inverted step pyramid, to expose the burial chamber (daily 8am–5pm; £E20). Its painted reliefs are faint, but you can see the governor, Khentika, his wife and son; people ploughing, driving cattle and sailing boats; and Wadjet eyes. It took forty workers 763 days to construct the tomb. The ticket is also valid for the ruins at **Ain Asil**, 1500m east of the necropolis, where a fortress and farming community whose name meant "Our Root is Lasting in the Oasis" existed from the Old Kingdom until Ptolemaic times. Both sites are reached by a track 100m east of Balat's teahouse, and from Ain Asil a back road continues to Bashendi – about 5km in all.

Bashendi

Minibuses either terminate at or pass the turning for the village of **BASHENDI**, 2km off the main road. Its name derives from Pasha Hindi, a medieval sheikh who is buried in the local cemetery, which dates back to Roman times. Tombs form the foundations of many of the houses, which are painted pale blue or buttercup yellow with floral friezes and hajj scenes, merging into the ground in graceful curves.

The cemetery is at the back, where the desert begins. Some empty sarcophagi separate the domed tomb of Pasha Hindi (where locals pray for the recovery of lost items) from the square **Tomb of Kitnes**. While both structures are of Roman origin, the latter still retains its original funerary reliefs, depicting Kitnes meeting the desert-gods Min, Seth and Shu. Its key is held by a villager who can be fetched, but since admission costs £E16, you might settle for viewing its pharaonic lintels.

There is also a **carpet-weaving** factory, established with the help of Helwan University of Fine Arts, to train youths in making rugs and kelims: Mut's tourist office can arrange a visit (£E1.50 entrance fee).

TENEIDA, on the eastern edge of the oasis, is a modern affair centred on a leafy square, whose only "sight" is a **cemetery** on the outskirts with weird tombstones resembling tiny houses. In desert lore, Teneida is known for the three Zwayah tribesmen who staggered out of the desert in 1931, alerting the authorities to a tragedy that was already weeks old. Bombed from their homes at Kufra Oasis in Libya by the Italians, five hundred Zwayah nomads had trekked 320km south over waterless desert to Jebel Uwaynat, where they found springs but no grazing. Faced with starvation, half the tribe struck out towards Dakhla without knowing the way, while the others remained to await their end. Thanks to the men's 21-day, 670-kilometre march (a feat of endurance with few parallels), search parties managed to rescue almost three hundred stragglers from the wilderness.

With a car, you can press on to see some **rock inscriptions** off the highway 10km beyond Teneida. The carvings include an ostrich at the base of the sandstone outcrop beside the road, while beyond some fields another rock shaped like a seated camel is covered in prehistoric and Bedouin drawings of giraffes, camels and hunters, as well as the name of Jarvis (British governor of Dakhla and Kharga in the 1930s) and many other visitors. In olden times, this marked the intersection of two caravan routes, the Darb al-Ghabari ("Dust Road") between Dakhla and Kharga, and another track that linked Teneida to the Forty Days Road.

The road to Kharga

Beyond Teneida's last flourish of greenery, wind-sculpted rocks give way to dune table-tops and gravelly sand, persisting for most of the way from Dakhla to Kharga (193km). Following the Darb el-Ghabari, the modern road skirts the phosphate-rich Abu Tartur Plateau that separates the two depressions. In the distance is a new township of 1500 flats, where almost nobody lives. The appearance of a phosphates factory and railroad 45km outside Kharga alerts you for a treat to follow. Golden **dunes** march across the depression, burying lines of telegraph poles and encroaching on the highway. Villagers faced with their advance have been known to add an extra storey to their house, live there while the dune consumes the ground floor, and move back downstairs once it has passed on. These dunes are outstretched fingers of the **Ghard Abu Muharrik** (see p.516), of the type known as "whalebacked". Folk wisdom asserts that the less common *barchan* or crescent-shaped dunes are always separate from whalebacks; you'll see a cluster of *barchans* in the desert to the left, nearer El-Kharga. There's no mobile phone signal between the two oases.

Kharga Oasis

Despite being the nearest of the oases to Luxor and the New Valley's capital, **Kharga Oasis** gets far fewer tourists than the others. This may start to change now that tourists can use the direct road from Luxor – which takes only two hours as opposed to the day-long journey via Assyut – but other disincentives remain. **El-Kharga** is a 1970s metropolis of 60,000 people with adequate facilities and a decent museum, but otherwise dull. While the oasis contains many ancient sites, most are only accessible by car, and the local police insist on accompanying tourists everywhere in town, even radioing HQ for permission before letting them step outside their hotel – which hardly makes for a comfortable atmosphere.

Submerged by the sea aeons ago, leaving fossils on the high plateau, the Kharga depression is hemmed in by great cliffs and broken up by massifs, with belts of dunes advancing across the oasis. It's thought that there were no dunes in Kharga during Roman times; myth has it that they erected a brass cow on the escarpment, which swallowed up the sand. Historically, Kharga's importance is due to the desert trade routes that converged on the oasis, notably the **Forty Days Road** (see p.538). Deserted Roman forts and entire villages that claim descent from Mamluke soldiers attest to centuries of firm control by Egypt's rulers, who have used Kharga as a place of exile since Bishop Aries of Alexandria was banished for heresy in the fourth century AD. In modern times, the founder of the popular newspaper *Al-Akhbar* was exiled by Nasser, and since 1994, Islamists have been incarcerated in the tuberculosis-ridden **Kharga Prison** (visible from the highway as one enters the oasis from the north).

Kharga is also seen by some as a portent that the New Valley spells ruin for the oases. The influx of *fellaheen* from the Nile Valley has changed agricultural practices; **rice** cultivation has proved more water-intensive than expected, depleting aquifers and turning land saline – leading to strict limits on its production.

It's indicative of the mixed antecedents of its citizens that the **name** Kharga may be pronounced "Harga" or "Harjah", depending on who's talking. Both the oasis and its capital are called Kharga; we've used the prefix "El-" to refer to the city.

El-Kharga

As the capital of the New Valley Governorate (comprising Kharga, Dakhla and Farafra oases), **EL-KHARGA** has grown into a sprawl of mid-rise buildings and highways, with the only reminder of its romantic oasis town origins being the souk. Banks and government buildings line the wide **Sharia Gamal Abdel Nasser**, which is too long and monotonous for pleasant walking, despite its ornamental obelisks, arches and shrubs. But **getting around** is easy, with green-and-white minibuses shuttling along Sharia Gamal Abdel Nasser, between Midan Showla and the Mabrouk Fountain, at either end of town (25pt flat fare). The only impediment to one's freedom of movement is the tourist police – though they might agree to withdraw their plainclothes escort if you write a letter stating that you don't need one.

Arrival and information

Arriving by bus, it makes sense to decide on a hotel and get dropped off at the nearest point, rather than riding on to the bus station off Midan Basateen. Kharga's **train station** is 5km south of town, off the road to Baris; a taxi from here into town costs about £E5. At the **tourist office,** by the Mabrouk Fountain on Sharia Gamal Abdel Nasser (Mon–Thurs & Sun 8.30am–2pm and maybe 7–10pm; ☎092/792-1206, ℻792-1205), Mohsen speaks good English but is chiefly into promoting his own tours of the oasis (see p.532). For a free **guided tour** of town, ask at the Tourist Friends Association on Sharia el-Nabawy (daily 5–10pm; ☎092/792-1451). The **tourist police** (☎092/792-1367; 24hr) are next door to the tourist office, with the regular **police** across the road.

You can change **money** and traveller's cheques at the Banque du Caire (which has the only **ATM** in the New Valley, taking Visa cards only) and Banque Misr (both daily except Fri 8.30am–2pm & 5.30-8pm). The **telephone** exchange is on Sharia el-Gumhorriya (24hr). The main **post office** (daily except Fri 8am–2.30pm) off Midan Showla has EMS post. There are four **Internet cafés** in a block's radius of Midan Basateen, plus a free facility (Mon–Thurs & Sun 8am–3pm & 6pm–midnight) in the Governorate building. The private Al-Salam **hospital** opposite the Museum of the New Valley is the better than the public one on Sharia el-Nabawy, where there are also several **pharmacies**. There are **petrol** stations on Sharia Bur Said, Midan Abdel Moniem Riad and Sharia el-Nabawy.

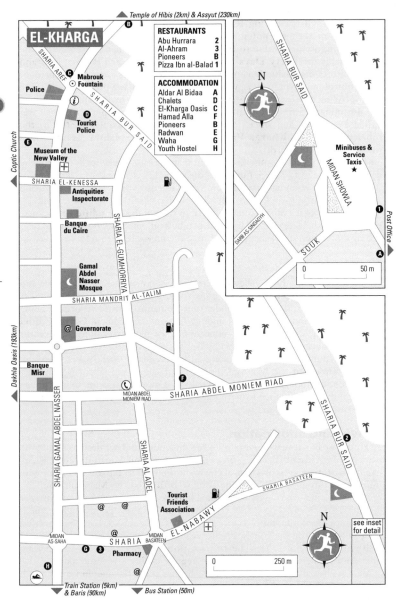

EL-KHARGA

Temple of Hibis (2km) & Assyut (230km)

RESTAURANTS
Abu Hurrara	2
Al-Ahram	3
Pioneers	B
Pizza Ibn al-Balad	1

ACCOMMODATION
Aldar Al Bidaa	A
Chalets	D
El-Kharga Oasis	C
Hamad Alla	F
Pioneers	B
Radwan	E
Waha	G
Youth Hostel	H

Mabrouk Fountain
Police
Tourist Police
Museum of the New Valley
Coptic Church
SHARIA AREF
SHARIA BUR SAID
SHARIA EL-KENESSA
Antiquities Inspectorate
Banque du Caire
SHARIA EL-GUMHORRIYA
Gamal Abdel Nasser Mosque
SHARIA MANDRIT AL-TALIM
Governorate
Dakhla Oasis (193km)
Banque Misr
SHARIA GAMAL ABDEL NASSER
MIDAN ABDEL MONIEM RIAD
SHARIA ABDEL MONIEM RIAD
SHARIA AL ADEL
Tourist Friends Association
MIDAN AS-SAHA
SHARIA BASATEEN
MIDAN BASATEEN
EL-NABAWY
Pharmacy
Train Station (5km) & Baris (90km)
Bus Station (50m)

SHARIA BUR SAID
Minibuses & Service Taxis
MIDAN SHOWLA
DARB AS-SINDADYH
SOUK
Post Office
N
0   50 m

SHARIA BUR SAID
SHARIA BASATEEN
N
0   250 m
see inset for detail

Accommodation

There's no problem with finding accommodation in El-Kharga, though it's not always great value. Staying outside town is feasible with a car, but rather impractical if you're relying on local transport to visit far-flung sites. All the places listed here are in El-Kharga.

Aldar Al Bidaa Off Midan Showla ℡092/792-
1717. Handy for the service taxi station but noisy,
with shabby rooms, some with fans and baths – the
Waha (see below) is similar, but half the price. ❶
Chalets or Villa A government resthouse behind
the tourist office (which handles reservations), with
four carpeted chalets (fan or a/c) sleeping up to
nine people, plus TV, bath and phone. ❷
El-Kharga Oasis Sharia Aref ℡092/792-1500.
Large a/c rooms with soft beds, bathrooms, and
balconies overlooking a huge palm garden – it
sounds great, but the hotel is always weirdly empty
and the garden rife with mosquitoes. Breakfast
included. ❷
Hamad Alla Off Sharia Abdel Moniem Riad
℡092/792-0638, ℻792-5017. On a quiet backstreet, this small, dark place has a/c rooms with
soft beds; some have bathrooms, fridges, TV,
heaters and balconies. There's also a restaurant
selling beer. ❷

Pioneers ℡092/792-9751, ℻792-7983, @www
.solymar-hotels.com. Out towards the Temple of
Hibis, Kharga's fanciest hotel has a/c rooms with
satellite TV, around a pool, a garden with a *qasr*-
style coffee shop, a restaurant and bar. Rates 25
percent lower over summer. Buffet breakfast and
dinner included. ❽
Radwan Sharia Radwan ℡010 345-7230. Simple,
clean a/c en-suite rooms and a rooftop with a view
of the mountains. ❷
Waha Off Midan as-Saha ℡092/792-0393. Within
walking distance of the bus station, the *Waha* has
basic rooms with grungy shared bathrooms; it's
worth paying £E6 more for private facilities. ❶
Youth Hostel Off Midan as-Saha ℡092/793-3854.
A new establishment with eight-bed dorms, each
with their own bathroom; a bed costs £E6, or £E20
in an a/c room. Guests can use a large pool in the
grounds for free. ❶

The Town

Prominently sited on Sharia Gamal Abdel Nasser, the **Museum of the New
Valley** (daily: summer 8.30am–6pm; winter 8am–5pm; £E20) is housed in a
modern building modelled on the tombs at Bagawat nearby, and contains artefacts from sites scattered across three oases. Of the exhibits on the ground floor
(labelled in English), the most impressive are Greco-Roman: painted sarcophagi
from Dakhla and from Maks al-Qibli to the south of El-Kharga; death masks
from Qasr el-Labeka to the north; and mummified rams, eagles and ibises from
the Muzawaka Tombs in Dakhla. The Old Kingdom is represented by an offerings tablet, scarabs and headrests from the tombs of the VI Dynasty governors
in Balat, also in Dakhla. Look out for the *ba* birds, representing the soul of the
deceased, unearthed by the French Mission at Dush Temple in the far south of
the oasis. Upstairs you'll find Coptic textiles and pottery, and floral friezes from
the Fatimid and Ottoman eras, mostly unlabelled.

While in the vicinity, check out the (dry) **Mabrouk Fountain**, just up the
road at the main junction, created by a local artist in three days. Its lusty figures
symbolize Mother Egypt dragging her unwilling child (the oases) towards its
destiny.

Aside from the **Gamal Abdel Nasser Mosque** (one of dozens that Nasser
built in provincial towns in the 1960s), and a **Coptic Church** discreetly located
off the high road, there's nothing else to see until you reach the lower part of
town (it's best to take a minibus, rather than walk the 2–3km). Here, dusty
Midan Showla is abuzz with people and traffic, a lively **souk** running off
into an old quarter of mud houses painted apricot or azure and daubed with
the Hand of Fatima. Turn right at the first crossroads and then left to find the
Darb as–Sindadyh, a dark, twisting street roofed with palm trunks, which
once extended over 4km; its oldest part dates from the tenth century. Only the
initial renovated stretch remains nowadays.

The tourist office can arrange visits to El-Kharga's **pottery and carpet
factory** and the **date factory** (both daily except Fri 8am–2pm; free), 50–100m
south of Midan as-Saha. Dates play an important part in the city's calendar, and
El-Kharga's **City Day** (October 3) celebrates the beginning of the date harvest
with a parade of floats along Sharia Gamal Abdel Nasser. The marriage season

is also timed to coincide with the flowering of the date crop (from July until harvest time). A more relaxing tourist activity is to chill out by the big **swimming pool** at the *Pioneers Hotel* (£E25 per person for non-residents) or the government pool by the *Youth Hostel* (negotiable).

Eating and drinking

The *Pioneers Hotel* **restaurant** features a lavish buffet supper (£E75) when tour groups are staying, and otherwise offers an à la carte menu of continental and Egyptian dishes, a well-stocked bar, and a terrace overlooking the pool. You can eat well for £E60 (excluding drinks). Other hotels offer variations on a three-course meal (£E30–50) of soup, chicken, rice and salad, as do cheap diners on Sharia Basateen and the *Al-Ahram* café on Sharia el-Nabawy, which sometimes also has *firik* (roasted green wheat served like rice or used as stuffing for chicken). *Abu Hurrara* on Sharia Bur Said is the best place for kebab or kofta. Alternatively, you can enjoy thin-crust pizza or sweet *fiteer* at *Pizza Ibn al-Balad* on Midan Showla (open daily 7–11pm). The only places selling **alcohol** are the bar at the *Pioneers* (with Egyptian beer, wine, spirits and cocktails) and the *Hamad Alla Hotel* (which just has Stella).

Moving on from El-Kharga

Buses to Cairo (7–8 hr; £E40–55) leave the terminal off Midan Basateen at 9pm, 10pm, 11pm and midnight, taking the Desert Road that bypasses the Nile Valley. On moonlit nights, try to get a seat on the left of the bus to see the magnificent escarpment en route to Assyut. It's almost worth travelling to Assyut (4–5 hr; £E8) by day just for the view; five buses depart between 6am and noon. Through-buses to Dakhla (£E9) leave Kharga at 2pm, 11pm and 1am. As a fallback, there are **service taxis** from Midan Showla to Assyut or Dakhla, though departures are irregular (your best bet is before 10am or just after 2pm; mid-morning or late afternoon are the worst times), and fares depend on how full the vehicle is when it finally leaves. Alternatively, Mohsen at the tourist office will take up to three people in his car to Dakhla for £E150, visiting Teneida, Bashendi and Balat (see p.527) en route. He'll even drive one or two people to Farafra or Bahariya with stopovers en route, for €40 per person per day.

As yet there are no buses or service taxis along the **direct road to Luxor** (275km), which leaves the oasis at Baghdad (see p.537). However, Mohsen will drive up to three people for £E350, and taxi drivers on Midan Showla may do the trip for £E350–500. The road is excellent and the journey takes only two hours. There are two first-aid stations with water, but no fuel, en route. The road meets the Nile Valley at Riziq, 15km south of Luxor.

Otherwise there's a third-class **train** that supposedly leaves Kharga station for Luxor every Friday at 7am. In reality, it may not operate for weeks, and when it does, the journey often takes far longer than the seven hours advertised. Used by workers in the phosphates industry, it doesn't even have a toilet on board.

An Egyptian petroleum company operates a weekly **flight to Cairo** from Kharga airfield (Wed 4pm; 1hr; $120 one-way), and accepts bookings (℡092/793-6900) in the Governorate building on Sharia Gamal Abdel Nasser.

Around the oasis

The size of the oasis, its minimal public transport and the remoteness of many sites means that you really need a car (if not a guide) to experience what Kharga has to offer. This can be arranged locally by a trio of moonlighting state employees – Mohsen at the tourist office (℡092/792-1206 or 010 180-6127, ℮mohsen_dl@yahoo.com); Mahmoud Youssef, director of the New Valley

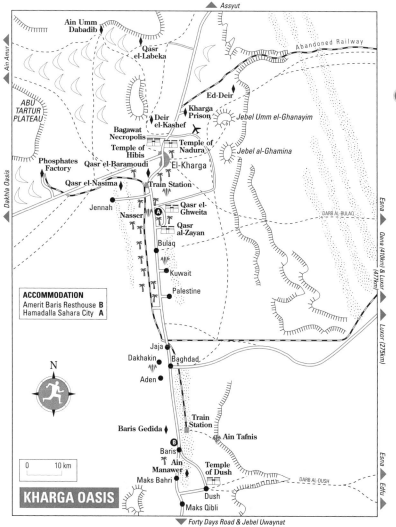

KHARGA OASIS

Museum (☎092/792-0084); and Mansour Osman, the director of Antiquities (☎012 374-5279). Both Mansour and Mahmoud have access to 4WD vehicles, and Mohsen can get almost anywhere with his taxi. Each can only take three passengers; the costs given below are the group rate.

Mahmoud asks €200 for a three-hundred-kilometre grand tour of all the sites (12hr), from Ain Umm Dabadib and Qasr al-Labeka in the north to Dush in the far south – or will guide people with their own 4WD for €120. Mohsen offers a shorter day-tour of Bagawat, Ed-Deir, Qasr al-Ghweita and Qasr al-Zayan for only $30, and half-day trips to Qasr el-Labeka (€60) or Ain Umm Dabadib (€150). Mansour's itineraries are negotiable; he also owns a **dirt-bike** and can guide bikers. A 2WD car should be able to reach most places using recently laid spur-roads or well-worn tracks – only Ain Umm Dabadib definitely needs 4WD.

North of El-Kharga

Two of the oasis' most evocative monuments lie just a few miles north of El-Kharga. While the **Temple of Hibis** has all but disappeared in recent years, the nearby **Bagawat Necropolis** is eerily impressive; one of the oldest Christian cemeteries in Egypt, it's backed by an imposing ruined monastery, **Deir el-Kashef**. Further north, the depression is littered with ruins of ancient towns and forts, with tunnels and other feats of Roman engineering waiting to be explored – these sites, however, such as **Ed-Deir**, **Qasr el-Labeka** and **Ain Umm Dabadib**, are difficult to reach and require a guide (see pp.532–533).

The Temple of Hibis

Although you can get there by catching a minibus from Midan Showla bound for El-Munira and asking to be dropped at *el-ma'abad* (the temple), it's fun to walk from the Mabrouk Fountain (2km) if the weather isn't too hot. En route, you'll catch sight of the ruined Ptolemaic **Temple of Nadura** atop a low hill in the desert to your right: its eroded sandstone wall and pronaos aren't worth the trek up to the top, though the view is.

Further on, you'll see what's left of the **Temple of Hibis** after a $20 million conservation fiasco. More accustomed to building bridges and factories, the contractors damaged eighty percent of the stone blocks when dismantling the temple to move it to higher ground due to rising groundwater, before it was found that the water table had fallen and the old site was better after all. The only part now standing is the **Persian Gate** of Darius I, originally erected circa 560 BC.

The vegetation roundabout covers the site of ancient Hibis, an XVIII Dynasty settlement that prospered under the Saïtes, Persians and Ptolemies. You don't need a ticket to see the temple itself, but the **kiosk** here is where you buy tickets for Bagawat and Deir el-Kashef (daily: summer 8am–6pm; winter 8am–5pm; £E20 for both sites).

△ The Bagawat Necropolis

The Bagawat Necropolis

The hilltop **Bagawat Necropolis** consists of 263 mud-brick chapels, used for Christian burials between the third and seventh centuries. They embody diverse forms of mud-brick vaulting or Roman-influenced portals, but are best known for their Coptic murals. Adam and Eve, Noah's Ark, Abraham and Isaac populate the dome of the **Chapel of Peace**, while Roman-looking pharaonic troops pursue the Jews, led by Moses, out of Egypt, in the **Chapel of the Exodus**. Flowery motifs and doves of peace can be seen inside **Tomb #25**, one of three adjacent family vaults on the ridge. The scenes are crudely executed but full of life and vividly coloured.

Deir el-Kashef

From the ticket kiosk, a track runs behind the hill, past an archeologists' rest-house and rows of rock-cut tombs, to reach the dramatic ruins of **Deir el-Kashef**, the Monastery of the Tax Collector. Named after a Mamluke governor, Mustafa, the five-storey monastery once housed hermits and travellers in its vaulted cells, nowadays choked by sand, and still commands a view of the point where the Darb al-Ghabari from Dakhla crossed the Forty Days Road. In the valley below you can see the ruins of a small **church** or hermitage, with Greek texts on the walls of the nave and the tiny cells where the monks slept. Beyond, four mighty crescent **dunes** to the north have spawned two infants downwind, either side of the Assyut road, near a crowd of whalebacks.

Other sights

For those with a sturdy car or dirt-bike and a local guide, there are many other sites to explore. A track from Bagawat skirts the foothills of the bat- and snake-infested **Jebel el-Teir** (Bird Mountain), whose wadis contain prehistoric, pharaonic and Coptic **inscriptions**. More intriguing are feats of ancient engineering nearer the escarpment. Here are **Roman fortresses** that once guarded, taxed and sheltered caravans on the road to Assyut. As a single caravan contained thousands of slaves and animals, they probably settled for the night in several forts. Fortresses were invariably sited near springs, either natural or man-made. Kharga has numerous underground aqueducts known as manafis, that drew on ground water like the *qanats* of ancient Persia (Ahmed Fakhry suggests that the system originated under Persian rule).

Qasr el-Labeka is reached via a spur-road off the highway facing a sign stating "Assyut 200km", that turns into a sandy track leading to a tiny oasis, where a farmer has cleared out the manafi to irrigate palms and plots. If you don't mind getting your feet wet, the shaft is narrow but tall enough to venture in; tiny tadpoles swim in the cool, pure, ankle-deep water. The vertical shafts allowing access from the surface give their name to such aqueducts (manafi means "shaft") and betray their presence.

You can tell where water lies near the surface from the scrub or palm trees on the plain beyond. Ruined houses and a temple (its walls still coloured blue and red) lie half-buried in the sand, with the fortress looming from a crag. Its twelve-metre walls enclose sand-choked chambers and the rear gate overlooks a palm grove. If Labeka's Arabic name ("Palm-wine Fort") signifies anything it wasn't the worst posting for a legionary.

Although **Ain Umm Dabadib** is only 18km from Labeka, the way is often blocked by sand and cars may have to backtrack as far as El-Kharga to find a corridor through the dunes. The site covers more than two hundred square kilometres and includes a ruined fortress, churches and tombs, but is most remarkable for its four underground aqueducts, with access shafts every 20m; the deepest is

53m underground; the longest runs for 4.6km. It's calculated that their builders cut and moved over 20,000 cubic metres of rock. When one of the manafis was cleared in the 1900s, water began to flow again. Now choked with sand and inhabited by snakes, scorpions and bats, they are dangerous to explore.

Further west, beyond the limits of the Kharga depression, the totally isolated, windblown spring of **Ain Amur** is situated 200m up the cliffs of the Abu Tartur Plateau. At 525m above sea level, this is the highest spring in the Western Desert and, like Ain Tafnis (see p.537), is fed by surface water trapped in the escarpment. Nearby are the **ruins** of a Roman fortress with Coptic graffiti, one of which relates how an early Christian traveller was "faint from thirst" when the spring saved him. Some believe that Ain Amur was the last watering hole of the legendary Lost Army of Cambyses (see box on p.517). Travel to Ain Amur requires **permission** and a recognized guide (see p.532).

Far across the oasis near the eastern scarp wall, **Ed-Deir** once guarded the shortest camel route to the Nile, which climbs out of the depression at the Abu Sighawal Pass. The fort lies 1km beyond the end of a track starting near Munira (the checkpoint on the road as you enter Kharga Oasis from the north); you must walk over the dunes at the end. Built in the reign of Diocletian, its twelve rounded towers are connected by a gallery, surrounding a well, and the surviving rooms covered in **graffiti** drawn by generations of soldiers: Turks in fezzes, tanks, airplanes, and obscenities. The **abandoned railway** in the distance was built by the British in 1906–8 and once carried special carriages with double roofs and wide eaves to protect passengers from the heat. Trips to Ed-Deir don't require permission.

South towards Baris

Exploring the **southern spur** of the oasis means flitting between sites off a highway. It's possible to negotiate with pick-up or **taxi** drivers on Midan Showla, who may agree to take you to the temples of Qasr el-Ghweita, Qasr al-Zayan and Dush for £E200–300. Buses to Baris township can drop you at the turn-off for Qasr el-Ghweita or Qasr al-Zayan – which are only 5km apart – but to visit Dush as well means staying overnight in Baris (see p.537 for details). **should we keep bus times** (2hr; £E3) leave El-Kharga at 9am and 2pm; the morning bus begins the return journey at noon, while the later one leaves Baris at 6am next day.

Five kilometres south of town you'll pass Kharga's **train station**, an Islamic-style edifice whose marble interior aspires to a grander role than the terminus of a train from Luxor which seldom runs even once a week.

Excavations, dunes and springs

Mahmoud or Mansour in El-Kharga will know about the ongoing **excavations** at two sites a few kilometres from the station and may be able to arrange a visit in the future. **Qasr al-Baramoudi** is a Roman fort with an oven-shaped pigeon tower, which once supplied the garrison with fowl. Such towers have been used in Egypt since antiquity and are still seen in the Nile Valley and Delta, but this is exceptional for being Roman and incorporated into military architecture. For reasons known to the architects, another fortress in the locality – **Qasr al-Nasima** – was equipped with an underground shaft for birds to roost in.

Further south and also off the highway, the village of **Jennah** backs onto a field of **dunes**, which tourists can admire at sunset before enjoying a soak in one of the **hot springs** in the palm groves on the far side of the highway, which vary in temperature up to 45°C. Usually the final stop on day-tours of the oasis, they're also visited by safari groups from Luxor en route to Dakhla Oasis.

You can **stay** at *Hamadalla Sahara City* (☎092/762-0240 or 010 255-0725, ⓔhamadallcity@yahoo.com; ❷), a garish complex located where the spur-road to Qasr el-Ghweita meets the highway, 17km from El-Kharga. There are domed air-conditioned rooms with a tepid spring-fed pool out back, and meals and beer are available.

Qasr el-Ghweita and Qasr al-Zayan

Visible from behind Hamadalla Sahara City, **Qasr el-Ghweita** (daily: summer 8am–6pm; winter 8am–5pm; £E20) is a fortified hilltop temple from the Late Period, with a commanding view of the area, which was intensively farmed in ancient times (its vineyards being mentioned in inscriptions in the Theban Necropolis). Its ten-metre-high walls enclose a sandstone temple dedicated to the Theban Triad, built by Darius I on the site of an older shrine, and modified by the Ptolemies. Its Hypostyle Hall contains scenes of Hapy the Nile-god holding symbols of the nomes of Upper and Lower Egypt. Nearby you can see the adobe remnants of a Ptolemaic settlement.

The spur-road continues 5km south to **Qasr al-Zayan** (daily: summer 8am–6pm; winter 8am–5pm; £E20), a Ptolemaic-Roman temple that lends its name to a village built over the ancient town of Tkhonemyris. This proximity to daily life helps you imagine it as a bustling settlement in antiquity. As at Qasr el-Ghweita, the temple is enclosed within a mud-brick fortress, together with living quarters for the garrison, a cistern and a bakery. Its portal bears the cartouches of Antonius Pius, who restored the temple in 138 AD. The plain hereabouts is 18m below sea level, the lowest point in Kharga Oasis.

As you return to the highway, the first large settlement, **Bulaq**, is divided into a picturesque old village to the west and a larger modern one to the east. Its **hot springs** are visible immediately before you enter town, on the right. Leaving Bulaq, you pass the whitewashed tomb of Sheikh Khalid shortly before the microwave tower that presages a string of New Valley settlements founded in the 1980s, named Kuwait, Palestine, Baghdad and Aden in a gesture of Arab solidarity. The **checkpoint** at the start of the **road to Luxor** (275km), near Baghdad, closes at 4pm.

Baris and beyond

Seventy kilometres south of El-Kharga, the township of **BARIS** (pronounced "Bar-ees") is named after the French capital, though its foraging goats and unpaved streets make a mockery of a billboard welcoming visitors to "Paris". Two kilometres before town, you'll pass the abandoned village of **Baris Gedida** (New Baris), begun in the early 1960s by architect Hassan Fathy and based on the principles of traditional oasis architecture, including wind shafts to cool the marketplace. Alas, work was halted by the Six Day War of 1967 and never resumed, so the initial settlers soon drifted away. Today, old Baris is set to develop further once the **Sheikh Zayed Canal** – drawing water from Lake Nasser (see p.406) – reaches Kharga, entering the depression at Baris.

Accommodation and **meals** are available at the laidback *Amiret Baris Rest-house* (☎092/797-5711 or 010 813-1472; ❷), beside the garage opposite the radio mast. Its staff can arrange **camel trips**, or a **pick-up** to take you to the Temple of Dush, 17km away (about £E30 round trip including waiting time), via a new road leaving Baris by the radio mast. With your own **4WD**, it's possible to make a scenic detour to **Ain Tafnis** (14km) by turning left at the first fork. Tafnis is one of two springs in the oasis that's nearly 200m above the floor of the depression, located on the slope of a mountain protruding from

The Forty Days Road

Of all the trade routes between North Africa and the tropical south, the **Forty Days Road** (Darb al-Arba'in) was the one most involved in **slavery** – the only business profitable enough to justify the risks and rigours of the thousand-mile journey. The slaves, purchased at the Dongola slave market or kidnapped by the fierce desert tribes, were assembled at **Kobbé**, a town (no longer existing) 60km northwest of El-Fasher, the capital of Sudan's Darfur Province, once an independent kingdom.

After a few days' march from Kobbé, the slaves were unchained from their yokes, for there was no way to escape. With no permanent water source until Bir Natrun, 530km away, they could only survive on the ox skins of water that burdened the camels. From **Bir Natrun**, caravans trekked 260km northeast across waterless, open sands, vulnerable to attack by bandits from the Arab Kababish and Bedayatt tribes, or the black Gor'an from Nukheila Oasis. The next stop, **Laqiya al-Arba'in**, had water but scant grazing for camels, and with their reserves of fodder exhausted they could easily weaken and stumble along the rocky 280-kilometre journey to **Selima Oasis**. While human losses were erased by the sands, the road gained definition from its Bactrian casualties; a 1946 survey of northwestern Sudan noted "a track about one mile wide marked with white camel bones".

W.G. Browne, the first European to complete the route, estimated the slave caravan's value at £115,000 sterling – a huge sum for the time (1762). Egyptian customs posts taxed caravans arriving in **Kharga Oasis**, the last stage before their ultimate destination, Assyut. As the caravans approached, small boys were hidden in empty water skins to evade tax, but officials would beat them to thwart this ploy. The most valuable slaves were young Nubian women – prized as concubines because their skin remained cool whatever the heat. Having sold their chattels at **Assyut**, traders bought "fabrics, jewellery, weaponry and kohl" for the return journey.

Traffic along the Forty Days Road effectively ended in 1884, after the rise of the Dervish Empire in Sudan closed the Egyptian–Sudanese border. When it reopened slavery had been prohibited, so the caravans ceased. As the illiterate slave-drivers died off, memories of the Darb al-Arba'in faded, as Michael Asher discovered when he tried to retrace the route from Darfur in the 1980s. Yet its name lives on, as geographers have designated the region through which it once ran as the **Darb al-Arba'in Desert**.

the escarpment. Greek, Coptic and Arabic **inscriptions** can be found in caves nearby, and the area is strewn with potsherds.

The spur-road to the temple passes **Ain Manawer**, three deep subterranean aqueducts buried by dunes which once supplied water to **Kysis**, a trading community straddling the Darb al-Dush to Esna and Edfu in the Nile Valley, and safeguarded with a hilltop Roman **fortress**. Its mud-brick walls are six metres high, with four or five storeys below ground. Abutting this, the **Temple of Dush** (daily: summer 8am–6pm; winter 8am–5pm; £E16) was built by Domitian and enlarged by Hadrian and Trajan, who added a monumental gateway. Reputedly once partly sheathed in gold, it is covered in dedications to the last two emperors, and the gateway in **graffiti** by Cailliaud and other nineteenth-century travellers. "Dush" is believed to derive from Kush, the name of the ancient Nubian kingdom with which the Egyptians traded along the Nile. A French archeological mission is in residence during the winter months.

From Dush, it's 32km by road to **MAKS BAHRI** ("Customs North"), a village that once lived off the infamous **Forty Days Road** (see box above), taxing each slave that entered the oasis, selling supplies and pandering to the slavemasters. Caravans going in the other direction were taxed at **MAKS QIBLI** ("Customs South"), where you can see a small mud-brick fort, the **Tabid**

△ The Temple of Dush

el-Darawish, built by the British after the Dervish invasion of 1893. Nowadays, the Forty Days Road has been paved as far south as Bir Tafarwi, to link up with the new agricultural project at East Oweinat, but cars can't go beyond the **checkpoint** 5km south of Maks Qibli without a permit from Cairo.

The Gilf Kebir, Jebel Uwaynat and the Great Sand Sea

Egypt's final frontier is the vast wilderness of the **Great Sand Sea** and the **Uwaynat Desert**, dominated by the huge plateau of the **Gilf Kebir**. Riven by *wadis* draining into lakes that dried out thousands of years ago, with colossal dunes leapfrogging each other to climb the 1000-metre-high escarpment, the Gilf is the closest environment on earth to the surface of Mars and has been studied by NASA since the 1970s. More recently, this obscure corner of Egypt was thrust into the limelight by the book and film *The English Patient*, dwelling on the exploits of the explorer László Almásy and his discovery of the **Cave of the Swimmers** at **Wadi Sura**. This magnificent example of **prehistoric rock art** is only one of thousands of engravings, drawings or paintings in the *wadis* of the

539
▬

Gilf Kebir and **Jebel Uwaynat**, a massif straddling the borders of Egypt, Libya and Sudan. In ancient times Jebel Uwaynat was inhabited by cattle pastoralist cultures which left equally amazing rock art at **Karkur Talh** and Ain Doua. Their depictions of giraffes, ostriches, lions and cattle – and people hunting and swimming – suggests what the environment was like before the decisive shift from savanna to desert occurred at the end of the Holocene wet period, around 5000 BC.

Since then, the Uwaynat Desert has become the **driest desert on earth**, with an aridity index of 200 (meaning that the solar energy received could evaporate 200 times the amount of precipitation received). Rainfall is less than a millimetre a year, and may fall only once a decade at Uwaynat and every five years on the Gilf. Barring a fluke rainfall such as allegedly saved Rohlfs in the Great Sand Sea, the nearest **water** supply is at least 500km away at Bir Tarfawi, where an experimental farm called East Oweinat draws on fossil water (trapped underground for millennia), and where the road to civilization begins. Beyond Bir Tarfawi there are only tracks or trackless desert: no fuel, food nor means of communication with the outside world (unless you bring a satphone); nor any people except a few survey or safari expeditions.

The websites Ⓦwww.fjexpeditions.com, Ⓦwww.zarzora.com and Ⓦwww .khalifaexp.com feature extensive photogalleries of the Gilf and Uwaynat, and news of recently discovered rock art. For an in-depth focus on Saharan rock art and prehistory, subscribe to the journal *Sahara* (Ⓦwww.saharajournal.com).

Travel practicalities

While the outermost dunes of the Great Sand Sea are easily accessible from Siwa (see p.550), crossing the Sand Sea or travelling to the Gilf Kebir or Jebel Uwaynat entails a deep-desert safari whose cost may be prohibitive. Even if it isn't, you need to **reserve** at least six months ahead to be sure of getting a place; expeditions only run from February to March and September to November, when the temperature is tolerable. Even so, **discomfort** is inevitable: sand gets into every crevice of your body, there's no water to spare for washing, and you start to stink – like everybody else in the vehicle. Unless you're willing to rough

△ Rock art from the Mestekawi-Foggini cave in the Gilf Kebir

it and muck in when needed, there's no point in coming at all. But if you do, you're sure to remember it for the rest of your life.

Safaris to the Uwaynat Desert are a major logistical effort, involving tangles of red tape, tonnes of supplies, high-tech communications and navigation gear. Don't think of going with fewer than three 4WD vehicles, or without a GPS set and satellite phone. Also essential is a **guide** who's done the trip enough times before to be confident; few of them use maps or compasses to chart the route, depending on their memory of landmarks, passed on from guide to guide. To prevent foolhardy ventures the authorities require all expeditions to have a permit from Military Intelligence in Cairo (see p.58), and since a 4WD ran over a landmine in 1999, that safaris are also accompanied by an **army escort** who knows where mines have been laid. They know lots about the desert, too, and often go into the safari business once their army careers are over, former colonel Mestekawi of Zarzora Expedition being the prime example. See p.474 and pp.507–508 for details of operators that specialize in the Gilf Kebir and Jebel Uwaynat.

Most safari outfits are willing to take people in their own 4WDs providing they're able to handle the **driving**, which needs experience, skill and nerve. If you have doubts on any of these scores then you should come as a **passenger** and let the safari team handle all the practicalities. Some safaris start from Cairo, others from Dakhla, Farafra or Bahariya oases; several firms are based in Europe and may organize package deals. Check that your travel **insurance** covers deep-desert journeys, and what (if any) back-up exists in case of **emergencies**; some outfits have contracts with an air-ambulance service whose light aircraft can land in the desert. Though the operator will supply meals, tents and bedding, you need to **bring** personal essentials such as sun block and skin cream and any luxuries like alcohol or cigarettes (the nearest supply is in Kharga or Dakhla oases). Binoculars are a must, too.

Approaches

There are two classic approaches to this corner of Egypt. One takes the Darb el-Tarfawi south from Dakhla Oasis and then a track to **Abu Ballas**, en route to the Gilf and then Uwaynat. The other assumes a more easterly starting point, from Kharga Oasis or even Aswan or Abu Simbel, and uses the Darb al-Arba'in – recently paved as far south as Bir Kiseba – to reach **Bir Tarfawi**, from where the first motorized explorers approached Uwaynat in the mid-1920s, finding the desert easier to cross than they'd expected. Approaching the Gilf from the north was – and is – more difficult due to the Great Sand Sea, but some safaris do it, in which case Regenfeld is a mandatory stopover (see p.549).

From Dakhla

Abu Ballas ("Father of Pots") is 240km from Dakhla, before the southeastern tip of the Great Sand Sea. Named by Prince Kemal el-Din in 1916, this hill is an ancient water cache strategically located between caravan trails and springs. Since 2000, German archeologists have excavated 27 way stations en route from Abu Ballas to the Gilf Kebir, seemingly part of a pharaonic trade route that may have led as far as Chad and possibly originated in Neolithic times.

Once there were hundreds of pots at Abu Ballas, each able to hold about thirty litres of water, some as old as the VI Dynasty, others stashed by Tebu nomads from the Libyan Desert to sustain their raids on Dakhla during Ottoman times. Eventually, men from Dakhla found the cache and smashed the pots; archeologists, explorers and tourists have removed most of the fragments, though a few remain photogenically posed. In the 1920s, geologist John Ball suggested that the "lost oasis" of Zerzura (see p.543) might actually be Abu Ballas and that the word *zerzura*, which is the Arabic name for a small black starling found in the Western Desert, might in this case refer to a *zir* or water jug. There is **rock art**, too, halfway up the southeast face: a cow suckling its calf, a bearded hunter and his dog chasing an antelope with a bow and arrows, and a man's profile. An hour's drive beyond Abu Ballas is a spectacular field of sedimentary *yardangs* resembling basking sea lions, dubbed the **Mud-Lions** (or Red Lions). Thereafter, dunes slope imperceptibly to the top of the plateau, impeding the way to the Gilf.

From Kharga

Depending on how far south you follow the Darb al-Arba'in and which roads you use, you may pass the ancient spring of **Bir Tarfawi**, in a depression surrounded by palms, acacias and tamarisks, once filled by two lakes ringed by Neolithic settlements. In 1981, Space Shuttle radar imaging revealed ancient riverbeds that convinced NASA scientist Farouk al-Baz (see p.550) that fossil water lay beneath the desert. His hypothesis proved to be correct, for the government has dug wells and established experimental farms near Bir Tarfawi. Collectively named **East Oweinat** (the English spelling differentiates it from Jebel Uwaynat, far away and unrelated to the project), they consist of circular fields irrigated by giant sprinklers, where high-value crops are grown for export to France from an airstrip. As the area is linked by road to Abu Simbel and Toshka, and there are plans to extend the Sheikh Zayed Canal to Kharga Oasis, it's possible to envisage a time when the middle of the Darb al-Arba'in Desert turns green – but not for decades.

The Gilf Kebir

For a hundred miles the great cliff went on. It seemed like the frontier of some "lost world" … unbroken except where the mouths of deep unlit gorges appeared as black slits, from the bottom of which an ancient debris of boulders spilled out fanwise for miles into the plain. It was tempting to go and explore one of those gorges. What might there not be far inland up the valleys which they drained? … But it was impossible to get close to the foot of the cliff without risking the cars.

Ralph Bagnold, *Libyan Sands: Travel in a Dead World*

Named the **Gilf Kebir** ("Great Barrier") by the first European to sight it, this 7770-square-kilometre limestone and sandstone plateau rises 1000m from the desert floor, an even more formidable obstacle than the Great Sand Sea. Early explorers only skirted its edges; it wasn't until the 1930s that they entered its valleys and found that the Gilf consists of two landmasses joined by an isthmus, almost cut through by a pass called Aqaba. Aeons ago in the late Tertiary age, the Gilf was a watershed draining water in all directions; its wadis were eroded by water and then by wind and sand over 100,000 years. The sheer cliffs on the south and southwest sides are the highest, while the northeasterly ones have been worn down by the Sand Sea: an unstoppable force meeting an unmovable object – and winning. **Dunes** have filled up the valleys and are climbing one on top of another to reach the plateau at Lama Pass; trillions of tonnes of sand on the march, white by the Sand Sea, or red around the middle of the plateau and its southern landmass. Despite being so arid, the top of the plateau gets just enough rainfall for hardy **flora and fauna** to survive. While its Barbary sheep have been hunted to the verge of extinction by Libyan poachers, nobody is endangering the foxes and lizards seen by the naturalist Xan Misonne in 1969, nor the wheatears, butterflies and Rose of Jericho flowers that the writer Cassandra

Vivian saw in 1998. And then there are the acacia trees that early explorers found, which were shrivelled when last seen but likely to survive until the next shower. Visitors may also find other surprises, too, like the wreck of a South African Air Force Blenheim bomber that turned up on the plateau in 2001 (thought to be one of five that took off from Kufra Oasis in 1942).

For many visitors the Gilf's allure has more to do with its fantastic **prehistoric rock art** – at Wadi Sura, Wadi Abd el-Malik and other sites – or the romance attached to the **explorers** who "discovered" it (Tebu and Gor'an nomads were fully aware of it all along, since it was their ancestors who created it). Almássy gets all the limelight, naturally, but Michael Ondaatje's novel also mentions other explorers of the 1920s and 1930s, such as the Egyptian Prince Kemal el-Din, the Englishmen Ralph Bagnold, Douglas Newbold and Kennedy Shaw, and the Irishman Patrick Clayton. During World War II, they set up the Long Range Desert Group (LRDG) that wreaked havoc behind Italian and German lines, while their former comrade Almássy served on the other side with the Afrika Korps. Since the 1960s the tradition of exploration has been revived by British, Belgian-Libyan, US, French and American-Egyptian expeditions, and by tourists from Germany, Italy, France, Hungary, Spain and Britain.

The "Zerzura" wadis

When Almássy and Lord Clayton took three cars and a plane to the Gilf in February 1932, the aim of their **Zerzura Expedition** was to find the legendary lost oasis of that name, which had obsessed Western explorers for generations (see p.544). Almássy was away visiting the Italians in Kufra when Clayton and Penderel flew over the northern Gilf and glimpsed "an acacia-dotted wadi" that they were unable to pinpoint on a map. After Almássy's return with a dozen bottles of wine to what was thereafter called Chianti Camp, they made further flights and spotted two such wadis from the air, but couldn't locate them on foot. Both Almássy and Clayton believed that these were two of the three valleys mentioned by Wilkinson in his 1835 list of unknown sites that set the European search for Zerzura rolling. But fate intervened in their plans, for Clayton died of polio on a visit to England, followed within a month by the expedition's sponsor, Prince Kemal el-Din, leaving Almássy to seek new sponsors and Clayton's widow to continue her husband's quest independently (see box, p.545).

Returning next spring in cars with balloon tyres, Almássy's party explored **Wadi Abd el-Malik**, the longest of the deep fissures in the northern Gilf. They found lots of acacia trees and sites of Tebu encampments and a large cave with **drawings** of longhorn cattle, men, and a prehistoric dwelling. (Another grotto was later found by Peel and Bagnold, containing **paintings** of cattle and a dog.) It was a Tebu caravan guide who told Almássy the name of the wadi and its side-valley, **Wadi Talh** ("Acacia Valley"), and spoke of a third valley called Wadi Hamra. When asked if he knew of Zerzura, he replied: "Oh, those silly Arab people, they do not know anything; they call these three wadis in the Gilf, Zerzura, but we local people know their real names." Almássy was sure that they had found Zerzura.

In 2002, an expedition exploring a valley to the west of Wadi Abd el-Malik climbed down three small canyons and found the largest cave yet discovered in the Gilf. Co-named after the expedition's leader and sponsor, the **Mestekawi–Foggini Cave** contains a peerless array of prehistoric art: **paintings** of humans and animals, **engravings** of cattle and ibexes, and the ghostly blown-outlines of dozens of **hands**. Some safari outfits now feature the cave on their itineraries (see p.474).

Zerzura: the "Lost Oasis"

With the "discovery" by motorized explorers of Selima, Merga and the Forty Day Road's water holes, the number of unlocated oases diminished until only the "Lost Oasis" of Zerzura remained. First mentioned in 1246 as an abandoned village in the desert beyond the Fayoum, it reappeared as a fabulous city in the fifteenth-century treasure-hunters' *Book of Hidden Pearls*:

This city is white like a pigeon, and on the door of it is carved a bird. Enter, and there you will find great riches, also the king and queen sleeping in their castle. Do not approach them, but take the treasure.

Citing native sources in 1835, Wilkinson placed the oasis "five days west of the road from El-Hayiz to Farafra", or "two or three days due west from Dakhleh". *Murray's Handbook* (1891) reported an "Oasis of the Blacks . . . also called Wady Zerzura" to the west of Farafra, and described it quite matter-of-factly. But Zerzura was still unlocated, and the stories placing it west of Dakhla gained credibility after Europeans "discovered" Kufra Oasis in Libya, which the same tales had mentioned. However, both the Rohlfs and Harding-King expeditions heard accounts of black men who periodically raided Dakhla from an oasis seven or eight days' journey to the southwest.

Having weighed the evidence for various speculative locations in the last chapter of *Libyan Sands*, Bagnold demarcated three zones. The "northern" one – encompassing the whole Sand Sea, but rating the areas west of Dakhla and Farafra as likeliest – was propounded by de Lancey Forth, citing the story of a town with iron gates, seven days' camel journey to the south, in the *Siwan Manuscript* (see p.551); plus tales of Bedouin chancing upon unknown oases while pursuing missing camels. Unfortunately, similar yarns also pointed towards the far south – that vast wilderness between Dakhla and the Selima and Merga oases in Sudan. Ball and Newbold favoured this area, largely free of dunes and often low enough to approach the subterranean water table; in addition, Newbold thought he glimpsed an oasis during a flight over the desert.

The third, "central" zone extended southwest from Dakhla as far as Jebel Uwaynat and was championed by Harding-King, who cited native accounts of incursions by "strange cows", Tebu raiders and a "black giantess". When Ball discovered a cache of water jars at Abu Ballas, southwest of Dakhla, it supported the stories but argued against an oasis; for if a water source existed, why bother to maintain a depot in the middle of nowhere? Then came Almássy and Lord Clayton, who were sure that three wadis in the northern Gilf Kebir were the legendary Zerzura – but they failed to convince others.

Accepting Ball's theory of a consistent water level beneath the Libyan Desert, Bagnold argued that Zerzura could only exist in low-lying areas or deep, wind-eroded hollows. As the desert was surveyed, the possibility of such sites escaping notice diminished, and Bagnold doubted that an undiscovered oasis existed. Perhaps Zerzura might once have been a water hole or an area favoured with periodic rainfall, but the fabled oasis of palms and ruins must be a figment of wishful thinking: a Bedouin Shangri-la that tantalized foreign explorers.

Wadi Hamra ("Red Valley"), on the eastern side of the plateau, is another must-see, named for its gorgeous red dunes drifting down a black mountainside – a Martian landscape found nowhere else in Egypt. The sandstone rocks bear **engravings** of giraffes, oryx, ostriches, gazelles and Barbary sheep – the prey that hunter-gatherers killed with dogs, lassos, bows and arrows during the Early Holocene epoch (8000–6000/5000 BC). This rock art is centuries if not thousands of years older than the images in the Cave of the Swimmers. Wadi Hamra was found in 1931 by Patrick Clayton, who noted plenty of trees and Barbary sheep, while Almássy discovered that it led up to the Gilf plateau. During the war, he reputedly tried to persuade Rommel to land glider-troops on top of the Gilf and bring them down into Wadi Hamra. Today, the wadi's **vegetation** is relatively prolific, following a downpour in 2005.

Wadi Sura and the Cave of the Swimmers

Although *The English Patient* transposes the Cave of the Swimmers to Ain Doua at Jebel Uwaynat, it actually lies in **Wadi Sura**, where Almássy found it in October 1933, with the Frobenius expedition that was searching for rock art at Uwaynat and in the western valleys of the Gilf that had been explored by Patrick Clayton two years earlier. Clayton's son believes that his father found the wadi and its other caves first, but it was Almássy's privilege to discover the Cave of the Swimmers and name the valley. The film, shot in Tunisia, took liberties by making the cave where Katherine Clifton died a deep, convoluted passage: it is, in fact, a shallow hollow on the lip of the wadi, and shockingly exposed to the elements.

László Almássy – the real "English Patient"

While Michael Ondaatje's novel *The English Patient* and the subsequent Oscar-winning film rescued Almássy's name from obscurity, both texts took liberties with the truth to cast "Count Ladislaus de Almasy" as a romantic hero whose love for another man's wife sealed their fates and left him dying of burns in an Italian villa. The real story is rather different – not least because Almássy was, in fact, homosexual.

Born in 1895, in Borostyánkő, Hungary (now Bernstein, Austria), **László Ede Almássy** learned to fly while at boarding school in England. During World War I he was a fighter ace and then an aide to the last Hapsburg monarch (who once mistakenly called him "Count" – a title that stuck), serving as his driver during two farcical attempts to regain the throne in 1921. Almássy then became a salesman for the off-road-car manufacturers Steyr, for whom he won many races, and in 1926 took Steyrs into the desert on the first of his numerous Sahara expeditions, about which he wrote several books. The Bedouin called him Abu Ramleh – Father of the Sands.

In February 1932 he initiated the **Zerzura Expedition** to the Gilf Kebir, the first to combine cars with light aircraft. His co-explorers were **Lord Robert** and **Lady Dorothy Clayton-East-Clayton** (the fictional Geoffrey and Katherine Clifton), the Irish desert surveyor **Patrick Clayton** (no relation) and Squadron Leader **Penderel**. Unlike in fiction, Lord Clayton died of a sudden illness back home in England, and although his widow returned to the desert to continue searching for Zerzura, she didn't meet Almássy again or share his discovery of the Cave of Swimmers – nor did she perish there in 1939, but rather in a fall from her plane in England six years earlier. Thus the motive for Almássy's collaboration with the Germans in *The English Patient* is pure invention.

As a reserve officer in the Hungarian Air Force, Almássy could hardly refuse being posted to Rommel's **Afrika Korps**, which used his expertise as a spotter and his photos for their official handbook – to the fury of his old companions in Egypt, many of whom were now in the LRDG (see box on p.546). Thanks to the codebreakers of Bletchley Park, the British knew of Almássy's infiltration of two German spies into Egypt, whom he guided through the Gilf to Kharga Oasis in 1941. He later made amends by visiting Patrick Clayton in an Italian POW camp and getting him moved to a better one. Almássy himself wound up in a Soviet camp where he lost his teeth from scurvy, before a Peoples' Court cleared him of being a Nazi sympathizer after testimony that he had sheltered Jewish neighbours in his flat in Budapest. His **final years** were spent in Africa, where he flew gliders and ran safaris. After catching dysentery in Egypt, he died in a clinic in Salzburg in 1951.

The **Cave of the Swimmers** harbours well over a hundred figures in diverse styles. The famous swimmers are 10cm long and painted in red, with small rounded heads on stalks, tadpole-shaped bodies and spidery arms and legs. Some are diving, implying that a lake once existed here (for which there's geological evidence). A second group of figures are depicted standing, with clumsy limbs, thick torsos and pea-shaped heads; hands only appear on the larger figures. Most are dark red, with bands of white around their ankles, wrists or waists, similar to the hunters at Karkur Talh. Still more intriguing are two yellow figures that seem to be stretching out their arms to welcome a third, smaller, red one, which may be a child and its parents. Cattle, giraffes, ostriches and dogs are also depicted on the walls.

Further along, the **Cave of the Archers** contains dark-red and white figures of naked men clutching bows, some of them shooting at cattle – whose presence dates these pictures to the Cattle Period (5000–2500 BC) of North African rock art. Hans Winkler of the 1938 Monod expedition termed the style of the male figures "balanced exaggeration", for they all have wide shoulders and hips, tiny waists and tapering limbs; feet and hands are rarely shown, and heads often omitted too – unlike the spear-carrying hunters depicted in Karkur Talh at Jebel Uwaynat, which are otherwise similar in style.

On the sandy plain before the wadi a huge fallen boulder covers the **Giraffe Cave**, found by Clayton in 1931. Inside are giraffes, cattle and dogs painted in black or white.

Other wadis

The southern part of the Gilf is riddled with wadis, some easy to enter, others nearly impossible. **Wadi Mashi** ("Walking Valley") gets its name because the mountains vanish and reappear as you approach, but has yet to yield any finds, unlike **Wadi Dayyiq** ("Narrow Valley"), where a large area is covered by stone-chippings left by prehistoric people manufacturing knives, blades and

The Long Range Desert Group (LRDG)

Founded by Ralph Bagnold in June 1940 to reconnoitre Axis forces and engage in "piracy on the high desert", the **Long Range Desert Group**'s motto was "Not by Strength, but Guile". Led by Bagnold and other prewar explorers such as Patrick Clayton, Kennedy Shaw and Douglas Newbold, it consisted mainly of New Zealanders, who soon learnt the arts of desert warfare. As with Special Forces ever since, the emphasis was on self-reliance and mobility. Each patrol took all it needed for a cross-desert journey of 1500 miles (which could be doubled by establishing a forward supply dump), in stripped-down Chevy trucks fitted with sand mats and channels (doubling as air markers for supply drops) and a sun compass invented by Bagnold. Patrols operated for up to eleven weeks as they espied convoys or delivered SAS commandos to attack airfields – in ten months, over 400 planes were thus destroyed (more than the RAF managed). British Foreign Secretary Anthony Eden called them "my mosquito army", while the Italians dubbed them the Ghost Army.

After Axis forces in North Africa surrendered in 1943, the LRDG were sent to the Balkans. They spoke a weird argot composed of English, Arabic, Hindi, German and Italian, and wore a mixture of uniforms, with a unit badge of a scorpion within a wheel, made by jewellers in Khan el-Khalili. You can **read** about the LRDG's exploits in Bagnold's *Sand, Wind and War: Memoirs of a Desert Explorer*, Saul Kelly's *The Hunt for Zerzura*, Peter Clayton's *Desert Explorer* (about his father, Patrick), or on the LRDG Preservation Society's website ⓦ www.lrdg.org.

arrow-heads from hard rocks; or **Wadi al-Bakht**, where four **prehistoric settlements** have been found. Besides ostrich eggs, grinding stones and bones, there's heaps of pottery dating back to 6930 BC – as old as the pottery at Nabta (see p.462) but different in style and colour. It's thought that people lived here for centuries, hunting ostriches and raising cattle around the shores of a lake until it disappeared by 5200 BC.

Nor is it just prehistory that has been preserved, for in 1991 a World War II ammunition truck was found in the desert to the east of Wadi Dayyiq. After being refuelled it started, and is now in the war museum at El-Alamein (see p.611). There are relics of the **Long Range Desert Group** (see box opposite) all over the region, from a Ford lorry and a GM stake-bed truck 10km southeast of the Gilf's southern tip, to hundreds of metal petrol cans with the Shell logo, laid out to form route markers. An evocative example is the **abandoned aerodrome** with a landing strip marked by concentric rings of petrol cans, near the wadi known as **Eight Bells**. This cluster of hills and depressions is the result of a vast prehistoric drainage system which carried water south into an even larger one that fed a super-lake stretching from Lake Chad to within 600km of the Gilf Kebir.

Circumventing the southern Gilf, cars pass through **Wadi Wassa** ("Wide Valley"), another ancient drainage valley with dozens of side wadis, islands, and a wrecked Chevy used by the LRDG. On the col that divides Wadi Wassa from **Wadi Faragh** ("Empty Valley"), Shaw found a cave containing engravings of cows and more ancient giraffes; it was thereafter shown on maps as **Shaw's Cave**, despite being known to caravan guides as the Cave of the Arch (Magharat el-Qantara). It's here that a military escort is most appreciated, for there are **mines** on the plain where two tracks cross about 5km west of the mouth of Wadi Faragh, and more are rumoured to have been laid at other strategic points. Wadi Faragh is also distinguished by a **Monument to Prince Kemal el-Din**, erected by Almásy to commemorate his patron's expeditions to Uwaynat, the Gilf and Merga Oasis, using caterpillar-tracked Citroëns in the 1920s.

The Clayton Craters and Jebels Peter and Paul

The two main tracks towards Jebel Uwaynat pass the **Clayton Craters**, discovered by Patrick Clayton on the second Bagnold expedition in 1931. Measuring up to 1km across, the twenty craters have sandstone rims rising about 30m from the desert floor, enclosing domes of greenish igneous rock or cork-shaped basalt formations, with dry stream-beds. While the baked and fused sandstone suggests a volcanic origin, the geologist Rushdi Said argues that springs caused the ground to collapse, forming the craters. Elsewhere in the Libyan Desert, remote sensing satellites have identified craters formed by meteor strikes, near Kufra Oasis in Libya and amid the Great Sand Sea (see p.548).

Otherwise, the chief landmarks are the twin mountains named **Jebels Peter and Paul**, steep-sided quartz trachyte plugs in the Precambrian bedrock, like the northern part of Uwaynat. Safari groups give them a wide berth, as **mines** have reputedly been laid roundabouts.

Jebel Uwaynat

On a map of North Africa, the ruler-straight borders of Libya, Egypt and Sudan intersect at **Jebel Uwaynat**, the highest point in the Libyan Desert. Surrounded by sand-sheets, it rises through a "vertical battlement" to 1898m above the desert floor and 600m above sea level, just high enough to attract a little rainfall, which percolates down to eight small pools or "springs" at its base (after which Uwaynat is named). The valleys there are fertile if watered, sustaining communities from prehistoric times until the early 1930s. Yet Uwaynat's location remained a mystery to the outside world until 1923, when it was reached by Hassanein Bey by camel from Kufra Oasis in Libya. With its coordinates established, the next challenge was to find a route from Egypt, which was accomplished in 1925 by Prince Kemal al-Din and John Ball, who followed in half-tracks from Bir Tarfawi. They were followed by Shaw, Almássy, Bagnold *et al.*, whose exploration of the Gilf was initally motivated by the desire to find a route to Uwaynat from the north.

After the Italians occupied Kufra and placed an outpost at Uwaynat, the possibility that it could be an unguarded back door into Egypt during wartime occurred to both Bagnold and the Italian commander Lorenzini – but not to the HQ staff-wallahs who turned down Bagnold's proposal for car patrols along the frontier. It wasn't until Italy declared war in June 1940 that the newly appointed General Wavell summoned him and learned that cars could easily drive from Uwaynat to Aswan in two days. The risk of a surprise attack that would cut links to Sudan and make all of Egypt hostage to a threat to blow up the Aswan Dam was too terrible to ignore, so Bagnold was authorized to set up long-range patrols to monitor any activity. In the event, the Italians never tried anything so bold, but Almássy later slipped through from Kufra via Uwaynat and the Gilf, to guide two German spies as far as Kharga Oasis, before returning to Libya.

Karkur Talh and other sites

Jebel Uwaynat covers 1500 square kilometres and consists of granite, sandstone and quartz trachyte formations. As in the Gilf, the northern slopes have borne the brunt of wind erosion and bizarre rock forms abound, while the wadis all around the base (called *karkurs*) contain engravings, drawings and paintings spanning thousands of years. One of the richest sites is **Karkur Talh** ("Acacia Valley"), where Hassanein Bey found images of lions, giraffes, ostriches, gazelles and cows engraved on the rocks at ground level – plus paintings of camels from a later epoch (camels reached Egypt in 525 BC). Higher up the valley, Shaw discovered ninety human figures drawn on the roof of a sandstone cave 1m high, whose figures were lither than the hunters in the Cave of the Archers at Wadi Sura but otherwise similar, leading Winkler to conclude that both were the work of the ancient Tebu, who once ranged across the Sahara from their mountainous homeland of Tibesti, in Chad. Besides the rock art in the main valley there are two hundred paintings and engravings in a lateral wadi, and over a thousand other locations in the areas that the Belgian expedition of 1968 called **Wadi Talh I** and **II**.

All the other rock-art sites lie over the partly mined border in Sudan or Libya and are currently **inaccessible** (except on safaris via Libya with Ancient World Tours or Fleigel Jerzerniczky Expeditions; see p.474). These include **Karkur Murr**, where Clayton found starving refugees from Kufra in 1931, and the massif's largest "spring", **Ain Doua**, which was the fictional location of the Cave of the Swimmers in *The English Patient* – though the rock art here was actually discovered by Almássy's driver.

The Great Sand Sea

Between the Gilf Kebir and Siwa Oasis lie 72,000 square kilometres of dune fields that the explorer Gerhard Rohlfs named the **Great Sand Sea** (Bahr er-Raml in Arabic). Though maps still define parts as beyond the "limits of reliable relief information", its overall configuration is known. From thick whalebacks and a mass of transverse dunes near Siwa, it washes south in parallel *seif* dunes (oriented north–south, with a slight northwest–southeast incline) as far as the eye can see.

Although its general existence was known at the time of Herodotus, the extent to which it stretched southwards wasn't realized until the Rohlfs expedition of 1874 headed west from Dakhla, bound for Kufra Oasis in Libya. With seventeen camels bearing water and supplies, they soon met the erg's outermost ranges: "an ocean" of sand-waves over 100m high, ranked 2–4km apart. Rohlfs estimated that their camels could scale six dunes and advance 20km westwards on the first and second days, but that their endurance would rapidly diminish thereafter, so with no prospect of water or an end to the dunes they were forced to turn north-northwest and follow the dune lanes towards Siwa. Their isolation was intense:

> If one stayed behind a moment and let the caravan out of one's sight, a loneliness could be felt in the boundless expanse such as brought fear even in the stoutest heart … Nothing but sand and sky! At sea the surface of the water is moved, unless there is a dead calm. Here in the sand ocean there is nothing to remind one of the great common life of the earth but the stiffened ripples of the last windstorm; all else is dead.

By the eighteenth day the expedition could no longer water every camel and the animals began dying. Then, according to the English version of his adventures, there was torrential rainfall in a spot where barely a drop falls for years, saving their lives and replenishing their water supply. Rohlfs called the spot **Regenfeld** ("Rainfield") and marked it with a cairn before he left, wondering "Will ever man's foot tread this place again?". However, in the German edition of his book, *Drei Monate in der libyschen Wüste*, he described a smaller expedition with no hint of supply problems – and whether or not a miraculous rainfall really saved their lives, Regenfeld has since been visited by scores of explorers and tourists. The message that he left in a bottle was removed by Hassanein Bey in 1923, who substituted a message of his own, followed decades later by Samir Lama and Jacques Monod. Now, all the messages, wine bottles and empty water tanks left by previous explorers have been taken by souvenir hunters.

Rohlfs' feat of trekking for 36 days over 675km (480km across the dunes) wasn't repeated until 1921–24, when Colonel de Lancey Forth entered the Sand Sea twice by camel from Dakhla and Siwa. Beneath a layer of sand he found campfires, charred ostrich eggs, flint knives and grinders from Neolithic times, when the desert was lush savanna.

Meanwhile, Ball and Moore had managed to round the Sand Sea's south-eastern tip (near latitude 24°) by car in 1917, while in 1923 Hassanein Bey circumvented its western edge as part of an extraordinary 3550-kilometre camel journey from Sollum on the Mediterranean to El-Fasher in Sudan's Darfur province. He also confirmed the existence of the hitherto legendary Jebel Uwaynat, whose water source encouraged motorized explorers to seek new routes to the southwest. For Prince Kemal el-Din in his fleet of caterpillar-tracked Citröens, and Bagnold and co. – who found customized Model-T Fords more effective – the next obstacle was the Gilf Kebir (see p.539), which barred the way to remoter Libyan oases.

Visiting the Great Sand Sea

Today, tourists can cross the Sand Sea on **deep-desert safaris** from Bahariya, Farafra or Cairo (see p.507 & p.474). Most itineraries feature Regenfeld and an area of desert strewn with pale green deposits of translucent **silica glass** – a material known to the Ancient Egyptians, for it was from this that the scarab on Tutankhamun's funerary pectoral cross was carved. In 2006, some Germans stole sixteen crateloads of silica glass with the help of a local safari agency. The silica glass deposits are thought to have originated in a prehistoric meteorite strike, whose impact fused sand into glass. Ground zero may have been the four-kilometre-wide **Al-Baz Crater**, 150km southeast of the silica glass region (the crater is named after its Egyptian-American discoverer, Farouk al-Baz, a pioneer in using satellites to search for water in arid areas).

If you can't afford a safari into the heart of the Sand Sea, a **brief excursion** from Siwa Oasis to **Bir Wahed** (see p.563) is enough to experience the utter desolation and colossal size of its dunes.

Siwa Oasis

Isolated by hundreds of kilometres of desert, **Siwa Oasis** remained virtually independent from Egypt until the late nineteenth century, sustaining a unique culture. Yet despite – or because of – its isolation, outsiders have been drawn here since antiquity. The legendary Army of Cambyses was heading this way when it disappeared into a sandstorm; Alexander the Great journeyed here to consult the famous Oracle of Amun; and Arabic tales of Santariyah (as the oasis was known) were common currency into the nineteenth century. In modern times, Siwa has received visits from kings and presidents, anthropologists and generals. Tourism only really began in the mid-1980s but has gathered steam since then, as Siwa has become a firm favourite with independent travellers and adventure tour groups.

The oasis offers all you could ask for in the way of desert **beauty spots**: thick palm groves clustered around freshwater springs and salt lakes; rugged massifs and enormous dunes. Equally impressive are the **ruins** of Shali and Aghurmi, labyrinthine mud-built towns that once protected the Siwans from desert raiders. Scattered around the oasis are ruined **temples** that attest to Siwa's fame and prosperity during Greco-Roman times; some claim that the tomb of Alexander the Great lies here. Visitors are also fascinated by **Siwan culture** and how it is reacting to outside influences like TV, schooling and tourism. Nowadays, it is mostly only older women who wear the traditional costume, silver jewellery and complex hair-braids; younger wives and unmarried women dress much the same as their counterparts in the Nile Valley. But the Siwans still observe their own festivals and wedding customs; and among themselves they speak Siwi, a Berber tongue (see p.553). Though things are changing, the Siwans remain sure of their identity and are determined to maintain it. Having weathered an invasion of 5000 rally cars and camp-followers when the Paris–Dakar–Cairo rally was routed via Siwa in 2003, and a horde of spectators for a solar eclipse in 2006, Siwans are bracing themselves for the arrival of holidaymakers on charter flights to Mersa Matrouh.

A little history

Beyond the fact that it sustained hunter-gatherers in Paleolithic times, little is known about Siwa Oasis before the XXVI Dynasty (525–404 BC), when the reputation of its **Oracle** spread throughout the Mediterranean world. Siwa's population seems to have been at risk from predatory desert tribes, so their first settlement was a fortified acropolis, about which classical accounts reveal little about this beyond its name, **Aghurmi**, and its position as a major caravan stop between Cyrenaica and Sudan. The Siwans are related to the Berbers of Algeria, Tunisia and Morocco, and their language is just a variant of the Berber tongues, so their society may have originally been matriarchal. Their later history is detailed in the *Siwan Manuscript*, its whereabouts are a closely guarded secret. A century-old compilation of oral histories, it relates how Siwa's rulers considered poisoning the springs with mummies in order to thwart the Muslim conquest (date uncertain), and how Bedouin and Berber raids had reduced Aghurmi's population to a mere two hundred by the twelfth century AD.

Shali and Siwan society

Round about 1203, seven families quit Aghurmi to found a new settlement called **Shali** (the Town). Their menfolk are still honoured as the "forty ancestors", and these pioneering families were probably the most vigorous of the surviving Siwans. Later, newcomers from Libya settled in the oasis, giving rise to the enduring distinction between the "Westerners" and the original, more numerous "Easterners", whose historic feud began after they disagreed over the route of a causeway that both had undertaken to build across the salt lake of Birket Siwa. Nonetheless, both coexisted within a single town built of *kharsif*: a salt-impregnated mud which dries cement-hard, but melts during downpours – fortunately, it rains heavily here only every fifty years or so. Fearful of raiders, Shali's *agwad* (elders) forbade families to live outside the walls, so as the population increased the town could only expand upwards. Siwan households added an extra floor with each generation, while the *agwad* regulated the width of alleys to one donkey's-breadth in an effort to ensure some light and air within the labyrinth.

Siwan bachelors aged between 20 and 40 were obliged to sleep in caves outside town, guarding the fields – hence their nickname, *zaggalah* ("club-bearers"). Noted for their love of palm liquor, song and dance, they shocked outsiders with their open **homosexuality**. Homosexual marriages were forbidden by King Fouad in 1928, but continued in secret until the late 1940s. Today, Siwans emphatically assert that homosexuality no longer exists in the oasis – whatever may be said on ⓦwww.gayegypt.com – and palm liquor has now been superseded by *arak* made from dates.

Another feature of Shali was the tradition of violent **feuds** between the Westerners and Easterners, in which all able-bodied males were expected to participate. Originally ritualized, with parallel lines of combatants exchanging blows between sunrise and sunset while their womenfolk threw stones at cowards and shouted encouragement, feuds became far deadlier with the advent of firearms, occasioning gun battles "on the slightest grounds". (Even now, Siwans know which clan they're descended from, and the town council is sited midway between the two neighbourhoods.) Yet they immediately closed ranks against outsiders – Bedouin raiders, *khedival* taxmen or European explorers.

Egyptian and British control

Visitors of the eighteenth and nineteenth centuries regularly experienced Siwan **xenophobia**. "Whenever I quitted my apartment, it was to be assailed with stones and a torrent of abusive language", Browne wrote in 1762. Having poked around the antiquities in Muslim guise, Frederick Hornemann was pursued into the desert, where "the braying of three hundred donkeys announced the arrival of the Siwan army", and only escaped thanks to his assistant's recitation of Koranic verses. Frederic Cailliaud was permitted to visit the gardens and ruins in 1819, but the town remained barred to strangers until six hundred troops sent by Mohammed Ali compelled the oasis to recognize **Egyptian authority** in 1820.

Although the Siwans subsequently revolted against their governor and defaulted on taxes (payable in dates) half a dozen times over the next sixty years, the oasis began to change. With the desert tribes suppressed, and Shali rendered unsafe by heavy rains, the *agwad* permitted families to settle outside the walls. From the 1850s onwards the great reformist preacher Mohammed Ibn Ali al-Senussi cast a spell over the desert peoples from Jaghbub Oasis just over the border, and Siwa – the site of his first *zawiya* – supported **Senussi** resistance to the Italian conquest of Libya (1912–30), until it became clear that their Senussi "liberators" would not restore Siwan independence. Thus in 1917, British forces were "welcomed by the cheering Siwans, who declared their loyalty as they always did with every new victorious conqueror", as Fakhry put it.

Anglo-Egyptian control of Siwa was maintained by the Frontier Camel Corps and Light Car Patrols. Agricultural advisors, a school and an orthodox imam were introduced following King Fouad's visit to the oasis in 1928. When the British withdrew as the Italians advanced across North Africa in 1942, the Siwans accepted Axis **occupation** with equal resignation. Unlike Rommel, who made a favourable impression during his flying visit, King Farouk dismayed the Siwans by wearing shorts and asking if they "still practised a certain vice" when he visited the oasis in 1945.

Modern Siwa

Paradoxical as it sounds, Siwa's biggest problem is an excess of fresh water, which gushes from springs and drains into salt lakes, increasing their volume and salinity. Smelly, mosquito-infested ponds all over town attest that the **water table** lies only twenty centimetres underground (less in winter). The water supply is saline or sandy, so residents have to collect water from springs by donkey. Foreign engineers are installing a drainage system and a water-purification plant at Dakhrour, outside town, but it will be some years before they're finished.

While Egyptian military bases exist here on sufferance, Siwans have welcomed developments in health care, education and communications. The road to Matrouh (completed in 1984) has encouraged exports of dates and olives, and tourism to the oasis, and in the 1990s the **economy** was boosted by new factories producing olive oil, mineral water and carpets. More recently, some five hundred Siwan **women** have been stitching traditional embroidery for an Italian couture house, earning twice the average Siwan wage for an agricultural labourer: the unmarried ones have saved so much money that they can be choosy about taking a husband.

Meanwhile, the Siwans' desire for breeze-block houses or low-rise flats with proper bathrooms rather than the traditional dusty mud-brick dwellings has alarmed conservationists. Britain's Prince Charles is among the VIPs backing the **Friends of Siwa Association**, a conservationist body set up by **Mounir Nematalla** (see p.563). An ordinance prohibiting the building of new houses was issued, but after public protests the governor in Mersa Matrouh ruled that people could build providing the exteriors were faced with mud in the traditional oasis style. Conversely, many locals regard the Friends of Siwa as a scam to embezzle donations, and Nematalla as a speculator who has bulldozed dozens of houses in pursuit of building a hotel beside Shali and annexing it as a lucrative private theme-park.

Visiting Siwa

The **best time** to come is during spring or autumn, when the Siwans hold festivals and the days are pleasantly warm. In winter, windless days can be nice, but nights – and gales – are chilling. From May onwards, rising temperatures keep people indoors between 11am and 7pm, and the nights are sultry and mosquito-ridden. Even when the **climate** is mild you'll probably feel like taking a midday siesta or a swim.

Unless you sign up with a desert safari – which might reach Siwa via the Qattara Depression – there are only two possible **approaches**, one via road from Bahariya Oasis (see p.499), the other from Alexandria or Mersa Matrouh – the route favoured by most visitors. There are three **buses** daily from Sidi Gaber in Alexandria to Siwa (8.30am, 11am & 6pm; 9hr; £E27), which call briefly at Moharrem Bey and take on extra passengers at Mersa Matrouh, four to five hours later. Matrouh is the starting point for an additional bus (£E12) leaving at 7.30am. You may also be able to catch a service taxi or **minivan** from Matrouh to Siwa; the fare is £E12 per person, or £E150–200 to rent the whole vehicle.

The three-hundred-kilometre journey from Matrouh to Siwa takes four hours by car or bus, with the Siwa road turning off the highway 20km west of Matrouh, at a checkpoint. Soon after, mobile phones cease to function until you reach a **resthouse** known as **Bir Nous** (Halfway Well), selling tea, soup and soft drinks. Its toilets are the nearest you get to the horrors of this route before the road was built. Until the nineteenth century there was only a camel trail (eight days from Matrouh) across this flat desert, and the few landmarks might be obscured by dust clouds or sandstorms. The sharp limestone ridges and hollows beneath the powdery surface of this *shabak* (net) desert also made the route hazardous for early motorists, who followed the line of telegraph poles. Nowadays the monotonous vistas – interspersed with army camps – keep going until the last 40km, when rock outcrops presage the appearance of the oasis.

Etiquette

Siwa is well known for its conservatism in matters of **dress** and **behaviour**. The tourist office requests visitors to refrain from public displays of affection or drinking alcohol, and women to keep their arms and legs covered – especially when bathing in pools. Women should also avoid wandering alone in places with few people around. Local people are generally more reserved than the Egyptians, and invitations home are less common.

Siwi

Siwi is an unwritten Berber dialect that is the mother tongue of all native Siwans, who also use Arabic in public life, so if you can get by in that language, you needn't deal with Siwi – unless you want to. Here are a few useful phrases to get you started.

yes	*mashi*	Give me ...	*ooshi ...*
no	*oola*	donkey(s)	*yeizite (zitan)*
How are you?	*Tanta elhalenik?*	horse	*agmare*
What's your name?	*Bit in insmitinik?*	camel(s)	*alghum*
Where are you going?	*Imani tehab?*	dates	*tenii*
What do you want?	*Tanta ekhsitta'?*	olives	*azumour*
I want ...	*ehk sehk ...*	water	*aman*
What's this?	*Tanta wook?*		

Visitors should respect Siwan feelings on **photography** (as well as the official ban on taking pictures of military installations – including the airport and sandbagged dugouts in unexpected locations). As a rule, local women are taboo subjects, whereas Siwan males – particularly the younger ones – don't mind being snapped (but always ask them first).

Siwa Town

Most visitors rate **SIWA TOWN** and the pools, rocks and ruins around as the oasis's main attractions, and not many bother to visit the outlying villages. Siwa Town has grown as its population has risen to 25,000 (at least 1000 of them from outside the oasis, mostly from two villages near Minya), and people have moved into modern housing, forsaking traditional mud-brick dwellings – just as their ancestors had previously abandoned the fortified hilltop city of **Shali**, whose ruins overlook the modern town. A triumphal arch and broad roads debouch onto a central market area, but the town slips away into a maze of alleyways, and loses itself amid the encircling palms. Boys driving donkey carts transport fodder and decorously wrapped Siwan women, and the braying of donkeys resounds from every quarter of town. After dark, a thousand stars emerge and Siwa's isolation from the world beyond the Great Sand Sea becomes almost palpable.

Arrival and information

Siwa's **tourist office** (summer daily 9am–2.30pm & 7–10pm, Fri 11am–1pm; winter daily except Fri 9am–2.30pm & 5–8pm; ☎ & ℱ046/460-1338 or 010 546-1992, ℮mahdi_hweiti@yahoo.com) is in the north of the town, opposite the Mother and Child Clinic and close to the bus station. It's run by English-speaking Mahdi Hweiti, a native Siwan who knows everything about the oasis and can arrange trips to outlying villages. Should you have any trouble in Siwa, go to him rather than the police.

There's a **pharmacy** in the centre and a grungy public **hospital** on the outskirts. Women patients may do better to head to the Mother and Child Clinic near the tourist office, where a gynaecologist and a paediatrician work mornings on alternate weeks. The **police** (☎046/460-1008) are next door to the **Banque du Caire** (Mon–Thurs & Sun 8.30am–2pm & 5–8pm, Fri & Sat 8–11am & 5–8pm), which has an ATM and can cash traveller's cheques. There are several **Internet cafés**, including a subsidized one for local youth (open to tourists; £E2/hr), in the lane behind the police station.

Accommodation

Siwa has both low-budget and upmarket **hotels**, including two lakeside ecolodges 13–16km from town. While it's worth reserving ahead if you're fussy about where you stay, the only time it's essential to do so is during Siwan festivals, when tour groups block-book hotels. On the whole, though, it's safe to assume that you'll find a bed. People wanting their own space can rent furnished **apartments** in the Engineers' Flats (from £E500 a month) or bungalows near the Hill of the Dead (£E100 a night) through Mahdi at the tourist office. Unless stated otherwise, **breakfast** is not included at hotels. Places out of town are marked on the map of Siwa Oasis on p.561.

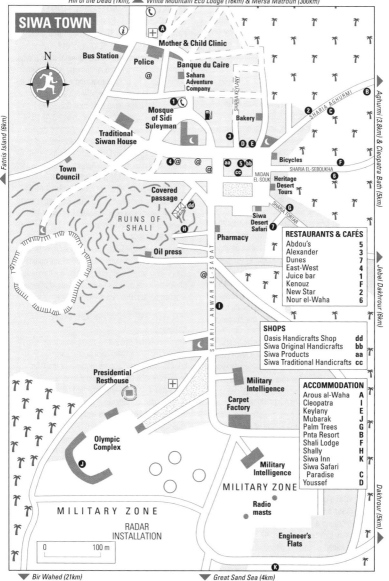

Hill of the Dead (1km), ▲ White Mountain Eco Lodge (16km) & Mersa Matrouh (300km)

SIWA TOWN

(i)

N

Bus Station

Police

@

Mother & Child Clinic

Banque du Caire

Sahara
Adventure
Company

Mosque
of Sidi
Suleyman

Bakery

Traditional
Siwan House

Town
Council

Bicycles

SHARIA EL-SEBOUKHA

MIDAN
EL-SOUK

Heritage
Desert
Tours

Covered
passage

RUINS OF
SHALI

Siwa
Desert
Safari

Pharmacy

Oil press

◄ Fatnis Island (6km)

Aghurmi (3.8km) & Cleopatra Bath (5km) ►

Jebel Dakhrour (6km) ►

Presidential
Resthouse

Military
Intelligence

Carpet
Factory

Olympic
Complex

Military
Intelligence

MILITARY ZONE

Radio
masts

MILITARY ZONE

RADAR
INSTALLATION

0   100 m

Engineer's
Flats

▼ Bir Wahed (21km)

▼ Great Sand Sea (4km)

◄ Dakhrour (5km) ►

RESTAURANTS & CAFÉS

Abdou's	5
Alexander	3
Dunes	7
East-West	4
Juice bar	1
Kenouz	F
New Star	2
Nour el-Waha	6

SHOPS

Oasis Handicrafts Shop	dd
Siwa Original Handicrafts	bb
Siwa Products	aa
Siwa Traditional Handicrafts	cc

ACCOMMODATION

Arous al-Waha	A
Cleopatra	I
Keylany	E
Mubarak	J
Palm Trees	G
Pnta Resort	B
Shali Lodge	F
Shally	H
Siwa Inn	K
Siwa Safari Paradise	C
Youssef	D

Siwa Town

Arous al-Waha Opposite the tourist office
☎046/460-0028. A state-owned hotel whose
name means "Bride of the Oasis", this has worn
but clean semi-carpeted rooms with fans, shower-
cabins and fridges. ❷

Cleopatra Sharia Anwar el-Sadat ☎ & ℱ046/460-
0421 or ☎010 334-0784, ⓦwww.cleopatra-siwa
.net. Clean, simple rooms, some with toilet, balcony
and fan; those in the quieter "chalet" block have all
three, but are plagued by mosquitoes. There's also
an a/c suite with TV and fridge (£E130). ❶

Keylany Midan el-Souk ☏ 046/460-1052 or 012 105-7977. Carpeted en-suite rooms with fan and balcony, a rooftop café and friendly management – the only drawback is the noise from the bazaar and nearby building sites. Reservations advised. ❷

Mubarak In the Olympic complex ☏ 046/460-0883, ☏ 460-0884. Antiseptic rooms with satellite TV, a/c and fridge; chalets (£E400) with large lounges and VIP suites (£E750) with multiple bedrooms and bathrooms. A Jacuzzi and sauna are available for guests. Rate includes breakfast. ❺

Palm Trees Off Midan el-Souk ☏ 046/460-1703 or 010 464-6529, ☏ 460-0006, ✉ ahmedsiwa88 @hotmail.com. Popular for its palm garden and quiet, central location, it has basic rooms with fans (a private bathroom costs £E10 extra) and an erratic water supply. ❶

Pnta Resort Sharia Aghurmi ☏ 010 254-8420. Four en-suite chalets in a palm grove with a spring-fed pool, outside town but only a 5min walk from the centre. Breakfast included. ❺

Shali Lodge Sharia el-Seboukha ☏ 046/460-1299, ☏ 460-1799, ✉ info@eqi.com.eg. A bijou hotel built of *kharsif* and palm-logs in the traditional oasis style, with palm trees growing out its rooftop restaurant: it was the prototype for the *Ecolodge* at Birket Siwa. ❺

Shally Off Sharia Anwar el-Sadat ☏ 046/460-1203. Small, tidy place; all the rooms have fans (£E20), and some baths, and balconies overlooking Shali – the view from the roof is superb. ❶

Siwa Inn Beyond the radio masts ☏ & ☏ 046/460-1287 or ☏ 010 617-6946, ✉ siwainn2000@yahoo.com. A rustic-style place 25 minutes' walk from the centre of town, whose ten slightly musty rooms with fans and baths over-look a garden with a cold pool. There's satellite TV and a restaurant. Breakfast included. ❸

Siwa Safari Paradise Sharia Aghurmi ☏ 046/460-1590, ☏ 460-1592, ⓦ www.siwaparadise.com. A tourist village of a/c rooms with fridges and satel-lite TV ($55), and bungalows with fan, heater and TV ($50) around a large cold spring pool for swim-ming. Rates include half board. ❺

Youssef Midan el-Souk ☏ 046/460-0678. Siwa's cheapest hotel has small, clean rooms with fans (£E16), some with balconies and/or bathrooms (£E8 extra), and a rooftop with a great view of town. ❶

East of town: Aghurmi and Jebel Dakhrour

Fata Morgana Jebel Dakhrour, 4km from Siwa Town ☏ & ☏ 046/460-0237 or ☏ 012 417-5188, ⓦ www.fatamorgana21.ch. Traditional-style rooms (some with fans and mosquito nets) with views of the Sand Sea or Dakhrour, and a garden with a small pool, in a remote, windswept setting. ❺

Qasr el-Zeytuna Jebel Dakhrour, 3.5km from town ☏ & ☏ 046/460-0037 or ☏ 012 372-2694. Spacious en-suite rooms, backing onto a garden and palm grove with goats and chickens, and a view of the Great Sand Sea. Breakfast included. ❺

Reem el-Waha 1km from Aghurmi, 3km from town ☏ 046/460-0071 or 010 268-9316, ☏ 046/493-3608. Pleasant rooms with TV, fridge and balcony, overlooking a bleak yard with a small circular swimming pool. Breakfast included. ❸

Siwa Shali Resort Jebel Dakhrour, 5km from town ☏ 046/921-0064 or 012 213-1983, ☏ 921-0103, ⓦ www.siwashaliresort.com. Yet more remote, this classy *kharsif*-style complex of a/c rooms boasts a 200m-long serpentine pool, another like the oasis's Cleopatra Bath, a Turkish bath, billiards, a piano and a desert library. Half board included. ❼

West of town: Birket Siwa

Adrar al-Milal Ecolodge 16km from town ☏ 010 166-2729, ✉ info@eqi.com.eg. An amazing mud-brick complex with superb views over the lake, lovely rooms, a big pool and palm garden. Guests pay $200 a day to enjoy unlimited meals prepared from organic ingredients, a 24hr bar and horse-riding. See p.563 for more about the *Ecolodge*. ❾

Taghaghien Touristic Island (aka *Safety Land*) 13km from town ☏ 046/921-0060 or 012 215-5596, ⓦ www.taghaghien-island.com. Reached by a causeway, this island campground has cosy en-suite huts, a circular pool, fab views at sunset, and alcohol. On the downside, its palm trees are dying and no transport is provided. Breakfast included. ❻

Taziry 15km from town ☏ 010 644-5881 or 010 112-2519, ⓦ www.taziry.com. Around the lake from the *Ecolodge*, this hotel (whose name means "Moon" in Siwi) is similar in style to its near neighbour, though on a smaller scale and with less greenery around its lakeside pool. Breakfast is included; other meals to order. Free transfers on arrival and departure. ❻

The Town

The **ruins of Shali**, looming above the centre and floodlit in the evening, are a constant invitation to explore. Until the 1890s, this hermetic labyrinth attained a height of over 60m, with many levels of chambers, passages and granaries. Its

Siwan festivals and weddings

Siwan festivals represent the most public side of a largely private culture, so it's worth making an effort to attend one. Since many Egyptians enjoy going to them, it's wise to reserve a room well in advance and get there several days early, as buses to the oasis fill up nearer the time.

The largest, most famous is **Siayha**, when 10,000 Siwans assemble at Jebel Dakhrour for three days of feasting, dancing and relaxation. A sheikh from Sidi Barrani on the Mediterranean coast comes in to bless the feast, and local children enjoy a school holiday and a truckload of ice cream, sweets and sugar cane. Many non-Siwans and foreigners come too, and are made welcome – though women shouldn't intrude on the *zikrs*. Siayha occurs during the period of the full moon in October, unless this coincides with Ramadan, in which case it's postponed until November.

Two other festivals are celebrated by Muslims everywhere: the **Lesser Bairam**, at the end of Ramadan; and the **Corban Bairam** (Great Feast), which starts earlier in Siwa than elsewhere in Egypt. The gathering of fuel and salt over the preceding nine days is reckoned to be as much a part of the event as the mass slaughter of sheep after festival prayers on the tenth day of Zoul Hagga. The sheep's hide is stewed together with its offal in an earthenware pot; its head and stomach are eaten the next day, when cuts of meat are distributed among relatives (new brides especially); and finally, any leftovers are preserved.

Ashura, on the tenth of Moharram, was once Siwa's principal feast, and fervently Shiite; the Fatimid Shia reached Egypt via the North African oases. Nowadays it's chiefly an event for children, who decorate their homes with palm stalks soaked in olive oil, and burn them at sunset, singing while the town is illuminated by torchlight. Afterwards the children go from house to house exchanging presents.

Sometimes on Thursday evenings, a handful of Siwans perform *zikrs* at the **tomb of Sidi Suleyman** beside the mosque that bears his name. Tourists may attend if they dress and behave appropriately; women must cover their hair. Siwans still tell tales about this local saint, whose miraculous powers were manifest even before he was born, for when his pregnant mother craved fish, a pigeon dropped a fully cooked one at her feet. He is also said to have once conjured up a sandstorm to bury an army of Tebu raiders.

Weddings

Although you might be invited to join the tea-drinking crowd outside the bridegroom's family house, foreigners rarely witness the intricate ritual of **Siwan weddings**, which used to last a week but now take two or three days. After reciprocal visits of kinsfolk, and a ritual bath that symbolizes the bride's abandonment of maidenhood, the bride is "kidnapped" by her spouse's family, returned, and then delivered wrapped in a sheet. The traditional wedding dress of embroidered shawls and skirts is as flamboyant as the outdoor garb of married women is drab. Although urban Egyptian styles were popular in the 1990s, traditional garb has made a comeback among brides, as has dancing, singing and drinking homemade wine and spirits at wedding banquets in the villages.

Traditionally, a Siwan widow commanded the same *mahr* (dowry) as a virgin since both were "daughters of the forty ancestors", but could only remarry after one year of bereavement. The Siwans regarded newly bereaved widows as "devourers of the soul" (*ghulah*), and forced them to spend forty days in solitary confinement before they were "cleansed" – a taboo now largely lapsed.

surreal remains cover the entire saddle of rock below a **mosque**, which is said to have been the last one in Egypt where the muezzin still shouted out the call to prayer without the benefit of a loudspeaker. Down behind the hill around the back of Shali is a donkey-driven **oil-press**, only used in December and January,

△ The entrance to the ruins of Shali

that dates back centuries. From vantage points in Shali, you can see the whole modern town, its palm groves, the salt lakes and table-top rocks beyond, and providing you don't peer too obviously into the houses below, it's possible to glimpse the Siwans at home. Downstairs, women busy themselves with cooking and childcare; a few mats and painted chests, used for storing the family valuables, constitute the only furniture.

You can get a closer look at home life at the sanitized **Traditional Siwan House** (Mon–Thurs & Sun 10am–noon; £E1.50); enquire at the town council if the custodian isn't there. Set up with funds raised by the wife of the Canadian ambassador, who feared that few such mud-brick dwellings would survive another deluge and the trend towards breeze-block housing, it serves as a museum of traditional dress, jewellery and toys, resembling a handicrafts shop. There are numerous handicrafts shops in the vicinity of the **market** on Midan el-Souk, which is busiest on Fridays, when villagers come in to buy and sell. The other focus of life is the **Mosque of Sidi Suleyman**, built by King Fouad next to the whitewashed **tomb** of Siwa's patron sheikh (see box on p.557).

By following the Mersa Matrouh road out of town and then bearing right, you'll reach the unmistakable Jebel al-Mawta, or **Hill of the Dead** (daily 9am–sunset; £E20), also known as the Ridge of the Mummified. Among scores of XXVI Dynasty and Ptolemaic tombs reused by the Romans, who cut loculi for their own burials, four locked ones still retain murals or inscriptions. The custodian might let you climb the hill to enjoy the view without paying, but you need a ticket to enter the tombs. In the **Tomb of Si-Amun**, murals depict with great artistry a bearded, Greek-looking merchant and his family worshipping Egyptian deities; unfortunately, they were vandalized by Allied soldiers after the tomb's discovery in 1940, when the Siwans dug into the necropolis to escape air raids and also found the **Tomb of Mesu-Isis**. Another third-century BC creation, this was used for two burials, although the decorators never got far beyond the entrance. Whereas Si-Amun's tomb bespeaks of Cyrenaic influence, the **Tomb of the Crocodile** reflects Siwa's longstanding ties to the Fayoum, where the crocodile cult flourished – with a dash of Hellenistic style in the painting of gazelles nibbling at a tree. The battered XXVI Dynasty **Tomb of Niperpathot** has a ruined court, side rooms, and a tiny burial chamber covered with red inscriptions, including praise of Niperpathot as "the straightforward one". The curator can unlock some other, unpainted tombs to show you **mummies** found at the Hill of the Dead, and a once-mummified skull, complete with hair.

Lastly, there's Siwa's incongruously pink and empty **Olympic complex**, built within an army base to the south of town. With seating for 20,000, it could accommodate most of the population of the oasis, but is currently only utilized by a few army officers, as it awaits its place in Egypt's bid to host the Olympic Games some time in the future. The complex incorporates the *Mubarak Hotel* and a resthouse for the Minister of Defence; on an outcrop stands a **Presidential resthouse** originally built for King Fouad. Both can be seen on the road out towards Bir Wahed.

Crafts

Traditional **crafts** still flourish in the oasis, particularly pottery, basketmaking, and embroidery, with almost all the handicrafts made by women. They produce traditional items such as black **robes** with orange or red piping, and embroidered **wedding dresses** embellished with antique coins, shells or beads, as well as cutting down old textiles into bags, tunics and waistcoats for the tourist market. Women also weave **carpets** and all kinds of **baskets** made from palm-fronds. The largest is the *tghara*, used for storing bread; smaller kinds include the red and green tasselled *nedibash* or platters like the *tarkamt*, traditionally used for serving sweets. They also mould **pottery** and fire it at home in bread-ovens: robust cooking and storage pots, delicate oil lamps, and a kind of baptismal crucible called the *shamadan en sebaa*. Popular buys include the *adjra*, used for washing hands, and *timjamait*, or incense burners; all of these are stocked at the Oasis Handicrafts Shop and Siwa Traditional Handicrafts.

Unlike the gold-loving Egyptians, Siwans have traditionally preferred **silver jewellery**, which served as bullion assets for a people mistrustful of banks and paper money. The designs are uniquely Siwan, influenced by Berber rather than Egyptian heritage. Local silversmiths once produced most of it, but in modern times it has largely come from Khan el-Khalili. Today, almost all the antique silver has ended up abroad and locals now prefer to buy gold jewellery from Alexandria, but Siwa Original Handicrafts, next to *Abdou's*, retains a few pieces (which you can't buy), and is one of several places selling modern replicas of traditional designs. Broad silver bracelets and oval rings wrought with geometric designs are the most popular items with visitors, while *Al-Salhat*, with its six pendants hung from silver and coral beads, is the easiest type of necklace to identify. You'll also recognize the *tiyalaqan*, a mass of chains tipped with bells, suspended from huge crescents; and an ornament for the head, consisting of silver hoops and bells suspended from matching chunks of bullion, called a *qasas*. Finally, there's the *aghraw*, a silver collar from which girls used to hang a decorative disc or *adrim*, that was removed on their wedding day – a custom that's no longer practised.

Eating and drinking

As the oases go, Siwa is good for eating, with several nice **restaurants** in the palm groves. *Kenouz*, on the rooftop of the *Shali Lodge*, has the fanciest menu, with spicy and sweet-and-sour dishes (£E10–30) as well as Egyptian staples, pizzas, a menu-of-the-day (£E40–50), and stuffed goat, lamb or turkey by special order. Alfresco alternatives where you can enjoy a full meal for £E25–40 include the Nour el-Waha, *New Star* and *Dunes*, whose chicken biryani is recommended.

At all of these places you can recline on cushions and smoke a *sheesha*; *Nour el-Waha* also has backgammon and dominoes. If you don't mind doing without a garden, *Abdou's* on Midan el-Souk is the place for soup, omelettes, *shish tawook* (chicken marinated in yogurt and spices) and people-watching. The *East-West* (named after the rival clans of Shali) is good for breakfast, while *Alexander* is the most peaceful of the cafés off the bazaar. Providing there are customers, all are open till around midnight. **Alcohol** is only available at the *Taghaghien Touristic Camp* (which charges non-residents £E10 entry and sells lukewarm Sakkara beer and Egyptian wine), or to residents of the *Ecolodge* (who can consume unlimited imported liquor). For fresh fruit juice, try the stand-up place near the Mosque of Sidi Suleyman.

The shops on Midan el-Souk are well supplied with canned goods, sweets, juices and bottled water, with fresh bread available at the bakery, while the **market** stocks seasonal vegetables, dates and olives galore, which you can sample before buying. Look out also for the sweets made from dates stuffed with chocolate or almonds, at Siwa Products.

Moving on from Siwa

Buses leave from a depot near the tourist office, where you should buy tickets the night before to be sure of getting a seat on the morning services. (Beware of being shortchanged.) Daily buses to **Alexandria** (9hr; £E27) depart at 7am, 10am and 5pm, stopping en route at **Mersa Matrouh** (4–5hr; £E12), where a fourth bus, leaving Siwa at 1pm, terminates. Additionally, there is usually a **minivan** to Matrouh (£E12) in the afternoon, leaving from the Sidi Suleyman mosque, or you can hire one to take you to Alex for £E500.

The journey to **Bahariya Oasis** (420km) currently takes seven or eight hours; once the entire road has been upgraded it should take five or six hours, depending on how much sand has blown across the tarmac – having to dig cars out of drifts isn't uncommon, and traffic is so rare that a breakdown can leave you stranded for ages. A **permit** is required to use the road (see p.561).

Tourists hoping to split the cost of a **ride** to Bahariya can advertise for fellow travellers at the tourist office. A pick-up truck is cheapest (£E800) but can only carry two passengers in comfort – ask at the the tourist office or the *Keylany Hotel* if you're interested. To travel by Jeep costs at least £E1200; to camp en route or travel straight on **to the White Desert** in Farafra Oasis, £E1500–1800. Those planning to **drive** themselves will need a 4WD with ample fuel and water, and must register the licence number when getting a permit. The turn-off for Bahariya is 6km north of town on the right-hand side of the Mersa Matrouh road. With your own 4WD you can visit four uninhabited **oases** along the way (covered on p.566).

Around Siwa Oasis

Although the **Siwa Oasis** depression is some 82km long and up to 28km wide, cultivated areas amount to less than 2000 acres and the total population is only 25,000; in some areas both population and cultivation have diminished since salination turned ancient gardens into barren *kharsif*. Nearer town, dense **palm groves** and wiry olive trees are carefully tended in mud- and palm-leaf-walled gardens: dates and olives are the chief crops. Siwa has as many as 80,000 olive trees and over 310,000 palm trees, of which around 23,000 are male palms, valued only for the white heart at the top of the tree, a local delicacy.

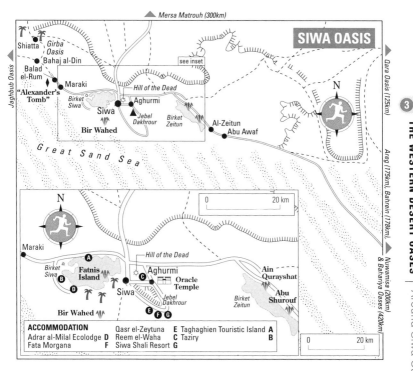

Palms form the backdrop to most places that you're likely to go, especially the **pools** or **baths**, which for many visitors are the highlight of the oasis. The nearer sites can be reached by bicycle, donkey *caretta* or on foot; just time your visit to avoid travelling in the hottest part of day. **Bicycles** can be rented from most hotels and handicraft shops for £E10–15 a day, but make sure you check the bike first before embarking on a long ride.

Though most of the oasis is freely accessible you need a **permit** from Military Intelligence to visit Bir Wahed, Shiatta or Qara Oasis, or use the road to Baharia. In each case there's a fee of $5 (payable in dollars only; check the latest price with the tourist office, as some safari firms overcharge) for the permit plus £E11 per individual. Your safari operator or the tourist office can arrange it a day before (Fri & Sat excepted), given a photocopy of your passport.

Shop around for **excursions**; the tourist office may be able to arrange trips to certain places more cheaply than **safari operators** based at hotels, shops or restaurants. Among those worth asking for a quote are Ramadan Abdel Aziz at the *Keylany* hotel, Ahmed at the *Palm Trees* hotel; Fathy Abdallah (☎010 656-6518) at *Abdou's* or Aloush (☎010 543-5455) at the *Nour el-Waha* restaurant. The Safari Adventure Company near the bank has a wide range of **equipment** for rent, from sleeping bags to dune-surfing boards.

Aghurmi and Jebel Dakhrour

This excursion is too far to walk in the heat, so it's best to hire a donkey *caretta* with a guide to ensure that you won't go astray on umarked roads and tracks.

Agree on a price beforehand; a two-hour circuit of the Oracle Temple, the Tamusi Bath and Jebel Dakhrour should cost £E25 for up to three people.

The road to Aghurmi begins at Siwa's main square and runs through the palm groves for 4km (a nice hour's walk if you're not going much further). Keep going straight on past the crossroads, and the modern village of **AGHURMI** appears shortly before the hill where the ancient Siwans built their first **fortified settlement** (daily 9am–sunset; £E20). Raised 12m above the plain and entered by a single gateway, Aghurmi had its own deep well (to the left, inside), making it impervious to sieges. The ruins are signposted as the "Alexander Crowning Hall", for it was here that the **Siwan Oracle** reposed in antiquity. Though some German architects have been criticized for crudely restoring the **temple** with concrete, it's no longer in danger of collapse and you can go inside. There's a fabulous view, encompassing two salt lakes, Dakhrour and Siwa Town in the distance, and a great mass of palms.

Fakhry dates the temple to the reign of Amasis the Drunkard (570–526 BC) but reckons it evolved from a seventh- or eighth-century BC site dedicated to Amun-Re, which others have attributed to the ram-headed Libyan god Ammon. Its history is subsequently much documented: a Persian army sent to destroy it was obliterated by the desert; emissaries sent by Cimon of Athens were told of his death as it happened; Eubotas of Cyrenaica, assured of success by the oracle, took his own victory statue to the 93rd Olympiad; and Lysander tried bribery to win the oracle's endorsement of his claim to the Spartan throne.

But the most famous petitioner was **Alexander the Great**. Having liberated Egypt from its hated Persian rulers and ordered the creation of a city on the Mediterranean, Alexander hurried to Siwa in the spring of 331 BC. It's thought that he sought confirmation that he was the son of Zeus (whom the Greeks identified with Amun), but the oracle's reply – whispered by a priest through an aperture in the wall of the sanctuary – is unrecorded, and Alexander kept it secret unto his death in Asia eight years later. Despite his personal wish to be buried near the oracle, he was probably interred in Alexandria, the capital he never saw – though two Greeks once claimed to have found his tomb in Siwa (see p.564).

From the ruins of Aghurmi you can gaze across thickets of palms to a cream-coloured pillar – part of a **ruined Temple of Amun** viewed side-on. It was probably founded by Nectanebo II (360–343 BC), who also rebuilt the Temple of Hibis at Kharga Oasis. To get there, continue along the road and take the signed turn to "Umm Ubayda", as it's known locally. A painted bas-reliefed wall and giant blocks of rubble are all that remain of this once-substantial XXX Dynasty creation after it was dynamited by a treasure-hunting governor in 1897.

Follow the path on to reach Ain Juba, known to tourists as the **Cleopatra Bath**, a deep circular pool of gently bubbling spring water, where local men bathe. Being fully visible to anyone passing along the trail, it's not a place where women can comfortably swim, and many prefer the **Tamusi Bath**, secluded 150m back along the path. *Ali's Garden* here serves tea and *sheeshas*, and by arrangement can offer special meals or host parties.

Heading on from the Cleopatra Bath, bear left at the fork and take the first path on the right. A ten-minute walk through clover fields and groves of palms will bring you out in the desert near **Jebel Dakhrour**. This rugged massif is the site for the Siyaha **festival** and affords stunning **views** from its summit. In contrast to the verdant oasis and the silvery salt lake, the southern horizon presents a desolate vista of crescent dunes and blackened mesas: the edge of the Great Sand Sea. The **hot sand** at Dakhrour is supposed to be good for rheumatic conditions and spinal problems, so sufferers come here to be buried up to their necks over three to five days during the summer months. The loop road encircling Dakhrour leads back to Siwa Town via a military zone.

Bir Wahed

One of the best excursions on offer is into the outer dunes of the Great Sand Sea, to **Bir Wahed**, 12km southwest of town. It's a magical spot, a **hot pool** the size of a large Jacuzzi, into which sulphurous water gushes; the run-off irrigates a garden around the pool. To soak up to your chest, puffing a *sheesha*, while the sun sets over the dunes and mesas all around, is a fantastic experience. You can climb outcrops or hunt for fossils in the vicinity, and on the way there or back you can plunge into a deep, jade-green **cold pool**, or sand-surf or roll down the sides of huge knife-edged dunes. The only downside is that mosquitoes are awful from dusk till dawn.

Most tourists visit Bir Wahed on a 4WD **excursion** organized by local safari operators. Expect to pay £E80–90 per person for a daytime visit, £E120–150 for an overnight stay, including supper and breakfast, blankets and tents – but not the obligatory **permit**, which costs extra (see p.561).

Alternatively, you could **walk**, provided it's not too hot and you carry at least four litres of water. It takes four hours, following the road out past the Olympic complex, fields and palm groves, and then Jeep tracks into the dunes. Don't attempt this if a sandstorm has occurred in the last few days, or is forecast. You can sleep in a tent (£E10) and buy water, *fuul* and feta cheese at Bir Wahed, but anyone considering staying more than one night should bring supplies from town. If you're walking, it's unlikely anyone will check your permit.

Fatnis Island and Birket Siwa

Another popular destination is "Fantasy" or **Fatnis Island**, on the salt lake of Birket Siwa, 6km west of town. An easy bike ride, it can also be reached by *caretta* (£E20–25) or on foot (1hr). Take the road out past the town council, then the left-hand road at the first fork. En route you'll pass the Abu Alif Bath, where farmhands wash; beyond the palm groves, follow a causeway across salt-encrusted pans onto Fatnis, where palms surround a large circular tiled **pool**, fed by fresh water welling up from clefts in the rock 15m below. There's a stall selling tea and *sheeshas*.

Actually, Fatnis is no longer an island; the **Birket Siwa** has receded and a barrage now divides it into a drainage reservoir and an intensely saline remnant, forming a thick crust that blackens the surrounding vegetation. Despite its faintly acrid smell the lake looks beautiful, with sculpted table-tops on the western horizon. The largest was bestowed the name **Jebel Beida** (White Mountain) by British cartographers; the Siwans call it Adrar al-Milal in their own language, while Egyptians know it as Sidi Jaffar.

On the far side of this is the extraordinary **Adrar al-Milal Ecolodge**, a vast, fantasy *qasr*-style hotel entirely built of *kharsif*, palm logs and translucent salt slabs (used instead of glass). The brainchild of Cairene environmental engineer Mounir Nematalla, the ecolodge uses local materials wherever possible – including olive wood and palm fibres for the furniture – and is designed to save energy and water, and recycle waste products on its organic farm. Since it often has no guests at all, they don't mind the occasional visitor looking around, providing you get written permission from the *Shali Lodge* in town first. On the far shore of the lake is the similar but smaller *Taziry* hotel. Both are reached by spur roads off the lakeside route to Maraki, which turns off the Mersa Matrouh highway 1km north of town. It's rather far to cycle (16km) so you'll need to take a car (£E30–40 return), or you could include it as a stopover on excursions to Balad el-Rum (see below).

Maraki and Shiatta

MARAKI is the collective name for several **villages** at the western end of the depression, separated from the main oasis by a rocky desert riddled with caves and tombs. The area was populous and intensively cultivated from Roman times until the fifteenth century, but is now mostly used for grazing by the **Bedouin** Al-Shihaybat tribe. Most buildings are quite new as the old settlements were destroyed by the deluge of 1982, which forced residents to shelter in caves at Balad el-Rum ("Town of the Romans"). In 1991, Maraki made news when Liana and Manos Souvaltzi announced their discovery of the "**Tomb of Alexander the Great**" beneath a ruined **Doric temple** near **Balad el-Rum**. Having endorsed their claim, the SCA backed off after the Greeks failed to refute criticism that they'd misread vital inscriptions. SCA boss Dr Hawass halted excavations, decreed that the Souvaltzis would never work in Egypt again, and moved all the stones to a depository – so there's nothing to see any more.

To travel beyond the checkpoint at Bahaj al-Din requires a **permit** (see p.561). Here a track runs off to **Girba Oasis**, occupied by the Bedouin settlement of **SHIATTA** and a detachment of Border Guards. For decades, this was a halt on the Masrab el-Ikhwan ("Road of the Brotherhood") from Jaghbub Oasis in Libya, whereby Senussi preachers reached the Western Desert oases. (*Masrab* is the Siwan word for a camel route, called a *darb* in other oases.) Today the border is crossed by **smugglers** of hashish, electrical goods and videos – hence the Border Guards. Shiatta's salt **spring** is thought to be the remnant of a lake that once spread towards Aghurmi. Seven metres underwater lies an **ancient boat** resembling the solar boats of the pharaohs; its discoverer, Dr Ashraf Sabri, speculates that it once sailed across the lake to the Oracle Temple. You can arrange to **dive** here through the *Keylany Hotel*, or Alexandra Dive in Alexandria (see p.603), but note that divers must be heavily weighted to counteract the buoyancy of the saline water.

Beyond Shiatta is **off-limits** to outsiders, but should access ever be permitted, there's an **underground river** waiting to be explored by divers. Further west are **minefields** along the Libyan border, sown by the British and Italians soon after they defined it in 1938 and by the Egyptians and Libyans since the 1970s. A corridor was cleared of mines to allow the passage of the 2003 Paris–Dakar Rally, but nonetheless an Italian team was injured by a landmine.

A full day's **excursion** to Maraki, Balad el-Rum and Shiatta can be arranged by the tourist office (£E120–160) or hotels such as the *Keylany* and *Palm Trees* (£E300).

Around Birket Zeitun

The largest salt lake in the oasis, **Birket Zeitun** is visible from Aghurmi and Jebel Dakhrour. Acres of mud the texture of dried cornflakes attest to the lake's slow recession. Only the far shore is inhabited, with villages that flourished in Roman times before centuries of slow decline set in, and US-aid-built houses that nobody has ever lived in. The lake's increasing salinity is both the cause and result of depopulation: as fewer irrigation works are maintained, more of the warm water from the **Ain Qurayshat** spring flows unused into the lake, crystallizing mineral salts as it evaporates. The source is enclosed by an industrial-sized concrete tank where you can bathe, though beware of the underwater ledges.

Better bathing, however, can be found around 35km southeast of Siwa Town at **ABU SHUROUF**, where there's a large, kidney-shaped pool of cool, clear, azure water with bug-eyed fishes swimming about, opposite the Hayat mineral water bottling plant. The village beyond the pool is remarkable for harbouring all the female **donkeys** in the oasis, which are kept and mated here. In Siwan parlance, "Have you been to Abu Shurouf?" is a euphemism for "Have you had sex?"

Further south along the lake, the village of **AL-ZEITUN** was once a model Senussi community tending the richest gardens in the oasis, until it was abandoned following an Italian bombing raid in 1940. Near the eastern end of the ruins is a small smoke-blackened kiosk-**temple** where the locals once sheltered from bombs, and which nowadays harbours bats. Two kilometres further on, the hillside is riddled with the eerie **Roman tombs** of **Abu Awaf**, overlooking the last **checkpoint** in the oasis before the *Darb Siwa* to Bahariya Oasis enters the deep desert (see p.566).

A half-day **tour** of these sites for three or four people can be arranged through the tourist office (£E40 per person) or safari operators such as *Shali Lodge* (£E200) and the *Keylany Hotel* (£E300), which charge by the car-load. Lunch is normally included.

Qara Oasis and the Qattara Depression

If you have the means and are seriously into desert travel, **Qara Oasis** has a compelling fascination. The smallest and poorest of the oases, populated by the descendants of runaway slaves, it has been described as "Siwa yesterday". Visitors are so rare that the villagers turn out to welcome them and serve a meal in their honour. Until flooding rendered it unsafe in 1982, the Qarawis occupied a Shali-like labyrinth atop "a solitary white mushroom of rock", edged by a "high smooth wall, impregnable to raiders, with one black tunnel for a street". Now, most families live in new houses on the plain. Legend states that Qarawi ancestors were once cursed by the Devil that their population would never exceed 317 – modern-day Qarawis deny this, pointing out that it is already well in excess of that figure.

The shortest **route** from Siwa to Qara is the Masrab Khidda (125km), but it's rough terrain and featureless mud flats make it essential to have someone who knows the way. Alternatively, you can head north towards Mersa Matrouh and turn off at the checkpoint just before the Bir Nous resthouse, onto a dirt road to Qara. Though it's not a regular **safari** destination, Ramadan at the *Keylany Hotel* can take you there and back by pick-up (£E350) or minibus (£E400). You'll need a **permit** (see p.561).

Northeast of Qara the land plummets into the **Qattara Depression**, which is seven times the size of all the Western Desert oases combined and may be the largest depression in the world. At 60–134m below sea level, it is one of the lowest places on earth, and the lowest point in Africa. Ever since Dr Ball first proposed it in the 1920s, Egyptian planners have dreamed of piping water 38km from the Mediterranean to the depression, utilizing the fall in height to generate hydroelectricity and run desalination plants and irrigation systems. But all attempts have foundered through lack of capital, and nothing seems likely to happen in the future. There is, however, exploration for **oil** at many points in the desert between Qattara and Mersa Matrouh, which explains the upgraded tracks that crisscross the wilderness. With a permit, even 2WDs can use the **El-Alamein–Bahariya desert road** (273km) that dips into the depression at **Naqb Abu Dweis** (mined on both sides of the wadi; don't leave the road), and carries on past a series of checkpoints and turn-offs to drilling facilities, before joining the Cairo–Bahariya highway. While crossing the depression, it passes the uninhabited **Maghra Oasis**, where Jurassic **fossils** of mastodons, reptiles, fish and mammals have been found; petrified wood lies around, and there's a salt lake.

Siwa to Bahariya

The ancient Darb Siwa caravan route to Bahariya Oasis has been upgraded to a **road** for some 200km from Siwa, with the rest due to be finished by 2008. Six **checkpoints** en route provide assurance that vehicles which break down will be missed, but otherwise there are no sources of water, nor any fuel for 420km – and mobile phones are beyond signal range. All travellers require a permit from Military Intelligence (see p.561).

If you are hiring someone to drive you from Siwa (see p.560), bear in mind that the quoted rate is for a nonstop journey, passing by a series of uninhabited oases off the road. Their beauty can only be appreciated by taking a longer 4WD excursion and camping **overnight** in one of the oases. Siwa Safari Paradise charges £E1200–1400 to travel via Qara and Areg, while other outfits quote around £E1500 for an overnight trip (meals included).

Areg Oasis lies 1km off the road, about 175km from Siwa, girdled by an escarpment which 4WDs should only descend with caution and in pairs, though it's easy to scramble down on foot, providing you avoid the brittle overhangs of the cliffs that ring the depression. The eroded floor resembles shredded cloth, surrounded by striated buff and white chalk buttes looking like giant brioches that have sat in the oven too long. The oasis was regarded as a haunt of bandits by nineteenth-century travellers, and its cliffs are riddled with **tombs**. A tablet from Alexandria records that the population of Siwa, Bahrein and other now-deserted oases numbered 400,000 in Persian times.

Bahrein Oasis lurks off the other side of the road, down a track from the third checkpoint. Just as you're wondering why you bothered to cross this dull stretch of desert, the oasis appears in all its glory. Named after its two azure salt lakes, Bahrein is awash with custard-coloured sand, hemmed in by giant croissant-like buttes. They're riddled with **tombs** where you can still find bones; their *loculi* date them from Greco-Roman times. In 2004, Italian archeologists unearthed a ruined **XXX Dynasty temple** here. Seductive as they look, the **salt lakes** are surrounded by mushy sand and salt crusts that can trap unwary vehicles, and if safari groups camp here, they usually do so in the palm groves on the far side, away from the mosquitoes and protected from sandstorms.

Nuwamisa Oasis looks equally lovely, with a salt lake rimmed by palms and crescent cliffs – but its name, "Oasis of the Mosquitoes", is all too true. Literally millions of **mosquitoes** swarm as soon as the sun goes down, making camping a nightmare, even if you're all zipped up in your tent. For that reason, travellers often hasten on to **Sitra Oasis**, which isn't so badly infested and used to be a watering hole for Bedouin smugglers bringing hashish into Egypt. During the last 45km of the journey to Bahariya the road skirts the **Ghard Kebir** ("Great Dunes"), whose sandy crests were likened by Bagnold to "unclipped horses' manes". The dunes are slowly making their way south from the Qattara Depression, destined to arrive in Bahariya in a few hundred years.

Alexandria and the Mediterranean coast

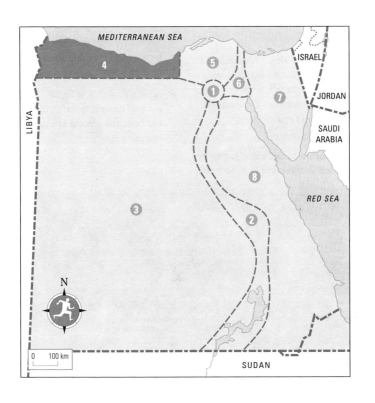

CHAPTER 4 # Highlights

✳ **Bibliotheca Alexandrina**
The city's library is a stunning example of contemporary architecture, aimed at reviving the legendary "Mother Library" of antiquity. See p.591

✳ **Catacombs of Kom es-Shoqafa** This eerie subterranean Roman necropolis is full of bizarre carvings, with a dining room for mourners. See p.593

✳ **Fresh seafood** Alexandria is famous for its seafood restaurants, where customers select their meal from a mound of fish and crustaceans. See p.598

✳ **Coffee houses and patisseries** *Trianon* and *Delices* have an old-world charm and literary associations. See p.600

✳ **Diving** Explore the underwater remains of Cleopatra's Palace, Roman galleys, French warships and German U-boats. See p.603

✳ **El-Alamein** The war museum and cemeteries are stark reminders of the decisive battle in 1942, and the hinterland harbours wrecked tanks and an abandoned field-hospital. See p.608

✳ **Agiiba Beach** The loveliest and easiest to reach of the beaches around Mersa Matrouh. See p.616

△ Fishing boats in Alexandria's Eastern Harbour, with Fort Qaitbey in the background

Alexandria and the Mediterranean coast

F or Ancient Egyptians, the **Mediterranean coast** marked the edge of the "Great Green", the measureless sea that formed the limits of the known world. Life and civilization meant the Nile Valley and the Delta – an outlook that still seems to linger in the country's subconscious. For, despite the white beaches, craggy headlands and turquoise sea that stretch for some five hundred kilometres, much of the Egyptian Med is eerily vacant and underpopulated.

Anywhere on the European side of the sea, package tourism would have taken hold decades ago. Here, however, partly due to a lack of fresh water, towns are few and generally small, and such tourism as exists is largely Egyptian, with no alcohol on sale and dress codes verging on the puritanical; conspicuous exceptions are resorts such as the *Hilton Burg el-Arab*, *Porto Marina* and **Almaza Bay**, aimed at European tourists. Aside from these, the main places worth noting are the World War II battlefield of **El-Alamein**, the Mediterranean Governorate capital of **Mersa Matrouh** (a jumping-off point for Siwa Oasis), and **wreck-diving** sites off **Sidi Abd el-Rahman**, **Sidi Barrani** and **Sollum**.

Alexandria, however, is an entirely different animal. Egypt's second city feels as Mediterranean and cosmopolitan as Athens or Marseille, its nineteenth-century architecture redolent of the colonial days immortalized by E.M. Forster, the poet Cavafy and, most famously, Lawrence Durrell. Its main sights, however, come from a different age, some dating from its time as the capital of Greco-Roman Egypt, and the seat of Cleopatra, the last of the Ptolemies; and others, such as the stunning modern library, the Bibliotheca Alexandrina, bringing the city bang into the twenty-first century. Antiquities from all eras can be viewed *in situ* underwater, as well as in local museums.

As for the **weather**, Egypt's Mediterranean coast gets hotter and drier the further west you travel, but Alexandria can be cold and windy in the winter, with torrential downpours and waves crashing over the Corniche for days on end. The Mediterranean Sea doesn't become warm enough for **swimming** till June, but you can be pretty sure of continuous sunshine from April until November.

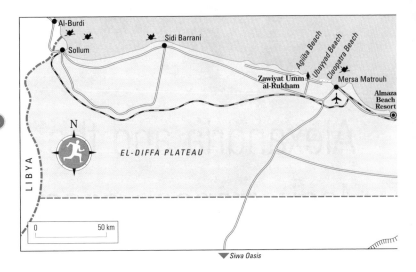

Siwa Oasis

Alexandria

Alexandria, princess and whore. The royal city and the anus mundi.

Lawrence Durrell, *The Alexandria Quartet*

A hybrid city dubbed the "Capital of Memory" by Durrell, **ALEXANDRIA** (El-Iskandariya in Arabic) turns its back on the rest of Egypt and faces the Mediterranean, as if contemplating its glorious past. One of the great cities of antiquity, Alex slumbered for 1300 years until it was revived by Mohammed Ali and transformed by Europeans, who gave the city its present shape and made it synonymous with cosmopolitanism and decadence. This era came to an end in the 1950s with the mass flight of non-Egyptians and a short-lived dose of revolutionary puritanism, but Alexandria's beaches, restaurants and breezy climate still attract hordes of Cairenes during the summer, while its jaded historical and literary mystique remains appealing to foreigners.

Alex is easily reached **from Cairo**, with a choice of train, bus, service taxi or plane. Buses and service taxis offer two routes, travelling by the verdant Desert Road past the turn-off for Wadi Natrun (whose monasteries are covered in Chapter 3), or by the hazardous, congested Delta Road, which is much slower, though the distance is roughly similar (about 225km). Remember that transport can get booked up from mid-June to late September, so reserve seats unless you're prepared to use service taxis.

The best **buses**, which do the journey in three hours, are operated by Superjet from outside Cairo's *Ramses Hilton* hotel; slightly cheaper and less comfortable services, run by the West Delta bus company, leave from the Turgoman Garage and the Aboud Terminal. The fastest **trains**, a/c Spanish and Turbini services, both leave three times daily and take just over two hours. There is also the so-called French service that has nine daily departures, takes thirty minutes longer and costs thirty percent less. **Service taxis** do the run in about three hours; in

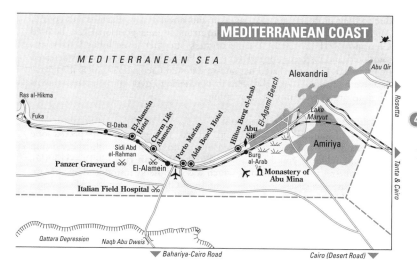

MEDITERRANEAN COAST

MEDITERRANEAN SEA

Ras al-Hikma

Fuka

El-Daba

El-Alamein
Charm Life
Alamein
Sidi Abd
el-Rahman

Panzer Graveyard ⚒ El-Alamein

Italian Field Hospital ⚒

Porto Marina

Aida Beach Hotel

Hilton Burg el-Arab

El-Agami Beach

Abu
Sir

Burg
al-Arab

Monastery of
Abu Mina

Alexandria

Abu Qir

Lake
Maryut

Amiriya

Rosetta

Tanta & Cairo

Qattara Depression   Naqb Abu Dweis

Bahariya-Cairo Road

Cairo (Desert Road)

Cairo both car- and minibus-taxis cluster outside Ramses Station and at the Aboud Terminal, their drivers bawling "Iskandariya! Iskandariya!". **Flying** from Cairo (50min) won't save you any time once you take getting to and from the airports into account, and there are also safety concerns about Alex's Nozha airport. For full details of bus, train, taxi and flight schedules and terminals, see the end of Chapter 1.

To reach Alex **from other parts of Egypt**, buses and/or service taxis are your best bet. Transport from the Delta and the Canal Zone is quite regular; from the Nile Valley, daily buses run from Beni Suef. See the relevant chapters for details.

Some history

When **Alexander the Great** wrested Egypt from the Persian empire in 332 BC at the age of 25, he decided against Memphis, the ancient capital, in favour of building a new city linked by sea to his Macedonian homeland. Choosing a site near the fishing village of **Rhakotis**, where two limestone spurs formed a natural harbour, he gave orders to his architect, Deinocrates, before travelling on to Siwa and thence to Asia, where he died eight years later. His corpse was subsequently returned to Egypt, where the priests refused burial at Memphis; its final resting place remains a mystery, although most archeologists believe it lies somewhere beneath Alexandria.

Thereafter Alexander's empire was divided amongst his Macedonian generals, one of whom took Egypt and adopted the title **Ptolemy I Soter**, founding a dynasty (323–30 BC). Avid promoters of Hellenistic culture, the **Ptolemies** made Alexandria an intellectual powerhouse: among its scholars were Euclid, the "father of geometry", and Eratosthenes, who accurately determined the circumference and diameter of the earth. Alexandria's great lighthouse, the **Pharos**, was literally and metaphorically a beacon, rivalled in fame only by the city's library, the **Bibliotheca Alexandrina** – the foremost centre of learning in the ancient world.

While the first three Ptolemies were energetic and enlightened, the later members of the dynasty are remembered as decadent and dissolute – perhaps due to their brother-sister marriages, in emulation of the pharaohs and gods of Ancient Egypt – and relied on Rome to maintain their position. Even the bold **Cleopatra VII** (51–30 BC) came unstuck after her lover, Julius Caesar, was murdered, and his successor in Rome (and her bed), Mark Antony, was defeated by Octavian. The latter hated her and so detested Cleopatra's capital at Alexandria that he banned Roman citizens from entering Egypt on the pretext that its religious orgies were morally corrupting.

Roman rule and Arab conquest

Whereas Alexandria's Egyptians and Greeks had previously respected one another's deities and even syncretized them into a common cult (the worship of Serapis), religious conflicts developed under **Roman rule** (30 BC–313 AD). The empire regarded Christianity, which was supposedly introduced by St Mark in 45 AD, as subversive, and the persecution of Christians from 250 AD onwards reached a bloody apogee under Emperor Diocletian, when the Copts maintain that 144,000 believers were martyred. (The Coptic Church dates its chronology from 284 AD, the "Era of Martyrs", rather than from Christ's birth.)

After the emperor Constantine made **Christianity** the state religion, a new controversy arose over the nature of Christ, the theological subtleties of which essentially masked a political rebellion by Egyptian **Copts** against Byzantine (ie Greek) authority. In Alexandria, the Coptic patriarch became supreme and his monks waged war against paganism, sacking the Serapis Temple and library in 391 and murdering the female scholar Hypatia in 415.

Local hatred of Byzantium disposed the Alexandrians to welcome the **Arab conquest** (641), whose commander, Amr, described the city as containing "4000 palaces, 4000 baths, 400 theatres, 1200 greengrocers and 40,000 Jews". But while the Arabs incorporated elements of Alexandrian learning into their own civilization, they cared little for a city which "seemed to them idolatrous and foolish", preferring to found a new capital at Fustat (now part of Cairo). Owing to neglect and the silting up of the waterways that connected it to the Nile, Alexandria inexorably declined over the next millennium, so that when Napoleon's expeditionary force arrived in 1798, they found a mere fishing village with four thousand inhabitants.

Mohammed Ali and colonial rule

Alexandria's **revival** sprang from the sultan Mohammed Ali's desire to make Egypt a commercial and maritime power, which necessitated a seaport. The Mahmudiya Canal, finished in 1820, once again linked Alexandria to the Nile, while a harbour, docks and arsenal were created with French assistance. European merchants erected mansions and warehouses, building outwards from the Place des Consuls (modern-day Midan Tahrir), and the city's population soared to 230,000.

Nationalist resentment of foreign influence fired the **Orabi revolt** of 1882, in retaliation for which British warships shelled the city, whose devastation was completed by arsonists and looters. Yet such was Alexandria's vitality and commercial importance that it quickly recovered.

Having survived bombing during World War II, Alexandria experienced new turmoil in the postwar era, as anti-British riots expressed rising **nationalism**. The **revolution** that forced King Farouk to sail into exile from Alexandria in 1952 didn't seriously affect the "foreign" community (many of whom had lived here for generations) until the Anglo-French-Israeli assault on Egypt during the Suez Crisis of 1956. The following year, Nasser expelled all French and British citizens and nationalized foreign businesses, forcing a hundred thousand

With few monuments to show for Alexandria's ancient lineage and much of the city's modern heritage spurned since Nasser's time, Alexandria's past is found in its faded coffee houses, minutiae such as old nameplates, the reminiscences of aged Arabs and Greeks, and in its **literary dimension**. E.M. Forster's *Alexandria: A History and a Guide* (1922) remains the classic source book, though Forster reckoned that the best thing he did was to publicize the work of Alexandrian-born Constantine Cavafy. Nostalgia, excess, loss and futility – the leitmotifs of Cavafy's poems – also pervade Lawrence Durrell's *The Alexandria Quartet*: indeed, Durrell used Cavafy as the basis for his character Balthazar. Generally, though, Durrell had little time for Egyptians, and his novels are not well regarded in Egypt. Michael Haag's *Alexandria – City of Memory* evokes the world of three writers inspired by the city's history and society, though bearing in mind the ancient adage that "a big book is a big nuisance", you might prefer Naguib Mahfouz's *Miramar*, a concise evocation of post-revolutionary Alex from an Egyptian standpoint. For foreign views of Alex, check out Charlie Pye-Smith's *The Other Nile*, Douglas Kennedy's *Beyond the Pyramids*, and Paul William Roberts' *River in the Desert*.

non–Egyptians to emigrate. Jewish residents also suffered after the discovery of an Israeli-controlled sabotage unit in the city, so that by the year's end only a few thousand Alexandrian Greeks and Jews remained. Foreign institutions, street names and suchlike were Egyptianized, and the custom of moving the seat of government to Alexandria during the hot summer months was ended.

Contemporary Alex

Though "old" Alexandrians undoubtedly regret the **changes** since Suez, Durrell's complaint that they produced "leaden uniformity" and rendered Alexandria "depressing beyond endurance" seems jaundiced and unjustified. Egypt's second city (pop. 5,500,000) has become more Egyptian and less patrician, but it doesn't lack contrasts and vitality. The difference is that middle-class Egyptians set the tone, not Greeks, Levantines and European expats. If Cavafy, *arak* and child-brothels represented the old days, *McDonald's*, Coke and Nike symbolize a new, brasher kind of cosmopolitanism. Overcrowding, pollution and traffic have all worsened, but the Med still keeps Alex cool.

Tension does, however, occasionally erupt. In 2005, hundreds of Muslim Brotherhood activists were arrested and one was shot dead during the run-up to the presidential election. Many see pent-up Islamist rage behind a knife attack by a "deranged" Muslim at a Coptic church in Sidi Gaber, which led to further assaults on churches and three days of sectarian **rioting** during which three people died, in April 2006. Fearing that Alexandria was sliding out of control, Mubarak appointed Adel Labib as city governor, to turn things around as he had in Qena (see p.334).

Arrival, orientation and information

West Delta and Superjet **buses** drop passengers at the **15th May Station** in Sidi Gaber, east of downtown, from where you can reach the centre by minibus #1, tram #2, #25 or #35 (25pt), or taxi (locals pay £E5, foreigners around £E10). Trains from Cairo usually stop at Sidi Gaber Station (north of the bus terminal) before terminating at **Masr Station**, about 1km south of downtown

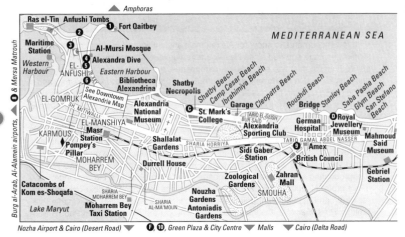

▲ Amphoras

Ras el-Tin Anfushi Tombs ❶ Fort Qaitbey

MEDITERRANEAN SEA

Maritime Station
Western Harbour
EL-ANFUSHI

❷
❸
❹ Al-Mursi Mosque
❺ Alexandra Dive
Bibliotheca Alexandrina
Eastern Harbour

EL-GOMRUK
See Downtown Alexandria Map
❻

SH. MITWALLI
EL-MANSHIYA
KARMOUS
Masr Station
Pompey's Pillar
MOHARREM BEY

Shatby Necropolis
Shatby Beach
Stanley Beach
Camp Cesar Beach
Ibrahimiya Beach

Alexandria National Museum
❼
Garage
Cleopatra Beach
Roushdi Beach
Bridge
Stanley Beach
Saba Pasha Beach
Glym Beach
San Stefano Beach

St. Mark's College
TARIQ EL-GEISH
BUR SAID
Alexandria Sporting Club
German Hospital
❽ Royal Jewellery Museum
Mahmoud Said Museum

Shallalat Gardens
SHARIA HORRIYA
Sidi Gaber Station
TARIQ GAMAL ABDEL NASSER
❾ Amex
British Council
Gebriel Station

Durrell House
Zoological Gardens
Zahran Mall
SMOUHA

Catacombs of Kom es-Shoqafa
SHARIA MOHARREM BEY
SHARIA AL-MA'MOUN
Nouzha Gardens
Antoniadis Gardens

Lake Maryut
Moharrem Bey Taxi Station

Nozha Airport & Cairo (Desert Road) ▼   ❻, ❿, Green Plaza & City Centre ▼   Malls   ▼ Cairo (Delta Road)

Midan Sa'ad Zaghloul, which you can reach by walking up Sharia Nabi Daniel (10–15min). **Service taxis** are likely to wind up on **Midan el-Gumhorriya**, outside Masr Station, but might terminate at the outlying **Moharrem Bey** depot; from there, catch a minibus (25pt to Midan el-Gumhorriya downtown) or a taxi (£E5) northwest to the centre.

Alexandria is served by three **airports**. EgyptAir use **Nozha**, 5km south of the city, as a stopover on some flights to Europe; other airlines use the new international terminals at **El-Alamein** or **Burg al-Arab** airport, respectively 130km and 60km from Alex. Public **transport** is limited to bus #555 (scheduled to coincide with flight arrivals and departures; £E6) from Burg al-Arab to Midan Sa'ad Zaghloul. A **taxi** to Alex from El-Alamein airport costs £E300, from Burg al-Arab £E80–100, from Nozha £E20.

Orientation and maps

Alexandria runs along the Mediterranean for 20km without ever venturing more than 8km inland – a true waterfront city. Its great **Corniche** sweeps around the **Eastern Harbour** and along the coast past a string of city **beaches** to **Montazah** and **Ma'amoura**, burning out before the final beach at **Abu Qir**. In the opposite direction, you need to get past the industrial zone of **Al-Max** to reach the western beaches of **Hannoville** and **El-Agami**. Away from the beach, visitors hang around the downtown quarter of **El-Manshiya** (see map, pp.580–581), where most of the restaurants, hotels and nightclubs are within a few blocks either side, or inland, of **Midan Sa'ad Zaghloul**.

The Corniche (and breezes blowing inland) make basic orientation quite simple, but the finer points can still be awkward. Unlike Cairo, downtown Alex has yet to be properly mapped, and the standard Lehnert & Landrock *Map of Alexandria* omits whole streets and blocks. **Street names** are also problematic, for signs don't always square with the latest official designation or popular usage (usually one change behind). Other street names have simply been Arabicized: Rue or Place to Sharia or Midan; "Alexandre le Grand" to "Iskander el-Akbar". In the downtown area, most of the signs are in English or Arabic, and people may use either when giving directions. A historical map of *Archeological Sites of Alexandria*, published by the Alexandria Preservation Trust, is on sale at bookshops (see p.603).

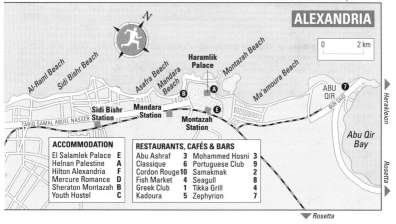

ACCOMMODATION		RESTAURANTS, CAFÉS & BARS			
El Salamlek Palace	E	Abu Ashraf	3	Mohammed Hosni	3
Helnan Palestine	A	Classique	6	Portuguese Club	9
Hilton Alexandria	F	Cordon Rouge	10	Samakmak	2
Mercure Romance	D	Fish Market	4	Seagull	8
Sheraton Montazah	B	Greek Club	1	Tikka Grill	4
Youth Hostel	C	Kadoura	5	Zephyrion	7

Information

The main **tourist office** off the southwest corner of Midan Sa'ad Zaghloul (daily 8.30am–6pm; Ramadan 9am–4pm; ☎03/485-1556) is staffed by very helpful English-speakers, who can answer most questions as well as provide a free booklet, *Alexandria Night and Day*. It has branches at Nozha airport (daily 8am–8pm; ☎03/425-0528), Masr Station (daily 8am–8pm; ☎03/392-5985) and Sidi Gaber Station (daily 8.30am–3pm; ☎03/426-3953) and a part-time one at the Maritime Station (irregular hours; no phone).

Though travel writers have ignored Alex since of late, books on the city's **archeology** and cultural heritage continue to be published. The French archeologist Jean-Yves Empereur of the Centre d'Etudes Alexandrines (CEA; ⊛www.cealex.org) has written two excellent guides to the city's sights and history, *Alexandria Revealed* and *Alexandria Rediscovered*, plus guide-books to the Greco-Roman Museum and the Catacombs; while the Hungarian Egyptologist Gyoző Vörös touches on the city's maritime history in his book *Taposiris Magna: Port of Isis*. All these books are available in local bookshops (see p.603) or can be consulted in the library of the Archeological Society of Alexandria, 6 Sharia Mahmoud Mokhtar (Mon–Wed & Sun 4.30–7.30pm; ☎03/486-0650). Among **websites** relating to Alex, ⊛www.touregypt.net has up-to-date listings under "Alexandria News", while ⊛www.houseofptolemy.org covers the city's ancient and modern history.

City transport

Downtown is compact enough to walk around, and along the Corniche to Fort Qaitbey makes a healthy constitutional (35–50min). However, you really need transport to reach other outlying areas. The main downtown terminals are **Ramleh** tram station; the square outside Masr Station, **Midan el-Gumhorriya**; and **Midan Khartoum**, to the east of the Greco-Roman Museum. Minibuses running along the Corniche can be boarded from the seafront side of both Midan Orabi and Sa'ad Zaghloul.

Useful public-transport services in Alexandria

Trams

#1	Ramleh to Victoria (near Sidi Bishr), via the Sporting Club and the Roushdi district
#2 (yellow)	Pompey's Pillar to El-Nozha (near the airport)
#2 (blue)	Ramleh to Victoria, via the Sporting Club and Roushdi
#4	Midan St Katerina to Moharrem Bey
#15	Ramleh to Ras el-Tin, via El-Gomruk and El-Anfushi (near Fort Qaitbey)
#16	Midan St Katerina to Pompey's Pillar and the Catacombs, and on to Moharrem Bey
#18	Midan Katerina to El-Nozha
#25	Midan Orabi (Unknown Soldier) to Sidi es-Sheikh (near Sidi Gaber station)

Buses

#3	Ramleh to Hannoville (El-Agami), via the Corniche
#11	Ras el-Tin to Ma'amoura, via the Corniche
#460	Midan Khartoum to Hannoville, via the Corniche
#555	Midan Sa'ad Zaghloul to Burg al-Arab airport
#709	Midan St Katerina to Pompey's Pillar

Minibuses

#1	Midan Sa'ad Zaghloul to the 15th May bus station/Sidi Gaber station and on to Sidi Bishr
#2	Ramleh to Hannoville
#3	Ramleh west to Abu Talaat (beyond El-Agami)
#731	Ras el-Tin to Sidi Bishr, via the Corniche
#735	Ras el-Tin to Montazah, via the Corniche
#736	Midan St Katerina to Ma'amoura, via Ramleh and the Corniche
#751	Moharrem Bey to Bitash
#765	Masr Station to Hannoville (El-Agami)
#766	Ras el-Tin to Abu Qir, via Sidi Gaber and the Corniche from Shatby onwards
#768	Masr Station to Abu Qir, inland

Trams, buses and minibuses

Trams are integral to Alex life, conveying all classes at a snail's pace and rattling past the houses of rich and poor alike. The original trams were built in Britain, but the ones currently in service were a gift from Denmark in the 1960s. Services run from 5.30am to 1am, with fares between 25pt and 35pt. Destinations and route numbers are in Arabic only, but you can get an idea from the vehicle's livery where it's heading: trams between Ramleh and Ras el-Tin (to the west) are painted yellow with a red trim; trams between Ramleh and points east (all of which stop at the Sporting Club), blue. On trams with three carriages, the middle one is **reserved for women**. Some have double-decker carriages, with a fab view from the top floor. Standing downstairs, you may have difficulty seeing the names of the tram stops, which are written in English on certain routes.

Run by the city and private operators, **buses** (50pt–£E1.50) are also numbered in Arabic and keep similar schedules to the trams, but are faster, with passengers boarding on the run between Sa'ad Zaghloul, Tahrir and El-Gumhorriya squares. However, city buses are very crowded, a situation made worse by gropers and pickpockets; whenever possible, use another form of transport. **Minibuses** offer a reasonably comfortable ride and cover many of the same routes. Those run by the municipality are blue and white (50pt–£E2.25), while privately operated ones are blue (£E1.50–2.25). Both run similar hours to trams and buses.

Taxis, calèches and car rental

Regular black-and-yellow **taxis** never use meters and will charge whatever they can get away with (especially going to Masr Station or any other departure point). You should pay about £E5 for a ride across downtown (say, to Shatby Beach), and £E20 for a trip all the way east to Montazah Beach. There are also new, rarely seen "City Taxis" (silver-grey Toyota Corollas) with meters, charging £E4 to start, £E1.50 per kilometre thereafter and £E10 an hour waiting time, which can be booked on free-phone ☏0800 999-9999.

Horse-drawn carriages solicit passengers with cries of "*calèche, calèche*" outside Masr Station and along the Corniche. Providing you don't get stuck in traffic jams or feel self-consciously "colonial", they can be a good way of touring the quieter parts of Alex and enjoying the sea breezes. You'll have to negotiate a price – reckon on £E15–20 an hour.

Renting a car makes sense if you're going to visit El-Alamein, west of Alexandria. For self-drive rental, El Lord, 6 Sharia Goul Gamal in Roushdi (☏03/546-4316), charges £E130–195 a day depending on the type of car, with 120km mileage included; Avis in the *Hotel Cecil* (daily 8am–8pm; ☏03/480-7055) has Toyotas ($50) and Mercedes ($90), with 100km mileage included. Thomas Cook on Midan Ramleh charges £E350 for a car with a driver to visit El-Alamein and the Monastery of St Mina, beating Avis, which asks £E450 for the same.

Accommodation

Alexandria's **hotels** include old *pensions* and glitzy citadels of *Sheraton*-style internationalism, though there are few mid-range establishments. A sea view is a big plus, and hotels charge accordingly – though in cheap hotels these rooms are freezing in wintertime. Two drawbacks that only later become apparent are **tram noise** and giant orange **cockroaches** – the twin banes of hotels near the waterfront. Basically, you either learn to live with them or move further inland. Bear in mind that the choice and availability of rooms is limited during high season, when **reservations** are advisable. The **price codes** quoted below are for the high season and refer to rooms without a sea view. You can count on hot water, and breakfast being included, unless stated otherwise. The downtown hotels are all marked on the map on pp.580–581. If you don't mind being out of the centre, there are some **upmarket hotels** at Montazah (see p.597) or out near the malls and International Garden on Alexandria's southern edge. Look for discount rates online.

Alexandria's **youth hostel** (☏03/592-5459) has triple-bed rooms (£E25) which are no cheaper than a double room in some budget hotels in the centre, and the location is extremely noisy and only really convenient for the library. The hostel is on a main road opposite St Mark's College in Shatby, 1km east of the downtown area. Take tram #1 or #2 from Ramleh to the College and turn towards the Corniche; the hostel is at 32 Sharia Bur Said, next to some Greco-Roman tombs.

If you're intending to stay a while, **renting a flat** makes sense. Most expats stay in the Roushdi district, a few kilometres east of the downtown area, where a well-furnished two-bedroom flat costs $300–400 a month. Rates are slightly cheaper downtown. Some properties are advertised online at ⓦ www.expatriates .com, ⓦ www.perfectplaces.com and (in Arabic) ⓦ www.chalihat.com.

Downtown

Acropole 27 Sharia Gamil el-Din Yassin, fourth floor ☎03/480-5980, ⓔ acropole_hotel@yahoo .com. Very central and within earshot of the trams, this old-fashioned hotel is smartening itself up. All rooms have washbasin and clean bedding; there's a surcharge for a side sea view (£E10) or private bath (£E25). Residents can use the kitchen. ❶

Cecil 16 Midan Sa'ad Zaghloul ☎03/448-7173, ⓕ 485-5655, ⓦ www.sofitel.com. Dead central, with fab views of the Eastern Harbour, the *Cecil* is an Alexandrian institution. Durrell, Churchill, Noël Coward and Somerset Maugham head the list of former guests, but modernization and *Sofitel* management have dispelled the old ambience. Regular rooms are cosy and a/c but nothing special. Amenities include French and Chinese restaurants, a nightclub, *Monty's Bar* and an Avis desk. You'll pay $50 extra for a sea view; a grand corner suite costs $280. Takes Amex, MC and Visa. ❽

Crillon 5 Sharia Adib Ishtak ☎03/480-0330. The best-preserved of Alex's prewar *pensions*, with a lobby full of stuffed birds. Its third floor has breezy Art Deco rooms with enclosed sea-view balconies and spotless shared bathrooms; don't bother with the small en-suite rooms on the sixth floor. In high season, half board is obligatory. ❷

Hyde Park 21 Sharia Amin Fikhry, eighth floor ☎03/487-5667. A scruffy *pension* whose card promises "water inside the room", "beans services 24 hours" and "to lament to inside the Repubic" (whatever that means), but fails to mention the glassed-in balconies with harbour views that are its only redeeming feature. A last resort. ❷

Metropole 52 Sharia Sa'ad Zaghloul ☎03/486-1467, ⓕ 486-2040, ⓔ resamet@paradiseinnegypt.com. Centrally located on the corner of Midan Ramleh, this wonderfully ornate 1900s hotel has been refurbished to four-star standards. All rooms have a/c and a fancy bathroom; the suites are furnished with antiques and have jacuzzis. It's worth paying $35 extra for a sea view. French restaurant. Takes Amex, DC, MC and Visa cards. ❼

New Hotel Welcome House 28 Sharia Gamil el-Din Yassin, fifth floor ☎03/480-6402. This shabby old place has the cheapest en-suite, sea-view rooms (£E30) in the centre and a kitchen for the use of guests – but the lift hasn't worked for years. ❶

Nile Excelsior 16 Sharia al-Bursa al-Qadima, second floor 03/480-0799, ⓔ nilehotel@hotmail .com. Just up the road from the *Spitfire Bar* (see

p.601), this outwardly grungy hotel has clean and comfortable high-ceilinged en-suite rooms. ❷

Normandie 28 Sharia Gamil el-Din Yassin, 4th floor ☎03/480-6830. One floor below the *New Hotel Welcome House*, this equally aged, fairly clean *pension* has sea-view rooms (£E25) with shared bathrooms (some lacking hot water). No breakfast. ❶

Sea Star 24 Sharia Amin Fikhry ☎03/480-5343, ⓕ 487-2388. A few blocks from Midan Ramleh, this hotel's top-floor rooms have distant sea views; the rest are quite dark and claustrophobic, but are en suite and clean. ❷

Triomphe 26 Sharia Gamil el-Din Yassin, 5th floor ☎03/480-7585, ⓔ adelabaza@hotmail.com. Attractively kitsch and, with side views of the sea from some rooms (£E30 extra), the *Triomphe* is one of the better budget options in Alex. No breakfast. ❷

Union 164 Sharia 26 July, 5th floor ☎03/480 7312, ⓕ 480-7350. Reservations are essential at this bright, clean Art Deco hotel three blocks along the Corniche from Midan Sa'ad Zaghloul, with a cool lounge facing the Eastern Harbour. It's worth paying £E20 more for a large carpeted room with a harbour view, balcony and private bathroom. Breakfast (£E9) is obligatory in high season. ❷

Windsor Palace 17 Sharia ash-Shohada ☎03/480-8123, ⓕ 480-9090, ⓔ resawin @paradiseinnegypt.com. This tastefully refurbished Edwardian hotel has three-star facilities (check out the Lady Spencer terrace and Prince Charles coffee shop), with soothing green and gold decor. Many of the rooms have fantastic views of the harbour. Takes all major cards. ❼

Outside the centre

El Salamlek Palace Montazah Gardens ☎03/547-7999, ⓕ 547-3585, ⓦ www.sangiovanni.com. This grandiose pseudo-Alpine chalet was once the residence of Khedive Abbas's mistress and is decorated in period style (suites from $370). Amenities include a private beach, the only casino in Alex (open to non-residents with passports), French and Italian restaurants. Takes all major cards. ❽

Helnan Palestine Near the Haramlik Palace ☎03/547-3500, ⓕ 547-3378, ⓦ www.helnan.com. Originally built to house Arab leaders attempting to solve the Palestinian problem in 1964, this hotel has been refurbished as a five-star conference venue. Spacious rooms overlook the palace or a lagoon where guests can fish or windsurf. Middle

Eastern, Italian and Asian cuisine are available. Discounts of around thirty percent off-season. ⑨

Hilton Alexandria 14th of May Bridge, Smouha ℡03/490-9120, Ⓕ420-9140, Ⓦwww.hilton.com. Opened in 2002, with first-rate amenities, though its motorway site on the outskirts (20min by taxi from the centre) is a big disadvantage. Takes all major cards. ⑥

Mercure Romance 303 Tariq el-Geish, Saba Pasha ℡03/584-0911, Ⓕ583-0526, Ⓦwww .accorhotels.com. On the Corniche, midway between Montazah and the centre, this four-star

Mercure is worth checking out. Rooms booked through *Longchamps Hotel* in Cairo (see p.99) can cost as little as $50 per person. Its Chinese restaurant and disco are also good. ⑧

Sheraton Montazah Montazah, on a busy junction outside the grounds of the palace ℡03/548-0550, Ⓕ540-1331, Ⓦwww.sheraton.com/montazah. A five-star tower featuring a nightclub, disco, small outdoor pool and tennis court. All rooms have a/c, minibar and satellite TV. Takes all major cards. Breakfast not included. ⑦

The City

I loved the shabbiness of the streets and cafés, the melancholy which hung over the city late of an evening, the slow decay (not destruction, mind you) of what the Europeans had left behind when they fled.

Charlie Pye-Smith, *The Other Nile*

Alex encourages nostalgia trips and random exploration, if only because the "sights" are limited and chance incidents often more revealing. Don't be afraid of following your nose and deviating from the usual itineraries, which could be completed in a day or so if you focus on the city's monumental **highlights**. The Roman Theatre and Villa of Birds at Kom el-Dikka and the spooky Catacombs of Kom es-Shoqafa are musts, as is the city's magnificent new library and Alexandria National Museum, exhibiting statues and other artefacts dredged from ancient cities on the seabed. If you also want to savour the ambience and literary mystique of the former European and "native" quarters, allow two or three days.

For convenience, these accounts start with the downtown area and work outwards, interweaving the ancient, remembered and existing cities. The **historical map** published by the Alexandria Preservation Trust helps make sense of the ancient city as you walk around, while anyone interested in **archeology** should check out the links on Ⓦwww.houseofptolemy.org.

South and east of Midan Sa'ad Zaghloul

Since E.M. Forster wrote his guide to Alexandria in 1922, the city's centre has shifted eastwards from the former Place Mohammed Ali (now Midan Tahrir) to the seafront **Midan Sa'ad Zaghloul**, a square named after the nationalist leader (1860–1927) whose **statue** gazes towards the Mediterranean. His deportation by the British to Malta provoked nationwide rioting (1919) and guaranteed Zaghloul a hero's return, though the independence he sought was denied for another generation. Zaghloul is referred to as "the Pasha" in Naguib Mahfouz's novel, *Miramar*.

With no trace of the Caesareum that stood here in ancient times (see p.582), the square today looks post-colonial; decrepit edifices that could have been lifted from Naples or Athens overshadow the tourist office. The dominant building is the pseudo-Moorish **Hotel Cecil**, where British Intelligence hatched the El-Alamein deception plan from a suite on the first floor. No longer the decadent and moribund establishment of *The Alexandria Quartet*, it now belongs to the *Sofitel* chain.

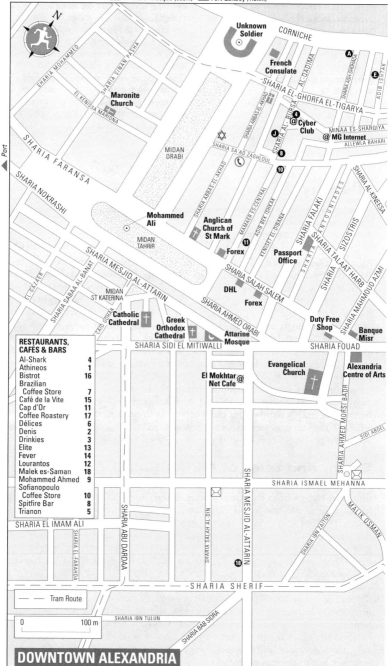

DOWNTOWN ALEXANDRIA

**RESTAURANTS,
CAFÉS & BARS**

Al-Shark	4
Athineos	1
Bistrot	16
Brazilian Coffee Store	7
Café de la Vite	15
Cap d'Or	11
Coffee Roastery	17
Délices	6
Denis	2
Drinkies	3
Elite	13
Fever	14
Lourantos	12
Malek es-Saman	18
Mohammed Ahmed	9
Sofianopoulo Coffee Store	10
Spitfire Bar	8
Trianon	5

Tram Route

0   100 m

▼ Pompey's Pillar & The Catacombs

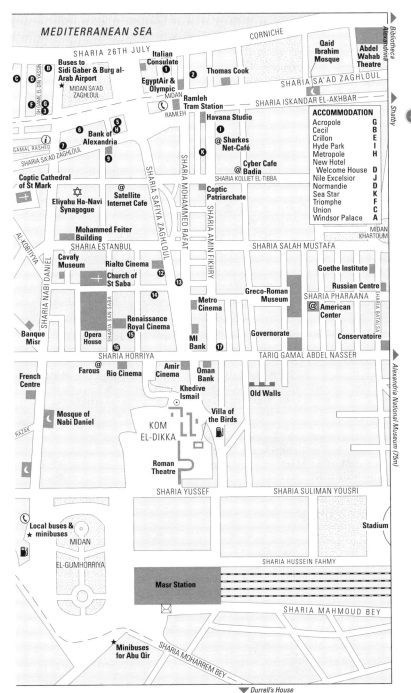

MEDITERRANEAN SEA

CORNICHE

SHARIA 26TH JULY

Buses to
Sidi Gaber & Burg al-
Arab Airport

Italian
Consulate ❶

EgyptAir &
Olympic

MIDAN SA'AD
ZAGHLOUL

MIDAN

RAMLEH

Ramleh
Tram Station

❷ Thomas Cook

Qaid
Ibrahim
Mosque

Abdel
Wahab
Theatre

SHARIA SA'AD ZAGHLOUL

SHARIA ISKANDAR EL-AKHBAR

Havana Studio

❿ Sharkes
Net-Café

Cyber Cafe
@ Badia

SHARIA KOLLIET EL-TIBBA

Bank of
Alexandria

Coptic Cathedral
of St Mark

Eliyahu Ha-Navi
Synagogue

Satellite
Internet Cafe

Coptic
Patriarchate

Mohammed Feiter
Building

SHARIA ESTANBUL

SHARIA SALAH MUSTAFA

Cavafy
Museum

Rialto Cinema ⓬

Church of
St Saba

⓭

Goethe Institute

Russian Centre

SHARIA PHARAANA

Greco-Roman
Museum

American
Center

Conservatoire

⓮

Metro
Cinema

Banque
Misr

Opera
House

Renaissance
Royal Cinema ⓯

⓰

MI
Bank ⓱

Governorate

SHARIA HORRIYA

TARIQ GAMAL ABDEL NASSER

Farous
French
Centre

Rio Cinema

Amir
Cinema

Oman
Bank

Khedive
Ismail

Old Walls

Mosque of
Nabi Daniel

KOM
EL-DIKKA

Villa of
the Birds

Roman
Theatre

SHARIA YUSSEF

SHARIA SULIMAN YOUSRI

Local buses &
minibuses

MIDAN

EL-GUMHORRIYA

Stadium

SHARIA HUSSEIN FAHMY

Masr Station

SHARIA MAHMOUD BEY

Minibuses
for Abu Qir

SHARIA MOHARREM BEY

Durrell's House

ACCOMMODATION

Acropole	G
Cecil	B
Crillon	E
Hyde Park	I
Metropole	H
New Hotel	
Welcome House	D
Nile Excelsior	J
Normandie	D
Sea Star	K
Triomphe	F
Union	C
Windsor Palace	A

A similar mystique once attended Alexandria's **patisseries**, of which there are a handful in the vicinity. *Délices*, established in 1922, is a tearoom with two long halls whose French name belies the fact that it was originally owned by Greeks, like the *Trianon* (where the poet Cavafy worked as a clerk for the First Circle of Irrigation on the floor above and scenes from the British war movie *Ice Cold in Alex* were filmed), and *Athineos* on Midan Ramleh (see p.600 for reviews of these and other patisseries). The *Trianon* stands just behind the former site of **Cleopatra's Needles**, two giant obelisks that once marked the entrance to the Caesareum (see below). Nineteenth-century visitors enjoyed sketching and photographing the one still standing and its fallen companion (toppled by an earthquake in 1301) until both were removed in the 1870s, to be re-erected on London's Embankment and in New York's Central Park. Their popular name is a misnomer, for they originated at Heliopolis fourteen centuries earlier, and were moved to Alexandria fifteen years after Cleopatra's death.

Sharia Nabi Daniel: the Synagogue and Coptic Cathedral

Starting as an inconspicuous backstreet beside the tourist office, **Sharia Nabi Daniel** grows wider as it runs south along the route of the ancient **Street of the Soma**. Paved in marble and flanked by marble colonnades, this dazzled the Arabs in 641, even though its finest buildings had already vanished. Before its destruction by feuding Christians in the fourth century, the north end of the street was crowned by the **Caesareum**, a temple begun by Cleopatra for Antony, which Octavian completed and dedicated to himself, filling it with paintings and statues.

A short way down Nabi Daniel, high wrought-iron gates and clusters of police guard the **Eliyahu Ha-Navi Synagogue**, entered via an alley to the north (admission may be possible on Saturday mornings; bring your passport and pretend to be Jewish if necessary). Built in 1885 by Baron Jacques de Menasce, its columned Italianate interior features stained-glass windows, giant menorahs and a collection of Torah scrolls from bygone neighbourhood synagogues that once served a Jewish community of seventy thousand, tracing its ancestry back to the city's foundation. Nowadays only a dozen or so, mostly elderly, Jews remain, six of whom look after the synagogue and its extensive archives.

Across the road, another set of gates marked by crosses betrays the **Coptic Cathedral of St Mark**, in a compound enclosed by taller buildings, entered from Sharia al-Kineesa al-Kobtiyya (once Rue de l'Eglise Copte), which joins Nabi Daniel further south. The cathedral is named after the Apostle martyred by pagans in 67 AD; kidnapped while giving Mass, he was dragged by horses through the streets of Alexandria, where his remains were held by a local church until 828, when the Venetians smuggled the body out of Muslim-ruled Alexandria in a barrel of salt pork, to reinter it at the Basilica di San Marco; the head was transferred to the custody of the Church of Mari Girgis in Cairo. In 1997, Pope John Paul II returned one of St Mark's fingers to Pope Shenouda III as a gesture of ecumenical reconciliation. A novel reinterpretation of this story was recently proposed by Andrew Chugg (see "Books", p.805), who argues that Alexander's body was secretly buried in the guise of St Mark's relics after Emperor Theodosius prohibited the worship of Alexander in 391 AD, and was later smuggled abroad by Venetians unaware of its true origin.

The cathedral itself is an early twentieth-century Byzantine pastiche, whose interior was unfairly described by Forster as "fatuously ugly". Remains of some of the first 47 patriarchs of the Alexandrian See are buried in a chapel to the left of the iconostasis. Daily services are held from 6 to 8pm and 8 to 10pm.

From the Cavafy Museum to the Opera House

Off Nabi Daniel on Sharia Estanbul, the flamboyant **Mohammed Feiter Building**, emblazoned with majolica panels and monogrammed coronets, serves as a landmark for locating a narrow lane across the road, formerly called Rue Lepsius and now Sharia Sharm el-Sheikh. At no. 4, near the far end, a tiny sign in Greek identifies the **Cavafy Museum** (Mon–Wed, Fri & Sat 10am–3pm, Thurs & Sun 10am–5pm; £E10), re-creating the second-floor flat where **Constantine Cavafy** (1863–1933) lived at the zenith of his poetic talent, above a bordello around the corner from the Greek Orthodox Church of St Saba. "Where could I live better?" he asked. "Below, the brothel caters for the flesh. And there is the church which forgives sin. And there is the hospital where we die." He died there indeed, and was buried in the Greek Cemetery at Shatby, where his grave bears the simple epitaph, *Poet*.

The museum was established by the Greek Consulate in 1992. Its custodian relates how "Cavafis" (as he is known) had nine brothers, loved candlelight, and died of throat cancer from drinking – but draws a veil over his homosexuality ("He never married"). Visitors can see his brass bed, icons, books and death mask, and the modest desk where he wrote *The Barbarians*, *Ithaca*, and his elegaic *The City*:

You won't find a new country, won't find another shore.
This city will always pursue you.
You'll walk the same streets, grow old
in the same neighbourhoods, turn grey in the same houses.
You'll always end up in this city. Don't hope for things elsewhere:
there's no ship for you, there's no road.
Now that you've wasted your life here, in this small corner,
you've destroyed it everywhere in the world.

There is also a room devoted to **Stratis Tsirkas**, a student of Cavafy's who wrote the trilogy *Drifting Cities*, about Greek underground politics in wartime Jerusalem, Cairo and Alexandria.

Across the road stands the Greek Orthodox **Church of St Saba** (daily 7.30am–12.30pm & 3.30–6pm), built over an ancient columnar temple of Apollo. The seventeenth-century church contains a marble columnar tablet on which St Catherine is said to have been beheaded, a giant bronze bell, and relics of Patriarch Petros VII, killed in a helicopter crash on Mount Athos in 2004. While Alexandria's Greek population has shrunk from 300,000 before 1957 to about 1000 today, the Patriarchate of Alexandria encompasses all Africa and its congregation throughout the continent has risen to 250,000 – a number unseen since Roman times.

From here, follow Sharia San Saba southwards past the **Opera House**, originally the Theatre Mohammed Ali and now better known as the **Sayed Darwish Theatre**. A splendid Beaux Arts edifice, it fuses elements of the Odéon Théâtre in Paris and the Vienna Opera House. Having peeked inside to admire its foyer, you can continue along one of the lanes on either side to emerge on Sharia Horriya. While in the vicinity, you could also check out the **Banque Masr** on Sharia Talaat Harb, occupying a copy of the Palazzo Farnese in Rome, which was built for an Italian bank in the 1920s; its lavish Gothic interior is worth seeing.

On to Midan el-Gumhorriya

The intersection of Nabi Daniel, Horriya and Fouad streets is classic **Durrell** territory. Durrell himself lived with Eve Cohen (the model for Justine) in a flat at 40 Sharia Fouad, while several of his fictional characters were located nearby:

Darley and Pombal on Nabi Daniel; Clea, Justine and Nessim on Rue Fuad Premier (now Sharia Fouad/Sharia Horriya).

The junction lies near the crossroads of ancient Alexandria, whose east–west axis, the **Canopic Way**, was lined by marble colonnades extending all the way from the Gate of the Sun, where visitors entered the city. Many scholars believe that this crossroads was the site of the **Mouseion** ("Shrine of the Muses"), an institution from which our word "museum" derives. Founded by Ptolemy I Soter (323–282 BC), it incorporated lecture halls, laboratories, observatories, and the legendary "Mother" Library (see p.592).

Across the way stood the **Soma** (meaning "dead body"), a temple where Alexander the Great was entombed alongside several Ptolemies. Alexander reposed in a gold sarcophagus until Ptolemy IX melted it down to mint coins during a crisis, but his body remained on view long after the dynasty had fallen. The victorious Octavian paid his respects to Alexandria's founder but disdained his heirs, stating "I wished to see a king, I did not wish to see corpses." According to one chronicler, Octavian accidentally broke Alexander's nose while bending to kiss the dead conqueror.

What happened to Alexander's body later remains a mystery. Some scholars believe that the Romans reburied him outside the Royal Quarter, in what is now Shatby, where the Christian cemeteries are today (see p.594). Reports from Mohammed Ali's time suggesting that Alexander's tomb lay deep beneath the nineteenth-century **Mosque of Nabi Daniel** (whose crypt holds the remains of the Sufi sheikh Mohammed Danyal al-Maridi) impelled the Egyptian Antiquities Organization to excavate in the 1990s, with no result. In 2002 two Greeks announced the discovery of Alexander's tomb at Siwa Oasis, to widespread derision (see p.564), while a more recent theory has it that his remains ended up in Venice as saintly relics of St Mark (see p.582).

Sharia Nabi Daniel ends at **Midan el-Gumhorriya**, a seething mass of bus and taxi ranks outside the neo-Baroque **Masr Station**, designed by a Greek and an Italian in 1927. You can beat a retreat into the Roman Theatre at Kom el-Dikka off Sharia Yussef.

Kom el-Dikka

In 1959 Polish archeologists searching for Alexander's tomb were licensed to excavate beneath the Turkish fort and slums on **Kom el-Dikka** ("Mound of Rubble"), revealing a substratum of **Roman remains** beneath a Muslim cemetery (daily 9am–5pm; Ramadan until 3pm; £E15). During Ptolemaic times this was the Park of Pan, a hilly pleasure-garden with a limestone summit carved into the shape of a pine cone, where Roman villas, baths and an amphitheatre were later built. The elegant **Roman Theatre** has marble seating for seven to eight hundred, cruder galleries for the plebs, and a forecourt with two patches of mosaic flooring. In Byzantine times, gladiatorial games were superseded by chariot races, with teams based on the Blues and Greens of Constantinople's hippodrome; some of the seats in the theatre bear graffiti supporting one of the teams (which were closely associated with political factions). Along the northern side of the theatre's portico are thirteen auditoria that might have been part of Alexandria's ancient **university**, with an annual enrolment of five thousand students.

A separate ticket, sold at the main entrance, entitles you to enter the **Villa of Birds** (£E5) – so called because of its mosaic floors, depicting nine different species of birds (and a panther). En route to the villa you'll pass a laboratory for cleaning antiques, with assorted masonry recently dredged from the seabed laid outside.

Further north within the compound, excavation work is taking place on a **residential quarter** (closed to visitors) whose jumbled arches and walls resolve into streets, shops and houses at close quarters. Many of the buildings were constructed from alternating courses of brick and stone, a technique called *opus mixtum* ("mixed work"). Five centuries later, the Arabs used the same method to build a wall around the shrunken city, which was reinforced by the Turks. The **east gate** (Bab Sharq) of the Arab city is embedded in the Stadium beyond Masr Station.

Sharia Safiya Zaghloul and the Quartier Grec

Exiting Kom el-Dikka and turning northwards round the corner of the site, you'll come to a **statue of Khedive Ismail** that once stood by the Corniche. It was removed in 1956 when he became reviled by nationalists as a dupe of colonialism, and has only now been granted a permanent home here. From the statue, cross over Sharia Horriya and head north along **Sharia Safiya Zaghloul**. In Cavafy's day this was called the Rue Missala and known for its billiard halls and rent boys; today it is named after the wife of the nationalist leader and noted for its shops and cinemas. The turning just beyond the Metro Cinema leads to the heart of what was once the **Quartier Grec**, or Greek Quarter, one of five urban zones allotted to different ethnic groups by Mohammed Ali, that became as rich and cosmopolitan as Alexandria itself. Many of its villas now house **cultural centres** (see p.604), along Sharia Batalsa (still identified by its old name of Rue de Ptolomees) and Sharia Phara'ana (signed Rue des Pharaons), including the American Center, previously owned by philanthropist and Zionist Georges Menasce.

The Greek Quarter's most famous building, however, is the **Greco–Roman Museum** (@www.grm.gov.eg), whose Classical facade by Leopold Deitrich Bey (1892) is visible at the far end of Rue du Musée. Home to Egypt's best collection of Classical antiquities, the museum is closed until 2008 for refurbishment. Its reopening date and future layout are uncertain, but some of its extensive collection will be on display at other museums in the meantime. When it reopens you will be able to see such treasures as a mummified crocodile, human mummies dating from *c*.100–250 AD, relics of the Serapis cult promoted by Ptolemy I, and death masks, statues and busts of Roman emperors, including Julius Caesar. In the museum garden are some tombs cut from rocks and a giant head of Mark Antony. While the Greco-Roman Museum is closed, the Alexandria National Museum has been making all the running.

The Alexandria National Museum

Back on Sharia Horriya (aka Tariq Gamal Abdel Nasser), head east beyond the governorate, passing en route a stratified section of the **old walls** behind some houses in an alley, and you'll reach the impressive **Alexandria National Museum**, at no. 110 near the corner of Midan Khartoum (daily 9am–5pm; £E30). Occupying an Italianate mansion once owned by a wood merchant, Assad Basily, the museum displays some of the amazing archeological finds made in and around the city during the past decade. Artfully lit and with English labelling, the museum also has an impressive art and history bookshop.

On the ground floor, pride of place is afforded to artefacts from **Herakleion** and **Canopus** (p.598). A diorite sphinx, a priest of Isis carrying a Canopic jar and a statue of the goddess share the spotlight with a granite stele of Nectanebo II that once stood at the mouth of the Canopic branch (see p.598) of the Nile. From **ancient Alexandria** come an effigy of Emperor Caracalla in pharaonic headgear, a **mosaic** of Medusa found beneath the Diana Cinema, a marble hand from an

△ Statuary at the Alexandria National Museum

unknown colossus and the **head of Briniky**, the wife of Ptolemy II. Upper Egypt is represented by a life-sized statue of Ben Menkh, lord of Dendara in Roman times.

Upstairs, splendid mother-of-pearl-inlaid doors and *mashrabiyas* precede **Coptic** stelae and friezes carved with lions, sheep or grapevines, followed by icons, priestly garments and accoutrements. The breadth of **Islamic** artefacts is even greater: sashes and capes of Persian or Turkish origin; gold coins minted under the Fatimid and Byzantine empires evincing trade between the two; and Mamluke and Ottoman weaponry (increasingly ceremonial and made in Europe as the balance of power tilted westwards). A final room upstairs entitled "Alexandria in the Twenty-First Century" juxtaposes photos of colonial street scenes and a satellite view of the city with crystal tableware, jewelled rings and medals from King Farouk's collection. Look out for the life-sized silver fish with a flexible body.

Around Midan Orabi and Midan Tahrir

The old heart of "European" Alexandria lies less than 500m west of Midan Sa'ad Zaghloul. To get there, you can catch a tram along Sharia el-Ghorfa el-Tigarya, or walk along **Sharia Sa'ad Zaghloul**, which starts as a busy shopping street aglow with neon, and ends as a shadowy alley. Along the way you can see traces of the past in Art Deco frontages and faded plaques bearing Greek, French or Armenian names, and perhaps be accosted by a seedy old guy who pimped for British soldiers in his youth and will regale you with sordid tales for the price of a drink in one of the backstreet **bars** (see p.601). Or you can delve into a warren of furniture and garment **workshops** across the square from the telephone exchange.

Emerging onto **Midan Orabi**, you'll see a Neoclassical **Monument of the Unknown Soldier** facing the seafront, where a naval guard of honour is changed every hour on the hour. No trace remains of the French Gardens where expatriates once strolled among the acacia trees and shrubs, but a derelict

synagogue on the corner of Sa'ad Zaghloul and a **Maronite Church** off the square attest to the area's social complexion a century ago.

Midan Tahrir

South of the French Gardens lay "Frank Square", the European city's social hub. "There is nothing in Alexandria but the Frank Square and the huts of the Alexandrians," wrote Florence Nightingale in 1849. Originally the Place des Consuls, it was renamed in honour of **Mohammed Ali**, whose equestrian **statue** (by Jacques Mart; 1868) now barely stands out against the scabrous facades in the background. After the Orabi Revolt of 1882, rebels were tied to the acacias, shot and buried there by British forces. Not surprisingly, its name was changed to Liberation Square – **Midan Tahrir** – following the Revolution.

Midan Tahrir also witnessed two crucial events of the Nasser era. In October 1954, a member of the Muslim Brotherhood fired on Nasser during a public speech; the botched (perhaps staged) assassination gave Nasser an excuse to ban the Brotherhood and supplant General Naguib (who was falsely implicated in the conspiracy) as Egypt's acknowledged leader. Two years later, on the fourth anniversary of King Farouk's abdication, Nasser delivered a three-hour speech broadcast live from here on national radio, climaxing in the announcement that Egypt had taken possession of the Suez Canal; the repetition of the name "Lesseps" earlier in his peroration was actually the codeword for the operation to begin.

Sharia Salah Salem and beyond

A few streets around Midan Tahrir deserve a mention, if not a ramble. Leading off to the southeast, the erstwhile Bond Street of Alexandria (as the British conceived it), Rue Chérif Pacha, was Cavafy's birthplace; on the corner stood the Cotton Exchange that once echoed with the cries of European merchants. Renamed **Sharia Salah Salem** after a colleague of Nasser's, the street is less chic than in colonial times, but is still the place to find **antiques** and **jewellery**, much of it once owned by "foreigners" dispossessed by Nasser. Its main landmark is the Moorish-Gothic **Anglican Church of St Mark**, whose congregation includes many Sudanese.

Seven blocks further along, the building at 2 Sharia Mahmoud Azmi is associated with Durrell (who worked at a propaganda bureau there in 1942) and the **Al-Fayeds**, who founded their first trading company there (its sign remains) and went on to become international business moguls – a far cry from their impoverished childhood in Alex's Sharbangi Alley. Mohammed Al-Fayed is best known for his ownership of Harrods in London and the relationship between his son Dodi and Princess Diana. His belief that they were murdered by British Intelligence is widely shared in Egypt.

The other main thoroughfare is **Sharia Mesjid al-Attarin**, named after the **Attarine Mosque** that stands on the site of the fourth-century Church of St Athanasius, who argued the "dual nature" of Christ against his theological opponent, Arius the Monophysite. The mosque has a lacy, multi-tiered minaret, reminiscent of Al-Nasir Mohammed's mosque in Cairo, and likewise dates from the fourteenth century. It was from here that Napoleon's forces removed a seven-ton sarcophagus, thought to be Alexander's, and later surrendered it to the British Museum, which attributed it to Nectanebo I.

Further west are two reminders of the city's multi-sectarian legacy. The **Greek Orthodox Cathedral** underpins a small Hellenistic enclave, while a **Catholic Cathedral** stands aloof from the bustling junction of Mesjid al-Attarin and Abu Dardaa streets. Northwest of Midan Tahrir, grandiose European architecture gives way to smaller-scale buildings that segue into the city's **souks**. Here, the main arteries are **Sharia Nokrashi** – heaving with fruit and vegetable stalls, butchers, bakeries and hardware stores – and **Sharia Faransa** (French Street), full of shops selling clothes, cloth and dressmaking materials. The network of alleys between the two thoroughfares is known as **Zinqat as-Sittat**, "The Women's Squeeze". Before the revolution, Nokrashi was notorious for its child bordellos. In *The Alexandria Quartet*, Justine sought her kidnapped daughter here, the diplomat Mountolive was mauled by child prostitutes, and Scobie (modelled on "Bimbashi" McPherson, the prewar head of the secret police) killed his neighbours with moonshine whisky.

Anfushi, Fort Qaitbey and the Pharos

Although the **Eastern Harbour** is no longer the busy port of ancient times, its graceful curve is definitely appealing. As it sweeps around towards Qaitbey's Fort, bureaucratic monoliths from the last decades of the twentieth century give way to stately palms and weathered colonial mansions, likened by Michael Palin to "Cannes with acne". Nearer the fort, fishermen cast rods and mend nets while the fresh catch is marketed and shipwrights work on hulls in a boatyard. Walking at least some of the way along the Corniche is highly recommended, but you may wish to use minibuses or trams for longer distances.

In ancient times, a seven-league dike – the **Heptastadion** – connected Alexandria with Pharos, then an island. Allowed to silt up after the Arab conquest, the Heptastadion gradually turned into a peninsula that the newcomers built over, creating the **Anfushi quarter** (or El-Anfushi) northwest of downtown. Its Ottoman mosques and some old *mashrabiya*'d houses are the only "sights" as such, but the variety of streetlife makes this an interesting area to explore. The best strategy is to hop on tram #15, running one block inland from the Corniche, which travels past most places of interest.

The **Terbana Mosque**, 700m along, is chiefly remarkable for its antique columns – no one knows where they came from. A huge pair with Corinthian capitals supports the minaret. Lesser columns are ranged eight to an arcade within and painted gloss white; there's also some fine tiling quietly going to pot – the mosque has been subject to slapdash "improvements" ever since it was built in 1685. The black-and-red-painted brickwork on the facade is a common Delta style.

The city's foremost religious building, the **Mosque of Abu al-Abbas al-Mursi**, is located the same distance again further north. It honours the patron saint of local fishermen and sailors, a thirteenth-century Andalusian sheikh. The existing structure was built in 1938 by an Italian architect, Mario Kossi, but its keel-arched panels, elaborately carved domes and cornices look as old as the sixteenth-century original. Women are only allowed into a room at the back of the mosque.

After a visit, have a drink in the arcade across the street and watch life go by. If you're feeling adventurous, you can investigate the maze of old houses behind the mosque; otherwise, press on to Qaitbey's fort.

Fort Qaitbey and the Pharos

One tram stop after Al-Mursi's mosque, take a short walk past the fishing port and repair yard full of brightly painted boats, and you will come to the promontory bearing Sultan Qaitbey's fort and the **Alexandra Yacht Club**, which holds an annual regatta in October. **Fort Qaitbey** (daily 9am–5pm; £E20) is an Alexandrian landmark, a Toytown citadel buffeted by wind-borne spray, its flag forever rippling. Built during the 1480s and later beefed up by Mohammed Ali, it commands great views of the city and the spume-flecked

△ Artist's impression of the Pharos

Mediterranean. Within the keep there's a mosque whose minaret was blown away by the British in 1882.

The fort occupies the site of the **Pharos**, Alexandria's great lighthouse, one of the Seven Wonders of the ancient world; the Pharos transcended its practical role as a navigational aid and early-warning system, becoming synonymous with the city itself. A combination of aesthetic beauty and technological audacity, it exceeded 125m – perhaps even 150m – in height, including the statue of Zeus at its summit.

Possibly conceived by Alexander himself, the Pharos took twelve years to build under the direction of an Asiatic Greek, Sostratus, and was completed in 283 BC. Its square base contained three hundred rooms, that, according to legend, once housed the seventy rabbis who translated the Hebrew scriptures into Greek for Ptolemy Philadelphus (*c*.200 BC), producing identical texts despite having worked alone. (In reality, this Septuagint version of the Bible wasn't completed until 130 BC, and the rabbis lived in huts on the island.) It is also thought to have housed hydraulic machinery for hauling the fuel up the second, octagonal storey; otherwise, this would have been accomplished by a procession of pack mules climbing a spiral ramp. The cylindrical third storey housed the lantern, whose light is thought to have been visible 56km away. Some chroniclers also mention a "mirror" that enabled the lighthouse keepers to observe ships far out at sea; a form of lens (whose secret was lost) has been postulated.

Around 700 AD the lantern collapsed, or was demolished by a treasure-hunting caliph; the base survived unscathed and Ibn Tulun restored the second level, until an earthquake in 1303 reduced the whole structure to rubble. The northwest section of the fort's enclosure walls incorporates some huge red-granite pillars that might have been part of the Pharos.

Since the 1990s, divers from the Centre d'Etudes Alexandrines have located over 2500 stone objects **underwater** at depths of 6–8m. These include the head of a colossus of Ptolemy as pharaoh and the base of an obelisk inscribed to Seti I, which have been brought to the surface; and several **monoliths**, weighing 50–70 tonnes apiece and embedded in the rock by the impact of their fall, that can only have belonged to the lighthouse. Five hundred metres offshore **wrecks** of Greek and Roman trading vessels laden with amphorae of wine and fish sauce have been found, and over fifty **anchors** of all eras – more pieces in the mosaic picture of ancient Alexandria that's emerging from surveys of the Eastern Harbour (see below). See p.603 for details of **diving** in the harbour.

The Anfushi Tombs, Ras el-Tin and the Western Harbour

Tram #15 runs on to the Ras el-Tin ("Cape of Figs") quarter, where you can alight at Sharia Ras el-Tin to find the rock-cut **Anfushi Tombs** (daily 9am–4.30pm; £E20), uncovered in 1901. Sited in pairs around a staircase leading to an open court, the four tombs are painted to simulate costly alabaster or marble and belonged to third-century BC Greek Alexandrians who adopted Ancient Egyptian funerary practices. The right-hand set has pictures of Egyptian gods, warships and feluccas; a Greek workman has also immortalized his mate's virtues in graffiti. Both the left-hand tombs have vestibules with benches for the deceased's relatives to eat and drink in their memory. Hang around and a keeper should appear to unlock the tombs.

It's possible that the necropolis extends beneath the gardens of **Ras el-Tin Palace**, overlooking the Western Harbour. The palace was built for Mohammed Ali, its audience hall sited so that he could watch his new fleet at anchor while reclining on his divan. Rebuilt and turned into the summer seat of government under Fouad I, it witnessed **King Farouk's abdication** on July 26, 1952. "What you have done to me I was getting ready to do to you," the king informed General Naguib, adding, "Your task will be difficult. It is not easy to govern Egypt." Wearing an admiral's uniform, Farouk departed on the royal yacht to a 21-gun salute; with him went the royal family, an English nursemaid, three Albanian bodyguards, a dog trainer and 244 trunks. The site is now off-limits as the palace is a Presidential residence; for a glimpse of the palace's Moorish **interior**, visit Ⓦ www.presidency.gov.eg. In the days when Pharos was an island, a Temple of Neptune stood here.

The **Western Harbour** has been Egypt's main port and naval base since the mid-nineteenth century, and witnessed the boldest Italian commando raid of World War II. On December 18, 1941, three manned torpedoes penetrated the harbour to lay charges beneath the battleships HMS *Valiant* and HMS *Queen Elizabeth*. The British pretended that the ships were still afloat when their hulls were resting on the sea bed. It took sixteen months' repairs before HMS *Valiant* was back in action; the *Queen Elizabeth* is still on the bottom. Unfortunately, diving isn't allowed in this naval harbour.

Inland, blocks of *shoonas* or warehouses with their foreign names still faintly visible are given over to the **cotton industry**, "greasy fluff" and rags littering the streets as in Forster's day. Another major industry is smuggling, for which the **port** is notorious; its 62 quays handle over 5000 ships every year, carrying about 75 percent of Egypt's import and export trade.

On the way back you could enjoy lunch at one of the many **fish restaurants** on Sharia Safar Pasha, between Ras el-Tin and Anfushi, or *Kadoura* along the Corniche back towards the centre (see p.599).

The submerged Royal Quarters

The opposite jaw of the Eastern Harbour is formed by a narrow promontory called **Silsileh** ("the Chain"), that's occupied by the navy and out of bounds. Aside from being the site of Naguib Mahfouz's fictional *Pension Miramar*, its interest lies in the **underwater** discoveries made since 1996 by Franck Goddio and the National French Centre for Studies, whose survey of the sea bed five metres down has revealed extensive submerged **ruins**, including granite columns, votive statues, sphinxes, pavements, ceramics and a pier from the **ancient Royal Quarters** of Alexandria. In 1998 they hauled up a sample to show the world: the largest and most striking objects were a metre-tall, black-granite figure of the goddess Isis holding a Canopic jar, and an intact 380kg diorite sphinx with the face of what is thought to be Ptolemy XII, Cleopatra's father. Samples of their salvage can be seen on Goddio's website, ⓦwww.underwaterdiscovery.org.

Goddio was quick to claim that they had found the site of **Cleopatra's palace** on the island of Antirrhodos (where she met her death), which had been plunged into the sea by a series of earthquakes and tidal waves some 1600 years ago. The Egyptians enthused about the idea of creating the world's first underwater museum – with Plexiglas tunnels that would allow visitors to stroll around below the surface. However, many archeologists felt that the site of the palace and the provenance of the ruins had only been tentatively established, until Goddio found inscriptions verifying his claim. As a marine treasure-hunter rather than an archeologist by profession, he has been criticized as a gadfly dashing from one project to another without completing any – yet still he turns up finds, not just in the Eastern Harbour, but also at Abu Qir (see p.598). His secret weapon is a nuclear resonance magnetometer that can detect likely antiquities through anomalies in the Earth's magnetic field, and plots them on a digital map fixed by GPS satellites. But though Goddio goes from triumph to triumph, the idea of an underwater museum has been quietly shelved after it was realized that the algal blooms would render Plexiglas tunnels opaque in summer.

Diving, however, is alluringly feasible, with visibility at its best (from 7–20 metres) from April to June and September to December. As well as seven or eight sphinxes (one 5m long), a giant obelisk and numerous columns, divers can see the wreck of an **Italian fighter** that was shot down and crashed on the ruins; the pilot's flight mask is fused into the rock. Contact Alexandra Dive (see p.603) for all arrangements.

The Bibliotheca Alexandrina

On the mainland beyond Silsileh, another wonder of antiquity has been resurrected in a new form. The **Bibliotheca Alexandrina** (Mon, Wed, Thurs & Sun 9am–7pm, Fri & Sat 3–7pm; ⓦwww.bibalex.gov.eg) resembles a giant discus embedded in the ground at an angle, representing a second sun rising beside the Mediterranean. Pictograms, hieroglyphs and letters from every alphabet are carved on its exterior, evoking the diversity of knowledge embodied in the ancient library and the aspirations of the new one.

The project to create a new Bibliotheca Alexandrina was approved by UNESCO in 1987 and cost some $355 million, mainly met by Egypt, Saudi Arabia, the Emirates and Iraq. Repeated setbacks delayed its inauguration ceremony until 2002, but now that it is open, it is recognized as one of Alexandria's must-visits, in particular for its architecture and museums. The complex, designed by a Norwegian–Austrian team of architects and built by Egyptian, British and Italian contractors, also includes a cultural centre (in the block opposite the entrance to the library).

Visiting the library

On the inland side facing Sharia Bur Said, a **colossus of Ptolemy II** dredged from the Eastern Harbour watches over a cloakroom (daily 11am–7pm) where all bags must be checked in, and kiosks selling **tickets** for the library (£E10; no children under 6), two museums inside it (£E20 each), and a combo ticket

Ancient Alexandria's library

Founded shortly after the city itself, on the advice of Ptolemy I's counselor Demetrius of Phalerum, in antiquity Alexandria's library stood beside the Mouseion in the heart of the city (see p.584). Dedicated to "the writings of all nations", it welcomed scholars and philosophers and supported research and debates. By law, all ships docking at Alexandria were obliged to allow any scrolls on board to be copied, if they were of interest. By the mid-first century BC it held 532,800 manuscripts (all catalogued by the Head Librarian, Callimachus), and later spawned a subsidiary attached to the **Temple of Serapis**; the two were known as the **"Mother"** and **"Daughter" libraries**, and together contained perhaps 700,000 scrolls (equivalent to about 100,000 printed books today).

As many as 40,000 (or even 400,000) were burned during Julius Caesar's assault on the city in 48 BC, when he supported Cleopatra against her brother Ptolemy XIII; as compensation, Mark Antony gave her the entire contents of the Pergamum Library in Greece (200,000 scrolls). But it was Christian mobs that destroyed this vast storehouse of "pagan" knowledge, torching the Mother Library in 293 and the Daughter Library in 391, though medieval Europe later mythologized its destruction as proof of Arab barbarism. An apocryphal tale had the Muslim leader Amr pronouncing: "If these writings of the Greeks agree with the Koran they are useless, and need not be preserved; if they disagree, they are pernicious, and ought to be destroyed."

covering them all (£E48; no student discount). **Photography** is permitted in the Antiquities and Manuscript museums (£E20; no flashes; video £E150), but not in the library itself. You can join a free **tour** in English just inside the entrance (at 11.15am, noon, 1.30pm, 2.15pm, 3pm, 3.45pm, 4.30pm and 5.15pm), or wander at will through the vast **reading area** – a stunning cascade of levels upheld by stainless-steel pillars suggestive of the columns in pharaonic temples. **Membership** (£E110 monthly; students & disabled £E55) requires ID, a photo and proof of address. **Events** and **exhibitions** are advertised in the lobby.

Start with the permanent **Impressions of Alexandria** exhibit (free), whose maps, engravings and photographs show how the city has evolved since antiquity and the ruins left after the British bombardment of 1882. You can then move onto the intriguing **Antiquities Museum** in the basement (Mon & Fri 1–7pm, Wed, Thurs & Sun 9am–7pm, Sat 11am–7pm). As well as a giant head of Serapis, a headless ibis statue and a black basalt Isis salvaged from Herakleion, it displays Thoth effigies from Tuna el-Gabel and Hermopolis, XI Dynasty model boats, and parts of two mosaic floors unearthed during the building of the present library, one depicting a dog beside a brass cup, the other a gladiator locked in combat. Back on the main entrance level, the **Manuscripts Museum** (same opening hours as the Antiquities Museum) is less intriguing, with its ancient scrolls and antiquarian tomes so dimly lit you can barely see any details. Lastly there's the **Planetarium**, a Death Star-like spheroid on the plaza facing the sea, whose shows *Cosmic Voyage*, *Human Body*, *Oasis in Space* and *Return to the Red Planet* (£E25) are the most child-friendly part of the complex (℡03/483-9999 ext 1739 for details).

Pompey's Pillar and the Catacombs

The poor **Karmous quarter** in the southwest of the city contains two of Alex's best-known ancient monuments. **Pompey's Pillar** can be reached by taxi (£E5–7) or bus #709 or tram #16 from Midan St Katerina. From Pompey's Pillar you can either ride the tram or walk on to the **Catacombs of Kom es-Shoqafa**. If you've just arrived in Egypt, the poverty of the slums that lie between the two might seem shocking. Tram #16 takes an extremely circuitous route back to its depot – returning to the centre, it's best to get off at Masr Station and walk from there.

Pompey's Pillar

Pompey's Pillar towers 25m above a limestone ridge and garden, surrounded by the fruits and pits of excavations. Despite its name, the red-granite column was actually raised to honour the Roman emperor Diocletian, who threatened to massacre the dissenting populace "until their blood reached his horse's knees", but desisted when his mount slipped and bloodied itself prematurely. The column is often erroneously described as coming from the **Temple of Serapis** that once stood nearby. Begun by the Greek architect Parmeniscos in the reign of Ptolemy III (246–221 BC), it rivalled the Soma and Caesareum in magnificence. Cleopatra later installed a "Daughter Library" of 42,800, which outlived the Mother Library by almost a century, only to be destroyed by Christian mobs in 391 AD.

Three subterranean galleries where the sacred Apis bulls were interred (see "Saqqara", p.226) are all that remain: you'll find them west of the ridge, which also features a Nilometer, three sphinxes (originally from Heliopolis) and some underground cisterns. Overall, however, the **site** (daily 9am–5pm, Ramadan 9am–3pm; £E15) is pretty disappointing considering what used to exist here.

The Catacombs of Kom es-Shoqafa

One of Alexandria's most memorable monuments, the **Catacombs of Kom es-Shoqafa** (daily 9am–5pm, Ramadan until 3pm; £E25), combine spookiness and kitsch, never mind their prosaic Arabic name, "Mound of Shards". To get there, turn right around the corner after leaving Pompey's Pillar and follow the road straight on for five minutes; the entrance to the catacombs is on the left 150m beyond a small square. Cameras must be left here, as photography is not allowed inside.

Egypt's largest known Roman burial site, the catacombs were discovered in 1900 when a donkey disappeared through the ground. The triple-level complex, hewn 35m into solid rock, is reached via a spiral stairway, past the shaft down which bodies were lowered. From the vestibule with its well and scalloped niches, you can squeeze through a fissure (right) into a lofty **hall** riddled with loculi, or family burial niches, each once sealed with a stone slab on which were painted the names and ages of the deceased. Scholars named it the Hall of Caracalla after the Roman emperor who massacred Alexandrian youths at a review in 215 AD. In the **Triclinium** (left), relatives toasted the dead from stone couches. When the first archeologists entered the chamber they found wine jars and tableware, and recently murals, only visible under ultraviolet light.

But the main attraction is the **Central Tomb** downstairs, whose vestibule is guarded by reliefs of bearded serpents with Medusa-headed shields. Inside are comically muscle-bound statues of Sobek and Anubis wearing Roman armour, dating from the second century AD when "the old faiths began to merge and melt" (Forster). Water has flooded the **Goddess Nemesis Hall** (still accessible) and submerged the lowest level, hastening the catacombs' decay. For more information, buy Jean-Yves Empereur's excellently illustrated *A Short Guide to the Catacombs of Kom es-Shoqafa*.

Moharrem Bey, Bab Sharq and Smouha

East of Karmous and southeast of El-Manshiya, **Moharrem Bey** is a once-affluent suburb of mansions and villas, now derelict and slummy. The district grew up in the mid-nineteenth century after the completion of the **Mahmudiya**

Canal, dug on the orders of Mohammed Ali at a cost of twenty thousand lives. Mohammed Ali died here in 1849, a year after being deposed for senility. The quarter was named after his son-in-law – the city's first governor – and was once home to Alexandria's mercantile elite. Its charm endured for a century, the final decades of which were embellished by the presence of residents like Cavafy (before he moved to Rue Lepsius) and **Durrell**. In 1943, Durrell and Eve Cohen rented the top floor of the turreted Ambron **house** at 19 Sharia al-Ma'amoun, where he wrote *Prospero's Cell* and *The Dark Labyrinth* (the *Alexandria Quartet* came later). Subsequently leased to the painter and sculptor Effat Nagui and her husband and fellow artist Sa'ad el-Khadem, the house is now owned by developers who've built ugly flats in the grounds and allowed the house to rot for nearly a decade. To see if it's still standing, catch a taxi (£E5) from Masr Station down Sharia Moharrem Bey (about 3km).

Bab Sharq

East of El-Manshiya, the affluent **Bab Sharq** district can be easily approached from the Quartier Grec (see p.585) or en route to the Corniche beaches (see overleaf). Its nexus is **Midan Khartoum**, an L-shaped park whose Ptolemaic **column** (erected to celebrate Britain's recapture of Khartoum in 1898) is a local landmark at the junction of Sharia Horriya and the Suez Canal Road.

Flanking this on two sides are the hilly **Shallalat Gardens**, ablaze with scarlet flame trees over summer. Their nineteenth-century French designer utilized remnants of the Arab city walls, Mohammed Ali's **Nahaseen Fort** and the Farkha Canal to create rockeries and ornamental ponds. Here, E.M. Forster had his first date with Mohammed el-Adl, a tram conductor whom he met at Ramleh in the winter of 1916–17. Before then, Forster's sexual passions had never been reciprocated. The racial, class and sexual barriers that their relationship challenged underlie the finale of *A Passage to India*, which Forster was struggling with when he learned of Mohammed's death from tuberculosis in 1922. Near the northwest corner of the Gardens is the **Ibn el-Nabih Cistern**, whose three levels are upheld by antique columns salvaged from older structures. Of the 700 underground reservoirs reported by the historian El-Makrisi, this is the only one that's accessible today (dawn–dusk; free).

Beyond the Suez Canal Road lies a sprawling necropolis of high-walled **cemeteries** consecrated to diverse faiths. Though most of the tombs date from the nineteenth or twentieth centuries, burials have occurred here since ancient times. Professor Faouzi Fakharani of Alexandria University thinks that a marble chamber found beneath the Greek cemetery may belong to a royal tomb, perhaps even that of Alexander – a theory that the Centre d'Etudes Alexandrines is investigating using ground-penetrating radar. Like the Greek compound, the Coptic, Catholic, Armenian, Maronite, Uniate, Protestant and Jewish cemeteries are full of lavish mausolea and sculptures, from the heyday of European supremacy. The necropolis extends nearly as far as St Mark's College in Shatby, in relation to which the Jewish cemetery is nearest.

During summer, affluent citizens hang out at the **Alexandria Sporting Club**, 1km east along Tariq Gamal Abdel Nasser. Its pool and tennis courts are the best in the city; polo and golf or billiards and movies at night-time are just some of the activities and entertainments (see p.603). All eastbound trams stop at the Sporting Club.

Smouha

The **Smouha** district in the southern suburbs is a magnet for wealthy Alexandrians. The **Zahran and Smouha Malls**, 300–400m from Sidi Gaber station, and the **Green Plaza Mall** and **City Center** superstore (run by the French chain Carrefour) by the 14th May Bridge, are popular hangouts. Smouha is also home to the **International Garden** and the **Jungle** theme park, full of attractions for children.

The district is named after the Baghdad-born Jewish architect Joseph Smouha, who moved to Egypt in the 1920s. His Smouha City (as it was originally called) was the local equivalent of Cairo's Heliopolis, a modern suburb for the upper-middle classes. Though all the "foreigners" were dispossessed by Nasser, their legacies – and names – survive in present-day Alexandria. The **Zoological Gardens** (closed at the time of writing as a precaution against bird flu) were opened in 1907. Next door, diverse trees planted by Khedive Ismail have grown to maturity in the **Nouzha Gardens** (daily: summer 9am–9pm; winter 9am–sunset; £E1), where military bands once played.

Nearby, flocks of egrets nest in the vine-entangled trees of the **Antoniaidis Gardens** (same hours; £E2). Embellished with Classical statuary, they were once the private grounds of a wealthy Greek family. In ancient times, the Nouzha area was a residential suburb inhabited by the likes of Callimachus (310–240 BC), the Head Librarian of the Bibliotheca Alexandrina. It was around here, too, that Amr's Muslim forces camped before entering the city in 641 AD.

Corniche beaches

Alexandria's beaches are an overworked asset. Hardly a square metre of sand goes unclaimed during high season, when literally millions of Egyptians descend on the city. Before June the beaches furthest out are relatively uncrowded, with predominantly local users; however, Alexandrians alone can number hundreds on Fridays, Saturdays and public holidays – days to be avoided.

The popularity of the beaches doesn't imply Western-style beach culture. On most you'll rarely see any woman past the age of puberty wearing a swimsuit – they wander into the sea fully clad. The only places that Western women can swim without the hindrance of a *galabiyya*, or a lot of attention, are the Venezia and Palestine beaches at Montazah (see p.597). Most beaches have parasols and chairs for rent, and sometimes public showers, while fish restaurants, soft-drink and snack vendors are ubiquitous.

The chief attractions on land are the **Royal Jewellery Museum** in Glym (if it's reopened), the **Mahmoud Said Museum** in San Stefano and the extensive grounds of the **Montazah** palace, further along the coast. Many visitors go beyond to **Abu Qir** for its seafood – though you can eat just as well closer in to Alexandria.

Travelling eastwards past the Corniche beaches looks simple on the map, but isn't so easy in practice. For the initial stretch as far as Cleopatra beach, minibuses #735, #736 and #768 run a block inland, and tram #2 three to five blocks in, leaving you with only the stops – mostly named after beaches – to go on. For transport beyond Cleopatra, see p.576. As most of the **city beaches** amount to an arc of sand overlooked by hotels and restaurants, they're hard to differentiate without a landmark in the vicinity. The following account includes some places a fair way inland.

Shatby to Stanley

The district known as **Shatby** (or Chatby) is overshadowed by **St Mark's College**, a massive, red-brick, neo-Baroque edifice whose dome is visible from afar. Founded to educate the city's Christian elite, it now forms part of Alexandria University. On the far side of Sharia Bur Said is the grandly named **Shatby**

Necropolis (daily 9am–4.30pm, Ramadan 9am–3pm; £E6), a small pit exposing some rock-cut ossuaries and sarcophagi from the third century BC, which can be viewed for free by peering over the wall of the nearby youth hostel. Shatby **beach** looks fit to spawn the "Swamp Thing", and the adjacent **Camp Cesar** is no better for its association with Julius Caesar (who camped here during the battle that left Cleopatra at his mercy). Hitler's deputy Führer, Rudolf Hess, was born in 1896 in neighbouring **Ibrahimiya**. When Alexandria was bombed in World War II, residents sheltered in the underground Roman cisterns between Ibrahimiya and Sidi Gaber.

Shortly before Cleopatra beach, tram #2 turns further inland, visiting **Sidi Gaber Station** and passing through the **Bacos** quarter where Gamal Abdel Nasser was born on January 15, 1918. He was 11 years old when he attended his first nationalist demonstration, got truncheoned and was jailed overnight. Tram #1 runs closer to **Cleopatra** beach, which has no connection with the lady herself, although the nearby **Roushdi** district was the site of Nikopolis, which Octavian (or Augustus Caesar, as he then styled himself) founded because he hated living in Alexandria. The British also built barracks and houses there, in the districts they named Stanley, Glym and San Stefano. Today, Roushdi is the centre of expat life in Alex, and many foreigners rent flats here – but a vestige of its origins remains in the form of the **Mustafa Kamel Necropolis** (daily 9am–4pm; £E20). Its four tombs, discovered in 1933, date from the second century BC; two are upheld by Doric columns and one contains a mural of a horseman. To get there, catch tram #2 from Ramleh to Roushdi tram station and walk towards the Corniche along Sharia al-Mo'asker al-Romani.

Travelling along the Corniche by minibus or taxi, traffic crosses the **Stanley Bridge**, opened in 2006, whose suspension towers mimic the Turko-Florentine architecture at Montazah. From the bridge, which takes only eastbound traffic, you can see Stanley Bay's tiers of concrete sun terraces and bathing cabins, built by the British in the 1920s.

The Royal Jewellery Museum

The **Royal Jewellery Museum**, at 27 Sharia Ahmed Yehia (daily 9am–5pm, Ramadan Mon–Thurs, Sat & Sun 9am–3pm, Fri 9–11.30am & 1.30–4pm, but check with tourist office first, as it may not have reopened after a recent refurbishment; £E35), is three blocks in from the Corniche, between Glym and San Stefano; it's also a short walk from the El-Fenoun el-Gamilia or Qasr el-Safa stops on the #2 tram line. The museum is housed in a mansion built for Mohammed Ali's granddaughter Princess Fatima el-Zaharaa (1903–83) and her husband Ali Heider, and is as splendidly vulgar as the treasures on display. Among the highlights are Mohammed Ali's diamond-inlaid snuffbox, King Farouk's gold chess-set, a platinum crown with 2159 diamonds, and his diamond-studded gardening tools. The main gallery downstairs is lined with stained-glass cameos of courtly love in eighteenth-century France, while images of Provençal farmers, milkmaids and food decorate the service corridors. Upstairs are the wildest his'n'hers bathrooms – hers with tiled murals of nymphs bathing in a waterfall, his with scenes of Côte d'Azur fishermen.

The Mahmoud Said Museum

Another treat in this part of town is the **Mahmoud Said Museum**, on Sharia Mahmoud Said Pasha (daily 10am–6pm; £E10): take tram #1 or #2 to Gianaclis (the stop after the Jewellery Museum), cross the tracks, head up the steps to the raised road and turn right. A judge who painted as a hobby, Mahmoud Said (1897–1964) was the first Egyptian artist to receive a state prize, yet disliked official commissions such as the wall-sized *Inaugural Ceremony of the Suez Canal* that greets visitors to the museum. He preferred to paint pensive, sensual women – *The Siren of Alexandria*, *Egyptian Country-Woman* and *Nabawiya With a Flowered Dress* – or landscapes of Alexandria, Lebanon and Stockholm.

Upstairs, six rooms are devoted to the brothers Seif (1906–79) and Adham (1908–59) Wanly, who founded the first Egyptian artists' studio in 1942 and taught Fine Arts at Alexandria University after the revolution. Seif was an Expressionist who depicted such bourgeois delights as casinos, nightclubs and horse-racing, with a prolific output including three thousand oil paintings, more than eighty thousand sketches, and theatre and opera sets; while Adham was into Cubism, abstraction and Socialist Realism, producing such polemical works as *Hunger*, *Peace* and *Palestine*. There are also two rooms showcasing the work of contemporary local artists such as Myriam Abdel Alim, Magda Sa'd el-Din and Abdel Hadfi al-Gazzar, as well as the odd abstract by Farouk Hosni, Egypt's Minister of Culture since 1987.

Sidi Bishr to Montazah

Fourteen kilometres east of the centre is the suburb of **Sidi Bishr**, served by minibuses from Midan Sa'ad Zaghloul in the centre, or Sidi Gaber. Sidi Bishr's mosque stands between two beaches with the same name, just east of which are the "Spouting Rocks" of **Bir Mas'ud**, where the waves rush into cavities to expel jets of water. Here the ancient Alexandrians, delighting in gadgetry, placed water-powered horns and mills, and the geometrician Hero invented the world's first coin-operated vending machine (dispensing holy water) in the first century AD.

Beyond Sidi Bishr, the Miami Casino gives way to two more sandy inlets, **Asafra** and **Mandara**, and, a couple of kilometres beyond, **Montazah**, the city's walled pleasure-grounds. The gates opposite the *Montazah Sheraton* give access to the well-tended grounds (daily 9am–midnight; £E5, £E6 Fri & Sun), with brass lamps, a clock tower, a bowling alley, and the flamboyant Turko-Florentine **Haramlik Palace** (closed to the public). Commissioned by King Fouad and designed by Ernesto Verruchi Bey, the palace served as a Red Cross hospital during World War I, and it was here that E.M. Forster worked as a nurse. It was also from here that King Farouk fled to Ras-el Tin before abdicating. The building was restored by Sadat, at a cost of £E7 million, and is now a presidential residence and guesthouse.

The largest of Montazah's bays is rimmed by the sandy **Venezia Beach** (£E10.50 admission; £E20 with a beach chair and umbrella), where dress standards for women are fairly relaxed. A promontory ending in an ornate "Turkish" **Belvedere** and a **lighthouse** encloses the bay, providing a sheltered spot for **windsurfing** and **snorkelling** in summer.

Inland stands the smaller **El Salamlek Palace**, built for the Austrian mistress of Khedive Abbas and now one of two luxury **hotels** in the grounds of Montazah (see p.578). **Palestine Beach**, attached to the *Helnan Palestine Hotel*, levies an admission charge of £E150 per person, including £E50 worth of food and drink.

Ma'amoura and Canopus

Round the headland to the east, **Ma'amoura** is a private enclave of holiday flats and villas, charging visitors £E3 admission before they've even glimpsed the **beach**, access to which costs a further £E20. Its sands are cleaner than most, but modest dress is recommended for women. The main beach entrance is off a roundabout on the Abu Qir road, about 1km east of the *Sheraton*. The #736 minibus will deliver you to the *Ma'amoura Palace Hotel*, within the enclave, which has its own private beach (£E25 admission).

Past Ma'amoura, the road runs inland of a swathe of military and naval bases, occupying the ancient site of **Canopus** – not that anything significant remains of this once-great Delta city, which flourished when a branch of the Nile reached the sea by the nearby "Canopic Mouth" but declined as this dried up and Alexandria arose. Classical mythology has it that Canopus was founded by a Greek navigator returning from the Trojan war, whom the locals later worshipped in the form of a jar with a human head. Nineteenth-century archeologists bestowed the title **Canopic jars** on similar receptacles used to preserve mummies' viscera. Each organ had its own protective deity (a minor son of Horus) whose visage adorned the stopper (human heads went out of fashion late in the XVIII Dynasty). Even after XXI Dynasty embalmers began replacing organs in the mummies, the practice of leaving Canopic jars in tombs continued. In 2004, marine archeologists found life-sized statues of Ptolemaic rulers and thousands of bronze pots, chandeliers and incense burners on the sea bed off Canopus.

Abu Qir

Beyond the naval bases is **Abu Qir** (pronounced Abu Ear), a former fishing village turned high-rise suburb, where Alexandrians come to enjoy its **beach** and outdoor **seafood restaurants** (see p.599).

Abu Qir is the site of two historic **battles**. Admiral Nelson's defeat of the French fleet at Abu Qir Bay (1798) effectively scuppered Napoleon's dream of an eastern empire and went down in British history as the Battle of the Nile, inspiring Mrs Hemans to write, "The boy stood on the burning deck …". Though the two fleets were evenly matched in numbers, Admiral Bruey had his ships cabled together in shallow water when Nelson's fleet charged them amidships, inflicting carnage at close quarters. The French lost eleven ships and seventeen thousand men, the English two ships and 218 sailors. In 1998–99, Franck Goddio's divers found the **wrecks** of the French flagship *L'Orient*, the *Sérieuse* and *Artémise* at a depth of 11m, 8km offshore. But Bonaparte had his revenge, when, in 1799, he personally led ten thousand cavalry against fifteen thousand Turks landed by the Royal Navy, pushing them back into the sea.

In 2001 Goddio's team announced the discovery of **Herakleion**, the fabled ancient entrepôt to Egypt that fell into the sea 1300 years ago. Buried by sediment for centuries in Abu Qir Bay, its identity was confirmed by a stele inscribed with the city's name, erected by Nectanebo I, and the pink-granite naos believed to belong to the temple of Heracles-Khonsu seen by Herodotus when he visited Herakleion in the fifth century BC. Divers also found three colossal statues of the Nile-god Hapy; in ancient times, the city stood at the mouth of a branch of the river.

Diving at these sites is a fantastic experience that Alexandra Dive (see p.603) can organize, though the bureaucracy involved requires four to five days' notice and at least four paying customers (or fewer willing to pay more) on each trip.

Eating and drinking

Alexandria can't match Cairo for culinary variety, but it beats the capital when it comes to **seafood and Greek restaurants** – and when these pall you can always fall back on Egyptian favourites like *shawarmas*, pizzas, *fuul* and falafel. **Coffee houses**, too, are an Alex speciality, and there are some good **bars** if you know where to look.

In addition, there are Western **fast-food outlets** all over town. *McDonald's* (daily 10am–11pm) is near the top of Sharia Safiya Zaghloul, near *Kentucky*

Fried Chicken and *Baskin-Robbins* (both daily 10am–2am) on the corner of Midan Ramleh; there's another *McDonald's* at Montazah, and a further branch of *KFC* on the Corniche in Roushdi.

Downtown venues appear on the map on pp.580–581, but there are also some recommendations far along the Corniche (marked on the city plan on pp.574–575) or in the western suburb of Agami.

Restaurants and cafés

The following establishments more or less represent the culinary and budgetary spectrum. Phone numbers are only given where reservations are advisable. Unless stated otherwise, credit cards are not accepted.

Downtown

Al-Shark Sharia al-Bursa al-Qadima. Serves kebab by the kilo and traditional Egyptian dishes such as *fatta* with mutton, rice with gizzards, and baked macaroni, to eat indoors or take away. Popular and inexpensive.

China House *Hotel Cecil*, Midan Sa'ad Zaghloul ☎03/487-7173. Nobody ever came to Alex to eat Chinese food, but if you're hankering for some, the chicken dumplings or grilled beef with garlic sauce are the best dishes on the menu. Takes all major cards. Daily 1pm–midnight.

Denis 1 Sharia Ibn Basaam, off Midan Ramleh. Faded 1950s-style fish bar where you select your fish or *calamari* from the freezer. A meal with a beer costs around £E40. Daily 10am–midnight.

Malek es-Samaan Off Sharia Mesjid al-Attarin. Look for the sign with a picture of a bird to find this humble open-air eatery in a yard that hosts a clothes market by day. Delicious spit-roast stuffed quail is all they serve. Daily 8pm–1am (or later).

Mohammed Ahmed 17 Sharia Shakor Pasha, off Sa'ad Zaghloul. One of the cheapest places for a takeaway or a quick meal downtown, it serves tasty *fuul*, falafel, and other vegetarian Egyptian dishes, with menus in English. Daily 6am–1am.

Further out

Abu Ashraf 28 Sharia Safar Pasha, Anfushi. Accessible by tram #15, this street is full of fish and kebab restaurants, tempting passers-by with their outdoor grills. *Abu Ashraf* is dearer than most and devoted to seafood, which is always excellent. Try the sea bass stuffed with garlic and herbs or the creamy shrimp *kishk* (casserole). Daily 24hr.

Cordon Rouge Green Plaza Mall, 14th May Bridge, Smouha. This slick, fairly pricey Mediterranean-style restaurant-cum-bar is popular with locals and expats. The menu features pasta, salads, grills and cocktails. Daily noon–2am.

Fish Market Sharia 26th July, Anfushi ☎03/480-5119. Sited above the *Tikka Grill*, this posh seafood restaurant has a/c and a fine view of the harbour. The mandatory salad platter (£E9 per person) is a meal in itself; wine and beer are available, though not listed on the menu. Daily 1pm–1am.

Greek Club Sharia Qasr Qaitbey, Anfushi (see map p.574). A good place to tuck into grilled squid or fish, *mezze* or moussaka, the *Greek Club* has spacious rooms and a large terrace that catches the afternoon breeze from the harbour. Daily noon–11pm.

Kadoura Sharia 26th July. An Alexandrian institution, *Kadoura* (pronounced Adoura) is quite scruffy, but great for seafood; all orders come with salad, rice and dips. If taking a taxi, make sure the driver knows you want this branch rather than the old one further inland. Expect to pay about £E50 for a meal. Daily noon–midnight.

Samakmak 42 Qasr Ras el-Tin, Anfushi ☎03/481-1560. Owned by retired belly-dancer Zizi Salem, this upscale fish place is renowned for its crab *tageen*, crayfish, and spaghetti with clams. In the summer you can eat outdoors in a large tent. Daily noon–midnight.

Seagull Sharia Agami, Al-Max ☎03/445-5575. Designed like a castle, and marking the spot where Napoleon landed in 1798, *Seagull* serves excellent seafood, and fruit and vegetables from its own farm. With a small zoo, a playground and pony rides, it's especially recommended for those with kids. Daily 10am–midnight.

Tikka Grill Underneath the *Fish Market*, Anfushi ☎03/547-4338. Plush surroundings and great service, with a free salad bar – a shame their tandoori grills and curries are so bland. Serves alcohol. Daily 1pm–1am.

Zephyrion Abu Qir beach. Fronted by a cactus garden, *Zephyrion* (Greek for "sea breeze") is the most identifiable of Abu Qir's seafood spots (some simply tables on the beach) and serves alcohol. Daily noon–midnight.

Coffee houses and patisseries

Before the Revolution, Alexandria's **coffee houses** and **patisseries** were the hub of bourgeois society. Artists, writers and socialites mingled and pursued affairs in such salons as *Athineos*, *The Trianon* and *Pastroudis*, where Durrell first met Eve Cohen. Since then some have closed (including *Pastroudis*) and others depend on tourists or a loyal, dwindling clientele of elderly Egyptian gentlemen. Younger Alexandrians prefer modern, Western-style places like *Bistrot* and *Coffee Roastery* or the terraced cafés in the Green Plaza Mall and other malls in Smouha (see p.594). For nocturnal types, there are **24-hour** coffee shops in the *Cecil* and *Montazah Sheraton* hotels. If you're into sipping tea surrounded by guys slapping down backgammon counters or dominoes between lung-charring tokes on *sheeshas*, there are dozens of traditional **Arab cafés** (*'ahwas*) in the sidestreets off Sharia Sa'ad Zaghloul.

Downtown

Athineos Midan Ramleh. Take a look inside, but don't eat there; its cakes are as flyblown as its classical motifs and mirrors, and the service is awful. Check out the gilded friezes and columns in the restaurant upstairs – the entrance is around the corner on the seafront. Daily 8am–midnight.

Bistrot 6 Sharia Fouad. One of the new breed of cafés, serving salads, sandwiches, tasty pasta dishes and fresh juices, with a pastry corner for breakfast and a shady terrace frequented by courting couples. Daily 9am–10pm.

Brazilian Coffee Store Corner of Nabi Daniel and Sa'ad Zaghloul, near the tourist office. Newly refurbished, with seating upstairs, this popular breakfast spot has an antique coffee-mill and a glass map of Brazil from 1929. Daily 6.30am–midnight.

Café de la Vite Off Sharia Horriya. A cosy coffee-house with ethno-arthouse decor, quiet by day but busy in the evenings, as people drop in after seeing a film or a performance at the nearby Opera House. Daily 11am–11pm.

Coffee Roastery 48 Sharia Fouad ☎ 03/483-4363. Come for the preppy MTV ambience and karaoke (Wed from 9.30pm; reservation required), as well as great smoothies and nonalcoholic cocktails, though the fajitas, salads and melts are disappointing. Daily 7.30am–1am.

Délices Between Midan and Sharia Sa'ad Zaghloul. Less inviting since they smartened it up, junked the teak bar and installed air-conditioning, but the tables outside have a fine view, and the cakes are as good as you'll get in Alex. They also serve savouries, soft drinks and beer (which must be drunk indoors). Daily 7am–11pm.

Sofianopoulo Coffee Store 18 Sharia Sa'ad Zaghloul. A vintage stand-up coffee shop furnished with silver grinders and allegorical statues. Six days a week they serve excellent cappuccino and croissants; on Sunday the only thing they sell is coffee beans. Daily 9am–11pm.

Trianon Corner of Sa'ad Zaghloul and Ramleh. The swankiest of Alexandria's patisseries boasts gilt columns and a splendidly ornate restaurant, whose food is rubbish. Stick to the Continental breakfast, pizzas, flambé dishes or alcohol. Daily 7am–midnight.

Further out

Classique 60 Sharia 26th July. This swanky new patisserie has a sumptuous array of European gateaux and Middle Eastern pastries, and is nonsmoking throughout. Daily 10am–11pm.

Drinking

Although Alex is the centre of Egypt's wine and spirits industry (the vineyards are at Gianaclis, near Lake Maryut), **bars** have a low profile. *Monty's Bar* (daily noon–2am) on the first floor of the *Hotel Cecil* is an anodyne place to sip beer or cocktails; if you're going to pay top prices, the *Fouad Bar* (daily 11am–4am) in the *El Salamlek Palace Hotel* at Montazah is plusher, with piano music in the evenings (smart dress required). But foreign residents and local drinkers tend to gather at the more characterful watering holes detailed below, where prices are lower. If you just want to buy booze, Drinkies (11am–midnight except Fri and Muslim holidays) on the corner of Sharia Gamil el-Din Yassin and Sharia el-Ghorfa el-Tigarya sells local wine and spirits and imported beer and alcopops; other foreign brands can be purchased within 48 hours of arrival in Egypt at the **duty-free**

shop, 31 Sharia Salah Salem (daily 11am–10pm; Ramadan 11am–2pm & 8–10pm), which accepts US dollars, sterling, euros or Visa cards only. All the places below are marked on the map on pp.580–581 unless stated otherwise.

Downtown

Cap d'Or Sharia Adib Bek Ishtak, off Sharia Sa'ad Zaghloul. A real slice of old Alex, furnished with Art Nouveau mouldings and engraved mirrors, where bohemians and expats rub shoulders over grilled sardines and bottles of whisky or tequila. It has a friendly atmosphere, and is popular with the gay community after midnight, when there may be live *oud* (lute) music. A full meal and a couple of beers costs about £E60. Daily noon–3am.

Elite 43 Sharia Safiya Zaghloul. Simple blue-painted extension to the restaurant of the same name (whose food is awful). Frequented by tourists, writers and oddballs; a place to talk and meet people, lubricated by Egyptian beer, *zibiba* or brandy. Usually open till midnight.

Fever Off Sharia Safiya Zaghloul. This preppy music bar serving Tex-Mex and Egyptian snacks, imported beer, spirits and cocktails is dead most nights, but packed out with fun-loving young Alexandrians on Thursdays. Daily 7am–4am.

Spitfire Bar Sharia al-Bursa al-Qadima. Small hangout covered in stickers from oil companies, warships and overland travel groups (the kind of foreigners that frequent the place), with Seventies rock music and TV sports. Mon–Sat noon–1am.

Further out

Greek Club Sharia Qasr Qaitbey, Anfushi. The breezy terrace here, overlooking the Eastern Harbour, is the perfect place for a cold beer or *zibiba* at sunset, and the food is good too. Daily noon–1am.

Portuguese Club (*Nady Portugali*) 42 Sharia Abd el-Qader Ragab, Roushdi ☏03/542-7599. A country club–cum–singles' bar frequented by expats, with pool or darts competitions (Tues), a disco (Thurs) and monthly party nights. Located 3km from the centre, off Tariq Gamal Abdel Nasser; catch tram #2 to the Egyptian-American Center and walk two blocks inland to find the first side-street off Sharia Kafr Abdou – which is the name to give if you take a taxi (£E5). There's no sign outside the club. Daily 3pm till the last customer leaves; open for breakfast from 10am on Fri.

Nightlife and entertainment

Thursday and Friday are the big nights out in Alex, but there's something happening all week. Several hotel **nightclubs** offer **bellydancing** and/or a Russian Show and DJ. It's wise to phone ahead and book a table at the ones in Montazah. At the *Helnan Palestine* (June–Sept daily 11.30pm–4.30am; Oct–May 3–4 nights weekly) they have a minimum charge of £E100 per person and only admit mixed-sex groups, while the *El Salamlek Palace* has a nightly programme (11pm–1am) in the summer (£E71 minimum charge). In the centre, the *Hotel Cecil's* nightclub (daily except Fri & Wed 11.30pm–4am) has two or three belly-dancers from midnight onwards (minimum charge £E75 per person), and the *Metropole* a Russian Show (nightly except Tues; free admission but you're expected to dine à la carte). A sleazier, more raucous nightclub is *Lourantos* at 44 Sharia Safiya Zaghloul (☏03/483-3576), best visited with an Egyptian friend to get past the doorman who might claim there's an entry charge (there isn't one), or to argue if they try to add it to your bill. The dancing starts at midnight and runs through till dawn if enough patrons are still paying.

Though most four- and five-star hotels have **discos**, they're moribund outside of summer, except for the *Mercure's*, which is busy on Thursday nights throughout the year. All of them, aside from the *Sheraton's*, restrict entry to mixed-sex groups, so if you're on your own, hang out at the *Portuguese Club* (see above) until a decent-sized group of people there decides to go dancing at the *Mercure* and tag along. If you prefer **karaoke**, there's a Wednesday-night bash at the *Coffee Roastery* (see p.600), though without any alcohol to loosen inhibitions.

Arts and festivals

After decades in the doldrums, Alexandria's cultural scene has seen a renaissance. The new library is naturally at the forefront, but money has also been spent on the city's historic opera house and other venues. The tourist office has details of their monthly programmes, also advertised *in situ* and at the *Elite* restaurant (see p.601).

The Cultural Centre at the **Bibliotheca Alexandrina** (see p.591) stages **classical music** (Arabic as well as European), modern **dance** and **drama**. Larger orchestral works and **ballet** are performed at the **Opera House** off Sharia Horriya (see p.583; ☎03/486-5106). A few blocks west of the opera, the one-time Mohammed Ali Club, where the city's elite mingled in colonial times, houses the **Alexandria Centre of Arts** (☎03/495-6633), whose blue-and-gold auditorium hosts occasional concerts by musicians from Egypt and abroad. Another, smaller venue for music is the **Conservatoire de Musique d'Alexandrie** at 90 Sharia Horriya (☎03/487-5086), under renovation at the time of writing. The most "alternative" venue is **Garage** in Sidi Gaber (☎03/544-3246, ✉tfetouh@yatfund.org), putting on performances by local and foreign youth theatre groups, in the former garage of the Jesuit Centre at 298 Sharia Bur Said (see map on p.574).

In August you can see **folk dances** by the Rida Troupe (Ballet Rida) or the National Troupe (El-Fir'a el-Qawmiyya) at the outdoor **Abdel Wahab Theatre** (☎03/486-3637), on the Corniche east of Midan Ramleh. During summer there's also a **circus** (☎03/592-3251), which sets up either at Azarita near the Abdel Wahab Theatre, or at St Mark's College in Shatby; check performance times with the tourist office.

In September, Alexandria's annual **International Film Festival** gives Egyptians a rare opportunity to see foreign movies in an uncensored state: the Convention Hall en route to the library is the main venue, but every cinema in town screens a few. Film-going is popular throughout the year, with extra screenings at all **cinemas** during Ramadan. Downtown, the three-screen Royal Renaissance (☎03/485-5725) by the Opera House and the six-screen Amir (☎03/392-7693) on the corner of Sharia Horriya and Safiya Zaghloul each screen English-language films you might have seen last year. These are trumped by first-releases at the scruffy old Rialto (☎03/486-4694) on Safiya Zaghloul, which far outclass the B-movies at the lovely Art Deco Metro (☎03/487-0432) down the road. Out in Smouha (15–25 minutes by taxi; £E7–10), the six-screen Green Plaza Mall Cineplex (☎03/490-9155), the five-screen Osman Group Cinema (☎03/424-5897) in Smouha Mall and the seven-screen Renaissance City Center (☎03/397-0156) in the City Center Mall vie to show the latest Hollywood blockbusters.

Other events include the two-week **Alexandria Biennial**, an exhibition of art from Mediterranean countries staged in November in odd-numbered years, and three annual sporting festivals: **long-distance swimming** in July, an annual **International Yachting Regatta** off the Eastern Harbour and an **International Marathon** along the Corniche from Ras el-Tin to Montazah, both staged in October.

During Ramadan, Alex revels in five **moulids** over five consecutive weeks, starting with *zikrs* outside the Mosque of Al-Mursi. The day after its "big night", the action shifts to Sidi Gaber's mosque, then Sidi Bishr's; these are followed by the moulids of Sidi Kamal and Sidi Mohammed al-Rahhal. And should you happen to be here over New Year, beware the blizzard of crockery that Alexandrians throw out of their windows at midnight.

Sport and activities

For those qualified to go **diving**, there are many **ancient ruins and wrecks** to be seen five to eighteen metres beneath the waters around Alexandria. Few other cities boast such a wealth of historic underwater sites, with blocks from the Pharos littering the sea bed near Qaitbey's fort, and Roman trading vessels lying 500m offshore. Some 11,000 artefacts and pieces of masonry remain from what was once the Royal Quarter in the Eastern Harbour, while Napoleonic wrecks and an ancient port lie beneath Abu Qir Bay.

Visibility in the Eastern Harbour declines as the water gets warmer, whereas other, less-sheltered sites are best dived in the summer, when the sea is calm. **Alexandra Dive** (T & F03/483-2045, Wwww.alexandra-dive.com), beside the *Tikka Grill* on the Corniche, can usually forecast conditions for the next 24 hours, and offers diving for a minimum of three people at two sites for €80 each (including lunch and the fee to the Underwater Archeology Department; equipment costs extra). As the Pharos and Cleopatra's palace are only 5–8m underwater, even uncertified divers may be accepted if they can pass a try-out and stick close to their "dive buddy" (Mahmoud is the guy to get) – though open-water diving courses (€250) are available. They can even arrange **underwater weddings** at Cleopatra's palace, while in summer, their dive centre at Almaza Bay (see p.612) offers World War II wreck-diving. It's worth contacting them in advance to discuss the feasibility of specific sites, as some require a permit that takes several days to obtain.

Other activities can be pursued at the **Sporting Club** (T03/543-3627). Alexandra Dive's owner, Dr Ashraf Sabri (T010 666-6514), can sign you in as a guest (£E25), after which you pay to use the **swimming pools** (£E25), tennis and squash courts, 18-hole **golf** course (£E250), or riding stables. Non-residents may use the **tennis** courts at the *Montazah Sheraton* (£E40/hr plus £E10 for each item of equipment). If you'd rather watch **football**, check who's playing at the Municipal Stadium, the home ground of **Al Ittihad**. Founded by students from Ras el-Tin in the 1920s, the club has won the Egyptian cup six times.

Directory

secondhand novels (abridged for students of English) on the pavement near the French Centre, which has a French bookshop in its grounds. Foreign newspapers are sold outside Ramleh telephone exchange and the *Metropole Hotel*.

Cigarettes The Rialto shop on Sharia Safiya Zaghloul, beside the Rialto cinema, sells a wide range of brands, including rolling tobacco and papers.

Consulates Ireland, 9 Sharia al-Batalssa (☎03/485-2672; Mon–Thurs & Sun 8am–1pm); Israel, 15 Sharia Mena, Roushdi (☎03/544-9501; Mon–Thurs & Sun 9.30am–3.30pm); UK, 3 Sharia Mena, Roushdi (☎03/546-7001; Mon–Thurs & Sun 8am–1pm); USA, 3 Sharia Phara'ana (☎02/797-2301; one day a month 9am–3pm). Australia, New Zealand and Canada have no consular representation; for other consulates, ask at the tourist office.

Cultural centres American Center, 3 Sharia Phara'ana (☎03/486-1009, ⓔAmericanCenter Alexandria@yahoo.com; Mon–Thurs & Sun 10am–4pm; Ramadan Mon–Thurs & Sun 10am–3pm); British Council, 11 Sharia Mahmoud El Ela, Roushdi (☎03/545-6512, ⓦwww.britishcouncil.org.eg; Mon–Thurs 10am–8pm, Fri–Sun 1–8pm); Cervantes Institute, 101 Sharia Horriya (☎03/392-0214, ⓦwww.elcairo.cervantes.es; daily 5–8pm); French Centre, 30 Sharia Nabi Daniel (☎03/391-8952, ⓦwww.ambafrance.eg.org/cfcc/alexandrie; daily except Fri 9am–9pm); Goethe Institute, 10 Sharia al-Batalssa (☎03/483-9870, ⓔgialex @internetalex.com; Mon & Wed noon–6pm, Tues & Sun 10am–4pm); Russian Centre, 5 Sharia Batalsa (☎03/486-5645; Mon–Thurs & Sun 10am–1pm & 5–8pm).

Dentist Alexandria Dental Centre, 321 Sharia Abu Qir, Cleopatra (☎03/427-7790); Medhat Naga, above the Bank of Alexandria on Sharia al-Keniset al-Dibana downtown (☎03/487-5551); or Dr Samuel, 51 Sharia Omar Lotfi, Camp Cesar (☎03/592-7216).

DHL 5 Sharia Salah Salem, beside the Banque du Caire (daily except Fri 9am–4.30pm).

Film processing Kodak film is sold and developed opposite the Rialto Cinema on Safiya Zaghloul; other places can be found on Sharia Sa'ad Zaghloul. The Havana Studio on Ramleh (daily 4–10pm) can burn digital images onto a CD for £E5.

Hospitals The German (Al-Almani) Hospital, 56 Sharia Abdel Salaam Aref, Saba Pasha

(☎03/585-7682), and the ICC Hospital, 24 Sharia Beha al-Din, Smouha (☎03/420-7320), are both well equipped.

International calls There are Menatel booths all over town. The 24hr exchange on Midan Ramleh has direct-dial phones and sells phonecards; the exchanges on Midan el-Gumhorriya and Sharia Sa'ad Zaghloul (both daily 8am–11pm) work on the pre-booking system.

Internet access Downtown are Cyber Club, Sharia al-Bursa al-Qadima (daily 24hr); Cyber Café Badia, 18 Sharia Kolliet el-Tiba (Sat–Thurs 8am–1am, Fri 3pm–1am); and Satellite Internet Café, Sharia Dr Hassan Fadaly, off Safiya Zaghloul (Mon–Sat 11am–11pm). Smouha's Zahran Mall has Click-It on the ground floor (daily 10.30am–1am), and Access Cybercafé on the floor above (daily 9am–midnight).

Passport office To renew your visa (£E12.50), go to kiosk #6 on the first floor of 25 Sharia Talaat Harb (☎03/484-7873; daily except Fri 8am–3pm), with one photo and a copy of the relevant pages of your passport (there's a photocopier on the street outside). No applications accepted after noon.

Pharmacies Khalil, on Sharia el-Ghorfa el-Tigarya, off Midan Sa'ad Zaghloul (daily except Fri 9am–midnight; ☎03/480-6710); Strand, by the intersection of Safiya and Sa'ad Zaghloul streets (daily 9am–1am; ☎03/486-5136), and others on Safiya Zaghloul and Nabi Daniel streets.

Post offices Midan Ramleh (daily 8am–3pm), Sharia el-Ghorfa el-Tigarya (same hours) and Masr Station (daily 8am–5pm). *Poste restante* is unreliable, so ask if you can have mail sent to your hotel. Express Mail Service is open till 2pm at all the main post offices.

Thomas Cook 15 Midan Sa'ad Zaghloul (☎03/484-7830, ⓕ487 4073, ⓦwww.thomascook.com.eg; daily 8am–5pm. Cashes and sells traveller's cheques, and deals with stolen ones. Daily 8am–5pm.

Tourist police Above the tourist office (☎03/485-0507), in the Maritime Station (no phone) and at the entrance to Montazah gardens (☎03/547-3814). All except the last are open 24hr.

Western Union Montazah Mall, beside the *Montazah Sheraton* (☎03/554-7572); Arab African International Bank, 73 Sharia Horriya, Sidi Gaber (☎03/392-0900). Both offices are open daily 8.30am–10pm.

Moving on

Most of the places covered in the remainder of this chapter can be reached from Alexandria by public transport. It's also feasible to make **day-excursions** to

Rosetta and Tanta in the Delta (see Chapter 5) or the Monasteries of Wadi Natrun (see Chapter 3).

Rail services between Alex and Cairo are detailed on p.270. At **Masr Station**, tickets for first-and second-class air-conditioned trains are sold from the office beside the tourist information booth on platform one, while ordinary second-and third-class tickets are sold in the front hall. Services to Tanta and Cairo can also be boarded at **Sidi Gaber Station**.

Buses

There are direct buses to Sinai, Hurghada and the Canal Zone, with the **15th May Terminal** behind Sidi Gaber Station (accessible by tram #2, and then an underpass) being the city's main bus station. It has two separate booking offices and terminals 50m apart, used by Superjet (5.30am–10.30pm; ☎03/429-8566) and West Delta (5.30am–10.30pm; ☎03/427-7822). From 7am till midnight, both run a/c services to **Cairo** (£E20–25) and its airport (£E25–31) every half hour. Hourly West Delta buses to **Mersa Matrouh** (£E15–23) run all year, supplemented by more comfortable Superjet services (daily 7.15am & 4pm; £E24) in the summer. Matrouh is a stopover for West Delta buses to **Siwa Oasis** (£E28) leaving Alex at 8.30am, 11am and 6pm; and for services to **Sollum** (6 daily; £E23). Heading for the oasis, you can travel there directly – an eleven-hour journey that makes it wise to catch the early-morning bus – or go as far as Mersa Matrouh, stay overnight and carry on to Siwa next day.

Other destinations served from Alex are **Port Said** (Superjet 6.45am; £E24; West Delta 6am, 8am, 11am, 4pm & 7pm; £E20–24); **Ismailiya** (West Delta 7am, 9am & 2.30pm; £E20); **Suez** (West Delta 6.30am, 9am, 2.30pm & 5.30pm; £E22); **El-Arish** (West Delta 9am; £E28); **Hurghada** (Superjet 8pm; £E85; West Delta 6.30pm; £E70); **Sharm el-Sheikh** (Superjet 7.30pm; £E88; West Delta 9pm; £E70); **Tanta** (West Delta hourly 6am–6pm; £E18) and **Zagazig** (West Delta 8am, 9am & 2pm; £E17). Tickets for West Delta buses can also be bought at their office on the corner of Midan Sa'ad Zaghloul and Sharia el-Ghorfa el-Tigarya (☎03/480-9685), provided the computer isn't down, which it frequently is.

Service taxis

The vast, shade-less **Moharrem Bey Terminal** (known as El-Mogaf Gedida, the "New Terminal") on the city's outskirts can be reached by minibus from the western side of Midan el-Gumhorriya (25pt) or by taxi (£E5). Its ranks of Peugeots, Toyota minibuses and minivans run to almost everywhere that's worth mentioning within 250km of Alexandria, including **Cairo** (£E10), **Wadi Natrun** resthouse (£E7), the **Monastery of Abu Mina** (£E2), **El-Alamein** (£E4), **Mersa Matrouh** (£E12), **Port Said** (£E15), **Rosetta** (£E4), **Tanta** (£E6) and **Zagazig** (£E13). Listen for the drivers shouting out destinations, or ask for directions to the right clump of service taxis.

The Mediterranean coast

Egypt's five-hundred-kilometre-long **Mediterranean coast** (known as Al-Sahel) has beautiful beaches and sparkling sea all the way to Libya. However, many stretches are still mined from World War II or off limits due to military bases, or simply hard to reach – while all the most accessible sites have been colonized by holiday villages. Unlike in Sinai and Hurghada, the majority of these cater to Egyptians, whose beach culture is significantly different from Westerners'. While the beach scene here may lack the atmosphere and the coral reefs found in the Red Sea, the Med is great for **wreck-diving**, with numerous warships and submarines to explore without the scrum of divers that you get at wrecks off Sinai, albeit only accessible through a single dive centre based at **Almaza Bay**.

Most foreign travellers heading this way aim for Siwa Oasis (see p.550) rather than the staid resort town of **Mersa Matrouh**. Aside from the **beaches** near Matrouh, other coastal sites are awkward to reach (or leave) without private transport, though you may consider it worth making the effort to get to the World War II battlefield of **El-Alamein**, which is also within taxi range of several luxurious beach hotels. In general, though, even the sea can seem reclusive here, hidden from sight of the coastal highway by gated **resorts** or barren ridges.

Swaths of the Mediterranean coast and its desert hinterland are still littered with **minefields** and **unexploded shells**. Never stray into wired-off areas or anything that resembles an abandoned camp or airfield, even if local goatherds seem unfazed by the risk.

Between Alexandria and El-Alamein

Travelling between Alexandria and El-Alamein, you'll pass a slew of **resorts** reserved for elite sections of Egyptian society such as the army, navy and diplomatic corps, and others open to anyone who can afford to stay. Their gorgeous beaches and middling-to-luxurious facilities draw well-heeled Egyptians or European package tourists, but for independent travellers they're simply blights on the landscape which make the colonial-era beach resort of **El-Agami** (20km from downtown Alexandria and serving as a commuter suburb) seem historic by comparison. Since the ancient city of Taposiris Magna and its coastal lighthouse were fenced off by the SCA, the only accessible "sight" is the **Monastery of Abu Mina**, inland of Burg al-Arab.

Abu Sir and Burg al-Arab

Heading west from Alex, you'll pass the oil refineries and steelworks of Al-Max, and the reedy expanse of **Lake Maryut**. Originally a freshwater lake linked to the Nile, it became ever more saline as the Canopic branch of the Nile silted up in Fatimid times, and the British later dug canals to flood it with sea water, to create a defensive barrier to the west of Alexandria. Nowadays, parts often dry out entirely in summer and others are used as drainage basins for industrial effluents, which have stained the water a livid pink.

Thirty kilometres beyond El-Agami the highway passes a fenced-off site called **Abu Sir**, better known to archeologists by its Roman name, **Taposiris Magna**. The limestone ridge south of the road bears the ruins of an ancient **city** that the Egyptians called Per Usiri ("Dwelling of Osiris") and the Greeks Busiris, which had one port on the Mediterranean and another on Lake Maryut. In Roman times, the Maryut region produced as much grain as the Fayoum and the Nile Valley, which was shipped to Italy to placate the potentially riotous plebs in the imperial capital.

Vital to this commerce was a chain of lighthouses from Alexandria to Cyrenaica (Libya), which warned sailors of the abrupt change from sea to sand along a coastline devoid of landmarks but plagued by reefs and shoals. While Alexandria's Pharos has disappeared, archeologists have gleaned clues to its shape from the sole surviving **lighthouse** in the chain, at Abu Sir. Most believe that this was a one-tenth scale replica of the Pharos, though Gyoző Vörös (excavator of the sun temple on Thoth Hill; see p.394) thinks it was the prototype for the Pharos rather than a scaled-down copy.

Confusingly, the lighthouse is often referred to as the **Burg al-Arab** ("Arab's Tower"), the name given to a coastal watchtower destroyed by the British in 1882, which was later bestowed on a model village designed by Wilfred Jennings-Bramly in 1915, on the opposite side of the lake from Abu Sir. Burg al-Arab served as RAF headquarters during the battle of El-Alamein and was later graced with a villa where President Sadat planned the October War of 1973. It still occupies a guarded enclave on the edge of the sprawling community.

To confuse things further, at km 52 on the highway there's a turn-off to the five-star **Hilton Burg el-Arab** on the coast (T03/374-0730, W www.hilton .com; ⑧), whose amenities include a vast white beach, a large pool and a children's splash pool, a gym and sauna. Rates are heavily discounted over winter, when foreign tour operators charge as little as \$85 for a double room booked as part of a package holiday. Package tourists fly into **Burg al–Arab airport**, twenty minutes' drive from the hotel, or El-Alamein International, an hour away; the hotel can arrange limo transfers (\$20/30).

The Monastery of Abu Mina

If you're hiring a car to visit El-Alamein, consider a side-trip to the Coptic **Monastery of Abu Mina**, 15km inland from Abu Sir, which can also be reached from Alexandria by minibus from the Moharrem Bey terminal. Deir Mari Mina, as it's known locally, honours **St Menas**, an Egyptian-born Roman legionary who was martyred in Asia Minor in 296 after refusing to renounce Christ. His ashes were buried here when the camel that was taking them home refused to go any further. Miraculous events on the spot persuaded others to exhume Menas in 350 and build a church over his grave, later enclosed within a huge basilica. A pilgrim city grew up as camel trains spread his fame (Menas is depicted between two camels), and "holy" water from local springs was exported throughout Christendom. But when these dried up in the twelfth century, the city and its vineyards were abandoned and soon buried by sand, only a small community of monks remaining.

While its belfry towers are visible from far away, high walls enclose the concrete buildings of the modern monastery, erected in 1959. Its **cathedral** is adorned with Italian marble, black and rose Aswan granite, and stained glass. Busloads of pilgrims arrive daily, particularly on November 11, **St Menas's Day**, when the cathedral overflows. In addition to Menas, the crypt houses the body of Pope Kyrillos VI (1959–71), whom Copts regard as a saint, writing petitions on his marble grave.

With permission from the monks, you may be allowed to explore the nearby **ruins** of the ancient monastery and pilgrim town. Fragments of marble paving, granite and basalt columns, and mosaics of semiprecious stones give some idea of how large and lavishly decorated the basilica of St Menas was, at a time when Christian churches in Europe were primitive structures. Until its water dried up, the pilgrim town even featured a hospice with hot and cold baths. Today the ruins are imperiled by rising groundwater and the site is on UNESCO's Endangered World Heritage list.

Beach resorts

The coastal road is flanked by wall-to-wall **resorts** that were reputedly to blame for the devaluation of the Egyptian currency in 2001. Speculators borrowed billions to construct resorts whose projected value was pledged as security for the loans but turned out to be grossly inflated. Over 80km of beaches and wildlife habitats disappeared under shoddy apartments and construction debris, ruining the coastline forever. As it costs more to improve substandard resorts than to start afresh on virgin ground, developers have simply moved on to new sites such as Almaza Bay (see p.612).

Each resort is presaged by an ostentatious gateway with armed guards. Moribund over winter, they come alive as BMW-borne families move in for the summer. Their **beach scene** is staid by Western standards; bikinis, cocktails and **discos** are only found at three resorts. The four-star *Aida Beach Hotel* at km 77 is popular with wealthy Cairenes (℡03/484-9017; ❼ including half board). At km 100, the Venetian-themed five-star *Porto Marina* (℡046/445-2711, ⓦwww .porto-marina.com; ❽) boasts canals, lagoons and gondolas, and Egypt's first international-class **marina** (able to accommodate 100-metre-long yachts), with an 18-hole **golf** course due in 2008. At Ghazala Bay past El-Alamein (km 140), the former *Mövenpick* is now the five-star *Charm Life Alamein* (℡02/266-8902, ⓦwww.charmlifehotels.com; ❼), featuring a heated indoor pool and freshwater outdoor ones, a dive centre, a French-managed health spa and child-oriented entertainments.

El-Alamein and around

Before Alamein we never had a victory. After Alamein we never had a defeat.

Winston Churchill, *The Hinge of Fate*

The utterly misnamed "city" of **EL-ALAMEIN** squats on a dusty plain 106km west of Alexandria, situated along a spur road that turns inland from the coastal highway. Anyone driving past could blink and see nothing except construction

△ Tanks at El-Alamein's War Museum

debris until they pass the Italian War Cemetery 9km down the highway. Still, El-Alamein ("Two Worlds") is an apt name for a place that witnessed the turning point of the North African campaign, determining the fate of Egypt and Britain's empire. When the Afrika Korps came within 111km of Alexandria on July 1, 1942, the city and the capital experienced "The Flap": documents were burned, civilians mobbed railway stations, and Egyptian nationalists prepared to welcome their Nazi "liberators". Control of Egypt, Middle Eastern oil and the Canal route to India seemed about to be wrested from the Allied powers by Germany and Italy. Instead, at El-Alamein, the Allied Eighth Army held, and then drove the Axis forces back, to ultimate defeat in Tunisia. Some eleven thousand soldiers were killed and seventy thousand wounded at El-Alamein alone; total casualties for the North African campaign (September 1940–March 1943) exceeded one hundred thousand. Travellers who wish to pay their respects to the dead or have an interest in military history should find the **cemeteries** and the **war museum** worth the effort of getting there. Commemorative **services** are held at El-Alamein each October; contact the British, Australian, Italian or German embassies in Cairo for details.

Sidi Abd el-Rahman, further along the coast, was at the heart of the Axis defences during the final battle of El-Alamein and witnessed the last stand of Rommel's rearguard. While its Panzer graveyard is too hazardous to visit, there are numerous wartime wrecks that can be explored on dive safaris from the deluxe resort of **Almaza Bay**, 50km further west. The intervening stretch of coast is earmarked for Egypt's first nuclear power station at El-Dabaa, which was announced in 2006 and is intended to be completed within a decade.

Visiting the cemeteries

The easiest way of visiting El-Alamein is by **renting a car** with a driver, through Thomas Cook in Alex for £E350 (see p.577); alternatively, you may be able to charter a **taxi** there for £E200–300, depending on your bargaining skills. Though comparatively expensive, a car enables you to reach the far-flung cemeteries and leave El-Alamein without difficulty – a major advantage over public transport. Hourly West Delta **buses** from Alex to Matrouh can drop you at the police checkpoint by the turn-off for the Allied War Cemetery, or 1km further west along the highway, closer to the War Museum (see below); you'll pay £E6–7 for the journey. The other way is to catch a **minibus** (£E4) from the Moharrem Bey terminal in Alex.

While getting there is straightforward enough, leaving can be harder. Basically, you walk back to the highway and flag down any bus or minibus heading in the right direction – but ensure they're going all the way to your destination. Vehicles heading towards Matrouh may turn off the highway to settlements such as Ras al-Hikma, from which there is no onward transport except for private taxis, while most minibuses heading in the direction of Alexandria actually terminate at the industrial satellite-city of **Amiriya** (from where it's £E10 by taxi or 25pt by minibus to downtown Alex).

The War Museum and cemeteries

While you can be sure of finding all the **cemeteries** open (daily: summer 8am–5pm; winter & Ramadan 9am–4pm), it's worth phoning ahead to check about the museum (⌀046/410-0021), as it closes now and again for some reason or another. All the Allied memorials lie beside a spur road off the highway, which begins just after the turn-off for the Qattara Depression (see p.611). First comes the **Greek Memorial**, followed 400m later by the **South**

The Battle of El-Alamein

Rather than the single, decisive clash of arms that many people imagine, the Battle of El-Alamein consisted of three savage bouts of mechanized warfare separated by relative lulls over a period of five months (July–November) in 1942. In the **First Battle** of El-Alamein, the **Afrika Korps'** advance was stymied by lack of fuel and munitions and stiff Allied resistance organized by General Auchinleck. Once resupplied, however, Field Marshal Erwin **Rommel** was able to press the advantage with 88-millimetre cannons that outranged the Allies' guns, as well as faster, better-armoured tanks, used with an élan that earned him the title "the Desert Fox".

In August, General Bernard **Montgomery** ("Monty") took over the Allied **Eighth Army**, vowing that it would retreat no further. He negated his army's weaknesses by siting its tanks "hull down" in pits with only their gun turrets above ground, protecting them until the Panzers came within range. Aware that the Allies were being resupplied, Rommel attacked the Alam Halfa Ridge in the **Second Battle** of El-Alamein (August 31 to September 6). Repulsed with heavy losses and desperately short of fuel, the Afrika Korps withdrew behind a field of five hundred thousand landmines. Monty patiently reorganized his forces, resisting pressure from his superiors to attack until he had amassed one thousand tanks. A stage illusionist, Jasper Maskelyne, concealed them in the desert and constructed fake tank parks as part of an elaborate deception plan to mislead Rommel as to where and when the Eighth Army's main offensive would occur.

Shortly after nightfall on October 23, Monty launched the **Third Battle** of El-Alamein with a barrage of 744 guns that was heard in Alexandria. Having cracked the Nazi Enigma code, the Allies knew that Rommel was convalescing in Italy; when the Eighth Army punched a corridor through the minefields of the central front on October 23, the Germans were taken unawares. Rommel managed to return two days later, but was obliged to concentrate his mobile units further north, stranding four Italian divisions in the south. The Allies had established a commanding position at Kidney Ridge, whence Monty launched the decisive strike on November 2, leaving Rommel with only 35 operational tanks by the end of the day. On November 5 the Eighth Army broke out and surged westwards; the Afrika Korps fought rearguard actions back through Libya until its inevitable surrender six months later.

African Memorial, and then the **Allied War Cemetery** secluded on the reverse slope of a hill. Planted with trees and flowers, it is a tranquil site for the graves of 7367 Allied soldiers (815 of them nameless, only "known unto God"), with memorial cloisters listing the names of 11,945 others whose bodies were never found. Though over half were Britons, the dead include Australians, New Zealanders, Indians, Malays, Melanesians, Africans, Canadians, French, Greeks and Poles. If you want to find a particular headstone, the Commonwealth War Graves Commission (Ⓦ www.cwgc.org) in London can tell you exactly where to look. Walking down to the cemetery, you'll pass the **Australian Memorial**, honouring the 9th Australian Division that stormed Point 29 and Thompson's Post during the penultimate phase of the Third Battle.

If you're coming by bus or service taxi, you're likely to be dropped further west along the highway, where a Sherman tank (not of World War II vintage, but captured from the Israelis) near a gas station marks the start of an uphill turn-off leading to the museum (El Mat-haf in Arabic). Follow this to a T-junction and turn left; the **War Museum** is 200m ahead (daily: summer 9am–5pm; winter & Ramadan 9am–4pm; £E10, camera £E5, video £E20), past a telephone exchange. Well presented, the museum has photos and models conveying the harsh conditions in the field. Due weight is given to the experience of both sides, and Egypt's role in the Allied struggle is deservedly credited. Notice the section on Almásy (of *The English Patient*; see p.545) and his role in guiding two German spies through the desert. Outside are two dozen tanks, cannons and trucks, including a lorry belonging to the Long Range Desert Group (see p.546) that was found in the desert in 1991. There's also a restored **Command Bunker** that was used by Monty during the battle, which you'll have to ask a guide to unlock.

On the highway west of El-Alamein is a **plaque** marking the furthest point of the Axis advance, which asserts: *Manco la Fortuna, Non il Valore* ("Lacking Fortune, Not Valour"), *1.7.1942, Alessandria 111km*. Further out you'll glimpse the **German Cemetery**, a squat octagonal ossuary housing the remains of 4280 soldiers and overlooking the sea from a peninsula to the north. An elegant white tower marks the **Italian Cemetery**, 3km further along the highway, which contains a small museum, and a chapel with the dedication: "To 4800 Italian soldiers, sailors and airmen. The desert and sea did not give back 38,000 who are missing." Do not wander around between these cemeteries; while the grounds themselves have been cleared, the intervening strips of land are still mined.

The battlefield

The battlefield itself is generally far too dangerous to explore, due to the **minefields** laid by both sides. A staggering 17.2 million landmines are estimated to remain in the Western Desert, which still kill and maim local Bedouin to this day. Casualties were highest in the 1950s, when a foreign scrap-metal dealer taught locals to make bombs from unexploded shells and blow derelict tanks into portable chunks. Germany, Britain and Italy have always rejected Egyptian and Libyan demands that they fund mine clearance programmes – the current excuse is that Egypt hasn't signed up to the Ottawa Convention banning the manufacture of mines. Although a few Bedouin with 4WDs are prepared to take people to such strategic strongpoints as **Kidney Ridge** (which the 51st Highland Division was disconcerted to find was actually a depression, leaving them exposed to enemy fire) and **Tell el-Issa** (stormed by the Australians), you would be foolish to rely on assurances that they know safe routes through the minefields.

However, two relics of the struggle can be seen without any risk from the road to the Qattara Depression that starts near the Greek Memorial. To the east of the road, **El-Alamein Station** looks much as it did in 1942, albeit no longer thronged with Allied troops (who dubbed the station "Heaven") and supplies; while 24km further south, the ridge on the western side is honeycombed with trenches and tunnels belonging to the **Italian Field Hospital** and defensive positions that were stormed by the Allied 30th Corps during "Operation Lightfoot" in October 1942. This road is well surfaced and eventually dips down into the Qattara Depression to meet up with the Cairo–Bahariya highway (see p.565) but you do need a **permit** to use it – and whatever you do, don't stray off the tarmac road, as the verges and surrounding areas are heavily mined.

The land war was waged in tandem with a battle for naval and air supremacy over the Mediterranean, as each side tried to cut the other's supply lines while protecting its own. Convoys and shipping losses were shrouded in secrecy and many wrecks were soon lost in the shifting sands, to be found by divers decades later. Only 100m off the coast of El-Alamein is the wreck of a British **troop carrier** sunk by the Luftwaffe, soldiers' helmets poignantly visible at a depth of ten metres. A twin-engined **bomber** whose nationality has yet to be established lies 55m underwater, about 10km off the coast. Both were found by Dr Ashraf Sabri, who runs Alexandra Dive and the Rommel Dive Centre (see p.603 and p.612), which organizes **wreck-diving** at these sites.

Sidi Abd el-Rahman

Nine kilometres past the last of the battlefield memorials, a spurt of housing announces **SIDI ABD EL-RAHMAN**, which is used as a pit-stop by buses going to Mersa Matrouh and Siwa. There's no point in lingering unless you're staying at the *El-Alamein Hotel* (℡046/468-0140 or 02/390-4701; ❸), a fancy resort with a stunning white **beach**, located 3km past a township established to settle Awlad Ali **Bedouin** who moved in from Libya in the nineteenth century. Many have abandoned their traditional goat's-hair tents for stone houses, but they still maintain flocks, which they graze on scrubland or pen behind their now-immobile homes. At Tell al-Aqaqir, 10km into the desert, is a **graveyard of Panzers**, destroyed in the final rout of the Afrika Korps from the battlefield; it was here that Von Thoma, the commander of the nearly obliterated 15th and 21st Panzer divisions, surrendered. Earlier in the campaign, the Afrika Korps' heaquarters and tank repair depot were located at Sidi Abd el-Rahman, behind a belt of minefields and gun emplacements 8km in depth. Though many mines were cleared by Eighth Army engineers, enough remain to make the interior too dangerous to explore.

Almaza Bay

The latest mega-resort is at **Almaza Bay**, 37km east of Mersa Matrouh, where the first of six planned hotels opened in 2006. The *Almaza Beach Resort* (℡02/737-8737, Ⓦwww.iberotel-eg.com; ❸) has a splendid bay for swimming and water-polo, a sauna, hammam and Jacuzzi. Guests can gain PADI or CMAS certification at the **Rommel Dive Centre** (℡ & Ⓕ03/483-2045, Ⓦwww.alexandra-dive.com) and, if suitably experienced, enjoy the thrill of **wreck-diving** sunken U-boats or warships off Mersa Matrouh, El-Alamein, Sidi Barrani or Sollum (see respective entries) for €80 per person per day. Facilities are set to expand, with the construction of an **Aqua Park** and yacht **marina**, a **tennis** academy, **horse-riding** circuit, an 18-hole **golf** course and a French-managed health and beauty **spa**. The resort is popular with Italian and German tourists, who fly into Mersa Matrouh International airport.

Mersa Matrouh and the road to Libya

Although **MERSA MATROUH** has grown phenomenally and sees itself as a sophisticated resort, it remains a hick town at heart, which is clogged with Egyptian and Libyan holidaymakers in summer. The town's silvery **beaches** are scrappy, with the best options being far from town at the magnificent cove at Agiiba and the neighbouring Ubbayad beach. Social norms are conservative: more women wear veils than headscarves, and sermons are broadcast from mosques every day, not only on Fridays. By no stretch of the imagination does Matrouh fit the tourist board's promise of a hedonist's playground – though nobody has seen fit to tell the package tourists that fly into its airport bound for Almaza Bay. However, travellers might consider Matrouh as an overnight stopover to break up the eleven-hour journey between Alexandria and Siwa.

Despite appearances, Mersa Matrouh ("Sheltered Anchorage") has a long **history**. Founded by Alexander the Great on his way to Siwa, it was the place where Mark Antony and Cleopatra sought solace after their defeat at Actium, and where her fleet put out to sea for its final battle against Octavian. During the Islamic era, Matrouh was a busy trading port with a sideline in smuggling; its other main industry (dating back to Roman times) was harvesting sponges, which only ceased in the 1980s. Divers came from as far away as the Cyclades – up to two thousand of them per year in the early twentieth century. To pluck the sponges from the sea bed 60–90m below, they used a stone to make themselves sink faster, which they jettisoned at the bottom. Today, cut-price Chinese goods at the Souk Libya outside town, and a record consignment of three hundred tonnes of hashish seized by the coastguard, suggest that cross-border trading and smuggling are flourishing again.

The 209-kilometre journey **from Alex** to Matrouh is best accomplished by bus; see p.605 for details of services, which are quicker and less scary than service taxis from the Moharrem Bey depot (£E12). The only trains from Alex are slow, filthy third-class services. Matrouh can be reached directly **from Cairo** in about six hours by West Delta buses from the Turgoman Terminal (see p.271); book seats a day beforehand. Mornings are the best time to catch sporadic service taxis (£E20) from outside Ramses Station, which take about seven hours; an alternative is to ride to Alex and pick up another service there. During summer, there are three sleeper-trains a week from Cairo ($62) to Matrouh plus one air-conditioned daytime service. EgyptAir flies from Cairo (1hr) on alternate days, landing at Mersa Matrouh International airport.

Arrival and information

On **arrival**, you can catch a microbus (25pt) or taxi (£E3–5) into the centre of town from Mersa Matrouh's bus and service-taxi station, train station or airport. Blue-and-white taxis are the mainstay of **transport** around town (£E3) and to the nearer beaches.

The **tourist office** (daily 9am–3pm; ☏046/493-1841) behind the Governorate building on Sharia Iskandariya has friendly, English-speaking staff who can answer most questions, and maybe interpret should you have a problem that requires the **tourist police** (☏046/493-5575) next door. Further east along Sharia ash-Shatta are the **post office** (daily except Fri 8.30am–2pm) and 24-hour **telephone exchange**, though it's easier to call from the Menatel card-phones along Sharia Iskandariya. Speed.Net, opposite the *Panyotis Greek Restaurant*, has **Internet access** (£E2.50/hr).

The National Bank on Sharia Galaa can **change money** and traveller's cheques and has an ATM, as does the Banque Misr, five blocks east on the corner of Sharia Zaher Galal, which also gives cash advances on MasterCard and Visa. The **passport office** (daily except Fri 9am–3pm; ☏046/493-5351) is near the train station. For medical emergencies, try the military **hospital** (closed Fri; ☏046/493-5286) on Sharia ash-Shatta rather than the public one (☏046/493-3355). There's a **pharmacy**, Al-Farghaly (daily: summer 8am–2am; winter 8am–9pm; ☏046/493-9390), on the corner of Sharia Iskandariya and Sharia Alam Rum.

Accommodation

Matrouh's **tourist season** runs from late June to early October, peaking in July and August, when it's essential to make **reservations** months in advance. Generally speaking, hotels are overpriced but have little problem filling their rooms over summer; some close down or slash their prices in winter. The **youth hostel** (☏046/493-2331; £E10 per person), 600m west of Sharia Iskandariya, has dinky shared rooms with bunk beds, with an 11pm curfew, but isn't suitable for women.

Where distances are given below, they refer to the distance from Sharia Iskandariya. All the places listed are open year-round; unless stated otherwise, breakfast is included. The rates quoted are for high season.

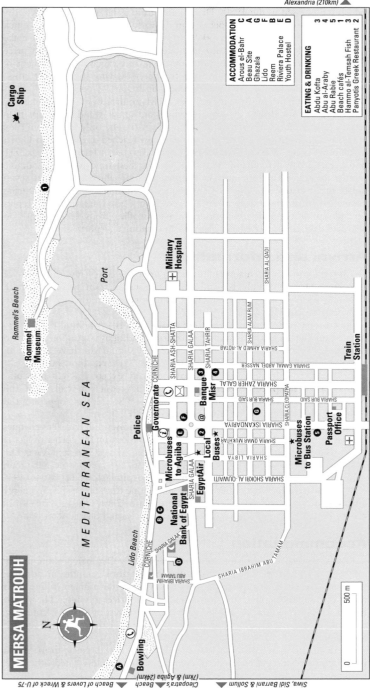

MERSA MATROUH

Alexandria (210km)

ACCOMMODATION
Arous el-Bahr	C
Beau Site	A
Ghazala	G
Lido	F
Reem	B
Riviera Palace	E
Youth Hostel	D

EATING & DRINKING
Abdu Kofta	3
Abu al-Araby	4
Abu Rabie	5
Beach cafés	1
Hammo al-Temsah Fish	3
Panyotis Greek Restaurant	2

Wreck of Volo

Rommel's Beach

Cargo Ship

Rommel Museum

Port

MEDITERRANEAN SEA

Lido Beach

CORNICHE

Police

Governorate

Military Hospital

Microbuses to Agiba

EgyptAir

Local Buses

National Bank of Egypt

SHARIA GALAA

SHARIA IBRAHIM ABU TAMAM

SHARIA ASH-SHATTA

SHARIA GALAA

SHARIA TAHRIR

SHARIA ALAM RUM

SHARIA AHMED AL-ROTAB

Banque Misr

Microbuses to Bus Station

Passport Office

SHARIA GAMAL ABDEL NASSER

SHARIA ZAHER GALAL

SHARIA BUR SAID

SHARIA BUR SAID

SHARIA CLEOPATRA

SHARIA ISKANDARIYA

SHARIA OMAR MUKHTAR

SHARIA LIBYA

SHARIA SHOKRI AL-QUWATII

SHARIA AL-QADI

Train Station

Bus & Service Taxi Station (1.5km), Airport (6km) & Alexandria (209km)

Bowling

Beach of Lovers & Wreck of U-75

Cleopatra's Beach (7km) & Agiba (24km)

Siwa, Sidi Barrani & Sollum

N

0   500 m

Arous el-Bahr Corniche ☎046/493-4420,
ℱ493-4419. The "Bride of the Sea" has pleasant
sea-facing a/c rooms with fridges, TV and
bathrooms, plus billiards, and a women-only gym
and sauna in the basement. Half board is obligatory
in high season; rates are fifty percent lower out of
season (when breakfast isn't included). ❺

Beau Site 1500m west along the Corniche
☎046/493-2066, ℱ493-3319, ⓦwww
.beausitehotel.com. Matrouh's best hotel has a/c
rooms overlooking a private beach and blue
lagoon; billiards, Internet access, a restaurant,
three bars and a summer disco. From June to Sept
half board is obligatory; off-season rates are forty
percent lower and include breakfast. Takes Master-
Card and Visa. ❼

Ghazala Sharia Alam Rum ☎046/493-3519.
Matrouh's cheapest hotel, with honest management, it has spartan rooms with washbasins but no
locks on the doors for £E15 per person, or £E20 for
a room to yourself. No hot water, nor running water
in the shared toilets/showers – they provide a
bucket of water for guests. No breakfast. ❶

Lido Sharia Galaa ☎ & ℱ046/493-2248. Rooms
are small but clean, with fans, TV, balconies, and
soap and towels in the bathroom. Breakfast
optional. ❷

Reem Corniche ☎046/493-3605, ℱ493-3608.
Less fancy than the *Beau Site*, but a lot cheaper for
a sea-facing room with a balcony, fridge and TV.
Half board included in high season; off-season
rates thirty percent lower. ❸

Riviera Palace Sharia Iskandariya
☎ & ℱ046/493-3045. Central three-star
hotel with a fake stuffed tiger in the lobby,
pleasant carpeted rooms with fridges, and a good
restaurant (no alcohol). Block-booked from July to
September. ❻

The town and the beaches

A grid of mould-poured blocks housing eighty thousand people, the **town**
spreads up from the coast towards a ridge festooned with radar dishes. As
Matrouh has gone from being a quiet fishing port to the booming capital of the
Mediterranean governorate, immigrants have poured in from other parts of
Egypt, inspiring mixed feelings amongst the locals.

Beaches are Matrouh's saving grace, so it's a shame that foreign women are
unlikely to enjoy them. As in Alex, Egyptian women sunbathe and swim fully
clothed, accompanied by male relations; a foreigner acting differently can be
subject to persistent staring and pestering. Only residents at the *Beau Site* can use
its private beach, free from hassle. The nearby municipal beaches are accessible by
bicycle, which can be rented from hotels and shops along Sharia Iskandariya
(£E10 per day). **Transport** to the western beaches varies with the season: from
June onwards you should be able to catch a microbus from the corner of Sharia
Galaa (£E3 to Agiiba), or an open-sided *tuf-tuf* bus (50pt) that shuttles back and
forth along the Corniche every hour or so from 6.30am to sunset, to Cleopatra
and Agiiba beaches. Additionally, local buses leaving from Sharia Tahrir run to
Zawiyat Umm al-Rukham. Alternatively, you can hire a taxi to take you to
Cleopatra and back, with an hour's waiting time, for about £E70.

For qualified divers, the coastal waters from Matrouh to the Gulf of Sollum
are as rewarding for **wreck-diving** as the Red Sea. Alas, since the Rommel
Dive Centre moved to Almaza Bay, you have to stay there to go on dive safaris.
Otherwise, only divers travelling with their own gear can explore the wrecks
off Rommel's Beach and the Beach of Lovers, in swimming range of the shore
(see below).

Town beaches

The three silvery-grey beaches around Matrouh's crescent-shaped bay are
separated by breakwaters and a small port further east. Beyond this, a spit of land
curves around to face the town, rimmed on the seaward side by **Rommel's
Beach**. The Desert Fox supposedly bathed here in between plotting the Alam
Halfa offensive from a nearby cave, now turned into a small **Rommel Museum**
(daily 9am–3pm except Fri; £E5). His maps, desk and leather greatcoat

(donated by his grandson, Manfred) are among the exhibits, which carry amusing captions like: "Rommel was the professor of contemporary military leaders to the extent that he was in every place at the same time."

Less than 100m off Rommel's Beach lies the stern half of the **Volo**, a 1567-tonne British freighter torpedoed en route from Tobruk to Alexandria by a German U-boat in December 1941; 28 of the 34 crew died. Further east is a sunken **cargo ship**, one of many supplied to Britain by the USA, which had numbers instead of names. Soon after sinking the *Volo*, U-boat **U-75** was holed by depth-charges from HMS *Kipling*; fourteen submariners drowned but thirty were rescued. The sub lies 600m off what is now the **Beach of Lovers** (Shaati al-Gharam), on the far side of Matrouh bay. A mile out in deeper water are **U-577**, sunk by a British Swordfish torpedo-bomber in 1942, and the destroyer **HMS Kipling**, crippled by Junkers-88s in May that year.

Back on land, you'd do better sunbathing at **Cleopatra Beach**, 7km west of town, which drops away sharply a metre offshore. Across the dunes on its far western side is **Cleopatra's Bath**, a hollow rock whirlpool bath where she and Mark Antony reputedly frolicked. Beyond the confines of the bath, heavy surf and sharp, slippery rocks make this a dangerous spot to swim.

Ubayyad and Agiiba beaches

Ubayyad Beach, 14km from town, is a vast expanse of silvery sand where the sea is calm and shallow up to 200m out. As you'd expect, it has been colonized: besides the Badr Tourist Village (open to the public) there is a private resort for army officers. Five kilometres further on, near the village of Umm Abraham, the sands have disgorged a tiny **ruined temple-fort** dedicated to Ramses II by his general Nebre, which marked Ancient Egypt's westernmost port. **Zawiyat Umm al-Rukham** (its local name) isn't signposted from the coastal road, and is currently off-limits while excavations continue. One find so far is a magnificent funerary statue of Nebre, now on display in the Luxor Museum (see p.350).

From the next headland, 24km from town, a path descends to **Agiiba Beach**. Agiiba ("Miraculous") is an apt name for this stunningly beautiful cove, but "beach" is rather a misnomer. To swim in the calm, crystal-clear turquoise water, you can dive off rocky shelves protruding into the sea or wade in off a tiny beach gunked up with algae. From July onwards, you'll have to walk around the headlands and along the shore to find an uncrowded spot. Bring food and drink as there's no guarantee of stalls operating on the cliff top, which overhangs some caves.

Eating

Matrouh's high street overflows with grocery stores and bakeries, and a fruit and veg **market** on nearby Sharia Omar Mukhtar – though many places are open year-round, they have longer hours in summertime. If you're looking for familiar fast food, there's a *KFC* beside the *Arous el-Bahr Hotel*. Of the hotel **restaurants**, the *Beau Site* and the *Riviera Palace* are the swankiest: otherwise, you're better off at one of the humbler places listed below. The opening hours given are for summertime; over winter, most places close before midnight, though coffee houses on the main drag and around the market stay open till the small hours.

Abdu Kofta Sharia Gamal Abdel Nasser. The best place in town for *kofta* or grilled meat (sold by weight), served with tasty *mezze* and salads, in a cool, clean upstairs room. Open year-round.

Abu al-Araby Sharia Tahrir. One of two simple fish restaurants on this street, where diners select their seafood from the freezer or wall-menu, specify grilled or fried, and sit back to await a delicious meal with all the trimmings.

Abu Rabie Sharia Iskandariya. Sit-down and takeaway diner offering *fuul*, *taamiya*, fried shrimp or *calamari* sandwiches, or any of those fillings served with rice and salad as a meal. Open till midnight year-round.

Hammo al-Temsah Fish Sharia Tahrir. Across the road from *Abu al-Araby*, this tiled diner specializes in fish rolled in a salty spice mixture that forms a charred crust when grilled, leaving the inside moist and tender. You can eat well for £E20–30, if you don't splurge on shrimp (£E140 per kilo).

Panyotis Greek Restaurant Sharia Iskandariya. Established in 1922, by one of the two families of Greek descent still living in Matrouh, in the summer it dishes up tasty fried fish or *calamari* with salad. Out of season no food is served, but alcohol is available year-round. Daily 8am–1am.

Drinking and entertainment

Matrouh is only lively over summer. The **Governorate Festival** (August 24) catches the season in full swing, with a parade of dancers, horses and camels down the main street and along the Corniche, and outdoor films and plays in the evening. In July and August, there's **live music** and **folklore shows** in the pleasure gardens near the *Beau Site Hotel*, and a Russian **circus** at the northern end of Sharia Iskandariya. Out of season, there's not much to do – the **bowling** alley near the *Beau Site* is open all year, and non-residents can play **billiards** (£E10/hr) and use the women-only **gym** and **sauna** (£E5/hr) at the *Arous el-Bahr Hotel*. Otherwise, you can watch TV in coffee houses or **drink**: inexpensive beers can be had downstairs at the *Panyotis Greek Restaurant* (spirits must be consumed upstairs or taken away wrapped), while the bars at the *Beau Site* are nice but pricey and a long walk from the centre. Reputedly, hashish can be obtained by asking around in any coffee house, but it would be foolhardy to do so.

Moving on

Three air-conditioned **buses** run daily from Matrouh to **Siwa Oasis** at 7.30am, 1.30pm and 4pm (£E12) – or you could catch the last through-bus from Alex, between 6.45 and 7.30pm. Allow half an hour to reach the bus station by microbus (25pt) from the junction of Omar Mukhtar and Cleopatra streets. There shouldn't be a problem getting a seat except around major Muslim or Siwan festivals; tickets can normally be bought on the bus. There may also be the odd **minibus** (£E12 per person for a full load) from the bus depot, but this should only be used as a last resort. Bring food and water for the four-and-a-half-hour journey. For details of buses to Sollum for the Libyan border, see p.618.

Siwa-bound **motorists** should avoid travelling in the midday heat and fill up before leaving, as there is only one petrol station along the three-hundred-kilometre Siwa route. The Siwa road is reached by following the Corniche west out of town, turning inland and passing the airport turn-off, and then heading south at the next junction, 20km from Matrouh. There's a police checkpoint, so you can't miss it. Don't stray far from the road if you stop for a leak; there are minefields on either side for miles into the desert.

Matrouh's **EgyptAir** office, on Sharia Galaa (Tues–Sun 9am–2pm & 6–9pm; ☎493-6573), is only open from June to September, when there are flights to Cairo (Thurs, Fri & Sun).

Sidi Barrani and Sollum

The **road to Libya** reflects relations between the Arab Republic of Egypt and the Libyan Jamahiriyah ("State of the Masses"). During the 1960s, when Gaddafi regarded Nasser's Egypt as the vanguard of Arab nationalism, people and goods flowed both ways, encouraging Gaddafi to propose that the two countries unite in 1973 – an ambition thwarted when Sadat cultivated the US and signed a peace treaty with Israel. In response, Libya severed relations, closed the border and began agitating for the overthrow of the Egyptian government; a cold war ensued, with sporadic incursions by Libyan warplanes and saboteurs during the 1980s.

It wasn't until 1990 that relations were restored and the border reopened. Despite an upturn in civilian traffic, there's still an overwhelming military presence along the 120km to **SIDI BARRANI** – a small port named after the Senussi missionary Sidi Mohammed el-Barrani, which was ferociously contested during the Western Desert campaign. In December 1940, the Eighth Army took 37,000 Italian prisoners for the loss of 600 of their own troops, only to be driven back by the Afrika Korps in 1942. At several sites along this coast, remnants from the war can be seen underwater. The Rommel Dive Centre at Almaza Bay (see p.612) offers **wreck-diving** trips to see the Royal Navy destroyer **HMS Defender**, which hunted four Italian submarines off the Libyan coast before being holed by a Junkers-88 in July 1941; the cruiser **HMS Niad** (torpedoed by a U-boat in 1942); the destroyer **HMS Gurka** (also sunk in 1942); and the German submarine **U-79** (depth-charged in 1941).

Sixty kilometres beyond Sidi Barrani, **SOLLUM** (pronounced "Sa-loom") overlooks the sea from a 180-metre cliff with a harbour at the bottom. A small **Allied War Cemetery** at the eastern entrance to town recalls the toll exacted at the Halfaya or "Hell Fire" Pass, where five waves of British tanks were destroyed by German guns dug into the ridge. Offshore lies an exciting dive site, the Italian submarine **Gondar**, containing three manned torpedoes of the type used against warships in Alexandria's Western Harbour (see p.590). The sub was forced to surface by depth charges and was scuttled by its crew in 1940; the Rommel Dive Centre can organize dives. Back on shore, Sollum boasts little more than a **bank**, a telephone office, a few grubby eating places and the *Sert* **hotel** (☎046/480-1113; ❷), which has en-suite rooms; its **restaurant** is the best place to eat in town.

The **border** crossing beyond the Halfaya Pass is officially open 24 hours, but its lethargic officials and sweltering queues of vehicles suggest otherwise. Foreigners must obtain Libyan **visas** beforehand (see p.264 for details of Libyan embassy in Cairo), and it's far easier to travel directly to Benghazi or Tripoli on a Superjet bus from the capital (see p.273) than catch a **bus** from Matrouh to Sollum (7am, 2pm, 3pm, 4.30pm, 6pm and 7.30pm; £E12; 4hr), and then a service taxi to the border crossing (£E4). On the Libyan side of the border, service taxis run to Al-Burdi, whence buses go to Tobruk and Benghazi.

5

The Delta

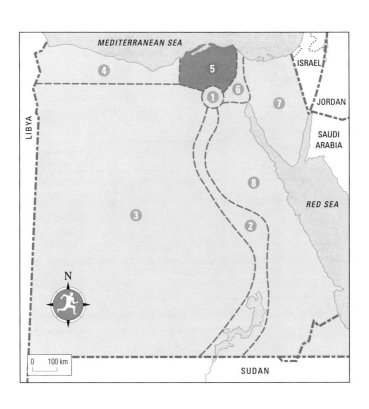

CHAPTER 5

Highlights

* **Rosetta's Delta-style architecture** The little town of Rosetta has been busy restoring its legacy of highly distinctive eighteenth- and nineteenth-century mansions, making it a very worthwhile stopover en route from Alexandria into the Delta. See p.623

* **Moulid of Saiyid Ahmed el-Bedawi** The city of Tanta becomes a seething mass of chanting Sufis, musicians, vendors, circus acts and spectators in the Delta's biggest festival of the year, held in October. See p.628

* **Tanis** The region's most interesting archeological site. See p.632

* **Lake Manzala** One of Egypt's top sites for birdwatching, where herons, spoonbills, pelicans and flamingos wade the shallows in search of fish. See p.637

△ Sarcophagus lids, Tanis

The Delta

W hile the Nile Valley's place in Ancient Egypt remains writ large in extraordinary monuments, the **Nile Delta**'s role has largely been effaced by time and other factors. Although several pharaonic dynasties arose and ruled from this region – Lower Egypt – little of their twenty provincial capitals remains beyond mounds of debris known as *tell* or *kom*. The pharaohs themselves set the precedent of plundering older sites of their sculptures and masonry – hard stone had to be brought to the Delta from distant quarries, so it was easier to recycle existing stocks – and nature performed the rest. With a yearly rainfall of nearly 20cm (the highest in Egypt, most of it during winter) and an annual inundation by the Nile that coated the land in silt, mud-brick structures were soon eroded or swept away. More recently, farmers have furthered the cycle of destruction by digging the mounds for a nitrate-enriched soil called *sebakh*, used for fertilizer; several sites catalogued by nineteenth-century archeologists have all but vanished since then.

Of the Delta's show of ancient monuments, the ruins of **Tanis**, **Avaris** and **Bubastis** are certainly worth knowing about, if not visiting. As for other sights, there's a sprinkling of "Delta-style" mansions in the coastal town of **Rosetta**, and an interesting museum in **Mansura**. Practically everywhere else on the map is an industrialized beehive or a teeming village, only worth visiting for **moulids** or popular festivals, of which the region has dozens. Combining piety, fun and commerce, the largest events draw crowds of over a million, with companies of *mawladiya* (moulid people) running stalls and rides, while the Sufi *tariqas* perform their *zikrs*. People camp outdoors and music blares into the small hours. Smaller, rural moulids tend to be heavier on the practical devotion, with people bringing their children or livestock for blessing, or the sick to be cured.

The great **Moulid of Saiyid el-Bedawi**, held at **Tanta** just after the cotton harvest in October, starts a cycle of Muslim festivals lasting well into November. At one- to two-week intervals, pilgrims and revellers congregate for week-long bashes at **Basyouni**, **Dasuq**, **Mahmudiya**, **Fuwa** and **Rosetta**. The Muslim month of Shawwal also occasions moulids at **Bilbeis** and **Zagazig**. During May, the remote **Monastery of St Damyanah** witnesses one of Egypt's largest **Christian moulids** and, come August, another event take place at the village of **Mit Damsis**. In January a unique **Jewish moulid** is held at **Damanhur**.

The Delta's other possible attraction is its flat, intensely green **landscape**, riven by waterways where feluccas glide past mud-brick villages and wallowing buffalo. The northern **lakes** are a wintering ground for herons, storks, great

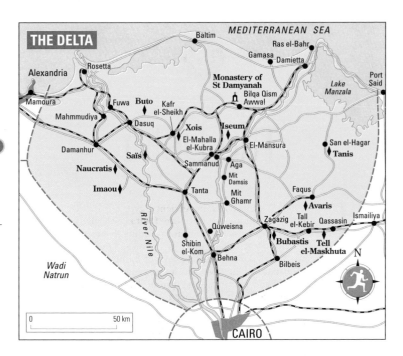

crested grebes and other water birds, while doves and pigeons – reared for human consumption in cotes shaped like Khmer temples – join other **birdlife** pecking around the cotton-, rice- and cornfields. In ancient times, wealthy Egyptians enjoyed going fowling in the reeds, using throwing sticks and hunting cats; their modern-day counterparts employ shotguns. The Delta is also still a habitat for wildcats and pygmy white-toothed shrews, but boars have been driven out and the last hippopotamus was shot in 1815.

More sombrely for the ecology, the Delta is one of the world regions most vulnerable to the effects of **global warming**. Oceanographers predict that a one-metre rise in the sea level would swamp Alexandria and submerge the Delta as far inland as Damanhur, destroying six percent of Egypt's cultivable land and displacing 3.3 million people. The freshwater Delta lagoons, which provide much of the nation's fish, would also be ruined. A more immediate threat is **erosion** by the Mediterranean. Now that the Delta is no longer renewed by silt from the Nile, its coastline is being worn away.

Visiting the Delta

As few visitors have time for more than one moulid or site, we've dealt with the region in less detail than other parts of Egypt. Depending on where you're aiming for, it might be better to start from Alex, Cairo or the Canal Zone: Rosetta and Damanhur are easiest to reach from Alex; Tanta from Cairo; and Zagazig from Ismailiya.

From Cairo, buses and service taxis to all parts of the Delta leave from Aboud terminal in Shubra (see p.271). There are direct buses from Cairo to the Delta resorts over summer. In some cases, a shortage of local **accommodation** makes day-trips more feasible than overnight stays. Trains are fine for reaching major towns, but service taxis and buses are the best way of getting around. Renting a car isn't necessarily a good idea: it's easy to have accidents on the Delta roads, and the unsurfaced ones are legally off-limits to foreign drivers – a hangover from 1960s spy-phobia. Should the police decide to make a fuss, you could conceivably spend a night in jail.

Rosetta, Damanhur and the Western Delta

The broader Rosetta branch of the Nile delineates one edge of the **Western Delta**, whose other flank fades into desert. Its cottonfields and mill towns are visible enough from the Delta Road or the Cairo–Alexandria railway, and few places merit closer inspection. **Rosetta** makes a nice day excursion from Alex, and **Damanhur** hosts two remarkable moulids, but you have to be pretty keen on archeology to bother with the *koms* off the Tanta road.

Rosetta (Rashid)

The coastal town of **ROSETTA** (Rashid in Arabic) has waxed and waned in counterpoint to the fortunes of Alexandria, 65km away. When Alex was moribund, Rosetta burgeoned as a port, entering its heyday after the Ottoman conquest of Egypt in the sixteenth century, only to decline after Alexandria's revival. The modern-day town is still "surrounded by groves of orange and lemon trees", as English traveller Eliza Fay wrote home in 1817, but its "appearance of cleanliness ... so gratifying to the English eye" has dissipated, and these days few tourists come to wander through its run-down, littered streets in search of once-elegant Ottoman mansions. It's certainly a far cry from the early nineteenth century, when travel writer E.D. Clarke saw "English ladies from the fleet and the army" wearing "long white dresses", riding "the asses of the country".

This earlier European fascination is due to the discovery of the **Rosetta Stone** by French soldiers in 1799. Their officer realized the significance of this second-century BC basalt slab inscribed with ancient hieroglyphs and demotic Egyptian and Greek script, which was forwarded to Napoleon's savants in Cairo. Although their archeological booty had to be surrendered in 1801 – which is how the Stone, "Alexander's Sarcophagus" and many other objects wound up in the British Museum – it was a French professor, Jean-François Champollion (1790–1832), who finally deciphered the hieroglyphs by comparison with the Greek text, and unlocked the secret of the Ancient Egyptian tongue.

The Town

Rosetta's main appeal lies in its **"Delta-style" architecture** dating from the Ottoman period of the eighteenth and nineteenth centuries. Many of the Delta-style mansions have recently been restored, their hallmarks being pointed brickwork (usually emphasized by white or red paint), inset beams and carved lintels, and a profusion of *mashrabiya*-work. with some also incorporating ancient columns. Though many of the Delta-style houses have been restored and look great from the outside, only one house, plus a Delta-style mill, are currently open to the public. **Tickets** to visit those, and Rosetta's other sights, are available from the Abu Shahim Mill (see p.624).

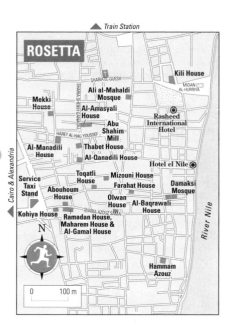

ROSETTA

▲ Train Station

SHARIA EL GUESH

Kili House

MIDAN
AL-HURRIYA

Ali al-Mahaldi
Mosque

Mekki
House

Al-Amasyali
House

Rasheed
International
Hotel

Abu
Shahim
Mill

HARET AL-HAG YOUSSEF

Al-Manadili
House

Thabet House

Al-Qanadili House

Hotel el Nile

Toqatli
House

Mizouni House

Service
Taxi
Stand

Abouhoum
House

Farahat House

Damaksi
Mosque

Olwan
House

Al-Baqrawali
House

Kohiya House

Ramadan House,
Maharem House &
Al-Gamal House

SHARIA AZOUZ SAMA

River Nile

N

0   100 m

Hammam
Azouz

Almost opposite the service taxi station, on Sharia Azouz Sama, you'll see some fine Delta-style houses, all dating from the eighteenth century. **Kohiya House** stands next to the mosque, while two doors further on is the trio of **Ramadan House**, **Maharem House** and **Al-Gamal House**, with **Abouhoum House** just across the street.

Further examples of Rosetta's Delta-style architecture lie on, or just off, Sharia Sheikh Qanadili, which runs north from Azouz Sama, parallel to the river, and is the second turning on your left past Abouhoum House. Just down the first turning on the right off Sheikh Qanadili is **Toqatli House**, held up by a recycled ancient column. Look upwards here to check out the *mashrabiya* window screens on the upper floors. Down the second right off Sheikh Qanadili are two more Delta-style residences, of which **Mizouni House**, built in 1740, is currently open to the public, though its interior isn't very exciting. The first house worth investigating along Sharia Sheikh Qanadili itself is **Al-Qanadili House**, on the left after 200m. **Thabet House**, 50m farther on the left, is one of the oldest of the Delta-style houses, built in 1709. Just around the corner, at the end of the next turning on the left (Haret al-Hag Youssef) is **Al-Manadili House**, its portico supported by two ancient columns of pharaonic or Greco-Roman origin. Inside, it boasts some wonderful ceilings, but is currently closed to the public.

Fifty metres further along Sheikh Qanadili is **Al-Amasyali House**, its upstairs reception room ennobled by a superb wooden ceiling and mother-of-pearl-inlaid *mashrabiyas*. Like the **Abu Shahim Mill** next door, it was built around 1808 for the Turkish Agha, Ali al-Topgi, who bequeathed them both to his servant Al-Amasyali. The mill, with its huge wooden grinders and delicately pointed keyhole arches, is open to the public, and it is here that you can buy tickets to visit all Rosetta's sights (all daily 9am–4pm, closing an hour earlier during Ramadan). Among them, a £E12 ticket (students £E6) allows you to visit the mill, the Beit al-Mizouni House (see opposite) and the Hammam Azouz bathhouse (see opposite).

Continuing along Sharia Sheikh Qanadili from here, a right turn after 100m takes you onto Sharia el-Guesh, with its small church. A left just before the church leads 500m to the train station, served by one morning train to Alex and eight trains a day to Mamoura (some connecting for Alexandria). Continuing straight ahead along El-Guesh past the church, you come to a junction, where the turning to the right, a busy market street, takes you past the **Ali al-Mahaldi Mosque**, worth popping in to check out the amazing miscellany of pilfered columns holding it up, some Greco-Roman, others looking suspiciously like the columns used to hold up the pulpits of Coptic churches.

If, instead of turning right at the junction on Sharia el-Guesh, you continue straight on (eastwards), you come out into **Midan al-Hurriya**, the town's main square, where the eighteenth-century **Kili House** contains a small **museum**, though its only notable exhibit is a diorama showing British soldiers being trounced by the locals. The museum has been closed for restoration, but when it reopens tickets (£E12, students £E6) should be available at Abu Shahim Mill.

Straight ahead of you at this point is the river, and if you continue south along the Corniche for 300m or so, and then take a right, you'll find the **Damaksi Mosque**, built in 1714, one storey above street level, next to another mansion, **Al-Baqrawali House**. Another couple of hundred metres south is a nineteenth-century bathhouse, **Hammam Azouz**. The marble interior, with its marble floors and fountains, has been lovingly restored, enabling you to see a fine example of a traditional bathhouse, though it is not in use today.

In addition to those described in the preceding section, we have marked one or two more Delta-style mansions on our map (**Olwan House**, **Farahat House** and **Mekki House**, the last dating, like Thabet House, from 1709), and you may wish to seek them out, though they are not open to the public, nor of any especially greater interest than those we have described.

Seven kilometres out of town is the **Fort of Qaitbey** (daily 9am–4pm, Ramadan 9am–3pm; £E12, students £E6). Built in 1479 to guard the mouth

△ Part of the facade of Ramadan House

of the Nile, it served as the first line of defence against the Crusaders and was later reinforced by the French, whose use of masonry imported from Upper Egypt led to the discovery of the Rosetta Stone. The fort can be reached from town by green-and-white taxi (£E30 round-trip) or fishing boat (£E50 after bargaining). For an alternative river trip, you can visit the tranquil old **Mosque of Abu Mandar**, 5km upriver from Rosetta; taxi-boats leave from the docks near Midan al-Horriya – expect to pay £E20–30 after haggling.

Around mid-November, the chain of festivals that started in Tanta the previous month should reach Rosetta. Don't despair if you come a few weeks earlier, since similar **moulids** occur at Fuwa, Mahmudiya and Dasuq, further inland. Salted fish (*fiseekh*) and hummus are the traditional snacks at these events.

Practicalities

The quickest way to reach the town from Alexandria is by **service taxi** from Midan el-Gumhorriya (1hr; £E3). There is also one **train** a day from Alex, which takes two hours. From Cairo, there is no direct transport, and the best way to get here is by train or service taxi to Damanhur, from where you can take a taxi (£E1) across town to pick up a service taxi to Rosetta (1hr 15min; £E2.25). There are no train services between Rosetta and Dasuq, Damanhur, Tanta or Cairo.

The best **place to stay** is the ⚓*Rasheed International Hotel* on the other side of the park south of Midan al-Horriya (☏045/239-4399, ✉rasheedhotel@yahoo.com; ❸), with air-conditioned en-suite rooms, some giving views over Midan al-Horriya or the river, while its **restaurant** offers the best food in town. The *Hotel el Nile* (☏045/292-2382; ❷), 300m along the Corniche south of the Beit Kili museum, is simple and clean, and some rooms have balconies overlooking the river.

Damanhur and around

Most of the land between Alex and Tanta is given over to **cotton**, Egypt's major cash crop, whose intensive cultivation began under Mohammed Ali. His French hydroengineer's scheme to regulate the flood waters by means of barrages across the Rosetta and Damietta branches of the Nile was ultimately realized by Sir Colin Scott-Moncrieff in 1880–90. The shift from flood to perennial irrigation enabled three or four cotton crops a year to be grown in the Delta, as is still the case.

Hardly surprising, then, that local towns are heavily into textiles, particularly the Beheira governorate capital, **DAMANHUR**, once Tmn-Hor, the City of Horus. This is also the main **transport** hub for the Western Delta, with regular trains to Cairo and Tanta, or to Alex, plus service taxis to all those places from Kubra Helu station, and to Rosetta or Dasuq (change there for Kafr el-Sheikh) from Kobri al-Felaqa station. A £E1 taxi ride will get you from one of these two service taxi stations to the other or to the train station.

Although much of Damanhur is drably functional, this city of 170,000 people gains a dash of colour from green-shuttered houses and bougainvillea-laden archways, and blossoms during its festival, **Moulid of Sheikh Abu Rish**, when turbaned Sufis perform *zikrs* and *munshids* to enthusiastic crowds. This occurs in late October and early November, a week after the festival at Dasuq, across the river. With venues so close together, the *mawladiya* (moulid people) can easily move on to the next event: barbers, circumcisers and all.

Egypt's only **Jewish moulid**, held over two days in January, is a very different scene. The shrine of **Abu Khatzeira**, a nineteenth-century mystic, has often been suspended in recent years, and when it is held, it's cordoned off by security police who rigorously exclude non-Jewish Egyptians, fearing a terrorist attack. Within the cordon a few thousand visitors, mostly French or Israeli, bring sick relatives or bottled water to be blessed, and "bid" for the key to Abu Khatzeira's shrine; the money raised supports its upkeep.

Two moulids: Dasuq and Fuwa

A week or so after Tanta's festival (see p.628), the agricultural town of **DASUQ** (the "q" is usually pronounced as a glottal stop) holds the **Moulid of Ibrahim al-Dasuqi** (starting October 10), drawing almost as many people to the eight-day event. Al-Dasuqi (1246–88) was the only native-born Egyptian to found a major Sufi order, the Burhamiya (whose chosen colour is green): the other brotherhoods originated abroad, or were started here by foreigners.

Dasuq is probably easiest to reach from Damanhur by bus or service taxi. You can also get to it by service taxi from Kafr el-Sheikh and Rosetta. Service taxis from Dasuq also serve **FUWA**, 13km northwest, where another **festival** occurs in late October or early November.

Between Damanhur and Tanta

A couple of **ancient sites** reduced to *kom* lie off the road between Damanhur and Tanta (64km). Roughly 23km out of Damanhur, a track leads 3km left off the main road to the village of El-Nibeirah, near two low mounds marking the site of **Naucratis**. During the XXVI Dynasty, when Egypt was ruled from the Delta, King Amasis (570–526 BC) granted this Greek colony a monopoly of trade between Egypt and Greece. Excavating the site for the British Museum in the nineteenth century, the great Egyptologist Flinders Petrie found it littered with shards of Greek pottery, and imagined that he was "wandering in the smashings of the Museum's vase-room".

At Itai El-Baroud, the last town before crossing the Rosetta branch of the Nile, another turn-off runs 14km south to El-Tud, by the "Mound of the Fort", Kom el-Hisn. This used to be **Imaou**, which became the capital of the Third Nome (an administrative district) during the New Kingdom, and was turned into a necropolis by the Hyksos pharaohs. A temple enclosure and numerous tombs are still evident.

Tanta and the Central Delta

Tanta, Egypt's fifth largest city, hosts the country's greatest moulid, which is worth experiencing for at least a day. The city also serves as a jumping-off point for practically everywhere else in the **Central Delta**, with several other moulids and a host of ancient sites scattered around the region. With regular trains and service taxis to Alex and Cairo running from early morning till nigh on midnight, you don't have to stay in Tanta; indeed, you'd be lucky to find a vacant room during the moulid. Elsewhere, tourist accommodation is virtually nonexistent anyway. Because the northwestern corner of this part of the Delta is easier to reach from Damietta or El-Mansura, we've allocated sites there to the "Eastern Delta" section (see p.630).

Tanta

A bustling industrial city with strong rural ties, **TANTA** marks the end of the cotton harvest in October with Egypt's largest festival, the **Moulid of Saiyid Ahmed el-Bedawi**. Tanta's population jumps from 250,000 to nearly three million as visitors pour in from the Delta villages, other parts of Egypt and the Arab world. Streets and squares fill with tents and stalls; Sufis prepare for *zikrs*, while musicians test their amps ("Allah, two, three"). Thousands camp out amid heaps of blankets and cooking pots, though sleep seems impossible. With music and chanting, vendors and devotees, a circus with lions and tigers and a levitation act, Tanta becomes a seething cacophony. If you plan to attend the week-long festival, it is best to leave all your valuables somewhere safe. Pickpocketing is rife and injuries may result from crushing or fist-fights in the dense crowd.

The moulid honours the founder of one of Egypt's largest Sufi brotherhoods. Born in Fès in Morocco in 1199, **Saiyid Ahmed el-Bedawi** was sent to Tanta in 1234 by the Iraqi Rifaiyah order, and later established his own *tariqa* ("brotherhood"), the Ahmediya. His name is invoked to ward off calamity – "Ya saiyid, ya Bedawi!" – but his moulid is anything but angst-ridden. "Although a religious festival, pleasure is the chief object of the pilgrims, and a few *fatahs* at the tomb of the saint are sufficient to satisfy every pious requirement", noted *Murray's Handbook* in 1891. The climax to the eight-day festival occurs on a Friday, when the Ahmediya – whose banners and turbans are red – parade with drums behind their mounted sheikh. Events focus on the triple-domed, Ottoman-style **mosque** wherein Bedawi and a lesser sheikh, Abd el-Al, are buried, which is located some 300m east of the railway station.

Tanta is known for its roasted chickpeas or garbanzo beans (*hummus* in Arabic, though it does not necessarily mean that they are mashed with garlic and tahini). They can be bought at any of the multitude of sweet shops surrounding the mosque.

Practicalities

As the **transport** hub of the Delta region, Tanta is well served, with regular buses to Cairo's Aboud terminal (half-hourly 6am–10pm; 1hr 30min). These serve the **Gomla bus station**, 2km north of the city centre (£E1–2 by taxi, or 30pt by microbus from opposite the rail station), where you will also find buses to Damanhur and Alexandria (every 45min till 7pm), and to Port Said (3 daily, all in the morning), and Suez (4 daily), plus service taxis to Cairo (1hr 15min), Damanhur (1hr) and Alex (2hr 15min). Buses to Mahalla el-Kubra leave every fifteen minutes from **Mura Shaha station**, which is connected with Gomla by microbus (30pt), and where you will also find service taxis to Mahalla (30min), Sammanud (40min), Mansura (1hr), Ismailiya (2hr) and Zagazig (1hr). Service taxis to Kafr el-Sheikh (1hr) leave from a place called Staad, which is on the microbus route between Gomla and Mura Shaha. From the handsome railway station in the city centre, there are nine air-conditioned **train** services a day to Benha, Cairo, Damanhur and Alexandria, plus innumerable slow ones to the above destinations, as well as to Mansura (1hr 30min), as well as ten to Damietta (2hr), but only one to Zagazig (1hr 30min).

Should you wish to **stay** in the vicinity during the moulid, book a room as far in advance as possible. The *New Arafa Hotel* on Midan al-Mahata, almost opposite the train station (☎040/340-5040 to 47; ❸), is conveniently located and good value, its decent-sized rooms equipped with a/c, TV and a minibar. Alternatively, the *Green House Hotel* on Sharia el-Borsa, off

Midan el-Gomhurriya, about 600m east of the station (☎040/333-0761 or 2, ⓕ333-0320; ☻), has similar facilities but smaller rooms and is not quite as comfortable, though its friendly staff can organize most things for you on request. On Midan el-Gomhurriya, diagonally opposite the street leading to the *Green House*, the Delta **Bank** cashes traveller's cheques, and there's an ATM for Visa and MasterCard outside the bank next door.

Around Tanta

Some of the places below are directly accessible from Tanta; to reach others you might have to change once or twice. For the committed, renting a private **taxi** gives the greatest scope for excursions.

As a footnote to bygone rulers, it's worth mentioning (but not visiting) the village of **Mit Abu el-Kom**, near the small town of Quweisna to the south of Tanta, as the **birthplace of Anwar Sadat**. Born in 1908, he escaped rural life by joining the army, became a nationalist and conspired with like-minded officers to overthrow King Farouk. As Nasser's heir, President Sadat waged war against, and then signed a peace treaty with, Israel; opened Egypt to Western capitalism – generating a consumer boom and massive corruption; and was ultimately assassinated by Islamic militants in 1981.

Buto and Xois

Only those with private transport and a consuming passion for **ancient sites** will bother trying to reach **Tell al-Faraoun** ("Mound of the Pharaoh"), on the edge of some marshes north of Ibtu village, itself 5km north off the Dasuq–Kafr el-Sheikh road. The site appears on maps as **Buto**, the Greek name for a dual city known to the Ancient Egyptians as Pr-Wadjet. **Wadjet**, the cobra-goddess of Lower Egypt (and whom the Greeks called Buto) was worshipped in the half of the city known as Dep. The other city, known as **Pe**, was dedicated to **Djbut**, the heron-god, who was later supplanted by Horus. Nothwithstanding all this, the 180-acre site had been obliterated down to its paving stones by the time Petrie excavated it.

Should you carry on to **Kafr el-Sheikh** and follow the Tanta road south, you'll pass the village of Sakha, occupying the site of **Xois**, ancient capital of the Sixth Nome.

Saïs

Nothing but a few pits filled with stagnant water remains of the once great city of **Saïs**, near the modern village of **Sa el-Hagar**, beside the Rosetta branch of the Nile. Founded at the dawn of Egyptian history, it was always associated with the goddess of war and hunting, **Neith**, whose cult emblem appeared on predynastic objects. In Egyptian cosmology, she was also the protectress of embalmed bodies; the Greeks identified her with Athena.

The city became Egypt's capital during the **Saïte Period**, when the XXVI Dynasty (664–525 BC) looked back to the Old Kingdom for inspiration, refurbishing the pyramid tombs and reviving archaic funerary rituals. In 525 BC the dynasty was overthrown by the Persian emperor Cambyses, who is said to have had the body of the penultimate Saïte king, Amasis "the Drunkard", removed from its tomb, whipped and burnt.

El-Mahalla el-Kubra and Sammanud

EL-MAHALLA EL-KUBRA, 24km northeast of Tanta, is Egypt's fourth largest city and a taxi staging-post for journeys to the riverside town – almost a suburb, these days – of **SAMMANUD**. Should you wish to stay in El-Mahalla, try the town's top **hotel**, the two-star *Omar Khayyam* on Midan Setta w'Ashreen Yulyu, 300m north of the train station along 26th July Street (☏040/223-4299; ❶), which is good value and well kept, with a choice of smaller rooms with shared bathrooms or larger en-suite rooms with a/c. Service taxis to Mansura, Damietta and Alexandria, along with frequent local buses to Tanta, leave from a depot round the corner from the train station, while service taxis for Tanta and Cairo leave from 500m south on 26th July Street, by a clock in the form of the Eiffel Tower: intercity buses also stop here.

Immediately west of the Sammanud taxi depot, near the hospital, a large mound and a scattering of red and black granite blocks mark the site of the Temple of Onuris-Shu, rebuilt by Nectanebo II to grace **Tjeboutjes**, the capital of the Twelfth Nome. Another city, **Busiris**, occupied a bluff overlooking the river further south, along the road out of Sammanud. However, part of a XXVI Dynasty basalt statue and fragments of a monumental gateway are all that remain of this reputed birthplace of Osiris.

The H8 road, which runs northeast from Sammanud to El-Mansura (see p.635), takes you past the site of ancient Pr-Hebeit, 10km to the west, better known by its Roman name, **Iseum**. Here, the great **Temple of Isis** which Nectanebo began and Ptolemy II completed has been reduced to an enclosure wall, some carved granite blocks and Hathor-headed capitals.

The Eastern Delta and the Delta resorts

The **Eastern Delta** scores on several counts: **Tanis**, **Avaris** and **Bubastis** are the best **pharaonic ruins** that Lower Egypt can offer; there are **moulids** aplenty, both Christian and Muslim; and if you include the places on the Central Delta coast, which are easier to reach from here, the region can also claim low-key beach resorts such as **Ras el-Bahr**, and some fine **bird-watching**. For some of these destinations it might be simpler to approach the Eastern Delta from Port Said or Ismailia, rather than Alex.

Zagazig and the ruins of Bubastis

The charmingly named **ZAGAZIG** (usually pronounced "Za'a'zi") is less appealing in reality, blighted by fumes from a soap factory. Only founded in 1830, it boasts of being the home town of Colonel **Ahmed Orabi** (1839–1911), leader of the 1882 revolt against British rule, whose statue stands outside the station. As a provincial capital with a thriving university, Zagazig is reticent about being the source of most of the **papyruses** sold in tourist shops throughout Egypt, which are manufactured in sweatshops and sold to dealers for as little as £E3–4 apiece. From a tourist's standpoint, its attractions are the **Moulid of Abu Khalil**, held outside the main mosque during the month of Shawwal (currently October or November), and the paltry ruins of Bubastis, to the southeast of town.

Whatever its shortcomings, Zagazig has the merit of being readily accessible. You can travel the 80km from Cairo by **bus** (every 20min; 1hr 30min; £E5) or **service taxi** (1hr 15min; £E3.50) from the Aboud terminal; coming back, service taxis for Cairo leave from just by the railway station. To find the bus station, cross the tracks via the pedestrian underpass, then turn left, and it's 200m ahead on the right. Buses from here also serve Benha (half-hourly; 45min), Cairo (half-hourly; 1hr 30min), Alexandria (4 daily; 3hr 30min), Ismailia (4 daily; 2hr) and Port Said (2 daily; 4hr). To find service taxis for Ismailia and Port Said, you'll have to go the Ismailia service taxi station,

5km from the town centre, reached by microbuses (50pt) from outside the train station. Buses and service taxis for Tanta, Mansura and Faqus leave from the Mansura bus station, which you can also get to by microbus from in front of the station (25pt). **Trains** from Zagazig serve Cairo (26 daily; 1hr 40min), Benha (26 daily; 40min), Ismailiya (18 daily; 1hr 20min), Mansura (14 daily; 1hr 30min) and Port Said (7 daily; 2hr 35min).

There are two cheap **hotels** opposite the train station; the better of the two by far is the *Opera* (℡055/230-3718; **①**), though it's slightly hidden away, with its entrance tucked away down a side alley and its sign in Arabic only. For something a little bit classier, try the three-star *Marina* at 58 Sharia Gamal Abdel Nasser, near al-Fatr Mosque (℡055/231-3934; **③**).

Bubastis

To reach the site of **BUBASTIS** (daily 9am–3pm; £E10, camera £E10, no student reductions), take the underpass on the left-hand side of the station and continue straight ahead (southeast) along Sharia Farouq for just under 1km, either on foot, or by microbus from the beginning of Farouq (25pt), or by taxi (£E1). The site is about 100m to your right at the end of the street. You are likely to get a thorough grilling on entry from the guards, who are not really used to foreign visitors, and may even follow you around the site, and there's little to see beyond the few displayed artefacts but scattered blocks and gaping pits. Nonetheless, archeologists have found here Old and New Kingdom cemeteries and vaulted catacombs full of feline mummies. The city was known to the Ancient Egyptians as Pr-Bastet ("House of Bastet"), after the cat-goddess whom they honoured with licentious festivals (see box below). Pilgrims sailed here in high spirits, saluting riverside towns with music, abuse and exposed loins. In the fifth century BC, Herodotus noted that 700,000 revellers consumed more wine than "during the whole of the rest of the year", and described how the city lay on raised ground encircling a canal-girt temple, "the

---

Bastet

The feline goddess **Bastet** was originally depicted as a lioness, her head surmounted by a solar disc and *uraeus* serpent. As the daughter of Re, she was associated with the destructive force of the sun-god's eye. This aggressive side of Bastet can be seen in texts and reliefs describing the pharaoh in battle. Her epithet, "Lady of Asheru", also linked her to the goddess Mut at Karnak, where temple reliefs show the pharaoh running ritual races in front of Bastet.

▲ Bastet

After about 1000 BC, however, this aspect of Bastet became subsumed by Sekhmet (see p.369), and the goddess herself was portrayed more commonly as a cat, often with a brood of kittens, and carrying a sacred rattle. The Coffin Texts of the Middle Kingdom frequently invoke her protection as the first-born daughter of Atum (another aspect of the sun-god). In return, the Egyptians venerated cats and mummified them at several sites, including Bubastis and Memphis. It was even a capital offence to kill a cat in Ancient Egypt, and when people's pet cats died, they were accorded funerary rites like those given to humans.

The Greeks later identified Bastet with Artemis, the Virgin Hunter, who was believed to be able to transform herself into a cat. The Egyptian association with cats remained strong even after the arrival of Christianity, and it was from Egypt that cats are thought to have arrived in Europe during or before the fourth century AD.

most pleasing to look at" in all of Egypt. Begun by the VI Dynasty pyramid-builders, Bubastis was enlarged and embellished for over 1700 years, attaining its apogee after its rulers established the XXII Dynasty, though the capital in this period was probably still Tanis (see below).

Bilbeis and Benha

To the south and southwest of Zagazig a couple of minor towns are worth a passing mention. **BILBEIS**, 10km away by road or rail, hosts a couple of festivals during Shawwal: its **moulids** of Abu Isa and Abu Alwan predate Abu Khalil's in Zagazig. Further west, beside the Damietta branch of the Nile, **BENHA**, at the junction of the Cairo–Alexandria and Cairo–Ismailiya train lines, is near another ancient site. To the northeast of town, 150m off the road, Kom el-Atrib is what remains of **Athribis**, once the capital of the Tenth Nome. This was the birthplace of Psammetichus I (664–610 BC), who restored pharaonic authority over Upper and Lower Egypt, replacing the so-called Dodekarchy with centralized government by the Saïte dynasty. Benha is served by six air-conditioned fast trains a day, plus numerous slower ones, and there are buses every twenty minutes from 6am to 9pm from Cairo's Aboud terminal, plus service taxis from Aboud.

Tanis, Avaris and the "Land of Goshen"

Early archeologists were drawn to the eastern marches of the Delta in search of clues to the Israelites' Biblical sojourn, but what they found proved more important to knowledge of Ancient Egypt. Fragmented statues and stelae, papyrus texts and layers of debris have shed light on dynastic chronologies and religious cults, the movement of Delta waterways and imperial borders, invasions and famines. Fresh discoveries are still being made – particularly at Avaris, a site associated with the Hyksos "Shepherd Kings" who seized control of the Delta after the collapse of the Middle Kingdom, and which could also have been inhabited by the Israelites during their sojourn in Egypt. The following accounts simplify a mass of contradictory evidence and theories thrown up by archeologists.

Tanis

One of the oldest-known sites is a huge *kom* near the village of **San el-Hagar** ("San of the Stones"), 167km northeast of Zagazig. Barring a stint by Petrie, the excavation has mostly been in French hands since the 1860s. Although best known by its Greek name, **TANIS**, the city was called *Zoan* in the Bible and known to the Ancient Egyptians as Djanet. It originally stood beside the Tanite branch of the Nile, which has long since dried up. In the film *Raiders of the Lost Ark*, it is here that Indiana Jones uncovers the Ark of the Covenant.

The **age and identity** of Tanis have been much debated, as scholars have frequently conflated it with Avaris, the capital of the Hyksos, or the much later city of Pi-Ramses, supposedly the "City of Bondage" from which the Israelites fled. In recent decades, however, both have been firmly identified with other sites (see p.634), and Tanis is now thought to have come into existence long afterwards, during the Third Intermediate Period. Some theorize that the XXI Dynasty founded Tanis as their capital at the same time as they abandoned the traditional cult of Seth in favour of the Theban Triad.

The desolate **site** looks as if the huge Ramessid **Temple of Amun** was shattered by a giant's hammer, scattering chunks of masonry and fragments of statues everywhere. Confusingly for scholars, the founders of Tanis plundered masonry from cities all over the Delta (some predating the Hyksos, who had earlier usurped it). In 1939, Pierre Montet discovered the **tombs** of **Psusennes II** and **Osorkon II**, containing the "Treasure of Tanis", which is now in the

Cairo Museum. Perplexingly, it was soon noted that the tomb of the XXI Dynasty ruler Psusennes seems to have been built *after* that of Osorkon, who is supposed to have lived well over a century later, during the XXII Dynasty. This anomaly is one of the cornerstones of controversial Egyptologist David Rohl's thesis that the conventional dating of events in Ancient Egypt is wrong by some centuries. Rohl argues that the two dynasties were actually contemporary, and that by assuming that they were sequential, archeologists have overestimated the duration of the Third Intermediate Period by at least 140 years. For more on this debate see the box on p.765.

While the site at Tanis can be wandered at will, **getting there** is awkward. The best jumping-off point is **FAQUS**, 37km to the south, which can be reached by service taxi from Ismailiya, Cairo or Zagazig, by bus from Zagazig or from Cairo's Aboud terminal (every 45min 7.30am–8.15pm; 2hr). From Faqus, you can catch a local bus or service taxi to San el-Hagar, or rent a private taxi for the round trip.

Avaris

Since 1966, excavations by Manfred Bietak at **Tell ed-Daba** ("Mound of the Hyena") have yielded many discoveries that have confirmed it as the site of **AVARIS**, the long-vanished **Hyksos** capital. The most sensational find, in 1991, were **Minoan-style frescoes** in a Hyksos-era palace on the western edge of the site, evincing strong links with the Minoan civilization on Crete, 500 miles away, even if not disproving the idea that the Hyksos originated in Palestine or Syria. (The term Hyksos derives from *hekau-khasut*, "princes of foreign lands".) Painted as Cretan civilization reached its zenith, the murals feature Cretan mountain landscapes and acrobats vaulting over bulls, as in the Minoan frescoes at Knossos. Both the Minoans and the Hyksos are thought to have associated bulls with the worship of storm gods.

However, the Hyksos finds are only half the story, for Avaris existed long before their invasion, and may hold the key to early Biblical history. Before finding the frescoes, Bietak's team excavated what had been a hilly residential quarter, uncovering grave goods that suggested that the bulk of the population originated from Palestine and Syria. This lay above a stratum of evidence for an older, more sophisticated community of non-Egyptians, where 65 percent of the burials were of children below the age of two. David Rohl (see p.765) argues that this represents the **Israelites** during their sojourn in Egypt and the culling of their male newborn by the "pharaoh who did not know Joseph", which would place the events of Exodus in the reign of Djudmose of the XIII Dynasty, *c.*1447 BC – two or three centuries earlier than is commonly accepted. The plagues that struck Egypt, followed by the Exodus, might then have been instrumental in leaving the Delta exposed to invasion by the warlike nomads later known as the Hyksos. Having been taken over by these newcomers, Avaris remained the Hyksos capital until its destruction by Ahmosis I, the founder of the New Kingdom.

Tell ed-Daba is only 7km from Faqus, and although the site is not yet officially open to tourists, those with a special interest can get permission to visit from the Supreme Council of Antiquities in Cairo.

The "Land of Goshen"

Many archeologists have striven to uncover the "**Land of Goshen**" where, according to the Biblical book of Exodus, the Israelites toiled for the pharaoh before Moses led them out of Egypt – though some shrewdly plugged the Biblical connection to raise money for digs with other aims (notably Petrie at Tanis). Public opinion was fixated on the Biblical "store cities of Pithom and Raamses", speculatively assigned to many locations between Avaris and the Bitter Lakes (the area through which the Suez Canal runs). "Raamses" has usually been identified as Pi-Ramses, the royal city of the XIX Dynasty pharaoh Ramses II – which is why his successor, Merneptah, regularly gets fingered as the pharaoh of the Exodus.

It is now certain that **Pi-Ramses** was centred on the modern-day village of **Qantir**, 3km northeast of Tell ed-Daba, but extended far enough to cover most of Avaris, which had been laid to waste centuries earlier. A mud-brick palace dating to the earliest phase of the city was discovered in 1929, and Bietak's excavations have revealed barracks and workshops, also from the Ramessid era. Unfortunately for those who believe that this was the "City of Bondage", no evidence of a foreign population was found in any of the strata associated with the New Kingdom – whereas at Tell ed-Daba, there are extensive traces from the Middle Kingdom, and even mass graves that fit the Biblical account of a calamity. Rather, Pi-Ramses was a parvenu city founded by Seti I and turned into a royal capital by Ramses II, which had dwindled in significance by the end of the New Kingdom. Much of its stonework was later taken to Tanis or Bubastis during the XXI and XXII dynasties; the most notable bits still *in situ* are the feet and one arm of a colossus of Ramses II, lying 50m apart in a field.

If the Israelites did flee from Avaris, what of the other cities mentioned in the book of Exodus – Pithom and Succoth? Here, the evidence is less conclusive, but they could well have been somewhere around **Tell el-Maskhuta**, an enormous *kom* off the road between Zagazig and Ismailiya. If Tell el-Maskhuta was really Pithom, then another *kom* a few kilometres to the west may have been Succoth.

To reach Sinai, the Israelites presumably went through Wadi Tumaylat, nowadays the route for traffic between Zagazig and Ismailiya (hourly buses). Before Tell el-Maskhuta, it passes **Tell el-Kebir**, where Orabi's rebellion was finally defeated by the British in September 1882. In the 1920s, the government sponsored a reforesting project in what was then virgin desert, and now supports plantations and orchards all the way to Ismailiya.

Mit Damsis and El-Mansura

Trains and inter-city buses take the shortest route **between Zagazig and El-Mansura**, and for most of the year that's a sensible option. In August, however, you might consider the alternative Mit Ghamr–Aga road in order to visit **Mit Damsis** village near the Damietta branch of the Nile, site of the Coptic **Moulid of St George**. Buses and service taxis **from Cairo** to El-Mansura, Zagazig and Faqus go mainly from the Aboud terminal; some minibus service taxis depart from outside Ramses train station, but these leave town by a more roundabout route and end up taking longer.

Mit Damsis

The **Moulid of St George** (August 2–28) is notable primarily for its **exorcisms**. Copts attribute demonic possession to improper baptism or deliberate curses, and specially trained priests bully and coax the *afrit* ("demon") to leave through its victim's fingers or toes rather than via the eyes, which is believed to cause blindness.

Egyptian Muslims likewise believe in possession, but don't always regard it as malign; in some cases they try to harmonize the relationship between the spirit and its human host rather than terminate it. Egyptians of both faiths take precautions against the Evil Eye. Christians put store in pictures of St George and the Virgin, while Muslims display the Hand of Fatima – literally hand-printed on the walls of dwellings – and perhaps the legend "*B'ismallah, masha' Allah*" ("In the name of God, whatever God wills").

Because the **moulid** is well attended there's a fair chance of lifts along the seven-kilometre track that turns west off the main road, 15km south of Aga. Mit Damsis rarely appears on maps; don't confuse it with Damas, which does.

El-Mansura

EL-MANSURA was founded as the camp of Sultan al-Kamil's army during the 1218–21 siege of Damietta, though its name ("The Victorious") was a premature boast, since the Crusaders reoccupied Damietta in 1247. Weakened by cancer and tuberculosis, Sultan Ayyub was unable to dislodge them, and died here in 1249 – a fact concealed by his widow, Shagar al-Durr, who issued orders in Ayyub's name, buying time until his heir could return from Iraq. Encouraged by the Mamlukes' withdrawal, France's Louis IX (later canonized as Saint Louis) led a sortie against the enemy camp, slaying their general in his bath. But with victory in sight, the Crusaders fell sick after eating corpse-fed fish, just before a devastating counterattack launched by Beybars the Crossbowman. Louis was captured and ransomed for Damietta's return, and later died in Tunisia while engaged on yet another ill-fated crusade.

The medieval house where Louis was imprisoned, Beit Ibn Luqman, is now the **Mansura National Museum** (Tues–Sun 8am–6pm; £E3), on Sharia Bur Said, 50m up from the Corniche, from which it is signposted. As well as the room where Louis was held prisoner, the museum has a hall of artworks portraying the events and characters of the defence of Mansura, most notably a wonderful tableau by Abdel Aziz Darwish in which a tired crusader knight is about to have his head hewn off by an Egyptian soldier, while a soldier to his left holds aloft a severed head and one to his right is busy throttling a crusader with his bare hands. There are also some swords and pieces of armour from the battle.

The rest of the town is mostly modern, with tree-lined avenues, a university, and a central mosque whose twin minarets are visible from afar. For outsiders, the town's most interesting feature is its delicious buffalo-milk **ice cream**, which can be sampled at the sweet shops on Sharia el-Habasy, a couple of blocks west of Sharia Bur Said.

Practicalities

Buses to Cairo (every 30 minutes 8.30am–9.30pm; 2hr) and Zagazig (every 30 minutes; 1hr 30min) run from the international bus station, which is 500m east of the train station down Sharia Gamal el-Din el-Afghani at the junction with Sharia el-Guesh. Buses from here also serve Sinai and the Canal Zone, with six a day to Sharm el-Sheikh (7hr) and nine to Suez (3hr 30min). **Service taxis** to Zagazig and Cairo leave from a station 1km further to the southeast. For Tanta, Alexandria, Mahalla el-Kubra, Kufr el-Sheikh, Damietta and Port Said, service taxis run from Talkha station across the river (cross the bridge at the Corniche end of Sharia Bur Said and continue straight ahead for about 1km to the end). **Trains** from Mansura are all pretty slow, and serve Cairo (7 daily; 2hr 30min–3hr), Zagazig (14 daily; 1hr 45min–2hr 05min), Damietta (14 daily; 1hr 30min), Tanta (25 daily; 1hr–1hr 30min) and Mahalla el-Kubra (25 daily; 45min).

El-Mansura has several **hotels** to choose from. The *Marshal el-Gezirah*, 2km west of the town centre on the Corniche (⊤ & Ⓕ 050/221-3000; ⓪), is the ritziest place in town, but there are several other decent choices that are both cheaper and more centrally located. The two-star ⚑ *Marshal Hotel* opposite the station on Midan Oum Kalthoum (☎050/233-3920; ❷) has very comfortable, carpeted rooms – ask for a big one as they all cost the same – and a **café** and pastry shop downstairs. One kilometre west at 13 Souk el-Toggar el-Gharby, off Sharia el-Habasy, is the *Cleopatra*, (☎050/223-6789 or 224-6789, Ⓕ224-1234; ❷), which has cosy rooms off its rather sombre wood-panelled corridors. Between the two, the *Abou Shama*, 300m west of the station on a little square halfway along Sharia el-Sawra (☎050/225-5810; ❷), is more modest, but still perfectly presentable.

The Monastery and Moulid of St Damyanah

Normally difficult to reach without private transport, the **Monastery of St Damyanah** becomes accessible during its namesake's **moulid** (May 15–20), when service taxis and private buses convey pilgrims across to the small town of **Bilqas Qisim Awwal**, whence it's 3km by track to Deir Sitt Damyanah. The monastery – whose four churches date from the nineteenth and twentieth centuries – is, in fact, rather less interesting than Damyanah's story and **festival**, which is one of the largest Christian moulids in Egypt. The daughter of a Roman governor under Diocletian, Damyanah refused to marry and insisted that her father build a palace into which she and forty other virgins could retire. All refused to worship Roman gods, and their example eventually converted her father – enraging Diocletian, who had the lot of them executed.

As with the Church of St George at Mit Damsis, Copts ascribe the building of Damyanah's shrine to St Helena, the mother of the Roman emperor Constantine. Pilgrims bring sick relatives (or livestock) to be blessed, and believe that Damyanah manifests herself at night as a pigeon, which can be distinguished from other birds by the trajectory of its flight. Icons and special pottery (inscribed "Happy returns, Damyanah") are popular buys at the fair, where Muslim tattooists do a brisk trade in St George, Christ on the cross, snakes, birds and other motifs, which punters select from display boards.

Damietta (Dumyat)

Sited near the mouth of the eastern branch of the Nile, the port city of **DAMIETTA** became prosperous in medieval times, through its trade in coffee, linen, dates and oil. However, it was always wide open to seaborne invasions and was seized by the Crusaders in 1167–68 and 1218–21, on the latter occasion accompanied by St Francis of Assisi – who ignorantly imagined that the Sultan al-Kamil knew nothing of Christianity, although he numbered Copts amongst his advisors. The main function of the Crusaders in Egypt, however, was pillage, and Damietta suffered heavily during its occupations. When Louis "the Pious" returned with a further crew in 1247, the inhabitants fled or deliberately sold the Crusaders contaminated fish – one cause of their defeat at El-Mansura (see p.635). Unfortunately, Damietta suffered a far worse attack under the Mamlukes, who razed the town and rendered its river impassable as a punishment for suspected disloyalty and a precaution against future invasions.

The town was revived by the Ottomans whose last pasha surrendered to the Beys here just before the rise of Mohammed Ali. With the opening of the Suez Canal, Damietta had to reorient its trade towards Port Said, some 70km away. Nowadays it's a thriving port city of 120,000 inhabitants, with the status of a provincial capital, and is known as a centre for the manufacture of furniture, which is the local cottage industry.

The only real reason to stay in Damietta is as a base for bird-watching or beachcombing. There are several modest **hotels** on the Nile-side Corniche, including the cheap but basic *Emad*, near Domiat el Ra'esy post office where the river bends (℡057/322-533; ❷). Just 200m away is the three-star *Soliman Inn* on Sharia el-Gala' (℡057/376-050, ℻377-050; ❷), with a/c, TV and fridge in every room, and 🍴 *El Manshy*, just off el-Gala' on Sharia el-Nokrashy (℡057/323-308; ❸), which is less well equipped but nonetheless good value and comfortable, with a decent **restaurant**. As for **transport**, Damietta is linked by rail with Tanta, Zagazig, Alex and Cairo, and by hourly buses (6am–5pm) or service taxis with Mansura and Cairo. Closer at hand are Port Said (30min drive along the causeway between Lake Manzala and the Med) and the beach resorts of the Central Delta, most importantly Ras el-Bahr.

Lake Manzala

East of Damietta lies **Lake Manzala**, a great place for **bird-watching** if you can find a boatman to take you through the reeds. In the nineteenth century, European visitors tended to be more interested in shooting wildfowl than observing it. "Their compact mass formed living islands upon the water; and when the wind took me to these, a whole island rose up with a loud and thrilling din to become a feathered cloud in the air", wrote one hunter.

Winter is the best time to see herons (*balashon* to locals), spoonbills (*midwas*), pelicans (*begga*) and flamingos (*basharus*). Along the Nile, these last are called "water camels" (*gamal el-bahr*).

Ras el-Bahr

RAS EL-BAHR, where the eastern branch of the Nile flows into the Med north of Damietta, is a pleasant beach resort. Across the river lies the busy fishing port of **Ezbet el-Bourg** (unmarked on most maps), named after an abandoned nineteenth-century **coastal fort** that's fun to explore. Hidden beneath a section of the walls is the **command bunker** (code-named Centre #10) containing seven small rooms in which Sadat's generals directed the October War of 1973.

From June to September, Ras el-Bahr is readily accessible from June to September by **service taxi** and **bus** (every 45min; 3hr 30min) from Cairo's Aboud terminal. Year-round, there are frequent service taxis from Damietta, and less frequent vehicles from El-Mansura. The town has several restaurants and **hotels**: try the *Abo Tabl* in the centre at 4 17th Street (℡057/528-166; ❷; June–Sept), the *El-Salam* on the seafront 1km north at 6 44th Street (℡057/529-156; ❸), or the smaller and more modest *El-Mobasher* six blocks further north and three east at 1 56th Street, where they prefer you to take half board (℡057/527-097; ❺; June–Aug).

6

The Canal Zone

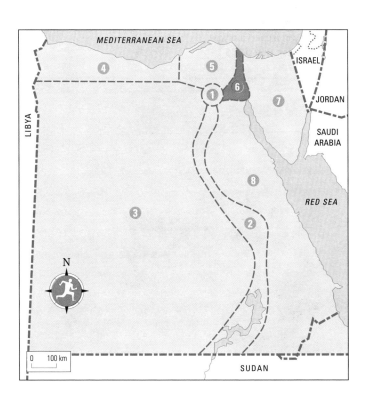

CHAPTER 6

Highlights

✳ **Birds of prey** Migrating vultures and eagles fly over Suez in spring. See p.647

✳ **Ismailiya** This European-style garden city was constructed for the builders of the canal. See p.648

✳ **Limbo Festival** Not what you might assume, this is a doll-burning festival, held annually in Ismailiya a week after Easter. See p.653

✳ **Mediterranean air** The fresh sea breeze, shopping and pleasant street cafés are a particular attraction of Port Said. See p.654

✳ **Ship-watching on the Suez Canal** International ferries are among the many giant ships that ply the Canal, still a crucial trade link between the West and the East. See p.657

△ A ship navigates the Suez Canal

The Canal Zone

Once feted as a triumph of nineteenth-century engineering and regarded as the linchpin of Britain's empire, the **Suez Canal** nowadays seems as Joseph Conrad described it: "a dismal but profitable ditch", connecting the Red Sea and the Mediterranean. Except around the harbour mouths or where ships are glimpsed between sandbanks, it's a pretty dull waterway relieved only by the Canal cities of Port Said and Ismailiya.

With its evocative waterfront, beaches and duty-free shopping, **Port Said** feels like Alexandria minus its cultural baggage – and a place that's somehow more authentic as a maritime city. By contrast, the Canal scarcely impinges on the leafy, villa-lined streets of **Ismailiya**, once the residence of the Suez Canal Company's European staff and now a popular honeymoon destination for Egyptians. Foreigners generally overlook both cities, prejudging them on the basis of **Suez**, a neglected and untidy place but a vital transport nexus between Cairo, the Sinai and the Red Sea coast.

Several trains serve the Suez Canal towns daily **from Cairo**, but the carriages are grimy and it's better to head here by bus or service taxi, which also represent your options if you're starting **from Alexandria**. **From Hurghada**, you can reach Suez rapidly by service taxi, but if you intend to head on to Sinai the same day, aim to arrive by in Suez noon to be sure of getting a bus connection. Travelling along the canal itself are half a dozen or so buses between Suez and Port Said. Drivers should be note that stretches of the canal are **off-limits** and should stick to main routes to avoid questioning by the military.

Heading on to **south Sinai** by road, you'll cross the canal at either the **Ahmed Hamdi Tunnel** (12km north of Suez) or the **car ferry** 7km north of Ismailiya. Destinations in **north Sinai** are served by a passenger ferry, at **Qantara**, and the new 4.1-kilometre **Ferdan Suspension Bridge** nearby. A couple of kilometres to the south is the **Ferdan Railway Bridge**, built on the site of an old track hastily constructed to transport army troops to Gaza during World War I, but dismantled by the Israelis in 1968. The largest retractable bridge in the world, with a span of 340m, it was devised in the late 1990s during a period of optimism in the Middle East, when a rail network running the Orient Express was planned, linking Egypt to Turkey and Europe via Palestine, Israel and Lebanon. This has been put on hold, but you can still see the bridge – which sits alongside the canal when not in use – closing daily from 9am to 11am and again from 9pm to 1am, a process which takes twenty minutes, to allow trains and cars to cross the canal.

The Canal's history

The **first attempts** to link the Red Sea and the Mediterranean by means of a canal are usually attributed to Necho II (610–595 BC) of the XXVI Dynasty.

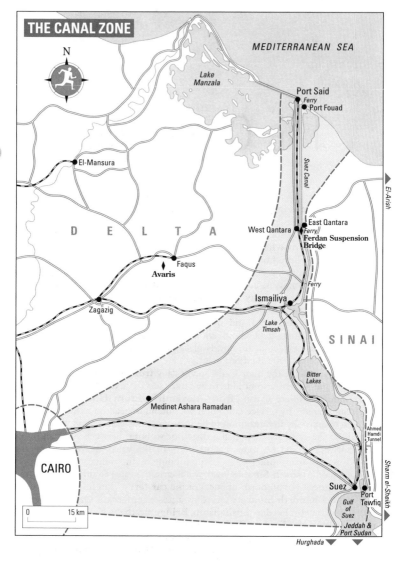

Herodotus claims that 120,000 workers had died before the project was abandoned after an oracle predicted that only Egypt's foes would benefit from it. Sure enough, it was the Persian emperor **Darius**, around 500 BC, who completed the first canal in the region, linking the Red Sea and the Great Bitter Lake, whence an older waterway created by Ramses II connected with Bubastis on the Nile and thence to the Mediterranean.

Refined by the Ptolemies and Trajan (who added an extension leading to Babylon-in-Egypt), this system of waterways was restored by **Amr** following the Muslim conquest and was used for shipping corn to Arabia until the eighth century, when it was deliberately abandoned to starve out rebels in Medina. Although the Venetians, Crusaders and Ottomans all considered renewing the old system, the idea of a canal running direct between the Red Sea and the Mediterranean was first mooted – and then vetoed – by Napoleon's engineers, who miscalculated a difference of ten metres between the two sea levels.

The discovery of their error, in the 1840s, encouraged a junior French consul, **Ferdinand de Lesseps**, to present his own plan to Said Pasha, who approved it despite British objections. ("It cannot be made, it shall not be made; but if it were made there would be a war between England and France for the possession of Egypt", Palmerston asserted.)

Work began at the Mediterranean end in 1859 and continued throughout the reign of Said's successor, Ismail (hence the names of Port Said and Ismailiya). Of the twenty thousand Egyptians employed in the **construction of the Suez Canal**, a great many died from accidents or cholera, while Ismail himself went bankrupt attempting to finance his one-third share of the £19 million sterling investment, most of which went on bankers' charges.

In 1875, Ismail was forced to sell his shares to Britain for a mere £4 million sterling and the Suez Canal effectively became an imperial concession. By appealing to the Rothschilds for a loan over dinner, Prime Minister Disraeli bought Ismail's shares before France could make an offer, and reported to Queen Victoria: "You have it, Madam". When the Canal finally opened in 1888, its vast profits went abroad with the **Suez Canal Company**, which acted as a state within a state, while two world wars saw the **Canal Zone** transformed into the largest military base on earth.

Following the end of World War II nationalist protests against the British presence grew, and guerrilla attacks in the Zone led to the British assault on Ismailiya's police barracks that sparked "Black Saturday" in Cairo (see p.121). After the 1952 Revolution, Egypt's new leaders demanded the withdrawal of British forces and a greater share of the Canal's revenue, and when the West refused to make loans to finance the Aswan High Dam, Nasser announced the Canal's **nationalization** (July 26, 1956). Britain and France tried to hamper this process, smearing Nasser as an "Arab Hitler". Israel's advance into Sinai that October became the agreed pretext for them to "safeguard" the Canal by bombarding and invading its cities. But by standing firm and appealing to outraged world opinion, Nasser emerged victorious from the **Suez Crisis**.

Suez Canal facts and figures

At 167km long, the Suez Canal is the third longest canal in the world and the longest without locks. It handles up to fifty ships a day, with seventy-five being its full capacity. The distance between Jeddah in Saudi Arabia and the port of Constanza on the Black Sea is 11,771 nautical miles via the Cape of Good Hope, but only 1,698 nautical miles via the Suez Canal. During its closure in the early 1970s, supertankers were built to travel around Africa – and proved too large to pass through Suez once it reopened. Since then the Canal has been widened in several places to accommodate the size of modern ships, and in places allows traffic to flow in both directions, but it is still not wide enough to allow continuous bi-directional traffic. For the most part the direction of traffic is alternated, with an average transit time of fifteen hours. The Canal is the Egypt's third largest source of income after the tourist industry and remittances from Egyptian expatriate workers employed in the Gulf. By mid-2006, it was earning more than $300 million annually from transit fees.

For more information on the Canal, visit ⓦ www.suezcanal.com.

The battered Canal cities had hardly recovered when the **1967 War** with Israel caused further damage and blocked the Canal with sunken vessels. The Canal was closed and Suez was evacuated during the "War of Attrition" that dragged on until 1969, while Israel fortified the **Bar-Lev Line** along the east bank, which the Egyptians stormed during the **October War** of 1973 (known as the 10th Ramadan or Yom Kippur War, respectively, to Arabs and Israelis). Although the Canal was reopened to shipping in 1975, both sides remained dug in on opposite banks until 1982, when Israel withdrew from Sinai.

⑥ Suez

Unlike Port Said and Ismailiya, **SUEZ** (Es-Suweis in Arabic) has a history long predating the Canal, going back to Ptolemaic Klysma. As Arabic Qulzum, the port prospered from the spice trade and pilgrimages to Mecca throughout medieval times, remaining a walled city until the eighteenth century, when Eliza Fay described it as "the Paradise of Thieves". The Canal brought modernization and assured revenues, later augmented by the discovery of oil in the Gulf of Suez. All this was lost during the wars with Israel. Almost the entire population was evacuated between 1967 and 1973, and the city was devastated by Israeli bombardments, subsequently requiring a massive reconstruction programme financed by the Gulf states. Today most of the city's 490,000 inhabitants have been rehoused in prefabricated estates or the patched-up remnants of older quarters, while noxious petrochemical refineries, cement and fertilizer plants ring the outskirts.

What Suez lacks in looks is made up for to some degree by the friendliness of the local people. For the foreign visitor, however, it's best to dress for the city wherever you are, saving your shorts and skimpy tops for the beaches of Sinai. The paucity of things to do in Suez is perhaps most keenly felt by the city's young people, many of whom spend their evenings hanging out, puffing on *sheesha* – the monotony broken only by their home team playing football in the city's stadium. Despite its important contribution to the Egyptian economy, Suez has yet to see significant investment in its infrastructure. Its residents seem to feel they have been largely forgotten by their government.

Arrival and information

Like the other Canal cities, Suez has regular bus and service-taxi connections with Cairo (every 30min 6am–8.30pm; 2hr; £E8). Both types of vehicle arrive at Suez's **Arba'in Terminal** (☏062/322-0753) on the Cairo road on the outskirts of town; from here you can take a taxi (£E5–10) or a microbus (50pt) into the town centre. The **train station**, 1500m west of the city centre's Arba'in Market (50pt by minibus), is served by six daily trains from Cairo (£E6) that take a little over two hours, and which run on to Ismailiya (6–7hr).

For the benefit of people arriving by ship, the **tourist office** (officially Mon–Wed & Sun 8am–8pm; ☏062/333-1141) and **tourist police** (24hr; ☏062/333-3543) are way out on the edge of **Port Tewfiq** (Bur Tewfiq in Arabic) on Suez Canal Street; you can catch a microbus out along Sharia el-Geish as far as the Passenger Terminal. The tourist office can supply a decent map of the city and other useful information but it's understaffed and not always open.

You can **change money** at the Bank of Alexandria on Sharia el-Geish (daily: summer 9am–2pm & 5–8pm; winter 8am–2pm & 6–9pm); the National Bank

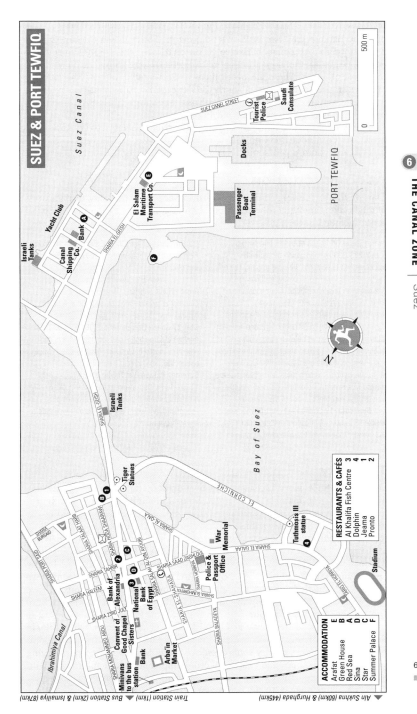

SUEZ & PORT TEWFIQ

Suez Canal

Bay of Suez

PORT TEWFIQ

Yacht Club

Israeli Tanks

Canal Shipping Co.

Bank Ⓐ

El Salam Maritime Transport Co. Ⓔ

SHARIA EL-GEISH

Ⓕ

Docks

Passenger Boat Terminal

SUEZ CANAL STREET

Tourist Police

Saudi Consulate

Ibrahimiya Canal

Israeli Tanks

SHARIA EL-GEISH

Tiger Statues

Ⓑ ①

SHARIA MOHAMMED ABDU

SHARIA BURGSAD

SHARIA PORT SAID

SHARIA TALAAT HARB

SHARIA MUSA SHARRAWI

SHARIA 23RD JULY

SHARIA HALEEM

SHARIA TAHRIR

Bank of Alexandria

② Ⓒ

Convent of Good Chapel Sisters

Ⓓ ③

National Bank of Egypt

SHARIA SALAH AL-DIN AYUBI

SHARIA SAAD ZAGHLOUL

SHARIA EL-SHAHADA

SHARIA GUMHURIYA

SHARIA HORRIA

SHARIA BALADIYA

Arba'in Market

Minivans to the bus station

Bank

SHARIA AL-QALA

War Memorial

Police & Passport Office

Ⓒ

EL CORNICHE

Tuthmosis III statue ④

Stadium

HANGE EL-TAHRIR

SHARIA EL GALAA

N

RESTAURANTS & CAFÉS

Al Khalifa Fish Centre	3
Dolphin	4
Jeama	1
Pronto	2

ACCOMMODATION

Arafat	E
Green House	B
Red Sea	A
Sina	D
Star	C
Summer Palace	F

0   500 m

▲ *Train Station (1km)* *Bus Station (2km) & Ismailiya (87km)*

▲ *Ain Sukhna (60km) & Hurghada (445km)*

of Egypt on Sharia Sa'ad Zaghloul (Mon–Thurs & Sun 8.30am–2pm & 5–8 pm); the Banque du Caire in Port Tewfiq (Mon–Thurs & Sun 8.30am–2pm & 5–8pm), or the Al Zahabeh Exchange on Sharia el-Geish (Sun–Thurs 8am–2pm & 6–10pm); there are also private exchanges in the souk. For ATMs, head to Sharia el-Geish. There are post offices in Port Tewfiq and on Sharia Hoda Sharawi, in the centre of town (both daily except Fri 8am–3pm), and you can make international calls from the **telephone exchange** (daily 8am–midnight) on the corner of Sa'ad Zaghloul and El-Shahada.

Visa extensions can be made at the **passport office** (daily except Fri 8am–2pm) inside **police** headquarters on Sharia Horriya; as always, arrive early with your passport and photo, a pen, something to read and a sense of humour.

Accommodation

Outside the hajj season, **finding a room** in Suez should be easy, though none of the hotels is anything to write home about. Except where indicated, breakfast is not included in the rate.

Arafat Hotel Off Sharia el-Geish, Port Tewfiq ☏062/333-8355. Clean, small rooms with balconies and fans, some with bathrooms. The only budget option if you need to stay in the port area. The manager has information about passenger ships for Saudi Arabia, etc. ❷

Green House Hotel Corner Sharia el-Geish and El Nabi Mousa St ☏062/333-1553, ✉green-house @link.net. The smartest hotel in Suez, with elaborate foyer and public areas, a swimming pool, and a very good restaurant and coffee and cake shop. The clean a/c rooms have Gulf views, but are in need of a revamp. Breakfast included. Popular with foreign engineers based in the area. ❻

Red Sea Hotel 13 Sharia Riad, Port Tewfiq ☏062/333-4302, ✉info@redseahotel.com. Clean and comfortable a/c rooms with bath, phone, balcony and satellite TV. The sixth-floor *Mermaid Restaurant* has great views of the canal. Breakfast included. ❻

Sina 21 Sharia Banque Misr ☏062/333-4181. Small rooms with fans, TV and clean shared bathrooms, with a fridge on each floor. A good, central, low-budget option. ❷

Star 17 Sharia Banque Misr ☏062/322-8737. A mixture of large and small rooms with fans and balconies; some have baths. Another good budget option. ❶

Summer Palace Port Tewfiq ☏062/322-1287, ☏332-1944. Run-to-seed three-star hotel, chiefly notable for its Gulf views and freshwater pool. Overpriced, but worth a visit to its al fresco café to enjoy the views. ❻

The City

Downtown Suez is readily accessible by microbus (50pt) or taxi (£E7–10) from the bus terminal. The main street, **Sharia el-Geish**, is a two-kilometre-long swath where cruising minibuses drop and collect passengers along the way to Port Tewfiq. Dusty palms and decrepit colonial-era buildings (including several churches) are followed by a strip of hotels, restaurants and currency exchanges. The **Convent of the Good Chapel Sisters** is an imposing colonial-style building given to the international sisterhood in 1872 by the Suez Canal Company after one of its directors recovered from a mystery illness while in their care. A decline in their numbers led the nuns to give their chapel over to the Coptic Church, but they still run a primary school and a dispensary for the poor.

The backstreets to the south of El-Geish harbour cheap cafés, while **Sharia Sa'ad Zaghloul** runs past consulates and a fun park towards the governorate. North of El-Geish, a tawdry souk overflows along **Sharia Haleem**, presaging a quarter of workshops and chandlers, crumbling century-old apartments with wooden balconies interspersed with modern government-built low-rises. There's a better **bazaar** to the northwest in Arba'in.

△ The Suez waterfront

An imposing statue of the pharaoh Tuthmosis III stands at the western end of El Corniche, which overlooks the Bay of Suez; meanwhile, on either side of the road at the eastern entrance, you'll see statues of two tigers growling and crouching as if ready to pounce. Signifying strength, they were built to guide ships through the canal. Similar tiger statues, destroyed by the Israelis in the 1967 War, originally stood on either side of the entrance to the canal.

The ultimate Suez activity is, of course, to take a trip to the port area to look at the enormous freighters and supertankers on the Canal. You'll notice young people swimming and families picnicking along Suez Canal Street. Don't be tempted to take photographs of the Canal, however; it's illegal, and the security officers stationed in the area will be sure to impose the law. In spring, migratory **birds of prey** make an arresting sight. Griffon vultures and imperial and steppe eagles overfly Suez to avoid crossing the Red Sea, which lacks the rising thermals on which they depend for flight. A more permanent resident is the Indian house crow – recognizable by its ear-splitting *caaarrrr* – which is thought to have arrived from India on ships during the course of the nineteenth century.

Eating and drinking

Eating options in Suez are very limited. Your best bet for seafood is the *Al Khalifa Fish Centre* (☎064/333-7303) at 320 Sharia el-Geish: there's no menu; just wait for the very friendly proprietor to bring out a platter of fish and simply point to what looks best. They often have *umm el-khaloul*, the popular local shellfish, on offer, though in hot weather avoid it if it looks as though it might have been left standing around. In the streets behind the restaurant you'll find a few simple shops selling snacks and fresh juice. Another good choice for simple fish dishes with salad is the *Dolphin* restaurant on Tariq El-Horiya, and for good-value *shawarma*, sandwiches or hot dogs, check out *Pronto*, a red-and-white canteen on Sharia el-Geish. The best restaurant in town is at the 🏃 *Green House Hotel*, a swanky hotel dining room with excellent service and a Continental menu. Try the good fish kebabs, from £E25, and finish off with one of the decadent cream cakes.

Suez transport connections

Suez is mainly used by travellers as an interchange between Cairo, Sinai and Hurghada. The bus station has three ticket kiosks: one for **Cairo**, one for East Delta buses to **Sinai, Alexandria** and **the Delta**, and one for Upper Egypt buses to **Hurghada**, **Luxor** and **Aswan**. Each kiosk has a timetable in Arabic. You will also find service taxis here that go to all major destinations, though fares vary widely according to demand.

- **Sinai** Most of the buses from Suez to Sinai start their journey in Cairo. There are seven buses daily from Suez to **Sharm el-Sheikh** (8.30am, 11am, 1.30pm, 3pm, 4.30pm 5.15pm & 6pm; 4hr; £E30). The 11am bus goes via Nuweiba and Dahab on the eastern coastal road and takes three hours longer. There are another two buses to **Nuweiba** and **Taba** daily (3pm, 5pm; 5hr; £E35). There is one bus daily to **St Catherine's Monastery** (2.30pm; 6hr; £E25). Service taxis are often quicker but will be packed and there's no a/c.
- **Ismailiya, Port Said and El-Arish** Buses and service taxis run every fifteen minutes to Ismailiya (6am–6.30pm; 45min–1hr; £E10), where you can change for a bus or taxi to El-Arish. There are also five buses daily from Suez to Port Said (7am, 9am, 11am, 12.15pm & 3.30pm; 2hr; £E10.50).
- **Alexandria** There are four buses daily to Alex (7am, 9am, 2.30pm & 5pm; 6hr; £E25); service taxis charge around £E20 and may be a little quicker.
- **Cairo** Buses leave every 30min (1hr 30min–2hr; £E8) throughout the day.
- **Hurghada** Fourteen buses daily (5am–11pm; 4–5hr; £E35–45), most of which stop at the **Ain Sukhna** (1hr; £E5), not far from Suez. There are also frequent service taxis.
- **Upper Egypt** Buses leave for Luxor (8am, 2pm & 8pm; 10hr; £E46–55) and Aswan (5am, 11am & 5pm; 8hr; £E54–62). These can also be taken only as far as Hurghada.

International ferries

Suez is the point of departure for passenger **boats to Saudi Arabia** used by migrant workers or pilgrims. Ferries to the Saudi port of **Jeddah** sail every day in theory, with additional sailings during the hajj season (six weeks either side of the month of Zoul Hagga). However, legal wranglings about safety issues following a spate of ferry disasters means that service has been severely disrupted of late. The journey takes around three days. Prices start at £E300 for deck space, rising to £E400–550 in a 2nd- or 1st-class cabin. Providing there's not a storm, sleeping on deck is fine.

Note that you can't buy a **ticket** unless you already have the right visa(s). The Saudi Consulate in Port Tewfiq has sections for work and hajj visas but tourist visas can be harder to obtain, so it might be a better idea to get a transit visa in Cairo, where you can also obtain a Sudanese visa – *inshallah*.

For up-to-date details on international ferry services, contact Telestar Travel in Cairo (1 Tahrir Square, ☎02/794-4600), or in Port Tewfiq enquire at El Salam Maritime Transport Co., 4 Mona St, next to Gate No. 5 of the port (☎062/332-6253, ⓦwww .elsalammaritime.com).

Drinking alcohol is impossible as Suez is a dry town, but for non-alcoholic beverages and *sheesha*, try the *Jeama* garden café next to the *Green House Hotel*, or the foyer coffee shop in the hotel itself.

Ismailiya

ISMAILIYA is popular with Egyptian tourists and honeymooners, who come to enjoy the beaches along Lake Timsah. While many might think that the place came into being with the building of the Suez Canal in 1862, recent historical research dates human settlement in the region to Biblical times – the area is mentioned in the Bible itself. Today the city has a schizoid character, defined by the rail line that cuts across it. South of the tracks lies the European-style **garden city** built for foreign employees of the Suez Canal Company, which extends to the verdant banks of the Sweetwater Canal. Following careful restoration, its leafy boulevards and placid streets, lined with colonial villas, look almost as they must have done in the 1930s, with bilingual street signs nourishing the illusion that the British Empire has just popped indoors for a quick cocktail. North of the train tracks is another world of hastily constructed flats grafted onto long-standing **slums**, and a quarter financed by the Gulf Emirates that provides a *cordon sanitaire* for the wealthy suburb of **Nemrah Setta** (Number Six).

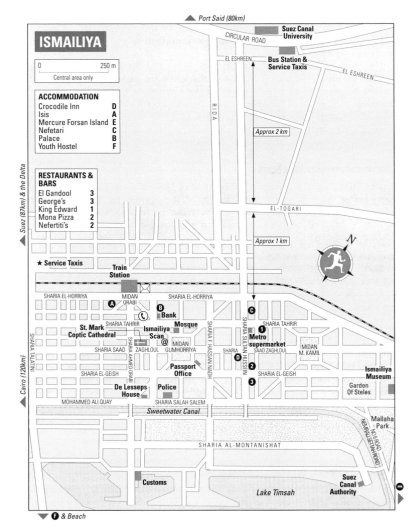

ISMAILIYA

0 _____ 250 m
Central area only

ACCOMMODATION
Crocodile Inn	D
Isis	A
Mercure Forsan Island	E
Nefetari	C
Palace	B
Youth Hostel	F

RESTAURANTS & BARS
El Gandool	3
George's	3
King Edward	1
Mona Pizza	2
Nefertiti's	2

Port Said (80km)

Suez Canal University
CIRCULAR ROAD
EL ESHREEN — Bus Station & Service Taxis
EL ESHREEN
RIDA
Approx 2 km
EL-TOGARI
Approx 1 km
N

Suez (87km) & the Delta

★ Service Taxis
Train Station
SHARIA EL-HORRIYA   MIDAN ORABI   SHARIA EL-HORRIYA
Bank
St. Mark Coptic Cathedral   SHARIA TAHRIR   Ismailiya Scan   Mosque   SHARIA TAHRIR
Metro supermarket
SHARIA SAAD AHMED ORABI   SHARIA SAAD   ZAGHLOUL   MIDAN GUMHORRIYA   SHARIA F. HASSAN NADH   SHARIA SULTAN HUSSEIN   SAAD ZAGHLOUL   MIDAN M. KAMIL
Passport Office
Cairo (120km)   SHARIA TALATINI   SHARIA EL-GEISH   SHARIA EL-GEISH   Ismailiya Museum
De Lesseps House   Police   Garden Of Steles
MOHAMMED ALI QUAY   SHARIA SALAH SALEM   Mallaha Park
Sweetwater Canal   NO.6 ROAD NEMRAH SETTA ROAD
SHARIA AL-MONTANISHAT
Customs   Suez Canal Authority
Lake Timsah

& Beach

Although Ismailiya can be reached from Cairo by train (6 daily; 3–5hr; £E11.50), buses or taxis are quicker and very frequent from the Turgoman Garage in **Cairo** (every 30min; 6.30am–8.30pm; 2hr; £E8), stopping en route at the Almaza terminal in Heliopolis. The 120-kilometre desert road from Cairo to Ismailiya runs through two places worth noting. **Khanka** contains Egypt's main asylum for the criminally insane, which has made its name a popular synonym for "totally crazy". Further out, a spate of country clubs presages **Medinet Ashara Ramadan** (10th of Ramadan City), a satellite city for the new breed of Cairene commuters, complete with quasi-American suburban homes and steak houses.

Arrival and information

All buses and service taxis wind up at the new **bus station** on the ring road outside Ismailiya, opposite the massive Suez Canal University building. From here take a taxi (£E5) or microbus (50pt) into the town centre. The old town's grid-plan and clearly named streets make **orientation** easy, which is just as well as there's no tourist office.

The **post office** (daily except Fri 9am–4pm) and the 24-hour **telephone exchange** are both just off Midan Orabi, while the **passport office** (daily except Fri 8am–2pm) is nearby on Midan Gummhorriya. You can **change money** at the Bank of Alexandria or the National Bank of Egypt – which takes Visa and MasterCard – both are just off Midan Orabi (both Mon–Thurs, Sat & Sun 8.30am–2pm & 5–8pm, Fri 8.30am–noon). For **Internet** access, try Ismailiya Scan opposite the mosque in Midan Gummhorriya.

Accommodation

Apart from a couple of smart hotels, most of Ismailiya's accommodation has seen better days. However, the majority of the options are safe, reasonably clean and cheap, and only really get busy during festivals and the summer season – May to September. Breakfast is included in rates given unless indicated otherwise.

Crocodile Inn 172 Sharia Sa'ad Zaghloul ⓣ064/391-2555, ⓕ391-2666. The only reasonably smart hotel in the town centre, with nice a/c rooms with balconies, plus a restaurant and 24hr coffee shop. ③

Isis Midan Orabi ⓣ064/392-2821. A range of budget rooms with fans. Staff are friendly and helpful, and there are reductions for long-staying guests. No breakfast. ①

Mercure Forsan Island 2km east of town ⓣ064/391-6316, ⓦwww.mercure.com. Leafy four-star resort set in fifty acres of grounds with a lake. Over 100 a/c rooms and 23 garden villas with satellite TV, minibar and international phone. Swimming pool and private beach with watersports. Special rates on online bookings. ⑦

Nefetari 41 Sharia Sultan Hussein ⓣ064/391-2822. A good choice with agreeable, albeit very pink, rooms, some with a/c and private baths. ②

Palace Midan Orabi ⓣ064/391-6327, ⓕ391-7761. A wonderfully pretentious nineteenth-century pile with a/c rooms, satellite TV and private baths. Popular with honeymooners, so it's often full. Good value. ③

Youth Hostel at Sharia Imhara Siyahi, 1km from the centre, £E2 by taxi ⓣ064/392-2850, ⓕ392-3429. Overlooking Lake Timsah, with its own beach, this hostel has 26 double, triple or six-person rooms with private baths. Non-members pay £E5 extra. It's just beyond the bridge on the left as you head south out of town. Dorm beds £E30. ②

The Town and around

Shaded by pollarded trees, Ismailiya's carefully restored old town is a pleasure to walk or bike around; most of the sights can be reached on foot within ten minutes. Heading to the sights outside town, catch a service taxi from the turn-off near Mallaha Park.

Starting on Mohammed Ali Quay, first on the trail is the large, vaguely Swiss-looking **House of Ferdinand de Lesseps**, who lived here during the Canal's construction. Disappointingly, you can only visit the interior if you're a VIP; it now serves as a private hotel for guests of the Suez Canal Authority. Lone visitors might chance a peek inside, however, if the rear gate is open. Books and photographs are scattered around de Lesseps' study, and the licence to dig the Canal hangs on one of the walls, while his carriage stands outdoors, encased in glass.

A pleasant fifteen minutes' walk down the street from the de Lesseps' House, the **Ismailiya Museum** (Mon–Thurs, Sat & Sun 9am–4pm, Fri and during Ramadan 9.30am–noon & 1.15–4pm; £E6, students £E3) leans towards ancient history, with four thousand Greco-Roman and pharaonic artefacts and an entire section devoted to the waterways of Ramses and Darius. One highlight is a lovely fourth-century mosaic depicting Phaedra, Dionysos, Eros and Hercules. Other sections cover the canal in modern history, the Battle of Ismailiya and the "Crossing" of October 1973.

The Muslim Brotherhood and the Battle of Ismailiya

Ismailiya – one of the most Europeanized of Egyptian towns – was the birthplace of the **Muslim Brotherhood** and its founder, **Hassan el-Banna**. As a child, el-Banna nailed up leaflets calling upon Muslims to renounce gold and silks, and awoke his neighbours before dawn prayers. When older, he campaigned against female emancipation, delivering fiery sermons in rented cafés. He founded the Ikhwan el-Muslimeen in 1928 and within fifteen years the Brotherhood had spread throughout Egypt and spawned offshoots across the Middle East, articulating an Islamic response to modernization on Western terms.

From campaigning for moral renewal it went on to organize paramilitary training and terrorist cells, and was outlawed by King Farouk (whose agents assassinated el-Banna) in 1949. Despite this, the Brotherhood mounted attacks against the British and an economic boycott in the Canal Zone. The British suspected that they received arms from sympathizers in the Egyptian police and tried to disarm the main barracks outside Ismailiya, whose garrison was ordered to resist by their superiors and only surrendered after fifty of them had been killed. The **Battle of Ismailiya** (January 25, 1952) outraged Egyptians and provoked an orgy of rioting in Cairo the following day – **"Black Saturday"** – when the police stood by as Brotherhood activists sped around in Jeeps, torching foreign properties.

Legalized after the 1952 Revolution, the Brotherhood was soon suppressed again for trying to kill Nasser in Alexandria. Hundreds of Brothers spent years in concentration camps, until amnestied by President Sadat, who sought to co-opt them as a counterweight to the left. Eventually, their growing influence and criticism of his policies led Sadat to jail them *en masse*, whereupon his assassination by Al-Jihad proved that other groups had grown up in the Brotherhood's shadow and surpassed it in radicalism. To isolate these new militants, Mubarak, too, wooed the Brotherhood with all kinds of concessions short of legalization. In **recent years** he has followed a less clear policy. While he ordered the arrest of scores of Brothers and the closure of their headquarters in Cairo, Brotherhood members who stood as independent candidates in the 2005 parliamentary elections won 88 seats (twenty percent of the total) – the legal opposition parties won only fourteen. Ironically, today the government appears to view the Brotherhood as a moderating influence within the Islamist movement, and their evident popularity has revived debate about whether it should remain banned.

With permission from the museum, you can also visit some plaques and obelisks from Ramses II's time in the **Garden of Steles** just to the west. It's nicer, however, to wander amid the 500 acres of exotic shrubs and trees of **Mallaha Park** to the south, or to stroll alongside the shady **Sweetwater Canal** that was dug to provide fresh water for labourers building the Suez Canal. Previously, supplies had to be brought across the desert by camels, or shipped across Lake Manzala to Port Said.

Lake Timsah

Notwithstanding its name, which translates as "Crocodile Lake", **Lake Timsah** has several nice **beaches**. Get there by taking a taxi or walking 1km out along Sharia Talatini. You can dine outside near picturesque fishing boats, or pay £E5–10 to use the manicured lawns and beaches of the private resorts and clubs (which may include snacks and drinks in the deal), though many of these places close outside high season. Wealthier citizens patronize the *Mercure Forsan Island* with its **waterskiing**, **windsurfing** and **tennis** facilities; you can use the beach and swimming pool here for a small fee.

The Bar-Lev Line

Service taxis turning off near Mallaha Park are usually bound for "Ferri Setta" (50pt), outside town, where locals use a **ferry crossing** (50pt) to the east bank of the Canal. Here, a vast sand rampart breached by deep cuts marks the former **Bar-Lev Line**, named after the Israeli general who designed it. Intended to stall any attack on Sinai for 48 hours, this 25-metre-high embankment was defended by forty mined strongpoints. In the event, they were totally surprised by Egypt's assault on **October 6, 1973**. As hidden artillery opened up at 2pm, eight thousand commandos dragged launches to the water's edge, roared across the 180-metre-wide canal and scaled the ramparts with ladders. Within hours, high-pressure hoses ordered from Bavaria "for the Cairo Fire Department" were blasting gaps for the Egyptian armour massing behind pontoon bridge layers.

However, although "The Crossing" was an Egyptian triumph (still remembered with pride), the war subsequently turned against them. An Israeli force under Ariel Sharon counterattacked across the canal between Lake Timsah and the Great Bitter Lake, wheeled inland to cut the Cairo–Suez road, and had virtually encircled the Egyptian army in Sinai by the time the superpowers imposed a ceasefire. Disengagement on the ground began with UN-sponsored talks at **Kilometre 101** – the nearest Israeli tanks came to Cairo.

Eating, nightlife and festivals

Ismailiya's dining options are adequate, if nothing special; when the weather's fine, locals head to the fishing port on Lake Timsah to dine al fresco; it's worth the cost of a taxi (£E5) out along Sharia Talatini to eat fish straight from the lake. You might even try the local shellfish specialty, *umm el-khaloul* – though note that's best avoided during hot weather when there's a greater risk of it going off. Otherwise, there are several decent restaurants clustered together in the centre. *George's* on Sharia Sultan Hussein is an established Greek place that has been going strong since 1950 and specializes in seafood and kebabs, while next door *El Gandool* serves up roast chicken or pigeon in a clean air-conditioned environment. Across the street, *Nefertiti's* (☏064/391-0494) offers fish main courses from £E25 and is open until midnight; *Mona Pizza* next door does reasonable pizzas with pitta bread bases.

The most popular **places to drink** are *King Edward*, 171 Sharia Tahrir (☏064/332-5451), an air-conditioned haunt favoured by expat engineers and which serves Continental and Egyptian food, and the bar at the *Mercure Forsan Island*; both attract an interesting crowd as the night wears on. The *Mercure* also has a nightly disco, and on Thursday evenings there's bellydancing and live music for a cover charge of £E125. Alternatively, most of the evening street life can be found around Sharia Talatini, Sharia Sa'ad Zaghloul and Sharia el-Geish, where shops, cafés and juice bars are open late into the night.

Festivals

Should you happen to be in town around Easter, Ismailiya is a good place to witness the spring festival of **Shams el-Nessim**, when families picnic in the park between the Sweetwater Canal and Lake Timsah, vehicles are decorated with flowers and little girls compete for the coveted title of "Miss Strawberry".

Even better is the "**Doll-Burning**" or **Limbo Festival**, held a week later. Its curious title refers to a hated nineteenth-century local governor – Limbo Bey – effigies of whom were torched by the citizenry. Ever since then, it has been customary to burn dolls resembling your pet hate: footballers are popular targets whenever Ismailiya's soccer club does poorly. The dolls are burned on the streets after dark.

Moving on

To get anywhere from Ismailiya, it's back to the bus station on the ring road opposite the Suez Canal University building. Private taxis (£E5) or service taxis (50pt) to the bus station leave from the rank on Sharia Talatini just north of the railway tracks.

- **To Cairo** Regular buses and service taxis throughout the day (6.30am–8.30pm; 2hr; £E8).
- **North Sinai** Buses leave eight times a day for **El-Arish** (8.30am–5pm; 3hr; £E10) as do frequent service taxis. There are also service taxis to **Rafah** – but only if the border is open (see p.29).
- **South Sinai** Buses and service taxis leave throughout the day and night to **Sharm el-Sheikh** (6.30am–midnight; 6hr; £E35). There's also a nightly bus to **Nuweiba** (9pm; 7–8hr; £E55).
- **Canal cities** Buses and service taxis travel regularly via Ismailiya and **Qantara** between **Port Said** (6.30am–6pm; 1hr; £E10) and **Suez** (6.30am–6pm; 1hr; £E10).

North of Ismailiya – Canal crossings

Seven kilometres north of Ismailiya, a **car ferry** crosses the canal more or less non-stop during daylight hours. Together with the Ahmed Hamdi Tunnel outside Suez, it used to carry almost all the traffic between mainland Egypt and Sinai until the opening of the Salaam (or Ferdan) Suspension Bridge in October 2001, which is now the most direct route from Cairo to Israel.

The only other crossing point is at **QANTARA**, 44km from Ismailiya and 80km from Port Said. As its name ("Bridge") suggests, this was the route used by pilgrims and armies to cross the marshy Isthmus of Suez before the canal was built. Since then, it has been spanned by pontoon bridges in wartime, but is now negotiated by a small passenger ferry, carrying locals, bikes and donkeys from one side of Qantara to the other. Most of the town is on the west bank, whose unpaved main drag has a busy souk and lines of service taxis going to Cairo and the canal cities; the battered, poorly rebuilt houses are a reminder that armies clashed here in 1973. There's a cafeteria on the east bank of the canal, along with

The New Kingdom war machine

Recent excavations in the Eastern Delta and Northern Sinai have cast light on the revolution in Egyptian warfare during the New Kingdom. The Hyksos invasion forced the Egyptians to adopt the weapons of their enemy – horses, chariots, composite bows, edged swords and bronze armour – and master cavalry tactics, hitherto unknown. **Chariots** became the key to their success, allowing rapid movement on the battlefield and over long distances. Light enough to be lifted over obstacles by their crew, they were kept on the road by mobile repair units and stables at the rear; one for 400 horses has been found at Tell ed-Daba in the Delta. Twelve **fortresses** along the **Great Horus military route** across Northern Sinai (depicted on Seti I's reliefs in the columned court at Karnak) provided defence in depth and stores for major campaigns; one at Tell Habouh, near Qantara, covers 12,000 square metres. Armies were supplied by donkeys or by galleys in coastal waters. Such logistics enabled Tuthmosis III to move 20,000 troops 400km in nine days – without being detected – while Ramses II extended Egypt's strategic reach to 2000km by pioneering the use of oxen (the mainstay of military logistics for the next thousand years). This formidable war machine made imperialism inevitable, and was fed by the spoils of war: 894 chariots, 2000 horses and 25,000 pack animals were taken at the battle of Meggido alone. The fortresses lie within what is still a sensitive military area, not yet open to tourists.

service taxis for El-Arish (2hr 30min; £E5), but it's easier to take one direct from Ismailiya.

Port Said

Founded at the start of the canal excavations, **PORT SAID** (Bur Said in Arabic) was by the late nineteenth century a major port where all the major maritime powers had consulates. It was long synonymous with smuggling and vice, and the adventurer De Monfreid was amused by the Arab cafés where "native policemen as well as coolies" smoked hashish in back rooms, supplied by primly respectable Greeks: "… every single one of them got his living from trafficking in hashish, either as a retail seller, or as a small-scale smuggler who haunted the liners."

Nowadays, this bustling city of 540,000 people earns its living as an important harbour; both for exports of Egyptian products like cotton and rice, but also as a fuelling station for ships that pass through the Suez Canal. A faintly raffish atmosphere lingers around its old streets, its timber-porched houses giving something of the feel of New Orleans's French Quarter.

Prior to the downturn in tourism caused by the unrest in Israel and the Occupied Territories, Port Said had been attempting to lure tourists away from Alexandria by promising better shops and less crowded beaches, cheap hotels and good restaurants. These days, aside from day-trippers from the cruise liners, foreign tourists seldom visit the city and hustlers are rare. It's an agreeable place to relax for a day or two if you don't mind the lack of "sights" and diversions, and are content to hang out on the beach or at one of the European-style street cafés.

Trains **from Cairo** (5 daily; £E18) take at least four hours to reach Port Said via Ismailiya, though it's more appealing to do the 220-kilometre journey by bus (3hr). Regular air-conditioned East Delta buses depart from near Ramses Station and from Turgoman Garage (every 30min; 6.30am–7pm;

PORT SAID

MEDITERRANEAN SEA

Beach

Beach

Pedestrian Promenade

Stadium

Governorate

Military Museum

El Salam Mosque

US Consulate

Shopping Centre

De Lesseps Plinth

Port Said National Museum

Tourist Port

Thomas Cook

Egypt Air

Afandy

North Africa Tours

Ferial Gardens

Tourist Police

Misr Travel

BAZAAR

Customs

Suez Canal Authority

Arsenal Basin

Sherif Basin

Train Station

Service Taxis

Suez Canal

PORT FOUAD

Yacht Basin

N

Streets

EL CORNICHE
SHARIA SAAD ZAGHLOUL
EL NASR ST
SHARIA ORABI
SHARIA 23RD JULY
SHARIA TARH EL-BAHR
SHARIA EL GUMHORIYA
SUEZ ST
SHARIA HASTIN
SHARIA SALAH SALEM
SHARIA SAFIA ZAGHLOUL
EL SHOHADA ST
SHARIA MUSTAFA KAMEL
NABIL MANSOR ST
ABU EL HASSAN ST
HAMED EL ALFY ST
EL RODA ST
EL GORY ST
FAHMY EL NOKRASHY ST
HASHMIN ST
EL DAKHLIA ST
AHMED ISMAIL ST
ESLAM ST
FARAMY EL ALFY ST
EL GIZA ST
ASWAN ST
EL MINIA ST
BEN SWEF ST
NABEH ST
EL SABAH ST
EL NASR ST
MOHAMED EL SAYED SARHAN ST
SHARIA SAAD ZAGHLOUL
EL QISI ST
SALAH EL DIN ST
SHARIA EN NAHDA

RESTAURANTS, CAFÉS & BARS

Abu Essam	2
Canal Cruise	7
Cecil Bar	10
Galal	8
Hamburger King	3
Kastan	1
KFC	5
Maxim	4
Pizza Hut	5
Pizza Pino	6
Popeye's Café	9
Reana House	10

ACCOMMODATION

Crystal	G
Helnan Port Said	A
Holiday	H
Hotel de la Poste	I
New Concorde	K
New Continental	J
Nora's Beach Hotel	B
Palace	E
Panorama	F
Sonesta	D
Youth Hostel	C

▲ Ashtoum El-Gamil & Tennis Island National Park   ▲ Bus Station (1.5km)

0   300 m

£E16.50). There are no direct trains **from Alexandria**, and seats on buses (4 daily; 6hr; £E20–22) are best reserved the day before. Service taxis provide the fastest transport **from Suez and Ismailiya** and augment buses **from the Delta**, where Damietta and El-Mansura have the best connections. Coming **from El-Arish** in north Sinai, you can catch a service taxi direct to the city.

Arrival and information

The main **point of arrival** is the bus station, which is on the outskirts of Port Said just off the main road from Ismailiya, from where you can catch a taxi (£E5) downtown. Orientation is straightforward, as most things of interest or use to tourists can be found on three thoroughfares: the waterfront Sharia Filastin; Sharia el-Gumhorriya, two blocks inland; or Sharia 23rd July.

The **tourist office** on Sharia Filastin (Mon–Thurs & Sat 9am–6pm, Fri 9am–2pm; ⓣ066/323-5289) can supply a useful map of the town with listings of hotels and services and some historical background. There's also a tourist booth at the train station (ⓣ066/322-3909), while the **tourist police** (ⓣ066/322-8570) is on the first floor of the post office building on Sharia El-Gumhorriya.

Accommodation

Most of Port Said's accommodation is very good value, with Sharia el-Gumhorriya offering the widest range of **hotels**, from modern tower blocks to old-style *pensions*. Rates given below include breakfast unless stated otherwise.

Crystal Hotel 12 Mohamed Makhmud ⓣ066/322-2747. A big complex which resembles a youth hostel, with 70 large en-suite a/c rooms at very low prices. The management is friendly enough, but the building itself is somewhat barren and dreary. ❷

Helnan Port Said El Corniche St ⓣ066/332-0890, ⓦwww.helnan.com. A five-star hotel right on the beach, with 203 rooms and suites and amenities including a pool, gym, sauna, coffee shop, nightclub, billiards room and Port Said's only bowling alley and roller-skating track. ❼

Holiday Hotel 23 Sharia el-Gumhorriya ⓣ066/322-0711. Imposing 72-room block with a streetside terrace and coffee shop, smart spacious lobby and friendly staff. Rooms a little shabby but comfortable, with satellite TV and fridge. Breakfast, taken in the seventh-floor restaurant, costs extra. ❺

Hotel de la Poste 46 Sharia el-Gumhorriya ⓣ066/322-9655. Rambling 1940s-style place offering high-ceilinged rooms with fans and baths. Overall it's very good value and has recently been renovated, though TV and fridge – and breakfast – cost extra. Restaurant, bar and patisserie. ❸

New Concorde Sharia Mustafa Kamel ⓣ066/323-5342, ⓕ323-5930. Carpeted rooms with baths, fans and TV, near the train station. Some of the rooms on the upper floors have views of the canal. ❹

New Continental 30 Sharia el-Gumhorriya ⓣ066/322-1355, ⓕ333-8088. Pleasant enough, though a bit shabby; a/c rooms with satellite TV, international phone and balconies. Breakfast costs extra. ❸

Nora's Beach Hotel El Corniche ⓣ066/332-9834, ⓕ332-9841. Huge 3-star beachside complex with 200 apartments and suites – a bit frayed at the edges but still comfortable – with a/c, private bathroom, satellite TV, minibar, balcony or terrace. With its three swimming pools, health club and disco, it's popular with Egyptian families. ❼

Palace 19 Sharia Ghandi, opposite the governorate building, near the beach ⓣ066/323-9450, ⓕ323-9464. Pleasantly furnished but very basic rooms with a/c and private bathrooms. ❷

Panorama Hotel Shari el-Gumhorriya ⓣ066/332-5101, ⓕ332-5103. A/c rooms with satellite TV, private bathrooms and big balconies. Great views, especially from the billiard room on the eleventh floor. A bit worn, but clean and comfortable, with a pizza restaurant on site. ❹

Sonesta Sharia Sultan Hussein, off Sharia Filastin ⓣ066/332-5511, ⓦwww.sonesta.com. A/c rooms with private bathrooms, satellite TV and minibar, overlooking the canal entrance and fishing harbour.

There's also a nice pool, and four restaurants including a good Italian place. Breakfast costs extra. ⑧

Youth Hostel Sharia al-Amin ☏ 066/322-8702. Not in a great location, near the stadium, this has clean but gloomy dorm rooms from £E12 and some plain doubles with shared bathrooms. ②

The City

Sharia el-Gumhorriya reflects Port Said's metamorphosis from a salty entrepôt to a slick commercial centre, plate-glass facades superceding early twentieth-century balconies as the street progresses from the Arsenal Basin to Sharia 23rd July. The adjacent **bazaar** quarter ranges from humble stalls on Salah El Din Street to smart boutiques on Sharia en-Nahda. These are joined by designer shops such as Hugo Boss and Timberland and sports stores like Nike and Adidas at the junction of Sharia el-Gumhorriya with Sharia 23rd July. Look carefully though; the latter shops are the genuine articles, while the Clarks shoe shop downtown and the Marks and Spencer in the shopping centre opposite the *Sonesta* are most definitely fakes.

The **Military Museum** on Sharia 23rd July (daily: summer 8am–2pm; winter 9am–2pm; Fri opening hours can be erratic; £E10) gives a strong sense of the Canal's embattled history. The 1956 Anglo-French-Israeli invasion is commemorated by lurid paintings and dioramas, while another room is dedicated to the October War of 1973. This gives pride of place to the storming of the Bar-Lev Line (see p.652), a heroic feat of arms ultimately wasted by the high command's failure to exploit Egypt's breakthrough in Sinai. Curiously absent from the large display of weaponry are the Soviet-made Strella and Molutka rockets that enabled Egyptian infantrymen to destroy Israeli jets and armour, rated by strategists as a minor revolution in modern warfare.

From here, it's about 15–20 minutes' walk east to the **Port Said National Museum** on Sharia Filastin. This however, has been closed for more than two years and no one seems to know if and when it will reopen. If it does and the original exhibits are still on display, highlights should include two mummies, an exquisitely worked faïence shroud and painted coffin, Ptolemaic funerary masks, Islamic tiles and *mashrabiyas*, Coptic textiles (especially a tunic adorned with images of the Apostles) and the coach of Khedive Ismail, used during the Canal's inauguration ceremonies.

Come evening, townsfolk and holidaymakers **stroll** along the Corniche and the parallel pedestrian promenade where a few calèches can be found for hire. From this coastal vantage point you can watch the dozens of vessels at anchor in the Mediterranean waiting to go through the Canal, their bulky hulls dwindling to lights bobbing far offshore. At the far end of the port area is a massive sandstone plinth that used to bear a huge **statue of de Lesseps**, before it was torn down following the 1952 Revolution. For an idea of the Canal's workings, take a dinner cruise on the Canal Cruise (see p.658) or catch the free **ferry** (every 15min) across to Port Fouad (see below).

You can rent chairs and parasols or windbreakers for about £E5 on Port Said's shell-strewn **beach**, which has public showers at 100m intervals. For calmer water and more relaxed sunbathing, consider paying about £E20 to use the **pools** at the *Sonesta* or the *Helnan*.

Port Fouad

Founded as a suburb for Canal bureaucrats in 1927, **PORT FOUAD** is quieter than its sister city. Residents describe their daily commutes to Port

Said as commuting between Asia and Africa; the battered ferry responsible offers an enjoyable ride, though it reeks of everything but intercontinental status. The suburb's decrepit but stylish **1930s architecture** can be appreciated by making a tour of Port Fouad's Art Deco flats, colonial villas and well-tended gardens. Travellers hoping to work their passage to the Med or the Indian Ocean could ask around at the **yacht basin**, although success is far from assured.

Ashtoum El-Gamil and Tennies Island National Park

Seven kilometres west of Port Said, straddling the Damietta coastal road, the **Ashtoum el-Gamil and Tennies Island National Park** is a small nature reserve, proclaimed in 1988. Covering roughly thirty square kilometres of inlets connecting the Mediterranean with Lake Manzala, it's a prime spot for bird-watching, its dunes and lagoons home to residents and winter migrants including flamingos, kingfishers, plovers and ducks. There are no fees or permits to visit the area and if driving, you can just pull off the road.

Eating and drinking

Eating out in Port Said is enjoyable, as fresh seafood abounds and most places have tables outdoors, allowing you to savour the bustling street life. Sharia el-Gumhorriya has plenty of **patisseries** and **coffee houses** to relax in. If you fancy a dinner excursion up the Suez Canal, make a reservation on the **Canal Cruise** (☎066/334-5222) at the entrance to the tourist port on the waterfront near the National Museum (5pm, 7pm & 10pm; 1hr 30min; $10 with soft drinks and pastries, $20 including dinner); schedules change, so check times at the booking office. On the other hand, if your tastes run to old-style atmosphere and the company of aged Greeks, head for the spit-and-sawdust *Cecil Bar* beneath the *Reana House*. The bar, open till midnight or later, is the only place in Port Said that serves alcohol, other than the restaurant in the *Helnan* hotel which offers one alcoholic cocktail made from local spirits. The *Helnan* also has a pricey but wide variety of continental dishes in the formal dining room. There are branches of both *KFC* and *Pizza Hut* on Sharia 23rd July.

Abu Essam El-Corniche St, diagonally opposite the *Helnan*. Excellent fish restaurant with moderate prices. A full meal costs £E20–30.

Galal El-Gumhorriya, diagonally across from the *Holiday Hotel*. A nice modern place to sit outside and eat *kofta* sandwiches or seafood (£E15–20). They also do *shawarma* takeaways and fresh juice. Daily 7am–1am; closed during Ramadan.

Hamburger King Corner of Sharia el-Gomhorriya and Sharia Tarh el-Bahr ☎066/322-4877. Burger bar popular with young Egyptians, also serving sandwiches, *shawarma* and pizza from £E8, along with fresh fruit juice. They can deliver to your hotel.

Kastan El-Corniche St, towards the stadium. Large and very busy 24hr seafood and fish restaurant on the beach. Around £E50 for a full meal.

Maxim In the shopping centre on the corner of el-Gumhorriya and el-Corniche. Port Said's most expensive fish restaurant, with splendid views of ships entering the Canal. A full meal costs £E40–60.

Pizza Pino On the corner of el-Gumhorriya and 23rd July streets. Popular, family-oriented joint with slick decor and quick service and a seductive range of Italian ice cream. Chefs work nonstop in the open kitchen to produce a wide range of authentic pizza/pasta dishes from £E18 and main fish courses for £E30.

Popeye's Café Sharia el-Gumhorriya, opposite the *Hotel de la Poste*. A pleasant Mediterranean-style street café with pretty terrace and a/c interior serving a wide selection of food, including huge banana splits. Daily 9am–2am.

Reana House 5 Sharia el-Gumhorriya, diagonally across from the *New Continental hotel*. On the scruffy side, serving tasty Korean and Chinese food including vegetarian dishes, at reasonable prices. Serves alcohol. Open till midnight or later.

Listings

Consulates UK, *Sonesta Hotel* Shopping Centre (℡066/323-1155); USA, Sharia el-Gumhorriya (℡066-322-6691).

Currency exchange There are numerous private exchanges around Sharia en-Nahda, and the shopping malls at the northern end of Sharia el-Gumhorriya can change money with less hassle than banks – and sometimes at a slightly better rate. Traveller's cheques can be cashed at Thomas Cook, 43 Sharia el-Gumhorriya (daily 8am–5pm; ℡066/322-7559, ⊛ww.thomascookegypt.com). Several of the banks along Sharia el-Gumhorriya have ATMs which accept Visa and MasterCard.

Hospitals The best-equipped and newest hospital is Al-Soliman, near the sports stadium (℡066/333-1533). Emergencies can also be treated at the Al-Mabarrah (℡066/322-0560) or El-Tadaman (℡066/323-1790) hospitals.

Internet access Afandy Internet Café is located opposite Nasco Tours on Sharia Filastin.

Pharmacy The 24-hr Hussein Pharmacy on Sharia el-Gumhorriya (℡066/333-9888) is diagonally opposite the *Hotel de la Poste*.

Post office The main branch (daily except Fri 9am–2pm) is near the southeast corner of Ferial Gardens.

Telephone exchange Just along from the tourist office on Sharia Filastin (24hr).

Travel agents Misr Travel near the tourist office on Sharia Filastin (℡066/322-6610).

Visa extensions The passport office is in the governorate building on Sharia 23rd July (Thurs & Sat 8am–2pm).

Moving on

East Delta **buses** to Cairo or Alexandria, Superjet a/c services to Cairo and buses to Ismailiya or the Delta all leave from the main bus station at the edge of town on the road to Ismailiya, about 3km from downtown. East Delta Bus Company (℡066/322-7883) has daily buses to Cairo (hourly 6am–8pm; 3hr; £E16.50), Alexandria (7am, 11am, 3.30pm & 7pm; 3hr; £E22), Ismailiya (hourly 6.30am–6.30pm; 1hr; £E10), which go on to Suez (2hr; £E10.50), and Luxor (1 daily; 8hr; £E53) via Hurghada (5hr; £E37). Superjet (℡066/321-1779) has one bus daily to Alexandria (4.30pm; 4hr; £E22) and several throughout the day to Cairo (3hr; £E17). **EgyptAir** has an office on Sharia el-Gumhorriya (℡066/322-0921), one block up from Thomas Cook.

Sinai

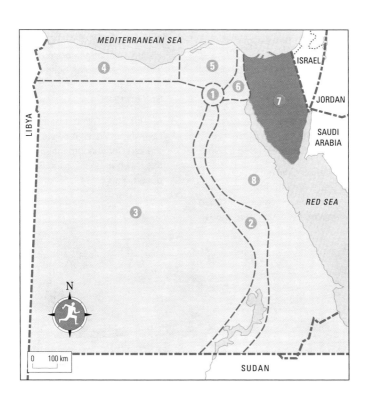

CHAPTER 7

Highlights

✳ **Reefs and wrecks** Check out the infamous blue hole, or go wreck-diving round the *Thistlegorm*. See p.673

✳ **Ras Mohammed** Egypt's first national park, sited at the tip of the Sinai peninsula, offers some world-class diving. See p.676

✳ **Na'ama Bay** Egypt's premier resort, its bars and clubs teem with revellers by night. See p.683

✳ **Nabeq National Park** Check out the spectacular scenery and the world's most northerly mangroves. See p.690

✳ **Dahab** Chill out in Asilah, renowned for its diving, laid-back beach cafés and cheap accommodation. See p.691

✳ **Bedouin culture** Moulids and weddings are held at full moon in the desert. See p.702

✳ **Desert safaris** Take a camel or Jeep safari to secluded palm-fringed wadis with Bedouin hosts. See p.709

✳ **St Catherine's Monastery** Built by Byzantine Empress Helena to commemorate the sight of the burning bush at the foot of Mount Sinai. See p.712

✳ **Mount Sinai** Climb the mountain where Moses received the Ten Commandments and see dawn break over the Sinai desert. See p.714

△ St Catherine's Monastery

7

Sinai

T he **Sinai** peninsula has been the gateway between Africa and Asia since time immemorial and a battleground for millennia. Prized for its strategic position and mineral wealth, Sinai is also revered by disparate cultures as the site of God's revelation to Moses, the wanderings of Exodus and the flight of the Holy Family. As Burton Bernstein wrote, "It has been touched, in one way or another by most of Western and Near Eastern history, both actual and mythic", being the supposed route by which the Israelites reached the Promised Land and Islam entered North Africa, then a theatre for Crusader-Muslim and Arab-Israeli conflicts, and finally transformed into an internationally monitored demilitarized zone.

Though mostly wilderness, Sinai looks far too dramatic – and too beautiful – to be dismissed as "24,000 square miles of nothing". The interior of southern Sinai is an arid moonscape of jagged ranges harbouring **Mount Sinai** and **St Catherine's Monastery**, where pilgrims climb the Steps of Repentance from the site of the Burning Bush to the summit where God delivered the Ten Commandments. Further north, the vast **Wilderness of the Wanderings** resembles a Jackson Pollock canvas streaked with colour and imprinted with tank tracks. The Sinai is also home to a remarkably high number of plants and wildlife; over sixty percent of Egypt's plant life thrives in this area, and 33 species are unique to it. Among a number of mammals that inhabit the region are the hyena, ibex and the rabbit-like hyrax. Venture into this "desert" on a **camel trek** or **Jeep safari** and you will also find remote springs and lush oases, providing some insights into **Bedouin culture** (for more on which, see the box on pp.668–689). Safaris can be organized at any of the resorts on the Aqaba coast; for an overview of safari destinations, see pp.709–710.

Above all, however, the south has the lure of exquisite coral reefs and tropical fish in the **Gulf of Aqaba**, one of the finest **diving** and **snorkelling** grounds in the world; a list of the best sites appears on p.673, along with practical information on dive courses and excursions, and there's an introduction to the reefs and their denizens in the separate colour section. The beach resorts at **Sharm el-Sheikh** (which includes **Na'ama Bay**), **Dahab** and **Nuweiba** cater to every taste and budget. From Sharm el-Sheikh you can make expeditions to Egypt's deepest reefs and most diverse aquatic life at **Ras Mohammed**, a mini-peninsula at the southern tip of Sinai, and the **Tiran Strait**, scattered with the wrecks of ships that have floundered on the reefs of this narrow passageway connecting the Red Sea to the Gulf of Aqaba. Northwest of here, the **Gulf of Suez** pales by comparison with its eastern counterpart – though year-round winds make it a great destination for diehard windsurfers and kiteboarders, there are no reefs and few sites to interest the general visitor. **Northern Sinai**,

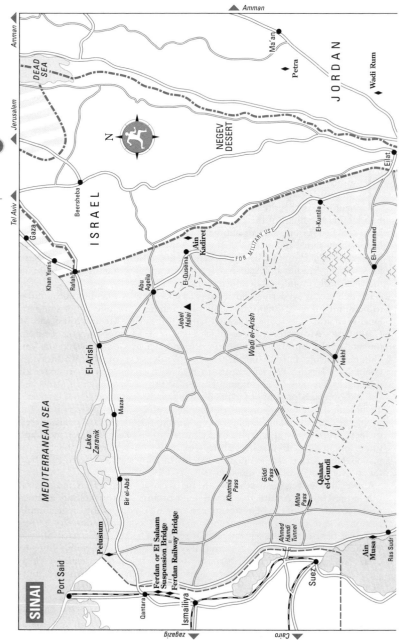

SINAI

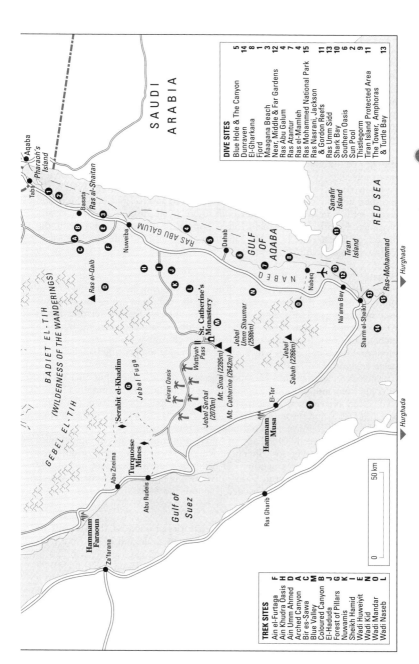

TREK SITES

Ain el-Furtaga	F
Ain Khudra Oasis	H
Ain Umm Ahmed	D
Arched Canyon	A
Bir es-Sawa	C
Blue Valley	M
Coloured Canyon	B
El-Haduda	J
Forest of Pillars	G
Nuwamis	I
Sheikh Hamid	K
Wadi Huweiyit	E
Wadi Kid	N
Wadi Mandar	O
Wadi Naseb	L

DIVE SITES

Blue Hole & The Canyon	5
Dunraven	14
El-Gharkana	8
Fjord	1
Maagana Beach	3
Near, Middle & Far Gardens	12
Ras Abu Galum	4
Ras Atantur	7
Ras el-Mamleh	4
Ras Mohammed National Park	15
Ras Nasrani, Jackson & Gordon Reefs	11
Ras Umm Sidd	13
Shark Bay	10
Southern Oasis	6
Sun Pool	2
Thistlegorm	9
Tiran Island Protected Area	11
The Tower, Amphoras & Turtle Bay	13

SINAI 7

visited by almost no Western tourists, has a barren coastline which you scarcely glimpse from the road, and a single town and focus in **El–Arish**, a laid-back if conservative place with a palm-fringed beach and a weekly Bedouin market.

Sinai's **climate** is extreme. On the coast, daytime temperatures can reach 50°C (120°F) during summer, while nights are sultry or temperate depending on the prevailing wind. In the mountains, which receive occasional snowfall over winter and the odd rainstorm during spring, nights are cooler – if not chilly or freezing. Outside of winter, you should wear a hat, use high-factor sunscreen and drink four to six litres of water a day (more if you're trekking) to avoid sunburn and heatstroke. During summer, the heat is likely to make you spend less time on the beach and more time in the water, and to forgo trekking or camel riding entirely.

The differences between Sinai and mainland Egypt can induce **culture shock**. For those accustomed to Egyptian towns and beaches, Sinai will seem amazingly uncrowded, laid-back and hassle-free – especially so for women. If you arrive from Israel or Jordan, of course, spending some days on a Sinai beach and then heading on to Cairo, you experience the reverse. Native Bedouin and recent settlers from the mainland both assert Sinai's distinctive character and disparage Egyptian government, often comparing it unfavourably with the period of Israeli rule. Even the customary salutation is different: "*kif halak*" ("How is your health/situation?") instead of "*izzayak*".

Some history

Fifty million years ago the Arabian Plate began shearing away from the African landmass, tearing the Sinai peninsula from the mainland while the Red Sea inundated the gap. Hot springs on the sea bed indicate that the tectonic forces which created Sinai are still active – the Gulf of Suez is widening by three inches each year. In **prehistoric times** the climate was less arid and Sinai supported herds of gazelles which Stone Age people trapped and slaughtered in stone enclosures.

Bronze Age Semites from Mesopotamia were the first to exploit Sinai's lodes of copper ore and turquoise, foreshadowing the peninsula's colonization by the III Dynasty pharaohs, who enslaved its Semitic population to work the mines and build roads and fortresses. According to Egyptian mythology, it was in Sinai that Isis sought the dismembered body of Osiris; Hathor, also associated with the region, was called "Our Lady of Sinai". **Pharaonic rule** continued until the invasion of the Hyksos "Shepherd Kings", whose occupation of northern Egypt lasted well over a century, till Ahmosis I drove them out and finally destroyed their last bastion in Gaza. This was subsequently the route by which Tuthmosis III and Ramses II invaded Palestine and Syria.

The Exodus

Enshrined in the Old Testament and by centuries of tradition, the **Exodus of the Israelites** is a historical conundrum, as no archeological evidence of their journey through Sinai has ever been found – though excavations at Avaris in the Delta (see p.633) suggest that this was the "City of Bondage" from which they fled. This is generally thought to have happened during the reign of the XIX Dynasty pharaoh, Merneptah (1236–1223 BC), although Egyptologist David Rohl argues that it occurred two centuries earlier (*c.*1447 BC), under Dudimose of the XIII Dynasty.

To identify their route and various crucial sites, scholars have compared Biblical descriptions with physical features and tried to reconcile myths with realities. The "**Red Sea**" found in the King James Bible is a mistranslation of the Hebrew *yam-suf*, or **Sea of Reeds**, which fits the salt lakes and marshes to the north of Suez, known today as the Bitter Lakes. From there, the Israelites proceeded down the coast to **Ain Musa** and followed **Wadi Feiran** inland towards **Mount Sinai**, although an alternative theory has them trekking across northern Sinai and receiving the Ten Commandments at **Jebel Halal**. Either way, the subsequent forty years in the wilderness are only explicable in terms of a lengthy stay at "Kadesh Barnea", identified as the oasis of **Ain Kedirat**, where there are extensive ruins.

Christianity and Islam

Over the next millennium or so, Sinai was invaded by Assyrians, Hittites and Babylonians, recaptured by Egypt, and conquered in turn by the Persians and Greeks. While the Ptolemies built ports along the Mediterranean coast, Semitic tribes from Petra established themselves between Aqaba and Gaza, both ultimately succumbing to the **Romans**. Whether or not the **Holy Family** had previously crossed Sinai to escape Herod's massacre, the region had begun to attract hermits even before Emperor Constantine legalized **Christianity**, which rooted itself in cathedrals and **monasteries** under Justinian's patronage.

In 639–40 the **Arabs** swept into Sinai, fired with the zeal of **Islam**. The new faith suited local tribes, which turned to plundering the desert monasteries while the Arabs sacked the cathedral cities. Northern Sinai eventually became a pawn in the **Crusades**, the area between Aqaba and Rafah belonging to the Frankish Kingdom until its collapse at Acre. After the Crusades, the victorious Mamlukes reopened Sinai's trade routes but the peninsula remained Egypt's Achilles heel, as the Ottoman Turks and Mohammed Ali demonstrated with their conquests of 1517 and 1831.

Twentieth-century Sinai

Sinai's strategic importance increased with the completion of the **Suez Canal**, and in 1892 Britain compelled Turkey to cede it as a buffer zone. Backed by Germany, the Turks retook it in 1914, laying roads and water pipelines along the northern coast and across the interior. Anglo-Egyptian forces only dislodged them – and went on to take Jerusalem – after a prolonged campaign.

During World War II Sinai witnessed little fighting, but the **creation of Israel** brought the territory right back into the front line. In 1948 the Israelis repulsed Arab attacks from all sides and took the **Gaza Strip** and **El-Arish** before an armistice was signed, only withdrawing under British pressure. Nasser brought together British and Israeli interests by closing the Gulf of Aqaba to Israeli shipping and nationalizing the Suez Canal. It was Israel's advance into Sinai in October 1956 that was the agreed pretext for Anglo-French intervention in the **Suez Crisis**; the three states, though militarily successful, were compelled to quit by international opposition, UN peace-keeping forces establishing a buffer zone in Gaza and guaranteeing free passage through the Gulf of Aqaba.

But further **Arab-Israeli wars** were inevitable. When Egypt ordered the UN to leave and resumed its blockade in 1967, Israel launched a pre-emptive strike and captured the entire peninsula, which it retained after the **Six Day War** and fortified with the Bar-Lev Line along the east bank of the Suez Canal. In the **October War of 1973**, Egypt broke through into Sinai but then suffered a devastating counterattack across the canal.

US-sponsored peace negotiations culminated in President Sadat's historic visit to Jerusalem, the **Camp David Accords** and a peace treaty signed in 1979, which led to Egypt's decade-long expulsion from the Arab League.

About 80,000 of Sinai's population are **Bedouin** who claim descent from the tribes of the Hejaz on the Arabian Peninsula, and thus rate themselves among the purest Arab genealogies. Only the Jebeliya tribe is anomalous, tracing its origins to the Caucasus.

Traditionally, each tribe roamed its own territory in search of grazing and settled around local oases. The Mizayna claimed the land between El-Tor and Nuweiba; the Tarabeen a swathe from Nuweiba to El-Arish; the Jebeliya the St Catherine's region, and so on. The number of **tribes** in Sinai is uncertain, ranging from 14 to 27 depending on which of their subdivisions are counted. Other tribes include the Sawalha, Alekat, Walad Shaheen and Tiyahah. Collectively, they are known as the Tawarah ("Arabs of Tor"), after the ancient name of the peninsula. For all the tribes, tribal and family honour were paramount, raids and camel-rustling a perpetual cause for blood feuds that might persist for generations. Agriculture or fishing was a hand-to-mouth activity, secondary to herding goats and camels – the latter being the measure of a tribe's wealth, with racing camels esteemed above all. Though devout Muslims, the Bedouin retained pagan superstitions and practices, with their own common law ('urf) instead of regular Islamic jurisprudence.

Unsurprisingly, the Bedouin took advantage of discarded weaponry to resist outside authority, attempts to settle the nomads having little success until the 1970s, when Israel constructed water tanks, schools and clinics at various sites. By providing employment and exposing the Bedouin to Western comforts, the coastal resorts had an equally profound effect on traditional lifestyles. Nowadays, many earn their living through tourism, taxi driving or construction work, and stone huts with corrugated iron roofs and TV antennae are more common than black tents. Although relations between the Bedouin and Egyptians are generally peaceful, grievances do arise; they usually focus on administrators and entrepreneurs from mainland Egypt, whom many Bedouin regard as here on sufferance, but who are steadily growing in numbers.

Bedouin culture

Although the provision of schools, medical posts and water tanks has enticed many Bedouin to forsake nomadic lives, others still roam the desert with their flocks. From the El-Arish road you can glimpse girls in peacock robes with hennaed tresses, aloof boys and men, and black-garbed women in veils or leather masks spangled with coins – the colour of the cross-stitched embroidery on their robes and hoods

Under its terms Israel evacuated all settlements founded during the occupation of Sinai and the territory reverted to Egypt. The phased transition was completed in 1982, except for the disputed enclave of Taba, finally resolved in 1989. The Multinational Force of Observers (**MFO**) based at Na'ama Bay monitors Sinai's "banded" demilitarized zones from orange-flagged outposts around the peninsula.

Tourism, introduced to Sinai by the Israelis, initially suffered from the hand-over, as the Camp David Accords forbade any development for five years. Since 1988, however, its recovery has shifted into overdrive: where the Aqaba coast once had just five hotels it now has more than 150, with more in the pipeline. While the areas of Ras Mohammed, Abu Galum and Nabeq are protected by their status as nature reserves, the entire coastline north of Nuweiba, and from Sharm el-Sheikh to Nabeq National Park, are highly developed. With plans to extend hotel development further into the desert, and ever more charter flights arriving from Europe into Sharm el-Sheikh, Sinai's days as a wilderness may well be numbered.

indicates whether they are married (red) or not (blue). On the horizon you may see black tents pitched in the desert; women are responsible for weaving the goat-hair *beit shaar* ("house of hair") and striking, unloading, packing and erecting them whenever the family moves on. In Bedouin divorces the husband gets the domestic animals while the woman keeps the tent.

The Bedouin are keen observers of the Sinai's furtive **wildlife**. Hares and foxes can lead them to water holes; desert sandgrouse, gazelles and the rare mountain ibex (*bedan*) make good hunting; and flocks must be guarded against the depredations of the jackal (*taaleb*), wolf (*dib*) and hyena (*dhaba*). The last has a mythological counterpart, the *dhabia*, believed to have the power to mesmerize solitary travellers into entering its lair. Other creatures imbued with supernatural significance are the dreaded horned viper, known as Abu Jenabiya ("Father of Going Sideways"), and the fox – personifying wisdom and cunning – who is a favourite character in children's tales.

Plants are even more important to the Bedouin, who feed their camels on a prickly tribulus called *ghraghada* and make extensive use of **herbal medicine**. Among the many remedies, *rabla* is an aromatic flower made into an essential oil that's used as a general pick-me-up, while *handl* seeds are ground into a paste, cooked in olive oil and applied in a bandage to aching joints, or mixed with garlic to treat snake or scorpion bites.

Storytelling holds a special place in Bedouin culture, where poetic imagery and Koranic rhetoric sprang naturally from the lips of shepherds exposed to a rich oral heritage since childhood. When food is lacking for guests, hospitality can still be rendered in words: "Had I known that you would honour me by walking this way, I should have strewn the path between your house and mine with mint and rose petals!". Although professional reciters of Arabic poetry are now rare, most Bedouin can reel off folk tales, which usually begin with their equivalent of "once upon a time", the phrase "kan ma kan . . ." ("there was, there was not").

Conversation is the expected reward for Bedouin **hospitality**, which traditionally stretched to three days, each named after a stage in the ritual: *salaam* ("greeting"), *ta'aam* ("eating") and *kelaam* ("speaking"). Before the rising of the morning star on the fourth day, hosts helped their guests prepare for departure; those who lingered beyond the drying of the dew were as welcome "as the spotted snake". Honour can now be satisfied by three servings of tea or coffee, and it's no longer mandatory to slaughter an animal.

The mercurial nature of Middle Eastern politics, however, means that tourism along the Sinai coast is a fickle business. Unrest in the West Bank and Gaza has greatly slowed tourist traffic from Israel, while the 2004 **terrorist attacks** in Taba, with more attacks in Sharm el-Sheikh and Dahab in 2005 and 2006 respectively, have worsened the situation further. While the Sharm el-Sheikh resorts and Dahab remain fairly busy with European package holiday-makers, the coast further north around Nuweiba and Taba that used to be the hangout for Israeli holiday-makers is very quiet; the airport at Taba is rarely used nowadays, and the Bedouin-run accommodation around Nuweiba is almost completely devoid of life.

Visiting Sinai

For the purposes of this guide, the peninsula divides into three zones – the **gulf coasts of Suez and Aqaba**, the **interior** and **northern Sinai**. Communications between the resorts along the coastal strip of the Gulf of Aqaba and the interior around St Catherine's are well established (these two areas make up the administrative region of **South Sinai**), but northern Sinai is effectively sundered from both, despite the upgrading of a route between El-Arish and Nekhl, inland. Transport to each zone **from mainland Egypt** is described at the start of each section, while the **approaches from Israel and Jordan** are covered in "Basics" (see pp.29–30). You can visit part of the peninsula on a free **Sinai-only visa**, valid for two weeks and covering South Sinai only (for more, see p.65). If you wish to visit Ras Mohammed, other parts of Sinai's interior or mainland Egypt, you'll need a **regular visa**, which can be obtained upon arrival at Sharm el-Sheikh airport.

Most travellers find it easy to get around, as **buses** are frequent and cheap and **service taxis** run to and from every resort. The sole exception is the **border at Taba**, which only has a few service taxis, whose drivers are notorious for taking financial advantage of the lack of buses. Foreign **motorists** are restricted to main roads; **hitchhiking** is a dubious proposition unless your destination is nearby or you're certain of a ride all the way (or at least to somewhere with shade and buses). Women should *never* hitch alone.

Accommodation and costs

Accommodation ranges from costly all-inclusive holiday villages at Na'ama Bay to cheap "campgrounds" at Nuweiba – not campgrounds in the usual sense, these consist of huts of stone, concrete, bamboo or palm leaves, and may or may not have electricity and bathrooms. Although tourism is a year-round business, there are definite peak periods when hotels charge higher prices and are liable to be full. To some extent this depends on the resort: Sharm el-Sheikh receives a surge of European package tourists over spring, autumn and Christmas. Before the political situation between Israel and the Palestinians deteriorated, the Bedouin-run camps between Taba and Dahab, especially those at Tarabeen and to the north, were flooded with Israelis during Jewish holidays. Also bear in mind **Egyptian holiday periods** – December 22–February 2, March 1–May 3 and July 19–October 31 – when you should try to book in advance. **Tap water** is not drinkable in Sinai, so you'll need to buy bottled water.

The **cost** of everyday items, meals and transport is higher in Sinai than elsewhere in Egypt, but still cheaper than in Israel or Europe. There are **banks** with ATMs in all the main resorts, while US dollars can be exchanged in many shops. Many dive centres and hotels will also take payments in euros, while Israeli shekels (NIS) are still sometimes accepted in many Gulf of Aqaba resorts.

Activities

Diving or **snorkelling** (see pp.671–674) can comfortably be done at any time of the year and constitute Sinai's greatest attraction. Details of dive centres, courses and trips are given under each resort as appropriate. There's a general rundown on **camel** and **Jeep safaris** on pp.709–710, with specifics in each relevant location. As a rule, sites near the coast can be visited at any time of the year by Jeep, and between October and April by camel. **Trekking** in the High Mountain Region (see p.716) is possible in winter if you are prepared to face chilly nights and possible snow flurries; in summer, it's only a matter of being fit enough to stand the heat.

Serious divers or trekkers should acquire the 1:250,000 *Sinai Map of Attractions*, an English-language tourist map based on Israeli army surveys, which is sold at the Taba border and most resorts. At a pinch, divers could make do with one of the maps produced by dive centres or travel agents, which outline the chief dive sites and Ras Mohammed National Park. For local information, pick up a copy of H^2O, (Ⓦ www.h2o-mag.com) a free quarterly **listings magazine** by the Red Sea Association with a particular slant on diving; it's available in Sharm el-Sheikh hotels, but harder to find in Nuweiba and Dahab.

The gulf coasts

Sinai rises and tapers as the peninsula runs towards its southern apex, red rock meeting golden sand and deep blue water along two gulf coasts. Even the **Gulf of Suez**, as E.M. Forster noted, looks enticing from offshore – "an exquisite corridor of tinted mountains and radiant water" – though it's nowadays transformed after dark into a vision of Hades by the flaming plumes of oil rigs.

For most travellers, however, Suez is merely an interlude before the **Gulf of Aqaba**, whose amazing coral reefs and tropical fish have given rise to a number of popular resorts. The beach scene here is the best Egypt can offer, and many resorts can organize trips into the wild **interior** by Jeep or camel. Even from the beach, the view of the mountains of Sinai and Saudi Arabia is magnificent.

Aside from those arriving from Israel or Jordan, most travellers approach the gulf coasts from Cairo, Suez or Hurghada. **From Cairo**, there are buses via the Sinai interior to Nuweiba (8 daily; 8hr; £E65), three of which carry on to Taba (9hr; £E75). Sharm el-Sheikh and Dahab buses use the southern road around the peninsula; to Sharm, there are Superjet buses (3 daily; 7hr; £E65) from Cairo's Turgoman Garage, and East Delta buses from the Sinai Terminal in Abbassiya (7 daily; 7hr; £E55), five of which continue to Dahab (9hr; £E65–75). There's also a service to St Catherine's Monastery (daily; 8hr; £E55). There are four daily EgyptAir **flights** from Cairo to Sharm (55min; $100 one-way). **Suez City** is the interchange for numerous buses coming from Hurghada, Cairo or northern Sinai; for details, see p.648.

EgyptAir operates indirect flights **from Luxor** to Sharm, via Cairo (Tues & Thurs 7.15am; $75). Travelling from the Nile Valley, you can also take a bus to **Hurghada**, from where you can continue by **catamaran** to Sharm (4 weekly; 1hr 30min) or charter a seven-seater **taxi** for the drive (£E800–900).

Diving

Much of the diving Sinai offers is easy to access and relatively sheltered from harsh winds and currents, making it a popular destination for those who have little or no experience. It's a cheap place to learn open-water diving and gain a PADI, BSAC or CMAS certificate, entitling you to dive anywhere in the world (NAUII, SSI or MDEA are less widely accepted). The initial step is a five-day **open-water** (OW) course, starting at around €300/$400 including equipment, plus €30/$40 or so for the certificate. Courses progress from classroom theory to your first dives in the hotel swimming pool or from the shore, finishing with a few boat dives at the end. Most centres offer a supervised introductory dive (from around €50/$65) for those uncertain about shelling out for a full course. Kids aged 8–10 years can try the PADI "**Bubble Maker**" course (€50/$65), which includes a short two-metre dive in the coral close to the shore. At the other end of the skill spectrum, you can be trained as an **instructor**

(€550/$700). Qualified divers can progress through **advanced open-water**, **dive master** and **instructor** certification, and take **specialized courses** in underwater rescue, night or wreck diving, to name but a few. Note that if you're certified but haven't logged a dive in the past three months, you might have to take a "check dive" as a refresher before you can go on a sea trip.

The type of diving and the degree of experience required at each dive site are mainly determined by underwater topography and currents. Around Sharm the chief activity is **boat diving** (you enter the water offshore) at sites ranging from novice-friendly to demanding. Up the coast past Dahab and Nuweiba this gives way to **shore diving**, where you wade or swim out to the reefs. **Liveaboards** (also called safari boats) allow you to spend days or weeks at sea, cruising the dive sites and shipwrecks of the north Red Sea around Ras Mohammed and the Tiran Strait (or the more southerly reefs beyond Hurghada, covered in Chapter 8). They also give access to less-visited sites out of "peak hours", and the chance to make up to five dives a day rather than the two dives offered by daily boats.

Boat trips to dive sites usually include tanks and weights; lunch on the boat is extra (about £E50). **Dive packages** can be a good deal, costing around €250/$325 for a five-day package (ten dives), with discounts sometimes available for advance or online bookings. Liveaboards can work out cheaper than staying in a hotel and buying a dive package separately, averaging around €100/$130 per person per day, including full board; airport transfers, diving equipment and alcohol are usually extra. Where equipment rental isn't covered, count on an extra €25/$35 per day. During quiet periods, bookings can be arranged at short notice (if you're interested in a liveaboard, try asking on the boat while it's at the marina), but to be sure of what you're getting it's best to book in advance through an agent.

Choosing a dive centre

Broadly speaking, most dive centres in Sharm el-Sheikh and Nuweiba are very good, but in Dahab, however, regulations are less likely to be adhered to and competition between dive centres is cut-throat, encouraging some divers to simply go for the cheapest option. When **choosing a dive centre**, ask around and then stick to those setups that have been there the longest and have proper links with organizations like PADI. Though centres associated with big hotels are safer bets than outfits on their own, smart premises are less important than the **equipment**. If left lying about, chances are it'll also be poorly maintained. Also note the location of the compressor used to fill the tanks; if it's near a road or other source of pollution, you'll be breathing it in underwater. Ask to see a card proving that the instructor is qualified to teach the course (PADI, BSAC or whatever), and not merely a dive master. Finally, many dive centres offer courses not only in English but also in various European languages; linguistic misunderstandings can be dangerous, so you need an instructor who speaks your language well.

Sinai dive sites

The following sites are all marked on the map at the start of this chapter.

Amphoras Between Ras Umm Sidd and Na'ama Bay, this is named after a Turkish galleon laden with amphoras of mercury that lies on the reef (indeed the site is also known as "Mercury"). **Blue Hole** 8km north of Dahab. The challenge of this 107m-deep hole in the reef is to swim through a passage 60m down and come up the other side – which is highly risky even for expert divers. Even dive masters and instructors who have successfully passed through before have met their fate at the Blue Hole. You can safely snorkel around the rim of the hole, however.

Canyon Near the Blue Hole. A narrow reef crack, 50m deep and only for experienced divers.

Dunraven The *Dunraven* was a ship which, en route from Bombay to Newcastle, steered onto a reef in fine weather on April 25, 1873 and sank 25m almost completely upside down. Though its 25 crew escaped, the captain was found negligent (he fatuously remarked, "Twenty-five is my lucky number!").

El-Gharkana A luxuriant reef, offshore from mangroves and lagoons with rare waterfowl and flora. Part of the Nabeq protected area.

Fjord 10km south of Taba. A picturesque cleft with underwater reefs.

Gordon Reef Off the coast of Ras Nasrani, in the shipwreck-littered Tiran Strait, with sharks and strong currents. Popular with experienced divers; not for beginners.

Jackson Reef A large reef between Tiran Island and the mainland, with a 70m drop-off, sharks and pelagic fish, and the shipwreck *Lara*. Strong currents; dangerous for beginners.

Maagana Beach 5–10km north of Nuweiba. The reef falls sheer around the "Devil's Head" to the north, getting shallower and less impressive further south.

Near, Middle and Far Gardens 1–5km north of Na'ama Bay. A series of lovely coral reefs, good for easy diving and snorkelling. The Near Gardens are within walking distance of Na'ama.

Pharaoh's Island Near Taba. There's superb under-water scenery, easy access by boat and a spectacular wall dive, but also strong currents; a diving guide is recommended. Israelis call it "Coral Island".

Ras Abu Galum 50km south of Nuweiba. A 400 square-kilometre protected area with a deep virgin reef wall and great fish. Access by 4WD or boat.

Ras Atantur Between Dahab and Nabeq. Colourful, abundant reef, with a shipwreck – the *Maria Schroeder* – 10km further south. Access by 4WD.

Ras el-Mamleh 20km south of Nuweiba. Another slab of virgin reef wall on the northern edge of the Ras Abu Galum protected area. Access by 4WD or boat.

Ras Mohammed National Park 25km southwest of Sharm el-Sheikh. Wonderful corals, mangrove lagoons, anemone gardens and crevice pools, with shark reefs offshore. It's also the site of the *Yolanda* shipwreck (see below).

Ras Nasrani Sheer reef wall riddled with shark caves; the Light and the Point are notable spots. Large turtles are a common sight on the reef slope. Beware of sharks and strong currents. Not for inexperienced divers.

Ras Umm Sidd Within walking distance of Sharm el-Sheikh at the north point of the harbour, this features exquisite fan corals and coral.

Shark Bay Colourful reef just off the beach of a small resort, 10km north of Na'ama Bay. Good for novices and experienced divers alike, and snorkellers.

Southern Oasis Gently sloping reef 7km to the south of Dahab, with easy diving and snorkelling.

Sun Pool 10–15km south of Taba. A gorgeous diving beach along a shallow reef extending as far north as the Fjord.

Thistlegorm Near El-Tor in the Gulf of Suez, this British ship, sunk by German bombers in 1941, was laden with rifles, uniforms, trucks and Jeeps – and also packed full of ammunition, which exploded, ripping the ship apart and killing most of the crew. To this day, the rear decks are peeled back towards the bridge leaving many a diver wondering what exactly they are looking at. Tubeworms grow out of the bathtub in the captain's cabin and you can still see much of the armoured vehicles she was carrying. Discovered by Jacques Cousteau, it's a popular dive from Sharm el-Sheikh.

Tiran Island Protected Area An archipelago with over twenty dive sites, all amazing. Sharks and strong currents; only for experienced divers unless explicitly stated otherwise.

The Tower South of Na'ama Bay is this sheer reef pillar dropping 60m. Easy access from the beach and mild currents; good for novice divers.

Turtle Bay Between Ras Umm Sidd and Amphoras, a shallow bay with turtles, easy to enjoy. Access is by boat.

Yolanda Off Ras Mohammed is this Cypriot freighter that struck a reef during a storm in 1981; its cargo includes a BMW and scores of porcelain lavatories.

Snorkelling

Snorkelling is also great fun and costs much less than diving. If you've never snorkelled before and find breathing through a tube unsettling, start with the baby reefs just off the beach, where the sea is only waist deep. By the time you've circled a reef and seen its profusion of rainbow-hued fish, snorkelling should feel like fun and you'll be ready to move on to bigger things.

Gear can be rented at most of Sinai's dive centres (daily rates: £E8 mask, £E8 snorkel, £E10 fins, £E10 protective rubber shoes). If you're planning to do a lot, it's cheaper to bring your own gear than to rent it from dive shops in Sinai (you might be able to sell it when you leave). Note that coral reefs and spiny urchins can rip unprotected feet to shreds; in all events you should only walk in designated "corridors" to protect the corals – if the water is too shallow to allow you to float above them. However cool the water may feel, the sun's rays can still burn exposed flesh, so always wear a T-shirt and use waterproof sunscreen.

Between Suez and Sharm el-Sheikh

The 338-kilometre journey between **Suez** and **Sharm el–Sheikh** takes only a few hours by bus or service taxi, and there's little point in stopping unless you've got private transport or you're an avid windsurfer. Such attractions as exist along (or off) the route are otherwise awkward to reach (or leave), so most travellers pass them by. Although the resort of **Ras Sudr** is essentially an oil town, its proximity to Cairo (130km) means it is becoming popular with Cairenes as a weekend get-away, while its year-round wind draws windsurfers from further afield. Further south, and inland, the pharaonic ruins at **Serabit el-Khadim** are also starting to attract larger numbers of visitors, most of them arriving from Sharm el-Sheikh or Dahab by Jeep. Beyond **El-Tor**, the area's administrative capital, there's little of interest until you reach the diving grounds of **Ras Mohammed**.

South along the Gulf of Suez

As you head south by road, the **Gulf of Suez** is sensed before it appears as a glint on the horizon, beyond the sands that rim the west for much of the way. Roughly 50km past the Ahmed Hamdi Tunnel, a dirt road turns off towards the coast to **AIN MUSA**, the **"Springs of Moses"**. According to scholastic conjecture and local legend, it was here that the Israelites halted after crossing the Red Sea, and Moses threw a tree in the bitter spring of Marah, which miraculously became drinkable (Exodus 15). Ain Musa is recognizable from the highway by the deposits of calcium and magnesium salts that surround the oasis, where only one of the twelve springs mentioned in Exodus remains, yielding water that has a strong chemical odour and acts as a powerful laxative. Many of the palm trees in the oasis were decapitated during various Sinai conflicts; an Israeli battery stationed here shelled Suez and Port Tewfiq during the War of Attrition, until Egypt recaptured Ain Musa in 1973. Camping is possible, although limited by the lack of food, water, and transport out. Ask at the village if you're interested, and you may find a Bedouin willing to guide you round.

Ras Sudr and Hammam Faraoun

Famed for the variety of seashells washed up on its beach, the resort of **RAS SUDR** (or Ras Sidr) is marred by a reeking oil refinery that doesn't seem to bother the middle-class Cairenes who patronize its holiday villages and **hotels**. The town itself offers little more than a few fly-blown **restaurants**, such as the *Manta Fish Market* next to the bus station, 300m south of the main road; a handful of shops and an **Internet café**, two blocks south of the main street.

This part of the coast is so windy it is often overlooked by travellers who seek the calmer reef-fringed shores of Sharm el-Sheikh, but the blemish-free beach and year-round and day-long cross-shore gusts make it a paradise for **windsurfers** and **kiteboarders**. Two resorts are both ideal for beginners, and can be reached by taxi from Ras Sudr's bus station. The

Ramada (☎010 171-7844, ⓦwww.ramada.com; ⓐ) 10km south of Ras Sudr has tidy chalets, some with kitchens, next to a wide sandy beach with restaurant, bar and minimarket. Lessons and equipment for windsurfing and kiteboarding can be organized, and activity packages can be booked through *Club Mistral* (ⓦwww.club-mistral.com). ⚓ *Moon Beach Retreat*, 40km south of Ras Sudr (☎069/340-1501, ⓦwww.moonbeachretreat .com; ⓐ), has accommodation in comfortable air-conditioned stone chalets; adjoining it and sharing the same management is the new *Green Hotel*, overlooking one of the lagoons, and with slightly smarter, pricier rooms than its neighbour. Boards and rigs can be hired from £E120 sterling per week, and there's also yoga instruction and mountain biking on offer.

Fifty-five kilometres south of Ras Sudr, a turn-off leads to **HAMMAM FARAOUN** ("Pharaoh's Bath"), several near-boiling **hot springs** which Arab folklore attributes to the pharaoh's struggles to extricate himself from the waves that engulfed his army as he chased Moses and the Israelites. Local Bedouin use the springs for curing rheumatism, and it is possible to bathe; a cave in the hill beside the shore leads into "the sauna", a warren of chambers awash with hot water, but it's more comfortable to bathe where the springs flow into the sea. There are plans to build a hotel nearby, but in the meantime the only option if you want to stay is to **camp**. You must inform the soldiers posted nearby, who enforce a ban on visiting the beach after 6pm.

Serabit el-Khadim and the turquoise mines

Built upon a 755-metre-high summit reached by a tortuous path, the rock-hewn temple known as **Serabit el-Khadim** is the only pharaonic temple in Sinai, surrounded by some of the region's grandest scenery. Erected during the XII Dynasty, when turquoise mining in the area was at its peak, it is an enduring symbol of pharaonic power over the nameless thousands who toiled in the mines of Sinai. Though Bedouin still glean some local turquoise by low-tech methods, the amount that remains isn't worth the cost of industrial extraction.

The scattered ruins of the temple itself consist of open courts and sanctuaries dedicated to the goddess Hathor in her aspect as "Mistress of Turquoise", and the god Soped, "Guardian of the Desert Ways". Both deities are invoked on rock-cut and freestanding stelae relating to mining expeditions. These were only possible for half of the year due to the heat and scarcity of water, and thus a permanent colony was never established. The temple (whose precincts were segregated from the mining area by a crude stone wall) was abandoned during the reign of Ramses VII. Known to the Bedouin for centuries, it was "discovered" by Reinhold Niebuhr in 1792, but not excavated until early in the nineteenth century.

Serabit el-Khadim is becoming a popular stop on **Jeep safaris** from points south, via a track leading off the road from St Catherine's into **Wadi Mukattab** – the Valley of Inscriptions. Here you can find dozens of hieroglyphic texts carved into the rocks, alongside Proto-Sinaitic **inscriptions** that continue into Wadi Maraghah, where ancient mine workings and stelae were damaged when the turquoise mines were revived by the British and before going bust in 1901. Most desert outfitters in Na'ama Bay, such as Sun 'n Fun (see p.686), can organize two- to three-day trips here for around $300 for a group of seven.

El-Tor

There's little to see along the coastal highway – which often veers inland, giving a wide berth to airstrips and oil terminals – besides a scattering of holiday resorts all the way to **EL-TOR** (or El-Tur), the administrative capital of South Sinai. The town itself consists of a mass of housing, a number of construction sites and a scattering of government buildings, and as with Ras Sudr, the main reason to come is for the **windsurfing and kiteboarding**. The only sight of note is the **Raithu Monastery**, commissioned by Byzantine emperor Justinian (527–565). Supplies were once sent by ship to El-Tor and were stored at Raithu before being transported to St. Catherine's Monastery in the interior. Today the monastery, next to the old port, is home to a very hospitable Greek Orthodox order that will allow you to visit and look at the remaining old stones of the original monastery; just knock on the door and ask nicely.

Most kiteboarders and windsurfers **stay** at ⚓ *Moses Bay* (☎069/377-4343, ⓦwww.mosesbayeltur.com; ❺), 2km north of the centre on the coast. It's the most attractive hotel in the area, with air-conditioned rooms with bath, satellite TV and a large sandy beach, as well as being home to the El-Tur Windsurfing Centre (ⓦwww.el-turwindsurfing.com), renting out windsurf boards and kiteboards and offering courses. Weekly hotel packages start from €160 per person sharing, including transfers from Sharm el-Sheikh airport and half board. Otherwise there's also the *Tur Sinai* (☎069/377-0059; ❸), in a modern white-washed building conveniently located next to the bus station and offering presentable rooms.

A couple of kilometres up the coast from *Moses Bay* are the **hot springs** of **Hammam Musa** (Moses's Bath; £E20), which lie in the shadow of the looming hill named after them. According to legend, Moses asked an elderly woman for a drink from the spring, but the woman refused him, so Moses called upon God to bless the water with therapeutic properties, making it unfit to drink. A path leading halfway up the hill affords spectacular views; facilities include changing rooms with towels and a cafeteria nearby selling snacks and drinks.

Ras Mohammed

At Sinai's southernmost tip is the not-to-be-missed **RAS MOHAMMED** peninsula, fringed with lagoons and reefs. Covering 480 square kilometres, it was declared a nature reserve in 1983, then Egypt's first marine **National Park** in 1989, and is home to a thousand-odd species of fish as well as 150 types of corals. Bordered to the west by the relatively shallow Gulf of Suez and to the east by the deep waters of the Gulf of Aqaba, it has strong currents throughout the year, making the waters very rich in nutrients. The age of this amazing ecosystem is evinced by marine fossils in the bedrock dating back twenty million years; on the shoreline are newcomers only 75,000 years old. Though the area is chiefly one for **divers**, there are calmer reefs for **snorkellers** to have a great time as well. The park is also home to terrestrial species such as foxes, reptiles and migratory birds such as the white stork.

Just over ten percent of the national park is accessible to visitors from sunrise to sunset, but you will need a full Egyptian **visa** and not just a Sinai-only one (they check). The €5 is usually included in the cost of excursions by Jeep or boat from Sharm el-Sheikh (bear in mind that as the number of dive boats allowed each day is limited, you can't be certain of a place on a boat at short notice). Alternatively, if you just plan to snorkel you could charter a taxi (about £E180) or self-drive car for the day. There are two perimeter gates on the road between El-Tor and Sharm el-Sheikh, leading to a main entrance, whence it's 20km to the nearest reefs.

Various trails – accessible by regular car – are marked by colour-coded arrows. The blue one leads to **Aqaba Beach**, the **Eel Garden**, the **Main**

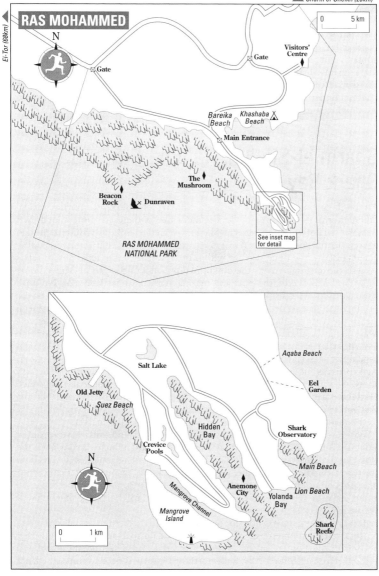

Beach and a **Shark Observatory** 50m up the cliffside, which affords distant views of the odd fin. Purple and then red shows the route to the **Hidden Bay**, **Anemone City** and **Yolanda Bay**, while green signifies the way to the **Crevice Pools** and the **Mangrove Channel**, where children can safely bathe in warm, sandy shallows. Divers head by boat to sites such as the **Shark Reefs** off Yolanda Bay (the place to see sharks, barracuda, giant Napoleon fish and manta rays), and **the Mushroom** or the **wreck** of the *Dunraven*, out towards

Beacon Rock. There's no dive centre at Ras Mohammed, so you need to visit on an organized dive.

A **visitor centre** (10am–sunset) off the road between the Sharm gate and the main entrance shows videos in English and Arabic on alternate hours and contains a library, shop and restaurant (11am–5pm). Free **telescopes** are located there, at the Shark Observatory, and at Suez Beach. To **camp** at the site near Khashaba Beach, pick up a form for a camping permit ($5 per person per night; children under 12 free) at the entrance to the park . Note that the nearest **shop** for supplies is in Sharm el-Sheikh, about thirty minutes away by car.

Sharm el-Sheikh, Na'ama Bay and Shark Bay

Although technically one destination, **Sharm el-Sheikh** comprises several different areas – and constant development means there are more added each year. You will often hear Sharm el-Sheikh referred to simply as **Sharm**, though if you are outside the resort that term refers to the whole resort, including Na'ama Bay, while once you are within the resort itself, the term Sharm refers only to the area that covers the downtown precinct of **Sharm el-Maya**, home to a large market area, the port and marina. It is a cheaper base than **Na'ama Bay**, 7km up the coast, where most of the best hotels and nightlife are based. Na'ama has an excellent wide sandy beach and top-class facilities; the general feel of the place is much like any Mediterranean coastal resort, while Sharm el-Maya retains a *baladi* ambience reminiscent of Suez or Cairo, which can come as a shock to package tourists leaving their resorts for the first time. Whereas beachwear is de rigueur at Na'ama, tourists staying in Sharm el-Maya would do well to **dress** modestly off the beach to avoid unwelcome attention. The cliff above Sharm el-Maya bay is home to a prosperous residential area called **Hadaba**; further north, roughly halfway between Sharm el-Maya and Na'ama Bay, you come to another largely residential area, **Hay el-Nur,** which is home to the main bus station, a hospital and a well-stocked supermarket.

Southeast of Sharm el-Maya bay, a string of hotels and villas have sprouted along the stretch of coast known as **Ras Umm Sidd**, which extends from the Ras Um Sidd dive site north to The Tower dive site. The swankiest resorts here are perched close to the coast, while cheaper hotels favoured by British tour operators fill up the land behind. It's a pretty bleak area, with poor beaches, and guests have to rely on shuttle buses to get them to the better amenities of Na'ama Bay.

Hotel development has not stopped at Na'ama Bay, and tourist villages, some up to a square kilometre in size, line the coast up to **Ras Nasrani** and even beyond to the borders of the **Nabeq** protected area. The once-beautiful and isolated retreat of **Shark Bay**, 8km north of Na'ama, is now swamped by large resorts – it still boasts a fine beach, however, and a view of Tiran Island.

Divers are no longer allowed to explore the reefs near Na'ama and Sharm el-Sheikh independently; all diving must now be done with a guide, which in practical terms means sticking with trips run by the dive operators. All of the Sharm and Na'ama Bay dive centres are members of the **South Sinai Association for Diving and Marine Activities** (T & F 069/366-0418, W www .southsinai.org), which regulates and promotes the diving industry in the region and organizes regular clean-ups of the sea. Before signing up for any courses, ask where you'll be doing your training: the water in Sharm el-Maya is less pleasant than in Na'ama Bay thanks to the former's proximity to the marina.

Sharm and Na'ama Bay tragically hit the headlines on July 24 2005, when the resort's tranquillity was shattered by a series of coordinated bomb attacks which killed around eighty people and injured more than two hundred. **Security measures** in the resort have been heightened since the attack, but travellers should always be vigilant.

Sharm el-Sheikh

A hunk of sterile buildings on a plateau commanding docks and other installations, **SHARM EL-SHEIKH** was developed by the Israelis after their capture of it in the 1967 War. Their main purpose was to thwart Egypt's blockade of the Tiran Strait and to control overland communications between the Aqaba and Suez coasts. Tourism was an afterthought – though an important one, helping to finance the Israeli occupation and settlements, which Egypt inherited between 1979 and 1982. Since then, Sharm's infrastructure seems to have expanded in fits and starts, without enhancing its appeal much. Despite some plush hotels and reams of propaganda about it being a slick resort, Sharm el-Sheikh is basically a **dormitory town** for the Egyptian workers who service neighbouring Na'ama Bay. Aside from package tourists conned by brochures, the only foreigners here are divers – drawn by the proximity of **Ras Umm Sidd** and other **reefs** – and a few backpackers who take advantage of its cheapish accommodation and commute into Na'ama Bay. Sharm has a beach, but its small bay doesn't match that of Na'ama, and the seedy downtown area also detracts from the hotels' "luxury" pretensions. In its defence, however,

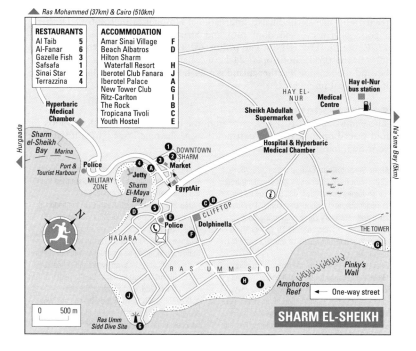

Sharm el–Maya has some good restaurants, snack bars and souvenir shops, and is the cheapest place in the area to go shopping for food.

Sharm also has an attraction for children in the **Dolphinella**, opposite the *Cliff Top Hotel* in Hadaba (Mon–Sat 10.30am–6pm; Ⓦ www.dolphinella.com), which puts on dolphin performances (3pm; £E100). In addition, throughout the day, you can swim with the dolphins for a hefty £E600 for thirty minutes, but that can be split among up to six people. All this said, the standards under which the animals are kept at the Dolphinella have been the subject of a campaign by the pressure group Marine Connection (Ⓦ www.marineconnection.org), which views the keeping of dolphins in captivity with distaste.

Arrival, information and transport

East Delta and Superjet buses from Cairo and Suez terminate at the Hay el-Nur **bus station** behind the Mobil station. The **port** where the catamaran arrives from Hurghada is 600m south of Sharm el-Maya. Sharm el-Sheikh **airport**, 10km north of Na'ama, is busy with charter flights from Europe, whose passengers are driven off to their holiday villages by bus; arriving on your own, you'll be dependent on taxis to get to Na'ama Bay (£E20) or Sharm (£E40).

Regular **minibuses** carry local workers between Sharm el-Maya and Na'ama (£E2 per person, possibly more if you have luggage). You can pick these up by flagging them down at any point along the main road, but bear in mind you won't be sharing space with cosmopolitan Egyptian holidaymakers, so it's advisable to be modestly dressed. Private **taxis** demand £E15–20 per carload.

The isolated and largely worthless **tourist office** (daily except Fri 9am–3pm; Ⓣ 069/366-4721) is a couple of kilometres northeast of the main facilities of the Hadaba clifftop, where an arcade contains three **banks** (daily 8am–2pm & 6–8pm), a **post office** (daily except Fri 8am–3pm), and a **pharmacy** (daily 9am–3pm & 6–11pm). There's also a bank at *Iberotel Palace*. For **medical treatment**, there's the Sharm International Hospital (Ⓣ 069/366-0894; there's a good pharmacy next door too) and Sharm Medical Centre (Ⓣ 069/366-1744), both in Hay el-Nur. The **police** (Ⓣ 069/366-0415) and **tourist police** (Ⓣ 069/366-0311), both open 24 hours, share a building near the arcade and beyond the mosque. Further inland is a 24-hour **telephone** exchange that sells international phonecards.

Accommodation

The windswept **clifftop** area, away from the beach, is the best place to look for mid-priced options. You can **camp** at Ras Mohammed (see p.678) if you have your own transport and tent.

Amar Sinai Village Clifftop area Ⓣ 069/366-2222, Ⓕ 366-2233. Eclectic, good-looking hotel, full of domes and arches, designed by its owner-in-residence, and with a "traditional" Egyptian farm and veterinary clinic around the back. Rooms have a/c and satellite TV. At lunchtime you can opt for a buffet meals or the à la carte fish menu. ❼

Beach Albatros On the cliff overlooking Sharm el-Maya, with access to the beach below by a very long staircase or lift Ⓣ 069/366-3922, Ⓦ www.pickalbatros.com. Construction of the beach here involved in-filling a stretch at the back of the reef, causing the latter's death. This hotel now has the best beach in this part of town, as well as a great view of the mountains and Ras Mohammed from the pool. Rates are all inclusive. ❼

Hilton Sharm Waterfall Resort On the beach at Ras Umm Sidd Ⓣ 069/366-3232, Ⓦ www.hiltonworldresorts.com. *Hilton*'s latest addition to Sharm has four hundred a/c rooms with all the trimmings, including an impressive waterfall feature and a small cable car to an even smaller beach. ❼

Iberotel Club Fanara On the beach at Ras Umm Sidd, next to the lighthouse Ⓣ 069/366-3966, Ⓦ www.iberotel-eg.com. Well-designed all-inclusive on one of the few good beaches in the area, especially for snorkelling.

Rooms have a/c, satellite TV and terrace, and there are pools and the latest in resort facilities. ❽

Iberotel Palace Sharm el-Maya ☎069/366-1111, ⓦwww.iberotel-eg.com. All-inclusive with over 240 rooms featuring luxurious mod-cons. There's a large section of beach, and lots of restaurants and sports facilities, including bicycle rental and a bank. ❽

Ritz-Carlton By the beach at Ras Umm Sidd ☎069/366-1919, ⓦwww.ritzcarlton.com. Trumpeted as the first *Ritz* in Africa, this huge resort has Internet access via the TV in each of the 320 large a/c rooms, a fitness centre, beauty salon and a spa. There is a beach with direct access to a reef (meaning it's good for snorkelling and diving but bad for swimming) and two pools with a "river" and waterfall. ❽

The Rock Clifftop area ☎069/366-1765, ⓦwww.hoteltherock.com. Neat a/c rooms with balconies or patios, TV and bath, plus a bar, swimming pool and shuttle bus. ❻

Tropicana Tivoli Clifftop area ☎069/366-1381, ⓦwww.tropicanahotels.com. Rooms with a/c and kitchenette, sited around a large pool. Also runs a shuttle bus to its sister hotel in Na'ama Bay and the beach at Ras Umm Sidd. Breakfast included. ❺

Youth Hostel Clifftop area ☎ & ⓕ069/366-0317. Cramped a/c triples and doubles, and cleanish bathrooms, some en suite. Facilities include a basketball and soccer court. May be full of young Egyptians or otherwise virtually empty. Non-members admitted (£E5 extra). Breakfast included. ❸

Diving and liveaboards

Most dive centres (generally daily 8.30am–6pm) are firmly attached to hotels, but the majority of them are happy to take non-guests for courses and daily boat diving. Dive boats set off at around 9am from the marina in Sharm el-Maya; most centres will collect you and drop you off again if necessary. (This is crucial if you're marooned at one of the hotels on the cliff in Ras Umm Sidd.)

Some of the dive centres listed below and on p.685 offer **liveaboards**. Alternatively, you can book directly with one of the operators or boats listed below. They all have offices in Hadaba, and set off from the marina in Sharm el-Maya.

In case of **diving emergencies**, contact Dr Adel Taher at the Hyperbaric Medical Centre near the Sharm el-Sheikh marina (☎069/366-0922 or ☎012 212-4292). There is also a 24-hour emergency hotline (☎012 333-1325) and a second decompression facility at the pyramid-shaped International Hospital in Hay el-Nur (☎069/366-8094). All dive schools charge an optional €6 per diver for three weeks' cover allowing emergency use of the chambers. For more information on emergency support for divers, visit ⓦwww.deco-international.com.

Dive centres

African Divers *Seti Sharm Hotel*, Ras Um Sidd ☎069/366-4884, ⓦwww.africandivers.com. PADI, CMAS, NAUI, SSI, French-speaking.

Colona Dive Club *Amar Sina*, Hadaba ☎069/366-3670, ⓦwww.colona.com. Caters primarily for Scandinavian clients. Liveaboards available. PADI Gold Palm Resort, SSI, Nitrox.

New Waves *Tropicana Tivoli* ☎012 220-0503, ⓦwww.divenewwaves.com. Five-day packages and liveaboards available. PADI Gold Palm Resort, SSI, BSAC, NAUI. Japanese- and Russian-speaking.

Rasta Divers Ras Umm Sidd ☎069/366-3328 or ☎012 213-3881, ⓔrasta@sinainet.com.eg. Rather

exclusive, catering mostly to private groups. Liveaboards available. PADI, CMAS, SSI.

Liveaboards

King Snefro Boats ☎069/366-1202 , ⓦwww.kingsnefro.com. Four boats and more than fifteen years' experience in the Red Sea. The cost, €75–115 per person per day, includes transfers and full board. Children under 7 go free and 7- to 12-year-olds are half price.

Sea Queen I, II and III ☎069/371-0506, ⓦwww.seaqueens.com. Liveaboards in opulent style.

Tornado Marine Fleet ⓦwww.tornadomarinefleet.com. Six boats offering week-long trips around the more popular dive sites and wrecks, from €1200.

Eating, drinking and nightlife

Aside from **eating and drinking** in hotels, Sharm el-Maya has its share of restaurants, cafés and *fuul* and *taamiya* stalls. **Seafood** is especially good; *Al Taib* (☎010 155-7686), set in the gardens on the hill leading up to Hadaba from

Sharm el-Maya, serves excellent and good-value fish, shrimps and *calamari*. They also do takeaways and home delivery. Two good seafood restaurants in the main market area are the *Sinai Star* (☏069/366-0323) and the more intimate *Safsafa* (☏069/366-0474), both popular with tour groups, and both charging £E30–60 for a meal. Recommended are the seafood platters, served with plenty of pitta bread, hummus and rice, and big enough to feed four or five people. Across from the *Sinai Star*, *Gazelle Fish* serves reasonably priced *calamari* at £E30 or a lobster for £E80. Next to the *Iberotel Palace* is the *Terrazzina* beach restaurant, which is popular with local residents and serves the catch-of-the-day in a relaxed atmosphere with cushions and loungers. The stunningly located and very romantic ⚓ *Al-Fanar* (☏069/366-2218) at Ras Umm Sidd lighthouse is housed in a tent, dishes up excellent Italian food and has a vast sea view taking in Ras Mohammed. **Nightlife** is limited to the organized entertainment in the hotels, though you could catch a taxi to the clubs in Na'ama Bay.

The best **supermarket** in Sharm is Sheikh Abdullah's in Hay el-Nur; fruit and vegetables are cheaper from the stalls in the main **market**.

Moving on from Sharm el-Sheikh

Sharm el-Sheikh is the transport hub of South Sinai, with bus services to Cairo, the Canal Zone and most points in the peninsula, boats to Hurghada, and domestic **flights** to Cairo (4 daily; 6.30am, 9.30am, 2.30pm & 11.30pm; $100), tickets for which can be bought from EgyptAir in Sharm (daily 9am–2pm & 6–9pm; ☏069/366-1058).

All **buses** leave from the Hay el-Nur bus station (☏069/366-0666). The Superjet night buses leaves for **Cairo** at 10pm, 11pm and 12pm (7hr; £E65), though you'll need to buy your ticket in advance in person at the bus station to be sure of getting a seat. These buses make fewer stops and tend to be quieter than the East Delta buses to Cairo (7.30am, 10.30am, 12.30am, 1.30pm, 2.30pm, 4.30pm, 7.30pm; 8hr; £E55), for which you have to reserve seats in person at the bus station in advance. The bus to **St Catherine's Monastery** leaves daily at 7.30am (£E28; it's worth turning up early) but won't get you there in time to see the monastery on the same day, as it closes at midday. The daily 9am service to **Taba** (£E26.50) and **Nuweiba** (£E21.50) stops at **Dahab** which can also be reached by direct buses at 2.30pm, 5pm and 8.30pm (£E11). Buses also run daily to the Canal cities of **Suez** (7 daily; 4hr; £E30) and **Ismailiya** (8am–7pm, hourly; £E35); as well as to **Luxor** (6.15pm; £E100) and **Alexandria** (9.15am; £E85). **Service taxis** serve Suez, Dahab and St Catherine's, though other destinations can be negotiated.

Finally, the ninety-minute **catamaran** trip from Sharm el-Sheikh to **Hurghada** departs on Mondays, Tuesdays, Thursdays and Saturdays at around 6pm (adults £E250 one way, £E475 return; children under 12 £E150 one way, £E285 return; children under 3 free but they don't get a seat); it's worth checking the latest schedules on ⓦwww.internationalfastferries.com. The catamaran also accommodates cars (£E245), motorbikes (£E125) and bicycles (£E50). Tickets can be bought at most of the hotels and travel agencies including Mena Tours (daily 10am–10pm except Fri from 1pm; ☏069/360-0190, ⓦwww.menatours.com.eg) in Na'ama Bay's *Marriott Hotel*, or at Sharm el-Sheikh port one hour before departure, though this is risky if you have a vehicle, as space is limited.

Between Sharm and Na'ama

The fabulous array of **dive spots** around Sharm and Na'ama is the chief attraction of both resorts, offering endless scope for boat or shore diving. The most accessible site is **Ras Umm Sidd**. The area is basically all coral reef without any natural sandy beaches – what sand there is has been imported by the hotels to create their own beaches. The endless construction has inevitably increased the debris many divers now encounter underwater in this area.

From Ras Umm Sidd, a paved road lined with holiday villages and hotels runs to **the Tower**, a fine diving beach colonized by the 120-roomed hotel, *New Tower Club* (☎069/360-0231, ⓕ360-1237; ❼) where the beach café is a good place for people-watching. The real lure, however, is a huge **coral pillar** just offshore, which drops 60m into the depths.

It's easy to get to the Tower by taxi from either Sharm or Na'ama, but it is no longer possible to access most of the reefs between Ras Umm Sidd and the Tower from land, as hotels along this stretch of coast now effectively block public access to the sea. Diving these reefs by boat, you come to (in order of appearance after Ras Umm Sidd) Fiasco, Paradise, Turtle Bay, Pinky's Wall and Amphoras. **Turtle Bay** has warm sun-dappled water that's lovely to swim in, even if there are fewer **green turtles** (*Chelonia myades*) than you'd wish for.

Na'ama Bay

With its fine beach and upmarket facilities, **NA'AMA BAY** has transformed itself so rapidly even the residents have trouble keeping up. In a few short years the bay has grown from a few huts on the beach and one lone hotel to what looks like a mini-city, especially at night when the electric lights blaze in the desert sky. **Diving** and **snorkelling** are still the main draws, with dive centres, hotels and malls being the only points of reference along the beachfront strip. The **beach** is divided into hotel-owned plots that are supposedly open to

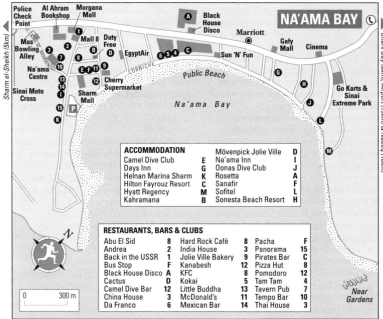

NA'AMA BAY

ACCOMMODATION

Camel Dive Club	E	Mövenpick Jolie Ville	D
Days Inn	G	Na'ama Inn	J
Helnan Marina Sharm	K	Oonas Dive Club	I
Hilton Fayrouz Resort	C	Rosetta	A
Hyatt Regency	M	Sanafir	F
Kahramana	B	Sofitel	L
		Sonesta Beach Resort	H

RESTAURANTS, BARS & CLUBS

Abu El Sid	8	Hard Rock Café	8	Pacha	F
Andrea	2	India House	8	Panorama	15
Back in the USSR	1	Jolie Ville Bakery	9	Pirates Bar	C
Bus Stop	F	Kanabesh	12	Pizza Hut	8
Black House Disco	A	KFC	8	Pomodoro	12
Cactus	D	Kokai	5	Tam Tam	4
Camel Dive Bar	12	Little Buddha	13	Tavern Pub	7
China House	3	McDonald's	11	Tempo Bar	10
Da Franco	6	Mexican Bar	14	Thai House	3

0 — 300 m

Near Gardens

anyone providing they don't use the parasols or chairs – though hippy-looking types may be hassled and topless bathing is highly unadvisable (not to mention illegal). There are two public beaches (£E5), though they are no more than narrow unkempt strips squeezed in next to the *Novotel* and the *Hilton* beaches.

Arrival, transport and accommodation

For details of the airport, bus station and transport from Sharm, see p.680. Since the 2005 terrorist attack, Na'ama Bay's tourist area has been paved and pedestrianized and vehicles are no longer permitted south of the main coast road; King of Bahrain Street and the Corniche now have a piazza-style atmosphere, especially at night. To get a **taxi** you will have to walk beyond the large hotel complexes to the main road or along King of Bahrain Street to the police checkpoint at the junction with the main road. **Mopeds** to get around Na'ama are available for a negotiable $50 per day from Red Sea Star Sports Centre (☎012 407-7216), in a kiosk near the *Tam Tam* restaurant; they also rent **push bikes** for £E20 per hour.

Luxurious **holiday villages** featuring acres of marble floors and lush landscaped gardens are the norm in Na'ama Bay. However, bargains can be had at the luxury hotels if booked as a **package** from the UK, but make sure you're not booked into one of the hotel "extensions", which often have a lower standard of accommodation and an awkward highway crossing to get to the sea. A few dive centres also offer rooms, and you don't necessarily have to do one of their courses to stay. Rates include breakfast unless otherwise stated.

Camel Dive Club Hotel On the main strip one block back from the beach ☎069/360-0700, ⓦwww.cameldive.com. Attached to one of Na'ama's best dive centres is this small, well-designed hotel. Its a/c rooms have satellite TV and are arranged around the pool, there's an award-winning Indian restaurant and the rooftop *Camel Bar* is popular with divers. Look out for room-and-dive packages on the website. ⑥

Days Inn Na'ama Bay ☎069/360-0210, ⓦwww.daysinn.com. This middling resort does not aspire to be Na'ama Bay's classiest, but the rooms are modern and spacious and it does get you right on the beach for a reasonable rate. ⑥

Four Seasons 9km north of Na'ama ☎069/360-3555, ⓦwww.fourseasons.com. Glitzy hotel designed for the jet set with stunning Arabian-style architecture. Expect six-star treatment and facilities such as spa and a vast heated pool with underwater music. Rooms from $360. ⑨

Helnan Marina Sharm At the southern end of Na'ama Bay, on the main strip ☎069/360-0170, ⓦwww.helnan.com. Na'ama's first hotel (Israeli-built) is showing its age but notable mainly for having one of the better beaches in Na'ama. Facilities include some disabled-friendly rooms plus Internet access and a computer games room, two pools and a watersports centre. ⑧

Hilton Fayrouz Resort On the beach ☎069/360-0136, ⓦwww.hiltonworldresorts .com. Comfortable and spacious a/c chalets set in

pretty landscaped gardens and with one of the largest beaches in Na'ama Bay. It's home to one of the locals' favourite pubs, *Pirates Bar*. Children under 12 stay free. ⑦

Hyatt Regency Just north of Na'ama Bay ☎069/360-1234, ⓦwww.sharm.hyatt.com. Expensively bedecked resort overlooking one of Na'ama Bay's premier diving sites, The Gardens. While the beach isn't great, guests can take advantage of beautiful landscaping, disabled rooms, a spa, non-allergenic sheets and towels, and an excellent if pricey Thai restaurant. ⑧

Kahramana Hotel Three blocks back from the beach ☎069/360-1071. Centrally located four-star complex built around a pool with a nice bar and pool table. ⑥

Mövenpick Golf and Resort 7km north of Na'ama ☎069/360-3200, ⓦwww.movenpickhotels.com. With over four hundred luxurious rooms, six villas with a pool, plus the best swimming pool in the area, a high-quality gym and health club, and of course an eighteen-hole championship golf course. The beach, however, is disappointing. ⑧

Mövenpick Jolie Ville In the middle of Na'ama ☎069/360-0100, ⓦwww.movenpickhotels.com. This hotel is so large it utilizes golf carts to shuttle occupants from one end to the other. Besides a popular beach bar and nightly cabaret entertainment, it boasts a casino and a good Italian restaurant. ⑧

Na'ama Inn Two blocks back from the beach ☎069/360-0801, ⓦwww.naamainn.com. Simple hotel with 38 rooms around a pool. Home to Easy Divers. Not the quietest of places, but conveniently located for clubbers or shopaholics. ⑤

Oonas Dive Club At the northern end of the bay ℡069/360-0581, Ⓦwww.oonasdiveclub.com. Rooms with a/c, balconies and decent views; guests are allowed to use the beach and pool at the nearby *Sonesta*. Ask about discounts for *Rough Guides* readers. ⑤

Rosetta Opposite the *Hilton*, on the other side of the highway ℡069/360-1888, Ⓦwww.tropicanahotels .com. Large a/c rooms with satellite TV and some apartments with fully equipped kitchens. Amenities include four pools, one especially for divers, a nice outdoor Egyptian restaurant, and the *Black House* disco. It's the base for Emperor Divers. ⑦

Sanafir One block back from the beach on the main strip ℡069/360-0197, Ⓔinfo@pachasharm .com. One of the first hotels in Na'ama, with a much-imitated white-domed compound of a/c rooms. There's a pool, and several restaurants and bars, which make it a popular evening venue. It's especially lively after midnight when *The Bus Stop* and *Pacha*, Na'ama's coolest clubs, gets going, so things can be noisy. Good buffet breakfast included. ⑥

Sofitel On the north hill overlooking Na'ama Bay ℡069/360-0081, Ⓦwww.sofitel.com. Impressive-looking resort with a/c rooms with terraces, one of the largest pools in Sharm, a beach, tennis courts, and stables for riding expeditions to the desert. ⑦

🏃 **Sonesta Beach Resort** At the northern end of Na'ama, on the beach ℡069/360-0725, Ⓦwww.sonesta.com. Beautifully designed place with over five hundred rooms, which manages to make you feel as if it were the only hotel on the beach. Facilities include tennis courts, two restaurants, seven swimming pools and a casino set around gardens. Each chalet is designed in traditional Arabic manner, with white-washed archways, domed roofs and spacious interiors. Nightly entertainment accompanies a buffet dinner. ⑧

Diving

Much of Na'ama's appeal lies in its plethora of **dive centres** (see below), which offer an extensive range of courses, trips and equipment rental. Though generally of a high standard, their prices and operating styles vary, so it's worth shopping around. All the dive centres listed here are open daily (mostly 8.30am–6pm). Dive boats leave at around 9am from the marina in **Sharm el-Maya**, and most dive centres will collect you from your hotel and drop you off again. Trips to the **Gordon** and **Jackson reefs** in the Tiran Strait (see p.673) or **Ras Mohammed** (p.676) will set you back around €65, a one-day **Thistlegorm** trip (see p.673) €125. Space permitting, **snorkellers** can join any boat for about €25. For **liveaboards** other than those offered by Na'ama Bay operators, see p.681.

Dive centres

Anthias *Sonesta Beach Resort* ℡069/360-0725, Ⓦwww.anthiasdivers.de. Austrian-run outfit that delivers proven service and options for just about any dive in the area, including liveaboards.

Camel Dive Club *Camel Dive Club Hotel* and with branches in other hotels ℡069/360-0700, Ⓦwww .cameldive.com. Good facilities and lots of daily dive trips, suitable for beginners up to instructor level. Popular with UK tourists.

Dive Africa *Sharm Holiday Hotel* ℡069/360-1388, Ⓦwww.diveafrica.com. Liveaboards available. PADI and SSI.

Divers International Near Gafy Mall ℡069/360-0865, Ⓦwww.diversintl.com. PADI, NAUI, SSI.

Easy Divers *Na'ama Inn* ℡069/360-0802, Ⓦwww.sharm.easydivers.com. A good-value place offering the usual courses and trips.

Emperor Divers & Red Sea Scuba Schools *Rosetta Hotel* ℡069/360-1734, Ⓦwww .emperordivers.com. Liveaboards, the usual range of courses, plus day-trips to the *Thistlegorm*.

Oonas Divers Near the *Sonesta* ℡069/360-0581, Ⓦwww.oonasdiveclub.com. Five-star PADI dive centre with its own accommodation (see above).

Red Sea Diving College Na'ama beach and in the *Hyatt* ℡069/360-0145, Ⓦwww.redseacollege .com Fine facilities and tuition, and liveaboards available. PADI.

Sinai Dive Club *Hilton Fayrouz Resort* ℡069/360-0136, Ⓦwww.dive-club.com. Liveaboards available. PADI, CMAS, SSI and NRC Nitrox courses.

Sinai Divers *Ghazala Hotel* ℡069/360-0697, Ⓦwww.sinaidivers.com. Efficient and experienced setup offering liveaboards. PADI, CMAS, SSI.

Snorkelling and watersports

While diving is the main pursuit, Na'ama is also great for **snorkelling**. Unfortunately, unless you're going to join a dive boat to get to further-flung sites (which is a very relaxing way of doing things; see p.681), visiting the local reefs involves some walking: drinking water, a hat and proper footwear are essential.

The best **reefs** – aptly known as coral gardens – run for several miles **north of Na'ama Bay**. They don't get many divers (being deemed inferior to The Tower or Shark Bay) but are ideal for snorkelling. Just look for a safe descent from the rocks and the shortest, smoothest reef flat, with dark water beyond its edge. Bear in mind that these reefs are regularly visited by glass-bottom boats, so you will need to take care while you're in the water. The **Near Gardens** can be reached on foot by following the coast beyond Oonas Dive Centre. Plummeting to unseen depths beyond its crest, the reef has spawned offshore pillars and fantastic encrustations, swarming with angelfish, parrotfish and blue snappers. From here you can swim to the equally amazing **Middle and Far gardens**, further up the coast.

Several agencies run overland snorkelling trips to the mangrove forests of **Nabeq** (see p.690), or boat trips to the less demanding reefs at **Ras Mohammed**, **Ras Nasrani** or **Shark Bay**. Sun 'n Fun, whose main office is on the Corniche near the *Hilton* (other branches in several hotels; ☎069/360-1623, ⓦwww .sunnfunsinai.com), offers a full-day boat trip to Ras Mohammed or Tiran for $35 (excluding the Ras Mohammed entry fee), as well as shorter one-to-two-hour snorkelling trips to the Near and Far gardens and White Knights from $10.

Apart from snorkelling, there's a wide variety of **watersports** on offer from most beachfront hotels, including sailing, windsurfing (instructors for both are available), water-skiing, parasailing, jetskiing, banana boat or tube rides and pedalos. There are also, of course, **glass-bottom boats** to view the depths without getting wet: Sun 'n Fun has boat trips leaving every two hours throughout the day from the beachfront near their office (1hr 30min; $16, children $9).

Overland trips and safaris

All the hotels and various safari companies can arrange tours by Jeep, camel, motorbike or quad bikes. Some of the most popular day excursions by Jeep are a mangrove-and-snorkelling visit to **Nabeq** (Sun 'n Fun does a half-day trip for $30); a 4WD trip to the **Coloured Canyon** followed by snorkelling at either Dahab or Nuweiba ($65); and **St Catherine's Monastery** (overnight trip including climbing **Mount Sinai** for $50). Nearer to Na'ama lies **Wadi Mandar**, visited on sunset trips by Jeep ($25) or camel ($30 with tea, $35 with dinner). If you see trips advertised for less, they probably involve travelling by bus rather than Jeep. A bit further up the road is **Wadi Ain Kid**, a long fertile canyon culminating in an oasis of palm trees, a well and Bedouin farm; overnight excursions cost around $60 including a Bedouin dinner. Several companies also offer excursions to **Serabit el-Khadim** (see p.675) and **Hammam Faraoun** (p.675).

For longer desert trips, **Madian Adventure** (☎069/366-0593, ⓔpeninsula @menanet.net), one of the most experienced guides in the area, offers Jeep safaris and mountain trekking from $60 per person per day. Remember if you're moving on, many of the sites, except for Nabeq, Wadi Mandar and Wadi Ain Kid, are cheaper to reach from Nuweiba or Dahab.

Horse-riding in the desert can be arranged at the *Sofitel* Equestrian Centre (☎069/360-0081) for $25 per hour, with overnight trips also available, starting from $100. **Quad bikes**, also known as ATVs (All-Terrain Vehicles), are another popular way of getting into the desert. Sun 'n Fun rents them ($35 for one person, $50 for two people, per hour) and also runs a popular guided quad-bike sunset trip which takes two hours and includes a Bedouin dinner. They also operate the **Sinai Moto Cross** quad-bike circuit (daily 9am–midnight; two rounds/15min costs $20 before 6pm, eves $25), with lots of sand dune ramps, off the main road to the west of the bowling alley.

If you fancy venturing out on your own **by car**, a Jeep Cherokee can be rented for $120 a day from Avis in Morgana Mall (☎069/360-0979). Prices for a smaller car such as a Ford Fiesta start from $50 a day: try Bita Car Rental (☎069/360-0826) at the *Falcon Hotel* on the beach south of the *Mövenpick Jolie Ville*; or, if you are over in Shark Bay and beyond, Budget (☎069/360-1610) at Coral Bay, past the airport. Bear in mind that it is illegal for unaccompanied foreigners to go **off-road**; there are still many unexploded landmines in Sinai and you won't know where they are.

Other activities

Thrill-seekers can try **go-kart racing** at the state-of-the-art Ghibli Raceway on the Airport Road (☎069/360-3939, ⓦwww.ghibliraceway.com), just before the entrance to the *Hyatt Regency*. For €20 during the day (1–5pm) or €27 at night (5pm–1am), you can have ten laps racing round one of the four circuits, including one for children over 7; all first-timers have to undergo a training session. If you still have energy to burn, head for the **bungee rocket** and **trampolines** at the nearby Sinai Extreme Park (☎010 669-6968), or the MAS **bowling alley** (☎069/360-2220, daily 7pm–1am; £E20 per game), a few hundred metres south of the *Hard Rock Café*.

Shopping

A number of **malls** and recreated "**souks**" compete to attract the attention of tourists, but there's little here you can't find in Cairo or Luxor – at lower prices. The Panorama, a large thatched souk near the *Helnan Marina Sharm*, sells just about every Egyptian souvenir imaginable. A few interesting specialist shops exist: Aladdin at the *Camel Dive Club Hotel* and Bashayer, in Sharm Mall, are worth a look for arts and crafts, mostly from Upper Egypt.

Eating

There are no really cheap places to eat in Na'ama. On the plus side, the quality of hotel cuisine is high, and ranges from Egyptian, Italian and seafood to Japanese and Thai. Prices tend to be higher along the **beach promenade** where every hotel offers at least one beachside restaurant, and along the lively inland King of Bahrain Street outside the *Sanafir* and *Camel Dive Club* hotels. Both these stretches are busy with holiday-makers, a handful of Egyptian touts and back-to-back restaurants and bars with tables spilling out onto the street. If you fancy eating on the beach, try the *Hilton*'s Italian restaurant, or the fish restaurant at *Shark Bay Bedouin Camp* (see p.690).

Standard **fast food** can be had at *McDonald's* on King of Bahrain Street and round the corner at *KFC* and *Pizza Hut* just past the *Hard Rock Café*. For **snacks and desserts**, head to the *Jolie Ville* bakery, at the northern end of the strip near *McDonald's,* for sweet and sticky delicacies and an espresso.

Restaurants

Abu El Sid On the roof of the *Hard Rock Café*. This atmospheric Egyptian restaurant has soft lighting and is decorated with tiles and Oriental musical instruments fixed to the walls. They serve reasonably priced grilled meat dishes including, a little oddly, a Western-style T-bone steak for £E45.

Andrea In the mall 200m northwest of the *Hard Rock Café*. One of many similar restaurants along this strip with mostly chicken-based Egyptian dishes, but also good-value pizzas and pasta dishes. There's an attractive terrace, too, slung with kilims.

Back in the USSR On the side of Morgana Mall near the highway. A throwback to the Soviet Union, with Marx, Engels and Lenin looming over blood-red decor while patrons dine on European-Russian dishes. Obviously, the best place in town for a vodka shot.

China House, Thai House and India House Second floor, Na'ama Centre. Three restaurants side-by-side under common ownership, that attempt to recreate the Far East on the Na'ama Bay strip. Main dishes in the £E35–55 range.

Da Franco *Hotel Ghazala*, on the promenade between the *Mövenpick* and *Hilton*. Excellent pizza and pasta restaurant with reasonably priced main dishes and a loaded seafood platter (good value at £E85).

Hard Rock Café ⓦ www.hardrock.com. Just around the corner from the main strip with an unmissable giant guitar above the door. Serves hamburgers with all the trimmings, and it's a hugely popular nightspot. Daily 12.30pm–2am (till 3am Sat).

Kanabesh King of Bahrain St, opposite *McDonald's*. Alfresco Lebanese cuisine; good value, especially if you're a meat lover. Open daily for lunch and dinner.

Kokai *Hotel Ghazala*, next to *Da Franco*. A Japanese restaurant with a pleasant terrace. The teppanyaki chefs will grill food at your table and there's a choice of Chinese too.

Pomodoro Camel Dive Club. Good if basic Italian restaurant, run by Italians. Some dishes attempt an Egyptian-Italian fusion, such as the kofta casserole.

Tam Tam *Hotel Ghazala* ☎ 069/360-0155. Tasty Egyptian food near the beach with rooftop seating and great views, plus a front lounge with low tables, rugs and cushions to sit on at the front. Excellent *karkaday*, lentil soup and Egyptian sweets; also *shawarmas* and *koftas*. Does takeaway. Twice a week there's also an Egyptian floor show (see below). Daily until 1am.

Tavern Pub In a small mall behind the Na'ama Centre. Tucked inside a pedestrian mall, this authentic British pub serves as a hangout for expats and football fans who come to watch sport on several big-screen TVs. There's classic pub grub including a "Sunday roast" (daily; £E45), curry and chilli.

Drinking and nightlife

Alcoholic drinks are widely available in bars and clubs at European prices, perhaps more so than anywhere else in Egypt; the Corniche is lined with open-air cocktail bars attached to the resorts. The **duty-free shop** in front of the *Kahramana Hotel* (daily 11am–2pm & 6–11pm; shorter hours during Ramadan) sells cheap booze, or try the kiosk on the Corniche near the *Days Inn*, which sells Stella from a fridge.

The *Sanafir* hotel qualifies as Na'ama's premier **nightspot**, with a variety of clubs, notably *Pacha* (see p.689). Its main competition, particularly popular with Italians, is the *Hard Rock Café*, just round the corner from the main strip (disco daily 8pm–2am, or Sat 3am). Other worthwhile discos include the *Black House Disco* at the *Rosetta*, and the *Cactus* at the *Mövenpick Jolie Ville*.

For a more Egyptian evening, the entire length of King of Bahrain Street is lined with countless **coffee shops** offering *sheeshas*. The best *sheesha* in town, however, can be had for £E10 at the outdoor café, the *Panorama,* with steps that climb up the hillside leading to private alcoves with tables, couches and great views. Most of the hotels offer Egyptian **floor shows**, but the best is at the *Tam Tam* restaurant, which holds an oriental dinner show featuring a lively team of dancers and musicians (Wed & Sun 7.30pm; £E90), plus a hot and cold *mezze* buffet or seafood, dessert and fruit.

Na'ama Bay also has several **casinos** that open late into the night, including the *Casino Royale* at the *Mövenpick*, and one at the *Sonesta*: you'll need to show your passport before entering.

Bars and clubs

Camel Dive Bar At the *Camel Dive Club*. A favourite starting point for the evening is this friendly affair decorated with flags and soccer

jerseys, and strewn with peanut shells on the floor; it's a good place to swap dive stories.

Little Buddha King of Bahrain St, ⓦ www .littlebuddha-sharm.com. Very elegant, with subtle lighting, burning incense and a cutting-edge sound system; this is the sister lounge/club to Paris's famous *Buddha Bar*. There's nothing little about the enormous circular bar and dance floor surrounding a downstairs dining area which serves sushi; a giant Buddha presides over the two storeys. Daily 1pm–3.30am.

Mexican Bar Next to the *Na'ama Inn*, under the cliff at the end of the main strip. A British hangout, this is unmissable thanks to the giant statue of a Mexican man on the roof. Resident DJ from midnight. Daily 1pm–3am.

Pacha Ⓦwww.pachasharm.com and *Bus Stop*, both at the *Sanafir* hotel. Both venues feature swimming pools, foam parties, international DJs, podiums supporting professional dancers and go on from midnight throughout the night. Entry fees vary depending on the event, but expect to pay £E150–200; tickets can be bought during the day from the office outside the hotel. On Fridays, they also run the *Echo Temple*, a desert venue at the foot of the Sinai Mountains that can accommodate four thousand people.

Pirates Bar In the *Hilton Fayrouz Resort*. A nautically themed venue that's popular with the expat dive crowd, and serves food. Happy hour 5.30–7.30pm.

Tavern Pub (see p.688). One of the main hangouts for British divers, this starts out as a bar-restaurant and later turns into a disco. Friday night sees a karaoke outbreak.

Tempo Bar In front of the Na'ama Centre, King of Bahrain St. A stylish place with tables spilling out onto the street and a long menu of cocktails, ice cream and *sheesha* pipes.

Directory

Banks and exchange Most hotels in Na'ama have banks (daily 8.30am–2pm & 6–9pm). The National Bank of Egypt has branches in the *Mövenpick* and *Hilton*. You can get cash advances on Visa and MasterCard at Banque Misr (9am–1.30pm & 5–8pm) in the Sharm Mall. Most banks have ATMs. For changing cash, Swiss Exchange in Morgana Mall (daily 9am–midnight) may offer slightly better rates than the banks.

Books and newspapers Most of the four- and five-star hotels have small bookshops and can provide international newspapers for their guests. Several have a "library" where you can pick up books left behind by past guests, though English-language books can be hard to find. Vendors pushing carts along the beachfront and around town sell international magazines and newspapers.

Cinema At the *Safir* hotel, on the edge of town on the Airport Road, screening relatively new Hollywood films for £E20.

Dentist Dr Hassan El Saarkawy, second floor, Mall 8 Ⓣ012 332-4160.

Doctor Dr Wael Habib, at the Mount Sinai Clinic in the *Mövenpick* Ⓣ069/360-0100. For diving emergencies, see p.681.

Hospitals The nearest hospitals are in Sharm el-Sheikh (see p.689).

Internet access Prices for using the Internet in Na'ama Bay are a little higher than the rest of Egypt, with cafés charging a standard £E10/hr. There are Internet cafés every few metres around King of Bahrain Street.

Pharmacy Towa, in the Sharm Mall (daily 10am–1am; Ⓣ069/360-0779), offers free home delivery. Another is Na'ama Bay Pharmacy (Ⓣ069/366-0338). The best-stocked pharmacy is next to the hospital in Hay el-Nur, back towards Sharm el-Sheikh.

Supermarkets Cherry, next to the *Mövenpick Jolie Ville* (daily 9am–midnight).

Telephones If you don't fancy calling from a card phone, you can make calls from Sharm No. 2, opposite the entrance to the *Sheraton*, about 1km north of Na'ama Bay (daily 10am–10pm).

Travel agents Thomas Cook, Gafy Mall (daily 9am–2pm & 6–8pm; Ⓣ069/360-1809), offers the usual range of travel services, plus Visa cash advances. Mena Tours at the *Marriott* (daily 10am–10pm except Fri from 1pm; Ⓣ069/360-0190, Ⓦwww.menatours.com.eg) can organize tours and book tickets for the Hurghada catamaran.

Western Union At the DHL office in the *Rosetta* (Mon–Thurs & Sun 9am–9pm; Ⓣ & Ⓕ069/360-2222).

Shark Bay

Ten kilometres up the coast from Na'ama, the once tranquil and secluded resort of **SHARK BAY** is now overlooked and overwhelmed by large holiday villages, and the sandy track that used to lead there has been replaced by a variety of surfaced roads servicing the hotels. But that hasn't deterred its many visitors, particularly the scores of day-visitors from Na'ama. Despite the bay's forbidding name (Beit el-Irsh, "House of the Shark" in Arabic), all the sharks have been scared away by divers, leaving a benign array of tropical fish and coral gardens just offshore, with deeper reefs and bigger fish further out. There's a £E10 charge to use the beach, which includes the use of showers and a soft drink.

You can **stay** here at *Shark's Bay Umbi Diving & Camp* (℡069/360-0942, 🅦www.sharksbay.net; ❹), a pleasant mix of bungalows and beach huts, some with air conditioning and en-suite bathrooms. It has its own private beach, jetty and a **dive centre** that runs boat trips to the Tiran Strait (day-dive €35; liveaboards €90 per day), while Bedouins who hang out there can arrange Jeep safaris into the interior. Its restaurant and Bedouin café are quiet nightspots that close around midnight; guests wanting more action can club together for a taxi into Na'ama. Package tourists generally stay at the nearby *Holiday Inn*, 1km south (℡069/360-2130, 🅦www.holidayinnsharm.com; ❼), which boasts 520 rooms, suites and villas and the usual luxury facilities, though its architecture is some of the least appealing in the area.

The Tiran Strait and Nabeq

The headland of Ras Nasrani beyond Shark Bay marks the beginning of the **Tiran Strait**, where the waters of the Gulf of Suez flow into the deeper Gulf of Aqaba, swirling around islands and reefs. In 1992, the Tiran archipelago was declared a protected area, but there are no admission charges or facilities; the only access is by boat from Sharm el-Maya or Shark Bay. This is *not* an excursion for novice divers, as the sea can be extremely rough and chilling (bring high-calorie drinks and snacks to boost your energy).

Sharks, manta rays, barracuda and Napoleon fish are typical of the deepwater sites around the **islands of Tiran** and **Sanafir**, though there are also shallow reefs like the Small Lagoon and Hushasha. The multitude of **shipwrecks** in the Gulf is due to treacherous reefs and currents, insurance fraud, and Egypt's blockade of the strait in the 1960s. The **Jackson Reef** has a spectacular seventy-metre drop-off and the wreck of the *Lara* to investigate, while the **Gordon Reef** boasts the hulk of the *Lucila*. Two notable sites at **Ras Nasrani** are the **Light**, with a forty-metre drop-off and pelagic fish; and the **Point**, with a dazzling array of reef fish.

Nabeq

Beyond the mouth of the Gulf of Aqaba, a ninety-kilometre swath of the coast as far north as Dahab City has been designated another protected area, named after the small oasis and **Bedouin village** of **NABEQ**. As few dive boats come here from Na'ama, the **reefs** are quieter than at Tiran or Ras Mohammed, but anyone considering staying in Nabeq should bear in mind that it is much windier here than in Na'ama, that transport connections are limited to shuttle buses and that the beaches can be poor. Most visitors are on half-day trips to see Nabeq's mangrove forests – the most northerly in the world. **Mangroves** can filter salt from sea water and thus survive in tropical coastal areas. As sediment traps, they reduce erosion and provide a habitat for mating fish and migratory birds (in summer and autumn), acting as the ecological interface between the coast and the interior, whose flood-prone wadis sustain ibex, hyrax, foxes and other **wildlife**.

All approaches to Nabeq are best made by someone who knows the way; wander off the track and you might inadvertently encounter **mines** left over from Israeli-Egyptian wars, which killed a Jeepload of tourists in 1995. Admission to the protected area costs €5; the only facilities are a **cafeteria** and visitors' centre.

One of the best of Nabeq's beachfront **hotels** is the *Radisson SAS* (☎069/371-0315, ⊛www.radissonsas.com; ➋), a luxurious resort 17km north of Na'ama, with six restaurants, three pools and a spa centre. Even better is the beautiful ⚓ *Nubian Village* next door (☎069/371-0200 ✉nubian@link.net; full-board ➋), designed to resemble a Nubian settlement, though it also has two pools, a nightclub, a spacious beach and a dive centre. It operates free shuttles to Na'ama.

Dahab and Asilah

Jagged mountains ranged inland of Na'ama Bay accompany the road 95km northwards, providing a magnificent backdrop for **Dahab**'s tawny beaches, from which its Arabic name – "gold" – derives. The resort divides into two localities: a cluster of holiday villages catering for affluent visitors, and the Bedouin settlement of **Asilah** 2.5km up the coast, where younger travellers hang out in a kind of "Goa by the Red Sea" – though as Asilah moves upmarket, the distinction between them is blurring. In recent years aquatic pursuits have begun to be taken as seriously in Dahab as in Na'ama, and a third area north of Asilah, near the dive sites of the Canyon and Blue Hole, is tipped for development should tourist numbers rebound after the recent downturn.

Like Sharm and Taba before, Dahab's relaxed ambience was shattered when three **bombs** went off in Asilah at 7.30pm on April 24, 2006. They destroyed several restaurants, shops and a supermarket, and killed 23 people, with 60 injured. A month later a man wanted in connection with the bombings was shot dead in El-Arish (see p.720). Today there is a noticable **security presence**, with plainclothes policemen and sniffer dogs. Whether you are on public or private transport, note that you will probably be asked to show your **passport** at checkpoints on leaving or entering Dahab.

Dahab City

Don't be discouraged by **DAHAB CITY**, the colony of municipal housing and government offices next to the holiday villages. The only reason to go there is to use its facilities: **petrol stations**, a **post office** and 24-hour **telephone exchange** (international calls with phonecards); a **supermarket** (daily 8am–10pm); and a **bank** with an ATM (Mon–Thurs & Sun 8.30am–2pm & 5–8pm, Sat 9am–2pm). The nearby *Swiss Inn Golden Palace Resort* has a bank that opens on Fridays (9am–noon & 6–9pm). The **tourist police** (☎069/364-0188) are located opposite the *Coralia Dahab*, while the **hospital** (☎069/364-6208) is to the southeast of the bus station.

Most budget travellers arrive at Dahab City's East Delta **bus station** and then head straight on to Asilah; every bus is met by **taxis** and **pick-ups** that charge £E5 per person to Asilah, £E10 for solo travellers. Few places are more than ten minutes' walk from the taxi drop-off point near the bridge in the middle of Asilah.

The **holiday villages** around Dahab Bay are self-contained, with private beaches and access to a coral reef on the headland. They all arrange **shuttles** for their guests directly from Sharm el-Sheik Airport for around €30 each way. At the eastern end of the string of resorts is the opulent ⚓ *Hilton Dahab*

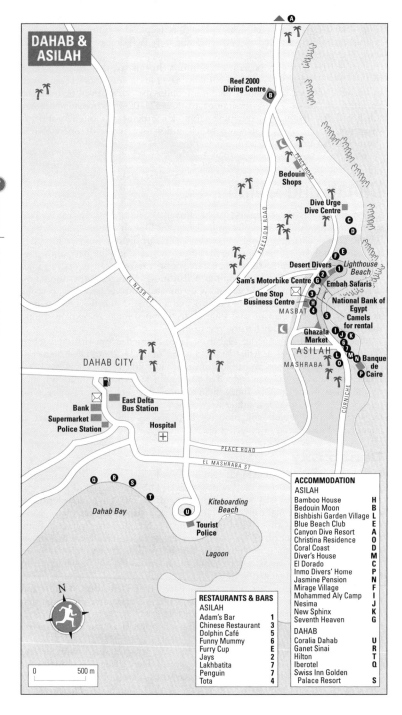

DAHAB & ASILAH

Reef 2000
Diving Centre **B**

Bedouin
Shops

Dive Urge
Dive Centre

C
D

F **E**
1 *Lighthouse
Beach*

Desert Divers **2**
G
Sam's Motorbike Centre **3** Embah Safaris
One Stop **H**
Business Centre **4** **National Bank of
Egypt**
MASBAT **5** **Camels
for rental**

I **J** **K**
Ghazala **6**
Market **L** **7** **M**
A S I L A H **N** **Banque
de**
MASHRABA **O** **Caire**
P

DAHAB CITY

Bank
Supermarket
Police Station

East Delta
Bus Station

Hospital

PEACE ROAD

EL MASHRABA ST

Q **R** **S**
T
*Kiteboarding
Beach*
U
Dahab Bay **Tourist
Police**

Lagoon

N

0   500 m

RESTAURANTS & BARS

ASILAH

Adam's Bar	**1**
Chinese Restaurant	**3**
Dolphin Café	**5**
Funny Mummy	**6**
Furry Cup	**E**
Jays	**2**
Lakhbatita	**7**
Penguin	**7**
Tota	**4**

ACCOMMODATION

ASILAH

Bamboo House	**H**
Bedouin Moon	**B**
Bishbishi Garden Village	**L**
Blue Beach Club	**E**
Canyon Dive Resort	**A**
Christina Residence	**O**
Coral Coast	**D**
Diver's House	**M**
El Dorado	**C**
Inmo Divers' Home	**P**
Jasmine Pension	**N**
Mirage Village	**F**
Mohammed Aly Camp	**I**
Nesima	**J**
New Sphinx	**K**
Seventh Heaven	**G**

DAHAB

Coralia Dahab	**U**
Ganet Sinai	**R**
Hilton	**T**
Iberotel	**Q**
Swiss Inn Golden
Palace Resort	**S**

(℡069/364-0310, Ⓦwww.hiltonworldresorts.com; ➐), the best of the upmarket resorts, with whitewashed Nubian-style chalets in a lush tract of garden surrounding a series of lagoons, plus extras such as WiFi Internet access; the beach is open to non-residents for £E40 a day. Next door, the *Swiss Inn Golden Palace Resort* (℡069/364-0054, Ⓦwww.swissinn.net; ➐) has its own dive and windsurfing centres. Next along the coast, the *Ganet Sinai Hotel* (℡069/364-0440, Ⓦwww.ganetsinai.com; ➐ including buffet breakfast), has air-conditioned rooms with TV and sea views, a private beach without coral (£E25 for non-guests, including a soft drink) and also a windsurfing and diving centre and a large yacht for dive trips. The most lavish hotel is the Greek-inspired *Iberotel Dahab* (℡069/364-1264, Ⓦwww.iberotel-eg.com; ➐), a 145-room palace with windsurfing and diving centres, plus a kids' club. Back at the eastern end of the bay, but accessed by a separate road near the lagoon, the charming *Coralia Dahab* (℡069/364-0301, Ⓦwww.accorhotels.com; ➏), monopolizes a windswept bay enclosed by a sandbar – a fabulous spot to learn how to windsurf.

Asilah

With its breathtaking views, quiet ambience and string of good beachside restaurants and hotels, the gentrified hippie colony of **ASILAH** is the Red Sea coast's best backpacker hangout. Its reputation as *the* place for hippie travellers emerged in the 1960s, when Israeli troops started coming here for a bit of R&R, introducing the Bedouin to a different way of life. Nowadays, the Bedouin village of tin shacks and scrawny goats has changed beyond recognition: concrete buildings stretch back behind scores of restaurants, small inns and bungalows, while local children wander beneath the palm trees selling Bedouin trousers (made in China), friendship bracelets and camel rides. Most of the palm huts were long ago replaced by hotels (some of which are very smart), while a section of the beach has been paved to create a pedestrian "corniche". As the tourist area has been cordoned off in Na'ama Bay, so the central streets in Asilah have been repaved and **pedestrianized**, and traffic will no longer be permitted into the area.

Drug smuggling and cultivation in Sinai

The Sinai Bedouin have a long tradition of **smuggling** hashish into Egypt. During colonial times the route followed the Mediterranean coast, until the militarization of El-Arish and the Canal Zone compelled smugglers to seek new routes across the interior. When this also became militarized due to war with Israel, they switched their attention to the mountains of South Sinai and the Aqaba coast. Under Israeli rule their activities were tolerated so long as the dope was bound for Egypt, but the emergence of an Israeli market caused a clampdown in the 1970s, when hash supplies from Lebanon were drying up.

Meanwhile, however, foreign hippies were flocking to Sinai and asking the Bedouin for grass (using the Indian term *ganja*, from which *bango*, the Egyptian word for marijuana, derives). Thus was planted the seed of a local **cultivation** industry, which really got going once Sinai was returned to Egypt and its police chief took a hand in the business for a decade. Today, Sinai is one of Egypt's main sources of *bango*, as cultivators can't be prosecuted owing to a loophole in the Camp David Accords – unlike dealers, who risk long-term imprisonment or even hanging, and rely on bribery to get off the hook. But the police must make *some* arrests, so it's rather like an auction where the lowest bidders are cast as scapegoats. This applies equally to foreigners – especially those who bring heroin or ecstasy to sell in Asilah.

Such is the lure of Asilah that visitors often stay longer than they'd expected, getting stuck in a daily routine of café life, or if they are more active, working at one of the dive centres. Given Asilah's reputation, it's important to stress the limitations on pure hedonism. Women can generally sunbathe here without any hassle, but **going topless** violates Egyptian law, and there are periodic crackdowns on **dope**: if you consume, it's at the risk of the police deciding they need to make up numbers on their arrest forms (see box, p.693). Finally, stick to bottled water to avoid the risk of **hepatitis** from contaminated cisterns; a dozen or so cases of infection occur every year.

Arrival and information

Arriving in Asilah, you'll be dropped at the parking lot in front of the **bridge** that divides **Masbat** to the north from **Mashraba** to the south. Both neighbourhoods extend for about a kilometre in each direction, strung out with restaurants and hotels along a pedestrian walkway, before petering out into the dust. **Lighthouse Beach**, at Masbat's northern headland, is the usual first stop for sunbathers and snorkellers. The bridge itself has recently been rebuilt (it was the location of one of the bombs) and beneath it an attractive tiled paddling pool is being laid out. **Bikes** can be rented from most of the dive centres (for around £E20/hr) to get up and down the beachfront Corniche.

There are a number of **Internet cafés** up and down the walkway, some doubling as **secondhand bookstores** where for a small fee you can also swap books. Most usually have **telephone**, **fax** and photocopying facilities too. There are a couple of **ATM** machines, one by *Jay's* restaurant and another outside the centrally located Ghazala Market (rebuilt after one of the bombs went off outside).

Opposite *Star of Dahab* is a Banque de Caire (daily 9am–12.30pm & 6–9pm). The One Stop Business Centre (7am–midnight) at *Bamboo House* has safety

△ Asilah's Corniche, with the *Tota* bar on the left

deposit boxes (£E20 per week or £E3 per day), and allows customers to make international calls and send faxes to most countries for £E7 per minute. You can buy stamps and post letters a couple of doors along at a kiosk simply called Post, next door to the *Chinese Restaurant*.

Accommodation

Asilah's accommodation ranges from simple, budget **campgrounds**, with basic concrete cells, usually with padlocks and electricity, and with showers, sinks and toilets in the yard, to **hotels** with en-suite facilities, sea views and air conditioning. Factors to consider when choosing a campground are whether and when they have hot showers, how they're rigged up to deal with mosquitoes, and noise levels (especially anywhere near the main strip at Masbat).

Bamboo House Hotel Masbat ℡069/364-0263. A hotel with neat, modern a/c rooms with TV and home to Emperor Divers. Sells beer on the front terrace. Rate includes breakfast. ❺

Bedouin Moon Hotel 3km north of Masbat ℡069/364-0695, ⓔ bedouinmoon@menanet.net. Attached to the Reef 2000 dive club, this is good for beachcombing and diving. Rooms come with a/c and fridge. They also have dorms (US$14 per bed). ❺

Bishbishi Garden Village Mashraba ℡069/364-0727, ⓦ www.bishbishi.com. Operated by the indefatigable Jimmy (who also runs the *Penguin* restaurant), this popular backpacker hangout has a range of rooms from basic cells to a/c rooms with private bath. It's a good place to meet other travellers looking to organize a desert trek. Bike rental available. ❷

Blue Beach Club 200m north of Lighthouse Beach ℡069/364-0411, ⓦ www .bluebeachclub.com. Friendly place with twenty neat rooms, hip, young European staff and an easy-going atmosphere. Yoga, massage, Arabic language lessons, reiki, riding and diving are available, as is the opportunity for heavy drinking at the *Furry Cup* bar. ❻

Canyon Dive Resort 11km north of Mashbat ℡012 437-3477. Attractive two-star place next to the Canyon dive site. Worth considering if all you want to do is dive, but otherwise a bit far from town. ❹

Christina Residence Mashraba ℡069/364-0390, ⓦ www.christinahotels.com. A hotel in two parts, one on the beach and another, less expensive building on the main road. Both premises have smart rooms, in whitewashed blocks with domed ceilings. Breakfast is included, but you pay extra for a/c. ❺

Coral Coast 300m north of Lighthouse Beach ℡069/364-1195, ⓦ www.coralcoast.com. Large concrete hotel block with thirty rooms with balconies or terraces on the beach, past the *Blue Beach Club*. Has a branch of Fantasea Divers attached. ❺

Diver's House Tucked away in the south of Mashraba ℡069/364-0451, ⓦ www.divershouse .com. Rambling hotel with attached dive school. A variety of quirky rooms with one to four beds on offer, including a dungeon-like double with a domed ceiling. Choice of fan or a/c. ❸

El Dorado 350m north of Lighthouse Beach ℡ & ℻069/364-1027, ⓦ www.eldoradodahab .com. Immaculate, recently refurbished a/c cabins, some with toilet and shower. Own dive centre and an excellent restaurant serving pizza. ❺

Inmo Divers' Home Mashraba ℡069/364-0370, ⓦ www.inmodivers.de. Stylish lodgings, all en suite, around a dive centre. Facilities include free Internet access, swimming pool and children's play area. Discounts for longer stays, divers and advance bookings. ❺

Jasmine Pension On the beach next to Diver's House ℡069/364-0852, ⓦ www.jasminepension .com. One of the best budget places around, with welcoming staff and tidy, good-value rooms, some with sea view and a/c, and a beachside café. ❷

Mirage Village Near Lighthouse Beach ℡069/364-0341, ⓦ www.mirage.com.eg. Tucked away behind a walled compound, this has pleasant a/c rooms, smart bathrooms, shady areas under palms to lounge in and a private beach. It's mosquito-free due to its windy position. The laid-back management organize regular fish barbecues. ❺

Mohammed Aly Camp On the beach where Masbat meets Mashraba ℡069/364-0268, ⓦ www.club-red.com. Though it's very central, only a few of the 110 rooms have much appeal. The best overlook the sea and have a/c and their own bathrooms. Run in association with the popular Club Red dive centre. ❸

Nesima Mashraba ℡069/364-0320, ⓦ www .nesima-resort.com. Possibly the most beautiful hotel in Asilah, with a great pool setting and spacious domed rooms with a/c. Used by British dive operators Regal and Crusader Travel. Discounts available in quiet periods. Has a branch of Western Union. ❻

New Sphinx Mashraba ☎069/364-0032, ⓦwww.sphinx-hotels-dive.com. Forty rooms with bath, a/c and satellite TV, plus a lovely pool and restaurant, the Funny Mummy, that's right on the waterfront. The older annexe next door is cheaper and shares the same facilities. Management are friendly and organize bar parties regularly. Breakfast included. ❹

Seventh Heaven Masbat ☎069/364-0080, ⓦwww.7heavenhotel.com. Another good backpacker hangout with inexpensive rooms and huts, and a good location between the bridge and Lighthouse Beach. There's a restaurant, though the breakfast is nothing to write home about. ❶

Eating, drinking and nightlife

A score of **restaurants** by the beach vie for customers. House, trance and chill-out music fill the air; floor cushions and posters reflect the mix of Bedouin and hippie influences. Cold drinks are always available, though not all places have alcohol licences, and you can sit around for hours without being required to eat (dishes take a long time to prepare, in any case). With menus displayed outside, it's easy to compare prices.

Pancakes with bananas, apples, ice cream or honey are popular for breakfast or late-night munchies, while main meals consist of pizzas, pasta or fish. Many places display a tempting heap of fresh fish and crustaceans outside. Unless you splash out on lobster, you can eat quite well in Asilah for £E40–60 a meal, including drinks and dessert. Most places are open until midnight or later, though the choice of food diminishes after 9pm. There are also numerous **supermarkets** (daily 7.30am–midnight, though the Ghazala Market is open 24hr), **fruit stalls** and *taamiya* stands.

Of the **restaurants**, *Jays* (evenings only), run by an Englishwoman, is popular with resident divers for pizza and pasta dishes and its great falafel sandwiches. Also busy is *Friends* nearby, one of a run of similar beachside places that stretch to the bridge and serve grills, juices and pancakes. South of the bridge, the *Chinese Restaurant* (☎069/364-0262) serves beer and large portions of authentic Chinese food. The *Dolphin Café*, just up from the police station, has reasonable Indian vegetarian baltis and noodles and coconut curries from £E25. Near the *New Sphinx* hotel, the new 🏃 *Funny Mummy* restaurant has an attractive roof terrace festooned with twinkly light and featuring hammocks, an Italian coffee machine, and *sheeshas* for £E5. Next door the very popular *Penguin* restaurant is good for a game of backgammon, a *sheesha,* and a decent fish platter from £E40, accompanied by great milkshakes. Close by, the *Lakhbatita* restaurant (☎069/364-1306) is worth a visit for its decor and atmosphere, though the food can be hit-or-miss; the *cioppino* (seafood stew; £E25) is the house speciality. It's decorated with tiles from old Coptic churches and doors from medieval warehouses from the Delta region, while the shelves are lined with giant jars of pickled vegetables and antiques collected from all over Egypt.

Unsurprisingly, **nightlife** centres on those hotels and restaurants serving alcohol. Both *Nesima* and the *New Sphinx* have popular bars with happy hours (6.30–7.30pm). The main place for the diving set is the *Furry Cup* bar at the *Blue Beach Club* (happy hour 6.30–8.30pm), while backpackers tend to hang out at the *Penguin* restaurant, or *Adam's Bar*, near Lighthouse Beach. The biggest bar in town is 🏃 *Tota*, recognizable by its ship-like facade, with satellite TV, a small dance floor, pool tables and a large, attractive beer garden in the back, serving very tasty garlic bread, steaming lasagne and passable pizza. Downstairs is the only place in Dahab where you can buy booze for a tipple in your room, though at the same prices as on the bar menu (£E65 for a bottle of wine, for example).

Egypt's underwater world

For snorkellers and scuba divers the Red Sea and the Gulf of Aqaba are heaven-sent destinations. Thanks to their relative isolation from the Indian Ocean, they harbour a high concentration of marine species found nowhere else on the planet, as well as many more common creatures, no less fascinating. Furthermore, the stable climate, shallow tides and exceptionally high salinity of the Red Sea provide perfect conditions for unusually brilliant corals and sponges to flourish – a revelation if you have previously snorkelled in such places as Hawaii or the Caribbean, whose reefs will ever after seem dull by comparison.

▲ A moray eel emerges from a crevice in the reef

Coral reefs

The **coral reefs** that fringe Egypt's Red Sea coastline have been created by generations of minuscule polyps depositing their limestone exoskeletons on the remains of their ancestors; living reefs can add 4–5cm of growth a year. As well as **hard corals** such as brain and fire coral, which have a rigid outer skeleton, the Red Sea is home to a remarkable abundance of **soft corals**, including dendronephyta, whip coral and sea fans. Many of these have a rubbery or feathery appearance; particularly eyecatching are the massive **gorgonian fans**, which can grow up to 2m across.

Most Red Sea reefs are of the **fringing** type, with a relatively flat area giving way to a seaward-facing slope, rich in life. Because most types of coral need a moderate amount of warm sunlight to flourish, the most spectacular formations are found within 30m of the surface. While reefs vary greatly in size, with some more encrusted with coral growths than others, the following description should give you an idea of their topography.

Just offshore, you'll sometimes find a shallow **lagoon**, its warm water and rubble-strewn, sandy bottom attracting starfish and sea slugs; clams and sea urchins hide in crevices and schools of damselfish and butterflyfish flit about. Forming the seaward boundary of the lagoon is the **reef flat**, the crest of which typically lies too close to the surface for coral to survive, and is usually a barren, rough-surfaced shelf. By contrast, the slightly deeper areas of the reef flat tend to be extremely rich in flora and fauna.

Beyond is the coral-encrusted **slope**, which may lead to a **drop-off**, similar to the edge of a cliff. The flatter areas may be dotted with coral pillars or knolls, their highly developed formations attracting anthias, snappers and wrasses, to name but a few. Lower down, the coral is sparser, and you may find sandy terraces overgrown with flora more commonly found on the bottom, such as seagrass, the habitat of sea horses and pipefish. Beyond the drop-off is open water.

Must-see species

Some of the Red Sea's most colourful and endearing marine creatures are gratifyingly easy to spot in the shallows, where the sunlight is brightest. Among the commonest and most vibrant species are **parrotfish**, easily recognizable by their beaky mouths,

▼ A parrotfish uses its beak-like mouth to nibble at coral

and jauntily striped **bufferflyfish**. Particularly exotic-looking are the **bannerfish**, whose long dorsal fins diminish to filaments.

Wherever soft stinging anemones cling to the reef, you're likely to see **clownfish** (also called anemone fish), immortalized in *Finding Nemo*. Equally commonplace but highly exotic-looking are **angelfish**, usually found close to the coral, singly or in pairs. Unmissable are the clouds of gold and vermillion anthias congregating around coral heads and fans.

Slopes and fore reefs are the habitat of snappers, goatfish and wrasses (the largest of these, the Napoleon wrasse, can dwarf a person). In deeper waters you may see sharks, including whitetip reef sharks, grey reef sharks and (occasionally) scalloped

▲ A diver shadows a Napoleon wrasse

hammerheads, while spotted reef stingrays are often seen on the sandy bottom.

Turtles, with their curious mixture of ugliness and grace, are among the most thrilling species to encounter underwater; the Red Sea has several species, including green turtles and hawksbill turtles. Dolphin encounters are much rarer, and those lucky enough to come across a pod of bottlenose or spinner dolphins are likely to count this among highlights of their trip.

Five best places to dive

Best for wreck-diving *Thistlegorm*, reached by liveaboard or from El Gouna or Sharm el-Sheikh
Best for dolphins and turtles El Gouna
Best for shore-diving with pristine coral Mersa Alam
Best for sharks The Brothers, reached by liveaboard or from El-Quseir or Hurghada
Best for beginners Na'ama Bay and Sharm el-Sheikh

Dangers of the deep

◀ Emperor angelfish and soft corals

Poisonous species include the spiny, bottom-dwelling **scorpion fish**, and the nocturnal **lionfish**, with its elaborate array of strikingly marked fins. The lethal **stonefish**, camouflaged as a gnarled rock, is harder to spot but fortunately rare. Very few Red Sea species behave aggressively towards people, however; you're more likely to have an unpleasant encounter with **anemones** or **fire coral**, both of which can sting or burn the skin, or with the spiny **sea urchin** – but only if you brush against any of these three creatures in a moment of carelessness. **Tiger sharks** have been known to attack, but are seldom found near the coast.

▲ The brilliantly coloured Klunzinger's wrasse

Common sense and conservation-mindedness should keep you from touching any underwater flora or fauna, particularly coral, which can be extremely sharp and is easily damaged (see below). It's also important to avoid aggravating any potentially dangerous creatures such as **moray eels**, which may bite when threatened, or **stingrays**, which can deliver a painful dose of venom. Certain times of the year see the arrival of hordes of **jellyfish**, contact with which can cause mild skin irritation; dive-centre staff can advise on the situation.

Protecting the reefs

While dive tourism enables you to witness the marvel of coral reefs and learn about the complex ecosystem that maintains them, the reefs are extremely fragile, being vulnerable to excessive sunlight, wave motion and accidental damage. Inexperienced or irresponsible divers who kick, trample or hold onto the coral pose one of the most serious **threats** to the reefs' existence. Many sites near Sharm el-Sheikh are now considered to be "over-dived", and other reefs have been damaged or destroyed by development projects, including the construction of hotels. Perhaps it's understandable that the most environmentally aware resort in the Sinai – *Basata*, north of Nuweiba – doesn't welcome divers.

For divers and snorkellers alike, the fundamental rule is: **look but don't touch**. If you're in one the marine parks, such as Ras Mohammed, you are also forbidden to feed the fish or remove anything from the sea. Don't buy **aquatic souvenirs**, the export of which is illegal. Even shells from the beach may be confiscated when you leave Egypt, with a hefty **fine** to pay.

▲ The lionfish, with its venomous spines

Diving, snorkelling and windsurfing

Shore diving is the norm in Dahab, with the reefs along the coast reached by pick-ups. The nicest reefs are to the north of Dahab Bay just past the lagoon; at Asilah the reefs are meagre, except for the area around the lighthouse, and much of the sea bed is covered in rubbish. Experienced divers should look out for occasional free "trash dives" advertised by dive schools; these are organized to clear the rubbish, mostly plastic bags blown into the sea, which sea turtles can mistake for jellyfish and choke on.

Most divers head 8km up the coast where you can find the Eel Garden, Canyon and Blue Hole dive sites, trips to which are arranged by most dive centres. The **Canyon** is a dark, narrow fissure that you reach from the shore by swimming along the reef and then diving to the edge of a coral wall. It can be frightening for inexperienced divers, as it sinks to a depth of 50m, but there's plenty to see at the top of the reef. Further north lies the notorious **Blue Hole**, which has claimed several lives (usually experienced divers who dive too deep for too long). This spectacular shaft in the reef plunges to 80m; the challenge involves descending 60m and swimming through a transverse passage to come up the other side. Divers who ascend too fast risk getting "bent"; inexperienced divers should not attempt this dive under any circumstances. Fortunately, the Hole can be enjoyed in safety by staying closer to the surface and working your way round to a dip in the reef known as the Bridge, which swarms with colourful fish and can even be viewed using snorkelling gear.

The main destination for day-long **dive safaris** is the Ras Abu Galum protected area, a thirty-kilometre stretch of coast with three diving beaches, accessible by Jeep or camel (see p.699). **Naqb Shahin** is the closest to Dahab of the three, and has fantastic coral and gold fish, but the sea is very turbulent, so many divers prefer **Ras Abu Galum** or **Ras el-Mamleh**, further north. All three sites have deep virgin reefs with a rich variety of corals and fish. Club Red does a one-day, two-dive trip by camel to Ras Abu Galum for €85 including all equipment, while Fantasea offers two standard shore dives near Dahab for €80, including tanks, weights and lunch. Trips to the *Thistlegorm* (see p.673) are available from Club Red for €100 including transport, food and three dives.

While renting equipment is costlier here than in Na'ama, **diving courses** are generally cheaper. Competition means cut-price deals, especially when business is quiet, but you should keep a sense of perspective – the rockbottom outlets are not necessarily going to be rigorous about your safety. Stick to the long-established centres like Club Red (open-water course €210, plus €30 for the certificate), INMO Divers (open-water course €300 including equipment, plus €30 for certification), or try Nesima, Dive Urge, Desert Divers or Divers International.

Dive centres

Canyon Dive Club 11km north of Mashbat ☎ 012 4373477. PADI.

Club Red *Mohammed Aly Camp* ☎ 069/364-0380. ⓦ www.club-red.com. PADI.

Dahab Divers Lighthouse Beach ☎ 069/364-0381, ⓦ www.dahab-divers.com. PADI.

Desert Divers Masbat ☎ 069/364-0500, ⓦ www .desert-divers.com. PADI courses; also organizes desert or snorkelling safaris, yoga sessions in Ras Abu Galum and rock climbing.

Dive Urge Masbat ☎ 069/364-0957, ⓦ www.dive-urge.com. PADI.

Divers House Mashraba ☎ 069/364-0885, ⓦ www.divershouse.com. PADI five-star.

El Dorado Masbat ☎ 069/364-1027, ⓦ www.eldoradodahab.com. PADI.

Fantasea Dive Club Lighthouse Beach ☎ 069/364-1373, ⓦ www.fantaseadiving.net. PADI, SSI.

INMO Mashraba ☎ 069/364-0370, ⓦ www.inmodivers.de. PADI.

Nesima Dive Centre *Nesima Hotel* ☎069/364-0320, ⓦwww.nesima-resort.com. PADI, BSAC.

Nirvana Dive Centre Near Lighthouse Beach ☎069/364-1261, ⓦwww.nirvanadivers.com. PADI, BSAC.

Planet Divers *Planet Oasis Hotel*, near Lighthouse Beach ☎069/364-1090, ⓦwww.planetdivers.com. PADI, CMAS, IANTD.

Red Sea Relax *Neptune Hotel*, just south of the footbridge between Mashbat and Masraba ☎069/364-1309, ⓦwww.red-sea-relax.com. CMAS, SSI, PDIC. Offers free dorm beds to divers.

Reef 2000 *Bedouin Moon Hotel* ☎069/364-0087, ⓦwww.reef2000.com. SSI.

Sinai Dive Club *Coralia Dahab* ☎069/364-0465, ⓦwww.dive-club.com. PADI.

Sub Sinai Mashraba ☎069/364-1317, ⓦwww.subsinai.com. PADI.

Free diving and snorkelling

The new watersport in Dahab is **free diving**, done on a single deep breath, without the aid of scuba gear. Expert training in the art is available from Lotta Ericson of Freedive Dahab (ⓦwww.freedivedahab.com), who offers courses of one to three days' duration (€75 for a one-day session), the longest of which includes a trip to the Blue Hole. Most participants find they can hold their breath for up to four minutes after three days of training, enabling them to dive to 15m or deeper. As for **snorkelling**, for a more ambitious jaunt than just wading out from the shore, arrange an excursion to the Blue Hole (£E25 for a half-day), which can be done through a number of operators, including Desert Divers.

Windsurfing

The wind blows at least two hundred days each year at Dahab, making this area a haven for windsurfers and kiteboarders. Both the *Hilton* and the *Swiss Inn* have windsurfing centres and rent boards for about €17/$22 per hour. Kiteboarding is also popular and equipment can be rented from a Russian outfit, Go Dahab (☎012 756-8358, ⓦwww.go-dahab.ru), at the lagoon near the *Ganet Sinai Hotel*. One-day introductory courses cost $195, while equipment can be rented by experienced kitesurfers for $50 for half a day.

Riding and safaris

If you fancy **riding** on the beach at Asilah, look out for the boys who rent out horses (£E50/hr) or camels (£E10–15/hr); they hang out by the restaurants on the beach near the palm trees in Masbat. Alternatively, the *Blue Beach Club* offers horse trips down the beach for £E90 per hour.

A more exciting option is to sign up for trips into the rugged interior, which can be organized at most campgrounds, through safari agencies, or by negotiating directly with guides. Itineraries and prices can vary widely so shop around. The most popular **day excursions** are by Jeep to the **Coloured Canyon** (see p.702), which costs €25 per person for a group of six; by camel to **Wadi Gnay**, a Bedouin hamlet with palms and a brackish spring (€35); or by camel to the mangrove forest of **Nabeq** (€16). Some outfits, including the Reef 2000 dive club and Desert Divers, also organize rock-climbing trips. Embah Safari near Lighthouse Beach (☎ & ℱ069/364-1690, ⓦwww.embah.com) offers diving, camel or Jeep safaris from €30/US$40 per person per day, as well as excursions to St. Catherine's and the Coloured Canyon, and trips further afield to Petra in Jordan. Sam's Motorbike Centre (☎010 111-2931) to the north of the bridge offers tours by either quad bike or motorbike (£E230 for two people; 2–3hr) into the desert, and longer trips that including snorkelling at various spots along the coast.

Ras Abu Galum

The coast between Dahab and Nuweiba is hidden from view as the road veers inland, but this remote area, the **Ras Abu Galum** Protectorate, harbours some of the richest wildlife in the Sinai. Access is limited to a coastal track (walking or camel only) from Dahab or an unpaved road (4WD) that branches off from the main road 20km short of Nuweiba. There are a couple of small shops and restaurants, but it's wise to bring food and water if you plan on staying a while. It is possible to walk from Dahab (Ras Abu Galum is approximately two hours from the Blue Hole) or you can rent a 4WD pick-up truck (£E20–30). Some of the tour operators stop here on the way to the Blue Hole, but for more in-depth exploration, the eco-tourism outfit Centre for Sinai (℡010 666-0835, ⓦwww.centre4sinai.com.eg), can introduce you to a Bedouin guide who organizes trips by Jeep or camel.

Moving on from Asilah and Dahab

Buses leave from Dahab City's East Delta bus station (℡069/364-1808). Of the buses to **Sharm** (9 daily; 1hr 30min; £E11), the 4pm bus continues to **Luxor** (18hr; £E100). There are five buses daily to **Cairo** (8.30am, 12.30pm, 2.30pm, 7.30pm, 10pm; 7–8 hr; £E62; £E75 for the 10pm bus). These don't stop in Suez but there is a direct bus to **Suez** at 8am (4–5hr; £E29). One bus daily at 8.30pm goes to **Zagazig** (6–7hr; £E42) and **Ismailiya** (6–7hr; £E38). There is a daily bus at 10.30am to **Nuweiba** (1hr; £E11), and **Taba** (3hr; £E22) with others to Nuweiba only at 3pm, 4pm and 6.30pm. The daily bus to **St Catherine's** (1hr; £E16) leaves around 9.30am, but unless you want to stay overnight and visit the monastery the next morning, it's best to go on an organized trip. **Shared taxis** can be booked in advance at any of the safari agencies and at most camps and hotels; it's worth asking around, as prices can vary for the same trip.

Nuweiba and Tarabeen

NUWEIBA is another resort on the Gulf of Aqaba, consisting of a **port** with nearby tourist complexes, followed 4km up the coast by **Nuweiba "City"**, an administrative and commercial centre grafted onto a former Israeli *moshav* (co-operative village). During the late 1970s, thousands of Israeli and Western backpackers flocked here to party and sleep on the beach – a heyday remembered fondly by shop and campground owners. Today tourism is at a virtual standstill and much of the year the campgrounds lie dormant. For most travellers, Nuweiba serves primarily as a stepping stone for onward travel by bus to Eilat in Israel or by ferry to Aqaba in Jordan. Nuweiba's neighbouring Bedouin settlement is called **TARABEEN**, after the local Bedouin tribe, and tends to attract younger travellers. Once there were more than twenty campgrounds and a few hotels on its wide and sandy beach, buzzing with restaurants and tourist bazaars; now the place is eerily empty, with only a few camps still functioning.

Arrival, transport and accommodation

Nuweiba's main **bus station** is at the port, though the Taba bus also stops on the highway close to Nuweiba City. **Taxis** charge £E15–20 from the port to Tarabeen, and £E5–10 from Nuweiba City to Tarabeen. You can walk from

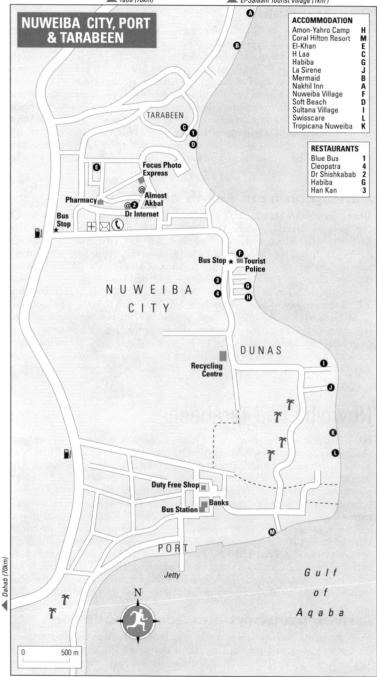

NUWEIBA CITY, PORT & TARABEEN

▲ Taba (70km)

▲ El-Salaam Tourist Village (1km)

Ⓐ

Ⓑ

TARABEEN

Ⓒ ❶
Ⓓ

Ⓔ

Focus Photo Express

@ **Almost Akbal**
Pharmacy
@ ❷ **Dr Internet**

Bus Stop ★

Ⓕ
Bus Stop ★ ■ **Tourist Police**

❸
❹

Ⓖ
Ⓗ

NUWEIBA CITY

DUNAS

Recycling Centre

Ⓘ

Ⓙ

Ⓚ

Ⓛ

Duty Free Shop ■
Banks
Bus Station

Ⓜ

PORT

Jetty

Gulf

of

Aqaba

N

0   500 m

ACCOMMODATION
Amon-Yahro Camp	H
Coral Hilton Resort	M
El-Khan	E
H Laa	C
Habiba	G
La Sirene	J
Mermaid	B
Nakhil Inn	A
Nuweiba Village	F
Soft Beach	D
Sultana Village	I
Swisscare	L
Tropicana Nuweiba	K

RESTAURANTS
Blue Bus	1
Cleopatra	4
Dr Shishkabab	2
Habiba	G
Han Kan	3

▲ Dahab (70km)

Nuweiba City to Tarabeen in twenty minutes along the beach; it takes slightly longer by road.

Accommodation is concentrated in three main locations: near the port, in Dunas along the beach south of Nuweiba City, and in Tarabeen, a couple of kilometres north. Tarabeen is the place to find cheap **campgrounds** (£E50–100), though these tend to come and go. Hotels generally include breakfast in the rate, but the campgrounds don't.

Amon-Yahro Camp The closest camp in Nuweiba to Dunas ☏069/350-0555, ⓦwww.amonyahro.net. A tidy camp with raised huts and electricity. It's run by Egyptologist Murad el Sayed, who also takes visitors on reliable and informative trips into the desert. Rates include breakfast. ❷

Coral Hilton Resort East of the port ☏069/352-0320, ⓦwww.hiltonworldresorts.com. Luxury holiday village with two heated pools and lots of sports facilities, including the Emperor Dive Centre. Non-residents can use the beach for £E25. ❻

El-Khan East of the road between Nuweiba City and Tarabeen ☏069/350-0316, ⓔanis@sinai4you .com. Bungalows, rooms, a good restaurant, and a Bedouin handicrafts exhibition and shop. Though not on the beach, it is handy for late-night bus arrivals and can arrange camel and Jeep safaris. ❹

H Laa Central Tarabeen ☏069/350-0679. The best of several similar camps in Tarabeen: the rooms are basic, a/c concrete boxes, but somewhat nicer than what's on offer in neighbouring camps. Breakfast included. ❷

Habiba Nuweiba City ☏069/350-0770, ⓔhabiba@sinai4you.com. Comfortable a/c bungalows and cheaper huts, some en suite, and boasting a very good restaurant on the beach. Breakfast included. ❺

La Sirene Between Nuweiba City and the port ☏069/350-0701, ⓕ350-0702. Attractive a/c bungalows dotted along a beautiful stretch of beach, with a dive centre, bar and restaurant. ❻

Mermaid North Tarabeen ☏069/350-0871, ⓦwww.redsea-mermaid.com. A mix of concrete huts with a/c and en-suite facilities, and simpler bamboo shelters. They're set among lawns and palms on a quiet stretch of private beach. ❹

Nakhil Inn North Tarabeen ☏069/350-0879, ⓦwww.nakhil-inn.com. Come here for smart, tastefully designed rooms, all with a/c, satellite TV and bath; children under 12 stay free. There's also a dive centre and occasional yoga instruction. ❺

Nuweiba Village In the centre of Nuweiba ☏069/350-0401-3, ⓦwww .nuweibavillageresort.com. Very comfortable a/c bungalows with TV, as well as a disco, dive centre, a spacious pool area and a private beach with a suitably laid-back bar. Free Internet access. ❼

Soft Beach At the southern end of Tarabeen's main street ☏010 364-7586, ⓦwww.softbeachcamp .com. More than forty classic Sinai beach shacks, plus hammocks and a restaurant on the sand. ❶

Sultana Village 2.5 km south of the *Nuweiba Village* ☏069/350-0490, ⓦwww.sinai4you /sultana. One of the sets of better beach bungalows in Dunas, the stylish stone huts are all equipped with bathroom and a/c. ❺

Swisscare 3km south of Nuweiba Village ☏069/352-0640, ⓦwww.swisscare-hotels.com. A pleasant new resort with a/c rooms arranged in two-storey whitewashed villas. Amenities include a pool, five restaurants, and extras such as massage and bicycle hire. ❻

Tropicana Nuweiba South of *Swisscare* ☏069/352-1056, ⓦwww.tropicanahotels.com. Comfortable four-star affair with a good beach, large pool, dive centre and kids' club. B&B and all-inclusive rates available. ❺

Diving and snorkelling

Diving in Nuweiba is mostly from the shore thanks to a lack of jetties or safe anchorages. There are several shallow **reefs** offshore, the best of which is the **Stone House**, beyond the southern promontory. Though fine for **snorkelling**, they're not so great for **diving** unless you're a novice, so the divers that come here usually travel to Ras Abu Galum (p.699) or sites north of Nuweiba (see p.705). These trips can be arranged by any of Nuweiba's **dive centres**: for example, Emperor Divers at the *Coral Hilton Resort* (☏069/352-0320, ⓦwww .emperordivers.com; PADI) has a Jeep dive trip to Ras Mamlach for €65. Other dive centres include Diving Camp Nuweiba at *Nuweiba Village*

(☏069/350-0401, ⓦwww.nuweibavillageresort.com; PADI, CMAS) and Scuba Divers at *La Sirene* (☏069/350-0705, ⓦwww.scuba-divers.de; SSI).

Jeep and camel safaris

Local Bedouin guides offer a wide range of **camel or Jeep safaris** into the interior, and these can be booked through any hotel or camp. Their duration depends on your destination and mode of transport; it usually takes two or three times as long by camel as it does by Jeep. Most guides charge £E150 per person per day by Jeep (camel journeys cost around £E30 more), which should include meals and the cost of registering the trip with the police. Drinking water may cost extra and be more expensive the further you get from shops, so it's wise to bring plenty along.

The nearest destinations are the palmy oasis of **Ain el-Furtaga** (which can be reached by regular car) and the colourful sandstone canyon of **Wadi Huweiyit** (by camel or 4WD). Slightly further north lies **Moyat el-Wishwashi**, a large rainwater catchment cistern hidden in a canyon between imposing boulders. All these sites can be reached by camel in a day. The most popular day excursion by Jeep is to the **Coloured Canyon** (about £E80 per person) via a trail from Ain el-Furtaga. Its name comes from the vivid striations on the steep walls of the canyon, which is sheltered from the wind and eerily silent. Having got there by 4WD, you can hike through the canyon in either direction. Other destinations include **Wadi Ghazala**, with its dunes and acacia groves where gazelles may be glimpsed; **Ain Umm Ahmed**, whose deep torrent fed by snow on the highest peaks of the Sinai shrinks to a stream as the seasons advance; and the oasis of **Ain Khudra**, supposedly the Biblical Hazeroth, where Miriam was stricken with leprosy for criticizing Moses.

Recommended **guides** include Anis Anisan at *El Khan* camp, who can arrange trips for small or large groups and will try to include a Bedouin wedding, camel race or a full moon *zwara* (traditional Bedouin meeting). The all-night **Bedouin weddings** are worth seeing as they provide a rare opportunity for young Bedouin men and women to mingle; the women wear beautiful wedding shawls decorated

△ Embarking on a camel safari

with sequins that catch the light of the full moon while the men perform dances to impress them. Also recommended is Morad Said at *Amon-Yahro Camp*, an English-speaking Egyptologist with plenty of insight into the Bedouin life. The *Habiba* camp runs a camel riding school (Ⓦ www.sinai4you.com/crs) which offers a three-day camel experience for €355, teaching you to ride a camel and also how to feed it, and imparting an insight into desert survival from the Bedouin.

Eating, drinking and nightlife

As an established backpacker hang-out, Tarabeen is home to a number of **budget cafés**, whose menus feature familiar dishes such as pizza, pasta and apple pancakes. Nuweiba City has less to offer, though its shops are good for self-caterers to stock up on fresh fruit and the like. **Nightlife** boils down to a disco in the *Nuweiba Village* (£E20 admission), or playing guitars, drums or backgammon and getting stoned at Tarabeen. If you want a beer, try the bars in upmarket hotels such as the *Hilton* or *Nuweiba Village*.

Restaurants

Blue Bus Tarabeen. One of the better beachside open-air restaurants, serving reasonable fish, pasta and pizza, and with plenty of cushions and rugs.

Cleopatra Nuweiba City, 220m south of Nuweiba Village. Egyptian-themed restaurant serving good seafood, *mezze* and chicken dishes from £E25. There's outdoor seating around a fountain strung with drying shark and various crustaceans. Beer is sold. Open until midnight.

Dr Shishkabab In Nuweiba City's bazaar ☏ 069/350-0273. A favourite with budget travellers, this serves sandwiches (£E15) and meat and vegetarian (from £E20) dishes. The gracious Dr Shishkabab, as the owner styles himself, is usually around in the evenings, when he's happy to talk to tourists, lend travel advice and put you in contact with guides for a desert safari. Daily 7am–11pm.

Habiba Nuweiba City. Well-prepared food is served at this camp's beachfront buffet restaurant, which gets very busy at lunchtimes serving tourists on day-trips from Sharm el-Sheikh and Na'ama. Daily 11am–midnight.

Han Kan Nuweiba City, close to *Nuweiba Village*. Excellent Chinese-Korean restaurant. Daily 11am–2pm & 6–10pm.

Directory

Banks and exchange There's a bank in the *Nuweiba Village* (daily except Fri 9am–1pm & 6–9pm), at the *Hilton*, and several in the port area with ATMs.

Doctor There is a doctor on call at the *Nuweiba Village*. The hospital in Nuweiba is poorly equipped, so head for Sharm el-Sheikh if you're seriously ill (see p.681).

Internet cafés Try *Almostakbal* on the main street, or *Dr Internet*, next to *Dr Shishkabab*.

Pharmacy Gasser, near Dr *Shishkabab* (☏ 069/350-0605; daily 10am–10pm).

Police Near the Town Council ☏ 069/350-0304; the Tourist Police (☏ 069/350-0231) are beside the parking lot outside the *Nuweiba Village*; both are open 24hr.

Post office In the centre two blocks east of the bus stop (daily except Fri 9am–2pm).

Telephones Next to the post office is a telephone office which takes phonecards.

Moving on

Some intercity **buses** trundle through Nuweiba City, but the only sure way of getting a bus south is to take a taxi to the main bus station (☏ 069/352-0371) at the port. Buses leave daily, roughly at 6.30am, 10.15am and 4.15pm for Dahab (1hr; £E11) and Sharm el-Sheikh (3hr; £E20), though schedules change from winter to summer, so it can be worth checking the times in advance. Services to Cairo (7–8hr; £E55) go via Taba (1hr) and depart daily from the bus station at 6am, 9am, 11am, 12pm & 3pm, and five to ten minutes' later from the bus stop on the highway near Nuweiba City.

You might also find **service taxis** hanging around Tarabeen, bound for Taba, Dahab, Sharm el-Sheikh or St Catherine's. Service taxis also meet the arrival of the boats from Aqaba.

Boats to Aqaba in Jordan

From Nuweiba's port (☏069/352-0427) you can catch a **ferry** or the **high-speed catamaran to Aqaba** in Jordan. Tickets are sold inside the port's entrance; you'll need to show your passport to go through the gates, and once inside you're not allowed to leave. Foreigners are assigned an official to guide them through customs and immigration and onto the boat. The office stops selling tickets about one hour before the ferries are scheduled to depart, so turn up a couple of hours early whichever service you want to travel on. There is a departure tax of £E50.

The **ferry** leaves daily at 2pm (an extra trip is put on in the afternoon during busy periods such as the hajj season) and takes three to five hours, depending on the weather. Foreigners must buy a 1st class **ticket** ($35 one-way, payable in dollars); children under 2 go free, under 5s pay a quarter of the full fare, and under 12s half. During Ramadan or the hajj season, it's a definite advantage to have access to the 1st class lounge, as the boat is crowded with Egyptian workers returning home or pilgrims bound for Mecca. The ferry also carries **vehicles** ($100). Don't be surprised if it leaves much later than scheduled. On boarding you'll be asked to hand over your passport, which will be returned at Aqaba customs or, if you go searching for it, on the boat.

Tickets for the **catamaran** cost $50 one-way and are worth the extra expense as this vessel is much more comfortable than the ferry and only takes an hour to Aqaba, though it doesn't take cars. Sailings are at 2pm except on Thursdays and Saturdays when it departs at 9am. Formalities are identical to those for the ferry.

Jordanian visas (valid for one month) are issued on board both the ferry and catamaran, or immediately after disembarkation; British, Canadian, US, Australian and New Zealand citizens shouldn't have any trouble getting one on the spot. Visa fees are around $15 (payable in US dollars or dinars) but can cost more depending on nationality. If there are five or more of you travelling, you can ask for a **group visa**, which is free of charge for a minimum stay of four nights. If you just want to visit Petra and return, you can book trips through *Habiba* camp (☏069/350-0770, Ⓦ www.sinai4you.com/habiba) – a three-day jaunt starts at €300 and includes B&B accommodation at Petra, though not ferry tickets or visas.

Between Nuweiba and Taba

The 70km of coastline between **Nuweiba** and the **Taba** border crossing into Israel was for a long while relatively untouched, scattered with just a few appealing low-key resorts. During the 1990s, these were joined by plenty of new holiday villages and a massive tourist development called **Taba Heights**. However, since September 11, 2001 many of these resorts have been virtually empty due to the dearth of Israeli visitors, with some closing down completely. Visitor numbers took a further knock after the events of October 7, 2004, when two massive car bombs destroyed a portion of the *Taba Hilton* hotel, killing 31 people and injuring more than 120. The attack coincided with a second bombing at Ras al-Shaitan that left three dead.

Time will tell if business will pick up again, but in the interim, independent travellers who venture this way will get long stretches of beautiful beaches more or less to themselves. The nicer places are signposted and may be visible from the highway, depending on the terrain. **Buses** can drop you at any point along the way if you ask the driver, but bear in mind that there are no **banks** until Taba, nor anywhere to buy **food** except the pricey resort restaurants.

The first spot worth noting is **MAAGANA BEACH**, whose southern end – called **Lami Beach** – begins 8km from Tarabeen. Though its reefs are quite shallow and unimpressive, the beach itself is nice, with public showers and toilets and striking rock formations. There's a **campground** with huts (❷) and a cafeteria frequented by Bedouin who run **camel and Jeep trips** to Wadi Huweiyit (see p.710) and other sites. Two kilometres further on lies the picturesque headland of **RAS AL-SHAITAN**, where the **reef** drops off sharply to the north, making it ideal for shore diving and snorkelling. *Castle Beach* resort (℡069/350-0926 or 012 220-6240; ❸) has **beach bungalows** with verandas, a good restaurant, and a shop selling souvenirs. There is a good reef for divers, and you can **rent camels** and guides for excursions to Moyat el-Wishwashi (see p.702). Several other camps nearby have a variety of accommodation, including *Ras Satan* camp (℡010 525-9109; 🅦www.ras-satan.com; ❷), a basic place of tents and bungalows run by the affable Ayash. If you are interested in exploring the desert, he can put you in contact with guides who take three- to four-day camel trips to places such as Ain Hudra and Wadi Ghazala for around £E100 per person per day, or who will take you to a traditional village near Gebel Gunna in the St Catherine's Protectorate.

Another 2km along the coast is the new *Tango Beach Resort* (℡012 217-1478, 🅦www.tangobeachresort.com; ❸) with neat en-suite rooms set around an attractive mosaic pool. Buffet meals, evening floor shows, and wind- and kitesurfing are on offer. A further 8km up the coast is the upmarket beach resort of *Bawaki* (℡069/350-0470, 🅦www.bawaki.com; ❺), boasting air-conditioned rooms with hot showers, a restaurant, bar and pool. It also has a few triple-bed huts. Breakfast is included in the price of accommodation, but other meals are expensive.

Just beyond Bawaki, there's more accommodation at **MAHASH**, which occupies a particularly fine stretch of white sandy beach with a cool breeze even on the hottest summer days. Camps here include *Yasmina*, *Ma'ayan* and *Eden*, with a small supermarket (all ❷).

Basata

The trendiest resort in these parts is **BASATA**, which lies by the headland of Ras el-Burqa. Created by the German-educated Sherif el-Ghamrawy, it is Egypt's most eco-friendly resort, with its own greenhouse, generator, bakery, desalination plant and school for local Bedouin children. Organic waste is fed to Basata's donkeys, goats, pigeons and ducks, or used to fertilize the fruit and vegetables. The huts are made entirely from natural materials; empty Baraka bottles are shredded and sent back to the company for recycling, and children can earn treats by collecting cigarette butts from the beach. Alcohol, drugs, television and loud music are forbidden lest they spoil the ambience, which is family-oriented with a New Age ethos. There's a communal vegetarian or fish dinner each night, and guests may help themselves in the kitchen and bakery: write down what you've taken and pay when you leave. You can store your own food in the fridge.

Such is Basata's popularity that it's advisable to **reserve ahead** (℡ & 🅕069/350-0480, 🅦www.basata.com; ❺). There are sixteen huts, some of them mud-brick, or you can pitch a tent on the beach. Guests can sign up for **inland safaris** (£E80 per person per day by Jeep, £E100 by camel) or rent **snorkelling** gear (£E28), but divers aren't welcome. You'll either feel at home with Basata's New Agers or find them unbearably cliquey.

Bir Swair and around

Five kilometres beyond Basata is *Club Aquasun* (☎010 667-8099, Ⓦwww .clubaquasun.com; ❻), a less eco-conscious mix of bungalows with air conditioning and bathrooms. The quiet sandy beach has a lovely **reef**, good for **snorkelling** and **diving. Jeep or camel trips** can also be arranged to Wadi Quseib and other destinations. A couple of kilometres further on is *Sallyland* (☎069/353-0380, ☯353-0381; £E150), a three-star hotel of little note except that it has one of the few **bars** in the area. Other similar newish hotels can be found along the coastal road, such as the *Sonesta* and *Safari Beach*.

Next is the Bedouin settlement of **BIR SWAIR**. Few of its camps survived the economic downturn, but *Antica* (☎010 508-0370; ❷), and *Alexandria* (☎010 166-1042, Ⓦwww.alexandriabeach.com; ❷) are up and running again. They both have basic but comfortable huts on one of Sinai's nicest beaches, as well as friendly staff and atmosphere. Guests here can visit the Bedouin village behind the camps in the mountains; you will be graciously received with tea and hospitality, but it's a good idea to give them a few Egyptian pounds in return and, as ever, always ask before taking photographs.

Another great beach, 3km north of Taba Heights, is the **Sun Pool**, which begins with a gentle slope and then plunges as it nears the **Fjord**, a beautiful inlet in the hills by the shore.

Taba Heights

Eighteen kilometres south of Taba, the **TABA HEIGHTS** development (Ⓦwww.tabaheights.com) covers 4.5 million square metres of land and boasts 5km of beach. Dubbed the "Red Sea Riviera", this huge resort complex is based around a "village", which features a casino, watersports, dive centre, restaurants, bars, cafés, shops, bazaars and a medical centre. The resort's five **hotels**, all luxurious, tend to be much cheaper if booked as part of a package. The newest addition is the striking green and orange ⚶ *Intercontinental* (☎069/358-0064, Ⓦwww.intercontinental.com; ❼) with over five hundred rooms around a man-made lake next to the beach, and surrounded by tropical gardens; amenities include a spa and indoor heated pool, a watersports centre and squash and tennis courts. Also here is the beautifully designed *Marriott* (☎069/358-0100, Ⓦwww.marriott.com; ❼), most of its rooms overlooking the Gulf of Aqaba, and featuring an Arabian spa. The huge five-star *Hyatt Regency Acacia* (☎069/358-0234, Ⓦwww.taba.hyatt.com; ❼) has six restaurants and bars, three pools, a private beach, kids' club, health centre, tennis courts, shuttle bus and car rental. The list of facilities is nearly as long at the slightly smaller *Sofitel* (☎069/358-0801, Ⓦwww.sofitel.com; ❼). A little less expensive than the rest is the all-inclusive *El Wekala Golf Resort* (☎069/360-1212, Ⓦwww.threecorners .com; ❼), which has smart rooms, three swimming pools, a spa and overlooks an eighteen-hole golf course, though the resort is a five-minute shuttle-bus ride from the beach. Though rates here include full board, guests can eat at other hotels using a "dine around" scheme.

Pharaoh's Island

Seven kilometres before Taba you'll see **Pharaoh's Island** (Gezirat Faraoun), known to Israelis as "Coral Island". Its barren rocks are crowned by the

7

SINAI | Between Nuweiba and Taba

△ The fort on Pharaoh's Island

renovated ruins of a **crusader fort** built in 1115 to levy taxes on Arab merchants while ostensibly protecting pilgrims travelling between Jerusalem and St Catherine's Monastery. The fort was subsequently captured by Salah al-Din but abandoned by the Arabs in 1183. Being only 250m offshore, it can be admired just as well from the mainland if you'd rather not pay the £E525 for a boat (from the *Salah al-Deen* hotel; see below) and another £E20 to tour the fort, which retains several towers and passageways along with a large cistern. There's also an expensive cafeteria that only opens when there are lots of tourists around.

The main reason to come here, however, is to dive or snorkel in the maze of **reefs** off the northeastern tip of the island. As the currents are strong and the reefs labyrinthine, it's best to be accompanied by a guide; this can be arranged at the *Salah al-Deen* **hotel** by the road on the mainland, opposite the island (☏069/353-0340, ✉tabarsrt@gega.net; half board ❻; under 12s stay free).

Taba and the border

Hugging the Gulf of Aqaba's northernmost reaches, the unassuming border town of **TABA** consists of little more than a handful of hotels, cafés, shops and a bus terminal. Its history, however, has been turbulent. Following its withdrawal from the Sinai, Israel claimed that Taba lay outside the jurisdiction of the Camp David Accords, and demanded US$60 million compensation for its return to Egypt. It took ten years of bitter negotiations until international arbitration finally returned the town to Egypt in 1989. After a period of relative calm, Taba's peace was shattered on October 7, 2004 when a massive car bomb tore away a side of the *Hilton Taba Hotel*, killing 32 people. Now open again, the hotel and its *Nelson Village* annexe (☏069/353-0140, ⊛www.hiltonworldresorts.com; ❼) have all the usual resort features including bike hire, pool and watersports. That said, a better accommodation option is the newer *Tobya Boutique Hotel* (☎069/353-0275, ⓦwww.tobyaboutiquehotel.com; ❼), on the highway 1km south of Taba. With a swimming pool, private beach and casino, this stylish complex is decked out in Egyptian-African themed hand-woven wool carpets, while the rooms are embellished with local crafts.

The East Delta **bus terminal** (☎069/353-0205) is a few hundred metres before the border. Buses run from here to **Nuweiba** (4 daily; 1hr; £E11), **Dahab** (2 daily; 2–3hr; £E22), **Sharm el-Sheikh** (2 daily; 3–4 hr; £E27), **Cairo** (4 daily; 6–7hr; £E55). **Service taxis** operate to Tarabeen and Nuweiba (£E50), Dahab (£E70) or Sharm (£E120).

Crossing the border

The **border with Israel** is open 24 hours except during Yom Kippur and Eid el-Adha. Avoid crossing after mid-morning on a Friday or any time on Saturday, however, as most public transport and businesses in Israel shut down over *shabbat*. The whole process can be very quick, unless you get caught behind a large group. For details of entering Egypt at Taba, and entry and departure taxes, see p.29. Don't listen to any taxi drivers who tell you that you need to take a taxi to the East Delta terminal – it is less than five minutes' walk.

The Israelis issue free three-month **visas** to EU, US, Australian and New Zealand citizens. However, if you plan on travelling to Syria or other Arab countries that do not recognize Israel, ask immigration on both sides of the border to leave your passport unstamped. Travellers must walk across a no-man's land between the Egyptian and Israeli checkpoints; from the Israeli checkpoint you catch a shared taxi or a #15 bus for the 10km into Eilat. If you need to **change money**, the exchange rate on the Egyptian side, at Bank Misr, which also has an ATM, is better than the Israeli bank where you pay your exit tax.

The interior

The **interior of Sinai** is a baking wilderness of jagged rocks, drifting sand and wind-scoured gravel pans, awesome in its desolation. Yet life flourishes around its isolated springs and water holes, or whenever rain falls, renewing the vegetation across vast tracts of semi-desert. Hinterland settlements bestride medieval pilgrimage routes, which the Turks transformed from camel tracks into dirt roads, then the Egyptians and Israelis improved and fought over. Both sides also built and bombed the airstrips which the MFO now use to monitor the Sinai's demilitarized zones.

As a result, the only readily accessible part of the interior is **St Catherine's Monastery**, **Mount Sinai** and **Feiran Oasis**, although some other, smaller oases can be reached by Jeep or camel from the Aqaba coast or St Catherine's (see opposite). That said, most buses from Cairo to Nuweiba traverse the **Wilderness of the Wanderings** via **Nekhl** and the **Mitla Pass**, allowing you to see something of the peninsula's interior. Because of the unexploded ordnance lying around, **independent motoring** is officially restricted outside the St Catherine's Feiran Oasis area.

Inland safaris and treks

Though most tourists are initially attracted by Sinai's beaches and reefs, even a brief trip into the interior should prove a memorable experience that'll whet your appetite for more. **Inland safaris** range from half-day excursions by Jeep or camel to treks lasting up to two weeks. Travelling by **Jeep** is obviously faster and makes few or no physical demands, but tends to distance you from the landscape and at worst can reduce the experience to a mere outing. This is rarely the case if you travel by **camel**, which feels totally in keeping with the terrain.

If you've never ridden a camel before, try a half-day excursion before committing yourself to a longer trip. Even a few hours in the saddle can leave you with aches in muscles that you never knew existed, so it's advisable to alternate between walking and riding. It's easy to get the hang of steering: pull firmly and gradually on the nose rope to change direction; a camel should stop if you turn its head to face sideways. Couching the animal – thrusting one's face close to its muzzle and growling "*kkhhurr, kkhhurr*" – is best left to the Bedouin guides. See "Riding" in Basics, p.56, for advice on posture.

For those with more time and stamina, the most rewarding option is to go **trekking on foot**. Treks can be arranged at the village of St Catherine's (where you can also obtain maps for one-day walks in the area from the protectorate) or at certain points along the roads into the interior – such as the village of Sheikh Hamid – and also through many of the Bedouin who run trips from the coastal resorts. The list of destinations below is by no means all-inclusive, but should give an idea of what's on offer.

Practicalities depend on your destination and mode of travel. Day excursions from the coast can be made on a Sinai-only visa, but to travel for any longer or explore the High Mountain Region beyond the immediate vicinity of St Catherine's Monastery and Mount Sinai you must have a regular Egyptian visa. To climb mountains you must also have a **permit** from the police, which can be obtained by your Bedouin guide. It is illegal – and highly risky – to go trekking without a guide. To help you select destinations and plot routes, buy the 1:250,000 *Sinai Map of Attractions*, sold at the main resorts on the coast. Other things to **bring** are listed in the "High Mountain Region and Feiran Oasis" section (p.716).

Finally, **respect the landscape** and leave it unspoiled. Bring plastic bags to remove your rubbish when you go, and burn any toilet paper left behind. Gathering firewood should be left to your guide, and gardens should never be entered without permission from the owners.

Safari destinations

The following are all shown on the map on pp.664–665.

Ain el-Furtaga 16km from Nuweiba by road. Palmy oasis at the crossroads of trails to the Coloured Canyon, Wadi Ghazala and Ain Khudra Oasis.

Ain Khudra Oasis One of the loveliest oases in Sinai, it can be reached by hiking from the St Catherine's road, with help from local Bedouin, or from the south by 4WD.

Ain Kid Oasis 14km off the road between Sharm el-Sheikh and Dahab; reached via Wadi Kid, a red-walled canyon where a spring appears in rainy years. The oasis has a freshwater well.

Ain Umm Ahmed Another beautiful oasis, accessible by 4WD or camel from Bir es-Sawa. Can serve as a base for climbing expeditions to Ras el-Qalb (see overleaf).

Arched Canyon Sinuous gorge that's only accessible on foot; drop-off and pick-up by 4WD from Ain el-Furtaga or Bir es-Sawa.

Bir es-Sawa Small oasis with a spring issuing from a cave, beside the El-Thammed road.

Blue Valley 12km from St Catherine's. A canyon painted blue by a Belgian artist in 1978.

Coloured Canyon 17km north of Ain el-Furtaga. Two rainbow-hued canyons, great for walking or rock-climbing (no water). One of the most popular day-trips from Nuweiba.

El-Haduda The biggest sand dune in eastern Sinai, reached from Sheikh Hamid (see below).

Feiran Oasis Over twelve thousand palm trees, monastic remains, and access to Jebel Serbal. Wadi Feiran may have been the route taken by the Israelites to reach Mount Sinai.

Forest of Pillars A unique natural phenomenon of petrified tree stumps on the cliffs of Jebel el-Tih, 15km northeast of Serabit el-Khadim. Access by 4WD or camel only; guide essential.

Jebel Sabah A 2266m peak in southern Sinai, from which Saudi Arabia and mainland Egypt are visible on clear days. For experienced hikers only, with abundant food and water. Permit required.

Jebel Serbal Near Feiran Oasis, this is one of the loveliest mountains in Sinai, with ruined chapels lining the trail to the summit (2070m). No climbing skills needed, but guide and permit required.

Jebel Umm Shaumar The second-highest peak in Sinai, whose summit (2586m) affords a view of the entire southern horn of the peninsula. Experienced climbers only. Permit required.

Nuwamis Prehistoric site with 5550-year-old graves and inscriptions 6km from Ain Khudra. Reached on foot (2hr 30min) from Sheikh Hamid, by appointment only.

Ras el-Qalb Isolated mountain (999m) associated in Bedouin folklore with the monster Ula. For climbers only; no water. Permit required.

Serabit el-Khadim Hilltop temple overlooking the Gulf of Suez, with ancient turquoise mines and inscriptions in the surrounding valleys; it's covered on p.675. Access by 4WD, then on foot.

Sheikh Hamid Bedouin settlement on the road to St Catherine's, 7km from the Dahab–Nuweiba road. This is the starting point for walking or camel treks to Ain Khudra, Nuwamis, El-Haduda, and remoter destinations (up to two weeks).

Wadi Ghazala Links Ain el-Furtaga and Ain Khudra Oasis. Acacia groves, dunes and gazelles.

Wadi Huweiyit North of Nuweiba. Colourful canyon with typical desert flora; easy hiking.

Wadi Mandar 40km north of Sharm el-Sheikh. Bedouin camel races occur here on January 1.

Wadi Naseb Runs down from Mount Catherine towards Dahab. The verdant upper reaches of the wadi are inhabited by Bedouin. 4WD essential.

St Catherine's Monastery and Mount Sinai

Venerated by Christians, Jews and Muslims as the site of God's revelation of the Ten Commandments, **Mount Sinai** overlooks the valley where Moses is said to have heard the Lord speaking from a burning bush.

The bush is now enshrined in **St Catherine's Monastery**, nestling in a valley at the foot of the Mount, surrounded by high walls and lush gardens. As tourists have followed pilgrims in ever greater numbers, the sacred mount has witnessed unseemly quarrels between Bedouin over the shrinking amount of sleeping space for the climbers at the peak, and the monastery itself shows signs of strain. Yet for most travellers it remains a compelling visit, while other seldom-visited peaks offer equally magnificent views if you're prepared to make the effort to reach them.

Despite its isolated location, St Catherine's is one of the most accessible parts of South Sinai. You can visit on **organized tours** from Na'ama Bay, Dahab, Nuweiba, Cairo, Hurghada or Eilat, or you can make your own way by bus or service taxi. A daily bus leaves Cairo's Abbassiya terminal at 11.30am for St Catherine's village via Feiran Oasis (7hr; £E37). Services from Sharm el-Sheikh (7.30am; £E28) and Dahab (9.30am; £E16) turn off the highway between Dahab and Nuweiba. All buses stop about 10km before the monastery at a petrol station/police checkpoint/ticket office for the St Catherine protectorate, where foreigners must purchase a **ticket** (£E20) to enter the area. For a group of travellers, another option is to engage a **service taxi** at Suez, Dahab, Nuweiba or Taba and split the cost. Taxis usually run in the morning and afternoon if enough customers are interested, raising their fares once the last bus has left. The same goes for taxis leaving St Catherine's, which run to Dahab and elsewhere, depending on demand.

The main drawback to buses, their variable schedules aside, is the fact that they rarely get to St Catherine's Monastery before it shuts at noon. If you are coming by bus and want to visit, consider **staying** at least one night; if you just want to climb Mount Sinai, ask to be dropped at the turn-off for the monastery, 1500m before St Catherine's village. Alternatively, you could take a **guided overnight trip** from Dahab or Sharm el-Sheikh, which includes a moonlit ascent of Mount Sinai, sleeping at the peak and returning to the monastery in the morning after sunrise. Most buses depart from the village between noon and 1pm.

St Catherine's village

While the monastery and Mount Sinai are the focus of interest, most of the facilities of use to tourists are in the **village of St Catherine**, 3km away. Shared taxis provide **transport** between the two, charging £E5. The road terminates at the village's main square. On one side is an arcade containing a **bank** (Mon–Thurs & Sun 8.30am–2pm & 6–9pm; no ATM), several supermarkets and restaurants; on the other side are the **tourist police** and a small and poorly equipped **hospital**. In the vicinity of the mosque are a **post office**, **telephone exchange** and the **bus station**. There's little to choose between the **restaurants** (6am–10pm), which do simple meals of chicken and rice or spaghetti bolognese; the *Panorama* also serves soup and pizzas (£E20–25).

For **short walks** in the area, guide maps can be purchased from the St Catherine Protectorate visitor centre and Bedouin museum (entry £E25) at the end of the road before the monastery. If you're planning to do any trekking in the High Mountain Region, ask locals to point you towards **El-Milga**, uphill past the main square of the village (about 150m northwest of the Co-op petrol station), where you'll find **Sheikh Mousa** (℡010 641-3575, ⊛www.sheikmousa.com), the chief of the Bedouin guides who lead expeditions. For more details, see "The High Mountain Region and Feiran Oasis", p.716.

Accommodation

Most people on tours arrive in the early hours to climb Mount Sinai and **catch the sunrise** before descending again. Independent travellers, however, can leave their packs in the monastery's storeroom (£E2) and ascend the camel path to **sleep out**. With nighttime temperatures around 10°C during summer and near zero over winter (when frosts and snow aren't uncommon), a sleeping bag is essential if you plan to do this; you can also rent blankets on the summit. Note, however, that with so many people wanting to sleep out, there is often little room at the top and it's very uncomfortable, and you may have to sleep further down the mountain at Elijah's Hollow (see p.715) and complete the journey before sunrise. The best bet for budget travellers is either of the **campgrounds** near St. Catherine's village, though most of those that are further away will arrange transport.

Catherine Plaza Just outside the village ℡069/347-0288. Smart four-star place with 147 a/c rooms, pool, 24hr coffee shop, restaurant and bar. Rates are half board. ❻
Daniela Village St Catherine's village ℡069/347-0379, ⊛www.daniela-hotels.com. Over 70 a/c rooms with baths, plus a restaurant, cafeteria, bar and TV room. Rates are full board. ❼

🏃 El Milga Bedouin Camp 150m past the Co-op petrol station ℡010 641-3575, ⊛www.sheikmousa.com. Welcoming lodge offering five basic double rooms and dorms (£E15), with mattresses on the floor. Bathrooms are clean, there's Internet access and free use of the washing machine, and space for camping (£E10 per person). Meals are available or you can use the kitchen to self-cater. Ask if you want to do some desert trekking. Dorms £E15, ②

El Wadi El Mouqudus Between *Catherine Plaza* and *Daniela Village* ☎069/347-0225. Friendly management and spacious three-star rooms with fridge and TV, plus a swimming pool in summer. B&B or half board. ④

Fox Desert Camp 800m from the village, near the main intersection ☎069/347-0344 or 010 565-9399. This backpacker hangout is the cheapest place in the area, with basic stone cabins and moth-eaten mattresses. You can also camp and use the communal showers and restaurant. ①

Morgenland Village 4km from the monastery ☎069/347-0700, ⑤347-0331. Offers dorms and large double rooms with showers, plus a restaurant, pool and craft shop. Dorms $10. ⑤

Safary Camp and Hotel 500m from the village behind Catherine Plaza, also known as "Moonland"

☎069/347-0085 or 347-0162, ⑥ mnland2002 @yahoo.com. The only budget place around where you can sleep on a bed rather than a mattress on the floor. Its doubles and triples are popular with backpackers and overlanders. Camping costs £E10 per person. ②

St Catherine's Monastery Guesthouse Just outside the monastery walls ☎069/347-0353. Sheltered by the towering red cliffs of Mount Sinai, this hotel has a dramatic setting unmatched in the Sinai. Such glorious views do not come cheap, however, and the en-suite twin-bedded rooms are small and basic, though basic meals are included. ⑥

St Catherine Tourist Village By the main road, 500m from the monastery ☎069/347-0333, ⑤347-0323. One of the better hotels in the area, with comfortable a/c apartments; breakfast and dinner included. ⑤

The Monastery of St Catherine

The **Monastery of St Catherine** is a Greek Orthodox foundation. Its origins date back to 337 AD, when the Byzantine **Empress Helena** ordered the construction of a chapel around the putative **Burning Bush**, already a focus for hermits and pilgrimages. During the sixth century, the site's vulnerability to raiders persuaded Emperor Justinian to finance a fortified enclosure and basilica, and to supply two hundred guards – half of them Greeks or Slavs – from whom the Jebeliya Bedouin claim descent.

Although the Prophet Mohammed is said to have guaranteed the monastery's protection after the Muslim conquest, the number of monks gradually dwindled until the "discovery" of St Catherine's relics (see p.716), which ensured a stream of pilgrims and bequests during the period of Crusader domination (1099–1270). Since then, it has had cycles of expansion and decline, on occasion being totally deserted. Most of the monks today have come here from the monasteries of Mount Athos in Greece.

Visiting the monastery

The monastery is **open** to visitors from 9am till noon. It's officially closed on Fridays, Sundays and on all Greek Orthodox holidays, but will sometimes open from 11am to noon on these days, in order to accommodate tourist demands. There is no admission charge, but visitors must be modestly dressed.

You enter through a small gate in the northern wall near **Kléber's Tower** (named after the Napoleonic general who ordered its reconstruction) rather than the main portal facing west, which has a funnel that was used for pouring boiling oil onto attackers. Built of granite, 10–15m high and 2–3m thick, St Catherine's **walls** are essentially unchanged since Stephanos Ailisios designed them in the sixth century.

As you emerge from the passage, a right turn takes you past **Moses' Well**, where the then fugitive from Egypt met Zipporah, one of Jethro's seven daughters, whom he married at the age of 40. Walking the other way and around the corner, you'll see a thorny evergreen bush outgrowing an enclosure. This is the transplanted descendant of the **Burning Bush** whence God spoke

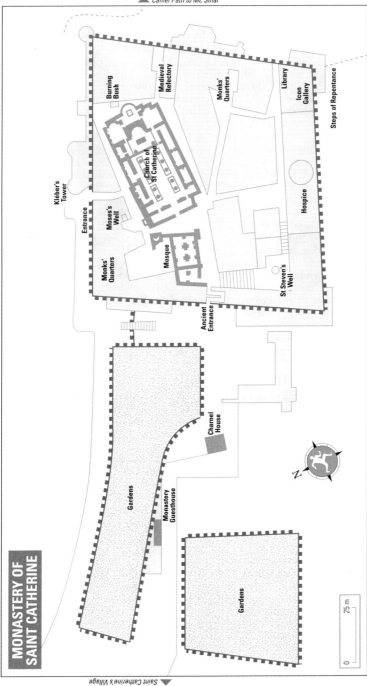

MONASTERY OF SAINT CATHERINE

Camel Path to Mt. Sinai

Mt. Sinai

Burning Bush

Medieval Refectory

Monks' Quarters

Library

Icon Gallery

Steps of Repentance

Kléber's Tower

Church of St Catherine

Entrance

Moses's Well

Hospice

Monks' Quarters

Mosque

St Steven's Well

Ancient Entrance

Charnel House

Gardens

Monastery Guesthouse

Gardens

N

25 m

0

Saint Catherine's Village

to Moses: "Come now therefore, and I will send thee unto Pharaoh, that thou mayest bring forth my people the children of Israel out of Egypt" (Exodus 3:10). Sceptics may be swayed by the fact that it's the only bush of its kind in the entire peninsula and that all attempts to grow cuttings from it elsewhere have failed. The bush was moved to its present site when Helena's chapel was built over its roots, behind the apse of St Catherine's Church.

A granite basilica, **St Catherine's Church** was erected by Justinian between 542 and 551; the walls and pillars and the cedarwood doors between the narthex and nave are all original. Its twelve pillars – representing the months of the year and hung with icons of the saints venerated during each one – have ornately carved capitals, loaded with symbolism. At the far end, a lavishly carved and gilded iconostasis rises towards a superb mosaic depicting Jesus flanked by Moses and Elijah, with Peter, John and James kneeling below. Unfortunately it's roped off and hard to see behind the ornate chandeliers suspended from the coffered, eighteenth-century ceiling. Behind the iconostasis is the **Chapel of the Burning Bush**, only viewable by special dispensation. The narthex displays a selection of the monastery's vast collection of **icons**, running the gamut of Byzantine styles and techniques, from encaustic wax to tempera. The church's **bell** is rung 33 times to rouse the monks before dawn.

Other parts of the monastery are usually closed to laypersons. Among them are an eleventh-century **mosque**, added to placate Muslim rulers; a **library** of over three thousand manuscripts and five thousand books, surpassed only by the Vatican's; and a **refectory** with Gothic arches and Byzantine murals. You can usually enter the **charnel house**, however, which is heaped with monks' skeletons; the cemetery itself is small, so corpses have to be disinterred after a year and moved into the ossuary. The cadaver in vestments is Stephanos, a sixth-century guardian of one of the routes to the Mount.

Mount Sinai

While some archeologists question whether **Mount Sinai** was really the Biblical mountain where Moses received the Ten Commandments, it's hard not to agree with the nineteenth-century American explorer John Lloyd Stephens that "among all the stupendous works of Nature, not a place can be selected more fitting for the exhibition of Almighty power". Its loftiest peak, a craggy, sheer-faced massif of grey and red granite "like a vengeful dagger that was dipped in blood many ages ago", rises 2285m above sea level. Strictly speaking, it's only this that the Bedouin call Jebel Musa ("Mount Moses"), though the name is commonly applied to the whole massif. Some Biblical scholars reckon that Moses proclaimed the Commandments from Ras Safsafa, at the opposite end of the ridge, which overlooks a wide valley where the Israelites could have camped.

Walking to the summit

Neither of the two **routes to the summit** requires a guide, but you shouldn't attempt the walk at night without a torch, and certainly not in winter – accidents are not uncommon. The longer but easier route is via the switchback **camel path**, starting 50m behind the monastery. It's possible to rent a camel for most of the ascent from Bedouins hanging out at the foot of the mount (£E40; £E15 at midday; 2hr), but it's really worth the effort of walking, which takes around two to three hours. You can stock up on water at the monastery shop before setting off, and there are refreshment stalls along the way. Prices rise the higher you go, but restocking on the mountain saves you carrying extra

△ Descending Mount Sinai

weight right at the start. Bedouin entrepreneurs at the peak rent out blankets and mattresses for the night (£E5–10).

Beyond the cleft below the summit, the path is joined by the other route, known as the Sikket Saiyidna Musa ("Path of Our Lord Moses") or **Steps of Repentance**. Hewn by a penitent monk, the 3750 steps make a much steeper ascent from the monastery (1hr 30min), which is hell on the leg muscles; some of the steps are a metre high.

Two buildings top the summit, a mosque and a Greek Orthodox church, both usually locked. Next to the mosque is the cave where God sheltered Moses: "I will put thee in a cleft of the rock, and will cover thee with my hand while I pass over" (Exodus 33:22). A little lower down the slope, a bunch of semi-permanent structures have sprung up, offering weary travellers a place to sleep.

Many people ascend by the camel path and descend by the steps. Start your ascent around 5pm (earlier during winter) to avoid the worst of the heat and arrive in time to watch the spellbinding sunset. With a torch, you could also climb the camel path (but not the steps) by night, though not during winter. Descending the steps, you'll enter a depression known as the Plain of Cypresses or **Elijah's Hollow**, where pilgrims pray and sing; a 500-year-old cypress tree stands here. This is also where Elijah is believed to have heard God's voice (I Kings 19:9–18) and hid from Jezebel, being fed by ravens. One of the two chapels is dedicated to him, the other to his successor, Elisha.

The High Mountain Region and Feiran Oasis

The area around St Catherine's is sometimes termed the **High Mountain Region**, as it contains numerous peaks over 2000m. Snow frequently covers the ground in winter and flash floods can occur at any time of the year. The scenery is fantastic, with phalanxes of serrated peaks looming above wadis full of tumbled boulders and wiry fruit trees; springs that are mere trickles in summer turn into waterfalls over winter. This harsh but beguiling land is the stamping ground of the Jebeliya and Aulad Said tribes, some of whom act as guides for **treks** on foot or by camel; with a few exceptions, the terrain is too rough for vehicles, even with 4WD. By law, foreigners are forbidden to embark on such expeditions without a Bedouin guide.

The trekking season runs from March to October, the main **starting point** being the village of **El-Milga** near St Catherine's (see p.711), where Sheikh Mousa will get things organized. He'll take your passport, register it with the police, purchase food and water, and work out all the details of the expedition. An all-inclusive trek, including guide, food and transport, costs around €30 per day. Even if you're going to walk, you'll need a camel to carry your baggage; surplus gear can be left at the sheikh's house. The ideal number of trekkers is three to five people; larger groups travel more slowly. You'll need comfortable hiking boots, warm clothes, a sleeping bag, sunglasses, sunscreen, lip salve, bug repellent and toilet paper. Though Sheikh Mousa can provide tents and eating utensils, you'll need to bring water purification tablets unless you're willing to drink from springs. To make sense of the landscape, it's essential to have a good map of South Sinai (see p.670) and a compass.

Mount Catherine, Blue Valley and other walks

Egypt's highest peak, **Mount Catherine** (Jebel Katerina; 2642m), lies roughly 6km south of Mount Sinai, and can be reached on foot in five to six hours. The path starts behind St Catherine's village and runs up the Wadi el-Leja on Mount Sinai's western flank, past the deserted Convent of the Forty and a Bedouin hamlet. Shortly afterwards the trail forks, the lower path winding off up a rubble-strewn canyon, Shagg Musa, which it eventually quits to ascend Mount Catherine – a straightforward but exhausting climb. On the summit are a chapel with water, a meteorological station and two rooms for pilgrims to stay overnight. The **panoramic view** encompasses most of the peninsula, from Hammam Faroun and the Wilderness of the Wanderings to the Arabian mountains beyond the Gulf of Aqaba.

According to tradition, it was on this peak that priests found the remains of **St Catherine** during the ninth or tenth century. Believers maintain that she was born in 294 AD in Alexandria of a noble family, converted to Christianity and subsequently lambasted Emperor Maxentius for idolatry, confounding fifty philosophers who tried to shake her faith. Following an attempt to break her on a spiked wheel (hence Catherine wheels), which shattered at her touch, Maxentius had her beheaded; her remains were transported to Sinai by angels. But some doubt that she ever existed and regard her cult as an invention of Western Catholicism, validated by "the land of her supposed sufferings" because of medieval France's demand for "holy oil" and other relics.

If climbing Mount Catherine seems too ambitious, consider visiting the **Blue Valley**, 5km southeast of the intersection of the roads to St Catherine's, Nuweiba and Feiran Oasis. You can do this as a day-trip from Dahab or in half a day from St Catherine's village by renting a Jeep and guide. The canyon's name derives from a Belgian who in 1978 painted its rocks a deep blue in emulation of the Bulgarian artist Christo, who hung drapes across the Grand Canyon and wrapped up the Reichstag in Berlin.

Longer treks

The two **four-day treks** outlined here give an idea of what can be done; some other possibilities are mentioned under "Feiran Oasis" (see below). The **first trek**, starting off in **El-Milga**, begins by taking the path through the **Abu Giffa Pass** down into Wadi Tubug, passing walled gardens en route to Wadi Shagg, where you'll find Byzantine ruins and huge boulders. From there you proceed to a grove of olive trees reputedly planted by the founder of the Jebeliya tribe, where you spend the night. The next day you follow the trail through Wadi Gibal and climb one of two peaks offering magnificent views, before descending to Farash Rummana, a camping spot with showers. On the third day you strike north through a canyon to the water holes of Galt al-Azraq, pushing on to camp out at Farsh Umm Sila or Farsh Tuweita. The final day begins with an easy hike down towards Wadi Tinya, before climbing Jebel Abbas Pasha (2383m), named after the paranoid ruler who built a palace there (now in ruins). Having retrieved your gear at the foot of the mountain, you follow a path down through the Zuweitun and Tubug valleys, back to Abu Giffa and El-Milga.

The **second trek** starts at **Abu Sila** village, 3km from El-Milga, where there are some rock inscriptions. You'll probably camp out near the sweetwater spring of Bustan el-Birka. Day two involves descending into Wadi Nugra, below Jebel el-Banat, where you can relax and bathe in pools fed by a twenty-metre-high waterfall. You then press on along the path through Wadi Gharba to the tomb of Sheikh Awad, where the Aulad Gundi tribe holds an annual feast in his honour. Having spent the night here, you have a choice of three routes to Farsh Abu Tuweita, the final night's camping spot. On the fourth day you follow the same route as the final leg of the other hike, visiting Abbas Pasha's ruined palace before returning to El-Milga.

Feiran Oasis

It's thought that the Ancient Israelites reached Mount Sinai by the same route that buses coming from the west use today, via Wadi Feiran and Wadi el-Sheikh. Travelling this road in the other direction, you might glimpse the **Tomb of Nabi Salah** near the **Watiyyah Pass**, where Bedouin converge for an annual **moulid** on the Prophet Mohammed's birthday. Celebrants smear themselves with "lucky" tomb dust, sacrifice sheep, race camels, bury their dead and pray, before enacting a rodeo and feasting on roast camel stuffed with lamb. Beyond the pass lies El-Tafra, a small and dismal oasis village.

Roughly 60km from St Catherine's the road passes a huge walled garden marking the start of **FEIRAN OASIS**. A twisting, granite-walled valley of palms and tamarisks, the oasis belongs to all the tribes of the Tawarah, who have houses and wells here. (Elsewhere, intertribal law permits the grazing of animals and pitching of tents on any land, but not the cutting of wood or building of stone houses.) Feiran was the earliest Christian stronghold in the Sinai, with its own bishop and convent, ruined during the seventh century but now rebuilt. Further back in time, this was reputedly the Rephidim of the Amalekites, who denied its wells to the thirsty Israelites, causing them to curse Moses until he smote the Rock of Horeb with his staff, making water gush forth. Refreshed, they joined battle with the Amalekites the next day, inspired by the sight of Moses standing on a hilltop, believed to have been the conical one that the Bedouin call **Jebel el-Tannuh**, with ruined chapels lining the track to its summit (1hr).

Other **hiking** possibilities in the area include **Jebel el-Banat** (1510m), further north, and the highly challenging ascent of **Jebel Serbal** (2070m), south of the oasis. This is approached via the rugged Wadi Aleyat, with a few springs at its upper end. From here you can either follow a goat track up a steep, boulder-strewn ravine called Abu Hamad (5hr), or take the longer but less precipitous Sikket er-Reshshah ("Path of the Sweaty") to the summit. From the main peak on the ridge there's a wonderful view of the oasis, countless mountains and wadis, with a narrow ledge jutting over a 1200m precipice.

As for finding a guide, make arrangements in El-Milga. A service taxi to Feiran costs £E90 for a group. Although Feiran Oasis lacks any **accommodation**, you could probably camp out somewhere in the palm groves with local consent.

The Wilderness of the Wanderings

Separating the granite peaks of South Sinai from the sandy wastes of the north is a huge tableland of gravel plains and fissured limestone, riven by wadis: the **Wilderness of the Wanderings** (Badiet el-Tih). Life exists in this desert thanks to sporadic rainfall between mid-October and mid-April; two or three downpours are enough to send yellow torrents surging down the wadis, rejuvenating the hardy vegetation that supports wildlife and refilling the cisterns that irrigate groves of palms and tamarisks. During Byzantine times, these cisterns sustained dozens of villages along the Sinai–Negev border; nowadays, the largest irrigated gardens are in Wadi Feiran and Wadi el-Arish.

Crossing the Wilderness via Nekhl and the Mitla Pass

The shortest route between Nuweiba and Cairo (470km; 6–7hr) crosses the great Wilderness via Nekhl and the Mitla Pass, more or less following the old Darb el-Hadi pilgrimage trail between Suez and Aqaba. By day the heat-hazed plateau is stupefyingly monotonous and it's hard not to fall asleep, which would mean missing a glimpse of several historic locations.

The road from Nuweiba heads north to El-Thammed before cutting west across Wadi el-Arish. **NEKHL**, at the heart of the peninsula, features a **derelict castle** built by Sultan al-Ghuri in 1516 and a big MFO observation post. South of one of the wadi's many tributaries lies **Qalaat el-Gundi** ("Fortress of the Soldier"), a **ruined fort** built by Salah al-Din; it can also be reached by a track from Ras Sudr on the Gulf of Suez. The fort stands atop a small mountain about one hour's climb from the road; be extremely careful when ascending the path, as there's a sheer drop on either side.

To the west, the road descends through the 480-metre-high **Mitla Pass**, one of three cleavages in the central plateau. When Ralph Bagnold attempted this route from Cairo by Model-T Ford in the early 1920s, it was choked with "yellow undulating cushions" of sand that buried the wire-mesh road laid by the British during World War I. The outcome of three Arab-Israeli conflicts was arguably determined at the Mitla Pass in some of the bloodiest **tank battles** in history. During the War of 1956, an Israeli parachute battalion seized and held the road until the arrival of armoured columns from El-Thammed, which dominated the interior. Having deployed their tanks in expectation of a similar strategy, the Egyptians were wrongfooted during the 1967 War, when the Israelis advanced from Abu Ageila to the northeast, captured the passes and then systematically annihilated their encircled foes, leaving the roadside littered with charred remains. In the October War of 1973, Egyptian forces failed to exploit their breakthrough along the Bar-Lev Line by rapidly seizing the Mitla and Giddi passes; many blamed their subsequent defeat on the cautiousness of the commander-in-chief, General Ismail.

Northern Sinai

While jagged mountains dominate the gulf coasts and interior of the peninsula, **northern Sinai** is awash with sand: pale dunes rising from coastal salt marshes and lagoons to meet gravel plains and wadis far inland. A succession of water holes along the coastal strip between Egypt and Palestine has made this Via Maris the favoured route for trade and invasions since late pharaonic times. Although the palmy beaches at **El-Arish** have spawned a popular domestic holiday resort, few of the settlements have ever amounted to much, nor deserve a visit nowadays. Most foreigners used to just zip through the region on direct buses between Cairo and Tel Aviv or Jerusalem, crossing the border at **Rafah** into the Palestinian Gaza Strip. But with recent unrest, the border here is open only sporadically, and for now travellers should use the crossing at Taba. Rafah, a divided frontier town, has been the subject of heated political tensions since 2003, when Egypt discovered thirty tunnels dug beneath its side of the border, which were widely regarded as the main conduit for smuggling weapons and drugs between Egypt and Gaza. The discovery led to a stepping up of patrols and arrests of alleged smugglers and tunnel diggers, many of whom had been operating since the 1980s.

No north–south transport is available to foreigners across the Sinai peninsula, so the only way to travel **between the Mediterranean and Aqaba coasts** is via Cairo and Suez. It's quickest to do this by **service taxi**, changing at Ismailiya and then again at Suez (or vice versa).

The road from Suez to El-Arish

The dominant impression of the road to El-Arish is of a string of **new towns** consisting of huge apartment buildings and named after hitherto insignificant villages based around wells. Whereas nineteenth-century guidebooks compared the merits of vital watering holes like **Bir el-Abd** ("brackish water and some telegraph-men's huts") and **Mazar** ("it is better not to camp near the well on account of the camel ticks"), modern travellers can drive past without a qualm. Between these towns lie ramshackle villages where the local Bedouin are being induced to settle, interspersed by golden **sand dunes** up to 50m high and 200m long.

Pelusium

Roughly 40km along the road to El-Arish from Qantara you pass a signposted turn-off for **PELUSIUM**. A fortress town that guarded Egypt's eastern border for many centuries, it's named after the Pelusiac branch of the Nile that once watered its surroundings. Many stories are attached to what the Bible records as the "Strength of Egypt". The Assyrian king Sennacherib lost 185,000 soldiers after swarms of rats ate their bows and quivers, while the army of Cambyses is said to have induced Pelusium's garrison to surrender without a fight by driving cats (the sacred animal of the goddess Bastet) before them. Here the Roman general Pompey was murdered on the orders of Ptolemy XII, and the Crusader king Baldwin I died of ptomaine poisoning after eating putrid fish.

Although the Pelusiac branch of the Nile started to dry up in the third century AD, the city remained inhabited well into the Islamic era, before being abandoned to the sands. In recent years, moves to bring 400,000 *feddans* of land under cultivation by digging the **Al-Salaam Canal** through this region have spurred a rash of **excavations** to recover archeological evidence before it is destroyed. The sites range from Qantara by the Suez Canal to Tell el-Mahraf near El-Arish. At Pelusium, they have uncovered parts of the pharaonic town and a **Roman amphitheatre** that can now be visited by tourists (daily 9am–5pm) – though since you need a car to get there, and official permission to tour the site, it seldom receives visitors.

El-Arish

Originally a Roman garrison town named Rhinocolorum ("Noses Cut Off") after the fate of dissidents exiled there, **EL-ARISH** has experienced more than its fair share of invasions. Rarely on the agenda for Western tourists, until recently this was a popular resort for domestic visitors, attracted by the palm-shaded beaches and bracing rollers. But events over the border in Gaza and the souring of relations between Israel and Egypt have meant that many Egyptians are eschewing El-Arish for other Mediterranean resorts such as Alexandria.

El-Arish is more **conservative** than the Aqaba coast resorts, with restrictions on booze and dress and a relatively subdued nightlife. Considered the back of beyond even by Egyptians, the quiet town has been thrust into the spotlight since October 2004 when it was discovered that the terrorist attacks in the southern Sinai were apparently masterminded from here. This led to a wave of arrests, and two days after the Dahab bombings of April 2006 there were two suicide bombs attacking police and MFO vehicles in El-Arish, though only the terrorists were killed. In May 2006 there were clashes between the police and members of the militant Tawhid w'al Jihad group, which reputedly pledges allegiance to Al-Qaeda. Their leader, Nasser Khamis Al-Mallahi, was shot dead and Egyptian security forces have claimed that he and his group were behind all the Sinai bombings.

Arrival, information and accommodation

El-Arish is served by East Delta **buses** from Cairo's Turgoman terminal (2 daily; 5hr; £E25–37) and from Ismailiya (6 daily; 3hr; £E10), as well as **service taxis**. Arriving from the west, you'll cruise along **Sharia El-Fateh** – parallel to the beach – until it swings inland and downhill to become **Sharia 23rd July**. This eventually turns into a **souk** of wooden-shuttered stores that look like a set from a Wild West movie, and terminates in **Midan Baladiya**, with its raucous mosque and fuming **bus station**. Minibuses and service taxis (50–75pt) constantly shuttle 2–3km between the souk and the beach.

El-ARISH map

MEDITERRANEAN SEA

SHARIA EL-FATEH

Basata Restaurant

Police Station & Hospital

SHARIA EL-GEISH

Multinational Force of Observers Store

SHARIA 23RD JULY

Museum & Zoo

Bank

Airport

ACCOMMODATION

El-Arish Resort	A
Mecca	E
Safa Hotel	F
Semiramis El-Arish	B
Sinai Beach	C
Sinai Sun	D

Bet 'A Bet

Aziz Restaurant

MIDAN BALADIYA

Service Taxis

EL-ARISH

0   500 m

Bus & Taxi Station

Bedouin Weekly Market

The **tourist police** (☏068/335-3400) and a largely useless **information** kiosk (☏068/336-3743; daily except Fri 9am–2pm) share a building on El-Fetah, in front of the *Sinai Beach Hotel*; the main **police** station (☏122) and **hospital** (☏068/336-1077) lie east along Sharia el-Geish, which forks off inland. There is a better equipped **Mubarak Military Hospital** (☏068/332-4018) near the North Sinai Governate in Dahiya. One block north of Sharia 23rd July, a side street leads to a **bank**, **post office** (daily except Fri 8am–2pm), and the 24-hour **telephone exchange** (international calls possible, but no card phones).

Accommodation

Outside of the July–September season there shouldn't be any problem finding somewhere to stay. The string of beachside hotels tend to be either overpriced or dirt-cheap hovels, so check out the town itself for good-value options.

El-Arish Resort Across from the beach on Sharia El-Fateh ☏068/335-1321, ⓕ335-2352. Well-kept singles, doubles and triples, all with sea views, with a nightclub in summer, pool, tennis courts and the only bar in El-Arish. Non-residents can pay a small fee to use the beach and pool. The rooms are expensive in peak season, but you can usually get a good discount out of season. ❼

Mecca Sharia El Salam ☏ & ⓕ068/335-2632. Welcoming hotel on a quiet street, one block east of

Sharia 23rd July. Probably the best value budget accommodation in town. Rates include breakfast. ❸

Safa Hotel Sharia 23rd July ☏068/335-3798. Rooms are reasonable, with shower and fan, and the staff friendly. Has a rooftop restaurant with nice views, and a laundry service. Look for the green "hotel" sign, 150m north of the Mr. Kodak store. ❹

Semiramis El-Arish Sharia El-Fateh ☏068/336-4167, ⓕ336-4168. Singles and doubles far from the beach, as well as pricier Med-facing suites. Despite the facilities, which include a pool, tennis court and restaurant, it's overpriced for what you get. ⑥

Sinai Beach Sharia El-Fateh ☎068/336-1713. Simple doubles and triples with private bathrooms and a/c, some with balconies overlooking the sea. ❸

Sinai Sun Sharia 23rd July ☎068/336-1855, ⑤336-3855. Faded but reasonably kept rooms of all sizes with balconies, bathrooms, a/c and TV. A good choice in its price bracket. ❸

The Town

Despite the huts and chalets lining several kilometres of **beach**, you can still find uncrowded stretches shaded by palm trees, the odd wrecked anti-aircraft gun adding a surreal touch. With cooler, rougher seas than the Aqaba coastline, and no reefs, El-Arish's beach is better for bracing dips and idle sunbathing than snorkelling or diving (there's no dive shop, anyway). Foreigners often get invited to join family gatherings, and for women travellers this can be a good way to avoid hassle from youths. Visitors are exhorted to stay off the beach after dark and dress modestly when in town – rules enforced by the police.

For a town of fifty thousand inhabitants, El-Arish offers few sights or entertainments. On Thursdays a **Bedouin market** sells fruit, vegetables and Bedouin handicrafts (9am–2pm); the latter are also available in tourist shops such as the Multinational Force of Observers store on Sharia 23rd July (☎068/335-1206). The only other attraction is a **Sinai Heritage Museum** (daily except Fri 9am–2pm; £E4) containing mostly stuffed wildlife and Bedouin handicrafts. It's just beyond the UN post along the coastal road to Rafah (catch a bus or service taxi).

Eating and nightlife

Midan Baladiya features several *fuul* and *taamiya* joints, while there are simple **restaurants** along Sharia 23rd July. *Aziz* (below the *El-Salaam Hotel*, beside Midan Baladiya) and *Bet 'A Bet* across the street do good *kofta* and salad, or chicken and chips, at reasonable rates. On the beach, try *Basata*, beyond the *El-Arish Resort*, for good seafood. With the exception of the well-stocked but expensive bar in the *El-Arish,* you'll be hard pressed to find any **alcohol**.

Smoking *sheeshas* over backgammon in one of the cafés on Sharia 23rd July is usually all that El-Arish can offer in the way of **nightlife** – and that's an exclusively male pursuit. Otherwise, in the summer the *El-Arish Resort* has a **nightclub** with live music and bellydancers.

The Red Sea Coast
and Eastern Desert

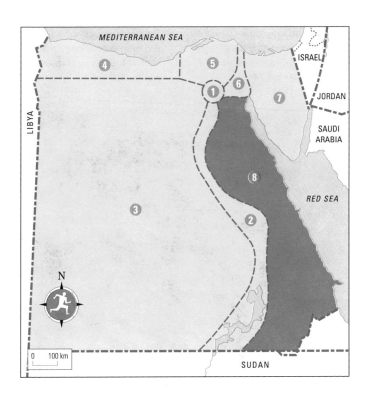

Highlights

* **Dive safaris** Hurghada is a good place to arrange diving trips or liveaboards, taking in the more remote reefs and wrecks of the south Red Sea. See p.714

* **Red Sea monasteries** Deep in the desert, St Paul's and St Anthony's were the world's first monasteries. See p.727

* **Hurghada nightlife** Die-hard clubbers can stay up all night at venues like the *Ministry of Sound*. See p.744

* **The Red Sea Mountains** Experience the wadis and Bedouin culture of the Red Sea Mountains, on camel or jeep safaris. See p.747

* **Mersa Alam** Camps and hotels here give access to some of the best, least-visited and most southerly dive sites in Egypt. See p.756

* **Prehistoric rock-art** Join a survey expedition to map sites in the Eastern Desert. See p.758

△ Red Sea Diving

8

The Red Sea Coast and Eastern Desert

For 1250km, from Suez to the Sudanese border, turquoise waves lap rocky headlands and windswept beaches along a coastline separated from the Nile Valley by the arid hills and mountains of the **Eastern Desert**. As in Sinai, the region's infertility and sparse population belie its mineral wealth and strategic location, and there are further points in common in the wildlife, Bedouin nomads and long monastic tradition. Tourism, too, has developed along similar lines, with holiday villages proliferating along the coast, and dive boats ranging down the Red Sea as far south as Eritrea.

An entrepôt since ancient times, the **Red Sea Coast** was once a microcosm of half the world, as Muslim pilgrims from as far away as Central Asia sailed to Arabia from its ports. Though piracy and slavery ceased towards the end of the nineteenth century, smuggling still drew adventurers like Henri de Monfried long after the Suez Canal had sapped the vitality of the Red Sea ports. Decades later, the coastline assumed new significance with the discovery of oil and its vulnerability to Israeli commando raids, which led to large areas being **mined** – one reason why tourism didn't arrive until the 1980s. It's worth being aware that large areas of the coastline and many wadis are still mined, and that any area with barbed-wire fencing (however rusty) is suspect. Never wander off public beaches or into the desert without a guide.

While Cairenes appreciate the beaches at **Ain Sukhna**, south of Suez, the real lure consists of fabulous island reefs off the coast of **Hurghada** – a booming, bold and brash resort town – and the less touristy settlements of **Port Safaga**, **El-Quseir** and **Mersa Alam** to the south. The coast south of Quseir is now subject to ambitious development plans and dive companies are also establishing supply bases for their dive boats along the southern coastline. Consequently "virgin" reefs in the south are opening up to divers, whose only option previously was a long journey by sea from Hurghada or from Sharm el-Sheikh in the Sinai. A list of dive sites accessible from Hurghada appears on p.741, while sites further to the south are mentioned on p.751 and p.756.

Crossing the Eastern Desert by bus gives little idea of its spectacular highlands. Apparently devoid of life, the granite ranges and limestone wadis harbour ancient rock-art, temples and quarries, gazelles and ibexes, and Bedouin. While you might not have the inclination, stamina or money for long excursions into the interior, thousands of Copts visit the **Red Sea**

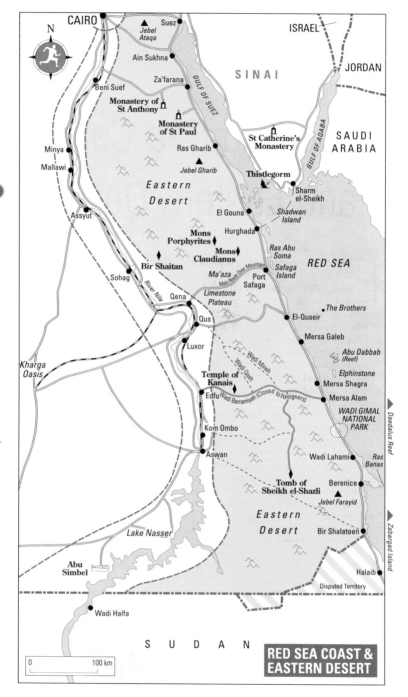

RED SEA COAST & EASTERN DESERT

0   100 km

monasteries. If totally off-the-beaten-track destinations are your thing, the Eastern Desert has more to offer than at first appears.

The Red Sea monasteries

Secreted amid the arid Red Sea Hills, Egypt's oldest **monasteries** – dedicated to **St Paul** and **St Anthony** – trace their origins back to the infancy of Christian monasticism, observing rituals that have scarcely changed over sixteen centuries. This tangible link with the primitive church gives them a special resonance for believers, but you don't have to be religious to appreciate their tranquil atmosphere and imposing setting – there's also scope for **bird-watching** in the vicinity.

Though neither monastery is directly accessible by public transport, they can be reached in several ways. The main thing to realize is that a quick visit is impossible, and no one is in any hurry once you get there. If you feel OK about travelling with devout believers, it's best to join the **pilgrim tours** arranged from Cairo by the Coptic Patriarchate (22 Sharia Ramses, Abbassiya; ☏02/396-0025) or the YMCA (72 Sharia al-Gumhorriya, downtown; ☏02/591-7360), which dispatches an occasional minibus. Coptic churches in Luxor or Hurghada may also run tours on a nonprofit basis. If you're travelling independently, chartering a **taxi** for the six- to eight-hour excursion should cost about £E400 from Suez, or £E700 from Cairo; taxis from Za'farana might do a four- to five-hour jaunt for around £E180. To drive from one monastery to the other (82km) takes about ninety minutes.

The cheapest way to see the monasteries combines **public transport**, **hitching** and **walking**. Outside of the hottest months, this shouldn't be dangerous providing you bring ample water and minimal luggage. Any bus from Cairo or Suez to Hurghada can drop you at the **turn-off for St Paul's Monastery** (26km south of Za'farana and 152km south of Suez), recognizable by its plastic-roofed bus shelter. Young Copts alight here, confident of hitching to the monastery, 13km uphill, for there's a fair amount of traffic along the well-paved road. Another place to try to cadge a lift is the cafeteria of the *Sahara Inn* motel (see p.731). Otherwise, you can approach St Anthony's Monastery on one of the service taxis running between Beni Suef and Za'farana. From the signposted turn-off 33km west of Za'farana, it's 15km uphill to the monastery, with some hitching prospects. It's also possible to hike between the two monasteries along a trail across the top of the plateau. This is quite demanding, so it's strongly recommended to engage a guide; you've a better chance of doing so at the Monastery of St Paul than at St Anthony.

Both monasteries are open daily from 9am to 5pm, but visitors are not permitted during Christmas or Lent. There are **dormitories** at the monasteries, though to stay in them you need written permission from the "residence" in Cairo (26 El-Kenisa El Morcosia St, Kolet Beck, Cairo; ☏02/590-0218), which is often refused, particularly if you are not part of a religious group. Both monasteries have **cafeterias**, and St Paul's has a shop selling basic foodstuffs, but you might want to bring your own supplies. Smoking and drinking alcohol are forbidden here, and you should respect the monasteries' conventions on dress and behaviour.

The Monastery of St Anthony

West of Za'farana, a wide valley cleaves the Galala Plateau and sets the road on course for the Nile, 168km away. Called **Wadi Arraba**, its name derives from the carts that once delivered provisions to the monastery, though legend attributes it to the pharaoh's chariots that pursued the Israelites towards the Red Sea. Turning off the road and south into the hills, it's possible to spot the monastery sited beneath a dramatic ridge of cliffs, known as Mount Qalah. If in doubt, ask anyone you encounter to point you towards Deir Amba Antonyos or Deir Qaddis Antwan.

Lofty walls with an interior catwalk surround the **Monastery of St Anthony**, whose lanes of two-storey dwellings, churches, mills and gardens of vines, olive and palms basically amount to a village. Formerly self-sufficient, the community now gets most of its food either from Cairo or its own farm near Beni Suef, but remains dependent on water from its **spring**, where Arab legend has it that Miriam, sister of Moses, bathed during the Exodus.

△ The Monastery of St Anthony

St Anthony

To many, **St Anthony** (251–356) is considered the "father of monasticism", and his life certainly coincided with a sea-change in Christianity's position. When Anthony was orphaned at the age of 18, he placed his sister in a convent, sold his possessions and became a hermit. Christians faced growing persecution at the time – the "Era of Martyrs" from which the Coptic calendar is dated – but the transformation of Christianity into a state religion in 313 caused many believers to view the Church as tainted by worldliness and foreign influences, and the hermit's life as a purer alternative. Admirers pursued Anthony ever deeper into the wilderness, camping out beneath Mount Qalah, where he dwelt in a cave until his death at the age of 105.

Icons depict the saint clothed in animal skins, barefoot and white-bearded, with an escort of lions. A century later, the Greek scholar Athanasius recounted his privations and visions in that prototypical work of Christian hagiography, the *Life of Anthony*, basis for the depictions of Anthony in the Wilderness throughout the next millennia of Coptic and Western art.

Some of the churches date from the early twentieth century and new ones are under construction. An English-speaking monk will give you a partial tour, which varies with each visitor; don't expect to see everything, as some areas are off limits. Highlights include the **keep**, a soot-blackened **bakery** and a **library** of over 1700 manuscripts. The oldest of the five churches is dedicated to the monastery's namesake, who may be buried underneath it. Be sure not to miss the wall paintings, some of which date back to the seventh century and have recently been restored to their former glory after years hidden under layers of soot, candle grease and grime. During Lent (when the gates are locked and deliveries are winched over the walls), monks celebrate the liturgy in the twelve-domed Church of St Luke, dating from 1776. A small **museum** details the monastery's history; next door is a well-stocked bookshop which sells books about the monastery and the Coptic Church in Egypt, as well as souvenirs and postcards.

All of these buildings are recent compared to the monastery's foundation, shortly after Anthony's death in 356. A sojourn by St John the Short (whose body was later stolen by other monks) is all that's recorded of its early **history**, but an influx of refugees from Wadi Natrun, and then Melkite monks, occurred during the sixth and seventh centuries. Subsequently pillaged by Bedouin and razed by Nasr al-Dawla, the monastery was restored during the twelfth century by Coptic monks, from whose ranks several Ethiopian bishops were elected. After a murderous revolt by the monastery servants, it was reoccupied by Coptic, Syrian and Ethiopian monks.

Today's permanent brethren, headed by Bishop Yustus, are university graduates and ex-professionals – not unlike the kind of people drawn to monasticism in the fourth century AD. A typical day at the monastery begins at 4am, with two hours of prayer and hymns followed by communion and Mass, all before breakfast.

St Anthony's Cave

Early morning or late afternoon is the best time to ascend to **St Anthony's Cave** (*maghara*), 2km from, and 276m above, the monastery (bring water). After passing a sculpture of St Anthony carved into the mountain rock, you'll face 1200 steps (45min) up to the cave, but the stunning views from 680m above the Red Sea reward your effort. Technicolour wadis and massifs spill down into the azure gulf, with Sinai's mountains rising beyond. The cave where Anthony spent his last 25 years contains medieval graffiti and modern *tilbas*, scraps of paper bearing supplications inscribed with "Remember, Lord, your servant", which pilgrims stick into cracks in the rock. **Birdlife** – hoopoes, desert larks, ravens, blue rock thrushes and pied wagtails – is surprisingly abundant, and you might glimpse shy **gazelles**.

The Monastery of St Paul

The **Monastery of St Paul** has always been overshadowed by St Anthony's. Its titular founder (not to be confused with the apostle Paul) was only 16 and an orphan when he fled Alexandria to escape Emperor Decius' persecutions, making him the earliest known hermit. Shortly before his death in 348, Paul was visited by Anthony and begged him to bring the robe of Pope Athanasius, for Paul to be buried in. Anthony departed to fetch this, but on the way back had a vision of Paul's soul being carried up to heaven by angels, and arrived to find him dead. While Anthony was wondering what to do, two lions appeared and dug a grave for the body, so Anthony shrouded it in the robe and took Paul's tunic of palm leaves as a gift for the pope, who subsequently wore it at Christmas, Epiphany and Easter.

The monastery (called Deir Amba Bula or Deir Mari Bolus) was a form of posthumous homage by Paul's followers: its turreted walls are built around the cave where he lived for decades. To a large extent, its fortunes have followed those of its more prestigious neighbour. In 1484 all its monks were slain by the Bedouin, who occupied St Paul's for eighty years. Rebuilt by Patriarch Gabriel VII, it was again destroyed near the end of the sixteenth century.

The monastery is much smaller than St Anthony's and a little more primitive looking. It boasts four churches, but the **Church of St Paul** is its spiritual centre, a cave-church housing the remains of the saint. The walls of the church are painted with murals generally thought inferior to those of St Anthony's, though they have been well preserved. A monk will show you round the chapels and identify their icons: notice the angel of the furnace with Shadrach, Meshach and Abednego, and the ostrich eggs hung from the ceiling – a symbol of the Resurrection. The southern sanctuary of the larger **Church of St Michael** contains a gilded icon of the head of John the Baptist on a dish. When Bedouin raided the monastery, its monks retreated into the five-storey **keep**, supplied with spring water by a hidden canal. Nowadays this is not enough to sustain the monks and their guests, so water is brought in from outside.

There is a small shop selling supplies and a reasonably priced cafeteria just outside the monastery grounds.

Ain Sukhna and El Gouna

Without private transport or a firm intention to visit the Red Sea monasteries (see p.727), it's hardly worth stopping between Suez and Hurghada. Heading south past the oil refineries and natural gas refineries that appear at intervals all along the coast, you'll see parched highlands rising inland. The **Jebel Ataqa** is the northernmost range in the Eastern Desert and an old Bedouin smuggling route by which hashish reached Cairo; Henri de Monfried sent his cargo this way.

From Suez, a seventy-kilometre series of beaches and coves marks the area around **AIN SUKHNA**, where middle-class Cairenes come to picnic at weekends. Ain Sukhna's name derives from the **hot springs** (35°C) that originate in the Jebel Ataqa, but it's the sea that attracts people. Light patches offshore indicate **coral reefs**, ideal for snorkelling, while rusty barbed-wire fences delineate areas sown with land mines (beneath the cliffs). There are paying **beaches** (£E20–40) in front of the *Ain Sukhna* and *Mena Oasis* hotels; other stretches are free.

If you haven't got a car, Ain Sukhna is best reached by **bus from Suez**. A growing number of **resorts** in the area attract plenty of affluent Egyptians, but hardly any foreigners. Ten kilometres south of Suez is the welcoming *Palmera* (T062/341-0816/7, Wwww.palmerabeachresort.com; ●), with three enormous swimming pools and several restaurants and bars. Other swish places to stay include *Portrait* (T062/332-5560, F333-2003; ●), 59km south of Suez, with a full range of facilities from a billiards room to a pastry shop, and the *Mena Oasis* (T062/329-0850, F329-0855; half board ●), 67km south of Suez, with a disco and over a kilometre of beach. The only budget accommodation in the area is the *Sahara Inn* motel (no phone or a/c; ●), about 10km south of **Za'farana** along the desolate, windblown highway.

The next stop for buses south of Ain Sukhna is at **Ras Gharib**, an oil town buffeted year-round by winds. The place holds little appeal, except perhaps to mountaineers interested in tackling **Jebel Gharib** (1757m).

El Gouna

Approximately 22km north of Hurghada lies the vast tourist resort of **El Gouna** (Wwww.elgouna.com), already popular with the Egyptian jet-set, although its Western clientele is not quite as well heeled, being more of a package-tour crowd who get good deals by booking in advance.

Built on a series of islands linked by purpose-built bridges and canals, El Gouna covers 17,000 square kilometres of land, supports 10,000 staff and includes four power plants, an international airport and several factories. The infrastructure includes a brewery that makes Sakkara and Löwenbrau beer, a winery producing Obelisque wine, a cheese factory making mozzarella, a state-of-the-art hospital with decompression chamber (T012 218-7550), plus an eighteen-hole **golf** course and a **casino**. There are two shopping centres, the main one having an open-air **cinema**, cafés, restaurants, bars, nightclubs, a school, **banks**, two travel agencies, a **museum**, **aquarium** and a **post office**. For those staying in Hurghada, there is a free half-hourly shuttle bus to the resort run by El Gouna Transport. Most hotels have **dive centres** attached (a list of dive sites in the vicinity appears on p.741), and water sports, horse-riding, go-karting, tennis, squash, and even flights in a microlight plane are also on offer. If you fancy a quick nip and tuck to complete your holiday, El Gouna even has its own plastic-surgery centre. The private **hospital** in El Gouna is recommended (emergencies T065/354-0011, Wwww.elgounahospital.com).

A **private airstrip** is served by two flights a week run by the charter company SunAir in Cairo (T02/335-7440, Wwww.sunair-eg.com). These leave Cairo on Thursday and Saturday at 6pm and return to the capital at 8pm.

Accommodation

There are more than a dozen **hotels** in the resort, ranging from three- to five-star, including a *Sheraton* and *Club Med*, as well as several clusters of private villas.

Mövenpick Resort T065/354-4501, Wwww
.moevenpick-elgouna.com. Luxurious a/c rooms with bath, balcony or patio overlooking the sea, pool or gardens, and satellite TV. There are four swimming pools, a dive centre (Wwww.divetribe.com),

kiteboarding, a 3km stretch of beach, and the latest addition is a health spa. ●
Sheraton Miramar T065/354-5606, Wwww
.sheraton.com/elgouna. Built on nine islands, its 338 a/c rooms have terraces, sea views and

8

THE RED SEA COAST AND EASTERN DESERT | Ain Sukhna and El Gouna

731

satellite TV. Two main swimming pools, three for children, with a kids' club and a dive centre. Wheelchair friendly. **❼**

🏌 **Steigenberger Golf Resort** ☎065/358-0140, Ⓦwww.steigenbergergolf-elgouna .com. German-owned, plush hotel with 18-hole championship golf course and a spa. It's won awards for both its outstanding architecture and environmental policies. **❽**

Three Corners Rihana Inn ☎065/358-0025, Ⓦwww.threecorners.com. A/c studios for two or four people, terraces with pool or mountain views, kitchenettes and satellite TV, and access to the beach and better facilities of its four-star sister hotel *Three Corners Rihana Resort*. It's home to the Colona Dive Centre (☎065/358-0113, Ⓦwww.corona.com) and the equally good Easy Divers (☎012 230-5202, Ⓦwww.easydivers-redsea.com). **❼**

Eating and drinking

Among the profusion of venues for eating, drinking and dancing are poolside cafés, karaoke joints, discos, Bedouin tents, formal bistros overlooking the marina, pastry shops and *sheesha* cafés. Holidaymakers on full-board packages can use the "dine around" system to patronize other hotels by getting a food credit from their own hotel; more details are listed in the "Dining" section of Ⓦwww.elgouna.com.

Hurghada (Ghardaka)

In the course of two decades, **HURGHADA** has been transformed from a humble fishing village of a few hundred souls into a booming town of over 150,000 people, drawn here from all over Egypt by the lure of making money. This phenomenal growth is almost entirely due to **tourism**, which accounts for 95 percent of the local economy. Yet it's worth taking Hurghada's claims to be a seaside resort with a handful of salt. Unlike Sinai, where soft sand and gorgeous reefs are within easy reach and women can bathe unhassled, Hurghada's public beaches are distant or uninviting, while the best marine life is far offshore. If you're not into diving or discos, you'll soon find that Hurghada lacks charm – though you have to admire its commercial gusto; many of the townsfolk come from Luxor's west bank, where tourism has been a way of life for generations.

While package tourists laze in their resorts, independent travellers often feel hard done by. Paying for boat trips and private beaches is unavoidable if you're

---

Russians in Hurghada

Hurghada's popularity with **Russian tourists** began in 1994, and was initially greeted with joy by hoteliers, whose occupancy rates had plummeted following terrorist attacks in the Nile Valley. Being inured to chaos and inflation back home, the Russians weren't deterred by bomb scares and proved to be big spenders. Sadly, however, cultural differences soon soured things, and many locals now regard them all as drunks or whores, while the Russians reciprocate with equal contempt. It doesn't help that some of the Russians really *are* mafiosi or prostitutes (the latter ply their trade in hotels as "personal assistants") – nor that the Egyptians are irked by the lack of a common language with which to hustle them.

Aside from filling up the holiday villages and replacing Egyptian bellydancers in the Oriental shows, the Russians haven't had much effect on other tourists – except perhaps for the bewilderment when they first see restaurant signs advertising *borsch* and *pelmeni*. As the Russians generally have little interest in diving (being content to make descents in the *Sindbad Submarine* (see p.742), or snorkelling trips to Giftun Island), not much mixing occurs, except in Hurghada's discos.

to enjoy Hurghada's assets, and although conditions for diving, windsurfing and deep-sea fishing are great, the **cost** is high, with real bargains limited to accommodation. Nor will you save much by self-catering; everything in the shops is more expensive than in Cairo or the Nile Valley. As tour groups come year round, there's no "off" season; **peak times** are the European Christmas and Easter holidays and the Russian vacation period of August and September. Budget hotels are most in demand over winter, when backpackers use Hurghada as a transit point between the Nile Valley and the Sinai.

The town itself is a hotchpotch of utilitarian structures, garish hotels, gaudy boutiques and sporadic patches of waste ground. Coming in from the north, look out for the windmill fields, built to harness wind power to generate electricity; until fairly recently, they stood alone in the desert, but today they nestle in among hotels and new construction sites.

Within Hurghada, most of the coastline from Ed-Dahar in the north to the so-called New Hurghada in the south is shielded from view by the line of resorts, so if you've come for the beach, be prepared to pay for the pleasure. While some may be put off by Hurghada's commercialism, other tourists will take solace in what they can discover underwater: a score of coral islands and reefs within a few hours' reach by boat, and many other amazing dive-sites that can be visited on liveaboards.

Approaches to Hurghada

Hurghada is more accessible by public transport than its location might suggest. Vehicles go flat out along the coastal highway and desert roads, but a full tank of petrol is essential – there are few pumps en route.

• **From Alexandria** Superjet has one **bus** daily to Hurghada (9hr; £E90).

• **From Cairo** There are frequent **buses** daily to Hurghada from the Turgoman terminal (6hr; £E60). El Gouna Transport Company (☏02/574-1533) also run about a dozen comfortable a/c buses throughout the day and night (6hr; £E60–70) from their office near the *Ramses Hilton*, just north of the Egyptian Antiquities Museum. You can also catch these buses half an hour later at Nasser City Station (Autostrad Road). EgyptAir **flights** (2–3 daily; 1hr; $120) should ideally be booked well in advance.

• **From Suez** The 410-kilometre journey from Suez can be covered in five hours by **service taxi** (£E30 per person), or at a less perilous speed by one of a dozen or so daily **buses** (5hr; £E35).

• **From Sinai** The **catamaran** trip from Sharm el-Sheikh is quick and convenient; see p.682 for details.

• **From the Nile Valley** During winter, hordes of travellers come to Hurghada by bus from Aswan (2 daily; 7hr; £E40) and Luxor (around 6 daily; 4–5hr; £E30) via Qena and Safaga. Alternatively, take a service taxi to Qena, walk to another taxi depot and catch a service taxi on to Hurghada (4hr; £E20). There are also a couple of buses daily from Assyut. A few service taxis cross the desert between Beni Suef and Za'farana, or Qift and El-Quseir but foreigners are not permitted to use these routes. EgyptAir may run flights from Luxor during peak travel periods.

Orientation

Although Hurghada stretches for nearly 40km along the coast, it's easily divisible into three zones. The town proper – known as **Ed-Dahar** – is separated from the coast by a barren rock massif known as Jebel el-Afish, so you rarely glimpse the sea. Ed-Dahar's evolution is apparent as administrative

HURGHADA

El Gouna (22km) & ⬤A

Police

See 'Ed-Dahar' map for detail

⬤B SHERATON ROAD

Superjet and El Gouna
Bus Stations

Naval Hyperbaric
Medical Centre

See inset map
for detail

N

Bowling Alley ⬤
⬤1

Duty Free Shop

✈

EgyptAir ⬤G
ℹ
Tourist
Police ⬤2 ⬤H ⬤I
Aquascope

HADABA

SHERATON ROAD

⬤C

⬤D

⬤E
⬤F

Duty Free Shop

⬤J

⬤K

El-Arabi ⬤L

⬤M

TARIQ AL-KURA

HURGHADA - SAFAGA ROAD

⬤N

⬤O

⬤3

RESTAURANTS, BARS & CLUBS

Abo Khadega	5
Agra	6
Alf Leila Wa Leila	3
Bonanza	13
Coppa Cabana	14
Dome	J
El-Joker	4
Far East Korea	16
Felfela's	18
Fish House	11
Hard Rock Café	2
KFC	1 & 12
Liquid Lounge	17
McDonald's	10
Moby Dick	7
Papa's Bar	15
Papa's Beach Bar	9
Pizza Hut	1
Spaghetti	8

El-Fanadir Reef

El-Fanous

Umm Gamar Island

Islands not to scale

Careless Reef

Big Giftun

Small Giftun

Abu Ramada

Abu Ramada
Gota

Magawish
Island

RED SEA

ACCOMMODATION

Andrea's	S
Conrad	O
Coral Beach Rotana	U
El-Samaka	H
Giftun Beach Resort	F
Golden Five	T
Golden Sun	P
Golf	Q
Hilton Hurghada Plaza	B
Hilton Resort	K
InterContinental	Z
Jasmin Village	J
La Perla	N
Magawish Village	D
Marine Sports Club	L
Marriott Beach Resort	G
Princess Club	C
Regina Style Resort	I
Sindbad Beach Resort	R
Sofitel	E
Youth hostel	M
	A

SIGALA

Airport

Duty Free

Misr
Travel
ℹ

Police
SIGALA
SQUARE
⬤P
⬤5
⬤6
Fedex
⬤Q

⬤4
Thomas
Cook

New
Harbour

Sharm

Old Harbour

N

⬤7
@⬤10
⬤8
⬤11
⬤R
⬤9

⬤12
⬤14
⬤13 El Gouna Bus Office
⬤15 *Public Beach*
⬤16
⬤S
Redcon
Mall
⬤17
⬤18

0 ——— 500 m

Abu Hashish
Cave

0 ——— 2 km

buildings give way to hotels, shops and a maze of mud-brick homes at the feet of Jebel el-Afish. Its amorphous downtown embraces the touristy bazaar quarter and a flourishing strip of restaurants, shops and hotels known as "**Hospital Street**", which spreads from Sharia Abdel Aziz Mustafa to the Aquarium on the Corniche. The main thoroughfare is **Tariq El-Nasr** (aka El-Nasr Way), whose busiest stretch lies between the bus station and Ed-Dahar's boarded-up telephone exchange (known as the *centraal*), which acts as a terminus for local public transport. The coastal Corniche is widely known as the Sheraton road, in reference to the now-closed landmark hotel that has long been its northernmost feature.

From Ed-Dahar, two main roads run 2–4km south to **Sigala**, which contains the modern **port** of Hurghada and a mass of restaurants and hotels, squeezed in wherever the terrain allows. Beyond Sigala is nothing but desert and an endless array of **coastal holiday villages** and construction sites, linked by slip roads to the Hurghada–Safaga road and dignified with the name of **New Hurghada**. This extends more than 30km south of Sigala and there seems nothing to prevent it from ultimately linking up with the resorts at Port Safaga, 50km south.

Arrival, information and transport

Most independent travellers **arrive** in Ed-Dahar at the **bus station** on the southern edge of the downtown area, though coming by Superjet or El Gouna buses, you'll arrive at their terminals about 1km further south along **Tariq El-Nasr**. If you arrive at the Superjet terminal and you're planning to stay in Ed-Dahar, you might want to hop into one of the ubiquitous white minivans (£E1) that ply Tariq El-Nasr. Service taxis from the Nile Valley wind up at the **taxi station** on Tariq El-Nasr, near the Police Station.

People arriving by boat from Sinai will disembark at the **harbour** in Sigala, whence you could walk to several mid-range places or catch a minivan (£E1) or taxi (£E10) to the centre of Ed-Dahar. Most package tourists who fly into the **airport** off the Hurghada–Safaga road are whisked to their resorts in buses; a taxi into Ed-Dahar will cost £E20–30.

Large and airy, with helpful staff, Hurghada's **tourist information centre** (daily 8.30am–8pm; ☎065/346-3221) is somewhat let down by a lack of useful leaflets; it's located opposite the faded *Grand Hotel* in New Hurghada. Look out for the *Connect Guide*, a monthly magazine with a **listings guide** and area map; it's free from most hotels. The free colour magazine *Red Sea Bulletin* (Ⓦwww .redseapages.com) comes out twice a month with articles and information about Hurghada in English, German and Russian, and can be picked up at hotels and dive centres, while *The Complete Map of Hurghada* shows the location of all the coastal resorts and can be bought from most souvenir shops for around £E20.

In addition, private agencies, hotels, dive centres and individual fixers are all ready to help – for a price. Information you're given by any of these in Hurghada should be regarded as suspect, since everyone earns a commission on whatever you can be induced to spend. Normally this doesn't matter too much – except when they steer you towards dodgy, potentially lethal, dive centres.

Transport

While **walking** is fine for getting around Ed-Dahar, transport is needed to reach Sigala or anywhere further south. **Private minibuses** run up and down the coast along the Corniche, as well as Tariq El-Nasr to the airport and beyond. You'll pay £E0.50 for a short hop or £E1 for rides between Ed-Dahar, Sigala and New Hurghada, and £E3 for a trip as far south as the *Jasmin Village*, 21km

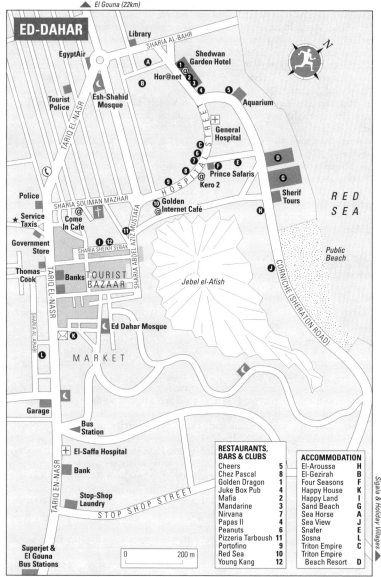

ED-DAHAR

El Gouna (22km)

Library

SHARIA AL-BAHR

EgyptAir

Shedwan
Garden Hotel

Hor@net

Esh-Shahid
Mosque

Tourist
Police

Aquarium

General
Hospital

Prince Safaris
Kero 2

Sherif
Tours

R E D
S E A

Police

Service
Taxis

SHARIA SOLIMAN MAZHAR

Come
In Cafe

Golden
Internet Café

Government
Store

SHARIA SHEIKH SEBAK

Thomas
Cook

Banks

TOURIST
BAZAAR

Jebel el-Afish

Public
Beach

Ed Dahar Mosque

M A R K E T

Garage

Bus
Station

El-Saffa Hospital

Bank

Stop-Shop
Laundry

STOP SHOP STREET

Superjet &
El Gouna
Bus Stations

0   200 m

RESTAURANTS, BARS & CLUBS		ACCOMMODATION	
Cheers	5	El-Aroussa	H
Chez Pascal	8	El-Gezirah	B
Golden Dragon	1	Four Seasons	F
Juke Box Pub	4	Happy House	K
Mafia	2	Happy Land	I
Mandarine	3	Sand Beach	G
Nirvana	7	Sea Horse	A
Papas II	4	Sea View	J
Peanuts	6	Snafer	E
Pizzeria Tarboush	11	Sosna	L
Portofino	9	Triton Empire	C
Red Sea	10	Triton Empire	
Young Kang	12	Beach Resort	D

Sigala & Holiday Villages

Sigala & New Hurghada Holiday Villages

away. The minibuses run 24 hours a day (though after midnight you may pay prices similar to that of a taxi), and can be flagged down at any point along their route. Some tourists scoot around on rented **bicycles**, which are okay in town if you can handle the traffic, but are not up to trips down the coastal highway, which is often buffeted by strong crosswinds. Lots of places around Ed-Dahar's bazaar rent bikes for £E15–25 per day; rates in Sigala are slightly higher.

Private taxis charge around £E5–10 for a ride in Ed-Dahar, £E10 to Sigala, and £E25–40 to the furthest holiday villages. The going rate to charter a taxi for the day is £E180 (for up to 6hr), provided you don't go any further than Safaga. If you want to go further afield, you could **rent a car**: local firms are the cheapest, though their deals tend to be for limited mileage on poorly maintained cars.

Accommodation

Well over a hundred **hotels** and **holiday villages** operate in Hurghada, with more being built: demand is generally so high that most villages boast occupancy rates of at least eighty percent. Arriving at Hurghada's bus station, you'll be mobbed by **hotel touts**, offering free transport to their establishment. If you're bent on locating a hotel on your own, bear in mind that few streets are named, and there are effectively no house numbers.

If you're coming for the diving, a **package deal** is the cheapest option, and you won't have to do the rounds of the dive centres. Hotels catering to **independent travellers** get a commission for each guest that they sign up for a diving course, so if you book one with your hotel when you get there, you may be able to negotiate a discount on the price of a room. As in Luxor and Aswan, many hotels make more on trips and commissions than on rooms.

Hurghada has a **youth hostel** (☏065/354-4989 or 350-0054; HI members £E30, non-HI £E35), on the beach 5km north of town and a long way from anything, next to the Marine Institute of Oceanic Studies. It has separate blocks for men and women, containing spartan rooms with fans, bunk beds, and clean shared bathrooms; there's a three-day maximum stay.

If you're hoping to stay and work, **renting an apartment** may make sense. Most rentals are arranged through dive centres or hotels that employ foreigners, but if you put the word out, prospective landlords – and housemates – should come forward. It's also worth checking the classifieds in the *Red Sea Pages Bulletin* (see p.735). Expect to pay about £E1500 per month (excluding bills) for a two-bedroom apartment near the beach, and a little less in the Amal district, between Ed-Dahar and Sigala.

Hurghada's **water** has to be piped from the Nile Valley, so depending on your hotel's storage capacity it might be cut off for several hours a day. Profligate consumption means that others go short. Foreigners who live here strongly advise against **drinking** the tap water, and if the thought of cooling down by standing under the sprinklers that irrigate the gardens of some of the upmarket hotels appeals, think again: this (barely) treated sewage is largely responsible for the stink that blankets the town.

Downtown Ed-Dahar

Most **budget places** cluster around the bazaar or the "strip" of cafés and shops between Sharia Abdel Aziz Mustafa and the Corniche, while **mid-range hotels** are sited off the main road near the Esh-Shahid Mosque and the coastal **holiday villages**. In general hotels are not as "luxury" as they claim to be – a good guide would be to subtract one star from their rating. Breakfast is included unless stated otherwise, and you can generally count on hot water. All the following places are marked on the map on p.736 except where noted.

El-Aroussa Corniche ☏ & ℱ 065/354-8434. Nice a/c rooms with bath, plus an indoor pool and music bar. Guests can use the beach at the pricier *Geisum Village* across the road. ❸

El-Gezirah Off Sharia al-Bahr ☏ 065/354-7785, ℱ 354-3708. Besides spacious a/c rooms with TV, this has a bar, restaurant and disco, friendly management, and offers free use of the pool and disco at the *Sand Beach*. Mainly German, Dutch and Russian groups. Discounts offered if it's quiet. ❻

Four Seasons Near the Corniche end of the strip ☏ & ⓕ 065/354-5456, ⓔ forseasonshurghada @hotmail.com. Simple, cleanish rooms, all with bath, balcony and partial sea views; some newly renovated rooms with a/c and satellite TV are also available for a large premium. ❻

Happy House Between the Ed-Dahar Mosque and Tariq El-Nasr ☏ 012 358-5016. Small, friendly hotel of long standing, with just four rooms (with fan) and a communal bathroom with one hot shower; there's also a kitchen. Inquire with Mustafa at the shop downstairs. ❷

Happy Land Sharia Sheikh Sebak ☏ 065/354-7373. Slightly shabby rooms, some en suite, in the noisy tourist bazaar. Mostly used by Egyptians, and within earshot of a mosque. ❶

Hilton Hurghada Plaza South end of the Corniche (see the main Hurghada map) ☏ 065/354-9745, ⓦ www.hiltonworldresorts.com. Massive but isolated five-star resort perched on an arid hill between Ed-Dahar and Sigala. Still, it does have a full range of facilities; if you're going to stay here, you probably won't bother leaving its confines. ❻

Sand Beach Corniche ☏ 065/354-7992. Four-star holiday village with three pools, a beach and diving centre, billiards room and disco. Popular with Russians. ❻

Sea Horse Off Sharia al-Bahr ☏ 065/354-8704. Comfortable rooms with private bath, a/c and balcony. There's a restaurant, bar, disco, billiards, backyard pool and sea views. Residents can use its beach, and the one at the *New Sea Horse*, by *Hilton Hurghada Plaza*. US$35

Sea View Corniche ☏ 065/354-5959, ⓕ 354-6779. Modern a/c rooms with baths and satellite TV, plus a tiny swimming pool, a seafood restaurant and free use of the *Sea Horse's* beach. ❹

🏃 **Snafer** Corniche ☏ & ⓕ 065/354-0260, ⓔ ashrafhurghada@hotmail.com. A pleasant hotel with courteous staff and well-kept rooms – probably Ed-Dahar's best-value hotel in its price bracket. The upper floors have good sea views, but reaching them means managing the stairs (there's no elevator). ❸

Sosna Off Tariq El-Nasr ☏ 065/354-6647. Carpeted rooms with fan and bedside lamps; private bathrooms are optional. With a relaxed atmosphere, it's used mainly by Egyptians. ❷

Triton Empire Hospital St ☏ 065/354-7186, ⓦ www.threecorners.com. Dominating the skyline, this large hotel has comfortable a/c en-suite rooms, satellite TV and balconies with sea views. Guests can use the beach at the nearby *Triton Empire Beach Resort*, though it's not advisable to walk between the two in beach wear. ❻

Triton Empire Beach Resort Corniche ☏ 065/354-7816, ⓦ www.threecorners.com. Comfortable a/c en-suite rooms with satellite TV, some with sea views. It's less opulent than some of the other hotels on this part of the beach, but the rooms are a shade cheaper. ❺

Sigala

Despite a relatively good range of places to eat and drink, it's hard to see why anyone would want to stay in Sigala, since there are better mid-range options in Ed-Dahar and ritzier holiday villages in New Hurghada. However, if everywhere else is full, you could try the following options.

Andrea's El-Hadaba Rd ☏ 065/344-2251. Pleasant Italian-owned place, home to the Bubbles dive centre, a/c rooms, three bars and a swimming pool. Popular with young English, German and French tourists. ❹

Golden Sun ☏ 065/394-3862, ⓕ 394-4403. Basic place with funky decor (check out the stuffed goat and fox in the lobby) and welcoming staff. Tucked into an alley near Misr Travel. ❷

Golf ☏ 065/344-2828, ⓕ 344-4328. Located on the main road by Misr Travel, with rambling, the dim hallways that open up to decent rooms, some with sea views. ❷

Regina Style Resort ☏ 065/344-2275. On the beach with two pools and a jetty, health club, tennis court and kids' club. There are more than four hundred a/c rooms and chalets, too. Half board ❻

New Hurghada

The **holiday villages** of New Hurghada take independent travellers if trade is slack. They're all fully self-contained, so there's zero incentive to leave their complexes. Unless stated otherwise, all the holiday villages reviewed (see map on p.734) have air-conditioning, at least one pool, a diving centre, beach and disco. Where the clientele is mainly from certain countries, you could feel at a disadvantage if you don't speak the right language. The distances stated below are measured from the bus station in Ed-Dahar.

Conrad International 22km ☏ 065/346-0020, ⓦ www.conradhotels.com. Five-star resort with an onyx-floored lobby and an outsized pool; Germans make up a large proportion of the clientele. ❼

Coral Beach Rotana 28km ☏ 065/346-1610, ⓦ www.coralbeachrotanaresorthurghada.com. Rooms are stylish and equipped with satellite TV and minibar; facilities include two pools, tennis, squash and horse-riding, and there's a large beach with reefs offshore. Mainly caters to Italians. ❼

El-Samaka 16km ☏ 065/346-5143, ⓦ www.elsamakabeach.com. Three hotels under the same management, the *Beach Hotel*, *Komfort Hotel* and *Desert Inn*. Accommodation is in bungalows (a/c midday and evenings only) with a small beach and windsurfing lagoon. Used by German and Russian tour groups. ❻

Giftun Beach Resort 14km ☏ 065/346-3040, ⓦ www.giftunbeachresort.com. Spanish-style chalets with fans, fronting a good beach and windsurfing lagoon. All-inclusive of meals and activities except for water sports. ❼

🏃 **Golden Five** 25km ☏ 065/344-7744, ⓦ www.golden5.com. A vast Vegas-style combination of theme park and hotel complex, with daily shows, a replica Egyptian village, an aqua park, enormous pools, a cable-car lift, and dozens of bars and restaurants. The disco at the main entrance is open to all from 11pm. ❼

Hilton Resort 17km ☏ 065/346-5036, ⓦ www.hiltonworldwideresorts.com. With a full range of facilities and the same five-star rating as its sister *Plaza* hotel (see p.738), but a bit older and pricier. ❼

InterContinental 17km ☏ 065/346-5100, ⓦ www.intercontinental.com. Opulent complex of rooms with bath, satellite TV and sea views. Amenities include a very large marina, health club and tennis courts. ❼

Jasmin Village 21km ☏ 065/346-0475, ⓔ info@alfa-travel.com. Simple rooms with satellite TV and fridge. Small beach with reef and windsurfing lagoons. Playground, zoo and aviary. Disabled access. Half board ❼

La Perla 6km ☏ & ⓕ 065/344-3280, ⓦ www.laperlahotel-eg.com. Pleasant and well managed, with a/c rooms and a swimming pool. A bit far from the action and the beach, but still popular with English groups. ❻

Magawish Village 19km ☏ 065/346-2621, ⓦ www.magawish.com. A former *Club Med*, with a big beach and good sports facilities, especially for wind- and kitesurfing, plus a children's playground. Half board ❼

Marine Sports Club 16km ☏ 065/346-3004, ⓕ 343-6007. Good-value a/c rooms with TV and fridge. Popular with Egyptian sport-fishing to aficionados. ❻

Marriott Beach Resort 11km ☏ 065/344-6950, ⓦ www.marriott.com. Five-star complex with a large pool and a small sandy beach, a marina, health club and residents-only disco. ❼

Princess Club 16km ☏ 065/344-7701, ⓕ 344-3109. Spacious a/c rooms with satellite TV and fridge, and three-storey villas equipped for self-catering. Small pool and windsurfing lagoon. ❻

Sindbad Beach Resort 13km ☏ 065/344-3261, ⓦ www.sindbad-group.com. Efficiently managed family-oriented four-star complex with lots of nightlife, a huge waterchute on the beach and an entertainment complex called Splash Park, offering dolphin shows. Also home to *Sindbad Submarine* (see p.742). Half board ❽

🏃 **Sofitel** 20km ☏ 065/344-4646, ⓦ www.sofitel.com. This classy pseudo-Moorish complex, with marble floors, lattice windows and a vast heated pool, is the best hotel on the strip. The management puts on events like themed dinners for which guests are encouraged to dress up. Used by Hayes & Jarvis tours. Half board ❼

Diving and snorkelling

It was **diving** that really put Hurghada on the map. The marine life here is broadly similar to that found off the coast of Sinai (see the *Egypt's underwater world* colour section), but the topography favours island corals over coastal reefs, with sharks, giant moray eels and manta rays in its deeper, rougher waters. The tide here is more dramatic, too; it drops by up to five metres from high to low tide, compared with a one-metre change in Sinai. Many islands have sheer-sided coral *ergs* (pillars) that are fantastic for drift diving, while others are shallow enough for snorkelling. There are about ten islands within day-trip range and over a score of sites that can be visited on extended dive safaris, or liveaboards.

As ever, dive **tourism** is its own worst enemy: once-rich coral and shellfish grounds have been devastated by the sheer weight of visitors. Hurghada welcomes hordes of tourists each week, and is home to more than one thousand tour boats. Anchoring on the reefs does irreparable damage to fragile corals, and those closest to the port have been hit especially hard. To help combat the problem, the **Underwater National Parks of the Red Sea and Protected Islands** (aka Marine Park) has introduced a new daily "environmental tax" for all divers (€3), snorkellers (€2) and those on diving safaris (€5), the proceeds of which are being ploughed back into Red Sea environmental projects. This is in addition to the standard per-person charge of €4 per day to dive the Giftun Islands and the nearby reefs and €5 per day for sites further south, such as Brothers and Zabargad. The problem is also being tackled by **HEPCA** (Hurghada Environmental Protection and Conservation Association; Ⓦ www .hepca.com), which is installing mooring buoys and trying to raise ecological awareness – but few of the local dive centres show much interest. Tourists can help by reporting any environmental or safety concerns to HEPCA, and by favouring dive centres which belong to HEPCA and which display a certificate from the **Egyptian Underwater Sports Federation**. You should also refrain from buying marine curios like clamshells (whose export is illegal).

A four- or five-day PADI Open Water course costs €300–350/$380–450 including the dive certificate; a two-day advanced course is €260–290/$340–375. Beginners can expect to pay around €75/$95 for two supervised dives. Scuba **equipment** is included in the price of courses, but otherwise costs around €25/$30 extra per day; renting snorkelling gear for a day costs about €6/$8. The average rate for a day's **boat diving** is €40–60/$50–75; most trips comprise two dives, separated by lunch, which is normally included in the price. Never hand over cash to someone on the street who promises to arrange a trip; book through a dive centre, where you can complain if things go wrong. You'll need to sign up and surrender your passport the night before; check that details are correctly noted, since wrongly documented passengers may be prevented from boarding. See p.741 for a list of reliable dive centres.

For longer trips, the Colona Dive Centre, based at *Magawish Village* (see p.739), can arrange **liveaboards** and diving packages (mostly lasting for a week) taking you further south to sites near Safaga, Mersa Alam, Wadi Gimal and Wadi Lahami, or even as far as the Zabargad Islands, about 100km southeast of Berenice and open only to boats with permits. The cost depends on factors like the vessel's amenities and the quality of the meals; expect to pay at least €80/$100 per person per day, though extra diving fees can add quite a bit to the cost depending on the location.

There are two **decompression chambers** in the Hurghada area: in El Gouna's hospital (see p.731) and the Mubarak Naval Hyperbaric & Emergency Medical Centre, in El-Dahar about 500 metres northwest of the police station (Ⓣ065/354-9150 or 354-4195).

Dive centres

Your life may depend on **choosing the right diving centre**; always check that the instructor is qualified, with valid ID and insurance, not merely photocopies. Many are freelancers who frequently change jobs, so even the best centres sometimes get bad ones. As a rule of thumb, it is safer to dive with the large outfits attached to holiday villages than with backstreet operators taking clients sent by budget hotels (whose recommendations can't be trusted). Of the one hundred or so dive centres in Hurghada, most are run by Europeans and tend to have higher standards than the locally managed outfits. The ones listed below are affiliated to HEPCA and thus subject to monitoring; in general, avoid those that aren't HEPCA-affiliated.

The thirty or so dive centres which are members of the **Diving Emergency Centre Organization** (DECO; ☎012 218-7550, ⓦ www.deco-international .de) encourage clients to pay €6 for three weeks' cover, which includes free use of the decompression chambers in Hurghada, El Gouna or Mersa Alam, doctor's fees, as well as equipment and medicines used in treatment, though not hospitalization or any transport for the injured person.

Aquanaut *Shedwan Golden Beach*, part of the same complex as the *Shedwan Garden*, Ed-Dahar ☎012 248-0463, ⓦ www.aquanaut.net.

Aquarius Diving Club *Marriott Beach Resort* ☎065/344-6950, ⓦ www.aquariusredsea.com.

Blue Heaven Divers *Regina Style Resort* ☎065/344-7833, ⓦ www.blueheaven-divers.com.

Colona *Magawish Village* ☎065/346-4631, ⓦ www .colona.com.

Divers International *Hilton Hurghada Plaza* ☎065/354-9745 ext 5507, ⓦ www.diversintl.com.

Dream Divers Corniche, close to *Cheers* bar; and in the *Shedwan Garden Hotel*, Ed-Dahar ☎010 631-0264, ⓦ www.dream-divers.info.

Easy Divers *Triton Empire Beach Resort* ☎012 230-5202, ⓦ www.easydivers-redsea.com.

El-Samaka *El-Samaka Beach Club* ☎065/346-5133, ⓦ www.el-samaka.com.

Emperor Divers *Hilton Resort* ☎065/344-4854, ⓦ www.emperordivers.com.

James & Mac *Giftun Beach Resort* ☎012 311-8923, ⓦ www.james-mac.com.

Jasmin Diving Center *Jasmin Village* ☎065/346-0475, ⓦ www.jasmin-diving.com.

Orca Tariq El-Nasr, between Ed-Dahar and Sigala ☎012 239-4784, ⓦ www.orca-diveclub-hurghada .com.

Sub Aqua *Sofitel* ☎065/346-4101, ⓦ www .subaqua-divecenter.com.

Subex Downtown, off the Corniche ☎065/354-8651, ⓦ www.subex.org.

Dive sites

Most sites within day-trip range are to the east and northeast of Hurghada. Inexperienced divers should be wary of the northerly reefs, where the currents are strongest. While many liveaboards go as far north as Ras Mohammed, sites to the south are regarded as more prestigious. All of the following are within day-trip range unless stated otherwise.

Abu Hashish Cave An underwater cave in the reef, once used as a dope-smugglers' cache.

Abu Ramada Three coral blocks covered in psychedelic-hued soft corals, off Giftun Island.

Abu Ramada Gota (aka "Aquarium"). Amazing standing *ergs* and 1500-year-old stony corals, with a profusion of bannerfish, sweetlips and spotted groupers.

Brothers Several *ergs* emerging from the deeps of the Red Sea, 80km northeast of El-Quseir. A popular liveaboard destination, now open only to boats with permits.

Careless Reef North of Giftun Island, and only accessible in mild weather conditions, this reef is the home of an extended community of moray eels.

Dolphin House A horseshoe-shaped reef 15km south of Mersa Alam, widely used by dolphins as a nursery for their young. HEPCA has recently installed buoys to prevent boats from entering. An excellent site for snorkelling.

El-Fanadir Beautiful reef slope and large table corals, to the north of Sigala.

El-Fanous Coral gardens just off Big Giftun Island, good for snorkelling as well as diving.

Giftun Island Most of the reefs on the Big and Small Giftun have been ruined by years of dive boats dropping their anchors onto the coral, and are now mostly visited by craft packed with snorkellers (€25/US$32 per person including equipment and lunch, but excluding entrance fee). Two notable spots are the Small Giftun Drift (fine reef-wall and lovely fan corals), and the Stone Beach on the northeast side of Big Giftun.

Shadwan Island Halfway to Sharm el-Sheikh, so out of day-trip range. Sheer walls and deep trenches here attract reef and oceanic sharks. Its lighthouse was of keen interest to de Monfried, when he navigated his boat through these waters in the early 1920s, with six hundred kilos of hashish secreted in its hold.

Thistlegorm This wreck (see p.673) is cheaper and slightly easier to reach from Sharm el-Sheikh.

Umm Gamar Island Sheer walls and caves, brilliant for drift diving. You can swim through a cave filled with thousands of silvery glassfish.

Snorkelling

The small reefs offshore from the *Shedwan* hotel complex in Ed-Dahar and the *Jasmin Village* in Hurghada have been subject to noticeable damage, though they do offer snorkellers a glimpse of fish and corals further out to sea. Most dive centres offer snorkelling trips and can recommend good locations at Giftun Island or elsewhere. An especially good deal is offered by Prince Safaris on Dr Sayed Koryem Street (℗065/354-9882 or ℗012 248-4015, Ⓦwww.prince-diving.com), behind the *Triton Empire Hotel*; it's run by friendly Bedouin brothers who grew up in Hurghada, and arranges snorkelling to Giftun Island for €15 (with lunch), which is around half the price charged by most of the other operators and agents.

Beaches, pools and water sports

Diving apart, Hurghada presents itself as an all-round beach resort. While the **public beach** in Sigala (daily 8am–sunset; £E5) has been transformed from a wasteland where no foreign tourist would be seen dead to a tidy shore with sunshades and a small refreshment kiosk, to sunbathe without unwanted attention, you'll have to go for the **private beaches**. In Ed-Dahar, the *Shedwan Golden Beach* (next to the *Shedwan Garden*), *Triton Empire Beach Resort* and *Sand Beach* open their beaches to outsiders for £E20–50 (you can also use the pools at the *Shedwan* and *Sand Beach*).

Further down the coast is the beach at *Liquid Lounge* (£E30), a trendy bar which has hammocks and sells beers; it's opposite the *Roma Hotel* in Sigala. Other holiday villages allow outsiders to use their beaches and **swimming pools** for a charge that ranges from £E35 at the *El-Samaka Beach Club* to £E60 at the *Magawish Village* (which has the nicest beach). Admission policies may change, so phone ahead to avoid a wasted journey. Buying beach or camping gear in Hurghada can be expensive; the Abu Ashara supermarket near *Papa's Bar* in Sigala has a good selection at low fixed prices.

Powerful gusts make Hurghada a great place for **windsurfing** and **kiteboarding**. Several holiday villages have lagoons and centres where you can rent boards (for around €12 per hour) or kites (€35 per hour), plus wetsuits, and some places offer instruction. Happy Surf (℗012 240-9888, Ⓦwww .happy-surf.de) organizes windsurfing and has branches at *Sofitel* and *Hilton Plaza*. For kiteboarding, try Pro Center at *Jasmin Village* (℗010 667-2811, Ⓦwww.procenterfriedl.com), and Colona Watersports at *Magawish Village* (℗010 344-1810, Ⓦwww.colonawatersports.com).

If you book one or two days ahead, *Marine Sports Club* (℗065/346-3004) can arrange **deep-sea fishing** day-trips with lunch for £E900 per boat (6–8 people) including equipment. An international fishing competition, sponsored by the Egyptian Fishing Federation, is held off Hurghada's shores every February.

The Aquarium, Sindbad Submarine and Aquascope

If you want a glimpse of the Red Sea's wonders without getting wet, visit the **Red Sea Aquarium** (daily 9am–10pm; £E5, camera £E2) on the Corniche. Its tanks are labelled in English, with diagrams of where to find each species on the reef. You can learn to recognize wrasses, triggerfish, sailfintangs, angelfish and many other types, but it's sad to see them in such cramped conditions when you know that millions of others are swimming freely not far away.

Alternatively, there are the much-hyped **Sindbad Submarines** ($50, children $25), two craft which can take 44 people to depths of 22m in comfort.

Disappointingly, however, half the time is spent getting to and from the sub's mooring offshore from the *Sindbad Beach Resort* in New Hurghada, and after submerging a diver swims alongside trailing bait to attract wrasses, groupers and parrotfish past the portholes. You'd do better to go on an introductory dive – but if the subs still appeal, bookings can be made at the resort (℡065/344-4688) or through the other holiday villages.

Another window on the underwater world can be seen from on board **Aquascope** ($30), a sort of space-age glass-bottomed boat. The two-hour trip leaves from the *Hor Palace Hotel* (℡065/346-3657) near the tourist office in New Hurghada and includes a fifty-minute tour of the coral reefs. A more traditional glass-bottomed boat experience can be had from most of the hotels for around £E40 per hour.

Eating

Hurghada is good for **eating out**, with a wide choice of cuisine suited to all budgets. There are dozens of restaurants in holiday villages, mostly upmarket and with **live music** (provided by cover bands or Egyptian floor shows) in the evening, while for a cheap meal, you can check out the many (sometimes nameless) fish restaurants and pizza parlours in Ed-Dahar and Sigala. **Opening hours** are generally mid-morning until 11pm or midnight (maybe later in high season), though the choice of food dwindles after 10pm. Almost everywhere adds around ten percent in **service taxes** to the bill – at some holiday villages they bump things up by as much as twenty percent.

For cheap eats, there are two good *fuul* and falafel stands on the street running south of, and parallel to, Sharia Sheikh Sebak; juice bars and nut stalls are scattered around the bazaar, and there are kushari diners near the bus station. In Sigala, there's a pair of falafel stands on Sigala Square near the police station, and a place with refrigerated carcasses outside that does tasty kebab, *kofta* and pizzas. Good-value Western cooked breakfasts (eggs, chips, beef sausages etc) can be had at the *Cheers* bar, near the Aquarium. For the less adventurous, there's the ubiquitous *Pizza Hut* and *KFC* near *Sindbad Beach Resort*, and *McDonald's* and another *KFC* in downtown Sigala.

Ed-Dahar

Chez Pascal Hospital St. Good Belgian-inspired food and service in a soothing and smart atmosphere; lobster thermidor or black pepper steak are both reasonably priced at around £E50. Sells alcohol.

 Golden Dragon *Shedwan Garden Hotel* ℡065/355-5051. One of a string of modern restaurants outside the *Shedwan* hotels with traditional red lanterns and replica Ming-vase decor, and authentic fare cooked by a Chinese chef. Meat dishes from £E50, seafood from £E60, and an extensive imported wine-list. The crab and corn soup is recommended.

Mafia *Shedwan Garden Hotel* ℡065/354-7007. With a shady terrace, this serves top-notch Italian pasta, wood-fired pizzas and a wide range of imported ice cream. Serves alcohol.

 Mandarine *Shedwan Garden Hotel* ℡065/354-7007. Excellent Lebanese restaurant with a pleasant street-side patio. Serves decent mixed grills, *shawarma* and kebabs from £E40.

Pizzeria Tarboush Sharia Abdel Aziz Mustafa. Small, simple pizzeria, with more than a dozen not-so-different-tasting varieties on the menu (from around £E10). Start with a margarita for £E1 and build on to that. No alcohol.

Portofino Hospital St. Pleasant terrace restaurant with a long menu of fish, pizza and pasta (main courses from around £E30), Stella and local wine by the glass.

 Red Sea Hospital St ℡065/354-9630. One of Hurghada's classiest seafood places, with a lovely rooftop terrace with pot plants and smart a/c dining downstairs. Main dishes start at £E20. Sells alcohol, including cocktails.

Young Kang Sharia Sheikh Sebak. Reasonable Chinese–Korean restaurant, with fair-sized portions at moderate prices. Sells beer.

Sigala

Abo Khadega East of Sigala Square. A small workers' café where you can get a tasty meal of soup, rice, salad, beans and grilled meat from £E8.

Agra Near the *Golf Hotel*. Excellent Indian restaurant serving a variety of dishes, including lamb biryani and tandoori murgh (barbecued chicken in yoghurt) for £E30–40.

Coppa Cabana Sheraton Rd. A corner café, popular with tourists, who come to enjoy real espresso and the very tempting range of ice-cream flavours.

El-Joker Near the police station in Sigala Square. Excellent seafood restaurant with generous portions at very good prices (£E25–35) – try the *calamari* soup. Daily 11pm–1am.

Far East Korea Redcon Mall ☏065/344-5207. Good-value Chinese–Korean restaurant with friendly staff; also does takeaway.

Felfela's Sheraton Rd, south of Redcon Mall ☏065/344-2410. This spacious branch of the famous Cairo chain serves decent Egyptian food at reasonable prices, and has a great view of the harbour. Sells beer and does takeaway. Good for vegetarians. Daily 8.30am–midnight.

Fish House Next to *McDonald's*. Reasonably priced sushi and formal fish restaurant upstairs with large picture windows looking out over Sheraton Rd, and a coffee shop downstairs; takeaways available. Daily 9am–10pm.

Moby Dick 150m north of *McDonald's*. Much patronised by tour groups, this restaurant serves both Egyptian and Western food, with very good falafel, as well as pizza, pasta and cold Stella. Daily noon–2am.

Spaghetti Near *McDonald's*. Steak and seafood restaurant with large outdoor seating area. Good value, and popular with families.

Drinking

As you'd expect in a major resort, lots of drinking goes on in discos, restaurants and hotels – though the number of actual bars isn't that large. Most restaurants don't sell alcohol during Ramadan and before 1pm on Fridays, but the holiday villages are exempt from these restrictions. There are **duty-free shops** in the AKA mall near the EgyptAir office in New Hurghada, in Sigala Square opposite the police station, and next to the *Ambassador Hotel* on the road to the airport. The following **bars** are open till midnight at least.

Ed-Dahar

Cheers Near the Aquarium. Open 24hr for serious drinking, with a wide range of cocktails for £E20 and very cold beer. The wide-ranging menu includes burgers for £E15 and good breakfasts.

Juke Box Pub On the Corniche. As a bar, it's pretty tacky, but it does have a rooftop beer garden with good views, and it serves food and stages sporadic bellydance shows.

Nirvana Hospital St. Dark pub-like bar with a few tall stools out front and a dart board. Stella is a reasonable £E10. Popular with Russians.

🏃 **Papas II** Below the *Juke Box Pub*. Similar to its older sister bar in Sigala, with live music from homegrown bands several nights a week. Food is reasonably priced and varies from stuffed jacket potatoes to *calamari*.

🏃 **Peanuts** Hospital St. Lively Dutch-run spot, with a modern interior and funky lighting, pub grub, and steaks from £E55 and sangría at £E5 a glass. Heineken on tap. Karaoke in five languages on Wed, disco on Sat, live pop and rock on Sun. Open until 2am.

New Hurghada

Hard Rock Café Across from the *El-Smaka* hotel ☏065/346-5170. Popular branch of this international chain decorated in rock memorabilia. A spacious outdoor area, pool tables, live music, DJs after midnight. Noon–3am.

Sigala

Papa's Bar Opposite the Redcon Mall ⊛www .papasbar.com. Dutch-run bar, full of diving instructors and popular with foreigners in general.

Nightlife

Hurghada has some of the liveliest nightlife in mainland Egypt, as hotels strive to outdo each other's discos and floor shows – but wild raves are unknown and the music is mostly mainstream. Posh places balk at shorts or trainers; smart-casual **dress** is universally acceptable. A £E20 minimum charge is standard almost everywhere, rising to £E50 in some venues. A Stella, Sakkara Gold or

Meister will set you back £E10–15, imported beer or a cocktail £E25–30. Few discos get going before 11pm, and while most are advertised as staying open till 4am, they do close early if things are quiet.

Papa's Beach Bar, one of the most popular hangouts at the time of writing, can be found in Sigala 350m south of the harbour (Ⓦwww.papasbar.com). Drawing both tourists and young Egyptian men, it doesn't really get going until midnight and has been a *Ministry of Sound* franchise since 2005, hosting both resident and international DJs. A more laid-back option is *Liquid Lounge* on Sheraton Road, opposite Sigala's *Roma Hotel*. A beachside venue popular with the diving fraternity, it plays different styles of music each night, which makes a welcome alternative to the techno at *Papa's Beach Bar*. Also in Sigala near *Papa's* is *Bonanza*, another popular tourist spot with Mexican–Western decor, a garden terrace and regular live music, including a salsa band. Other favourites are in holiday villages; try the *Dome* at the *InterContinental* or the discos at the *Sand Beach*, *Princess Club*, *Sindbad Beach Resort*, *Giftun Beach Resort* or the *Sofitel*.

Occasionally you can see **bellydancing** at some clubs, with one of the best shows at *Alf Leila Wa Leila* ("1001 Nights"), on the southern outskirts of Hurghada. Tickets including transport can be bought at most hotels ($35 including dinner, $25 with soft drinks; 8–10.30pm). Some resort discos also put on "Russian shows" featuring tawdry dance troupes between songs.

Directory

Banks Of the two close together on Tariq El-Nasr in Ed-Dahar, the Banque Misr (daily 9am–9pm) has an ATM outside and gives cash advances on Visa and MasterCard, while the National Bank of Egypt (Mon–Thurs & Sun 8.30am–2pm & 6–9pm, Fri 9–11am & 2–5pm) takes traveller's cheques. There's also an ATM in the *Empire* and *La Pacha Cataract* in Sigala. In New Hurghada there are ATMs at the HSBC near *KFC*, at the *InterContinental* and at Banque Misr just north of the tourist office.

Bowling There's a bowling alley near the *Pizza Hut* in New Hurghada (☎065/344-3693).

Car rental Avis, opposite *Aqua Village* (☎065/344-4146), has a good range of 4WDs. There's also CRC Rent-a-Car just south of the Marine Sports Club in New Hurghada (☎065/344-4885, Ⓔcrc_hurghada @yahoo.com); Hertz at the airport (☎065/344-4146); and Max Car Rental, on Sheraton Rd in Sigala (☎065/344-4050), above *McDonald's*.

Couriers Federal Express is on Sheraton Rd in Sigala (daily except Fri 9am–5pm; ☎065/344-2444).

Hospitals The general hospital in Ed-Dahar (☎065/334-6740) and the private El-Saffa on El-Nasr St (☎065/354-6965) have improved, but it's better to try the El-Salam Hospital (☎065/354-8787, Ⓦwww.elsalamhospital.com) near the *Arabia Village Hotel*, on the Corniche between the *Hilton* and the port, or the hospital in El Gouna (see p.731). Holiday villages have physicians on call, and other doctors can be found listed in the *Connect Guide*.

Internet cafés There are a couple of 24hr Internet places in Ed-Dahar, namely the friendly Golden

Internet Café, a few metres northeast of the bazaar down a side alley; and Come In Café on Sharia Soliman Mazhar. Also open long hours is Hor@net in the mall at the *Shedwan Garden Hotel* (daily 10am–midnight). Sigala has dozens of Internet cafés, particularly around *McDonald's*, including Stargate next door and Fastdot upstairs.

Laundry In Ed-Dahar, try Stop-Shop off Tariq El-Nasr (daily 8am–8pm), 300m south of the bus station. Most hotels can have your washing sent out for £E2–10 per item.

Pharmacies There are several on Sharia Abdel Aziz Mustafa and Tariq el-Nasr in Ed-Dahar, and outside the hospitals.

Post office On Tariq el-Nasr, 200m north of the bus station (daily except Fri 8am–2pm), with an Express Mail Service.

Telephones Direct-dial phones in the 24hr *centraal* in Sigala, just south of *McDonald's*, as well as at several points on the street; phonecards are sold at the *centraal*.

Thomas Cook In Sigala at 8 Sheraton Rd (daily 9am–2pm & 6–9pm; ☎065/344-3338) and in Ed-Dahar at 2 Tariq el-Nasr (same hours; ☎065/354-1807). Both offices offer all the usual services, including Moneygram cash transfers, and also handles MasterCard emergencies.

Tourist police Next to the tourist office in New Hurghada (24hr; ☎065/344-7773). To contact the police in Ed-Dahar, call ☎065/354-3365.

Tours Most hotels and scores of travel agencies offer excursions to Luxor, Sinai or Cairo as day-trips or overnight packages, and can book tickets for the catamaran to Sharm el-Sheikh. Among the contenders it's worth mentioning Misr Travel on Sheraton Road in Sigala (daily 8.30am–10pm; ☎065/344-2131, ⓦ www.misrtravel.net) for its day-trips to the Red Sea monasteries (€55), among other tours. Other long-established agents include Prince Safaris in Ed-Dahar near the *Triton Empire* hotel (☎065/354-9882, ⓦ www.prince-diving.com), who run very long day-trips to Luxor (€45), taking in Karnak and the West Bank; and Cairo (€50), visiting the Egyptian Antiquities Museum and pyramids.

Work Distinctly feasible if you have diving qualifications (Divemaster upwards) or foreign languages (especially Japanese or Russian). Hotels and dive centres need people to work at reception or drum up clients. Ask other foreigners working here which firms are dodgy, and don't hand over your passport lightly. Whatever you do, do not invest any money in Hurghada – the biggest sharks aren't found in the Red Sea.

Moving on

EgyptAir **flights** are the quickest way of reaching **Cairo** (2–3 daily; around $120). You can book flights at the airline's offices in New Hurghada (☎065/346-3034) or Ed-Dahar (☎065/354-7891); both are open daily 8am–8pm. The **airport** (☎065/344-3974) is 15km south of Ed-Dahar, off the Hurghada–Safaga road (£E20–30 by taxi, plus £E4 airport entry tax).

Buses

For travel by **bus** to Cairo and Luxor, it's a good idea to buy your tickets in advance from the main bus station (☎065/354-7582). **East Delta** runs eleven a/c buses daily to Cairo's Turgoman garage (8am, 10am, 11.30am, 1pm, 2pm, 4pm, 5.30pm, 10pm, 11.30pm, 1am & 2am; 6–8hr; £E60–70). The **El Gouna Transport Company** (☎065/354-1561) has twelve buses from Hurghada, via El Gouna, throughout the night and day to Cairo (7hr; £E60–70).

Suez is served by a dozen buses daily (5hr; £E35) and tickets are sold on the bus. Buses to Luxor (5hr; £E30) leave at 10.30am, 10.30pm, 12am, 1am, 3am and 4.30am, and are routed via Safaga and Qena, with a couple of services continuing to Aswan. Other buses travel to Safaga hourly (7am–2am; 1hr; £E5), which is also accessible by buses bound for Mersa Alam (8hr; £E30) via El-Quseir (4hr; £E15) at 8pm, 1am and 3.30am. Other buses go daily to Assyut (8am; £E37) and Sohag (7am; £E35).

Besides the above, a/c **Superjet** buses depart four times a day for Cairo (12pm, 2.30pm, 5pm & 12am; £E70) from the Superjet station (☎065/354-4722), 1km south of Ed-Dahar's main bus station; the 2.30pm bus carries on to Alexandria (£E85). Buy tickets in advance to be sure of a seat.

Taxis

Mornings are the best time to catch seven-seater **service taxis** to Suez (5hr; £E25), Cairo (6–7hr; £E35), Port Safaga (45min; £E5), El-Quseir (1hr 30min; £E15) or Mersa Alam (3–4hr; £E25). A fair price for seven people to hire a **taxi** to Luxor is £E200; don't believe anyone who says there's a "convoy charge" for foreigners. Groups can also consider taking one all the way to Sharm el-Sheikh (about £E800) – which is one way to avoid a tedious interlude at Suez (see p.648).

By sea

The **catamaran** to **Sharm el-Sheikh** is run by International Fast Ferries (ⓦ www.internationalfastferries.com) and takes an hour and a half to complete the journey (Mon & Sat at 5am, Tues & Thurs at 8am; adults £E250/475 one way/return, children £E150/285, under-3s free). Space for cars (£E245) must be booked in advance. Tickets can be bought from a wide variety of outlets: Sherif Tours (☎065/354-5147), next to the *Sand Beach Hotel* on the Corniche; any travel agent (including Thomas Cook); EgyptAir; most of the hotels; the El Gouna office at their bus station in Ed-Dahar; or the kiosk near *Papa's Bar* in Sigala. There's also a **ferry** three times a week to **Duba** in Saudi Arabia (3 weekly at 9am; 3hr; £E400), but note that Saudi visas have to be obtained in Cairo.

The Red Sea Mountains

Inland of Hurghada, the barren plains erupt into the **Red Sea Mountains**, which follow the coast southwards towards Ethiopia. This geologically primitive range of granite, porphyry and breccia contains Egypt's highest mountains outside Sinai, rearing up to 2187m above sea level. During winter, peaks exceeding 1500m draw moisture from rising masses of air, while in summertime they precipitate brief, localized storms accompanied by violent lightning and flash floods. Hardy desert plants flourish in their wake, providing grazing for feral ruminants and the flocks of a few thousand nomads. Roaming their vast tribal lands, these Bedouin are perfectly at home in the wilderness – unlike isolated groups of miners and soldiers, who feel almost as exiled as the slaves who quarried here in ancient times.

As far as Europeans are concerned, the Red Sea Mountains were first climbed in the 1920s and 1930s, and have hardly been scaled since; as Sinai becomes increasingly commercialized, this may become the next wilderness to attract tourists.

Exploring the mountains

Short of befriending some Bedouin and tagging along with them, the Red Sea Mountains are most easily accessible via **day-excursions from Hurghada**. Most companies offer half-day camel or jeep safaris at sundown, including a barbecue and Bedouin entertainments for around €30/$40. Prince Safaris (see p.742) offers a sunset safari comprising a thirty-minute Land Cruiser journey to a Bedouin village for a camel ride, followed by tea, some Bedouin music and a buffet dinner, which makes a good introduction to the Bedouin and the majestic landscape they live in. They also offer two-hour morning quad-bike rides in the desert (€20/$25), including a short camel ride, and run longer desert camping trips on request.

The government is trying to promote **adventure tourism** in the Eastern Desert, so the opportunities for organized treks and mountain-climbing are improving. Red Sea Adventures at Shagra Village in Mersa Alam (see p.755) have spent over two years mapping rock-art sites by GPS and offers tailor-made trips into the desert. From October to March, for example, they offer jeep and camel safaris and hikes for groups of five or more, including a six-day jeep safari from Hurghada to Mons Claudianus and Mons Porphyrites; the price (€850/$1100) includes hotel accommodation, transport, safari, food and drink. Various half-, full-day and overnight hikes or camel or jeep trips are also available, starting from around €35/$45 per person. From Mersa Alam they also organize stargazing trips to a desert amphitheatre where images from a telescope are projected on to a large screen (€25/$32).

Mons Porphyrites

Twenty kilometres north of Hurghada, a piste quits the highway and climbs inland towards **Jebel Abu Dukhaan**, the 1161-metre-high "Mountain of

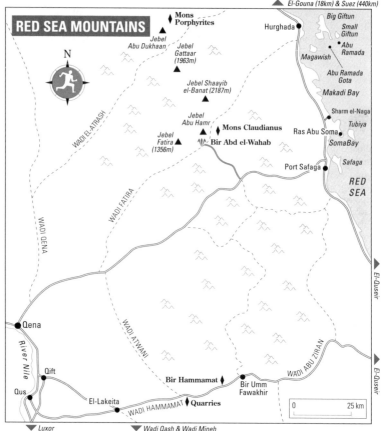

RED SEA MOUNTAINS

El-Gouna (18km) & Suez (440km)

Mons Porphyrites

Jebel Abu Dukhaan

Jebel Gattaar (1963m)

Jebel Shaayib el-Banat (2187m)

Jebel Abu Hamr

Jebel Fatira (1356m)

Mons Claudianus

Bir Abd el-Wahab

WADI EL-ATRASH

WADI FATIRA

WADI QENA

WADI ATWANI

WADI HAMMAMAT

WADI ABU ZIRAN

Hurghada

Big Giftun

Small Giftun

Abu Ramada

Magawish

Abu Ramada Gota

Makadi Bay

Sharm el-Naga

Tubiya

Ras Abu Soma

SomaBay

Port Safaga

Safaga

RED SEA

El-Quseir

El-Quseir

Qena

River Nile

Qift

Qus

El-Lakeita

Bir Hammamat

Bir Umm Fawakhir

Quarries

0   25 km

Luxor

Wadi Qash & Wadi Mineh

Smoke". Anciently known as **Mons Porphyrites**, this was the Roman Empire's main source of fine red porphyry, used for columns and ornamentation. Blocks were dragged 150km to the Nile, or by a shorter route to the coast, whence they were shipped to far-flung sites such as Baalbek in Lebanon, or Constantinople. Round about the extensive quarries lies a **ruined town** of rough-hewn buildings with two large cisterns and an unfinished Ionic temple. Rock hyraxes used to live in dens around Jebel Abu Dukhaan until all its trees were cut down for fuel. From the ruins, the piste follows Wadi el-Atrash and Wadi Qena down to the Nile Valley.

Mons Claudianus

Although **Mons Claudianus** is only 50km distant from Mons Porphyrites as the crow flies, lofty massifs necessitate more roundabout approaches. Coming from Hurghada, you need to follow a piste that starts between the port and Magawish Village. There are also two routes off the Port Safaga–Qena road: a well-surfaced one, 41km from the coast, and a longer, rougher piste nearer Qena.

Under the emperors Trajan and Hadrian, the pale, black-flecked granite quarried at Mons Claudianus was used to construct the Pantheon and Trajan's

Forum in Rome. Around the **quarries**, beneath Jebel Fatira and Jebel Abu Hamr, you'll find numerous unformed capitals and abandoned columns. Wadi Fatira contains a cracked, 200-tonne monster, dubbed the "**Mother of Columns**" by the Arabs, while in the quarries of Hydreuma lies a giant unfinished **sarcophagus**. There's also a sizeable ruined town, **Fons Trajanus**.

Jebel Gattaar and Jebel Shaayib el-Banat

Between the two quarries rise the highest mountains in the Eastern Desert: Jebel Gattaar and Jebel Shaayib el-Banat. Jebel Gattaar (1963m) is esteemed by the Bedouin for its permanent springs and comparatively abundant vegetation. Umm Yasar and other wadis draining from Gattaar contain hundreds of acacia and ben trees, a remnant of once-extensive forests that were ravaged by charcoaling. As late as the 1880s, E.A. Floyer found Wadi Gattaar "thickly studded with big mimosa trees, some twenty and thirty feet high", whose reckless felling compelled the Bedouin to cut down live acacias for fodder when drought struck in the 1950s.

Further south, the loftier **Jebel Shaayib el–Banat** (2187m) rises to a summit that the geographer and mountaineer George Murray likened to a "monstrous webbed hand of seven smoothed fingers". The highest mountain in mainland Egypt, it was first climbed by Murray in 1922. In Bedouin folklore, Shaayib harbours a "Tree of Light" whose leaves can cure blindness; the world's only other one is believed to be in Lebanon.

The coast south of Hurghada

Down the coast from Hurghada, the stream of holiday resorts becomes less dense until three belated spurts of development on the outskirts of **Port Safaga** (58km), **El-Quseir** (a further 85km), and **Mersa Alam** (a further 132km). Little more than an overgrown, grubby port, Safaga has few charms though it is within boat range of some stunning offshore reefs, while El-Quseir retains a sleepy quality unlike anywhere else on the Red Sea. The region around Mersa Alam is home to a few isolated diving camps and not much else, but this is set to change as a new tourist development, **Port Ghalib**, is presently under construction.

Further south, communications become tenuous and bureaucratic obstacles loom as you head towards the Sudanese border. From Shalateen, you need military permission to proceed further south, or into the mountains, and the allure of the far south depends primarily on its reefs, which can be reached by dive boats operating out of Hurghada, Safaga, El-Quseir and Mersa Alam.

The highway initially runs several kilometres inland before regaining the coast. About 40km after Hurghada and 18km before Safaga, a signpost indicates the turn-off for **SHARM EL-NAGA**, a wide bay where the attractive *Sharm El-Naga Resort and Diving Centre* (☏010 111-2942, ⓦ www.sharmelnaga.com; ❻) has forty comfortable en-suite chalets, a vast swimming pool, bar and restaurant (rates are all-inclusive). The main attraction here is the **beach diving** and **snorkelling** (the dive centre can be contacted on ☏010 123-4540) and daytrippers from overcrowded Hurghada often come here to use the beach (£E25 fee for non-guests).

The luxury development of **Soma Bay**, 2km further south (ⓦ www .sombabay.com), boasts a Gary Player–designed eighteen-hole golf course and Les Thermes Marins des Cascades, a spa and thalasso-therapy centre, among other delights. There are several top-notch hotels offering similar facilities, of which the *Sheraton Soma Bay* (☎065/354-5845, Ⓦ www.sheraton-somabay .com; ❾) is the most appealing, with over three hundred rooms, several restaurants and bars, a nightclub and elaborate mosaic pool. Further south, just before Safaga, is **Makadi Bay**, a similar-style complex with a *Meridien* and several four- and five-star *Iberotel* hotels; the *Iberotel Makadi Beach* has the best range of facilities and a choice of half or full board (☎065/359-0000, Ⓦ www .iberotel.com; ❼).

Port Safaga

PORT SAFAGA (Bur Safaga in Arabic) amounts to very little. Coming in from the north, you pass a slip road curving off to six holiday villages on a headland, which cater to groups on diving holidays. The town begins 3km later and consists of a single windswept avenue running straight on past concrete boxes with bold signs proclaiming their function, until the bus station and a final mosque, 4km south. Silos and cranes identify the port, which runs alongside (but remains out of bounds) for most of this distance. Safaga's only attraction is the **reefs** to the north, and there's not much reason to hang around otherwise. As buses and taxis travelling between Hurghada and Luxor use the desert highway from Safaga to Qena/Qift, passengers can see all there is to see as they drive through town.

The **bus station** is near to the port, while most of Safaga's facilities are along the main drag, including the **police station** and **EgyptAir**, 200m south of the City Council, followed by a **hospital** 500m on. There's a **petrol station** beyond the next turn-off, across the main road from the Bank of Alexandria; further south on the other side are Banque Misr and the National Bank of Egypt, and a **telephone exchange**. Tourists staying at the holiday villages can change money at the **bank** inside *Shams Safaga* or at the Banque du Caire in the shopping arcade near the *Holiday Inn*. There is no tourist office.

Accommodation

In Safaga itself, accommodation includes several pricey **hotels** near the beach and a few mid-range options on the Corniche. If you're diving, you'll probably be staying at one of the cluster of holiday resorts with dive centres, all of which are around 3–5km north of town unless otherwise stated; minibuses (£E1–2) run out to the *Shams Safaga*, the furthest of the resort complexes.

Amira Safaga On the Corniche between the port and the town ☎065/325-3821, Ⓦ www .amirasafaga.com. Smart hotel with its own beach and a decent range of facilities, but isolated from the other tourist villages. Half board ❻

Cleopatra Opposite EgyptAir, in town ☎065/253-3926. Reasonable, carpeted rooms with TV and baths, off dingy corridors. Caters mainly for Egyptians. ❷

Holiday Inn Resort ☎065/326-0100, Ⓦ www .ichotelsgroup.com. Safaga's most stylish tourist village, with an outsized pool and fine sea views; rooms have a/c, fridge and satellite TV. Happy hour for cocktails in the *Windsurf Bar* is 8–10pm. ❼

Lotus Bay Resort & Gardens ☎065/325-1040, Ⓦ www.lotusbay.com. This spacious array of villas in a nice garden has all mod cons, plus tennis,

squash, pool, billiards, a kids' club, and a dive and windsurfing centre on site. Italian/Swiss clientele. Half board ❻

Menaville Village ☎065/326-0064, Ⓦ www .menaville.com. A decent place, not too flashy, with a large pool and gardens and reasonable rates. The clientele are mainly Swiss, Italian and French. It's also home to the Thermal Karlovy Vary Centre, which offers treatment for psoriasis and rheumatism, capitalizing on Safaga's supposedly propitious natural circumstances – including high UV levels in the sunshine and some radioactivity in the sands. ❼

Nemo ☎065/325-6777, Ⓦ www.nemodive .com. This European-owned, Disney-themed hotel, located on the Corniche (coming from Hurghada, take the first left before entering town), has an eager management, bright rooms and sea views. There's also a colourful children's playground and chess and dominoes in the bar. Weekly All-inclusive packages start from €200. **⑤**

🏃 **Shams Safaga** ☎065/325-1781, ⓦwww .shams-dive.com. Lavish resort with 340 rooms, a private reef, good sports facilities and a children's playground. Popular with British tour

groups. A Mistral windsurfing and kiteboarding centre is based here (ⓦwww.club-mistral.com). Half or full board; rates include local alcoholic drinks. **⑦**

Solymar Resort Paradise 4km north of town ☎065/326-0016, ⓦwww.solymar-hotels.com. Safaga's first resort, it's been renovated nicely and attracts a largely Slavic clientele. Half board **⑦**

Diving and snorkelling

Boats and instructors at the main **dive centres** tend to be committed to groups, though they will take on independent travellers if they have space: expect to pay around €300/$385 for a four-day PADI Open Water course, or €45/$60 for two boat dives. As in Hurghada, an **environmental fee** of €3 a day is levied on all diving and snorkelling trips.

The main diving grounds lie 6–8km offshore from the holiday villages between Safaga Island and the Ras Abu Soma headland to the north. **Tubiya Island** is ringed with corals only just off its beach, while dive boats drop their clients directly over the sunken **North and South Fairway Reefs** or the twin pairs of sites known as **Tubiya Kebir**, **Tubiya Soraya**, **Gamul Soraya** and **Gamul Kebir**. Other sites include the **Seven Pillars** off Ras Abu Soma, and the **Panorama Reef** and **Shark Point**, 10km east of Safaga Island. Most of them are notable for their coral pillars and strong currents.

Dive centres in the vicinity include the Alpha Red Sea at the *Amira Safaga Hotel* and *Menaville Village* (☎065/325-3229, ⓦwww.alpharedsea.com); Barakuda at *Lotus Bay* (☎065/325-3911, ⓦwww.barakuda-diving.com); Ducks, *Holiday Inn Resort* (☎065/326-0100, ⓦwww.ducks-dive-center-de); Orca at *Sun Beach* (☎065/326-0111, ⓦwww.orca-red-sea.com); and Shams Safaga at the *Shams Safaga* ☎065/325-1781, ⓦwww.shams-dive.com).

△ A meal break on a Red Sea liveaboard

Among the big fish prevalent in these waters are aggressive **hammerhead sharks**. Research suggests that they track their victims with two forms of biological sensor. At long range and when closing in on its kill, the hammerhead senses vibrations in the water, but in the final seconds it tunes into electromagnetic fields "bounced" off its target.

Eating

Aside from the **restaurants** at the holiday resorts, there are several **cafés** offering sandwiches or *shawarmas* on the main drag. For grilled meat, pasta, salads and pizzas, however, you're better off at the *Aly Baba* restaurant (daily noon–10pm), 2km north of the town centre, or the *El-Joker* restaurant (T065/326-0575), 3km north of town opposite the *Lotus Bay*.

Moving on from Safaga

There are around nine **buses** daily to Hurghada (6am–11.30pm; £E5) and seven to Cairo (6am–11.30pm; £E70). Sticking to the Red Sea Coast, three buses a day (9pm, 2am & 4.30am) run down to El-Quseir (£E10) and Mersa Alam (£E30). There are six buses a day (5.30am–11.30pm) that ply the desert road to Qena (£E20) and Luxor (£E25), a couple of which go all the way to Aswan (£E45). **Service taxis** leave from the depot 500m south of the port entrance and run in between buses to Hurghada and Qena for similar rates, though it can take a long time to muster enough passengers for El-Quseir.

El-Quseir

EL-QUSEIR, 85km from Safaga, is also a phosphates extraction centre, though with fewer inhabitants and more appeal. In pharaonic times, it was from here that boats sailed to the "Land of Punt" (thought to be Yemen or Somalia), as depicted in reliefs within Hatshepsut's temple at Deir el-Bahri. The Romans knew it as Leukos Limen ("White Harbour"), while under Arab rule El-Quseir was the largest port on the Red Sea until the tenth century, and remained a major transit point for pilgrims until the 1840s, when Flaubert caught its last flickers of exoticism. Crude pearl-fishers' pirogues resembling dug-out tree trunks shared the harbour with graceful Arab dhows, whose outsize sterns and high prows mimicked calligraphic flourishes, while Arabs and Africans jostled with Tartars from Bukhara and Crimea.

Today, El-Quseir is a sleepy place that seems mostly unaffected by tourism, despite the presence of holiday villages on its outskirts. The main **orientation** point is a traffic roundabout where service taxis drop and wait for passengers, near a Co-op garage and the *Sea Princess Hotel*. The road bearing off to the right leads to a small **harbour** where you can watch men building boats on the beach, or stroll past shuttered and balconied houses to reach a **mosque** dating back to the thirteenth century and a **quarantine hospital** built to screen pilgrims in the nineteenth century.

Smack in the centre of town, just past the main traffic roundabout, sits El-Quseir's most impressive landmark, the sixteenth-century crumbling **walled fortress** (daily 9am–5pm; £E10), now housing a museum. Designed to protect trade routes used by the Ottomans, the fortress fell into decline after trade was diverted around the Cape of Good Hope. Napoleon's army raised the French flag here in 1799, only to attract the attention of British warships, the HMS *Daedalus* and HMS *Fox*, sailing off the coast. The French survived a brief assault by the British, but abandoned the fort two years later for engagements elsewhere in the country. The fort's most recent occupant was the Egyptian army, stationed here until 1975.

The fortress entrance is through a gate on the southern side of the building, where you can buy a ticket for a guided tour, which lasts about forty minutes. The cistern, the watchtower (which you can climb for excellent views), and rooms built into the walls of the fortress each contain small exhibits on the history and traditions of the Red Sea Coast, including displays on Bedouin life, the Coptic monasteries, Roman mines and ship building.

Aside from the fortress, El-Quseir's main diversion is strolling along the beach-side **promenade** where cafés serve snacks and cold drinks. Life moves at a pretty slow pace, except on Fridays, when Ma'aza and Ababda Bedouin flock into town for the weekly **market**. The best **dive sites** near the town are the Brothers, east of El-Quseir, and the Elphinstone and Abu Dabbab reefs, down towards Mersa Alam, although the Quei and Wizr reefs are closer. All the **dive centres** are attached to the resort hotels, and may not allow outside divers to join their trips. If you want to dive here, it's best to book a package deal from the start.

Practicalities

The **bus station** and the **service taxi stand** are side-by-side in the heart of town, a ten-minute walk or a short minibus hop (50pt) from the main roundabout. There are three a/c buses daily to **Cairo** (7.30am, 9am & 8.30pm; 10hr; £E80) and two non-a/c (6am & 7pm; 11hr; £E60); all services stop at Safaga (2hr; £E10) and Hurghada (3hr; £E15). Heading south, there are five buses daily to **Mersa Alam** via the coastal route (5am, 9am, 7pm & 8pm; 2hr; £E10). **Service taxis** depart when full for Cairo (£E40–50), Hurghada (£E10), Safaga (£E8) and Mersa Alam (£E10). To reach **Luxor**, you could charter a taxi via Safaga (expect to pay £E250–300 for seven people) or get a bus to Safaga and an onward bus from there.

El-Quseir's **bank** (no ATM) is on Sharia el-Gumhorriya, 150m north of the roundabout, while the road that turns right at this point leads to an old-fashioned **telephone exchange** (24hr). For **Internet access**, Hotline is about 100m east of the *Sea Princess* on Sharia Port Said, just south of the roundabout.

Accommodation

Accommodation is limited to two hotels in the centre and a clutch of holiday villages outside town. The central *Sea Princess* on Sharia Port Said (℡065/333-1880; ❷) is an odd, tatty little hotel decorated with film posters and vintage banknotes, whose friendly staff and clean shared bathrooms just fail to make the rabbit-hutch rooms tolerable. A far better option is the ⚓ *El Quseir Hotel* further along Sharia Port Said (℡065/333-2301; ❸), a refurbished period 1920s home with charming rooms. Though rates may seem a bit high for rooms that aren't en suite, the hotel is a welcome break for mid-range travellers tired of boxy concrete bungalows, and the ocean views from the balcony also help compensate. The hotel isn't signed, so look for the "Diving world – Red Sea Egypt" emblem above the door.

About 10km north of town is *Rocky Valley Diver's Camp* (℡065/326-0055, ⓦwww.rockyvalleydiverscamp.com; ❺), a handful of Bedouin-style bungalows and tents and a restaurant run by Hassan who also rents out snorkelling and diving gear. At the luxury end, it's hard to beat the newish, beautifully designed ⚓ *Radisson SAS Resort*, 3km north of town on the Safaga road (℡065/335-0260, ⓦwww .radisson.com; ❼). Built Bedouin-style with domed roofs, it features several pools, a dive centre, riding stables and spa. Also good is the ⚓ *Mövenpick Resort El Quseir* (℡065/333-2100, ⓦwww.movenpick-hotels.com; ❻), a spacious five-star resort

7km north of town (£E15–20 by taxi) with every facility imaginable, including a dive centre and spa. The European-managed, Nubian-style resort is one of the few in this part of Egypt that has managed to blend with the local environment and native culture, while running development projects such as computer training. Five hundred metres north is the three-star *Flamenco Beach Resort* (℡065/335-0200, Ⓦwww.flamencohotels.com; ⑤), a garish pink complex with reasonable diving packages including half board accommodation.

Eating and drinking

Among the handful of **places to eat** around El-Quseir, the best is the *Old Restaurant*, a popular Bedouin-themed place some 50m north of the *El-Quseir Hotel*, with offerings ranging from inexpensive grilled chicken to a seafood platter (£E60). The *Citadel Restaurant*, on the main road near the fortress, is more of a local place but serves excellent meals. For drinks and snacks, head down to the string of cafés by the Corniche. **Alcohol** and nightlife are confined to the holiday villages, which sometimes feature a bellydancer; non-residents may attend at the management's discretion.

South to Mersa Alam

The coastal road south of El-Quseir (sections of which are currently being moved slightly further inland to protect the coast and wildlife) runs through some of the most amazing landscape and desert in Egypt. It's sprinkled with holiday resorts all along the 132km stretch to Mersa Alam. Although this southern Red Sea Coast is growing in popularity with holidaymakers and divers, its tourist infrastructure is far from developed. Telephone use is limited and some resorts have to rely on expensive satellite communications, though mobile-phone coverage is reasonable in the area.

A few of the **resorts** along the coast, such as *Helio* and *Utopia*, won't take independent travellers, but others will, such as the huge *Akassia*, 26km south of El-Quseir (℡012 745-5049, Ⓦwww.akassia.com; half board ⑦), with 360 rooms, an enormous domed lobby, and five swimming pools, including a wave pool. Alternatively, there's the three-star *Mangrove Bay Resort*, 30km south of El-Quseir (Cairo ℡02/748-6748, Ⓦwww.mangrovebayresort.com; half board ⑦), with its own beautiful, white sandy beach.

Further south, 50km north of Mersa Alam, is **Mersa Alam International Airport** (Ⓦwww.marsa-alam-airport.com), served by several flights from Europe daily. There's no public transport from the airport, and most arrivals are ferried to their resorts in shuttle buses.

Adjacent to the airport is the **Port Ghalib** development (Ⓦwww.portghalib .com), presently under construction. Essentially a new town (similar to El Gouna north of Hurghada), when completed it will occupy 18km of coast, and comprise shops, a golf course, accommodation units, hotels, a promenade and a three-hundred-berth yacht marina. Like the airport, the project is being funded by a Kuwaiti investment company which is also funding similar projects in the Gulf States. A few resorts are already open, such as the *Coral Beach Diving Hotel* (℡065/370-0222, Ⓦwww.millenniumhotels.com; ⑦), proffering four-star luxury in bright, modern rooms, and a dive centre (Ⓦwww.emperordivers.com).

Twenty-five kilometres north of Mersa Alam is the German-run *Oasis* (Ⓦwww .mersa-oasis.com; ⑤) with twenty bungalows, each with different decor and assembled to mimic a small village; it also features a restaurant, bar and pool. A little to the south is the five-star *Kahramana* (℡012 745-4105; ⑦), whose Mexican-inspired architecture is set against beautiful and empty sandy beaches.

Slightly cheaper rooms can be had at *Club Amaraya* at the resort's entrance (⑥), which shares the *Kahramana*'s facilities and has a dive centre (☎065/333-4510, ⓦwww.ducks-dive-centre.de).

A ten-minute walk south of the *Kahramana*, at **Mersa Shagra**, is the northernmost of three "ecolodges" run by Red Sea Diving Safari. 🏃 *Shagra Village* (☎02/338-0022, ⓦwww.redsea-divingsafari.com; ⑥) is a beachside dive-centre with environmentally friendly accommodation, ranging from tents on the beach to smart bungalows, both sharing facilities, as well as more luxurious en-suite chalets. Rates include all meals and unlimited soft drinks, and beer is available; underwater weddings are a speciality, with the bride and groom in full scuba gear for the ceremony. It's also home to Red Sea Desert Adventures (☎012 399-3860, ⓦwww.redseadesertadventures.com), whose jeep and camel safaris run from October to March (see p.747), as well as Egypt's most southerly decompression chamber, the Hyperbaric Medical Centre (☎012 165-3806); divers are encouraged to take out cover in case they have to use it (€6 for three weeks).

Mersa Alam

The town of **MERSA ALAM** itself is undistinguished, consisting of a large army base, some government buildings and new apartment blocks constructed for the expected influx of hotel staff to the area, grafted onto a fishing port where liveaboards now moor. Opposite is a coffee shop patronized by local divers. The **bus station** is on the edge of town, 800m west of the traffic circle, with daily buses to Hurghada (5am, 12.30pm, 2.30pm & 5pm; 5hr; £E30) via El-Quseir (2hr; £E10) and irregular buses and **service taxis** to Shalateen (4hr; £E20). There is also regular transport to Edfu and Aswan in the Nile Valley, but foreigners aren't allowed to travel the road through the mountains independently. Travellers heading for the tomb of Sheikh el-Shazli (see p.756) risk being turned back,

Ⓐ, Ⓑ & El-Quseir ▲

MERSA ALAM AREA

Ⓒ
Ⓓ
Ⓔ

Mersa Shagra

Hyperbaric Medical Centre

N

RED SEA

Mersa Alam

Edfu ◄

Bus Station/ Service Taxis

Ⓕ
Ⓖ
Ⓗ

0   5 km

ACCOMMODATION
Awlad Baraka Diving Camp	F
Club Amaraya	D
Coral Beach Diving	B
Iberotels	A
Kahramana	D
Oasis	C
Nakari Village	H
Shagra Village	E
Shams Alam	I
Umtondoba Ecolodge	G

Wadi Gimal National Park Headquarters Ⓘ

Wadi Gimal Island

WADI GIMAL NATIONAL PARK

Wadi Lahami & Berenice ▼

too – Red Sea Desert Adventures is the best source of information on this route. The only bank, with an ATM, is 25km away at the *Kahramana Hotel*.

South of Mersa Alam

For keen divers that have made it this far, there are several camps and two hotels to the south of town offering **accommodation**. All arrange transfers from either Mersa Alam or Hurghada airports. This eerily empty and barren region of just mountains, ocean and reefs is far removed from the commercialized northern Red Sea Coast but it does give the opportunity to explore the most remote dive-sites in the south Red Sea, such as **Samaduy**, **Abu Dabab**, **Elphinstone** and the **Fury Shoal**.

Twelve kilometres south of Mersa Alam, *Awlad Baraka Diving Camp* (T021/248 8062, W www.aquariusredsea.com; full board ❻) has twenty comfortable "African" huts, a restaurant and café, and offers PADI Open Water courses. A similar set-up can be found at *Umtondoba Ecolodge* (T012 792-3336, W www .ecolodge-redsea.com; ❻), 14km south of town, where the diving is run by Deep South Diving (T010 395-9492, W www.deep-south-diving.com), which organizes day-trips (€35/$45 for two dives including lunch) and open-water diving courses. There's another Red Sea Diving Safari "ecolodge" at *Nakari Village*, 18km south of Mersa Alam (T02/337-1833, W www.Mersanakari.com; full board ❻), with accommodation in tents or domed Bedouin huts, all with communal bathrooms.

Fifty kilometres south of Mersa Alam is *Shams Alam Hotel* (T012 2444932, W www.shams-dive.com; full board ❼), with 160 fully equipped rooms surrounding a pool and a dive school offering trips to **Wadi Gimal National Park**, a unique protected area covering 6000 square kilometres of land and 4000 square kilometres of sea; its entrance is just 100m beyond the hotel. Inside the park's borders, three ranger stations, built to look like ancient Roman domiciles, are used as base camps by scientists surveying the land and studying plant and animal species. Spring and autumn are particularly good times to observe bird migrations, including osprey, falcons, white-eyed gulls and the occasional flamingo. The park headquarters, next to the Wadi Gimal Diving Centre, is not yet equipped for travellers, but there are plans to build an on-site information centre. To **camp** in the park, foreigners need permission from the Coast Guard

---

The Moulid of Abul Hassan al-Shazli

Outside Egypt, **Abul Hassan al-Shazli** (who died in 1258) is known as al-Shadhili, hence the name of his Sufi order, the Shadhiliyya. According to believers, al-Shazli asked God to let him die in a place where nobody had ever sinned, and the Prophet Mohammed buried him deep in the mountains at **Wadi Humaysara**, roughly midway between Aswan and Berenice. The remoteness of his tomb has never deterred pilgrims, for whom the journey has become much easier since a local entrepreneur built a road to the site as a gift. It turns off the Edfu road at the tomb of another Sufi sheikh, Salim, which pilgrim trucks circle three times to avoid incurring his jealousy, before driving on to Wadi Humaysara (100km).

Al-Shazli's **moulid** starts ten days before the Muslim feast of Eid al-Adha and reaches its climax the day before the Eid. Twenty thousand Sufis from all over Egypt gather to perform *zikrs* outside his tomb, and hundreds of tents and snack stalls are pitched for the occasion. You shouldn't have any problem identifying the pilgrim trucks, festooned with banners and loudspeakers. At other times of the year, Red Sea Desert Adventures (see p.755) organize trips into the desert for groups of five or more.

in Mersa Alam; Red Sea Desert Adventures (see p.755) may be able to help with these, or you could contact Mohamed Abbas (@matahoon2004@yahoo.com), a researcher at the park.

Around 80km south of the park, and 5km south of the village of **Hamata**, is the new *Zabargad Dive Resort* (☎012 746-8823, ⓦwww.orca-diveclub-hamata .com; ❺), which has attractive, fully equipped Nubian-style domed bungalows with pool, restaurant and bar, and is popular with German divers. Four kilometres further south is the third of the Red Sea Diving Safari "ecolodges", *Wadi Lahami Village* (Cairo ☎02/338-0021, ⓦwww.redsea-divingsafari.com; ❺), which caters for experienced divers only and has full-board accommodation in tents. Just beyond the turn-off for the *Wadi Lahami Village* is the southernmost resort on the Red Sea Coast, the five-star ⚓ *Lahami Bay* (Cairo ☎02/753-7100, ⓦwww .lahamibay.com; ❺), which offers excellent amenities despite its remote location, including an Italian restaurant, pool bar, tennis courts, sauna and fitness centre, as well as diving and windsurfing centres. Its dive area is a further 50km south at the port of **Ras Banata**, whose island reefs are home to one of the few undisturbed breeding grounds for **sea turtles** on the Red Sea Coast.

The far south: Berenice to the Sudanese border

As the coast road heads southwards to the Sudanese border, the seemingly endless coastline is almost completely empty except for the occasional mangrove, herd of grazing camels or cluster of tanks left by the military. One hundred and forty-five kilometres south of Mersa Alam is the town of **BERENICE**, named after the wife of Ptolemy II, on whose suggestion a trading port was established here in 275 BC. Abandoned during the fifth century AD, the site was excavated in 1818 by Belzoni, who found a Temple of Semiramis and other ruins. Nowadays, Berenice amounts to a few characterless buildings clustered together in a windswept bay, with little to interest tourists, though the hinterland of Berenice has several would-be attractions. For climbers, there is the challenge of Egypt's "most aggressive peaks", **Jebel Farayid** (whose highest point was reached by Murray in 1925) and the **Berenice Bodkin** – one of the largest rock spires in the whole of North Africa and the Middle East. Here, too, are the ancient **Emerald Mines of Wadi Sakait**, worked from pharaonic to Roman times and under the caliphs; Mohammed Ali had them reopened, but few gems remained to be found and the mines were soon abandoned. Nearby is a small Ptolemaic rock temple, dedicated to Isis and Serapis. Red Sea Desert Adventures (see p.755) can organize a six-day safari from Mersa Alam, taking in both Berenice and Wadi Sakait.

The reasons why this area has long been off-limits are geopolitical. Following the Iranian Revolution, the **Ras Banas air base** was earmarked for use by the US Rapid Deployment Force and war games were held in the Eastern Desert, simulating an Allied response to an Iranian attack on the Saudi oil fields. Such manoeuvres waned after Iran was embroiled in war with Iraq, and the US "forward base" withdrew to Diego Garcia – so that when Iraq invaded Kuwait in 1990, the only unit available for immediate airlift into Saudi Arabia was a single battalion of Egyptian commandos.

More recently, the **far south** has been a bone of contention between Egypt and Sudan, whose common border was arbitrarily set by the British in 1899 on the basis of the twenty-second parallel. After independence, both countries agreed that this was unfair on the Bishari nomads whose tribal grounds straddled the border, so a slice of Egyptian territory was placed under Sudanese administration – a compromise that worked fine until Sudan granted a Canadian oil company offshore exploration rights, and Egypt responded by sending in troops to reassert its sovereignty. Since 1992, the region from **Bir Shalateen** down to **Halaib** has been under military rule, and Egypt has launched a crash programme of "development" to cement its hold on this previously neglected, potentially oil-rich region.

In 1999, some restrictions were lifted and tourists can now travel at least as far as **Shalateen**, which has a daily camel market that attracts plenty of Sudanese traders. A lot of haggling goes on between the traders, but it won't make much sense without a local guide: with some advance warning, Red Sea Desert Adventures (see p.755) will run a very informative day-trip to the village. As yet there is no tourist accommodation in the area, and official permission must be obtained from police in Berenice or Shalateen if you wish to **camp**. Your best chance for a camping permit is through Red Sea Desert Adventures. The area is still a very sensitive military zone and anyone not obtaining permission is likely to be treated with extreme suspicion.

Off the coast 100km southeast of Berenice is **Zabargad Island**, whose deep reefs teem with oceanic fish and corals. It's a favourite long-haul destination for liveaboards setting out from Hurghada and other diving centres.

Rock-art sites in the Eastern Desert

The **rock art** of the Eastern Desert is one of Egypt's best-kept secrets, overlooked due to the abundance of pharaonic monuments in the Nile Valley and the difficulty of reaching many of the sites, spread over 24,000 square kilometres of desert to the east of Luxor and Edfu. Though small by comparison with the Western Desert, the dangers of this terrain shouldn't be underestimated: it's easy to get lost in the labyrinth of waterless wadis, and at least one 4WD group has died there. The **sites** vary from a single boulder to swathes of cliff face dotted with pictures of people and animals, flotillas of boats and herds of giraffes, ostriches and elephants.

For climatic reasons, the rock-art sites are best explored from mid-September till mid-May. Broadly speaking there are three areas of interest. Two are partially accessible by 2WD, using the roads between El-Quseir and Qift or Mersa Alam and Edfu, but all of the wadis between them require 4WD. Vehicles must travel in pairs and carry all water and fuel needed for the journey. Due to gold mining in the area and the need to protect vulnerable sites, access is only allowed from the Red Sea Coast, not the Nile Valley. Military Intelligence and SCA **permits** for off-road travel are only issued to a single foreign tour-operator, Ancient World Tours (Ⓦ www.ancient.co.uk), in conjunction with the Egyptian firm Pan Arab Tours.

The importance of rock art

While pharaonic and Roman inscriptions have revealed much about mining and trade, it's the rock art created before the unification of Egypt (*c*.3100 BC) that's really intriguing for the light it sheds on the origins of Egyptian civilization. **Dating** predynastic rock art is highly speculative, involving stylistic comparisons and analysis of patination (the extent to which inscriptions and rock faces darken with exposure to sunlight, dew and other factors). Since wadis often subside, some scholars date art by its height above the valley floor, assigning **spirals** to the earliest phase (7000–6000 BC), followed by **wildlife** and hunting scenes. Giraffes, crocodiles, hippos and ibexes plainly belong to a time when the region was moister than today (*c*.4000–2700 BC). Camels didn't reach Egypt until 625 BC, whereas elephants lived here in predynastic times and were later imported by the Romans, so their presence can be ambiguous. Cattle reflect the pastoralism that took hold between 5500 and 4000 BC, and probably inspired the bovine iconography of pharaonic civilization.

The oldest **human figures** are gods or chieftains in ostrich-feather headdresses, brandishing maces; intriguingly similar to the "Conquering Hero" motif in pre- and Early Dynastic art at Hierakonpolis in the Nile Valley. They often appear standing in **boats**, which come in four types and are frequently surrounded by ostriches, elephants or cattle. Both Hans Winkler, who did seminal research in the 1930s, and David Rohl who recently studied the rock art, believe that the oldest boats represent "**Eastern Invaders**" from Mesopotamia, who reached Egypt by the Red Sea and conquered the indigenous people of the Nile Valley, kick-starting Egyptian civilization. Boat motifs were employed throughout the pharaonic era.

In pharaonic times the Eastern Desert was inhabited, as it was an important source of gold, porphyry and breccia, so there are plenty of **hieroglyphs**, cartouches of great pharaohs, and images of Min (the local deity of Coptos, and god of the desert). For the Romans, the road to Berenice was an important trade route, well protected with forts and scribbled with diverse **graffiti**, while Bedouin filtering in from Sinai and up from Sudan left their own tribal markers.

The sites

The road from El-Quseir to Qift (just north of Qus) in the Nile Valley passes lots of rock art and inscriptions, especially from pharaonic times. The quarries at **Wadi Hammamat** (see the Red Sea Mountains map, p.748) are full of beautiful **hieroglyphs**, some overlaying dancing goddesses and ibexes. Predynastic boats and pharaonic inscriptions appear on the rocks either side of the road between Wadi Hammamat and El-Lakeita. Both these localities mark the start of trails to predynastic sites in **Wadi Qash** and **Wadi Atwan**, and require a 4WD and a guide who really knows the way.

Wadi Mineh (marked on the map on p.748), accessible by 4WD from either main road, but impenetrable without GPS, is a ravishing terrain of broad wadis and dunes containing the greatest wealth of petroglyphs and rock art in Egypt. At the northern end of Wadi Mineh is everything from pharaonic boats and **Horus figures** to Roman graffiti extolling the virtues of a prostitute. Farther south in Wadi Abu Wasil, a secluded area that Winkler called **Site 26** is covered with pictures of **chieftains**, boats, ostriches and cattle. One appears to show a man bleeding a cow, a practice found among pastoralist tribes even today.

Finally, the Mersa Alam–Edfu road runs straight through **Wadi Barramiyah** (see map on p.726), where the rock-cut **Temple of Kanais**, 50km from Edfu, contains scenes of Seti I smiting Shasu (a nomadic group from the Levant) and Nubian foes, and inscriptions lauding the well that he had dug along this desolate route. East of the temple, predynastic **boats** appear on both sides of the road; some are huge, with up to seventy crewmen. Notice the pictograms of a hippo, an elephant, and a pharaonic standard resembling the hieroglyph "to bore", appropriate for a mining area. There are more boats and animals within walking distance of the road, and up side-wadis. **Wadi Umm Salam** has been dubbed the "Canyon of the Boats" and also contains lines and squiggles that match up to modern maps of the wadi systems – a **predynastic map** of the area, some believe.

Contexts

Contexts

The historical framework

The present borders of Egypt are almost identical to those in pharaonic times, territories such as Sinai and Nubia being essentially marginal to the heartland of the Nile Valley and its Delta, where Egyptian civilization emerged some five thousand years ago. The historical continuity is staggering: the pharaonic era alone lasted thirty centuries before being appropriated by Greek and Roman emperors.

Egypt's significance in the ancient world was paramount, and the country has never been far from the front line of world history. Although neither Christianity nor Islam was born in Egypt, both are stamped with its influence. In modern times, when the Arab world sought to rid itself of European masters, Egypt was at the forefront of the anti-colonial struggle, while its peace treaty with Israel altered the geopolitics of the Middle East.

The beginnings

Stone tools from the gravel beds of Upper Egypt, El-Qaf and the Gilf Kebir in the Western Desert attest to the presence of **hunter–gathering hominids** in the area over 250,000 years ago, when the Sahara was a lush savanna that supported zebras, elephants and other game. Between the **Late Middle Paleolithic** (*c.*70,000 BC) and **Upper Paleolithic** (*c.*24,000 BC) eras there were fluctuating wet and dry periods, when lakes rose or shrank and grasslands expanded or receded, and tribes are assumed to have moved backwards and forwards between the Nile and the oases. While most still lived by hunting and fishing, herding cattle emerged even before cereal cultivation, sheep and goat herding filtered through from the Near East (*c.*7000 BC).

During the **Neolithic** era, Middle Egypt and the Delta had **settled communities** that cultivated wheat and flax, herded flocks and wove linen. Although some reverted to a nomadic lifestyle after the rains of the Neolithic era checked the process of desertification, others remained to develop into agricultural societies. It was during the **Middle and Late Neolithic periods** (6600–5100 and 5100–4700 BC respectively) that human occupation of the Western Desert reached its peak, giving rise to the rock art in the Cave of the Swimmers and other sites at the Gilf Kebir and Jebel Uwaynat.

Predynastic Egypt

The impetus for development came from southern Egypt. At **Nabta Playa**, 100km west of Abu Simbel, archeologists have identified the world's **oldest calendar** of standing stones and sculpted monoliths – dating from around 6000 BC – that attests to a Neolithic culture with a knowledge of astronomy and the resources and organization to create such a site. And then there are the mysterious **boats** drawn in the Eastern Desert perhaps a thousand years later, which Rohl believes represent "Eastern Invaders" who conquered the indigenous people of the Nile Valley. However, evidence of later agricultural societies is less impressive, and there is disagreement over the categorization of cultures. The earliest is known as the **Badarian**, after the village of El-Badari where Brunton carried out excavations in the 1920s. The Badarians were farmers, hunters and miners; they made fine pottery, carved bone and ivory, and traded for turquoise and wood.

The **Naqada I** period, from about 4000 BC onwards, was characterized by larger settlements and a distinctive style of pottery: burnished red clayware with black rims or white zoomorphic decorations. Clay and ivory figurines show Naqada menfolk sporting beards and penis shields, raising a possible ethnic connection with their Libyan neighbours. More extraordinary are the narrow-necked vases carved from basalt, which can't be reproduced by twenty-first-century technology but were supposedly made by the Stone Age Naqada I culture.

In the conventional scheme of things, graves from the **Naqada II** period contain copper tools and glazed beads that signify advances in technology, and extraneous materials such as lapis lazuli, indicating trade with Asia. The graves themselves evolved from simple pits into painted tombs lined with mats and wood and, later still, brick. The development of extensive irrigation systems (*c*.3300 BC) boosted productivity and promoted links between communities.

The Two Lands

By this time, the communities of Upper and Lower Egypt existed in two loose **confederations**. As power coalesced around Naqada in the south and Behdet in the Delta, each confederation became identified with a chief deity and a symbol of statehood: Seth and the White Crown with **Upper Egypt**, Horus and the Red Crown with the **Delta**.

Later, each acquired a new capital (Hierakonpolis and Buto, respectively) and strove for domination over the entire region. The eventual triumph of the southern kingdom resulted in the **unification of the Two Lands** (*c*.3100 or 2090 BC) under the quasi-mythical ruler **Menes** (aka Narmer), and the start of Egypt's Dynastic period. Some identify him as pharaoh Aha, whose tomb is the earliest found at Saqqara, but if the Greek name "Menes" is derived from the Egyptian *mena* ("Establisher"), it may not refer to any actual individual.

The Archaic Period

The **Early Dynastic** or **Archaic Period** was the formative epoch of Egyptian civilization. Its beginnings are a mix of history and myth, relating to the foundation – supposedly by Menes – of the city of **Memphis**, located at the junction between Upper and Lower Egypt: the first imperial city on earth.

From this base, Djer and Den, the third and fifth kings of the **I Dynasty** (*c*.3100–2890 or 2920–2770 BC), attempted to bring Sinai under Egyptian control. Writing, painting and architecture became increasingly sophisticated, while royal tombs at Saqqara and Abydos developed into complex mastabas, thought to have been modelled on the palaces of living kings. At this time, royal burials were accompanied by the deceased's servants – a practice that later dynasties abandoned.

Also indicative of future trends was the dissolution of the unified kingdom as centralized authority waned towards the end of the dynasty. Although this was restored by **Raneb** (or Hotepsekhemwy), founder of a new line of rulers, regional disputes persisted throughout the **II Dynasty** (*c*.2890–2686 or 2770–2645 BC).

These disputes probably inspired the **contendings of Seth and Horus**, a major theme in Egyptian mythology. The Stele of Peribsen shows a temple

Egyptology is riddled with uncertainties, not least in its chronology of dynasties and kingdoms (not an Egyptian concept, but a modern invention enabling scholars to get a handle on three thousand years of history). Two critics have assailed conventional chronology from opposite directions. Their arguments deserve to be read in full, but can be summarized as follows.

In *A Test of Time*, **David Rohl** examines the "Four Pillars" of synchronicity between Ancient Egyptian and Biblical history and judges only one to be impeccable. In Rohl's opinion, anomalies such as the royal burials at Tanis and Deir el-Bahri, Israelite chariots on the Ashkelon Wall at Karnak, and evidence of their sojourn at Avaris call for a revision of the chronology of the Third Intermediate Period, with knock-on effects on earlier times. Rohl's **New Chronology** puts the Exodus in the XIII rather than the XIX Dynasty, and makes Akhenaten a contemporary of David and Saul. The sceptical response from other archeologists can be read on ⓦmembers.aol.com/IanWade%20/Waste/Index.html.

Unlike Rohl, **Anthony West** is not a professional Egyptologist, and his *Serpent in the Sky* – propounding that the Egyptian temples embody the legacy of an older, greater civilization dating back to Atlantis – was laughed off until two geologists agreed that the erosion in the bedrock of the Sphinx shows that it was created at least 2600 years earlier than had hitherto been assumed. Egyptologists failed to refute their evidence in a showdown at the 1992 conference of the American Association for the Advancement of Science, but have since taken comfort from a study by the Getty Institute, which concludes that the erosion proves nothing of the kind.

As both debates are unresolved, we've stuck to **orthodox chronologies**, about which even mainstream Egyptologists differ and acknowledge margins of error. These are up to a hundred years in the period around 3000 BC, seventy-five years around 2000 BC, and between ten and fifteen years around 1000 BC. From 500 BC onwards, dates are fairly precise until the Ptolemaic era, when the chronology gets hazy, only firming up again in Roman times.

facade surmounted by the figure of Seth, rather than Horus, the traditional symbol of kings. However, the rivalry between the two regions and their respective deities appears to have been resolved under **Khasekhemwy**, the last king of the dynasty – paving the way for an era of assurance.

During the **III Dynasty** (*c*.2686–2613 or 2649–2575 BC), advances in technology and developments in culture raised Egypt to an unprecedented level of civilization. The main figure of the III Dynasty was **King Zoser** (or Djoser), whose architect, **Imhotep**, built the first **Step Pyramid** at Saqqara in the 27th century BC. The pyramid's conception and construction were a landmark, and later generations deified Imhotep as the ultimate sage. On the economic and political front, the III Dynasty also sent expeditions into Sinai, to seek turquoise and copper and to subjugate the local Bedouin.

The Old Kingdom

Pyramid-building and expansionism were likewise pursued during the **IV Dynasty** (*c*.2613–2494 or 2575–2465 BC). The Dynasty's first king, **Snofru** (aka Sneferu), raised two pyramids at Dahshur and made incursions into Nubia and Libya. His successors, **Cheops** (Khufu), **Chephren** (Khafre) and **Mycerinus** (Menkaure), erected the **Pyramids of Giza**, expanded trade relations with the Near East, and developed mining activities in Nubia, where a copper-smelting factory was established at the Second Cataract. Though Snofru's line expired with the death of **Shepseskaf**, his widow Queen **Khentkawes** is believed to have married a high priest to produce an heir.

This trend continued during the **VI Dynasty** (*c*.2345–2181 or 2465–2323 BC), when nobles were buried in their own **nomes** (provinces). While punitive expeditions carried the pharaoh's banner deep into Nubia, Libya and Palestine, domestic power ebbed to the nomarchs, the situation reaching the point of no return under **Pepi II** (aka Neferkare), whose death heralded the **end of the Old Kingdom**.

The First Intermediate Period

After Pepi's death, decades of provincial rivalry and chaos ensued, with petty dynasties claiming the mantle of the Old Kingdom. The Greek historian Manetho records seventy rulers during the brief **VII Dynasty** (*c*.2181–2173 or 2150–2134 BC), while an unknown number of kings vainly asserted their claims from Memphis during the **VIII Dynasty** (*c*.2173–2160 or 2150–2134 BC).

When rains failed over the Ethiopian highlands, famine struck Egypt, exacerbating civil disorder. Weak principalities sought powerful allies such as **Herakleopolis**, the dominant city of the Twentieth Nome, whose ruler, **Achthoes**, gained control of Middle Egypt, assumed the throne name Meryibre, and founded the **IX Dynasty** in 2160 or 2154 BC.

Whereas most of the north came under the control of the IX and **X Dynasty** (*c*.2130–2040 or 2154–2040 BC) kings of Herakleopolis, Upper Egypt was contested by the rulers of **Edfu** and Luxor (known to history as **Thebes**, which would later be the capital of the New Kingdom). After vanquishing his rival, the Theban ruler Inyotef Sehertowy tried to extend his power beyond Upper Egypt, founding the **XI Dynasty** (*c*.2133–1991 or 2134–2040 BC). The struggle between north and south was only finally resolved by **Nebhepetre Mentuhotpe II**, who reunited the whole country under one authority in 2055 or 2050 BC, establishing the Middle Kingdom.

The Middle Kingdom

During Mentuhotpe's fifty-year reign the mines and trade routes were reopened; incursions into Libya, Nubia and Sinai resumed; and arts and crafts flourished again. His successors, Mentuhotpe III and IV, were most notable for their expeditions to the Land of Punt. Inscriptions from Wadi Hammamat name the vizier in charge of the second expedition as **Amenemhat** (or Ammenemes), who subsequently founded the **XII Dynasty** (*c*.1991–1786 or 1985–1955 BC).

Amenemhat returned the capital to Memphis and safeguarded the Nile Delta from raiders by constructing the Walls of the Prince, a fortified *cordon sanitaire*. Northern Nubia was annexed, and trade extended further into Palestine and Syria.

Under Amenemhat's son, **Senusert I** (aka Sesostris I), the administrative capital was transferred to the **Fayoum**, where massive waterworks were undertaken. Amenemhat II curbed the power of the nomarchs, while Senusert III may have abolished the office completely. These kings also built **the last pyramids**, at Lahun, El-Lisht and Hawara, where the final pyramid was erected by Amenemhat III, alongside the Labyrinth described by Herodotus.

According to Rohl's New Chronology, it was **Amenemhat III** who took **Joseph** as his vizier and let the **Israelites** settle in the Delta (*c.*1662 BC). Graves at Avaris suggest a large Semitic population stricken by calamities, akin to the Biblical account of the events leading up to the Exodus, which Rohl assigns to the reign of the XIII Dynasty pharaoh **Dudimose** (*c.*1447 BC). Both these dates are utterly at variance with the conventional chronology, which places the Exodus two centuries later, during the New Kingdom.

However, there is no disagreement that the late XII Dynasty was a **troubled time**, with the Nile flooding at record levels, bringing poor harvests and famine in its wake. The faces of the statues of pharaohs of this era are uniquely stern and careworn. Whether or not Egypt was also smitten by plagues and disrupted by an exodus from the Delta, it was obviously in poor shape to resist an invasion.

The Second Intermediate Period

Under the **XIII Dynasty** Egypt slid towards an era of disorder that archeologists term the **Second Intermediate Period**, when the pharaohs lost control of Nubia and the Delta. For the first time, Lower Egypt fell into the hands of "rulers of foreign lands" or *heka kaswt* – later rendered by the Ptolematic historian Manetho as **Hyksos**. While Manetho relates that "peoples of an obscure race" appeared "like a blast of God" in the reign of Dudimose, most archeologists believe that they filtered into the eastern Delta as immigrants or slaves during the late Middle Kingdom, and only took over later. There's less doubt that they had weapons and technology which gave them an edge over the Egyptians: chariots, bronze armour, helmets and swords, and recurved bows that outranged the Egyptian ones.

For a time, the western Delta remained independent, under the **XIV or Xois Dynasty**, which was contemporaneous with the **Hyksos XV Dynasty** until about 1650 BC. After capturing Memphis, the Hyksos established relations with Thebes and traded up and down the Nile, but continued to rule from the Delta city of **Avaris** and maintain links with Palestine, Crete and Persia. Relations deteriorated after the **Theban XVII Dynasty** began harassing their caravans and ships, and the Hyksos king **Apophis** sent an insult to Sekenenre Tao II of Thebes, who used it as a pretext to declare war (*c.*1560 BC). Sekenenre Tao's son **Khamose** continued the struggle on two fronts (after the Hyksos forged an alliance with Nubia) and was within striking distance of Avaris when he died, whereupon his brother, **Ahmosis I**, finally expelled the Hyksos from Egypt (in 1567 or 1550 BC), ushering in a new era.

Although Egyptian chronicles describe their rule as anarchic, evidence such as the *Rhind Mathematical Papyrus* suggests that the Hyksos fostered native culture, took Egyptian names and ruled as pharaohs, while their introduction of the *shaduf* (counterweighted draw-well) irrigation device proved of lasting benefit to Egyptian agriculture. Many think that their dismissive sobriquet, the "Shepherd Kings", is a mistranslation of Manetho's rendering of the original Egyptian name.

The New Kingdom

The **XVIII Dynasty** (*c.*1567–1320 or 1550–1307 BC) founded by Ahmosis inaugurated the **New Kingdom**, a period of stability, wealth and expansion, whose rulers include some of the most famous names in Egyptian history. During this era **Nubia** was brought under Egyptian control, yielding gold, ivory, ebony, gems and, most importantly, slaves. The professional armies of the pharaohs also invaded the Near East, Syria and Palestine, establishing colonies governed by Egyptian viceroys or local satraps. One result was an influx of immigrants into Egypt, bringing new customs, ideas and technology.

The effects are evident at **Thebes**, capital of the New Kingdom, where a spate of temples and tombs symbolize the pre-eminence of the god **Amun** and the power of the pharaohs. While **Tuthmosis I** (*c.*1525–1512 BC) built the first tomb in the Valley of the Kings, his daughter **Hatshepsut** raised the great mortuary temple of Deir el-Bahri, ruling as pharaoh (*c.*1503–1482 BC) despite her stepson's claim on the throne. Having belatedly assumed power, **Tuthmosis III** embarked on imperial conquests, extending Egyptian power beyond the Fourth Cataract in Nubia, and across the Euphrates to the boundaries of the Hittite Empire. His successor **Amenophis II** (*c.*1459–1425 BC) penetrated deeper into Nubia, and **Tuthmosis IV** (*c.*1425–1417 BC) further strengthened the empire by marrying a princess of Mitanni, a state bordering the Hittites.

The zenith of Egyptian power coincided with the reign of **Amenophis III** (*c.*1417–1379 BC). With the empire secure and prosperity at home, the king devoted himself to the arts and the construction of great edifices such as Luxor Temple. During the same period, a hitherto minor aspect of the sun-god was increasingly venerated in royal circles: the **cult of Aten**, which the pharaoh's son would subsequently enshrine above all others.

The Amarna Revolution

By changing his name from Amenophis IV to **Akhenaten** and founding a new capital at Tell el-Amarna, the young king underlined his commitment to a new **monotheistic religion** that challenged the existing priesthood and bureaucracy. Since the story of Akhenaten and **Nefertiti** is related in detail on p.297, here it suffices to say that the **Amarna Revolution** barely outlasted his reign (*c.*1379–1362 BC) and that of his mysterious successor, **Smenkhkare**, who died the following year.

The boy king **Tutankhamun** (1361–1352 BC) was easily persuaded to abjure Aten's cult and return the capital to Thebes, heralding a **Theban counter-revolution** that continued under **Ay** and **Horemheb**. Though Horemheb (*c.*1348–1320 BC) effectively restored the *status quo ante*, his lack of royal blood and, more importantly, an heir, brought the XVIII Dynasty to a close.

The XIX Dynasty

The **XIX Dynasty** (*c.*1320–1200 or 1307–1196 BC) began with the reign of Horemheb's vizier, **Ramses I** (*c.*1320–1318 BC), whose family was to produce several warrior-kings who would recapture territories lost under Akhenaten. **Seti I** (*c.*1318–1304 BC) reasserted pharaonic authority in Nubia, Palestine and the Near East, and began a magnificent temple at Abydos. His son **Ramses II** (*c.*1304–1237 BC) completed the temple and the reconquest of Asia Minor, commemorating his dubious victory at Qadesh with numerous reliefs, but later concluding a treaty with the Hittites. At home, Ramses usurped temples and statues built by others, and raised his own monumental edifices – notably the Ramesseum at Thebes and the sun temples at Abu Simbel.

His son **Merneptah** (*c.*1236–1217 BC) faced invasions by the "Sea Peoples" from the north and Libyans from the west, but eventually defeated the latter at Pi-yer in the western Delta. He is also popularly believed to be the pharaoh of the **Exodus**, though the only known pharaonic reference to the Israelites describes an Egyptian victory against these "nomads". The XIX Dynasty expired with **Seti II** (*c.*1210 BC), to be followed by a decade without a ruling dynasty.

The XX Dynasty

The **XX Dynasty** (*c.*1200–1085 or 1196–1070 BC), begun by Sethnakhte, was the last of the New Kingdom. His successor **Ramses III** (*c.*1198–1166 BC) repulsed three great invasions by the Libyans and Sea Peoples, and built the vast temple-cum-pleasure palace of **Medinet Habu**. But strikes by workmen at the royal necropolis and an assassination plot within the king's harem presaged problems to come. Under the eight kings who followed (all called Ramses), Egypt lost the remains of its Asiatic Empire, and thieves plundered the necropolis. **Ramses XI** (*c.*1114–1085 BC) withdrew to his residence in the Delta, delegating control of Upper Egypt to **Herihor**, high priest of Amun, and Lower Egypt to Vizier **Smendes**.

The Third Intermediate Period

This division was consolidated under the **XXI Dynasty** (*c.*1069–945 BC), the successors of Herihor and Smendes ruling their respective halves of Egypt from **Thebes** and **Tanis**. The two ruling houses (both designated as the XXI Dynasty) seem to have coexisted in harmony, with the Theban priest-kings acknowledging the Tanite pharaohs' superiority. Towards the end of this era, a powerful new dynasty of **Libyan** extraction was founded by **Shoshenk I**. This **XXII Dynasty** (*c.*945–715 BC) ruled Egypt from Bubastis in the Delta until a rival line seized power in Upper Egypt, precipitating civil war between the Bubastite monarchs and the Theban **XXIII Dynasty** (818–720 BC), which was further complicated by a brief **XXIV Dynasty** (727–715 BC) of Ethiopian kings.

The lifespan of these four dynasties – termed the **Third Intermediate Period** (TIP) – is one of the murkiest eras of Egyptian history, yet crucial to the New Chronology hypothesis, as the accepted dates for the New Kingdom hinge on the length of the TIP. Rohl contends that the XXI and XXII dynasties overlapped for generations, and that the duration of the TIP should therefore be reduced accordingly – with knock-on effects down the line. Even mainstream Egyptologists differ over the next significant dynasty, which some assign to the final phase of the TIP, and others regard as the start of the Late Period – but at least they all more or less agree on dates from this point onwards.

The Late Period

In 747 BC, Egypt's prolonged instability was brought to an end by the intervention of neighbouring Nubia. The Nubian king Piankhi advanced as far north as Memphis, while his brother Shabaka went on to conquer the Delta and reunite the Two Lands. The **XXV Dynasty of Nubian Kings** (*c.*747–656 BC) was marked by a revival of artistic and cultural life and renewed devotion to Amun (as evinced by reliefs at Karnak and Luxor). The dynasty's later, Ethiopian, rulers had to contend with the Assyrians, who were thrown back from the gates of **Thebes** in 671 BC and eventually sacked the city in 664 BC.

Egypt became a province of the Assyrian Empire, ruled by local princes who paid tribute to the Assyrians until they withdrew from Egypt to defend their empire from the Babylonians, leaving a vacuum that was filled by **Psammetichus I**, the fourth ruler of the **XXVI Dynasty** (664–525 BC). Known as the *Saïte Dynasty* after its capital at **Saïs** in the Delta, this was the last great age of pharaonic civilization, harking back to the glories of the Old Kingdom in art and architecture, but also adopting new technologies and allowing colonies of Greek merchants at Naucratis and Jewish mercenaries at Elephantine.

Necho II (610–595 BC) defeated Josiah, King of Judah, at Megiddo, but was routed by the Babylonians. He is also credited with starting to build a canal to link the Nile with the Red Sea. Though **Psammetichus II** (595–589 BC) enjoyed several victories, his successor **Apries** was overthrown following defeat in Cyrenaica, the throne passing to **Amasis** "the Drunkard", who relied on Greek allies to stave off the Persian Empire.

Persian rule

The **Persian invasion** of 525 BC began a new era of rule by foreigners that essentially lasted until Nasser eventually overthrew Egypt's monarchy in 1952.

Mindful of the Assyrians' mistake, the Persian emperors **Cambyses** and **Darius I** kept a tight grip on Egypt. Besides completing Necho's canal and founding a new city near Memphis, called **Babylon-in-Egypt** (today's "Old Cairo"), they built and restored temples to enhance their legitimacy. But **rebellions** against Xerxes and Artaxerxes testified to Egyptian hatred of this foreign **XXVII Dynasty** (*c.*525–404 BC).

The Persians, ousted by Amyrtaeus, sole ruler of the **XXVIII Dynasty**, constantly assailed the native rulers that followed. Though **Nectanebo I** of the **XXX Dynasty** (*c.*380–343 BC) managed to repulse them with Greek help, his successor's campaign in Phoenicia failed. Finally, bereft of allies, **Nectanebo II** (360–343 BC) was crushingly defeated by Artaxerxes III, and fled to Nubia. Egypt remained under Persian control until 332 BC, when their entire empire succumbed to **Alexander the Great**.

The Ptolemies

Alexander's stay in Egypt was brief, though long enough for him to adopt local customs. He offered sacrifices to the gods of Memphis and visited Amun's temple at Siwa; reorganized the country's administration, installing himself as pharaoh; and founded the coastal city of **Alexandria**; he then went off to conquer what remained of the known world. Upon his death in 323 BC, Alexander's Macedonian generals divided the empire, Ptolemy becoming ruler of Egypt and establishing the **Ptolemaic Dynasty** in 332.

Under Ptolemy I, **Greek** became the official language, and Hellenistic ideas had a profound effect on Egyptian art, religion and technology. Although Greek deities were also introduced, the Ptolemies cultivated the Egyptian gods and ruled much like Egyptian pharaohs, erecting great cult temples such as Edfu and Kom Ombo. They also opened new ports, established the great Library of Alexandria and had Hebrew scriptures translated into Greek by rabbis. The first synagogue in Egypt was founded at Leontopolis in the Delta.

It was dynastic disputes that led to the loss of Ptolemaic control. **Roman intervention** in Egypt grew until, under Ptolemy XII Auletes (80–51 BC), Egypt was almost totally dependent on Rome. **Julius Caesar** attacked Egypt in 54 BC, taking Alexandria by force.

The most famous queen of Egypt, **Cleopatra VII** (51–30 BC), was also the last of the Ptolemies. Under the protection of Julius Caesar – by whom she bore a son, Caesarion – Cleopatra managed to prolong her family's rule. After Caesar's death, she formed a similar alliance with **Mark Antony** to preserve Egyptian independence. Their joint fleets, however, suffered disaster against **Octavian** at the Battle of Actium, and both committed suicide rather than face captivity. Subsequently Egypt was reduced to the status of a province of the Roman Empire (30 BC).

Roman rule and the rise of Christianity

The **Roman emperors**, like the Ptolemies, adopted many of the Egyptian cults, building such monuments as Trajan's kiosk at Philae and temples at Dendara and Esna. Their main interest in the new colony, however, lay in its potential as grain supplier to Rome. With this end constantly in mind, trade routes were ensured by Roman garrisons at Alexandria, Babylon (Old Cairo) and Syene (Aswan). In terms of culture, language and administration, **Hellenistic influence** barely diminished and Alexandria continued to thrive as an important centre of Greek and Hebrew learning.

Although the **Holy Family's flight to Egypt** from Palestine cannot be proven, Egypt's Jewish colonies would have been a natural place of refuge, and many sites remain associated with the episode. According to Coptic tradition, **Christianity** was brought to Egypt by **St Mark**, who arrived in the time of Nero. Mark converted many to the new underground faith, founding the Patriarchate of Alexandria in 61 AD.

Politically, the most significant ruler was **Trajan** (98–117), who reopened Necho's Red Sea Canal. Trade flourished with the export of glass, linen, papyrus and precious stones. But the *fellaheen* were growing increasingly discontented with heavy taxation and forced recruitment into the Roman army.

The Copts

First-century Egypt was fertile ground for the spread of Christianity. The religion of the old gods had lost its credibility over the millennia of political manipulations and disasters, while the population – Egyptians and Jews alike – was becoming increasingly anti-Roman and nationalistic in its outlook. The core of Christianity, too, had a resonance in ancient traditions, with its emphasis on resurrection, divine judgement and the cult of the great mother.

Inevitably, as Egypt's Christians – who became known as **Copts** – grew in political confidence, there was conflict with the Roman authorities. In 202, **persecutions** began, reaching their height under **Diocletian** (284–305), when thousands of Coptic Christians were massacred. Copts date their calendar from the massacres in 284.

The legalization of Christianity and its adoption as the imperial religion by **Constantine** in 313 did little to help the Copts. The Roman leaders, from their new capital at **Byzantium**, embraced an orthodox faith that differed fundamentally from that of their Egyptian co-religionists – and persecutions continued. An attempt to reconcile differences at the **Council of Nicaea** (325) failed, and the split had become irrevocable by the time it was formalized at the **Council of Chalcedon** (451), following which the Copts established their own completely separate Patriarchate at Alexandria.

The same period also saw the emergence of **monasticism**, which took root in the Egyptian deserts. The monasteries of St Catherine in the Sinai, those of Wadi Natrun and Sohag, and St Anthony's and St Paul's in the Red Sea Mountains, all originated in these years.

The coming of Islam

Apart from a brief invasion in 616, Egypt remained under **Byzantine rule** until the **advance of Islam** in the seventh century. The Muslim armies, led by the Prophet Mohammed's successor, Abu Bakr, defeated the Byzantine army in 636. General Amr Ibn al-As then advanced towards the fortress town of Babylon-in-Egypt, which surrendered after a brief siege, to be followed by Heliopolis (640) and finally the imperial capital of Alexandria (642).

Amr built his capital, **Fustat**, north of Babylon-in-Egypt, in what is today Old Cairo. However, Egypt was merely a province in the vast Islamic empire that was governed from Damascus and Baghdad. As in Roman times, Egypt's primary role was as a bread basket for the empire.

Arabization and Islamicization was a gradual and uneven process, with intermittent periods of religious toleration and discrimination. Much depended on the character of the caliphs and their own power struggles, whose impact was felt throughout the Islamic empire. In 750, the empire's ruling **Umayyad** dynasty was defeated by the armies of Abu al-Abbas (a descendant of Abu Bakr), and an **Abbassid** caliphate came to power in Baghdad, administering Egypt, along with its other territories, for the next two centuries.

The Tulunids (868–905) and Ikhshidids (935–969)

In 868, **Ahmed Ibn Tulun**, sent to administer Egypt on behalf of Caliph al-Mu'tazz, declared the territory independent. He and his successors, the **Tulunids**, ruled for 37 years, during which time economic stability and order were restored. Like previous rulers, Ibn Tulun built a new capital city, **Al-Qitai**, whose vast mosque still remains. The dynasty did not long outlive him, however. His spendthrift son, Khomaruya, was assassinated, as were his heirs, and by 905 Abbassid rule was reimposed.

Egypt remained under the direct control of Baghdad until 935, when Mohammed Ibn Tughj was appointed governor and granted the title Ikhshid (ruler or king) by the caliph. Like the Tulunids, the **Ikhshidid dynasty** functioned virtually independently of the caliphate. Severe taxation, though, led to popular discontent. The death in 965 of Tughj's second son, Ali, combined with famine, drought and political instability, opened the way for an invasion of the **Shia Fatimids** from Tunisia.

The Fatimid Era (969–1171)

The early **Fatimid caliphs** ruled half the Muslim world, with Egypt forming the central portion of an empire that included North Africa, Sicily, Syria and western Arabia. **Gohar**, commander of the caliphal forces, built the city of **Al-Qahira** (the Triumphant) as a new capital in 969, its walls containing opulent palaces and the prestigious mosque-university of Al-Azhar. **Caliph al-Muizz** installed himself in the city and from there ruled the empire. Trade with India, Africa and Europe expanded, the burdensome tax system was abolished, and a vast multi-racial army that included Europeans, Berbers, Sudanese and Turks was formed.

Whereas Al-Muizz and his successor Al-Aziz were efficient and tolerant rulers, under whom Egypt's economy prospered and the arts flourished, the third caliph – **Al-Hakim** (996–1021) – was a mad and capricious despot. His laws outraged the population, while his support of Byzantine against Latin Christians, and destruction of the Church of the Holy Sepulchre in Jerusalem, later provided a pretext for the First Crusade. His mysterious disappearance (see p.140) was taken by his followers as proof of messianic stature.

By the long reign of Al-Hakim's grandson, **Al-Mostansir** (1035–94), decay had set in. The empire was largely controlled by army commanders, administration was chaotic and famine added to the troubles. A series of governors imposed control over the army and restored peace and prosperity to Egypt for a further hundred years, but the loss of Syria to the Seljuk Turks, and new forces in Europe, left the empire increasingly vulnerable.

The **First Crusade** (1097–99), and those that followed, were motivated as much by the desire to acquire estates as to restore Christian dominance to the Holy Land. Egypt was not attacked until 1167, by which time the Crusader kingdom held the former Fatimid coastal area of Palestine. Outraged at the fraternization between Franks and Fatimids, the Seljuk Sultan, Nur al-Din, sent an expedition to Cairo to repel them. The sultan's deputy, Shirkoh, occupied Upper Egypt, while his nephew, Salah al-Din al-Ayyubi – known to Europe as Saladin – took possession of Alexandria.

The Ayyubids (1171–1250)

On the death of the last Fatimid caliph in 1171, **Salah al-Din** became ruler of Egypt. To this day he remains a hero in the Arab world, a ruler renowned for his personal modesty, generosity, culture and political acumen. Having no pretensions to religious leadership, Salah al-Din chose for himself the secular title of Al-Sultan ("The Power") rather than that of caliph, giving his family's name to the dynasty that succeeded him. Of his 24-year reign, he spent only eight years in Cairo, the rest being spent in liberating Crusader-held territory. By 1183, Syria had been won back and in 1187 Jerusalem was recaptured.

In Cairo, Salah al-Din built a fortress – today's Citadel – and expanded the Fatimid walls to enclose the city. In order to propagate Sunni orthodoxy, he also introduced the Seljuk institution of the **madrassa** or teaching mosque, thus turning Cairo into a great centre of learning. Hospitals were endowed, too, and the pharaonic canal at Fayoum was reopened.

Following his peaceful death in Damascus in 1193, Salah al-Din's eastern territories fragmented into principalities, though Egypt remained united under the Ayyubids. His nephew, **Al-Kamil** (1218–38), repulsed the Fifth Crusade. The last of the dynasty, **Ayyub** (1240–49), built up a formidable army of Turkish-speaking Qipchak slaves from the Black Sea region, and he himself married a slave girl, **Shagar al-Durr** ("Tree of Pearls").

It was Shagar al-Durr who took power following Ayyub's death, ruling openly as sultana until the Abbassid caliphs insisted that she take a husband, quoting the Prophet's words: "Woe to the nations ruled by women." Jealous of her power and warned by astrologers that he would die at a woman's hands, her husband, Aybak, planned to take a second wife, whereupon she had him murdered. She herself was assassinated soon afterwards, but her henchman, **Beybars the Crossbowman**, clawed his way to power.

The Mamlukes (1250–1517)

Beybars was a commander (amir) among the **Mamlukes**, the foreign troops on whom the later Ayyubids depended. Recruits originally came from Central Asia but were later drawn from all over the Near East and the Balkans. Their price in the slave markets reflected the "value" of ethnic stock (130–140 ducats for a Tartar, 110–120 for a Circassian, 50–80 for a Slav or Albanian) plus individual traits: sturdy, handsome youths were favoured.

Following Beybars' accession, the Mamlukes became a self-perpetuating warrior caste whose amirs ruled Egypt for the next three centuries, each sultan intriguing his way through the ranks to assume the throne by *coup d'état* or assassination. As the Mamlukes were forbidden to marry until they reached a certain rank, their sexual relations with peers and superiors also played a part in their advancement. With the support of the right amirs, the most ruthless Mamluke could aspire to being sultan. Frequent changes of ruler were actually preferred, since contenders had to spread around bribes, not least to arrange assassinations.

Bahri Mamlukes (1250–1382)

The **Bahri** ("River") **Mamlukes**, named after their garrison by the Nile and predominantly Turkic, formed the first of these military dynasties. The dynasty was founded by **Qalaoun**, who poisoned Beybars' heirs to inherit the throne. He sponsored numerous buildings in Cairo, and established relations as far afield as Ceylon and East Africa, concluding treaties with the Hapsburg Emperor Rudolph and other European princes. In 1291 his son, **Khalil**, forced the remaining Crusaders from their stronghold in Acre, Palestine.

Qalaoun's son **Mohammed al-Nasir** (1294–1340) was another great builder and power-broker. He concluded treaties with the Mongols, after defeating them in Syria, and strengthened political and trade ties with Europe. After his death a series of weak relatives were barely able to hold the throne in the face of conflicts between rival Mamluke factions.

Burgi Mamlukes (1382–1517)

In 1382 the sultanate was seized by **Barquq**, one of the Circassian **Burgi** ("Tower") **Mamlukes** from the garrison below the Citadel. To finance his campaigns against the **Mongols**, who by 1387 were on the borders of Syria, he had to impose punitive taxes that beggared the economy. Hardships were exacerbated by famine and plague during the reign of his son, **Farag** (1399–1405), and it was only under Sultan **Barsbey** (1422–37) that Egypt regained some of its power. Barsbey established friendly relations with the new power in the north, the Ottoman Turks, and expanded trade in the Indian Ocean. But although the next hundred years saw relative peace and security, the Egyptian economy remained shaky.

The country experienced a brief revival under the rule of **Qaitbey** (1468–95), though his lavish building programme imposed a huge burden. The 46th (and penultimate) sultan, **Qansuh al-Ghuri** (1501–16), suffered the loss of customary revenues after Vasco da Gama discovered the Cape of Good Hope, dealing a crippling blow to Egypt's spice trade monopoly. Worse was to come, as the **Ottoman Turks** consolidated their northern empire, defeating the Shiite Persians and then attacking Mamluke territory in northern Syria. In 1516, Al-Ghuri was killed in battle and his successor, Tumanbey, was executed in Cairo by the Ottomans in 1517.

Ottoman Egypt (1517–1798)

Even after the Turkish conquest, the Mamlukes remained powerful figures, running the administration of what was now a province of the vast **Ottoman Empire**. Government was provided by a series of **pashas**, career officials trained in Istanbul. As long as taxes were received, the Ottomans interfered little with Egyptian affairs and Cairo retained its importance as a religious, if not cultural or commercial, centre.

The Mamluke army continued to grow with the import of Caucasian slaves and by the end of the sixteenth century had become powerful enough to depose a pasha, although the Ottomans still held overall control. The growing power of the highest rank of the military corps – the **Beys** – posed a challenge to that of the pashas. Their arbitrary taxes, profligate ways and internal rivalry dominated events.

Meanwhile, economic decline, accelerated by changes in European shipping routes, and an outbreak of plague in 1719, left the country in a sorry shape. The French traveller Volney, visiting around 1784, described a depopulated country, whose capital was crumbling and surrounded by mounds of rubbish.

French Occupation (1798–1802)

At the end of the eighteenth century, Egypt became a pawn in the struggle for power between France and Britain. **Napoleon** saw Egypt as a means to disrupt British commerce and eventually overthrow their rule in India. In 1798, his fleet landed at Alexandria, where he issued a proclamation that began with the Islamic *bismillah* ("In the name of God . . ."). He stated his aim of liberating Egypt from the "riffraff of slaves", and concluded that he respected Allah, his Prophet and the Koran more than the Mamlukes did.

Although Napoleon routed the Mamlukes at Imbaba and occupied Cairo, he left his fleet exposed at Abu Qir Bay, where it was attacked and destroyed by the British under Nelson. With his grand vision in tatters, and facing a declaration of war from the Ottoman sultan, Napoleon returned secretly to France. General Kléber, whom he left in charge, had a victory over the Ottomans, but was then assassinated. When his successor, General Menou, took charge, declared his conversion to Islam, and proclaimed Egypt a **French protectorate**, the British invaded from Abu Qir and occupied Alexandria. Combined Ottoman-British forces then took Damietta and Cairo, and the French were forced to surrender. Under the Capitulation Agreement, the archeological treasures gathered by Napoleon's savants were surrendered to Britain – which is why the **Rosetta Stone** ended up in the British Museum rather than the Louvre.

Mohammed Ali and his heirs (1805–92)

After the expulsion of the French a power struggle ensued, which was won by **Mohammed Ali**, whose dynasty was to change Egypt more radically than any ruler since Salah al-Din. An officer in the Albanian Corps of the Ottoman forces, Mohammed Ali is widely regarded as the founder of modern Egypt. The Ottomans confirmed him as **Pasha** in 1805, whereupon he proceeded to decapitate – literally and figuratively – what remained of the Mamluke power structure. The first time was on the occasion of his accession, where he tricked them into a coup attempt; six years later, he dispensed with the rest of the Mamluke leadership, inviting 470 Beys to a feast at the Citadel and slaughtering the lot.

Though nominally a vassal of the Ottoman sultan, Mohammed Ali's control was absolute. He confiscated private land for his own use and set about modernizing Egypt with European expertise, building railways, factories and canals. Meanwhile, his son Ibrahim led a murderous campaign to subjugate northern **Sudan**, of which the only positive result was the introduction of a special kind of **cotton** – henceforth Egypt's major cash crop.

When Mohammed Ali died insane in 1849, his power greatly reduced after disastrous adventurism in Greece and Syria, he was succeeded by **Abbas** (1848–54), who closed the country's factories and schools and opened Egypt to free trade, thus delaying the country's industrial development for the next century. Abbas's successor, **Said Pasha** (1854–63), granted a concession to a French engineer, **Ferdinand de Lesseps**, to build the **Suez Canal**. The project was completed in 1869, by which time **Khedive Ismail** (1863–79) was in power. An ambitious and enlightened ruler, Ismail transformed Cairo, spending lavishly on modernization. However, exorbitant interest rates had to be paid on loans from European lenders. Egyptian indebtedness spiralled and, to stave off bankruptcy, Ismail sold his Suez Canal shares to the British government in 1875.

He was deposed and succeeded by his son **Tewfiq** (1879–92), whose own financial control was limited by the French and British, to the disgust of patriotic Egyptians. A group of army officers forced him to make power-sharing concessions and to appoint their leader, **Ahmed Orabi**, as Minister of War. France and Britain responded by sending in the gunboats, shelling Alexandria and landing an army at Ismailiya, which subsequently routed Orabi's forces at Tell el-Kebir and restored Tewfiq as a puppet ruler under British control.

British occupation and Egyptian nationalism

Britain's stated intention was to set Egyptian affairs in order and then withdraw, but its interests dictated a more active and permanent involvement. From 1883 to 1907, Egypt was controlled by the British Consul-General, Sir Evelyn Baring, later **Lord Cromer**, who coined the term "Veiled Protectorate" to describe the relationship between the two countries.

The emergence of the **Mahdi** in Sudan accelerated the trend towards direct British involvement in military and civil affairs. Sudan was nominally an Egyptian *khedival* possession – a status quo which the British, ostensibly, moved to protect. However, Britain was clearly pursuing its own interests and dominating Egyptian government to the extent of replacing its key officials with British colonial personnel. Egyptian resentment at this usurpation of authority found expression both under Tewfiq's son, **Abbas II**, who came to power in 1892, and in a nationalist movement led by a young lawyer, **Mustafa Kamel**. To ameliorate the situation, the British made a series of reforms and allowed Ahmed Orabi to return from exile in Ceylon.

Economically, however, Egypt was effectively a colony, with Britain supplying all the country's manufactured goods, and in turn encouraging Egyptian dependence on cotton exports. In order to grow cotton, the *fellaheen* had to take out loans; when prices fell, many were forced to sell up to large landowners.

Towards independence

Politically, things came to a head when Turkey entered **World War I** on the side of Germany, in November 1916. Egypt was still nominally a province of the Ottoman Empire, so to protect its interests – the Suez Canal and free passage to the East – Britain declared Egypt a protectorate. By 1917, **Fouad**, the sixth son of Ismail, was *khedive* of Egypt, with Sir Reginald Wingate its High Commissioner.

The **nationalist movement** flourished under wartime conditions. In 1918, its leader, **Sa'ad Zaghloul**, presented the High Commissioner with a demand for autonomy, which was rejected. The request to send a delegation (*wafd*) to London led to Zaghloul's arrest and deportation to Malta, a decision rescinded after nationwide anti-British riots. In 1922 Britain abolished the protectorate and recognized Egypt as an independent state, but kept control of the legal system, communications, defence and the Suez Canal. In March 1922, Fouad assumed the title of king.

The years between independence and World War II saw a struggle for power between the king, the British and the nationalist **Wafd Party**. Backed by the masses, the Wafd won landslide elections, but King Fouad retained power and the backing of the British. His son, **King Farouk**, succeeded him to the throne in 1935 and a year later signed a twenty-year **Anglo–Egyptian treaty**, which ended British occupation but empowered British forces to remain in the Suez Canal Zone. In 1937, Egypt joined the League of Nations, but the outbreak of World War II halted its move to complete independence.

World War II and postwar manoeuvrings

World War II saw Rommel's **Afrika Korps** coming within 111km of Alexandria, though they were repulsed by the **Eighth Army** under General

Montgomery at the **Battle of El-Alamein** in October 1942. Thereafter the tide of war turned in the Western Desert campaign and the Allies continued to advance across North Africa, through Libya and Tunisia.

During the war, Egypt served a vital strategic role as a British base in the Middle East. The Wafd leadership went along with support for the Allies, keeping internal tensions controlled on the tacit understanding that full independence would be granted after the war. Cairo became a centre of international power-broking, with its British political-military command and exiled Balkan royals. On conclusion of the war, the Wafd demanded the evacuation of British troops and unification with Sudan – in opposition to British plans for the latter's self-government. Popular resentment was expressed in anti-British riots and strikes, supported by the **Muslim Brotherhood**, which led to clashes with British troops. In January 1947, British troops were evacuated from Alexandria and the Canal Zone.

Following the declaration of the state of **Israel** in May 1948, Egypt joined Iraq, Syria and Jordan in a military invasion. The defeat of the Arab forces was followed by a UN-organized treaty in February 1949 that left the coastal **Gaza Strip** of Palestine under Egyptian administration. Many of the Egyptian officers who fought in this war were disgusted by the incompetence and corruption of their superiors: it was from the officers' ranks that many of the leading lights of the 1952 Revolution were to emerge.

The 1952 Revolution

For the time being, the country experimented with democracy, holding its first **elections** in ten years. The Wafd won a majority and formed a government with Nahas Pasha as prime minister. A course for crisis was set, as the **Suez Canal** – which the British still controlled – loomed increasingly large. In 1952, Nahas was dismissed by King Farouk after abrogating the 1936 treaty with Britain, and the army was sent out onto the streets to quell anti-British protests.

Reaction was swift. On July 23, 1952, a group of conspiratorial **Free Officers** seized power and forced the **abdication of King Farouk**. General Naguib, the official leader of the group, was made commander of the armed forces and became prime minister, but real power lay in the hands of the nine officers of the **Revolutionary Command Council** (RCC), foremost among whom was Colonel **Gamal Abdel Nasser**.

Under RCC direction, the constitution was revoked, political parties dissolved, the monarchy abolished and Egypt declared a **republic** (July 26, 1953). Meanwhile, a struggle for power was taking place behind the scenes, as Naguib attempted to step beyond his figurehead status and moderate the revolutionary impulses of the RCC. After being implicated in an attempt on Nasser's life at Alexandria in 1954, Naguib was placed under house arrest; Nasser became acting head of state and in June 1956 was confirmed as president.

The Nasser Era (1956–70)

President Nasser dominated Egypt and the Arab world until his death in 1970, his ideology of Arab nationalism and socialism making him supremely popular with the masses (if not always their governments) from Iraq to Morocco. Under his leadership, Egypt was at the forefront of **anti-colonialism**, lending support to liberation struggles in Algeria, sub-Saharan Africa and other regions. Nasser also helped to set up the Non-Aligned Movement with Yugoslavia, India and Indonesia in 1955.

Nasser's most urgent priority, from the start, was to assert Egyptian control over the **Suez Canal**. In 1954 he reached agreement for the withdrawal of British troops from the Canal Zone, though the Canal's management and profits were to remain in foreign hands. At the same time he was seeking credits from the World Bank to finance construction of the Aswan High Dam and weapons to rearm Egyptian forces, depleted from the 1948 War. When the Soviet Union offered to supply the latter, the United States vetoed loans for the dam. Committed to the Aswan plan, Nasser had little alternative but to nationalize the Suez Canal in order to secure revenue. This he did in July 1956.

His action was regarded by the West, and especially by Britain, as a threat to vital interests, and an unholy alliance was formed to combat the "Arab Hitler". Britain and France concluded a secret agreement with Israel, whose **invasion of Sinai** in October 1956 was to provide the pretext for their own military intervention. Following massive bombardment of the zone and British paratroop landings in Port Said, the United States stepped in to impose a solution, threatening to destabilize the British economy unless their forces were withdrawn. The American motivation was to keep Britain and France from gaining control of the Middle East, and the Arabs from moving en masse into the Soviet camp. In the event, the Canal was reopened under full Egyptian control and Nasser emerged from the **Suez Crisis** as a champion of Arab nationalism.

On a wave of **pan–Arab** sentiment, Egypt and Syria united to form the **United Arab Republic** (UAR) in 1958, an unworkable arrangement that foundered within three years. Nasser also intervened in the **Yemen civil war**, supporting the revolutionary faction, to the extent of authorizing the use of poison gas against royalist forces. On a broader political front, he moved closer to the Soviet Union, accepting technical and military assistance on a massive scale, to help build the Aswan Dam and to counter an increasingly well-armed, US-supplied Israel. Meeting in Cairo in 1964, the **Arab League** set aside funds for the formation of the **Palestine Liberation Organization**.

The Six Day War

War was again on the horizon. When Israel threatened to invade Syria in 1967, Nasser sent Egyptian forces into Sinai, ordered UN monitors to withdraw, and blockaded the Tiran Straits, cutting shipping to the Israeli port of Eilat. Israel responded with a pre-emptive strike, destroying the Egyptian Air Force on the ground and seizing the entire Sinai. This **Six Day War** resulted in the Israeli occupation of Sinai and the Gaza Strip, the West Bank and the Golan Heights. It was a shattering defeat for the Arabs, and Nasser in particular, who proffered his resignation to the public, only resuming the presidency after vast demonstrations of support on the streets.

The Six Day War had no official resolution, merely subsiding into a **War of Attrition**, which was to drag on for the next two years. From their positions in Sinai, Israeli forces bombarded Egypt's Canal cities, and even Cairo and Middle Egypt suffered bombing raids. Egypt, meanwhile, was rearming with Soviet assistance and struggling to deal with millions of refugees from the Canal Zone and the newly occupied Gaza Strip.

Progress and repression

Amid the political drama of Suez and the wars with Israel, it is easy to overlook the **social achievements** of the Nasser era. One of the first acts of the Revolutionary Command Council was to break up the old feudal estates, transferring **land** to the *fellaheen*. As a result of the **Aswan Dam**, the amount of land under cultivation increased by fifteen percent – exceeding Egypt's population growth for the first time. The dam's electricity also powered a huge new **industrial base**, which was established virtually from scratch. Similarly radical progress was made in the fields of **education and health care**. The number of pupils in school doubled, and included both sexes for the first time. As a result of a huge programme of local health centres and the doubling of the number of doctors, average life expectancy rose from 43 to 52 years.

The downside of Nasserism was a heavily bureaucratic, Soviet-modelled system. Political life was stifled by the merging of all parties into the **Arab Socialist Union** (ASU). Opponents of the regime were not tolerated: censorship, torture, show trials and political internment were widespread.

Nevertheless, **Nasser's death** – from a heart attack – in September 1970 came as a profound shock to the whole Arab world. His funeral procession in Cairo was the largest the country has ever seen.

Egypt under Sadat (1970–81)

Nasser's successor was his vice president, **Anwar Sadat**, whom the ASU hierarchy confirmed as president in October 1970. His role was to reform an Egypt demoralized by defeat in the 1967 War, economic stagnation and austerity. His first significant act was to announce a "**corrective revolution**", reversing the policy of centralized economic control and expelling over a thousand Soviet advisors.

Again, however, domestic affairs were overshadowed by military ones. In concert with Syria and Jordan, Egypt launched a new campaign against Israel. On October 6, 1973, Egyptian forces crossed the Suez Canal, storming the "invincible" Bar-Lev Line to enter Israeli-occupied Sinai. This **October War** (aka 10th Ramadan/Yom Kippur War) ultimately turned against the Arabs, but enhanced their bargaining position and dealt a blow to Israeli self-confidence. In addition, Egypt regained a strip of territory to the east of the Suez Canal.

The open-door policy

After the war, extensive changes took place in Egypt. An amnesty was granted to political prisoners, press censorship was lifted and some political parties, including the Muslim Brotherhood, were allowed. Equally important was Sadat's economic policy of *infitah* or "**open door**", designed to encourage private and foreign investment and to reduce the role of the state in the economy.

Helped by Gulf Arab investments – a reward for the October War – and stimulated by the reconstruction of the Canal cities, the economy boomed. However, the benefits were distributed unevenly: while the number of millionaires rose from 500 to 17,000 between 1975 and 1981 and an affluent middle class developed, the condition of the urban poor and *fellaheen* worsened. Some five million families subsisted on less than $30 a month, and one and a half million Egyptians migrated to work in the Gulf states.

Camp David and afterwards

In 1977, when the International Monetary Fund insisted on the removal of subsidies on basic foodstuffs, there were nationwide **food riots**. Sadat saw the crunch coming and needed a major injection of Western capital. That year Sadat went to Jerusalem, the first Arab leader to visit Israel. This dramatic step, accompanied by a total realignment of Egyptian foreign policy towards the United States, reflected Sadat's need for US investment and his belief that Israel's acquisition of nuclear weapons made a military solution to the conflict impossible.

Under the US-sponsored **Camp David Agreement** of 1978, Egypt recognized Israel's right to exist and Israel agreed to withdraw from Sinai. This independent peace treaty, which failed to resolve the Palestinian issue, outraged Arab opinion. The Arab League Council, meeting in Baghdad, decided to withdraw their ambassadors to Egypt, sever economic and political links, and transfer the League's headquarters from Cairo to Tunis.

At home, Sadat encouraged the rise of Islamic political forces to counter leftist influences. But as the Muslim Brotherhood grew stronger and protested against the economic slump and the Camp David accord, Sadat clamped down, ordering wholesale arrests of his critics. This resulted in a highly charged atmosphere, and ultimately **Sadat's assassination** by Islamic militants in October 1981.

Mubarak's Egypt

Sadat's policies have for the most part been continued, more cautiously, by his successor **Hosni Mubarak**, who took office in 1981 and remains in power at the time of writing. While his sheer survival counts for something, the country's situation is almost as precarious as it was in the early 1970s, when the writer Naguib Mahfouz likened Egypt to a group of drowning men struggling to reach the water's surface.

The economy

Egypt's **economy** was in dire straits by the end of the Sadat era, and its root problems seem intractable. Only three percent of Egypt's land is useable for agriculture, while the **population** rises by a million every nine months (at the time of writing, it stands at 76 million). Since the mid-1980s, Egypt has had to import half the food it needs, and its **foreign debt** has reached over $33 billion. Without $2 billion a year in **US aid** (Egypt is the largest recipient after Israel), the economy would collapse. It is this situation that has led to such schemes as the Toshka Project, which aims to make 5700 square kilometres of desert fertile by irrigating it with water pumped from Lake Nasser (see p.467).

Domestic revenues depend on a narrow base that's vulnerable to regional instability: remittances from Egyptians working abroad, crude-oil production, tolls on shipping through the Suez Canal, and tourism. All were badly hit by the **Gulf War** of 1990–91, which led to over a million refugees returning from Kuwait and Iraq and wiped out the tourist industry for a year. The government's support for US action against Iraq was rewarded by the writing-off of $7 billion in debts, further military and economic aid, and the promise of contracts and jobs for Egyptians in the Gulf States, but prospects had hardly begun to improve when terrorist attacks on tourists exposed another aspect of the economy's vulnerablity. **Tourism** had only just recovered from the crippling effects of the 1997 Luxor massacre when the 9/11 attacks in the US sent it plunging again.

Even before this, the economy's fragility was evident, as speculation against the Egyptian pound and a liquidity crisis in the banking system led to a six percent **devaluation** of the national currency in 2001, and its flotation in 2003. Things could have been worse had Egypt not been attracting new investments from foreign and domestic sources since the mid-1990s, while the prospect of Egypt becoming a major exporter of **natural gas** over the next decade offers some hope to economists.

For most ordinary Egyptians, however, living standards are no higher than in Nasser's time, and the need for housing, jobs and land is greater than ever. Discontent is also fostered by widespread **corruption**, extending from local government to central ministries and the private sector. While cases of buildings collapsing due to contractors cutting corners have become all too familiar, the whole nation was shocked by a catastrophic **train fire** in 2002 that killed 363 third-class passengers – exposing the ramshackle state of Egypt's railways and officialdom's indifference to the lives of the poor.

In February 2006 the arrival of bird flu in Egypt caused widespread alarm. At the time of writing, most of the fatalities from the H5N1 virus have been women, who rear poultry at home and employ an ancient method of feeding, whereby they chew grain and blow it into the birds' mouths. With five million households rearing ducks or chickens, the government has refused to compensate them for birds culled and terminated payments to commercial breeders after some were discovered to be passing sick birds to one another so all could claim. Instead, the authorities are offering free flu vaccinations in the Delta and the Fayoum and asking foreign donors to fund a nationwide vaccination programme. The World Health Organization fears that Egypt offers ideal conditions for the H5N1 virus to mutate into a deadlier strain, and has accused the government of complacency – to which it has responded by blaming donors for failing to pay funds already pledged.

Domestic politics

Mubarak's pseudo-liberalization of the media and parliamentary politics has given a democratic gloss to an authoritarian system, essentially unchanged since Nasser's time. Under the **emergency laws** passed after Sadat's murder – still in force today – demonstrations are illegal unless licensed by the police (who violently suppress unauthorized ones), and **censorship** of the media extends to the removal of "atheist" works from the Cairo Book Fair. **Torture** and other abuses of power by the police and security forces go unpunished, while human rights activists and political opponents are arrested.

Prodded by US rhetoric about spreading democracy, Mubarak had to open the presidential election to other candidates when he ran for a fifth term of office in September 2005. However, opposition candidates were vilified and persecuted: Cairene lawyer **Ayman Nour** was jailed (and later freed) on charges of forging signatures as MP of a new liberal party, Al-Ghad ("Tomorrow"), while meetings of the reformist alliance **Kifaya** ("Enough") were broken up by government thugs. As everyone expected, Mubarak was re-elected by a huge majority – and might have won even in a fair election thanks to his track record and the perception of Nour as a self-interested oligarch backed by the US.

Government manipulation was less successful in the three-stage ballot for the National Assembly in the last months of 2005. Despite being banned, and police

As the third president to have emerged from the armed forces, Mubarak is even more beholden to them than his predecessors. Ex-military and police officers hold top jobs in civilian life, and **internal security** is a constant preoccupation.

Between 1992 and 1998, **Islamic militants** and the security forces fought a vicious, low-level war in Middle Egypt. Human rights organizations estimate that over 1200 people were killed, 10,000 wounded and scores of thousands detained under the emergency laws during the six-year insurgency. Ironically, the **Luxor massacre** that made headlines around the world in 1997 proved to be the swansong of the extremist Gamaat Islamiya – whose imprisoned leaders denounced the massacre and announced a ceasefire – while the other militant group, Jihad Islami, had by this time decamped to Afghanistan, where they forged an alliance with Al-Qaida.

To Egyptians' dismay, there has since been a resurgence of **terrorism**. In October 2004, car bombs killed 34 tourists at the Sinai resorts of **Taba** and **Ras al-Shaitun**. The government blamed it on a Palestinian angered by events in Gaza, but the interrogation of 2500 residents of North Sinai suggested that the culprits were local Bedouin sympathizers of Al-Qaida. By holding families hostage and cracking down on drug smuggling, the police angered many other Bedouin and inadvertently helped the terrorists gain support. A triple bombing at **Sharm el-Sheikh** in July 2005 left 70 dead and a hitherto unknown group, Al-Tawhid w'al Jihad, claimed responsibility, stating: "Our war has begun by targeting the axis of Zionist evil and immorality in Sinai, where Moses spoke to God." Only after a further bombing at **Dahab** in April 2006 did security forces storm the terrorists' bases at Jebel Halal and Jebel Magarah in the hinterland of El-Arish, dubbed the "Tora Bora of Sinai". However, the discovery of huge caches of TNT near Rafah and Ismailiya and the arrest of a Palestinian wearing an explosive belt in 2007 suggests that terrorists are still active in Egypt.

violence that claimed eleven lives, the Muslim Brotherhood won a quarter of the seats under the guise of independent candidates – an unpredecented protest vote that the regime had to swallow (see pp.788–790 for more on Islamist politics in Egypt). Since then the government has tried to weaken the opposition by arresting the Brotherhood's financial backers, and Internet bloggers who have publicized scandals ignored by the state media, such as torture in police stations, or the crowds of young men who ran amok in downtown Cairo during Eid al-Fitr in 2006, molesting women – an outrage against traditional norms that provoked nationwide soul-searching. In 2007, the Alexandrian blogger Abdel Kareem Soliman was sentenced to four years in prison for "insulting Islam" and Mubarak, after calling Al-Azhar University "a nursery of terrorism" and Egypt's president a despot.

Although a taboo subject in the media, it's widely believed that the ailing president, in his late 70s at the time of writing, wants his younger son, **Gamal Mubarak**, to succeed him, despite assertions that "Egypt is not Syria". A small Westernized minority may consider Gamal a modernizer like King Mohammed VI of Morocco, but most Egyptians view him as a playboy set to inherit the family fortune. Few doubt that a succession crisis looms in the not so distant future.

Foreign affairs

Though he managed to restore ties with Arab states that had boycotted Egypt after Sadat's détente with Israel, and Egypt was able to rejoin the Arab League in 1990, Mubarak has maintained a "cold peace" with the Jewish state. His

foreign policy involves a delicate balancing act, as Egypt remains impaled on the contradictions of its relationships with America, Israel and the rest of the Arab world. The US is Egypt's prime financial underwriter and arms supplier, but consistently favours Israel, which Arab states and peoples universally regard as the main source of instability and danger in the Middle East. To an uncomfortable degree, the regime's stability hangs on the decisions of other governments and the outcome of US and Israeli elections – as the tortuous **peace process** in the Middle East has faltered or revived.

The terrorist attacks of **9/11** crystallized the Bush administration's view of world affairs as a struggle between good and evil, with Palestinians cast as terrorists unless proven otherwise, while the identification of two of the hijackers as Egyptians and most of the rest as Saudis – not to mention the nationality of Al-Qaida's leaders – further undermined relations between the US and its closest Arab allies, Egypt and Saudi Arabia. While both countries managed to keep a lid on domestic opposition to America's war in Afghanistan and the invasion of Iraq, they resented being told that they should become democratic when the US also expected them to ignore the outrage of their peoples resulting from its actions or those of Israel. During the Lebanon war of mid-2006, Egypt's government made impotent noises while cracking down on protests, yet again, while the Shia militia Hezbollah won universal Arab acclaim by withstanding Israeli attacks and launching rockets at Israeli towns.

The US failure in Iraq, the election of a Hamas government in the Palestinian territories and Hezbollah's defiance in Lebanon all benefited Iran, whose bid for nuclear power and, many suspect, nuclear weapons, rung alarm bells from Washington to Cairo. Tellingly, Bush granted Mubarak's heir-apparent Gamal a meeting at the White House shortly before Egypt announced that it would build a nuclear power station on the Mediterranean coast, which could give Egypt the means to produce nuclear weapons should Iran do so – though this aim has yet to be openly stated.

Islam

slam was a new religion born of the wreckage of the Greco-Roman world around the south of the Mediterranean. Its founder, a merchant named **Mohammed** from the wealthy city of Mecca (in what is now Saudi Arabia), was chosen as God's Prophet; in about 609 AD, he began to hear divine messages, which were later transcribed into the **Koran**, Islam's holy book. This was the same God worshipped by Jews and Christians – Jesus is one of the minor prophets in Islam – but Muslims claim he had been misunderstood by both earlier religions.

The distinctive feature of this new faith was directness – a reaction to the increasing complexity of established religions and an obvious attraction. In Islam there is no intermediary between humans and God (**Allah**) in the form of an institutionalized priesthood or complicated liturgy; and worship, in the form of prayer, is a direct and personal communication with God.

The Pillars of Faith

Believers face five essential requirements, the so-called "**Pillars of Faith**": prayer five times daily, the pilgrimage (hajj) to Mecca, the Ramadan fast, a religious levy, and – most fundamental of all – the acceptance that "there is no God but Allah and Mohammed is His Prophet". The Pillars of Faith are still central to Muslim life, articulating and informing daily existence. Ritual **prayers** are the most visible. Bearing in mind that the Islamic day begins at sunset, the five daily prayer times are sunset, after dark, dawn, noon and afternoon. Prayers can be performed anywhere, but preferably in a mosque. In the past, and even today in some places, a muezzin (prayer crier) would climb his minaret each time and summon the faithful.

Nowadays, the call is likely to be pre-recorded; even so, this most distinctive of Islamic sounds has a beauty all of its own. The message is simplicity itself: "God is most great (*Allahu Akbar*). I testify that there is no God but Allah. I testify that Mohammed is His Prophet. Come to prayer, come to security. God is great." Another phrase is added in the morning: "Prayer is better than sleep."

Prayers are preceded by ritual washing and are spoken with the feet bare. The worshipper, facing Mecca (the direction indicated in a mosque by the *mihrab* or niche), recites the *Fatihah*, the first chapter of the Koran: "Praise be to God, Lord of the worlds, the Compassionate, the Merciful, King of the Day of Judgement. Only thee do we worship and thine aid do we seek. Guide us on the straight path, the path of those on whom thou hast bestowed thy grace, not the path of those who incur thine anger nor of those who go astray." The same words are then repeated twice in the prostrate position, with some interjections of *Allahu Akbar*. It is a highly ritualized procedure, the prostrate position symbolic of the worshipper's role as servant (Islam literally means "submission"), and the sight of thousands of people going through the same motions simultaneously in a mosque is a powerful one. On Islam's holy day, Friday, all believers are expected to attend prayers in their local grand mosque. Here the whole community comes together in worship led by an *imam,* who may also deliver the *khutba*, or sermon.

Ramadan is the name of the ninth month in the lunar Islamic calendar, the month in which the Koran was revealed to Mohammed. For the whole of the month, believers must obey a rigorous fast (the custom was originally modelled on Jewish and Christian practice), forsaking all forms of consumption between sunrise and sundown; this includes food, drink, cigarettes and any form of sexual contact. Only a few categories of people are exempted: travellers, children, pregnant women and warriors engaged in a *jihad*, or holy war. Given the climates in which many Muslims live, the fast is a formidable undertaking, but in practice it becomes a time of intense celebration.

The pilgrimage, or **hajj**, to Mecca is an annual event, with millions flocking to Mohammed's birthplace from all over the world. Here they go through several days of rituals, the central one being a sevenfold circumambulation of the Ka'ba shrine, before kissing a black stone set in its wall. Islam requires that all believers go on a hajj as often as is practically possible, but for the poor it may well be a once-in-a-lifetime occasion, and is sometimes replaced by a series of visits to lesser, local shrines – in Egypt, for instance, to the mosques of Saiyida Zeinab or El-Hussein in Cairo.

Based on these central articles, the new Islamic faith proved to be inspirational. Mohammed's own Arab nation was soon converted, and the Arabs then proceeded to carry their religion far and wide in an extraordinarily rapid territorial expansion.

Development in Egypt

Islam's **arrival in Egypt**, in 640, coincided with widespread native resentment of Byzantine rule and its particular version of Christianity. By promising to respect Egyptian Christians and Jews as "people of the Book", the Muslim leader **Amr** got acquiescence, if not immediate support, from the population, in the wake of the Arab conquest. For many Egyptians who had found Christianity a more valid religion than the old pagan, polytheistic theology, Islam must have seemed a logical simplification, capturing the essence of human relationships with an all-powerful god.

Early on, the spread of Islam was accompanied by a practical conflict of interest. The Arabs wished to spread the faith, yet their administration depended on finance raised by a poll tax (*jizia*) levied on non-Muslims. A balance was maintained for a while, but towards the end of the ninth century, rulers began to use the tax as a punitive measure, alongside a series of repressive acts directed against the Christian and Jewish faiths. Caliph al-Hakim, in particular, embarked on a programme of destroying churches and synagogues. However, it was not until the eleventh century that Cairo attained a **Muslim majority**, and not until the thirteenth century for Egypt as a whole.

The original Arab dynasties of Egypt subscribed to **Sunni Islam** – the more "orthodox" branch of the religion, dominant then, as now, in most parts of the Arab world. However, the Fatimid dynasty, which took control of Egypt in 969, signalled a shift to **Shiite Islam**, which was to continue (among the rulers, at least) until late in the twelfth century. Under the Ayyubid dynasty that followed, Egypt reverted, permanently as it turned out, to Sunni adherence, with orthodoxy propagated through the new institution of the **madrassa** – a theological college attached to a mosque.

Orthodoxy, by its nature, has to be an urban-based tradition. Learned men – lawyers, Koranic scholars and others – could only congregate in the cities where, gathered together and known collectively as the **ulema**, they regulated the faith. In Sunni Islam, the *ulema* divide into four schools (*madhahib*): Hanbali,

Maliki, Hanafi and Shafi'i – the last two of which predominate in Egypt. The Grand Sheikh of Cairo's great **Mosque of Al–Azhar** is regarded as the ultimate theological authority by most Sunnis outside the Gulf Arab states, and issues *fatwas* (opinions) on a range of questions submitted by believers, from family matters to financial affairs – in person, by post or email (⊛www.alazhar .org). However, the Grand Sheikh is not the only religious authority in Egypt; there is also a Grand Mufti, or supreme jurist, who is formally separate from Al–Azhar, although in practice he is bound to have studied or taught there at some point.

Sheikhs and Sufis

Alongside this formal religious establishment, Egypt also developed **a popular religious culture**, manifested in the veneration of sheikhs and the formation of Sufi brotherhoods – both of which remain important today. **Sheikhs** are basically local holy men: people who developed reputations for sanctity and learning. There is no set process for their sanctification in Islam – only acclamation – so the names change with the locality. Similar to sheikhs are individuals revered simply as **saiyid** ("lord") or **saiyida** ("lady"), due to their direct descent from the Prophet's line. Important Egyptian examples include Saiyid el-Hussein, Mohammed's grandson and the son of Ali, and the Prophet's granddaughters, Saiyida Zeinab and Saiyida Nafisa.

Although the Koran prohibits monasticism and isolation from the community, Islam soon developed religious orders dedicated to asceticism and a mystical experience of God. Collectively known as the **Sufis**, these groups generally coalesced around a charismatic teacher, from whom they derived their name. The largest of these brotherhoods (*tariqas*) in Egypt are the **Rifai**, the **Ahmediya** and the **Shadhiliyya** – who can be seen at moulids ("saint's day" festivals) parading with their distinctive banners.

Towards crisis

Unlike Christianity (at least Protestant Christianity), which has accepted the separation of church and state, Islam sees no such distinction. Civil law was provided by the Sharia, the religious law contained in the Koran, and intellectual life by the madrassas and Al-Azhar University. The religious basis of Arab study and intellectual life did not prevent its **scholars and scientists** from producing work that was hundreds of years ahead of contemporary "Dark Age" Europe. The medical treatises of Ibn Sina (who is known in Europe as Avicenna) and the piped water and sewage systems of Fustat are just two Egyptian examples. Arab work in developing and transmitting Greco-Roman culture was vital to the whole development of the European Renaissance.

By this time, however, the Islamic world was beginning to move away from the West. The **Crusades** were one enduring influence towards division. Another was the Islamic authorities themselves, who were increasingly suspicious (like the Western Church) of any challenge and actively discouraging of innovation. At first it did not matter in political terms that Islamic culture became static. But by the end of the eighteenth century, Europe was ready to take advantage. Napoleon's expedition to Egypt in 1798 marked the beginning of a century in which virtually every Islamic country came under the control of a **European power**.

Islam cannot be held solely responsible for the Muslim world's material decline, but because it influences every part of its believers' lives, and East–West rivalry had always been viewed in primarily religious terms, the nineteenth and twentieth centuries saw something of a **crisis in religious confidence**. Why had Islam's former power now passed to infidel foreigners?

The Islamist response

Responses to this question veered between two extremes. There were those who felt that Islam should try to incorporate some of the West's secularism and materialism; on the other side, there were movements holding that Islam should turn its back on the West, purify itself of all corrupt additions and thus rediscover its former power.

The earliest exponent of the latter view was the **Muslim Brotherhood** (Il-Ikhwan il-Muslimeen), founded in Ismailiya by **Hassan el-Banna** in 1928. The Brotherhood preached a moral renewal of Islam, established a network of schools and training centres, and later set up clandestine paramilitary groups. It was aimed as much against the corrupt feudal institutions as against Western imperialism.

Within fifteen years, the Brotherhood had spread throughout Egypt and spawned offshoots across the Middle East. Its terrorist activities prompted a violent state response, with its banning by King Farouk, whose bodyguards assassinated el-Banna in 1949. His mantle was assumed by **Sayyid Qutb**, whose conversion to radical Islam followed two years in the USA, where he was appalled by American women, the "animal-like" mixing of sexes and jazz music "created by Negroes to satisfy their love of noise and whet their sexual desires".

After the 1952 Revolution, the legitimized Brotherhood rapidly became disillusioned with Nasser's secular nationalism. In 1954, two Brothers attempted to assassinate him during a public meeting in Alexandria. Mass arrests followed and Qutb was jailed for ten years, writing a manifesto, *Milestones*, that was smuggled out of prison. His most influential idea was that Muslim states had reverted to Jahiliyya (the pagan era before Islam) by failing to apply Sharia law. True Muslims would experience "poverty, difficulty, frustration, torment and sacrifice" until Jahiliyya was overthrown. On the day of Qutb's execution in 1966, a 15-year-old follower vowed to continue his work by forging an Islamist vanguard: Ayman al-Zawahiri, the future founder of Jihad Islami and Al-Qaida's deputy leader, whose 2001 tract *Knights Under the Prophet's Banner* paid homage to Qutb.

In Egypt, the Brotherhood remained underground until the Sadat era, when the government regarded it as a useful counterweight to the Left. By this time the Brotherhood had abjured violence and its tacit cooperation with the state led to the emergence of more radical groups. Al-Takfir w'al-Hijra ("Excommunication and Exodus") attacked boutiques and nightclubs in Cairo during the 1977 food riots. Another group within Egypt's Military Academy planned a *coup d'état* but was nipped in the bud. The most effective was **Al-Jihad**, which assassinated Sadat and attempted to launch a revolution in Assyut in 1981. While the killers were hanged their "spiritual leader", the blind Sheikh Omar Abd el-Rahman, was acquitted and later moved to the USA (see box on p.306).

Under Mubarak, the mainstream Islamic opposition was allowed to establish clinics and schools for the poor, achieving greater influence over cultural life. In the late 1980s, **Gamaat Islamiya** ("Islamic Societies") captured the professional unions, and thousands of Egyptians put their savings into Islamic investment houses, which offered higher returns than ordinary banks. When these went bankrupt amid accusations of fraud, the Islamic movement's credibility was badly dented, but its prompt distribution of aid after the 1991 Cairo earthquake redeemed its reputation amongst the urban poor.

The following year, **Islamic militants** began a terrorist campaign in Middle Egypt, attacking tourists, policemen and Copts. Gamaat Islamiya (not to be confused with the aforementioned Islamic Societies, despite their overlapping membership and ideology) and the smaller Jihad Islami ("Islamic Jihad") both claimed Sheikh Abd el-Rahman and Al-Jihad as their exemplars, and divine sanction for attacks on the "Pharaonic regime", "infidel" tourists, and Copts who refused to pay *jizia* – the tax that non-Muslims had to pay under the caliphate. In practice, this involved local groups of extortionists, some of them traditional criminal families, or simply one clan revenging itself on another.

While Copts complained that the security forces were riddled with Islamist sympathizers, Muslims in Middle Egypt were subjected to curfews, searches, arbitrary arrest and torture by the security forces. In other ways, however, the authorities deferred to the Islamist agenda, jailing three hundred Egyptians for converting to Christianity, and ruling that a Cairo professor convicted of "apostasy" must separate from his wife.

By the time the imprisoned leadership of the Gamaat Islamiya announced a ceasefire after the Luxor massacre, the leaders of the Jihad Islami, **Ayman al-Zawahiri** and Mohammed Atef, had joined Osama Bin Laden in Afghanistan, merging with Al-Qaida to form the "World Islamic Front Against Jews and Crusaders". Their assault on the World Trade Center on September 11, 2001, was a devastating reprise of Abd el-Rahman's followers' attack on the Twin Towers in 1993. In Egypt, a new terrorist group called Al-Tawhid w'al Jihad has wreaked havoc on Sinai's resorts since 2004. That its members were Sinai Bedouin – a people who have previously showed no radical inclinations – especially alarmed the authorities.

Since the 2005 elections the Muslim Brotherhood – led by the sprightly octogenarian Mahdi Akef – has had 88 out of 454 seats in the National Assembly. While some credit them with being a responsible opposition, nudging Egypt towards parliamentary democracy, others reckon that their true agenda is summed up by the phrase "One man, one vote, once" – meaning that, having taken power by democratic means, the Brotherhood would abolish democracy. Their English-language website (@www.ikhwanweb.com) is couched in more moderate terms than their Arabic one.

While many Egyptians doubt that Islam offers a solution for *everything* – and the lifestyle aspirations of Egyptian youth are far from fundamentalist – the Islamists' view of world events is broadly shared at every level of society, from janitors to generals. The Brotherhood has a large following in universities and legal associations, with activists willing to risk arrest and torture. Besides using intimidation, the authorities have tried to marginalize them by changing the laws regulating professional associations and attempting to introduce a unified nationwide **azan** (call to prayer) in place of the cacophony of individual muezzins (which critics fear could provide a pretext to silence preachers linked to the Brotherhood). The training of **female imams** at Al-Azhar University is another aspect of the government's strategy to "modernize" Islam and move it away from radicalism (Morocco is likewise training women to be imams).

Though believers were united in outrage at cartoons of the Prophet in a Danish newspaper and Pope Benedict's characterization of Islam as violent, other controversies have been divisive. In 2007 Grand Mufti Ali Gomaa dismayed liberals by declaring statues idolatrous and outraged conservatives by ruling that women who lost their virginity before marriage could have reconstructive hymen surgery without telling their husbands, and even keep silent about adultery. Conservatives also deplored the Minister of Culture calling the veil "regressive" and the liberal theologian Gamal el-Banna (brother of Hassan el-Banna) arguing that the prohibition on smoking during Ramadan had no basis in Sharia law.

Egypt's most popular cleric is Sheikh Yusuf al-Qaradawi, who opines on the Al Jazeera show *Sharia and Life* and on ⊛www.islamonline.net. In the West he has been condemned for stating that homosexuals deserve the same punishment as fornicators, and that suicide bombings against Israeli soldiers and civilians in the Occupied Territories are a legitimate form of resistance. Yet he has also been denounced by Saudi clerics for saying that "The enmity that is between us and the Jews is for the sake of land only, not for the sake of religion", and for favouring Sufism and music – all of which are anathema to hardline Wahhabis.

Chronology

The chronology below is designed for general reference of monuments and dynasties or rulers. For simplicity, only the **major figures of each dynasty** or era are listed, and likewise with monuments and artefacts.

The following **abbreviations** are used: EAM (Egyptian Antiquities Museum in Cairo), IAM (Islamic Arts Museum in Cairo) and BM (British Museum in London).

c.250,000 BC ▶ **Hunter-gathering hominids** roam the savannas. Stone tools from this time have been discovered in gravel beds of Upper Egypt and Nubia.

c.25,000 BC ▶ **Late Paleolithic era**. Onset of desertification, until rains of Neolithic era. Ostrich eggs and flints have been found beneath dunes of Great Sand Sea.

c.6000 BC ▶ **Middle Neolithic era**. Intensive occupation of the Western Desert by hunter-gatherers. Rock art at the Gilf Kebir; solar calendar at Nabta Playa.

Predynastic Egypt

c.5000 BC ▶ Pastoralism becomes widespread in the Eastern and Western deserts, while **Badarian culture** takes root in the Nile Valley. Pottery, jewellery and ivory excavated at village of El-Badari in Upper Egypt.

c.4000 BC ▶ **Naqada I culture** Burnished pottery and granite mace heads have been found near Qus in Upper Egypt.

Early Dynastic or Archaic Period (c.3100–2686 or 2920–2575 BC)

c.2920–2770 BC ▶ **I Dynasty** Aha; Djer; Den.c.2920 or 3100 BC ▶ **Unification of the Two Lands** (Upper and Lower Egypt) by **Menes**. Foundation of Memphis; Palette of Narmer (EAM); Stele of Peribsen (BM); Scorpion Macehead (Ashmolean Museum, Oxford).

2686–2613 or 2469–2575 BC ▶ **III Dynasty** Zoser; Sekhemkhet; Huni. Step Pyramid and Unfinished Pyramid built at Saqqara; Collapsed Pyramid at Maidum.

Old Kingdom (c.2686–2181 or 2575–2134 BC)

2613–2494 or 2575–2465 BC ▶ **IV Dynasty** Snofru; Cheops; Chephren; Mycerinus. Bent Pyramid at Dahshur; Great Pyramids of Giza.

2494–2345 or 2465–2323 BC ▶ **V Dynasty** Userkaf; Sahure; Neferefre; Nyuserre; *Unas*. Sun Temples and Pyramids at Abu Sir; several further pyramids at Saqqara.

2345–2181 or 2323–2150 BC ▶ **VI Dynasty** Teti; Pepi I; Pepi II. More pyramids at Saqqara.

First Intermediate Period (c.2181–2050 or 2134–2040 BC)

2181–2160 or 2150–2134 BC
▶ **VII and VIII dynasties** Period of anarchy and fragmentation of power.

2160–2130 or 2154–2040 BC
▶ **IX and X dynasties** Achthoes. Capital at Herakleopolis, near Beni Suef.

2133–1991 BC ▶ **XI Dynasty** Inyotef Sehertowy; Nebhepetre Mentuhotpe II reunites Two Lands in 2050 BC. Ruined mortuary temple at Deir el-Bahri; Mentuhotpe's statue (EAM).

Middle Kingdom (c.2055–1650 or 2050–1786 BC)

1991–1786 or 1985–1955 BC
▶ **XII Dynasty** Amenemhat I; Senusert I and II; Amenemhat III. Pyramids at Lahun, Lisht and

Hawara; rock tombs at Beni Hassan and Aswan; site of Medinet Madi.

1955–1650 BC ▶ **XIII Dynasty**

Second Intermediate Period (c.1786–1567 or 1650–1950 BC)

1786–1603 or 1650–1550 BC
▶ **XIV Dynasty**

1674–1567 BC ▶ **XV and XVI (Hyksos) dynasties** Khyam; Apophis I and II. Capital at Avaris in the

Delta (with Minoan frescoes); Rhind Mathematical Papyrus (BM).

1684–1567 BC ▶ **XVII Dynasty** Expulsion of the Hyksos by Ahmosis. Tombs at Qarat Hilwah.

New Kingdom (c.1567–1085 or 1550–1070 BC)

1567–1320 or 1550–1307 BC
▶ **XVIII Dynasty** Two Lands reunited; period of imperial expansion. Ahmosis; Amenophis I; Tuthmosis I and II; Hatshepsut; Tuthmosis III; Amenophis II and III; Akhenaten; Smenkhkare; Tutankhamun; Ay; Horemheb. Temple of Deir el-Bahri; site of Tell el-Amarna; royal tombs in the valleys of the Kings and Queens at Thebes; Luxor and Karnak temples; Tutankhamun's gold (EAM).

1320–1200 or 1307–1196 BC
▶ **XIX Dynasty** Ramses I; Seti I; Ramses II; Merneptah; Seti II. Serapeum at Saqqara; temples at Abydos and Abu Simbel; Ramesseum and royal tombs at Thebes.

1200–1085 or 1196–1070 BC
▶ **XX Dynasty** Sethnakhte; Ramses III (and eight other minor and hopeless Ramses). Temple of Medinet Habu and further royal tombs at Thebes; some are plundered by workmen.

Third Intermediate Period (c.1069–747 BC)

1069–945 BC ▶ **XXI Dynasty** Authority divided between Tanis and Thebes. Smendes; Herihor; Psusennes I and II. Capital at Tanis; Treasure of Tanis (EAM); *Book of the Dead* (BM).

945–715 BC ▶ **XXII Dynasty** Shoshenk; Osorkon. Ruins at Tanis; Shoshenk's relief at Karnak.

818–715 BC ▶ **XXIII and XXIV dynasties**

Late Period (747–332 BC)

747–656 BC ▶ **XXV (Nubian) Dynasty** Piankhi; Shabaka; Taharqa; Tanutamun. Reliefs at Luxor; Kiosk of Taharqa at Karnak; statue of Amenirdis (EAM).

664–525 BC ▶ **XXVI (Saïte) Dynasty** Psammetichus I; Necho II; Psammetichus II; Apries; Amasis. Ruins of Naucratis; steles at Ismailiya.

525–404 BC ▶ **XXVII (Persian) Dynasty** Persian invasion. Cambyses; Darius I; Xerxes; Artaxerxes I. Temple

of Hibis at Kharga Oasis; completion of Nile–Red Sea Canal; foundation of Babylon-in-Egypt (Cairo).

404–380 BC ▶ **XXVIII and XXIX dynasties** Amyrtaeus; Amasis "The Drunkard". Temple of El-Ghweeta, Kharga Oasis; tomb of Amunhotep Huy, Bahariya Oasis.

380–343 BC ▶ **XXX Dynasty** Nectanebo I and II. Additions to Philae and Karnak; ruined temple of Amun at Siwa Oasis.

Ptolemaic Era (332–30 BC)

332–30 BC ▶ **Alexander the Great** conquers Egypt and founds Alexandria. His successors, the **Ptolemies**, make the city a beacon for the Mediterranean world, where Hellenistic and Judaistic culture mingles. Their line expires with Cleopatra VII (51–30 BC), vanquished by the power of Rome. In Nubia,

the kingdom of Meröe reaches its apogee. Construction (or modification) of temples of Edfu, Esna, Kom Ombo, Dendara and Philae; catacombs in Alexandria; Sanctuary of Amun at Siwa Oasis; ruins of Karanis and Qasr Qaroun in the Fayoum; Valley of the Mummies at Bahariya Oasis; Temple of Dakka, Lake Nasser.

Roman and Byzantine Period (30 BC–640 AD)

30 BC ▶ Octavian (Augustus) annexes Egypt to the **Roman Empire**. Tomb of Kitnes and Temple of Dush in Kharga Oasis.

45 AD ▶ St Mark brings **Christianity** to Egypt. Muzawaka Tombs in Dakhla Oasis.

249–305 ▶ **Persecution of Coptic Christians** under Decius and Diocletian. "Pompey's Pillar" at Alexandria.

313 ▶ Edict of Milan **legalizes Christianity**. Foundation of

monasteries of Wadi Natrun, St Anthony, St Paul and St Catherine.

395 ▶ Partition of Roman Empire into East and West; Egypt falls under Eastern, **Byzantine**, sphere. Necropolis of El-Bagawat at Kharga Oasis.

451 ▶ Council of Chalcedon leads to **expulsion of Copts from Orthodox Church**. Numerous objects in Coptic Museum (Cairo).

Arab Dynasties (640–1517)

640–642 ▶ **Arab conquest** of Egypt; introduction of **Islam**. Mosque of Amr and ruins of Fustat in Cairo.

661–750 ▶ Egypt forms part of **Umayyad Caliphate**, ruled from

the dynasty's capital at Damascus. Ceramics and pottery (IAM).

750–935 ▶ **Abbassids** depose Umayyads and form new dynasty, ruling from Baghdad. In 870 Egypt's governor, **Ibn Tulun**, declares independence, founding a dynasty which rules until 905. Mosque of Ibn Tulun in Cairo.

935–969 ▶ **Ikhshidid dynasty** takes power in Egypt.

969–1171 ▶ **Shiite Fatimid dynasty** conquers Egypt and seizes the Islamic Caliphate, which it rules from Cairo. Mosques of Al-Azhar, Al-Hakim and Al-Aqmar, Mausoleum of

Imam Al-Shafi'i, and various fortified gates, in Cairo.

1171–1250 ▶ **Salah al-Din** founds **Ayyubid dynasty** and liberates land conquered by the Crusaders. Egypt returns to **Sunni Islam**. Intrigues of **Shagar al-Durr** open the way to **Mamluke** takeover. Madrassa-Mausoleum of Al-Silah Ayyub and the Aqueduct in Cairo; ruins of Shali in Siwa Oasis. Mausoleum of Shagar al-Durr in Cairo.

Mamluke Dynasties (1250–1517)

1250–1382 ▶ **Bahri Mamlukes** Qalaoun; Khalil; Mohammed al-Nasir. In Cairo: Qalaoun's Maristan-Mausoleum-Madrassa, Mosques of Al-Nasir, House of Uthman Katkhuda, and Qasr Bashtak.

1382–1517 ▶ **Burgi Mamlukes** Barquq; Farag; Barsbey; Qaitbey; Qansuh al-Ghuri. In Cairo: Barquq's Mausoleum, Madrassa and Khanqah of Barsbey, Mosque of Qaitbey, and the Ghuriya. Also, Fort Qaitbey in Alexandria.

Ottoman Period (1517–1798)

1517 ▶ **Selim the Grim conquers Egypt**. For the next three centuries the country is ruled as an Ottoman province from Istanbul. In Cairo: Mosques of Suleyman al-Silahdar and Suleyman Pasha; Sabil-Kuttab of Abd al-Rahman Katkhuda. Terbana Mosque in Alex.

1798–1802 ▶ French occupation of Egypt. Capitulation Agreement of 1802 leaves British in effective control of the country. Treasures shipped off to Louvre/British Museum. European graffiti left on numerous temples.

Pashas, khedives and kings (1805–1952)

1805 ▶ **Mohammed Ali** seizes power and begins a programme of ruthless **modernization**. Mohammed Ali Mosque in Cairo; Ras el-Tin Palace and Mahmudiya Canal in Alexandria. Belzoni, Mariette and others pioneer digs at pharaonic sites in the Nile Valley and Delta.

1848–54 ▶ Reign of **Abbas I**.

1854–63 ▶ Reign of **Said Pasha**. Suez Canal begun.

1863–79 ▶ Reign of **Khedive Ismail**. Completion of Suez Canal; Central Cairo boulevards constructed.

1879–92 ▶ Reign of **Khedive Tewfiq**. British crush the **Orabi Revolt** (1882–83). Tewfiq reinstated as a puppet ruler under British control. Howard Carter discovers Tutankhamun's tomb at Thebes (1922) at the tail end of a period of intensive excavations throughout Egypt.

1935–52 ▶ Reign of King Farouk; during World War II Egypt stays under British control.

1952–53 ▶ Farouk overthrown by Free Officers. Egypt declared a republic. Construction of Midan Tahrir in Cairo.

Modern Egypt (1952–)

1956 ▶ **Nasser** becomes president; **Suez Crisis**. Major industrialization programme, and construction of schools, hospitals and public housing.

1967 ▶ **Six Day War** with Israel; massive damage to Canal cities.

1970 ▶ **Nasser dies** and is succeeded as president by **Sadat**. High Dam at Aswan completed (1970).

1973 ▶ **October War** with Israel.

1977–78 ▶ Food riots. Sadat's trip to Jerusalem leads to **Camp David** agreement. Mohandiseen district of Cairo built, along with hundreds of new hotels, shops, etc. First line of Cairo metro completed.

1981 ▶ **Assassination of Sadat**. Presidency assumed by **Mubarak**.

1990 ▶ **Gulf War**.

1991 ▶ **Cairo earthquake** Many buildings damaged, but the second metro line is pushed to completion.

1994 ▶ **Underwater finds at Alexandria** Divers and archeologists begin exploration of the ruins of the ancient Lighthouse of Pharos and the royal quarters in the harbour at Alexandria.

1995 ▶ Tomb of Ramses II's sons found in the Valley of the Kings.

1996 ▶ **Valley of the Mummies** Egypt's largest cache of mummies is discovered in Bahariya Oasis.

1997 ▶ Fifty-eight foreigners killed by Islamic militants at Hatshepsut's Temple, near Luxor. **Toshka Project** inaugurated.

2000 ▶ The interior of the **Red Pyramid** at Dahshur is reopened after many years.

2001 ▶ Discovery of the underwater city of **Herakleion** at Abu Qir on the Mediterranean coast.

2002 ▶ Inauguration of the **Bibliotheca Alexandrina**, and the completion of the main branch of the **Sheikh Zayid Canal** at Toshka.

2004 ▶ Opening of the Alexandria National Museum. Bombing of *Taba Hilton* in Sinai.

2005 ▶ **Mubarak** wins a fifth term as president. Bombings at Sharm el-Sheikh in Sinai.

2006 ▶ Discovery of **tomb KV63** at the Valley of the Kings. Bombings at Dahab in Sinai.

Music

Egypt's traditions in music, as with other cultural spheres, date back to pharaonic times, though the primary influences are Arab and Islamic. Given Egypt's status in the Arab world, it's no surprise that Cairo is the centre of the Arab recording industry – a dominance partly acquired thanks to the decline of its rivals in Lebanon, Libya and Kuwait, but one which is at the same time being challenged by new studios and labels in Saudi Arabia and the Emirates. Still, Egypt's vast and youthful population (over thirty million Egyptians are under 25) makes it the most important market for Arab music; what follows is the briefest of introductions to the various major musical genres.

Ancient Egyptian music

You won't hear **Ancient Egyptian music** played anywhere – indeed, nobody is sure what it sounded like – but enough is known about the instruments for musicologists to have tried to recreate the hymns and processional songs that accompanied religious rituals and court life in ancient times. Flutes and clarinet-type instruments go back to the Old Kingdom (if not Predynastic times), as do harps (which evolved from hand-held instruments to large, freestanding ones), trumpets, cymbals and castanets. By the Middle Kingdom, harps were accompanied by the *sistrum* (a kind of rattle associated with the goddess Hathor and often carved with her face), tambourines, clappers and a type of guitar. The lute and lyre appeared during the Second Intermediate Period and were probably introduced by the Hyksos, while other instruments came into Egypt as a result of the various foreign invasions after the fall of the New Kingdom.

Religious music

Although the call to prayer and the recitation of the Koran are not regarded in Egypt as music, they are certainly musical and listened to for pleasure – especially during Ramadan and other religious festivals. The *tajwid*, or musically elaborate style of Koranic recitation, reached its apogee in Egypt; virtuosity is maintained by rigorously testing reciters before they are awarded the title of moqri. Among the masters of this genre are **Sheikh Mohammed Mahmoud al-Tablawi**, **Sheikh Abdelbasset Abdessamad** and **Mohammed Rifaat**.

Performers may be **munshids** – professionals who move from one festival to another – or simply the **muezzin** or **imam** of the local mosque. In everyday life, all muezzins have their individual styles of phrasing, and the government's proposal to replace diverse voices with a single nationwide **azan** has been fiercely resisted (though many city-dwellers would welcome a ban on amplifiers). Recitals at **moulids** are often more participation than performance, with lines of Sufi devotees chanting and swaying to the accompaniment of a drum. These recitals, known as **zikrs**, can last for days. **Sufi music** gained a wider following in Egypt in the late 1990s thanks to **Yassin al-Tuhami**, who revitalized a once-forgotten moulid in the Muqattam Hills that now draws *fellaheen*, Cairene and foreign Sufi enthusiasts alike.

Coptic liturgical music is quite different in spirit and only to be heard at church services. Some maintain that it is descended from Ancient Egyptian temple chants, as the Coptic language has many similarities with Ancient Egyptian and cymbals are played during the liturgy (distinguishing Coptic from the Orthodox ritual music, which is purely choral). Much Coptic music on the Web actually hails from churches in the US rather than Egypt (see links on ⓦwww.copticchurch.org and ⓦwww.coptic.org), but CDs of local Coptic choirs are sold at churches and monasteries in Egypt.

Another form – which many would deny is religious at all – is **zar** music, performed at rituals that are often likened to exorcisms, though their aim is not to expel a spirit from its host but to harmonize relations between them. *Zars* are usually private events reserved for women but occasionally occur at public moulids.

Classical Arabic music

The antecedents of **classical Arabic music** can be traced back to the **Bedouin** war bards of the Arabian peninsula, whose metre matched that of a camel's stride, but also to the refined **court music** of the great caliphal cities of Baghdad and Damascus, and Ottoman Constantinople, which nurtured instrumental and compositional skills for generations.

During the twentieth century the form was characterized by oriental scales, orchestras and male choirs, bravura rhetoric and soloists filled with yearning. **Sayyid Darwish** was its father, blending Western instruments and harmony with Arab musical forms and Egyptian folklore, but its greatest exponent was **Umm Kalthoum**, whose fifty-year career spanned the advent of gramophones, radio and long-distance broadcasting, making her the most popular singer in the Arab world. In Egypt she was a national institution, accorded a weekly concert on radio and, later, TV; her funeral in 1975 drew the largest crowd since that of President Nasser, who used her nationalist songs to keep the masses behind him and timed his speeches around her broadcasts.

Almost as revered was **Mohammed Abdel Wahab**, indelibly associated with the nightclubs of Cairo's Tawfiqiyya district, who composed the music for Egypt's national anthem, "Biladi, Biladi". His career was linked to the birth of the Egyptian film industry in the 1930s, which also saw the rise of Lebanese-born **Farid al-Atrache** and his sister **Asmahan** (killed in a car crash in 1944). Another superstar was the actor/singer **Abdel Halim Hafez**, the "Nightingale of the Nile", whose film recordings are still loved though he died in 1977. Mohammed Abdel Wahab survived all of the above, but lay low for nearly twenty years before releasing his last song shortly before his death in 1991. His protégée, **Warda al-Jaza'iriya**, is a true Mediterranean – French, Algerian, Lebanese and Egyptian by birth, heritage and residency – who has been at the forefront of Arab music for decades but rejects comparisons with Umm Kalthoum.

Regional/ethnic music

The different types of folk or popular music you'll come across vary greatly with the region and environment: Cairo, the Nile Valley, the Delta and the desert all have their own characteristic sounds, rhythms and instruments. Often their songs reflect the rituals of everyday life: weddings, harvest festivals, old stories of village life or triumphs.

Saiyidi

The music of Upper Egypt – known, like its people, as **Saiyidi** – has a characteristic rhythm, which horses are trained to dance to. It is based upon two instruments: the *nahrasan*, a two-sided drum hung over the chest and beaten with sticks; and the *mismar saiyidi*, a kind of wooden trumpet. Performances often involve monologues, ripe with puns and wit. One of the famous names of the genre, **Omar Gharzawi**, is known for his rebuttals of the stereotyped image of stupid, hot-headed Saiyidis. **Sayed Rekaby El-Genena** revels in poetic rapping competitions, a tradition in his home village of Jaafra, while **Rabia el-Bakaria**'s music and lyrics are likened by admirers to Egyptian reggae. On a more official standing is *Raïs* ("Boss") **Met'al Gnawi**, the head of a Luxor family of musicians who has represented Egypt at music festivals abroad, with a band promoted as **Les Musiciens du Nil**. At home he is best known for his hit "Ya Farula!" (My Strawberry), full of fruity sexual allusions.

Fellahi

The northern counterpart to Saiyidi music, found in the Delta, is known as **fellahi** (peasant) music. It is generally softer, with a fondness for the *matsoum* (4/4) rhythm, and use of instruments like the *rababa*, a two-stringed viol, and the *mismar*, a kind of oboe.

Sawaheeli

Found along the Mediterranean coast and in the Canal Zone, **Sawaheeli** music is characterized by the use of a harp-like stringed instrument, the *simsimiya*. Another form, specific to Alexandria, also features the accordion, the result of the city's Greek and Turkish influences. The most famous Sawaheeli singers are **Aid el-Gannirni** from Suez and **Abdou el-Iskanrani** from Alex, while Port Said is home to Zakaria Ibrahim's band **El Tanbura**.

Bedouin

There are two kinds of **Bedouin** music in Egypt: one found in the Western Desert, towards Libya, the other in the Eastern Desert and Sinai. Both have songs recounting old intrigues, activities and stories to a strong rhythmic accompaniment featuring handclapping and frame drums called *duf* or *darabukka*, depending on their size. This polyrhythmic sound has been a major influence on *shababi* music (see p.800), but **Awad al-Malki** aside, Bedouin artists have yet to achieve widespread popularity in Egypt or the international success of Nubian musicians. You won't find Bedouin music cassettes on sale in Cairo, but may strike lucky in Sinai or Mersa Matrouh.

Nubian

Nubian music found a global audience in the 1990s, when **Ali Hassan Kuban** hit the world-music charts with the albums *From Nubia To Cairo* and *Walk Like A Nubian*. Born in 1933, he sang on boats as a child, played at weddings and founded a succession of bands that introduced brass sections, electric guitars and soul vocals to Nubian music, releasing his last album shortly before his death in 2001. Kuban, the female vocalist **Tété Alhinho** and other Nubian musicians cut several CDs under the name **Salamat** for the Piranha label (@www.piranha.de).

Drummer **Mahmoud Fadl** began his career as a limbo dancer at weddings and has produced four albums of his own plus *Umm Kalthoum 7000*, a Nubian homage to the Arab diva featuring the singer **Salma Abu Greisha**, who also appears on Fadl's *The Drummers of the Nile Go South*, with drummers **Gaafar Hargal** and **Hamdi Matoul**. Fadl divides his time between Cairo and Berlin, where his Tribal House project "United Nubians" has been a big hit at the annual Love Parade.

Until his death in 2006, another international star was **Hamza al-Din**, whose compositions for the *oud* (lute) and *tar* (single-skinned frame drum) were influenced by his Sufi beliefs and conservatory training. His haunting *Escalay* ("The Waterwheel") was a lament to his birthplace, drowned by Lake Nasser; he also wrote pieces for ballet companies and the Kronos Quartet.

Pop music

In Cairo and other cities, rural traditions have mixed with more elite styles and adapted to reflect urban preoccupations and the faster pace of life. By the mid-1980s two main types of music had developed: **shaabi** and **shababi**. Nowadays, some would say that the distinction between them is moot, and artists such as Hakim can rightfully claim to have a foot in each camp, while pop idol Amr Diab has spearheaded attempts to stake a claim on the world market. In Egypt, *shaabi* and *shababi* stars release their hits at peak sales periods such as Ramadan and St Valentine's Day. Satellite music channels such as Mazika, Dream and Melody have an insatiable appetite for new talents and video clips are pushing the boundaries of sexual morality, with female stars like Ruby asserting a new mood of empowerment among young urban women. For news and clips of *shaabi* and *shababi* stars, visit **websites** @www.mazika.com, @www.albawaba .com and @www.sotwesoora.com, or Internet **radio stations** like Al Madina FM (@www.almadinafm.com).

Shaabi

Shaabi ("people") music was born in the working-class quarters of Cairo, where millions of second- and third-generation rural migrants live. It blends the traditional form of the *mawal* (plaintive vocal improvisations) with a driving beat; the lyrics are often raunchy or satirical, politically and socially provocative. You will rarely hear this music via the media, though it is not so much banned as beneath the contempt of the middle classes and respectable society, who see its rudeness and social criticism as coming from another Egypt. It is to be heard, however, at weddings and parties throughout working-class Cairo and at some of the nightclubs along Pyramids Road – and played on battered cassettes in taxis, buses and cafés.

The original *shaabi* singer was **Ahmed Adaweyah**, who, from 1971 on, introduced the idea of street language and subsequently broke every rule in the book. Later exponents introduced elements of rap and disco into the *shaabi* sound, in the manner of Algerian *raï* music. The genre is still frowned upon in official cultural circles, but commands a wide following. **Sha'ban Abdel Rahim** was a laundry ironer until a television appearance catapulted him to stardom. His earthy persona infuriated Egypt's cultural arbiters, while his song "I Hate Israel" was cited in the Knesset as proof of anti-Semitism in the Egyptian media. After his next bestseller, "Don't Hit Iraq", Sha'ban was embraced by the government and recorded "The Word of Truth", a paean to Mubarak crediting him with making running water and mobile phones readily available to the masses. His most recent hit at the time of writing was an attack on Pope Benedict for insulting Islam. Meanwhile, rival *shaabi* superstar **Hakim** has tried to reach an international crossover audience with a remix of his hits by Transglobal Underground, following the example of Amr Diab (see below).

Shababi

Shababi or "youthful" music – also known as **al-jeel** ("the generation") music – followed hot on the heels of *shaabi* in the 1980s. It took disco elements like drum tracks and synthesized backing and mixed them with Nubian and Bedouin rhythms. The latter came in large part through the influence of Libyan musicians who had fled to Cairo after Gaddafi's "cultural revolution", one such being **Hamid el-Shaeri**, whose 1988 back-room recording of "Lolaiki" sung by **Ali Hamaida** sold in millions, launching the genre. Some fans and critics now call *shababi* "Mediterranean" music, acknowledging the crosscurrents of influences within the Arab world and its European diaspora – while others simply see it as classic Arabic pop.

Whatever the name, it's big business – though not exactly as in the West. Piracy means that most artists receive relatively little from sales of tapes and CDs, earning their money from appearances at weddings and concerts instead. That said, Egypt's foremost pop idol, **Amr Diab**, broke into the international market with the song "Nour el Ain", and had another international hit with "Akhtar Wahed" in 2002. He was also the first Egyptian artist to release a pop video and make collaborative recordings with the *raï* star Khaled and the Greek singer Angela Dimitriu, launching the so-called "Mediterranean" sound.

Mohammed Mounir is almost as popular in the Arab world, and rated ahead of the rest of the pack for his plaintive songs of city life and pan-Arab yearning. His music alternates between his Nubian roots and more mainstream love ballads, but since he sings in Arabic rather than Nubian it is not regarded as specifically Nubian music.

Shababi has a galaxy of female stars that compete on satellite channels across the Arab world. Many are foreigners – the Moroccan **Samira Saeed** or the Lebanese **Elissa**, **Nancy Ajram** and **Haifa Wahbe** – who are based in Cairo or at least sing in the Egyptian dialect, but the most controversial singer is homegrown. Born in the Islamist stronghold of Assyut (whose citizens stress that that she was raised in Cairo), **Ruby** has set Egyptian eyes agog with the sexuality of her videos and the assertiveness of her lyrics. Her message of "girl power" is at the cutting edge of Egyptian gender politics and got her expelled from Egypt's musicians' union in 2007. By contrast, **Shireen Abdel Wahab** is seen as respectable and performs at official functions and benefit concerts, besides collaborating with other artists. Other popular artists include the musician and actor **Mustafa Amar** and the lutist and singer **Ehab Tawfik**.

Discography

Although CDs are catching on fast in Egypt, cassettes remain the medium of choice for recorded music, being robust, cheap and very easy to copy – piracy is such a problem that it has its own special police division in Cairo. For details of music outlets in Egypt's capital, see p.255, and if you have a special interest in traditional music, check out the recordings issued by the Centre for Culture and Art (ⓦwww.egyptmusic.org), Egypt's foremost institute of ethnomusicology. In Europe or North America you can find a more limited range of vintage albums – mostly Umm Kalthoum and the like – with a few more contemporary releases on world music labels such as Mondo Melodia, Piranha or Axiom.

Ancient Egyptian music

Michael Atherton *Ankh: The Sound of Ancient Egypt* (Celestial Harmonies). Haunting suites developed from songs or poems.

Religious music

Mohammed Rifaat and Sheikh Abdelbasset Addessamad *Le Saint Coran* (Clube du Disque Arabe). Two masters of Koranic recitation featured on a series of CDs issued in France.

Al-Hamidiyah Brotherhood *Saint Egypt: La Châdhiliya – Sufi Chants from Cairo* (Institut de Monde Arabe).

An offshoot of the Shadhiliyya Sufi order.

Umm Sameh, Umm Hassan and Nour el-Sabah *Mazaher*. Three *zar* priestesses on CD and video, available in Cairo from the Egyptian Center for Culture and Art.

Classical Arabic music

🏃 **Umm Kalthoum** *Al-Awia fil Gharam; Al-Atlaal; Enta Omri* (Sono Cairo). Three of her greatest live recordings, available in CD or DVD format.

Sayyid Dervish *Cheikh Sayed Darwiche – L'Immortel* (Baidaphone). A rare, crackly recording of three vocal improvisations, made shortly before Dervish's death.

🏃 **Mohammed Abdel Wahab** *Treasures* (EMI Arabia). A double CD featuring works from his later period including "The Last Blessing", an amazing 40-minute recital.

Abdel Halim Hafez *Abdel Halim Hafez – Twentieth Anniversary Memorial Edition* (EMI Arabia). This double CD includes some of his 1930s film-score songs and experimental arrangements from the 1960s.

Farid al-Atrache *Les Années '30* (Clube Du Disque Arabe). Remastered songs from the 1930s when Farid was at his hottest.

Asmahan *Asmahan* (Baidaphone). A CD compilation of her best-loved songs.

Warda *Warda* (EMI Hemisphere). A CD compilation of her more recent work.

Saiyidi music

🏃 **Les Musiciens du Nil** *Charcoal Gypsies* (Real World). On this album Met'al Gnawi's ensemble fuses African and Middle Eastern percussion with traditional Saiyidi sounds, to irresistible effect.

Sayed Rekaby El-Genena *Jaafra*. Poetic rapping, *oud* and *duf* music from a Bedouin village in the Aswan governorate, available on CD from the Egyptian Center for Culture and Art.

Nubian music

🏃 **Ali Hassan Kuban** *From Nubia to Cairo, Walk Like a Nubian* and *Real Nubian* (Piranha). An infectious mix of wedding songs, brass bands and African percussion.

🏃 **Hamza ad-Din** *Escalay* (Nonesuch). Classical oud music inspired by Nubian sounds and Sufism.

🏃 **Mahmoud Fadl** *The Drummers of the Nile Go South; The*

Drummers of the Nile in Town (Piranha). The Nubian master-percussionist whips up a storm with Saiyidi musicians and the Hasaballah brass band.

🏃 **Salamat** *Mambo El Soudani – Nubian Al Jeel Music from Cairo and Ezzayakoum* (Piranha). Stonking percussion and frenzied sax and trumpet riffs.

Sawaheeli

El Tanbura *The Simsimiya of Port Said* (Institut du Monde Arabe); *Between the Desert and the Sea* (World Village). The former is their debut, featuring Sufi and traditional

songs; the latter, their latest release at the time of writing, celebrates the fiftieth anniversary of the nationalization of the Suez Canal.

Shaabi

🏃 **Ahmed Adaweyah** *Al-Tareek; Adaweat*. Two soulful albums featuring the father of it all at his best, widely available in Egypt.

Hakim *Lela* (EMI Arabia). Sizzling *shaabi* with guest appearances by Stevie Wonder and the late James Brown.

Shababi

🏃 **Amr Diab** *Akhtar Wahed; Kemmel Kalamak* (Rotana). The first is an excellent introduction to Diab's singing, while the second marks his debut as a composer.

Mohammed Mounir *Ahmar Shafayef* (Mondo Melodia). Plaintive

songs of life and the city with a political edge.

Ruby *Fein Habibi* (MSM Egypt). This 2004 album set a new benchmark for the daringness of its lyrics and video clips. Ruby has since been banned from releasing her recordings in Egypt.

Books

Most of the books listed below are in print; those that are out of print (o/p) should be easy to track down in secondhand bookstores. Books that are only published in Egypt are generally most easily available in Cairo. The American University in Cairo Press is abbreviated to AUC in the reviews.

Books aside, there are a handful of **periodicals** which are worth seeking out if you are seriously into Egyptology. The *Journal of Egyptian Archaeology*, published annually by the Egyptian Exploration Society (EES, ⓦwww.ees.ac.uk) is the world's leading forum for all matters Egyptological: all the new theories and discoveries get printed here first. The EES also publishes the magazine *Egyptian Archeology*, illustrated and with a popular slant. Annual membership of the EES entitles you to receive the journal and two issues of the magazine; for details contact the Secretary, Egyptian Exploration Society, 3 Doughty Mews, London WC1N 2PG. Finally, *Ancient Egypt* is a magazine featuring easy-to-read articles by academics, plus listings of lectures, conferences and events held by Egyptology societies in Britain; articles from back issues appear on the magazine's website, ⓦwww.ancientegyptmagazine.com.

Travel

General

Jonathan Cott *The Search for Omm Sety: A Story of Eternal Love* (Olympic). A biography of Dorothy Eady, who believed herself to be the reincarnation of a temple priestess and lover of Seti I at Abydos, where the book is sold today.

Amelia Edwards *A Thousand Miles up the Nile* (Darf). Verbose, patronizing classic from the 1870s. All books on Egypt have their Amelia quotes – the *Rough Guide To Egypt* included.

🏃 **Gustave Flaubert** *Flaubert in Egypt* (Penguin). A romp through the brothels, baths and "native quarters" by the future author of *Madame Bovary*, who cared little for monuments but delighted in Egyptian foibles and vices.

🏃 **Amitav Ghosh** *In An Antique Land* (Granta). Wry tales of contemporary life in a Delta village,

interspersed with snippets of less absorbing historical research.

Douglas Kennedy *Beyond the Pyramids* (Abacus). A dour, Paul Theroux-ish jaunt around Egypt in the late 1980s; the Alex and Assyut sections stand out.

🏃 **E.W. Lane** *Manners and Customs of the Modern Egyptians* (Cosimo). Facsimile edition of this encyclopedic study of life in Mohammed Ali's Cairo, first published in 1836. Highly browsable.

Henri de Monfreid *Hashish* (Penguin). A latter-day swash-buckler, de Monfreid followed a spell in Djibouti jail by smuggling hash on the Red Sea during the 1920s.

Gerard de Nerval *Journey to the Orient* (Peter Owen). De Nerval thrilled to the splendour, squalor, cruelty and eroticism of Mohammed

Ali's Egypt, and was stoned for much of his visit. A wild read.

Florence Nightingale *Letters from Egypt* (Parkway). A stuffier view of Egypt, by a 29-year-old English-woman who had yet to make herself famous in the Crimean War. Illustrated with paintings and drawings by David Roberts, Edward Lear and other artists of the period.

Christopher Pick *Egypt: A Traveller's Anthology* (Murray). By a mixed bag of observers from the eighteenth and nineteenth centuries, including Disraeli, Mark Twain, Vita Sackville-West, Flaubert, E.M. Forster and Freya Stark.

Charlie Pye-Smith *The Other Nile* (o/p). Witty and insightful account of a tour in the early 1980s, interwoven with recollections of trips into Sudan and Ethiopia, before coups and famine made them inaccessible.

Paul William Roberts *River in the Desert* (Tauris Parke). Chiefly interesting for its eyewitness account of a *zar* (exorcism) and a chapter on the Kushmaan Bedouin of the Eastern Desert.

Anthony Sattin *The Pharaoh's Shadow* (Orion). Fascinating discourse on the "survival" of Ancient Egyptian religious beliefs and practices in modern-day Egypt.

Stanley Stewart *Old Serpent Nile: A Journey to the Source* (o/p). Stewart managed to travel from the Nile Delta to the Mountains of the Moon in Uganda in the late 1980s, and relates his adventures in spare, taut prose.

Cairo

Mamluk Art: The Splendour and Magic of the Sultans (Museum With No Frontiers). A European Union-funded guide to Mamluke architecture in Cairo, Alexandria and Rosetta, with concise essays illustrated with colour photos, plans and walking routes.

James Aldridge *Cairo* (o/p). Highly readable history of the city from ancient times until the mid-1960s, including several fine maps and photographs.

Artemis Cooper *Cairo in the War* (o/p). Excellent account of a febrile era, with vignettes of Evelyn Waugh, Olivia Manning and other postwar luminaries. Secondhand copies are quite valuable.

Maria Golia *Cairo: City of Sand* (Reaktion Books). Focuses on the domestic life, housing and nitty-gritty of contemporary Cairo, including its satellite cities, ring road and other prestige projects.

Richard Parker *Islamic Monuments of Cairo: A Practical Guide* (AUC). A detailed handbook to the monuments and history of seventh- to nineteenth-century Cairo, illustrated with black and white photos.

Max Rodenbeck *Cairo: The City Victorious* (Picador/ Vintage). This superb history of Cairo includes the best anecdotes from earlier histories by Aldridge and Stewart (see above and below), and follows events up until 1999.

Desmond Stewart *Great Cairo, Mother of the World* (AUC). Entertaining and erudite history of the city, from pharaonic times through to the Nasser era.

Alexandria

Andrew Chugg *The Lost Tomb of Alexander the Great* (Periplus); *Alexander's Lovers* (Lulu.com). Chugg's theory, expounded in *The Lost Tomb*, that Alexander's body is buried in Venice under the guise of St Mark caused a stir in 2004. The follow-up focuses on Alexander's wives and lovers.

Jean-Yves Empereur *Alexandria Revealed*; *Alexandria Rediscovered* (AUC). As director of the Centre d'Etudes Alexandrines, responsible for excavating the Pharos, the Catacombs and lesser-known sites, Empereur has unearthed a mass of evidence about the ancient city. In *Alexandria Rediscovered* he writes about the problems of working in a city whose buried past is all too fragile. Both books are very readable and profusely illustrated.

E.M. Forster *Alexandria: A History and a Guide* (Andre Deutsch). This 2004 Abinger Edition is replete with erudite notations to Forster's 1922 guidebook, and includes his collection of essays on Alexandrian life, *Pharos and Pharillon*.

Michael Hagg *Alexandria: Capital of Memory* (Yale University Press). An evocative and beautifully written account of the city as experienced by Forster, Cavafy and Durrell, illustrated with many rare photographs from the 1920s, 1930s and 1940s.

Roy MacLeod *The Library of Alexandria: Center of Learning in the Ancient World* (AUC). A history of the legendary library that delves into the city's Greek heritage, the book trade in antiquity, Neoplatonist philosophers, Mystery Schools and many other topics. An introduction by the director of the Bibliotheca Alexandrina brings the story full circle.

The desert

Wael Abed *The Other Egypt: Travels in No Man's Land* (Zarzora Expedition). A *tour d'horizon* of the natural wonders of the Western Desert, by one of Egypt's leading safari guides and desert ecologists. Illustrated with eighty colour photos, plus rare black-and-white photos taken by explorers in the 1920s and 1930s. Sold in Cairo and Bahariya.

R.A. Bagnold *Sand, Wind and War: Memoirs of a Desert Explorer* (Tucson); *Libyan Sands: Travels in a Dead World* (o/p). One of a band of motorized explorers of the Western Desert during the 1920s and 1930s, Bagnold later wrote a seminal work on dune-formation (continuously in print since 1939) and led the Long Range Desert Group. Despite Bagnold's restrained prose, his exploits are compelling and the sheer range of journeys – to all the oases, Uwaynat, the Great Sand Sea and the Forty Days Road – make for essential reading.

Burton Bernstein *Sinai: The Great and Terrible Wilderness* (o/p). Mixture of travel writing and history, describing Sinai on the eve of its handover to Egypt in 1979. Dated, but still the best book on the region.

Peter Clayton *Desert Explorer* (Zerzura). A biography of the author's father, Patrick Clayton, who mapped the Western Desert at the same time as Bagnold and was likewise active in the LRDG until his capture by the Italians.

Ahmed Fakhry *The Oases of Egypt* (AUC; 2 vols.). Volume I, covering Siwa, is fascinating and has been republished in paperback; Volume II, on Bahariya and Farafra, is heavier going and remains out of print, but can be found in Cairo bookshops. A volume on Dakhla and Kharga was aborted after Fakhry's death in 1973.

Zahi Hawass *Valley of the Golden Mummies: The Greatest Egyptian Discovery since Tutankhamun* (Virgin Books/AUC). Written by the chief of Egypt's Supreme Council for Antiquities, with superb photos of his excavation of the Greco-Roman necropolis in Bahariya Oasis. The book's omission of others' doubts about his methodology is perhaps understandable.

Saul Kelly *The Hunt for Zerzura: The Lost Oasis and the Desert War* (Murray). A detailed account of the real drama that inspired *The English Patient*. It's likely to remain the last word in English until somebody translates Almásy's own account from German, or his biography from Hungarian.

David Rohl (ed.) *Followers of Horus Eastern Desert Survey Vol. 1* (ISIS). Profusely illustrated study of the rock art of the Eastern Desert, by the Followers of Horus (see p.758). Order by post from Mike Rowland, ISIS Treasurer, 127 Porter Rd, Basingstoke, Hants RG22 4JT, England. The editor is better known for his controversial books and TV series *A Test of Time* and *Legend* (see "Ancient History", below).

Cassandra Vivian *The Western Desert of Egypt: An Explorer's Handbook* (AUC). The best guidebook on the subject, ranging from geology to folklore and petroglyphs to safaris. It covers all the oases and off-the-beaten-track sites, complete with maps and GPS waypoints. Fits the dashboard of a 4WD, but too heavy for a rucksack. Sold in Cairo and Bahariya Oasis.

Ancient history

General

Margaret Bunson *Encyclopedia of Ancient Egypt* (Facts on File). Over 1500 entries, with useful subject indexes, charts and chronologies – though not as comprehensive as the *British Museum Dictionary of Ancient Egypt* (see p.807).

Mark Collier & Bill Manley *How to Read Egyptian Hieroglyphics: A Step-By-Step Guide To Teach Yourself* (British Museum Press). Just what the title says – and an unexpected bestseller, thanks to its clarity and the exciting sense of knowledge that it confers.

Aidan Dodson & Dyan Hilton *The Complete Royal Families of Ancient Egypt* (Thames & Hudson). An engrossing study of the family lives and personal relations of Egypt's rulers, from the Old Kingdom up until the Ptolemies.

George Hart *British Museum Pocket Dictionary of Egyptian Gods and Goddesses* (British Museum

Press); *Routledge Dictionary of Egyptian Gods and Goddesses* (Routledge). Both are highly useful guides to the deities and myths of Ancient Egypt, illustrated with line drawings. The former is easier to carry when visiting temples in Egypt.

Colin J. Humphreys *The Miracles of Exodus: A Scientist's Discovery of the Extraordinary Natural Causes of the Biblical Stories* (HarperCollins). With a title like that, who could resist a look? Some of the explanations therein seem quite plausible, others less so.

T.G.H. James *The British Museum Concise Introduction: Ancient Egypt* (British Museum Press). As former keeper of the Egyptian Antiquities department of the British Museum, James has written scores of books; this one is a useful general introduction to Ancient Egypt, illustrated with material from the museum's collection.

Dieter Kurth *Edfu Temple: A Guide by an Ancient Egyptian Priest* (AUC). A complete translation of the hieroglyphic inscriptions on the enclosure wall of Edfu Temple, describing the rituals and daily life within its walls.

Jaromir Malek *The Cat in Ancient Egypt* (British Museum Press). A charming monograph with delightful illustrations.

Dimitri Meeks & Christine Favard-Meeks *Daily Life of the Egyptian Gods* (Murray). Scholarly study of the rituals and beliefs surrounding the gods; a TV spin-off focused on the more salacious bits.

Stephen Quirke and Jeffrey Spencer (eds.) *The British Museum Book of Ancient Egypt* (British Museum Press). A good general survey, lavishly illustrated with material from the museum's Egyptian collection.

Gay Robins *Women in Ancient Egypt* (British Museum Press). Interesting study of a subject largely ignored

until the 1990s, focusing on queens and priestesses, fertility rituals and much else.

David Rohl *A Test of Time: The Bible – From Myth to History*; *Legend: Genesis of Civilisation* (Arrow). The former is a stimulating argument for revising the chronology of Ancient Egyptian and Biblical history; the latter advances an unusual theory of Egypt's pre-dynastic era. Both are closely argued and worth reading even if you're sceptical (as most Egyptologists are).

Ian Shaw *The Oxford History of Ancient Egypt* (Oxford University Press). An excellent survey taking in theories and discoveries up until 2003, with many fine illustrations and site plans.

Ian Shaw & Paul Nicholson *British Museum Dictionary of Ancient Egypt* (British Museum Press). Richly illustrated, paperback-sized dictionary, especially good for site plans and assessments of fairly recent discoveries.

John Ray *The Rosetta Stone and the Rebirth of Ancient Egypt* (Profile). Relates the discovery of the crib that enabled Champollion to decipher Ancient Egyptian hieroglyphs – without which, their civilization would still be a mystery. Ray argues that more credit for their deciphering is due to a rival English scholar, Thomas Young.

John Taylor *Egypt and Nubia* (British Museum Press). Covers the history of Nubia from 4000 BC to the dawning of the Christian era, focusing on ancient Nubian art and relations with Egypt.

Joyce Tyldesley *Hatshepsut: The Female Pharaoh*; *Nefertiti: Egypt's Sun Queen*; *Ramses: Egypt's Greatest Pharaoh* (all Penguin). Readable and illuminating biographies of some of the most famous rulers of the New Kingdom.

Jean Vercoutter *The Search for Ancient Egypt* (Thames & Hudson). Pocket-size account of Egypt's "discovery" by foreigners, packed with drawings, photos and engravings.

🏃 **Kent Weeks** *The Lost Tomb* (Phoenix Press); *The Treasures of Luxor and the Valley of the Kings* (Art Guides); *Atlas of the Valley of the Kings* (AUC). The first describes Weeks' discovery and excavation of the mass tomb of the sons of Ramses II; the second is an illustrated guide to treasures from Luxor and its necropolis; and the third is the first volume of an ongoing magnum opus,

showcased on the Theban Mapping Project's website, ⓦ www.kv5.com.

John Anthony West *Serpent in the Sky: High Wisdom of Ancient Egypt* (Quest); *The Traveler's Key to Ancient Egypt: A Guide to the Sacred Places of Ancient Egypt* (Quest). West's symbolic, New Age interpretation of Ancient Egyptian culture is based on the theories of Schwaller de Lubicz, who spent 15 years measuring and studying Luxor Temple. *Serpent* is quite heavy going and marred by rants, but *Traveler's Key* is a lively on-site guide that points out inconsistencies in orthodox Egyptology and presents alternative theories.

Pyramidology

Guillemette Andreu *Egypt in the Age of the Pyramids* (Cornell University Press). Nicely illustrated study of the pyramids' evolution in the context of Ancient Egyptian life and culture, by a French Egyptologist.

Robert Bauval *The Orion Mystery* (Mandarin). Postulates that the Giza Pyramids corresponded to the three stars in Orion's Belt as it was in 10,500 BC – a theory shot down in a BBC documentary that was later ruled by adjudicators to be unfair.

I.E.S. Edwards *The Pyramids of Egypt* (Penguin). Lavishly illustrated, closely argued survey of all the major pyramids, overdue for an update since it was last revised in 1991.

Graham Hancock *Fingerprints of the Gods* (Mandarin); *The Message of the Sphinx*; *The Mars Mystery* (Heinemann); *Heaven's Mirror* (Penguin). Picking up where Bauval left off, Hancock asserts that the

Egyptian and pre-Columbian pyramids, Angkor Wat Temple and the stone figures of Easter Island were all created by a lost civilization propagated by extraterrestrials.

Peter Hodges *How the Pyramids were Built* (Arris & Phillips). As a professional stonemason, Hodges has practical experience, rather than academic qualifications, on his side. An easy read and quite persuasive.

Britta Le Va & Salima Ikram *Egyptian Pyramids* (Zeitouna). A slim booklet of evocative sepia photos and brief accounts of the major pyramids, sold in Cairo.

Kurt Mendelssohn *The Riddle of the Pyramids* (o/p). An attempt to resolve the enigma of the Maidum and Dahshur pyramids, which postulates a "pyramid production line" and caused a stir in the world of Egyptology during the 1980s.

The Amarna Period/Tutankhamun

Cyril Aldred *Akhenaten, King of Egypt* (Thames & Hudson). A conventional

account of the Amarna period by one of Britain's leading Egyptologists.

Christiane Desroches-Noblecourt *Tutankhamen: Life and Death of a Pharaoh* (Penguin). Superbly illustrated, detailed study of all aspects of the boy-pharaoh and his times.

🏃 **Michael Haag** *The Rough Guide to Tutankhamun* (Rough Guides). A pocket-sized guide, covering not just the life of its subject but also the history of the Valley of the Kings and the lives of Howard Carter and Lord Carnarvon. Illustrated throughout with both archive and modern photographs.

T.G.H. James *Tutankhamun* (White Star). Another illustrated tome which devotes equal space to Tut's life and times and the excavation of his tomb.

Dominic Montserrat *Akhenaten: History, Fantasy and Ancient Egypt*

(Routledge). An interesting study of how Akhenaten's image has evolved and resonated in popular culture since he was "discovered" in the nineteenth century.

Ahmed Osman *Moses and Akhenaten; Stranger in the Valley of the Kings* (both Bear & Co.). These two books argue that Akhenaten was actually Moses, and his grandfather Yuya the Biblical Joseph, in a substantial rewrite of the Exodus story.

Julia Samson *Nefertiti and Cleopatra* (Rubicon). Fascinating account of Egypt's most famous queens, by an expert on Amarna civilization. Samson concludes that Smenkhkare, Akhenaten's mysterious successor, was actually Nefertiti; her coverage of Cleopatra is rather less controversial.

Ptolemaic, Roman and Coptic Egypt

Alan Bowman *Egypt After the Pharaohs* (British Museum Press). Scholarly, nicely illustrated study of an often overlooked period.

Christian Cannuyer *Coptic Egypt – The Christians of the Nile* (Thames & Hudson). A pocket-sized, easy to read study of Coptic history and culture, fully illustrated throughout.

Lucy Hughes-Hallett *Cleopatra: Histories, Dreams and Distortions* (o/p). Arresting deconstructive analysis of Cleopatra in history and myth down through the ages.

Dominic Montserrat *Sex and Society in Graeco-Roman Egypt* (Kegan Paul). In-depth study of sexual mores and practices in a famously licentious era.

Gyoző Vörös *Taposiris Magna: Port of Isis*. A richly illustrated look at the ancient port city whose lighthouse is commonly thought to be a scaled-down copy of the Pharos at Alexandria, though Vörös argues it was actually a prototype.

Claudia Yvonne *Coptic Life in Egypt* (AUC). A concise historical and contemporary narrative, illustrated with some superb photos.

Medieval and modern history

The Crusades

🏃 **Amin Maalouf** *The Crusades through Arab Eyes* (Saqi Books). A Lebanese Copt, Maalouf has used

the writings of contemporary Arab chroniclers to retrace two centuries of Middle Eastern history, and concludes that present-day relations between the Arab world and the West are still marked by the battle that ended seven centuries ago.

🏃 Steven Runciman *A History of the Crusades* (Penguin). Highly readable three-volume narrative, laced with anecdote and scandal. Runciman's hero is Salah al-Din, rather than Richard the Lionheart, who is depicted (like most of the other traditional Western good guys) in all his murderous ferocity.

Colonial Era

George Annesley *The Rise of Modern Egypt* (Pentland Press). A readable survey of the period from Napoleon's invasion to the Suez Crisis, marred by Annesley's colonialist attitudes.

🏃 John Bierman & Colin Smith *Alamein: War Without Hate* (Penguin). A superb account of the North African campaign, quoting extensively from the recollections of soldiers on all sides, and conclusively laying the myth of Italian cowardice to rest.

🏃 Stephen Bungay *Alamein* (Aurum Press). Concise, highly readable, and enlightening on the interplay between strategy, tactics, logistics and intelligence during the Western Desert campaign.

Derek Hopwood *Sexual Encounters in the Middle East: The British, the French and the Arabs* (Ithaca Press). An interesting study of fascination for "the other" and the mutual miscomprehensions it engendered.

🏃 Anthony Sattin *Lifting the Veil: British Society in Egypt 1768–1956* (o/p). A fascinating slice of social history, charting the rise and fall of British tourists and expatriates in Egypt. Classic photographs, too.

Post-Independence

🏃 Said K. Aburish *Nasser: The Last Arab* (Duckworth). A new look at an old hero, who embodied the aspirations and contradictions of Arab nationalism. As the author of books on Saddam Hussein, Arafat and the House of Saud, Aburish mourns the lack of a new Nasser to inspire the Arabs today.

Raymond William Baker *Islam Without Fear: Egypt and the New Islamists* (Harvard University Press); *Sadat and After* (I. B. Tauris). The first is a social profile of Egypt's contemporary Islamists, the second a critique of Egyptian society from six different perspectives, including those of the Muslim Brotherhood, Nasserists, Marxists and the entrepreneur Osman Ahmed Osman, each presented sympathetically.

Mohammed Heikal *Cutting the Lion's Tail*; *The Road to Ramadan*; *The Autumn of Fury* (all o/p). These three books cover, respectively, the Suez Crisis, the 1973 War, and Sadat's rise and fall. As a confidante of Nasser's since the Revolution, one-time editor of *Al-Ahram* and Minister of Information, Heikal provides a genuine inside view.

David Hirst & Irene Beeson *Sadat* (o/p). Revealing political biography of the man whom Kissinger described as "the greatest since Bismarck", but which stops short of his assassination.

🏃 Derek Hopwood *Egypt: Politics and Society 1945–90* (Routledge). Accessible and useful survey of the modern era, now in its third edition.

Anwar Sadat *In Search of Identity* (Buccaneer). An anodyne, ghosted autobiography that reveals less about the character of Egypt's assassinated president than either Heikal or Hirst and Beeson.

Anthropology, sociology and feminism

Gamal Amin *Whatever Happened to the Egyptians?; Whatever Else Happened to the Egyptians?* (AUC). Two insightful, wryly readable accounts of social changes from the 1950s to the present. Subjects covered range from car ownership and Westernization in the first book, to TV, fashions and weddings in the second.

Nayra Atiya (ed.) *Khul-Khaal: Five Egyptian Women Tell Their Stories* (Syracuse University Press). Gripping biographical accounts by women from diverse backgrounds, revealing much about Egyptian life a generation ago that still holds true today. Widely sold in Egypt.

Nicolaas Biegman *Egypt's Side-Shows* (Thames & Hudson). Engaging colour photos of moulids, weddings and other rituals of Egyptian life.

R. Critchfield *Shahhat: An Egyptian* (AUC). A wonderful book, based on several years' resident research with the Nile Valley *fellaheen*, across the river from Luxor. Moving,

amusing and shocking, by turn. Widely sold in Egypt.

Smadar Lavie *The Poetics of Military Occupation: Mzeina Allegories of Bedouin Identity under Israeli and Egyptian Rule* (University of California Press). Interesting study of the Bedouin tribe most affected by the changes in Sinai under both regimes, by an Israeli anthropologist.

Lila Abu Lughod *Veiled Sentiments: Honour and Poetry in a Bedouin Society* (University of California Press). Another anthropological study, devoted to the Awlad Ali tribe of the Western Desert.

Nawal el-Saadawi *The Hidden Face of Eve* (Zed). Egypt's best-known woman writer, Saadawi has been in conflict with the Egyptian authorities most of her life. This is her major polemic, covering a wide range of topics – sexual aggression, female circumcision, prostitution, divorce and sexual relationships. Her website (www.nawalsaadawi.net) embraces literature, sociology and politics (see also p.813).

Islam

A.J. Arberry (trans.) *The Koran* (Oxford University Press). This translation is the best English-language version of Islam's holy book, whose revelations and prose style form the basis of the Muslim faith and Arab literature.

Karen Armstrong *Muhammed: A Prophet for Our Times* (HarperPress); *Islam: A Short History*

(Weidenfeld & Nicolson). Two widely acclaimed books by a religious scholar and former nun, which dispel many falsehoods and misconceptions about Islam and its Prophet.

🐾 **Titus Burckhardt** *Art of Islam: Language and Meaning* (o/p). Superbly illustrated, intellectually penetrating overview of Islamic art and architecture.

Wildlife

🐾 **Bertel Bruun** *Common Birds of Egypt* (AUC). Slim illustrated guide.

🐾 **Guy Buckles** *Dive Guide: The Red Sea* (New Holland). An illustrated guide to over 125 diving and snorkelling sites from Sinai to Eritrea, with notes on access, visibility and diving conditions, as well as the species that you'll see.

David Cottridge & Richard Porter *A Photographic Guide to Birds of Egypt and the Middle East* (New

Holland). This ornithology guide is better illustrated than Brunn's, but heavier to carry around.

Richard Hoath *Natural Selections: A Year of Egypt's Wildlife* (AUC). Enlightening and charming study of Egypt's birds, land and sea creatures, illustrated with the author's drawings.

Edward Lieske & Robert F. Myers *Coral Reef Guide* (Collins). A full-colour guide to more than 1200 species in the Red Sea, with brief details of a few dive sites.

Egyptian fiction

André Aciman *Out of Egypt: A Memoir* (Harvill); *Call Me by Your Name* (Farrar Strauss Giroux). The scion of a flamboyant Jewish family who emigrated to Alex at the turn of the century and left three generations later, Aciman came of age in Italy and France and his sensibility is more European than Egyptian.

🐾 **Alaa Al-Aswany** *The Yacoubian Building* (Fourth Estate/Harper Perennial). Four entwined stories about the tenants of a Cairo apartment block. A doorkeeper's son with a chip on his shoulder, a gay newspaper editor and a fallen aristocrat seeking their own kind of love, and a power-hungry politician provide an insight into the joys and frustrations of Cairene life. A controversial bestseller and hit movie in Egypt.

🐾 **Salwa Bakr** *The Golden Chariot* (Garnet); *The Wiles of Men and*

Other Stories (Quartet). A novel set in a women's prison near Cairo, seen through the eyes of an Alexandrian aristocrat jailed for murder, and a collection of stories highlighting different facets of women's oppression in contemporary Egypt, both touching and disturbing.

André Chedid *The Sixth Day; From Sleep Unbound* (Swallow). Another émigré author, whose metaphor-laden plots and clinical prose are not exactly beach reading.

🐾 **Gamal al-Ghitani** *Incidents in Zafraani Alley* (o/p); *Zayni Barakat* (AUC); *Pyramid Texts* (AUC). *Incidents* is a highly accessible, darkly humorous read, which could be interpreted as a satire on state paranoia and credulous fundamentalism. Its ending is confused by the fact that the page order has been scrambled in the English-language edition, which can be found in Cairo. *Zayni Barakat* is a convoluted, elliptical drama set in the last years of Mamluke rule, which reached a wider audience at home when it was adapted for Egyptian television. His latest novel, *Pyramid Texts*, is a series of Sufistic parables about the human condition, inspired by the Sphinx and the Giza Pyramids.

Nabil Naoum Gorgy *The Slave's Dream and Other Stories* (Quartet). The amorality of man and nature is the main theme of this collection of tales, influenced by Borges and Bowles.

 Yusuf Idris *The Cheapest Nights* (Peter Owen); *Rings of Burnished Brass* (o/p). Two superb collections by Egypt's finest writer of short stories, who died in 1991. Uncompromisingly direct, yet ironic.

 Naguib Mahfouz *Palace Walk*; *Palace of Desires*; *Sugar Street*; *Miramar*. The late Nobel laureate's novels have a rather nineteenth-century feel, reminiscent in plot and characterization of Balzac or Victor Hugo. His "Cairo Trilogy", comprising the first three books listed here, is a tri-generational saga set during the British occupation, while *Miramar* looks back on the 1952 Revolution from the twilight of the Nasser era. Favoured themes include the discrepancy between ideology and human problems, and hypocrisy and injustice.

Yusuf al-Qa'id *War in the Land of Egypt* (Arris). A Gogol-esque satire of corruption and hypocrisy in 1970s rural Egypt, which was first published in a Russian translation and only later in Arabic.

 Nawal el-Saadawi *Woman at Point Zero* (Zed); *The Fall of the Imam* (Minerva); *God Dies by the Nile* (Zed); and others. Saadawi's novels are informed by her work as a doctor and psychiatrist in Cairo, and by her feminist and socialist beliefs, on subjects that are virtually taboo in Egypt. *Point Zero*, her best, is a powerful and moving story of a woman condemned to death for killing a pimp. You will find very few of her books on sale in Egypt, though *The Fall of the Imam* is the only one officially banned (see also p.811).

Ahdaf Soueif *Aisha*; *In the Eye of the Sun*; *The Map of Love*; *I Think of You* (Bloomsbury). Born in Cairo, Souief was educated in Egypt and England. Her semi-autobiographical novels are acclaimed for their sensibility: *In the Eye of the Sun* explores love and destiny in the Middle East during the 1960s and 1970s; *The Map of Love* (shortlisted for the Booker Prize) and *I Think of You* focus on sexual politics.

 Bahaa Taher *Aunt Safiyya and the Monastery* (University of California Press). Beautifully crafted novella set in a village in Upper Egypt, where a blood feud is challenged by a Muslim farmer and a Coptic monk.

Anthologies

Margot Badran and Miriam Cooke (eds.) *Opening the Gates: a Century of Arab Feminist Writing* (Virago). Mix of fiction and polemic, including a fair number of Egyptian contributors.

 Inea Bushnaq *Arab Folktales* (o/p). Great collection of folk stories from across the Arab world, including many from Egypt, with interesting thematic pieces putting them in context.

W.M. Hutchins (ed./trans.) *Egyptian Tales and Short Stories of the 1970s & 80s* (AUC). Includes various stories by Nawal el-Saadawi, Amira

Nowaira, Gamal al-Ghitani and Fouad Higazy.

Joyce Tyldesley *Stories from Ancient Egypt: Egyptian Truths and Legends for* *Children* (Rutherford Press). Retold by a respected scholar with drawings of myths and deities by Julian Heath, this book is an easy way to learn some Egyptology.

Poetry and biography

C.P. Cavafy *The Collected Poems of C.P. Cavafy: A New Translation* (Norton). Elegiac evocations of the Alexandrian myth by the city's most famous poet, in a new translation by Aliki Barnstone.

Tawfiq al-Hakim *The Prison of Life* (AUC). An autobiographical essay by one of the formative figures of modern Egyptian literature, covering the first thirty years of Al-Hakim's life.

Robert Liddell *Cavafy: A Biography* (Duckworth). Steeped in Classicism and Egypt, Liddell is a penetrating critic and connoisseur of Cavafy's poetry and milieu, who has also written novels set in Egypt (see p.815).

Foreign fiction

Michael Asher *The Eye of Ra; Firebird* (HarperCollins). Two gung-ho thrillers with a supernatural edge, involving outlaw desert tribes and the lost oasis of Zerzura, written by an explorer with an SAS background.

Noel Barber *A Woman of Cairo* (Hodder). Ill-starred love and destiny amongst the Brits and westernized Egyptians of King Farouk's Cairo, interwoven with historical events and characters. From that perspective, a good insight into those times.

Moyra Caldecott *Hatshepsut: Daughter of Amun* (Bladud). A romantic account of the rise and fall of Queen Hatshepsut.

Agatha Christie *Death Comes at the End; Death on the Nile* (Collins). The latter is a classic piece of skull-duggery solved by Hercule Poirot aboard a Nile cruiser, which Christie wrote while staying at the *Old Cataract Hotel* in Aswan. *Death Comes at the End* is a lamer effort, set around Luxor and the Valley of the Kings.

Len Deighton *City of Gold* (o/ p). Hard-boiled thriller set in 1941, when vital information was being leaked to Rommel.

Paul Doherty *The Mask of Ra* (Headline). Set at the time of Hatshepsut's accession, this pharaonic whodunit is in a similar vein to Gill's trilogy (see below).

Lawrence Durrell *The Alexandria Quartet* (Faber). Endless sexual and metaphysical ramblings, occasionally relieved by a dollop of Alex atmosphere or a profound psychological insight.

Ken Follet *The Key to Rebecca* (Pan). Fast-paced thriller based on the true story of a German spy, Eppler, who operated in Cairo during 1942. Follet exercises artistic licence when describing the outcome, but the bellydancer Sonia, and Sadat's involvement, are largely faithful to history.

Anton Gill *City of the Horizon; City of Dreams; City of the Dead*

(Bloomsbury). Gill's trilogy pits the scribe Huy against diverse conspirators during the reigns of Tutankhamun and Horemheb, in the aftermath of the Amarna era.

Robert Irwin *The Arabian Nightmare* (Dedalus). Brilliant, paranoid fantasy set in the Cairo of Sultan Qaitbey, where a Christian spy contracts the affliction of the title. As his madness deepens, reality and illusion spiral inwards like an opium-drugged walk through a *medina* of the mind.

Robert Liddell *Unreal City*; *The Rivers of Babylon* (Peter Owen). Two ironic novels of expat life, the first set in wartime Alexandria, the second in Cairo prior to the Suez Crisis.

Olivia Manning *The Levant Trilogy* (Penguin). The second half of this six-volume blockbuster of love and war finds the Pringles in Egypt, and is based on the experiences of Manning and her husband Reggie.

Glenn Meade *The Sands of Sakkara* (Coronet). *The Eagle Has Landed* transplanted to Egypt, with a plot to kill Roosevelt and Churchill at the *Mena House* near the Pyramids.

Michael Ondaatje *The English Patient* (Picador). The novel takes liberties with the truth when portraying Almásy and his co-explorers (see p.545) but its brilliance is undeniable, and its equal focus on Kip and Dorothy make it richer and more multi-layered than the film.

Michael Pearce *The Mamur Zapt and the Donkey-vous*; *The Mamur Zapt and the Girl in the Nile*; *The Mamur Zapt and the Men Behind*; *The Mamur Zapt and the Return of the Carpet*; *The Mamur Zapt and the Spoils of Egypt* (Fontana/HarperCollins). A series of cracking yarns set in *khedival* Egypt, featuring the chief of Cairo's secret police.

William Smethurst *Sinai* (o/p). Political skullduggery, ancient history and the paranormal keep you hooked and baffled till the end. Mostly set in Sinai, so an ideal read for the beach at Dahab.

Wilbur Smith *River God*; *The Seventh Scroll*; *Warlock* (Pan). A blockbuster trilogy that crams the Hyksos invasion and liberation of Ancient Egypt into two volumes, interspersed by the search for the lost tomb of pharaoh Mamose in modern times. Enjoyable, if lines like "By the festering foreskin of Seth …." don't make you snort with derision.

Paul Sussman *The Lost Army of Cambyses* (Bantam). An archeological-cum-terrorist thriller that centres on the legendary Persian army which vanished in a sandstorm (see p.517).

Language

Language

Language

Although Arabic is the common and official language of 23 countries, the spoken dialect of each can vary considerably. **Egyptian Arabic**, however, is the most widely understood in the Arab world, because of Egypt's vast film, television and music industry.

Egyptians are well used to tourists who speak only their own language, but an attempt to tackle at least a few words in Arabic is invariably greeted with great delight and encouragement and as often as not the exclamation "You speak Arabic better than I do!" Although most educated and urban Egyptians will have been taught some English and are only too happy to practise it on you, a little Arabic is a big help in the more remote areas. French may also come in handy in some cities, such as Alexandria, where Greek is also spoken by older folk; German, too, is increasingly understood in tourist-related spheres.

Transliteration from Arabic script into English presents some problems, since some letters have no equivalents. The phonetic guide below should help with **pronunciation**:

ai as in *eye*	**ey/ay** as in *day*
aa as in *bad* but lengthened	**ee** as in *feet*
aw as in *rose*	**gh** like the French r (back of the throat)
'a glottal stop as in *bottle*	**kh** as in Scottish *loch*
'a as when asked to say *ah* by the doctor	

Note that every letter should be pronounced, and that double consonants should always be pronounced separately.

Vocabulary

Whatever else you do, at least make an effort to learn the Arabic numerals and polite greetings. The phrases and terms in this section represent only the most common bits of vocabulary you might need; for a comprehensive list, try the *Rough Guide Egyptian Arabic Phrasebook*.

Basics

aiwa or **na'am**	Yes	**itfaddal (m) /**	
la	No	**itfaddali (f)**	Come in, please (to m/f)
shukran	Thank you	**low samaht (m) /**	
afwan	You're welcome	**samahti (f)**	Excuse me
min fadlak (m) /		**aasif (m) / asfa (f)**	Sorry
fadlik (f)	Please (to m/f)	**inshallah**	God willing
		Shokran	Thank you

Greetings and farewells

ahlan w-sahlan	Welcome/hello
ahlan bik (m) / biki (f) / bikum (pl)	(response)
assalaamu aleikum	Hello (formal)
wa-aleikum assalaam	(response)
marhaba or sa'eeda	Greetings
fursa sa'eeda	Nice to meet you
sabah il-kheer	Good morning (morning of goodness)
sabah in-nur	(response: morning of light)

masa' il-kheer	Good evening (evening of goodness)
masa' in-nur	(response: evening of light)
izzayak (m) / izzayik (f)	How are you (m/f) ?
kwayyis (m) / kwayyisa (f)	[I'm] Fine, good (m/f)
il-hamdu lillah	Thanks be to God
tisbah (m) / tisbahi (f) 'ala kheer	Good night
wenta (m) / wenti (f) bikheer	And to you (m/f)
ma'a salaama	Goodbye

Directions

feyn...	Where is...
funduk (name) ?	Hotel (name) ?
mat'am (name)?	(name) restaurant?
mahattat il-autobees?	the bus station?
mahattat il-atr?	the train station?
el-mogaf?	the service taxi depot?
il-mataar?	the airport?
il-mustashfa?	the hospital?
il-twalet?	the toilet?
shimaal/yimeen/ 'ala tool	Left/right/straight ahead

areeb/ba'eed	Near/far
hina/hinak	Here/there
il-autobees yisafir imta?	When does the bus leave?
il-atr yisafir imta?	When does the train leave?
... yoosal?	... arrive?
issa'a kam?	What time (is it)?
il-awwil/il-akhir/ et-tani	First/last/next
wallahaaga	Nothing
lissa	Not yet

Shopping

fi 'andak (m) / 'andik (f) ... ?	Do you (m/f) have ...?
... sigaara/sagayir	... cigarette(s)
... kibreet	... matches
... gurnal	... newspaper
ayyiz (m) / ayyza (f) haaga ...	I (m/f) want something ...
tanya	else
... ahsan min da	... better than this
... arkhas min da	... cheaper

... zay da	... like this
(wa-laakin)	(but)
akbar/asghar	bigger/smaller
bi-kam (da)?	How much (is it)?
da ghaali awi	It's too expensive
kebeer	big
sughayyar	small
maashi	That's fine
fi?	There is/is there?
di/da	This/that

Accommodation

fi 'andak (m) / 'andik (f) ouda?	Do you (m/f) have a room?

ayyiz/ayyza ashuf il-owad	I (m/f) would like to see the room

mumkin ashuf il-owad?	Can I see the rooms?	… balcona?	… a balcony?
fi … ?	Is there …?	… takyeef hawa?	… air conditioning?
… mayya sukhna?	… hot water?	… telifoon?	… a telephone?
… doush?	… a shower?	kam il-hisab?	How much is the bill?

Useful phrases

ismak (m) / ismik (f) ey?	What is your (m/f) name?	ana gaw'aan (m) / gaw'aana (f)	I (m/f) am hungry
ismi …	My name is …	ana 'atshaan (m) / 'atshaana (f)	I (m/f) am thirsty
titkallim (m) / titkallimi … (f)	Do you (m/f) speak …	(mush) ayyiz (m) / ayyza (f) …	I (m/f) (don't) want …
'arabi?	Arabic?	ana (mush)	I (m/f) am (not)
ingleezi?	English?	mitgawwiz (m) /	married
fransawi?	French?	mitgawwiza (f)	
ana batkallim ingleezi	I speak English	mush shughlak	It's not your business
ana ma-batkallim		sibni le wadi!	Don't touch me!
'arabi	I don't speak Arabic	yalla	Let's go
ana fahem (shwaiya)	I understand (a little)	baraahah	Slowly
ya'ani ey bil-ingleezi?	What's that in English?	khalas	Enough! Finished!
ana mush fahem (m) / fahma (f)	I (m/f) don't understand	maalesh	Never mind
ana mush 'aarif (m) / 'aarfa (f)	I (m/f) don't know	mush muhim	It doesn't matter
ana ta'abaan (m) /		ma feesh mushkila	There's no problem
ta'abaana (f)	I (m/f) am tired/ unwell	mumkin?	May I/is it possible?
		mush mumkin	It's not possible

Calendar

youm	day	ba'deen	later
leyla	night	youm is-sabt	Saturday
usboo'a	week	youm il-ahad	Sunday
shahr	month	youm il-itnayn	Monday
sana	year	youm it-talaata	Tuesday
innaharda	today	youm il-arb'a	Wednesday
bukra	tomorrow	youm il-khamees	Thursday
imbaarih	yesterday	youm il-gum'a	Friday

Money

feyn il-bank?	Where's the bank?	… shikaat siyahiyya	… traveller's cheques
ayyiz/ayyza aghayyar …	I (m/f) want to change …	giney	Egyptian pound
… floos	… money	nuss giney	half pound
… ginay sterlini	… British pounds	roba' giney	quarter pound
… dolar amrikani	… US dollars	irsh	piastre
… euro	… euros	irshayn	2 piastres
		khamsa irsh	5 piastres

Numbers and fractions

Though Arabic numerals may seem confusing at first, they are not hard to learn and with a little practice you should soon be able to read bus numbers without any problems. The one and the nine are easy enough; the confusing ones are the five, which looks like a Western zero; the six, which looks like a Western seven; and the four, which looks like a three written backwards. In practice, once you've got the hang of it, the trickiest are the two and the three, which are sufficiently similar to be easily confused. Note that unlike the rest of the Arabic language, the numerals are written from left to right.

sifr	·	0	wahid wa 'ashreen	٢١		21
wahid	١	1	talaateen	٣·		30
itnayn	٢	2	arb'aeen	٤·		40
talaata	٣	3	khamseen	٥·		50
arb'a	٤	4	sitteen	٦·		60
khamsa	٥	5	sab'aeen	٧·		70
sitta	٦	6	tamaneen	٨·		80
sab'a	٧	7	tis'een	٩·		90
tamaanya	٨	8	miyya	١··		100
tes'a	٩	9	miyya wa-wahid			
'ashara	١·	10	wa 'ashreen	١٢١		121
hidarsha	١١	11	mitayn	٢··		200
itnarsha	١٢	12	talaata miyya	٣··		300
talatarsha	١٣	13	arb'at miyya	٤··		400
arb'atarsha	١٤	14	alf	١···		1000
khamastarsha	١٥	15	alfayn	٢···		2000
sittarsha	١٦	16	talaat alaaf	٣···		3000
sab'atarsha	١٧	17	arb'at alaaf	٤···		4000
tamantarsha	١٨	18	nuss			1/2
tis'atarsha	١٩	19	roba'			1/4
'ashreen	٢·	20	tumna			1/8

Egyptian food and drink terms

Basics

'Aish	Bread	Firakh	Chicken
Zibda	Butter	Zeit	Oil
Beyd	Eggs	Zeitun	Olives
Samak	Fish	Filfil	Pepper
Gibna	Cheese	Melh	Salt
Gibna rumi	Yellow cheese	Sukkar	Sugar
Gibna beyda	White cheese	Khudaar	Vegetables
Murabba	Jam	Salata	Salad
'Asal	Honey	Fawaakih	Fruit
Lahma	Meat	Zabaadi	Yoghurt

Shurba	Soup	Mala'a	Spoon
Izaaza	Bottle	Tarabeyza	Table
Kubbaaya	Glass	Garson	Waiter
Showka	Fork	Lista/menoo	Menu
Sikkeena	Knife	El-hisaab	The bill (check)

Drinks

Shai	Tea	Beera	Beer
Shai bi-na'ana	Tea with mint	Nibeet	Wine
Shai bi-laban	Tea with milk	Zibiba	Ouzo
Shai kushari	Tea made with loose-leaf	'Aseer	Juice
		'Aseer asab	Sugar-cane juice
Shai lipton	Tea made with a tea bag	'Aseer burtu'an	Orange juice
		'Aseer limoon	Lemon juice
Laban	Milk	'Aseer manga	Mango juice
Ahwa	Coffee (usually Turkish)	Karkaday	Hibiscus
Ziyaada	very sweet	Tamar hindi	Tamarind (cordial)
Mazboot	medium	'Er' sous	Liquorice-water
'Ariha	little sugar	Helba	Fenugreek infusion
Saada	no sugar	Irfa	Cinnamon infusion
Ahwa fransawi	Instant or filter coffee	Yansoon	Aniseed infusion
Mayya	Water	Sahleb	Milky drink made with ground orchid root
Mayya ma'adaniyya	Mineral water		

Soups, salads and vegetables

Shurba	Soup	Fasuliyya	Beans
Shurbit firakh	Chicken soup	Gazar	Carrots
Shurbit 'adas	Lentil soup	Baamya	Okra (gumbo, ladies' fingers)
Shurbit khudaar	Vegetable soup		
Salata	Salad	Bisilla	Peas
Salatit khiyaar	Cucumber salad	Bataatis	Potatoes
Salatit tamatim	Tomato salad	Ruz	Rice
Salatit khadra	Mixed green salad	Torshi	Pickled vegetables
Basal	Onion	Bidingaan	Eggplant (aubergine)

Main dishes

Kofta	Mincemeat flavoured with spices and onions, grilled on a skewer	Firakh	Chicken grilled or stewed and served with vegetables
		Fatta	Mutton or chicken stew, cooked with bread
Kebab	Chunks of meat, usually lamb, grilled with onions and tomatoes	Hamam mashwi	Grilled pigeon
Molukhiyya	Jew's mallow, a leafy vegetable stewed with meat or chicken broth and garlic to make a slimy, spinach-like dish	Lahm dani	Lamb
		Kibda	Liver
		Kalewi	Kidney
		Mokh	(Sheep) brains

| Dik rumi | Turkey | Gambari | Prawns |
| Samak mashwi | Grilled fish served with salad, bread and dips | Calamari | Squid |

Appetizers and fast food

Fuul	Fava beans served with oil and lemon, sometimes also with onions, meat, eggs or tomato sauce	Kushari	Mixture of noodles, lentils and rice, topped with fried onions and a spicy tomato sauce
Taamiya	Falafel; balls of deep-fried mashed chickpeas and spices	Shakshouka	Chopped meat and tomato sauce, cooked with an egg on top
Shawarma	Slivers of pressed, spit-roasted lamb, served in pitta bread	Makarona	Macaroni "cake" baked in a white sauce or mincemeat gravy
Tahina	Sesame-seed paste mixed with spices, garlic and lemon, eaten with pitta bread	Mahshi	Literally "stuffed", variety of vegetables (peppers, tomatoes, aubergines, courgettes) filled with mincemeat and/or rice, herbs and pine nuts
Hummus	Chickpea paste mixed with tahini, garlic and lemon, sometimes served with pine nuts and/or meat (but also just the Arabic for chickpeas/garbanzo beans; indeed, more commonly used with that meaning in Egypt)	Wara einab	Vine leaves filled as above and flavoured with lemon juice
		Fiteer	A sort of pancake/pizza made of layers of flaky filo pastry with sweet or savoury fillings
Babaghanoug	Paste of aubergines mashed with tahina		

Desserts, sweets, fruits and nuts

Mahallabiyya	Sweet rice or cornflour pudding, topped with pistachios	'Ishta	Cream
		Tuffah	Apples
		Mishmish	Apricots
Balila	Milk dish with nuts, raisins and wheat	Mawz	Bananas
		Balah	Dates
Baklava	Flaky filo pastry, honey and nuts	Teen	Figs
		Teen shawqi	Prickly pear (cactus fruit)
Basbousa	Pastry of semolina, honey and nuts		
Umm (or Om) Ali	Corn cake soaked in milk, sugar, raisins, coconut and cinnamon, usually served hot	Shammam	Melon
		Battikh	Watermelon
		Farawla	Strawberries
		Fuul sudaani	Peanuts
		Lib batteekh	Watermelon seeds
Gelati or ays krim	Ice cream	Lawz	Almonds

Some phrases

Ayyzeen el-menu min fadlak	We'd like the menu please	Da mush ...	This is not ...
Sukkar aleel	With little sugar	... taaza	... fresh
Ihna ayyzeen ...	We'd like to have ...	... lahm	... meat
Ana makulsh ...	I can't/don't eat ...	... mistiwi kwayyis	... cooked enough
Bidoon sukkar	Without sugar	Da lazeez awi	This is very tasty
'Ey da?	What is this?	Iddini/iddina ...	Give me/us ...
Ma'alabtish da	I didn't order this	El-hisaab, minfadlak (m) / minfadlik (f)	The bill, please
Ihna mush ayyzeen da	We don't want this	... taba'	... a plate
		... futa	... a napkin

Glossary

Common alternative spellings are given in brackets.

Ablaq Striped. An effect achieved by painting, or laying courses of different-coloured masonry (the costlier method); usually white with red or buff. A Bahri Mamluke innovation, possibly derived from the Roman technique of *opus mixtum* – an alternation of stone and brickwork.

Abu "Father of"; an honorific accorded to men, also used metaphorically, as in Abu Ballas, "Father of Pots", an ancient water cache in the Western Desert.

AH *Anno Hegirae*. The year of the Prophet Mohammed's exodus (*hijra*) from Mecca is the starting point of Islamic chronology (622 AD by the Western reckoning).

Ain (Ayn, Ein) Spring.

Amir (Emir) Commander, prince.

Ba The Ancient Egyptian equivalent of the soul or personality, often represented by a human-headed bird; also used to describe the physical manifestation of certain gods.

Bab Gate or door, as in the medieval city walls.

Bahr River, sea, canal.

Baksheesh Alms or tips.

Baladi National, local, rural or countrified; from *balad*, meaning country or land.

Bango Marijuana.

Baraka Blessing.

Beit (Beyt) House. Segregated public and private quarters, the *malqaf, maq'ad* and *mashrabiya* are typical features of old Cairene mansions.

Benzin Petrol (gasoline).

Bey (Bay) Lord or noble; an Ottoman title, now a respectful form of address to anyone in authority.

Bir (Beer) Well.

Birka (Birqa, Birket) Lake.

Burg (Borg) Tower.

Cadi (Qadi) Judge.

Calèche Horse-drawn carriage.

Caliph Successor to the Prophet Mohammed and spiritual and political leader of the Muslim empire. A struggle over this office caused the Sunni–Shia schism of 656 AD. Most caliphs ruled from Baghdad or Damascus and delegated control of imperial provinces like Egypt.

Canopic jar Sealed receptacle used in funerary rituals to preserve the viscera of the deceased after embalming. The stomach, intestines, liver and lungs each had a patron deity, sculpted on the Canopic jar's lid.

Cloisonné A multi-step enamelling process used to produce jewellery, vases and other decorative objects.

Corniche Seafront or riverfront promenade.

Dahabiya Nile houseboat.

Darb Path or way; can apply to alleyways, thoroughfares, or desert caravan routes.

Deir Monastery or convent.

Djed pillar Ancient Egyptian symbol of stability, in the shape of a pillar with three or four horizontal flanges, possibly derived from a pole around which grain was tied.

Egyptian Antiquities Organization (EAO) The former name of the agency responsible for Egypt's historic monuments and other antiquities, now called the Supreme Council for Antiquities.

Egyptian Environmental Affairs Agency (EEAA) The agency responsible for Egypt's nature reserves.

Ezba A hamlet or village.

Feddan A traditional measure of land equivalent to 4200 square kilometres; it derives from the Arabic word for a yoke of oxen, implying the area of ground that could be tilled in a certain time.

Fellaheen (sing. fellah) Peasant farmers who work their own land or as sharecroppers or hired labourers for wealthier farmers.

Felucca Nile sailing boat.

Finial Ornamental crown of a dome or minaret, often topped by an Islamic crescent.

Galabiyya Loose flowing robe worn by men.

Gam'a Large congregational mosque, as opposed to a *masgid*.

Gezira Island.

Ghard (Ghird) Extended belt of sand dunes.

Gumhorriya Republic.

Hajj (Hadj) Pilgrimage to Mecca.

Hagg/Hagga One who has visited Mecca.

Haikal Sanctuary of a Coptic church.

Hammam Turkish bathhouse.

Hantour A Middle Egypt term for a *calèche*.

Haramlik Literally the "forbidden" area, ie women's or private apartments in a house or palace.

Heb The Ancient Egyptian word for festival. Its hieroglyph depicted a reed hut on a bowl.

Heb-Sed An Ancient Egyptian festival symbolizing the renewal of the king's physical and magical powers, celebrated in the thirtieth year of his reign and every three years thereafter.

Ikhwan Familiar name for the Muslim Brotherhood (Il-Ikhwan il-Muslimeen), Egypt's oldest Islamic organization (founded in 1928 and banned since 1954).

Islamist(s) Groups aiming to replace secular with Sharia law (see p.829) and realign Egypt's foreign policy – some by peaceful means, others violently. The term is preferred to "fundamentalist", since almost all Muslims have a fundamental belief in the literal truth of the Koran.

Ithyphallic Decorous term for a god with an erection; Min, Amun and Osiris were often depicted thus by the Ancient Egyptians.

Jebel (Gebel, Gabal, etc) Hill or mountain in Arabic.

Jedid/Jedida (Gadid/Gadia) "New" in Arabic; the ending depends on whether the subject of the adjective is masculine or feminine. In Upper Egypt, the first syllable is pronounced as a soft *je*; in Lower Egypt, as a hard *ga* sound.

Jihad Often translated as "Holy War", this Arabic term can also describe non-violent striving in the cause of Islam, or a believer's inner, spiritual battle with temptation or moral weakness.

Ka Ancient Egyptians believed that an individual's life-force served as the "double" of his or her physical being and required sustenance after their death, through offerings to the deceased's *ka* statue, sometimes secluded in a *serdab*.

Karkur Gorge.

Khalig Gulf or canal.

Khan Place where goods were made, stored and sold, which also provided accommodation for travellers and merchants, like a *wikala*.

Khanqah Sufi hostel, analagous to a monastery.

Khedive Viceroy.

Kom Mound of rubble and earth covering an ancient settlement.

Kubri Bridge.

Kufic The earliest style of Arabic script. Foliate *kufic* was a more elaborate form, superseded by *naskhi* script.

Kuttab Koranic school, usually for boys or orphans.

Leyla kebira "Big night": the climactic night of a popular religious festival.

Liwan An arcade or vaulted space off a courtyard in mosques and *madrassas*; originally, the term meant a sitting room opening onto a covered court.

Madrassa Literally a "place of study" but generally used to designate theological schools. Each *madrassa* propagates a particular rite of Islamic jurisprudence.

Mahalla A neighbourhood inhabited by a particular religious or ethnic community.

Mahwagi Local laundryman or woman.

Malqaf Wind scoop for directing cool breezes into houses; in Egypt, they always face north, towards the prevailing wind.

Mamissi Birth House. A pseudo-Coptic term coined to describe a structure attached to temples from the Late Period to Roman times, where rituals celebrating the birth of Horus and the reigning king were performed.

Maq'ad The Arabic word for an arch-fronted "sitting place" on the second floor of old Cairene houses, overlooking the courtyard.

Maristan The medieval term for a public hospital.

Mashrabiya An alcove in lattice windows where jars of water can be cooled by the wind; by extension, the projecting balcony and screened window itself, which enabled women to watch street-life or the *salamlik* without being observed.

Mesjid (Mesgid, Masjid) A small local mosque, as opposed to a *gam'a*.

Mashhad An Islamic sanctuary or oratory.

Masr (Misr, Musr) Popular name for Egypt, and Cairo, dating back to antiquity.

Mastaba Mud-brick benches outside buildings, which Mohammed Ali removed in Cairo to reduce idling and speed up the traffic. Egyptologists use the word to describe the flat-roofed, multi-roomed tombs of the Old Kingdom, found at Saqqara and other sites.

Melkites (Melchites) Christians from Egypt, Syria and Palestine who rejected the doctrine of Monophysism at the Council of Chalcedon (451) and aligned themselves with the Byzantine rather than the Coptic Church.

Merlons Indentations and raised portions along a parapet. Fatimid merlons were angular; Mamluke ones crested, trilobed (like a fleur-de-lis) or in fancier leaf patterns.

Mida'a Fountain for the ritual ablutions that precede prayer, located in a mosque's vestibule or courtyard.

Midan The Arabic term for an open space or square; in Tulunid Cairo and Mogul India, most were originally polo grounds.

Mihrab Niche indicating the direction of Mecca, to which all Muslims pray.

Minaret Tower from which the call to prayer is given; derived from *minara*, the Arabic word for "beacon" or "lighthouse".

Minbar Pulpit from which an address to the Friday congregation is given. Often superbly inlaid or carved in variegated marble or wood.

Mit Village or hamlet.

Mosque A simple enclosure facing Mecca

in its original form, the mosque acquired minarets, *riwaqs*, *madrassas* and mausolea as it was developed by successive dynasties. Large congregational mosques are called *gam'a*; smaller, local "places of prostration" are known as *mesjid* – a very old distinction. Very small mosques, often associated with Sufi orders or Senussis, are known as *zawiyas*.

Moulid Popular festival marking an event in the Koran or the birthday of a Muslim saint. The term also applies to the name-days of Coptic saints.

Muezzin A prayer-crier (who nowadays is more likely to broadcast by loudspeaker than to climb up and shout from the minaret).

Muhazafat Governorate, or province; Egypt is divided into 26 of them.

Muhtasib An official responsible for overseeing markets, commercial transactions, public hygiene and morals during the era of the caliphs and sultans.

Mukhabarat Military Intelligence.

Multinational Force of Observers (MFO) Contingents of foreign troops stationed in Sinai to monitor compliance with the Camp David Agreement of 1978.

Munshid Professional reciter of Koranic verses and praises to Allah.

Muqarnas Stalactites, pendants or honeycomb ornamentation of portals, domes or squinches.

Naos The core and sanctuary of a Coptic or Byzantine church, where the liturgy is performed.

Naskhi Form of Arabic script with joined-up letters, introduced by the Ayyubids.

National Democratic Party (NDP) Egypt's ruling party since 1978, when it was created by Sadat to replace the Arab Socialist Union; called Hizb il-Watani il-Dimuqrati in Arabic.

Nemset A vessel employed in rituals such as the Closing of the Mouth ceremony.

Nomarch A term used to describe a provincial governor in Ancient Egypt.

Nome A Greek term, used to describe a province of Ancient Egypt.

Nomen The name that a pharaoh was given at birth, which equates more or less with a family name, eg Tuthmosis in the XVIII Dynasty or Ramses in the XIX Dynasty.

Ostracon (pl. ostraca) A Greek term used by archeologists to describe potsherds or flakes of limestone bearing texts and drawings, often consisting of personal jottings, letters or scribal exercises.

Pasha (Pacha) Ruler – a lord or prince. Nowadays, a respectful term of address for anyone in authority, pronounced "basha".

Petroglyph Images created by incising, bruising or abrading rock surfaces, as opposed to pictographs, which are images drawn or painted on rock. Both terms are commonly associated with prehistoric rock art.

Prenomen The "throne name" assumed by a pharaoh at his coronation. When inscribed in a cartouche it is usually preceded by the symbols for Upper and Lower Egypt, and followed by the suffix Re.

Pronaos Vestibule of a Greek or Roman temple, enclosed by side walls and a row of columns in front.

Pylon A broad, majestic gateway that formed the entrance to temples from the XVIII Dynasty onwards, or a series of gateways within large complexes such as Karnak. Typically incised with giant images of deities and pharaohs, and notched for flagstaffs.

Qa'a An Arabic term for a large hall or reception room.

Qadim/Qadima (masc./fem.) "Old", as in Masr al-Qadima, or Old Cairo.

Qalaa Fortress, citadel.

Qarat Peak, ridge, spur.

Qasr Palace, fortress, mansion. Also used to describe semi-fortified villages in the oases, such as Qasr al-Farafra.

Qibla The direction in which Muslims pray, indicated in mosques by the wall where the *mihrab* is located.

Qubba Dome, and by extension any domed tomb or shrine.

Raïs Boss, chief.

Ras Cape, headland, peak.

Repoussé A technique in which malleable metal is ornamented by hammering from the reverse side to form a raised design on the front, which is often combined with the opposite technique of chasing (hammering from the front) to form a finished piece.

Riwaq Arcaded aisle around a mosque's *sahn*, originally used as residential quarters for theological students; ordinary folk may also take naps here.

Sabil Public fountain or water cistern. During the nineteenth century it was often combined with a Koranic school to make a *sabil-kuttab*.

Sahn Central courtyard of a mosque, frequently surrounded by *riwaqs* or *liwans*.

Salamlik The "greeting" area of a house; ie the public and men's apartments.

Sanctuary The *liwan* incorporating the *qibla* wall in a mosque, or the shrine of a deity in an Ancient Egyptian temple.

Senet An Ancient Egyptian board game for two players, using counters on a grid of 30 squares. Moves were determined by throwing sticks or knuckle-bones.

Senussis An Islamist movement, strong in the Libyan Desert between 1830 and 1930, which resisted British and Italian colonialism in Egypt and Libya.

Serdab The Arabic word for a cellar beneath a mosque. Also used by Egyptologists to describe the room in *mastaba* tombs where statues of the deceased's *ka* were placed, often with eye-holes or a slit in the wall enabling the *ka* to leave the chamber, and offerings to be made to the statue from the tomb's chapel.

Shabti (ushabti) Ancient funerary figurines, whose purpose was to spare their owner from having to perform menial tasks in the afterlife. By the New Kingdom, tombs contained one figure for each day of the year, plus 36 "overseers" to supervise them.

Sharia Street (literally "way"). With the Arabic feminine ending added (the resulting word is sometimes transliterated Shariah), it refers to laws based on Koranic precepts.

Sharm Bay.

Shorta Police.

Soffits Undersides of arches, often decorated with stripes (*ablaq*) or formalized plant designs (an Ottoman motif).

Squinch An arch spanning the right angle formed by two walls, so as to support a dome.

Sufis Islamic mystics who seek to attain union with Allah through trance-inducing *zikrs* and dances. Whirling Dervishes belong to one of the Sufi sects.

Supreme Council for Antiquities (SCA) The state organization responsible for Egypt's ancient monuments, formerly called the Egyptian Antiquities Organization.

Tabut An Ottoman-era cenotaph or grave marker, sometimes embellished with a "hat" indicating the deceased's rank.

Tariqa A Sufi order or dervish brotherhood.

Tell Another word for *kom*.

Tir Canal.

Thuluth Script whose vertical strokes are three times larger than its horizontal ones; *Thuluth* literally means "third".

Tuf-tuf A form of transport in some tourist areas, consisting of an engine pulling open-sided carriages, but running along roads; similar to a Noddy train.

Ulema Collective name for Islamic scholars and jurists.

Umm "Mother of"; an honorific accorded to women, also used metaphorically, as in *Umm al-Dunya*, "Mother of the World" – a sobriquet bestowed on Cairo.

Uraeus (pl. uraei) The rearing-cobra symbol of the Delta goddess Wadjet, worn as part of the royal crown and often identified with the destructive "Eye of Re".

Wadi Valley or watercourse (usually dry).

Wahah Oasis.

Waqf The endowment of some religious, educational or charitable institution in perpetuity. In Egypt, thousands of such bequests are overseen by the Ministry of Awqaf.

Wikala Bonded warehouse with rooms for merchants upstairs. Here they bought trading licences from the *muhtasib* and haggled over sales in the courtyard. *Okel* is another term for a *wikala*.

Yardang Freestanding, wind-eroded rock formations, typical of the White Desert.

Zaar Exorcism.

Zawiya Originally a *khanqah* centred around a particular sheikh or Sufi order (*tariqa*), but nowadays used to mean a very small mosque.

Zebaleen Rubbish-collectors and recyclers, once active in Egyptian towns and cities but nowadays largely superseded by commercial waste-collection companies.

Zikr Marathon session of chanting and swaying, intended to induce communion with Allah.

Ziyada Outer courtyard separating early mosques from their surroundings; literally "an addition".

Zuqaq Narrow cul-de-sac, from the Turkish word for "street".

Travel store

ROUGH GUIDES Complete Listing

UK & Ireland
Britain
Devon & Cornwall
Dublin **D**
Edinburgh **D**
England
Ireland
The Lake District
London
London **D**
London Mini Guide
Scotland
Scottish Highlands & Islands
Wales

Europe
Algarve **D**
Amsterdam
Amsterdam **D**
Andalucía
Athens **D**
Austria
Baltic States
Barcelona
Barcelona **D**
Belgium & Luxembourg
Berlin
Brittany & Normandy
Bruges **D**
Brussels
Budapest
Bulgaria
Copenhagen
Corfu
Corsica
Costa Brava **D**
Crete
Croatia
Cyprus
Czech & Slovak Republics
Denmark
Dodecanese & East Aegean Islands
Dordogne & The Lot
Europe
Florence & Siena
Florence **D**
France
Germany
Gran Canaria **D**
Greece
Greek Islands
Hungary
Ibiza & Formentera **D**
Iceland
Ionian Islands
Italy
The Italian Lakes
Languedoc & Roussillon
Lanzarote & Fuerteventura **D**
Lisbon **D**
The Loire Valley
Madeira **D**
Madrid **D**
Mallorca **D**
Mallorca & Menorca
Malta & Gozo **D**
Menorca
Moscow
The Netherlands
Norway
Paris
Paris **D**
Paris Mini Guide
Poland
Portugal
Prague
Prague **D**
Provence & the Côte D'Azur
Pyrenees
Romania
Rome
Rome **D**
Sardinia
Scandinavia
Sicily
Slovenia
Spain
St Petersburg
Sweden
Switzerland
Tenerife & La Gomera **D**
Turkey
Tuscany & Umbria
Venice & The Veneto
Venice **D**
Vienna

Asia
Bali & Lombok
Bangkok
Beijing
Cambodia
China
Goa
Hong Kong & Macau
Hong Kong & Macau **D**
India
Indonesia
Japan
Kerala
Laos
Malaysia, Singapore & Brunei
Nepal
The Philippines
Rajasthan, Dehli & Agra
Singapore
Singapore **D**
South India
Southeast Asia
Sri Lanka
Taiwan
Thailand
Thailand's Beaches & Islands
Tokyo
Vietnam

Australasia
Australia
Melbourne
New Zealand
Sydney

North America
Alaska
Baja California
Boston
California
Canada
Chicago
Colorado
Florida
The Grand Canyon
Hawaii
Honolulu **D**
Las Vegas **D**
Los Angeles
Maui **D**
Miami & South Florida
Montréal
New England
New Orleans **D**
New York City
New York City **D**
New York City Mini Guide
Orlando & Walt Disney World® **D**
Pacific Northwest
San Francisco
San Francisco **D**
Seattle
Southwest USA
Toronto
USA
Vancouver
Washington DC
Washington DC **D**
Yellowstone & The Grand Tetons
Yosemite

Caribbean & Latin America
Antigua & Barbuda **D**
Argentina
Bahamas
Barbados **D**
Belize
Bolivia
Brazil
Cancùn & Cozumel **D**
Caribbean
Central America
Chile
Costa Rica
Cuba
Dominican Republic
Dominican Republic **D**
Ecuador
Guatemala
Jamaica
Mexico
Peru
St Lucia **D**
South America
Trinidad & Tobago
Yúcatan

Africa & Middle East
Cape Town & the Garden Route
Dubai **D**
Egypt
Gambia
Jordan

D: Rough Guide **DIRECTIONS** for short breaks

Available from all good bookstores

ROUGH GUIDES

Complete Listing

For more information go to www.roughguides.com

Visit us online

www.roughguides.com

Information on over 25,000 destinations around the world

- **Read** Rough Guides' trusted travel info
- **Access** exclusive articles from Rough Guides authors
- **Update** yourself on new books, maps, CDs and other products
- **Enter** our competitions and win travel prizes
- **Share** ideas, journals, photos & travel advice with other users
- **Earn** points every time you contribute to the Rough Guide
  community and get rewards

BROADEN YOUR HORIZONS

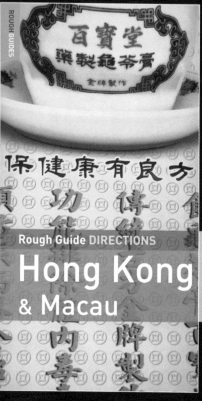

DesertshipSafari

Jeep, Camel and Trekking trips to the Western Desert

We offer preplanned trips for individuals and groups, but we can also tailore trips based on your preferences. Baharia Oasis and surroundings, White Desert and all places in the Western Desert like Siwa, Gilf Kebir, Sand Sea and Luxor. During the tour we offer full board with local dishes.

Yahia Kandil   Baharia Oasis
Email:yahiakandil@yahoo.de
Phone: 002-02-8496754
Mobile:002-012-3216790
Web: www.desertshipsafari.com

Avoid Guilt Trips

Buy fair trade coffee + bananas ✓

Save energy – use low energy bulbs ✓

– don't leave tv on standby ✓

Offset carbon emissions from flight to Madrid ✓

Send goat to Africa ✓

Join Tourism Concern today ✓

Slowly, the world is changing.
Together we can, and will, make a difference.

Tourism Concern is the only UK registered charity fighting exploitation in one of the largest industries on earth: people forced from their homes in order that holiday resorts can be built, sweatshop labour conditions in hotels and destruction of the environment are just some of the issues that we tackle.

Sending people on a guilt trip is not something we do. We know as well as anyone that holidays are precious. But you can help us to ensure that tourism always benefits the local communities involved.

Call 020 7133 3330
or visit **tourismconcern.org.uk** to find out how.

A year's membership of Tourism Concern costs just £20 (£12 unwaged)
- that's 38 pence a week, less than the cost of a pint of milk, organic of course.

Fighting Exploitation in Tourism

TourismConcern

Small print and

Index

A Rough Guide to Rough Guides

Published in 1982, the first Rough Guide – to Greece – was a student scheme that became a publishing phenomenon. Mark Ellingham, a recent graduate in English from Bristol University, had been travelling in Greece the previous summer and couldn't find the right guidebook. With a small group of friends he wrote his own guide, combining a highly contemporary, journalistic style with a thoroughly practical approach to travellers' needs.

The immediate success of the book spawned a series that rapidly covered dozens of destinations. And, in addition to impecunious backpackers, Rough Guides soon acquired a much broader and older readership that relished the guides' wit and inquisitiveness as much as their enthusiastic, critical approach and value-for-money ethos.

These days, Rough Guides include recommendations from shoestring to luxury and cover more than 200 destinations around the globe, including almost every country in the Americas and Europe, more than half of Africa and most of Asia and Australasia. Our ever-growing team of authors and photographers is spread all over the world, particularly in Europe, the USA and Australia.

In the early 1990s, Rough Guides branched out of travel, with the publication of Rough Guides to World Music, Classical Music and the Internet. All three have become benchmark titles in their fields, spearheading the publication of a wide range of books under the Rough Guide name.

Including the travel series, Rough Guides now number more than 350 titles, covering: phrasebooks, waterproof maps, music guides from Opera to Heavy Metal, reference works as diverse as Conspiracy Theories and Shakespeare, and popular culture books from iPods to Poker. Rough Guides also produce a series of more than 120 World Music CDs in partnership with World Music Network.

Visit www.roughguides.com to see our latest publications.

Rough Guide travel images are available for commercial licensing at www.roughguidespictures.com

Rough Guide credits

Text editors: Richard Lim, Samantha Cook and Alice Park
Layout: Sachin Tanwar
Cartography: Rajesh Mishra
Picture editor: Sarah Cummins
Production: Aimee Hampson
Proofreader: Anna Leggett and Diane Margolis
Cover design: Chloë Roberts
Photographer: Eddie Gerald
Editorial: **London** Kate Berens, Claire Saunders, Ruth Blackmore, Polly Thomas, Alison Murchie, Karoline Densley, Andy Turner, Keith Drew, Edward Aves, Nikki Birrell, Alice Park, Sarah Eno, Lucy White, Jo Kirby, James Smart, Natasha Foges, Roisin Cameron, Joe Staines, Duncan Clark, Peter Buckley, Matthew Milton, Tracy Hopkins, Ruth Tidball; **New York** Andrew Rosenberg, Steven Horak, AnneLise Sorensen, Amy Hegarty, April Isaacs, Ella Steim, Anna Owens, Joseph Petta, Sean Mahoney
Design & Pictures: **London** Scott Stickland, Dan May, Diana Jarvis, Mark Thomas, Jj Luck, Harriet Mills, Nicole Newman; **Delhi** Umesh Aggarwal, Ajay Verma, Jessica Subramanian, Ankur Guha, Pradeep Thapliyal, Anita Singh, Madhavi Singh, Karen D'Souza

Production: Katherine Owers
Cartography: **London** Maxine Repath, Ed Wright, Katie Lloyd-Jones; **Delhi** Jai Prakash Mishra, Rajesh Chhibber, Ashutosh Bharti, Animesh Pathak, Jasbir Sandhu, Karobi Gogoi, Amod Singh, Alakananda Bhattacharya, Athokpam Jotinkumar
Online: **New York** Jennifer Gold, Kristin Mingrone; **Delhi** Manik Chauhan, Narender Kumar, Rakesh Kumar, Amit Kumar, Amit Verma, Rahul Kumar, Ganesh Sharma, Debojit Borah
Marketing & Publicity: **London** Liz Statham, Niki Hanmer, Louise Maher, Jess Carter, Vanessa Godden, Vivienne Watton, Anna Paynton, Rachel Sprackett; **New York** Geoff Colquitt, Megan Kennedy, Katy Ball; **Delhi** Reem Khokhar
Special Projects Editor: Philippa Hopkins
Manager India: Punita Singh
Series Editor: Mark Ellingham
Reference Director: Andrew Lockett
Publishing Coordinator: Megan McIntyre
Publishing Director: Martin Dunford
Commercial Manager: Gino Magnotta
Managing Director: John Duhigg

Publishing information

This seventh edition published August 2007 by
Rough Guides Ltd,
80 Strand, London WC2R 0RL
345 Hudson St, 4th Floor,
New York, NY 10014, USA
14 Local Shopping Centre, Panchsheel Park,
New Delhi 110017, India
Distributed by the Penguin Group
Penguin Books Ltd,
80 Strand, London WC2R 0RL
Penguin Group (USA)
375 Hudson Street, NY 10014, USA
Penguin Group (Australia)
250 Camberwell Road, Camberwell,
Victoria 3124, Australia
Penguin Books Canada Ltd,
10 Alcorn Avenue, Toronto, Ontario,
Canada M4V 1E4
Penguin Group (NZ)
67 Apollo Drive, Mairangi Bay, Auckland 1310,
New Zealand

Cover concept by Peter Dyer.

Typeset in Bembo and Helvetica to an original design by Henry Iles.

Printed and bound in China

© Dan Richardson 2007

856pp includes index

A catalogue record for this book is available from the British Library

ISBN: 978-1-84353-782-3

3 5 7 9 8 6 4 2

Help us update

We've gone to a lot of effort to ensure that the seventh edition of **The Rough Guide to Egypt** is accurate and up to date. However, things change – places get "discovered", opening hours are notoriously fickle, restaurants and rooms raise prices or lower standards. If you feel we've got it wrong or left something out, we'd like to know, and if you can remember the address, the price, the time, the phone number, so much the better. We'll credit all contributions, and send a copy of the next edition (or any other Rough Guide if you prefer) for the best letters. Everyone who writes to us and isn't already a subscriber will receive a copy of our full-colour thrice-yearly newsletter. Please mark letters: "**Rough Guide Egypt Update**" and send to: Rough Guides, 80 Strand, London WC2R 0RL, or Rough Guides, 345 Hudson St, 4th Floor, New York, NY 10014. Or send an email to **mail@roughguides.com** Have your questions answered and tell others about your trip at
www.roughguides.atinfopop.com

Acknowledgements

Thanks from **Dan Richardson** to Hagg Ibrahim, Hamada, Karin and Tayeb el-Khalifa and Aladin Al-Sahaby for their hospitality and friendship in Luxor; and the assistance of outstanding tourist officials, namely Mrs Selwa (Luxor), Shukri Sa'ad and Hakeem Hussein (Aswan), Hussein Farag and Mahmoud Abd el-Samir (Minya), Ramadan Osman and Mohammed Abd el-Hamid (Assyut), Hassan Rifat (Sohag), Maha Hamdy (Alexandria), Mahdi Hweiti (Siwa) and Omar Ahmed (Dakhla). Also thanks to Mahmoud Yussef and Mohsen in Kharga Oasis; Talat Mulah, Yehiya Kandil and Ashraf Lotfi in Bahariya Oasis, and the staff of the *Crillon Hotel* in Alexandria. In London, thanks are due to Richard Lim for his Horus-eyed scrutiny and incisive pruning of the text.

Daniel Jacobs thanks Hisham Youssef (*Berlin Hotel*, Cairo), Salah Mohammed, Hamdi Shora, Caroline Evanoff, Carmen Weinstein and Lizzie Williams

Readers' letters

SMALL PRINT

Thanks to the following who took the trouble to write in with updates and corrections (and apologies to anyone whose name we've inadvertently omitted or misspelled):

Mohammed Abbas; Jane Akshar; Simon Allen; Zahraa Adel Awad; Geoffrey Bailey; Oldriska Balouskova; E. Baylis; Boen & Esther; James Bothamley; Diana and David Bruce; Geff Brown; Vicky Bullard; Kathleen Cameron; Rob Cameron; Alicia Choo; Julie Colburn; Jennie Cole; Clive Collins; Judy Collins; Vivien Conrad; Sherard Cowper-Coles; John Davis; Gordon Dawes; Mike Dean; Matthew Deane; Jan Deckers; B.M. Dobson; Moyra Elliott; Martin Empson; Jacqui Evans; Christopher Fitz-Simon; Jorge Forero; Pamela Garelick; Doreen Green; Libby Hakim; Dorothy & Brian Hodgson Smith; Dick Hoek; Bel Jackson; Helen Jackson; William Jamieson; Ben Johnson; Cathy Kinnear; Justine Kirby; Koteiba; Geoffrey Lenox-Smith; Joe Levy; Rena Maguire; Diana Mason; Roy Messenger; M.A. McLoughlin; Maria Luckhurst; Oscar Merne; John Molteno; Sana Mukhtar; Tom Muldoon; M.G. Nightingale; Patrick Ostyn; Harold Otness; Nancy Priestley; Bdelsalam Ragab; Peter J. Rial; Toby Randall; Jimena Rojas; Simone Rutkowitz; El-Sayed; Ed Schoch; Sylvia Smith; Svetlana and Andrija; Bob Turner; Anne Vanbrabant; Neil van der Linden; H.J. van Vliet; Erik Weijers.

Photo credits

All photos © Rough Guides except the following:

Full page
Camels at the Great Pyramids © Paul Hardy/ Corbis
Souk al-Tawfiqia, Cairo © Daniel Jacobs

Introduction
Street sign, Cairo © Gary Cook/Alamy
Ibis © Roger Wood/Corbis
Snorkeller off Golden Beach, Dahab © Nick Hanna/Alamy

Things not to miss
01 Feluccas on the Nile, Aswan © Ellen Rooney/ Getty
02 Mount Sinai © Jon Arnold/Alamy
03 *Dahabiya* © Jean Dominique Dallet/Alamy
05 Corals and diver © F. Jack Jackson/Alamy
06 Bedouins on camels and windsurfers at Dahab © Simon Miles/Corbis
07 Bent Pyramid at Dahshur © Peter Wilson/ DKImages
08 Moulid © dkpix/Alamy
10 A *mezze* spread © Jean Dominique Dallet/ Alamy
11 Bellydancer © Roger Ressmeyer/Corbis
12 Islamic Cairo © Gary Cook/Alamy
13 Batfish, Ras Mohammed © Ivor Fulcher/ Corbis
14 Sphinx, Giza © Guy Midkiff/Alamy
15 Siwa © James Morris/Axiom
16 Al-Qasr © Seran de Leede
18 White Desert © Peter Wilson/DKimages
19 Bedouin weavers, Western Desert © Sarah Errington/Hutchinson
20 Taweret statue, Egyptian Antiquities Museum © Roger Wood/Corbis
21 Feluccas © Christine Osbourne – Worldwide Picture Library/Alamy
22 Abu Simbel © Richard Passmore/Getty
24 Egret, Wadi Rayan © Amjad el-Geoushi/Alamy
25 Library at Alexandria © Sandro Vannini/Corbis
26 Catacombs of Kom es-Shoqafa © Stuart Franklin/Magnum
27 Monastery of St Paul © Bojan Brecelj/Corbis
28 Abydos, Tomb of Seti I © James Morris/Axiom
30 Jeep safari © Hugh Sitton/Alamy
31 St Catherine's Monastery © Joerg Hardtke/ Getty
32 Floorshow at Na'ama Bay © Sanafir Hotel
33 Great Sand Sea © Sylvain Grandadam/Robert Harding
34 Tomb of Ramses I, Valley of the Kings © James Morris/Axiom
35 Ballooning over the West Bank, Luxor © Max Alexander/DKImages

Islamic architecture colour section
Cairo's Northern Cemeteries © Daniel Jacobs
Portal in Islamic Cairo © Gary Cook/Alamy
Mashrabiya window, Beit al-Sihaymi, Cairo © Gary Cook/Alamy

Temple architecture colour section
Karnak temple © Anthony Cassidy/JAI/Corbis
Bas-relief of festival procession, Ramesseum © Richard Lim

Egypt's underwater world colour section
Clownfish © Blickwinkel/Alamy
Moray Eel © Liquid-Light Underwater Photography/Alamy
Parrotfish © Adam Butler/Alamy
Napoleon wrasse © Reinhard Dirscherl/Alamy
Angelfish © Fabrice Bettex/Alamy
Klunzinger's wrasse © Blickwinkel/Alamy
Lionfish © Reinhard Dirscherl/Alamy

Black and whites
p.119 Midan Talaat Harb © Gary Cook/Alamy
p.240 Café chess © Jon Spaull/Axiom
p.250 Copper ware © Chris Caldicott/Axiom
p.276 Jeweller's, Aswan © Richard Lim
p.320 Feluccas on the Nile © BL Images Ltd/ Alamy
p.333 Temple of Hathor © Alistair Duncan/ DKImages
p.386 Opening the tomb of Tutankhamun © Hulton-Deutsch Collection/Corbis
p.446 View over Sehel Island © Richard Lim
p.470 Siwa © Peter Wilson/DKImages
p.534 Bagawat Necropolis © Max Alexander/ DKImages
p.539 Temple of Dush © Seran de Leede
p.540 Rock art © Mike P. Shepherd/Alamy
p.568 Fishing boats, Alexandria © Gary Cook/ Alamy
p.589 Engraving of the Pharos lighthouse © Philip de Bay/Corbis
p.620 Tanis Coffins © Ian M. Butterfield/Alamy
p.640 Ship on the Suez Canal © Jack Jackson/ Robert Harding Picture Library Ltd/Alamy
p.647 Suez © Horst Ossinger/Corbis
p.662 St Catherine's Monastery © Hanan Isachar/Corbis
p.707 Pharaoh's Island © Jon Spaull/DKImages
p.724 Diving in the Red Sea © Alamy
p.727 Monastery of St Anthony © Gordon Sinclair/Alamy
p.751 Meal break on liveaboard © Nick Hanna/ Alamy

ROUGH GUIDES

SMALL PRINT

Selected images from our guidebooks are available for licensing from:

ROUGHGUIDESPICTURES.COM

Index

Map entries are in colour.

INDEX

INDEX

I

INDEX

853

Map symbols

maps are listed in the full index using coloured text

– – –	Chapter division boundary	Lighthouse
– ∎ – ∎ –	International boundary	Battlefield
═══	Main road	Shipwreck
───	Minor road	Restaurant
∷∷∷	Tunnel	Hotel
– – – –	Footpath/track	Statue
───	River	★ Transport stop
— —	Ferry route	Garage/fuel station
—∎—	Railway	Telephone
—Ⓜ—	Metro line & station	Post office
▪▪▪▪	Wall	Information point
◆	Point of interest	@ Internet access
✈	Airport	Hospital
⋔⋔	Cliff face/escarpment	Parking
☾	Crescent dune	Temple
⍡	Oasis/palm grove	Tomb
⋔⋔	Spring	Monastery/convent
⚘	Waterfall	Synagogue
ⵜ	Fountain	Building
⊛	Swimming Pool	Stadium
⭭	Viewpoint	Church
⌃⌃	Mountain range	Mosque
▲	Mountain peak	Christian cemetery
ⱳⱳ	Reef	Muslim cemetery
☀	Crater	Park/national park
◿	Pyramid	Farmland
◓	Cave	Beach/dunes
≋	Mountain pass	Delta
♦	Checkpoint	Saltpan